The OXFORD PAPERBACK FRENCH DICTIONARY

SECOND EDITION

French–English
English–French
Français–anglais
Anglais–français

MICHAEL JANES

DORA CARPENTER

EDWIN CARPENTER

D0348584

Oxford N
OXFORD UNIVERSITY PRESS

Oxford University Press, Walton Street, Oxford OX2 6DP

Oxford New York
Athens Auckland Bangkok Bombay
Calcutta Cape Town Dar es Salaam Delhi
Florence Hong Kong Istanbul Karachi
Kuala Lumpur Madras Madrid Melbourne
Mexico City Nairobi Paris Singapore
Taipei Tokyo Toronto

and associated companies in
Berlin Ibadan

Oxford is a trade mark of Oxford University Press

© Oxford University Press 1986, 1993
Second edition first published 1993
as The Oxford French Minidictionary
First issued as an Oxford University Press paperback 1994

British Library Cataloguing in Publication Data

Data available

Library of Congress Cataloging in Publication Data
Janes, Michael.
The Oxford French dictionary : French–English, English–French : français–
anglais, anglais–français / Michael Janes, Dora Carpenter, Edwin
Carpenter.—2nd ed.
p. cm.
1. French language—Dictionaries—English. 2. English
language—Dictionaries—French. I. Carpenter, Dora. II. Carpenter,
Edwin. III. Title.
443'.21—dc20 PC2640.J26 1994 93–29653
ISBN 0–19–280014–0

7 9 10 8

Printed in Great Britain by
Mackays
Chatham, Kent

Preface

This is the second edition of *The Oxford Paperback French Dictionary*. It remains largely the work of Michael Janes, the compiler of the first edition, but some entries have been substantially revised and we have been able to incorporate a large proportion of new material. We hope to have kept to the aim of the original: to provide users requiring a compact dictionary with the maximum amount of useful material.

Dora Latiri-Carpenter
Edwin Carpenter

Introduction

When you look up a word, you will find a pronunciation, a grammatical part of speech, and the translation. Sometimes more than one translation is given, and material in brackets in *italics* is included to help you choose the right one. For example, under **cabin** you will see (*hut*) and (*in ship, aircraft*). When a word has more than one part of speech, this can affect the translation. For example **praise** is translated one way when it is a verb (*v.t.*) and another way when it is a noun (*n.*).

A swung dash (∼) represents the entry word, or the part of it that comes before a vertical bar (as in **libert|y**). You will see it in examples using the entry word and words based on it. For example, under **good** you will find **as ∼ as** and **∼-looking**.

Translations are given in their basic form. You will find tables at the end showing verb forms. Irregular verbs are marked on the French to English side with †. This side also shows the plurals of nouns and the feminine forms of adjectives when they do not follow the normal rules.

Abbreviations · Abréviations

abbreviation	*abbr., abrév.*	abréviation
adjective(s)	*a. (adjs.)*	adjectif(s)
adverb(s)	*adv(s).*	adverbe(s)
American	*Amer.*	américain
anatomy	*anat.*	anatomie
approximately	*approx.*	approximativement
archaeology	*archaeol., archéol.*	archéologie
architecture	*archit.*	architecture
motoring	*auto.*	automobile
auxiliary	*aux.*	auxiliaire
aviation	*aviat.*	aviation
botany	*bot.*	botanique
computing	*comput.*	informatique
commerce	*comm.*	commerce
conjunction(s)	*conj(s).*	conjonction(s)
cookery	*culin.*	culinaire
electricity	*electr., électr.*	électricité
feminine	*f.*	féminin
familiar	*fam.*	familier
figurative	*fig.*	figuré
geography	*geog., géog.*	géographie
geology	*geol., géol.*	géologie
grammar	*gram.*	grammaire
humorous	*hum.*	humoristique
interjection(s)	*int(s).*	interjection(s)
invariable	*invar.*	invariable
legal, law	*jurid.*	juridique
language	*lang.*	langue
masculine	*m.*	masculin
medicine	*med., méd.*	médecine
military	*mil.*	militaire
music	*mus.*	musique
noun(s)	*n(s).*	nom(s)
nautical	*naut.*	nautique
oneself	*o.s.*	se, soi-même
proprietary term	*P.*	marque déposée
pejorative	*pej., péj.*	péjoratif
philosophy	*phil.*	philosophie
photography	*photo.*	photographie
plural	*pl.*	pluriel
politics	*pol.*	politique
possessive	*poss.*	possessif

past participle	*p.p.*	participe passé
prefix	*pref., préf.*	préfixe
preposition(s)	*prep(s)., prép(s).*	préposition(s)
present participle	*pres. p.*	participe présent
pronoun	*pron.*	pronom
relative pronoun	*pron. rel.*	pronom relatif
psychology	*psych.*	psychologie
past tense	*p.t.*	passé
something	*qch.*	quelque chose
someone	*qn.*	quelqu'un
railway	*rail.*	chemin de fer
religion	*relig.*	religion
relative pronoun	*rel. pron.*	pronom relatif
school, scholastic	*schol., scol.*	scolaire
singular	*sing.*	singulier
slang	*sl.*	argot
someone	*s.o.*	quelqu'un
something	*sth.*	quelque chose
technical	*techn.*	technique
television	*TV*	télévision
university	*univ.*	université
auxiliary verb	*v. aux.*	verbe auxiliaire
intransitive verb	*v.i.*	verbe intransitif
pronominal verb	*v. pr.*	verbe pronominal
transitive verb	*v.t.*	verbe transitif

Proprietary terms

This dictionary includes some words which are, or are asserted to be, proprietary terms or trade marks. The presence or absence of such assertions should not be regarded as affecting the legal status of any proprietary name or trade mark.

Pronunciation of French

Phonetic symbols

Vowels

i	v*ie*	y	vêt*u*
e	pr*é*	ø	p*eu*
ɛ	l*ai*t	œ	p*eu*r
a	pl*a*t	ə	d*e*
ɑ	b*a*s	ɛ̃	mat*in*
ɔ	m*o*rt	ɑ̃	s*ans*
o	m*o*t	ɔ̃	b*on*
u	gen*ou*	œ̃	l*un*di

Consonants and semi-consonants

p	*p*ayer	ʒ	*j*e
b	*b*on	m	*m*ain
t	*t*erre	n	*n*ous
d	*d*ans	l	*l*ong
k	*c*ou	r	*r*ue
g	*g*ant	ɲ	a*gn*eau
f	*f*eu	ŋ	campi*ng*
v	*v*ous	j	*y*eux
s	*s*ale	w	*ou*i
z	*z*éro	ɥ	h*u*ile
ʃ	*ch*at		

Note: ' before the pronunciation of a word beginning with*h* indicates no liaison or elision.

An asterisk immediately following an apostrophe in some words like **qu'*** shows that this form of the word is used before a vowel or mute 'h'.

A

a /a/ *voir* **avoir**.

à /a/ *prép.* (*à + le = au, à + les = aux*) in, at; (*direction*) to; (*temps*) at; (*jusqu'à*) to, till; (*date*) on; (*époque*) in; (*moyen*) by, on; (*prix*) for; (*appartenance*) of; (*mesure*) by. **donner**/*etc.* **à qn.**, give/*etc.* to s.o. **apprendre**/*etc.* **à faire**, learn/*etc.* to do. **l'homme à la barbe**, the man with the beard. **à la radio**, on the radio. **c'est à moi**/*etc.*, it is mine/*etc.* **c'est à vous**/*etc.* **de**, it is up to you/*etc.* to, (*en jouant*) it is your/*etc.* turn to. **à six km d'ici**, six km. away. **dix km à l'heure**, ten km. an *ou* per hour. **il a un crayon à la main**, he's got a pencil in his hand.

abaissement /abɛsmɑ̃/ *n.m.* (*baisse*) drop, fall.

abaisser /abese/ *v.t.* lower; (*levier*) pull *ou* push down; (*fig*) humiliate. **s'~** *v. pr.* go down, drop; (*fig.*) humiliate o.s. **s'~ à**, stoop to.

abandon /abɑ̃dɔ̃/ *n.m.* abandonment; desertion; (*sport*) withdrawal; (*naturel*) abandon. **à l'~**, in a state of neglect. **~ner** /-ɔne/ *v.t.* abandon, desert; (*renoncer à*) give up, abandon; (*céder*) give (à, to). **s'~ner à**, give o.s. up to.

abasourdir /abazurdir/ *v.t.* stun.

abat-jour /abaʒur/ *n.m. invar.* lampshade.

abats /aba/ *n.m. pl.* offal.

abattement /abatmɑ̃/ *n.m.* dejection; (*faiblesse*) exhaustion; (*comm.*) allowance.

abattis /abati/ *n.m. pl.* giblets.

abattoir /abatwar/ *n.m.* slaughterhouse, abattoir.

abattre† /abatr/ *v.t.* knock down; (*arbre*) cut down; (*animal*) slaughter; (*avion*) shoot down; (*affaiblir*) weaken; (*démoraliser*) dishearten. **s'~** *v. pr.* come down, fall (down). **se laisser ~**, let things get one down.

abbaye /abei/ *n.f.* abbey.

abbé /abe/ *n.m.* priest; (*supérieur d'une abbaye*) abbot.

abcès /apsɛ/ *n.m.* abscess.

abdi|quer /abdike/ *v.t./i.* abdicate. **~cation** *n.f.* abdication.

abdom|en /abdɔmɛn/ *n.m.* abdomen. **~inal** (*m. pl.* **~inaux**) *a.* abdominal.

abeille /abɛj/ *n.f.* bee.

aberrant, ~e /abɛrɑ̃, -t/ *a.* absurd.

aberration /abɛrɑsjɔ̃/ *n.f.* aberration; (*idée*) absurd idea.

abêtir /abetir/ *v.t.* make stupid.

abhorrer /abɔre/ *v.t.* loathe, abhor.

abîme /abim/ *n.m.* abyss.

abîmer /abime/ *v.t.* damage, spoil. **s'~** *v. pr.* get damaged *ou* spoilt.

abject /abʒɛkt/ *a.* abject.

abjurer /abʒyre/ *v.t.* abjure.

ablation /ablasjɔ̃/ *n.f.* removal.

ablutions /ablysjɔ̃/ *n.f. pl.* ablutions.

aboiement /abwamɑ̃/ *n.m.* bark(ing). **~s**, barking.

abois (aux) /(oz)abwa/ *adv.* at bay.

abol|ir /abɔlir/ *v.t.* abolish. **~ition** *n.f.* abolition.

abominable /abɔminabl/ *a.* abominable.

abond|ant, ~ante /abɔ̃dɑ̃, -t/ *a.* abundant, plentiful. **~amment** *adv.* abundantly. **~ance** *n.f.* abundance; (*prospérité*) affluence.

abonder /abɔ̃de/ *v.i.* abound (**en**, in). **~ dans le sens de qn.**, completely agree with s.o.

abonn|er (s') /(s)abɔne/ *v. pr.* subscribe (à, to). **~é, ~ée** *n.m., f.* subscriber; season-ticket holder. **~ement** *n.m.* (*à un journal*) subscription; (*de bus, théâtre, etc.*) season-ticket.

abord /abɔr/ *n.m.* access. **~s**, surroundings. **d'~**, first.

abordable /abɔrdabl/ *a.* (*prix*) reasonable; (*personne*) approachable.

abordage /abɔrdaʒ/ *n.m.* (*accident: naut.*) collision. **prendre à l'~**, (*navire*) board, attack.

aborder /abɔrde/ *v.t.* approach; (*lieu*) reach; (*problème etc.*) tackle. —*v.i.* reach land.

aborigène /abɔriʒɛn/ *n.m.* aborigine, aboriginal.

aboutir /abutir/ *v.i.* succeed, achieve a result. **∼ à**, end (up) in, lead to. **n'∼ à rien**, come to nothing.

aboutissement /abutismɑ̃/ *n.m.* outcome.

aboyer /abwaje/ *v.i.* bark.

abrasi|f, **∼ve** /abrazif, -v/ *a. & n.m.* abrasive.

abrégé /abreʒe/ *n.m.* summary.

abréger /abreʒe/ *v.t.* (*texte*) shorten, abridge; (*mot*) abbreviate, shorten; (*visite*) cut short.

abreuv|er /abrœve/ *v.t.* water; (*fig.*) overwhelm (**de**, with). **s'∼er** *v. pr.* drink. **∼oir** *n.m.* watering-place.

abréviation /abrevjɑsjɔ̃/ *n.f.* abbreviation.

abri /abri/ *n.m.* shelter. **à l'∼**, under cover. **à l'∼ de** sheltered from.

abricot /abriko/ *n.m.* apricot.

abriter /abrite/ *v.t.* shelter; (*recevoir*) house. **s'∼** *v. pr.* (take) shelter.

abroger /abrɔʒe/ *v.t.* repeal.

abrupt /abrypt/ *a.* steep, sheer; (*fig.*) abrupt.

abruti, **∼e** /abryti/ *n.m., f.* (*fam.*) idiot.

abrutir /abrytir/ *v.t.* make *ou* drive stupid, dull the mind of.

absence /apsɑ̃s/ *n.f.* absence.

absent, **∼e** /apsɑ̃, -t/ *a.* absent, away; (*chose*) missing. —*n.m., f.* absentee. **il est toujours ∼**, he's still away. **d'un air ∼**, absently. **∼éisme** /-teism/ *n.m.* absenteeism. **∼éiste** /-teist/ *n.m./f.* absentee.

absenter (s') /(s)apsɑ̃te/ *v. pr.* go *ou* be away; (*sortir*) go out, leave.

absolu /apsɔly/ *a.* absolute. **∼ment** *adv.* absolutely.

absolution /apsɔlysjɔ̃/ *n.f.* absolution.

absor|ber /apsɔrbe/ *v.t.* absorb; (*temps etc.*) take up. **∼bant**, **∼bante** *a.* (*travail etc.*) absorbing; (*matière*) absorbent. **∼ption** *n.f.* absorption.

absoudre /apsudr/ *v.t.* absolve.

absten|ir (s') /(s)apstənir/ *v. pr.* abstain. **s'∼ir de**, refrain from. **∼tion** /-ɑ̃sjɔ̃/ *n.f.* abstention.

abstinence /apstinɑ̃s/ *n.f.* abstinence.

abstr|aire /apstrɛr/ *v.t.* abstract. **∼action** *n.f.* abstraction. **faire ∼action de**, disregard. **∼ait**, **∼aite** *a. & n.m.* abstract.

absurd|e /apsyrd/ *a.* absurd. **∼ité** *n.f.* absurdity.

abus /aby/ *n.m.* abuse, misuse; (*injustice*) abuse. **∼ de confiance**, breach of trust. **∼ sexuel**, sexual abuse.

abuser /abyze/ *v.t.* deceive. —*v.i.* go too far. **s'∼** *v. pr.* be mistaken. **∼ de**, abuse, misuse; (*profiter de*) take advantage of; (*alcool etc.*) over-indulge in.

abusi|f, **∼ve** /abyzif, -v/ *a.* excessive; (*usage*) mistaken.

acabit /akabi/ *n.m.* **du même ∼**, of that sort.

académicien, **∼ne** /akademisjɛ̃, -jɛn/ *n.m., f.* academician.

académ|ie /akademi/ *n.f.* academy; (*circonscription*) educational district. **A∼ie**, Academy. **∼ique** *a.* academic.

acajou /akaʒu/ *n.m.* mahogany.

acariâtre /akarjɑtr/ *a.* cantankerous.

accablement /akablǝmɑ̃/ *n.m.* despondency.

accabl|er /akable/ *v.t.* overwhelm. **∼er d'impôts**, burden with taxes. **∼er d'injures**, heap insults upon. **∼ant**, **∼ante** *a.* (*chaleur*) oppressive.

accalmie /akalmi/ *n.f.* lull.

accaparer /akapare/ *v.t.* monopolize; (*fig.*) take up all the time of.

accéder /aksede/ *v.i.* **∼ à**, reach; (*pouvoir, requête, trône, etc.*) accede to.

accélér|er /akselere/ *v.i.* (*auto.*) accelerate. —*v.t.*, **s'∼er** *v. pr.* speed up. **∼ateur** *n.m.* accelerator. **∼ation** *n.f.* acceleration; speeding up.

accent /aksɑ̃/ *n.m.* accent; (*sur une syllabe*) stress, accent; (*ton*) tone. **mettre l'∼ sur**, stress.

accentu|er /aksɑ̃tɥe/ *v.t.* (*lettre, syllabe*) accent; (*fig.*) emphasize, accentuate. **s'∼uer** *v. pr.* become more pronounced, increase. **∼uation** *n.f.* accentuation.

accept|er /aksɛpte/ *v.t.* accept. **∼er de**, agree to. **∼able** *a.* acceptable. **∼ation** *n.f.* acceptance.

acception /aksɛpsjɔ̃/ *n.f.* meaning.

accès /aksɛ/ *n.m.* access; (*porte*) entrance; (*de fièvre*) attack; (*de colère*) fit; (*de joie*) (out)burst. **les ∼ de**, (*voies*) the approaches to. **facile d'∼**, easy to get to.

accessible /aksesibl/ *a.* accessible; (*personne*) approachable.

accession /aksɛsjɔ̃/ *n.f.* **∼ à**, accession to.

accessit /aksesit/ *n.m.* honourable mention.

accessoire /akseswar/ *a.* secondary. —*n.m.* accessory; (*théâtre*) prop.

accident /aksidɑ̃/ *n.m.* accident. **∼ de train/d'avion**, train/plane crash. **par ∼**, by accident. **∼é** /-te/ *a.* damaged *ou* hurt (in an accident); (*terrain*) uneven, hilly.

accidentel, **∼le** /aksidɑ̃tɛl/ *a.* accidental.

acclam|er /aklame/ *v.t.* cheer, acclaim. **∼ations** *n.f. pl.* cheers.

acclimat|er /aklimate/ *v.t.*, **s'∼er** *v. pr.* acclimatize; (*Amer.*) acclimate. **∼ation** *n.f.* acclimatization; (*Amer.*) acclimation.

accolade /akɔlad/ *n.f.* embrace; (*signe*) brace, bracket.

accommodant, **∼e** /akɔmɔdɑ̃, -t/ *a.* accommodating.

accommodement /akɔmɔdmɑ̃/ *n.m.* compromise.

accommoder /akɔmɔde/ *v.t.* adapt (**à**, to); (*cuisiner*) prepare; (*assaisonner*) flavour. **s'∼ de**, put up with.

accompagn|er /akɔ̃paɲe/ *v.t.* accompany. **s'∼er de**, be accompanied by. **∼ateur**, **∼atrice** *n.m., f.* (*mus.*) accompanist; (*guide*) guide. **∼ement** *n.m.* (*mus.*) accompaniment.

accompli /akɔ̃pli/ *a.* accomplished.

accompl|ir /akɔ̃plir/ *v.t.* carry out, fulfil. **s'∼ir** *v. pr.* be carried out, happen. **∼issement** *n.m.* fulfilment.

accord /akɔr/ *n.m.* agreement; (*harmonie*) harmony; (*mus.*) chord. **être d'∼**, agree (**pour**, to). **se mettre d'∼**, come to an agreement, agree. **d'∼!**, all right!, OK!

accordéon /akɔrdeɔ̃/ *n.m.* accordion.

accord|er /akɔrde/ *v.t.* grant; (*couleurs etc.*) match; (*mus.*) tune. **s'∼er** *v. pr.* agree. **s'∼er avec**, (*s'entendre avec*) get on with. **∼eur** *n.m.* tuner.

accoster /akɔste/ *v.t.* accost; (*navire*) come alongside.

accotement /akɔtmɑ̃/ *n.m.* roadside, verge; (*Amer.*) shoulder.

accoter (**s'**) /(s)akɔte/ *v. pr.* lean (**à**, against).

accouch|er /akuʃe/ *v.i.* give birth (**de**, to); (*être en travail*) be in labour. —*v.t.* deliver. **∼ement** *n.m.* childbirth; (*travail*) labour. (*médecin*) **∼eur** *n.m.* obstetrician. **∼euse** *n.f.* midwife.

accoud|er (**s'**) /(s)akude/ *v. pr.* lean (one's elbows) on. **∼oir** *n.m.* armrest.

accoupl|er /akuple/ *v.t.* couple; (*faire copuler*) mate. **s'∼er** *v. pr.* mate. **∼ement** *n.m.* mating; coupling.

accourir /akurir/ *v.i.* run up.

accoutrement /akutrəmɑ̃/ *n.m.* (strange) garb.

accoutumance /akutymɑ̃s/ *n.f.* habituation; (*méd.*) addiction.

accoutum|er /akutyme/ *v.t.* accustom. **s'∼er** *v. pr.* get accustomed. **∼é** *a.* customary.

accréditer /akredite/ *v.t.* give credence to; (*personne*) accredit.

accro /akro/ *n.m./f.* (*drogué*) addict; (*amateur*) fan.

accroc /akro/ *n.m.* tear, rip; (*fig.*) hitch.

accroch|er /akrɔʃe/ *v.t.* (*suspendre*) hang up; (*attacher*) hook, hitch; (*déchirer*) catch; (*heurter*) hit; (*attirer*) attract. **s'∼er** *v. pr.* cling, hang on; (*se disputer*) clash. **∼age** *n.m.* hanging; hooking; (*auto.*) collision; (*dispute*) clash; (*mil.*) encounter.

accroissement /akrwasmɑ̃/ *n.m.* increase (**de**, in).

accroître /akrwatr/ *v.t.*, **s'∼** *v. pr.* increase.

accroup|ir (**s'**) /(s)akrupir/ *v. pr.* squat. **∼i** *a.* squatting.

accru /akry/ *a.* increased, greater.

accueil /akœj/ *n.m.* reception, welcome.

accueill|ir /akœjir/ *v.t.* receive, welcome; (*aller chercher*) meet. **∼ant**, **∼ante** *a.* friendly.

acculer /akyle/ *v.t.* corner. **∼ à**, force *ou* drive into *ou* against *ou* close to.

accumul|er /akymyle/ *v.t.*, **s'∼er** *v. pr.* accumulate, pile up. **∼ateur** *n.m.* accumulator. **∼ation** *n.f.* accumulation.

accus /aky/ *n.m. pl.* (*fam.*) battery.

accusation /akyzasjɔ̃/ *n.f.* accusation; (*jurid.*) charge. **l'∼**, (*magistrat*) the prosecution.

accus|er /akyze/ *v.t.* accuse (**de**, of); (*blâmer*) blame (**de**, for); (*jurid.*) charge (**de**, with); (*fig.*) show, emphasize. **∼er réception de**, acknowledge receipt of. **∼ateur**, **∼atrice** *a.* incriminating; *n.m., f.* accuser. **∼é**, **∼ée** *a.* marked; *n m, f.* accused.

acerbe /asɛrb/ *a.* bitter.

acéré /asere/ *a.* sharp.

achalandé /aʃalɑ̃de/ *a.* **bien ∼**, well-stocked.

acharn|é /aʃarne/ *a.* relentless, ferocious. **∼ement** *n.m.* relentlessness.

acharner (**s'**) /(s)aʃarne/ *v. pr.* **s'∼ sur**, set upon; (*poursuivre*) hound. **s'∼ à faire**, keep on doing.

achat /aʃa/ *n.m.* purchase. **∼s**, shopping. **faire l'∼ de**, buy.

acheminer /aʃmine/ *v.t.* dispatch, convey. **s'∼ vers**, head for.

achet|er /aʃte/ *v.t.* buy. **∼er à**, buy from; (*pour*) buy for. **∼eur**, **∼euse** *n.m., f.* buyer; (*client de magasin*) shopper.

achèvement /aʃɛvmɑ̃/ *n.m.* completion.

achever /aʃve/ v.t. finish (off). **s'~** v. pr. end.

acid|e /asid/ a. acid, sharp. —n.m. acid. **~ité** n.f. acidity. **~ulé** a. slightly acid.

acier /asje/ n.m. steel. **aciérie** n.f. steelworks.

acné /akne/ n.f. acne.

acolyte /akɔlit/ n.m. (péj.) associate.

acompte /akɔ̃t/ n.m. deposit, part-payment.

à-côté /akote/ n.m. side-issue. **~s**, (argent) extras.

à-coup /aku/ n.m. jolt, jerk. **par ~s**, by fits and starts.

acoustique /akustik/ n.f. acoustics. —a. acoustic.

acqu|érir† /akerir/ v.t. acquire, gain; (biens) purchase, acquire. **~éreur** n.m. purchaser. **~isition** n.f. acquisition; purchase.

acquiescer /akjese/ v.i. acquiesce, agree.

acquis, **~e** /aki, -z/ n.m. experience. —a. acquired; (fait) established; (faveurs) secured. **~ à**, (projet) in favour of.

acquit /aki/ n.m. receipt. **par ~ de conscience,** for peace of mind.

acquitt|er /akite/ v.t. acquit; (dette) settle. **s'~er de**, (promesse, devoir) carry out. **s'~er envers**, repay. **~ement** n.m. acquittal; settlement.

âcre /ɑkr/ a. acrid.

acrobate /akrɔbat/ n.m./f. acrobat.

acrobatie /akrɔbasi/ n.f. acrobatics. **~ aérienne**, aerobatics. **acrobatique** /-tik/ a. acrobatic.

acte /akt/ n.m. act, action, deed; (théâtre) act; (de naissance, mariage) certificate. **~s**, (compte rendu) proceedings. **prendre ~ de**, note.

acteur /aktœr/ n.m. actor.

acti|f, **~ve** /aktif, -v/ a. active. —n.m. (comm.) assets. **avoir à son ~f**, have to one's credit ou name. **~vement** adv. actively.

action /aksjɔ̃/ n.f. action; (comm.) share; (jurid.) action. **~naire** /-jɔnɛr/ n.m./f. shareholder.

actionner /aksjɔne/ v.t. work, activate.

activer /aktive/ v.t. speed up; (feu) boost. **s'~** v. pr. hurry, rush.

activiste /aktivist/ n.m./f. activist.

activité /aktivite/ n.f. activity. **en ~**, active.

actrice /aktris/ n.f. actress.

actualiser /aktɥalize/ v.t. update.

actualité /aktɥalite/ n.f. topicality. **l'~**, current events. **les ~s**, news. **d'~**, topical.

actuel, **~le** /aktɥɛl/ a. present; (d'actualité) topical. **~lement** adv. at the present time.

acuité /akɥite/ n.f. acuteness.

acupunct|ure /akypɔ̃ktyr/ n.f. acupuncture. **~eur** n.m. acupuncturist.

adage /adaʒ/ n.m. adage.

adapt|er /adapte/ v.t. adapt; (fixer) fit. **s'~er** v. pr. adapt (o.s.); (techn.) fit, **~ateur**, **~atrice** n.m., f. adapter; n.m. (électr.) adapter. **~ation** n.f. adaptation.

additif /aditif/ n.m. (note) rider; (substance) additive.

addition /adisjɔ̃/ n.f. addition; (au café etc.) bill; (Amer.) check. **~nel**, **~nelle** /-jɔnɛl/ a. additional. **~ner** /-jɔne/ v.t. add; (totaliser) add (up).

adepte /adɛpt/ n.m./f. follower.

adéquat, **~e** /adekwa, -t/ a. suitable.

adhérent, **~e** /aderɑ̃, -t/ n.m., f. member.

adhé|rer /adere/ v.i. adhere, stick (à, to). **~rer à**, (club etc.) be a member of; (s'inscrire à) join. **~rence** n.f. adhesion. **~sif**, **~sive** a. & n.m. adhesive. **~sion** n.f. membership; (accord) adherence.

adieu (pl. **~x**) /adjø/ int. & n.m. goodbye, farewell.

adipeu|x, **~se** /adipø, -z/ a. fat; (tissu) fatty.

adjacent, **~e** /adʒasɑ̃, -t/ a. adjacent.

adjectif /adʒɛktif/ n.m. adjective.

adjoindre /adʒwɛ̃dr/ v.t. add, attach; (personne) appoint. **s'~** v. pr. appoint.

adjoint, **~e** /adʒwɛ̃, -t/ n.m., f. & a. assistant. **~ au maire**, deputy mayor.

adjudant /adʒydɑ̃/ n.m. warrant-officer.

adjuger /adʒyʒe/ v.t. award; (aux enchères) auction. **s'~** v. pr. take.

adjurer /adʒyre/ v.t. beseech.

admettre† /admɛtr/ v.t. let in, admit; (tolérer) allow; (reconnaître) admit; (candidat) pass.

administrati|f, **~ve** /administratif, -v/ a. administrative.

administr|er /administre/ v.t. run, manage; (justice, biens, antidote, etc.) administer. **~ateur**, **~atrice** n.m., f. administrator, director. **~ation** n.f. administration. **A~ation**, Civil Service.

admirable /admirabl/ a. admirable.

admirati|f, **~ve** /admiratif, -v/ a. admiring.

admir|er /admire/ v.t. admire. **~ateur**, **~atrice** n.m., f. admirer. **~ation** n.f. admiration.

admissible /admisibl/ *a.* admissible; (*candidat*) eligible.

admission /admisjɔ̃/ *n.f.* admission.

adolescen|t, ~te /adɔlesɑ̃, -t/ *n.m., f.* adolescent. **~ce** *n.f.* adolescence.

adonner (s') /(s)adɔne/ *v. pr.* **s'~ à,** devote o.s. to; (*vice*) take to.

adopt|er /adɔpte/ *v.t.* adopt. **~ion** /-psjɔ̃/ *n.f.* adoption.

adopti|f, ~ve /adɔptif, -v/ *a.* (*enfant*) adopted; (*parents*) adoptive.

adorable /adɔrabl/ *a.* delightful, adorable.

ador|er /adɔre/ *v.t.* adore; (*relig.*) worship, adore. **~ation** *n.f.* adoration; worship.

adosser /adose/ *v.t.* **s'~** *v. pr.* lean back (**à, contre,** against)

adouci|r /adusir/ *v.t.* soften; (*boisson*) sweeten; (*personne*) mellow; (*chagrin*) ease. **s'~r** *v. pr.* soften; mellow; ease; (*temps*) become milder. **~ssant** *n.m.* (fabric) softener.

adresse /adrɛs/ *n.f.* address; (*habileté*) skill.

adresser /adrese/ *v.t.* send, (*écrire l'adresse sur*) address; (*remarque etc.*) address. **~ la parole à,** speak to. **s'~ à,** address; (*aller voir*) go and ask *ou* see; (*bureau*) enquire at; (*viser, intéresser*) be directed at.

adroit, ~e /adrwa, -t/ *a.* skilful, clever. **~ement** /-tmã/ *adv.* skilfully, cleverly.

aduler /adyle/ *v.t.* adulate.

adulte /adylt/ *n.m./f.* adult. **—**a.* adult; (*plante, animal*) fully-grown.

adultère /adyltɛr/ *a.* adulterous. **—***n.m.* adultery.

advenir /advənir/ *v.i.* occur.

adverbe /advɛrb/ *n.m* adverb.

adversaire /advɛrsɛr/ *n.m.* opponent, adversary.

adverse /advɛrs/ *a.* opposing.

adversité /advɛrsite/ *n.f.* adversity.

aérateur /aeratœr/ *n m* ventilator.

aér|er /aere/ *v.t.* air; (*texte*) lighten. **s'~er** *v. pr.* get some air. **~ation** *n.f* ventilation. **~é** *a.* airy.

aérien, ~ne /aerjɛ̃, -jɛn/ *a.* air; (*photo*) aerial; (*câble*) overhead; (*fig.*) airy.

aérobic /aerɔbik/ *m.* aerobics.

aérodrome /aerɔdrom/ *n.m.* aerodrome.

aérodynamique /aerɔdinamik/ *a.* streamlined, aerodynamic.

aérogare /aerɔgar/ *n.f.* air terminal.

aéroglisseur /aerɔglisœr/ *n.m.* hovercraft.

aérogramme /aerɔgram/ *n.m.* airmail letter; (*Amer.*) aerogram.

aéronautique /aerɔnotik/ *a.* aeronautical. **—***n.f.* aeronautics.

aéronavale /aerɔnaval/ *n.f.* Fleet Air Arm; (*Amer.*) Naval Air Force.

aéroport /aerɔpɔr/ *n.m.* airport.

aéroporté /aerɔpɔrte/ *a.* airborne.

aérosol /aerɔsɔl/ *n.m.* aerosol.

aérospat|ial (*m. pl.* **~iaux**) /aerɔspasjal, -jo/ *a.* aerospace.

affable /afabl/ *a.* affable.

affaibl|ir /afeblir/ *v.t.*, **s'~ir** *v. pr.* weaken. **~issement** *n m* weakening.

affaire /afɛr/ *n.f.* matter, affair; (*histoire*) affair; (*transaction*) deal; (*occasion*) bargain; (*firme*) business; (*jurid.*) case. **~s,** affairs; (*comm.*) business; (*effets*) belongings. **avoir ~ à,** (have) to deal with. **c'est mon ~, ce sont mes ~s,** that is my business. **faire l'~,** do the job. **tirer qn. d'~,** help s.o. out. **se tirer d'~,** manage.

affair|er (s') /(s)afere/ *v pr.* bustle about. **~é** *a.* busy.

affaiss|er (s') /(s)afese/ *v. pr.* (*sol*) sink, subside; (*poutre*) sag; (*personne*) collapse. **~ement** /-ɛsmã/ *n.m.* subsidence.

affaler (s') /(s)afale/ *v. pr.* slump (down), collapse.

affam|er /afame/ *v.t.* starve. **~é** *a.* starving.

affect|é /afɛkte/ *a.* affected. **~ation[1]** *n f* affectation.

affect|er /afɛkte/ *v.t.* (*feindre, émouvoir*) affect; (*destiner*) assign; (*nommer*) appoint, post. **~ation[2]** *n.f.* assignment; appointment, posting.

affecti|f, ~ve /afɛktif, -v/ *a.* emotional.

affection /afɛksjɔ̃/ *n.f.* affection; (*maladie*) ailment. **~ner** /-jɔne/ *v.t.* be fond of

affectueu|x, ~se /afɛktɥø, -z/ *a.* affectionate.

affermir /afɛrmir/ *v.t.* strengthen.

affiche /afiʃ/ *n.f.* (public) notice; (*publicité*) poster; (*théâtre*) bill.

affich|er /afiʃe/ *v.t.* (*announce*) put up; (*événement*) announce; (*sentiment etc.*, *comput.*) display. **~age** *n.m.* billposting; (*électronique*) display.

affilée (d') /(d)afile/ *adv.* in a row, at a stretch.

affiler /afile/ *v.t.* sharpen.

affil|ier (s') /(s)afilje/ *v. pr.* become affiliated. **~iation** *n.f.* affiliation.

affiner /afine/ *v.t.* refine.

affinité /afinite/ *n.f.* affinity.

affirmati|f, **~ve** /afirmatif, -v/ *a.* affirmative. —*n.f.* affirmative.

affirm|er /afirme/ *v.t.* assert. **~ation** *n.f.* assertion.

affleurer /aflœre/ *v.i.* appear on the surface.

affliction /afliksjɔ̃/ *n.f.* affliction.

afflig|er /afliʒe/ *v.t.* grieve. **~é** *a.* distressed. **~é de,** afflicted with.

affluence /aflyɑ̃s/ *n.f.* crowd(s).

affluent /aflyɑ̃/ *n.m.* tributary.

affluer /aflye/ *v.i.* flood in; (*sang*) rush.

afflux /afly/ *n.m.* influx, flood; (*du sang*) rush.

affol|er /afɔle/ *v.t.* throw into a panic. **s'~er** *v. pr.* panic. **~ant,** **~ante** *a.* alarming. **~ement** *n.m.* panic.

affranch|ir /afrɑ̃ʃir/ *v.t.* stamp; (*à la machine*) frank; (*esclave*) emancipate; (*fig.*) free. **~issement** *n.m.* (*tarif*) postage.

affréter /afrete/ *v.t.* charter.

affreu|x, **~se** /afrø, -z/ *a.* (*laid*) hideous; (*mauvais*) awful. **~sement** *adv.* awfully, hideously.

affriolant, **~e** /afrijɔlɑ̃, -t/ *a.* enticing.

affront /afrɔ̃/ *n.m.* affront.

affront|er /afrɔ̃te/ *v.t.* confront. **s'~er** *v. pr.* confront each other. **~ement** *n.m.* confrontation.

affubler /afyble/ *v.t.* rig out (**de,** in).

affût /afy/ *n.m.* **à l'~,** on the watch (**de,** for).

affûter /afyte/ *v.t.* sharpen.

afin /afɛ̃/ *prép. & conj.* **~ de/que,** in order to/that.

africain, **~e** /afrikɛ̃, -ɛn/ *a. & n.m.,* *f.* African.

Afrique /afrik/ *n.f.* Africa. **~ du Sud,** South Africa.

agacer /agase/ *v.t.* irritate, annoy.

âge /ɑʒ/ *n.m.* age. **quel ~ avez-vous?,** how old are you? **~ adulte,** adulthood. **~ mûr,** middle age. **d'un certain ~,** past one's prime.

âgé /ɑʒe/ *a.* elderly. **~ de cinq ans/***etc.*, five years/*etc.* old.

agence /aʒɑ̃s/ *n.f.* agency, bureau, office; (*succursale*) branch. **~ d'interim,** employment agency. **~ de voyages,** travel agency.

agenc|er /aʒɑ̃se/ *v.t.* organize, arrange. **~ement** *n.m.* organization.

agenda /aʒɛ̃da/ *n.m.* diary; (*Amer.*) datebook.

agenouiller (s') /(s)aʒnuje/ *v. pr.* kneel (down).

agent /aʒɑ̃/ *n.m.* agent; (*fonctionnaire*) official. **~ (de police),** policeman. **~ de change,** stockbroker.

agglomération /aglɔmerɑsjɔ̃/ *n.f.* built-up area, town.

aggloméré /aglɔmere/ *n.m.* (*bois*) chipboard.

agglomérer /aglɔmere/ *v.t.,* **s'~** *v. pr.* pile up.

agglutiner /aglytine/ *v.t.,* **s'~** *v. pr.* stick together.

aggraver /agrave/ *v.t.,* **s'~** *v. pr.* worsen.

agil|e /aʒil/ *a.* agile, nimble. **~ité** *n.f.* agility.

agir /aʒir/ *v.i.* act. **il s'agit de faire,** it is a matter of doing; (*il faut*) it is necessary to do. **dans ce livre il s'agit de,** this book is about. **dont il s'agit,** in question.

agissements /aʒismɑ̃/ *n.m. pl.* (*péj.*) dealings.

agité /aʒite/ *a.* restless, fidgety; (*troublé*) agitated; (*mer*) rough.

agit|er /aʒite/ *v.t.* (*bras etc.*) wave; (*liquide*) shake; (*troubler*) agitate; (*discuter*) debate. **s'~er** *v. pr.* bustle about; (*enfant*) fidget; (*foule, pensées*) stir. **~ateur,** **~atrice** *n.m., f.* agitator. **~ation** *n.f.* bustle; (*trouble*) agitation.

agneau (*pl.* **~x**) /aɲo/ *n.m.* lamb.

agonie /agɔni/ *n.f.* death throes.

agoniser /agɔnize/ *v.i.* be dying.

agraf|e /agraf/ *n.f.* hook; (*pour papiers*) staple. **~er** *v.t.* hook (up); staple. **~euse** *n.f.* stapler.

agrand|ir /agrɑ̃dir/ *v.t.* enlarge. **s'~ir** *v. pr.* expand, grow. **~issement** *n.m.* extension; (*de photo*) enlargement.

agréable /agreabl/ *a.* pleasant. **~ment** /-əmɑ̃/ *adv.* pleasantly.

agré|er /agree/ *v.t.* accept. **~er à,** please. **~é** *a.* authorized.

agrég|ation /agregɑsjɔ̃/ *n.f.* agrégation (*highest examination for recruitment of teachers*). **~é,** **~ée** /-ʒe/ *n.m., f.* agrégé (*teacher who has passed the agrégation*).

agrément /agremɑ̃/ *n.m.* charm; (*plaisir*) pleasure; (*accord*) assent.

agrémenter /agremɑ̃te/ *v.t.* embellish (**de,** with).

agrès /agrɛ/ *n.m. pl.* (gymnastics) apparatus.

agress|er /agrese/ *v.t.* attack. **~eur** /-ɛsœr/ *n.m.* attacker; (*mil.*) aggressor. **~ion** /-ɛsjɔ̃/ *n.f.* attack; (*mil.*) aggression.

agressi|f, **~ve** /agresif, -v/ *a.* aggressive. **~vité** *n.f.* aggressiveness.

agricole /agrikɔl/ *a.* agricultural; (*ouvrier etc.*) farm.

agriculteur /agrikyltœr/ *n.m.* farmer.

agriculture /agrikyltyr/ *n.f.* agriculture, farming.

agripper /agripe/ *v.t.*, **s'~ à**, grab, clutch.

agroalimentaire /agrɔalimɑ̃tɛr/ *n.m.* food industry.

agrumes /agrym/ *n.m. pl.* citrus fruit(s).

aguerrir /agerir/ *v.t.* harden.

aguets (aux) /(oz)agɛ/ *adv.* on the look-out.

aguicher /agiʃe/ *v.t.* entice.

ah /a/ *int.* ah, oh.

ahur|ir /ayrir/ *v.t.* dumbfound. **~issement** *n.m.* stupefaction.

ai /e/ *voir* **avoir**.

aide /ɛd/ *n.f.* help, assistance, aid. —*n.m./f.* assistant. **à l'~ de**, with the help of. **~ familiale**, home help. **~-mémoire** *n.m. invar.* handbook of facts. **~ sociale**, social security; (*Amer.*) welfare. **~ soignant, ~ soignante** *n.m., f.* auxiliary nurse. **venir en ~ à**, help.

aider /ede/ *v.t./i.* help, assist. **~ à faire**, help to do. **s'~ de**, use.

aïe /aj/ *int.* ouch, ow.

aïeul, ~e /ajœl/ *n.m., f.* grand-parent.

aïeux /ajø/ *n.m. pl.* forefathers.

aigle /ɛgl/ *n.m.* eagle.

aigr|e /ɛgr/ *a.* sour, sharp; (*fig.*) sharp. **~e-doux, ~e-douce** *a.* bitter-sweet. **~eur** *n.f.* sourness; (*fig.*) sharpness. **~eurs d'estomac**, heartburn.

aigrir /egrir/ *v.t.* embitter; (*caractère*) sour. **s'~** *v. pr.* turn sour; (*personne*) become embittered.

aigu, ~ë /egy/ *a.* acute; (*objet*) sharp; (*voix*) shrill. (*mus.*) **les ~s**, the high notes.

aiguillage /eguijaʒ/ *n.m.* (*rail.*) points; (*rail., Amer.*) switches.

aiguille /eguij/ *n.f.* needle; (*de montre*) hand; (*de balance*) pointer.

aiguill|er /eguije/ *v.t.* shunt; (*fig.*) steer. **~eur** *n.m.* pointsman; (*Amer.*) switchman. **~eur du ciel**, air traffic controller.

aiguillon /eguijɔ̃/ *n.m.* (*dard*) sting; (*fig.*) spur. **~ner** /-jɔne/ *v.t.* spur on.

aiguiser /eg(ɥ)ize/ *v.t.* sharpen; (*fig.*) stimulate.

ail (*pl.* **~s**) /aj/ *n.m.* garlic.

aile /ɛl/ *n.f.* wing.

ailé /ele/ *a.* winged.

aileron /ɛlrɔ̃/ *n.m.* (*de requin*) fin.

ailier /elje/ *n.m.* winger; (*Amer.*) end.

aille /aj/ *voir* **aller**[1].

ailleurs /ajœr/ *adv.* elsewhere. **d'~**, besides, moreover. **par ~**, moreover, furthermore. **partout ~**, everywhere else.

ailloli /ajɔli/ *n.m.* garlic mayonnaise.

aimable /ɛmabl/ *a.* kind. **~ment** /-əmɑ̃/ *adv.* kindly.

aimant[1] /ɛmɑ̃/ *n.m.* magnet. **~er** /-te/ *v.t.* magnetize.

aimant[2]**, ~e** /ɛmɑ̃, -t/ *a.* loving.

aimer /eme/ *v.t.* like; (*d'amour*) love. **j'aimerais faire**, I'd like to do. **~ bien**, quite like. **~ mieux** *ou* **autant**, prefer.

aine /ɛn/ *n.f.* groin.

aîné, ~e /ene/ *a.* eldest; (*entre deux*) elder. —*n.m., f.* eldest (child); elder (child). **~s** *n.m. pl.* elders. **il est mon ~**, he is older than me *ou* my senior.

ainsi /ɛ̃si/ *adv.* thus; (*donc*) so. **~ que**, as well as; (*comme*) as. **et ~ de suite**, and so on. **pour ~ dire**, so to speak, as it were.

air /ɛr/ *n.m.* air; (*mine*) look, air; (*mélodie*) tune. **~ conditionné**, air-conditioning. **avoir l'~ de**, look like. **avoir l'~ de faire**, appear to be doing. **en l'~**, (up) in the air; (*promesses etc.*) empty.

aire /ɛr/ *n.f.* area. **~ d'atterrissage**, landing-strip.

aisance /ɛzɑ̃s/ *n.f.* ease; (*richesse*) affluence.

aise /ɛz/ *n.f.* joy. —*a.* **bien ~ de/que**, delighted about/that. **à l'~**, (*sur un siège*) comfortable; (*pas gêné*) at ease; (*fortuné*) comfortably off. **mal à l'~**, uncomfortable; ill at ease. **aimer ses ~s**, like one's comforts. **se mettre à l'~**, make o.s. comfortable.

aisé /eze/ *a.* easy; (*fortuné*) well-off. **~ment** *adv.* easily.

aisselle /ɛsɛl/ *n.f.* armpit.

ait /ɛ/ *voir* **avoir**.

ajonc /aʒɔ̃/ *n.m.* gorse.

ajourn|er /aʒurne/ *v.t.* postpone; (*assemblée*) adjourn. **~ement** *n.m.* postponement; adjournment.

ajout /aʒu/ *n.m.* addition.

ajouter /aʒute/ *v.t.*, **s'~** *v. pr.* add (à, to). **~ foi à**, lend credence to.

ajust|er /aʒyste/ *v.t.* adjust; (*coup*) aim; (*cible*) aim at; (*adapter*) fit. **s'~er** *v. pr.* fit. **~age** *n.m.* fitting. **~é** *a.* close-fitting. **~ement** *n.m.* adjustment. **~eur** *n.m.* fitter.

alambic /alɑ̃bik/ *n.m.* still.

alanguir (s') /(s)alɑ̃gir/ *v. pr.* grow languid.

alarme /alarm/ *n.f.* alarm. **donner l'~,** sound the alarm.

alarmer /alarme/ *v.t.* alarm. **s'~** *v. pr.* become alarmed (**de,** at).

alarmiste /alarmist/ *a. & n.m.* alarmist.

albâtre /albɑtr/ *n.m.* alabaster.

albatros /albatros/ *n.m.* albatross.

album /albɔm/ *n.m.* album.

albumine /albymin/ *n.f.* albumin.

alcali /alkali/ *n.m.* alkali.

alcool /alkɔl/ *n.m.* alcohol; (*eau de vie*) brandy. **~ à brûler,** methylated spirit. **~ique** *a. & n.m./f.* alcoholic. **~isé** *a.* (*boisson*) alcoholic. **~isme** *n.m.* alcoholism.

alcootest /alkɔtɛst/ *n.m.* (P.) breath test; (*appareil*) breathalyser.

alcôve /alkov/ *n.f.* alcove.

aléa /alea/ *n.m.* hazard.

aléatoire /aleatwar/ *a.* uncertain; (*comput.*) random.

alentour /alɑ̃tur/ *adv.* around. **~s** *n.m. pl.* surroundings. **aux ~s de,** round about.

alerte /alɛrt/ *a.* agile. —*n.f.* alert. **~ à la bombe,** bomb scare.

alerter /alɛrte/ *v.t.* alert.

algarade /algarad/ *n.f.* altercation.

algèbre /alʒɛbr/ *n.f.* algebra. **~ébrique** *a.* algebraic.

Alger /alʒe/ *n.m./f.* Algiers.

Algérie /alʒeri/ *n.f.* Algeria.

algérien, ~ne /alʒerjɛ̃, -jɛn/ *a. & n.m., f.* Algerian.

algue /alg/ *n.f.* seaweed. **les ~s,** (*bot.*) algae.

alias /aljɑs/ *adv.* alias.

alibi /alibi/ *n.m.* alibi.

aliéné, ~e /aljene/ *n.m., f.* insane person.

alién|er /aljene/ *v.t.* alienate; (*céder*) give up. **s'~er** *v. pr.* alienate. **~ation** *n.f.* alienation.

aligner /aliɲe/ *v.t.* (*objets*) line up, make lines of; (*chiffres*) string together. **~ sur,** bring into line with. **s'~** *v. pr.* line up. **s'~ sur,** align o.s. on. **alignement** /-əmɑ̃/ *n.m.* alignment.

aliment /alimɑ̃/ *n.m.* food. **~aire** /-tɛr/ *a.* food; (*fig.*) bread-and-butter.

aliment|er /alimɑ̃te/ *v.t.* feed; (*fournir*) supply; (*fig.*) sustain. **~ation** *n.f.* feeding; supply(ing); (*régime*) diet; (*aliments*) groceries.

alinéa /alinea/ *n.m.* paragraph.

aliter (s') /(s)alite/ *v. pr.* take to one's bed.

allaiter /alete/ *v.t.* feed. **~ au biberon,**

bottle-feed. **~ au sein,** breast-feed; (*Amer.*) nurse.

allant /alɑ̃/ *n.m.* verve, drive.

allécher /aleʃe/ *v.t.* tempt.

allée /ale/ *n.f.* path, lane; (*menant à une maison*) drive(way). **~s et venues,** comings and goings.

allégation /alegasjɔ̃/ *n.f.* allegation.

allég|er /aleʒe/ *v.t.* make lighter; (*poids*) lighten; (*fig.*) alleviate. **~é** *a.* (*diététique*) light.

allègre /alɛgr/ *a.* gay; (*vif*) lively, jaunty.

allégresse /alegrɛs/ *n.f.* gaiety.

alléguer /alege/ *v.t.* put forward.

Allemagne /almaɲ/ *n.f.* Germany. **~ de l'Ouest,** West Germany.

allemand, ~e /almɑ̃, -d/ *a. & n.m., f.* German. —*n.m.* (*lang.*) German.

aller[1]† /ale/ (*aux. être*) go. **s'en ~** *v. pr.* go away. **~ à,** (*convenir à*) suit; (*s'adapter à*) fit. **~ faire,** be going to do. **comment allez-vous?, (comment) ça va?,** how are you? **ça va!,** all right! **il va bien,** he is well. **il va mieux,** he's better. **allez-y!,** go on! **allez!,** come on! **allons-y!,** let's go!

aller[2] /ale/ *n.m.* outward journey; **~ (simple),** single (ticket); (*Amer.*) one-way (ticket). **~ (et) retour,** return journey; (*Amer.*) round trip; (*billet*) return (ticket); (*Amer.*) round trip (ticket).

allerg|ie /alɛrʒi/ *n.f.* allergy. **~ique** *a.* allergic.

alliage /aljaʒ/ *n.m.* alloy.

alliance /aljɑ̃s/ *n.f.* alliance; (*bague*) wedding-ring; (*mariage*) marriage.

allié, ~e /alje/ *n.m., f.* ally; (*parent*) relative (by marriage).

allier /alje/ *v.t.* combine; (*pol.*) ally. **s'~** *v. pr.* combine; (*pol.*) become allied; (*famille*) become related (**à,** to).

alligator /aligatɔr/ *n.m.* alligator.

allô /alo/ *int.* hallo, hello.

allocation /alɔkasjɔ̃/ *n.f.* allowance. **~ (de) chômage,** unemployment benefit. **~s familiales,** family allowance.

allocution /alɔkysjɔ̃/ *n.f.* speech.

allongé /alɔ̃ʒe/ *a.* elongated.

allongement /alɔ̃ʒmɑ̃/ *n.m.* lengthening.

allonger /alɔ̃ʒe/ *v.t.* lengthen; (*bras, jambe*) stretch (out). **s'~** *v. pr.* get longer; (*s'étendre*) stretch (o.s.) out.

allouer /alwe/ *v.t.* allocate.

allum|er /alyme/ *v.t.* light; (*radio, lampe, etc.*) turn on; (*pièce*) switch the light(s) on in; (*fig.*) arouse. **s'~er** *v. pr.* (*lumière*) come on. **~age** *n.m.* lighting;

(*auto.*) ignition. **~e-gaz** *n.m. invar.* gas lighter.

allumette /alymɛt/ *n.f.* match.

allure /alyr/ *n.f.* speed, pace; (*démarche*) walk; (*prestance*) bearing; (*air*) look. **à toute ~**, at full speed. **avoir de l'~**, have style.

allusion /alyzjɔ̃/ *n.f.* allusion (**à**, to); (*implicite*) hint (**à**, at). **faire ~ à**, allude to; hint at.

almanach /almana/ *n.m.* almanac.

aloi /alwa/ *n.m.* **de bon ~**, sterling; (*gaieté*) wholesome.

alors /alɔr/ *adv.* then. —*conj.* so, then. **~ que**, when, while; (*tandis que*) whereas. **ça ~!**, well! **et ~?**, so what?

alouette /alwɛt/ *n.f.* lark.

alourdir /alurdir/ *v.t.* weigh down.

aloyau (*pl.* **~x**) /alwajo/ *n.m.* sirloin.

alpage /alpaʒ/ *n.m.* mountain pasture.

Alpes /alp/ *n.f. pl.* **les ~**, the Alps.

alpestre /alpɛstr/ *a.* alpine.

alphab|et /alfabɛ/ *n.m.* alphabet. **~étique** *a.* alphabetical.

alphabétiser /alfabetize/ *v.t.* teach to read and write.

alphanumérique /alfanymerik/ *a.* alphanumeric.

alpin, ~e /alpɛ̃, -in/ *a.* alpine.

alpinis|te /alpinist/ *n.m./f.* mountaineer. **~me** *n.m.* mountaineering.

altér|er /altere/ *v.t.* falsify; (*abîmer*) spoil; (*donner soif à*) make thirsty. **s'~er** *v. pr.* deteriorate. **~ation** *n.f.* deterioration.

alternati|f, ~ve /alternatif, -v/ *a.* alternating. —*n.f.* alternative. **~vement** *adv.* alternately.

altern|er /alterne/ *v.t./i.* alternate. **~ance** *n.f.* alternation. **en ~ance**, alternately. **~é** *a.* alternate.

Altesse /altɛs/ *n.f.* Highness.

alt|ier, ~ière /altje, -jɛr/ *a.* haughty.

altitude /altityd/ *n.f.* altitude, height.

alto /alto/ *n.m.* viola.

aluminium /alyminjɔm/ *n.m.* aluminium; (*Amer.*) aluminum.

alvéole /alveɔl/ *n.f.* (*de ruche*) cell.

amabilité /amabilite/ *n.f.* kindness.

amadouer /amadwe/ *v.t.* win over.

amaigr|ir /amegrir/ *v.t.* make thin(ner). **~issant, ~issante** *a.* (*régime*) slimming.

amalgam|e /amalgam/ *n.m.* combination. **~er** *v.t.* combine, amalgamate.

amande /amɑ̃d/ *n.f.* almond; (*d'un fruit à noyau*) kernel.

amant /amɑ̃/ *n.m.* lover.

amarr|e /amar/ *n.f.* (mooring) rope. **~es**, moorings. **~er** *v.t.* moor.

amas /ama/ *n.m.* heap, pile.

amasser /amase/ *v.t.* amass, gather; (*empiler*) pile up. **s'~** *v. pr.* pile up; (*gens*) gather.

amateur /amatœr/ *n.m.* amateur. **~ de**, lover of. **d'~**, amateur; (*péj.*) amateurish. **~isme** *n.m.* amateurism.

amazone (en) /(ɑ̃)amazon/ *adv.* side-saddle.

Amazonie /amazoni/ *n.f.* Amazonia.

ambages (sans) /(sɑ̃z)ɑ̃baʒ/ *adv.* in plain language.

ambassade /ɑ̃basad/ *n.f.* embassy.

ambassa|deur, ~drice /ɑ̃basadœr, -dris/ *n.m., f.* ambassador.

ambiance /ɑ̃bjɑ̃s/ *n.f.* atmosphere.

ambiant, ~e /ɑ̃bjɑ̃, -t/ *a.* surrounding.

ambigu, ~ë /ɑ̃bigy/ *a.* ambiguous. **~ité** /-ɥite/ *n.f.* ambiguity.

ambitieu|x, ~se /ɑ̃bisjø, -z/ *a.* ambitious.

ambition /ɑ̃bisjɔ̃/ *n.f.* ambition. **~ner** /-jɔne/ *v.t.* have as one's ambition (**de**, to).

ambivalent, ~e /ɑ̃bivalɑ̃, -t/ *a.* ambivalent.

ambre /ɑ̃br/ *n.m.* amber.

ambulanc|e /ɑ̃bylɑ̃s/ *n.f.* ambulance. **~ier, ~ière** *n.m., f.* ambulance driver.

ambulant, ~e /ɑ̃bylɑ̃, -t/ *a.* itinerant.

âme /am/ *n.f.* soul. **~ sœur**, soul mate.

amélior|er /ameljɔre/ *v.t.*, **s'~er** *v. pr.* improve. **~ation** *n.f.* improvement.

aménag|er /amenaʒe/ *v.t.* (*arranger*) fit out; (*transformer*) convert; (*installer*) fit up; (*territoire*) develop. **~ement** *n.m.* fitting out; conversion; fitting up; development; (*modification*) adjustment.

amende /amɑ̃d/ *n.f.* fine. **faire ~ honorable**, make an apology.

amend|er /amɑ̃de/ *v.t.* improve; (*jurid.*) amend. **s'~er** *v. pr.* mend one's ways. **~ement** *n.m.* (*de texte*) amendment.

amener /amne/ *v.t.* bring; (*causer*) bring about. **~ qn. à faire**, cause sb. to do. **s'~** *v. pr.* (*fam.*) come along.

amenuiser (s') /(s)amənɥize/ *v. pr.* dwindle.

amer, amère /amɛr/ *a.* bitter.

américain, ~e /amerikɛ̃, -ɛn/ *a. & n.m., f.* American.

Amérique /amerik/ *n.f.* America. **~ centrale/latine**, Central/Latin America. **~ du Nord/Sud**, North/South America.

amertume /amɛrtym/ *n.f.* bitterness.

ameublement /amœbləmɑ̃/ n.m. furniture.

ameuter /amøte/ v.t. draw a crowd of; (fig.) stir up.

ami, ~e /ami/ n.m., f. friend; (de la nature, des livres, etc.) lover. —a. friendly.

amiable /amjabl/ a. amicable. à l'~ adv. amicably; a. amicable.

amiante /amjɑ̃t/ n.m. asbestos.

amic|al (m. pl. ~aux) /amikal, -o/ a. friendly. ~alement adv. in a friendly manner.

amicale /amikal/ n.f. association.

amidon /amidɔ̃/ n.m. starch. ~ner /-ɔne/ v.t. starch.

amincir /amɛ̃sir/ v.t. make thinner. s'~ v. pr. get thinner.

amir|al (pl. ~aux) /amiral, -o/ n.m. admiral.

amitié /amitje/ n.f. friendship. ~s, kind regards. prendre en ~, take a liking to.

ammoniac /amɔnjak/ n.m. (gaz) ammonia.

ammoniaque /amɔnjak/ n.f. (eau) ammonia.

amnésie /amnezi/ n.f. amnesia.

amnistie /amnisti/ n.f. amnesty.

amniocentèse /amniɔsɛ̃tɛz/ n.f. amniocentesis.

amocher /amɔʃe/ v.t. (fam.) mess up.

amoindrir /amwɛ̃drir/ v.t. diminish.

amollir /amɔlir/ v.t. soften.

amonceler /amɔ̃sle/ v.t., s'~ v.pr. pile up.

amont (en) /(ɑ̃n)amɔ̃/ adv. upstream.

amorc|e /amɔrs/ n.f. bait; (début) start; (explosif) fuse, cap; (de pistolet d'enfant) cap. ~er v.t. start; (hameçon) bait; (pompe) prime.

amorphe /amɔrf/ a. (mou) listless.

amortir /amɔrtir/ v.t. (choc) cushion; (bruit) deaden; (dette) pay off; (objet acheté) make pay for itself.

amortisseur /amɔrtisœr/ n.m. shock absorber.

amour /amur/ n.m. love. pour l'~ de, for the sake of. ~-propre n.m. self-respect.

amouracher (s') /(s)amuraʃe/ v. pr. become infatuated (de, with).

amoureu|x, ~se /amurø, -z/ a. (ardent) amorous; (vie) love. —n.m., f. lover. ~x de qn., in love with s.o.

amovible /amɔvibl/ a. removable.

ampère /ɑ̃pɛr/ n.m. amp(ere).

amphibie /ɑ̃fibi/ a. amphibious.

amphithéâtre /ɑ̃fiteatr/ n.m. amphitheatre; (d'université) lecture hall.

ample /ɑ̃pl/ a. ample; (mouvement) broad. ~ment /-əmɑ̃/ adv. amply.

ampleur /ɑ̃plœr/ n.f. extent, size; (de vêtement) fullness.

ampli /ɑ̃pli/ n.m. amplifier.

amplif|ier /ɑ̃plifje/ v.t. amplify; (fig.) expand, develop. s'~ier v.pr. expand, develop. ~icateur n.m. amplifier.

ampoule /ɑ̃pul/ n.f. (électrique) bulb; (sur la peau) blister; (de médicament) phial.

ampoulé /ɑ̃pule/ a. turgid.

amput|er /ɑ̃pyte/ v.t. amputate; (fig.) reduce. ~ation n.f. amputation; (fig.) reduction.

amuse-gueule /amyzgœl/ n.m. invar. appetizer.

amus|er /amyze/ v.t. amuse; (détourner l'attention de) distract. s'~er v. pr. enjoy o.s.; (jouer) play. ~ant, ~ante a. (blague) funny; (soirée) enjoyable, entertaining. ~ement n.m. amusement; (passe-temps) diversion. ~eur n.m. (péj.) entertainer.

amygdale /amidal/ n.f. tonsil.

an /ɑ̃/ n.m. year. avoir dix/etc. ans, be ten/etc. years old.

anachronisme /anakrɔnism/ n.m. anachronism.

analgésique /analʒezik/ a. & n.m. analgesic.

analog|ie /analɔʒi/ n.f. analogy. ~ique a. analogical, (comput.) analogue.

analogue /analɔg/ a. similar.

analphabète /analfabɛt/ a. & n.m./f. illiterate.

analy|se /analiz/ n.f. analysis; (de sang) test. ~ser v.t. analyse. ~ste n.m./f. analyst. ~tique a. analytical.

ananas /anana(s)/ n.m. pineapple.

anarch|ie /anarʃi/ n.f. anarchy. ~ique a. anarchic. ~iste n.m./f. anarchist.

anatom|ie /anatɔmi/ n.f. anatomy. ~ique a. anatomical.

ancestr|al (m. pl. ~aux) /ɑ̃sɛstral, -o/ a. ancestral.

ancêtre /ɑ̃sɛtr/ n.m. ancestor.

anche /ɑ̃ʃ/ n.f. (mus.) reed.

anchois /ɑ̃ʃwa/ n.m. anchovy.

ancien, ~ne /ɑ̃sjɛ̃, -jɛn/ a. old; (de jadis) ancient; (meuble) antique; (précédent) former, ex- , old; (dans une fonction) senior. —n.m., f. senior; (par l'âge) elder. ~ combattant, ex-serviceman. ~nement /-jɛnmɑ̃/ adv. formerly. ~neté /-jɛnte/ n.f. age; seniority.

ancr|e /ɑ̃kr/ n.f. anchor. **jeter/lever**

l'~e, cast/weigh anchor. ~er v.t.
anchor; (fig.) fix. s'~er v.pr. anchor.
andouille /ãduj/ n.f. sausage filled with
chitterlings; (idiot: fam.) nitwit.
âne /ɑn/ n.m. donkey, ass; (imbécile)
ass.
anéantir /aneãtir/ v.t. destroy;
(exterminer) annihilate; (accabler)
overwhelm.
anecdot|e /anɛkdɔt/ n.f. anecdote.
~ique a. anecdotal.
ané|mie /anemi/ n.f. anaemia. ~ié,
~ique adjs. anaemic.
ânerie /ɑnri/ n.f. stupidity; (parole)
stupid remark.
ânesse /ɑnɛs/ n.f. she-ass.
anesthés|ie /anɛstezi/ n.f. (opération)
anaesthetic. ~ique a. & n.m (substance) anaesthetic.
ang|e /ãʒ/ n.m. angel. aux ~es, in
seventh heaven. ~élique a. angelic.
angélus /ãʒelys/ n.m. angelus.
angine /ãʒin/ n.f. throat infection.
anglais, ~e /ãglɛ, -z/ a. English. —n.m.,
f. Englishman, Englishwoman. — n.m.
(lang.) English.
angle /ãgl/ n.m. angle; (coin) corner.
Angleterre /ãglətɛr/ n.f. England.
anglicisme /ãglisism/ n.m. anglicism.
angliciste /ãglisist/ n.m./f. English
specialist.
anglo- /ãglɔ/ préf. Anglo-.
anglophone /ãglɔfɔn/ a. English-speak-
ing. —n.m./f. English speaker.
anglo-saxon, ~e /ãglɔsaksɔ̃, -ɔn/ a.
& n.m., f. Anglo-Saxon.
angoiss|e /ãgwas/ n.f. anxiety. ~ant,
~ante a. harrowing. ~é a. anxious.
~er v.t. make anxious.
anguille /ãgij/ n.f. eel.
anguleux, ~se /ãgylø, z/ a. (traits)
angular.
anicroche /anikrɔʃ/ n.f. snag.
anim|al (pl. ~aux) /animal, -o/ n.m.
animal. —a. (m. pl. ~aux) animal.
anima|teur, ~trice /animatœr, -tris/
n.m., f. organizer, leader; (TV) host,
hostess.
anim|é /anime/ a. lively; (affairé) busy,
(être) animate. ~ation n.f. liveliness;
(affairement) activity; (cinéma) anima-
tion.
animer /anime/ v.t. liven up; (mener)
lead; (mouvoir, pousser) drive;
(encourager) spur on. s'~ v. pr. liven
up.
animosité /animozite/ n.f. animosity.
anis /anis/ n.m. (parfum, boisson)
aniseed.

ankylos|er (s') /(s)ãkiloze/ v. pr. go stiff.
~é a. stiff.
anneau (pl. ~x) /ano/ n.m. ring; (de
chaîne) link.
année /ane/ n.f. year.
annexe /anɛks/ a. attached; (question)
related; (bâtiment) adjoining. —n.f.
annexe; (Amer.) annex.
annex|er /anɛkse/ v.t. annex; (document)
attach. ~ion n.f. annexation.
annihiler /aniile/ v.t. annihilate.
anniversaire /anivɛrsɛr/ n.m. birthday;
(d'un événement) anniversary. —a.
anniversary.
annonc|e /anɔ̃s/ n.f. announcement;
(publicitaire) advertisement; (indice)
sign. ~er v.t. announce; (dénoter)
indicate. s'~er bien/mal, look
good/bad. ~eur n.m. advertiser;
(speaker) announcer.
Annonciation /anɔ̃sjasjɔ̃/ n.f. l'~, the
Annunciation.
annuaire /anɥɛr/ n.m. year book. ~
(téléphonique), (telephone) directory.
annuel, ~le /anɥɛl/ a. annual, yearly.
~lement adv. annually, yearly.
annuité /anɥite/ n.f. annual payment.
annulaire /anylɛr/ n.m. ringfinger.
annul|er /anyle/ v.t. cancel; (contrat)
nullify; (jugement) quash. s'~er v. pr.
cancel each other out. ~ation n.f. can-
cellation.
anodin, ~e /anɔdɛ̃, -in/ a. insignificant; (blessure) harmless.
anomalie /anɔmali/ n.f. anomaly.
ânonner /anɔne/ v.t./i. mumble, drone.
anonymat /anɔnima/ n.m. anonymity.
anonyme /anɔnim/ a. anonymous.
anorak /anɔrak/ n.m. anorak.
anorexie /anɔreksi/ n.f. anorexia.
anorm|al (m, pl. ~aux) /anɔrmal, -o/
a. abnormal.
anse /ãs/ n.f. handle; (baie) cove.
antagonis|me /ãtagɔnism/ n.m. an-
tagonism. ~te n.m./f. antagonist; a.
antagonistic.
antan (d') /(d)ãtã/ a. of long ago.
antarctique /ãtarktik/ a. & n.m.
Antarctic.
antenne /ãtɛn/ n.f. aerial; (Amer.)
antenna; (d'insecte) antenna; (succursale) agency; (mil.) outpost; (auto.,
méd.) emergency unit. à l'~, on the air.
sur l'~ de, on the wavelength of.
antérieur /ãterjœr/ a. previous, earlier;
(placé devant) front. ~ à, prior to.
~ement adv. earlier. ~ement à, prior
to. **antériorité** /-jɔrite/ n.f. precedence.
anthologie /ãtɔlɔʒi/ n.f. anthology.

anthropolo|gie /ɑ̃trɔpɔlɔʒi/ *n.f.* anthropology. **~gue** *n.m./f.* anthropologist.

anthropophage /ɑ̃trɔpɔfaʒ/ *a.* cannibalistic. —*n.m./f.* cannibal.

anti- /ɑ̃ti/ *préf.* anti-.

antiadhési|f, ~ve /ɑ̃tiaedzif, -v/ *a.* non-stick.

antiaérien, ~ne /ɑ̃tiaerjɛ̃, -jɛn/ *a.* anti-aircraft. **abri ~,** air-raid shelter.

antiatomique /ɑ̃tiatɔmik/ *a.* **abri ~,** fall-out shelter.

antibiotique /ɑ̃tibjɔtik/ *n.m.* antibiotic.

anticancéreu|x, ~se /ɑ̃tikɑ̃serø, -z/ *a.* (anti-)cancer.

antichambre /ɑ̃tiʃɑ̃br/ *n.f.* waiting-room, antechamber.

anticipation /ɑ̃tisipasjɔ̃/ *n.f.* **d'~,** (*livre, film*) science fiction. **par ~,** in advance.

anticipé /ɑ̃tisipe/ *a.* early.

anticiper /ɑ̃tisipe/ *v.t./i.* **~ (sur),** anticipate.

anticonceptionnel, ~le /ɑ̃tikɔ̃sɛpsjɔnɛl/ *a.* contraceptive.

anticorps /ɑ̃tikɔr/ *n.m.* antibody.

anticyclone /ɑ̃tisyklon/ *n.m.* anticyclone.

antidater /ɑ̃tidate/ *v.t.* backdate, antedate.

antidote /ɑ̃tidɔt/ *n.m.* antidote.

antigel /ɑ̃tiʒɛl/ *n.m.* antifreeze.

antihistaminique /ɑ̃tiistaminik/ *a. & n.m.* antihistamine.

antillais, ~e /ɑ̃tijɛ, -z/ *a. & n.m., f.* West Indian.

Antilles /ɑ̃tij/ *n.f. pl.* **les ~,** the West Indies.

antilope /ɑ̃tilɔp/ *n.f.* antelope.

antimite /ɑ̃timit/ *n.m.* moth repellent.

antipath|ie /ɑ̃tipati/ *n.f.* antipathy. **~ique** *a.* unpleasant.

antipodes /ɑ̃tipɔd/ *n.m. pl.* antipodes. **aux ~ de,** (*fig.*) poles apart from.

antiquaire /ɑ̃tikɛr/ *n.m./f.* antique dealer.

antiqu|e /ɑ̃tik/ *a.* ancient. **~ité** *n.f.* antiquity; (*objet*) antique.

antirouille /ɑ̃tiruj/ *a. & n.m.* rustproofing.

antisémit|e /ɑ̃tisemit/ *a.* anti-Semitic. **~isme** *n.m.* anti-Semitism.

antiseptique /ɑ̃tisɛptik/ *a. & n.m.* antiseptic.

antithèse /ɑ̃titɛz/ *n.f.* antithesis.

antivol /ɑ̃tivɔl/ *n.m.* anti-theft lock *ou* device.

antre /ɑ̃tr/ *n.m.* den.

anus /anys/ *n.m.* anus.

anxiété /ɑ̃ksjete/ *n.f.* anxiety.

anxieu|x, ~se /ɑ̃ksjø, -z/ *a.* anxious. —*n.m., f.* worrier.

août /u(t)/ *n.m.* August.

apais|er /apeze/ *v.t.* calm down, (*douleur, colère*) soothe (*faim*) appease. **s'~er** *v. pr.* (*tempête*) die down. **~ement** *n.m.* appeasement; soothing. **~ements** *n.m. pl.* reassurances.

apanage /apanaʒ/ *n.m.* **l'~ de,** the privilege of.

aparté /aparte/ *n.m.* private exchange; (*théâtre*) aside. **en ~,** in private.

apath|ie /apati/ *n.f.* apathy. **~ique** *a.* apathetic.

apatride /apatrid/ *n.m./f.* stateless person.

apercevoir† /apɛrsəvwar/ *v.t.* see. **s'~ de,** notice. **s'~ que,** notice *ou* realize that.

aperçu /apɛrsy/ *n.m.* general view *ou* idea; (*intuition*) insight.

apéritif /aperitif/ *n.m.* aperitif.

à-peu-près /apøprɛ/ *n.m. invar.* approximation.

apeuré /apœre/ *a.* scared.

aphone /afɔn/ *a.* voiceless.

aphte /aft/ *n.m.* mouth ulcer.

apit|oyer /apitwaje/ *v.t.* move (to pity). **s'~oyer sur,** feel pity for. **~oiement** *n.m.* pity.

aplanir /aplanir/ *v.t.* level; (*fig.*) smooth out.

aplatir /aplatir/ *v.t.* flatten (out). **s'~** *v. pr.* (*s'allonger*) lie flat; (*s'humilier*) grovel; (*tomber: fam.*) fall flat on one's face.

aplomb /aplɔ̃/ *n.m.* balance; (*fig.*) self-possession. **d'~,** (*en équilibre*) steady, balanced.

apogée /apɔʒe/ *n.m.* peak.

apologie /apɔlɔʒi/ *n.f.* vindication.

a posteriori /apɔsterjɔri/ *adv.* after the event.

apostolique /apɔstɔlik/ *a.* apostolic.

apostroph|e /apɔstrɔf/ *n.f.* apostrophe; (*appel*) sharp address. **~er** *v.t.* address sharply.

apothéose /apɔteoz/ *n.f.* final triumph.

apôtre /apotr/ *n.m.* apostle.

apparaître† /aparɛtr/ *v.i.* appear. **il apparaît que,** it appears that.

apparat /apara/ *n.m.* pomp. **d'~,** ceremonial.

appareil /aparɛj/ *n.m.* apparatus; (*électrique*) appliance; (*anat.*) system; (*téléphonique*) phone; (*dentaire*) brace; (*auditif*) hearing-aid; (*avion*) plane; (*culin.*) mixture. **l'~ du parti,** the party machinery. **c'est Gabriel à l'~,** it's

Gabriel on the phone. ∿(-photo), camera. ∿ électroménager, household electrical appliance.

appareiller¹ /apareje/ *v.i.* (*navire*) cast off, put to sea.

appareiller² /apareje/ *v.t.* (*assortir*) match.

apparemment /aparamã/ *adv.* apparently.

apparence /aparãs/ *n.f.* appearance. **en ∿**, outwardly; (*apparemment*) apparently.

apparent, ∿e /aparã, -t/ *a.* apparent; (*visible*) conspicuous.

apparenté /aparãte/ *a.* related; (*semblable*) similar.

appariteur /aparitœr/ *n.m.* (*univ.*) attendant, porter.

apparition /aparisjɔ̃/ *n.f.* appearance; (*spectre*) apparition.

appartement /apartəmã/ *n.m.* flat; (*Amer.*) apartment.

appartenance /apartənãs/ *n.f.* membership (à, of), belonging (à, to).

appartenir† /apartənir/ *v.i.* belong (à, to). **il lui/vous/***etc.* **appartient de**, it is up to him/you/*etc.* to.

appât /apa/ *n.m.* bait; (*fig.*) lure. **∿er** /-te/ *v.t.* lure.

appauvrir /apovrir/ *v.t.* impoverish. **s'∿** *v. pr.* grow impoverished.

appel /apɛl/ *n.m.* call; (*jurid.*) appeal; (*mil.*) call-up. **faire ∿**, appeal. **faire ∿ à**, (*recourir à*) call on; (*invoquer*) appeal to; (*évoquer*) call up; (*exiger*) call for. **faire l'∿**, (*scol.*) call the register; (*mil.*) take a roll-call. **∿ d'offres**, (*comm.*) invitation to tender. **faire un ∿ de phares**, flash one's headlights.

appelé /aple/ *n.m.* conscript.

appel|er /aple/ *v.t.* call; (*nécessiter*) call for. **s'∿er** *v. pr.* be called. **∿é à**, (*désigné à*) marked out for. **en ∿er à**, appeal to. **il s'appelle**, his name is. **∿lation** /apelasjɔ̃/ *n.f.* designation.

appendic|e /apɛ̃dis/ *n.m.* appendix. **∿ite** *n.f.* appendicitis.

appentis /apãti/ *n.m.* lean-to.

appesantir /apəzãtir/ *v.t.* weigh down. **s'∿** *v. pr.* grow heavier. **s'∿ sur**, dwell upon.

appétissant, ∿e /apetisã, -t/ *a.* appetizing.

appétit /apeti/ *n.m.* appetite.

applaud|ir /aplodir/ *v.t./i.* applaud. **∿ir à**, applaud. **∿issements** *n.m. pl.* applause.

applique /aplik/ *n.f.* wall lamp.

appliqué /aplike/ *a.* painstaking.

appliquer /aplike/ *v.t.* apply; (*loi*) enforce. **s'∿** *v. pr.* apply o.s. (à, to). **s'∿ à**, (*concerner*) apply to. **applicable** /-abl/ *a.* applicable. **application** /-asjɔ̃/ *n.f.* application.

appoint /apwɛ̃/ *n.m.* contribution. **d'∿**, extra. **faire l'∿**, give the correct money.

appointements /apwɛ̃tmã/ *n.m. pl.* salary.

apport /apɔr/ *n.m.* contribution.

apporter /apɔrte/ *v.t.* bring.

apposer /apoze/ *v.t.* affix.

appréciable /apresjabl/ *a.* appreciable.

apprécI|er /apresje/ *v.t.* appreciate; (*évaluer*) appraise. **∿iation** *n.f.* appreciation; appraisal.

appréhen|der /apreãde/ *v.t.* dread, fear; (*arrêter*) apprehend. **∿sion** *n.f.* apprehension.

apprendre† /aprãdr/ *v.t./i.* learn; (*être informé de*) hear of. **∿ qch. à qn.**, teach s.o. sth.; (*informer*) tell s.o. sth. **∿ à faire**, learn to do. **∿ à qn. à faire**, teach s.o. to do. **∿ que**, learn that, (*être informé*) hear that.

apprenti, ∿e /aprãti/ *n.m., f.* apprentice.

apprentissage /aprãtisaʒ/ *n.m.* apprenticeship; (*d'un sujet*) learning.

apprêté /aprete/ *a.* affected.

apprêter /aprete/ *v.t., s'∿** *v. pr.* prepare.

apprivoiser /aprivwaze/ *v.t.* tame.

approba|teur, ∿trice /aprɔbatœr, -tris/ *a.* approving.

approbation /aprɔbasjɔ̃/ *n.f.* approval.

approchant, ∿e /aprɔʃã, -t/ *a.* close, similar.

approche /aprɔʃ/ *n.f.* approach.

approché /aprɔʃe/ *a.* approximate.

approcher /aprɔʃe/ *v.t.* (*objet*) move near(er) (**de**, to); (*personne*) approach. **—***v.i.* **∿ (de)**, approach. **s'∿ de**, approach, move near(er) to.

approfond|ir /aprɔfɔ̃dir/ *v.t.* deepen; (*fig.*) go into thoroughly. **∿i** *a.* thorough.

approprié /aprɔprije/ *a.* appropriate.

approprier (s') /(s)aprɔprije/ *v. pr.* appropriate.

approuver /apruve/ *v.t.* approve; (*trouver louable*) approve of; (*soutenir*) agree with.

approvisionn|er /aprɔvizjɔne/ *v.t.* supply. **s'∿er** *v. pr.* stock up. **∿ement** *n.m.* supply.

approximati|f, ∿ve /aprɔksimatif, -v/ *a.* approximate. **∿vement** *adv.* approximately.

approximation /aprɔksimɑsjɔ̃/ *n.f.* approximation.

appui /apɥi/ *n.m.* support; (*de fenêtre*) sill; (*pour objet*) rest. **à l'~ de,** in support of. **prendre ~,** support o.s. on.

appuie-tête /apɥitɛt/ *n.m.* headrest.

appuyer /apɥije/ *v.t.* lean, rest; (*presser*) press; (*soutenir*) support, back. —*v.i.* **~ sur,** press (on); (*fig.*) stress. **s'~ sur,** lean on; (*compter sur*) rely on.

âpre /ɑpr/ *a.* harsh, bitter. **~ au gain,** grasping.

après /aprɛ/ *prép.* after; (*au-delà de*) beyond. —*adv.* after(wards); (*plus tard*) later. **~ avoir fait,** after doing. **~ qu'il est parti,** after he left. **~ coup,** after the event. **~ tout,** after all. **d'~,** (*selon*) according to. **~-demain** *adv.* the day after tomorrow. **~-guerre** *n.m.* postwar period. **~-midi** *n.m./f. invar.* afternoon. **~-rasage** *n.m.* aftershave. **~-ski** *n.m.* moonboot. **~-vente** *a.* after-sales.

a priori /aprijɔri/ *adv.* in principle, without going into the matter. —*n.m.* preconception.

à-propos /aprɔpo/ *n.m.* timeliness; (*fig.*) presence of mind.

apte /apt/ *a.* capable (**à,** of).

aptitude /aptityd/ *n.f.* aptitude, ability.

aquarelle /akwarɛl/ *n.f.* water-colour, aquarelle.

aquarium /akwarjɔm/ *n.m.* aquarium.

aquatique /akwatik/ *a.* aquatic.

aqueduc /akdyk/ *n.m.* aqueduct.

arabe /arab/ *a.* Arab; (*lang.*) Arabic; (*désert*) Arabian. —*n.m./f.* Arab. —*n.m.* (*lang.*) Arabic.

Arabie /arabi/ *n.f.* **~ Séoudite,** Saudi Arabia.

arable /arabl/ *a.* arable.

arachide /araʃid/ *n.f.* peanut.

araignée /areɲe/ *n.f.* spider.

arbitraire /arbitrɛr/ *a.* arbitrary.

arbitr|e /arbitr/ *n.m.* referee; (*cricket, tennis*) umpire; (*maître*) arbiter; (*jurid.*) arbitrator. **~age** *n.m.* arbitration; (*sport*) refereeing. **~er** *v.t.* (*match*) referee; (*jurid.*) arbitrate.

arborer /arbɔre/ *v.t.* display; (*vêtement*) sport.

arbre /arbr/ *n.m.* tree; (*techn.*) shaft.

arbrisseau (*pl.* **~x**) /arbriso/ *n.m.* shrub.

arbuste /arbyst/ *n.m.* bush.

arc /ark/ *n.m.* (*arme*) bow; (*voûte*) arch. **~ de cercle,** arc of a circle.

arcade /arkad/ *n.f.* arch. **~s,** arcade, arches.

arc-boutant (*pl.* **arcs-boutants**) /arkbutɑ̃/ *n.m.* flying buttress.

arc-bouter (s') /(s)arkbute/ *v. pr.* lean (for support), brace o.s.

arceau (*pl.* **~x**) /arso/ *n.m.* hoop; (*de voûte*) arch.

arc-en-ciel (*pl.* **arcs-en-ciel**) /arkɑ̃sjɛl/ *n.m.* rainbow.

archaïque /arkaik/ *a.* archaic.

arche /arʃ/ *n.f.* arch. **~ de Noé,** Noah's ark.

archéolo|gie /arkeɔlɔʒi/ *n.f.* archaeology. **~gique** *a.* archaeological. **~gue** *n.m./f.* archaeologist.

archer /arʃe/ *n.m.* archer.

archet /arʃɛ/ *n.m.* (*mus.*) bow.

archétype /arketip/ *n.m.* archetype.

archevêque /arʃəvɛk/ *n.m.* archbishop.

archi- /arʃi/ *préf.* (*fam.*) tremendously.

archipel /arʃipɛl/ *n.m.* archipelago.

architecte /arʃitɛkt/ *n.m.* architect.

architecture /arʃitɛktyr/ *n.f.* architecture.

archiv|es /arʃiv/ *n.f. pl.* archives. **~iste** *n.m./f.* archivist.

arctique /arktik/ *a. & n.m.* Arctic.

ardemment /ardamɑ̃/ *adv.* ardently.

ard|ent, ~ente /ardɑ̃, -t/ *a.* burning; (*passionné*) ardent; (*foi*) fervent. **~eur** *n.f.* ardour; (*chaleur*) heat.

ardoise /ardwaz/ *n.f.* slate.

ardu /ardy/ *a.* arduous.

are /ar/ *n.m.* are (= *100 square metres*).

arène /arɛn/ *n.f.* arena. **~(s),** (*pour courses de taureaux*) bullring.

arête /arɛt/ *n.f.* (*de poisson*) bone; (*bord*) ridge.

argent /arʒɑ̃/ *n.m.* money; (*métal*) silver. **~ comptant,** cash. **prendre pour ~ comptant,** take at face value. **~ de poche,** pocket money.

argenté /arʒɑ̃te/ *a.* silver(y); (*métal*) (silver-)plated.

argenterie /arʒɑ̃tri/ *n.f.* silverware.

argentin, ~e /arʒɑ̃tɛ̃, -in/ *a. & n.m., f.* Argentinian, Argentine.

Argentine /arʒɑ̃tin/ *n.f.* Argentina.

argil|e /arʒil/ *n.f.* clay. **~eux, ~euse** *a.* clayey.

argot /argo/ *n.m.* slang. **~ique** /-ɔtik/ *a.* (*terme*) slang; (*style*) slangy.

arguer /argɥe/ *v.i.* **~ de,** put forward as a reason.

argument /argymɑ̃/ *n.m.* argument. **~er** /-te/ *v.i.* argue.

aride /arid/ *a.* arid, barren.

aristocrate /aristɔkrat/ *n.m./f.* aristocrat.

aristocrat|ie /aristɔkrasi/ *n.f.* aristocracy. ~**ique** /-atik/ *a.* aristocratic.

arithmétique /aritmetik/ *n.f.* arithmetic. —*a.* arithmetical.

armateur /armatœr/ *n.m.* shipowner.

armature /armatyr/ *n.f.* framework; (*de tente*) frame.

arme /arm/ *n.f.* arm, weapon. ~**s**, (*blason*) arms. ~ **à feu**, firearm.

armée /arme/ *n.f.* army. ~ **de l'air**, Air Force. ~ **de terre**, Army.

armement /arməmɑ̃/ *n.m.* arms.

armer /arme/ *v.t.* arm; (*fusil*) cock; (*navire*) equip; (*renforcer*) reinforce; (*photo.*) wind on. ~ **de**, (*garnir de*) fit with. **s'**~ **de**, arm o.s. with.

armistice /armistis/ *n.m.* armistice.

armoire /armwar/ *n.f.* cupboard; (*penderie*) wardrobe; (*Amer.*) closet.

armoiries /armwari/ *n.f. pl.* (coat of) arms.

armure /armyr/ *n.f.* armour.

arnaque /arnak/ *n.f.* (*fam.*) swindling. **c'est de l'**~, it's a swindle *ou* con (*fam.*). ~**r** *v.t.* swindle, con (*fam.*).

arnica /arnika/ *n.f.* (*méd.*) arnica.

aromate /arɔmat/ *n.m.* herb, spice.

aromatique /arɔmatik/ *a.* aromatic.

aromatisé /arɔmatize/ *a.* flavoured.

arôme /arom/ *n.m.* aroma.

arpent|er /arpɑ̃te/ *v.t.* pace up and down; (*terrain*) survey. ~**eur** *n.m.* surveyor.

arqué /arke/ *a.* arched; (*jambes*) bandy.

arraché (à l') /(al)araʃe/ *adv.* with a struggle, after a hard struggle.

arrache-pied (d') /(d)araʃpje/ *adv.* relentlessly.

arrach|er /araʃe/ *v.t.* pull out *ou* off; (*plante*) pull *ou* dig up; (*cheveux, page*) tear *ou* pull out; (*par une explosion*) blow off. ~**er à**, (*enlever a*) snatch from; (*fig.*) force *ou* wrest from. **s'**~**er qch.**, fight over sth. ~**age** /-aʒ/ *n.m.* pulling *ou* digging up.

arraisonner /arɛzɔne/ *v.t.* inspect.

arrangeant, ~e /arɑ̃ʒɑ̃, -t/ *a.* obliging.

arrangement /arɑ̃ʒmɑ̃/ *n.m.* arrangement.

arranger /arɑ̃ʒe/ *v.t.* arrange, fix up; (*réparer*) put right; (*régler*) sort out; (*convenir à*) suit. **s'**~ *v. pr.* (*se mettre d'accord*) come to an arrangement; (*se débrouiller*) manage (**pour**, to).

arrestation /arɛstasjɔ̃/ *n.f.* arrest.

arrêt /arɛ/ *n.m.* stopping (**de**, of); (*lieu*) stop; (*pause*) pause; (*jurid.*) decree. ~**s**, (*mil.*) arrest. **à l'**~, stationary. **faire un** ~, (make a) stop. **sans** ~,

without stopping. ~ **maladie**, sick leave. ~ **de travail**, (*grève*) stoppage; (*méd.*) sick leave. **rester** *ou* **tomber en** ~, stop short.

arrêté /arete/ *n.m.* order.

arrêter /arete/ *v.t./i.* stop; (*date, regard*) fix; (*appareil*) turn off; (*appréhender*) arrest. **s'**~ *v. pr.* stop. (**s'**)~ **de faire**, stop doing.

arrhes /ar/ *n.f. pl.* deposit.

arrière /arjer/ *n.m.* back, rear; (*football*) back. —*a. invar.* back, rear. **à l'**~, **in** *ou* at the back. **en** ~, behind; (*marcher*) backwards. **en** ~ **de**, behind. ~**boutique** *n.f.* back room (of the shop). ~**garde** *n.f.* rearguard. ~**goût** *n.m.* after-taste. ~**grand-mère** *n.f.* great-grandmother. ~**grand-père** (*pl.* ~**grands-pères**) *n.m.* great-grandfather. ~**pays** *n.m.* backcountry. ~**pensée** *n.f.* ulterior motive. ~**plan** *n.m.* background.

arriéré /arjere/ *a.* backward. —*n.m.* arrears.

arrimer /arime/ *v.t.* rope down; (*cargaison*) stow.

arrivage /arivaʒ/ *n.m.* consignment.

arrivant, ~e /arivɑ̃, -t/ *n.m., f.* new arrival.

arrivée /arive/ *n.f.* arrival; (*sport*) finish.

arriver /arive/ *v.i.* (*aux. être*) arrive, come; (*réussir*) succeed; (*se produire*) happen. ~ **à**, (*atteindre*) reach. ~ **à faire**, manage to do. **en** ~ **à faire**, get to the stage of doing. **il arrive que**, it happens that. **il lui arrive de faire**, he (sometimes) does.

arriviste /arivist/ *n.m./f.* self-seeker.

arrogan|t, ~te /arɔgɑ̃, -t/ *a.* arrogant. ~**ce** *n.f.* arrogance.

arroger (s') /(s)arɔʒe/ *v. pr.* assume (*without justification*).

arrondir /arɔ̃dir/ *v.t.* (make) round; (*somme*) round off. **s'**~ *v. pr.* become round(ed).

arrondissement /arɔ̃dismɑ̃/ *n.m.* district.

arros|er /arɔze/ *v.t.* water; (*repas*) wash down; (*rôti*) baste; (*victoire*) celebrate with a drink. ~**age** *n.m.* watering. ~**oir** *n.m.* watering-can.

arsen|al (*pl.* ~**aux**) /arsənal, -o/ *n.m.* arsenal; (*naut.*) dockyard.

arsenic /arsənik/ *n.m.* arsenic.

art /ar/ *n.m.* art. ~**s et métiers**, arts and crafts. ~**s ménagers**, domestic science.

artère /arter/ *n.f.* artery. (**grande**) ~, main road.

artériel, ~le /arterjɛl/ *a.* arterial.

arthrite /artrit/ *n.f.* arthritis.
arthrose /artroz/ *n.f.* osteoarthritis.
artichaut /artiʃo/ *n.m.* artichoke.
article /artikl/ *n.m.* article; (*comm.*) item, article. **à l'~ de la mort,** at death's door. **~ de fond,** feature (article). **~s d'ameublement,** furnishings. **~s de voyage,** travel requisites *ou* goods.
articul|er /artikyle/ *v.t.,* **s'~er** *v. pr.* articulate. **~ation** *n.f.* articulation; (*anat.*) joint.
artifice /artifis/ *n.m.* contrivance.
artificiel, ~le /artifisjɛl/ *a.* artificial. **~lement** *adv.* artificially.
artill|erie /artijri/ *n.f.* artillery. **~eur** *n.m.* gunner.
artisan /artizã/ *n.m.* artisan, craftsman. **l'~ de,** (*fig.*) the architect of. **~al** (*m. pl.* **~aux**) /-anal, -o/ *a.* of *ou* by craftsmen, craft; (*amateur*) homemade. **~at** /-ana/ *n.m.* craft; (*classe*) artisans.
artist|e /artist/ *n.m./f.* artist. **~ique** *a.* artistic.
as[1] /a/ *voir* **avoir**.
as[2] /as/ *n.m.* ace.
ascendant[1], **~e** /asãdã, -t/ *a.* ascending, upward.
ascendant[2] /asãdã/ *n.m.* influence. **~s,** ancestors.
ascenseur /asãsœr/ *n.m.* lift; (*Amer.*) elevator.
ascension /asãsjõ/ *n.f.* ascent. **l' A~,** Ascension.
ascète /asɛt/ *n.m./f.* ascetic.
ascétique /asetik/ *a.* ascetic.
aseptique /asɛptik/ *a.* aseptic.
aseptis|er /asɛptize/ *v.t.* disinfect; (*stériliser*) sterilize. **~é** (*péj.*) sanitized.
asiatique /azjatik/ *a. & n.m./f.,* **Asiate** /azjat/ *n.m./f.* Asian.
Asie /azi/ *n.f.* Asia.
asile /azil/ *n.m.* refuge; (*pol.*) asylum; (*pour malades, vieillards*) home.
aspect /aspɛ/ *n.m.* appearance; (*fig.*) aspect. **à l'~ de,** at the sight of.
asperge /aspɛrʒ/ *n.f.* asparagus.
asper|ger /aspɛrʒe/ *v.t.* spray. **~sion** *n.f.* spray(ing).
aspérité /asperite/ *n.f.* bump, rough edge.
asphalt|e /asfalt/ *n.m.* asphalt. **~er** *v.t.* asphalt.
asphyxie /asfiksi/ *n.f.* suffocation.
asphyxier /asfiksje/ *v.t.,* **s'~** *v. pr.* suffocate, asphyxiate; (*fig.*) stifle.
aspic /aspik/ *n.m.* (*serpent*) asp.

aspirateur /aspiratœr/ *n.m.* vacuum cleaner.
aspir|er /aspire/ *v.t.* inhale; (*liquide*) suck up. —*v.i.* **~er à,** aspire to. **~ation** *n.f.* inhaling; suction; (*ambition*) aspiration.
aspirine /aspirin/ *n.f.* aspirin.
assagir /asaʒir/ *v.t.,* **s'~** *v. pr.* sober down.
assaill|ir /asajir/ *v.t.* assail. **~ant** *n.m.* assailant.
assainir /asenir/ *v.t.* clean up.
assaisonn|er /asɛzɔne/ *v.t.* season. **~ement** *n.m.* seasoning.
assassin /asasɛ̃/ *n.m.* murderer; (*pol.*) assassin.
assassin|er /asasine/ *v.t.* murder; (*pol.*) assassinate. **~at** *n.m.* murder; (*pol.*) assassination.
assaut /aso/ *n.m.* assault, onslaught. **donner l'~ à, prendre d'~,** storm.
assécher /aseʃe/ *v.t.* drain.
assemblée /asãble/ *n.f.* meeting; (*gens réunis*) gathering; (*pol.*) assembly.
assembl|er /asãble/ *v.t.* assemble, put together; (*réunir*) gather. **s'~er** *v. pr.* gather, assemble. **~age** *n.m.* assembly; (*combinaison*) collection; (*techn.*) joint. **~eur** *n.m.* (*comput.*) assembler.
assener /asene/ *v.t.* (*coup*) deal.
assentiment /asãtimã/ *n.m.* assent.
asseoir† /aswar/ *v.t.* sit (down), seat; (*affermir*) establish; (*baser*) base. **s'~** *v. pr.* sit (down).
assermenté /asɛrmãte/ *a.* sworn.
assertion /asɛrsjõ/ *n.f.* assertion.
asservir /asɛrvir/ *v.t.* enslave.
assez /ase/ *adv.* enough; (*plutôt*) quite, fairly. **~ grand/rapide** *etc.,* big/fast/ *etc.* enough (**pour,** to). **~ de,** enough. **j'en ai ~ (de),** I've had enough (of).
assid|u /asidy/ *a.* (*zélé*) assiduous; (*régulier*) regular. **~u auprès de,** attentive to. **~uité** /-ɥite/ *n.f.* assiduousness; regularity. **~ûment** *adv.* assiduously.
assiéger /asjeʒe/ *v.t.* besiege.
assiette /asjɛt/ *n.f.* plate; (*équilibre*) seat. **~ anglaise,** assorted cold meats. **~ creuse/plate,** soup/dinner-plate. **ne pas être dans son ~,** feel out of sorts.
assiettée /asjete/ *n.f.* plateful.
assigner /asiɲe/ *v.t.* assign; (*limite*) fix.
assimil|er /asimile/ *v.t.,* **s'~er** *v. pr.* assimilate. **~er à,** liken to; (*classer*) class as. **~ation** *n.f.* assimilation; likening; classification.
assis, ~e /asi, -z/ *voir* **asseoir.** —*a.* sitting (down), seated.

assise /asiz/ n.f. (base) foundation. ∼s, (tribunal) assizes; (congrès) conference, congress.

assistance /asistãs/ n.f. audience; (aide) assistance. l'A∼ (publique), government child care service.

assistant, ∼e /asistã, -t/ n.m., f. assistant; (univ.) assistant lecturer. ∼s, (spectateurs) members of the audience. ∼ social, ∼e sociale, social worker.

assist|er /asiste/ v.t. assist. —v.i. ∼er à, attend, be (present) at; (scène) witness. ∼é par ordinateur, computer-assisted.

association /asɔsjasjɔ̃/ n.f. association.

associé, ∼e /asɔsje/ n.m., f. partner, associate. —a. associate.

associer /asɔsje/ v.t. associate; (mêler) combine (à, with). ∼ qn. à, (projet) involve s.o. in; (bénéfices) give s.o. a share of. s'∼ v. pr. (sociétés personnes) become associated, join forces (à, with); (s'harmoniser) combine (à, with). s'∼ à, (joie de qn.) share in; (opinion de qn.) share; (projet) take part in.

assoiffé /aswafe/ a. thirsty.

assombrir /asɔ̃brir/ v.t. darken; (fig.) make gloomy. s'∼ v. pr. darken; become gloomy.

assommer /asɔme/ v.t. knock out; (tuer) kill; (animal) stun; (fig.) overwhelm; (ennuyer: fam.) bore.

Assomption /asɔ̃psjɔ̃/ n.f. Assumption.

assorti /asɔrti/ a. matching; (objets variés) assorted.

assort|ir /asɔrtir/ v.t. match (à, with, to). ∼ir de, accompany with. s'∼ir (à), match. ∼iment n.m. assortment.

assoup|ir (s') /(s)asupir/ v. pr. doze off, (s'apaiser) subside. ∼i a. dozing.

assouplir /asuplir/ v.t. make supple; (fig.) make flexible.

assourdir /asurdir/ v.t. (personne) deafen; (bruit) deaden.

assouvir /asuvir/ v.t. satisfy.

assujettir /asyʒetir/ v.t. subject, subdue. ∼ à, subject to.

assumer /asyme/ v.t. assume.

assurance /asyrãs/ n.f. (self-)assurance; (garantie) assurance; (contrat) insurance. ∼-maladie n.f. health insurance. ∼s sociales, National Insurance. ∼-vie n.f. life assurance ou insurance.

assuré, ∼e /asyre/ a. certain, assured; (sûr de soi) (self-)confident, assured. —n.m., f. insured. ∼ment adv. certainly.

assurer /asyre/ v.t. ensure; (fournir) provide; (exécuter) carry out; (comm.) insure; (stabiliser) steady; (frontières) make secure. ∼ à qn. que, assure s.o. that. ∼ qn. de, assure s.o. of. ∼ la gestion de, manage. s'∼ de/que, make sure of/that. s'∼ qch., (se procurer) secure ou ensure sth. **assureur** /-œr/ n.m. insurer.

astérisque /asterisk/ n.m. asterisk.

asthm|e /asm/ n.m. asthma. ∼atique a. & n.m./f. asthmatic.

asticot /astiko/ n.m. maggot.

astiquer /astike/ v.t. polish.

astre /astr/ n.m. star.

astreignant, ∼e /astrɛɲɑ̃, -t/ a. exacting.

astreindre /astrɛ̃dr/ v.t. ∼ qn. à qch., force sth. on s.o. ∼ à faire, force to do.

astringent, ∼e /astrɛ̃ʒɑ̃, -t/ a. astringent.

astrolo|gie /astrɔlɔʒi/ n.f. astrology. ∼gue n.m./f. astrologer.

astronaute /astrɔnot/ n.m./f. astronaut.

astronom|ie /astrɔnɔmi/ n.f. astronomy. ∼e n.m./f. astronomer. ∼ique a. astronomical.

astuce /astys/ n.f. smartness; (truc) trick; (plaisanterie) wisecrack.

astucieu|x, ∼se /astysjø, -z/ a. smart, clever.

atelier /atəlje/ n.m. workshop; (de peintre) studio.

athée /ate/ n.m./f. atheist. —a. atheistic. ∼isme n.m. atheism.

athl|ète /atlɛt/ n.m./f. athlete. ∼étique a. athletic. ∼étisme n.m. athletics.

atlantique /atlɑ̃tik/ a. Atlantic. —n.m. A∼, Atlantic (Ocean).

atlas /atlas/ n.m. atlas.

atmosph|ère /atmosfɛr/ n.f. atmosphere. ∼érique a. atmospheric.

atome /atom/ n.m. atom.

atomique /atomik/ a. atomic.

atomiseur /atomizœr/ n.m. spray.

atout /atu/ n.m. trump (card); (avantage) great asset.

âtre /atr/ n.m. hearth.

atroc|e /atrɔs/ a. atrocious. ∼ité n.f. atrocity.

atroph|ie /atrɔfi/ n.f. atrophy. ∼ié a. atrophied.

attabler (s') /(s)atable/ v. pr. sit down at table.

attachant, ∼e /ataʃɑ̃, -t/ a. likeable.

attache /ataʃ/ n.f. (agrafe) fastener; (lien) tie.

attach|é /ataʃe/ a. être ∼é à, (aimer) be attached to. —n.m., f. (pol.) attaché.

~é-case *n.m.* attaché case. ~ement *n.m.* attachment.

attacher /ataʃe/ *v.t.* tie (up); (*ceinture, robe, etc.*) fasten; (*étiquette*) attach. ~ à, (*attribuer à*) attach to. —*v.i.* (*culin.*) stick. s'~ à, (*se lier à*) become attached to; (*se consacrer à*) apply o.s. to.

attaque /atak/ *n.f.* attack. ~ (cérébrale), stroke. il va en faire une ~, he'll have a fit. ~ à main armée, armed attack.

attaqu|er /atake/ *v.t./i.*, s'~er à, attack; (*problème, sujet*) tackle. ~ant, ~ante *n.m.*, *f.* attacker; (*football*) striker; (*football, Amer.*) forward.

attardé /atarde/ *a.* backward; (*idées*) outdated; (*en retard*) late.

attarder (s') /(s)atarde/ *v. pr.* linger.

atteindre† /atɛ̃dr/ *v.t.* reach; (*blesser*) hit; (*affecter*) affect.

atteint, ~e /atɛ̃, -t/ *a.* ~ de, suffering from.

atteinte /atɛ̃t/ *n.f.* attack (à, on). porter ~ à, make an attack on.

attel|er /atle/ *v.t.* (*cheval*) harness; (*remorque*) couple. s'~er à, get down to. ~age *n.m.* harnessing; coupling; (*bêtes*) team.

attelle /atɛl/ *n.f.* splint.

attenant, ~e /atnã, -t/ *a.* ~ (à), adjoining.

attendant (en) /(ãn)atãdã/ *adv.* meanwhile.

attendre /atãdr/ *v.t.* wait for; (*bébé*) expect; (*être le sort de*) await; (*escompter*) expect. —*v.i.* wait. ~ que qn. fasse, wait for s.o. to do. s'~ à, expect.

attendr|ir /atãdrir/ *v.t.* move (to pity). s'~ir *v. pr.* be moved to pity. ~issant, ~issante *a.* moving.

attendu /atãdy/ *a.* (*escompté*) expected; (*espéré*) long-awaited. ~ que, considering that.

attentat /atãta/ *n.m.* murder attempt. ~ (à la bombe), (bomb) attack.

attente /atãt/ *n.f.* wait(ing); (*espoir*) expectation.

attenter /atãte/ *v.i.* ~ à, make an attempt on; (*fig.*) violate.

attenti|f, ~ve /atãtif, -v/ *a.* attentive; (*scrupuleux*) careful. ~f à, mindful of; (*soucieux*) careful of. ~vement *adv.* attentively.

attention /atãsjõ/ *n.f.* attention; (*soin*) care. ~ (à)!, watch out (for)! faire ~ à, (*professeur*) pay attention to; (*marche*) mind. faire ~ à faire, be careful to do. ~né /-jɔne/ *a.* considerate.

attentisme /atãtism/ *n.m.* wait-and-see policy.

atténuer /atenɥe/ *v.t.* (*violence*) tone down; (*douleur*) ease; (*faute*) mitigate. s'~ *v. pr.* subside.

atterrer /atere/ *v.t.* dismay.

atterr|ir /aterir/ *v.i.* land. ~issage *n.m.* landing.

attestation /atɛstasjõ/ *n.f.* certificate.

attester /atɛste/ *v.t.* testify to. ~ que, testify that.

attifé /atife/ *a.* (*fam.*) dressed up.

attirail /atiraj/ *n.m.* (*fam.*) gear.

attirance /atirãs/ *n.f.* attraction.

attirant, ~e /atirã, -t/ *a.* attractive.

attirer /atire/ *v.t.* draw, attract; (*causer*) bring. s'~ *v. pr.* bring upon o.s.; (*amis*) win.

attiser /atize/ *v.t.* (*feu*) poke; (*sentiment*) stir up.

attitré /atitre/ *a.* accredited; (*habituel*) usual.

attitude /atityd/ *n.f.* attitude; (*maintien*) bearing.

attraction /atraksjõ/ *n.f.* attraction.

attrait /atrɛ/ *n.m.* attraction.

attrape-nigaud /atrapnigo/ *n.m.* (*fam.*) con.

attraper /atrape/ *v.t.* catch; (*habitude, style*) pick up; (*duper*) take in; (*gronder*: *fam.*) tell off.

attrayant, ~e /atrɛjã, -t/ *a.* attractive.

attrib|uer /atribɥe/ *v.t.* award; (*donner*) assign; (*imputer*) attribute. s'~uer *v. pr.* claim. ~ution *n.f.* awarding; assignment. ~utions *n.f. pl.* attributions.

attrister /atriste/ *v.t.* sadden.

attroup|er (s') /(s)atrupe/ *v. pr.* gather. ~ement *n.m.* crowd.

au /o/ *voir* à.

aubaine /obɛn/ *n.f.* (stroke of) good fortune.

aube /ob/ *n.f.* dawn, daybreak.

aubépine /obepin/ *n.f.* hawthorn.

auberg|e /obɛrʒ/ *n.f.* inn. ~e de jeunesse, youth hostel. ~iste *n.m./f.* innkeeper.

aubergine /obɛrʒin/ *n.f.* aubergine; (*Amer.*) egg-plant.

aucun, ~e /okœ̃, okyn/ *a.* no, not any; (*positif*) any. —*pron.* none, not any; (*positif*) any. ~ des deux, neither of the two. d'~s, some. ~ement /okynmã/ *adv.* not at all.

audace /odas/ *n.f.* daring; (*impudence*) audacity.

audacieu|x, ~se /odasjø, -z/ *a.* daring.

au-delà /odla/ *adv.*, ~ de *prép.* beyond.

au-dessous /odsu/ *adv.*, **∼ de** *prép.* below; (*couvert par*) under.

au-dessus /odsy/ *adv.*, **∼ de** *prép.* above.

au-devant (de) /odvɑ̃(də)/ *prép.* **aller ∼ de qn.**, go to meet s.o.

audience /odjɑ̃s/ *n.f.* audience; (*d'un tribunal*) hearing; (*intérêt*) attention.

Audimat /odimat/ *n.m.* (P.) **l'∼**, the TV ratings.

audiotypiste /odjotipist/ *n.m./f.* audio typist.

audio-visuel, ∼le /odjovizɥɛl/ *a.* audio-visual.

audi|teur, ∼trice /oditœr, -tris/ *n.m.*, *f.* listener.

audition /odisjɔ̃/ *n.f.* hearing; (*théâtre, mus.*) audition. **∼ner** /-jone/ *v.t./i.* audition.

auditoire /oditwar/ *n.m.* audience.

auditorium /oditorjom/ *n.m.* (*mus., radio*) recording studio.

auge /oʒ/ *n.f.* trough.

augment|er /ogmɑ̃te/ *v.t./i.* increase; (*employé*) increase the pay of. **∼ation** *n.f.* increase. **∼ation (de salaire)**, (pay) rise; (*Amer.*) raise.

augure /ogyr/ *n.m.* (*devin*) oracle. **être de bon/mauvais ∼**, be a good/bad sign.

auguste /ogyst/ *a.* august.

aujourd'hui /oʒurdɥi/ *adv.* today.

aumône /omon/ *n.f.* alms.

aumônier /omonje/ *n.m.* chaplain.

auparavant /oparavɑ̃/ *adv.* before(hand).

auprès (de) /oprɛ(də)/ *prép.* by, next to; (*comparé à*) compared with; (*s'adressant à*) to.

auquel, ∼le /okɛl/ *voir* lequel.

aura, aurait /ora, orɛ/ *voir* avoir.

auréole /oreol/ *n.f.* halo.

auriculaire /orikylɛr/ *n.m.* little finger.

aurore /oror/ *n.f.* dawn.

ausculter /oskylte/ *v.t.* examine with a stethoscope.

auspices /ospis/ *n.m. pl.* auspices.

aussi /osi/ *adv.* too, also; (*comparaison*) as; (*tellement*) so. —*conj.* (*donc*) therefore. **∼ bien que,** as well as.

aussitôt /osito/ *adv.* immediately. **∼ que,** as soon as. **∼ arrivé/levé/***etc.*, as soon as one has arrived/got up/*etc.*

aust|ère /ostɛr/ *a.* austere. **∼érité** *n.f.* austerity.

austral (*m. pl.* **∼s**) /ostral/ *a.* southern.

Australie /ostrali/ *n.f.* Australia.

australien, ∼ne /ostraljɛ̃, -jɛn/ *a.* & *n.m.*, *f.* Australian.

autant /otɑ̃/ *adv.* (*travailler, manger,*

etc.) as much (**que,** as). **∼ (de),** (*quantité*) as much (**que,** as); (*nombre*) as many (**que,** as); (*tant*) so much; so many. **∼ faire,** one had better do. **d'∼ plus que,** all the more since. **en faire ∼,** do the same. **pour ∼,** for all that.

autel /otɛl/ *n.m.* altar.

auteur /otœr/ *n.m.* author. **l'∼ du crime,** the person who committed the crime.

authentifier /otɑ̃tifje/ *v.t.* authenticate.

authenti|que /otɑ̃tik/ *a.* authentic. **∼cité** *n.f.* authenticity.

auto /oto/ *n.f.* car. **∼s tamponneuses,** dodgems, bumper cars.

auto- /oto/ *préf.* self-, auto-.

autobiographie /otobjografi/ *n.f.* autobiography.

autobus /otobys/ *n.m.* bus.

autocar /otokar/ *n.m.* coach.

autochtone /otokton/ *n.m./f.* native.

autocollant, ∼e /otokolɑ̃, -t/ *a.* self-adhesive. —*n.m.* sticker.

autocratique /otokratik/ *a.* autocratic.

autocuiseur /otokyizœr/ *n.m.* pressure cooker.

autodéfense /otodefɑ̃s/ *n.f.* self-defence.

autodidacte /otodidakt/ *a.* & *n.m./f.* self-taught (person).

auto-école /otoekol/ *n.f.* driving school.

autographe /otograf/ *n.m.* autograph.

automate /otomat/ *n.m.* automaton, robot.

automatique /otomatik/ *a.* automatic. **∼ment** *adv.* automatically.

automat|iser /otomatize/ *v.t.* automate. **∼ion** /-masjɔ̃/ *n.f.* **∼isation** *n.f.* automation.

automne /oton/ *n.m.* autumn; (*Amer.*) fall.

automobil|e /otomobil/ *a.* motor, car. —*n.f.* (motor) car. **l'∼e,** (*sport*) motoring. **∼iste** *n.m./f.* motorist.

autonom|e /otonom/ *a.* autonomous. **∼ie** *n.f.* autonomy.

autopsie /otopsi/ *n.f.* post-mortem, autopsy.

autoradio /otoradjo/ *n.m.* car radio.

autorail /otoraj/ *n.m.* railcar.

autorisation /otorizasjɔ̃/ *n.f.* permission, authorization; (*permis*) permit.

autoris|er /otorize/ *v.t.* authorize, permit; (*rendre possible*) allow (of). **∼é** *a.* (*opinions*) authoritative.

autoritaire /otoritɛr/ *a.* authoritarian.

autorité /otorite/ *n.f.* authority. **faire ∼,** be authoritative.

autoroute /otorut/ *n.f.* motorway; (*Amer.*) highway.

auto-stop /otɔstɔp/ *n.m.* hitch-hiking. **faire de l'~,** hitch-hike. **prendre en ~,** give a lift to. **~peur, ~peuse** *n.m., f.* hitch-hiker.

autour /otur/ *adv.,* **~ de** *prép.* around. **tout ~,** all around.

autre /otr/ *a.* other. **un ~ jour/***etc.,* another day/*etc.* —*pron.* **un ~, une ~,** another (one). **l'~,** the other (one). **les autres,** the others; (*autrui*) others. **d'~s,** (some) others. **l'un l'~,** each other. **l'un et l'~,** both of them. **~ chose/part,** sth./somewhere else. **qn./rien d'~,** s.o./nothing else. **quoi d'~?,** what else? **d'~ part,** on the other hand. **vous ~s Anglais,** you English. **d'un jour/***etc.* **à l'~,** (*bientôt*) any day/*etc.* now. **entre ~s,** among other things.

autrefois /otrəfwa/ *adv.* in the past.

autrement /otrəmã/ *adv.* differently; (*sinon*) otherwise; (*plus*) far more. **~ dit,** in other words.

Autriche /otriʃ/ *n.f.* Austria.

autrichien, ~ne /otriʃjɛ̃, -jɛn/ *a.* & *n.m., f.* Austrian.

autruche /otryʃ/ *n.f.* ostrich.

autrui /otrɥi/ *pron.* others.

auvent /ovã/ *n.m.* canopy.

aux /o/ *voir* **à.**

auxiliaire /oksiljɛr/ *a.* auxiliary. —*n.m./f.* (*assistant*) auxiliary. —*n.m.* (*gram.*) auxiliary.

auxquel|s, ~les /okɛl/ *voir* **lequel.**

aval (en) /(ãn)aval/ *adv.* downstream.

avalanche /avalãʃ/ *n.f.* avalanche.

avaler /avale/ *v.t.* swallow.

avance /avãs/ *n.f.* advance; (*sur un concurrent*) lead. **~ (de fonds),** advance. **à l'~, d'~,** in advance. **en ~,** early; (*montre*) fast. **en ~ (sur),** (*menant*) ahead (of).

avancement /avãsmã/ *n.m.* promotion.

avanc|er /avãse/ *v.i.* move forward, advance; (*travail*) make progress; (*montre*) be fast; (*faire saillie*) jut out. —*v.t.* (*argent*) advance; (*montre*) put forward. **s'~er** *v. pr.* move forward, advance; (*se hasarder*) commit o.s. **~é,** **~ée** *a.* advanced; *n.f.* projection.

avanie /avani/ *n.f.* affront.

avant /avã/ *prép* & *adv.* before. —*a. invar.* front. —*n.m.* front; (*football*) forward. **~ de faire,** before doing. **~ qu'il (ne) fasse,** before he does. **en ~,** (*mouvement*) forward. **en ~ (de),** (*position, temps*) in front (of). **~ peu,** before long. **~ tout,** above all. **bien ~ dans,** very deep(ly) *ou* far into. **~-bras**

n.m. invar. forearm. **~-centre** *n.m.* centre-forward. **~-coureur** *a. invar.* precursory, foreshadowing. **~-dernier, ~-dernière** *a.* & *n.m., f.* last but one. **~-garde** *n.f.* (*mil.*) vanguard; (*fig.*) avant-garde. **~-goût** *n.m.* foretaste. **~-guerre** *n.m.* pre-war period. **~-hier** /-tjɛr/ *adv.* the day before yesterday. **~-poste** *n.m.* outpost. **~-première** *n.f.* preview. **~-propos** *n.m.* foreword. **~-veille** *n.f.* two days before.

avantag|e /avãtaʒ/ *n.m.* advantage; (*comm.*) benefit. **~er** *v.t.* favour; (*embellir*) show off to advantage.

avantageu|x, ~se /avãtaʒø, -z/ *a.* attractive.

avar|e /avar/ *a.* miserly. —*n.m./f.* miser. **~e de,** sparing of. **~ice** *n.f.* avarice.

avarié /avarje/ *a.* (*aliment*) spoiled.

avaries /avari/ *n.f. pl.* damage.

avatar /avatar/ *n.m.* (*fam.*) misfortune.

avec /avɛk/ *prép.* with; (*envers*) towards. —*adv.* (*fam.*) with it *ou* them.

avenant, ~e /avnã, -t/ *a.* pleasing.

avenant (à l') /(al)avnã/ *adv.* in a similar style.

avènement /avɛnmã/ *n.m.* advent; (*d'un roi*) accession.

avenir /avnir/ *n.m.* future. **à l'~,** in future. **d'~,** with (future) prospects.

aventur|e /avãtyr/ *n.f.* adventure; (*sentimentale*) affair. **~eux, ~euse** *a.* adventurous; (*hasardeux*) risky. **~ier, ~ière** *n.m., f.* adventurer.

aventurer (s') /(s)avãtyre/ *v. pr.* venture.

avenue /avny/ *n.f.* avenue.

avérer (s') /(s)avere/ *v. pr.* prove (to be).

averse /avɛrs/ *n.f.* shower.

aversion /avɛrsjõ/ *n.f.* aversion.

avert|ir /avɛrtir/ *v.t.* inform; (*mettre en garde, menacer*) warn. **~i** *a.* informed. **~issement** *n.m.* warning.

avertisseur /avɛrtisœr/ *n.m.* (*auto.*) horn. **~ d'incendie,** fire-alarm.

aveu (*pl.* **~x**) /avø/ *n.m.* confession. **de l'~ de,** by the admission of.

aveugl|e /avœgl/ *a.* blind. —*n.m./f.* blind man, blind woman. **~ement** *n.m.* blindness. **~ément** *adv.* blindly. **~er** *v.t.* blind.

aveuglette (à l') /(al)avœglɛt/ *adv.* (*à tâtons*) blindly.

avia|teur, ~trice /avjatœr, -tris/ *n.m., f.* aviator.

aviation /avjasjõ/ *n.f.* flying; (*industrie*) aviation; (*mil.*) air force. **d'~,** air.

avid|e /avid/ *a.* greedy (**de,** for);

(*anxieux*) eager (**de,** for). ～**e de faire,** eager to do. ～**ité** *n.f.* greed; eagerness.

avilir /avilir/ *v.t.* degrade. —*v.i.*

avion /avjɔ̃/ *n.m.* plane, aeroplane, aircraft; (*Amer.*) airplane. ～ **à réaction,** jet.

aviron /avirɔ̃/ *n.m.* oar. l'～, (*sport*) rowing.

avis /avi/ *n.m.* opinion; (*renseignement*) notification; (*comm.*) advice. **à mon ～,** in my opinion. **changer d'～,** change one's mind. **être d'～ que,** be of the opinion that.

avisé /avize/ *a.* sensible. **bien/mal ～ de,** well-/ill-advised to.

aviser /avize/ *v.t.* notice; (*informer*) advise. —*v.i.* decide what to do (**à,** about). **s'～ de,** suddenly realize. **s'～ de faire,** take it into one's head to do.

aviver /avive/ *v.t.* revive.

avocat[1], ～**e** /avɔka, -t/ *n.m., f.* barrister; (*Amer.*) attorney; (*fig.*) advocate. ～ **de la défense,** counsel for the defence.

avocat[2] /avɔka/ *n.m.* (*fruit*) avocado (pear).

avoine /avwan/ *n.f.* oats.

avoir† /avwar/ *v. aux.* have. —*v.t.* have; (*obtenir*) get; (*duper: fam.*) take in. —*n.m.* assets. **je n'ai pas de café,** I haven't (got) any coffee; (*Amer.*) I don't have any coffee. **est-ce que tu as du café?,** have you (got) any coffee?; (*Amer.*) do you have any coffee? ～ **à faire,** have to do. **tu n'as qu'à l'appeler,** all you have to do is call her. ～ **chaud/faim**/*etc.*, be hot/hungry/*etc.* ～ **dix**/*etc.* **ans,** be ten/*etc.* years old. ～ **lieu,** take place. ～ **lieu de,** have good reason to. **en ～ contre qn.,** have a grudge against s.o. **en ～ assez,** have had enough. **en ～ pour une minute**/*etc.*, be busy for a minute/*etc.* **il en a pour cent francs,** it will cost him one hundred francs. **qu'est-ce que vous avez?,** what is the matter with you? **on m'a eu!,** I've been had.

avoisin|er /avwazine/ *v.t.* border on. ～**ant,** ～**ante** *a.* neighbouring.

avort|er /avɔrte/ *v.i.* (*projet etc.*) miscarry. (**se faire**) ～**er,** have an abortion. ～**é** *a.* abortive. ～**ement** *n.m.* (*méd.*) abortion.

avou|er /avwe/ *v.t.* confess (to). —*v.i.* confess. ～**é** *a.* avowed; *n.m.* solicitor; (*Amer.*) attorney.

avril /avril/ *n.m.* April.

axe /aks/ *n.m.* axis; (*essieu*) axle; (*d'une*

politique) main line(s), basis. ～ (**routier**), main road.

axer /akse/ *v.t.* centre.

axiome /aksjom/ *n.m.* axiom.

ayant /ɛjɑ̃/ *voir* **avoir.**

azimuts /azimyt/ *n.m. pl.* **dans tous les ～,** (*fam.*) all over the place.

azote /azɔt/ *n.m.* nitrogen.

azur /azyr/ *n.m.* sky-blue.

B

ba-ba /beaba/ *n.m.* **le ～ (de),** the basics (of).

baba /baba/ *n.m.* ～ (**au rhum**), rum baba. **en rester ～,** (*fam.*) be flabbergasted.

babil /babi(l)/ *n.m.* babble. ～**ler** /-ije/ *v.i.* babble.

babines /babin/ *n.f. pl.* **se lécher les ～,** lick one's chops.

bablole /babjɔl/ *n.f.* knick-knack.

bâbord /babɔr/ *n.m.* port (side).

babouin /babwɛ̃/ *n.m.* baboon.

baby-foot /babifut/ *n.m. invar.* table football.

baby-sitt|er /bebisitœr/ *n.m./f.* baby-sitter. ～**ing** *n.m.* **faire du ～ing,** babysit.

bac[1] /bak/ *n.m.* = **baccalauréat.**

bac[2] /bak/ *n.m.* (*bateau*) ferry; (*récipient*) tub; (*plus petit*) tray.

baccalauréat /bakalɔrea/ *n.m.* school leaving certificate.

bâch|e /baʃ/ *n.f.* tarpaulin. ～**er** *v.t.* cover (with a tarpaulin).

bachel|ier, ～**ière** /baʃəlje, -jɛr/ *n.m., f.* holder of the *baccalauréat.*

bachot /baʃo/ *n.m.* (*fam.*) = **baccalauréat.** ～**er** /-ɔte/ *v.i.* cram (for an exam).

bâcler /bakle/ *v.t.* botch (up).

bactérie /bakteri/ *n.f.* bacterium.

badaud, ～**e** /bado, -d/ *n.m., f.* (*péj.*) onlooker.

badigeon /badiʒɔ̃/ *n.m.* whitewash. ～**ner** /-ɔne/ *v.t.* whitewash; (*barbouiller*) daub.

badin, ～**e** /badɛ̃, -in/ *a.* light-hearted.

badiner /badine/ *v.i.* joke (**sur, avec,** about).

badminton /badmintɔn/ *n.m.* badminton.

baffe /baf/ *n.f.* (*fam.*) slap.

baffle /bafl/ *n.m.* speaker.

bafouer /bafwe/ *v.t.* scoff at.

bafouiller /bafuje/ *v.t./i.* stammer.
bâfrer /bɑfre/ *v.i.* (*fam.*) gobble. **se ∼**
v.pr. stuff o.s.
bagage /bagaʒ/ *n.m.* bag; (*fig.*) (store of)
knowledge. **∼s,** luggage, baggage. **∼s**
à main, hand luggage.
bagarr|e /bagar/ *n.f.* fight. **∼er** *v.i.*, **se**
∼er *v. pr.* fight.
bagatelle /bagatɛl/ *n.f.* trifle; (*somme*)
trifling amount.
bagnard /baɲar/ *n.m.* convict.
bagnole /baɲɔl/ *n.f.* (*fam.*) car.
bagou(t) /bagu/ *n.m.* **avoir du ∼,** have
the gift of the gab.
bagu|e /bag/ *n.f.* (*anneau*) ring. **∼er** *v.t.*
ring.
baguette /bagɛt/ *n.f.* stick; (*de chef*
d'orchestre) baton; (*chinoise*) chopstick; (*magique*) wand; (*pain*) stick of
bread. **∼ de tambour,** drumstick.
baie /bɛ/ *n.f.* (*géog.*) bay; (*fruit*) berry.
∼ (vitrée), picture window.
baign|er /beɲe/ *v.t.* bathe; (*enfant*) bath.
—*v.i.* **∼er dans,** soak in; (*être*
enveloppé dans) be steeped in. **se ∼er**
v. pr. go swimming (*ou*) bathing. **∼é**
de, bathed in; (*sang*) soaked in. **∼ade**
/beɲad/ *n.f.* bathing, swimming. **∼eur,**
∼euse /beɲœr, -øz/ *n.m.*, *f.* bather.
baignoire /beɲwar/ *n.f.* bath(-tub).
bail (*pl.* **baux** /baj, bo/ *n.m.* lease.
bâill|er /baje/ *v.i.* yawn; (*être ouvert*)
gape. **∼ement** *n.m.* yawn.
bailleur /bajœr/ *n.m.* **∼ de fonds,**
(*comm.*) backer.
bâillon /bajɔ̃/ *n.m.* gag. **∼ner** /bajɔne/
v.t. gag.
bain /bɛ̃/ *n.m.* bath; (*de mer*) bathe. **∼(s)**
de soleil, sunbathing. **∼-marie** (*pl.*
∼s-marie) *n.m.* double boiler. **∼ de**
bouche, mouthwash. **mettre qn. dans**
le ∼, (*compromettre*) drop s.o. in it; (*au*
courant) put s.o. in the picture. **se**
remettre dans le ∼, get back into the
swim of things. **prendre un ∼ de foule,**
mingle with the crowd.
baiser /beze/ *n.m.* kiss. —*v.t.* (*main*)
kiss; (*fam.*) screw.
baisse /bɛs/ *n.f.* fall, drop. **en ∼,** falling.
baisser /bese/ *v.t.* lower; (*radio, lampe,*
etc.) turn down. —*v.i.* go down, fall;
(*santé, forces*) fail. **se ∼** *v. pr.* bend
down.
bajoues /baʒu/ *n.f. pl.* chops.
bakchich /bakʃiʃ/ *n.m.* (*fam.*) bribe.
bal (*pl.* **∼s**) /bal/ *n.m.* dance; (*habillé*)
ball; (*lieu*) dance-hall. **∼ costumé,**
fancy-dress ball.
balad|e /balad/ *n.f.* stroll; (*en auto*)
drive. **∼er** *v.t.* take for a stroll. **se ∼er**

v. pr. (go for a) stroll; (*excursionner*)
wander around. **se ∼er (en auto),** go
for a drive.
baladeur /baladœr/ *n.m.* personal
stereo.
balafr|e /balafr/ *n.f.* gash; (*cicatrice*)
scar. **∼er** *v.t.* gash.
balai /balɛ/ *n.m.* broom. **∼-brosse** *n.m.*
garden broom.
balance /balɑ̃s/ *n.f.* scales. **la B∼,** Libra.
balancer /balɑ̃se/ *v.t.* swing; (*douce-*
ment) sway; (*lancer: fam.*) chuck; (*se*
débarrasser de: fam.) chuck out. —*v.i.*,
se ∼ *v. pr.* swing; sway. **se ∼ de,** (*fam.*)
not care about.
balancier /balɑ̃sje/ *n.m.* (*d'horloge*)
pendulum; (*d'équilibriste*) pole.
balançoire /balɑ̃swar/ *n.f.* swing;
(*bascule*) see-saw.
balay|er /baleje/ *v.t.* sweep (up);
(*chasser*) sweep away; (*se débarrasser*
de) sweep aside. **∼age** *n.m.* sweeping;
(*cheveux*) highlights. **∼eur, ∼euse**
n.m., *f.* road sweeper.
balbut|ier /balbysje/ *v.t./i.* stammer.
∼iement *n.m.* stammering.
balcon /balkɔ̃/ *n.m.* balcony; (*théâtre*)
dress circle.
baleine /balɛn/ *n.f.* whale.
balis|e /baliz/ *n.f.* beacon; (*bouée*) buoy;
(*auto.*) (road) sign. **∼er** *v.t.* mark out
(with beacons); (*route*) signpost.
balistique /balistik/ *a.* ballistic.
balivernes /balivɛrn/ *n.f. pl.* balder-
dash.
ballade /balad/ *n.f.* ballad.
ballant, ∼e /balɑ̃, -t/ *a.* dangling.
ballast /balast/ *n.m.* ballast.
balle /bal/ *n.f.* (*projectile*) bullet; (*sport*)
ball; (*paquet*) bale.
ballerine /balrin/ *n.f.* ballerina.
ballet /balɛ/ *n.m.* ballet.
ballon /balɔ̃/ *n.m.* balloon; (*sport*) ball.
∼ de football, football.
ballonné /balɔne/ *a.* bloated.
ballot /balo/ *n.m.* bundle; (*nigaud: fam.*)
idiot.
ballottage /balɔtaʒ/ *n.m.* second ballot
(*due to indecisive result*).
ballotter /balɔte/ *v.t./i.* shake about, toss.
balnéaire /balneɛr/ *a.* seaside.
balourd, ∼e /balur, -d/ *n.m.*, *f.* oaf.
—*a.* oafish.
balustrade /balystrad/ *n.f.* railing(s).
bambin /bɑ̃bɛ̃/ *n.m.* tot.
bambou /bɑ̃bu/ *n.m.* bamboo.
ban /bɑ̃/ *n.m.* round of applause. **∼s,** (*de*
mariage) banns. **mettre au ∼ de,** cast
out from. **publier les ∼s,** have the
banns called.

banal (*m. pl.* ~s) /banal/ *a.* commonplace, banal. ~ité *n.f.* banality.

banane /banan/ *n.f.* banana.

banc /bɑ̃/ *n.m.* bench; (*de poissons*) shoal. ~ **des accusés**, dock. ~ **d'essai**, test bed; (*fig.*) testing-ground.

bancaire /bɑ̃kɛr/ *a.* banking; (*chèque*) bank.

bancal (*m. pl.* ~s) /bɑ̃kal/ *a.* wobbly; (*raisonnement*) shaky.

bandage /bɑ̃daʒ/ *n.m.* bandage. ~ **herniaire**, truss.

bande[1] /bɑ̃d/ *n.f.* (*de papier etc.*) strip; (*rayure*) stripe; (*de film*) reel; (*radio*) band; (*pansement*) bandage. ~ (**magnétique**), tape. ~ **dessinée**, comic strip. ~ **sonore**, sound-track. **par la** ~, indirectly.

bande[2] /bɑ̃d/ *n.f.* (*groupe*) bunch, band, gang.

bandeau (*pl.* ~x) /bɑ̃do/ *n.m.* headband; (*sur les yeux*) blindfold.

bander /bɑ̃de/ *v.t.* bandage; (*arc*) bend; (*muscle*) tense. ~ **les yeux à**, blindfold.

banderole /bɑ̃drɔl/ *n.f.* banner.

bandit /bɑ̃di/ *n.m.* bandit. ~**isme** /-tism/ *n.m.* crime.

bandoulière (en) /(ɑ̃)bɑ̃duljɛr/ *adv.* across one's shoulder.

banjo /bɑ̃(d)ʒo/ *n.m.* banjo.

banlieue|e /bɑ̃ljø/ *n.f.* suburbs. **de** ~**e**, suburban. ~**sard**, ~**sarde** /-zar, -zard/ *n.m., f.* (suburban) commuter.

bannière /banjɛr/ *n.f.* banner.

bannir /banir/ *v.t.* banish.

banque /bɑ̃k/ *n.f.* bank; (*activité*) banking. ~ **d'affaires**, merchant bank.

banqueroute /bɑ̃krut/ *n.f.* (fraudulent) bankruptcy.

banquet /bɑ̃kɛ/ *n.m.* dinner; (*fastueux*) banquet.

banquette /bɑ̃kɛt/ *n.f.* seat.

banquier /bɑ̃kje/ *n.m.* banker.

baptême /batɛm/ *n.m.* baptism; christening. ~**iser** *v.t.* baptize, christen; (*appeler*) christen.

baquet /bakɛ/ *n.m.* tub.

bar /bar/ *n.m.* (*lieu*) bar.

baragouin /baragwɛ̃/ *n.m.* gibberish, gabble. ~**er** /-wine/ *v.t./i.* gabble; (*langue*) speak a few words of.

baraque /barak/ *n.f.* hut, shed; (*boutique*) stall; (*maison: fam.*) house. ~**ments** *n.m. pl.* huts.

baratin /baratɛ̃/ *n.m.* (*fam.*) sweet *ou* smooth talk. ~**er** /-ine/ *v.t.* (*fam.*) chat up; (*Amer.*) sweet-talk.

barbar|e /barbar/ *a.* barbaric. —*n.m./f.* barbarian. ~**ie** *n.f.* (*cruauté*) barbarity.

barbe /barb/ *n.f.* beard. ~ **à papa**, candy-floss; (*Amer.*) cotton candy. **la** ~!, (*fam.*) blast (it)! **quelle** ~!, (*fam.*) what a bore!

barbecue /barbəkju/ *n.m.* barbecue.

barbelé /barbəle/ *a.* **fil** ~, barbed wire.

barber /barbe/ *v.t.* (*fam.*) bore.

barbiche /barbiʃ/ *n.f.* goatee.

barbiturique /barbityrik/ *n.m.* barbiturate.

barboter[1] /barbɔte/ *v.i.* paddle, splash.

barboter[2] /barbɔte/ *v.t.* (*voler: fam.*) pinch.

barbouill|er /barbuje/ *v.t.* (*peindre*) daub; (*souiller*) smear; (*griffonner*) scribble. **avoir l'estomac** ~**é** ou **se sentir** ~**é** feel liverish.

barbu /barby/ *a.* bearded.

barda /barda/ *n.m.* (*fam.*) gear.

barder /barde/ *v.i.* **ça va** ~, (*fam.*) sparks will fly.

barème /barɛm/ *n.m.* list, table; (*échelle*) scale.

baril /baril(l)/ *n.m.* barrel; (*de poudre*) keg.

bariolé /barjɔle/ *a.* motley.

barman /barman/ *n.m.* barman; (*Amer.*) bartender.

baromètre /barɔmɛtr/ *n.m.* barometer.

baron, ~**ne** /barɔ̃, -ɔn/ *n.m., f.* baron, baroness.

baroque /barɔk/ *a.* (*fig.*) weird; (*archit., art*) baroque.

baroud /barud/ *n.m.* ~ **d'honneur**, gallant last fight.

barque /bark/ *n.f.* (small) boat.

barrage /baraʒ/ *n.m.* dam; (*sur route*) road-block.

barre /bar/ *n.f.* bar; (*trait*) line, stroke; (*naut.*) helm.

barreau (*pl.* ~x) /baro/ *n.m.* bar; (*d'échelle*) rung. **le** ~, (*jurid.*) the bar.

barrer /bare/ *v.t.* block; (*porte*) bar; (*rayer*) cross out; (*naut.*) steer. **se** ~ *v. pr.* (*fam.*) hop it.

barrette /barɛt/ *n.f.* (hair-)slide.

barricad|e /barikad/ *n.f.* barricade. ~**er** *v.t.* barricade. **se** ~**er** *v. pr.* barricade o.s.

barrière /barjɛr/ *n.f.* (*porte*) gate; (*clôture*) fence; (*obstacle*) barrier.

barrique /barik/ *n.f.* barrel.

baryton /baritɔ̃/ *n.m.* baritone.

bas, basse /bɑ, bɑs/ *a.* low; (*action*) base. —*n.m.* bottom; (*chaussette*) stocking. —*n.f.* (*mus.*) bass. —*adv.* low. **à** ~, down with. **au** ~ **mot**, at the lowest estimate. **en** ~, down below; (*dans une maison*) downstairs. **en** ~ **âge**, young. **en** ~ **de**, at the bottom of. **plus** ~, further *ou* lower down. ~-**côté** *n.m.* (*de*

route) verge; (*Amer.*) shoulder. ～ **de
casse** *n.m. invar.* lower case. ～ **de laine,**
nest-egg. ～**-fonds** *n.m. pl.* (*eau*)
shallows; (*fig.*) dregs. ～ **morceaux,**
(*viande*) cheap cuts. ～**-relief** *n.m.* low
relief. ～**-ventre** *n.m.* lower abdomen.
mettre ～, give birth (to).

basané /bazane/ *a.* tanned.

bascule /baskyl/ *n.f.* (*balance*) scales.
cheval/fauteuil à ～, rocking-horse/
-chair.

basculer /baskyle/ *v.t./i.* topple over;
(*benne*) tip up.

base /baz/ *n.f.* base; (*fondement*) basis;
(*pol.*) rank and file. **de** ～, basic.

baser /baze/ *v.t.* base. **se** ～ **sur,** base o.s.
on.

basilic /bazilik/ *n.m.* basil.

basilique /bazilik/ *n.f.* basilica.

basket(-ball) /baskɛt(bol)/ *n.m.* basketball.

basque /bask/ *a.* & *n.m./f.* Basque.

basse /bɑs/ *voir* **bas.**

basse-cour (*pl.* **basses-cours**) /bɑskur/
n.f. farmyard.

bassement /bɑsmɑ̃/ *adv.* basely.

bassesse /bɑsɛs/ *n.f.* baseness;
(*action*) base act.

bassin /basɛ̃/ *n.m.* bowl; (*pièce d'eau*)
pond; (*rade*) dock; (*géog.*) basin;
(*anat.*) pelvis. ～ **houiller,** coalfield.

basson /bɑsɔ̃/ *n.m.* bassoon.

bastion /bastjɔ̃/ *n.m.* bastion.

bat /ba/ *voir* **battre.**

bât /ba/ *n.m.* **là où le** ～ **blesse,** where
the shoe pinches.

bataill|e /batɑj/ *n.f.* battle; (*fig.*) fight.
～**er** *v.i.* fight.

bataillon /batajɔ̃/ *n.m.* battalion.

bâtard, ～**e** /batar, -d/ *n.m.*, *f.*
bastard. —*a.* (*solution*) hybrid.

bateau (*pl.* ～**x**) /bato/ *n.m.* boat. ～**-
mouche** (*pl.* ～**x-mouches**) *n.m.*
sightseeing boat.

bâti /bati/ *a.* **bien** ～, well-built.

batifoler /batifɔle/ *v.i.* fool about.

bâtiment /batimɑ̃/ *n.m.* building;
(*navire*) vessel; (*industrie*) building
trade.

bâtir /batir/ *v.t.* build; (*coudre*) baste.

bâtisse /batis/ *n.f.* (*péj.*) building.

bâton /batɔ̃/ *n.m.* stick. **à** ～**s rompus,**
jumping from subject to subject. ～ **de
rouge,** lipstick.

battage /bataʒ/ *n.m.* (*publicité*: *fam.*)
(hard) plugging.

battant /batɑ̃/ *n.m.* (*vantail*) flap.
porte à deux ～**s,** double door.

battement /batmɑ̃/ *n.m.* (*de cœur*)
beat(ing); (*temps*) interval.

batterie /batri/ *n.f.* (*mil.*, *électr.*)
battery; (*mus.*) drums. ～ **de cuisine,**
pots and pans.

batteur /batœr/ *n.m.* (*mus.*) drummer; (*culin.*) whisk.

battre† /batr/ *v.t./i.* beat; (*blé*) thresh;
(*cartes*) shuffle; (*parcourir*) scour;
(*faire du bruit*) bang. **se** ～ *v. pr.* fight. ～
des ailes, flap its wings. ～ **des mains,**
clap. ～ **en retraite,** beat a retreat. ～ **la
semelle,** stamp one's feet. ～ **pavillon
britannique/**etc., fly the British/*etc.*
flag. ～ **son plein,** be in full swing.

battue /baty/ *n.f.* (*chasse*) beat; (*de
police*) search.

baume /bom/ *n.m.* balm.

bavard, ～**e** /bavar, -d/ *a.* talkative.
—*n.m.*, *f.* chatterbox.

bavard|er /bavarde/ *v.i.* chat; (*jacasser*)
chatter, gossip. ～**age** *n.m.* chatter,
gossip.

bav|e /bav/ *n.f.* dribble, slobber; (*de
limace*) slime. ～**er** *v.i.* dribble, slobber.
～**eux,** ～**euse** *a.* dribbling; (*omelette*)
runny.

bav|ette /bavɛt/ *n.f.*, ～**oir** *n.m.* bib.
tailler une ～**ette,** (*fam.*) have a chat.

bavure /bavyr/ *n.f.* smudge; (*erreur*)
mistake. ～ **policière,** (*fam.*) police
cock-up. **sans** ～, flawless(ly).

bazar /bazar/ *n.m.* bazaar; (*objets*: *fam.*)
clutter.

bazarder /bazarde/ *v.t.* (*vendre*: *fam.*)
get rid of, flog.

BCBG *abrév.* (*bon chic bon genre*)
posh.

BD *abrév.* (*bande dessinée*) comic
strip.

béant, ～**e** /beɑ̃, -t/ *a.* gaping.

béat, ～**e** /bea, -t/ *a.* (*hum.*) blissful;
(*péj.*) smug. ～**itude** /-tityd/ *n.f.*
(*hum.*) bliss.

beau *ou* **bel*, belle** (*m. pl.* ～**x**) /bo, bɛl/
a. fine, beautiful; (*femme*) beautiful;
(*homme*) handsome; (*grand*) big.
—*n.f.* beauty; (*sport*) deciding game.
au ～ **milieu,** right in the middle. **bel et
bien,** well and truly. **de plus belle,** more
than ever. **faire le** ～, sit up and beg. **on
a** ～ **essayer/insister/**etc., however
much one tries/insists/*etc.*, it is no use
trying/insisting/*etc.* ～**x-arts** *n.m. pl.*
fine arts. ～**-fils** (*pl.* ～**x-fils**) *n.m.* son-
in-law; (*remariage*) stepson. ～**-frère**
(*pl.* ～**x-frères**) *n.m.* brother-in-law.
～**-père** (*pl.* ～**x-pères**) *n.m.* father-in-
law; stepfather. ～**x-parents** *n.m. pl.*
parents-in-law.

beaucoup /boku/ *adv.* a lot, very much.
—*pron.* many (people). ～ **de,** (*nombre*)

many; (*quantité*) a lot of. **pas ∼ (de)**, not many; (*quantité*) not much. **∼ plus**/*etc.*, much more/*etc.* **∼ trop**, much too much. **de ∼**, by far.

beauté /bote/ *n.f.* beauty. **en ∼**, magnificently. **tu es en ∼**, you are looking good.

bébé /bebe/ *n.m.* baby. **∼-éprouvette**, test-tube baby.

bec /bɛk/ *n.m.* beak; (*de plume*) nib; (*de bouilloire*) spout; (*de casserole*) lip; (*bouche*: *fam.*) mouth. **∼-de-cane** (*pl.* **∼s-de-cane**)door-handle. **∼ de gaz**, gas lamp (*in street*).

bécane /bekan/ *n.f.* (*fam.*) bike.

bécasse /bekas/ *n.f.* woodcock.

bêche /bɛʃ/ *n.f.* spade.

bêcher /beʃe/ *v.t.* dig.

bécoter /bekɔte/ *v.t.*, **se ∼** *v. pr.* (*fam.*) kiss.

becquée /beke/ *n.f.* **donner la ∼ à**, (*oiseau*) feed; (*fig.*) spoonfeed.

bedaine /bədɛn/ *n.f.* paunch.

bedeau (*pl.* **∼x**) /bədo/ *n.m.* beadle.

bedonnant, ∼e /bədɔnɑ̃, -t/ *a.* paunchy.

beffroi /befrwa/ *n.m.* belfry.

bégayer /begeje/ *v.t./i.* stammer.

bègue /bɛg/ *n.m./f.* stammerer. **être ∼**, stammer.

bégueule /begœl/ *a.* prudish.

béguin /begɛ̃/ *n.m.* **avoir le ∼ pour**, (*fam.*) have a crush on.

beige /bɛʒ/ *a.* & *n.m.* beige.

beignet /bɛɲɛ/ *n.m.* fritter.

bel /bɛl/ *voir* **beau**.

bêler /bele/ *v.i.* bleat.

belette /bəlɛt/ *n.f.* weasel.

belge /bɛlʒ/ *a.* & *n.m./f.* Belgian.

Belgique /bɛlʒik/ *n.f.* Belgium.

bélier /belje/ *n.m.* ram. **le B∼**, Aries.

belle /bɛl/ *voir* **beau**.

belle-fille (*pl.* **∼s-filles**) /bɛlfij/ *n.f.* daughter-in-law; (*remariage*) step-daughter. **∼-mère** (*pl.* **∼s-mères**) *n.f.* mother-in-law; stepmother. **∼-sœur** (*pl.* **∼-sœurs**) *n.f.* sister-in-law.

belligérant, ∼e /beliʒerɑ̃, -t/ *a.* & *n.m.* belligerent.

belliqueu|x, ∼se /belikø, -z/ *a.* warlike.

belote /bəlɔt/ *n.f.* belote (*card game*).

belvédère /bɛlvedɛr/ *n.m.* (*lieu*) viewing spot, viewpoint.

bémol /bemɔl/ *n.m.* (*mus.*) flat.

bénédiction /benediksjɔ̃/ *n.f.* blessing.

bénéfice /benefis/ *n.m.* (*gain*) profit; (*avantage*) benefit.

bénéficiaire /benefisjɛr/ *n.m./f.* beneficiary.

bénéficier /benefisje/ *v.i.* **∼ de**, benefit from; (*jouir de*) enjoy, have.

bénéfique /benefik/ *a.* beneficial.

Bénélux /benelyks/ *n.m.* Benelux.

benêt /bənɛ/ *n.m.* simpleton.

bénévole /benevɔl/ *a.* voluntary.

bén|in, ∼igne /benɛ̃, -iɲ/ *a.* mild, slight; (*tumeur*) benign.

bén|ir /benir/ *v.t.* bless. **∼it, ∼ite** *a.* (*eau*) holy; (*pain*) consecrated.

bénitier /benitje/ *n.m.* stoup.

benjamin, ∼e /bɛ̃ʒamɛ̃, -in/ *n.m., f.* youngest child.

benne /bɛn/ *n.f.* (*de grue*) scoop; (*amovible*) skip. **∼ (basculante)**, dump truck.

benzine /bɛ̃zin/ *n.f.* benzine.

béotien, ∼ne /beɔsjɛ̃, -jɛn/ *n.m., f.* philistine.

béquille /bekij/ *n.f.* crutch; (*de moto*) stand.

bercail /bɛrkaj/ *n.m.* fold.

berceau (*pl.* **∼x**) /bɛrso/ *n.m.* cradle.

bercer /bɛrse/ *v.t.* (*balancer*) rock; (*apaiser*) lull; (*leurrer*) delude.

berceuse /bɛrsøz/ *n.f.* lullaby.

béret /berɛ/ *n.m.* beret.

berge /bɛrʒ/ *n.f.* (*bord*) bank.

berg|er, ∼ère /bɛrʒe, -ɛr/ *n.m., f.* shepherd, shepherdess. **∼erie** *n.f.* sheep-fold.

berlingot /bɛrlɛ̃go/ *n.m.* boiled sweet; (*emballage*) carton.

berne (en) /(ɑ̃)bɛrn/ *adv.* at half mast.

berner /bɛrne/ *v.t.* hoodwink.

besogne /bəzɔɲ/ *n.f.* task, job, chore.

besoin /bəzwɛ̃/ *n.m.* need. **avoir ∼ de**, need. **au ∼**, if need be.

best|ial (*m. pl.* **∼iaux**) /bɛstjal, -jo/ *a.* bestial.

bestiaux /bɛstjo/ *n.m. pl.* livestock.

bestiole /bɛstjɔl/ *n.f.* creepy-crawly.

bétail /betaj/ *n.m.* farm animals.

bête[1] /bɛt/ *n.f.* animal. **∼ noire**, pet hate, pet peeve. **∼ sauvage**, wild beast. **chercher la petite ∼**, be overfussy.

bête[2] /bɛt/ *a.* stupid. **∼ment** *adv.* stupidly.

bêtise /betiz/ *n.f.* stupidity; (*action*) stupid thing.

béton /betɔ̃/ *n.m.* concrete. **∼ armé**, reinforced concrete. **∼nière** /-ɔnjɛr/ *n.f.* cement-mixer, concrete-mixer.

betterave /bɛtrav/ *n.f.* beetroot. **∼ sucrière**, sugar-beet.

beugler /bøgle/ *v.i.* bellow, low; (*radio*) blare.

beur /bœr/ *n.m./f.* & *a.* (*fam.*) young French North African.

beurr|e /bœr/ *n.m.* butter. **∼er** *v.t.*

butter. **~ier** *n.m.* butter-dish. **~é,** *a.* buttered; (*fam.*) drunk.

bévue /bevy/ *n.f.* blunder.

biais /bjɛ/ *n.m.* (*fig.*) expedient; (*côté*) angle. **de ~, en ~,** at an angle. **de ~,** (*fig.*) indirectly.

biaiser /bjeze/ *v.i.* hedge.

bibelot /biblo/ *n.m.* curio.

biberon /bibrɔ̃/ *n.m.* (feeding-)bottle. **nourrir au ~,** bottle-feed.

bible /bibl/ *n.f.* bible. **la B~,** the Bible.

bibliographie /biblijɔgrafi/ *n.f.* bibliography.

bibliophile /biblijɔfil/ *n.m./f.* booklover.

biblioth|èque /biblijɔtɛk/ *n.f.* library; (*meuble*) bookcase; **~écaire** *n.m./f.* librarian.

biblique /biblik/ *a.* biblical.

bic /bik/ *n.m.* (P.) biro (P.).

bicarbonate /bikarbɔnat/ *n.m.* **~ (de soude),** bicarbonate (of soda).

biceps /bisɛps/ *n.m.* biceps.

biche /biʃ/ *n.f.* doe.

bichonner /biʃɔne/ *v.t.* doll up.

bicoque /bikɔk/ *n.f.* shack.

bicyclette /bisiklɛt/ *n.f.* bicycle.

bide /bid/ *n.m.* (*ventre*: *fam.*) belly; (*théâtre*: *fam.*) flop.

bidet /bidɛ/ *n.m.* bidet.

bidon /bidɔ̃/ *n.m.* can.—*a. invar.* (*fam.*) phoney. **c'est pas du ~,** (*fam.*) it's the truth, it's for real.

bidonville /bidɔ̃vil/ *n.f.* shanty town.

bidule /bidyl/ *n.m.* (*fam.*) thing.

bielle /bjɛl/ *n.f.* connecting rod.

bien /bjɛ̃/ *adv.* well; (*très*) quite, very. —*n.m.* good; (*patrimoine*) possession. —*a. invar.* good; (*passable*) all right; (*en forme*) well; (*à l'aise*) comfortable; (*beau*) attractive; (*respectable*) nice, respectable. —*conj.* **~ que,** (al)though. **~ que ce soit/que ça ait,** although it is/it has. **~ du,** (*quantité*) a lot of, much. **~ des,** (*nombre*) many. **il l'a ~ fait,** (*intensif*) he did do it. **ce n'est pas ~ de,** it is not right to. **~ sûr,** of course. **~s de consommation,** consumer goods. **~-aimé, ~-aimée** *a.* & *n.m.*, *f.* beloved. **~-être** *n.m.* well-being. **~-fondé** *n.m.* soundness. **~-pensant, ~-pensante** *a.* & *n.m.*, *f.* (*péj.*) right-thinking.

bienfaisan|t, -te /bjɛ̃fəzɑ̃, -t/ *a.* beneficial. **~ce** *n.f.* charity. **fête de ~ce,** fête.

bienfait /bjɛ̃fɛ/ *n.m.* (kind) favour; (*avantage*) benefit.

bienfai|teur, ~trice /bjɛ̃fɛtœr, -tris/ *n.m.*, *f.* benefactor.

bienheureu|x, ~se /bjɛ̃nœrø, -z/ *a.* happy, blessed.

bienséan|t, ~te /bjɛ̃seɑ̃, -t/ *a.* proper. **~ce** *n.f.* propriety.

bientôt /bjɛ̃to/ *adv.* soon. **à ~,** see you soon.

bienveillan|t, ~te /bjɛ̃vɛjɑ̃, -t/ *a.* kind(ly). **~ce** *n.f.* kind(li)ness.

bienvenu, ~e /bjɛ̃vny/ *a.* welcome. —*n.f.* welcome.—*n.m.*, *f.* **être le ~, être la ~e,** be welcome. **souhaiter la ~e à,** welcome.

bière /bjɛr/ *n.f.* beer; (*cercueil*) coffin. **~ blonde,** lager. **~ brune,** stout, brown ale. **~ pression,** draught beer.

biffer /bife/ *v.t.* cross out.

bifteck /biftɛk/ *n.m.* steak.

bifur|quer /bifyrke/ *v.i.* branch off, fork. **~cation** *n.f.* fork, junction.

bigam|e /bigam/ *a.* bigamous. —*n.m./f.* bigamist. **~ie** *n.f.* bigamy.

bigarré /bigare/ *a.* motley.

big-bang /bigbɑ̃g/ *n.m.* big bang.

bigot, ~e /bigo, -ɔt/ *n.m.*, *f.* religious fanatic. —*a.* over-pious.

bigoudi /bigudi/ *n.m.* curler.

bijou (*pl.* **~x**) /biʒu/ *n.m.* jewel. **~terie** *n.f.* (*boutique*) jeweller's shop; (*comm.*) jewellery. **~tier, ~tière** *n.m.*, *f.* jeweller.

bikini /bikini/ *n.m.* bikini.

bilan /bilɑ̃/ *n.m.* outcome; (*d'une catastrophe*) (casualty) toll; (*comm.*) balance sheet. **faire le ~ de,** assess. **~ de santé,** check-up.

bile /bil/ *n.f.* bile. **se faire de la ~,** (*fam.*) worry.

bilieu|x, ~se /biljø, -z/ *a.* bilious; (*fig.*) irascible.

bilingue /bilɛ̃g/ *a.* bilingual.

billard /bijar/ *n.m.* billiards; (*table*) billiard-table.

bille /bij/ *n.f.* (*d'enfant*) marble; (*de billard*) billiard-ball.

billet /bijɛ/ *n.m.* ticket; (*lettre*) note; (*article*) column. **~ (de banque),** (bank)note. **~ d'aller et retour,** return ticket; (*Amer.*) round trip ticket. **~ de faveur,** complimentary ticket. **~ aller simple,** single ticket; (*Amer.*) one-way ticket.

billetterie /bijɛtri/ *n.f.* cash dispenser.

billion /biljɔ̃/ *n.m.* billion (= 10^{12}); (*Amer.*) trillion.

billot /bijo/ *n.m.* block.

bimensuel, ~le /bimɑ̃sɥɛl/ *a.* fortnightly, bimonthly.

bin|er /bine/ *v.t.* hoe. **~ette** *n.f.* hoe; (*fam.*) face.

biochimie /bjɔʃimi/ *n.f.* biochemistry.

biodégradable /bjɔdegradabl/ *a.* biodegradable.

biograph|ie /bjɔgrafi/ n.f. biography. **~e** n.m./f. biographer.

biolog|ie /bjɔlɔʒi/ n.f. biology. **~ique** a. biological. **~iste** n.m./f. biologist.

bipède /bipɛd/ n.m. biped.

bis¹, bise /bi, biz/ a. greyish brown.

bis² /bis/ a.invar. (numéro) A, a. —n.m. & int. encore.

bisbille (en) /(ã)bisbij/ adv. (fam.) at loggerheads (**avec**, with).

biscornu /biskɔrny/ a. crooked; (bizarre) weird.

biscotte /biskɔt/ n.f. rusk.

biscuit /biskɥi/ n.m. (salé) biscuit; (Amer.) cracker; (sucré) biscuit; (Amer.) cookie. **~ de Savoie,** sponge-cake.

bise¹ /biz/ n.f. (fam.) kiss.

bise² /biz/ n.f. (vent) north wind.

bison /bizɔ̃/ n.m. (American) buffalo, bison.

bisou /bizu/ n.m. (fam.) kiss.

bisser /bise/ v.t. encore.

bistouri /bisturi/ n.m. lancet.

bistre /bistr/ a. & n.m. dark brown.

bistro(t) /bistro/ n.m. café, bar.

bit /bit/ n.m. (comput.) bit.

bitume /bitym/ n.m. asphalt.

bizarre /bizar/ a. odd, peculiar. **~ment** adv. oddly. **~rie** n.f. peculiarity.

blafard, ~e /blafar, -d/ a. pale.

blagu|e /blag/ n.f. joke. **~e à tabac,** tobacco-pouch. **~er** v.i. joke; v.t. tease. **~eur, ~euse** n.m., f. joker; a. jokey.

blaireau (pl. **~x**) /blɛro/ n.m. shaving-brush; (animal) badger.

blâm|e /blɑm/ n.m. rebuke, blame. **~able** a. blameworthy. **~er** v.t. rebuke, blame.

blanc, blanche /blã, blãʃ/ a. white; (papier, page) blank. —n.m. white; (espace) blank. —n.m., f. white man, white woman. —n.f. (mus.) minim. **~ (de poulet),** breast, white meat (of the chicken). **le ~,** (linge) whites. **laisser en ~,** leave blank.

blancheur /blãʃœr/ n.f. whiteness.

blanch|ir /blãʃir/ v.t. whiten; (linge) launder; (personne: fig.) clear; (culin.) blanch. **~ir (à la chaux),** whitewash. —v.i. turn white. **~issage** n.m. laundering. **~isserie** n.f. laundry. **~isseur, ~isseuse** n.m., f. laundry-man, laundress.

blasé /blaze/ a. blasé.

blason /blazɔ̃/ n.m. coat of arms.

blasph|ème /blasfɛm/ n.m. blasphemy. **~ématoire** a. blasphemous. **~émer** v.t./i. blaspheme.

blatte /blat/ n.f. cockroach.

blazer /blɛzœr/ n.m. blazer.

blé /ble/ n.m. wheat.

bled /blɛd/ n.m. (fam.) dump, hole.

blême /blɛm/ a. (sickly) pale.

bless|er /blese/ v.t. injure; hurt; (par balle) wound; (offenser) hurt, wound. **se ~er** v. pr. injure ou hurt o.s. **~ant, ~ante** /blesã, -t/ a. hurtful. **~é, ~ée** n.m., f. casualty, injured person.

blessure /blesyr/ n.f. wound.

blet, ~te /blɛ, blɛt/ a. over-ripe.

bleu /blø/ a. blue; (culin.) very rare. **~ marine,** navy blue. —n.m. blue; (contusion) bruise. **~(s),** (vêtement) overalls. **~ir** v.t./i. turn blue.

bleuet /bløɛ/ n.m. cornflower.

bleuté /bløte/ a. slightly blue.

blind|er /blɛ̃de/ v.t. armour(-plate); (fig.) harden. **~é** a. armoured; (fig.) immune (**contre,** to); n.m. armoured car, tank.

blizzard /blizar/ n.m. blizzard.

bloc /blɔk/ n.m. block; (de papier) pad; (système) unit; (pol.) bloc. **à ~,** hard, tight. **en ~,** all together. **~-notes** (pl. **~s-notes**) n.m. note-pad.

blocage /blɔkaʒ/ n.m. (des prix) freeze, freezing; (des roues) locking; (psych.) block.

blocus /blɔkys/ n.m. blockade.

blond, ~e /blɔ̃, -d/ a. fair, blond. —n.m., f. fair-haired ou blond man ou woman. **~eur** /-dœr/ n.f. fairness.

bloquer /blɔke/ v.t. block; (porte, machine) jam; (freins) slam on; (roues) lock; (prix, crédits) freeze; (grouper) put together. **se ~** v. pr. jam; (roues) lock.

blottir (se) /(sə)blɔtir/ v. pr. snuggle, huddle.

blouse /bluz/ n.f. smock.

blouson /bluzɔ̃/ n.m. lumber-jacket; (Amer.) windbreaker.

blue-jean /bludʒin/ n.m. jeans.

bluff /blœf/ n.m. bluff. **~er** v.t./i. bluff.

blush /blœʃ/ n.m. blusher.

boa /bɔa/ n.m. boa.

bobard /bɔbar/ n.m. (fam.) fib.

bobine /bɔbin/ n.f. reel; (sur machine) spool; (électr.) coil.

bobo /bobo/ n.m. (fam.) sore, cut. **avoir ~,** have a pain.

bocage /bɔkaʒ/ n.m. grove.

boc|al (pl. **~aux**) /bɔkal, -o/ n.m. jar.

bock /bɔk/ n.m. beer glass; (contenu) glass of beer.

body /bodi/ n.m. leotard.

bœuf (pl. **~s**) /bœf, bø/ n.m. ox; (viande) beef. **~s,** oxen.

bogue /bɔg/ n.m. (comput.) bug.

bohème /bɔɛm/ a. & n.m./f. unconventional.

boire† /bwar/ *v.t./i.* drink; (*absorber*) soak up. ～ **un coup,** have a drink.
bois¹ /bwa/ *voir* **boire.**
bois² /bwa/ *n.m.* (*matériau, forêt*) wood. **de ～, en ～,** wooden.
boisé /bwaze/ *a.* wooded.
bois|er /bwaze/ *v.t.* (*chambre*) panel. ～**eries** *n.f. pl.* panelling.
boisson /bwasɔ̃/ *n.f.* drink.
boit /bwa/ *voir* **boire.**
boîte /bwat/ *n.f.* box; (*de conserves*) tin, can; (*firme: fam.*) firm. ～ **à gants,** glove compartment. ～ **aux lettres,** letter-box. ～ **de nuit,** night-club. ～ **postale,** post-office box. ～ **de vitesses,** gear box.
boiter /bwate/ *v.i.* limp; (*meuble*) wobble.
boiteu|x, ～**se** /bwatø, -z/ *a.* lame; (*meuble*) wobbly; (*raisonnement*) shaky.
boîtier /bwatje/ *n.m.* case.
bol /bɔl/ *n.m.* bowl. **un ～ d'air,** a breath of fresh air. **avoir du ～,** (*fam.*) be lucky.
bolide /bɔlid/ *n.m.* racing car.
Bolivie /bɔlivi/ *n.f.* Bolivia.
bolivien, ～ne /bɔlivjɛ̃, -jɛn/ *a. & n.m., f.* Bolivian.
bombance /bɔ̃bɑ̃s/ *n.f.* faire ～, (*fam.*) revel.
bombard|er /bɔ̃barde/ *v.t.* bomb; (*par obus*) shell; (*nommer: fam.*) appoint unexpectedly (as). ～**er qn. de,** (*fig.*) bombard s.o. with. ～**ement** *n.m.* bombing; shelling. ～**ier** *n.m.* (*aviat.*) bomber.
bombe /bɔ̃b/ *n.f.* bomb; (*atomiseur*) spray, aerosol.
bombé /bɔ̃be/ *a.* rounded; (*route*) cambered.
bomber /bɔ̃be/ *v.t.* ～ **la poitrine,** throw out one's chest.
bon, bonne /bɔ̃, bɔn/ *a.* good; (*qui convient*) right; (*prudent*) wise. ～ **à/pour,** (*approprié*) fit to/for. **tenir ～,** stand firm. —*n.m.* (*billet*) voucher, coupon; (*comm.*) bond. **du ～,** some good. **pour de ～,** for good. **à quoi ～?,** what's the good *ou* point? **bonne année,** happy New Year. ～ **anniversaire,** happy birthday. ～ **appétit/voyage,** enjoy your meal/trip. **bonne chance/nuit,** good luck/night. **bonne femme,** (*péj.*) woman. **bonne-maman** (*pl.* **bonnes-mamans**) *n.f.* (*fam.*) granny. ～**-papa** (*pl.* ～**s-papas**) *n.m.* (*fam.*) grand-dad. ～ **sens,** common sense. ～ **vivant,** bon viveur. **de bonne heure,** early.
bonbon /bɔ̃bɔ̃/ *n.m.* sweet; (*Amer.*) candy. ～**nière** /-ɔnjɛr/ *n.f.* sweet box; (*Amer.*) candy box.

bonbonne /bɔ̃bɔn/ *n.f.* demijohn; (*de gaz*) canister.
bond /bɔ̃/ *n.m.* leap. **faire un ～,** leap in the air; (*de surprise*) jump.
bonde /bɔ̃d/ *n.f.* plug; (*trou*) plughole.
bondé /bɔ̃de/ *a.* packed.
bondir /bɔ̃dir/ *v.i.* leap; (*de surprise*) jump.
bonheur /bɔnœr/ *n.m.* happiness; (*chance*) (good) luck. **au petit ～,** haphazardly. **par ～,** luckily.
bonhomme¹ (*pl.* **bonshommes**) /bɔnɔm, bɔ̃zɔm/ *n.m.* fellow. ～ **de neige,** snowman.
bonhom|me² /bɔnɔm/ *a. invar.* good-hearted. ～**ie** *n.f.* good-heartedness.
bonifier (se) /(sə)bɔnifje/ *v. pr.* improve.
boniment /bɔnimɑ̃/ *n.m.* smooth talk.
bonjour /bɔ̃ʒur/ *n.m. & int.* hallo, hello, good morning *ou* afternoon.
bon marché /bɔ̃marʃe/ *a. invar.* cheap. —*adv.* cheap(ly).
bonne¹ /bɔn/ *a.f. voir* **bon.**
bonne² /bɔn/ *n.f.* (*domestique*) maid. ～ **d'enfants,** nanny.
bonnement /bɔnmɑ̃/ *adv.* **tout ～,** quite simply.
bonnet /bɔnɛ/ *n.m.* hat; (*de soutien-gorge*) cup. ～ **de bain,** swimming cap.
bonneterie /bɔnɛtri/ *n.f.* hosiery.
bonsoir /bɔ̃swar/ *n.m. & int.* good evening; (*en se couchant*) good night.
bonté /bɔ̃te/ *n.f.* kindness.
bonus /bɔnys/ *n.m.* (*auto.*) no claims bonus.
boom /bum/ *n.m.* (*comm.*) boom.
boots /buts/ *n.m. pl.* ankle boots.
bord /bɔr/ *n.m.* edge; (*rive*) bank. **à ～ (de),** on board. **au ～ de la mer,** at the seaside. **au ～ des larmes,** on the verge of tears. ～ **de la route,** roadside. ～ **du trottoir,** kerb; (*Amer.*) curb.
bordeaux /bɔrdo/ *n.m. invar.* Bordeaux (wine), claret. —*a. invar.* maroon.
bordée /bɔrde/ *n.f.* ～ **d'injures,** torrent of abuse.
bordel /bɔrdɛl/ *n.m.* brothel; (*désordre: fam.*) shambles.
border /bɔrde/ *v.t.* line, border; (*tissu*) edge; (*personne, lit*) tuck in.
bordereau (*pl.* ～**x**) /bɔrdəro/ *n.m.* (*liste*) note, slip; (*facture*) invoice.
bordure /bɔrdyr/ *n.f.* border. **en ～ de,** on the edge of.
borgne /bɔrɲ/ *a.* one-eyed; (*fig.*) shady.
borne /bɔrn/ *n.f.* boundary marker. ～ **(kilométrique),** (*approx.*) milestone. ～**s,** limits.
borné /bɔrne/ *a.* narrow; (*personne*) narrow-minded.

borner /bɔrne/ v.t. confine. se ~ v. pr. confine o.s. (à, to).

bosquet /bɔske/ n.m. grove.

bosse /bɔs/ n.f. bump; (de chameau) hump. **avoir la ~ de**, (fam.) have a gift for. **avoir roulé sa ~**, have been around.

bosseler /bɔsle/ v.t. emboss; (endommager) dent.

bosser /bɔse/ v.i. (fam.) work (hard). —v.t. (fam.) work (hard) at.

bossu, ~e /bɔsy/ n.m., f. hunch-back.

botani|que /bɔtanik/ n.f. botany. —a. botanical. ~ste n.m./f. botanist.

bott|e /bɔt/ n.f. boot; (de fleurs, légumes) bunch; (de paille) bundle, bale. ~es de caoutchouc, wellingtons. ~ier n.m. boot-maker.

botter /bɔte/ v.t. (fam.) ça me botte, I like the idea.

Bottin /bɔtɛ̃/ n.m. (P.) phone book.

bouc /buk/ n.m. (billy-)goat; (barbe) goatee. ~ émissaire, scapegoat.

boucan /bukɑ̃/ n.m. (fam.) din.

bouche /buʃ/ n.f. mouth. ~ bée, open-mouthed. ~ d'égout, manhole. ~ d'incendie, (fire) hydrant. ~ de métro, entrance to the underground ou subway (Amer.). ~-à-bouche n.m. mouth-to-mouth resuscitation.

bouché /buʃe/ a. c'est ~, (profession, avenir) it's a dead end.

bouchée /buʃe/ n.f. mouthful.

boucher[1] /buʃe/ v.t. block; (bouteille) cork. se ~ v. pr. get blocked. se ~ le nez, hold one's nose.

bouch|er[2], ~ère /buʃe, -ɛr/ n.m., f. butcher. ~erie n.f. butcher's (shop); (carnage) butchery.

bouche-trou /buʃtru/ n.m. stopgap.

bouchon /buʃɔ̃/ n.m. stopper; (en liège) cork; (de bidon, tube) cap; (de pêcheur) float, (de circulation: fig.) hold-up.

boucle /bukl/ n.f. (de ceinture) buckle; (forme) loop; (de cheveux) curl. ~ d'oreille, ear-ring.

boucl|er /bukle/ v.t. fasten; (terminer) finish off; (enfermer: fam.) shut up; (encercler) seal off; (budget) balance. —v.i. curl. ~é a. (cheveux) curly.

bouclier /buklije/ n.m. shield.

bouddhiste /budist/ a. & n.m./f. Buddhist.

boud|er /bude/ v.i. sulk. —v.t. steer clear of. ~erie n.f. sulkiness. ~eur, ~euse a. & n.m., f. sulky (person).

boudin /budɛ̃/ n.m. black pudding.

boudoir /budwar/ n.m. boudoir.

boue /bu/ n.f. mud.

bouée /bwe/ n.f. buoy. ~ de sauvetage, lifebuoy.

boueu|x, ~se /bwø, -z/ a. muddy.

—n.m. dustman; (Amer.) garbage collector.

bouff|e /buf/ n.f. (fam.) food, grub. ~er v.t./i. (fam.) eat; (bâfrer) gobble.

bouffée /bufe/ n.f. puff, whiff; (méd.) flush; (d'orgueil) fit.

bouffi /bufi/ a. bloated.

bouffon, ~ne /bufɔ̃, -ɔn/ a. farcical. —n.m. buffoon.

bouge /buʒ/ n.m. hovel; (bar) dive.

bougeoir /buʒwar/ n.m. candlestick.

bougeotte /buʒɔt/ n.f. la ~, (fam.) the fidgets.

bouger /buʒe/ v.t./i. move, (agir) stir. se ~ v. pr. (fam.) move.

bougie /buʒi/ n.f. candle; (auto.) spark(ing)-plug.

bougon, ~ne /bugɔ̃, -ɔn/ a. grumpy. ~ner /-ɔne/ v.i. grumble.

bouillabaisse /bujabɛs/ n.f. bouillabaisse.

bouillie /buji/ n.f. porridge; (pour bébé) baby food; (péj.) mush. **en ~**, crushed, mushy.

bouill|ir† /bujir/ v.i. boil. —v.t. (faire) ~ir, boil. ~ant, ~ante a. boiling; (très chaud) boiling hot.

bouilloire /bujwar/ n.f. kettle.

bouillon /bujɔ̃/ n.m. (aliment) stock. ~ cube, stock cube. ~ner /-ɔne/ v.i. bubble.

bouillotte /bujɔt/ n.f. hot-water bottle.

boulang|er, ~ère /bulɑ̃ʒe, -ɛr/ n.m., f, baker. ~erie n.f. bakery. ~erie-pâtisserie n.f. baker's and confectioner's shop.

boule /bul/ n.f. ball; (de machine à écrire) golf ball. ~s, (jeu) bowls. **jouer aux ~s**, play bowls. **une ~ dans la gorge**, lump in one's throat. ~ de neige, snowball. **faire ~ de neige**, snowball.

bouleau (pl. ~x) /bulo/ n.m. (silver) birch.

bouledogue /buldɔg/ n.m. bulldog.

boulet /bulɛ/ n.m. (de canon) cannon-ball; (de forçat: fig.) ball and chain.

boulette /bulɛt/ n.f. (de papier) pellet; (aliment) meat ball.

boulevard /bulvar/ n.m. boulevard.

boulevers|er /bulvɛrse/ v.t. turn upside down; (pays, plans) disrupt; (émouvoir) distress, upset. ~ant, ~ante a. deeply moving. ~ement n.m. upheaval.

boulier /bulje/ n.m. abacus.

boulimie /bulimi/ n.f. compulsive eating; (méd.) bulimia.

boulon /bulɔ̃/ n.m. bolt.

boulot[1] /bulo/ n.m. (travail: fam.) work.

boulot[2], ~te /bulo, -ɔt/ a. (rond: fam.) dumpy.

boum /bum/ *n.m. & int.* bang. —*n.f.* (*réunion: fam.*) party.

bouquet /bukɛ/ *n.m.* (*de fleurs*) bunch, bouquet; (*d'arbres*) clump. **c'est le ∼!**, (*fam.*) that's the last straw!

bouquin /bukɛ̃/ *n.m.* (*fam.*) book. **∼er** /-ine/ *v.t./i.* (*fam.*) read. **∼iste** /-inist/ *n.m./f.* second-hand bookseller.

bourbeu|x, ∼se /burbø, -z/ *a.* muddy.

bourbier /burbje/ *n.m.* mire.

bourde /burd/ *n.f.* blunder.

bourdon /burdɔ̃/ *n.m.* bumble-bee.

bourdonn|er /burdɔne/ *v.i.* buzz. **∼ement** *n.m.* buzzing.

bourg /bur/ *n.m.* (market) town.

bourgade /burgad/ *n.f.* village.

bourgeois, ∼e /burʒwa, -z/ *a. & n.m., f.* middle-class (person); (*péj.*) bourgeois. **∼ie** /-zi/ *n.f.* middle class(es).

bourgeon /burʒɔ̃/ *n.m.* bud. **∼ner** /-ɔne/ *v.i.* bud.

bourgogne /burgɔɲ/ *n.m.* burgundy. —*n.f.* **la B∼**, Burgundy.

bourlinguer /burlɛ̃ge/ *v.i.* (*fam.*) travel about.

bourrade /burad/ *n.f.* prod.

bourrage /buraʒ/ *n.m.* **∼ de crâne**, brainwashing.

bourrasque /burask/ *n.f.* squall.

bourrati|f, ∼ve /buratif, -v/ *a.* filling, stodgy.

bourreau (*pl.* **∼x**) /buro/ *n.m.* executioner. **∼ de travail**, workaholic.

bourrelet /burlɛ/ *n.m.* weather-strip, draught excluder; (*de chair*) roll of fat.

bourrer /bure/ *v.t.* cram (**de**, with); (*pipe*) fill. **∼ de**, (*nourriture*) stuff with. **∼ de coups**, thrash. **∼ le crâne à qn.**, fill s.o.'s head with nonsense.

bourrique /burik/ *n.f.* ass.

bourru /bury/ *a.* surly.

bours|e /burs/ *n.f.* purse; (*subvention*) grant. **la B∼e**, the Stock Exchange. **∼ier, ∼ière** *a.* Stock Exchange; *n.m., f.* holder of a grant.

boursoufler /bursufle/ *v.t., se ∼ v. pr.* puff up, swell.

bouscul|er /buskyle/ *v.t.* (*pousser*) jostle; (*presser*) rush; (*renverser*) knock over. **∼ade** *n.f.* rush; (*cohue*) crush.

bouse /buz/ *n.f.* (cow) dung.

bousiller /buzije/ *v.t.* (*fam.*) mess up.

boussole /busɔl/ *n.f.* compass.

bout /bu/ *n.m.* end; (*de langue, bâton*) tip; (*morceau*) bit. **à ∼**, exhausted. **à ∼ de souffle**, out of breath. **à ∼ portant**, point-blank. **au ∼ de**, (*après*) after. **∼ filtre**, filter-tip. **venir à ∼ de**, (*finir*) manage to finish.

boutade /butad/ *n.f.* jest; (*caprice*) whim.

boute-en-train /butɑ̃trɛ̃/ *n.m. invar.* joker, live wire.

bouteille /butɛj/ *n.f.* bottle.

boutique /butik/ *n.f.* shop; (*de mode*) boutique.

bouton /butɔ̃/ *n.m.* button; (*pustule*) pimple; (*pousse*) bud; (*de porte, radio, etc.*) knob. **∼ de manchette**, cuff-link. **∼-d'or** *n.m.* (*pl.* **∼s-d'or**) buttercup. **∼ner** /-ɔne/ *v.t.* button (up). **∼nière** /-ɔnjɛr/ *n.f.* buttonhole. **∼-pression** (*pl.* **∼s-pression**) *n.m.* press-stud; (*Amer.*) snap.

boutonneu|x, ∼se /butɔnø, -z/ *a.* pimply.

bouture /butyr/ *n.f.* (*plante*) cutting.

bovin, ∼e /bɔvɛ̃, -in/ *a.* bovine. **∼s** *n.m. pl.* cattle.

bowling /bɔliŋ/ *n.m.* bowling; (*salle*) bowling-alley.

box (*pl.* **∼ ou boxes**) /bɔks/ *n.m.* lock-up garage; (*de dortoir*) cubicle; (*d'écurie*) (loose) box; (*jurid.*) dock.

box|e /bɔks/ *n.f.* boxing. **∼er** *v.t./i.* box. **∼eur** *n.m.* boxer.

boyau (*pl.* **∼x**) /bwajo/ *n.m.* gut; (*corde*) catgut; (*galerie*) gallery; (*de bicyclette*) tyre; (*Amer.*) tire.

boycott|er /bɔjkɔte/ *v.t.* boycott. **∼age** *n.m.* boycott.

BP *abrév.* (*boîte postale*) PO Box.

bracelet /braslɛ/ *n.m.* bracelet; (*de montre*) strap.

braconn|er /brakɔne/ *v.i.* poach. **∼ier** *n.m.* poacher.

brad|er /brade/ *v.t.* sell off. **∼erie** *n.f.* open-air sale.

braguette /bragɛt/ *n.f.* fly.

braille /braj/ *n.m. & a.* Braille.

brailler /braje/ *v.t./i.* bawl.

braire /brɛr/ *v.i.* bray.

braise /brɛz/ *n.f.* embers.

braiser /breze/ *v.t.* braise.

brancard /brɑ̃kar/ *n.m.* stretcher; (*bras*) shaft. **∼ier** /-dje/ *n.m.* stretcher-bearer.

branch|e /brɑ̃ʃ/ *n.f.* branch. **∼ages** *n.m. pl.* (cut) branches.

branché /brɑ̃ʃe/ *a.* (*fam.*) trendy.

branch|er /brɑ̃ʃe/ *v.t.* connect; (*électr.*) plug in. **∼ement** *n.m.* connection.

branchies /brɑ̃ʃi/ *n.f. pl.* gills.

brandir /brɑ̃dir/ *v.t.* brandish.

branle /brɑ̃l/ *n.m.* **mettre en ∼**, set in motion. **se mettre en ∼**, get started. **∼-bas (de combat)** *n.m. invar.* bustle.

branler /brɑ̃le/ *v.i.* be shaky. —*v.t.* shake.

braquer /brake/ *v.t.* aim; (*regard*) fix; (*roue*) turn; (*banque: fam.*) hold up. **∼ qn. contre**, turn s.o. against. —*v.i.*

(*auto.*) turn (the wheel). —*v. pr.* **se ~,** dig one's heels in.

bras /bra/ *n.m.* arm. —*n.m. pl.* (*fig.*) labour, hands. **à ~-le-corps** *adv.* round the waist. **~ dessus bras dessous,** arm in arm. **~ droit,** (*fig.*) right-hand man. **en ~ de chemise,** in one's shirtsleeves.

brasier /brazje/ *n.m.* blaze.

brassard /brasar/ *n.m.* arm-band.

brasse /bras/ *n.f.* (breast-)stroke; (*mesure*) fathom.

brassée /brase/ *n.f.* armful.

brass|er /brase/ *v.t.* mix; (*bière*) brew; (*affaires*) handle a lot of. **~age** *n.m.* mixing; brewing. **~erie** *n.f.* brewery; (*café*) brasserie. **~eur** *n.m.* brewer. **~eur d'affaires,** big businessman.

brassière /brasjɛr/ *n.f.* (baby's) vest.

bravache /bravaʃ/ *n.m.* braggart.

bravade /bravad/ *n.f.* **par ~,** out of bravado.

brave /brav/ *a.* brave; (*bon*) good. **~ment** *adv.* bravely.

braver /brave/ *v.t.* defy.

bravo /bravo/ *int.* bravo. —*n.m.* cheer.

bravoure /bravur/ *n.f.* bravery.

break /brɛk/ *n.m.* estate car; (*Amer.*) station-wagon.

brebis /brəbi/ *n.f.* ewe. **~ galeuse,** black sheep.

brèche /brɛʃ/ *n.f.* gap, breach. **être sur la ~,** be on the go.

bredouille /brəduj/ *a.* empty-handed.

bredouiller /brəduje/ *v.t./i.* mumble.

bref, brève /brɛf, -v/ *a.* short, brief. —*adv.* in short. **en ~,** in short.

Brésil /brezil/ *n.m.* Brazil.

brésilien, ~ne /breziljɛ̃, -jɛn/ *a. & n.m., f.* Brazilian.

Bretagne /brətaɲ/ *n.f.* Brittany.

bretelle /brətɛl/ *n.f.* (shoulder)strap; (*d'autoroute*) access road. **~s,** (*pour pantalon*) braces; (*Amer.*) suspenders.

breton, ~ne /brətɔ̃, -ɔn/ *a. & n.m., f.* Breton.

breuvage /brœvaʒ/ *n.m.* beverage.

brève /brɛv/ *voir* **bref.**

brevet /brəvɛ/ *n.m.* diploma. **~ (d'invention),** patent.

brevet|er /brəvte/ *v.t.* patent. **~é** *a.* patented.

bribes /brib/ *n.f. pl.* scraps.

bric-à-brac /brikabrak/ *n.m. invar.* bric-à-brac.

bricole /brikɔl/ *n.f.* trifle.

bricol|er /brikɔle/ *v.i.* do odd (do-it-yourself) jobs. —*v.t.* fix (up). **~age** *n.m.* do-it-yourself (jobs). **~eur, ~euse** *n.m., f.* handyman, handywoman.

brid|e /brid/ *n.f.* bridle. **tenir en ~e,** keep

in check. **~er** *v.t.* (*cheval*) bridle; (*fig.*) keep in check, bridle; (*culin.*) truss.

bridé /bride/ *a.* **yeux ~s,** slit eyes.

bridge /bridʒ/ *n.m.* (*cartes*) bridge.

briève|ment /brijɛvmɑ̃/ *adv.* briefly. **~té** *n.f.* brevity.

brigad|e /brigad/ *n.f.* (*de police*) squad; (*mil.*) brigade; (*fig.*) team. **~ier** *n.m.* (*de police*) sergeant.

brigand /brigɑ̃/ *n.m.* robber. **~age** /-daʒ/ *n.m.* robbery.

briguer /brige/ *v.t.* seek (after).

brill|ant, ~ante /brijɑ̃, -t/ *a.* (*couleur*) bright; (*luisant*) shiny; (*remarquable*) brilliant. —*n.m.* (*éclat*) shine; (*diamant*) diamond. **~amment** *adv.* brilliantly.

briller /brije/ *v.i.* shine.

brim|er /brime/ *v.t.* bully, harass. **se sentir brimé,** feel put down. **~ade** *n.f.* vexation.

brin /brɛ̃/ *n.m.* (*de corde*) strand; (*de muguet*) sprig. **~ d'herbe,** blade of grass. **un ~ de,** a bit of.

brindille /brɛ̃dij/ *n.f.* twig.

bringuebaler /brɛ̃gbale/ *v.i.* (*fam.*) wobble about.

brio /brijo/ *n.m.* brilliance. **avec ~,** brilliantly.

brioche /brijɔʃ/ *n.f.* brioche (*small round sweet cake*); (*ventre: fam.*) paunch.

brique /brik/ *n.f.* brick.

briquer /brike/ *v.t.* polish.

briquet /brikɛ/ *n.m.* (cigarette-)lighter.

brisant /brizɑ̃/ *n.m.* reef.

brise /briz/ *n.f.* breeze.

bris|er /brize/ *v.t.* break. **se ~er** *v. pr.* break. **~e-lames** *n.m. invar.* breakwater. **~eur de grève** *n.m.* strikebreaker.

britannique /britanik/ *a.* British. *n.m./f.* Briton. **les B ~s,** the British.

broc /bro/ *n.m.* pitcher.

brocant|e /brokɑ̃t/ *n.f.* second-hand goods. **~eur, ~euse** *n.m., f.* second-hand goods dealer.

broche /brɔʃ/ *n.f.* brooch; (*culin.*) spit. **à la ~,** spit-roasted.

broché /brɔʃe/ *a.* paperback(ed).

brochet /brɔʃɛ/ *n.m.* (*poisson*) pike.

brochette /brɔʃɛt/ *n.f.* skewer.

brochure /brɔʃyr/ *n.f.* brochure, booklet.

brod|er /brɔde/ *v.t.* embroider. —*v.i.* (*fig.*) embroider the truth. **~erie** *n.f.* embroidery.

broncher /brɔ̃ʃe/ *v.i.* **sans ~,** without turning a hair.

bronch|es /brɔ̃ʃ/ *n.f. pl.* bronchial tubes. **~ite** *n.f.* bronchitis.

bronze /brɔ̃z/ *n.m.* bronze.

bronz|er /brɔ̃ze/ *v.i.,* **se ~er** *v. pr.* get a

(sun-)tan. **~age** *n.m.* (sun-)tan. **~é** *a.* (sun-)tanned.

brosse /brɔs/ *n.f.* brush. **~** **à dents,** toothbrush. **~** **à habits,** clothes-brush. **en ~,** (*coiffure*) in a crew cut.

brosser /brɔse/ *v.t.* brush; (*fig.*) paint. **se ~ les dents/les cheveux,** brush one's teeth/hair.

brouette /bruɛt/ *n.f.* wheelbarrow.

brouhaha /bruaa/ *n.m.* hubbub.

brouillard /brujar/ *n.m.* fog.

brouille /bruj/ *n.f.* quarrel.

brouill|er /bruje/ *v.t.* mix up; (*vue*) blur; (*œufs*) scramble; (*radio*) jam; (*amis*) set at odds. **se ~er** *v. pr.* become confused; (*ciel*) cloud over; (*amis*) fall out. **~on¹, ~onne** *a.* untidy.

brouillon² /brujɔ̃/ *n.m.* (rough) draft.

broussailles /brusaj/ *n.f. pl.* undergrowth.

brousse /brus/ *n.f.* **la ~,** the bush.

brouter /brute/ *v.t./i.* graze.

broutille /brutij/ *n.f.* trifle.

broyer /brwaje/ *v.t.* crush; (*moudre*) grind.

bru /bry/ *n.f.* daughter-in-law.

bruin|e /brɥin/ *n.f.* drizzle. **~er** *v.i.* drizzle.

bruire /brɥir/ *v.i.* rustle.

bruissement /brɥismã/ *n.m.* rustling.

bruit /brɥi/ *n.m.* noise; (*fig.*) rumour.

bruitage /brɥitaʒ/ *n.m.* sound effects.

brûlant, **~e** /brylã, -t/ *a.* burning (hot); (*sujet*) red-hot; (*ardent*) fiery.

brûlé /bryle/ *a.* (*démasqué*: *fam.*) blown. **—***n.m.* burning. **ça sent le ~,** I can smell sth. burning.

brûle-pourpoint (à) /(a)brylpurpwɛ̃/ *adv.* point-blank.

brûl|er /bryle/ *v.t./i.* burn; (*essence*) use (up); (*signal*) go through *ou* past (without stopping); (*dévorer*: *fig.*) consume. **se ~er** *v. pr.* burn o.s. **~eur** *n.m.* burner.

brûlure /brylyr/ *n.f.* burn. **~s** **d'estomac,** heartburn.

brum|e /brym/ *n.f.* mist. **~eux, ~euse** *a.* misty; (*idées*) hazy.

brun, ~e /brœ̃, bryn/ *a.* brown, dark. **—***n.m.* brown. **—***n.m., f.* dark-haired person. **~ir** /brynir/ *v.i.* turn brown; (*se bronzer*) get a tan.

brunch /brœnʃ/ *n.m.* brunch.

brushing /brœʃiŋ/ *n.m.* blow-dry.

brusque /brysk/ *a.* (*soudain*) sudden, abrupt; (*rude*) abrupt. **~ment** /-əmã/ *adv.* suddenly, abruptly.

brusquer /bryske/ *v.t.* rush.

brut /bryt/ *a.* (*diamant*) rough; (*soie*) raw; (*pétrole*) crude; (*comm.*) gross.

brut|al (*m. pl.* **~aux**) /brytal, -o/ *a.* brutal. **~aliser** *v.t.* treat roughly *ou* violently, manhandle. **~alité** *n.f.* brutality.

brute /bryt/ *n.f.* brute.

Bruxelles /brysɛl/ *n.m./f.* Brussels.

bruy|ant, ~ante /brɥijã, -t/ *a.* noisy. **~amment** *adv.* noisily.

bruyère /bryjɛr/ *n.f.* heather.

bu /by/ *voir* **boire**.

bûche /byʃ/ *n.f.* log. **~** **de Noël,** Christmas log. **(se) ramasser une ~,** (*fam.*) come a cropper.

bûcher¹ /byʃe/ *n.m.* (*supplice*) stake.

bûch|er² /byʃe/ *v.t./i.* (*fam.*) slog away (at). **~eur, ~euse** *n.m., f.* (*fam.*) slogger.

bûcheron /byʃrɔ̃/ *n.m.* woodcutter.

budg|et /bydʒɛ/ *n.m.* budget. **~étaire** *a.* budgetary.

buée /bɥe/ *n.f.* mist, condensation.

buffet /byfɛ/ *n.m.* sideboard; (*réception, restaurant*) buffet.

buffle /byfl/ *n.m.* buffalo.

buis /bɥi/ *n.m.* (*arbre, bois*) box.

buisson /bɥisɔ̃/ *n.m.* bush.

buissonnière /bɥisɔnjɛr/ *a.f.* **faire l'école ~,** play truant.

bulbe /bylb/ *n.m.* bulb.

bulgare /bylgar/ *a. & n.m./f.* Bulgarian.

Bulgarie /bylgari/ *n.f.* Bulgaria.

bulldozer /byldozɛr/ *n.m.* bulldozer.

bulle /byl/ *n.f.* bubble.

bulletin /byltɛ̃/ *n.m.* bulletin, report; (*scol.*) report; (*billet*) ticket. **~** **d'information,** news bulletin. **~ météorologique,** weather report. **~ (de vote),** ballot-paper. **~ de salaire,** payslip. **~-réponse** *n.m.* (*pl.* **~s-réponses**) reply slip.

buraliste /byralist/ *n.m./f.* tobacconist; (*à la poste*) clerk.

bureau (*pl.* **~x**) /byro/ *n.m.* office; (*meuble*) desk; (*comité*) board. **~ de location,** booking-office; (*théâtre*) box-office. **~ de poste,** post office. **~ de tabac,** tobacconist's (shop). **~ de vote,** polling station.

bureaucrate /byrokrat/ *n.m./f.* bureaucrat.

bureaucrat|ie /byrokrasi/ *n.f.* bureaucracy. **~ique** /-tik/ *a.* bureaucratic.

bureautique /byrotik/ *n.f.* office automation.

burette /byrɛt/ *n.f.* (*de graissage*) oilcan.

burin /byrɛ̃/ *n.m.* (cold) chisel.

burlesque /byrlɛsk/ *a.* ludicrous; (*théâtre*) burlesque.

bus /bys/ *n.m.* bus.
busqué /byske/ *a.* hooked.
buste /byst/ *n.m.* bust.
but /by(t)/ *n.m.* target; (*dessein*) aim, goal; (*football*) goal. **avoir pour ∼ de,** aim to. **de ∼ en blanc,** point-blank. **dans le ∼ de,** with the intention of.
butane /bytan/ *n.f.* butane, Calor gas (P.).
buté /byte/ *a.* obstinate.
buter /byte/ *v.i.* **∼ contre,** knock against; (*problème*) come up against. —*v.t.* antagonize. **se ∼** *v. pr.* (*s'entêter*) become obstinate.
buteur /bytœr/ *n.m.* striker.
butin /bytɛ̃/ *n.m.* booty, loot.
butiner /bytine/ *v.i.* gather nectar.
butoir /bytwar/ *n.m.* **∼ (de porte),** doorstop.
butor /bytɔr/ *n.m.* (*péj.*) lout.
butte /byt/ *n.f.* mound. **en ∼ à,** exposed to.
buvard /byvar/ *n.m.* blotting-paper.
buvette /byvɛt/ *n.f.* (refreshment) bar.
buveu|r, ∼se /byvœr, -øz/ *n m , f.* drinker.

C

c' /s/ *voir* **ce**[1].
ça /sa/ *pron.* it, that; (*pour désigner*) that; (*plus près*) this. **ça va?,** (*fam.*) how's it going? **ça va!,** (*fam.*) all right! **où ça?,** (*fam.*) where? **quand ça?,** (*fam.*) when? **c'est ça,** that's right.
çà /sa/ *adv.* **çà et là,** here and there.
caban|e /kaban/ *n.f.* hut; (*à outils*) shed. **∼on** *n.m.* hut; (*en Provence*) cottage.
cabaret /kabarɛ/ *n.m.* night-club.
cabas /kaba/ *n.m.* shopping bag.
cabillaud /kabijo/ *n.m.* cod.
cabine /kabin/ *n.f.* (*à la piscine*) cubicle; (*à la plage*) (beach) hut; (*de bateau*) cabin; (*de pilotage*) cockpit; (*de camion*) cab; (*d'ascenseur*) cage. **∼ (téléphonique),** phone-booth, phone-box.
cabinet /kabinɛ/ *n.m.* (*de médecin*) surgery; (*Amer.*) office; (*d'avocat*) office; (*clientèle*) practice; (*pol.*) Cabinet; (*pièce*) room. **∼s,** (*toilettes*) toilet. **∼ de toilette,** toilet.
câble /kabl/ *n.m.* cable; (*corde*) rope.
câbler /kable/ *v.t.* cable.
cabosser /kabɔse/ *v.t.* dent.
cabot|age /kabɔtaʒ/ *n.m.* coastal navigation. **∼eur** *n.m.* coaster.

cabotin, ∼e /kabɔtɛ̃, -in/ *n.m., f.* (*théâtre*) ham; (*fig.*) play-actor. **∼age** /-inaʒ/ *n.m.* ham acting; (*fig.*) play-acting.
cabrer /kabre/ *v.t.*, **se ∼** *v. pr.* (*cheval*) rear up. **se ∼ contre,** rebel against.
cabri /kabri/ *n.m.* kid.
cabriole /kabrijɔl/ *n.f.* (*culbute*) somersault. **faire des ∼s,** caper about.
cacahuète /kakaɥɛt/ *n.f.* peanut.
cacao /kakao/ *n m* cocoa.
cachalot /kaʃalo/ *n.m.* sperm whale.
cache /kaʃ/ *n.m.* mask; (*photo.*) lens cover.
cachemire /kaʃmir/ *n.m.* cashmere.
cach|er /kaʃe/ *v.t.* hide, conceal (**à,** from). **se ∼er** *v. pr.* hide; (*se trouver caché*) be hidden. **∼e-cache** *n m invar.* hide-and-seek. **∼-nez** *n.m. invar.* scarf. **∼-pot** *n.m.* cache-pot.
cachet /kaʃɛ/ *n.m.* seal; (*de la poste*) postmark; (*comprimé*) tablet; (*d'artiste*) fee; (*fig.*) style.
cacheter /kaʃte/ *v.t.* seal.
cachette /kaʃɛt/ *n.f.* hiding-place. **en ∼,** in secret.
cachot /kaʃo/ *n.m.* dungeon.
cachott|eries /kaʃɔtri/ *n.f. pl.* secrecy. **faire des ∼eries,** be secretive. **∼ier, ∼ière** *a.* secretive.
cacophonie /kakɔfɔni/ *n.f.* cacophony.
cactus /kaktys/ *n.m.* cactus.
cadavérique /kadaverik/ *a.* (*teint*) deathly pale.
cadavre /kadavr/ *n.m.* corpse.
caddie /kadi/ *n.m.* trolley.
cadeau (*pl.* **∼x**) /kado/ *n.m.* present, gift. **faire un ∼ à qn.,** give s.o. a present.
cadenas /kadna/ *n.m.* padlock. **∼ser** /-ase/ *v.t.* padlock.
cadenc|e /kadɑ̃s/ *n.f.* rhythm, cadence; (*de travail*) rate. **en ∼e,** in time. **∼é** *a.* rhythmic(al).
cadet, ∼te /kadɛ, t/ *a.* youngest; (*entre deux*) younger. —*n.m., f.* youngest (child); younger (child).
cadran /kadrɑ̃/ *n.m.* dial. **∼ solaire,** sundial.
cadre /kadr/ *n.m.* frame; (*milieu*) surroundings; (*limites*) scope; (*contexte*) framework. —*n.m./f.* (*personne: comm.*) executive. **les ∼s,** (*comm.*) the managerial staff.
cadrer /kadre/ *v.i.* **∼ avec,** tally with. —*v.t.* (*photo*) centre.
cadu|c, ∼que /kadyk/ *a.* obsolete.
cafard /kafar/ *n.m.* (*insecte*) cockroach.

avoir le ~, (*fam.*) be feeling low. **~er** /-de/ *v.i.* (*fam.*) tell tales.

caf|é /kafe/ *n.m.* coffee; (*bar*) café. **~é au lait,** white coffee. **~etière** *n.f.* coffee-pot.

caféine /kafein/ *n.f.* caffeine.

cafouiller /kafuje/ *v.i.* (*fam.*) bumble, flounder.

cage /kaʒ/ *n.f.* cage; (*d'escalier*) well; (*d'ascenseur*) shaft.

cageot /kaʒo/ *n.m.* crate.

cagibi /kaʒibi/ *n.m.* storage room.

cagneu|x, ~se /kaɲø, -z/ *a.* knock-kneed.

cagnotte /kaɲɔt/ *n.f.* kitty.

cagoule /kagul/ *n.f.* hood.

cahier /kaje/ *n.m.* notebook; (*scol.*) exercise-book.

cahin-caha /kaɛ̃kaa/ *adv.* **aller ~,** (*fam.*) jog along.

cahot /kao/ *n.m.* bump, jolt. **~er** /kaɔte/ *v.t./i.* bump, jolt. **~eux, ~euse** /kaɔtø, -z/ *a.* bumpy.

caïd /kaid/ *n.m.* (*fam.*) big shot.

caille /kɑj/ *n.f.* quail.

cailler /kaje/ *v.t./i.*, **se ~** *v. pr.* (*sang*) clot; (*lait*) curdle.

caillot /kajo/ *n.m.* (blood) clot.

caillou (*pl.* **~x**) /kaju/ *n.m.* stone; (*galet*) pebble. **~teux, ~teuse** *a.* stony. **~tis** *n.m.* gravel.

caisse /kɛs/ *n.f.* crate, case; (*tiroir, machine*) till; (*guichet*) pay-desk; (*bureau*) office; (*mus.*) drum. **~ enregistreuse,** cash register. **~ d'épargne,** savings bank. **~ de retraite,** pension fund.

caiss|ier, ~ière /kesje, -jɛr/ *n.m., f.* cashier.

cajol|er /kaʒole/ *v.t.* coax. **~eries** *n.f. pl.* coaxing.

cake /kɛk/ *n.m.* fruit-cake.

calamité /kalamite/ *n.f.* calamity.

calandre /kalɑ̃dr/ *n.f.* radiator grill.

calanque /kalɑ̃k/ *n.f.* creek.

calcaire /kalkɛr/ *a.* (*sol*) chalky; (*eau*) hard.

calciné /kalsine/ *a.* charred.

calcium /kalsjɔm/ *n.m.* calcium.

calcul /kalkyl/ *n.m.* calculation; (*scol.*) arithmetic; (*différentiel*) calculus. **~ biliaire,** gallstone.

calcul|er /kalkyle/ *v.t.* calculate. **~ateur** *n.m.* (*ordinateur*) computer, calculator. **~atrice** *n.f.* (*ordinateur*) calculator. **~ette** *n.f.* (pocket) calculator.

cale /kal/ *n.f.* wedge; (*de navire*) hold. **~ sèche,** dry dock.

calé /kale/ *a.* (*fam.*) clever.

caleçon /kalsɔ̃/ *n.m.* underpants; (*de femme*) leggings. **~ de bain,** (bathing) trunks.

calembour /kalɑ̃bur/ *n.m.* pun.

calendrier /kalɑ̃drije/ *n.m.* calendar; (*fig.*) timetable.

calepin /kalpɛ̃/ *n.m.* notebook.

caler /kale/ *v.t.* wedge; (*moteur*) stall. **—***v.i.* stall.

calfeutrer /kalføtre/ *v.t.* stop up the cracks of.

calibr|e /kalibr/ *n.m.* calibre; (*d'un œuf, fruit*) grade. **~er** *v.t.* grade.

calice /kalis/ *n.m.* (*relig.*) chalice; (*bot.*) calyx.

califourchon (à) /(a)kalifurʃɔ̃/ *adv.* astride. **—***prép.* **à ~ sur,** astride.

câlin, ~e /kalɛ̃, -in/ *a.* endearing, cuddly. **~er** /-ine/ *v.t.* cuddle.

calmant /kalmɑ̃/ *n.m.* sedative.

calm|e /kalm/ *a.* calm **—***n.m.* calm(ness). **du ~e!,** calm down! **~er** *v.t.*, **se ~** *v. pr.* (*personne*) calm (down); (*diminuer*) ease.

calomn|ie /kalɔmni/ *n.f.* slander; (*écrite*) libel. **~ier** *v.t.* slander; libel. **~ieux, ~ieuse** *a.* slanderous; libellous.

calorie /kalɔri/ *n.f.* calorie.

calorifuge /kalɔrifyʒ/ *a.* (heat-)insulating. **—***n.m.* lagging.

calot /kalo/ *n.m.* (*mil.*) forage-cap.

calotte /kalɔt/ *n.f.* (*relig.*) skullcap; (*tape: fam.*) slap.

calqu|e /kalk/ *n.m.* tracing; (*fig.*) exact copy. **~er** *v.t.* trace; (*fig.*) copy. **~er sur,** model on.

calvaire /kalvɛr/ *n.m.* (*croix*) calvary; (*fig.*) suffering.

calvitie /kalvisi/ *n.f.* baldness.

camarade /kamarad/ *n.m./f.* friend; (*pol.*) comrade. **~ de jeu,** playmate. **~rie** *n.f.* good companionship.

cambiste /kɑ̃bist/ *n.m./f.* foreign exchange dealer.

cambouis /kɑ̃bwi/ *n.m.* (engine) oil.

cambrer /kɑ̃bre/ *v.t.* arch. **se ~** *v. pr.* arch one's back.

cambriol|er /kɑ̃brijole/ *v.t.* burgle. **~age** *n.m.* burglary. **~eur, ~euse** *n.m., f.* burglar.

cambrure /kɑ̃bryr/ *n.f.* curve.

came /kam/ *n.f.* **arbe à ~s,** camshaft.

camée /kame/ *n.m.* cameo.

camelot /kamlo/ *n.m.* street vendor.

camelote /kamlɔt/ *n.f.* junk.

camembert /kamɑ̃bɛr/ *n.m.* Camembert (cheese).

caméra /kamera/ *n.f.* (*cinéma, télévision*) camera.

caméra|man (*pl.* ~**men**) /kameraman, -mɛn/ *n.m.* cameraman.

camion /kamjɔ̃/ *n.m.* lorry, truck. ~**citerne** *n.m.* tanker. ~**nage** /-jɔnaʒ/ *n.m.* haulage. ~**nette** /-jɔnɛt/ *n.f.* van. ~**neur** /-jɔnœr/ *n.m.* lorry *ou* truck driver; (*entrepreneur*) haulage contractor.

camisole /kamizɔl/ *n.f.* ~ (**de force**), strait-jacket.

camoufl|er /kamufle/ *v.t.* camouflage. ~**age** *n.m.* camouflage.

camp /kɑ̃/ *n.m.* camp; (*sport*)side.

campagn|e /kɑ̃paɲ/ *n.f.* country(side); (*mil., pol.*) campaign. ~**ard**, ~**arde** *a.* country; *n.m.*, *f.* countryman, countrywoman.

campanile /kɑ̃panil/ *n.m.* belltower.

camp|er /kɑ̃pe/ *v.i.* camp. —*v.t.* plant boldly; (*esquisser*) sketch. **se** ~**er** *v. pr.* plant o.s. ~**ement** *n.m.* encampment. ~**eur**, ~**euse** *n.m., f.* camper.

camphre /kɑ̃fr/ *n.m.* camphor.

camping /kɑ̃piŋ/ *n.m.* camping. **faire du** ~, go camping. ~**car** *n.m.* camper van; (*Amer.*) motorhome. ~**gaz** *n.m. invar.* (P.) camping-gaz. (**terrain de**) ~, campsite.

campus /kɑ̃pys/ *n.m.* campus.

Canada /kanada/ *n.m.* Canada.

canadien, ~**ne** /kanadjɛ̃, -jɛn/ *a.* & *n.m.*, *f.* Canadian. —*n.f.* fur-lined jacket.

canaille /kanɑj/ *n.f.* rogue.

can|al (*pl.* ~**aux**) /kanal, -o/ *n.m.* (*artificiel*) canal; (*bras de mer*) channel; (*techn., TV*) channel. **par le** ~**al de,** through.

canalisation /kanalizɑsjɔ̃/ *n.f.* (*tuyaux*) main(s).

canaliser /kanalize/ *v.t.* (*eau*) canalize; (*fig.*) channel.

canapé /kanape/ *n.m.* sofa.

canard /kanar/ *n.m.* duck; (*journal*: *fam.*) rag.

canari /kanari/ *n.m.* canary.

cancans /kɑ̃kɑ̃/ *n.m. pl.* malicious gossip.

canc|er /kɑ̃sɛr/ *n.m.* cancer. **le C**~**er,** Cancer. ~**éreux**, ~**éreuse** *a.* cancerous. ~**érigène** *a.* carcinogenic.

cancre /kɑ̃kr/ *n.m.* dunce.

cancrelat /kɑ̃krɔla/ *n.m.* cockroach.

candélabre /kɑ̃delabr/ *n.m.* candelabrum.

candeur /kɑ̃dœr/ *n.f.* naïvety.

candidat, ~**e** /kɑ̃dida, -t/ *n.m.*, *f.* candidate; (*à un poste*) applicant, candidate (**à, for**). ~**ure** /-tyr/ *n.f.*

application; (*pol.*) candidacy. **poser sa** ~ **pour,** apply for.

candide /kɑ̃did/ *a.* naïve.

cane /kan/ *n.f.* (female) duck. ~**ton** *n.m.* duckling.

canette /kanɛt/ *n.f.* (*de bière*) bottle.

canevas /kanva/ *n.m.* canvas; (*plan*) framework, outline.

caniche /kaniʃ/ *n.m.* poodle.

canicule /kanikyl/ *n.f.* hot summer days.

canif /kanif/ *n.m.* penknife.

canin, ~**e** /kanɛ̃, -in/ *a.* canine. —*n.f.* canine (tooth).

caniveau (*pl.* ~**x**) /kanivo/ *n.m.* gutter.

cannabis /kanabis/ *n.m.* cannabis.

canne /kan/ *n.f.* (walking-)stick. ~ **à pêche**, fishing-rod. ~ **à sucre**, sugar-cane.

cannelle /kanɛl/ *n.f.* cinnamon.

cannibale /kanibal/ *a.* & *n.m./f.* cannibal.

canoë /kanɔe/ *n.m.* canoe; (*sport*) canoeing.

canon /kanɔ̃/ *n.m.* (big) gun; (*d'une arme*) barrel; (*principe, règle*) canon. ~**nade** /-ɔnad/ *n.f.* gunfire. ~**nier** /-ɔnje/ *n.m.* gunner.

canot /kano/ *n.m.* boat. ~ **de sauvetage,** lifeboat. ~ **pneumatique,** rubber dinghy.

canot|er /kanɔte/ *v.i.* boat. ~**age** *n.m.* boating. ~**ier** *n.m.* boater.

cantate /kɑ̃tat/ *n.f.* cantata.

cantatrice /kɑ̃tatris/ *n.f.* opera singer.

cantine /kɑ̃tin/ *n.f.* canteen.

cantique /kɑ̃tik/ *n.m.* hymn.

canton /kɑ̃tɔ̃/ *n.m.* (*en France*) district; (*en Suisse*) canton.

cantonade (à la) /(ala)kɑ̃tɔnad/ *adv.* for all to hear.

cantonner /kɑ̃tɔne/ *v.t.* (*mil.*) billet. **se** ~ **dans,** confine o.s. to.

cantonnier /kɑ̃tɔnje/ *n.m.* roadman, road mender.

canular /kanylar/ *n.m.* hoax.

caoutchou|c /kautʃu/ *n.m.* rubber; (*élastique*) rubber band. ~**c mousse,** foam rubber. ~**té** *a.* rubberized. ~**teux**, ~**teuse** *a.* rubbery.

cap /kap/ *n.m.* cape, headland; (*direction*) course. **doubler** *ou* **franchir le** ~ **de,** go beyond (the point of). **mettre le** ~ **sur,** steer a course for.

capable /kapabl/ *a.* able, capable. ~ **de qch.,** capable of sth. ~ **de faire,** able to do, capable of doing.

capacité /kapasite/ *n.f.* ability; (*contenance*) capacity.

cape /kap/ *n.f.* cape. **rire sous** ∼, laugh up one's sleeve.

capillaire /kapilɛr/ *a.* (*lotion, soins*) hair. (**vaisseau**) ∼, capillary.

capilotade (en) /(ɑ̃)kapilɔtad/ *adv.* (*fam.*) reduced to a pulp.

capitaine /kapitɛn/ *n.m.* captain.

capit|al, ∼**ale** (*m. pl.* ∼**aux**) /kapital, -o/ *a.* major, fundamental; (*peine, lettre*) capital. —*n.m.* (*pl.* ∼**aux**) (*comm.*) capital; (*fig.*) stock. ∼**aux,** (*comm.*) capital. —*n.f.* (*ville, lettre*) capital.

capitalis|te /kapitalist/ *a.* & *n.m./f.* capitalist. ∼**me** *n.m.* capitalism.

capiteu|x, ∼**se** /kapitø, -z/ *a.* heady.

capitonné /kapitɔne/ *a.* padded.

capitul|er /kapityle/ *v.i.* capitulate. ∼**ation** *n.f.* capitulation.

capor|al (*pl.* ∼**aux**) /kapɔral, -o/ *n.m.* corporal.

capot /kapo/ *n.m.* (*auto.*) bonnet; (*auto., Amer.*) hood.

capote /kapɔt/ *n.f.* (*auto.*) hood; (*auto., Amer.*) (convertible) top; (*fam.*) condom.

capoter /kapɔte/ *v.i.* overturn.

câpre /kɑpr/ *n.f.* (*culin.*) caper.

capric|e /kapris/ *n.m.* whim, caprice. ∼**ieux,** ∼**ieuse** *a.* capricious; (*appareil*) temperamental.

Capricorne /kaprikɔrn/ *n.m.* **le** ∼, Capricorn.

capsule /kapsyl/ *n.f.* capsule; (*de bouteille*) cap.

capter /kapte/ *v.t.* (*eau*) tap; (*émission*) pick up; (*fig.*) win, capture.

capti|f, ∼**ve** /kaptif, -v/ *a.* & *n.m.,* *f.* captive.

captiver /kaptive/ *v.t.* captivate.

captivité /kaptivite/ *n.f.* captivity.

captur|e /kaptyr/ *n.f.* capture. ∼**er** *v.t.* capture.

capuch|e /kapyʃ/ *n.f.* hood. ∼**on** *n.m.* hood; (*de stylo*) cap.

caquet /kakɛ/ *n.m.* **rabattre le** ∼ **à qn.,** take s.o. down a peg or two.

caquet|er /kakte/ *v.i.* cackle. ∼**age** *n.m.* cackle.

car[1] /kar/ *conj.* because, for.

car[2] /kar/ *n.m.* coach; (*Amer.*) bus.

carabine /karabin/ *n.f.* rifle.

caracoler /karakɔle/ *v.i.* prance.

caract|ère /karaktɛr/ *n.m.* (*nature, lettre*) character. ∼**ères d'imprimerie,** block letters. ∼**ériel,** ∼**érielle** *a.* character; *n.m., f.* disturbed child.

caractérisé /karakterize/ *a.* well-defined.

caractériser /karakterize/ *v.t.* characterize. **se** ∼ **par,** be characterized by.

caractéristique /karakteristik/ *a.* & *n.f.* characteristic.

carafe /karaf/ *n.f.* carafe; (*pour le vin*) decanter.

caraïbe /karaib/ *a.* Caribbean. **les C**∼**s,** the Caribbean.

carambol|er (se) /(sə)karɑ̃bɔle/ *v. pr.* (*voitures*) smash into each other. ∼**age** *n.m.* multiple smash-up.

caramel /karamɛl/ *n.m.* caramel. ∼**iser** *v.t./i.* caramelize.

carapace /karapas/ *n.f.* shell.

carat /kara/ *n.m.* carat.

caravane /karavan/ *n.f.* (*auto.*) caravan; (*auto., Amer.*) trailer; (*convoi*) caravan.

carbone /karbɔn/ *n.m.* carbon; (*double*) carbon (copy). (**papier**) ∼, carbon (paper).

carboniser /karbɔnize/ *v.t.* burn (to ashes).

carburant /karbyrɑ̃/ *n.m.* (motor) fuel.

carburateur /karbyratœr/ *n.m.* carburettor; (*Amer.*) carburetor.

carcan /karkɑ̃/ *n.m.* (*contrainte*) yoke.

carcasse /karkas/ *n.f.* carcass; (*d'immeuble, de voiture*) frame.

cardiaque /kardjak/ *a.* heart. —*n.m./f.* heart patient.

cardigan /kardigɑ̃/ *n.m.* cardigan.

cardin|al (*m. pl.* ∼**aux**) /kardinal, -o/ *a.* cardinal. —*n.m.* (*pl.* ∼**aux**) cardinal.

Carême /karɛm/ *n.m.* Lent.

carence /karɑ̃s/ *n.f.* inadequacy; (*manque*) deficiency.

caressant, ∼**e** /karɛsɑ̃, -t/ *a.* endearing.

caress|e /karɛs/ *n.f.* caress. ∼**er** /-ese/ *v.t.* caress, stroke; (*espoir*) cherish.

cargaison /kargɛzɔ̃/ *n.f.* cargo.

cargo /kargo/ *n.m.* cargo boat.

caricatur|e /karikatyr/ *n.f.* caricature. ∼**al** (*m. pl.* ∼**aux**) *a.* caricature-like.

car|ie /kari/ *n.f.* cavity. **la** ∼**ie** (**dentaire**), tooth decay. ∼**ié** *a.* (*dent*) decayed.

carillon /karijɔ̃/ *n.m.* chimes; (*horloge*) chiming clock. ∼**ner** /-jɔne/ *v.i.* chime, peal.

caritati|f, ∼**ve** /karitatif, -v/ *a.* **association** ∼**ve,** charity.

carlingue /karlɛ̃g/ *n.f.* (*d'avion*) cabin.

carnage /karnaʒ/ *n.m.* carnage.

carnass|ier, ∼**ière** /karnasje, -jɛr/ *a.* flesh-eating.

carnaval (*pl.* ∼**s**) /karnaval/ *n.m.* carnival.

carnet /karnɛ/ *n.m.* notebook; (*de tickets*

etc.) book. ~ **de chèques,** cheque-book. ~ **de notes,** school report.
carotte /karɔt/ *n.f.* carrot.
carotter /karɔte/ *v.t.* (*argot*) swindle. ~ **qch. à qn.,** (*argot*) wangle sth. from s.o.
carpe /karp/ *n.f.* carp.
carpette /karpɛt/ *n.f.* rug.
carré /kare/ *a.* (*forme, mesure*) square; (*fig.*) straightforward. —*n.m.* square; (*de terrain*) patch.
carreau (*pl.* ~x) /karo/ *n.m.* (window) pane; (*par terre, au mur*) tile; (*dessin*) check; (*cartes*) diamonds. **à ~x,** check(ed).
carrefour /karfur/ *n.m.* crossroads.
carreler /karle/ *v.t.* tile. ~**age** *n.m.* tiling; (*sol*) tiles.
carrelet /karlɛ/ *n.m.* (*poisson*) plaice.
carrément /karemɑ̃/ *adv.* straight; (*dire*) straight out.
carrer (se) /(sə)kare/ *v. pr.* settle firmly (**dans,** in).
carrière /karjɛr/ *n.f.* career; (*terrain*) quarry.
carrossable /karɔsabl/ *a.* suitable for vehicles.
carrosse /karɔs/ *n.m.* (horse-drawn) coach.
carrosserie /karɔsri/ *n.f.* (*auto.*) body(work). ~**ier** *n.m.* (*auto.*) body-builder.
carrure /karyr/ *n.f.* build; (*fig.*) calibre.
cartable /kartabl/ *n.m.* satchel.
carte /kart/ *n.f.* card; (*géog.*) map; (*naut.*) chart; (*au restaurant*) menu. ~**s,** (*jeu*) cards. **à la ~,** (*manger*) à la carte. ~ **blanche,** a free hand. ~ **de crédit,** credit card. ~ **des vins,** wine list. ~ **de visite,** (business) card. ~ **grise,** (car) registration card. ~ **postale,** postcard.
cartel /kartɛl/ *n.m.* cartel.
cartilage /kartilaʒ/ *n.m.* cartilage.
carton /kartɔ̃/ *n.m.* cardboard; (*boîte*) (cardboard) box. ~ **à dessin,** portfolio. **faire un ~,** (*fam.*) take a pot-shot. ~**nage** /-ɔnaʒ/ *n.m.* cardboard packing. ~**-pâte** *n.m.* pasteboard. **en ~-pâte,** cardboard.
cartonné /kartɔne/ *a.* (*livre*) hardback.
cartouche /kartuʃ/ *n.f.* cartridge; (*de cigarettes*) carton. ~**ière** *n.f.* cartridge-belt.
cas /kɑ/ *n.m.* case. **au ~ où,** in case. ~ **urgent,** emergency. **en aucun ~,** on no account. **en ~ de,** in the event of, in case of. **en tout ~,** in any case. **faire ~ de,** set great store by. ~ **de conscience** matter of conscience.

casanier, ~ière /kazanje, -jɛr/ *a.* home-loving.
casaque /kazak/ *n.f.* (*de jockey*) shirt.
cascade /kaskad/ *n.f.* waterfall; (*fig.*) spate.
cascadeur, ~euse /kaskadœr, -øz/ *n.m., f.* stuntman, stuntgirl.
case /kɑz/ *n.f.* hut; (*compartiment*) pigeon-hole; (*sur papier*) square.
caser /kaze/ *v.t.* (*mettre*) put; (*loger*) put up; (*dans un travail*) find a job for; (*marier: péj.*) marry off.
caserne /kazɛrn/ *n.f.* barracks.
cash /kaʃ/ *adv.* **payer ~,** pay (in) cash.
casier /kazje/ *n.m.* pigeon-hole, compartment; (*meuble*) cabinet; (*à bouteilles*) rack. ~ **judiciaire,** criminal record.
casino /kazino/ *n.m.* casino.
casque /kask/ *n.m.* helmet; (*chez le coiffeur*) (hair-)drier. ~**e (à écouteurs),** headphones. ~**é** *a.* wearing a helmet.
casquette /kaskɛt/ *n.f.* cap.
cassant, ~e /kasɑ̃, -t/ *a.* brittle; (*brusque*) curt.
cassation /kasasjɔ̃/ *n.f.* **cour de ~,** appeal court.
casse /kɑs/ *n.f.* (*objets*) breakages. **mettre à la ~,** scrap.
casser /kase/ *v.t./i.* break; (*annuler*) annul. **se ~** *v. pr.* break. ~**er la tête à,** (*fam.*) give a headache to. ~**e cou** *n.m. invar.* daredevil. ~**e-croûte** *n.m. invar.* snack. ~**e-noisettes** *ou* ~**e-noix** *n.m. invar.* nutcrackers. ~**e-pieds** *n.m./f. invar.* (*fam.*) pain (in the neck). ~**e-tête** *n.m. invar.* (*problème*) headache; (*jeu*) brain teaser.
casserole /kasrɔl/ *n.f.* saucepan.
cassette /kasɛt/ *n.f.* casket; (*de magnétophone*) cassette, (*de vidéo*) video tape.
cassis¹ /kasis/ *n.m.* blackcurrant.
cassis² /kasi/ *n.m.* (*auto.*) dip.
cassoulet /kasulɛ/ *n.m.* stew (of beans and meat).
cassure /kɑsyr/ *n.f.* break.
caste /kast/ *n.f.* caste.
castor /kastɔr/ *n.m.* beaver.
castrer /kastre/ *v.t.* castrate. ~**ation** *n.f.* castration.
cataclysme /kataklism/ *n.m.* cataclysm.
cataloguer /katalɔg/ *n.m.* catalogue. ~**er** *v.t.* catalogue; (*personne: péj.*) label.
catalyseur /katalizœr/ *n.m.* catalyst.
cataphote /katafɔt/ *n.m.* reflector.
cataplasme /kataplasm/ *n.m.* poultice.

catapult|e /katapylt/ *n.f.* catapult. ~**er**
v.t. catapult.
cataracte /katarakt/ *n.f.* cataract.
catastroph|e /katastrɔf/ *n.f.* disaster,
catastrophe. ~**ique** *a.* catastrophic.
catch /katʃ/ *n.m.* (all-in) wrestling.
~**eur,** ~**euse** *n.m., f.* (all-in) wrestler.
catéchisme /kateʃism/ *n.m.* catechism.
catégorie /kategɔri/ *n.f.* category.
catégorique /kategɔrik/ *a.* categorical.
cathédrale /katedral/ *n.f.* cathedral.
catholi|que /katɔlik/ *a.* Catholic.
~**cisme** *n.m.* Catholicism. **pas très**
~**que,** a bit fishy.
catimini (en) /(ɑ̃)katimini/ *adv.* on the
sly.
cauchemar /koʃmar/ *n.m.* nightmare.
cause /koz/ *n.f.* cause; (*jurid.*) case. **à** ~
de, because of. **en** ~, (*en jeu, concerné*)
involved. **pour** ~ **de,** on account
of.
caus|er /koze/ *v.t.* cause. —*v.i.* chat.
~**erie** *n.f.* talk. ~**ette** *n.f.* **faire la**
~**ette,** have a chat.
caustique /kostik/ *a.* caustic.
caution /kosjɔ̃/ *n.f.* surety; (*jurid.*) bail;
(*appui*) backing; (*garantie*) deposit.
sous ~, on bail.
cautionn|er /kosjone/ *v.t.* guarantee;
(*soutenir*) back.
cavalcade /kavalkad/ *n.f.* (*fam.*) stampede, rush.
cavalerie /kavalri/ *n.f.* (*mil.*) cavalry;
(*au cirque*) horses.
caval|ier, ~**ière** /kavalje, -jɛr/ *a.*
offhand. —*n.m., f.* rider; (*pour danser*)
partner. —*n.m.* (*échecs*) knight.
cave[1] /kav/ *n.f.* cellar.
cave[2] /kav/ *a.* sunken.
caveau (*pl.* ~**x**) /kavo/ *n.m.* vault.
caverne /kavɛrn/ *n.f.* cave.
caviar /kavjar/ *n.m.* caviare.
cavité /kavite/ *n.f.* cavity.
CD (*abrév.*) (*compact disc*) CD.
ce[1]**, c'*** /sə, s/ *pron.* it, that. **c'est,** it *ou*
that is. **ce sont,** they are. **c'est moi,** it's
me. **c'est un chanteur/une chan-
teuse/***etc.*, he/she is a singer/*etc.* **ce qui,**
ce que, what. **ce que c'est bon/***etc.***!,**
how good/*etc.* it is! **tout ce qui, tout ce
que,** everything that.
ce[2] *ou* **cet***, **cette** (*pl.* **ces**) /sə, sɛt, se/ *a.*
that; (*proximité*) this. **ces,** those;
(*proximité*) these.
CE *abrév.* (Communauté européenne)
EC.
ceci /səsi/ *pron.* this.
cécité /sesite/ *n.f.* blindness.
céder /sede/ *v.t.* give up. —*v.i.* (*se*

rompre) give way; (*se soumettre*) give
in.
cédille /sedij/ *n.f.* cedilla.
cèdre /sɛdr/ *n.m.* cedar.
CEE *abrév.* (*Communauté économique
européenne*) EEC.
ceinture /sɛ̃tyr/ *n.f.* belt; (*taille*) waist;
(*de bus, métro*) circle (line). ~ **de
sauvetage,** lifebelt. ~ **de sécurité,** seat-
belt.
ceinturer /sɛ̃tyre/ *v.t.* seize round the
waist; (*entourer*) surround.
cela /səla/ *pron.* it, that; (*pour désigner*)
that. ~ **va de soi,** it is obvious.
célèbre /selɛbr/ *a.* famous.
célébr|er /selebre/ *v.t.* celebrate. ~**ation**
n.f. celebration (**de,** of).
célébrité /selebrite/ *n.f.* fame;
(*personne*) celebrity.
céleri /sɛlri/ *n.m.* (*en branches*) celery.
~**(-rave),** celeriac.
céleste /selɛst/ *a.* celestial.
célibat /seliba/ *n.m.* celibacy.
célibataire /selibatɛr/ *a.* unmarried.
—*n.m.* bachelor. —*n.f.* unmarried
woman.
celle, celles /sɛl/ *voir* **celui.**
cellier /selje/ *n.m.* store-room (*for wine*).
cellophane /selɔfan/ *n.f.* (P.) Cellophane
(P.).
cellul|e /selyl/ *n.f.* cell. ~**aire** *a.* cell.
fourgon ou voiture ~**aire,** prison van.
celui, celle (*pl.* **ceux, celles**) /səlɥi, sɛl,
sø/ *pron.* the one. ~ **de mon ami,** my
friend's. ~**-ci,** this (one). ~**-là,** that
(one). **ceux-ci,** these (ones). **ceux-là,**
those (ones).
cendr|e /sɑ̃dr/ *n.f.* ash. ~**é** *a.* (*couleur*)
ashen. **blond** ~**é,** ash blond.
cendrier /sɑ̃drije/ *n.m.* ashtray.
censé /sɑ̃se/ *a.* **être** ~ **faire,** be supposed
to do.
censeur /sɑ̃sœr/ *n.m.* censor; (*scol.*)
assistant headmaster.
censur|e /sɑ̃syr/ *n.f.* censorship. ~**er** *v.t.*
censor; (*critiquer*) censure.
cent (*pl.* ~**s**) /sɑ̃/ (*generally* /sɑ̃t/ *pl.*
/sɑ̃z/ *before vowel*) *a.* & *n.m.* (a)
hundred. ~ **un** /sɑ̃œ̃/ a hundred and
one.
centaine /sɑ̃tɛn/ *n.f.* hundred. **une** ~
(de), (about) a hundred.
centenaire /sɑ̃tnɛr/ *n.m.* (*anniversaire*)
centenary.
centième /sɑ̃tjɛm/ *a.* & *n.m./f.*
hundredth.
centigrade /sɑ̃tigrad/ *a.* centigrade.
centilitre /sɑ̃tilitr/ *n.m.* centilitre.
centime /sɑ̃tim/ *n.m.* centime.

centimètre /sɑ̃timɛtr/ *n.m.* centimetre; (*ruban*) tape-measure.

centr|al, **~ale** (*m. pl.* **~aux**) /sɑ̃tral, -o/ *a.* central. —*n.m.* (*pl.* **~aux**). **~al** (**téléphonique**), (telephone) exchange. —*n.f.* power-station. **~aliser** *v.t.* centralize.

centr|e /sɑ̃tr/ *n.m.* centre. **~e-ville** *n.m.* town centre. **~er** *v.t.* centre.

centuple /sɑ̃typl/ *n.m.* le **~** (**de**), a hundredfold. **au ~**, a hundredfold.

cep /sɛp/ *n.m.* vine stock.

cépage /sepaʒ/ *n.m.* (variety of) vine.

cèpe /sɛp/ *n.m.* (edible) boletus.

cependant /səpɑ̃dɑ̃/ *adv.* however.

céramique /seramik/ *n.f.* ceramic; (*art*) ceramics.

cerceau (*pl.* **~x**) /sɛrso/ *n.m.* hoop.

cercle /sɛrkl/ *n.m.* circle; (*cerceau*) hoop. **~ vicieux**, a vicious circle.

cercueil /sɛrkœj/ *n.m.* coffin.

céréale /sereal/ *n.f.* cereal.

cérébr|al (*m. pl.* **~aux**) /serebral, -o/ *a.* cerebral.

cérémonial (*pl.* **~s**) /seremɔnjal/ *n.m.* ceremonial.

cérémon|ie /seremɔni/ *n.f.* ceremony. **~ie(s)**, (*façons*) fuss. **~ieux**, **~ieuse** *a.* ceremonious.

cerf /sɛr/ *n.m.* stag.

cerfeuil /sɛrfœj/ *n.m.* chervil.

cerf-volant (*pl.* **cerfs-volants**) /sɛrvɔlɑ̃/ *n.m.* kite.

ceris|e /sriz/ *n.f.* cherry. **~ier** *n.m.* cherry tree.

cerne /sɛrn/ *n.m.* ring.

cern|er /sɛrne/ *v.t.* surround; (*question*) define. **les yeux ~és**, with rings under one's eyes.

certain, **~e** /sɛrtɛ̃, -ɛn/ *a.* certain; (*sûr*) certain, sure (**de**, of; **que**, that). —*pron.* **~s**, certain people. **d'un ~ âge**, past one's prime. **un ~ temps**, some time.

certainement /sɛrtɛnmɑ̃/ *adv.* certainly.

certes /sɛrt/ *adv.* indeed.

certificat /sɛrtifika/ *n.m.* certificate.

certif|ier /sɛrtifje/ *v.t.* certify. **~ier qch. à qn.**, assure s.o. of sth. **~ié** *a.* (*professeur*) qualified.

certitude /sɛrtityd/ *n.f.* certainty.

cerveau (*pl.* **~x**) /sɛrvo/ *n.m.* brain.

cervelas /sɛrvəla/ *n.m.* saveloy.

cervelle /sɛrvɛl/ *n.f.* (*anat.*) brain; (*culin.*) brains.

ces /se/ *voir* **ce²**.

césarienne /sezarjɛn/ *n.f.* Caesarean (section).

cessation /sesasjɔ̃/ *n.f.* suspension.

cesse /sɛs/ *n.f.* **n'avoir de ~ que**, have no rest until. **sans ~**, incessantly.

cesser /sese/ *v.t./i.* stop. **~ de faire**, stop doing.

cessez-le-feu /seselfø/ *n.m. invar.* cease-fire.

cession /sesjɔ̃/ *n.f.* transfer.

c'est-à-dire /setadir/ *conj.* that is (to say).

cet, cette /sɛt/ *voir* **ce²**.

ceux /sø/ *voir* **celui**.

chacal (*pl.* **~s**) /ʃakal/ *n.m.* jackal.

chacun, **~e** /ʃakœ̃, -yn/ *pron.* each (one), every one; (*tout le monde*) everyone.

chagrin /ʃagrɛ̃/ *n.m.* sorrow. **avoir du ~**, be distressed. **~er** /-ine/ *v.t.* distress.

chahut /ʃay/ *n.m.* row, din. **~er** /-te/ *v.i.* make a row; *v.t.* be rowdy with. **~eur**, **~euse** /- tœr, -tøz/ *n.m.*, *f.* rowdy.

chaîn|e /ʃɛn/ *n.f.* chain; (*de télévision*) channel. **~e de montagnes**, mountain range. **~e de montage/fabrication**, assembly/production line. **~e hi-fi**, hi fi system. **en ~e**, (*accidents*) multiple. **~ette** *n.f.* (small) chain. **~on** *n.m.* link.

chair /ʃɛr/ *n.f.* flesh. **bien en ~**, plump. **en ~ et en os**, in the flesh. **~ à saucisses**, sausage meat. **la ~ de poule**, goose-flesh. —*a. invar.* (**couleur**) **~**, flesh-coloured.

chaire /ʃɛr/ *n.f.* (d'*église*) pulpit. (*univ.*) chair.

chaise /ʃɛz/ *n.f.* chair. **~ longue**, deck-chair.

chaland /ʃalɑ̃/ *n.m.* barge.

châle /ʃal/ *n.m.* shawl.

chalet /ʃalɛ/ *n.m.* chalet.

chaleur /ʃalœr/ *n.f.* heat; (*moins intense*) warmth; (*d'un accueil, d'une couleur*) warmth. **~eux**, **~euse** *a.* warm.

challenge /ʃalɑ̃ʒ/ *n.m.* contest.

chaloupe /ʃalup/ *n.f.* launch, boat.

chalumeau (*pl.* **~x**) /ʃalymo/ *n.m.* blowlamp; (*Amer.*) blowtorch.

chalut /ʃaly/ *n.m.* trawl-net **~ier** /-tje/ *n.m.* trawler.

chamailler (**se**) /(sə)ʃamaje/ *v. pr.* squabble.

chambarder /ʃɑ̃barde/ *v.t.* (*fam.*) turn upside down.

chambre /ʃɑ̃br/ *n.f.* (bed)room; (*pol., jurid.*) chamber. **faire ~ à part**, sleep in different rooms. **~ à air**, inner tube. **~ d'amis**, spare *ou* guest room. **~ à coucher**, bedroom. **~ à un lit/deux lits**, single/double room. **~ forte**, strong-room.

chambrer /ʃɑ̃bre/ *v.t.* (*vin*) bring to room temperature.

chameau (*pl.* ∼x) /ʃamo/ *n.m.* camel.

chamois /ʃamwa/ *n.m.* chamois. **peau de** ∼, chamois leather.

champ /ʃɑ̃/ *n.m.* field. ∼ **de bataille,** battlefield. ∼ **de courses,** racecourse.

champagne /ʃɑ̃paɲ/ *n.m.* champagne.

champêtre /ʃɑ̃pεtr/ *a.* rural.

champignon /ʃɑ̃piɲɔ̃/ *n.m.* mushroom; (*moisissure*) fungus. ∼ **de Paris,** button mushroom.

champion, ∼**ne** /ʃɑ̃pjɔ̃, -jɔn/ *n.m.,* *f.* champion. ∼**nat** /-jɔna/ *n.m.* championship.

chance /ʃɑ̃s/ *n.f.* (good) luck; (*possibilité*) chance. **avoir de la** ∼, be lucky. **quelle** ∼!, what luck!

chanceler /ʃɑ̃sle/ *v.i.* stagger; (*fig.*) falter.

chancelier /ʃɑ̃səlje/ *n.m.* chancellor.

chanceu|x, ∼**se** /ʃɑ̃sø, -z/ *a.* lucky.

chancre /ʃɑ̃kr/ *n.m.* canker.

chandail /ʃɑ̃daj/ *n.m.* sweater.

chandelier /ʃɑ̃dəlje/ *n.m.* candlestick.

chandelle /ʃɑ̃dεl/ *n.f.* candle. **dîner aux** ∼s, candlelight dinner.

change /ʃɑ̃ʒ/ *n.m.* (foreign) exchange.

changeant, ∼**e** /ʃɑ̃ʒɑ̃, -t/ *a.* changeable.

changement /ʃɑ̃ʒmɑ̃/ *n.m.* change. ∼ **de vitesses** (*dispositif*) gears.

changer /ʃɑ̃ʒe/ *v.t./i.* change. **se** ∼ *v. pr.* change (one's clothes). ∼ **de nom/voiture,** change one's name/car. ∼ **de place/train,** change places/trains. ∼ **de direction,** change direction. ∼ **d'avis** *ou* **d'idée,** change one's mind. ∼ **de vitesses,** change gear.

changeur /ʃɑ̃ʒœr/ *n.m.* ∼ **automatique,** (money) change machine.

chanoine /ʃanwan/ *n.m.* canon.

chanson /ʃɑ̃sɔ̃/ *n.f.* song.

chant /ʃɑ̃/ *n.m.* singing; (*chanson*) song; (*religieux*) hymn.

chantage /ʃɑ̃taʒ/ *n.m.* blackmail. ∼ **psychologique,** emotional blackmail.

chant|er /ʃɑ̃te/ *v.t./i.* sing. **si cela vous** ∼**e,** (*fam.*) if you feel like it. **faire** ∼, (*délit*) blackmail. ∼**eur,** ∼**euse** *n.m., f.* singer.

chantier /ʃɑ̃tje/ *n.m.* building site. ∼ **naval,** shipyard. **mettre en** ∼, get under way, start.

chantonner /ʃɑ̃tɔne/ *v.t./i.* hum.

chanvre /ʃɑ̃vr/ *n.m.* hemp.

chao|s /kao/ *n.m.* chaos. ∼**tique** /kaɔtik/ *a.* chaotic.

chaparder /ʃaparde/ *v.t.* (*fam.*) filch.

chapeau (*pl.* ∼x) /ʃapo/ *n.m.* hat. ∼!, well done!

chapelet /ʃaplε/ *n.m.* rosary; (*fig.*) string.

chapelle /ʃapεl/ *n.f.* chapel. ∼ **ardente,** chapel of rest.

chapelure /ʃaplyr/ *n.f.* breadcrumbs.

chaperon /ʃaprɔ̃/ *n.m.* chaperon. ∼**ner** /-ɔne/ *v.t.* chaperon.

chapiteau (*pl.* ∼x) /ʃapito/ *n.m.* (*de cirque*) big top; (*de colonne*) capital.

chapitre /ʃapitr/ *n.m.* chapter; (*fig.*) subject.

chapitrer /ʃapitre/ *v.t.* reprimand.

chaque /ʃak/ *a.* every, each.

char /ʃar/ *n.m.* (*mil.*) tank; (*de carnaval*) float; (*charrette*) cart; (*dans l'antiquité*) chariot.

charabia /ʃarabja/ *n.m.* (*fam.*) gibberish.

charade /ʃarad/ *n.f.* riddle.

charbon /ʃarbɔ̃/ *n.m.* coal. ∼ **de bois,** charcoal. ∼**nages** /-ɔnaʒ/ *n.m. pl.* coalmines.

charcut|erie /ʃarkytri/ *n.f.* porkbutcher's shop; (*aliments*) (cooked) pork meats. ∼**ier,** ∼**ière** *n.m., f.* porkbutcher.

chardon /ʃardɔ̃/ *n.m.* thistle.

charge /ʃarʒ/ *n.f.* load, burden; (*mil.,* *électr., jurid.*) charge; (*mission*) responsibility. ∼**s,** expenses; (*de locataire*) service charges. **être à la** ∼ **de,** be the responsibility of. ∼**s sociales,** social security contributions. **prendre en** ∼, take charge of; (*transporter*) give a ride to.

chargé /ʃarʒe/ *a.* (*journée*) busy; (*langue*) coated. —*n.m., f.* ∼ **de mission.** head of mission. ∼ **d'affaires,** chargé d'affaires, ∼ **de cours,** lecturer.

charger /ʃarʒe/ *v.t.* load; (*attaquer*) charge; (*batterie*) charge. —*v.i.* (*attaquer*) charge. **se** ∼ **de,** take charge *ou* care of. ∼ **qn. de,** weigh. s.o. down with; (*tâche*) entrust s.o. with. ∼ **qn. de faire,** instruct s.o. to do. **chargement** /-əmɑ̃/ *n.m.* loading; (*objets*) load.

chariot /ʃarjo/ *n.m.* (*à roulettes*) trolley; (*charrette*) cart.

charitable /ʃaritabl/ *a.* charitable.

charité /ʃarite/ *n.f.* charity. **faire la** ∼, give to charity. **faire la** ∼ **à,** give to.

charlatan /ʃarlatɑ̃/ *n.m.* charlatan.

charmant, ∼**e** /ʃarmɑ̃, -t/ *a.* charming.

charm|e /ʃarm/ *n.m.* charm. ∼**er** *v.t.* charm. ∼**eur,** ∼**euse** *n.m., f.* charmer.

charnel, ∼**le** /ʃarnεl/ *a.* carnal.

charnier /ʃarnje/ *n.m.* mass grave.

charnière /ʃarnjɛr/ *n.f.* hinge. **à la ~ de,** at the meeting point between.
charnu /ʃarny/ *a.* fleshy.
charpent|e /ʃarpɑ̃t/ *n.f.* framework; (*carrure*) build. **~é** *a.* built.
charpentier /ʃarpɑ̃tje/ *n.m.* carpenter.
charpie (en) /(ɑ̃)ʃarpi/ *adv.* in(to) shreds.
charretier /ʃartje/ *n.m.* carter.
charrette /ʃarɛt/ *n.f.* cart.
charrier /ʃarje/ *v.t.* carry.
charrue /ʃary/ *n.f.* plough.
charte /ʃart/ *n.f.* charter.
charter /ʃartɛr/ *n.m.* charter flight.
chasse /ʃas/ *n.f.* hunting; (*au fusil*) shooting; (*poursuite*) chase; (*recherche*) hunt. **~ (d'eau),** (toilet) flush. **~ sous-marine,** underwater fishing.
châsse /ʃɑs/ *n.f.* shrine, reliquary.
chass|er /ʃase/ *v.t./i.* hunt; (*faire partir*) chase away; (*odeur, employé*) get rid of. **~e-neige** *n.m. invar.* snow-plough. **~eur, ~euse** *n.m., f.* hunter; *n.m.* page-boy; (*avion*) fighter.
châssis /ʃɑsi/ *n.m.* frame; (*auto.*) chassis.
chaste /ʃast/ *a.* chaste. **~té** /-əte/ *n.f.* chastity.
chat, ~te /ʃa, ʃat/ *n.m., f.* cat.
châtaigne /ʃɑtɛɲ/ *n.f.* chestnut.
châtaignier /ʃatɛɲe/ *n.m.* chestnut tree.
châtain /ʃɑtɛ̃/ *a. invar.* chestnut (brown).
château (*pl.* **~x**) /ʃɑto/ *n.m.* castle; (*manoir*) manor. **~ d'eau,** water-tower. **~ fort,** fortified castle.
châtelain, ~e /ʃatlɛ̃, -ɛn/ *n.m., f.* lord of the manor, lady of the manor.
châtier /ʃɑtje/ *v.t.* chastise; (*style*) refine.
châtiment /ʃɑtimɑ̃/ *n.m.* punishment.
chaton /ʃatɔ̃/ *n.m.* (*chat*) kitten.
chatouill|er /ʃatuje/ *v.t.* tickle. **~ement** *n.m.* tickling.
chatouilleu|x, ~se /ʃatujø, -z/ *a.* ticklish; (*susceptible*) touchy.
chatoyer /ʃatwaje/ *v.i.* glitter.
châtrer /ʃɑtre/ *v.t.* castrate.
chatte /ʃat/ *voir* **chat.**
chaud, ~e /ʃo, ʃod/ *a.* warm; (*brûlant*) hot; (*vif: fig.*) warm. —*n.m.* heat. **au ~,** in the warm(th). **avoir ~,** be warm; be hot. **il fait ~,** it is warm; it is hot. **pour te tenir ~,** to keep you warm. **~ement** /-dmɑ̃/ *adv.* warmly; (*disputé*) hotly.
chaudière /ʃodjɛr/ *n.f.* boiler.
chaudron /ʃodrɔ̃/ *n.m.* cauldron.
chauffage /ʃofaʒ/ *n.m.* heating. **~ central,** central heating.
chauffard /ʃofar/ *n.m.* (*péj.*) reckless driver.
chauff|er /ʃofe/ *v.t./i.* heat (up). **se ~er** *v. pr.* warm o.s. (up). **~e-eau** *n.m. invar.* water-heater.
chauffeur /ʃofœr/ *n.m.* driver; (*aux gages de qn.*) chauffeur.
chaum|e /ʃom/ *n.m.* (*de toit*) thatch.
chaussée /ʃose/ *n.f.* road(way).
chauss|er /ʃose/ *v.t.* (*chaussures*) put on; (*enfant*) put shoes on (to). **se ~er** *v. pr.* put one's shoes on. **~er bien,** (*aller*) fit well. **~er du 35/*etc.***, take a size 35/*etc.* shoe. **~e-pied** *n.m.* shoehorn. **~eur** *n.m.* shoemaker.
chaussette /ʃosɛt/ *n.f.* sock.
chausson /ʃosɔ̃/ *n.m.* slipper; (*de bébé*) bootee. **~ (aux pommes),** (apple) turnover.
chaussure /ʃosyr/ *n.f.* shoe. **~s de ski,** ski boots. **~s de marche,** hiking boots.
chauve /ʃov/ *a.* bald.
chauve-souris (*pl.* **chauves-souris**) /ʃovsuri/ *n.f.* bat.
chauvin, ~e /ʃovɛ̃, -in/ *a.* chauvinistic. *n.m., f.* chauvinist. **~isme** /-inism/ *n.m.* chauvinism.
chaux /ʃo/ *n.f.* lime.
chavirer /ʃavire/ *v.t./i.* (*bateau*) capsize.
chef /ʃɛf/ *n.m.* leader, head; (*culin.*) chef; (*de tribu*) chief. **~ d'accusation,** (*jurid.*) charge. **~ d'équipe,** foreman; (*sport*) captain. **~ d'État,** head of State. **~ de famille,** head of the family. **~ de file,** (*pol.*) leader. **~ de gare,** station-master. **~ d'orchestre,** conductor. **~ de service,** department head. **~-lieu** (*pl.* **~s-lieux**) *n.m.* county town.
chef-d'œuvre (*pl.* **chefs-d'œuvre**) /ʃɛdœvr/ *n.m.* masterpiece.
cheik /ʃɛk/ *n.m.* sheikh.
chemin /ʃmɛ̃/ *n.m.* path, road; (*direction, trajet*) way. **beaucoup de ~ à faire,** a long way to go. **~ de fer,** railway. **en** *ou* **par ~ de fer,** by rail. **~ de halage,** towpath. **~ vicinal,** by-road. **se mettre en ~,** start out.
cheminée /ʃmine/ *n.f.* chimney; (*intérieure*) fireplace; (*encadrement*) mantelpiece; (*de bateau*) funnel.
chemin|er /ʃmine/ *v.i.* plod; (*fig.*) progress. **~ement** *n.m.* progress.
cheminot /ʃmino/ *n.m.* railwayman; (*Amer.*) railroad man.
chemis|e /ʃmiz/ *n.f.* shirt; (*dossier*) folder; (*de livre*) jacket. **~e de nuit,** night-dress. **~ette** *n.f.* short-sleeved shirt.
chemisier /ʃmizje/ *n.m.* blouse.
chen|al (*pl.* **~aux**) /ʃənal, -o/ *n.m.* channel.
chêne /ʃɛn/ *n.m.* oak.

chenil /ʃni(l)/ *n.m.* kennels.
chenille /ʃnij/ *n.f.* caterpillar.
chenillette /ʃnijɛt/ *n.f.* tracked vehicle.
cheptel /ʃɛptɛl/ *n.m.* livestock.
chèque /ʃɛk/ *n.m.* cheque. ～ **de voyage**, traveller's cheque.
chéquier /ʃekje/ *n.m.* cheque-book.
cher, chère /ʃɛr/ *a.* (*coûteux*) dear, expensive; (*aimé*) dear. —*adv.* (*coûter, payer*) a lot (of money). —*n.m., f.* **mon ～, ma chère**, my dear.
chercher /ʃɛrʃe/ *v.t.* look for; (*aide, paix, gloire*) seek. **aller ～**, go and get *ou* fetch, go for. ～ **à faire**, attempt to do. ～ **la petite bête**, be finicky.
chercheu|r, ～se /ʃɛrʃœr, -øz/ *n.m., f.* research worker.
chèrement /ʃɛrmɑ̃/ *adv.* dearly.
chéri|, ～e /ʃeri/ *a.* beloved. —*n.m., f.* darling.
chérir /ʃerir/ *v.t.* cherish.
cherté /ʃɛrte/ *n.f.* high cost.
chéti|f, ～ve /ʃetif, -v/ *a.* puny.
chev|al (*pl.* ～**aux**) /ʃval, -o/ *n.m.* horse. ～**al** (**vapeur**), horsepower. **à ～al**, on horseback. **à ～al sur**, straddling. **faire du ～al**, ride (a horse). ～**al-d'arçons** *n.m. invar.* (*gymnastique*) horse.
chevaleresque /ʃvalrɛsk/ *a.* chivalrous.
chevalerie /ʃvalri/ *n.f.* chivalry.
chevalet /ʃvalɛ/ *n.m.* easel.
chevalier /ʃvalje/ *n.m.* knight.
chevalière /ʃvaljɛr/ *n.f.* signet ring.
chevalin, ～e /ʃvalɛ̃, -in/ *a.* (*boucherie*) horse; (*espèce*) equine.
chevauchée /ʃvoʃe/ *n.f.* (horse-)ride.
chevaucher /ʃvoʃe/ *v.t.* straddle. —*v.i.*, **se ～** *v. pr.* overlap.
chevelu /ʃəvly/ *a.* hairy.
chevelure /ʃəvlyr/ *n.f.* hair.
chevet /ʃvɛ/ *n.m.* **au ～ de**, at the bedside of.
cheveu (*pl.* ～**x**) /ʃvø/ *n.m.* (*poil*) hair. ～**x**, (*chevelure*) hair. **avoir les ～x longs**, have long hair.
cheville /ʃvij/ *n.f.* ankle; (*fiche*) peg, pin; (*pour mur*) (wall) plug.
chèvre /ʃɛvr/ *n.f.* goat.
chevreau (*pl.* ～**x**) /ʃəvro/ *n.m.* kid.
chevreuil /ʃəvrœj/ *n.m.* roe(-deer); (*culin.*) venison.
chevron /ʃəvrɔ̃/ *n.m.* (*poutre*) rafter. **à ～s**, herring-bone.
chevronné /ʃəvrɔne/ *a.* experienced, seasoned.
chevrotant, ～e /ʃəvrɔtɑ̃, -t/ *a.* quavering.

chewing-gum /ʃwiŋgɔm/ *n.m.* chewing-gum.
chez /ʃe/ *prép.* at *ou* to the house of; (*parmi*) among; (*dans le caractère ou l'œuvre de*) in. ～ **le boucher**/*etc.*, at the butcher's/*etc.* ～ **soi**, at home; (*avec direction*) home. ～**-soi** *n.m. invar.* home.
chic /ʃik/ *a. invar.* smart; (*gentil*) kind. **sois ～**, do me a favour. ～ **style.** **avoir le ～ pour**, have the knack of. ～ (**alors**)!, great!
chicane /ʃikan/ *n.f.* zigzag. **chercher ～ à qn**, needle s.o.
chiche /ʃiʃ/ *a.* mean (**de**, with). ～ (**que je le fais**)!, (*fam.*) I bet you I will, can, *etc.*
chichis /ʃiʃi/ *n.m. pl.* (*fam.*) fuss.
chicorée /ʃikɔre/ *n.f.* (*frisée*) endive; (*à café*) chicory.
chien, ～ne /ʃjɛ̃, ʃjɛn/ *n.m.* dog. —*n.f.* dog, bitch. ～ **de garde**, watch-dog. ～**-loup** *n.m.* (*pl.* ～**s-loups**) wolfhound.
chiffon /ʃifɔ̃/ *n.m.* rag.
chiffonner /ʃifɔne/ *v.t.* crumple; (*préoccuper*) bother.
chiffonnier /ʃifɔnje/ *n.m.* rag-and-bone man.
chiffre /ʃifr/ *n.m.* figure; (*code*) code. ～**s arabes/romains**, Arabic/Roman numerals. ～ **d'affaires**, turnover.
chiffrer /ʃifre/ *v.t.* set a figure to, assess; (*texte*) encode. **se ～ à**, amount to.
chignon /ʃiɲɔ̃/ *n.m.* bun, chignon.
Chili /ʃili/ *n.m.* Chile.
chilien, ～ne /ʃiljɛ̃, -jɛn/ *a. & n.m., f.* Chilean.
chim|ère /ʃimɛr/ *n.f.* fantasy. ～**érique** *a.* fanciful.
chim|ie /ʃimi/ *n.f.* chemistry. ～**ique** *a.* chemical. ～**iste** *n.m./f.* chemist.
chimpanzé /ʃɛ̃pɑ̃ze/ *n.m.* chimpanzee.
Chine /ʃin/ *n.f.* China.
chinois, ～e /ʃinwa, -z/ *a. & n.m., f.* Chinese. —*n.m.* (*lang.*) Chinese.
chiot /ʃjo/ *n.m.* pup(py).
chiper /ʃipe/ *v.t.* (*fam.*) swipe.
chipoter /ʃipɔte/ *v.i.* (*manger*) nibble; (*discuter*) quibble.
chips /ʃips/ *n.m. pl.* crisps; (*Amer.*) chips.
chiquenaude /ʃiknod/ *n.f.* flick.
chiromanc|ie /kirɔmɑ̃si/ *n.f.* palmistry. ～**ien, ～ienne** *n.m., f.* palmist.
chirurgic|al (*m. pl.* ～**aux**) /ʃiryrʒikal, -o/ *a.* surgical.
chirurg|ie /ʃiryrʒi/ *n.f.* surgery. ～**ie esthétique**, plastic surgery. ～**ien** *n.m.* surgeon.
chlore /klɔr/ *n.m.* chlorine.

choc /ʃɔk/ *n.m.* (*heurt*) impact, shock; (*émotion*) shock; (*collision*) crash; (*affrontement*) clash; (*méd.*) shock.

chocolat /ʃɔkɔla/ *n.m.* chocolate; (*à boire*) drinking chocolate. ∼ **au lait**, milk chocolate. ∼ **chaud**, hot chocolat.

chœur /kœr/ *n.m.* (*antique*) chorus; (*chanteurs, nef*) choir. **en** ∼, in chorus.

chois|ir /ʃwazir/ *v.t.* choose, select. ∼**i** *a.* carefully chosen; (*passage*) selected.

choix /ʃwa/ *n.m.* choice, selection. **au** ∼, according to preference. **de** ∼, choice. **de premier** ∼, top quality.

choléra /kɔlera/ *n.m.* cholera.

chômage /ʃomaʒ/ *n.m.* unemployment. **en** ∼, unemployed. **mettre en** ∼ **technique**, lay off.

chôm|er /ʃome/ *v.i.* be unemployed; (*usine*) lie idle. ∼**eur**, ∼**euse** *n.m., f.* unemployed person. **les** ∼**eurs**, the unemployed.

chope /ʃɔp/ *n.f.* tankard.

choper /ʃɔpe/ *v.t.* (*fam.*) catch.

choquer /ʃɔke/ *v.t.* shock; (*commotionner*) shake.

choral, ∼**e** (*m. pl.* ∼**s**) /kɔral/ *a.* choral. —*n.f.* choir, choral society.

chorégraph|ie /kɔregrafi/ *n.f.* choreography. ∼**e** *n.m./f.* choreographer.

choriste /kɔrist/ *n m /f.* (*à l'église*) chorister; (*opéra, etc.*) member of the chorus *ou* choir.

chose /ʃoz/ *n.f.* thing. (**très**) **peu de** ∼, nothing much.

chou (*pl.* ∼**x**) /ʃu/ *n.m.* cabbage. ∼ (**à la crème**), cream puff. ∼**x de Bruxelles**, Brussels sprouts. **mon petit** ∼, (*fam.*) my little dear.

choucas /ʃuka/ *n.m.* jackdaw.

chouchou, ∼**te** /ʃuʃu, −t/ *n.m., f.* pet, darling. **le** ∼ **du prof.**, the teacher's pet.

choucroute /ʃukrut/ *n.f.* sauerkraut.

chouette¹ /ʃwɛt/ *n.f.* owl.

chouette² /ʃwɛt/ *a.* (*fam.*) super.

chou fleur (*pl.* **choux-fleurs**) /ʃuflœr/ *n.m.* cauliflower.

choyer /ʃwaje/ *v.t.* pamper.

chrétien, ∼**ne** /kretjɛ̃, −jɛn/ *a. & n.m., f.* Christian.

Christ /krist/ *n.m.* **le** ∼, Christ.

christianisme /kristjanism/ *n.m.* Christianity.

chrom|e /krom/ *n.m.* chromium, chrome. ∼**é** *a.* chromium-plated.

chromosome /krɔmozom/ *n.m.* chromosome.

chronique /krɔnik/ *a.* chronic. —*n.f.* (*rubrique*) column; (*nouvelles*) news; (*annales*) chronicle. ∼**eur** *n.m.* columnist; (*historien*) chronicler.

chronolog|ie /krɔnɔlɔʒi/ *n.f.* chronology. ∼**ique** *a.* chronological.

chronom|ètre /krɔnɔmɛtr/ *n.m.* stopwatch. ∼**étrer** *v.t.* time.

chrysanthème /krizɑ̃tɛm/ *n.m.* chrysanthemum.

chuchot|er /ʃyʃɔte/ *v.t./i.* whisper. ∼**ement** *n.m.* whisper(ing).

chuinter /ʃwɛ̃te/ *v.i.* hiss.

chut /ʃyt/ *int.* shush.

chute /ʃyt/ *n.f.* fall; (*déchet*) scrap. ∼ (**d'eau**), waterfall. ∼ **du jour**, nightfall. ∼ **de pluie**, rainfall. **la** ∼ **des cheveux**, hair loss.

chuter /ʃyte/ *v.i.* fall.

Chypre /ʃipr/ *n.f.* Cyprus.

-ci /si/ *adv.* (*après un nom précédé de ce, cette, etc.*) **cet homme-ci**, this man. **ces maisons-ci**, these houses.

ci- /si/ *adv.* here. **ci-après**, hereafter. **ci-contre**, opposite. **ci-dessous**, below. **ci-dessus**, above. **ci-gît**, here lies. **ci-inclus**, **ci-incluse**, **ci-joint**, **ci-jointe**, enclosed.

cible /sibl/ *n.f.* target.

ciboul|e /sibul/ *n.f.*, ∼**ette** *n.f.* chive(s).

cicatrice /sikatris/ *n.f.* scar.

cicatriser /sikatrize/ *v.t.*, **se** ∼ *v. pr.* heal (up).

cidre /sidr/ *n.m.* cider.

ciel (*pl.* **cieux, ciels**) /sjɛl, sjø/ *n m* sky; (*relig.*) heaven. **cieux**, (*relig.*) heaven.

cierge /sjɛrʒ/ *n.m.* candle.

cigale /sigal/ *n.f.* cicada.

cigare /sigar/ *n.m.* cigar.

cigarette /sigarɛt/ *n.f.* cigarette.

cigogne /sigɔɲ/ *n.f.* stork.

cil /sil/ *n.m.* (*eye*)lash.

ciller /sije/ *v.i.* blink.

cime /sim/ *n.f.* peak, tip.

ciment /simɑ̃/ *n.m.* cement. ∼**er** − te/ *v.t.* cement.

cimetière /simtjɛr/ *n.m.* cemetery. ∼ **de voitures**, breaker's yard.

cinéaste /sineast/ *n.m./f.* film-maker.

ciné-club /sineklœb/ *n.m.* film society.

cinéma /sinema/ *n.m.* cinema. ∼**tographique** *a.* cinema.

cinémathèque /sinematɛk/ *n.f.* film library; (*salle*) film theatre.

cinéphile /sinefil/ *n.m./f.* film lover.

cinétique /sinetik/ *a.* kinetic.

cinglant, ∼**e** /sɛ̃glɑ̃, −t/ *a.* biting.

cinglé /sɛ̃gle/ *a.* (*fam.*) crazy.

cingler /sɛ̃gle/ *v.t.* lash.

cinq /sɛ̃k/ *a. & n.m.* five. ∼**ième** *a. & n.m./f.* fifth.

cinquantaine /sɛ̃kãtɛn/ *n.f.* une ～ **(de),** about fifty.

cinquant|e /sɛ̃kãt/ *a. & n.m.* fifty. ～**ième** *a. & n.m./f.* fiftieth.

cintre /sɛ̃tr/ *n.m.* coat-hanger; (*archit.*) curve.

cintré /sɛ̃tre/ *a.* (*chemise*) fitted.

cirage /siraʒ/ *n.m.* (wax) polish.

circoncision /sirkɔ̃sizjɔ̃/ *n.f.* circumcision.

circonférence /sirkɔ̃ferãs/ *n.f.* circumference.

circonflexe /sirkɔ̃flɛks/ *a.* circumflex.

circonscription /sirkɔ̃skripsjɔ̃/ *n.f.* district. ～ **(électorale),** constituency.

circonscrire /sirkɔ̃skrir/ *v.t.* confine; (*sujet*) define.

circonspect /sirkɔ̃spɛkt/ *a.* circumspect.

circonstance /sirkɔ̃stãs/ *n.f.* circumstance; (*occasion*) occasion. ～**s atténuantes,** mitigating circumstances.

circonstancié /sirkɔ̃stãsje/ *a.* detailed.

circonvenir /sirkɔ̃vnir/ *v.t.* circumvent.

circuit /sirkɥi/ *n.m.* circuit; (*trajet*) tour, trip.

circulaire /sirkylɛr/ *a. & n.f.* circular.

circul|er /sirkyle/ *v.i.* circulate; (*train, automobile, etc.*) travel; (*piéton*) walk. **faire ～er,** (*badauds*) move on. ～**ation** *n.f.* circulation; (*de véhicules*) traffic.

cire /sir/ *n.f.* wax.

ciré /sire/ *n.m.* oilskin; waterproof.

cir|er /sire/ *v.t.* polish, wax. ～**euse** *n.f.* (*appareil*) floor-polisher.

cirque /sirk/ *n.m.* circus; (*arène*) amphitheatre; (*désordre:* fig.) chaos.

cirrhose /siroz/ *n.f.* cirrhosis.

cisaille(s) /sizaj/ *n.f.* (*pl.*) shears.

ciseau (*pl.* ～**x**) /sizo/ *n.m.* chisel. ～**x,** scissors.

ciseler /sizle/ *v.t.* chisel.

citadelle /sitadɛl/ *n.f.* citadel.

citadin, ～**e** /sitadɛ̃, -in/ *n.m., f.* city dweller. —*a.* city.

cité /site/ *n.f.* city. ～ **ouvrière,** (workers') housing estate. ～ **universitaire,** (university) halls of residence. ～**-dortoir** *n.f.* (*pl.* ～**s-dortoirs**) dormitory town.

cit|er /site/ *v.t.* quote, cite; (*jurid.*) summon. ～**ation** *n.f.* quotation; (*jurid.*) summons.

citerne /sitɛrn/ *n.f.* tank.

cithare /sitar/ *n.f.* zither.

citoyen, ～**e** /sitwajɛ̃, -jɛn/ *n.m., f.* citizen. ～**neté** /-jɛnte/ *n.f.* citizenship.

citron /sitrɔ̃/ *n.m.* lemon. ～ **vert,** lime. ～**nade** /-ɔnad/ *n.f.* lemon squash *ou* drink, (still) lemonade.

citrouille /sitruj/ *n.f.* pumpkin.

civet /sivɛ/ *n.m.* stew. ～ **de lièvre/lapin,** jugged hare/rabbit.

civette /sivɛt/ *n.f.* (*culin.*) chive(s).

civière /sivjɛr/ *n.f.* stretcher.

civil /sivil/ *a.* civil; (*non militaire*) civilian; (*poli*) civil. —*n.m.* civilian. **dans le ～,** in civilian life. **en ～,** in plain clothes.

civilisation /sivilizasjɔ̃/ *n.f.* civilization.

civiliser /sivilize/ *v.t.* civilize. **se ～** *v. pr.* become civilized.

civi|que /sivik/ *a.* civic. ～**sme** *n.m.* civic sense.

clair /klɛr/ *a.* clear; (*éclairé*) light, bright; (*couleur*) light; (*liquide*) thin. —*adv.* clearly. —*n.m.* ～ **de lune,** moonlight. **le plus ～ de,** most of. ～**ement** *adv.* clearly.

claire-voie (à) /(a)klɛrvwa/ *adv.* with slits to let the light through.

clairière /klɛrjɛr/ *n.f.* clearing.

clairon /klɛrɔ̃/ *n.m.* bugle. ～**ner** /-ɔne/ *v.t.* trumpet (forth).

clairsemé /klɛrsəme/ *a.* sparse.

clairvoyant, ～**e** /klɛrvwajã, -t/ *a.* clear-sighted.

clamer /klame/ *v.t.* utter aloud.

clameur /klamœr/ *n.f.* clamour.

clan /klã/ *n.m.* clan.

clandestin, ～**e** /klãdɛstɛ̃, -in/ *a.* secret; (*journal*) underground. **passager ～,** stowaway.

clapet /klapɛ/ *n.m.* valve.

clapier /klapje/ *n.m.* (rabbit) hutch.

clapot|er /klapɔte/ *v.i.* lap. ～**is** *n.m.* lapping.

claquage /klakaʒ/ *n.m.* strained muscle.

claque /klak/ *n.f.* slap. **en avoir sa ～ (de),** (*fam.*) be fed up (with).

claqu|er /klake/ *v.i.* bang; (*porte*) slam, bang; (*fouet*) snap, crack; (*se casser:* fam.) conk out; (*mourir:* fam.) snuff it. —*v.t.* (*porte*) slam, bang; (*dépenser:* fam.) blow; (*fatiguer:* fam.) tire out. ～**er des doigts,** snap one's fingers. ～**er des mains,** clap one's hands. **il claque des dents,** his teeth are chattering. ～**ement** *n.m.* bang(ing); slam(ming); snap(ping).

claquettes /klakɛt/ *n.f. pl.* tap-dancing.

clarifier /klarifje/ *v.t.* clarify.

clarinette /klarinɛt/ *n.f.* clarinet.

clarté /klarte/ *n.f.* light, brightness; (*netteté*) clarity.

classe /klɑs/ *n.f.* class; (*salle:* scol.) class(-room). **aller en ～,** go to school. ～ **ouvrière/moyenne,** working/middle class. **faire la ～,** teach.

class|er /klɑse/ v.t. classify; (par mérite) grade; (papiers) file; (affaire) close. **se ~er premier/ dernier,** come first/last. **~ement** n.m. classification; grading; filing; (rang) place, grade; (de coureur) placing.

classeur /klɑsœr/ n.m. filing cabinet; (chemise) file.

classif|ier /klasifje/ v.t. classify. **~ication** n.f. classification.

classique /klasik/ a. classical; (de qualité) classic(al); (habituel) classic. —n.m. classic; (auteur) classical author.

clause /kloz/ n.f. clause.

claustration /klostrɑsjɔ̃/ n.f. confinement.

claustrophobie /klostrofobi/ n.f. claustrophobia.

clavecin /klavsɛ̃/ n.m. harpsichord.

clavicule /klavikyl/ n.f. collar-bone.

clavier /klavje/ n.m. keyboard.

claviste /klavist/ n.m /f keyboarder.

clé, clef /kle/ n.f. key; (outil) spanner; (mus.) clef. —a. invar. key. **~ anglaise,** (monkey-)wrench. **~ de contact,** ignition key. **~ de voûte,** keystone. **prix ~s en main,** (voiture) on-the-road price.

clémen|t, **~te** /klemɑ̃, -t/ a. (doux) mild; (indulgent) lenient. **~ce** n.f. mildness; leniency.

clémentine /klemɑ̃tin/ n.f. clementine.

clerc /klɛr/ n.m. (d'avoué etc.) clerk; (relig.) cleric.

clergé /klɛrʒe/ n.m. clergy.

cléric|al (m. pl. **~aux**) /klerikal, -o/ a. clerical.

cliché /kliʃe/ n.m cliché; (photo.) negative.

client, **~e** /klijɑ̃, -t/ n.m., f. customer; (d'un avocat) client; (d'un médecin) patient; (d'hôtel) guest. **~èle** /-tɛl/ n.f. customers, clientele; (d'un avocat) clientele, clients, practice; (d'un médecin) practice, patients; (soutien) custom.

cligner /kliɲe/ v.i. **~ des yeux,** blink. **~ de l'œil,** wink.

clignot|er /kliɲote/ v.i. blink; (lumière) flicker; (comme signal) flash. **~ant** n.m. (auto.) indicator; (auto., Amer.) directional signal.

climat /klima/ n.m. climate. **~ique** /-tik/ a. climatic.

climatis|ation /klimatizɑsjɔ̃/ n.f. air-conditioning. **~é** a. air-conditioned.

clin d'œil /klɛ̃dœj/ n.m. wink. **en un ~,** in a flash.

clinique /klinik/ a. clinical. —n.f. (private) clinic.

clinquant, **~e** /klɛ̃kɑ̃, -t/ a. showy.

clip /klip/ n.m. video.

clique /klik/ n.f. clique; (mus., mil.) band.

cliquet|er /klikte/ v.i. clink. **~is** n.m. clink(ing).

clitoris /klitoris/ n.m. clitoris.

clivage /klivaʒ/ n.m. cleavage.

clochard, **~e** /klɔʃar, -d/ n.m., f. tramp.

cloch|e¹ /klɔʃ/ n.f. bell; (fam.) idiot. **~ à fromage,** cheese cover. **~ette** n.f. bell.

cloche² /klɔʃ/ n.f. (fam.) idiot.

cloche-pied (à) /(a)klɔʃpje/ adv. hopping on one foot.

clocher¹ /klɔʃe/ n.m. bell-tower; (pointu) steeple. **de ~,** parochial.

clocher² /klɔʃe/ v.i. (fam.) be wrong.

cloison /klwazɔ̃/ n.f. partition; (fig.) barrier. **~ner** /-ɔne/ v.t. partition; (personne) cut off.

cloître /klwatr/ n.m. cloister.

cloîtrer (se) /(sə)klwatre/ v. pr. shut o.s. away.

clopin-clopant /klɔpɛ̃klɔpɑ̃/ adv. hobbling.

cloque /klɔk/ n.f. blister.

clore /klɔr/ v.t. close.

clos, **~e** /klo, -z/ a. closed.

clôtur|e /klotyr/ n.f. fence; (fermeture) closure. **~er** v.t. enclose; (festival, séance, etc.) close.

clou /klu/ n.m. nail; (furoncle) boil; (de spectacle) star attraction. **~ de girofle,** clove. **les ~s,** (passage) zebra ou pedestrian crossing. **~** (fig.) pin down. **être cloué au lit,** be confined to one's bed **~er le bec à qn.,** shut s.o. up.

clouté /klute/ a. studded.

clown /klun/ n.m. clown.

club /klœb/ n.m. club.

coaguler /kɔagyle/ v.t./i., **se ~** v. pr. coagulate.

coaliser (se) /(sə)kɔalize/ v. pr. join forces.

coalition /kɔalisjɔ̃/ n.f. coalition.

coasser /kɔase/ v.i. croak.

cobaye /kɔbaj/ n.m. guinea-pig.

coca /kɔka/ n.m. (P.) Coke.

cocagne /kɔkaɲ/ n.f. **pays de ~,** land of plenty.

cocaïne /kɔkain/ n.f. cocaine.

cocarde /kɔkard/ n.f. rosette.

cocard|ier, **~ière** /kɔkardje, -jɛr/ a. chauvinistic.

cocasse /kɔkas/ a. comical.

coccinelle /kɔksinɛl/ n.f. ladybird; (*Amer.*) ladybug; (*voiture*) beetle.

cocher[1] /kɔʃe/ v.t. tick (off), check.

cocher[2] /kɔʃe/ n.m. coachman.

cochon, ～ne /kɔʃɔ̃, -ɔn/ n.m. pig. —n.m., f. (*personne: fam.*) pig. —a. (*fam.*) filthy. **～nerie** /-ɔnri/ n.f. (*saleté: fam.*) filth; (*marchandise: fam.*) rubbish.

cocktail /kɔktɛl/ n.m. cocktail; (*réunion*) cocktail party.

cocon /kɔkɔ̃/ n.m. cocoon.

cocorico /kɔkɔriko/ n.m. cock-a-doodle-doo.

cocotier /kɔkɔtje/ n.m. coconut palm.

cocotte /kɔkɔt/ n.f. (*marmite*) casserole. **～ minute**, (P.) pressure-cooker. **ma ～**, (*fam.*) my sweet, my dear.

cocu /kɔky/ n.m. (*fam.*) cuckold.

code /kɔd/ n.m. code. **～s, phares ～**, dipped headlights. **～ de la route**, Highway Code. **se mettre en ～**, dip one's headlights.

coder /kɔde/ v.t. code.

codifier /kɔdifje/ v.t. codify.

coéquip|ier, ～ière /kɔekipje, -jɛr/ n.m., f. team-mate.

cœur /kœr/ n.m. heart; (*cartes*) hearts. **～ d'artichaut**, artichoke heart. **～ de palmier**, heart of palm. **à ～ ouvert**, (*opération*) open-heart; (*parler*) freely. **avoir bon ～**, be kind-hearted. **de bon ～**, with a good heart. **par ～**, by heart. **avoir mal au ～**, feel sick. **je veux en avoir le ～ net**, I want to be clear in my own mind (about it).

coexist|er /kɔɛgziste/ v.i. coexist. **～ence** n.f. coexistence.

coffre /kɔfr/ n.m. chest; (*pour argent*) safe; (*auto.*) boot; (*auto., Amer.*) trunk. **～-fort** (*pl.* **～s-forts**) n.m. safe.

coffrer /kɔfre/ v.t. (*fam.*) lock up.

coffret /kɔfrɛ/ n.m. casket, box.

cognac /kɔɲak/ n.m. cognac.

cogner /kɔɲe/ v.t./i. knock. **se ～** v. pr. knock o.s.

cohabit|er /kɔabite/ v.i. live together. **～ation** n.f. living together.

cohérent, ～e /kɔerɑ̃, -t/ a. coherent.

cohésion /kɔezjɔ̃/ n.f. cohesion.

cohorte /kɔɔrt/ n.f. troop.

cohue /kɔy/ n.f. crowd.

coi, coite /kwa, -t/ a. silent.

coiffe /kwaf/ n.f. head-dress.

coiff|er /kwafe/ v.t. do the hair of; (*chapeau*) put on; (*surmonter*) cap. **～er qn. d'un chapeau**, put a hat on s.o. **se ～er** v. pr. do one's hair. **～é de**, wearing. **bien/mal ～é**, with tidy/untidy

hair. **～eur, ～euse** n.m., f. hairdresser; n.f. dressing-table.

coiffure /kwafyr/ n.f. hairstyle; (*chapeau*) hat; (*métier*) hairdressing.

coin /kwɛ̃/ n.m. corner; (*endroit*) spot; (*cale*) wedge; (*pour graver*) die. **au ～ du feu**, by the fireside. **dans le ～**, locally. **du ～**, local. **le boulanger du ～**, the local baker.

coincer /kwɛ̃se/ v.t. jam; (*caler*) wedge; (*attraper: fam.*) catch. **se ～** v. pr. get jammed.

coïncid|er /kɔɛ̃side/ v.i. coincide. **～ence** n.f. coincidence.

coing /kwɛ̃/ n.m. quince.

coït /kɔit/ n.m. intercourse.

coite /kwat/ *voir* **coi**.

coke /kɔk/ n.m. coke.

col /kɔl/ n.m. collar; (*de bouteille*) neck; (*de montagne*) pass. **～ roulé**, polo-neck; (*Amer.*) turtle-neck. **～ de l'utérus**, cervix.

coléoptère /kɔleɔptɛr/ n.m. beetle.

colère /kɔlɛr/ n.f. anger; (*accès*) fit of anger. **en ～**, angry. **se mettre en ～**, lose one's temper.

colér|eux, ～euse /kɔlerø, -z/, **～ique** adjs. quick-tempered.

colibri /kɔlibri/ n.m. humming-bird.

colifichet /kɔlifiʃɛ/ n.m. trinket.

colimaçon (en) /(ɑ̃)kɔlimasɔ̃/ adv. spiral.

colin /kɔlɛ̃/ n.m. (*poisson*) hake.

colin-maillard /kɔlɛ̃majar/ n.m. **jouer à ～**, play blind man's buff.

colique /kɔlik/ n.f. diarrhoea; (*méd.*) colic.

colis /kɔli/ n.m. parcel.

collabor|er /kɔlabɔre/ v.i. collaborate (à, on). **～er à**, (*journal*) contribute to. **～ateur, ～atrice** n.m., f. collaborator; contributor. **～ation** n.f. collaboration (à, on); contribution (à, to).

collant, ～e /kɔlɑ̃, -t/ a. skin-tight; (*poisseux*) sticky. —n.m. (*bas*) tights; (*de danseur*) leotard.

collation /kɔlasjɔ̃/ n.f. light meal.

colle /kɔl/ n.f. glue; (*en pâte*) paste; (*problème: fam.*) poser; (*scol., argot*) detention.

collect|e /kɔlɛkt/ n.f. collection. **～er** v.t. collect.

collecteur /kɔlɛktœr/ n.m. (*égout*) main sewer.

collecti|f, ～ve /kɔlɛktif, -v/ a. collective; (*billet, voyage*) group. **～vement** adv. collectively.

collection /kɔlɛksjɔ̃/ n.f. collection.

collectionn|er /kɔlɛksjɔne/ *v.t.* collect. **~eur, ~euse** *n.m., f.* collector.

collectivité /kɔlɛktivite/ *n.f.* community.

coll|ège /kɔlɛʒ/ *n.m.* (secondary) school; (*assemblée*) college. **~égien, ~égienne** *n.m., f.* schoolboy, schoolgirl.

collègue /kɔlɛg/ *n.m./f.* colleague.

coll|er /kɔle/ *v.t.* stick; (*avec colle liquide*) glue; (*affiche*) stick up; (*mettre: fam.*) stick; (*scol., argot*) keep in; (*par une question: fam.*) stump. —*v.i.* stick (à, to); (*être collant*) be sticky. **~er à,** (*convenir à*) fit, correspond to. **être ~é à,** (*examen: fam.*) fail.

collet /kɔlɛ/ *n.m.* (*piège*) snare. **~ monté,** prim and proper. **prendre qn. au ~,** collar s.o.

collier /kɔlje/ *n.m.* necklace; (*de chien*) collar.

colline /kɔlin/ *n.f.* hill.

collision /kɔlizjɔ̃/ *n.f.* (*choc*) collision; (*lutte*) clash. **entrer en ~** (**avec**), collide (with).

colloque /kɔlɔk/ *n.m.* symposium.

collyre /kɔlir/ *n.m.* eye drops.

colmater /kɔlmate/ *v.t.* seal; (*trou*) fill in.

colombe /kɔlɔ̃b/ *n.f.* dove.

Colombie /kɔlɔ̃bi/ *n.f.* Colombia.

colon /kɔlɔ̃/ *n.m.* settler.

colonel /kɔlɔnɛl/ *n.m.* colonel.

colon|ial, ~iale (*m. pl. ~iaux*) /kɔlɔnjal, -jo/ *a.* & *n.m., f.* colonial.

colonie /kɔlɔni/ *n.f.* colony. **~ de vacances,** children's holiday camp.

coloniser /kɔlɔnize/ *v.t.* colonize.

colonne /kɔlɔn/ *n.f.* column. **~ vertébrale,** spine. **en ~ par deux,** in double file.

color|er /kɔlɔre/ *v.t.* colour; (*bois*) stain. **~ant** *n.m.* colouring. **~ation** *n.f.* (*couleur*) colour(ing).

colorier /kɔlɔrje/ *v.t.* colour (in).

coloris /kɔlɔri/ *n.m.* colour.

coloss|al (*m. pl. ~aux*) /kɔlɔsal, -o/ *a.* colossal.

colosse /kɔlɔs/ *n.m.* giant.

colport|er /kɔlpɔrte/ *v.t.* hawk. **~eur, ~euse** *n.m., f.* hawker.

colza /kɔlza/ *n.m.* rape(-seed).

coma /kɔma/ *n.m.* coma. **dans le ~,** in a coma.

combat /kɔ̃ba/ *n.m.* fight; (*sport*) match. **~s,** fighting.

combati|f, ~ve /kɔ̃batif, -v/ *a.* eager to fight; (*esprit*) fighting.

combatt|re† /kɔ̃batr/ *v.t./i.* fight. **~ant,**

~ante *n.m., f.* fighter; batant.

combien /kɔ̃bjɛ̃/ *adv.* **~ (de),** (*quantité*) how much; (*nombre*) how many; (*temps*) how long. **~ il a changé!,** (*comme*) how he has changed! **~y a-t-il d'ici à . . .?,** how far is it to . . .?

combinaison /kɔ̃binɛzɔ̃/ *n.f.* combination; (*manigance*) scheme; (*de femme*) slip; (*bleu de travail*) boiler suit; (*Amer.*) overalls; (*de plongée*) wetsuit. **~ d'aviateur,** flying-suit.

combine /kɔ̃bin/ *n.f.* trick; (*fraude*) fiddle.

combiné /kɔ̃bine/ *n.m.* (*de téléphone*) receiver.

combiner /kɔ̃bine/ *v.t.* (*réunir*) combine; (*calculer*) devise.

comble[1] /kɔ̃bl/ *a.* packed.

comble[2] /kɔ̃bl/ *n.m.* height. **~s,** (*mansarde*) attic, loft. **c'est le ~!,** that's the (absolute) limit!

combler /kɔ̃ble/ *v.t.* fill; (*perte, déficit*) make good; (*désir*) fulfil, (*personne*) gratify. **~ qn. de cadeaux/etc.,** lavish gifts/*etc.* on s.o.

combustible /kɔ̃bystibl/ *n.m.* fuel.

combustion /kɔ̃bystjɔ̃/ *n.f.* combustion.

comédie /kɔmedi/ *n.f.* comedy. **~ musicale,** musical. **jouer la ~,** put on an act.

comédien, ~ne /kɔmedjɛ̃, -jɛn/ *n.m., f.* actor, actress.

comestible /kɔmɛstibl/ *a.* edible. **~s** *n.m. pl.* foodstuffs.

comète /kɔmɛt/ *n.f.* comet.

comique /kɔmik/ *a.* comical; (*genre*) comic. —*n.m.* (*acteur*) comic; (*comédie*) comedy; (*côté drôle*) comical aspect.

comité /kɔmite/ *n.m.* committee.

commandant /kɔmɑ̃dɑ̃/ *n.m.* commander; (*armée de terre*) major. **~ (de bord),** captain. **~ en chef,** Commander-in-Chief.

commande /kɔmɑ̃d/ *n.f.* (*comm.*) order. **~s,** (*d'avion etc.*) controls.

command|er /kɔmɑ̃de/ *v.t.* command; (*acheter*) order. —*v.i.* be in command. **~er à,** (*maîtriser*) control. **~er à qn. de,** command s.o. to. **~ement** *n.m.* command; (*relig.*) commandment.

commando /kɔmɑ̃do/ *n.m.* commando.

comme /kɔm/ *conj.* as. —*prép.* like. —*adv.* (*exclamation*) how. **~ ci comme ça,** so-so. **~ d'habitude, ~ à l'ordinaire,** as usual. **~ il faut,** proper(ly). **~ pour faire,** as if to do. **~ quoi,** to the effect that. **qu'avez-vous ~**

amis/**etc.?**, what have you in the way of friends/*etc.*? ~ **c'est bon!**, it's so good! ~ **il est mignon!** isn't he sweet!

commémor|er /kɔmemɔre/ *v.t.* commemorate. ~**ation** *n.f.* commemoration.

commenc|er /kɔmɑ̃se/ *v.t.* begin, start. ~**er à faire**, begin *ou* start to do. ~**ement** *n.m.* beginning, start.

comment /kɔmɑ̃/ *adv.* how. ~**?**, (*répétition*) pardon?; (*surprise*) what? ~ **est-il?**, what is he like? **le ~ et le pourquoi**, the whys and wherefores.

commentaire /kɔmɑ̃tɛr/ *n.m.* comment; (*d'un texte*) commentary.

comment|er /kɔmɑ̃te/ *v.t.* comment on. ~**ateur**, ~**atrice** *n.m.*, *f.* commentator.

commérages /kɔmeraʒ/ *n.m. pl.* gossip.

commerçant, ~**e** /kɔmɛrsɑ̃, -t/ *a.* (*rue*) shopping; (*personne*) business-minded. —*n.m.*, *f.* shopkeeper.

commerce /kɔmɛrs/ *n.m.* trade, commerce; (*magasin*) business. **faire du ~**, trade.

commerc|ial (*m. pl.* ~**iaux**) /kɔmɛrsjal, -jo/ *a.* commercial. ~**ialiser** *v.t.* market. ~**ialisable** *a.* marketable.

commère /kɔmɛr/ *n.f.* gossip.

commettre /kɔmɛtr/ *v.t.* commit.

commis /kɔmi/ *n.m.* (*de magasin*) assistant; (*de bureau*) clerk.

commissaire /kɔmisɛr/ *n.m.* (*sport*) steward. ~ **(de police)**, (police) superintendent. ~**-priseur** (*pl.* ~**s-priseurs**) *n.m.* auctioneer.

commissariat /kɔmisarja/ *n.m.* ~ **(de police)**, police station.

commission /kɔmisjɔ̃/ *n.f.* commission; (*course*) errand; (*message*) message. ~**s**, shopping. ~**naire** /-jɔnɛr/ *n.m.* errand-boy.

commod|e /kɔmɔd/ *a.* handy; (*facile*) easy. **pas** ~**e**, (*personne*) a difficult customer. —*n.f.* chest (of drawers). ~**ité** *n.f.* convenience.

commotion /kɔmosjɔ̃/ *n.f.* ~ **(cérébrale)**, concussion. ~**né** /-jɔne/ *a.* shaken.

commuer /kɔmɥe/ *v.t.* commute.

commun, ~**e** /kɔmœ̃, -yn/ *a.* common; (*effort*, *action*) joint; (*frais*, *pièce*) shared. —*n.f.* (*circonscription*) commune. ~**s** *n.m. pl.* outhouses, outbuildings. **avoir** *ou* **mettre en** ~, share. **le ~ des mortels**, ordinary mortals. ~**al** (*m. pl.* ~**aux**) /-ynal, -o/ *a.* of the commune, local. ~**ément** /-ynemɑ̃/ *adv.* commonly.

communauté /kɔmynote/ *n.f.* community. ~ **des biens** (*entre époux*) shared estate.

commune /kɔmyn/ *voir* **commun**.

communiant, ~**e** /kɔmynjɑ̃, -t/ *n.m.*, *f.* (*relig.*) communicant.

communicati|f, ~**ve** /kɔmynikatif, -v/ *a.* communicative.

communication /kɔmynikasjɔ̃/ *n.f.* communication; (*téléphonique*) call. ~ **interurbaine**, long-distance call.

commun|ier /kɔmynje/ *v.i.* (*relig.*) receive communion; (*fig.*) commune. ~**ion** *n.f.* communion.

communiqué /kɔmynike/ *n.m.* communiqué.

communiquer /kɔmynike/ *v.t.* pass on, communicate; (*mouvement*) impart. —*v.i.* communicate. **se** ~ **à**, spread to.

communis|te /kɔmynist/ *a.* & *n.m./f.* communist. ~**me** *n.m.* communism.

commutateur /kɔmytatœr/ *n.m.* (*électr.*) switch.

compact /kɔ̃pakt/ *a.* dense; (*voiture*) compact.

compact disc /kɔ̃paktdisk/ *n.m.* (P.) compact disc.

compagne /kɔ̃paɲ/ *n.f.* companion.

compagnie /kɔ̃paɲi/ *n.f.* company. **tenir** ~ **à**, keep company.

compagnon /kɔ̃paɲɔ̃/ *n.m.* companion; (*ouvrier*) workman. ~ **de jeu**, playmate.

comparaître /kɔ̃parɛtr/ *v.i.* (*jurid.*) appear (**devant**, before).

compar|er /kɔ̃pare/ *v.t.* compare. ~**er qch./qn. à** *ou* **et** compare sth./s.o. with *ou* and; **se** ~**er** *v. pr.* be compared. ~**able** *a.* comparable. ~**aison** *n.f.* comparison; (*littéraire*) simile. ~**atif**, ~**ative** *a.* & *n.m.* comparative. ~**é** *a.* comparative.

comparse /kɔ̃pars/ *n.m./f.* (*péj.*) stooge.

compartiment /kɔ̃partimɑ̃/ *n.m.* compartment. ~**er** /-te/ *v.t.* divide up.

comparution /kɔ̃parysjɔ̃/ *n.f.* (*jurid.*) appearance.

compas /kɔ̃pa/ *n.m.* (pair of) compasses; (*boussole*) compass.

compassé /kɔ̃pase/ *a.* stilted.

compassion /kɔ̃pasjɔ̃/ *n.f.* compassion.

compatible /kɔ̃patibl/ *a.* compatible.

compatir /kɔ̃patir/ *v.i.* sympathize. ~ **à**, share in.

compatriote /kɔ̃patrijɔt/ *n.m./f.* compatriot.

compens|er /kɔ̃pɑ̃se/ *v.t.* compensate for, make up for. ~**ation** *n.f.* compensation.

compère /kɔ̃pɛr/ *n.m.* accomplice.

compéten|t, ~**te** /kɔpetɑ̃, -t/ a. competent. ~**ce** n.f. competence.

compétiti|f, ~**ve** /kɔpetitif, -v/ a. competitive.

compétition /kɔpetisjɔ̃/ n.f. competition; (*sportive*) event. **de** ~, competitive.

complainte /kɔplɛ̃t/ n.f. lament.

complaire (se) /(sə)kɔplɛr/ v. pr. **se** ~ **dans**, delight in.

complaisan|t, ~**te** /kɔplɛzɑ̃, -t/ a. kind; (*indulgent*) indulgent. ~**ce** n.f. kindness; indulgence.

complément /kɔplemɑ̃/ n.m. complement; (*reste*) rest. ~ (**d'objet**), (*gram.*) object. ~ **d'information,** further information. ~**aire** /-tɛr/ a. complementary; (*renseignements*) supplementary.

compl|et[1], ~**ète** /kɔplɛ, -t/ a. complete; (*train, hôtel, etc.*) full. ~**ètement** adv. completely.

complet[2] /kɔplɛ/ n.m. suit.

compléter /kɔplete/ v.t. complete; (*agrémenter*) complement. **se** ~ v. pr. complement each other.

complex|e[1] /kɔplɛks/ a. complex. ~**ité** n.f. complexity.

complex|e[2] /kɔplɛks/ n.m. (*sentiment, bâtiments*) complex. ~**é** a. hung up.

complication /kɔplikasjɔ̃/ n.f. complication; (*complexité*) complexity.

complic|e /kɔplis/ n.m. accomplice. ~**ité** n.f. complicity.

compliment /kɔplimɑ̃/ n.m. compliment. ~**s**, (*félicitations*) congratulations. ~**er** /-te/ v.t. compliment.

compliqu|er /kɔplike/ v.t. complicate. **se** ~**er** v. pr. become complicated. ~**é** a. complicated.

complot /kɔplo/ n.m. plot. ~**er** /-ɔte/ v.t./i. plot.

comporter[1] /kɔpɔrte/ v.t. contain; (*impliquer*) involve.

comport|er[2] (**se**) /(sə)kɔpɔrte/ v. pr. behave; (*joueur*) perform. ~**ement** n.m. behaviour, (*de joueur*) performance.

composé /kɔpoze/ a. compound; (*guindé*) stilted. —n.m. compound.

compos|er /kɔpoze/ v.t. make up, compose; (*chanson, visage*) compose; (*numéro*) dial. —v.i. (*scol.*) take an exam; (*transiger*) compromise. **se** ~**er de,** be made up *ou* composed of. ~**ant** n.m., ~**ante** n.f. component.

composi|teur, ~**trice** /kɔpozitœr, -tris/ n.m., f. (*mus.*) composer.

composition /kɔpozisjɔ̃/ n.f. composition; (*examen*) test, exam.

composter /kɔpɔste/ v.t. (*billet*) punch.

compot|e /kɔpɔt/ n.f. stewed fruit. ~**e de pommes,** stewed apples. ~**ier** n.m. fruit dish.

compréhensible /kɔpreɑ̃sibl/ a. understandable.

compréhensi|f, ~**ve** /kɔpreɑ̃sif, -v/ a. understanding.

compréhension /kɔpreɑ̃sjɔ̃/ n.f. understanding, comprehension.

comprendre† /kɔprɑ̃dr/ v.t. understand; (*comporter*) comprise. **ça se comprend,** that is understandable.

compresse /kɔprɛs/ n.f. compress.

compression /kɔprɛsjɔ̃/ n.f. (*physique*) compression, (*réduction*) reduction. ~ **de personnel,** staff cuts.

comprimé /kɔprime/ n.m. tablet.

comprimer /kɔprime/ v.t. compress; (*réduire*) reduce.

compris, ~**e** /kɔpri, -z/ a. included; (*d'accord*) agreed. ~ **entre**, (contained) between. **service (non)** ~, service (not) included, (not) including service. **tout** ~, (all) inclusive. **y** ~, including.

compromettre /kɔprɔmɛtr/ v.t. compromise.

compromis /kɔprɔmi/ n.m. compromise.

comptab|le /kɔtabl/ a. accounting. —n.m. accountant. ~**ilité** n.f. accountancy; (*comptes*) accounts; (*service*) accounts department.

comptant /kɔtɑ̃/ adv. (*payer*) (in) cash; (*acheter*) for cash.

compte /kɔt/ n.m. count; (*facture, à la banque, comptabilité*) account; (*nombre exact*) right number. **demander/rendre des** ~**s**, ask for/give an explanation. **à bon** ~, cheaply. **s'en tirer à bon** ~, get off lightly. **à son** ~, (*travailler*) for o.s., on one's own. **faire le** ~ **de,** count. **pour le** ~ **de,** on behalf of. **sur le** ~ **de,** about. ~ **à rebours,** countdown. ~**-gouttes** n.m. invar. (*méd.*) dropper. **au** ~**-gouttes,** (*fig.*) in dribs and drabs. ~ **rendu,** report; (*de film, livre*) review. ~**-tours** n.m. invar. rev counter.

compter /kɔte/ v.t. count; (*prévoir*) reckon; (*facturer*) charge for; (*avoir*) have; (*classer*) consider. —v.i. (*calculer, importer*) count. ~ **avec,** reckon with. ~ **faire,** expect to do. ~ **parmi,** (*figurer*) be considered among. ~ **sur,** rely on.

compteur /kɔtœr/ n.m. meter. ~ **de vitesse,** speedometer.

comptine /kɔtin/ n.f. nursery rhyme.

comptoir /kɔ̃twar/ *n.m.* counter; (*de café*) bar.

compulser /kɔ̃pylse/ *v.t.* examine.

comt|e, ~esse /kɔ̃t, -ɛs/ *n.m.*, *f.* count, countess.

comté /kɔ̃te/ *n.m.* county.

con, conne /kɔ̃, kɔn/ *a.* (*argot*) bloody foolish. —*n.m.*, *f.* (*argot*) bloody fool.

concave /kɔ̃kav/ *a.* concave.

concéder /kɔ̃sede/ *v.t.* grant, concede.

concentr|er /kɔ̃sɑ̃tre/ *v.t.*, **se ~er** *v. pr.* concentrate. **~ation** *n.f.* concentration. **~é** *a.* concentrated; (*lait*) condensed; (*personne*) absorbed; *n.m.* concentrate.

concept /kɔ̃sɛpt/ *n.m.* concept.

conception /kɔ̃sɛpsjɔ̃/ *n.f.* conception.

concerner /kɔ̃sɛrne/ *v.t.* concern. **en ce qui me concerne,** as far as I am concerned.

concert /kɔ̃sɛr/ *n.m.* concert. **de ~,** in unison.

concert|er /kɔ̃sɛrte/ *v.t.* organize, prepare. **se ~er** *v. pr.* confer. **~é** *a.* (*plan etc.*) concerted.

concerto /kɔ̃sɛrto/ *n.m.* concerto.

concession /kɔ̃sesjɔ̃/ *n.f.* concession; (*terrain*) plot.

concessionnaire /kɔ̃sesjɔnɛr/ *n.m./f.* (authorized) dealer.

concevoir† /kɔ̃svwar/ *v.t.* (*imaginer, engendrer*) conceive; (*comprendre*) understand.

concierge /kɔ̃sjɛrʒ/ *n.m./f.* caretaker.

concile /kɔ̃sil/ *n.m.* council.

concil|ier /kɔ̃silje/ *v.t.* reconcile. **se ~ier** *v. pr.* (*s'attirer*) win (over). **~iation** *n.f.* conciliation.

concis, ~e /kɔ̃si, -z/ *a.* concise. **~ion** /-zjɔ̃/ *n.f.* concision.

concitoyen, ~ne /kɔ̃sitwajɛ̃, -jɛn/ *n.m.*, *f.* fellow citizen.

concl|ure† /kɔ̃klyr/ *v.t./i.* conclude. **~ure** *a*, conclude in favour of. **~uant, ~uante** *a.* conclusive. **~usion** *n.f.* conclusion.

concocter /kɔ̃kɔkte/ *v.t.* (*fam.*) cook up.

concombre /kɔ̃kɔ̃br/ *n.m.* cucumber.

concorde /kɔ̃kɔrd/ *n.f.* concord.

concord|er /kɔ̃kɔrde/ *v.i.* agree. **~ance** *n.f.* agreement; (*analogie*) similarity. **~ant, ~ante** *a.* in agreement.

concourir /kɔ̃kurir/ *v.i.* compete. **~ à,** contribute towards.

concours /kɔ̃kur/ *n.m.* competition; (*examen*) competitive examination; (*aide*) aid; (*de circonstances*) combination.

concr|et, ~ète /kɔ̃krɛ, -t/ *a.* concrete. **~ètement** *adv.* in concrete terms.

concrétiser /kɔ̃kretize/ *v.t.* give concrete form to. **se ~** *v. pr.* materialize.

conçu /kɔ̃sy/ *a.* **bien/mal ~,** (*appartement etc.*) well/badly planned.

concubinage /kɔ̃kybinaʒ/ *n.m.* cohabitation.

concurrenc|e /kɔ̃kyrɑ̃s/ *n.f.* competition. **faire ~e à,** compete with. **jusqu'à ~e de,** up to. **~er** *v.t.* compete with.

concurrent, ~e /kɔ̃kyrɑ̃, -t/ *n.m.*, *f.* competitor; (*scol.*) candidate. —*a.* competing.

condamn|er /kɔ̃dɑne/ *v.t.* (*censurer, obliger*) condemn; (*jurid.*) sentence; (*porte*) block up. **~ation** *n.f.* condemnation; (*peine*) sentence. **~é** *a.* (*fichu*) without hope, doomed.

condens|er /kɔ̃dɑ̃se/ *v.t.*, **se ~er** *v. pr.* condense. **~ation** *n.f.* condensation.

condescendre /kɔ̃desɑ̃dr/ *v.i.* condescend (**à,** to).

condiment /kɔ̃dimɑ̃/ *n.m.* condiment.

condisciple /kɔ̃disipl/ *n.m.* classmate, schoolfellow.

condition /kɔ̃disjɔ̃/ *n.f.* condition. **~s,** (*prix*) terms. **à ~ de** *ou* **que,** provided (that). **sans ~,** unconditional(ly). **sous ~,** conditionally. **~nel, ~nelle** /-jɔnɛl/ *a.* conditional. **~nel** *n.m.* conditional (tense).

conditionnement /kɔ̃disjɔnmɑ̃/ *n.m.* conditioning; (*emballage*) packaging.

conditionner /kɔ̃disjɔne/ *v.t.* condition; (*emballer*) package.

condoléances /kɔ̃dɔleɑ̃s/ *n.f. pl.* condolences.

conduc|teur, ~trice /kɔ̃dyktœr, -tris/ *n.m.*, *f.* driver.

conduire† /kɔ̃dɥir/ *v.t.* lead; (*auto.*) drive; (*affaire*) conduct. —*v.i.* drive. **se ~** *v. pr.* behave. **~ à,** (*accompagner à*) take to.

conduit /kɔ̃dɥi/ *n.m.* (*anat.*) duct.

conduite /kɔ̃dɥit/ *n.f.* conduct; (*auto.*) driving; (*tuyau*) main. **~ à droite,** (*place*) right-hand drive.

cône /kon/ *n.m.* cone.

confection /kɔ̃fɛksjɔ̃/ *n.f.* making. **de ~,** ready-made. **la ~,** the clothing industry. **~ner** /-jɔne/ *v.t.* make.

confédération /kɔ̃federasjɔ̃/ *n.f.* confederation.

conférenc|e /kɔ̃ferɑ̃s/ *n.f.* conference; (*exposé*) lecture. **~e au sommet,** summit conference. **~ier, ~ière** *n.m.*, *f.* lecturer.

conférer /kɔ̃fere/ *v.t.* give; (*décerner*) confer.

confess|er /kɔ̃fese/ *v.t.*, **se ~er** *v. pr.*

confess. ~eur *n.m.* confessor. ~ion *n.f.* confession; (*religion*) denomination. ~ionnal (*pl.* ~ionnaux) *n.m.* confessional. ~ionnel, ~ionnelle *a.* denominational.

confetti /kɔ̃feti/ *n.m. pl.* confetti.

confiance /kɔ̃fjɑ̃s/ *n.f.* trust. avoir ~ en, trust.

confiant, ~e /kɔ̃fjɑ̃, -t/ *a.* (*assure*) confident; (*sans défiance*) trusting. ~ en *ou* dans, confident in.

confiden|t, ~te /kɔ̃fidɑ̃, -t/ *n.m., f.* confidant, confidante. ~ce *n.f.* confidence.

confidentiel, ~le /kɔ̃fidɑ̃sjɛl/ *a.* confidential.

confier /kɔ̃fje/ *v.t.* ~ à qn., entrust s.o. with; (*secret*) confide to s.o. se ~ à, confide in.

configuration /kɔ̃figyrɑsjɔ̃/ *n.f.* configuration.

confiner /kɔ̃fine/ *v.t.* confine. —*v.i.* ~ à, border on. se ~ *v. pr.* confine o.s. (à, dans, to).

confins /kɔ̃fɛ̃/ *n.m. pl.* confines.

confirm|er /kɔ̃firme/ *v.t.* confirm. ~ation *n.f.* confirmation.

confis|erie /kɔ̃fizri/ *n.f.* sweet shop. ~eries, confectionery. ~eur, ~euse *n.m., f.* confectioner.

confis|quer /kɔ̃fiske/ *v.t.* confiscate. ~cation *n.f.* confiscation.

confit, ~e /kɔ̃fi, -t/ *a.* (*culin.*) candied. fruits ~s, crystallized fruits. —*n.m.* ~ d'oie, goose liver conserve.

confiture /kɔ̃fityr/ *n.f.* jam.

conflit /kɔ̃fli/ *n.m.* conflict.

confondre /kɔ̃fɔ̃dr/ *v.t.* confuse, mix up; (*consterner, étonner*) confound. se ~ *v. pr.* merge. se ~ en excuses, apologize profusely.

confondu /kɔ̃fɔ̃dy/ *a.* (*déconcerté*) overwhelmed, confounded.

conforme /kɔ̃fɔrm/ *a.* ~ à, in accordance with.

conformément /kɔ̃fɔrmemɑ̃/ *adv.* ~ à, in accordance with.

conform|er /kɔ̃fɔrme/ *v.t.* adapt. se ~er à, conform to. ~ité *n.f.* conformity.

conformis|te /kɔ̃fɔrmist/ *a.* & *n.m./f.* conformist. ~me *n.m.* conformism.

confort /kɔ̃fɔr/ *n.m.* comfort. tout ~, with all mod cons. ~able /-tabl/ *a.* comfortable.

confrère /kɔ̃frɛr/ *n.m.* colleague.

confrérie /kɔ̃freri/ *n.f.* brotherhood.

confront|er /kɔ̃frɔ̃te/ *v.t.* confront; (*textes*) compare. se ~er à *v. pr.* confront. ~ation *n.f.* confrontation.

confus, ~e /kɔ̃fy, -z/ *a.* confused; (*gêné*) embarrassed.

confusion /kɔ̃fyzjɔ̃/ *n.f.* confusion; (*gêné*) embarrassment.

congé /kɔ̃ʒe/ *n.m.* holiday; (*arrêt momentané*) time off; (*mil.*) leave; (*avis de départ*) notice. ~ de maladie, sick-leave. ~ de maternité, maternity leave. jour de ~, day off. prendre ~ de, take one's leave of.

congédier /kɔ̃ʒedje/ *v.t.* dismiss.

cong|eler /kɔ̃ʒle/ *v.t.* freeze. les ~elés, frozen food. ~élateur *n.m.* freezer.

congénère /kɔ̃ʒenɛr/ *n.m./f.* fellow creature.

congénit|al (*m. pl.* ~aux) /kɔ̃ʒenital, -o/ *a.* congenital.

congère /kɔ̃ʒɛr/ *n.f.* snow-drift.

congestion /kɔ̃ʒɛstjɔ̃/ *n.f.* congestion. ~ cérébrale, stroke, cerebral haemorrhage. ~ner /-jɔne/ *v.t.* congest; (*visage*) flush.

congrégation /kɔ̃greyɑsjɔ̃/ *n.f.* congregation.

congrès /kɔ̃grɛ/ *n.m.* congress.

conifère /kɔnifɛr/ *n.m.* conifer.

conique /kɔnik/ *a.* conic(al).

conjectur|e /kɔ̃ʒɛktyr/ *n.f.* conjecture. ~er *v.t./i.* conjecture.

conjoint, ~e[1] /kɔ̃ʒwɛ̃, -t/ *n.m., f.* spouse.

conjoint, ~e[2] /kɔ̃ʒwɛ̃, -t/ *a.* joint. ~ement /-tmɑ̃/ *adv.* jointly.

conjonction /kɔ̃ʒɔ̃ksjɔ̃/ *n.f.* conjunction.

conjonctivite /kɔ̃ʒɔ̃ktivit/ *n.f.* conjunctivitis.

conjoncture /kɔ̃ʒɔ̃ktyr/ *n.f.* circumstances; (*économique*) economic climate.

conjugaison /kɔ̃ʒygɛzɔ̃/ *n.f.* conjugation.

conjug|al (*m. pl.* ~aux) /kɔ̃ʒygal, -o/ *a.* conjugal.

conjuguer /kɔ̃ʒyge/ *v.t.* (*gram.*) conjugate; (*efforts*) combine. se ~ *v. pr.* (*gram.*) be conjugated.

conjur|er /kɔ̃ʒyre/ *v.t.* (*éviter*) avert; (*implorer*) entreat. ~ation *n.f.* conspiracy. ~é, ~ée *n.m., f.* conspirator.

connaissance /kɔnɛsɑ̃s/ *n.f.* knowledge; (*personne*) acquaintance. ~s, (*science*) knowledge. faire la ~ de, meet; (*personne connue*) get to know. perdre ~, lose consciousness. sans ~, unconscious.

connaisseur /kɔnɛsœr/ *n.m.* connoisseur.

connaître† /kɔnɛtr/ *v.t.* know; (*avoir*) have. se ~ *v. pr.* (*se rencontrer*) meet.

faire ∼, make known. **s'y** ∼ **à** *ou* **en,** know (all) about.

conne|cter /kɔnɛkte/ *v.t.* connect. ∼**xion** *n.f.* connection.

connerie /kɔnri/ *n.f.* (*argot*) (*remarque*) rubbish. **faire une** ∼, do sth. stupid. **dire une** ∼, talk rubbish. **quelle** ∼**!,** how stupid!

connivence /kɔnivɑ̃s/ *n.f.* connivance.

connotation /kɔnɔtɑsjɔ̃/ *n.f.* connotation.

connu /kɔny/ *a.* well-known.

conquér|ir /kɔ̃kerir/ *v.t.* conquer. ∼**ant,** ∼**ante** *n.m.,* *f.* conqueror.

conquête /kɔ̃kɛt/ *n.f.* conquest.

consacrer /kɔ̃sakre/ *v.t.* devote; (*relig.*) consecrate; (*sanctionner*) establish. **se** ∼ *v. pr.* devote o.s. (**à,** to).

consciemment /kɔ̃sjamɑ̃/ *adv.* consciously.

conscience /kɔ̃sjɑ̃s/ *n.f.* conscience; (*perception*) consciousness. **avoir/prendre** ∼ **de,** be/become aware of. **perdre** ∼**,** lose consciousness. **avoir bonne/mauvaise** ∼**,** have a clear/guilty conscience.

conscencieu|x, ∼**se** /kɔ̃sjɑ̃sjø, -z/ *a.* conscientious.

conscient, ∼**e** /kɔ̃sjɑ̃, -t/ *a.* conscious. ∼ **de,** aware *ou* conscious of.

conscrit /kɔ̃skri/ *n.m.* conscript.

consécration /kɔ̃sekrɑsjɔ̃/ *n.f.* consecration.

consécuti|f, ∼**ve** /kɔ̃sekytif, -v/ *a.* consecutive. ∼**f à,** following upon. ∼**vement** *adv.* consecutively.

conseil /kɔ̃sɛj/ *n.m.* (piece of) advice; (*assemblée*) council, committee; (*séance*) meeting; (*personne*) consultant. ∼ **d'administration,** board of directors. ∼ **des ministres,** Cabinet. ∼ **municipal,** town council.

conseiller[1] /kɔ̃seje/ *v.t.* advise. ∼ **à qn. de,** advise s.o. to. ∼ **qch. à qn.,** recommend sth. to s.o.

conseill|er[2], ∼**ère** /kɔ̃seje, -ɛjɛr/ *n.m., f.* adviser, counsellor. ∼**er municipal,** town councillor.

consent|ir /kɔ̃sɑ̃tir/ *v.i.* agree (**à,** to). —*v.t.* grant. ∼**ement** *n.m.* consent.

conséquence /kɔ̃sekɑ̃s/ *n.f.* consequence. **en** ∼**,** consequently; (*comme il convient*) accordingly.

conséquent, ∼**e** /kɔ̃sekɑ̃, -t/ *a.* logical; (*important*: *fam.*) sizeable. **par** ∼**,** consequently.

conserva|teur, ∼**trice** kɔ̃sɛrvatœr, -tris/ *a.* conservative. —*n.m., f.* (*pol.*) conservative. —*n.m.* (*de musée*) curator. ∼**tisme** *n.m.* conservatism.

conservatoire /kɔ̃sɛrvatwar/ *n.m.* academy.

conserve /kɔ̃sɛrv/ *n.f.* tinned *ou* canned food. **en** ∼**,** tinned, canned.

conserv|er /kɔ̃sɛrve/ *v.t.* keep; (*en bon état*) preserve; (*culin.*) preserve. **se** ∼**er** *v. pr.* (*culin.*) keep. ∼**ation** *n.f.* preservation.

considérable /kɔ̃siderabl/ *a.* considerable.

considération /kɔ̃siderɑsjɔ̃/ *n.f.* consideration; (*respect*) regard. **prendre en** ∼**,** take into consideration.

considérer /kɔ̃sidere/ *v.t.* consider; (*respecter*) esteem. ∼ **comme,** consider to be.

consigne /kɔ̃siɲ/ *n.f.* (*de gare*) left luggage (office); (*Amer.*) (baggage) checkroom; (*scol.*) detention; (*somme*) deposit; (*ordres*) orders. ∼ **automatique,** (left-luggage) lockers; (*Amer.*) (baggage) lockers.

consigner /kɔ̃siɲe/ *v.t.* (*comm.*) charge a deposit on; (*écrire*) record; (*élève*) keep in; (*soldat*) confine.

consistan|t, ∼**te** /kɔ̃sistɑ̃, -t/ *a.* solid; (*épais*) thick. ∼**ce** *n.f.* consistency; (*fig.*) solidity.

consister /kɔ̃siste/ *v.i.* ∼ **en/dans,** consist of/in. ∼ **à faire,** consist in doing.

consœur /kɔ̃sœr/ *n.f.* colleague; fellow member.

consol|er /kɔ̃sole/ *v.t.* console. **se** ∼**er** *v. pr.* be consoled (**de,** for). ∼**ation** *n.f.* consolation.

consolider /kɔ̃sɔlide/ *v.t.* strengthen; (*fig.*) consolidate.

consomma|teur, ∼**trice** /kɔ̃sɔmatœr, -tris/ *n.m., f.* (*comm.*) consumer; (*dans un café*) customer.

consommé[1] /kɔ̃sɔme/ *a.* consummate.

consommé[2] /kɔ̃sɔme/ *n.m.* (*bouillon*) consommé.

consomm|er /kɔ̃sɔme/ *v.t.* consume; (*user*) use, consume; (*mariage*) consummate. —*v.i.* drink. ∼**ation** *n.f.* consumption; consummation; (*boisson*) drink. **de** ∼**ation,** (*comm.*) consumer.

consonne /kɔ̃sɔn/ *n.f.* consonant.

consortium /kɔ̃sɔrsjɔm/ *n.m.* consortium.

conspir|er /kɔ̃spire/ *v.i.* conspire. ∼**ateur,** ∼**atrice** *n.m., f.* conspirator. ∼**ation** *n.f.* conspiracy.

conspuer /kɔ̃spɥe/ *v.t.* boo.

const|ant, ∼**ante** /kɔ̃stɑ̃, -t/ *a.*

constant. —*n.f.* constant. ∼**amment**
/-amã/ *adv.* constantly. ∼**ance** *n.f.*
constancy.
constat /kɔ̃sta/ *n.m.* (official) report.
constat|er /kɔ̃state/ *v.t.* note; (*certifier*)
certify. ∼**ation** *n.f.* observation, statement of fact.
constellation /kɔ̃stelasjɔ̃/ *n.f.* constellation.
constellé /kɔ̃stele/ *a.* ∼ **de,** studded with.
constern|er /kɔ̃stɛrne/ *v.t.* dismay.
∼**ation** *n.f.* dismay.
constip|é /kɔ̃stipe/ *a.* constipated; (*fig.*)
stilted. ∼**ation** *n.f.* constipation.
constitu|er /kɔ̃stitɥe/ *v.t.* make up,
constitute; (*organiser*) form; (*être*)
constitute. **se** ∼**er prisonnier,** give o.s.
up. ∼**é de,** made up of.
constituti|f, ∼**ve** /kɔ̃stitytif, -v/ *a.*
constituent.
constitution /kɔ̃stitysjɔ̃/ *n.f.* formation;
(*d'une équipe*) composition; (*pol.,
méd.*) constitution. ∼**nel,** ∼**nelle**
/-jɔnɛl/ *a.* constitutional.
constructeur /kɔ̃stryktœr/ *n.m.* manu-
facturer.
constructi|f, ∼**ve** /kɔ̃stryktif, -v/ *a.*
constructive.
constr|uire† /kɔ̃strɥir/ *v.t.* build;
(*système, phrase, etc*) construct.
∼**uction** *n.f.* building; (*structure*)
construction.
consul /kɔ̃syl/ *n.m.* consul. ∼**aire** *a.*
consular. ∼**at** *n.m.* consulate.
consult|er /kɔ̃sylte/ *v.t.* consult. —*v.i.*
(*médecin*) hold surgery; (*Amer.*) hold
office hours. **se** ∼**er** *v. pr.* confer.
∼**ation** *n.f.* consultation; (*réception:
méd.*) surgery; (*Amer.*) office.
consumer /kɔ̃syme/ *v.t.* consume. **se** ∼
v. pr. be consumed.
contact /kɔ̃takt/ *n.m.* contact; (*toucher*)
touch. **au** ∼ **de,** on contact with;
(*personne*) by contact with, by seeing.
mettre/couper le ∼, (*auto.*) switch
on/off the ignition. **prendre** ∼ **avec,**
get in touch with. ∼**er** *v.t.* contact.
contag|ieux, ∼**ieuse** /kɔ̃taʒjø, -z/ *a.*
contagious. ∼**ion** *n.f.* contagion.
container /kɔ̃tɛnɛr/ *n.m.* container. .
contamin|er /kɔ̃tamine/ *v.t.* con-
taminate. ∼**ation** *n.f.* contamination.
conte /kɔ̃t/ *n.m.* tale. ∼ **de fées,** fairy
tale.
contempl|er /kɔ̃tɑ̃ple/ *v.t.* contemplate.
∼**ation** *n.f.* contemplation.
contemporain, ∼**e** /kɔ̃tɑ̃pɔrɛ̃, -ɛn/ *a.*
& *n.m.*, *f.* contemporary.
contenance /kɔ̃tnɑ̃s/ *n.f.* (*contenu*)

capacity; (*allure*) bearing; (*sang-froid*)
composure.
conteneur /kɔ̃tnœr/ *n.m.* container.
contenir† /kɔ̃tnir/ *v.t.* contain; (*avoir
une capacité de*) hold. **se** ∼ *v. pr.*
contain o.s.
content, ∼**e** /kɔ̃tɑ̃, -t/ *a.* pleased (**de,**
with). ∼ **de faire,** pleased to do.
content|er /kɔ̃tɑ̃te/ *v.t.* satisfy. **se** ∼**er
de,** content o.s. with. ∼**ement** *n.m.*
contentment.
contentieux /kɔ̃tɑ̃sjø/ *n.m.* matters in
dispute; (*service*) legal department.
contenu /kɔ̃tny/ *n.m.* (*de contenant*)
contents; (*de texte*) content.
conter /kɔ̃te/ *v.t.* tell, relate.
contestataire /kɔ̃tɛstatɛr/ *n.m./f.* protester.
conteste (sans) /(sã)kɔ̃tɛst/ *adv.* indis-
putably.
contest|er /kɔ̃tɛste/ *v.t.* dispute;
(*s'opposer*) protest against. —*v.i.*
protest. ∼**able** *a.* debatable. ∼**ation** *n.f.*
dispute; (*opposition*) protest.
conteu|r, ∼**se** /kɔ̃tœr, øz/ *n.m.*, *f.*
story-teller.
contexte /kɔ̃tɛkst/ *n.m.* context.
contigu, ∼**ë** /kɔ̃tigy/ *a.* adjacent (**à,** to).
continent /kɔ̃tinɑ̃/ *n.m.* continent. ∼**al**
(*m. pl.* ∼**aux**) /-tal, -to/ *a.*
continental.
contingences /kɔ̃tɛ̃ʒɑ̃s/ *n.f. pl.* contin-
gencies.
contingent /kɔ̃tɛ̃ʒɑ̃/ *n.m.* (*mil.*) contingent; (*comm.*) quota.
continu /kɔ̃tiny/ *a.* continuous.
continuel, ∼**le** /kɔ̃tinɥɛl/ *a.* continual.
∼**lement** *adv.* continually.
contin|uer /kɔ̃tinɥe/ *v.t.* continue. —*v.i.*
continue, go on. ∼**uer à** *ou* **de faire,**
carry on *ou* go on *ou* continue doing
∼**uation** *n.f.* continuation.
continuité /kɔ̃tinɥite/ *n.f.* continuity.
contorsion /kɔ̃tɔrsjɔ̃/ *n.f.* contortion. **se**
∼**ner** *v. pr.* wriggle.
contour /kɔ̃tur/ *n.m.* outline, contour.
∼**s,** (*d'une route etc.*) twists and turns,
bends.
contourner /kɔ̃turne/ *v.t.* go round;
(*difficulté*) get round.
contracepti|f, ∼**ve** /kɔ̃trasɛptif, -v/ *a.*
& *n.m.* contraceptive.
contraception /kɔ̃trasɛpsjɔ̃/ *n.f.* contraception.
contract|er /kɔ̃trakte/ *v.t.* (*maladie,
dette*) contract; (*muscle*) tense, contract; (*assurance*) take out. **se** ∼**er** *v. pr.*
contract. ∼**é** *a.* tense. ∼**ion** /-ksjɔ̃/ *n.f.*
contraction.

contractuel, ∼**le** /kɔ̃traktɥɛl/ *n.m., f.*
(*agent*) traffic warden.
contradiction /kɔ̃tradiksjɔ̃/ *n.f.* contradiction.
contradictoire /kɔ̃tradiktwar/ *a.* contradictory; (*débat*) open.
contraignant, ∼**e** /kɔ̃trɛɲɑ̃, -t/ *a.*
restricting.
contraindre† /kɔ̃trɛ̃dr/ *v.t.* compel.
contraint, ∼**e** /kɔ̃trɛ̃, -t/ *a.* constrained. —*n.f.* constraint.
contraire /kɔ̃trɛr/ *a. & n.m.* opposite. ∼
à, contrary to. **au** ∼, on the contrary.
∼**ment** *adv.* ∼**ment à,** contrary to.
contralto /kɔ̃tralto/ *n.m.* contralto.
contrar|**ier** /kɔ̃trarje/ *v.t.* annoy;
(*action*) frustrate. ∼**iété** *n.f.* annoyance.
contrast|**e** /kɔ̃trast/ *n.m.* contrast. ∼**er**
v.i. contrast.
contrat /kɔ̃tra/ *n.m.* contract.
contravention /kɔ̃travɑ̃sjɔ̃/ *n.f.* (parking-)ticket. **en** ∼, in contravention (à,
of).
contre /kɔ̃tr(ə)/ *prép.* against; (*en
échange de*) for. **par** ∼, on the other
hand. **tout** ∼, close by. ∼-**attaque** *n.f.,*
∼-**attaquer** *v.t.* counter-attack. ∼-
balancer *v.t.* counterbalance. ∼-
courant *n.m.* **aller à** ∼-**courant de,**
swim against the current of. ∼-**indiqué**
a. (*méd.*) contra-indicated; (*déconseillé*)
not recommended. **à** ∼-**jour** *adv.*
against the (sun)light. ∼-**offensive** *n.f.*
counter-offensive. **prendre le** ∼-**pied,**
do the opposite; (*opinion*) take the
opposite view. **à** ∼-**pied** *adv.* (*sport*) on
the wrong foot. ∼-**plaqué** *n.m.*
plywood. ∼-**révolution** *n.f.* counter-
revolution. ∼-**torpilleur** *n.m.*
destroyer.
contreband|**e** /kɔ̃trəbɑ̃d/ *n.f.* contraband. **faire la** ∼**e de, passer en** ∼**e,**
smuggle. ∼**ier** *n.m.* smuggler.
contrebas (en) /(ɑ̃)kɔ̃trəba/ *adv. &
prép.* **en** ∼ **(de),** below.
contrebasse /kɔ̃trəbas/ *n.f.* double-bass.
contrecarrer /kɔ̃trəkare/ *v.t.* thwart.
contrecœur (à) /(a)kɔ̃trəkœr/ *adv.*
reluctantly.
contrecoup /kɔ̃trəku/ *n.m.* consequence.
contredire† /kɔ̃trədir/ *v.t.* contradict. **se**
∼ *v. pr.* contradict o.s.
contrée /kɔ̃tre/ *n.f.* region, land.
contrefaçon /kɔ̃trəfasɔ̃/ *n.f.* (*objet imité,
action*) forgery.
contrefaire /kɔ̃trəfɛr/ *v.t.* (*falsifier*)
forge; (*parodier*) mimic; (*déguiser*)
disguise.

contrefait, ∼**e** /kɔ̃trəfɛ, -t/ *a.*
deformed.
contreforts /kɔ̃trəfɔr/ *n.m. pl.* foothills.
contremaître /kɔ̃trəmɛtr/ *n.m.* foreman.
contrepartie /kɔ̃trəparti/ *n.f.* compensation. **en** ∼, in exchange, in return.
contrepoids /kɔ̃trəpwa/ *n.m.* counterbalance.
contrer /kɔ̃tre/ *v.t.* counter.
contresens /kɔ̃trəsɑ̃s/ *n.m.* misinterpretation; (*absurdité*) nonsense. **à** ∼,
the wrong way.
contresigner /kɔ̃trəsiɲe/ *v.t.* countersign.
contretemps /kɔ̃trətɑ̃/ *n.m.* hitch. **à** ∼,
at the wrong time.
contrevenir /kɔ̃trəvnir/ *v.i.* ∼ **à,**
contravene.
contribuable /kɔ̃tribɥabl/ *n.m./f.* taxpayer.
contribuer /kɔ̃tribɥe/ *v.t.* contribute (à,
to, towards).
contribution /kɔ̃tribɥsjɔ̃/ *n.f.* contribution. ∼**s,** (*impôts*) taxes; (*administration*) tax office.
contrit, ∼**e** /kɔ̃tri, -t/ *a.* contrite.
contrôl|**e** /kɔ̃trol/ *n.m.* check; (*des prix,
d'un véhicule*) control; (*poinçon*)
hallmark; (*scol.*) test. ∼**e continu,**
continuous assessment. ∼**e de soi-
même,** self-control. ∼**e des changes,**
exchange control. ∼**e des naissances**
birth-control. ∼**er** *v.t.* check;
(*surveiller, maîtriser*) control. **se** ∼**er**
v. pr. control o.s.
contrôleu|**r,** ∼**se** /kɔ̃trolœr, -øz/ *n.m.,*
f. (*bus*) conductor *ou* conductress; (*de
train*) (ticket) inspector.
contrordre /kɔ̃trɔrdr/ *n.m.* change of
orders.
controvers|**e** /kɔ̃trɔvɛrs/ *n.f.* controversy. ∼**é** *a.* controversial.
contumace (par) /(par)kɔ̃tymas/ *adv.* in
one's absence.
contusion /kɔ̃tyzjɔ̃/ *n.f.* bruise. ∼**né**
/-jɔne/ *a.* bruised.
convaincre† /kɔ̃vɛ̃kr/ *v.t.* convince. ∼
qn. de faire, persuade s.o. to do.
convalescen|**t,** ∼**te** /kɔ̃valesɑ̃, -t/ *a. &*
n.m., f. convalescent. ∼**ce** *n.f.* convalescence. **être en** ∼**ce,** convalesce.
convenable /kɔ̃vnabl/ *a.* (*correct*)
decent, proper; (*approprié*) suitable.
convenance /kɔ̃vnɑ̃s/ *n.f.* **à sa** ∼, to
one's satisfaction. **les** ∼**s,** the
proprieties.
convenir† /kɔ̃vnir/ *v.i.* be suitable. ∼ **à**
suit. ∼ **de/que,** (*avouer*) admit
(to)/that. ∼ **de qch.,** (*s'accorder sur*)

agree on sth. ⁓ **de faire,** agree to do. **il convient de,** it is advisable to; (*selon les bienséances*) it would be right to.

convention /kɔ̃vɑ̃sjɔ̃/ *n.f.* convention. ⁓**s,** (*convenances*) convention. **de** ⁓, conventional. ⁓ **collective,** industrial agreement. ⁓**né** *a.* (*prix*) official; (*médecin*) health service (*not private*). ⁓**nel,** ⁓**nelle** /-jɔnɛl/ *a.* conventional.

convenu /kɔ̃vny/ *a.* agreed.

converger /kɔ̃vɛrʒe/ *v.i.* converge.

convers|er /kɔ̃vɛrse/ *v.i.* converse. ⁓**ation** *n.f.* conversation.

conver|tir /kɔ̃vɛrtir/ *v.t.* convert (à, to; en, into). **se** ⁓**tir** *v. pr.* be converted, convert. ⁓**sion** *n.f.* conversion. ⁓**tible** *a.* convertible.

convexe /kɔ̃vɛks/ *a.* convex.

conviction /kɔ̃viksjɔ̃/ *n.f.* conviction.

convier /kɔ̃vje/ *v.t.* invite.

convive /kɔ̃viv/ *n.m./f.* guest.

conviv|ial (*m. pl.* ⁓**iaux**) /kɔ̃vivjal, -jo/ *a.* convivial; (*comput.*) user-friendly.

convocation /kɔ̃vɔkasjɔ̃/ *n.f.* summons to attend; (*d'une assemblée*) convening; (*document*) notification to attend.

convoi /kɔ̃vwa/ *n.m.* convoy; (*train*) train. ⁓ **(funèbre),** funeral procession.

convoit|er /kɔ̃vwate/ *v.t.* desire, covet, envy. ⁓**ise** *n.f.* desire, envy.

convoquer /kɔ̃vɔke/ *v.t.* (*assemblée*) convene; (*personne*) summon.

convoy|er /kɔ̃vwaje/ *v.t.* escort. ⁓**eur** *n.m.* escort ship. ⁓**eur de fonds,** security guard.

convulsion /kɔ̃vylsjɔ̃/ *n.f.* convulsion.

cool /kul/ *a. invar.* cool, laidback.

coopérati|f, ⁓**ve** /kɔɔperatif, -v/ *a.* co-operative. —*n.f.* co-operative (society).

coopér|er /kɔɔpere/ *v.i.* co-operate (à, in). ⁓**ation** *n.f.* co-operation. **la C**⁓**ation,** civilian national service.

coopter /kɔɔpte/ *v.t.* co-opt.

coordination /kɔɔrdinasjɔ̃/ *n.f.* co-ordination

coordonn|er /kɔɔrdɔne/ *v.t.* co-ordinate. ⁓**ées** *n.f. pl.* co-ordinates; (*adresse: fam.*) particulars.

copain /kɔpɛ̃/ *n.m.* (*fam.*) pal; (*petit ami*) boyfriend.

copeau (*pl.* ⁓**x**) /kɔpo/ *n.m.* (*lamelle de bois*) shaving.

cop|ie /kɔpi/ *n.f.* copy; (*scol.*) paper. ⁓**ier** *v.t./i.* copy. ⁓**ier sur,** (*scol.*) copy *ou* crib from.

copieu|x, ⁓**se** /kɔpjø, -z/ *a.* copious.

copine /kɔpin/ *n.f.* (*fam.*) pal; (*petite amie*) girlfriend.

coproduction /kɔprɔdyksjɔ̃/ *n.f.* co-production.

copiste /kɔpist/ *n.m./f.* copyist.

copropriété /kɔprɔprijete/ *n.f.* co-ownership.

copulation /kɔpylasjɔ̃/ *n.f.* copulation.

coq /kɔk/ *n.m.* cock. ⁓**-à-l'âne** *n.m. invar.* abrupt change of subject.

coque /kɔk/ *n.f.* shell; (*de bateau*) hull.

coquelicot /kɔkliko/ *n.m.* poppy.

coqueluche /kɔklyʃ/ *n.f.* whooping cough.

coquet, ⁓**te** /kɔkɛ, -t/ *a.* flirtatious; (*élégant*) pretty; (*somme: fam.*) tidy. ⁓**terie** /-tri/ *n.f.* flirtatiousness.

coquetier /kɔktje/ *n.m.* egg-cup.

coquillage /kɔkijaʒ/ *n.m.* shellfish; (*coquille*) shell.

coquille /kɔkij/ *n.f.* shell; (*faute*) misprint. ⁓ **Saint-Jacques,** scallop.

coquin, ⁓**e** /kɔkɛ̃, -in/ *a.* naughty. —*n.m., f.* rascal.

cor /kɔr/ *n.m.* (*mus.*) horn, (*au pied*) corn.

cor|ail (*pl.* ⁓**aux**) /kɔraj, -o/ *n.m.* coral.

Coran /kɔrɑ̃/ *n.m.* Koran.

corbeau (*pl.* ⁓**x**) /kɔrbo/ *n.m.* (*oiseau*) crow.

corbeille /kɔrbɛj/ *n.f.* basket. ⁓ **à papier,** waste-paper basket.

corbillard /kɔrbijar/ *n.m.* hearse.

cordage /kɔrdaʒ/ *n.m.* rope. ⁓**s,** (*naut.*) rigging.

corde /kɔrd/ *n.f.* rope; (*d'arc, de violon, etc.*) string. ⁓ **à linge,** washing line. ⁓ **à sauter,** skipping-rope. ⁓ **raide,** tightrope. ⁓**s vocales,** vocal cords.

cordée /kɔrde/ *n.f.* roped party.

cord|ial (*m. pl.* ⁓**iaux**) /kɔrdjal, -jo/ *a.* warm, cordial. ⁓**ialité** *n.f.* warmth.

cordon /kɔrdɔ̃/ *n.m.* string, cord. ⁓ **bleu** (*pl.* ⁓**s-bleus**) *n.m.* first-rate cook. ⁓ **de police,** police cordon.

cordonnier /kɔrdɔnje/ *n.m.* shoe mender.

Corée /kɔre/ *n.f.* Korea.

coreligionnaire /kɔrɔliʒjɔnɛr/ *n.m./f.* person of the same religion.

coriace /kɔrjas/ *a.* (*aliment*) tough. —*a. & n.m.* tenacious and tough (person).

corne /kɔrn/ *n.f.* horn.

cornée /kɔrne/ *n.f.* cornea.

corneille /kɔrnɛj/ *n.f.* crow.

cornemuse /kɔrnəmyz/ *n.f.* bagpipes.

corner[1] /kɔrne/ *v.t.* (*page*) make dog-eared. —*v.i.* (*auto.*) hoot; (*auto., Amer.*) honk.

corner[2] /kɔrnɛr/ *n.m.* (*football*) corner.

cornet /kɔrnɛ/ n.m. (paper) cone; (*crème glacée*) cornet, cone.

corniaud /kɔrnjo/ n.m. (*fam.*) nitwit.

corniche /kɔrniʃ/ n.f. cornice; (*route*) cliff road.

cornichon /kɔrniʃɔ̃/ n.m. gherkin.

corollaire /kɔrɔlɛr/ n.m. corollary.

corporation /kɔrpɔrasjɔ̃/ n.f. professional body.

corporel, ~le /kɔrpɔrɛl/ a. bodily; (*châtiment*) corporal.

corps /kɔr/ n.m. body; (*mil., pol.*) corps. **~ à corps**, hand to hand. **~ électoral**, electorate. **~ enseignant**, teaching profession. **faire ~ avec**, form part of.

corpulen|t, ~te /kɔrpylɑ̃, -t/ a. stout. **~ce** n.f. stoutness.

correct /kɔrɛkt/ a. proper, correct; (*exact*) correct; (*tenue*) decent. **~ement** adv. properly; correctly; decently.

correc|teur, ~trice /kɔrɛktœr, -tris/ n.m., f. (*d'épreuves*) proof-reader; (*scol.*) examiner. **~teur d'orthographe**, spelling checker.

correction /kɔrɛksjɔ̃/ n.f. correction; (*punition*) beating.

corrélation /kɔrelasjɔ̃/ n.f. correlation.

correspondan|t, ~te /kɔrɛspɔ̃dɑ̃, -t/ a. corresponding. —n.m., f. correspondent; (*au téléphone*) caller. **~ce** n.f. correspondence; (*de train, d'autobus*) connection. **vente par ~ce**, mail order.

correspondre /kɔrɛspɔ̃dr/ v.i. (*s'accorder, écrire*) correspond; (*chambres*) communicate.

corrida /kɔrida/ n.f. bullfight.

corridor /kɔridɔr/ n.m. corridor.

corrig|er /kɔriʒe/ v.t. correct; (*devoir*) mark, correct; (*punir*) beat; (*guérir*) cure. **se ~er de**, cure o.s. of. **~é** n.m. (*scol.*) correct version, model answer.

corroborer /kɔrɔbɔre/ v.t. corroborate.

corro|der /kɔrɔde/ v.t. corrode. **~sion** /-ozjɔ̃/ n.f. corrosion.

corromp|re† /kɔrɔ̃pr/ v.t. corrupt; (*soudoyer*) bribe. **~u** a. corrupt.

corrosi|f, ~ve /kɔrozif, -v/ a. corrosive.

corruption /kɔrypsjɔ̃/ n.f. corruption.

corsage /kɔrsaʒ/ n.m. bodice; (*chemisier*) blouse.

corsaire /kɔrsɛr/ n.m. pirate.

Corse /kɔrs/ n.f. Corsica.

corse /kɔrs/ a. & n.m./f. Corsican.

corsé /kɔrse/ a. (*vin*) full-bodied; (*scabreux*) spicy.

corset /kɔrsɛ/ n.m. corset.

cortège /kɔrtɛʒ/ n.m. procession.

cortisone /kɔrtizon/ n.f. cortisone.

corvée /kɔrve/ n.f. chore.

cosaque /kɔzak/ n.m. Cossack.

cosmétique /kɔsmetik/ n.m. cosmetic.

cosmique /kɔsmik/ a. cosmic.

cosmonaute /kɔsmɔnot/ n.m./f. cosmonaut.

cosmopolite /kɔsmɔpɔlit/ a. cosmopolitan.

cosmos /kɔsmɔs/ n.m. (*espace*) (outer) space; (*univers*) cosmos.

cosse /kɔs/ n.f. (*de pois*) pod.

cossu /kɔsy/ a. (*gens*) well-to-do; (*demeure*) opulent.

costaud, ~e /kɔsto, -d/ a. (*fam.*) strong. —n.m. (*fam.*) strong man.

costum|e /kɔstym/ n.m. suit; (*théâtre*) costume. **~é** a. dressed up.

cote /kɔt/ n.f. (classification) mark; (*en Bourse*) quotation; (*de cheval*) odds (**de**, on); (*de candidat, acteur*) rating. **~ d'alerte**, danger level.

côte /kot/ n.f. (*littoral*) coast; (*pente*) hill; (*anat.*) rib; (*de porc*) chop. **~ à côte**, side by side. **la C~ d'Azur**, the (French) Riviera.

côté /kote/ n.m. side; (*direction*) way. **à ~**, nearby; (*voisin*) nextdoor. **à ~ de**, next to; (*comparé à*) compared to; (*cible*) wide of. **aux ~s de**, by the side of. **de ~**, aside; (*regarder*) sideways. **mettre de ~**, put aside. **de ce ~**, this way. **de chaque ~**, on each side. **de tous les ~s**, on every side; (*partout*) everywhere. **du ~ de**, towards; (*proximité*) near; (*provenance*) from.

coteau (*pl. ~x*) /kɔto/ n.m. hill.

côtelette /kotlɛt/ n.f. chop.

coter /kɔte/ v.t. (*comm.*) quote; (*apprécier, noter*) rate.

coterie /kɔtri/ n.f. clique.

côt|ier, ~ière /kotje, -jɛr/ a. coastal.

cotis|er /kɔtize/ v.i. pay one's contributions (**à**, to); (*à un club*) pay one's subscription. **se ~er** v. pr. club together. **~ation** n.f. contribution(s); subscription.

coton /kɔtɔ̃/ n.m. cotton. **~ hydrophile**, cotton wool.

côtoyer /kotwaje/ v.t. skirt, run along; (*fréquenter*) rub shoulders with; (*fig.*) verge on.

cotte /kɔt/ n.f. (*d'ouvrier*) overalls.

cou /ku/ n.m. neck.

couchage /kuʃaʒ/ n.m. sleeping arrangements.

couchant /kuʃɑ̃/ n.m. sunset.

couche /kuʃ/ n.f. layer; (*de peinture*)

coat; (*de bébé*) nappy. **~s**, (*méd.*) childbirth. **~s sociales**, social strata.

coucher /kuʃe/ *n.m.* **~ (du soleil)**, sunset. —*v.t.* put to bed; (*loger*) put up; (*étendre*) lay down. **~ (par écrit)**, set down. —*v.i.* sleep. **se ~** *v. pr.* go to bed; (*s'étendre*) lie down; (*soleil*) set. **couché** *a.* in bed; (*étendu*) lying down.

couchette /kuʃɛt/ *n.f.* (*rail.*) couchette; (*naut.*) bunk.

coucou /kuku/ *n.m.* cuckoo.

coude /kud/ *n.m.* elbow; (*de rivière etc.*) bend. **~ à coude**, side by side.

cou-de-pied (*pl.* **cous-de-pied**) /kudpje/ *n.m.* instep.

coudoyer /kudwaje/ *v.t.* rub shoulders with.

coudre† /kudr/ *v.t./i.* sew.

couenne /kwan/ *n.f.* (*de porc*) rind.

couette /kwɛt/ *n.f.* duvet, continental quilt.

couffin /kufɛ̃/ *n.m.* Moses basket.

couiner /kwine/ *v.i.* squeak.

coulant, ~e /kulɑ̃, -t/ *a.* (*indulgent*) easy-going; (*fromage*) runny.

coulée /kule/ *n.f.* **~ de lave**, lava flow.

couler[1] /kule/ *v.i.* flow, run; (*fromage, nez*) run; (*fuir*) leak. —*v.t.* (*sculpture, métal*) cast; (*vie*) pass, lead. **se ~** *v. pr.* (*se glisser*) slip.

couler[2] /kule/ *v.t./i.* (*bateau*) sink.

couleur /kulœr/ *n.f.* colour; (*peinture*) paint; (*cartes*) suit. **~s**, (*teint*) colour. **de ~**, (*homme, femme*) coloured. **en ~s**, (*télévision, film*) colour.

couleuvre /kulœvr/ *n.f.* (grass *ou* smooth) snake.

coulis /kuli/ *n.m.* (*culin.*) coulis.

couliss|e /kulis/ *n.f.* (*de tiroir etc.*) runner. **~es**, (*théâtre*) wings. **à ~e**, (*porte, fenêtre*) sliding. **~er** *v.i.* slide.

couloir /kulwar/ *n.m.* corridor; (*de bus*) gangway; (*sport*) lane.

coup /ku/ *n.m.* blow; (*choc*) knock; (*sport*) stroke; (*de crayon, chance, cloche*) stroke; (*de fusil, pistolet*) shot; (*fois*) time; (*aux échecs*) move. **à ~ sûr**, definitely. **après ~**, after the event. **boire un ~**, have a drink. **~ de chiffon**, wipe (with a rag). **~ de coude**, nudge. **~ de couteau**, stab. **~ d'envoi**, kick-off. **~ d'état** (*pol.*) coup. **~ de feu**, shot. **~ de fil**, phone call. **~ de filet**, haul. **~ de frein**, sudden braking. **~ de grâce**, coup de grâce. **~ de main**, helping hand. **avoir le ~ de main**, have the knack. **~ d'œil**, glance. **~ de pied**, kick. **~ de poing**, punch. **~ de sang**, (*méd.*) stroke. **~ de soleil**, sunburn. **~**

de sonnette, ring (on a bell). **~ de téléphone**, (tele)phone call. **~ de tête**, wild impulse. **~ de théâtre**, dramatic event. **~ de tonnerre**, thunderclap. **~ de vent**, gust of wind. **~ franc**, free kick. **~ sur coup**, in rapid succession. **d'un seul ~**, in one go. **du premier ~**, first go. **sale ~**, dirty trick. **sous le ~ de**, under the influence of. **sur le ~**, immediately. **tenir le coup**, take it.

coupable /kupabl/ *a.* guilty. —*n.m./f.* culprit.

coupe[1] /kup/ *n.f.* cup; (*de champagne*) goblet; (*à fruits*) dish.

coupe[2] /kup/ *n.f.* (*de vêtement etc.*) cut; (*dessin*) section. **~ de cheveux**, haircut.

coupé /kupe/ *n.m.* (*voiture*) coupé.

coup|er /kupe/ *v.t./i.* cut; (*arbre*) cut down; (*arrêter*) cut off; (*voyage*) break; (*appétit*) take away; (*vin*) water down. **~er par**, take a short cut via. **se ~er** *v. pr.* cut o.s.; (*routes*) intersect. **~er la parole à**, cut short. **~e-papier** *n.m. invar.* paper-knife.

couperosé /kuproze/ *a.* blotchy.

couple /kupl/ *n.m.* couple.

coupler /kuple/ *v.t.* couple.

couplet /kuplɛ/ *n.m.* verse.

coupole /kupɔl/ *n.f.* dome.

coupon /kupɔ̃/ *n.m.* (*étoffe*) remnant; (*billet, titre*) coupon.

coupure /kupyr/ *n.f.* cut; (*billet de banque*) note; (*de presse*) cutting. **~ (de courant)**, power cut.

cour /kur/ *n.f.* (court)yard; (*de roi*) court; (*tribunal*) court. **~ (de récréation)**, playground. **~ martiale**, court martial. **faire la ~ à**, court.

courag|e /kuraʒ/ *n.m.* courage. **~eux, ~euse** *a.* courageous.

couramment /kuramɑ̃/ *adv.* frequently; (*parler*) fluently.

courant[1], **~e** /kurɑ̃, -t/ *a.* standard, ordinary; (*en cours*) current.

courant[2] /kurɑ̃/ *n.m.* current; (*de mode, d'idées*) trend. **~ d'air**, draught. **dans le ~ de**, in the course of. **être/mettre au ~ de**, know/tell about; (*à jour*) be/bring up to date on.

courbatur|e /kurbatyr/ *n.f.* ache. **~é** *a.* aching.

courbe /kurb/ *n.f.* curve. —*a.* curved.

courber /kurbe/ *v.t./i.*, **se ~** *v. pr.* bend.

coureu|r, ~se /kurœr, -øz/ *n.m., f.* (*sport*) runner. **~r automobile**, racing driver. —*n.m.* womanizer.

courge /kurʒ/ *n.f.* marrow; (*Amer.*) squash.

courgette /kurʒɛt/ n.f. courgette;
(*Amer.*) zucchini.
courir† /kurir/ v.i. run; (*se hâter*) rush;
(*nouvelles etc.*) go round. —*v.t.*
(*risque*) run; (*danger*) face; (*épreuve
sportive*) run *ou* compete in;
(*fréquenter*) do the rounds of; (*files*)
chase.
couronne /kurɔn/ n.f. crown; (*de fleurs*)
wreath.
couronn|er /kurɔne/ v.t. crown.
~**ement** n.m. coronation, crowning;
(*fig.*) crowning achievement.
courrier /kurje/ n.m. post, mail; (*à
écrire*) letters; (*de journal*) column.
courroie /kurwa/ n.f. strap; (*techn.*) belt.
courroux /kuru/ n.m. wrath.
cours /kur/ n.m. (*leçon*) class; (*série de
leçons*) course; (*prix*) price; (*cote*) rate;
(*déroulement, d'une rivière*) course;
(*allée*) avenue. **au** ~ **de,** in the course
of. **avoir** ~, (*monnaie*) be legal tender;
(*fig.*) be current; (*scol.*) have a lesson.
~ **d'eau,** river, stream. ~ **du soir,**
evening class. ~ **magistral,** (*univ.*)
lecture. **en** ~, current; (*travail*) in
progress. **en** ~ **de route,** on the way.
course /kurs/ n.f. run(ning); (*épreuve de
vitesse*) race; (*entre rivaux*: fig.) race;
(*de projectile*) flight; (*voyage*) journey;
(*commission*) errand. ~**s,** (*achats*)
shopping; (*de chevaux*) races.
cours|ier, ~**ère** /kursje, -jɛr/ n.m., f.
messenger.
court¹, ~**e** /kur, -t/ a. short. —*adv.*
short. **à** ~ **de,** short of. **pris de** ~,
caught unawares. ~**-circuit** (*pl.* ~**s-
circuits**) n.m. short circuit.
court² /kur/ n.m. ~ **(de tennis),** (tennis)
court.
court|ier, ~**ière** /kurtje, -jɛr/ n.m., f.
broker.
courtisan /kurtizɑ̃/ n.m. courtier.
courtisane /kurtizan/ n.f. courtesan.
courtiser /kurtize/ v.t. court.
courtois, ~**e** /kurtwa, -z/ a. courteous.
~**ie** /-zi/ n.f. courtesy.
couscous /kuskus/ n.m. couscous.
cousin, ~**e** /kuzɛ̃, -in/ n.m., f. cousin.
~ **germain,** first cousin.
coussin /kusɛ̃/ n.m. cushion.
coût /ku/ n.m. cost.
couteau (*pl.* ~**x**) /kuto/ n.m. knife. ~ **à
cran d'arrêt,** flick-knife.
coutellerie /kutɛlri/ n.f. (*magasin*)
cutlery shop.
coût|er /kute/ v.t./i. cost. ~**e que coûte,**
at all costs. **au prix** ~**ant,** at cost
(price). ~**eux,** ~**euse** a. costly.

coutum|e /kutym/ n.f. custom. ~**ier,**
~**ière** a. customary.
coutur|e /kutyr/ n.f. sewing; (*métier*)
dressmaking; (*points*) seam. ~**ier** n.m.
fashion de-signer. ~**ière** n.f.
dressmaker.
couvée /kuve/ n.f. brood.
couvent /kuvɑ̃/ n.m. convent; (*de
moines*) monastery.
couver /kuve/ v.t. (*œufs*) hatch;
(*personne*) pamper; (*maladie*) be
coming down with, be sickening for.
—*v.i.* (*feu*) smoulder; (*mal*) be
brewing.
couvercle /kuvɛrkl/ n.m. (*de marmite,
boîte*) lid; (*d'objet allongé*) top.
couvert¹, ~**e** /kuvɛr, -t/ a. covered
(**de,** with); (*habillé*) covered up; (*ciel*)
overcast. —*n.m.* (*abri*) cover. **à** ~,
(*mil.*) under cover. **à** ~ **de,** (*fig.*) safe
from.
couvert² /kuvɛr/ n.m. (*à table*) place-
setting; (*prix*) cover charge. ~**s,**
(*couteaux etc.*) cutlery. **mettre le** ~,
lay the table.
couverture /kuvɛrtyr/ n.f. cover; (*de lit*)
blanket; (*toit*) roofing. ~ **chauffante,**
electric blanket.
couveuse /kuvøz/ n.f. ~ **(artificielle),**
incubator.
couvreur /kuvrœr/ n.m. roofer.
couvr|ir† /kuvrir/ v.t. cover. **se** ~**ir** v.
pr. (*s'habiller*) cover up; (*se coiffer*)
put one's hat on; (*ciel*) become
overcast. ~**e-chef** n.m. hat. ~**e-feu** (*pl.*
~**e-feux**) n.m. curfew. ~**e-lit** n.m.
bedspread.
cow-boy /kɔbɔj/ n.m. cowboy.
crabe /krab/ n.m. crab.
crachat /kraʃa/ n.m. spit(tle).
cracher /kraʃe/ v.i. spit; (*radio*) crackle.
—*v.t.* spit (out).
crachin /kraʃɛ̃/ n.m. drizzle.
crack /krak/ n.m. (*fam.*) wizard, ace,
prodigy.
craie /krɛ/ n.f. chalk.
craindre† /krɛ̃dr/ v.t. be afraid of, fear;
(*être sensible à*) be easily damaged by.
crainte /krɛ̃t/ n.f. fear. **de** ~ **de/que,** for
fear of/that.
crainti|f, ~**ve** /krɛtif, -v/ a. timid.
cramoisi /kramwazi/ a. crimson.
crampe /krɑ̃p/ n.f. cramp.
crampon /krɑ̃pɔ̃/ n.m. (*de chaussure*)
stud.
cramponner (se) /(sə)krɑ̃pɔne/ v. *pr.*
~ **à,** cling to.
cran /krɑ̃/ n.m. (*entaille*) notch; (*trou*)
hole; (*courage*: fam.) pluck.

crâne /krɑn/ n.m. skull.

crâner /krɑne/ v.i. (fam.) swank.

crapaud /krapo/ n.m. toad.

crapul|e /krapyl/ n.f. villain. ~eux, ~euse a. sordid, foul.

craqu|er /krake/ v.i. crack, snap; (plancher) creak; (couture) split; (fig.) break down; (céder) give in. —v.t. ~er une allumette, strike a match. ~ement n.m. crack(ing), snap(ping); creak(ing); striking.

crass|e /kras/ n.f. grime. ~eux, ~euse a. grimy.

cratère /kratɛr/ n.m. crater.

cravache /kravaʃ/ n.f. horsewhip.

cravate /kravat/ n.f. tie.

crawl /krol/ n.m. (nage) crawl.

crayeu|x, ~se /krejø, -z/ a. chalky.

crayon /krejɔ̃/ n.m. pencil. ~ (de couleur), crayon. ~ à bille, ball-point pen. ~ optique, light pen.

créanc|ier, ~ière /kreɑ̃sje, -jɛr/ n.m., f. creditor.

créa|teur, ~trice /kreatœr, -tris/ a. creative. —n.m., f. creator.

création /kreasjɔ̃/ n.f. creation; (comm.) product.

créature /kreatyr/ n.f. creature.

crèche /krɛʃ/ n.f. day nursery; (relig.) crib.

crédibilité /kredibilite/ n.f. credibility.

crédit /kredi/ n.m. credit; (banque) bank. ~s, funds. à ~, on credit. faire ~, give credit (à, to). ~er /-te/ v.t. credit. ~eur, ~euse /-tœr, -tøz/ a. in credit.

credo /kredo/ n.m. creed.

crédule /kredyl/ a. credulous.

créer /kree/ v.t. create.

crémation /kremasjɔ̃/ n.f. cremation.

crème /krɛm/ n.f. cream; (dessert) cream dessert —a. invar. cream —n.m. (café) ~, white coffee. ~ anglaise, fresh custard. ~ à raser, shaving-cream.

crémeu|x, ~se /kremø, -z/ a. creamy.

crém|ier, ~ière /kremje, -jɛr/ n.m., f. dairyman, dairywoman. ~erie /kremri/ n.f. dairy.

créneau (pl. ~x) /kreno/ n.m. (trou, moment) slot; (dans le marché) gap; faire un ~, park between two cars.

créole /kreɔl/ n.m./f. Creole.

crêpe[1] /krɛp/ n.f. (galette) pancake. ~rie n.f. pancake shop.

crêpe[2] /krɛp/ n.m. (tissu) crêpe; (matière) crêpe (rubber).

crépit|er /krepite/ v.i. crackle. ~ement n.m. crackling.

crépu /krepy/ a. frizzy.

crépuscule /krepyskyl/ n.m. twilight, dusk.

crescendo /kreʃɛndo/ adv. & n.m. invar. crescendo.

cresson /kresɔ̃/ n.m. (water)cress.

crête /krɛt/ n.f. crest; (de coq) comb.

crétin, ~e /kretɛ̃, -in/ n.m., f. cretin.

creuser /krøze/ v.t. dig; (évider) hollow out; (fig.) go deeply into. se ~ (la cervelle), (fam.) rack one's brains.

creuset /krøze/ n.m. (lieu) melting-pot.

creu|x, ~se /krø, -z/ a. hollow; (heures) off peak. n.m. hollow; (de l'estomac) pit.

crevaison /krəvɛzɔ̃/ n.f. puncture.

crevasse /krəvas/ n.f. crack; (de glacier) crevasse; (de la peau) chap.

crevé /krəve/ a. (fam.) worn out.

crève-cœur /krɛvkœr/ n.m. invar. heart-break.

crever /krəve/ v.t./i. burst; (pneu) puncture burst; (exténuer: fam.) exhaust; (mourir: fam.) die; (œil) put out.

crevette /krəvɛt/ n.f. ~ (grise), shrimp. ~ (rose), prawn.

cri /kri/ n.m. cry; (de douleur) scream, cry.

criant, ~e /krijɑ̃, -t/ a. glaring.

criard, ~e /krijar, -d/ a. (couleur) garish; (voix) bawling.

crible /kribl/ n.m. sieve, riddle.

criblé /krible/ a. ~ de, riddled with.

cric /krik/ n.m. (auto.) jack.

crier /krije/ v.i. (fort) shout, cry (out); (de douleur) scream; (grincer) creak. —v.t. (ordre) shout (out).

crim|e /krim/ n.m. crime; (meurtre) murder. ~inalité n.f. crime. ~inel, ~inelle a. criminal; n.m., f. criminal; (assassin) murderer.

crin /krɛ̃/ n.m. horsehair.

crinière /krinjɛr/ n.f. mane.

crique /krik/ n.f. creek.

criquet /krike/ n.m. locust.

crise /kriz/ n.f. crisis; (méd.) attack; (de colère) fit. ~ cardiaque, heart attack. ~ de foie, bilious attack.

crisp|er /krispe/ v.t., se ~er v. pr. tense; (poings) clench. ~ation n.f. tenseness; (spasme) twitch. ~é a. tense.

crisser /krise/ v.i. crunch; (pneu) screech.

crist|al (pl. ~aux) /kristal, -o/ n.m. crystal.

cristallin, ~e /kristalɛ̃, -in/ a. (limpide) crystal-clear.

cristalliser /kristalize/ v.t./i., se ~ v. pr. crystallize.

critère /kritɛr/ n.m. criterion.
critique /kritik/ a. critical. —n.f.
criticism; (*article*) review. —n.m.
critic. **la ~,** (*personnes*) the critics.
critiquer /kritike/ v.t. criticize.
croasser /krɔase/ v.i. caw.
croc /kro/ n.m. (*dent*) fang; (*crochet*)
hook.
croc-en-jambe (*pl.* **crocs-en-jambe**)
/krɔkɑ̃ʒɑ̃b/ n.m. = **croche-pied.**
croche /krɔʃ/ n.f. quaver. **double ~,**
semiquaver.
croche-pied /krɔʃpje/ n.m. **faire un ~ à,**
trip up.
crochet /krɔʃɛ/ n.m. hook; (*détour*)
detour; (*signe*) (square) bracket;
(*tricot*) crochet. **faire au ~,** crochet.
crochu /krɔʃy/ a. hooked.
crocodile /krɔkɔdil/ n.m. crocodile.
crocus /krɔkys/ n.m. crocus.
croire† /krwar/ v.t./i. believe (**à, en,** in);
(*estimer*) think, believe (**que,** that).
croisade /krwazad/ n.f. crusade.
croisé /krwaze/ a. (*veston*) double-
breasted. —n.m. crusader.
croisée /krwaze/ n.f. window. **~ des
chemins,** crossroads.
crois|er[1] /krwaze/ v.t., **se ~er** v. pr.
cross; (*passant, véhicule*) pass (each
other). **(se) ~er les bras,** fold one's
arms. **(se) ~er les jambes,** cross one's
legs. **~ement** n.m. crossing; passing;
(*carrefour*) crossroads.
crois|er[2] /krwaze/ v.i. (*bateau*) cruise.
~eur n.m. cruiser. **~ière** n.f. cruise.
croissan|t[1] /krwasɑ̃, -t/ a.
growing; (*lune*) wax. **~ce** n.f. growth.
croissant[2] /krwasɑ̃/ n.m. crescent;
(*pâtisserie*) croissant.
croître† /krwatr/ v.i. grow; (*lune*) wax.
croix /krwa/ n.f. cross. **~ gammée,**
swastika. **C~-Rouge,** Red Cross.
croque-monsieur /krɔkməsjø/ n.m. *invar.* toasted ham and cheese sandwich.
croque-mort /krɔkmɔr/ n.m. undertaker's assistant.
croqu|er /krɔke/ v.t./i. crunch;
(*dessiner*) sketch. **chocolat à ~er,**
plain chocolate. **~ant, ~ante** a.
crunchy.
croquet /krɔkɛ/ n.m. croquet.
croquette /krɔkɛt/ n.f. croquette.
croquis /krɔki/ n.m. sketch.
crosse /krɔs/ n.f. (*de fusil*) butt;
(*d'évêque*) crook.
crotte /krɔt/ n.f. droppings.
crotté /krɔte/ a. muddy.
crottin /krɔtɛ̃/ n.m. (horse) dung.

crouler /krule/ v.i. collapse; (*être en
ruines*) crumble.
croupe /krup/ n.f. rump; (*de colline*)
brow. **en ~,** pillion.
croupier /krupje/ n.m. croupier.
croupir /krupir/ v.i. stagnate.
croustill|er /krustije/ v.i. be crusty.
~ant, ~ante a. crusty; (*fig.*) spicy.
croûte /krut/ n.f. crust; (*de fromage*)
rind; (*de plaie*) scab. **en ~,** (*culin.*) en
croûte.
croûton /krutɔ̃/ n.m. (*bout de pain*)
crust; (*avec potage*) croûton.
croyable /krwajabl/ a. credible.
croyan|t, ~te /krwajɑ̃, -t/ n.m., f.
believer. **~ce** n.f. belief.
CRS *abrév.* (*Compagnies républicaines
de sécurité*) French state security
police.
cru[1] /kry/ *voir* **croire.**
cru[2] /kry/ a. raw; (*lumière*) harsh;
(*propos*) crude. —n.m. vineyard; (*vin*)
wine.
crû /kry/ *voir* **croître.**
cruauté /kryote/ n.f. cruelty.
cruche /kryʃ/ n.f. pitcher.
cruc|ial (*m. pl.* **~iaux**) /krysjal, -jo/ a.
crucial.
crucif|ier /krysifje/ v.t. crucify. **~ixion**
n.f. crucifixion.
crucifix /krysifi/ n.m. crucifix.
crudité /krydite/ n.f. (*de langage*)
crudeness. **~s,** (*culin.*) raw vegetables.
crue /kry/ n.f. rise in water level. **en ~,**
in spate.
cruel, ~le /kryɛl/ a. cruel.
crûment /krymɑ̃/ adv. crudely.
crustacés /krystase/ n.m. pl. shellfish.
crypte /kript/ n.f. crypt.
Cuba /kyba/ n.m. Cuba.
cubain, ~e /kybɛ̃, -ɛn/ a. & n.m., f.
Cuban.
cub|e /kyb/ n.m. cube. —a. (*mètre etc.*)
cubic. **~ique** a. cubic.
cueill|ir† /kœjir/ v.t. pick, gather;
(*personne: fam.*) pick up. **~ette** n.f.
picking, gathering.
cuill|er, ~ère /kɥijɛr/ n.f. spoon. **~er à
soupe,** soup-spoon; (*mesure*) table-
spoonful. **~erée** n.f. spoonful.
cuir /kɥir/ n.m. leather. **~ chevelu,**
scalp.
cuirassé /kɥirase/ n.m. battleship.
cuire /kɥir/ v.t./i. cook; (*picoter*) smart.
~ (au four), bake. **faire ~,** cook.
cuisine /kɥizin/ n.f. kitchen; (*art*)
cookery, cooking; (*aliments*) cooking.
faire la ~, cook.
cuisin|er /kɥizine/ v.t./i. cook;

(*interroger*: *fam.*) grill. ~ier, ~ière
n.m., *f.* cook; *n.f.* (*appareil*) cooker,
stove.

cuisse /kɥis/ *n.f.* thigh; (*de poulet*,
mouton) leg.

cuisson /kɥisɔ̃/ *n.m.* cooking.

cuit, ~e /kɥi, -t/ *a.* cooked. bien ~,
well done *ou* cooked. trop ~,
overdone.

cuivr|e /kɥivr/ *n.m.* copper. ~e (jaune),
brass. ~es, (*mus.*) brass. ~é *a.*
coppery.

cul /ky/ *n.m.* (*derrière*: *fam.*) backside,
bum.

culasse /kylas/ *n.f.* (*auto.*) cylinder head;
(*arme*) breech.

culbut|e /kylbyt/ *n.f.* somersault; (*chute*)
tumble. ~er *v.i.* tumble; *v.t.* knock
over.

cul-de-sac (*pl.* culs-de-sac) /kydsak/
n.m. cul-de-sac.

culinaire /kylinɛr/ *a.* culinary; (*recette*)
cooking.

culminer /kylmine/ *v.i.* reach the highest
point.

culot[1] /kylo/ *n.m.* (*audace*: *fam.*) nerve,
cheek.

culot[2] /kylo/ *n.m.* (*fond*: *techn.*) base.

culotte /kylɔt/ *n.f.* (*de femme*) knickers;
(*Amer.*) panties. ~ (de cheval), (riding)
breeches. ~ courte, short trousers.

culpabilité /kylpabilite/ *n.f.* guilt.

culte /kylt/ *n.m.* cult, worship; (*religion*)
religion; (*protestant*) service.

cultivé /kyltive/ *a.* cultured.

cultiv|er /kyltive/ *v.t.* cultivate;
(*plantes*) grow. ~ateur, ~atrice *n.m.*,
f. farmer.

culture /kyltyr/ *n.f.* cultivation; (*de
plantes*) growing; (*agriculture*) farming; (*éducation*) culture. ~s, (*terrains*)
lands under cultivation. ~ physique,
physical training.

culturel, ~le /kyltyrɛl/ *a.* cultural.

cumuler /kymyle/ *v.t.* (*fonctions*) hold
simultaneously.

cupide /kypid/ *a.* grasping.

cure /kyr/ *n.f.* (*course of*) treatment,
cure.

curé /kyre/ *n.m.* (parish) priest.

cur|er /kyre/ *v.t.* clean. se ~er les
dents/ongles, clean one's teeth/nails.
~e-dent *n.m.* toothpick. ~e-pipe *n.m.*
pipe-cleaner.

curieu|x, ~se /kyrjø, -z/ *a.* curious.
—*n.m.*, *f.* (*badaud*) onlooker.
~sement *adv.* curiously.

curiosité /kyrjozite/ *n.f.* curiosity;
(*objet*) curio; (*spectacle*) unusual sight.

curriculum vitae /kyrikylɔm vite/ *n.m.*
invar. curriculum vitae.

curseur /kyrsœr/ *n.m.* cursor.

cutané /kytane/ *a.* skin.

cuve /kyv/ *n.f.* tank.

cuvée /kyve/ *n.f.* (*de vin*) vintage.

cuvette /kyvɛt/ *n.f.* bowl; (*de lavabo*)
(wash-)basin; (*des cabinets*) pan, bowl.

CV /seve/ *n.m.* CV.

cyanure /sjanyr/ *n.m.* cyanide.

cybernétique /sibɛrnetik/ *n.f.* cybernetics.

cycl|e /sikl/ *n.m.* cycle. ~ique *a.*
cyclic(al).

cyclis|te /siklist/ *n.m./f.* cyclist. —*a.*
cycle. ~me *n.m.* cycling.

cyclomoteur /syklɔmɔtœr/ *n.m.* moped.

cyclone /syklon/ *n.m.* cyclone.

cygne /siɲ/ *n.m.* swan.

cylindr|e /silɛ̃dr/ *n.m.* cylinder. ~ique *a.*
cylindrical.

cylindrée /silɛ̃dre/ *n.f.* (*de moteur*)
capacity.

cymbale /sɛ̃bal/ *n.f.* cymbal.

cynique /sinik/ *a.* cynical. —*n.m.* cynic.
~sme *n.m.* cynicism.

cyprès /siprɛ/ *n.m.* cypress.

cypriote /siprijɔt/ *a.* & *n.m./f.* Cypriot.

D

d' /d/ *voir* de.

d'abord /dabɔr/ *adv.* first; (*au début*) at
first.

dactylo /daktilo/ *n.f.* typist. ~(graphie) *n.f.* typing. ~graphe *n.f.* typist.
~graphier *v.t.* type.

dada /dada/ *n.m.* hobby horse.

dahlia /dalja/ *n.m.* dahlia.

daigner /deɲe/ *v.t.* deign.

daim /dɛ̃/ *n.m.* (fallow) deer; (*cuir*)
suede.

dall|e /dal/ *n.f.* paving stone, slab. ~age
n.m. paving.

daltonien, ~ne /daltɔnjɛ̃, -jɛn/ *a.*
colour-blind.

dame /dam/ *n.f.* lady; (*cartes*, *échecs*)
queen. ~s, (*jeu*) draughts; (*jeu*: *Amer.*)
checkers.

damier /damje/ *n.m.* draught-board;
(*Amer.*) checker-board. à ~, chequered.

damn|er /dane/ *v.t.* damn. ~ation *n.f.*
damnation.

dancing /dɑ̃siɲ/ *n.m.* dance-hall.

dandiner (se) /(sə)dãdine/ v. pr. waddle.

Danemark /danmark/ n.m. Denmark.

danger /dãʒe/ n.m. danger. **en ～,** in danger. **mettre en ～,** endanger.

dangereu|x, ～se /dãʒrø, -z/ a. dangerous.

danois, ～e /danwa, -z/ a. Danish. —n.m., f. Dane. —n.m. (lang.) Danish.

dans /dã/ prép. in; (mouvement) into; (à l'intérieur de) inside, in; (approximation) about. **～ dix jours,** in ten days' time. **prendre/boire/**etc. **～,** take/ drink/etc. out of ou from.

dans|e /dãs/ n.f. dance; (art) dancing. **～er** v.t./i. dance. **～eur, ～euse** n.m., f. dancer.

dard /dar/ n.m. (d'animal) sting.

darne /darn/ n.f. steak (of fish).

dat|e /dat/ n.f. date. **～e limite,** deadline; **～e limite de vente,** sell-by date; **～e de péremption,** expiry date. **～er** v.t./i. date. **à ～er de,** as from.

datt|e /dat/ n.f. (fruit) date. **～ier** n.m. date-palm.

daube /dob/ n.f. casserole.

dauphin /dofɛ̃/ n.m. (animal) dolphin.

davantage /davãtaʒ/ adv. more; (plus longtemps) longer. **～ de,** more. **～ que,** more than; longer than.

de, d'＊ /də, d/ prép. (de + le = du, de + les = des) of; (provenance) from; (moyen, manière) with; (agent) by. —article some; (interrogation) any, some. **le livre de mon ami,** my friend's book. **un pont de fer,** an iron bridge. **dix mètres de haut,** ten metres high. **du pain,** (some) bread; **une tranche de pain,** a slice of bread. **des fleurs,** (some) flowers.

dé /de/ n.m. (à jouer) dice; (à coudre) thimble. **dés,** (jeu) dice.

dealer /dilər/ n.m. (drug) dealer.

débâcle /debakl/ n.f. (mil.) rout.

déball|er /debale/ v.t. unpack; (montrer, péj.) spill out. **～age** n.m. unpacking.

débarbouiller /debarbuje/ v.t. wash the face of. **se ～** v. pr. wash one's face.

débarcadère /debarkadɛr/ n.m. landing-stage.

débardeur /debardœr/ n.m. docker; (vêtement) tank top.

débarqu|er /debarke/ v.t./i. disembark, land; (arriver: fam.) turn up. **～ement** n.m. disembarkation.

débarras /debara/ n.m. junk room. **bon ～!,** good riddance!

débarrasser /debarase/ v.t. clear (**de,** of). **～ qn. de,** take from s.o.; (défaut, ennemi) rid s.o. of. **se ～ de,** get rid of, rid o.s. of.

débat /deba/ n.m. debate.

débattre†[1] /debatr/ v.t. debate. —v.i. **～ de,** discuss.

débattre†[2] (se) /(sə)debatr/ v. pr. struggle (to get free).

débauch|e /deboʃ/ n.f. debauchery; (fig.) profusion. **～er**[1] v.t. debauch.

débaucher[2] /deboʃe/ v.t. (licencier) lay off.

débile /debil/ a. weak; (fam.) stupid. —n.m./f. moron.

débit /debi/ n.m. (rate of) flow; (de magasin) turnover; (élocution) delivery; (de compte) debit. **～ de tabac,** tobacconist's shop; **～ de boissons,** licensed premises.

débi|ter /debite/ v.t. cut up; (fournir) produce; (vendre) sell; (dire: péj.) spout; (compte) debit. **～teur, ～trice** n.m., f. debtor; a. (compte) in debit.

débl|ayer /debleje/ v.t. clear. **～aiement, ～ayage** n.m. clearing.

déblo|quer /debloke/ v.t. (prix, salaires) free. **～cage** n.m. freeing.

déboires /debwar/ n.m. pl. disappointments.

déboiser /debwaze/ v.t. clear (of trees).

déboîter /debwate/ v.i. (véhicule) pull out. —v.t. (membre) dislocate.

débord|er /deborde/ v.i. overflow. —v.t. (dépasser) extend beyond. **～er de,** (joie etc.) be overflowing with. **～é à,** snowed under (**de,** with). **～ement** n.m. overflowing.

débouché /debuʃe/ n.m. opening; (carrière) prospect; (comm.) outlet; (sortie) end, exit.

déboucher /debuʃe/ v.t. (bouteille) uncork; (évier) unblock. —v.i. emerge (**de,** from). **～ sur,** (rue) lead into.

débourser /deburse/ v.t. pay out.

déboussolé /debusole/ a. (fam.) disorientated, disoriented.

debout /dəbu/ adv. standing; (levé, éveillé) up. **être ～, se tenir ～,** be standing, stand. **se mettre ～,** stand up.

déboutonner /debutone/ v.t. unbutton. **se ～** v. pr. unbutton o.s.; (vêtement) come undone.

débraillé /debraje/ a. slovenly.

débrancher /debrãʃe/ v.t. unplug, disconnect.

débray|er /debreje/ v.i. (auto.) declutch; (faire grève) stop work. **～age** /debrɛjaʒ/ n.m. (pédale) clutch; (grève) stoppage.

débris /debri/ *n.m. pl.* fragments; (*détritus*) rubbish, debris.

débrouill|er /debruje/ *v.t.* disentangle; (*problème*) sort out. **se ~er** *v. pr.* manage. **~ard, ~arde** *a.* (*fam.*) resourceful.

débroussailler /debrusaje/ *v.t.* clear (of brushwood).

début /deby/ *n.m.* beginning. **faire ses ~s**, (*en public*) make one's début.

début|er /debyte/ *v.i.* begin; (*dans un métier etc.*) start out. **~ant, ~ante** *n.m., f.* beginner.

déca /deka/ *n.m.* decaffeinated coffee.

décaféiné /dekafeine/ *a.* decaffeinated. **—***n.m.* **du ~**, decaffeinated coffee.

deçà (en) /(ã)dəsa/ *adv.* this side. **—***prép.* **en ~ de**, this side of.

décacheter /dekaʃte/ *v.t.* open.

décade /dekad/ *n.f.* ten days; (*décennie*) decade.

décaden|t, ~te /dekadã, -t/ *a.* decadent. **~ce** *n.f.* decadence.

décalcomanie /dekalkɔmani/ *n.f.* transfer; (*Amer.*) decal.

décal|er /dekale/ *v.t.* shift. **~age** *n.m.* (*écart*) gap. **~age horaire,** time difference.

décalquer /dekalke/ *v.t.* trace.

décamper /dekɑ̃pe/ *v.i.* clear off.

décanter /dekɑ̃te/ *v.t.* allow to settle. **se ~** *v. pr.* settle.

décap|er /dekape/ *v.t.* scrape down; (*surface peinte*) strip. **~ant** *n.m.* chemical agent; (*pour peinture*) paint stripper.

décapotable /dekapɔtabl/ *a.* convertible.

décapsul|er /dekapsyle/ *v.t.* take the cap off. **~eur** *n.m.* bottle-opener.

décarcasser (se) /(sə)dekarkase/ *v. pr.* (*fam.*) work o.s. to death.

décathlon /dekatlɔ̃/ *n.m.* decathlon.

décéd|er /desede/ *v.i.* die. **~é** *a.* deceased.

décel|er /desle/ *v.t.* detect; (*démontrer*) reveal. **~able** *a.* detectable.

décembre /desɑ̃br/ *n.m.* December.

décennie /deseni/ *n.f.* decade.

déc|ent, ~ente /desã, -t/ *a.* decent. **~emment** /-amã/ *adv.* decently. **~ence** *n.f.* decency.

décentralis|er /desãtralize/ *v.t.* decentralize. **~ation** *n.f.* decentralization.

déception /desɛpsjɔ̃/ *n.f.* disappointment.

décerner /desɛrne/ *v.t.* award.

décès /desɛ/ *n.m.* death.

décev|oir† /desvwar/ *v.t.* disappoint. **~ant, e** *a.* disappointing.

déchaîn|er /deʃene/ *v.t.* (*violence etc.*) unleash; (*enthousiasme*) arouse a good deal of. **se ~er** *v. pr.* erupt. **~ement** /-ɛnmã/ *n.m.* (*de passions*) outburst.

décharge /deʃarʒ/ *n.f.* (*salve*) volley of shots. **~ (électrique),** electrical discharge. **~ (publique),** rubbish tip.

décharg|er /deʃarʒe/ *v.t.* unload; (*arme, accusé*) discharge. **~er de,** release from. **se ~er** *v. pr.* (*batterie, pile*) go flat. **~ement** *n.m.* unloading.

décharné /deʃarne/ *a.* bony.

déchausser (se) /(sə)deʃose/ *v. pr.* take off one's shoes; (*dent*) work loose.

dèche /dɛʃ/ *n.f.* **dans la ~,** broke.

déchéance /deʃeãs/ *n.f.* decay.

déchet /deʃɛ/ *n.m.* (*reste*) scrap; (*perte*) waste. **~s,** (*ordures*) refuse.

déchiffrer /deʃifre/ *v.t.* decipher.

déchiqueter /deʃikte/ *v.t.* tear to shreds.

déchir|ant, ~ante /deʃirã, -t/ *a.* heart-breaking. **~ement** *n.m.* heart-break; (*conflit*) split.

déchir|er /deʃire/ *v.t.* tear; (*lacérer*) tear up; (*arracher*) tear off *ou* out; (*diviser*) tear apart; (*oreilles: fig.*) split. **se ~er** *v. pr.* tear. **~ure** *n.f.* tear.

déch|oir /deʃwar/ *v.i.* demean o.s. **~oir de,** (*rang*) lose, fall from. **~u** *a.* fallen.

décibel /desibel/ *n.m.* decibel.

décid|er /deside/ *v.t.* decide on; (*persuader*) persuade. **~er que/de,** decide that/to. **—***v.i.* decide. **~er de qch.,** decide on sth. **se ~er** *v. pr.* make up one's mind (**à,** to). **~é** *a.* (*résolu*) determined; (*fixé, marqué*) decided. **~ément** *adv.* really.

décim|al, ~ale /desimal, -o/ *a.* & *n.f.* decimal.

décimètre /desimɛtr/ *n.m.* decimetre.

décisi|f, ~ve /desizif, -v/ *a.* decisive.

décision /desizjɔ̃/ *n.f.* decision.

déclar|er /deklare/ *v.t.* declare; (*naissance*) register. **se ~er** *v. pr.* (*feu*) break out. **~er forfait,** (*sport*) withdraw. **~ation** *n.f.* declaration; (*commentaire politique*) statement. **~ation d'impôts,** tax return.

déclasser /deklase/ *v.t.* (*coureur*) relegate; (*hôtel*) downgrade.

déclench|er /deklãʃe/ *v.t.* (*techn.*) release, set off; (*lancer*) launch; (*provoquer*) trigger off. **se ~er** *v. pr.* (*techn.*) go off. **~eur** *n.m.* (*photo.*) trigger.

déclic /deklik/ *n.m.* click; (*techn.*) trigger mechanism.

déclin /deklɛ̃/ n.m. decline.

déclin|er[1] /dekline/ v.i. decline. ∼**aison** n.f. (lang.) declension.

décliner[2] /dekline/ v.t. (refuser) decline; (dire) state.

déclivité /deklivite/ n.f. slope.

décocher /dekɔʃe/ v.t. (coup) fling; (regard) shoot.

décoder /dekɔde/ v.t. decode.

décoiffer /dekwafe/ v.t. (ébouriffer) disarrange the hair of.

décoincer /dekwɛ̃se/ v.t. free.

décoll|er[1] /dekɔle/ v.i. (avion) take off. ∼**age** n.m. take-off.

décoller[2] /dekɔle/ v.t. unstick.

décolleté /dekɔlte/ a. low-cut. —n.m. low neckline.

décolor|er /dekɔlɔre/ v.t. fade; (cheveux) bleach. **se** ∼**er** v. pr. fade. ∼**ation** n.f. bleaching.

décombres /dekɔ̃br/ n.m. pl. rubble.

décommander /dekɔmɑ̃de/ v.t. cancel.

décompos|er /dekɔ̃poze/ v.t. break up; (substance) decompose; (visage) contort. **se** ∼**er** v. pr. (pourrir) decompose. ∼**ition** n.f. decomposition.

décompt|e /dekɔ̃t/ n.m. deduction; (détail) breakdown. ∼**er** v.t. deduct.

déconcerter /dekɔ̃sɛrte/ v.t. disconcert.

décongel|er /dekɔ̃ʒle/ v.t. thaw. ∼**ation** n.f. thawing.

décongestionner /dekɔ̃ʒɛstjɔne/ v.t. relieve congestion in.

déconseill|er /dekɔ̃seje/ v.t. ∼**er qch. à qn.**, advise s.o. against sth. ∼**é** a. not advisable, inadvisable.

décontenancer /dekɔ̃tnɑ̃se/ v.t. disconcert.

décontract|er /dekɔ̃trakte/ v.t., **se** ∼ v. pr. relax. ∼**é** a. relaxed.

déconvenue /dekɔ̃vny/ n.f. disappointment.

décor /dekɔr/ n.m. (paysage, théâtre) scenery; (cinéma) set; (cadre) setting; (de maison) décor.

décorati|f, ∼**ve** /dekɔratif, -v/ a. decorative.

décor|er /dekɔre/ v.t. decorate. ∼**ateur,** ∼**atrice** n.m., f. (interior) decorator. ∼**ation** n.f. decoration.

décortiquer /dekɔrtike/ v.t. shell; (fig.) dissect.

découdre (se) /(sə)dekudr/ v. pr. come unstitched.

découler /dekule/ v.i. ∼ **de,** follow from.

découp|er /dekupe/ v.t. cut up; (viande) carve; (détacher) cut out. **se** ∼**er sur,**

stand out against. ∼**age** n.m. (image) cut-out.

décourag|er /dekuraʒe/ v.t. discourage. **se** ∼**er** v. pr. become discouraged. ∼**ement** n.m. discouragement. ∼**é** a. discouraged.

décousu /dekuzy/ a. (vêtement) falling apart; (idées etc.) disjointed.

découvert, ∼**e** /dekuvɛr, -t/ a. (tête etc.) bare; (terrain) open. —n.m. (de compte) overdraft. —n.f. discovery. **à** ∼, exposed; (fig.) openly. **à la** ∼**e de,** in search of.

découvrir† /dekuvrir/ v.t. discover; (enlever ce qui couvre) uncover; (voir) see; (montrer) reveal. **se** ∼ v. pr. uncover o.s.; (se décoiffer) take one's hat off; (ciel) clear.

décrasser /dekrase/ v.t. clean.

décrépit, ∼**e** /dekrepi, -t/ a. decrepit. ∼**ude** n.f. decay.

décret /dekrɛ/ n.m. decree. ∼**er** /-ete/ v.t. decree.

décrié /dekrije/ v.t. decried.

décrire† /dekrir/ v.t. describe.

décrisp|er (se) /(sə)dekrispe/ v. pr. become less tense. ∼**ation** n.f. lessening of tension.

décroch|er /dekrɔʃe/ v.t. unhook; (obtenir: fam.) get. —v.i. (abandonner: fam.) give up. ∼**er (le téléphone),** pick up the phone. ∼**é** a. (téléphone) off the hook.

décroître /dekrwatr/ v.i. decrease.

décrue /dekry/ n.f. going down (of river water).

déçu /desy/ a. disappointed.

décupl|e /dekypl/ n.m. **au** ∼**e,** tenfold. **le** ∼**e de,** ten times. ∼**er** v.t./i. increase tenfold.

dédaign|er /dedeɲe/ v.t. scorn. ∼**er de faire,** consider it beneath one to do. ∼**eux,** ∼**euse** /dedeɲø, -z/ a. scornful.

dédain /dedɛ̃/ n.m. scorn.

dédale /dedal/ n.m. maze.

dedans /dədɑ̃/ adv. & n.m. inside. **au** ∼ **(de),** inside. **en** ∼, on the inside.

dédicac|e /dedikas/ n.f. dedication, inscription. ∼**er** v.t. dedicate, inscribe.

dédier /dedje/ v.t. dedicate.

dédommag|er /dedɔmaʒe/ v.t. compensate (**de,** for). ∼**ement** n.m. compensation.

dédouaner /dedwane/ v.t. clear through customs.

dédoubler /deduble/ v.t. split into two. ∼ **un train,** put on a relief train.

déd|uire† /dedɥir/ v.t. deduct;

(*conclure*) deduce. **~uction** *n.f.* deduction; **~uction d'impôts** tax deduction.

déesse /dees/ *n.f.* goddess.

défaillance /defajɑ̃s/ *n.f.* weakness; (*évanouissement*) black-out; (*panne*) failure.

défaill|ir /defajir/ *v.i.* faint; (*forces etc.*) fail. **~ant, ~ante** *a.* (*personne*) faint; (*candidat*) defaulting.

défaire† /defɛr/ *v.t.* undo; (*valise*) unpack; (*démonter*) take down; (*débarrasser*) rid. **se ~** *v. pr.* come undone. **se ~ de,** rid o.s. of.

défait, ~e /defɛ, -t/ *a.* (*cheveux*) ruffled; (*visage*) haggard.

défaite /defɛt/ *n.f.* defeat.

défaitisme /defetizm/ *n.m.* defeatism.

défaitiste /defetist/ *a. & n.m./f.* defeatist.

défalquer /defalke/ *v.t.* (*somme*) deduct.

défaut /defo/ *n.m.* fault, defect; (*d'un verre, diamant, etc.*) flaw; (*carence*) lack; (*pénurie*) shortage. **à ~ de,** for lack of. **en ~,** at fault. **faire ~,** (*argent etc.*) be lacking. **par ~,** (*jurid.*) in one's absence.

défav|eur /defavœr/ *n.f.* disfavour. **~orable** *a.* unfavourable.

défavoriser /defavɔrize/ *v.t.* put at a disadvantage.

défection /defɛksjɔ̃/ *n.f.* desertion. **faire ~,** desert.

défect|ueux, ~ueuse /defɛktɥø, -z/ *a.* faulty, defective. **~uosité** *n.f.* faultiness; (*défaut*) fault.

défendre /defɑ̃dr/ *v.t.* defend; (*interdire*) forbid. **~ à qn. de,** forbid s.o. to. **se ~** *v. pr.* defend o.s.; (*se débrouiller*) manage; (*se protéger*) protect o.s. **se ~ de,** (*refuser*) refrain from.

défense /defɑ̃s/ *n.f.* defence; (*d'éléphant*) tusk. **~ de fumer/**etc., no smoking/etc.

défenseur /defɑ̃sœr/ *n.m.* defender.

défensi|f, ~ve /defɑ̃sif, -v/ *a. & n.f.* defensive.

déféren|t, ~te /deferɑ̃, -t/ *a.* deferential. **~ce** *n.f.* deference.

déférer /defere/ *v.t.* (*jurid.*) refer. —*v.i.* **~ à,** (*avis etc.*) defer to.

déferler /defɛrle/ *v.i.* (*vagues*) break; (*violence etc.*) erupt.

défi /defi/ *n.m.* challenge; (*refus*) defiance. **mettre au ~,** challenge.

déficeler /defisle/ *v.t.* untie.

déficience /defisjɑ̃s/ *n.f.* deficiency.

déficient /defisjɑ̃/ *a.* deficient.

déficit /defisit/ *n.m.* deficit. **~aire** *a.* in deficit.

défier /defje/ *v.t.* challenge; (*braver*) defy. **se ~ de,** mistrust.

défilé¹ /defile/ *n.m.* procession; (*mil.*) parade; (*fig.*) (continual) stream. **~ de mode,** fashion parade.

défilé² /defile/ *n.m.* (*géog.*) gorge.

défiler /defile/ *v.i.* march (past); (*visiteurs*) stream; (*images*) flash by. **se ~** *v. pr.* (*fam.*) sneak off.

défini /defini/ *a.* definite.

définir /definir/ *v.t.* define.

définissable /definisabl/ *a.* definable.

définiti|f, ~ve /definitif, -v/ *a.* final; (*permanent*) definitive. **en ~ve,** in the final analysis. **~vement** *adv.* definitively, permanently.

définition /definisjɔ̃/ *n.f.* definition; (*de mots croisés*) clue.

déflagration /deflagrasjɔ̃/ *n.f.* explosion.

déflation /deflɑsjɔ̃/ *n.f.* deflation. **~niste** /-jɔnist/ *a.* deflationary.

défoncer /defɔ̃se/ *v.t.* (*porte etc.*) break down; (*route, terrain*) dig up; (*lit*) break the springs of. **se ~** *v. pr.* (*fam.*) work like mad; (*drogué*) get high.

déform|er /deforme/ *v.t.* put out of shape; (*membre*) deform; (*faits, pensée*) distort. **~ation** *n.f.* loss of shape; deformation; distortion.

défouler (se) /(sə)defule/ *v. pr.* let off steam.

défraîchir (se) /(sə)defreʃir/ *v. pr.* become faded.

défrayer /defreje/ *v.t.* (*payer*) pay the expenses of.

défricher /defriʃe/ *v.t.* clear (for cultivation).

défroisser /defrwase/ *v.t.* smooth out.

défunt, ~e /defœ̃, -t/ *a.* (*mort*) late. —*n.m., f.* deceased.

dégagé /degaʒe/ *a.* clear; (*ton*) free and easy.

dégag|er /degaʒe/ *v.t.* (*exhaler*) give off; (*désencombrer*) clear; (*délivrer*) free; (*faire ressortir*) bring out. —*v.i.* (*football*) kick the ball (down the pitch *ou* field). **se ~er** *v. pr.* free o.s.; (*ciel, rue*) clear; (*odeur etc.*) emanate. **~ement** *n.m.* giving off; clearing; freeing; (*espace*) clearing; (*football*) clearance.

dégainer /degene/ *v.t./i.* draw.

dégarnir /degarnir/ *v.t.* clear, empty. **se ~** *v. pr.* clear, empty; (*crâne*) go bald.

dégâts /dega/ *n.m. pl.* damage.

dégel /deʒɛl/ *n.m.* thaw. **~er** /deʒle/ *v.t./i.* thaw (out). **(faire) ~er,** (*culin.*) thaw.

dégénér|er /deʒenere/ v.i. degenerate. **~é, ~ée** a. & n.m., f. degenerate.

dégingandé /deʒɛ̃gɑ̃de/ a. gangling.

dégivrer /deʒivre/ v.t. (auto.) de-ice; (frigo) defrost.

déglacer /deglase/ v.t. (culin.) deglaze.

déglingu|er /deglɛ̃ge/ (fam.) v.t. knock about. **se ~er** v. pr. fall to bits. **~é** adj. falling to bits.

dégonfl|er /degɔ̃fle/ v.t. let down, deflate. **se ~er** v. pr. (fam.) get cold feet. **~é** a. (pneu) flat; (lâche: fam.) yellow.

dégorger /degɔrʒe/ v.i. **faire ~**, (culin.) soak.

dégouliner /deguline/ v.i. trickle.

dégourdi /degurdi/ a. smart.

dégourdir /degurdir/ v.t. (membre, liquide) warm up. **se ~ les jambes**, stretch one's legs.

dégoût /degu/ n.m. disgust.

dégoût|er /degute/ v.t. disgust. **~er qn. de qch.**, put s.o. off sth. **~ant**, **~ante** a. disgusting. **~é** a. disgusted. **~é de**, sick of. **faire le ~é**, look disgusted.

dégradant /degradɑ̃/ a. degrading.

dégrader /degrade/ v.t. degrade; (abîmer) damage. **se ~** v. pr. (se détériorer) deteriorate.

dégrafer /degrafe/ v.t. unhook.

degré /dəgre/ n.m. degree; (d'escalier) step.

dégressi|f, **~ve** /degresif, -v/ a. gradually lower.

dégrèvement /degrɛvmɑ̃/ n.m. **~ fiscal** ou **d'impôts**, tax reduction.

dégrever /degrəve/ v.t. reduce the tax on.

dégringol|er /degrɛ̃gɔle/ v.i. tumble (down). —v.t. rush down. **~ade** n.f. tumble.

dégrossir /degrosir/ v.t. (bois) trim; (projet) rough out.

déguerpir /degɛrpir/ v.i. clear off.

dégueulasse /degœlas/ a. (argot) disgusting, lousy.

dégueuler /degœle/ v.t. (argot) throw up.

déguis|er /degize/ v.t. disguise. **se ~er** v. pr. disguise o.s.; (au carnaval etc.) dress up. **~ement** n.m. disguise; (de carnaval etc.) fancy dress.

dégust|er /degyste/ v.t. taste, sample; (savourer) enjoy. **~ation** n.f. tasting, sampling.

déhancher (se) /(sə)deɑ̃ʃe/ v. pr. sway one's hips.

dehors /dəɔr/ adv. & n.m. outside. —n.m. pl. (aspect de qn.) exterior. **au ~ (de)**, outside. **en ~ de**, outside;

(hormis) apart from. **jeter/mettre**/etc. **~**, throw/put/etc. out.

déjà /deʒa/ adv. already; (avant) before, already.

déjà-vu /deʒavy/ n.m. inv. déjà vu.

déjeuner /deʒœne/ v.i. (have) lunch; (le matin) (have) breakfast. —n.m. lunch. **(petit) ~**, breakfast.

déjouer /deʒwe/ v.t. thwart.

delà /dəla/ adv. & prép. **au ~ (de)**, **en ~ (de)**, **par ~**, beyond.

délabrer (se) /(sə)delɑbre/ v. pr. become dilapidated.

délacer /delase/ v.t. undo.

délai /delɛ/ n.m. time-limit; (attente) wait; (sursis) extension (of time). **sans ~**, without delay. **dans les plus brefs ~s**, as soon as possible.

délaisser /delese/ v.t. desert.

délass|er /delase/ v.t., **se ~er** v. pr. relax. **~ement** n.m. relaxation.

délation /delasjɔ̃/ n.f. informing.

délavé /delave/ a. faded.

délayer /deleje/ v.t. mix (with liquid); (idée) drag out.

delco /dɛlko/ n.m. (P., auto.) distributor.

délecter (se) /(sə)delɛkte/ v. pr. **se ~ de**, delight in.

délégation /delegasjɔ̃/ n.f. delegation.

délégu|er /delege/ v.t. delegate. **~é, ~ée** n.m., f. delegate.

délibéré /delibere/ a. deliberate; (résolu) determined. **~ment** adv. deliberately.

délibér|er /delibere/ v.i. deliberate. **~ation** n.f. deliberation.

délicat /delika/ a. /delika, -t/ a. delicate; (plein de tact) tactful; (exigeant) particular. **~ement** /-tmɑ̃/ adv. delicately; tactfully. **~esse** /-tɛs/ n.f. delicacy; tact. **~esses** /-tɛs/ n.f. pl. (kind) attentions.

délice /delis/ n.m. delight. **~s** n.f. pl. delights.

délicieu|x, **~se** /delisjø, -z/ a. (au goût) delicious; (charmant) delightful.

délié /delje/ a. fine, slender; (agile) nimble.

délier /delje/ v.t. untie; (délivrer) free. **se ~** v. pr. come untied.

délimit|er /delimite/ v.t. determine, demarcate. **~ation** n.f. demarcation.

délinquan|t, **~te** /delɛ̃kɑ̃, -t/ a. & n.m., f. delinquent. **~ce** n.f. delinquency.

délire /delir/ n.m. delirium; (fig.) frenzy.

délir|er /delire/ v.i. be delirious (**de**, with); (déraisonner) rave. **~ant**,

~ante *a.* delirious; (*frénétique*) frenzied; (*fam.*) wild.

délit /deli/ *n.m.* offence, crime.

délivr|er /delivre/ *v.t.* free, release; (*pays*) deliver; (*remettre*) issue. ~ance *n.f.* release; deliverance; issue.

déloger /deloʒe/ *v.t.* force out.

déloy|al (*m. pl.* ~aux) /delwajal, -jo/ *a.* disloyal; (*procédé*) unfair.

delta /dɛlta/ *n.m.* delta.

deltaplane /dɛltaplan/ *n.m.* hang-glider.

déluge /delyʒ/ *n.m.* flood; (*pluie*) downpour.

démagogie /demagɔʒi/ *n.m.* demagogy.

démagogue /demagɔg/ *n.m./f.* demagogue.

demain /dmɛ̃/ *adv.* tomorrow.

demande /dmɑ̃d/ *n.f.* request; (*d'emploi*) application; (*exigence*) demand. ~ **en mariage,** proposal (of marriage).

demandé /dmɑ̃de/ *a.* in demand.

demander /dmɑ̃de/ *v.t.* ask for; (*chemin, heure*) ask; (*emploi*) apply for; (*nécessiter*) require. ~ **que/si,** ask that/if. ~ **qch. à qn.,** ask s.o. for sth. ~ **à qn. de,** ask s.o. to. ~ **en mariage,** propose to. se ~ **si/où**/*etc.*, wonder if/where/*etc.*

demandeu|r ~se /dmɑ̃dœr, -øz/ *n.m., f.* les ~rs **d'emploi** job seekers.

démangl|er /demɑ̃ʒe/ *v.t./i.* itch. ~eaison *n.f.* itch(ing).

démanteler /demɑ̃tle/ *v.t.* break up.

démaquill|er (se) /(sə)demakije/ *v. pr.* remove one's make-up. ~ant *n.m.* make-up remover.

démarcation /demarkasjɔ̃/ *n.f.* demarcation.

démarchage /demarʃaʒ/ *n.m.* door-to-door selling.

démarche /demarʃ/ *n.f.* walk, gait, (*procédé*) step. **faire des** ~s **auprès de,** make approaches to.

démarcheu|r ~se /demarʃœr, -øz/ *n.m., f.* (door-to-door) canvasser.

démarr|er /demare/ *v.i.* (*moteur*) start (up); (*partir*) move off; (*fig.*) get moving. —*v.t.* (*fam.*) get moving. ~age *n.m.* start. ~eur *n.m.* starter.

démasquer /demaske/ *v.t.* unmask.

démêlant /demɛlɑ̃/ *n.m.* conditioner.

démêler /demele/ *v.t.* disentangle.

démêlés /demele/ *n.m. pl.* trouble.

déménag|er /demenaʒe/ *v.i.* move (house). —*v.t.* (*meubles*) remove. ~ement *n.m.* move; (*de meubles*) removal. ~eur *n.m.* removal man; (*Amer.*) furniture mover.

démener (se) /(sə)demne/ *v. pr.* move about wildly; (*fig.*) exert o.s.

démen|t, ~te /demɑ̃, -t/ *a.* insane. —*n.m., f.* lunatic. ~ce *n.f.* insanity.

démenti /demɑ̃ti/ *n.m.* denial.

démentir /demɑ̃tir/ *v.t.* refute; (*ne pas être conforme à*) belie. ~ **que,** deny that.

démerder (se) /(sə)demɛrde/ (*fam.*) manage.

démesuré /demazyre/ *a.* inordinate.

démettre /demɛtr/ *v.t.* (*poignet etc.*) dislocate. ~ **qn. de,** dismiss s.o. from. se ~ *v. pr.* resign (**de,** from).

demeure /dəmœr/ *n.f.* residence. **mettre en** ~ **de,** order to.

demeurer /dəmœre/ *v.i.* live; (*rester*) remain.

demi, ~e /dmi/ *a.* half(-). —*n.m., f.* half. —*n.m.* (*bière*) (half-pint) glass of beer; (*football*) half-back. —*n.f.* (*à l'horloge*) half-hour. —*adv.* à ~, half; (*ouvrir, fermer*) half-way. **à la** ~e, at half-past. **une heure et** ~e, an hour and a half; (*à l'horloge*) half past one. **une** ~**-journée/-livre**/*etc.*, half a day/pound/*etc.*, a half-day/-pound/*etc.* ~**-cercle** *n.m.* semicircle. ~**-finale** *n.f.* semifinal. ~**-frère** *n m* stepbrother ~**-heure** *n.f.* half-hour, half an hour. ~**-jour** *n.m.* half-light. ~**-mesure** *n f* half-measure. **à** ~**-mot** *adv.* without having to express every word. ~**-pension** *n.f.* half-board. ~**-pensionnaire** *n.m./f.* day-boarder. ~**-sel** *a. invar.* slightly salted. ~**-sœur** *n.f.* stepsister. ~**-tarif** *n.m.* half-fare. ~**-tour** *n.m.* about turn; (*auto.*) U-turn. **faire** ~**-tour,** turn back.

démis, ~e /demi, -z/ *a.* dislocated. ~ **de ses fonctions,** removed from his post.

démission /demisjɔ̃/ *n.f.* resignation. ~ner /-jɔne/ *v.i.* resign.

démobiliser /demɔbilize/ *v.t.* demobilize.

démocrate /demɔkrat/ *n.m./f.* democrat. —*a.* democratic.

démocrat|ie /demɔkrasi/ *n.f.* democracy. ~ique /-atik/ *a.* democratic.

démodé /demɔde/ *a.* old-fashioned.

démographi|e /demɔgrafi/ *n.f.* demography. ~que *a.* demographic.

demoiselle /dəmwazɛl/ *n.f.* young lady; (*célibataire*) spinster. ~ **d'honneur,** bridesmaid.

démol|ir /demɔlir/ *v.t.* demolish. ~ition *n.f.* demolition.

démon /demɔ̃/ *n.m.* demon. **le D~**, the Devil.

démoniaque /demɔnjak/ *a.* fiendish.

démonstra|teur, ~trice /demɔ̃stratœr, -tris/ *n.m., f.* demonstrator. **~tion** /-asjɔ̃/ *n.f.* demonstration; (*de force*) show.

démonstrati|f, ~ve /demɔ̃stratif, -v/ *a.* demonstrative.

démonter /demɔ̃te/ *v.t.* take apart, dismantle; (*installation*) take down; (*fig.*) disconcert. **se ~** *v. pr.* come apart.

démontrer /demɔ̃tre/ *v.t.* show, demonstrate.

démoraliser /demɔralize/ *v.t.* demoralize.

démuni /demyni/ *a.* impoverished. **~ de,** without.

démunir /demynir/ *v.t.* **~ de,** deprive of. **se ~ de,** part with.

démystifier /demistifje/ *v.t.* enlighten.

dénaturer /denatyre/ *v.t.* (*faits etc.*) distort.

dénégation /denegasjɔ̃/ *n.f.* denial.

dénicher /deniʃe/ *v.t.* (*trouver*) dig up; (*faire sortir*) flush out.

dénigr|er /denigre/ *v.t.* denigrate. **~ement** *n.m.* denigration.

dénivellation /denivɛlasjɔ̃/ *n.f.* (*pente*) slope.

dénombrer /denɔ̃bre/ *v.t.* count; (*énumérer*) enumerate.

dénomination /denɔminasjɔ̃/ *n.f.* designation.

dénommé, ~e /denɔme/ *n. m., f.* **le ~ X,** the said X.

dénonc|er /denɔ̃se/ *v.t.* denounce; (*scol.*) tell on. **se ~er** *v. pr.* give o.s. up. **~iateur, ~iatrice** *n.m., f.* informer; (*scol.*) tell-tale. **~iation** *n.f.* denunciation.

dénoter /denɔte/ *v.t.* denote.

dénouement /denumɑ̃/ *n.m.* outcome; (*théâtre*) dénouement.

dénouer /denwe/ *v.t.* unknot, undo. **se ~** *v. pr.* (*nœud*) come undone.

dénoyauter /denwajote/ *v.t.* stone; (*Amer.*) pit.

denrée /dɑ̃re/ *n.f.* foodstuff.

dens|e /dɑ̃s/ *a.* dense. **~ité** *n.f.* density.

dent /dɑ̃/ *n.f.* tooth; (*de roue*) cog. **faire ses ~s,** teethe. **~aire** /-tɛr/ *a.* dental.

dentelé /dɑ̃tle/ *a.* jagged.

dentelle /dɑ̃tɛl/ *n.f.* lace.

dentier /dɑ̃tje/ *n.m.* denture.

dentifrice /dɑ̃tifris/ *n.m.* toothpaste.

dentiste /dɑ̃tist/ *n.m./f.* dentist.

dentition /dɑ̃tisjɔ̃/ *n.f.* teeth.

dénud|er /denyde/ *v.t.* bare. **~é** *a.* bare.

dénué /denɥe/ *a.* **~ de,** devoid of.

dénuement /denymɑ̃/ *n.m.* destitution.

déodorant /deɔdɔrɑ̃/ *a.m. & n.m.* (**produit**) **~,** deodorant.

déontologi|e /deɔ̃tɔlɔʒi/ *n.f.* code of practice. **~que** *a.* ethical.

dépann|er /depane/ *v.t.* repair; (*fig.*) help out. **~age** *n.m.* repair. **de ~age,** (*service etc.*) breakdown. **~euse** *n.f.* breakdown lorry; (*Amer.*) wrecker.

dépareillé /depareje/ *a.* odd, not matching.

départ /depar/ *n.m.* departure; (*sport*) start. **au ~,** at the outset.

départager /departaʒe/ *v.t.* settle the matter between.

département /departəmɑ̃/ *n.m.* department.

dépassé /depase/ *a.* outdated.

dépass|er /depase/ *v.t.* go past, pass; (*véhicule*) overtake; (*excéder*) exceed; (*rival*) surpass; (*dérouter: fam.*) be beyond. —*v.i.* stick out; (*véhicule*) overtake. **~ement** *n.m.* overtaking.

dépays|er /depeize/ *v.t.* disorientate, disorient. **~ant, ~e** *a.* disorientating. **~ement** *n.m.* disorientation; (*changement*) change of scenery.

dépêch|e /depɛʃ/ *n.f.* dispatch. **~er**[1] /-eʃe/ *v.t.* dispatch.

dépêcher[2] (**se**) /(sə)depeʃe/ *v. pr.* hurry (up).

dépeindre /depɛ̃dr/ *v.t.* depict.

dépendance /depɑ̃dɑ̃s/ *n.f.* dependence; (*bâtiment*) outbuilding.

dépendre /depɑ̃dr/ *v.t.* take down. —*v.i.* depend (**de,** on). **~ de,** (*appartenir à*) belong to.

dépens (**aux**) /(o)depɑ̃/ *prép.* **aux ~ de,** at the expense of.

dépens|e /depɑ̃s/ *n.f.* expense; expenditure. **~er** *v.t./i.* spend; (*énergie etc.*) expend. **se ~er** *v. pr.* exert o.s.

dépens|ier, ~ière /depɑ̃sje, -jɛr/ *a.* **être ~ier,** be a spendthrift.

dépérir /deperir/ *v.i.* wither.

dépêtrer (**se**) /(sə)depetre/ *v. pr.* get o.s. out (**de,** of).

dépeupler /depœple/ *v.t.* depopulate. **se ~** *v. pr.* become depopulated.

déphasé /defaze/ *a.* (*fam.*) out of touch.

dépilatoire /depilatwar/ *a. & n.m.* depilatory.

dépist|er /depiste/ *v.t.* detect; (*criminel*) track down; (*poursuivant*) throw off the scent. **~age** *n.m.* detection.

dépit /depi/ *n.m.* resentment. **en ~ de,** despite. **en ~ du bon sens,** against all common sense. **~é** /-te/ *a.* vexed.

déplacé /deplase/ *a.* out of place.

déplac|er /deplase/ *v.t.* move. **se ~er** *v. pr.* move; (*voyager*) travel. **~ement** *n.m.* moving; travel(-ling).

déplaire /depler/ *v.i.* **~ à**, (*irriter*) displease. **ça me déplaît**, I dislike that.

déplaisant, ~e /depleza, -t/ *a.* unpleasant, disagreeable.

déplaisir /deplezir/ *n.m.* displeasure.

dépliant /deplijã/ *n.m.* leaflet.

déplier /deplije/ *v.t.* unfold.

déplor|er /deplore/ *v.t.* (*trouver regrettable*) deplore; (*mort*) lament. **~able** *a.* deplorable.

dépl|oyer /deplwaje/ *v.t.* (*ailes, carte*) spread; (*courage*) display; (*armée*) deploy. **~oiement** *n.m.* display; deployment.

déport|er /deporte/ *v.t.* (*exiler*) deport; (*dévier*) carry off course. **~ation** *n.f.* deportation.

déposer /depoze/ *v.t.* put down; (*laisser*) leave; (*passager*) drop; (*argent*) deposit; (*installation*) dismantle; (*plainte*) lodge; (*armes*) lay down; (*roi*) depose. —*v.i.* (*jurid.*) testify. **se ~** *v. pr.* settle.

dépositaire /depoziter/ *n.m./f.* (*comm.*) agent.

déposition /depozisjɔ̃/ *n.f.* (*jurid.*) statement.

dépôt /depo/ *n.m.* (*garantie, lie*) deposit; (*entrepôt*) warehouse; (*d'autobus*) depot; (*d'ordures*) dump. **laisser en ~**, give for safe keeping.

dépotoir /depotwar/ *n.m.* rubbish dump.

dépouille /depuj/ *n.f.* skin, hide. **~ (mortelle)**, mortal remains. **~s**, (*butin*) spoils.

dépouiller /depuje/ *v.t.* go through; (*votes*) count; (*écorcher*) skin. **~ de**, strip of.

dépourvu /depurvy/ *a.* **~ de**, devoid of. **prendre au ~**, catch unawares.

dépréc|ier /depresje/ *v.t.*, **se ~ier** *v. pr.* depreciate. **~iation** *n.f.* depreciation.

déprédations /depredasjɔ̃/ *n.f. pl.* damage.

dépr|imer /deprime/ *v.t.* depress. **~ession** *n.f.* depression. **~ession nerveuse**, nervous breakdown.

depuis /dəpчi/ *prép.* since; (*durée*) for; (*à partir de*) from. —*adv.* (ever) since. **~ que**, since. **~ quand attendez-vous?**, how long have you been waiting?

députation /depytasjɔ̃/ *n.f.* deputation.

député, ~e /depyte/ *n.m., f.* Member of Parliament.

déraciné, ~e /derasine/ *a. & n.m., f.* rootless (person).

déraciner /derasine/ *v.t.* uproot.

déraill|er /deraje/ *v.i.* be derailed; (*fig., fam.*) be talking nonsense. **faire ~er**, derail. **~ement** *n.m.* derailment. **~eur** *n.m.* (*de vélo*) gear mechanism, *dérailleur*.

déraisonnable /derezɔnabl/ *a.* unreasonable.

dérang|er /derãʒe/ *v.t.* (*gêner*) bother, disturb; (*dérégler*) upset, disrupt. **se ~er** *v. pr.* put o.s. out. **ça vous ~e si . . .?**, do you mind if . . .? **~ement** *n.m.* bother; (*désordre*) disorder, upset. **en ~ement**, out of order.

dérap|er /derape/ *v.i.* skid; (*fig.*) get out of control. **~age** *n.m.* skid.

déréglé /deregle/ *a.* (*vie*) dissolute; (*estomac*) upset; (*pendule*) (that is) not running properly.

dérégler /deregle/ *v.t.* put out of order. **se ~** *v. pr.* go wrong.

dérision /derizjɔ̃/ *n.f.* mockery. **par ~**, derisively. **tourner en ~**, mock.

dérisoire /derizwar/ *a.* derisory.

dérivatif /derivatif/ *n.m.* distraction.

dériv|e /deriv/ *n.f.* **aller à la ~e**, drift. **~er** *v.i.* (*bateau*) drift; *v.t.* (*détourner*) divert.

dériv|er² /derive/ *v.i.* **~er de**, derive from. **~é** *a.* derived; *n.m.* derivative; (*techn.*) by-product.

dermatolo|gie /dɛrmatɔlɔʒi/ *n.f.* dermatology. **~gue** /-g/ *n.m./f.* dermatologist.

dern|ier, ~ière /dɛrnje, -jɛr/ *a.* last; (*nouvelles, mode*) latest; (*étage*) top. *n.m., f.* last (one). **ce ~ier**, the latter. **en ~ier**, last. **le ~ier cri**, the latest fashion.

dernièrement /dɛrnjɛrmɑ̃/ *adv.* recently.

dérobé /derobe/ *a.* hidden. **à la ~e**, stealthily.

dérober /derobe/ *v.t.* steal; (*cacher*) hide (**à, from**). **se ~** *v. pr.* slip away. **se ~ à**, (*obligation*) shy away from; (*se cacher à*) hide from.

dérogation /derɔgasjɔ̃/ *n.f.* exemption.

déroger /derɔʒe/ *v.i.* **~ à**, go against.

dérouiller (se) /(sə)deruje/ *v. pr.* **se ~ les jambes** to stretch one's legs.

déroul|er /derule/ *v.t.* (*fil etc.*) unwind. **se ~er** *v. pr.* unwind; (*avoir lieu*) take place; (*récit, paysage*) unfold. **~ement** *n.m.* (*d'une action*) development.

déroute /derut/ *n.f.* (*mil.*) rout.

dérouter /derute/ *v.t.* disconcert.

derrière /dɛrjɛr/ *prép. & adv.* behind.

—*n.m.* back, rear; (*postérieur*) behind. **de ~,** back, rear; (*pattes*) hind. **par ~,** (from) behind, at the back *ou* rear.

des /de/ *voir* **de.**

dès /dɛ/ *prép.* (right) from, from the time of. **~ lors,** from then on. **~ que,** as soon as.

désabusé /dezabyze/ *a.* disillusioned.

désaccord /dezakɔr/ *n.m.* disagreement. **~é** /-de/ *a.* out of tune.

désaffecté /dezafɛkte/ *a.* disused.

désaffection /dezafɛksjɔ̃/ *n.f.* alienation (**pour,** from).

désagréable /dezagreabl/ *a.* unpleasant.

désagréger (se) /(sə)dezagreʒe/ *v. pr.* disintegrate.

désagrément /dezagremɑ̃/ *n.m.* annoyance.

désaltérant /dezalterɑ̃/ *a.* thirst-quenching, refreshing.

désaltérer /dezaltere/ *v.i.,* **se ~** *v. pr.* quench one's thirst.

désamorcer /dezamɔrse/ *v.t.* (*situation, obus*) defuse.

désappr|ouver /dezapruve/ *v.t.* disapprove of. **~obation** *n.f.* disapproval.

désarçonner /dezarsɔne/ *v.t.* disconcert, throw; (*jockey*) unseat, throw.

désarmant /dezarmɑ̃/ *a.* disarming.

désarm|er /dezarme/ *v.t./i.* disarm. **~ement** *n.m.* (*pol.*) disarmament.

désarroi /dezarwa/ *n.m.* confusion.

désarticulé /dezartikyle/ *a.* dislocated.

désastr|e /dezastr/ *n.m.* disaster. **~eux, ~euse** *a.* disastrous.

désavantag|e /dezavɑ̃taʒ/ *n.m.* disadvantage. **~er** *v.t.* put at a disadvantage. **~eux, ~euse** *a.* disadvantageous.

désaveu (*pl.* **~x**) /dezavø/ *n.m.* repudiation.

désavouer /dezavwe/ *v.t.* repudiate.

désaxé, ~e /dezakse/ *a.* & *n.m., f.* unbalanced (person).

descendan|t, ~te /desɑ̃dɑ̃, -t/ *n.m., f.* descendant. **~ce** *n.f.* descent; (*enfants*) descendants.

descendre /desɑ̃dr/ *v.i.* (*aux. être*) go down; (*venir*) come down; (*passager*) get off *ou* out; (*nuit*) fall. **~ de,** (*être issu de*) be descended from. **~ à l'hôtel,** go to a hotel. —*v.t.* (*aux. avoir*) (*escalier etc.*) go *ou* come down; (*objet*) take down; (*abattre, fam.*) shoot down.

descente /desɑ̃t/ *n.f.* descent; (*pente*) (downward) slope; (*raid*) raid. **~ de lit,** bedside rug.

descripti|f, ~ve /dɛskriptif, -v/ *a.* descriptive.

description /dɛskripsjɔ̃/ *n.f.* description.

désemparé /dezɑ̃pare/ *a.* distraught.

désemplir /dezɑ̃plir/ *v.i.* **ne pas ~,** be always crowded.

désendettement /dezɑ̃dɛtmɑ̃/ *n.m.* getting out of debt.

désenfler /dezɑ̃fle/ *v.i.* go down.

déséquilibre /dezekilibr/ *n.m.* imbalance. **en ~,** unsteady.

déséquilibr|er /dezekilibre/ *v.t.* throw off balance. **~é, ~ée** *a.* & *n.m., f.* unbalanced (person).

désert[1] **~e** /dezɛr, -t/ *a.* deserted.

désert[2] /dezɛr/ *n.m.* desert. **~ique** /-tik/ *a.* desert.

déserter /dezɛrte/ *v.t./i.* desert. **~eur** *n.m.* deserter. **~ion** /-ɛrsjɔ̃/ *n.f.* desertion.

désespér|er /dezɛspere/ *v.i.,* **se ~er** *v. pr.* despair. **~er de,** despair of. **~ant, ~ante** *a.* utterly disheartening. **~é** *a.* in despair; (*état, cas*) hopeless; (*effort*) desperate. **~ément** *adv.* desperately.

désespoir /dezɛspwar/ *n.m.* despair. **au ~,** in despair. **en ~ de cause,** as a last resort.

déshabill|er /dezabije/ *v.t.* **se ~er** *v. pr.* undress, get undressed. **~é** *a.* undressed; *n.m.* négligée.

déshabituer (se) /(sə)dezabitɥe/ *v. pr.* **se ~ de,** get out of the habit of.

désherb|er /dezɛrbe/ *v.t.* weed. **~ant** *n.m.* weed-killer.

déshérit|er /dezerite/ *v.t.* disinherit. **~é** *a.* (*région*) deprived. **les ~és** *n.m. pl.* the underprivileged.

déshonneur /dezɔnœr/ *n.m.* dishonour.

déshonor|er /dezɔnɔre/ *v.t.* dishonour. **~ant, ~ante** *a.* dishonourable.

déshydrater /dezidrate/ *v.t.,* **se ~** *v. pr.* dehydrate.

désigner /deziɲe/ *v.t.* (*montrer*) point to *ou* out; (*élire*) appoint; (*signifier*) indicate.

désillusion /dezilyzjɔ̃/ *n.f.* disillusionment.

désincrust|er /dezɛ̃kryste/ *v. pr.* (*chaudière*) descale; (*peau*) exfoliate. **~ant** *a.* **produit ~ant,** (skin) scrub.

désinence /dezinɑ̃s/ *n.f.* (*gram.*) ending.

désinfect|er /dezɛ̃fɛkte/ *v.t.* disinfect. **~ant** *n.m.* disinfectant.

désinfection /dezɛ̃fɛksjɔ̃/ *n.f.* disinfection.

désintégrer /dezɛ̃tegre/ *v.t.,* **se ~** *v. pr.* disintegrate.

désintéressé /dezɛ̃terese/ *a.* disinterested.

désintéresser (se) /(sə)dezɛ̃terese/ *v. pr.* **se ∼ de**, lose interest in.

désintoxication /dezɛ̃tɔksikasjɔ̃/ *n.f.* detoxification. **cure de ∼**, detoxification course.

désintoxiquer /dezɛ̃tɔksike/ *v.t.* cure of an addiction; (*régime*) purify.

désinvolt|e /dezɛ̃vɔlt/ *a.* casual. **∼ure** *n.f.* casualness.

désir /dezir/ *n.m.* wish, desire; (*convoitise*) desire.

désirer /dezire/ *v.t.* want; (*convoiter*) desire. **∼ faire**, want *ou* wish to do.

désireu|x, ∼se /dezirø, -z/ *a.* **∼x de**, anxious to.

désist|er (se) /(sə)deziste/ *v. pr.* withdraw. **∼ement** *n.m.* withdrawal.

désobéir /dezɔbeir/ *v.i.* **∼ (à)**, disobey.

désobéissan|t, ∼te /dezɔbeisɑ̃, -t/ *a.* disobedient. **∼ce** *n.f.* disobedience.

désobligeant, ∼e /dezɔbliʒɑ̃, -t/ *a.* disagreeable, unkind.

désodé /desɔde/ *a.* sodium-free.

désodorisant /dezɔdɔrizɑ̃/ *n.m.* air freshener.

désœuvr|é /dezœvre/ *a.* idle. **∼ement** *n.m.* idleness.

désolé /dezɔle/ *a.* (*région*) desolate.

désol|er /dezɔle/ *v.t.* distress. **être ∼é**, (*regretter*) be sorry. **∼ation** *n.f.* distress.

désopilant, ∼e /dezɔpilɑ̃, -t/ *a.* hilarious.

désordonné /dezɔrdɔne/ *a.* untidy; (*mouvements*) uncoordinated.

désordre /dezɔrdr/ *n.m.* disorder; (*de vêtements, cheveux*) untidiness. **mettre en ∼**, make untidy.

désorganiser /dezɔrganize/ *v.t.* disorganize.

désorienté /dezɔrjɑ̃te/ *a.* disorientated.

désorienter /dezɔrjɑ̃te/ *v.t.* disorientate, disorient.

désormais /dezɔrmɛ/ *adv.* from now on.

désosser /dezɔse/ *v.t.* bone.

despote /dɛspɔt/ *n.m.* despot.

desquels, desquelles /dekɛl/ *voir* **lequel**.

dessécher /desefe/ *v.t.*, **se ∼** *v. pr.* dry out *ou* up.

dessein /desɛ̃/ *n.m.* intention. **à ∼**, intentionally.

desserrer /desere/ *v.t.* loosen. **sans ∼ les dents**, without opening his/her mouth. **se ∼** *v. pr.* come loose.

dessert /desɛr/ *n.m.* dessert.

desserte /desɛrt/ *n.f.* (*transports*) service, servicing.

desservir /desɛrvir/ *v.t./i.* clear away; (*autobus*) provide a service to, serve.

dessin /desɛ̃/ *n.m.* drawing; (*motif*) design; (*contour*) outline. **∼ animé**, (*cinéma*) cartoon. **∼ humoristique**, cartoon.

dessin|er /desine/ *v.t./i.* draw; (*fig.*) outline. **se ∼er** *v. pr.* appear, take shape. **∼ateur, ∼atrice** *n.m., f.* artist; (*industriel*) draughtsman.

dessoûler /desule/ *v.t./i.* sober up.

dessous /dəsu/ *adv.* underneath. **—***n.m.* under-side, underneath. **—***n.m. pl.* underclothes. **du ∼**, bottom; (*voisins*) downstairs. **en ∼, par ∼**, underneath. **∼-de-plat** *n.m. invar.* (*heat-resistant*) table-mat. **∼-de-table** *n.m. invar.* backhander.

dessus /dəsy/ *adv.* on top (of it), on it. **—***n.m.* top. **du ∼**, top; (*voisins*) upstairs. **en ∼**, above. **par ∼**, over (it). **avoir le ∼**, get the upper hand. **∼-de-lit** *n.m. invar.* bedspread.

destabilis|er /destabilize/ *v.t.* destabilize. **∼ation** *n.f.* destabilization.

destin /destɛ̃/ *n.m.* (*sort*) fate; (*avenir*) destiny.

destinataire /dɛstinatɛr/ *n.m./f.* addressee.

destination /dɛstinasjɔ̃/ *n.f.* destination; (*emploi*) purpose. **à ∼ de**, (going) to.

destinée /dɛstine/ *n.f.* (*sort*) fate; (*avenir*) destiny.

destin|er /dɛstine/ *v.t.* **∼er à**, intend for; (*vouer*) destine for; (*affecter*) earmark for. **être ∼é à faire**, be intended to do; (*condamné, obligé*) be destined to do. **se ∼er à**, (*carrière*) intend to take up.

destit|uer /dɛstitɥe/ *v.t.* dismiss (from office). **∼ution** *n.f.* dismissal.

destruc|teur, ∼trice /dɛstryktœr, -tris/ *a.* destructive.

destruction /dɛstryksjɔ̃/ *n.f.* destruction.

dés|uet, ∼uète /desɥɛ, -t/ *a.* outdated.

désunir /dezynir/ *v.t.* divide.

détachant /detaʃɑ̃/ *n.m.* stain-remover.

détach|é /detaʃe/ *a.* detached. **∼ement** *n.m.* detachment.

détacher /detaʃe/ *v.t.* untie; (*ôter*) remove, detach; (*déléguer*) send (on assignment *ou* secondment). **se ∼** *v. pr.* come off, break away; (*nœud etc.*) come undone; (*ressortir*) stand out.

détail /detaj/ *n.m.* detail; (*de compte*) breakdown; (*comm.*) retail. **au ∼**, (*vendre etc.*) retail. **de ∼**, (*prix etc.*) retail. **en ∼**, in detail.

détaillé /detaje/ *a.* detailed.

détaill|er /detaje/ *v.t.* (*articles*) sell in small quantities, split up. **∼ant, ∼ante** *n.m., f.* retailer.

détaler /detale/ *v.i.* (*fam.*) make tracks, run off.

détartrant /detartrã/ *n.m.* descaler.

détaxer /detakse/ *v.t.* reduce the tax on.

détect|er /detɛkte/ *v.t.* detect. ⁓**eur** *n.m.* detector. ⁓**ion** /-ksjɔ̃/ *n.f.* detection.

détective /detɛktiv/ *n.m.* detective.

déteindre /detɛ̃dr/ *v.i.* (*couleur*) run (**sur**, on to). ⁓ **sur**, (*fig.*) rub off on.

détend|re /detɑ̃dr/ *v.t.* slacken; (*ressort*) release; (*personne*) relax. **se** ⁓**re** *v. pr.* become slack, slacken; be released; relax. ⁓**u** *a.* (*calme*) relaxed.

détenir† /detnir/ *v.t.* hold; (*secret*, *fortune*) possess.

détente /detɑ̃t/ *n.f.* relaxation; (*pol.*) détente; (*saut*) spring; (*gâchette*) trigger; (*relâchement*) release.

déten|teur, ⁓**trice** /detɑ̃tœr, -tris/ *n.m.*, *f.* holder.

détention /detɑ̃sjɔ̃/ *n.f.* ⁓ **préventive**, custody.

détenu, ⁓**e** /detny/ *n.m.*, *f.* prisoner.

détergent /detɛrʒɑ̃/ *n.m.* detergent.

détérior|er /deterjore/ *v.t.* damage. **se** ⁓**er** *v. pr.* deteriorate. ⁓**ation** *n.f.* damaging; deterioration.

détermin|er /detɛrmine/ *v.t.* determine. **se** ⁓**er** *v. pr.* make up one's mind (**à**, to). ⁓**ation** *n.f.* determination. ⁓**é** *a.* (*résolu*) determined; (*précis*) definite.

déterrer /detere/ *v.t.* dig up.

détersif /detɛrsif/ *n.m.* detergent.

détestable /detɛstabl/ *a.* foul.

détester /detɛste/ *v.t.* hate. **se** ⁓ *v. pr.* hate each other.

déton|er /detone/ *v.i.* explode, detonate. ⁓**ateur** *n.m.* detonator. ⁓**ation** *n.f.* explosion, detonation.

détonner /detone/ *v.i.* clash.

détour /detur/ *n.m.* bend; (*crochet*) detour; (*fig.*) roundabout means.

détourné /deturne/ *a.* roundabout.

détourn|er /deturne/ *v.t.* divert; (*tête*, *yeux*) turn away; (*avion*) hijack; (*argent*) embezzle. **se** ⁓**er de**, stray from. ⁓**ement** *n.m.* hijack(ing); embezzlement.

détrac|teur, ⁓**trice** /detraktœr, -tris/ *n.m.*, *f.* critic.

détraquer /detrake/ *v.t.* break, put out of order; (*estomac*) upset. **se** ⁓ *v. pr.* (*machine*) go wrong.

détresse /detrɛs/ *n.f.* distress.

détriment /detrimɑ̃/ *n.m.* detriment.

détritus /detritys/ *n.m. pl.* rubbish.

détroit /detrwa/ *n.m.* strait.

détromper /detrɔ̃pe/ *v.t.* undeceive, enlighten.

détruire† /detrɥir/ *v.t.* destroy.

dette /dɛt/ *n.f.* debt.

deuil /dœj/ *n.m.* mourning; (*perte*) bereavement. **porter le** ⁓, be in mourning.

deux /dø/ *a.* & *n.m.* two. ⁓ **fois**, twice. **tous** (**les**) ⁓, both. ⁓**-pièces** *n.m. invar.* (*vêtement*) two-piece; (*logement*) two-room flat *or* apartment. ⁓**-points** *n.m. invar.* (*gram.*) colon. ⁓**-roues** *n.m. invar.* two-wheeled vehicle.

deuxième /døzjɛm/ *a.* & *n.m./f.* second. ⁓**ment** *adv.* secondly.

dévaler /devale/ *v.t./i.* hurtle down.

dévaliser /devalize/ *v.t.* rob, clean out.

dévaloriser /devalorize/ *v.t.*, **se** ⁓ *v. pr.* reduce in value.

dévalorisant, ⁓**e** /devalorizɑ̃, -t/ *a.* demeaning.

déval|uer /devalɥe/ *v.t.*, **se** ⁓**uer** *v. pr.* devalue. ⁓**uation** *n.f.* devaluation.

devancer /dəvɑ̃se/ *v.t.* be *ou* go ahead of; (*arriver*) arrive ahead of; (*prévenir*) anticipate.

devant /dəvɑ̃/ *prép.* in front of; (*distance*) ahead of; (*avec mouvement*) past; (*en présence de*) before; (*face à*) in the face of. —*adv.* in front; (*à distance*) ahead. —*n.m.* front. **prendre les** ⁓**s**, take the initiative. **de** ⁓, front. **par** ⁓, at *ou* from the front, in front. **aller au** ⁓ **de qn.**, go to meet sb. **aller au** ⁓ **des désirs de qn.**, anticipate sb.'s wishes.

devanture /dəvɑ̃tyr/ *n.f.* shop front; (*étalage*) shop-window.

dévaster /devaste/ *v.t.* devastate.

déveine /devɛn/ *n.f.* bad luck.

développ|er /devlope/ *v.t.*, **se** ⁓**er** *v. pr.* develop. ⁓**ement** *n.m.* development; (*de photos*) developing.

devenir† /dəvnir/ *v.i.* (*aux. être*) become. **qu'est-il devenu?**, what has become of him?

dévergondé /devɛrgɔ̃de/ *a.* shameless.

déverser /devɛrse/ *v.t.*, **se** ⁓ *v. pr.* empty out, pour out.

dévêtir /devetir/ *v.t.*, **se** ⁓ *v. pr.* undress.

déviation /devjɑsjɔ̃/ *n.f.* diversion.

dévier /devje/ *v.t.* divert; (*coup*) deflect. —*v.i.* (*ballon*, *balle*) veer; (*personne*) deviate.

devin /dəvɛ̃/ *n.m.* fortune-teller.

deviner /dvine/ *v.t.* guess; (*apercevoir*) distinguish.

devinette /dvinɛt/ *n.f.* riddle.

devis /dvi/ *n.m.* estimate.

dévisager /devizaʒe/ *v.t.* stare at.

devise /dviz/ *n.f.* motto. ⁓**s**, (*monnaie*) (foreign) currency.

dévisser /devise/ *v.t.* unscrew.

dévitaliser /devitalize/ *v.t.* (*dent*) kill the nerve in.

dévoiler /devwale/ *v.t.* reveal.

devoir¹ /dvwar/ *n.m.* duty; (*scol.*) homework; (*fait en classe*) exercise.

devoir†² /dvwar/ *v.t.* owe. —*v. aux.* ~ **faire,** (*nécessité*) must do, have (got) to do; (*intention*) be due to do. ~ **être,** (*probabilité*) must be. **vous devriez,** you should. **il aurait dû,** he should have.

dévolu /devɔly/ *n.m.* **jeter son** ~ **sur,** set one's heart on. —*a.* ~ **à,** allotted to.

dévorer /devɔre/ *v.t.* devour.

dévot, ~**e** /devo, -ɔt/ *a.* devout.

dévotion /devosjɔ̃/ *n.f.* (*relig.*) devotion.

dévouer (se) /(sə)devwe/ *v. pr.* devote o.s. (**à,** to); (*se sacrifier*) sacrifice o.s. ~**é** *a.* devoted. ~**ement** /-vumɑ̃/ *n.m.* devotion.

dextérité /dɛksterite/ *n.f.* skill.

diab|ète /djabɛt/ *n.m.* diabetes. ~**étique** *a. & n.m./f.* diabetic.

diab|le /djabl/ *n.m.* devil. ~**olique** *a.* diabolical.

diagnosti|c /djagnɔstik/ *n.m.* diagnosis. ~**quer** *v.t.* diagnose.

diagon|al, ~**ale** (*m. pl.* ~**aux**) /djagɔnal, -o/ *a. & n.f.* diagonal. **en** ~**ale,** diagonally.

diagramme /djagram/ *n.m.* diagram; (*graphique*) graph.

dialecte /djalɛkt/ *n.m.* dialect.

dialogu|e /djalɔg/ *n.m.* dialogue. ~**er** *v.i.* (*pol.*) have a dialogue.

diamant /djamɑ̃/ *n.m.* diamond.

diamètre /djamɛtr/ *n.m.* diameter.

diapason /djapazɔ̃/ *n.m.* tuning-fork.

diaphragme /djafragm/ *n.m.* diaphragm.

diapo /djapo/ *n.f.* (*colour*) slide.

diapositive /djapozitiv/ *n.f.* (*colour*) slide.

diarrhée /djare/ *n.f.* diarrhoea.

dictat|eur /diktatœr/ *n.m.* dictator. ~**ure** *n.f.* dictatorship.

dict|er /dikte/ *v.t.* dictate. ~**ée** *n.f.* dictation.

diction /diksjɔ̃/ *n.f.* diction.

dictionnaire /diksjɔnɛr/ *n.m.* dictionary.

dicton /diktɔ̃/ *n.m.* saying.

dièse /djɛz/ *n.m.* (*mus.*) sharp.

diesel /djezɛl/ *n.m. & a. invar.* diesel.

diète /djɛt/ *n.f.* (*régime*) diet.

diététicien, ~**ne** /djetetisjɛ̃, -jɛn/ *n.m., f.* dietician.

diététique /djetetik/ *n.f.* dietetics. —*a.* **produit** *ou* **aliment** ~, dietary product.

dieu (*pl.* ~**x**) /djø/ *n.m.* god. **D**~, God.

diffamatoire /difamatwar/ *a.* defamatory.

diffam|er /difame/ *v.t.* slander; (*par écrit*) libel. ~**ation** *n.f.* slander; libel.

différé (en) /(ɑ̃)difere/ *adv.* (*émission*) recorded.

différemment /diferamɑ̃/ *adv.* differently.

différence /diferɑ̃s/ *n.f.* difference. **à la** ~ **de,** unlike.

différencier /diferɑ̃sje/ *v.t.* differentiate. **se** ~ **de,** (*différer de*) differ from.

différend /diferɑ̃/ *n.m.* difference (of opinion).

différent, ~**e** /diferɑ̃, -t/ *a.* different (**de,** from).

différentiel, ~**le** /diferɑ̃sjɛl/ *a. & n.m.* differential.

différer¹ /difere/ *v.t.* postpone.

différer² /difere/ *v.i.* differ (**de,** from).

difficile /difisil/ *a.* difficult. ~**ment** *adv.* with difficulty.

difficulté /difikylte/ *n.f.* difficulty.

difform|e /difɔrm/ *a.* deformed. ~**ité** *n.f.* deformity.

diffus, ~**e** /dify, -z/ *a.* diffuse.

diffus|er /difyze/ *v.t.* broadcast; (*lumière, chaleur*) diffuse. ~**ion** *n.f.* broadcasting; diffusion.

dig|érer /diʒere/ *v.t.* digest; (*endurer; fam.*) stomach. ~**este,** ~**estible** *adjs.* digestible. ~**estion** *n.f.* digestion.

digesti|f, ~**ve** /diʒɛstif, -v/ *a.* digestive. —*n.m.* after-dinner liqueur.

digit|al (*m. pl.* ~**aux**) /diʒital, -o/ *a.* digital.

digne /diɲ/ *a.* (*noble*) dignified; (*honnête*) worthy. ~ **de,** worthy of. ~ **de foi,** trustworthy.

dignité /diɲite/ *n.f.* dignity.

digression /digresjɔ̃/ *n.f.* digression.

digue /dig/ *n.f.* dike.

diktat /diktat/ *n.m.* diktat.

dilapider /dilapide/ *v.t.* squander.

dilat|er /dilate/ *v.t.*, **se** ~**er** *v. pr.* dilate. ~**ation** /-asjɔ̃/ *n.f.* dilation.

dilemme /dilɛm/ *n.m.* dilemma.

dilettante /diletɑ̃t/ *n.m., f.* amateur.

diluant /dilyɑ̃/ *n.m.* thinner.

diluer /dilɥe/ *v.t.* dilute.

diluvien, ~**ne** /dilyvjɛ̃, -ɛn/ *a.* (*pluie*) torrential.

dimanche /dimɑ̃ʃ/ *n.m.* Sunday.

dimension /dimɑ̃sjɔ̃/ *n.f.* (*taille*) size; (*mesure*) dimension.

dimin|uer /diminɥe/ *v.t.* reduce, decrease; (*plaisir, courage, etc.*) lessen;

(*dénigrer*) lessen. —*v.i.* decrease.
~ution *n.f.* decrease (**de**, in).
diminutif /diminytif/ *n.m.* diminutive;
(*surnom*) pet name *ou* form.
dinde /dɛ̃d/ *n.f.* turkey.
dindon /dɛ̃dɔ̃/ *n.m.* turkey.
dîn|er /dine/ *n.m.* dinner. —*v.i.* have
dinner. ~**eur**, ~**euse** *n.m.*, *f.* diner.
dingue /dɛ̃g/ *a.* (*fam.*) crazy.
dinosaure /dinozɔr/ *n.m.* dinosaur.
diocèse /djɔsɛz/ *n.m.* diocese.
diphtérie /difteri/ *n.f.* diphtheria.
diphtongue /diftɔ̃g/ *n.f.* diphthong.
diplomate /diplɔmat/ *n.m.* diplomat.
—*a.* diplomatic.
diplomat|ie /diplɔmasi/ *n.f.* diplomacy.
~**ique** /-atik/ *a.* diplomatic.
diplôm|e /diplom/ *n.m.* certificate,
diploma; (*univ.*) degree. ~**é** *a.*
qualified.
dire† /dir/ *v.t.* say; (*secret*, *vérité*, *heure*)
tell; (*penser*) think. ~ **que**, say that. ~
à qn. que/de, tell s.o. that/to. **se** ~ *v. pr.*
(*mot*) be said; (*fatigué etc.*) say that one
is. **ça me/vous**/*etc.* **dit de faire**,
I/you/*etc.* feel like doing. **on dirait que**,
it would seem that, it seems that.
dis/dites donc!, hey! —*n.m.* **au** ~ **de**,
selon les ~**s de**, according to.
direct /dirɛkt/ *a.* direct. **en** ~,
(*émission*) live. ~**ement** *adv.* directly.
direc|teur, ~**trice** /dirɛktœr, -tris/
n.m., *f.* director; (*chef de service*)
manager, manageress; (*d'école*) headmaster, headmistress.
direction /dirɛksjɔ̃/ *n.f.* (*sens*) direction;
(*de société etc.*) management; (*auto.*)
steering. **en** ~ **de**, (going) to.
directive /dirɛktiv/ *n.f.* instruction.
dirigeant, ~**e** /diriʒã, -t/ *n.m.*, *f.* (*pol.*)
leader; (*comm.*) manager. —*a.* (*classe*)
ruling.
diriger /diriʒe/ *v.t.* run, manage, direct;
(*véhicule*) steer; (*orchestre*) conduct;
(*braquer*) aim; (*tourner*) turn. **se** ~ *v.
pr.* guide o.s. **se** ~ **vers**, make one's
way to.
dirigis|me /diriʒism/ *n.m.* interven-
tionism. ~**te** /-ist/ *a.* & *n.m./f.*
interventionist.
dis /di/ *voir* **dire**.
discern|er /disɛrne/ *v.t.* discern.
~**ement** *n.m.* discernment.
disciple /disipl/ *n.m.* disciple.
disciplin|e /disiplin/ *n.f.* discipline.
~**aire** *a.* disciplinary. ~**er** *v.t.*
discipline.
discontinu /diskɔ̃tiny/ *a.* intermittent.

discontinuer /diskɔ̃tinɥe/ *v.i.* **sans** ~,
without stopping.
discordant, ~**e** /diskɔrdã, -t/ *a.*
discordant.
discorde /diskɔrd/ *n.f.* discord.
discothèque /diskɔtɛk/ *n.f.* record
library; (*club*) disco(thèque).
discount /diskunt/ *n.m.* discount.
discourir /diskurir/ *v.i.* (*péj.*) hold forth,
ramble on.
discours /diskur/ *n.m.* speech.
discréditer /diskredite/ *v.t.* discredit.
discr|et, ~**ète** /diskrɛ, -t/ *a.* discreet.
~**ètement** *adv.* discreetly.
discrétion /diskresjɔ̃/ *n.f.* discretion. **à**
~, as much as one desires.
discrimination /diskriminɑsjɔ̃/ *n.f.* discrimination.
discriminatoire /diskriminatwar/ *a.*
discriminatory.
disculper /diskylpe/ *v.t.* exonerate. **se** ~
v. pr. prove o.s. innocent.
discussion /diskysjɔ̃/ *n.f.* discussion;
(*querelle*) argument.
discuté /diskyte/ *a.* controversial.
discut|er /diskyte/ *v.t.* discuss;
(*contester*) question. —*v.i.* (*parler*)
talk; (*répliquer*) argue. ~**er de**,
discuss. ~**able** *a.* debatable.
disette /dizɛt/ *n.f.* (food) shortage.
diseuse /dizøz/ *n.f.* ~ **de bonne
aventure**, fortune-teller.
disgrâce /disgrɑs/ *n.f.* disgrace.
disgracieu|x, ~**se** /disgrasjø, -z/ *a.*
ungainly.
disjoindre /disʒwɛ̃dr/ *v.t.* take apart. **se**
~ *v. pr.* come apart.
dislo|quer /dislɔke/ *v.t.* (*membre*)
dislocate; (*machine etc.*) break (apart).
se ~**quer** *v. pr.* (*parti*, *cortège*) break
up; (*meuble*) come apart. ~**cation** *n.f.*
(*anat.*) dislocation.
dispar|aître† /disparɛtr/ *v.i.* disappear;
(*mourir*) die. **faire** ~**aître**, get rid of.
~**ition** *n.f.* disappearance; (*mort*)
death. ~**u**, ~**ue** *a.* (*soldat etc.*)
missing. *n.m.*, *f.* missing person; (*mort*)
dead person.
disparate /disparat/ *a.* ill-assorted.
disparité /disparite/ *n.f.* disparity.
dispensaire /dispɑ̃sɛr/ *n.m.* clinic.
dispense /dispɑ̃s/ *n.f.* exemption.
dispenser /dispɑ̃se/ *v.t.* exempt (**de**,
from). **se** ~ **de** (**faire**), avoid (doing).
disperser /dispɛrse/ *v.t.* (*éparpiller*)
scatter; (*répartir*) disperse. **se** ~ *v. pr.*
disperse.
disponib|le /dispɔnibl/ *a.* available.
~**ilité** *n.f.* availability.

dispos, ~e /dispo, -z/ *a.* **frais et ~,** fresh and alert.

disposé /dispoze/ *a.* **bien/mal ~,** in a good/bad mood. **~ à,** prepared to. **~ envers,** disposed towards.

disposer /dispoze/ *v.t.* arrange. **~ à,** (*engager à*) incline to. **—*v.i.* ~ de,** have at one's disposal. **se ~ à,** prepare to.

dispositif /dispozitif/ *n.m.* device; (*plan*) plan of action. **~ anti-parasite,** suppressor.

disposition /dispozisjɔ̃/ *n.f.* arrangement; (*humeur*) mood; (*tendance*) tendency. **~s,** (*préparatifs*) arrangements; (*aptitude*) aptitude. **à la ~ de,** at the disposal of.

disproportionné /disprɔpɔrsjɔne/ *a.* disproportionate.

dispute /dispyt/ *n.f.* quarrel.

disputer /dispyte/ *v.t.* (*match*) play; (*course*) run in; (*prix*) fight for; (*gronder; fam.*) tell off. **se ~** *v. pr.* quarrel; (*se battre pour*) fight over; (*match*) be played.

disquaire /diskɛr/ *n.m./f.* record dealer.

disqualif|ier /diskalifje/ *v.t.* disqualify. **~ication** *n.f.* disqualification.

disque /disk/ *n.m.* (*mus.*) record; (*sport*) discus; (*cercle*) disc, disk. **~ dur,** hard disk.

disquette /diskɛt/ *n.f.* (floppy) disk.

dissection /disɛksjɔ̃/ *n.f.* dissection.

dissemblable /disablabl/ *a.* dissimilar.

disséminer /disemine/ *v.t.* scatter.

disséquer /diseke/ *v.t.* dissect.

dissertation /disɛrtasjɔ̃/ *n.f.* (*scol.*) essay.

disserter /disɛrte/ *v.i.* **~ sur,** comment upon.

dissiden|t, ~te /disidã, -t/ *a. & n.m., f.* dissident. **~ce** *n.f.* dissidence.

dissimul|er /disimyle/ *v.t.* conceal (à, from). **se ~er** *v. pr.* conceal o.s. **~ation** *n.f.* concealment; (*fig.*) deceit.

dissipé /disipe/ *a.* (*élève*) unruly.

dissip|er /disipe/ *v.t.* (*fumée, crainte*) dispel; (*fortune*) squander; (*personne*) lead into bad ways. **se ~er** *v. pr.* disappear. **~ation** *n.f.* squandering; (*indiscipline*) misbehaviour.

dissolution /disɔlysjɔ̃/ *n.f.* dissolution.

dissolvant /disɔlvã/ *n.m.* solvent; (*pour ongles*) nail polish remover.

dissonant, ~e /disɔnã, -t/ *a.* discordant.

dissoudre† /disudr/ *v.t.,* **se ~** *v. pr.* dissolve.

dissua|der /disɥade/ *v.t.* dissuade (de,

from). **~sion** /-ɥazjɔ̃/ *n.f.* dissuasion. **force de ~sion,** deterrent force.

dissuasi|f, ~ve /disɥazif, -v/ *a.* dissuasive.

distance /distãs/ *n.f.* distance; (*écart*) gap. **à ~,** at *ou* from a distance.

distancer /distãse/ *v.t.* leave behind.

distant, ~e /distã, -t/ *a.* distant.

distendre /distãdr/ *v.t.,* **se ~** *v. pr.* distend.

distill|er /distile/ *v.t.* distil. **~ation** *n.f.* distillation.

distillerie /distilri/ *n.f.* distillery.

distinct, ~e /distɛ̃(kt), -ɛkt/ *a.* distinct. **~ement** /-ɛktəmã/ *adv.* distinctly.

distincti|f, ~ve /distɛ̃ktif, -v/ *a.* distinctive.

distinction /distɛ̃ksjɔ̃/ *n.f.* distinction.

distingué /distɛ̃ge/ *a.* distinguished.

distinguer /distɛ̃ge/ *v.t.* distinguish.

distraction /distraksjɔ̃/ *n.f.* absent-mindedness; (*oubli*) lapse; (*passe-temps*) distraction.

distraire† /distrɛr/ *v.t.* amuse; (*rendre inattentif*) distract. **se ~** *v. pr.* amuse o.s.

distrait, ~e /distrɛ, -t/ *a.* absent-minded. **~ement** *a.* absent-mindedly.

distrayant, ~e /distrɛjã, -t/ *a.* entertaining.

distrib|uer /distribɥe/ *v.t.* hand out, distribute; (*répartir, amener*) distribute; (*courrier*) deliver. **~uteur** *n.m.* (*auto., comm.*) distributor. **~uteur (automatique),** vending-machine; (*de billets*) (cash) dispenser. **~ution** *n.f.* distribution; (*du courrier*) delivery; (*acteurs*) cast.

district /distrikt/ *n.m.* district.

dit¹, dites /di, dit/ *voir* **dire.**

dit², ~e /di, dit/ *a.* (*décidé*) agreed; (*surnommé*) called.

diurétique /djyretik/ *a. & n.m.* diuretic.

diurne /djyrn/ *a.* diurnal.

divag|uer /divage/ *v.i.* rave. **~ations** *n.f. pl.* ravings.

divan /divã/ *n.m.* divan.

divergen|t, ~te /divɛrʒã, -t/ *a.* divergent. **~ce** *n.f.* divergence.

diverger /divɛrʒe/ *v.i.* diverge.

divers, ~e /divɛr, -s/ *a.* (*varié*) diverse; (*différent*) various. **~ement** /-səmã/ *adv.* variously.

diversifier /divɛrsifje/ *v.t.* diversify.

diversion /divɛrsjɔ̃/ *n.f.* diversion.

diversité /divɛrsite/ *n.f.* diversity.

divert|ir /divɛrtir/ *v.t.* amuse. **se ~ir**

v. pr. amuse o.s. ~**issement** *n.m.* amusement.

dividende /dividãd/ *n.m.* dividend.

divin, ~**e** /divɛ̃, -in/ *a.* divine.

divinité /divinite/ *n.f.* divinity.

divis|er /divize/ *v.t.,* **se** ~**er** *v. pr.* divide. ~**ion** *n.f.* division.

divorc|e /divɔrs/ *n.m.* divorce. ~**é** ~**ée** *a.* divorced; *n.m., f.* divorcee. ~**er** *v.i.* ~**er (d'avec),** divorce.

divulguer /divylge/ *v.t.* divulge.

dix /dis/ (/di/ *before consonant,* /diz/ *before vowel*) *a. & n.m.* ten. ~**ième** /dizjɛm/ *a. & n.m./f.* tenth.

dix-huit /dizɥit/ *a. & n.m.* eighteen. ~**ième** *a. & n.m./f.* eighteenth.

dix-neu|f /diznœf/ *a. & n.m.* nineteen. ~**vième** *a. & n.m./f.* nineteenth.

dix-sept /disɛt/ *a. & n.m.* seventeen. ~**ième** *a. & n.m./f.* seventeenth.

dizaine /dizɛn/ *n.f.* (about) ten.

docile /dɔsil/ *a.* docile.

docilité /dɔsilite/ *n.f.* docility.

dock /dɔk/ *n.m.* dock.

docker /dɔkɛr/ *n.m.* docker.

doct|eur /dɔktœr/ *n.m.* doctor. ~**oresse** *n.f.* (*fam.*) lady doctor.

doctorat /dɔktɔra/ *n.m.* doctorate.

doctrin|e /dɔktrin/ *n.f.* doctrine. ~**aire** *a.* doctrinaire.

document /dɔkymã/ *n.m.* document. ~**aire** -tɛr/ *a. & n.m.* documentary.

documentaliste /dɔkymãtalist/ *n.m./f.* information officer.

document|er /dɔkymãte/ *v.t.* document. **se** ~**er** *v. pr.* collect information. ~**ation** *n.f.* information, literature. ~**é** *a.* well-documented.

dodo /dodo/ *n.m.* **faire** ~, (*langage enfantin*) go to byebyes.

dodu /dɔdy/ *a.* plump.

dogm|e /dɔgm/ *n.m.* dogma. ~**atique** *a.* dogmatic.

doigt /dwa/ *n.m.* finger. **un** ~ **de,** a drop of. **à deux** ~**s de,** a hair's breadth away from. ~ **de pied,** toe.

doigté /dwate/ *n.m.* (*mus.*) fingering, touch; (*adresse*) tact.

dois, doit /dwa/ *voir* **devoir**[2].

Dolby /dɔlbi/ *n.m. & a.* (P.) Dolby (P.).

doléances /dɔleãs/ *n.f. pl.* grievances.

dollar /dɔlar/ *n.m.* dollar.

domaine /dɔmɛn/ *n.m.* estate, domain; (*fig.*) domain.

dôme /dom/ *n.m.* dome.

domestique /dɔmɛstik/ *a.* domestic. —*n.m./f.* servant.

domestiquer /dɔmɛstike/ *v.t.* domesticate.

domicile /dɔmisil/ *n.m.* home. **à** ~, at home; (*livrer*) to the home.

domicilié /dɔmisilje/ *a.* resident.

domin|er /dɔmine/ *v.t./i.* dominate; (*surplomber*) tower over, dominate; (*équipe*) dictate the game (to). ~**ant,** ~**ante** *a.* dominant; *n.f.* dominant feature. ~**ation** *n.f.* domination.

domino /dɔmino/ *n.m.* domino.

dommage /dɔmaʒ/ *n.m.* (*tort*) harm. ~**(s),** (*dégâts*) damage. **c'est** ~, it's a pity. **quel** ~, what a shame. ~**s-intérêts** *n.m. pl.* (*jurid.*) damages.

dompt|er /dõte/ *v.t.* tame. ~**eur,** ~**euse** *n.m., f.* tamer.

don /dõ/ *n.m.* (*cadeau, aptitude*) gift.

dona|teur, ~**trice** /dɔnatœr, -tris/ *n.m., f.* donor.

donation /dɔnasjõ/ *n.f.* donation.

donc /dõ(k)/ *conj.* so, then; (*par conséquent*) so, therefore.

donjon /dõʒõ/ *n.m.* (*tour*) keep.

donné /dɔne/ *a.* (*fixé*) given; (*pas cher: fam.*) dirt cheap. **étant** ~ **que,** given that.

données /dɔne/ *n.f. pl.* (*de science*) data; (*de problème*) facts.

donner /dɔne/ *v.t.* give; (*vieilles affaires*) give away; (*distribuer*) give out; (*récolte etc.*) produce; (*film*) show; (*pièce*) put on. —*v.i.* ~ **sur,** look out on to. ~ **dans,** (*piège*) fall into. **ça donne soif/faim,** it makes one thirsty/hungry. ~ **à réparer/***etc.*, take to be repaired/*etc.* ~ **lieu à,** give rise to. **se** ~ **à,** devote o.s. to. **se** ~ **du mal,** go to a lot of trouble (**pour faire,** to do).

donneu|r, ~**se** /dɔnœr, -øz/ *n.m., f.* (*de sang*) donor.

dont /dõ/ *pron. rel.* (*chose*) whose, of which; (*personne*) whose; (*partie d'un tout*) of whom; (*chose*) of which; (*provenance*) from which; (*manière*) in which. **le père** ~ **la fille,** the father whose daughter. **ce** ~, what. ~ **il a besoin,** which he needs. **l'enfant** ~ **il est fier,** the child he is proud of. **trois enfants** ~ **deux sont jumeaux,** three children, two of whom are twins.

dopage /dɔpaʒ/ *n.m.* doping.

doper /dɔpe/ *v.t.* dope. **se** ~ *v. pr.* take dope.

doré /dɔre/ *a.* (*couleur d'or*) golden; (*avec dorure*) gold. **la bourgeoisie** ~**e** the affluent middle class.

dorénavant /dɔrenavã/ *adv.* henceforth.

dorer /dɔre/ *v.t.* gild; (*culin.*) brown.

dorloter /dɔrlɔte/ *v.t.* pamper.

dorm|ir† /dɔrmir/ *v.i.* sleep; (*être*

endormi) be asleep. ~eur, ~euse *n.m.*, *f.* sleeper. il dort debout, he can't keep awake. une histoire à ~ir debout, a cock-and-bull story.

dortoir /dɔrtwar/ *n.m.* dormitory.

dorure /dɔryr/ *n.f.* gilding.

dos /do/ *n.m.* back; (*de livre*) spine. à ~ de, riding on. de ~, from behind. ~ crawlé, backstroke.

dos|e /doz/ *n.f.* dose. ~age *n.m.* (*mélange*) mixture. faire le ~age de, measure out; balance. ~er *v.t.* measure out; (*équilibrer*) balance.

dossard /dɔsar/ *n.m.* (*sport*) number.

dossier /dɔsje/ *n.m.* (*documents*) file; (*de chaise*) back.

dot /dɔt/ *n.f.* dowry.

doter /dɔte/ *v.t.* ~ de, equip with.

douan|e /dwan/ *n.f.* customs. ~ier, ~ière *a.* customs; *n.m.*, *f.* customs officer.

doubl|e /dubl/ *a. & adv.* double. —*n.m.* (*copie*) duplicate; (*sosie*) double. le ~e (de), twice as much *ou* as many (as). le ~ emessieurs, the men's doubles. ~e décimètre, ruler. ~ement[1] *adv.* doubly.

doubl|er /duble/ *v.t./i.* double; (*dépasser*) overtake; (*vêtement*) line; (*film*) dub; (*classe*) repeat; (*cap*) round. ~ement[2] *n.m.* doubling. ~ure *n.f.* (*étoffe*) lining; (*acteur*) understudy.

douce /dus/ *voir* doux.

douceâtre /dusɑtr/ *a.* sickly sweet.

doucement /dusmɑ̃/ *adv.* gently.

douceur /dusœr/ *n.f.* (*mollesse*) softness; (*de climat*) mildness; (*de personne*) gentleness; (*joie, plaisir*) sweetness. ~s, (*friandises*) sweet things. en ~, smoothly.

douch|e /duʃ/ *n.f.* shower. ~er *v.t.* give a shower to. se ~er *v. pr.* have *ou* take a shower.

doudoune /dudun/ *n.f.* (*fam.*) anorak.

doué /dwe/ *a.* gifted. ~ de, endowed with.

douille /duj/ *n.f.* (*électr.*) socket.

douillet, ~te /dujɛ, -t/ *a.* cosy, comfortable; (*personne: péj.*) soft.

doul|eur /dulœr/ *n.f.* pain; (*chagrin*) grief. ~oureux, ~oureuse *a.* painful. la ~oureuse *n.f.* the bill.

doute /dut/ *n.m.* doubt. sans ~, no doubt. sans aucun ~, without doubt.

douter /dute/ *v.i.* ~ de, doubt. se ~ de, suspect.

douteu|x, ~se /dutø, -z/ *a.* doubtful.

Douvres /duvr/ *n.m./f.* Dover.

doux, douce /du, dus/ *a.* (*moelleux*) soft;

(*sucré*) sweet; (*clément, pas fort*) mild; (*pas brusque, bienveillant*) gentle.

douzaine /duzɛn/ *n.f.* about twelve; (*douze*) dozen. une ~ d'œufs/*etc.*, a dozen eggs/*etc.*

douz|e /duz/ *a. & n.m.* twelve. ~ième *a. & n.m./f.* twelfth.

doyen, ~ne /dwajɛ̃, -jɛn/ *n.m.*, *f.* dean; (*en âge*) most senior person.

dragée /draʒe/ *n.f.* sugared almond.

dragon /dragɔ̃/ *n.m.* dragon.

dragu|e /drag/ *n.f.* (*bateau*) dredger. ~er *v.t.* (*rivière*) dredge; (*filles: fam.*) chat up, try to pick up.

drain /drɛ̃/ *n.m.* drain.

drainer /drene/ *v.t.* drain.

dramatique /dramatik/ *a.* dramatic; (*tragique*) tragic. —*n.f.* (television) drama.

dramatiser /dramatize/ *v.t.* dramatize.

dramaturge /dramatyrʒ/ *n.m./f.* dramatist.

drame /dram/ *n.m.* drama.

drap /dra/ *n.m.* sheet; (*tissu*) (woollen) cloth. ~-housse /draus/ *n.m.* fitted sheet.

drapeau (*pl.* ~x) /drapo/ *n.m.* flag.

draper /drape/ *v.t.* drape.

dress|er /drese/ *v.t.* put up, erect; (*tête*) raise; (*animal*) train; (*liste*) draw up. se ~er *v. pr.* (*bâtiment etc.*) stand; (*personne*) draw o.s. up. ~er l'oreille, prick up one's ears. ~age /dresaʒ/ *n.m.* training. ~eur, ~euse /drescœr, -øz/ *n.m.*, *f.* trainer.

dribbler /drible/ *v.t./i.* (*sport*) dribble.

drille /drij/ *n.m.* un joyeux ~, a cheery character.

drive /drajv/ *n.m.* (*comput.*) drive.

drogue /drɔg/ *n.f.* drug. la ~, drugs.

drogu|er /drɔge/ *v.t.* (*malade*) drug heavily, dose up; (*victime*) drug. se ~er *v. pr.* take drugs. ~é, ~ée *n.m.*, *f.* drug addict.

drogu|erie /drɔgri/ *n.f.* hardware and chemist's shop; (*Amer.*) drugstore. ~iste *n.m./f.* owner of a *droguerie*.

droit[1], ~e /drwa, -t/ *a.* (*non courbe*) straight; (*loyal*) upright; (*angle*) right. —*adv.* straight. *n.f.* straight line.

droit[2] ~e /drwa, -t/ *a.* (*contraire de gauche*) right. à ~e, on the right; (*direction*) (to the) right. la ~e, the right (side); (*pol.*) the right (wing). ~ier, ~ière /-tje, -tjɛr/ *a. & n.m.*, *f.* right-handed (person).

droit[3] /drwa/ *n.m.* right. ~(s), (*taxe*) duty; (*d'inscription*) fee(s). le ~, (*jurid.*) law. avoir ~ à, be entitled to.

avoir le ⁓ de, be allowed to. être dans
son ⁓, be in the right. ⁓ d'auteur,
copyright. ⁓s d'auteur, royalties.

drôle /drol/ *a.* funny. ⁓ d'air, funny
look. ⁓ment *adv.* funnily; (*extrêmement: fam.*) dreadfully.

dromadaire /drɔmadɛr/ *n.m.* dromedary.

dru /dry/ *a.* thick. **tomber** ⁓, fall thick
and fast.

drugstore /drœgstɔr/ *n.m.* drugstore.

du /dy/ *voir* **de**.

dû, due /dy/ *voir* **devoir**². —*a.* due.
—*n.m.* due; (*argent*) dues. **du à,** due to.

duc, duchesse /dyk, dyʃɛs/ *n.m., f.* duke,
duchess.

duel /dɥɛl/ *n.m.* duel.

dune /dyn/ *n.f.* dune.

duo /dɥo/ *n.m.* (*mus.*) duet; (*fig.*) duo.

dup|e /dyp/ *n.f.* dupe. ⁓er *v.t.* dupe.

duplex /dyplɛks/ *n.m.* split-level apartment; (*Amer.*) duplex; (*émission*) link-
up.

duplicata /dyplikata/ *n.m. invar.* duplicate.

duplicité /dyplisite/ *n.f.* duplicity.

duquel /dykɛl/ *voir* **lequel**.

dur /dyr/ *a.* hard; (*sévère*) harsh, hard;
(*viande*) tough, hard; (*col, brosse*) stiff.
—*adv.* hard. —*n.m.* tough guy. ⁓
d'oreille, hard of hearing.

durable /dyrabl/ *a.* lasting.

durant /dyrã/ *prép.* during; (*mesure de
temps*) for.

durc|ir /dyrsir/ *v.t./i.*, **se** ⁓**ir** *v. pr.*
harden. ⁓issement *n.m.* hardening.

dure /dyr/ *n.f.* à la ⁓, the hard way.

durée /dyre/ *n.f.* length; (*période*)
duration.

durement /dyrmã/ *adv.* harshly.

durer /dyre/ *v.i.* last.

dureté /dyrte/ *n.f.* hardness; (*sévérité*)
harshness.

duvet /dyvɛ/ *n.m.* down; (*sac*) (down-
filled) sleeping-bag.

dynami|que /dinamik/ *a.* dynamic.
⁓sme *n.m.* dynamism.

dynamit|e /dinamit/ *n.f.* dynamite. ⁓er
v.t. dynamite.

dynamo /dinamo/ *n.f.* dynamo.

dynastie /dinasti/ *n.f.* dynasty.

dysenterie /disãtri/ *n.f.* dysentery.

E

eau (*pl.* ⁓**x**) /o/ *n.f.* water. ⁓

courante/dormante, running/still
water. ⁓ de Cologne, eau-de-Cologne.
⁓ dentifrice, mouthwash. ⁓ de
toilette, toilet water. ⁓-de-vie (*pl.* ⁓x-
de-vie) *n.f.* brandy. ⁓ douce/salée,
fresh/salt water. ⁓-forte (*pl.* ⁓x-
fortes) *n.f.* etching. ⁓ potable, drinking
water. ⁓ de Javel, bleach. ⁓ minérale,
mineral water. ⁓ gazeuse, fizzy water.
⁓ plate, still water. ⁓x usées, dirty
water. **tomber à l'**⁓, (*fig.*) fall through.
prendre l'⁓, take in water.

ébahi /ebai/ *a.* dumbfounded.

ébattre (s') /(s)ebatr/ *v. pr.* frolic.

ébauch|e /eboʃ/ *n.f.* outline. ⁓er *v.t.*
outline. **s'**⁓**er** *v. pr.* form.

ébène /ebɛn/ *n.f.* ebony.

ébéniste /ebenist/ *n.m.* cabinet-maker.

éberlué /ebɛrlɥe/ *a.* flabbergasted.

éblou|ir /ebluir/ *v.t.* dazzle. ⁓issement
n.m. dazzle, dazzling; (*malaise*) dizzy
turn.

éboueur /ebwœr/ *n.m.* dustman; (*Amer.*)
garbage collector.

ébouillanter /ebujãte/ *v.t.* scald.

éboul|er (s') /(s)ebule/ *v. pr.* crumble,
collapse. ⁓ement *n.m.* landslide. ⁓is
n.m. pl. fallen rocks and earth.

ébouriffé /eburife/ *a.* dishevelled.

ébranler /ebrɑ̃le/ *v.t.* shake. **s'**⁓ *v. pr.*
move off.

ébrécher /ebreʃe/ *v.t.* chip.

ébriété /ebrijete/ *n.f.* intoxication.

ébrouer (s') /(s)ebrue/ *v. pr.* shake o.s.

ébruiter /ebrɥite/ *v.t.* spread about.

ébullition /ebylisjɔ̃/ *n.f.* boiling. **en** ⁓,
boiling.

écaille /ekaj/ *n.f.* (*de poisson*) scale; (*de
peinture, roc*) flake; (*matière*) tortoiseshell.

écailler /ekaje/ *v.t.* (*poisson*) scale. **s'**⁓
v. pr. flake (off).

écarlate /ekarlat/ *a. & n.f.* scarlet.

écarquiller /ekarkije/ *v.t.* ⁓ les yeux,
open one's eyes wide.

écart /ekar/ *n.m.* gap; (*de prix etc.*)
difference; (*embardée*) swerve; (*de
conduite*) lapse (**de,** in). **à l'**⁓, out of
the way. **tenir à l'**⁓, (*participant*) keep
out of things. **à l'**⁓ **de,** away from.

écarté /ekarte/ *a.* (*lieu*) remote. **les
jambes** ⁓**es,** (with) legs apart. **les bras**
⁓**s,** with one's arms out.

écartement /ekartəmã/ *n.m.* gap.

écarter /ekarte/ *v.t.* (*objets*) move apart;
(*ouvrir*) open; (*éliminer*) dismiss. ⁓
qch. de, move sth. away from. ⁓ **qn.
de,** keep s.o. away from. **s'**⁓ *v. pr.*
(*s'éloigner*) move away; (*quitter son*

chemin) move aside. **s'~ de,** stray from.

ecchymose /ekimoz/ *n.f.* bruise.

ecclésiastique /eklezjastik/ *a.* ecclesiastical. —*n.m.* clergyman.

écervelé, **~e** /esɛrvəle/ *a.* scatter-brained. —*n.m., f.* scatter-brain.

échafaud|age /eʃafodaʒ/ *n.m.* scaffolding; (*amas*) heap. **~er** *v.t.* (*projets*) construct.

échalote /eʃalɔt/ *n.f.* shallot.

échang|e /eʃɑ̃ʒ/ *n.m.* exchange. **en ~e (de),** in exchange (for). **~er** *v.t.* exchange (**contre,** for).

échangeur /eʃɑ̃ʒœr/ *n.m.* (*auto.*) interchange.

échantillon /eʃɑ̃tijɔ̃/ *n.m.* sample. **~nage** /-jɔnaʒ/ *n.m.* range of samples.

échappatoire /eʃapatwar/ *n.f.* (*clever*) way out.

échappée /eʃape/ *n.f.* (*sport*) breakaway.

échappement /eʃapmɑ̃/ *n.m.* exhaust.

échapp|er /eʃape/ *v.i.* **~ à,** escape; (*en fuyant*) escape (from). **s'~** *v. pr.* escape. **~ des mains de** *ou* **à,** slip out of the hands of. **l'~ belle,** have a narrow *ou* lucky escape.

écharde /eʃard/ *n.f.* splinter.

écharpe /eʃarp/ *n.f.* scarf; (*de maire*) sash. **en ~,** (*bras*) in a sling.

échasse /eʃas/ *n.f.* stilt.

échassier /eʃasje/ *n.m.* wader.

échaud|er /eʃode/ *v.t.* **se faire ~er, être ~é,** get one's fingers burnt.

échauffer /eʃofe/ *v.t.* heat; (*fig.*) excite. **s'~** *v. pr.* warm up.

échauffourée /eʃofure/ *n.f.* (*mil.*) skirmish; (*bagarre*) scuffle.

échéance /eʃeɑ̃s/ *n.f.* due date (for payment); (*délai*) deadline; (*obligation*) (financial) commitment.

échéant (le cas) /(ləkaz)eʃeɑ̃/ *adv.* if the occasion arises, possibly.

échec /eʃɛk/ *n.m.* failure. **~s,** (*jeu*) chess. **~ et mat,** checkmate. **en ~,** in check.

échelle /eʃɛl/ *n.f.* ladder; (*dimension*) scale.

échelon /eʃlɔ̃/ *n.m.* rung; (*de fonctionnaire*) grade; (*niveau*) level.

échelonner /eʃlɔne/ *v.t.* spread out, space out.

échevelé /eʃəvle/ *a.* dishevelled.

échine /eʃin/ *n.f.* backbone.

échiquier /eʃikje/ *n.m.* chessboard.

écho /eko/ *n.m.* echo. **~s,** (*dans la presse*) gossip.

échographie /ekɔgrafi/ *n.f.* ultrasound (scan).

échoir /eʃwar/ *v.i.* (*dette*) fall due; (*délai*) expire.

échoppe /eʃɔp/ *n.f.* stall.

échouer¹ /eʃwe/ *v.i.* fail.

échouer² /eʃwe/ *v.t.* (*bateau*) ground. —*v.i.,* **s'~** *v. pr.* run aground.

échu /eʃy/ *a.* (*delai*) expired.

éclabouss|er /eklabuse/ *v.t.* splash. **~ure** *n.f.* splash.

éclair /eklɛr/ *n.m.* (flash of) lightning; (*fig.*) flash; (*gâteau*) éclair. —*a. invar.* lightning.

éclairag|e /eklɛraʒ/ *n.m.* lighting; (*point de vue*) light. **~iste** /-aʒist/ *n.* lighting technician.

éclaircie /eklɛrsi/ *n.f.* sunny interval.

éclairc|ir /eklɛrsir/ *v.t.* make lighter; (*mystère*) clear up. **s'~ir** *v. pr.* (*ciel*) clear; (*mystère*) become clearer. **~issement** *n.m.* clarification.

éclairer /eklere/ *v.t.* light (up); (*personne*) give some light to; (*fig.*) enlighten; (*situation*) throw light on. —*v.i.* give light. **s'~** *v. pr.* become clearer. **s'~ à la bougie,** use candle-light.

éclaireu|r, **~se** /eklɛrœr, -øz/ *n.m., f.* (boy) scout, (girl) guide. —*n.m.* (*mil.*) scout.

éclat /ekla/ *n.m.* fragment; (*de lumière*) brightness; (*de rire*) (out)burst; (*splendeur*) brilliance.

éclatant, **~e** /eklatɑ̃, -t/ *a.* brilliant.

éclat|er /eklate/ *v.i.* burst; (*exploser*) go off; (*verre*) shatter; (*guerre*) break out; (*groupe*) split up. **~er de rire,** burst out laughing. **~ement** *n.m.* bursting; (*de bombe*) explosion; (*scission*) split.

éclipse /eklips/ *n.f.* eclipse.

éclipser /eklipse/ *v.t.* eclipse. **s'~** *v. pr.* slip away.

écl|ore /eklɔr/ *v.i.* (*œuf*) hatch; (*fleur*) open. **~osion** *n.f.* hatching; opening.

écluse /eklyz/ *n.f.* (*de canal*) lock.

écœurant, **~e** /ekœrɑ̃, -t/ *a.* (*gâteau*) sickly; (*fig.*) disgusting.

écœurer /ekœre/ *v.t.* sicken.

école /ekɔl/ *n.f.* school. **~ maternelle/ primaire / secondaire,** nursery/ primary / secondary school. **~ normale,** teachers' training college.

écol|ier, **~ière** /ekɔlje, -jɛr/ *n.m., f.* schoolboy, schoolgirl.

écolo /ekɔlo/ *a. & n.m./f.* green.

écolog|ie /ekɔlɔʒi/ *n.f.* ecology. **~ique** *a.* ecological, green.

écologiste /ekɔlɔʒist/ *n.m./f.* ecologist.
éconduire /ekɔ̃dyir/ *v.t.* dismiss.
économat /ekɔnɔma/ *n.m.* bursary.
économe /ekɔnɔm/ *a.* thrifty. —*n.m./f.* bursar.
économ|ie /ekɔnɔmi/ *n.f.* economy. **∼ies,** (*argent*) savings. **une ∼ie de,** (*gain*) a saving of. **∼ie politique,** economics. **∼ique** *a.* (*pol.*) economic; (*bon marché*) economical. **∼iser** *v.t./i.* save. **∼iste** *n.m./f.* economist.
écoper /ekɔpe/ *v.t.* bail out. **∼ (de),** (*fam.*) get.
écorce /ekɔrs/ *n.f.* bark; (*de fruit*) peel.
écorch|er /ekɔrʃe/ *v.t.* graze; (*animal*) skin. **s'∼er** *v. pr.* graze o.s. **∼ure** *n.f.* graze.
écossais, ∼e /ekɔsɛ, -z/ *a.* Scottish. —*n.m., f.* Scot.
Écosse /ekɔs/ *n.f.* Scotland.
écosser /ekɔse/ *v.t.* shell.
écosystème /ekɔsistɛm/ *n.m.* ecosystem.
écouler[1] /ekule/ *v.t.* dispose of, sell.
écoul|er[2] **(s')** /(s)ekule/ *v. pr.* flow (out), run (off); (*temps*) pass. **∼ement** *n.m.* flow.
écourter /ekurte/ *v.t.* shorten.
écoute /ekut/ *n.f.* listening. **à l'∼ (de),** listening in to. **aux ∼s,** attentive. **heures de grande ∼,** peak time. **∼s téléphoniques,** phone tapping.
écout|er /ekute/ *v.t.* listen to; (*radio*) listen (in) to. —*v.i.* listen. **∼eur** *n.m.* earphones; (*de téléphone*) receiver.
écran /ekrɑ̃/ *n.m.* screen. **∼ total,** sunblock.
écrasant, ∼e /ekrɑzɑ̃, -t/ *a.* overwhelming.
écraser /ekraze/ *v.t.* crush; (*piéton*) run over. **s'∼** *v. pr.* crash (**contre,** into).
écrémé /ekreme/ *a.* **lait ∼,** skimmed milk. **lait demi-∼,** semi-skimmed milk.
écrevisse /ekrəvis/ *n.f.* crayfish.
écrier (s') /(s)ekrije/ *v. pr.* exclaim.
écrin /ekrɛ̃/ *n.m.* case.
écrire† /ekrir/ *v.t./i.* write; (*orthographier*) spell. **s'∼** *v. pr.* (*mot*) be spelt.
écrit /ekri/ *n.m.* document; (*examen*) written paper. **par ∼,** in writing.
écriteau (*pl.* **∼x**) /ekrito/ *n.m.* notice.
écriture /ekrityr/ *n.f.* writing. **∼s,** (*comm.*) accounts. **l'É∼ (sainte),** the Scriptures.
écrivain /ekrivɛ̃/ *n.m.* writer.
écrou /ekru/ *n.m.* nut.
écrouer /ekrue/ *v.t.* imprison.
écrouler (s') /(s)ekrule/ *v. pr.* collapse.

écru /ekry/ *a.* (*couleur*) natural; (*tissu*) raw.
Écu /eky/ *n.m. invar.* ecu.
écueil /ekœj/ *n.m.* reef; (*fig.*) danger.
éculé /ekyle/ *a.* (*soulier*) worn at the heel; (*fig.*) well-worn.
écume /ekym/ *n.f.* foam; (*culin.*) scum.
écum|er /ekyme/ *v.t.* skim; (*piller*) plunder. —*v.i.* foam. **∼oire** *n.f.* skimmer.
écureuil /ekyrœj/ *n.m.* squirrel.
écurie /ekyri/ *n.f.* stable.
écuy|er, ∼ère /ekɥije, -jɛr/ *n.m., f.* (horse) rider.
eczéma /ɛgzema/ *n.m.* eczema.
édenté /edɑ̃te/ *a.* toothless.
édifice /edifis/ *n.m.* building.
édif|ier /edifje/ *v.t.* construct; (*porter à la vertu, éclairer*) edify. **∼ication** *n.f.* construction; edification.
édit /edi/ *n.m.* edict.
édi|ter /edite/ *v.t.* publish; (*annoter*) edit. **∼teur, ∼trice** *n.m., f.* publisher; editor.
édition /edisjɔ̃/ *n.f.* edition; (*industrie*) publishing.
éditor|ial (*pl.* **∼iaux**) /editɔrjal, -jo/ *n.m.* editorial.
édredon /edrədɔ̃/ *n.m.* eiderdown.
éducateur, ∼trice /edykatœr, -tris/ *n.m., f.* teacher.
éducati|f, ∼ve /edykatif, -v/ *a.* educational.
éducation /edykasjɔ̃/ *n.f.* education; (*dans la famille*) upbringing; (*manières*) manners. **∼ physique,** physical education.
édulcorant /edylkɔrɑ̃/ *n.m. & a.* (**produit**) **∼,** sweetener.
éduquer /edyke/ *v.t.* educate; (*à la maison*) bring up.
effac|é /efase/ *a.* (*modeste*) unassuming. **∼ement** *n.m.* unassuming manner; (*suppression*) erasure.
effacer /efase/ *v.t.* (*gommer*) rub out; (*par lavage*) wash out; (*souvenir etc.*) erase. **s'∼** *v. pr.* fade; (*s'écarter*) step aside.
effar|er /efare/ *v.t.* alarm. **∼ement** *n.m.* alarm.
effaroucher /efaruʃe/ *v.t.* scare away.
effecti|f[1]**, ∼ve** /efɛktif, -v/ *a.* effective. **∼vement** *adv.* effectively; (*en effet*) indeed.
effectif[2] /efɛktif/ *n.m.* size, strength. **∼s,** numbers.
effectuer /efɛktɥe/ *v.t.* carry out, make.
efféminé /efemine/ *a.* effeminate.
effervescen|t, ∼te /efɛrvesɑ̃, -t/ *a.*

comprimé ~**t,** effervescent tablet. ~**ce**
n.f. excitement.
effet /efɛ/ *n.m.* effect; (*impression*)
impression. ~**s,** (*habits*) clothes,
things. **en** ~, indeed. **faire de l'**~, have
an effect, be effective. **faire
bon/mauvais** ~, make a good/bad
impression.
efficac|e (s') /efikas/ *a.* effective; (*personne*)
efficient. ~**ité** *n.f.* effectiveness;
efficiency.
effigie /efiʒi/ *n.f.* effigy.
effilocher (s') /(s)efiloʃe/ *v. pr.* fray.
cfflanqué /eflɑ̃ke/ *a.* emaciated.
effleurer /eflœre/ *v.t.* touch lightly;
(*sujet*) touch on; (*se présenter à*) occur
to.
effluves /eflyv/ *n.m. pl.* exhalations.
effondr|er (s') /(s)efɔ̃dre/ *v. pr.* collapse.
~**ement** *n.m.* collapse.
efforcer (s') /(s)eforse/ *v. pr.* try (hard)
(**de,** to).
effort /efor/ *n.m.* effort.
effraction /efraksjɔ̃/ *n.f.* **entrer par** ~,
break in.
effray|er /efreje/ *v.t.* frighten;
(*décourager*) put off. **s'**~**er** *v. pr.* be
frightened. ~**ant,** ~**ante** *a.* frighten-
ing; (*fig.*) frightful.
effréné /efrene/ *a.* wild.
effriter (s') /(s)efrite/ *v. pr.* crumble.
effroi /efrwa/ *n.m.* dread.
effronté /efrɔ̃te/ *a.* impudent.
effroyable /efrwajabl/ *a.* dreadful.
effusion /efyzjɔ̃/ *n.f.* ~ **de sang,**
bloodshed.
ég|al, ~**ale** (*m. pl.* ~**aux**) /egal, -o/
equal; (*surface, vitesse*) even. —*n.m.,*
f. equal. **ça m'est/lui est** ~**al,** it is all
the same to me/him. **sans égal,**
matchless. **d'**~ **à égal,** between equals.
également /egalmɑ̃/ *adv.* equally,
(*aussi*) as well.
égaler /egale/ *v.t.* equal.
égaliser /egalize/ *v.t./i.* (*sport*) equalize;
(*niveler*) level out; (*cheveux*) trim.
égalit|é /egalite/ *n.f.* equality; (*de
surface, d'humeur*) evenness. **à** ~**é** (**de
points**), equal. ~**aire** *a.* egalitarian.
égard /egar/ *n.m.* regard. ~**s,** consideration. **à cet** ~, in this respect. **à l'**~ **de,**
with regard to; (*envers*) towards. **eu** ~
à, in view of.
égar|er /egare/ *v.t.* mislay; (*tromper*)
lead astray. **s'**~**er** *v. pr.* get lost; (*se
tromper*) go astray. ~**ement** *n.m.* loss;
(*affolement*) confusion.
égayer /egeje/ *v.t.* (*personne*) cheer up;
(*pièce*) brighten up.

égide /eʒid/ *n.f.* aegis.
églantier /eglɑ̃tje/ *n.m.* wild
rose(-bush).
églefin /egləfɛ̃/ *n.m.* haddock.
église /egliz/ *n.f.* church.
égoïs|te /egoist/ *a.* selfish. —*n.m./f.*
egoist. ~**me** *n.m.* selfishness, ego-
ism.
égorger /egɔrʒe/ *v.t.* slit the throat of.
égosiller (s') /(s)egozije/ *v. pr.* shout
one's head off.
égout /egu/ *n.m.* sewer.
égoutt|er /egute/ *v.t./i.,* **s'**~**er** *v. pr.*
(*vaisselle*) drain. ~**oir** *n.m.* draining-
board; (*panier*) dish drainer.
égratign|er /egratiɲe/ *v.t.* scratch. ~**ure**
n.f. scratch.
égrener /egrəne/ *v.t.* (*raisins*) pick off;
(*notes*) sound one by one.
Égypte /eʒipt/ *n.f.* Egypt.
égyptien, ~**ne** /eʒipsjɛ̃, -jɛn/ *a. & n.m.,*
f. Egyptian.
eh /e/ *int.* hey. **eh bien,** well.
éjacul|er /eʒakyle/ *v.i.* ejaculate. ~**ation**
n.f. ejaculation.
éjectable *a.* **siège** ~, ejector seat.
éjecter /eʒɛkte/ *v.t.* eject.
élabor|er /elabɔre/ *v.t.* elaborate.
~**ation** *n.f.* elaboration.
élaguer /elage/ *v.t.* prune.
élan[1] /elɑ̃/ *n.m.* (*sport*) run-up; (*vitesse*)
momentum; (*fig.*) surge.
élan[2] /elɑ̃/ *n.m.* (*animal*) moose.
élancé /elɑ̃se/ *a.* slender.
élancement /elɑ̃smɑ̃/ *n.m.* twinge.
élancer (s') /(s)elɑ̃se/ *v. pr.* leap forward,
dash; (*se dresser*) soar.
élarg|ir /elarʒir/ *v.t.,* **s'**~**ir** *v. pr.* widen.
~**issement** *n.m.* widening.
élasti|que /elastik/ *a.* elastic. —*n.m.*
elastic band; (*tissu*) elastic. ~**cité** *n.f.*
elasticity.
élec|teur, ~**trice** /elɛktœr, -tris/ *n.m.,*
f. voter, elector.
élection /elɛksjɔ̃/ *n.f.* election.
élector|al (*m. pl.* ~**aux**) /elɛktɔral, -o/
a. (*réunion etc.*) election; (*collège*)
electoral.
électorat /elɛktɔra/ *n.m.* electorate,
voters.
électricien /elɛktrisjɛ̃/ *n.m.* electrician.
électricité /elɛktrisite/ *n.f.* electricity.
électrifier /elɛktrifje/ *v.t.* electrify.
électrique /elɛktrik/ *a.* electric(al).
électrocuter /elɛktrɔkyte/ *v.t.* electrocute.
électroménager /elɛktrɔmenaʒe/ *n.m.*
l'~, household appliances.
électron /elɛktrɔ̃/ *n.m.* electron.

électronique /elɛktrɔnik/ *a.* electronic.
—*n.f.* electronics.

électrophone /elɛktrɔfɔn/ *n.m.* record-player.

élég|ant, ~ante /elegɑ̃, -t/ *a.* elegant.
~amment *adv.* elegantly. **~ance** *n.f.*
elegance.

élément /elemɑ̃/ *n.m.* element; (*meuble*)
unit. **~aire** /-tɛr/ *a.* elementary.

éléphant /elefɑ̃/ *n.m.* elephant.

élevage /ɛlvaʒ/ *n.m.* (stock-)breeding.

élévation /elevɑsjɔ̃/ *n.f.* raising; (*hausse*)
rise; (*plan*) elevation.

élève /elɛv/ *n.m./f.* pupil.

élevé /ɛlve/ *a.* high; (*noble*) elevated.
bien ~, well-mannered.

élever /ɛlve/ *v.t.* raise; (*enfants*) bring up,
raise; (*animal*) breed. **s'~** *v. pr.* rise;
(*dans le ciel*) soar up. **s'~ à,** amount to.

éleveu|r, ~se /ɛlvœr, -øz/ *n.m., f.*
(stock-)breeder.

éligible /eliʒibl/ *a.* eligible.

élimé /elime/ *a.* worn thin.

élimin|er /elimine/ *v.t.* eliminate.
~ation *n.f.* elimination. **~atoire** *a.*
eliminating; *n.f.* (*sport*) heat.

élire† /elir/ *v.t.* elect.

élite /elit/ *n.f.* élite.

elle /ɛl/ *pron.* she; (*complément*) her;
(*chose*) it. **~-même** *pron.* herself;
itself.

elles /ɛl/ *pron.* they; (*complément*) them.
~-mêmes *pron.* themselves.

ellip|se /elips/ *n.f.* ellipse. **~tique** *a.*
elliptical.

élocution /elɔkysjɔ̃/ *n.f.* diction.

élog|e /elɔʒ/ *n.m.* praise. **faire l'~e de,**
praise. **~ieux, ~ieuse** *a.* laudatory.

éloigné /elwaɲe/ *a.* distant. **~ de,** far
away from. **parent ~,** distant relative.

éloign|er /elwaɲe/ *v.t.* take away *ou*
remove (**de,** from); (*personne aimée*)
estrange (**de,** from); (*danger*) ward off;
(*visite*) put off. **s'~er** *v. pr.* go *ou* move
away (**de,** from); (*affectivement*) become estranged (**de,** from). **~ement**
n.m. removal; (*distance*) distance;
(*oubli*) estrangement.

élongation /elɔ̃gɑsjɔ̃/ *n.f.* strained
muscle.

éloquen|t, ~te /elɔkɑ̃, -t/ *a.* eloquent.
~ce *n.f.* eloquence.

élu, ~e /ely/ *a.* elected. —*n.m., f.* (*pol.*)
elected representative.

élucider /elyside/ *v.t.* elucidate.

éluder /elyde/ *v.t.* elude.

émacié /emasje/ *a.* emaciated.

ém|ail (*pl.* **~aux**) /emaj, -o/ *n.m.*
enamel.

émaillé /emaje/ *a.* enamelled. **~ de,**
studded with.

émancip|er /emɑ̃sipe/ *v.t.* emancipate.
s'~er *v. pr.* become emancipated.
~ation *n.f.* emancipation.

éman|er /emane/ *v.i.* emanate. **~ation**
n.f. emanation.

émarger /emarʒe/ *v.t.* initial.

emball|er /ɑ̃bale/ *v.t.* pack, wrap;
(*personne: fam.*) enthuse. **s'~er** *v. pr.*
(*moteur*) race; (*cheval*) bolt;
(*personne*) get carried away. **~age** *n.m.*
package, wrapping.

embarcadère /ɑ̃barkadɛr/ *n.m.* landing-
stage.

embarcation /ɑ̃barkɑsjɔ̃/ *n.f.* boat.

embardée /ɑ̃barde/ *n.f.* swerve.

embargo /ɑ̃bargo/ *n.m.* embargo.

embarqu|er /ɑ̃barke/ *v.t.* embark;
(*charger*) load; (*emporter: fam.*) cart
off. —*v.i.*, **s'~er** *v. pr.* board, embark.
s'~er dans, embark upon. **~ement**
n.m. embarkation; loading.

embarras /ɑ̃bara/ *n.m.* obstacle; (*gêne*)
embarrassment; (*difficulté*) difficulty.

embarrasser /ɑ̃barase/ *v.t.* clutter (up);
(*gêner dans les mouvements*) hinder;
(*fig.*) embarrass. **s'~ de,** burden o.s.
with.

embauch|e /ɑ̃boʃ/ *n.f.* hiring; (*emploi*)
employment. **~er** *v.t.* hire, take on.

embauchoir /ɑ̃boʃwar/ *n.m.* shoe tree.

embaumer /ɑ̃bome/ *v.t./i.* (make) smell
fragrant; (*cadavre*) embalm.

embellir /ɑ̃belir/ *v.t.* brighten up; (*récit*)
embellish.

embêt|er /ɑ̃bete/ *v.t.* (*fam.*) annoy.
s'~er *v. pr.* (*fam.*) get bored. **~ant,
~ante** *a.* (*fam.*) annoying. **~ement**
/ɑ̃bɛtmɑ̃/ *n.m.* (*fam.*) annoyance.

emblée (d') /(d)ɑ̃ble/ *adv.* right away.

emblème /ɑ̃blɛm/ *n.m.* emblem.

embobiner /ɑ̃bɔbine/ *v.t.* (*fam.*) get
round.

emboîter /ɑ̃bwate/ *v.t.*, **s'~** *v. pr.* fit
together. **(s')~ dans,** fit into. **~ le pas à
qn.,** (*imiter*) follow suit.

embonpoint /ɑ̃bɔ̃pwɛ̃/ *n.m.* stoutness.

embouchure /ɑ̃buʃyr/ *n.f.* (*de fleuve*)
mouth; (*mus.*) mouthpiece.

embourber (s') /(s)ɑ̃burbe/ *v. pr.* get
bogged down.

embourgeoiser (s') /(s)ɑ̃burʒwaze/ *v.
pr.* become middle-class.

embout /ɑ̃bu/ *n.m.* tip.

embouteillage /ɑ̃butɛjaʒ/ *n.m.* traffic
jam.

emboutir /ɑ̃butir/ *v.t.* (*heurter*) crash
into.

embranchement /ɑ̃brɑ̃ʃmɑ̃/ *n.m.* (*de routes*) junction.

embraser /ɑ̃brɑze/ *v.t.* set on fire, fire. **s'~** *v. pr.* flare up.

embrass|er /ɑ̃brɑse/ *v.t.* kiss; (*adopter, contenir*) embrace. **s'~er** *v. pr.* kiss. **~ades** *n.f. pl.* kissing.

embrasure /ɑ̃brazyr/ *n.f.* opening.

embray|er /ɑ̃breje/ *v.i.* let in the clutch. **~age** /ɑ̃brɛjaʒ/ *n.m.* clutch.

embrigader /ɑ̃brigade/ *v.t.* enrol.

embrocher /ɑ̃brɔʃe/ *v.t.* (*viande*) spit.

embrouiller /ɑ̃bruje/ *v.t.* mix up; (*fils*) tangle. **s'~** *v pr* get mixed up.

embroussaillé /ɑ̃brusaje/ *a.* (*poils, chemin*) bushy.

embryon /ɑ̃brijɔ̃/ *n.m.* embryo. **~naire** /-jɔnɛr/ *a.* embryonic.

embûches /ɑ̃byʃ/ *n.f. pl.* traps.

embuer /ɑ̃bɥe/ *v.t.* mist up.

embuscade /ɑ̃byskad/ *n.f.* ambush.

embusquer (s') /(s)ɑ̃byske/ *v. pr.* lie in ambush.

éméché /emeʃe/ *a.* tipsy.

émeraude /ɛmrod/ *n.f.* emerald.

émerger /emɛrʒe/ *v.i.* emerge; (*fig.*) stand out.

émeri /ɛmri/ *n.m.* emery.

émerveill|er /emɛrveje/ *v.t.* amaze. **s'~er de,** marvel at, be amazed at. **~ement** /-vɛjmɑ̃/ *n.m.* amazement, wonder.

émett|re /emɛtr/ *v.t.* give out; (*message*) transmit; (*timbre, billet*) issue; (*opinion*) express. **~eur** *n.m.* transmitter.

émeut|e /emøt/ *n.f.* riot. **~ier,** **~ière** *n.m., f.* rioter.

émietter /cmjete/ *v.t.,* **s'~** *v. pr.* crumble.

émigrant, **~e** /emigrɑ̃, -t/ *n.m., f.* emigrant.

émigr|er /emigre/ *v.i.* emigrate. **~ation** *n.f.* emigration.

émincer /emɛ̃se/ *v.t.* cut into thin slices.

émin|ent, **~ente** /eminɑ̃, -t/ *a.* eminent. **~emment** /-amɑ̃/ *adv.* eminently. **~ence** *n.f.* eminence; (*colline*) hill. **~ence grise,** éminence grise.

émissaire /emisɛr/ *n.m.* emissary.

émission /emisjɔ̃/ *n.f.* emission; (*de message*) transmission; (*de timbre*) issue; (*programme*) broadcast.

emmagasiner /ɑ̃magazine/ *v.t.* store.

emmanchure /ɑ̃mɑ̃ʃyr/ *n.f.* armhole.

emmêler /ɑ̃mele/ *v.t.* tangle. **s'~** *v. pr.* get mixed up.

emménager /ɑ̃menaʒe/ *v.i.* move in. **~ dans,** move into.

emmener /ɑ̃mne/ *v.t.* take; (*comme prisonnier*) take away.

emmerder /ɑ̃mɛrde/ *v.t.* (*argot*) bother. **s'~** *v. pr.* (*argot*) get bored.

emmitoufler /ɑ̃mitufle/ *v.t.,* **s'~** *v. pr.* wrap up (warmly).

émoi /emwa/ *n.m.* excitement.

émoluments /emɔlymɑ̃/ *n.m. pl.* remuneration.

émonder /emɔ̃de/ *v.t.* prune.

émoti|f, **~ve** /emɔtif, -v/ *a.* emotional.

émotion /emosjɔ̃/ *n f.* emotion; (*peur*) fright. **~nel,** **~nelle** /-jɔnɛl/ *a.* emotional.

émousser /emuse/ *v.t.* blunt.

émouv|oir /emuvwar/ *v.t.* move. **s'~oir** *v. pr.* be moved. **~ant,** **~ante** *a.* moving.

empailler /ɑ̃paje/ *v.t.* stuff.

empaqueter /ɑ̃pakte/ *v.t.* package.

emparer (s') /(s)ɑ̃pare/ *v. pr.* **s'~ de,** seize.

empâter (s') /(s)ɑ̃pɑte/ *v. pr.* fill out, grow fatter.

empêchement /ɑ̃pɛʃmɑ̃/ *n.m.* hitch, difficulty.

empêcher /ɑ̃peʃe/ *v.t.* prevent. **~ de faire,** prevent *ou* stop (from) doing. **il ne peut pas s'~ de penser,** he cannot help thinking. **(il) n'empêche que,** still.

empêch|eur, **~euse** /ɑ̃peʃœr, -øz/ *n.m., f.* **~eur de tourner en rond,** spoilsport.

empeigne /ɑ̃pɛɲ/ *n.f.* upper.

empereur /ɑ̃prœr/ *n.m.* emperor.

empeser /ɑ̃pəze/ *v.t.* starch.

empester /ɑ̃peste/ *v.t.* make stink, stink out; (*essence etc.*) stink of, **—** *v.i.* stink.

empêtrer (s') /(s)ɑ̃petre/ *v. pr.* become entangled.

emphase /ɑ̃faz/ *n.f.* pomposity.

empiéter /ɑ̃pjete/ *v.i.* **~ sur,** encroach upon.

empiffrer (s') /(s)ɑ̃pifre/ *v pr.* (*fam.*) gorge o.s.

empil|er /ɑ̃pile/ *v.t.,* **s'~** *v. pr.* pile (up).

empire /ɑ̃pir/ *n.m.* empire; (*fig.*) control.

empirer /ɑ̃pire/ *v.i.* worsen.

empirique /ɑ̃pirik/ *a.* empirical.

emplacement /ɑ̃plasmɑ̃/ *n.m.* site.

emplâtre /ɑ̃plɑtr/ *n.m.* (*méd.*) plaster.

emplettes /ɑ̃plɛt/ *n.f. pl.* purchase. **faire des ~,** do one's shopping.

emplir /ɑ̃plir/ *v.t.,* **s'~** *v. pr.* fill.

emploi /ɑ̃plwa/ *n.m.* use; (*travail*) job. **~ du temps,** timetable. **l'~,** (*pol.*) employment.

employ|er /ɑ̃plwaje/ *v.t.* use; (*personne*) employ. **s'~er** *v. pr.* be used. **s'~er à**, devote o.s. to. **~é, ~ée** *n.m.*, *f.* employee. **~eur, ~euse** *n.m.*, *f.* employer.

empocher /ɑ̃pɔʃe/ *v.t.* pocket.

empoigner /ɑ̃pwaɲe/ *v.t.* grab. **s'~** *v. pr.* come to blows.

empoisonn|er /ɑ̃pwazɔne/ *v.t.* poison; (*empuantir*) stink out; (*embêter: fam.*) annoy. **~ement** *n.m.* poisoning.

emport|é /ɑ̃pɔrte/ *a.* quicktempered. **~ement** *n.m.* anger.

emporter /ɑ̃pɔrte/ *v.t.* take (away); (*entraîner*) carry away; (*prix*) carry off; (*arracher*) tear off. **~ un chapeau**/*etc.*, (*vent*) blow off a hat/*etc.* **s'~** *v. pr.* lose one's temper. **l'~**, get the upper hand (**sur**, of). **plat à ~**, take-away.

empoté /ɑ̃pɔte/ *a.* silly.

empourpré /ɑ̃purpre/ *a.* crimson.

empreint, **~e** /ɑ̃prɛ̃, -t/ *a.* **~ de**, marked with. —*n.f.* mark. **~e** (**digitale**), fingerprint. **~e de pas**, footprint.

empress|er (s') /(s)ɑ̃prese/ *v. pr.* **s'~er auprès de**, be attentive to. **s'~er de**, hasten to. **~é** *a.* eager, attentive. **~ement** /ɑ̃prɛsmɑ̃/ *n.m.* eagerness.

emprise /ɑ̃priz/ *n.f.* influence.

emprisonn|er /ɑ̃prizɔne/ *v.t.* imprison. **~ement** *n.m.* imprisonment.

emprunt /ɑ̃prœ̃/ *n.m.* loan. **faire un ~**, take out a loan.

emprunté /ɑ̃prœ̃te/ *a.* awkward.

emprunt|er /ɑ̃prœ̃te/ *v.t.* borrow (**à**, from); (*route*) take; (*fig.*) assume. **~eur, ~euse** *n.m.*, *f.* borrower.

ému /emy/ *a.* moved; (*apeuré*) nervous; (*joyeux*) excited.

émulation /emylɑsjɔ̃/ *n.f.* emulation.

émule /emyl/ *n.m./f.* imitator.

émulsion /emylsjɔ̃/ *n.f.* emulsion.

en[1] /ɑ̃/ *prép.* in; (*avec direction*) to; (*manière, état*) in, on; (*moyen de transport*) by; (*composition*) made of. **en cadeau/médecin**/*etc.*, as a present/doctor/*etc.* **en guerre**, at war. **en faisant**, by ou on *ou* while doing.

en[2] /ɑ̃/ *pron.* of it, of them; (*moyen*) with it; (*cause*) from it; (*lieu*) from there. **en avoir/vouloir**/*etc.*, have/want/*etc.* some. **ne pas en avoir/vouloir**/*etc.*, not have/want/*etc.* any. **où en êtes-vous?**, where are you up to?, how far have you got? **j'en ai assez**, I've had enough. **en êtes-vous sûr?**, are you sure?

encadr|er /ɑ̃kadre/ *v.t.* frame; (*entourer d'un trait*) circle; (*entourer*) surround.

~ement *n.m.* framing; (*de porte*) frame.

encaiss|er /ɑ̃kese/ *v.t.* (*argent*) collect; (*chèque*) cash; (*coups: fam.*) take. **~eur** /ɑ̃kesœr/ *n.m.* debt-collector.

encart /ɑ̃kar/ *n.m.* **~ publicitaire**, (advertising) insert.

en-cas /ɑ̃ka/ *n.m.* (stand-by) snack.

encastré /ɑ̃kastre/ *a.* built-in.

encaustiqu|e /ɑ̃kɔstik/ *n.f.* wax polish. **~er** *v.t.* wax.

enceinte[1] /ɑ̃sɛ̃t/ *a.f.* pregnant. **~ de 3 mois**, 3 months pregnant.

enceinte[2] /ɑ̃sɛ̃t/ *n.f.* enclosure. **~ (acoustique)**, loudspeaker.

encens /ɑ̃sɑ̃/ *n.m.* incense.

encercler /ɑ̃sɛrkle/ *v.t.* surround.

en haîn|er /ɑ̃ʃene/ *v.t.* chain (up); (*coordonner*) link (up). —*v.i.* continue. **s'~er** *v. pr.* be linked (up). **~ement** /ɑ̃ʃɛnmɑ̃/ *n.m.* (*suite*) chain; (*liaison*) link(ing).

enchant|er /ɑ̃ʃɑ̃te/ *v.t.* delight; (*ensorceler*) enchant. **~é** *a.* (*ravi*) delighted. **~ement** *n.m.* delight; (*magie*) enchantment.

enchâsser /ɑ̃ʃase/ *v.t.* set.

enchère /ɑ̃ʃɛr/ *n.f.* bid. **mettre** *ou* **vendre aux ~s**, sell by auction.

enchevêtrer /ɑ̃ʃvetre/ *v.t.* tangle. **s'~** *v. pr.* become tangled.

enclave /ɑ̃klav/ *n.f.* enclave.

enclencher /ɑ̃klɑ̃ʃe/ *v.t.* engage.

enclin, ~e /ɑ̃klɛ̃, -in/ *a.* **~ à**, inclined to.

enclore /ɑ̃klɔr/ *v.t.* enclose.

enclos /ɑ̃klo/ *n.m.* enclosure.

enclume /ɑ̃klym/ *n.f.* anvil.

encoche /ɑ̃kɔʃ/ *n.f.* notch.

encoignure /ɑ̃kɔɲyr/ *n.f.* corner.

encoller /ɑ̃kɔle/ *v.t.* paste.

encolure /ɑ̃kɔlyr/ *n.f.* neck.

encombre *n.m.* **sans ~**, without any problems.

encombr|er /ɑ̃kɔ̃bre/ *v.t.* clutter (up); (*gêner*) hamper. **s'~er de**, burden o.s. with. **~ant, ~ante** *a.* cumbersome. **~ement** *n.m.* congestion; (*auto.*) traffic jam; (*volume*) bulk.

encontre de (à l') /(al)ɑ̃kɔ̃trədə/ *prép.* against.

encore /ɑ̃kɔr/ *adv.* (*toujours*) still; (*de nouveau*) again; (*de plus*) more; (*aussi*) also. **~ mieux/plus grand**/*etc.*, even better/larger/*etc.* **~ une heure/un café**/*etc.*, another hour/coffee/*etc.* **pas ~**, not yet. **si ~**, if only.

encourag|er /ɑ̃kuraʒe/ *v.t.* encourage. **~ement** *n.m.* encouragement.

encourir /ãkurir/ v.t. incur.

encrasser /ãkrase/ v.t. clog up (with dirt).

encr|e /ãkr/ n.f. ink. ~**er** v.t. ink.

encrier /ãkrije/ n.m. ink-well.

encroûter (s') /(s)ãkrute/ v. pr. become doggedly set in one's ways. s'~ **dans**, sink into.

encyclopéd|ie /ãsiklɔpedi/ n.f. encyclopaedia. ~**ique** a. encyclopaedic.

endetter /ãdete/ v.t., s'~ v. pr. get into debt.

endeuiller /ãdœje/ v.t. plunge into mourning.

endiablé /ãdjable/ a. wild.

endiguer /ãdige/ v.t. dam; (fig.) check.

endimanché /ãdimãʃe/ a. in one's Sunday best.

endive /ãdiv/ n.f. chicory.

endocrinolo|gie /ãdɔkrinɔlɔʒi/ n.f. endocrinology. ~**gue** n.m./f. endocrinologist.

endoctrin|er /ãdɔktrine/ v.t. indoctrinate. ~**ement** n.m. indoctrination.

endommager /ãdɔmaʒe/ v.t. damage.

endorm|ir /ãdɔrmir/ v.t. send to sleep; (atténuer) allay. s'~**ir** v. pr. fall asleep. ~**i** a. asleep; (apathique) sleepy.

endosser /ãdose/ v.t. (vêtement) put on; (assumer) assume; (comm.) endorse.

endroit /ãdrwa/ n.m. place; (de tissu) right side. à l'~, the right way round, right side out.

end|uire /ãdɥir/ v.t. coat. ~**uit** n.m. coating.

endurance /ãdyrãs/ n.f. endurance.

endurant, ~**e** /ãdyrã, -t/ a. tough.

endurci /ãdyrsi/ a. **célibataire** ~, confirmed bachelor.

endurcir /ãdyrsir/ v.t. harden. s'~ v. pr. become hard(ened).

endurer /ãdyre/ v.t. endure.

énerg|ie /enɛrʒi/ n.f. energy; (techn.) power. ~**étique** a. energy. ~**ique** a. energetic.

énervant, ~**e** /enɛrvã, -t/ a. irritating, annoying.

énerver /enɛrve/ v.t. irritate. s'~ v. pr. get worked up.

enfance /ãfãs/ n.f. childhood. **la petite** ~, infancy.

enfant /ãfã/ n.m./f. child. ~ **en bas âge**, infant. ~**illage** /-tijaʒ/ n.m. childishness. ~**in**, ~**ine** /-tɛ̃, -tin/ a. childlike; (puéril) childish; (jeu, langage) children's.

enfanter /ãfãte/ v.t./i. give birth (to).

enfer /ãfɛr/ n.m. hell.

enfermer /ãfɛrme/ v.t. shut up. s'~ v. pr. shut o.s. up.

enferrer (s') /(s)ãfere/ v. pr. become entangled.

enfiévré /ãfjevre/ a. feverish.

enfilade /ãfilad/ n.f. string, row.

enfiler /ãfile/ v.t. (aiguille) thread; (anneaux) string; (vêtement) slip on; (rue) take; (insérer) insert.

enfin /ãfɛ̃/ adv. at last, finally; (en dernier lieu) finally; (somme toute) after all; (résignation, conclusion) well.

enflammer /ãflame/ v.t. set fire to; (méd.) inflame. s'~ v. pr. catch fire.

enfl|er /ãfle/ v.t./i., s'~**er** v. pr. swell. ~**é** a. swollen. ~**ure** n.f. swelling.

enfoncer /ãfɔ̃se/ v.t. (épingle etc.) push ou drive in; (chapeau) push down; (porte) break down; (mettre) thrust, put. —v.i., s'~ v. pr. sink (**dans**, into).

enfouir /ãfwir/ v.t. bury.

enfourcher /ãfurʃe/ v.t. mount.

enfourner /ãfurne/ v.t. put in the oven.

enfreindre /ãfrɛ̃dr/ v.t. infringe.

enfuir (s') /(s)ãfɥir/ v. pr. run off.

enfumer /ãfyme/ v.t. fill with smoke.

engagé /ãgaʒe/ a. committed.

engageant, ~**e** /ãgaʒã, -t/ a. attractive.

engag|er /ãgaʒe/ v.t. (lier) bind, commit; (embaucher) take on; (commencer) start, (introduire) insert, (entraîner) involve; (encourager) urge; (investir) invest. s'~**er** v. pr. (promettre) commit o.s.; (commencer) start; (soldat) enlist; (concurrent) enter. s'~**er à faire**, undertake to do. s'~**er dans**, (voie) enter. ~**ement** n.m. (promesse) promise; (pol., comm.) commitment; (début) start; (inscription, sport) entry.

engelure /ãʒlyr/ n.f. chilblain.

engendrer /ãʒãdre/ v.t. beget; (causer) generate.

engin /ãʒɛ̃/ n.m. machine; (outil) instrument; (projectile) missile. ~ **explosif**, explosive device.

englober /ãglɔbe/ v.t. include.

engloutir /ãglutir/ v.t. swallow (up). s'~ v. pr. (navire) be engulfed.

engorger /ãgɔrʒe/ v.t. block.

engou|er (s') /(s)ãgwe/ v. pr. s'~**er de**, become infatuated with. ~**ement** /-umã/ n.m. infatuation.

engouffrer /ãgufre/ v.t. devour. s'~ **dans**, rush into (with force).

engourd|ir /ãgurdir/ v.t. numb. s'~**ir** v. pr. go numb. ~**i** a. numb.

engrais /ɑ̃grɛ/ *n.m.* manure; (*chimique*) fertilizer.

engraisser /ɑ̃grese/ *v.t.* fatten. **s'~** *v. pr.* get fat.

engrenage /ɑ̃grənaʒ/ *n.m.* gears; (*fig.*) chain (of events).

engueuler /ɑ̃gœle/ *v.t.* (*argot*) curse, swear at, hurl abuse at.

enhardir (s') /(s)ɑ̃ardir/ *v. pr.* become bolder.

énième /ɛnjɛm/ *a.* (*fam.*) umpteenth.

énigm|e /enigm/ *n.f.* riddle, enigma. **~atique** *a.* enigmatic.

enivrer /ɑ̃nivre/ *v.t.* intoxicate. **s'~** *v. pr.* get drunk.

enjamb|er /ɑ̃ʒɑ̃be/ *v.t.* step over; (*pont*) span. **~ée** *n.f.* stride.

enjeu (*pl.* **~x**) /ɑ̃ʒø/ *n.m.* stake(s).

enjôler /ɑ̃ʒole/ *v.t.* wheedle.

enjoliver /ɑ̃ʒolive/ *v.t.* embellish.

enjoliveur /ɑ̃ʒolivœr/ *n.m.* hub-cap.

enjoué /ɑ̃ʒwe/ *a.* cheerful.

enlacer /ɑ̃lase/ *v.t.* entwine.

enlaidir /ɑ̃ledir/ *v.t.* make ugly. —*v.i.* grow ugly.

enlèvement /ɑ̃lɛvmɑ̃/ *n.m.* removal; (*rapt*) kidnapping.

enlever /ɑ̃lve/ *v.t.* (*emporter*) take (away), remove (**à**, from); (*vêtement*) take off, remove; (*tache, organe*) take out, remove; (*kidnapper*) kidnap; (*gagner*) win.

enliser (s') /(s)ɑ̃lize/ *v. pr.* get bogged down.

enluminure /ɑ̃lyminyr/ *n.f.* illumination.

enneig|é /ɑ̃neʒe/ *a.* snow-covered. **~ement** /ɑ̃nɛʒmɑ̃/ *n.m.* snow conditions.

ennemi /ɛnmi/ *n.m. & a.* enemy. **~ de,** (*fig.*) hostile to. **l'~ public numéro un,** public enemy number one.

ennui /ɑ̃nɥi/ *n.m.* boredom; (*tracas*) trouble, worry. **il a des ~s,** he's got problems.

ennuyer /ɑ̃nɥije/ *v.t.* bore; (*irriter*) annoy; (*préoccuper*) worry. **s'~** *v. pr.* get bored.

ennuyeu|x, ~se /ɑ̃nɥijø, -z/ *a.* boring; (*fâcheux*) annoying.

énoncé /enɔ̃se/ *n.m.* wording, text; (*gram.*) utterance.

énoncer /enɔ̃se/ *v.t.* express, state.

enorgueillir (s') /(s)ɑ̃nɔrgœjir/ *v. pr.* **s'~ de,** pride o.s. on.

énorm|e /enɔrm/ *a.* enormous. **~ément** *adv.* enormously. **~ément de,** an enormous amount of. **~ité** *n.f.*
enormous size; (*atrocité*) enormity; (*bévue*) enormous blunder.

enquérir (s') /(s)ɑ̃kerir/ *v. pr.* **s'~ de,** enquire about.

enquêt|e /ɑ̃kɛt/ *n.f.* investigation; (*jurid.*) inquiry; (*sondage*) survey. **mener l'~e,** lead the inquiry. **~er** /-ete/ *v.i.* **~er (sur),** investigate. **~eur, ~euse** *n.m., f.* investigator.

enquiquin|er /ɑ̃kikine/ *v.t.* (*fam.*) bother. **~ant, ~ante** *a.* irritating. **c'est ~ant,** it's a nuisance.

enraciné /ɑ̃rasine/ *a.* deep-rooted.

enrag|er /ɑ̃raʒe/ *v.i.* be furious. **faire ~er,** annoy. **~é** *a.* furious; (*chien*) mad; (*fig.*) fanatical. **~eant, ~eante** *a.* infuriating.

enrayer /ɑ̃reje/ *v.t.* check.

enregistr|er /ɑ̃rʒistre/ *v.t.* note, record; (*mus.*) record. (**faire**) **~er,** (*bagages*) register, check in. **~ement** *n.m.* recording; (*des bagages*) registration.

enrhumer (s') /(s)ɑ̃ryme/ *v. pr.* catch a cold.

enrich|ir /ɑ̃riʃir/ *v.t.* enrich. **s'~ir** *v. pr.* grow rich(er). **~issement** *n.m.* enrichment.

enrober /ɑ̃rɔbe/ *v.t.* coat (**de,** with).

enrôler /ɑ̃role/ *v.t.*, **s'~** *v. pr.* enlist, enrol.

enrou|er (s') /(s)ɑ̃rwe/ *v. pr.* become hoarse. **~é** *a.* hoarse.

enrouler /ɑ̃rule/ *v.t.*, **s'~** *v. pr.* wind. **s'~ dans une couverture,** roll o.s. up in a blanket.

ensabler /ɑ̃sable/ *v.t.*, **s'~** *v. pr.* (*port*) silt up.

ensanglanté /ɑ̃sɑ̃glɑ̃te/ *a.* bloodstained.

enseignant, ~e /ɑ̃sɛɲɑ̃, -t/ *n.m., f.* teacher. —*a.* teaching.

enseigne /ɑ̃sɛɲ/ *n.f.* sign.

enseignement /ɑ̃sɛɲmɑ̃/ *n.m.* teaching; (*instruction*) education.

enseigner /ɑ̃seɲe/ *v.t./i.* teach. **~ qch. à qn.,** teach s.o. sth.

ensemble /ɑ̃sɑ̃bl/ *adv.* together. —*n.m.* unity; (*d'objets*) set; (*mus.*) ensemble; (*vêtements*) outfit. **dans l'~,** on the whole. **d'~,** (*idée etc.*) general. **l'~ de,** (*totalité*) all of, the whole of.

ensemencer /ɑ̃smɑ̃se/ *v.t.* sow.

enserrer /ɑ̃sere/ *v.t.* grip (tightly).

ensevelir /ɑ̃səvlir/ *v.t.* bury.

ensoleill|é /ɑ̃sɔleje/ *a.* sunny. **~ement** /ɑ̃sɔlɛjmɑ̃/ *n.m.* (period of) sunshine.

ensommeillé /ɑ̃sɔmeje/ *a.* sleepy.

ensorceler /ɑ̃sɔrsəle/ *v.t.* bewitch.

ensuite /ɑ̃sɥit/ *adv.* next, then; (*plus tard*) later.

ensuivre (s') /(s)ãsɥivr/ *v. pr.* follow. **et tout ce qui s'ensuit,** and so on.

entaill|e /ãtaj/ *n.f.* notch; (*blessure*) gash. ∼**er** *v.t.* notch; gash.

entamer /ãtame/ *v.t.* start; (*inciser*) cut into; (*ébranler*) shake.

entass|er /ãtɑse/ *v.t.*, **s'**∼**er** *v. pr.* pile up. **(s')**∼**er dans,** cram (together) into. ∼**ement** *n.m.* (*tas*) pile.

entendement /ãtãdmã/ *n.m.* understanding. **ça dépasse l'**∼, it defies one's understanding.

entendre /ãtãdr/ *v.t.* hear; (*comprendre*) understand; (*vouloir*) intend, mean; (*vouloir dire*) mean. **s'**∼ *v. pr.* (*être d'accord*) agree. ∼ **dire que,** hear that. ∼ **parler de,** hear of. **s'**∼ **(bien),** get on (**avec,** with). **(cela) s'entend,** of course.

entendu /ãtãdy/ *a.* (*convenu*) agreed; (*sourire, air*) knowing. **bien** ∼, of course. **(c'est)** ∼!, all right!

entente /ãtãt/ *n.f.* understanding. **à double** ∼, with a double meaning.

entériner /ãterine/ *v.t.* ratify.

enterr|er /ãtere/ *v.t.* bury. ∼**ement** /ãtɛrmã/ *n.m.* burial, funeral.

entêtant, ∼**e** /ãtetã, -t/ *a.* heady.

en-tête /ãtɛt/ *n.m.* heading. **à** ∼, headed.

entêt|é /ãtete/ *a.* stubborn. ∼**ement** /ãtɛtmã/ *n.m.* stubbornness.

entêter (s') /(s)ãtete/ *v. pr.* persist (**à, dans,** in).

enthousias|me /ãtuzjasm/ *n.m.* enthusiasm. ∼**mer** *v.t.* enthuse. **s'**∼**mer pour,** enthuse over. ∼**te** *a.* enthusiastic.

enticher (s') /(s)ãtiʃe/ *v. pr.* **s'**∼ **de,** become infatuated with.

ent|ier, ∼**ière** /ãtje, -jɛr/ *a.* whole; (*absolu*) absolute; (*entêté*) unyielding. —*n.m.* whole. **en** ∼**ier,** entirely. ∼**ièrement** *adv.* entirely.

entité /ãtite/ *n.f.* entity.

entonner /ãtɔne/ *v.t.* start singing.

entonnoir /ãtɔnwar/ *n.m.* funnel; (*trou*) crater.

entorse /ãtɔrs/ *n.f.* sprain. ∼ **à,** (*loi*) infringement of.

entortiller /ãtɔrtije/ *v.t.* wrap (up); (*enrouler*) wind, wrap; (*duper*) deceive.

entourage /ãturaʒ/ *n.m.* circle of family and friends; (*bordure*) surround.

entourer /ãture/ *v.t.* surround (**de,** with); (*réconforter*) rally round. ∼ **de,** (*écharpe etc.*) wrap round.

entracte /ãtrakt/ *n.m.* interval.

entraide /ãtrɛd/ *n.f.* mutual aid.

entraider (s') /(s)ãtrede/ *v. pr.* help each other.

entrailles /ãtraj/ *n.f. pl.* entrails.

entrain /ãtrɛ̃/ *n.m.* zest, spirit.

entraînant, ∼**e** /ãtrɛnã, -t/ *a.* rousing.

entraînement /ãtrɛnmã/ *n.m.* (*sport*) training.

entraîn|er /ãtrene/ *v.t.* carry away *ou* along; (*emmener, influencer*) lead; (*impliquer*) entail; (*sport*) train; (*roue*) drive. ∼**eur** /ãtrɛnœr/ *n.m.* trainer.

entrav|e /ãtrav/ *n.f.* hindrance. ∼**er** *v.t.* hinder.

entre /ãtr(ə)/ *prép.* between; (*parmi*) among(st). ∼ **autres,** among other things. **l'un d'**∼ **nous/vous/eux,** one of us/you/ them.

entrebâillé /ãtrəbaje/ *a.* ajar.

entrechoquer (s') /(s)ãtrəʃɔke/ *v. pr.* knock against each other.

entrecôte /ãtrəkot/ *n.f.* rib steak.

entrecouper /ãtrəkupe/ *v.t.* ∼ **de,** intersperse with.

entrecroiser (s') /(s)ãtrəkrwaze/ *v. pr.* (*routes*) intersect.

entrée /ãtre/ *n.f.* entrance; (*accès*) admission, entry; (*billet*) ticket; (*culin.*) first course; (*de données: techn.*) input. ∼ **interdite,** no entry.

entrefaites (sur ces) /(syrsez)ãtrəfɛt/ *adv.* at that moment.

entrefilet /ãtrəfilɛ/ *n.m.* paragraph.

entrejambe /ãtrəʒãb/ *n.m.* crotch.

entrelacer (s') /(s)ãtrəlase/ *v.t.*, **s'**∼ *v. pr.* intertwine.

entremêler /ãtrəmele/ *v.t.*, **s'**∼ *v. pr.* (inter)mingle.

entremets /ãtrəmɛ/ *n.m.* dessert.

entremetteu|r, ∼**se** /ãtrəmɛtœr, -øz/ *n m , f* (*péj.*) go-between.

entre|mettre (s') /(s)ãtrəmɛtr/ *v. pr.* intervene. ∼ **mise** *n.f.* intervention. **par l'**∼**mise de,** through.

entreposer /ãtrəpoze/ *v.t.* store.

entrepôt /ãtrəpo/ *n.m.* warehouse.

entreprenant, ∼**e** /ãtrəprənã, -t/ *a.* (*actif*) enterprising; (*séducteur*) forward.

entreprendre† /ãtrəprãdr/ *v.t.* start on; (*personne*) buttonhole. ∼ **de faire,** undertake to do.

entrepreneur /ãtrəprənœr/ *n.m.* ∼ **(de bâtiments),** (building) contractor.

entreprise /ãtrəpriz/ *n.f.* undertaking; (*société*) firm.

entrer /ãtre/ *v.i.* (*aux. être*) go in, enter; (*venir*) come in, enter. ∼ **dans,** go *ou* come into, enter; (*club*) join. ∼ **en collision,** collide (**avec,** with). **faire** ∼, (*personne*) show in. **laisser** ∼, let in.

entresol /ãtrəsɔl/ *n.m.* mezzanine.

entre-temps /ãtrətã/ *adv.* meanwhile.

entretenir† /ãtrətnir/ *v.t.* maintain; (*faire durer*) keep alive. ∼ **qn. de,** converse with s.o. about. **s'∼** *v. pr.* speak (**de,** about; **avec,** to).

entretien /ãtrətjɛ̃/ *n.m.* maintenance; (*discussion*) talk; (*audience pour un emploi*) interview.

entrevoir /ãtrəvwar/ *v.t.* make out; (*brièvement*) glimpse.

entrevue /ãtrəvy/ *n.f.* interview.

entrouvrir /ãtruvrir/ *v.t.* half-open.

énumér|er /enymere/ *v.t.* enumerate. ∼**ation** *n.f.* enumeration.

envah|ir /ãvair/ *v.t.* invade, overrun; (*douleur, peur*) overcome. ∼**isseur** *n.m.* invader.

enveloppe /ãvlɔp/ *n.f.* envelope; (*emballage*) covering; (*techn.*) casing.

envelopper /ãvlɔpe/ *v.t.* wrap (up); (*fig.*) envelop.

envenimer /ãvnime/ *v.t.* embitter. **s'∼** *v. pr.* become embittered.

envergure /ãvɛrgyr/ *n.f.* wing-span; (*importance*) scope; (*qualité*) calibre.

envers /ãvɛr/ *prép.* toward(s), to. —*n.m.* (*de tissu*) wrong side. **à l'∼,** upside down; (*pantalon*) back to front; (*chaussette*) inside out.

enviable /ãviabl/ *a.* enviable. **peu ∼,** unenviable.

envie /ãvi/ *n.f.* desire, wish; (*jalousie*) envy. **avoir ∼ de,** want, feel like. **avoir ∼ de faire,** want to do, feel like doing.

envier /ãvje/ *v.t.* envy.

envieu|x, ∼**se** /ãvjø, -z/ *a.* & *n.m.,* f. envious (person).

environ /ãvirɔ̃/ *adv.* (round) about. ∼**s** *n.m. pl.* surroundings. **aux ∼s de,** round about.

environnement /ãvirɔnmã/ *n.m.* environment.

environn|er /ãvirɔne/ *v.t.* surround. ∼**ant,** ∼**ante** *a.* surrounding.

envisager /ãvizaʒe/ *v.t.* consider. ∼ **de faire,** consider doing.

envoi /ãvwa/ *n.m.* dispatch; (*paquet*) consignment.

envol /ãvɔl/ *n.m.* flight; (*d'avion*) take-off.

envoler (s') /(s)ãvɔle/ *v. pr.* fly away; (*avion*) take off; (*papiers*) blow away.

envoûter /ãvute/ *v.t.* bewitch.

envoyé, ∼**e** /ãvwaje/ *n.m.,* f. envoy; (*de journal*) correspondent.

envoyer† /ãvwaje/ *v.t.* send; (*lancer*) throw. ∼ **promener qn.,** give s.o. the brush-off.

enzyme /ãzim/ *n.m.* enzyme.

épagneul, ∼**e** /epaɲœl/ *n.m.,* f. spaniel.

épais, ∼**se** /epɛ, -s/ *a.* thick. ∼**seur** /-sœr/ *n.f.* thickness.

épaissir /epesir/ *v.t./i.,* **s'∼** *v. pr.* thicken.

épanch|er (s') /(s)epãʃe/ *v. pr.* pour out one's feelings; (*liquide*) pour out. ∼**ement** *n.m.* outpouring.

épanoui /epanwi/ *a.* (*joyeux*) beaming, radiant.

épan|ouir (s') /(s)epanwir/ *v. pr.* (*fleur*) open out; (*visage*) beam; (*personne*) blossom. ∼**ouissement** *n.m.* (*éclat*) blossoming, full bloom.

épargne /eparɲ/ *n.f.* saving; (*somme*) savings. **caisse d'∼,** savings bank.

épargn|er /eparɲe/ *v.t./i.* save; (*ne pas tuer*) spare. ∼**er qch. à qn.,** spare s.o. sth. ∼**ant,** ∼**ante** *n.m.,* f. saver.

éparpiller /eparpije/ *v.t.* scatter. **s'∼** *v. pr.* scatter; (*fig.*) dissipate one's efforts.

épars, ∼**e** /epar, -s/ *a.* scattered.

épat|er /epate/ *v.t.* (*fam.*) amaze. ∼**ant,** ∼**ante** *a.* (*fam.*) amazing.

épaule /epol/ *n.f.* shoulder.

épauler /epole/ *v.t.* (*arme*) raise; (*aider*) support.

épave /epav/ *n.f.* wreck.

épée /epe/ *n.f.* sword.

épeler /ɛple/ *v.t.* spell.

éperdu /epɛrdy/ *a.* wild, frantic. ∼**ment** *adv.* wildly, frantically.

éperon /eprɔ̃/ *n.m.* spur. ∼**ner** /-ɔne/ *v.t.* spur (on).

épervier /epɛrvje/ *n.m.* sparrow-hawk.

éphémère /efemɛr/ *a.* ephemeral.

éphéméride /efemerid/ *n.f.* tear-off calendar.

épi /epi/ *n.m.* (*de blé*) ear. ∼ **de cheveux,** tuft of hair.

épic|e /epis/ *n.f.* spice. ∼**é** *a.* spicy. ∼**er** *v.t.* spice.

épic|ier, ∼**ière** /episje, -jɛr/ *n.m.,* f. grocer. ∼**erie** *n.f.* grocery shop; (*produits*) groceries.

épidémie /epidemi/ *n.f.* epidemic.

épiderme /epidɛrm/ *n.m.* skin.

épier /epje/ *v.t.* spy on.

épilep|sie /epilɛpsi/ *n.f.* epilepsy. ∼**tique** *a.* & *n.m./f.* epileptic.

épiler /epile/ *v.t.* remove unwanted hair from; (*sourcils*) pluck.

épilogue /epilɔg/ *n.m.* epilogue; (*fig.*) outcome.

épinard /epinar/ *n.m.* (*plante*) spinach. ∼**s,** (*nourriture*) spinach.

épin|e /epin/ *n.f.* thorn, prickle; (*d'animal*) prickle, spine. ∼**e dorsale,** backbone. ∼**eux,** ∼**euse** *a.* thorny.

épingl|e /epɛ̃gl/ n.f. pin. **~e de nourrice,**
~e de sûreté, safety-pin. **~er** v.t. pin;
(arrêter: fam.) nab.

épique /epik/ a. epic.

épisod|e /epizɔd/ n.m. episode. **à ~es,**
serialized. **~ique** a. occasional.

épitaphe /epitaf/ n.f. epitaph.

épithète /epitɛt/ n.f. epithet.

épître /epitr/ n.f. epistle.

éploré /eplɔre/ a. tearful.

épluche-légumes /eplyʃlegym/ n.m.
invar. (potato) peeler.

épluch|er /eplyʃe/ v.t. peel; (examiner:
fig.) scrutinize. **~age** n.m. peeling;
(fig.) scrutiny. **~ure** n.f. piece of peel
ou peeling. **~ures** n.f. pl. peelings.

épong|e /epɔ̃ʒ/ n.f. sponge. **~er** v.t.
(liquide) sponge up; (surface) sponge
(down); (front) mop; (dettes) wipe out.

épopée /epɔpe/ n.f. epic.

époque /epɔk/ n.f. time, period. **à l'~,** at
the time. **d'~,** period.

épouse /epuz/ n.f. wife.

épouser[1] /epuze/ v.t. marry.

épouser[2] /epuze/ v.t. (forme, idée)
assume, embrace, adopt.

épousseter /epuste/ v.t. dust.

époustouflant, ~e /epustuflɑ̃, -t/ a.
(fam.) staggering.

épouvantable /epuvɑ̃tabl/ a. appalling.

épouvantail /epuvɑ̃taj/ n.m. scarecrow.

épouvant|e /epuvɑ̃t/ n.f. terror. **~er** v.t.
terrify.

époux /epu/ n.m. husband. **les ~,** the
married couple.

éprendre (s') /(s)eprɑ̃dr/ v. pr. **s'~ de,**
fall in love with.

épreuve /eprœv/ n.f. test; (sport) event;
(malheur) ordeal; (photo.) print;
(d'imprimerie) proof. **mettre à l'~,** put
to the test.

éprouvé /epruve/ a. (well-)proven.

éprouv|er /epruve/ v.t. test; (ressentir)
experience; (affliger) distress. **~ante** a. testing.

éprouvette /epruvɛt/ n.f. test-tube.
bébé-~, test-tube baby.

épuis|er /epɥize/ v.t. (fatiguer, user)
exhaust. **s'~er** v. pr. become exhausted. **~é** a. exhausted; (livre) out of
print. **~ement** n.m. exhaustion.

épuisette /epɥizɛt/ n.f. fishing-net.

épur|er /epyre/ v.t. purify; (pol.) purge.
~ation n.f. purification; (pol.) purge.

équat|eur /ekwatœr/ n.m. equator.
~orial (m. pl. **~oriaux**) a. equatorial.

équation /ekwasjɔ̃/ n.f. equation.

équerre /ekɛr/ n.f. (set) square. **d'~,**
square.

équilibr|e /ekilibr/ n.m. balance. **être** ou
se tenir en ~e, (personne) balance;
(objet) be balanced. **~é** a. well-
balanced. **~er** v.t. balance. **s'~er** v. pr.
(forces etc.) counterbalance each other.

équilibriste /ekilibrist/ n.m./f. tightrope
walker.

équinoxe /ekinɔks/ n.m. equinox.

équipage /ekipaʒ/ n.m. crew.

équlpe /ekip/ n.f. team. **~ de nuit/jour,**
night/day shift.

équipé /ekipe/ a. **bien/mal ~,** well/
poorly equipped.

équipée /ekipe/ n.f. escapade.

équipement /ekipmɑ̃/ n.m. equipment.
~s, (installations) amenities, facilities.

équiper /ekipe/ v.t. equip (de, with). **s'~**
v. pr. equip o.s.

équip|ier, ~ière /ekipje, -jɛr/ n.m., f.
team member.

équitable /ekitabl/ a. fair. **~ment**
/-əmɑ̃/ adv. fairly.

équitation /ekitasjɔ̃/ n.f. (horse-)riding.

équlté /ekite/ n.f. equity.

équivalen|t, ~te /ekivalɑ̃, -t/ a.
equivalent. **~ce** n.f. equivalence.

équivaloir /ekivalwar/ v.i. **~ à,** be
equivalent to.

équivoque /ekivɔk/ a. equivocal;
(louche) questionable. **—**n.f. ambiguity.

érable /erabl/ n.m. maple.

érafl|er /erafle/ v.t. scratch. **~ure** n.f.
scratch.

éraillé /eraje/ a. (voix) raucous.

ère /ɛr/ n.f. era.

érection /erɛksjɔ̃/ n.f. erection.

éreinter /erɛ̃te/ v.t. exhaust; (fig.)
criticize severely.

ergoter /ɛrgɔte/ v.i. quibble.

ériger /eriʒe/ v.t. erect. **(s')~ en,** set
(o.s.) up as.

ermite /ɛrmit/ n.m. hermit.

éroder /erɔde/ v.t. erode.

érosion /erozjɔ̃/ n.f. erosion.

éroti|que /erɔtik/ a. erotic. **~sme** n.m.
eroticism.

errer /ɛre/ v.i. wander.

erreur /ɛrœr/ n.f. mistake, error. **dans**
l'~, mistaken. **par ~,** by mistake. **~**
judiciaire, miscarriage of justice.

erroné /ɛrɔne/ a. erroneous.

ersatz /ɛrzats/ n.m. ersatz.

érudit, ~e /erydi, -t/ a. scholarly.
—n.m., f. scholar. **~ion** /-sjɔ̃/ n.f.
scholarship.

éruption /erypsjɔ̃/ n.f. eruption; (méd.)
rash.

es /ɛ/ voir **être.**

escabeau (*pl.* ~x) /ɛskabo/ *n.m.* stepladder; (*tabouret*) stool.

escadre /ɛskadr/ *n.f.* (*naut.*) squadron.

escadrille /ɛskadrij/ *n.f.* (*aviat.*) flight, squadron.

escadron /ɛskadrɔ̃/ *n.m.* (*mil.*) squadron.

escalad|e /ɛskalad/ *n.f.* climbing; (*pol.*, *comm.*) escalation. ~er *v.t.* climb.

escalator /ɛskalatɔr/ *n.m.* (P.) escalator.

escale /ɛskal/ *n.f.* (*d'avion*) stopover; (*port*) port of call. **faire ~ à**, (*avion*, *passager*) stop over at; (*navire*, *passager*) put in at.

escalier /ɛskalije/ *n.m.* stairs. ~ **mécanique** *ou* **roulant**, escalator.

escalope /ɛskalɔp/ *n.f.* escalope.

escamotable /ɛskamɔtabl/ *a.* (*techn.*) retractable.

escamoter /ɛskamɔte/ *v.t.* make vanish; (*éviter*) dodge.

escargot /ɛskargo/ *n.m.* snail.

escarmouche /ɛskarmuʃ/ *n.f.* skirmish.

escarpé /ɛskarpe/ *a.* steep.

escarpin /ɛskarpɛ̃/ *n.m.* pump.

escient /esjɑ̃/ *n.m.* **à bon ~**, with good reason.

esclaffer (s') /(s)ɛsklafe/ *v. pr.* guffaw, burst out laughing.

esclandre /ɛsklɑ̃dr/ *n.m.* scene.

esclav|e /ɛsklav/ *n.m./f.* slave. ~**age** *n.m.* slavery.

escompte /ɛskɔ̃t/ *n.m.* discount.

escompter /ɛskɔ̃te/ *v.t.* expect; (*comm.*) discount.

escort|e /ɛskɔrt/ *n.f.* escort. ~**er** *v.t.* escort. ~**eur** *n.m.* escort (ship).

escouade /ɛskwad/ *n.f.* squad.

escrim|e /ɛskrim/ *n.f.* fencing. ~**eur**, ~**euse** *n.m.*, *f.* fencer.

escrimer (s') /(s)ɛskrime/ *v. pr.* struggle.

escroc /ɛskro/ *n.m.* swindler.

escroqu|er /ɛskrɔke/ *v.t.* swindle. ~**er qch. à qn.**, swindle s.o. out of sth. ~**erie** *n.f.* swindle.

espace /ɛspas/ *n.m.* space. ~**s verts**, gardens, parks.

espacer /ɛspase/ *v.t.* space out. **s'**~ *v. pr.* become less frequent.

espadrille /ɛspadrij/ *n.f.* rope sandals.

Espagne /ɛspaɲ/ *n.f.* Spain.

espagnol, ~e /ɛspaɲɔl/ *a.* Spanish. —*n.m.*, *f.* Spaniard. —*n.m.* (*lang.*) Spanish.

espagnolette /ɛspaɲɔlɛt/ *n.f.* (window) catch.

espèce /ɛspɛs/ *n.f.* kind, sort; (*race*) species. ~**s**, (*argent*) cash. ~

d'idiot/de brute/*etc.***!**, you idiot/brute/ *etc.*!

espérance /ɛsperɑ̃s/ *n.f.* hope.

espérer /ɛspere/ *v.t.* hope for. ~ **faire/que**, hope to do/that. —*v.i.* hope. ~ **en**, have faith in.

espiègle /ɛspjɛgl/ *a.* mischievous.

espion, ~ne /ɛspjɔ̃, -jɔn/ *n.m.*, *f.* spy.

espionn|er /ɛspjɔne/ *v.t./i.* spy (on). ~**age** *n.m.* espionage, spying.

esplanade /ɛsplanad/ *n.f.* esplanade.

espoir /ɛspwar/ *n.m.* hope.

esprit /ɛspri/ *n.m.* spirit; (*intellect*) mind; (*humour*) wit. **perdre l'**~, lose one's mind. **reprendre ses** ~**s**, come to. **vouloir faire de l'**~, try to be witty.

Esquimau, ~de (*m. pl.* ~x) /ɛskimo, -d/ *n.m.*, *f.* Eskimo.

esquinter /ɛskɛ̃te/ *v.t.* (*fam.*) ruin.

esquiss|e /ɛskis/ *n.f.* sketch; (*fig.*) suggestion. ~**er** *v.t.* sketch; (*geste etc.*) make an attempt at.

esquiv|e /ɛskiv/ *n.f.* (*sport*) dodge. ~**er** *v.t.* dodge. **s'**~**er** *v. pr.* slip away.

essai /ese/ *n.m.* testing; (*épreuve*) test, trial; (*tentative*) try; (*article*) essay. **à l'**~, on trial.

essaim /esɛ̃/ *n.m.* swarm. ~**er** /eseme/ *v.i.* swarm; (*fig.*) spread.

essayage /esejaʒ/ *n.m.* (*de vêtement*) fitting. **salon d'**~, fitting room.

essayer /eseje/ *v.t./i.* try; (*vêtement*) try (on); (*voiture etc.*) try (out). ~ **de faire**, try to do.

essence[1] /esɑ̃s/ *n.f.* (*carburant*) petrol; (*Amer.*) gas.

essence[2] /esɑ̃s/ *n.f.* (*nature*, *extrait*) essence.

essentiel, ~le /esɑ̃sjɛl/ *a.* essential. —*n.m.* **l'**~, the main thing; (*quantité*) the main part. ~**lement** *adv.* essentially.

essieu (*pl.* ~x) /esjø/ *n.m.* axle.

essor /esɔr/ *n.m.* expansion. **prendre son** ~, expand.

essor|er /esɔre/ *v.t.* (*linge*) spin-dry; (*en tordant*) wring. ~**euse** *n.f.* spin-drier.

essouffler *v.t.* make breathless. **s'**~ *v. pr.* get out of breath.

ess|uyer[1] /esɥije/ *v.t.* wipe. **s'**~**uyer** *v. pr.* dry *ou* wipe o.s. ~**uie-glace** *n.m. invar.* windscreen wiper; (*Amer.*) windshield wiper. ~**uie-mains** *n.m. invar.* hand-towel.

essuyer[2] /esɥije/ *v.t.* (*subir*) suffer.

est[1] /ɛ/ *voir* **être**.

est[2] /ɛst/ *n.m.* east. —*a. invar.* east; (*partie*) eastern; (*direction*) easterly.

estampe /ɛstɑ̃p/ *n.f.* print.

estampille /ɛstɑ̃pij/ n.f. stamp.

esthète /ɛstɛt/ n.m./f. aesthete.

esthéticienne /ɛstetisjɛn/ n.f. beautician.

esthétique /ɛstetik/ a. aesthetic.

estimable /ɛstimabl/ a. worthy.

estimation /ɛstimasjɔ̃/ n.f. valuation.

estime /ɛstim/ n.f. esteem.

estim|er /ɛstime/ v.t. (objet) value; (calculer) estimate; (respecter) esteem; (considérer) consider. **~ation** n.f. valuation; (calcul) estimation.

estiv|al (m. pl. **~aux**) /ɛstival, -o/ a. summer. **~ant, ~ante** n.m., f. summer visitor, holiday-maker.

estomac /ɛstɔma/ n.m. stomach.

estomaqué /ɛstɔmake/ a. (fam.) stunned.

estomper (s') /(s)ɛstɔ̃pe/ v. pr. become blurred.

estrade /ɛstrad/ n.f. platform.

estragon /ɛstragɔ̃/ n.m. tarragon.

estropi|er /ɛstrɔpje/ v.t. cripple; (fig.) mangle. **~ié, ~iée** n.m., f. cripple.

estuaire /ɛstɥɛr/ n.m. estuary.

estudiantin, ~e /ɛstydjɑ̃tɛ̃, -in/ a. student.

esturgeon /ɛstyrʒɔ̃/ n.m. sturgeon.

et /e/ conj. and. **et moi/lui/etc.?**, what about me/him/etc.?

étable /etabl/ n.f. cow-shed.

établi[1] /etabli/ a. established. **un fait bien ~**, a well-established fact.

établi[2] /etabli/ n.m. work-bench.

établir /etablir/ v.t. establish; (liste, facture) draw up; (personne, camp, record) set up. **s'~** v. pr. (personne) establish o.s. **s'~ épicier/etc.**, set (o.s.) up as a grocer/etc. **s'~ à son compte**, set up on one's own.

établissement /etablismɑ̃/ n.m. (bâtiment, institution) establishment.

étage /etaʒ/ n.m. floor, storey; (de fusée) stage. **à l'~**, upstairs. **au premier ~**, on the first floor.

étager (s') /(s)etaʒe/ v. pr. rise at different levels.

étagère /etaʒɛr/ n.f. shelf; (meuble) shelving unit.

étai /etɛ/ n.m. prop, buttress.

étain /etɛ̃/ n.m. pewter.

étais, était /etɛ/ voir être.

étal (pl. **~s**) /etal/ n.m. stall.

étalag|e /etalaʒ/ n.m. display; (vitrine) shop-window. **faire ~e de**, show off **~iste** n.m./f. window-dresser.

étaler /etale/ v.t. spread; (journal) spread (out); (vacances) stagger; (exposer) display. **s'~** v. pr. (s'étendre) stretch out; (tomber: fam.)

fall flat. **s'~ sur**, (paiement) be spread over.

étalon /etalɔ̃/ n.m. (cheval) stallion; (modèle) standard.

étanche /etɑ̃ʃ/ a. watertight; (montre) waterproof.

étancher /etɑ̃ʃe/ v.t. (soif) quench; (sang) stem.

étang /etɑ̃/ n.m. pond.

étant /etɑ̃/ voir être.

étape /etap/ n.f. stage; (lieu d'arrêt) stopover.

état /eta/ n.m. state; (liste) statement; (métier) profession; (nation) State. **en bon/mauvais ~**, in good/bad condition. **en ~ de**, in a position to. **hors d'~ de**, not in a position to. **en ~ de marche**, in working order. **~ civil**, civil status. **~-major** (pl. **~s-majors**) n.m. (officiers) staff. **faire ~ de**, (citer) mention. **être dans tous ses ~s**, be in a state. **~ des lieux**, inventory.

étatisé /etatize/ a. State-controlled.

États-Unis /etazyni/ n.m. pl. **~ (d'Amérique)**, United States (of America).

étau (pl. **~x**) /eto/ n.m. vice.

étayer /eteje/ v.t. prop up.

été[1] /ete/ voir être.

été[2] /ete/ n.m. summer.

étein|dre[†] /etɛ̃dr/ v.t. put out, extinguish; (lumière, radio) turn off. **s'~dre** v. pr. (feu) go out; (mourir) die. **~t, ~te** /etɛ̃, -t/ a. (feu) out; (volcan) extinct.

étendard /etɑ̃dar/ n.m. standard.

étendre /etɑ̃dr/ v.t. spread; (journal, nappe) spread out; (bras, jambes) stretch (out); (linge) hang out; (agrandir) extend. **s'~** v. pr. (s'allonger) stretch out; (se propager) spread; (plaine etc.) stretch. **s'~ sur**, (sujet) dwell on.

étendu, ~e /etɑ̃dy/ a. extensive. —n.f. area; (d'eau) stretch; (importance) extent.

éternel, ~le /etɛrnɛl/ a. eternal. **~lement** adv. eternally.

éterniser (s') /(s)etɛrnize/ v. pr. (durer) drag on.

éternité /etɛrnite/ n.f. eternity.

étern|uer /etɛrnɥe/ v.i. sneeze. **~uement** /-ymɑ̃/ n.m. sneeze.

êtes /ɛt/ voir être.

éthique /etik/ a. ethical. —n.f. ethics.

ethn|ie /ɛtni/ n.f. ethnic group. **~ique** a. ethnic.

éthylisme /etilism/ n.m. alcoholism.

étinceler /etɛ̃sle/ v.i. sparkle.

étincelle /etɛ̃sɛl/ *n.f.* spark.

étioler (s') /(s)etjɔle/ *v. pr.* wilt.

étiqueter /etikte/ *v.t.* label.

étiquette /etikɛt/ *n.f.* label; (*protocole*) etiquette.

étirer /etire/ *v.t.*, **s'~** *v. pr.* stretch.

étoffe /etɔf/ *n.f.* fabric.

étoffer /etɔfe/ *v.t.*, **s'~** *v. pr.* fill out.

étoil|e /etwal/ *n.f.* star. **à la belle ~e**, in the open. **~e de mer**, starfish. **~é** *a.* starry.

étonn|er /etɔne/ *v.t.* amaze. **s'~er** *v. pr.* be amazed (**de**, at). **~ant, ~ante** *a.* amazing. **~ement** *n.m.* amazement.

étouffée /etufe/ *n.f.* **cuire à l'~**, braise.

étouff|er /etufe/ *v.t./i.* suffocate; (*sentiment, révolte*) stifle; (*feu*) smother; (*bruit*) muffle. **on ~e**, it is stifling. **s'~er** *v. pr.* suffocate; (*en mangeant*) choke. **~ant, ~ante** *a.* stifling.

étourd|i, ~ie /eturdi/ *a.* unthinking, scatter-brained. —*n.m., f.* scatter-brain. **~erie** *n.f.* thoughtlessness; (*acte*) thoughtless act.

étourd|ir /eturdir/ *v.t.* stun; (*griser*) make dizzy. **~issant, ~issante** *a.* stunning. **~issement** *n.m.* (*syncope*) dizzy spell.

étourneau (*pl.* **~x**) /eturno/ *n.m.* starling.

étrange /etrɑ̃ʒ/ *a.* strange. **~ment** *adv.* strangely. **~té** *n.f.* strangeness.

étrang|er, ~ère /etrɑ̃ʒe, -ɛr/ *a.* strange, unfamiliar; (*d'un autre pays*) foreign. —*n.m., f.* foreigner; (*inconnu*) stranger. **à l'~er**, abroad. **de l'~er**, from abroad.

étrangler /etrɑ̃gle/ *v.t.* strangle; (*col*) stifle. **s'~** *v. pr.* choke.

être† /ɛtr/ *v.i.* be. —*v. aux.* (*avec aller, sortir, etc.*) have. **~ donné/fait par**, (*passif*) be given/done by. —*n.m.* (*personne, créature*) being. **~ humain**, human being **~ médecin/tailleur**/*etc.*, be a doctor/a tailor/*etc.* **~ à qn.**, be s.o.'s. **c'est à faire**, it needs to be *ou* should be done. **est-ce qu'il travaille?**, is he working?, does he work? **vous travaillez, n'est-ce pas?**, you are working, aren't you?, you work, don't you? **il est deux heures**/*etc.*, it is two o'clock/*etc.* **nous sommes le six mai**, it is the sixth of May.

étrein|dre /etrɛ̃dr/ *v.t.* grasp; (*ami*) embrace. **~te** /-ɛ̃t/ *n.f.* grasp; embrace.

étrenner /etrene/ *v.t.* use for the first time.

étrennes /etrɛn/ *n.f. pl.* (*cadeau*) New Year's gift.

étrier /etrije/ *n.m.* stirrup.

étriqué /etrike/ *a.* tight; (*fig.*) small-minded.

étroit, ~e /etrwa, -t/ *a.* narrow; (*vêtement*) tight; (*liens, surveillance*) close. **à l'~**, cramped. **~ement** /-tmɑ̃/ *adv.* closely. **~esse** /-tɛs/ *n.f.* narrowness.

étude /etyd/ *n.f.* study; (*bureau*) office. (**salle d'**)**~**, (*scol.*) prep room; (*scol., Amer.*) study hall. **à l'~**, under consideration. **faire des ~s (de)**, study.

étudiant, ~e /etydjɑ̃, -t/ *n.m., f.* student.

étudier /etydje/ *v.t./i.* study.

étui /etyi/ *n.m.* case.

étuve /etyv/ *n.f.* steamroom. **quelle étuve!**, it's like a hothouse in here.

étuvée /etyve/ *n.f.* **cuire à l'~**, braise.

etymologie /etimɔlɔʒi/ *n.f.* etymology.

eu, eue /y/ *voir* **avoir**.

eucalyptus /økaliptys/ *n.m.* eucalyptus.

euphémisme /øfemism/ *n.m.* euphemism.

euphorie /øfɔri/ *n.f.* euphoria.

Europe /ørɔp/ *n.f.* Europe.

européen, ~ne /ørɔpeɛ̃, -ɛɛn/ *a. & n.m., f.* European.

euthanasie /øtanazi/ *n.f.* euthanasia.

eux /ø/ *pron.* they; (*complément*) them. **~-mêmes** *pron.* themselves.

évac|uer /evakɥe/ *v.t.* evacuate. **~uation** *n.f.* evacuation.

évad|er (s') /(s)evade/ *v. pr.* escape. **~é, ~ée** *a.* escaped; *n.m., f.* escaped prisoner.

éval|uer /evalɥe/ *v.t.* assess. **~uation** *n.f.* assessment.

évang|ile /evɑ̃ʒil/ *n.m.* gospel. **l'Évangile**, the Gospel. **~élique** *a.* evangelical.

évan|ouir (s') /(s)evanwir/ *v. pr.* faint; (*disparaître*) vanish. **~ouissement** *n.m.* (*syncope*) fainting fit.

évapor|er /evapɔre/ *v.t.*, **s'~er** *v. pr.* evaporate. **~ation** *n.f.* evaporation.

évasi|f, ~ve /evazif, -v/ *a.* evasive.

évasion /evazjɔ̃/ *n.f.* escape; (*par le rêve etc.*) escapism.

éveil /evɛj/ *n.m.* awakening. **donner l'~ à**, arouse the suspicions of. **en ~**, alert.

éveill|er /eveje/ *v.t.* awake(n); (*susciter*) arouse. **s'~er** *v. pr.* awake(n); be aroused. **~é** *a.* awake; (*intelligent*) alert.

événement /evɛnmɑ̃/ *n.m.* event.

éventail /evɑ̃taj/ *n.m.* fan; (*gamme*) range.

éventaire /evɑ̃tɛr/ *n.m.* stall, stand.

éventé /evɑ̃te/ *a.* (*gâté*) stale.

éventrer /evɑ̃tre/ *v.t.* (*sac etc.*) rip open.

éventualité /evɑ̃tɥalite/ *n.f.* possibility. **dans cette ∼,** in that event.

éventuel, ∼le /evɑ̃tɥɛl/ *a.* possible. **∼lement** *adv.* possibly.

évêque /evɛk/ *n.m.* bishop.

évertuer (s') /(s)evɛrtɥe/ *v. pr.* **s'∼ à,** struggle hard to.

éviction /eviksjɔ̃/ *n.f.* eviction.

évidemment /cvidamɑ̃/ *adv.* obviously; (*bien sûr*) of course.

évidence /evidɑ̃s/ *n.f.* obviousness; (*fait*) obvious fact. **être en ∼,** be conspicuous. **mettre en ∼,** (*fait*) highlight.

évident, ∼e /evidɑ̃, -t/ *a.* obvious, evident.

évider /evide/ *v.t.* hollow out.

évier /evje/ *n.m.* sink.

évincer /evɛ̃se/ *v.t.* oust.

éviter /evite/ *v.t.* avoid (**de faire,** doing). **∼ à qn.,** (*dérangement etc.*) spare s.o.

évoca|teur ∼trice /evɔkatœr, -tris/ *a.* evocative.

évocation /evɔkɑsjɔ̃/ *n.f.* evocation.

évolué /evɔlɥe/ *a.* highly developed.

évol|uer /evɔlɥe/ *v.i.* develop; (*se déplacer*) move, manœuvre; (*Amer.*) maneuver. **∼ution** *n.f.* development; (*d'une espèce*) evolution; (*déplacement*) movement.

évoquer /evɔke/ *v.t.* call to mind, evoke.

ex- /ɛks/ *préf.* ex-.

exacerber /ɛgzasɛrbe/ *v.t.* exacerbate.

exact, ∼e /ɛgza(kt), -akt/ *a.* exact, accurate; (*correct*) correct; (*personne*) punctual. **∼ement** /-ktəmɑ̃/ *adv.* exactly. **∼itude** /-ktityd/ *n.f.* exactness; punctuality.

ex aequo /ɛgzeko/ *adv.* (*classer*) equal. **être ∼,** be equally placed.

exagéré /ɛgzaʒere/ *a.* excessive.

exagér|er /ɛgzaʒere/ *v.t./i.* exaggerate; (*abuser*) go too far. **∼ation** *n.f.* exaggeration.

exaltation /ɛgzaltɑsjɔ̃/ *n.f.* elation.

exalté, ∼e /ɛgzalte/ *n.m., f.* fanatic.

exalter /ɛgzalte/ *v.t.* excite; (*glorifier*) exalt.

examen /ɛgzamɛ̃/ *n.m.* examination; (*scol.*) exam(ination).

examin|er /ɛgzamine/ *v.t.* examine. **∼ateur, ∼atrice** *n.m., f.* examiner.

exaspér|er /ɛgzaspere/ *v.t.* exasperate. **∼ation** *n.f.* exasperation.

exaucer /ɛgzose/ *v.t.* grant; (*personne*) grant the wish(es) of.

excavateur /ɛkskavatœr/ *n.m.* digger.

excavation /ɛkskavɑsjɔ̃/ *n.f.* excavation.

excédent /ɛksedɑ̃/ *n.m.* surplus. **∼ de bagages,** excess luggage. **∼ de la balance commerciale,** trade surplus. **∼aire** /-tɛr/ *a.* excess, surplus.

excéder[1] /ɛksede/ *v.t.* (*dépasser*) exceed.

excéder[2] /ɛksede/ *v.t.* (*agacer*) irritate.

excellen|t, ∼te /ɛksɛlɑ̃, -t/ *a.* excellent. **∼ce** *n.f.* excellence.

exceller /ɛksele/ *v.i.* excel (**dans,** in).

excentri|que /ɛksɑ̃trik/ *a.* & *n.m./f.* eccentric. **∼cité** *n.f.* eccentricity.

excepté /ɛksɛpte/ *a.* & *prép.* except.

excepter /ɛksɛpte/ *v.t.* except.

exception /ɛksɛpsjɔ̃/ *n.f.* exception. **à l'∼ de,** except for. **d'∼,** exceptional. **faire ∼,** be an exception. **∼nel, ∼nelle** /-jɔnɛl/ *a.* exceptional. **∼nellement** /-jɔnɛlmɑ̃/ *adv.* exceptionally.

excès /ɛksɛ/ *n.m.* excess. **∼ de vitesse,** speeding.

excessi|f, ∼ve /ɛksesif, -v/ *a.* excessive. **∼vement** *adv.* excessively.

excitant /ɛksitɑ̃/ *n.m.* stimulant.

excit|er /ɛksite/ *v.t.* excite; (*encourager*) exhort (**à,** to); (*irriter: fam.*) annoy. **∼ation** *n.f.* excitement.

exclam|er (s') /(s)ɛksklame/ *v. pr.* exclaim. **∼ation** *n.f.* exclamation.

exclu|re† /ɛksklyr/ *v.t.* exclude; (*expulser*) expel; (*empêcher*) preclude. **∼sion** *n.f.* exclusion.

exclusi|f, ∼ve /ɛksklyzif, -v/ *a.* exclusive. **∼vement** *adv* exclusively. **∼vité** *n.f.* (*comm.*) exclusive rights. **en ∼vité à,** (*film*) (showing) exclusively at.

excrément(s) /ɛkskremɑ̃/ *n.m.* (*pl.*). excrement.

excroissance /ɛkskrwasɑ̃s/ *n.f.* (*out*) growth, excrescence.

excursion /ɛkskyrsjɔ̃/ *n.f.* excursion; (*à pied*) hike.

excuse /ɛkskyz/ *n.f.* excuse. **∼s,** apology. **faire des ∼s,** apologize.

excuser /ɛkskyze/ *v.t.* excuse. **s'∼** *v. pr.* apologize (**de,** for). **je m'excuse,** (*fam.*) excuse me.

exécrable /ɛgzekrabl/ *a.* abominable.

exécrer /ɛgzekre/ *v.t.* loathe.

exécut|er /ɛgzekyte/ *v.t.* carry out, execute; (*mus.*) perform; (*tuer*) execute. **∼ion** /-sjɔ̃/ *n.f.* execution; (*mus.*) performance.

exécuti|f, **~ve** /ɛgzekytif, -v/ *a.* & *n.m.*
(*pol.*) executive.

exemplaire /ɛgzɑ̃plɛr/ *a.* exemplary.
—*n.m.* copy.

exemple /ɛgzɑ̃pl/ *n.m.* example. **par ~**,
for example. **donner l'~**, set an
example.

exempt, **~e** /ɛgzɑ̃, -t/ *a.* **~ de**, exempt
from.

exempt|er /ɛgzɑ̃te/ *v.t.* exempt (**de**,
from). **~ion** /-psjɔ̃/ *n.f.* exemption.

exercer /ɛgzɛrse/ *v.t.* exercise;
(*influence, contrôle*) exert; (*métier*)
work at; (*former*) train, exercise. **s'~**
(**à**), practise.

exercice /ɛgzɛrsis/ *n.m.* exercise; (*mil.*)
drill; (*de métier*) practice. **en ~**, in
office; (*médecin*) in practice.

exhaler /ɛgzale/ *v.t.* emit.

exhausti|f, **~ve** /ɛgzostif, -v/ *a.*
exhaustive.

exhiber /ɛgzibe/ *v.t.* exhibit.

exhibitionniste /ɛgzibisjɔnist/ *n.m./f.*
exhibitionist.

exhorter /ɛgzɔrte/ *v.t.* exhort (**à**, to).

exigence /ɛgziʒɑ̃s/ *n.f.* demand.

exig|er /ɛgziʒe/ *v.t.* demand. **~eant**,
~eante *a.* demanding.

exigu, **~ë** /ɛgzigy/ *a.* tiny.

exil /ɛgzil/ *n.m.* exile. **~é**, **~ée** *n.m.*, *f.*
exile. **~er** *v.t.* exile. **s'~er** *v. pr.* go into
exile.

existence /ɛgzistɑ̃s/ *n.f.* existence.

exist|er /ɛgziste/ *v.i.* exist. **~ant**, **~ante**
a. existing.

exode /ɛgzɔd/ *n.m.* exodus.

exonér|er /ɛgzɔnere/ *v.t.* exempt (**de**,
from). **~ation** *n.f.* exemption.

exorbitant, **~e** /ɛgzɔrbitɑ̃, -t/ *a.*
exorbitant.

exorciser /ɛgzɔrsize/ *v.t.* exorcize.

exotique /ɛgzɔtik/ *a.* exotic.

expansi|f, **~ve** /ɛkspɑ̃sif, -v/ *a.*
expansive.

expansion /ɛkspɑ̃sjɔ̃/ *n.f.* expansion.

expatr|ier (s') /(s)ɛkspatrije/ *v. pr.* leave
one's country. **~ié**, **~iée** *n.m.*, *f.*
expatriate.

expectative /ɛkspɛktativ/ *n.f.* **dans l'~**,
still waiting.

expédient, **~e** /ɛkspedjɑ̃, -t/ *a.* & *n.m.*
expedient. **vivre d'~s**, live by one's
wits. **user d'~s**, resort to expedients.

expéd|ier /ɛkspedje/ *v.t.* send, dispatch;
(*tâche: péj.*) dispatch. **~iteur**, **~itrice**
n.m., *f.* sender. **~ition** *n.f.* dispatch;
(*voyage*) expedition.

expéditi|f, **~ve** /ɛkspeditif, -v/ *a.*
quick.

expérience /ɛksperjɑ̃s/ *n.f.* experience;
(*scientifique*) experiment.

expérimenté /ɛksperimɑ̃te/ *a.* experienced.

expériment|er /ɛksperimɑ̃te/ *v.t.* test,
experiment with. **~al** (*m. pl.* **~aux**) *a.*
experimental. **~ation** *n.f.* experimenta-
tion.

expert, **~e** /ɛkspɛr, -t/ *a.* expert.
—*n.m.* expert; (*d'assurances*) valuer;
(*Amer.*) appraiser. **~-comptable** (*pl.*
~s-comptables) *n.m.* accountant.

expertis|e /ɛkspɛrtiz/ *n.f.* expert ap-
praisal. **~er** *v.t.* appraise.

expier /ɛkspje/ *v.t.* atone for.

expir|er /ɛkspire/ *v.i.* breathe out; (*finir,
mourir*) expire. **~ation** *n.f.* expiry.

explicati|f, **~ve** /ɛksplikatif, -v/ *a.*
explanatory.

explication /ɛksplikɑsjɔ̃/ *n.f.* explanation; (*fig.*) discussion; (*scol.*) commentary. **~ de texte**, (*scol.*) literary
commentary.

explicite /ɛksplisit/ *a.* explicit.

expliquer /ɛksplike/ *v.t.* explain. **s'~** *v.
pr.* explain o.s.; (*discuter*) discuss
things; (*être compréhensible*) be understandable.

exploit /ɛksplwa/ *n.m.* exploit.

exploitant /ɛksplwatɑ̃/ *n.m.* **~
(agricole)**, farmer.

exploit|er /ɛksplwate/ *v.t.* (*personne*)
exploit; (*ferme*) run; (*champs*) work.
~ation *n.f.* exploitation; running;
working; (*affaire*) concern. **~eur**,
~euse *n.m.*, *f.* exploiter.

explor|er /ɛksplɔre/ *v.t.* explore.
~ateur, **~atrice** *n.m.*, *f.* explorer.
~ation *n.f.* exploration.

explos|er /ɛksploze/ *v.i.* explode. **faire
~er**, explode; (*bâtiment*) blow up.
~ion *n.f.* explosion.

explosi|f, **~ve** /ɛksplozif, -v/ *a.* & *n.m.*
explosive.

export|er /ɛkspɔrte/ *v.t.* export. **~ateur**,
~atrice *n.m.*, *f.* exporter; *a.* exporting.
~ation *n.f.* export.

exposant, **~e** /ɛkspozɑ̃, -t/ *n.m.*, *f.*
exhibitor.

exposé /ɛkspoze/ *n.m.* talk (**sur**, on);
(*d'une action*) account. **faire l'~ de la
situation**, give an account of the
situation.

expos|er /ɛkspoze/ *v.t.* display, show;
(*expliquer*) explain; (*soumettre, mettre
en danger*) expose (**à**, to); (*vie*)
endanger. **~é au nord**/*etc.*, facing
north/*etc.* **s'~er à**, expose o.s. to.

exposition /ɛkspozisjɔ̃/ *n.f.* display; (*salon*) exhibition. ~ **à,** exposure to.

exprès[1] /ɛksprɛ/ *adv.* specially; (*délibérément*) on purpose.

expr|ès[2], **~esse** /ɛksprɛs/ *a.* express. **~essément** *adv.* expressly.

exprès[3] /ɛkspres/ *a. invar. & n.m.* **lettre** ~, express letter. **(par)** ~, sent special delivery.

express /ɛksprɛs/ *a. & n.m. invar.* **(café)** ~, espresso. **(train)** ~, fast train.

expressi|f, **~ve** /ɛkspresif, -v/ *a.* expressive.

expression /ɛkspresjɔ̃/ *n.f.* expression. ~ **corporelle,** physical expression.

exprimer /ɛksprime/ *v.t.* express. **s'~** *v. pr.* express o.s.

expuls|er /ɛkspylse/ *v.t.* expel; (*locataire*) evict; (*joueur*) send off. **~ion** *n.f.* expulsion; eviction.

expurger /ɛkspyrʒe/ *v.t.* expurgate.

exquis, **~e** /ɛkski, -z/ *a.* exquisite.

extase /ɛkstɑz/ *n.f.* ecstasy.

extasier (s') /(s)ɛkstɑzje/ *v. pr.* **s'~ sur,** be ecstatic about.

extensible /ɛkstɑ̃sibl/ *a.* expandable, extendible. **tissu** ~, stretch fabric.

extensi|f, **~ve** /ɛkstɑ̃sif, -v/ *a.* extensive.

extension /ɛkstɑ̃sjɔ̃/ *n.f.* extension; (*expansion*) expansion.

exténuer /ɛkstenɥe/ *v.t.* exhaust.

extérieur /ɛksterjœr/ *a.* outside; (*signe, gaieté*) outward; (*politique*) foreign. —*n.m.* outside, exterior; (*de personne*) exterior. **à l'~ (de),** outside. **~ement** *adv.* outwardly.

extérioriser /ɛksterjɔrize/ *v.t.* show, externalize.

extermin|er /ɛkstɛrmine/ *v.t.* exterminate. **~ation** *n.f.* extermination.

externe /ɛkstɛrn/ *a.* external. —*n.m./f.* (*scol.*) day pupil.

extincteur /ɛkstɛ̃ktœr/ *n.m.* fire extinguisher.

extinction /ɛkstɛ̃ksjɔ̃/ *n.f.* extinction. ~ **de voix,** loss of voice.

extirper /ɛkstirpe/ *v.t.* eradicate.

extor|quer /ɛkstɔrke/ *v.t.* extort. **~sion** *n.f.* extortion.

extra /ɛkstra/ *a. invar.* first-rate. —*n.m. invar.* (*repas*) (special) treat.

extra- /ɛkstra/ *préf.* extra-.

extrad|er /ɛkstrade/ *v.t.* extradite. **~ition** *n.f.* extradition.

extr|aire† /ɛkstrɛr/ *v.t.* extract. **~action** *n.f.* extraction.

extrait /ɛkstrɛ/ *n.m.* extract.

extraordinaire /ɛkstraɔrdinɛr/ *a.* extraordinary.

extravagan|t, **~te** /ɛkstravagɑ̃, -t/ *a.* extravagant. **~ce** *n.f.* extravagance.

extraverti, **~e** /ɛkstravɛrti/ *n.m.,* *f.* extrovert.

extrême /ɛkstrɛm/ *a. & n.m.* extreme. **E~-Orient** *n.m.* Far East. **~ment** *adv.* extremely.

extrémiste /ɛkstremist/ *n.m.,* *f.* extremist.

extrémité /ɛkstremite/ *n.f.* extremity, end; (*misère*) dire straits. **~s,** (*excès*) extremes.

exubéran|t, **~te** /ɛgzyberɑ̃, -t/ *a.* exuberant. **~ce** *n.f.* exuberance.

exulter /ɛgzylte/ *v.i.* exult.

exutoire /ɛgzytwar/ *n.m.* outlet.

F

F *abrév.* (*franc, francs*) franc, francs.

fable /fɑbl/ *n.f.* fable.

fabrique /fabrik/ *n.f.* factory.

fabri|quer /fabrike/ *v.t.* make; (*industriellement*) manufacture; (*fig.*) make up. **~cant,** **~cante** *n.m.,* *f.* manufacturer. **~cation** *n.f.* making; manufacture.

fabul|er /fabyle/ *v.i.* fantasize. **~ation** *n.f.* fantasizing.

fabuleu|x, **~se** /fabylø, -z/ *a.* fabulous.

fac /fak/ *n.f.* (*fam.*) university.

façade /fasad/ *n.f.* front; (*fig.*) façade.

face /fas/ *n.f.* face; (*d'un objet*) side. **en** ~ **(de), d'en** ~, opposite. **en** ~ **de,** (*fig.*) faced with. ~ **à, facing;** (*fig.*) faced with. **faire** ~ **à,** face.

facétie /fasesi/ *n.f.* joke.

facette /fasɛt/ *n.f.* facet.

fâch|er /faʃe/ *v.t.* anger. **se ~er** *v. pr.* get angry; (*se brouiller*) fall out. **~é** *a.* angry; (*désolé*) sorry.

fâcheu|x, **~se** /faʃø, -z/ *a.* unfortunate.

facil|e /fasil/ *a.* easy; (*caractère*) easygoing. **~ement** *adv.* easily. **~ité** *n.f.* easiness; (*aisance*) ease; (*aptitude*) ability; (*possibilité*) facility. **~ités de paiement,** easy terms.

faciliter /fasilite/ *v.t.* facilitate.

façon /fasɔ̃/ *n.f.* way; (*de vêtement*) cut. **~s,** (*chichis*) fuss. **de cette** ~, in this way. **de** ~ **à,** so as to. **de toute** ~, anyway.

façonner /fasɔne/ *v.t.* shape; (*faire*) make.

facteur¹ /faktœr/ *n.m.* postman.

facteur² /faktœr/ *n.m.* (*élément*) factor.

factice /faktis/ *a.* artificial.

faction /faksjɔ̃/ *n.f.* faction. **de** ∼, (*mil.*) on guard.

factur|e /faktyr/ *n.f.* bill; (*comm.*) invoice. ∼**er** *v.t.* invoice.

facultati|f, ∼ve /fakyltatif, -v/ *a.* optional.

faculté /fakylte/ *n.f.* faculty; (*possibilité*) power; (*univ.*) faculty.

fade /fad/ *a.* insipid.

fagot /fago/ *n.m.* bundle of firewood.

fagoter /fagɔte/ *v.t.* (*fam.*) rig out.

faibl|e /fɛbl/ *a.* weak; (*espoir, quantité, écart*) slight; (*revenu, intensité*) low. —*n.m.* weakling; (*penchant, défaut*) weakness. ∼**e d'esprit,** feeble-minded. ∼**esse** *n.f.* weakness. ∼**ir** *v.i.* weaken.

faïence /fajɑ̃s/ *n.f.* earthenware.

faille /faj/ *n.f.* (*géog.*) fault; (*fig.*) flaw.

faillir /fajir/ *v.i.* **j'ai failli acheter**/*etc.*, I almost bought/*etc.*

faillite /fajit/ *n.f.* bankruptcy; (*fig.*) collapse.

faim /fɛ̃/ *n.f.* hunger. **avoir** ∼, be hungry.

fainéant, ∼e /feneɑ̃, -t/ *a.* idle. —*n.m., f.* idler.

faire† /fɛr/ *v.t.* make; (*activité*) do; (*rêve, chute, etc.*) have; (*dire*) say. **ça fait 20 F,** that's 20 F. **ça fait 3 ans,** it's been 3 years. —*v.i.* do; (*paraître*) look. **se** ∼, *v. pr.* (*petit etc.*) make o.s.; (*amis, argent*) make; (*illusions*) have; (*devenir*) become. ∼ **du rugby/du violon**/*etc.*, play rugby/the violin/*etc.* ∼ **construire/punir**/*etc.*, have *ou* get built/punished/*etc.*, ∼ **pleurer/tomber**/ *etc.*, make cry/fall/*etc.* **se** ∼ **tuer**/*etc.*, get killed/*etc.* **se** ∼ **couper les cheveux,** have one's hair cut. **il fait beau/chaud**/*etc.*, it is fine/hot/*etc.* ∼ **l'idiot,** play the fool. **ne** ∼ **que pleurer**/*etc.*, (*faire continuellement*) do nothing but cry/*etc.* **ça ne fait rien,** it doesn't matter. **se** ∼ **à,** get used to. **s'en** ∼, worry. **ça se fait,** that is done. ∼**-part** *n.m. invar.* announcement.

fais, fait¹ /fɛ/ *voir* **faire.**

faisable /fəzabl/ *a.* feasible.

faisan /fəzɑ̃/ *n.m.* pheasant.

faisandé /fəzɑ̃de/ *a.* high.

faisceau (*pl.* ∼**x**) /fɛso/ *n.m.* (*rayon*) beam; (*fagot*) bundle.

fait², ∼**e** /fɛ, fɛt/ *a.* done; (*fromage*) ripe. ∼ **pour,** made for. **tout** ∼, ready made. **c'est bien** ∼ **pour toi,** it serves you right.

fait³ /fɛ/ *n.m.* fact; (*événement*) event. **au** ∼ **(de),** informed (of). **de ce** ∼, therefore. **du** ∼ **de,** on account of. ∼ **divers,** (trivial) news item. ∼ **nouveau,** new development. **sur le** ∼, in the act.

faîte /fɛt/ *n.m.* top; (*fig.*) peak.

faites /fɛt/ *voir* **faire.**

faitout /fɛtu/ *n.m.* stew-pot.

falaise /falɛz/ *n.f.* cliff.

falloir† /falwar/ *v.i.* **il faut qch./qn.,** we, you, *etc.* need sth./so. **il lui faut du pain,** he needs bread. **il faut rester,** we, you, *etc.* have to *ou* must stay. **il faut que j'y aille,** I have to *ou* must go. **il faudrait que tu partes,** you should leave. **il aurait fallu le faire,** we, you, *etc.* should have done it. **il s'en faut de beaucoup que je sois,** I am far from being. **comme il faut,** properly; *a.* proper.

falot, ∼e /falo, falɔt/ *a.* grey.

falsifier /falsifje/ *v.t.* falsify.

famélique /famelik/ *a.* starving.

fameu|x, ∼se /famø, -z/ *a.* famous; (*excellent: fam.*) first-rate. ∼**sement** *adv.* (*fam.*) extremely.

famil|ial (*m. pl.* ∼**iaux**) /familjal, -jo/ *a.* family.

familiar|iser /familjarize/ *v.t.* familiarize (**avec,** with). **se** ∼**iser** *v. pr.* familiarize o.s. ∼**isé** *a.* familiar. ∼**ité** *n.f.* familiarity.

famil|ier, ∼ière /familje, -jɛr/ *a.* familiar; (*amical*) informal. —*n.m.* regular visitor. ∼**ièrement** *adv.* informally.

famille /famij/ *n.f.* family. **en** ∼, with one's family.

famine /famin/ *n.f.* famine.

fanati|que /fanatik/ *a.* fanatical. —*n.m./f.* fanatic. ∼**sme** *n.m.* fanaticism.

faner (se) /(sə)fane/ *v. pr.* fade.

fanfare /fɑ̃far/ *n.f.* brass band; (*musique*) fanfare.

fanfaron, ∼ne /fɑ̃farɔ̃, -ɔn/ *a.* boastful. —*n.m., f.* boaster.

fanion /fanjɔ̃/ *n.m.* pennant.

fantaisie /fɑ̃tezi/ *n.f.* imagination, fantasy; (*caprice*) whim. **(de)** ∼, (*boutons etc.*) fancy.

fantaisiste /fɑ̃tezist/ *a.* unorthodox.

fantasme /fɑ̃tasm/ *n.m.* fantasy.

fantasque /fɑ̃task/ *a.* whimsical.

fantastique /fɑ̃tastik/ *a.* fantastic.

fantoche /fɑ̃tɔʃ/ *n.m.* puppet.

fantôme /fɑ̃tom/ *n.m.* ghost. —*a.* (*péj.*) bogus.

faon /fɑ̃/ *n.m.* fawn.

faramineux, **∼se** /faraminø, -z/ *a.*
astronomical.

farc|e¹ /fars/ *n.f.* (practical) joke;
(*théâtre*) farce. **∼eur**, **∼euse** *n.m.*, *f.*
joker.

farc|e² /fars/ *n.f.* (*hachis*) stuffing. **∼ir**
v.t. stuff.

fard /far/ *n.m.* make-up. **piquer un ∼**,
blush. **∼er** /-de/ *v.t.*, **se ∼er** *v. pr.* make
up.

fardeau (*pl.* **∼x**) /fardo/ *n.m.* burden.

farfelu, **∼e** /farfəly/ *a. & n.m.*, *f.*
eccentric.

farin|e /farin/ *n.f.* flour. **∼eux**, **∼euse** *a.*
floury. **les ∼eux** *n.m. pl.* starchy food.

farouche /faruʃ/ *a.* shy; (*peu sociable*)
unsociable; (*violent*) fierce. **∼ment**
adv. fiercely.

fascicule /fasikyl/ *n.m.* volume.

fascin|er /fasine/ *v.t.* fascinate. **∼ation**
n.f. fascination.

fascis|te /faʃist/ *a. & n.m./f.* fascist. **∼me**
n.m. fascism.

fasse /fas/ *voir* **faire**.

faste /fast/ *n.m.* splendour.

fast-food /fastfud/ *n.m.* fast-food place.

fastidieu|x, **∼se** /fastidjø, -z/ *a.*
tedious.

fat|al (*m. pl.* **∼als**) /fatal/ *a.* inevitable;
(*mortel*) fatal. **∼alement** *adv.* inevitably. **∼alité** *n.f.* (*destin*) fate.

fataliste /fatalist/ *n.m./f.* fatalist.

fatidique /fatidik/ *a.* fateful.

fatigant, **∼e** /fatigã, -t/ *a.* tiring;
(*ennuyeux*) tiresome.

fatigue /fatig/ *n.f.* fatigue, tiredness.

fatigu|er /fatige/ *v.t.* tire; (*yeux, moteur*)
strain. —*v.i.* (*moteur*) labour. **se ∼er** *v.*
pr. get tired, tire (**de**, of). **∼é** *a.* tired.

fatras /fatra/ *n.m.* jumble.

faubourg /fobur/ *n.m.* suburb.

fauché /foʃe/ *a.* (*fam.*) broke.

faucher /foʃe/ *v.t.* (*herbe*) mow; (*voler:*
fam.) pinch. **∼ qn.**, (*véhicule, tir*) mow
s.o. down.

faucille /fosij/ *n.f.* sickle.

faucon /fokõ/ *n.m.* falcon, hawk.

faudra, **faudrait** /fodra, fodrɛ/ *voir*
falloir.

faufiler (se) /(sə)fofile/ *v. pr.* edge one's
way.

faune /fon/ *n.f.* wildlife, fauna.

faussaire /fosɛr/ *n.m.* forger.

fausse /fos/ *voir* **faux²**.

faussement /fosmã/ *adv.* falsely,
wrongly.

fausser /fose/ *v.t.* buckle; (*fig.*) distort.
∼ compagnie à, sneak away from.

fausseté /foste/ *n.f.* falseness.

faut /fo/ *voir* **falloir**.

faute /fot/ *n.f.* mistake; (*responsabilité*)
fault; (*délit*) offence; (*péché*) sin. **en ∼**,
at fault. **∼ de**, for want of. **∼ de quoi**,
failing which. **sans faute**, without fail.
∼ de frappe, typing error. **∼ de goût**,
bad taste. **∼ professionelle**, professional misconduct.

fauteuil /fotœj/ *n.m.* armchair; (*de*
président) chair; (*théâtre*) seat. **∼**
roulant, wheelchair.

fauti|f, **∼ve** /fotif, -v/ *a.* guilty; (*faux*)
faulty. —*n.m.*, *f.* guilty party.

fauve /fov/ *a.* (*couleur*) fawn. —*n.m.*
wild cat.

faux¹ /fo/ *n.f.* scythe.

faux², **fausse** /fo, fos/ *a.* false; (*falsifié*)
fake, forged; (*numéro, calcul*) wrong;
(*voix*) out of tune. **c'est ∼!**, that is
wrong! **∼ témoignage**, perjury. **faire**
∼ bond à qn., stand s.o. up. —*adv.*
(*chanter*) out of tune. —*n.m.* forgery.
fausse alerte, false alarm. **fausse**
couche, miscarriage. **∼-filet** *n.m.*
sirloin. **∼ frais**, *n.m. pl.* incidental expenses. **∼-monnayeur** *n.m.* forger.

faveur /favœr/ *n.f.* favour. **de ∼**,
(*régime*) preferential. **en ∼ de**, in
favour of.

favorable /favɔrabl/ *a.* favourable.

favori, **∼te** /favɔri, -t/ *a. & n.m.*, *f.*
favourite. **∼tisme** *n.m.* favouritism.

favoriser /favɔrize/ *v.t.* favour.

fax /faks/ *n.m.* fax. **∼er** *v.t.* fax.

fébrile /febril/ *a.* feverish.

fécond, **∼e** /fekõ, -d/ *a.* fertile. **∼er**
/-de/ *v.t.* fertilize. **∼ité** /-dite/ *n.f.*
fertility.

fédér|al (*m. pl.* **∼aux**) /federal, -o/ *a.*
federal.

fédération /federasjõ/ *n.f.* federation.

fée /fe/ *n.f.* fairy.

féer|ie /fe(e)ri/ *n.f.* magical spectacle.
∼ique *a.* magical.

feindre† /fɛdr/ *v.t.* feign. **∼ de**, pretend
to.

feinte /fɛt/ *n.f.* feint.

fêler /fele/ *v.t.*, **se ∼** *v. pr.* crack.

félicit|er /felisite/ *v.t.* congratulate (**de**,
on). **∼ations** *n.f. pl.* congratulations
(**pour**, on).

félin, **∼e** /felɛ, -in/ *a. & n.m.* feline.

fêlure /felyr/ *n.f.* crack.

femelle /fəmɛl/ *a. & n.f.* female.

fémin|in, **∼ine** /feminɛ, -in/ *a.*
feminine; (*sexe*) female; (*mode,*
équipe) women's. —*n.m.* feminine.
∼ité *n.f.* femininity.

féministe /feminist/ *n.m./f.* feminist.

femme /fam/ n.f. woman; (*épouse*) wife.
~ **au foyer,** housewife. ~ **de
chambre,** chambermaid. ~ **de
ménage,** cleaning lady.
fémur /femyr/ n.m. thigh-bone.
fendiller /fɑ̃dije/ v.t., **se** ~ v. pr. crack.
fendre /fɑ̃dr/ v.t. (*couper*) split;
(*fissurer*) crack; (*foule*) push through.
se ~ v. pr. crack.
fenêtre /fənɛtr/ n.f. window.
fenouil /fənuj/ n.m. fennel.
fente /fɑ̃t/ n.f. (*ouverture*) slit, slot;
(*fissure*) crack.
féod|al (m. pl. ~**aux**) /feɔdal, -o/ a.
feudal.
fer /fɛr/ n.m. iron. ~ **(à repasser),** iron.
~ **à cheval,** horseshoe. ~**-blanc** (pl.
~**s-blancs**) n.m. tinplate. ~ **de lance,**
spearhead. ~ **forgé,** wrought iron.
fera, ferait /fəra, fərɛ/ *voir* **faire.**
férié /ferje/ a. **jour** ~, public holiday.
ferme¹ /fɛrm/ a. firm. —*adv.*
(*travailler*) hard. ~**ment** /-əmɑ̃/ adv.
firmly.
ferme² /fɛrm/ n.f. farm; (*maison*)
farm(house).
fermé /fɛrme/ a. closed; (*gaz, radio,
etc.*) off.
ferment /fɛrmɑ̃/ n.m. ferment.
ferment|er /fɛrmɑ̃te/ v.i. ferment.
~**ation** n.f. fermentation.
fermer /fɛrme/ v.t./i. close, shut; (*cesser
d'exploiter*) close *ou* shut down; (*gaz,
robinet*) turn off. **se** ~ v. pr. close, shut.
fermeté /fɛrməte/ n.f. firmness.
fermeture /fɛrmətyr/ n.f. closing;
(*dispositif*) catch. ~ **annuelle,** annual
closure. ~ **éclair,** (P.) zip(-fastener).
(*Amer.*) zipper.
ferm|ier, ~ière /fɛrmje, -jɛr/ n.m.
farmer. —n.f. farmer's wife. —a. farm.
fermoir /fɛrmwar/ n.m. clasp.
féroc|e /ferɔs/ a. ferocious. ~**ité** n.f.
ferocity.
ferraille /fɛraj/ n.f. scrap-iron.
ferré /fɛre/ a. (*canne*) steel-tipped.
ferrer /fɛre/ v.t. (*cheval*) shoe.
ferronnerie /fɛrɔnri/ n.f. ironwork.
ferroviaire /fɛrɔvjɛr/ a. rail(way).
ferry(-boat) /fɛri(bot)/ n.m. ferry.
fertil|e /fɛrtil/ a. fertile. ~**e en,** (*fig.*)
rich in. ~**iser** v.t. fertilize. ~**ité** n.f.
fertility.
féru, ~e /fery/ a. ~ **de,** passionate
about.
ferv|ent, ~ente /fɛrvɑ̃, -t/ a. fervent.
—n.m., f. enthusiast (**de,** of). ~**eur** n.f.
fervour.
fesse /fɛs/ n.f. buttock.

fessée /fese/ n.f. spanking.
festin /fɛstɛ̃/ n.m. feast.
festival (pl. ~**s**) /fɛstival/ n.m. festival.
festivités /fɛstivite/ n.f. pl. festivities.
festoyer /fɛstwaje/ v.i. feast.
fêtard /fɛtar/ n.m. merry-maker.
fête /fɛt/ n.f. holiday; (*religieuse*) feast;
(*du nom*) name-day; (*réception*) party;
(*en famille*) celebration; (*foire*) fair;
(*folklorique*) festival. ~ **des Mères,**
Mother's Day. ~ **foraine,** fun-fair.
faire la ~, make merry. **les** ~**s (de fin
d'année),** the Christmas season.
fêter /fete/ v.t. celebrate; (*personne*)
give a celebration for.
fétiche /fetiʃ/ n.m. fetish; (*fig.*) mascot.
fétide /fetid/ a. fetid.
feu¹ (pl. ~**x**) /fø/ n.m. fire; (*lumière*)
light; (*de réchaud*) burner. ~**x
(rouges),** (traffic) lights. **à** ~ **doux/vif,**
on a low/ high heat. **du** ~, (*pour
cigarette*) a light. **au** ~!, fire! ~
d'artifice, firework display. ~ **de joie,**
bonfire. ~ **rouge/vert/orange,** red/
green/amber *ou* yellow (*Amer.*). ~ **de
position,** sidelight. **mettre le** ~ **à,** set
fire to. **prendre** ~, catch fire. **jouer
avec le** ~, play with fire. **ne pas faire
long** ~, not last.
feuillage /fœjaʒ/ n.m. foliage.
feuille /fœj/ n.f. leaf; (*de papier, bois,
etc.*) sheet; (*formulaire*) form.
feuillet /fœjɛ/ n.m. leaf.
feuilleter /fœjte/ v.t. leaf through.
feuilleton /fœjtɔ̃/ n.m. (*à suivre*) serial;
(*histoire complète*) series.
feuillu /fœjy/ a. leafy.
feutre /føtr/ n.m. felt; (*chapeau*) felt hat;
(*crayon*) felt-tip (pen).
feutré /føtre/ a. (*bruit*) muffled.
fève /fɛv/ n.f. broad bean.
février /fevrije/ n.m. February.
fiable /fjabl/ a. reliable.
fiançailles /fjɑ̃saj/ n.f. pl. engagement.
fianc|er (se) /(sə)fjɑ̃se/ v. pr. become
engaged (**avec,** to). ~**é,** ~**ée** a.
engaged; n.m. fiancé; n.f. fiancée.
fiasco /fjasko/ n.m. fiasco.
fibre /fibr/ n.f. fibre. ~ **de verre,**
fibreglass.
ficeler /fisle/ v.t. tie up.
ficelle /fisɛl/ n.f. string.
fiche /fiʃ/ n.f. (index) card; (*formulaire*)
form, slip; (*électr.*) plug.
ficher¹ /fiʃe/ v.t. (*enfoncer*) drive (**dans,**
into).
ficher² /fiʃe/ v.t. (*faire: fam.*) do;
(*donner: fam.*) give; (*mettre: fam.*) put.
se ~ **de,** (*fam.*) make fun of. ~ **le**

camp, (*fam.*) clear off. **il s'en fiche,** (*fam.*) he couldn't care less.
fichier /fiʃje/ *n.m.* file.
fichu /fiʃy/ *a.* (*mauvais: fam.*) rotten; (*raté: fam.*) done for. **mal ~,** (*fam.*) terrible.
ficti|f, ~ve /fiktif, -v/ *a.* fictitious.
fiction /fiksjɔ̃/ *n.f.* fiction.
fidèle /fidɛl/ *a.* faithful. —*n.m./f.* (*client*) regular; (*relig.*) believer. **~s,** (*à l'église*) congregation. **~ment** *adv.* faithfully.
fidélité /fidelite/ *n.f.* fidelity.
fier[1], **fière** /fjɛr/ *a.* proud (**de,** of). **fièrement** *adv.* proudly. **~té** *n.f.* pride.
fier[2] (**se**) /(sə)fje/ *v. pr.* **se ~ à,** trust.
fièvre /fjɛvr/ *n.f.* fever.
fiévreu|x, ~se /fjevrø, -z/ *a.* feverish.
figé /fiʒe/ *a.* fixed, set; (*manières*) stiff.
figer /fiʒe/ *v.t./i.*, **se ~** *v. pr.* congeal. **~ sur place,** petrify.
fignoler /fiɲɔle/ *v.t.* refine (upon), finish off meticulously.
figu|e /fig/ *n.f.* fig. **~ier** *n.m.* fig-tree.
figurant, ~e /figyrɑ̃, -t/ *n.m., f.* (*cinéma*) extra.
figure /figyr/ *n.f.* face; (*forme, personnage*) figure; (*illustration*) picture.
figuré /figyre/ *a.* (*sens*) figurative. **au ~,** figuratively.
figurer /figyre/ *v.i.* appear. —*v.t.* represent. **se ~** *v. pr.* imagine.
fil /fil/ *n.m.* thread; (*métallique, électrique*) wire; (*de couteau*) edge; (*à coudre*) cotton. **au ~ de,** with the passing of. **au ~ de l'eau,** with the current. **~ de fer,** wire. **au bout du ~,** on the phone.
filament /filamɑ̃/ *n.m.* filament
filature /filatyr/ *n.f.* (*textile*) mill; (*surveillance*) shadowing.
file /fil/ *n.f.* line; (*voie: auto.*) lane. **~ (d'attente),** queue; (*Amer.*) line. **en ~ indienne,** in single file. **se mettre en ~,** line up.
filer /file/ *v.t.* spin; (*suivre*) shadow. **~ qch. à qn.,** (*fam.*) slip s.o. sth. —*v.i.* (*bas*) ladder, run; (*liquide*) run; (*aller vite: fam.*) speed along, fly by; (*partir: fam.*) dash off. **~ doux,** do as one's told. **~ à l'anglaise,** take French leave.
filet /file/ *n.m.* net; (*d'eau*) trickle; (*de viande*) fillet. **~ (à bagages),** (luggage) rack. **~ à provisions,** string bag (*for shopping*).
fil|ial, ~iale (*m. pl.* **~iaux**) /filjal, -jo/ *a.* filial. —*n.f.* subsidiary (company).
filière /filjɛr/ *n.f.* (official) channels; (*de*

trafiquants) network. **passer par** *ou* **suivre la ~,** (*employé*) work one's way up.
filigrane /filigran/ *n.m.* watermark. **en ~,** between the lines.
filin /filɛ̃/ *n.m.* rope.
fille /fij/ *n.f.* girl; (*opposé à fils*) daughter. **~-mère** (*pl.* **~s-mères**) *n.f.* (*péj.*) unmarried mother.
fillette /fijɛt/ *n.f.* little girl.
filleul /fijœl/ *n.m.* godson. **~e** *n.f.* god-daughter.
film /film/ *n.m.* film. **~ d'épouvante/ muet/parlant,** horror/silent/talking film. **~ dramatique,** drama. **~er** *v.t.* film.
filon /filɔ̃/ *n.m.* (*géol.*) seam; (*situation*) source of wealth.
filou /filu/ *n.m.* crook.
fils /fis/ *n.m.* son.
filtr|e /filtr/ *n.m.* filter. **~er** *v.t./i.* filter; (*personne*) screen.
fin[1] /fɛ̃/ *n.f.* end. **à la ~,** finally. **en ~ de compte,** all things considered. **~ de semaine,** weekend. **mettre ~ à,** put an end to. **prendre ~,** come to an end.
fin[2], **fine** /fɛ̃, fin/ *a.* fine; (*tranche, couche*) thin; (*taille*) slim; (*plat*) exquisite; (*esprit, vue*) sharp. —*adv.* (*couper*) finely. **~es herbes,** herbs.
fin|al, ~ale (*m. pl.* **~aux** *ou* **~als**) /final, -o/ *a.* final. —*n.f.* (*sport*) final; (*gram.*) final syllable. —*n.m.* (*pl.* **~aux** *ou* **~als**) (*mus.*) finale. **~alement** *adv.* finally; (*somme toute*) after all.
finaliste /finalist/ *n.m./f.* finalist.
financ|e /finɑ̃s/ *n.f.* finance. **~er** *v.t.* finance. **~ier, ~ière** *a.* financial; *n.m.* financier
finesse /finɛs/ *n.f.* fineness; (*de taille*) slimness; (*acuité*) sharpness. **~s,** (*de langue*) niceties.
fini /fini/ *a.* finished; (*espace*) finite. —*n.m.* finish.
finir /finir/ *v.t./i.* finish, end; (*arrêter*) stop; (*manger*) finish (up). **en ~ avec,** have done with. **~ par faire,** end up doing. **ça va mal ~,** it will turn out badly.
finition /finisjɔ̃/ *n.f.* finish.
finlandais, ~e /fɛ̃lɑ̃dɛ, -z/ *a.* Finnish. —*n.m., f.* Finn.
finlande /fɛ̃lɑ̃d/ *n.f.* Finland.
finnois, ~e /finwa, -z/ *a.* Finnish. —*n.m.* (*lang.*) Finnish.
fiole /fjɔl/ *n.f.* phial.
firme /firm/ *n.f.* firm.
fisc /fisk/ *n.m.* tax authorities. **~al** (*m. pl.*

~aux) *a.* tax, fiscal. ~alité *n.f.* tax system.

fission /fisjɔ̃/ *n.f.* fission.

fissur|e /fisyr/ *n.f.* crack. ~er *v.t.*, se ~er *v. pr.* crack.

fiston /fistɔ̃/ *n.m.* (*fam.*) son.

fixation /fiksɑsjɔ̃/ *n.f.* fixing; (*complexe*) fixation.

fixe /fiks/ *a.* fixed; (*stable*) steady. à heure ~, at a set time. menu à prix ~, set menu.

fix|er /fikse/ *v.t.* fix. ~er (du regard), stare at. se ~er *v. pr.* (*s'installer*) settle down. être ~é, (*personne*) have made up one's mind.

flacon /flakɔ̃/ *n.m.* bottle.

flageolet /flaʒɔlɛ/ *n.m.* (*haricot*) (dwarf) kidney bean.

flagrant, ~e /flagrɑ̃, -t/ *a.* flagrant. en ~ délit, in the act.

flair /flɛr/ *n.m.* (sense of) smell; (*fig.*) intuition. ~er /flere/ *v.t.* sniff at; (*fig.*) sense.

flamand, ~e /flamɑ̃, -d/ *a.* Flemish. —*n.m.* (*lang.*) Flemish. —*n.m., f.* Fleming.

flamant /flamɑ̃/ *n.m.* flamingo.

flambant /flɑ̃bɑ̃/ *adv.* ~ neuf, brand-new.

flambé, ~e /flɑ̃be/ *a.* (*culin.*) flambé.

flambeau (*pl.* ~x) /flɑ̃bo/ *n.m.* torch.

flambée /flɑ̃be/ *n.f.* blaze; (*fig.*) explosion.

flamber /flɑ̃be/ *v.i.* blaze; (*prix*) shoot up. —*v.t.* (*aiguille*) sterilize; (*volaille*) singe.

flamboyer /flɑ̃bwaje/ *v.i.* blaze.

flamme /flam/ *n.f.* flame; (*fig.*) ardour. en ~s, ablaze.

flan /flɑ̃/ *n.m.* custard-pie.

flanc /flɑ̃/ *n.m.* side; (*d'animal, d'armée*) flank.

flancher /flɑ̃ʃe/ *v.i.* (*fam.*) give in.

Flandre(s) /flɑ̃dr/ *n.f.* (*pl.*) Flanders.

flanelle /flanɛl/ *n.f.* flannel.

flân|er /flane/ *v.i.* stroll. ~erie *n.f.* stroll.

flanquer /flɑ̃ke/ *v.t.* flank; (*jeter: fam.*) chuck; (*donner: fam.*) give. ~ à la porte, kick out.

flaque /flak/ *n.f.* (*d'eau*) puddle; (*de sang*) pool.

flash (*pl.* ~es) /flaʃ/ *n.m.* (*photo.*) flash; (*information*) news flash.

flasque /flask/ *a.* flabby.

flatt|er /flate/ *v.t.* flatter. se ~er de, pride o.s. on. ~erie *n.f.* flattery. ~eur, ~euse *a.* flattering; *n.m., f.* flatterer.

fléau (*pl.* ~x) /fleo/ *n.m.* (*désastre*) scourge; (*personne*) bane.

flèche /flɛʃ/ *n.f.* arrow; (*de clocher*) spire. monter en ~, spiral. partir en ~, shoot off.

flècher /fleʃe/ *v.t.* mark *ou* signpost (with arrows).

fléchette /fleʃɛt/ *n.f.* dart.

fléchir /fleʃir/ *v.t.* bend; (*personne*) move. —*v.i.* (*faiblir*) weaken; (*poutre*) sag, bend.

flegmatique /flɛgmatik/ *a.* phlegmatic.

flemm|e /flɛm/ *n.f.* (*fam.*) laziness. j'ai la ~e de faire, I can't be bothered doing. ~ard, ~arde *a.* (*fam.*) lazy; *n.m., f.* (*fam.*) lazy-bones.

flétrir /fletrir/ *v.t.*, se ~ *v. pr.* wither.

fleur /flœr/ *n.f.* flower. à ~ de terre/d'eau, just above the ground/water. à ~s, flowery. ~ de l'âge, prime of life. en ~s, in flower.

fleur|ir /flœrir/ *v.i.* flower; (*arbre*) blossom; (*fig.*) flourish. —*v.t.* adorn with flowers. ~i *a.* flowery.

fleuriste /flœrist/ *n.m./f.* florist.

fleuve /flœv/ *n.m.* river.

flexible /flɛksibl/ *a.* flexible.

flexion /flɛksjɔ̃/ *n.f.* (*anat.*) flexing.

flic /flik/ *n.m.* (*fam.*) cop.

flipper /flipœr/ *n.m.* pinball (machine).

flirter /flœrte/ *v.i.* flirt.

flocon /flɔkɔ̃/ *n.m.* flake.

flopée /flɔpe/ *n.f.* (*fam.*) une ~ de, masses of.

floraison /flɔrɛzɔ̃/ *n.f.* flowering.

flore /flɔr/ *n.f.* flora.

florissant, ~e /flɔrisɑ̃, -t/ *a.* flourishing.

flot /flo/ *n.m.* flood, stream. être à ~, be afloat. les ~s, the waves.

flottant, ~e /flɔtɑ̃, -t/ *a.* (*vêtement*) loose; (*indécis*) indecisive.

flotte /flɔt/ *n.f.* fleet; (*pluie: fam.*) rain; (*eau: fam.*) water.

flottement /flɔtmɑ̃/ *n.m.* (*incertitude*) indecision.

flott|er /flɔte/ *v.i.* float; (*drapeau*) flutter; (*nuage, parfum, pensées*) drift; (*pleuvoir: fam.*) rain. ~eur *n.m.* float.

flou /flu/ *a.* out of focus; (*fig.*) vague.

fluct|uer /flyktɥe/ *v.i.* fluctuate. ~uation *n.f.* fluctuation.

fluet, ~te /flyɛ, -t/ *a.* thin.

fluid|e /flɥid/ *a.* & *n.m.* fluid. ~ité *n.f.* fluidity.

fluor /flyɔr/ *n.m.* (*pour les dents*) fluoride.

fluorescent, ~e /flyɔresɑ̃, -t/ *a.* fluorescent.

flût|e /flyt/ *n.f.* flute; (*verre*) champagne

glass. **~iste** *n.m./f.* flautist; (*Amer.*) flutist.

fluv|ial (*m. pl.* **~iaux**) /flyvjal, -jo/ *a.* river.

flux /fly/ *n.m.* flow. **~ et reflux,** ebb and flow.

FM /ɛfɛm/ *abrév. f.* FM.

foc /fɔk/ *n.m.* jib.

fœtus /fetys/ *n.m.* foetus.

foi /fwa/ *n.f.* faith. **être de bonne/mauvaise ~,** be acting in good/bad faith. **ma ~!,** well (indeed)! **digne de ~,** reliable.

foie /fwa/ *n.m.* liver. **~ gras,** foie gras.

foin /fwɛ̃/ *n.m.* hay. **faire tout un ~,** (*fam.*) make a fuss.

foire /fwar/ *n.f.* fair. **faire la ~,** (*fam.*) make merry.

fois /fwa/ *n.f.* time. **une ~,** once. **deux ~,** twice. **à la ~,** at the same time. **des ~,** (*parfois*) sometimes. **une ~ pour toutes,** once and for all.

foison /fwazɔ̃/ *n.f.* abundance. **à ~,** in abundance. **~ner** /-ɔne/ *v.i.* abound (**de,** in).

fol /fɔl/ *voir* **fou.**

folâtrer /fɔlɑtre/ *v.i.* frolic.

folichon, ~ne /fɔliʃɔ̃, -ɔn/ *a.* **pas ~,** (*fam.*) not much fun.

folie /fɔli/ *n.f.* madness; (*bêtise*) foolish thing, folly.

folklor|e /fɔlklɔr/ *n.m.* folklore. **~ique** *a.* folk, (*fam.*) picturesque.

folle /fɔl/ *voir* **fou.**

follement /fɔlmɑ̃/ *adv.* madly.

fomenter /fɔmɑ̃te/ *v.t.* foment.

fonc|er[1] /fɔ̃se/ *v.t./i.* darken. **~é a.** dark.

foncer[2] /fɔ̃se/ *v.i.* (*fam.*) dash along. **~ sur,** (*fam.*) charge at.

fonc|ier, ~ière /fɔ̃sje, -jɛr/ *a.* fundamental; (*comm.*) real estate. **~ièrement** *adv.* fundamentally.

fonction /fɔ̃ksjɔ̃/ *n.f.* function; (*emploi*) position. **~s,** (*obligations*) duties. **en ~ de,** according to. **~ publique,** civil service. **voiture de ~,** company car.

fonctionnaire /fɔ̃ksjɔnɛr/ *n.m./f.* civil servant.

fonctionnel, ~le /fɔ̃ksjɔnɛl/ *a.* functional.

fonctionn|er /fɔ̃ksjɔne/ *v.i.* work. **faire ~er,** work. **~ement** *n.m.* working.

fond /fɔ̃/ *n.m.* bottom; (*de salle, magasin, etc.*) back; (*essentiel*) basis; (*contenu*) content; (*plan*) background. **à ~,** thoroughly. **au ~,** basically. **de ~,** (*bruit*) background; (*sport*) long-distance. **de ~ en comble,** from top to bottom. **au** *ou* **dans le ~,** really.

fondament|al (*m. pl.* **~aux**) /fɔ̃damɑ̃tal, -o/ *a.* fundamental.

fondation /fɔ̃dasjɔ̃/ *n.f.* foundation.

fond|er /fɔ̃de/ *v.t.* found; (*baser*) base (**sur,** on). (**bien**) **~é,** well-founded. **~é à,** justified in. **se ~er sur,** be guided by, place one's reliance on. **~ateur, ~atrice** *n.m., f.* founder.

fonderie /fɔ̃dri/ *n.f.* foundry.

fondre /fɔ̃dr/ *v.t./i.* melt; (*dans l'eau*) dissolve; (*mélanger*) merge. **se ~** *v. pr.* merge. **faire ~,** melt; dissolve. **~ en larmes,** burst into tears. **~ sur,** swoop on.

fondrière /fɔ̃drijɛr/ *n.f.* pot-hole.

fonds /fɔ̃/ *n.m.* fund. —*n.m. pl.* (*capitaux*) funds. **~ de commerce,** business.

fondu /fɔ̃dy/ *a.* melted; (*métal*) molten.

fontaine /fɔ̃tɛn/ *n.f.* fountain; (*source*) spring.

fonte /fɔ̃t/ *n.f.* melting; (*fer*) cast iron. **~ des neiges,** thaw.

foot /fut/ *n.m.* (*fam.*) football.

football /futbol/ *n.m.* football. **~eur** *n.m.* footballer.

footing /futiŋ/ *n.m.* fast walking.

forage /fɔraʒ/ *n.m.* drilling.

forain /fɔrɛ̃/ *n.m.* fairground entertainer. (**marchand**) **~,** stall-holder (*at a fair or market*).

force /fɔrs/ *n.f.* force; (*physique*) strength; (*hydraulique etc.*) power. **~s,** (*physiques*) strength. **à ~ de,** by sheer force of. **de ~, par la ~,** by force. **~ de dissuasion,** deterrent. **~ de frappe,** strike force, deterrent. **~ de l'âge,** prime of life. **~s de l'ordre,** police (force).

forcé /fɔrse/ *a.* forced; (*inévitable*) inevitable.

forcément /fɔrsemɑ̃/ *adv.* necessarily; (*évidemment*) obviously.

forcené, ~e /fɔrsəne/ *a.* frenzied —*n.m., f.* maniac.

forceps /fɔrsɛps/ *n.m.* forceps.

forcer /fɔrse/ *v.t.* force (**à faire,** to do); (*voix*) strain. —*v.i.* (*exagérer*) overdo it. **se ~** *v. pr.* force o.s.

forcir /fɔrsir/ *v.i.* fill out.

forer /fɔre/ *v.t.* drill.

forest|ier, ~ière /fɔrestje, -jɛr/ *a.* forest.

foret /fɔrɛ/ *n.m.* drill.

forêt /fɔrɛ/ *n.f.* forest.

forfait /fɔrfɛ/ *n.m.* (*comm.*) inclusive price. **~aire** /-tɛr/ *a.* (*prix*) inclusive.

forge /fɔrʒ/ n.f. forge.
forger /fɔrʒe/ v.t. forge; (inventer) make up.
forgeron /fɔrʒərɔ̃/ n.m. blacksmith.
formaliser (se) /(sə)fɔrmalize/ v. pr. take offence (de, at).
formalité /fɔrmalite/ n.f. formality.
format /fɔrma/ n.m. format.
formater /fɔrmate/ v.t. (comput.) format.
formation /fɔrmasjɔ̃/ n.f. formation; (de médecin etc.) training; (culture) education. **~ permanente** ou **continue**, continuing education. **~ professionnelle**, professional training.
forme /fɔrm/ n.f. form; (contour) shape, form. **~s**, (de femme) figure. **en ~**, (sport) in good shape, on form. **en ~ de**, in the shape of. **en bonne et due ~**, in due form.
formel, **~le** /fɔrmɛl/ a. formal; (catégorique) positive. **~lement** adv. positively.
former /fɔrme/ v.t. form; (instruire) train. **se ~** v. pr. form.
formidable /fɔrmidabl/ a. fantastic.
formulaire /fɔrmylɛr/ n.m. form.
formul|**e** /fɔrmyl/ n.f. formula; (expression) expression; (feuille) form. **~e de politesse**, polite phrase, letter ending. **~er** v.t. formulate.
fort¹, **~e** /fɔr, -t/ a. strong; (grand) big; (pluie) heavy; (bruit) loud; (pente) steep; (élève) clever. —adv. (frapper) hard; (parler) loud; (très) very; (beaucoup) very much. —n.m. strong point. **au plus ~ de**, at the height of. **c'est une ~e tête**, she/he's headstrong.
fort² /fɔr/ n.m. (mil.) fort.
forteresse /fɔrtərɛs/ n.f. fortress.
fortifiant /fɔrtifjɑ̃/ n.m. tonic.
fortif|**ier** /fɔrtifje/ v.t. fortify. **~ication** n.f. fortification.
fortiori /fɔrsjɔri/ **a ~**, even more so.
fortuit, **~e** /fɔrtɥi, -t/ a. fortuitous.
fortune /fɔrtyn/ n.f. fortune. **de ~**, (improvisé) makeshift. **faire ~**, make one's fortune.
fortuné /fɔrtyne/ a. wealthy.
fosse /fos/ n.f. pit; (tombe) grave. **~ d'aisances**, cesspool. **~ d'orchestre**, orchestral pit. **~ septique**, septic tank.
fossé /fose/ n.m. ditch; (fig.) gulf.
fossette /fosɛt/ n.f. dimple.
fossile /fosil/ n.m. fossil.
fossoyeur /foswajœr/ n.m. gravedigger.
fou ou **fol***, **folle** /fu, fɔl/ a. mad; (course, regard) wild; (énorme: fam.) tremendous. **~ de**, crazy about. —n.m.

madman; (bouffon) jester. —n.f. madwoman; (fam.) gay. **le ~ rire**, the giggles.
foudre /fudr/ n.f. lightning.
foudroy|**er** /fudrwaje/ v.t. strike by lightning; (maladie etc.) strike down; (atterrer) stagger. **~ant**, **~ante** a. staggering; (mort, maladie) violent.
fouet /fwɛ/ n.m. whip; (culin.) whisk.
fouetter /fwete/ v.t. whip; (crème etc.) whisk.
fougère /fuʒɛr/ n.f. fern.
fougu|**e** /fug/ n.f. ardour. **~eux**, **~euse** a. ardent.
fouill|**e** /fuj/ n.f. search; (archéol.) excavation. **~er** v.t./i. search; (creuser) dig. **~er dans**, (tiroir) rummage through.
fouillis /fuji/ n.m. jumble.
fouine /fwin/ n.f. beech-marten.
fouiner /fwine/ v.i. nose about.
foulard /fular/ n.m. scarf.
foule /ful/ n.f. crowd. **une ~ de**, (fig.) a mass of.
foulée /fule/ n.f. stride. **il l'a fait dans la ~**, he did it while he was at it.
fouler /fule/ v.t. press; (sol) tread. **se ~ le poignet/le pied** sprain one's wrist/foot. **ne pas se ~**, (fam.) not strain o.s.
foulure /fulyr/ n.f. sprain.
four /fur/ n.m. oven; (de potier) kiln; (théâtre) flop. **~ à micro-ondes**, microwave oven. **~ crématoire**, crematorium.
fourbe /furb/ a. deceitful.
fourbu /furby/ a. exhausted.
fourche /furʃ/ n.f. fork; (à foin) pitchfork.
fourchette /furʃɛt/ n.f. fork; (comm.) margin.
fourchu /furʃy/ a. forked.
fourgon /furgɔ̃/ n.m. van; (wagon) wagon. **~ mortuaire**, hearse.
fourgonnette /furgɔnɛt/ n.f. (small) van.
fourmi /furmi/ n.f. ant. **avoir des ~s**, have pins and needles.
fourmiller /furmije/ v.i. swarm (de, with).
fournaise /furnɛz/ n.f. (feu, endroit) furnace.
fourneau (pl. **~x**) /furno/ n.m. stove.
fournée /furne/ n.f. batch.
fourni /furni/ a. (épais) thick.
fourn|**ir** /furnir/ v.t. supply, provide; (client) supply; (effort) put in. **~ir à qn.**, supply s.o. with. **se ~ir chez**, shop at. **~isseur** n.m. supplier. **~iture** n.f. supply.

fourrage /furaʒ/ n.m. fodder.
fourré¹ /fure/ n.m. thicket.
fourré² /fure/ a. (vêtement) fur-lined; (gâteau etc.) filled (with jam, cream, etc.).
fourreau (pl. ⌐x) /furo/ n.m. sheath.
fourr|er /fure/ v.t. (mettre: fam.) stick. ⌐e-tout n.m. invar. (sac) holdall.
fourreur /furœr/ n.m. furrier.
fourrière /furjɛr/ n.f. (lieu) pound.
fourrure /furyr/ n.f. fur.
fourvoyer (se) /(sə)furvwaje/ v. pr. go astray.
foutaise /futɛz/ n.f. (argot) rubbish.
foutre /futr/ v.t. (argot) = **ficher²**.
foutu, ⌐e /futy/ a. (argot) = **fichu**.
foyer /fwaje/ n.m. home; (âtre) hearth; (club) club; (d'étudiants) hostel; (théâtre) foyer; (photo.) focus; (centre) centre.
fracas /fraka/ n.m. din; (de train) roar; (d'objet qui tombe) crash.
fracass|er /frakase/ v.t., se ⌐er v. pr. smash. ⌐ant, ⌐ante a. (bruyant, violent) shattering.
traction /fraksjɔ̃/ n.f. fraction. ⌐ner /-jɔne/ v.t., se ⌐ner v. pr. split (up).
fractur|e /fraktyr/ n.f. fracture. ⌐er v.t. (os) fracture; (porte etc.) break open.
fragil|e /fraʒil/ a fragile. ⌐ité n.f. fragility.
fragment /fragmɑ̃/ n.m. bit, fragment. ⌐aire /-tɛr/ a. fragmentary. ⌐er /-te/ v.t. split, fragment.
fraîche /frɛʃ/ voir **frais¹**.
fraîchement /frɛʃmɑ̃/ adv. (récemment) freshly; (avec froideur) coolly.
fraîcheur /frɛʃœr/ n.f. coolness; (nouveauté) freshness.
fraîchir /frɛʃir/ v.i. freshen.
frais¹, fraîche /frɛ, -ʃ/ a. fresh; (temps, accueil) cool; (peinture) wet. —adv. (récemment) newly. —n.m. **mettre au** ⌐, put in a cool place. **prendre le** ⌐, take a breath of cool air. ⌐ **et dispos,** fresh. **il fait** ⌐, it is cool.
frais² /frɛ/ n.m. pl. expenses; (droits) fees. ⌐ **généraux,** (comm.) overheads, running expenses. ⌐ **de scolarité,** school fees.
frais|e /frɛz/ n.f. strawberry. ⌐ier n.m. strawberry plant.
frambois|e /frɑ̃bwaz/ n.f. raspberry. ⌐ier n.m. raspberry bush.
fran|c¹, ⌐che /frɑ̃, -ʃ/ a. frank; (regard) open; (net) clear; (cassure) clean; (libre) free; (véritable) downright. ⌐c-maçon (pl. ⌐cs-maçons) n.m. Freemason. ⌐c-maçon-

nerie n.f. Freemasonry. ⌐-parler n.m. inv. outspokenness.
franc² /frɑ̃/ n.m. franc.
français, ⌐e /frɑ̃sɛ, -z/ a. French. —n.m., f. Frenchman, Frenchwoman. —n.m. (lang.) French.
France /frɑ̃s/ n.f. France.
franche /frɑ̃ʃ/ voir **franc¹**.
franchement /frɑ̃ʃmɑ̃/ adv. frankly; (nettement) clearly; (tout à fait) really.
franchir /frɑ̃ʃir/ v.t. (obstacle) get over; (traverser) cross; (distance) cover; (limite) exceed.
franchise /frɑ̃ʃiz/ n.f. frankness; (douanière) exemption (from duties).
franco /frɑ̃ko/ adv. postage paid.
franco- /frɑ̃ko/ préf. Franco-.
francophone /frɑ̃kɔfɔn/ a. French-speaking. —n.m./f. French speaker.
frange /frɑ̃ʒ/ n.f. fringe.
franquette (à la bonne) /(alabɔn)frɑ̃kɛt/ adv. informally.
frappant, ⌐e /frapɑ̃, -t/ a. striking.
frappe /frap/ n.f. (de courrier etc.) typing; (de dactylo) touch.
frappé, ⌐e /frape/ a. chilled.
frapp|er /frape/ v.t./i. strike; (battre) hit, strike; (monnaie) mint; (à la porte) knock, bang. ⌐é **de panique,** panic-stricken.
frasque /frask/ n.f. escapade.
fratern|el, ⌐elle /fratɛrnɛl/ a. brotherly. ⌐iser v.i. fraternize. ⌐ité n.f. brotherhood.
fraude /frod/ n.f. fraud; (à un examen) cheating.
frauder /frode/ v.t./i. cheat.
frauduleu|x, ⌐se /frodylø, -z/ a. fraudulent.
frayer /freje/ v.t. open up. se ⌐ un passage, force one's way (dans, through).
frayeur /frejœr/ n.f. fright.
fredonner /frədɔne/ v.t. hum.
free-lance /frilɑ̃s/ a. & n.m./f. freelance.
freezer /frizœr/ n.m. freezer.
frégate /fregat/ n.f. frigate.
frein /frɛ̃/ n.m. brake. **mettre un** ⌐ **à,** curb. ⌐ **à main,** hand brake.
frein|er /frene/ v.t. slow down; (modérer, enrayer) curb. —v.i. (auto.) brake. ⌐age /frenaʒ/ n.m. braking.
frelaté /frəlate/ a. adulterated.
frêle /frɛl/ a. frail.
frelon /frəlɔ̃/ n.m. hornet.
freluquet /frəlykɛ/ n.m. (fam.) weed.
frémir /fremir/ v.i. shudder, shake; (feuille, eau) quiver.
frêne /frɛn/ n.m. ash.

fréné|sie /frenezi/ n.f. frenzy. **~tique** a. frenzied.

fréqu|ent, **~ente** /frekɑ̃, -t/ a. frequent. **~emment** /-amɑ̃/ adv. frequently. **~ence** n.f. frequency.

fréquenté /frekɑ̃te/ a. crowded.

fréquent|er /frekɑ̃te/ v.t. frequent; (école) attend; (personne) see. **~ation** n.f. frequenting. **~ations** n.f. pl. acquaintances.

frère /frɛr/ n.m. brother.

fresque /frɛsk/ n.f. fresco.

fret /frɛ/ n.m. freight.

frétiller /fretije/ v.i. wriggle.

fretin /frɔtɛ̃/ n.m. menu **~**, small fry.

friable /frijabl/ a. crumbly.

friand, **~e** /frijɑ̃, -d/ a. **~** de, fond of.

friandise /frijɑ̃diz/ n.f. sweet; (Amer.) candy; (gâteau) cake.

fric /frik/ n.m. (fam.) money.

fricassée /frikase/ n.f. casserole.

friche (en) /(ɑ̃)friʃ/ adv. fallow. **être en ~**, lie fallow.

friction /friksjɔ̃/ n.f. friction; (massage) rub-down. **~ner** /-jɔne/ v.t. rub (down).

frigidaire /friʒidɛr/ n.m. (P.) refrigerator.

frigid|e /friʒid/ a. frigid. **~ité** n.f. frigidity.

frigo /frigo/ n.m. (fam.) fridge.

frigorif|ier /frigɔrifje/ v.t. refrigerate. **~ique** a. (vitrine etc.) refrigerated.

frileu|x, **~se** /frilø, -z/ a. sensitive to cold.

frime /frim/ n.f. (fam.) show off. **~r** v.i. (fam.) putting on a show.

frimousse /frimus/ n.f. (sweet) face.

fringale /frɛ̃gal/ n.f. (fam.) ravenous appetite.

fringant, **~e** /frɛ̃gɑ̃, -t/ a. dashing.

fringues /frɛ̃g/ n.f. pl. (fam.) togs.

friper /fripe/ v.t., **se ~** v. pr. crumple.

fripon, **~ne** /fripɔ̃, -ɔn/ n.m., f. rascal. —a. rascally.

fripouille /fripuj/ n.f. rogue.

frire /frir/ v.t./i. fry. **faire ~**, fry.

frise /friz/ n.f. frieze.

fris|er /frize/ v.t./i. (cheveux) curl; (personne) curl the hair of. **~é** a. curly.

frisquet /friskɛ/ a.m. (fam.) chilly.

frisson /frisɔ̃/ n.m. (de froid) shiver; (de peur) shudder. **~ner** /-ɔne/ v.i. shiver; shudder.

frit, **~e** /fri, -t/ a. fried. —n.f. chip. **avoir la ~e,** (fam.) feel good.

friteuse /fritøz/ n.f. (deep-)fryer.

friture /frityr/ n.f. fried fish; (huile) (frying) oil ou fat.

frivol|e /frivɔl/ a. frivolous. **~ité** n.f. frivolity.

froid, **~e** /frwa, -d/ a. & n.m. cold. **avoir/prendre ~,** be/catch cold. **il fait ~,** it is cold. **~ement** /-dmɑ̃/ adv. coldly; (calculer) coolly. **~eur** /-dœr/ n.f. coldness.

froisser /frwase/ v.t. crumple; (fig.) offend. **se ~** v. pr. crumple; (fig.) take offence. **se ~ un muscle,** strain a muscle.

frôler /frole/ v.t. brush against, skim; (fig.) come close to.

fromag|e /frɔmaʒ/ n.m. cheese. **~er,** **~ère** a. cheese; n.m., f. cheese maker; (marchand) cheesemonger.

froment /frɔmɑ̃/ n.m. wheat.

froncer /frɔ̃se/ v.t. gather. **~ les sourcils,** frown.

fronde /frɔ̃d/ n.f. sling; (fig.) revolt.

front /frɔ̃/ n.m. forehead; (mil., pol.) front. **de ~,** at the same time; (de face) head-on; (côte à côte) abreast. **faire ~ à,** face up to. **~al** (m. pl. **~aux**) /-tal, -to/ a. frontal.

frontali|er, ère /frɔ̃talje, -ɛr/ a. border. **(travailleur) ~er,** commuter from across the border.

frontière /frɔ̃tjɛr/ n.f. border, frontier.

frott|er /frɔte/ v.t./i. rub; (allumette) strike. **~ement** n.m. rubbing.

frottis /frɔti/ n.m. **~ vaginal,** smear test.

frouss|e /frus/ n.f. (fam.) fear. **avoir la ~e,** (fam.) be scared. **~ard,** **~arde** n.m., f. (fam.) coward.

fructifier /fryktifje/ v.i. faire **~**, put to work.

fructueu|x, **~se** /fryktɥø, -z/ a. fruitful.

frug|al (m. pl. **~aux**) /frygal, -o/ a. frugal. **~alité** n.f. frugality.

fruit /frɥi/ n.m. fruit. **des ~s,** (some) fruit. **~s de mer,** seafood. **~é** /-te/ a. fruity. **~ier,** **~ière** /-tje, -tjɛr/ a. fruit; n.m., f. fruiterer.

fruste /fryst/ a. coarse.

frustr|er /frystre/ v.t. frustrate. **~ant,** **~ante** a. frustrating. **~ation** n.f. frustration.

fuel /fjul/ n.m. fuel oil.

fugiti|f, **~ve** /fyʒitif, -v/ a. (passager) fleeting. —n.m., f. fugitive.

fugue /fyg/ n.f. (mus.) fugue. **faire une ~,** run away.

fuir† /fɥir/ v.i. flee, run away; (eau, robinet, etc.) leak. —v.t. (éviter) shun.

fuite /fɥit/ n.f. flight; (de liquide, d'une nouvelle) leak. **en ~,** on the run. **mettre**

en ~, put to flight. **prendre la ~**, take (to) flight.

fulgurant, ~e /fylgyrɑ̃, -t/ a. (*vitesse*) lightning.

fumée /fyme/ n.f. smoke; (*vapeur*) steam.

fum|er /fyme/ v.t./i. smoke. **~e-cigarette** n.m. invar. cigarette- holder. **~é** a. (*poisson, verre*) smoked. **~eur, ~euse** n.m., f. smoker.

fumet /fymɛ/ n.m. aroma.

fumeu|x, ~se /fymø, -z/ a. (*confus*) hazy.

fumier /fymje/ n.m. manure.

fumiste /fymist/ n.m./f. (*fam.*) shirker.

funambule /fynɑ̃byl/ n.m./f. tightrope walker.

funèbre /fynɛbr/ a. funeral; (*fig.*) gloomy.

funérailles /fyneraj/ n.f. pl. funeral.

funéraire /fynerɛr/ a. funeral.

funeste /fynɛst/ a. fatal.

funiculaire /fynikylɛr/ n.m. funicular.

fur /fyr/ n.m. **au ~ et à mesure**, as one goes along, progressively. **au ~ et à mesure que,** as.

furet /fyrɛ/ n.m. ferret.

fureter /fyrte/ v.i. nose (about).

fureur /fyrœr/ n.f. fury; (*passion*) passion. **avec ~,** furiously; passionately. **mettre en ~,** infuriate. **faire ~,** be all the rage.

furibond, ~e /fyribɔ̃, -d/ a. furious.

furie /fyri/ n.f. fury; (*femme*) shrew.

furieu|x, ~se /fyrjø, -z/ a. furious.

furoncle /fyrɔ̃kl/ n.m. boil.

furti|f, ~ve /fyrtif, -v/ a. furtive.

fusain /fyzɛ̃/ n.m. (*crayon*) charcoal; (*arbre*) spindle-tree.

fuseau (pl. ~x) /fyzo/ n.m. ski trousers; (*pour filer*) spindle. **~ horaire,** time zone.

fusée /fyze/ n.f. rocket.

fuselage /fyzlaʒ/ n.m. fuselage.

fuselé /fyzle/ a. slender.

fusible /fyzibl/ n.m. fuse.

fuser /fyze/ v.i. issue forth.

fusil /fyzi/ n.m. rifle, gun; (*de chasse*) shotgun. **~ mitrailleur,** machine-gun.

fusill|er /fyzije/ v.t. shoot. **~ade** n.f. shooting.

fusion /fyzjɔ̃/ n.f. fusion; (*comm.*) merger. **~ner** /-jɔne/ v.t./i. merge.

fut /fy/ *voir* **être**.

fût /fy/ n.m. (*tonneau*) barrel; (*d'arbre*) trunk.

futé /fyte/ a. cunning.

futil|e /fytil/ a. futile. **~ité** n.f. futility.

futur /fytyr/ a. & n.m. future. **~e femme/maman,** wife-/mother-to-be.

fuyant, ~e /fɥijɑ̃, -t/ a. (*front, ligne*) receding; (*personne*) evasive.

fuyard, ~e /fɥijar, -d/ n.m., f. runaway.

G

gabardine /gabardin/ n.f. gabardine; raincoat.

gabarit /gabari/ n.m. dimension; (*patron*) template; (*fig.*) calibre.

gâcher /gɑʃe/ v.t. (*gâter*) spoil; (*gaspiller*) waste.

gâchette /gɑʃɛt/ n.f. trigger.

gâchis /gɑʃi/ n.m. waste.

gadoue /gadu/ n.f. sludge.

gaff|e /gaf/ n.f. blunder. **faire ~e,** (*fam.*) be careful (**à,** of). **~er** v.i. blunder.

gag /gag/ n.m. gag.

gage /gaʒ/ n.m. pledge; (*de jeu*) forfeit. **~s,** (*salaire*) wages. **en ~ de,** as a token of. **mettre en ~,** pawn.

gageure /gaʒyr/ n.f. wager (against all the odds).

gagn|er /gaɲe/ v.t. (*match, prix, etc.*) win; (*argent, pain*) earn; (*temps, terrain*) gain; (*atteindre*) reach; (*convaincre*) win over. —v.i. win, (*fig.*) gain. **~er sa vie,** earn one's living. **~ant, ~ante,** a. winning; n.m., f. winner. **~e-pain** n.m. invar. job.

gai /ge/ a. cheerful; (*ivre*) merry. **~ement** adv. cheerfully. **~eté** n.f. cheerfulness. **~etés** n.f. pl. delights.

gaillard, ~e /gajar, -d/ a. hale and hearty; (*grivois*) coarse. —n.m. hale and hearty fellow; (*type: fam.*) fellow.

gain /gɛ̃/ n.m. (*salaire*) earnings; (*avantage*) gain; (*économie*) saving. **~s,** (*comm.*) profits; (*au jeu*) winnings.

gaine /gɛn/ n.f. (*corset*) girdle; (*étui*) sheath.

gala /gala/ n.m. gala.

galant, ~e /galɑ̃, -t/ a. courteous; (*scène, humeur*) romantic.

galaxie /galaksi/ n.f. galaxy.

galb|e /galb/ n.m. curve. **~é** a. shapely.

gale /gal/ n.f. (*de chat etc.*) mange.

galéjade /galeʒad/ n.f. (*fam.*) tall tale.

galère /galɛr/ n.f. (*navire*) galley. **c'est la ~!,** (*fam.*) what an ordeal!

galérer /galere/ v.i. (*fam.*) have a hard time.

galerie /galri/ n.f. gallery; (théâtre) circle; (de voiture) roof- rack.

galet /galɛ/ n.m. pebble.

galette /galɛt/ n.f. flat cake.

galeu|x, ∼se /galø, -z/ a. (animal) mangy.

galipette /galipɛt/ n.f. somersault.

Galles /gal/ n.f. pl. **le pays de ∼**, Wales.

gallois, ∼e /galwa, -z/ a. Welsh. —n.m., f. Welshman, Welshwoman. —n.m. (lang.) Welsh.

galon /galɔ̃/ n.m. braid; (mil.) stripe. **prendre du ∼**, be promoted.

galop /galo/ n.m. gallop. **aller au ∼**, gallop. **∼ d'essai**, trial run. **∼er** /-ɔpe/ v.i. (cheval) gallop; (personne) run.

galopade /galɔpad/ n.f. wild rush.

galopin /galɔpɛ̃/ n.m. (fam.) rascal.

galvaudé /galvode/ a. worthless.

gambad|e /gɑ̃bad/ n.f. leap. **∼er** v.i. leap about.

gamelle /gamɛl/ n.f. (de soldat) mess bowl ou tin; (d'ouvrier) food-box.

gamin, ∼e /gamɛ̃, -in/ a. playful. —n.m., f. (fam.) kid.

gamme /gam/ n.f. (mus.) scale; (série) range. **haut de ∼**, up-market, top of the range. **bas de ∼**, down-market, bottom of the range.

gang /gɑ̃g/ n.m. gang.

ganglion /gɑ̃glijɔ̃/ n.m. swelling.

gangrène /gɑ̃grɛn/ n.f. gangrene.

gangster /gɑ̃gstɛr/ n.m. gangster; (escroc) crook.

gant /gɑ̃/ n.m. glove. **∼ de toilette**, face-flannel, face-cloth. **∼é** /gɑ̃te/ a. (personne) wearing gloves.

garag|e /garaʒ/ n.m. garage. **∼iste** n.m. garage owner; (employé) garage mechanic.

garant, ∼e /garɑ̃, -t/ n.m., f. guarantor. —n.m. guarantee. **se porter ∼ de**, guarantee, vouch for.

garant|ie /garɑ̃ti/ n.f. guarantee; (protection) safeguard. **∼ies**, (de police d'assurance) cover. **∼ir** v.t. guarantee; (protéger) protect (de, from).

garce /gars/ n.f. (fam.) bitch.

garçon /garsɔ̃/ n.m. boy; (célibataire) bachelor. **∼ (de café)**, waiter. **∼ d'honneur**, best man.

garçonnière /garsɔnjɛr/ n.f. bachelor flat.

garde¹ /gard/ n.f. guard; (d'enfants, de bagages) care; (service) guard (duty); (infirmière) nurse. **de ∼**, on duty. **∼ à vue**, (police) custody. **mettre en ∼**,

warn. **prendre ∼**, be careful (à, of). **(droit de) ∼**, custody (de, of).

garde² /gard/ n.m. (personne) guard; (de propriété, parc) warden. **∼ champêtre**, village policeman. **∼ du corps**, bodyguard.

gard|er /garde/ v.t. (conserver, maintenir) keep; (vêtement) keep on; (surveiller) look after; (défendre) guard. **se ∼er** v. pr. (denrée) keep. **∼er le lit**, stay in bed. **se ∼er de faire**, be careful not to do. **∼e-à-vous** int. (mil.) attention. **∼e-boue** n.m. invar. mudguard. **∼e-chasse** (pl. **∼es-chasses**) n.m. gamekeeper. **∼e-fou** n.m. railing. **∼e-manger** n.m. invar. (food) safe; (placard) larder. **∼e-robe** n.f. wardrobe.

garderie /gardəri/ n.f. crèche.

gardien, ∼ne /gardjɛ̃, -jɛn/ n.m., f. (de prison, réserve) warden; (d'immeuble) caretaker; (de musée) attendant; (garde) guard. **∼ de but**, goalkeeper. **∼ de la paix**, policeman. **∼ de nuit**, night watchman. **∼ne d'enfants**, childminder.

gare¹ /gar/ n.f. (rail.) station. **∼ routière**, coach station; (Amer.) bus station.

gare² /gar/ int. **∼ (à toi)**, watch out!

garer /gare/ v.t., **se ∼** v. pr. park.

gargariser (se) /(sə)gargarize/ v. pr. gargle.

gargarisme /gargarism/ n.m. gargle.

gargouille /garguj/ n.f. (water-)spout; (sculptée) gargoyle.

gargouiller /garguje/ v.i. gurgle.

garnement /garnəmɑ̃/ n.m. rascal.

garn|ir /garnir/ v.t. (décorer) decorate; (couvrir) cover; (doubler) line; (culin.) garnish. **∼i** a. (plat) served with vegetables. **bien ∼i**, (rempli) well-filled.

garnison /garnizɔ̃/ n.f. garrison.

garniture /garnityr/ n.f. (légumes) vegetables; (ornement) trimming; (de voiture) trim.

garrot /garo/ n.m. (méd.) tourniquet.

gars /gɑ/ n.m. (fam.) fellow.

gas-oil /gazɔjl/ n.m. diesel oil.

gaspill|er /gaspije/ v.t. waste. **∼age** n.m. waste.

gastrique /gastrik/ a. gastric.

gastronom|e /gastrɔnɔm/ n.m./f. gourmet. **∼ie** n.f. gastronomy.

gâteau (pl. **∼x**) /gɑto/ n.m. cake. **∼ sec**, biscuit; (Amer.) cookie. **un papa ∼**, a doting dad.

gâter /gate/ v.t. spoil. se ~ v. pr. (dent, viande) go bad; (temps) get worse.

gâterie /gatri/ n.f. little treat.

gâteu|x, ~se /gatø, -z/ a. senile.

gauch|e¹ /goʃ/ a. left. à ~e, on the left; (direction) (to the) left. la ~e, the left (side); (pol.) the left (wing). ~er, ~ère a. & n.m., f. left-handed (person). ~iste a. & n.m./f. (pol.) leftist.

gauche² /goʃ/ a. (maladroit) awkward. ~rie n.f. awkwardness.

gaufre /gofr/ n.f. waffle.

gaufrette /gofrɛt/ n.f. wafer.

gaulois, ~e /golwa, -z/ a. Gallic; (fig.) bawdy. —n.m., f. Gaul.

gausser (se) /(sə)gose/ v. pr. se ~ de, deride, scoff at.

gaver /gave/ v.t. force-feed; (fig.) cram. se ~ de, gorge o.s. with.

gaz /gaz/ n.m. invar. gas. ~ lacrymogène, tear-gas.

gaze /gaz/ n.f. gauze.

gazelle /gazɛl/ n.f. gazelle.

gaz|er /gaze/ v.i. (fam.) ça ~e, it's going all right.

gazette /gazɛt/ n.f. newspaper.

gazeu|x, ~se /gazø, -z/ a. (boisson) fizzy.

gazoduc /gazodyk/ n.m. gas pipeline.

gazomètre /gazomɛtr/ n.m. gasometer.

gazon /gazõ/ n.m. lawn, grass.

gazouiller /gazuje/ v.i. (oiseau) chirp; (bébé) babble.

geai /ʒɛ/ n.m. jay.

géant, ~e /ʒeã, -t/ a. & n.m., f. giant.

geindre /ʒɛ̃dr/ v.i. groan.

gel /ʒɛl/ n.m. frost; (pâte) gel; (comm.) freezing.

gélatine /ʒelatin/ n.f. gelatine.

gel|er /ʒəle/ v.t./i. freeze. on gèle, it's freezing. ~é a. frozen; (membre abîmé) frost-bitten. ~ée n.f. frost, (culin.) jelly. ~ée blanche, hoar-frost.

gélule /ʒelyl/ n.f. (méd.) capsule.

Gémeaux /ʒemo/ n.m. pl. Gemini.

gém|ir /ʒemir/ v.i. groan. ~issement n.m. groan(ing).

gênant, ~e /ʒɛnã, -t/ a. embarrassing; (irritant) annoying.

gencive /ʒãsiv/ n.f. gum.

gendarme /ʒãdarm/ n.m. policeman, gendarme. ~rie /-əri/ n.f. police force; (local) police station.

gendre /ʒãdr/ n.m. son-in-law.

gène /ʒɛn/ n.m. gene.

gêne /ʒɛn/ n.f. discomfort; (confusion) embarrassment; (dérangement) trouble. dans la ~, in financial straits.

généalogie /ʒenealɔʒi/ n.f. genealogy.

gên|er /ʒene/ v.t. bother, disturb; (troubler) embarrass; (encombrer) hamper; (bloquer) block. ~é a. embarrassed.

génér|al (m. pl. ~aux) /ʒeneral, -o/ a. general. —n.m. (pl. ~aux) general. en ~al, in general. ~alement adv. generally.

généralis|er /ʒeneralize/ v.t./i. generalize. se ~er v. pr. become general. ~ation n.f. generalization.

généraliste /ʒeneralist/ n.m./f. general practitioner, GP.

généralité /ʒeneralite/ n.f. majority. ~s, general points.

génération /ʒenerasjõ/ n.f. generation.

génératrice /ʒeneratris/ n.f. generator.

génére|ux, ~se /ʒenerø, -z/ a. generous. ~sement adv. generously.

générique /ʒenerik/ n.m. (cinéma) credits. —a. generic.

générosité /ʒenerozite/ n.f. generosity.

genêt /ʒənɛ/ n.m. (plante) broom.

génétique /ʒenetik/ a. genetic. —n.f. genetics.

Genève /ʒənɛv/ n.m./f. Geneva.

gén|ial (m. pl. ~iaux) /ʒenjal, -jo/ a. brilliant; (fam.) fantastic.

génie /ʒeni/ n.m. genius. ~ civil, civil engineering.

genièvre /ʒənjɛvr/ n.m. juniper.

génisse /ʒenis/ n.f. heifer.

génit|al (m. pl. ~aux) /ʒenital, -o/ a. genital.

génocide /ʒenɔsid/ n.m. genocide.

génoise /ʒenwaz/ n.f. sponge (cake).

genou (pl. ~x) /ʒnu/ n.m. knee. à ~x, kneeling. se mettre à ~x, kneel.

genre /ʒãr/ n.m. sort, kind; (attitude) manner; (gram.) gender. ~ de vie, life-style.

gens /ʒã/ n.m./f. pl. people.

genti|l, ~lle /ʒãti, -j/ a. kind, nice; (agréable) nice; (sage) good. ~llesse /-jɛs/ n.f. kindness. ~ment adv. kindly.

géograph|ie /ʒeɔgrafi/ n.f. geography. ~e n.m./f. geographer. ~ique a. geographical.

geôl|ier, ~ière /ʒolje, -jɛr/ n.m., f. gaoler, jailer.

géolo|gie /ʒeɔlɔʒi/ n.f. geology. ~gique a. geological. ~gue n.m./f. geologist.

géomètre /ʒeɔmɛtr/ n.m. surveyor.

géométr|ie /ʒeɔmetri/ n.f. geometry. ~ique a. geometric.

géranium /ʒeranjɔm/ n.m. geranium.

géran|t, ~te /ʒerã, -t/ n.m., f. manager, manageress. ~t d'immeuble, landlord's agent. ~ce n.f. management.

gerbe /ʒɛrb/ n.f. (de fleurs, d'eau) spray; (de blé) sheaf.

gercé /ʒɛrse/ a. chapped.

ger|cer /ʒɛrse/ v.t./i., **se ~cer** v. pr. chap. **~çure** n.f. chap.

gérer /ʒere/ v.t. manage.

germain, ~e /ʒɛrmɛ̃, -ɛn/ a. **cousin ~,** first cousin.

germanique /ʒɛrmanik/ a. Germanic.

germ|e /ʒɛrm/ n.m. germ. **~er** v.i. germinate.

gésier /ʒezje/ n.m. gizzard.

gestation /ʒɛstɑsjɔ̃/ n.f. gestation.

geste /ʒɛst/ n.m. gesture.

gesticul|er /ʒɛstikyle/ v.i. gesticulate. **~ation** n.f. gesticulation.

gestion /ʒɛstjɔ̃/ n.f. management.

geyser /ʒezɛr/ n.m. geyser.

ghetto /ʒeto/ n.m. ghetto.

gibecière /ʒibsjɛr/ n.f. shoulder-bag.

gibet /ʒibɛ/ n.m. gallows.

gibier /ʒibje/ n.m. (animaux) game.

giboulée /ʒibule/ n.f. shower.

gicl|er /ʒikle/ v.i. squirt. **faire ~er,** squirt. **~ée** n.f. squirt.

gifl|e /ʒifl/ n.f. slap (in the face). **~er** v.t. slap.

gigantesque /ʒigɑ̃tɛsk/ a. gigantic.

gigot /ʒigo/ n.m. leg (of lamb).

gigoter /ʒigɔte/ v.i. (fam.) wriggle.

gilet /ʒilɛ/ n.m. waistcoat; (cardigan) cardigan. **~ de sauvetage,** life-jacket.

gin /dʒin/ n.m. gin.

gingembre /ʒɛ̃ʒɑ̃br/ n.m. ginger.

gingivite /ʒɛ̃ʒivit/ n.f. gum infection.

girafe /ʒiraf/ n.f. giraffe.

giratoire /ʒiratwar/ a. **sens ~,** round-about.

giroflée /ʒirɔfle/ n.f. wallflower.

girouette /ʒirwɛt/ n.f. weathercock, weather-vane.

gisement /ʒizmɑ̃/ n.m. deposit.

gitan, ~e /ʒitɑ̃, -an/ n.m., f. gypsy.

gîte /ʒit/ n.m. (maison) home; (abri) shelter. **~ rural,** holiday cottage.

givr|e /ʒivr/ n.m. (hoar-)frost. **~er** v.t., **se ~er** v. pr. frost (up).

givré /ʒivre/ a. (fam.) nuts.

glace /glas/ n.f. ice; (crème) ice-cream; (vitre) window; (miroir) mirror; (verre) glass.

glac|er /glase/ v.t. freeze; (gâteau, boisson) ice; (papier) glaze; (pétrifier) chill. **se ~er** v. pr. freeze. **~é** a. (vent, accueil) icy.

glac|ial (m. pl. **~iaux**) /glasjal, -jo/ a. icy.

glacier /glasje/ n.m. (géog.) glacier; (vendeur) ice-cream man.

glacière /glasjɛr/ n.f. icebox.

glaçon /glasɔ̃/ n.m. (pour boisson) ice-cube; (péj.) cold fish.

glaïeul /glajœl/ n.m. gladiolus.

glaise /glɛz/ n.f. clay.

gland /glɑ̃/ n.m. acorn; (ornement) tassel.

glande /glɑ̃d/ n.f. gland.

glander /glɑ̃de/ v.i. (fam.) laze around.

glaner /glane/ v.t. glean.

glapir /glapir/ v.i. yelp.

glas /glɑ/ n.m. knell.

glauque /glok/ a. (fig.) gloomy.

glissant, ~e /glisɑ̃, -t/ a. slippery.

gliss|er /glise/ v.i. slide; (sur l'eau) glide; (déraper) slip; (véhicule) skid. **—v.t., se ~er** v. pr. slip (dans, into). **~ade** n.f. sliding; (endroit) slide. **~ement** n.m. sliding; gliding; (fig.) shift. **~ement de terrain,** landslide.

glissière /glisjɛr/ n.f. groove. **à ~,** (porte, système) sliding.

glob|al (m. pl. **~aux**) /glɔbal, -o/ a. (entier, général) overall. **~alement** adv. as a whole.

globe /glɔb/ n.m. globe. **~ oculaire,** eyeball. **~ terrestre,** globe.

globule /glɔbyl/ n.m. (du sang) corpuscle.

gloire /glwar/ n.f. glory.

glorieu|x, ~se /glɔrjø, -z/ a. glorious. **~sement** adv. gloriously.

glorifier /glɔrifje/ v.t. glorify.

glose /gloz/ n.f. gloss.

glossaire /glɔsɛr/ n.m. glossary.

glouss|er /gluse/ v.i. chuckle; (poule) cluck. **~ement** n.m. chuckle; cluck.

glouton, ~ne /glutɔ̃, -ɔn/ a. gluttonous. —n.m., f. glutton.

gluant, ~e /glyɑ̃, -t/ a. sticky.

glucose /glykoz/ n.m. glucose.

glycérine /gliserin/ n.f. glycerine.

glycine /glisin/ n.f. wisteria.

gnome /gnom/ n.m. gnome.

go /go/ **tout de go,** straight out.

GO (abrév. grandes ondes) long wave.

goal /gol/ n.m. goalkeeper.

gobelet /gɔblɛ/ n.m. tumbler, mug.

gober /gɔbe/ v.t. swallow (whole). **je ne peux pas le ~,** (fam.) I can't stand him.

godasse /gɔdas/ n.f. (fam.) shoe.

godet /gɔdɛ/ n.m. (small) pot.

goéland /gɔelɑ̃/ n.m. (sea)gull.

goélette /gɔelɛt/ n.f. schooner.

gogo (à) /(a)gɔgo/ adv. (fam.) galore, in abundance.

goguenard, ~e /gɔgnar, -d/ a. mocking.

goguette (en) /(ã)gɔgɛt/ adv. (fam.) having a binge ou spree.

goinfr|e /gwɛ̃fr/ n.m. (glouton: fam.) pig. **se ~er** v. pr. (fam.) stuff o.s. like a pig (**de**, with).

golf /gɔlf/ n.m. golf; golf course.

golfe /gɔlf/ n.m. gulf.

gomm|e /gɔm/ n.f. rubber; (Amer.) eraser; (résine) gum. **~er** v.t. rub out.

gond /gɔ̃/ n.m. hinge. **sortir de ses ~s**, go mad.

gondol|e /gɔ̃dɔl/ n.f. gondola. **~ier** n.m. gondolier.

gondoler (se) /(sə)gɔ̃dɔle/ v. pr. warp, (rire: fam.) split one's sides.

gonfl|er /gɔ̃fle/ v.t./i. swell; (ballon, pneu) pump up, blow up; (exagérer) inflate. **se ~er** v. pr. swell. **~é** a. swollen. **il est ~é**, (fam.) he's got a nerve. **~ement** n.m. swelling.

gorge /gɔrʒ/ n.f. throat; (poitrine) breast; (vallée) gorge.

gorgée /gɔrʒe/ n.f. sip, gulp.

gorg|er /gɔrʒe/ v.t. fill (**de**, with). **se ~er** v. pr. gorge o.s. (**de**, with). **~é de**, full of.

gorille /gɔrij/ n.m. gorilla; (garde: fam.) bodyguard.

gosier /gozje/ n.m. throat.

gosse /gɔs/ n.m./f. (fam.) kid.

gothique /gɔtik/ a. Gothic.

goudron /gudrɔ̃/ n.m. tar. **~ner** /-ɔne/ v.t. tar; (route) surface. **à faible teneur en ~**, low tar.

gouffre /gufr/ n.m. gulf, abyss.

goujat /guʒa/ n.m. lout, boor.

goulot /gulo/ n.m. neck. **boire au ~**, drink from the bottle.

goulu, **~e** /guly/ a. gluttonous. —n.m., f. glutton.

gourde /gurd/ n.f. (à eau) flask; (idiot: fam.) chump.

gourdin /gurdɛ̃/ n.m. club, cudgel.

gourer (se) /(sə)gure/ v. pr. (fam.) make a mistake.

gourmand, **~e** /gurmã, -d/ a. greedy. —n.m., f. glutton. **~ise** /-diz/ n.f. greed; (mets) delicacy.

gourmet /gurmɛ/ n.m. gourmet.

gourmette /gurmɛt/ n.f. chain bracelet.

gousse /gus/ n.f. **~ d'ail**, clove of garlic.

goût /gu/ n.m. taste.

goûter /gute/ v.t. taste; (apprécier) enjoy. —v.i. have tea. —n.m. tea, snack. **~ à** ou **de**, taste.

goutt|e /gut/ n.f. drop; (méd.) gout. **~er** v.i. drip.

goutte-à-goutte /gutagut/ n.m. drip.

gouttelette /gutlɛt/ n.f. droplet.

gouttière /gutjɛr/ n.f. gutter.

gouvernail /guvɛrnaj/ n.m. rudder; (barre) helm.

gouvernante /guvɛrnãt/ n.f. governess.

gouvernement /guvɛrnəmã/ n.m. government. **~al** (m. pl. **~aux**) /-tal, -to/ a. government.

gouvern|er /guvɛrne/ v.t./i. govern. **~eur** n.m. governor.

grâce /grɑs/ n.f. (charme) grace; (faveur) favour; (jurid.) pardon; (relig.) grace. **~ à**, thanks to.

gracier /grasje/ v.t. pardon.

gracieu|x, ~se /grasjø, -z/ a. graceful; (gratuit) free. **~sement** adv. gracefully; free (of charge).

gradation /gradɑsjɔ̃/ n.f. gradation.

grade /grad/ n.m. rank. **monter en ~**, be promoted.

gradé /grade/ n.m. non-commissioned officer.

gradin /gradɛ̃/ n.m. tier, step. **en ~s**, terraced.

gradué /gradye/ a. graded, graduated.

graduel, **~le** /gradɥɛl/ a. gradual.

grad|uer /gradɥe/ v.t. increase gradually. **~uation** n.f. graduation.

graffiti /grafiti/ n.m. pl. graffiti.

grain /grɛ̃/ n.m. grain; (naut.) squall; (de café) bean; (de poivre) pepper corn. **~ de beauté**, beauty spot. **~ de raisin**, grape.

graine /grɛn/ n.f. seed.

graissage /grɛsaʒ/ n.m. lubrication.

graiss|e /grɛs/ n.f. fat; (lubrifiant) grease. **~er** v.t. grease. **~eux, ~euse** a. greasy.

gramm|aire /gramɛr/ n.f. grammar. **~atical** (m. pl. **~aticaux**) a. grammatical.

gramme /gram/ n.m. gram.

grand, **~e** /grã, -d/ a. big, large; (haut) tall; (mérite, distance, ami) great; (bruit) loud; (plus âgé) big. —adv. (ouvrir) wide. **~ ouvert**, wide open. **voir ~**, think big. —n.m., f. (adulte) grown-up; (enfant) older child. **au ~ air**, in the open air. **au ~ jour**, in broad daylight; (fig.) in the open. **de ~e envergure**, large-scale. **en ~e partie**, largely. **~-angle**, n.m. wide angle. **~e banlieue**, outer suburbs. **G~e-Bretagne** n.f. Great Britain. **pas ~-chose**, not much. **~ ensemble**, housing estate. **~es lignes**, (rail.) main lines. **~ magasin**, department store. **~-mère** (pl. **~s-mères**) n.f. grandmother. **~s-parents** n.m. pl. grandparents. **~-père** (pl. **~s-pères**) n.m. grandfather. **~e**

personne, grown-up. ⁓ **public,** general public. ⁓**-rue** *n.f.* high street. ⁓**e surface,** hypermarket. ⁓**es vacances,** summer holidays.

grandeur /grɑ̃dœr/ *n.f.* greatness; (*dimension*) size. **folie des** ⁓**s,** delusions of grandeur.

grandiose /grɑ̃djoz/ *a.* grandiose.

grandir /grɑ̃dir/ *v.i.* grow; (*bruit*) grow louder. —*v.t.* make taller.

grange /grɑ̃ʒ/ *n.f.* barn.

granit /granit/ *n.m.* granite.

granulé /granyle/ *n.m.* granule.

graphique /grafik/ *a.* graphic. —*n.m.* graph.

graphologie /grafɔlɔʒi/ *n.f.* graphology.

grappe /grap/ *n.f.* cluster. ⁓ **de raisin,** bunch of grapes.

grappin /grapɛ̃/ *n.m.* **mettre le** ⁓ **sur,** get one's claws into.

gras, ⁓**se** /grɑ, -s/ *a.* fat; (*aliment*) fatty; (*surface*) greasy; (*épais*) thick; (*caractères*) bold. —*n.m.* (*culin.*) fat. **faire la** ⁓**se matinée,** sleep late. ⁓**sement payé,** highly paid.

gratification /gratifikasjɔ̃/ *n.f.* bonus, satisfaction.

gratifi|er /gratifje/ *v.t.* favour, reward (**de,** with). ⁓**ant,** ⁓**ante** *a.* rewarding.

gratin /gratɛ̃/ *n.m.* baked dish with cheese topping; (*élite: fam.*) upper crust.

gratis /gratis/ *adv.* free.

gratitude /gratityd/ *n.f.* gratitude.

gratt|er /grate/ *v.t./i.* scratch; (*avec un outil*) scrape. **se** ⁓**er** *v. pr.* scratch o.s. **ça me** ⁓**e,** (*fam.*) it itches. ⁓**e-ciel** *n.m. invar.* skyscraper. ⁓**-papier** *n.m. invar.* (*péj.*) pen pusher.

gratuit, ⁓**e** /gratɥi, -t/ *a.* free; (*acte*) gratuitous. ⁓**ement** /-tma/ *adv.* free (of charge).

gravats /grava/ *n.m. pl.* rubble.

grave /grav/ *a.* serious; (*solennel*) grave; (*voix*) deep; (*accent*) grave. ⁓**ment** *adv.* seriously; gravely.

grav|er /grave/ *v.t.* engrave; (*sur bois*) carve. ⁓**eur** *n.m.* engraver.

gravier /gravje/ *n.m.* gravel.

gravir /gravir/ *v.t.* climb.

gravitation /gravitasjɔ̃/ *n.f.* gravitation.

gravité /gravite/ *n.f.* gravity.

graviter /gravite/ *v.i.* revolve.

gravure /gravyr/ *n.f.* engraving; (*de tableau, photo*) print, plate.

gré /gre/ *n.m.* (*volonté*) will; (*goût*) taste. **à son** ⁓, (*agir*) as one likes. **de bon** ⁓, willingly. **bon** ⁓ **mal gré,** like

it or not. **je vous en saurais** ⁓, I'll be grateful for that.

grec, ⁓**que** /grɛk/ *a. & n.m.,* f. Greek. —*n.m.* (*lang.*) Greek.

Grèce /grɛs/ *n.f.* Greece.

greff|e /grɛf/ *n.f.* graft; (*d' organe*) transplant. ⁓**er** /grefe/ *v.t.* graft; transplant.

greffier /grefje/ *n.m.* clerk of the court.

grégaire /greger/ *a.* gregarious.

grêle[1] /grɛl/ *a.* (*maigre*) spindly; (*voix*) shrill.

grêl|e[2] /grɛl/ *n.f.* hail. ⁓**er** /grele/ *v.i.* hail. ⁓**on** *n.m.* hailstone.

grelot /grəlo/ *n.m.* (little) bell.

grelotter /grəlɔte/ *v.i.* shiver.

grenade[1] /grənad/ *n.f.* (*fruit*) pomegranate.

grenade[2] /grənad/ *n.f.* (*explosif*) grenade.

grenat /grəna/ *a. invar.* dark red.

grenier /grənje/ *n.m.* attic; (*pour grain*) loft.

grenouille /grənuj/ *n.f.* frog.

grès /grɛ/ *n.m.* sandstone; (*poterie*) stoneware.

grésiller /grezije/ *v.i.* sizzle; (*radio*) crackle.

grève[1] /grɛv/ *n.f.* strike. **se mettre en** ⁓, go on strike. ⁓ **du zèle,** work-to-rule; (*Amer.*) rule-book slow-down. ⁓ **de la faim,** hunger strike. ⁓ **sauvage,** wildcat strike.

grève[2] /grɛv/ *n.f.* (*rivage*) shore.

gréviste /grevist/ *n.m./f.* striker.

gribouill|er /gribuje/ *v.t./i.* scribble. ⁓**is** /-ji/ *n.m.* scribble.

grief /grijɛf/ *n.m.* grievance.

grièvement /grijɛvmɑ̃/ *adv.* seriously.

griff|e /grif/ *n.f.* claw; (*de couturier*) label. ⁓**er** *v.t.* scratch, claw.

griffonner /grifɔne/ *v.t./i.* scrawl.

grignoter /griɲɔte/ *v.t./i.* nibble.

gril /gril/ *n.m.* grill, grid(iron).

grillade /grijad/ *n.f.* (*viande*) grill.

grillage /grijaʒ/ *n.m.* wire netting.

grille /grij/ *n.f.* railings; (*portail*) (metal) gate; (*de fenêtre*) bars; (*de cheminée*) grate; (*fig.*) grid.

grill|er /grije/ *v.t./i.* burn; (*ampoule*) blow; (*feu rouge*) go through. **(faire)** ⁓**er,** (*pain*) toast; (*viande*) grill; (*café*) roast. ⁓**e-pain** *n.m. invar.* toaster.

grillon /grijɔ̃/ *n.m.* cricket.

grimace /grimas/ *n.f.* (funny) face; (*de douleur, dégoût*) grimace.

grimer /grime/ *v.t.,* **se** ⁓ *v. pr.* make up.

grimper /grɛ̃pe/ *v.t./i.* climb.

grinc|er /grɛ̃se/ *v.i.* creak. ⁓**er des**

dents, grind one's teeth. **~ement** *n.m.* creak(ing).

grincheu|x, **~se** /grɛ̃ʃø, -z/ *a.* grumpy.

gripp|e /grip/ *n.f.* influenza, flu. **être ~é**, have (the) flu; (*mécanisme*) be seized up *ou* jammed.

gris, **~e** /gri, -z/ *a.* grey; (*saoul*) tipsy.

grisaille /grizaj/ *n.f.* greyness, gloom.

grisonner /grizɔne/ *v.i.* go grey.

grisou /grizu/ *n.m.* **coup de ~**, firedamp explosion.

grive /griv/ *n.f.* (*oiseau*) thrush.

grivois, **~e** /grivwa, -z/ *a.* bawdy.

grog /grɔg/ *n.m.* grog.

grogn|er /grɔɲe/ *v.i.* growl; (*fig.*) grumble. **~ement** *n.m.* growl; grumble.

grognon, **~ne** /grɔɲɔ̃, -ɔn/ *a.* grumpy.

groin /grwɛ̃/ *n.m.* snout.

grommeler /grɔmle/ *v.t./i.* mutter.

grond|er /grɔ̃de/ *v.i.* rumble; (*chien*) growl; (*conflit etc.*) be brewing. —*v.t.* scold. **~ement** *n.m.* rumbling; growling.

groom /grum/ *n.m.* page(-boy).

gros, **~se** /gro, s/ *a.* big, large; (*gras*) fat; (*important*) great; (*épais*) thick; (*lourd*) heavy. —*n.m.*, *f.* fat man, fat woman. —*n.m.* **le ~ de**, the bulk of. **de ~**, (*comm.*) wholesale. **en ~**, roughly; (*comm.*) wholesale. **~ bonnet**, (*fam.*) bigwig. **~ lot**, jackpot. **~ mot**, rude word. **~ plan**, close-up. **~ titre**, headline. **~se caisse**, big drum.

groseille /grozɛj/ *n.f.* (*red ou white*) currant. **~ à maquereau**, gooseberry.

grosse /gros/ *voir* **gros**.

grossesse /grosɛs/ *n.f.* pregnancy.

grosseur /grosœr/ *n.f.* (*volume*) size; (*enflure*) lump.

gross|ier, **~ière** /grosje, -jɛr/ *a.* coarse, rough; (*imitation, instrument*) crude; (*vulgaire*) coarse; (*insolent*) rude; (*erreur*) gross. **~ièrement** *adv.* (*sommairement*) roughly; (*vulgairement*) coarsely. **~ièreté** *n.f.* coarseness; crudeness; rudeness; (*mot*) rude word.

grossir /grosir/ *v.t./i.* swell; (*personne*) put on weight; (*au microscope*) magnify; (*augmenter*) grow; (*exagérer*) magnify.

grossiste /grosist/ *n.m./f.* wholesaler.

grosso modo /grosomɔdo/ *adv.* roughly.

grotesque /grotɛsk/ *a.* grotesque; (*ridicule*) ludicrous.

grotte /grɔt/ *n.f.* cave, grotto.

grouill|er /gruje/ *v.i.* be swarming (**de**, with). **~ant**, **~ante** *a.* swarming.

groupe /grup/ *n.m.* group; (*mus.*) band.

~ électrogène, generating set. **~ scolaire**, school block.

group|er /grupe/ *v.t.*, **se ~er** *v.pr.* group (together). **~ement** *n.m.* grouping.

grue /gry/ *n.f.* (*machine, oiseau*) crane.

grumeau (*pl.* **~x**) /grymo/ *n.m.* lump.

gruyère /gryjɛr/ *n.m.* gruyère (cheese).

gué /ge/ *n.m.* ford. **passer** *ou* **traverser à ~**, ford.

guenon /gənɔ̃/ *n.f.* female monkey.

guépard /gepar/ *n.m.* cheetah.

guêp|e /gɛp/ *n.f.* wasp. **~ier** /gepje/ *n.m.* wasp's nest; (*fig.*) trap.

guère /gɛr/ *adv.* (**ne**) **~**, hardly. **il n'y a ~ d'espoir**, there is no hope.

guéridon /geridɔ̃/ *n.m.* pedestal table.

guérill|a /gerija/ *n.f.* guerrilla warfare. **~ero** /-jero/ *n.m.* guerrilla.

guér|ir /gerir/ *v.t.* (*personne, maladie, mal*) cure (**de**, of); (*plaie, membre*) heal. —*v.i.* get better; (*blessure*) heal. **~ir de**, recover from. **~ison** *n.f.* curing; healing; (*de personne*) recovery. **~isseur**, **~isseuse** *n.m.*, *f.* healer.

guérite /gerit/ *n.f.* (*mil.*) sentry-box.

guerre /gɛr/ *n.f.* war. **en ~**, at war. **faire la ~**, wage war (**à**, against). **~ civile**, civil war. **~ d'usure**, war of attrition.

guerr|ier, **~ière** /gɛrje, -jɛr/ *a.* warlike. —*n.m.*, *f.* warrior.

guet /gɛ/ *n.m.* watch. **faire le ~**, be on the watch. **~-apens** /gɛtapɑ̃/ *n.m. invar.* ambush.

guetter /gete/ *v.t.* watch; (*attendre*) watch out for.

gueule /gœl/ *n.f.* mouth; (*figure: fam.*) face. **ta ~!**, (*fam.*) shut up!

gueuler /gœle/ *v.i.* (*fam.*) bawl.

gueuleton /gœltɔ̃/ *n.m.* (*repas: fam.*) blow-out, slap-up meal.

gui /gi/ *n.m.* mistletoe.

guichet /giʃɛ/ *n.m.* window, counter; (*de gare*) ticket-office (window), (*de théâtre*) box-office (window).

guide /gid/ *n.m.* guide. —*n.f.* (*fille scout*) girl guide. **~s** *n.f. pl.* (*rênes*) reins.

guider /gide/ *v.t.* guide.

guidon /gidɔ̃/ *n.m.* handlebars.

guignol /giɲɔl/ *n.m.* puppet; (*personne*) clown; (*spectacle*) puppet-show.

guili-guili /giligili/ *n.m.* (*fam.*) tickle. **faire ~ à**, tickle.

guillemets /gijmɛ/ *n.m. pl.* quotation marks, inverted commas. **entre ~**, in inverted commas.

guilleret, ∼**te** /gijʀɛ, -t/ a. sprightly, jaunty.

guillotin|e /gijɔtin/ n.f. guillotine. ∼**er** v.t. guillotine.

guimauve /gimov/ n.f. marshmallow. **c'est de la** ∼, (fam.) it's mush.

guindé /gɛ̃de/ a. stilted.

guirlande /girlɑ̃d/ n.f. garland.

guise /giz/ n.f. **à sa** ∼, as one pleases. **en** ∼ **de,** by way of.

guitar|e /gitar/ n.f. guitar. ∼**iste** n.m./f. guitarist.

gus /gys/ n.m. (fam.) bloke.

guttur|al (m. pl. ∼**aux**) /gytyral, -o/ a. guttural.

gym /ʒim/ n.f. gym.

gymnas|e /ʒimnɑz/ n.m. gym(nasium). ∼**te** /-ast/ n.m./f. gymnast. ∼**tique** /-astik/ n.f. gymnastics.

gynécolo|gie /ʒinekɔlɔʒi/ n.f. gynaecology. ∼**gique** a. gynaecological. ∼**gue** n.m./f. gynaecologist.

gypse /ʒips/ n.m. gypsum.

H

habile /abil/ a. skilful, clever. ∼**té** n.f. skill.

habilité /abilite/ a. ∼ **à faire,** entitled to do.

habill|er /abije/ v.t. dress (de, in); (équiper) clothe; (recouvrir) cover (de, with). **s'**∼**er** v. pr. dress (o.s.), get dressed; (se déguiser) dress up. ∼**é** a. (costume) dressy. ∼**ement** n.m. clothing.

habit /abi/ n.m. dress, outfit; (de cérémonie) tails. ∼**s,** clothes.

habitable /abitabl/ a. (in)habitable.

habitant, ∼**e** /abitɑ̃, -t/ n.m., f. (de maison) occupant; (de pays) inhabitant.

habitat /abita/ n.m. housing conditions; (d'animal) habitat.

habitation /abitasjɔ̃/ n.f. living; (logement) house.

habit|er /abite/ v.i. live. —v.t. live in; (planète, zone) inhabit. ∼**é** a. (terre) inhabited.

habitude /abityd/ n.f. habit. **avoir l'**∼ **de faire,** be used to doing. **d'**∼, usually. **comme d'**∼, as usual.

habitué, ∼**e** /abitɥe/ n.m., f. regular visitor; (client) regular.

habituel, ∼**le** /abitɥɛl/ a. usual. ∼**lement** adv. usually.

habituer /abitɥe/ v.t. ∼ **à,** accustom to. **s'**∼ **à,** get used to.

hache /'aʃ/ n.f. axe.

haché /'aʃe/ a. (viande) minced; (phrases) jerky.

hacher /'aʃe/ v.t. mince; (au couteau) chop.

hachette /'aʃɛt/ n.f. hatchet.

hachis /'aʃi/ n.m. minced meat; (Amer.) ground meat.

hachisch /'aʃiʃ/ n.m. hashish.

hachoir /'aʃwar/ n.m. (appareil) mincer; (couteau) chopper; (planche) chopping board.

hagard, ∼**e** /'agar, -d/ a. wild(-looking).

haie /'ɛ/ n.f. hedge; (rangée) row. **course de** ∼**s,** hurdle race.

haillon /'ajɔ̃/ n.m. rag.

hain|e /'ɛn/ n.f. hatred. ∼**eux,** ∼**euse** a. full of hatred.

haïr /'air/ v.t. hate.

hâl|e /'al/ n.m. (sun-)tan. ∼**é** a. (sun-)tanned.

haleine /alɛn/ n.f. breath. **hors d'**∼, out of breath. **travail de longue** ∼, long job.

hal|er /'ale/ v.t. tow. ∼**age** n.m. towing.

haleter /'alte/ v.i. pant.

hall /'ol/ n.m. hall; (de gare) concourse.

halle /'al/ n.f. (covered) market. ∼**s,** (main) food market.

hallucination /alysinasjɔ̃/ n.f. hallucination.

halo /'alo/ n.m. halo.

halte /'alt/ n.f. stop; (repos) break; (escale) stopping place. —int. stop; (mil.) halt. **faire** ∼, stop.

halt|ère /altɛr/ n.m. dumb-bell. ∼**érophilie** n.f. weight-lifting.

hamac /'amak/ n.m. hammock.

hamburger /ɑ̃burgœr/ n.m. hamburger.

hameau (pl. ∼**x**) /'amo/ n.m. hamlet.

hameçon /amsɔ̃/ n.m. (fish-)hook.

hanche /'ɑ̃ʃ/ n.f. hip.

hand-ball /'ɑ̃dbal/ n.m. handball.

handicap /'ɑ̃dikap/ n.m. handicap. ∼**é,** ∼**ée** a. & n.m., f. handicapped (person). ∼**er** v.t. handicap.

hangar /'ɑ̃gar/ n.m. shed; (pour avions) hangar.

hanneton /'antɔ̃/ n.m. May-bug.

hanter /'ɑ̃te/ v.t. haunt.

hantise /'ɑ̃tiz/ n.f. obsession (de, with).

happer /'ape/ v.t. snatch, catch.

haras /'arɑ/ n.m. stud-farm.

harasser /'arase/ v.t. exhaust.

harcèlement /arsɛlmɑ̃/ n.m. ∼ **sexuel,** sexual harassment.

harceler /'arsəle/ *v.t.* harass.
hardi /'ardi/ *a.* bold. **∼esse** /-djɛs/ *n.f.*
boldness. **∼ment** *adv.* boldly.
hareng /'arã/ *n.m.* herring.
hargn|e /'arɲ/ *n.f.* (aggressive) bad
temper. **∼eux, ∼euse** *a.* bad-tempered.
haricot /'ariko/ *n.m.* bean. **∼ vert,**
French *ou* string bean; (*Amer.*) green
bean.
harmonica /armɔnika/ *n.m.* harmonica.
harmon|ie /armɔni/ *n.f.* harmony.
∼ieux, ∼ieuse *a.* harmonious.
harmoniser /armɔnize/ *v.t.,* **s'∼** *v. pr.*
harmonize.
harnacher /'arnaʃe/ *v.t.* harness.
harnais /'arnɛ/ *n.m.* harness.
harp|e /'arp/ *n.f.* harp. **∼iste** *n.m./f.*
harpist.
harpon /'arpɔ̃/ *n.m.* harpoon. **∼ner**
/-ɔne/ *v.t.* harpoon; (*arrêter: fam.*)
detain.
hasard /'azar/ *n.m.* chance; (*coïnci-
dence*) coincidence. **∼s,** (*risques*)
hazards. **au ∼,** (*choisir etc.*) at random;
(*flâner*) aimlessly. **∼eux, ∼euse** /-dø,
-z/ *a.* risky.
hasarder /'azarde/ *v.t.* risk; (*remarque*)
venture. **se ∼ dans,** risk going into. **se
∼ à faire,** risk doing.
hâte /'ɑt/ *n.f.* haste. **à la ∼, en ∼,**
hurriedly. **avoir ∼ de,** be eager to.
hâter /'ɑte/ *v.t.* hasten. **se ∼** *v. pr.* hurry
(**de, to**).
hât|if, ∼ve /'ɑtif, v/ *a.* hasty;
(*précoce*) early.
hauss|e /'os/ *n.f.* rise (**de,** in). **∼e des
prix,** price rises. **en ∼,** rising. **∼er** *v.t.*
raise; (*épaules*) shrug. **se ∼er** *v. pr.*
stand up, raise o.s. up.
haut, ∼e /'o, 'ot/ *a.* high; (*de taille*) tall.
—*adv.* high; (*parler*) loud(ly); (*lire*)
aloud. —*n.m.* top. **à ∼e voix,** aloud.
des ∼s et des bas, ups and downs. **en
∼,** (*regarder, jeter*) up; (*dans une
maison*) upstairs. **en ∼ (de),** at the top
(of). **∼ en couleur,** colourful. **plus ∼,**
further up, higher up; (*dans un texte*)
above. **en ∼ lieu,** in high places. **∼-de-
forme** (*pl.* **∼s-de-forme**) *n.m.* top hat.
∼-fourneau (*pl.* **∼s-fourneaux**) *n.m.*
blast-furnace. **∼-le-cœur** *n.m. invar.*
nausea. **∼-parleur** *n.m.* loudspeaker.
hautain, ∼e /'otɛ̃, -ɛn/ *a.* haughty.
hautbois /'obwa/ *n.m.* oboe.
hautement /'otmã/ *adv.* highly.
hauteur /'otœr/ *n.f.* height; (*colline*)
hill; (*arrogance*) haughtiness. **à la ∼,**
(*fam.*) up to it. **à la ∼ de,** level with;
(*tâche, situation*) equal to.

hâve /'ɑv/ *a.* gaunt.
havre /'avr/ *n.m.* haven.
Haye (La) /(la)'ɛ/ *n.f.* The Hague.
hayon /'ɛjɔ̃/ *n.m.* (*auto.*) rear opening,
tail-gate.
hebdo /ɛbdɔ/ *n.m.* (*fam.*) weekly.
hebdomadaire /ɛbdɔmadɛr/ *a. & n.m.*
weekly.
héberg|er /ebɛrʒe/ *v.t.* accommodate,
take in. **∼ement** *n.m.* accommodation.
hébété /ebete/ *a.* dazed.
hébraïque /ebraik/ *a.* Hebrew.
hébreu (*pl.* **∼x**) /ebrø/ *a.m.* Hebrew.
—*n.m.* (*lang.*) Hebrew. **c'est de l'∼!,**
it's double Dutch.
hécatombe /ekatɔ̃b/ *n.f.* slaughter.
hectare /ɛktar/ *n.m.* hectare (= *10,000
square metres*).
hégémonie /eʒemɔni/ *n.f.* hegemony.
hein /'ɛ̃/ *int.* (*fam.*) eh.
hélas /'elas/ *int.* alas. —*adv.* sadly.
héler /'ele/ *v.t.* hail.
hélice /elis/ *n.f.* propeller.
hélicoptère /elikɔptɛr/ *n.m.* helicopter.
helvétique /ɛlvetik/ *a.* Swiss.
hématome /ematom/ *n.m.* bruise.
hémisphère /emisfɛr/ *n.m.* hemisphere.
hémorragie /emɔraʒi/ *n.f.* haemorrhage.
hémorroïdes /emɔrɔid/ *n.f. pl.* piles,
haemorrhoids.
henn|ir /'enir/ *v.i.* neigh. **∼issement**
n.m. neigh.
hepatite /epatit/ *n.f.* hepatitis.
herbage /ɛrbaʒ/ *n.m.* pasture.
herb|e /ɛrb/ *n.f.* grass; (*méd., culin.*)
herb. **en ∼ e,** green; (*fig.*) budding.
∼eux, ∼euse *a.* grassy.
herbicide /ɛrbisid/ *n.m.* weed-killer.
hérédit|é /eredite/ *n.f.* heredity. **∼aire** *a.*
hereditary.
héré|sie /erezi/ *n.f.* heresy. **∼tique** *a.*
heretical; *n.m./f.* heretic.
hériss|er /'erise/ *v.t.,* **se ∼er** *v. pr.*
bristle. **∼er qn.,** ruffle s.o. **∼é** *a.*
bristling (**de,** with).
hérisson /'erisɔ̃/ *n.m.* hedgehog.
héritage /eritaʒ/ *n.m.* inheritance;
(*spirituel etc.*) heritage.
hérit|er /erite/ *v.t./i.* inherit (**de,** from).
∼er de qch., inherit sth. **∼ier, ∼ière**
n.m., f. heir, heiress.
hermétique /ɛrmetik/ *a.* airtight; (*fig.*)
unfathomable. **∼ment** *adv.* hermetic-
ally.
hermine /ɛrmin/ *n.f.* ermine.
hernie /'ɛrni/ *n.f.* hernia.
héroïne[1] /erɔin/ *n.f.* (*femme*) heroine.
héroïne[2] /erɔin/ *n.f.* (*drogue*) heroin.

héroï|que /erɔik/ a. heroic. **∼sme** n.m. heroism.

héron /'erɔ̃/ n.m. heron.

héros /'ero/ n.m. hero.

hésit|er /ezite/ v.i. hesitate (à, to). **en ∼ant**, hesitantly. **∼ant**, **∼ante** a. hesitant. **∼ation** n.f. hesitation.

hétéro /eterɔ/ n.m. & a. (fam.) straight.

hétéroclite /eterɔklit/ a. heterogeneous.

hétérogène /eterɔʒɛn/ a. heterogeneous.

hétérosexuel, ∼le /eterɔsɛksyɛl/ n.m., f. & a. heterosexual.

hêtre /'ɛtr/ n.m. beech.

heure /œr/ n.f. time; (mesure de durée) hour; (scol.) period. **quelle ∼ est-il?,** what time is it? **il est dix**/etc. **∼s,** it is ten/etc. o'clock. **à l'∼,** (venir, être) on time. **d'∼ en heure,** hourly. **∼ avancée,** late hour. **∼ d'affluence, ∼ de pointe,** rush-hour. **∼ indue,** ungodly hour. **∼s creuses,** off-peak periods. **∼s supplémentaires,** overtime.

heureusement /œrøzmɑ̃/ adv. fortunately, luckily.

heureu|x, ∼se /œrø, -z/ a. happy; (chanceux) lucky, fortunate.

heurt /'œr/ n.m. collision; (conflit) clash.

heurter /'œrte/ v.t. (cogner) hit; (mur etc.) bump into, hit; (choquer) offend. **se ∼ à,** bump into, hit; (fig.) come up against.

hexagone /ɛgzagɔn/ n.m. hexagon. **l'∼,** France.

hiberner /ibɛrne/ v.i. hibernate.

hibou (pl. **∼x**) /'ibu/ n.m. owl.

hideu|x, ∼se /'idø, -z/ a. hideous.

hier /jɛr/ adv. yesterday. **∼ soir,** last night, yesterday evening.

hiérarch|ie /'jerarʃi/ n.f. hierarchy. **∼ique** a. hierarchical.

hi-fi /'ifi/ a. invar. & n.f. (fam.) hi-fi.

hilare /ilar/ a. merry.

hilarité /ilarite/ n.f. laughter.

hindou, ∼e /ɛ̃du/ a. & n.m., f. Hindu.

hippi|que /ipik/ a. horse, equestrian. **∼sme** n.m. horse-riding.

hippodrome /ipɔdrom/ n.m. racecourse.

hippopotame /ipɔpɔtam/ n.m. hippopotamus.

hirondelle /irɔ̃dɛl/ n.f. swallow.

hirsute /irsyt/ a. shaggy.

hisser /'ise/ v.t. hoist, haul. **se ∼** v. pr. raise o.s.

histoire /istwar/ n.f. (récit, mensonge) story; (étude) history; (affaire) business. **∼(s),** (chichis) fuss. **∼s,** (ennuis) trouble.

historien, ∼ne /istɔrjɛ̃, -jɛn/ n.m., f. historian.

historique /istɔrik/ a. historical.

hiver /ivɛr/ n.m. winter. **∼nal** (m. pl. **∼naux**) a. winter; (glacial) wintry. **∼ner** v.i. winter.

H.L.M. /'aʃɛlɛm/ n.m./f. (= habitation à loyer modéré) block of council flats; (Amer.) (government-sponsored) low-cost apartment building.

hocher /'ɔʃe/ v.t. **∼ la tête,** (pour dire oui) nod; (pour dire non) shake one's head.

hochet /'ɔʃɛ/ n.m. rattle.

hockey /'ɔkɛ/ n.m. hockey. **∼ sur glace,** ice hockey.

hold-up /'ɔldœp/ n.m. invar. (attaque) hold-up.

hollandais, ∼e /'ɔlɑ̃dɛ, -z/ a. Dutch. —n.m., f. Dutchman, Dutchwoman. —n.m. (lang.) Dutch.

Hollande /'ɔlɑ̃d/ n.f. Holland.

hologramme /ɔlɔgram/ n.m. hologram.

homard /'ɔmar/ n.m. lobster.

homéopathie /ɔmeɔpati/ n.f. homoeopathy.

homicide /ɔmisid/ n.m. homicide. **∼ involontaire,** manslaughter.

hommage /ɔmaʒ/ n.m. tribute. **∼s,** (salutations) respects. **rendre ∼ à,** pay tribute.

homme /ɔm/ n.m. man; (espèce) man(kind). **∼ d'affaires,** businessman. **∼ de la rue,** man in the street. **∼ d'État,** statesman. **∼ de paille,** stooge. **∼-grenouille** (pl. **∼s-grenouilles**) n.m. frogman. **∼ politique,** politician.

homog|ène /ɔmɔʒɛn/ a. homogeneous. **∼énéité** n.f. homogeneity.

homologue /ɔmɔlɔg/ n.m./f. counterpart.

homologué /ɔmɔlɔge/ a. (record) officially recognized; (tarif) official.

homologuer /ɔmɔlɔge/ v.t. recognize (officially), validate.

homonyme /ɔmɔnim/ n.m. (personne) namesake.

homosex|uel, ∼uelle /ɔmɔsɛksyɛl/ a. & n.m., f. homosexual. **∼ualité** n.f. homosexuality.

Hongrie /'ɔ̃gri/ n.f. Hungary.

hongrois, ∼e /'ɔ̃grwa, -z/ a. & n.m., f. Hungarian.

honnête /ɔnɛt/ a. honest; (satisfaisant) fair. **∼ment** adv. honestly; fairly. **∼té** n.f. honesty.

honneur /ɔnœr/ n.m. honour; (mérite) credit. **d'∼,** (invité, place) of honour; (membre) honorary. **en l'∼ de,** in honour of. **en quel ∼?,** (fam.) why? **faire ∼ à,** (équipe, famille) bring credit to.

honorable /ɔnɔrabl/ *a.* honourable; (*convenable*) respectable. **~ment** /-əmã/ *adv.* honourably; respectably.

honoraire /ɔnɔrɛr/ *a.* honorary. **~s** *n.m. pl.* fees.

honorer /ɔnɔre/ *v.t.* honour; (*faire honneur à*) do credit to. **s'~ de**, pride o.s. on.

honorifique /ɔnɔrifik/ *a.* honorary.

hont|e /'ɔ̃t/ *n.f.* shame. **avoir ~e**, be ashamed (**de**, of). **faire ~e à**, make ashamed. **~eux, ~euse** *a.* (*personne*) ashamed (**de**, of); (*action*) shameful. **~eusement** *adv.* shamefully.

hôpit|al (*pl.* **~aux**) /ɔpital, -o/ *n.m.* hospital.

hoquet /'ɔkɛ/ *n.m.* hiccup. **le ~**, (the) hiccups.

horaire /ɔrɛr/ *a.* hourly. **—n.m.** timetable. **~ flexible**, flexitime.

horizon /ɔrizɔ̃/ *n.m.* horizon; (*perspective*) view.

horizont|al (*m. pl.* **~aux**) /ɔrizɔtal, -o/ *a.* horizontal. **~alement** *adv.* horizontally.

horloge /ɔrlɔʒ/ *n.f.* clock.

horlog|er, ~ère /ɔrlɔʒe, -ɛr/ *n.m., f.* watchmaker.

hormis /'ɔrmi/ *prép.* save.

hormon|al (*m. pl.* **~aux**) /ɔrmɔnal, -no/ *a.* hormonal, hormone.

hormone /ɔrmɔn/ *n.f.* hormone.

horoscope /ɔrɔskɔp/ *n.m.* horoscope.

horreur /ɔrœr/ *n.f.* horror. **avoir ~ de**, detest.

horrible /ɔribl/ *a.* horrible. **~ment** /-əmã/ *adv.* horribly.

horrifier /ɔrifje/ *v.t.* horrify.

hors /'ɔr/ *prép.* **~ de**, out of; (*à l'extérieur de*) outside. **~-bord** *n.m. invar.* speedboat. **~ d'atteinte**, out of reach. **~ d'haleine**, out of breath. **~ d'œuvre** *n.m. invar.* hors- d'œuvre. **~ de prix**, exorbitant. **~ de soi**, beside o.s. **~-jeu** *a. invar.* offside. **~-la-loi** *n.m. invar.* outlaw. **~ pair**, outstanding. **~-taxe** *a. invar.* duty-free.

hortensia /ɔrtɑ̃sja/ *n.m.* hydrangea.

horticulture /ɔrtikyltyr/ *n.f.* horticulture.

hospice /ɔspis/ *n.m.* home.

hospital|ier, ~ière¹ /ɔspitalje, -jɛr/ *a.* hospitable. **~ité** *n.f.* hospitality.

hospital|ier, ~ière² /ɔspitalje, -jɛr/ *a.* (*méd.*) hospital. **~iser** *v.t.* take to hospital.

hostie /ɔsti/ *n.f.* (*relig.*) host.

hostil|e /ɔstil/ *a.* hostile. **~ité** *n.f.* hostility.

hosto /ɔstɔ/ *n.m.* (*fam.*) hospital.

hôte /ot/ *n.m.* (*maître*) host; (*invité*) guest.

hôtel /otɛl/ *n.m.* hotel. **~ (particulier)**, (private) mansion. **~ de ville**, town hall. **~ier, ~ière** /otəlje, -jɛr/ *a.* hotel; *n.m., f.* hotelier. **~lerie** *n.f.* hotel business; (*auberge*) country hotel.

hôtesse /otɛs/ *n.f.* hostess. **~ de l'air**, air hostess.

hotte /'ɔt/ *n.f.* basket; (*de cuisinière*) hood.

houblon /'ublɔ̃/ *n.m.* **le ~**, hops.

houill|e /'uj/ *n.f.* coal. **~e blanche**, hydroelectric power. **~er, ~ère** *a.* coal; *n.f.* coalmine.

houl|e /'ul/ *n.f.* (*de mer*) swell. **~eux, ~euse** *a.* stormy.

houligan /uligan/ *n.m.* hooligan.

houppette /'upɛt/ *n.f.* powder-puff.

hourra /'ura/ *n.m. & int.* hurrah.

housse /'us/ *n.f.* dust-cover.

houx /'u/ *n.m.* holly.

hovercraft /ɔverkraft/ *n.m.* hovercraft.

hublot /'yblo/ *n.m.* porthole.

huche /'yʃ/ *n.f.* **~ à pain**, breadbin.

huer /'ɥe/ *v.t.* boo. **huées** *n.f. pl.* boos.

huil|e /ɥil/ *n.f.* oil; (*personne: fam.*) bigwig. **~er** *v.t.* oil. **~eux, ~euse** *a.* oily.

huis /ɥi/ *à ~ clos*, in camera.

huissier /ɥisje/ *n.m.* (*appariteur*) usher; (*jurid.*) bailiff.

huit /'ɥi(t)/ *a.* eight. **—n.m.** eight. **~ jours**, a week. **lundi en ~**, a week on Monday. **~aine** /'ɥiten/ *n.f.* (*semaine*) week. **~ième** /'ɥitjɛm/ *a. & n.m./f.* eighth.

huître /ɥitr/ *n.f.* oyster.

humain, ~e /ymɛ̃, ymɛn/ *a.* human; (*compatissant*) humane. **~ement** /ymɛnmã/ *adv.* humanly; humanely.

humanitaire /ymaniter/ *a.* humanitarian.

humanité /ymanite/ *n.f.* humanity.

humble /œbl/ *a.* humble.

humecter /ymɛkte/ *v.t.* moisten.

humer /'yme/ *v.t.* smell.

humeur /ymœr/ *n.f.* mood; (*tempérament*) temper. **de bonne/mauvaise ~**, in a good/bad mood.

humid|e /ymid/ *a.* damp; (*chaleur, climat*) humid; (*lèvres, yeux*) moist. **~ité** *n.f.* humidity.

humil|ier /ymilje/ *v.t.* humiliate. **~iation** *n.f.* humiliation.

humilité /ymilite/ *n.f.* humility.

humorist|e /ymɔrist/ *n.m./f.* humorist. **~ique** *a.* humorous.

humour /ymur/ n.m. humour; (sens) sense of humour.

huppé /'ype/ a. (fam.) high-class.

hurl|er /'yrle/ v.t./i. howl. **~ement** n.m. howl(ing).

hurluberlu /yrlybɛrly/ n.m. scatterbrain.

hutte /'yt/ n.f. hut.

hybride /ibrid/ a. & n.m. hybrid.

hydratant, ~e /idratã, -t/ a. (lotion) moisturizing.

hydrate /idrat/ n.m. **~ de carbone,** carbohydrate.

hydraulique /idrolik/ a. hydraulic.

hydravion /idravjɔ̃/ n.m. seaplane.

hydro-electrique /idroelɛktrik/ a. hydroelectric.

hydrogène /idrɔʒɛn/ n.m. hydrogen.

hyène /jɛn/ n.f. hyena.

hyg|iène /iʒjɛn/ n.f. hygiene. **~iénique** /iʒjenik/ a. hygienic.

hymne /imn/ n.m. hymn. **~ national,** national anthem.

hyper- /iper/ préf. hyper-.

hypermarché /ipɛrmarʃe/ n.m. (supermarché) hypermarket.

hypermétrope /ipɛrmetrɔp/ a. longsighted.

hypertension /ipɛrtãsjɔ̃/ n.f. high blood-pressure.

hypno|se /ipnoz/ n.f. hypnosis. **~tique** /-ɔtik/ a. hypnotic. **~tisme** /-ɔtism/ n.m. hypnotism.

hypnotis|er /ipnotize/ v.t. hypnotize. **~eur** n.m. hypnotist.

hypocrisie /ipɔkrizi/ n.f. hypocrisy.

hypocrite /ipɔkrit/ a. hypocritical. **—**n.m./f. hypocrite.

hypoth|èque /ipɔtɛk/ n.f. mortgage. **~équer** v.t. mortgage.

hypoth|èse /ipɔtez/ n.f. hypothesis. **~étique** a. hypothetical.

hystér|ie /isteri/ n.f. hysteria. **~ique** a. hysterical.

I

iceberg /isbɛrg/ n.m. iceberg.

ici /isi/ adv. (espace) here; (temps) now. **d'~ demain,** by tomorrow. **d'~ là,** in the meantime. **d'~ peu,** shortly. **~ même,** in this very place.

icône /ikon/ n.f. icon.

idé|al (m. pl. **~aux**) /ideal, -o/ a. ideal. **—**n.m. (pl. **~aux**) ideal. **~aliser** v.t. idealize.

idéalis|te /idealist/ a. idealistic. **—**n.m./f. idealist. **~me** n.m. idealism.

idée /ide/ n.f. idea; (esprit) mind. **~ fixe,** obsession. **~ reçue,** conventional opinion.

identif|ier /idãtifje/ v.t., **s'~ier** v. pr. identify (à, with). **~ication** n.f. identification.

identique /idãtik/ a. identical.

identité /idãtite/ n.f. identity.

idéolog|ie /ideɔlɔʒi/ n.f. ideology. **~ique** a. ideological.

idiom|e /idjom/ n.m. idiom. **~atique** /idjɔmatik/ a. idiomatic.

idiot, ~e /idjo, idjɔt/ a. idiotic. **—**n.m., f. idiot. **~ie** /idjɔsi/ n.f. idiocy; (acte, parole) idiotic thing.

idiotisme /idjɔtism/ n.m. idiom.

idolâtrer /idɔlatre/ v.t. idolize.

idole /idɔl/ n.f. idol.

idyll|e /idil/ n.f. idyll. **~ique** a. idyllic.

if /if/ n.m. (arbre) yew.

igloo /iglu/ n.m. igloo.

ignare /iɲar/ a. ignorant. **—**n.m./f. ignoramus.

ignifugé /iɲifyʒe/ a. fireproof.

ignoble /iɲɔbl/ a. vile.

ignoran|t, ~te /iɲorã, -t/ a. ignorant. **—**n.m., f. ignoramus. **~ce** n.f. ignorance.

ignorer /iɲore/ v.t. not know; (personne) ignore.

il /il/ pron. he; (chose) it. **il est vrai/**etc. **que,** it is true/etc. that. **il neige/pleut/**etc., it is snowing/raining/ etc. **il y a,** there is; (pluriel) there are; (temps) ago; (durée) for. **il y a 2 ans,** 2 years ago. **il y a plus d'une heure que j'attends,** I've been waiting for over an hour.

île /il/ n.f. island. **~ déserte,** desert island. **~ anglo-normandes,** Channel Islands. **~s Britanniques,** British Isles.

illég|al (m. pl. **~aux**) /ilegal, -o/ a. illegal. **~alité** n.f. illegality.

illégitim|e /ileʒitim/ a. illegitimate. **~ité** n.f. illegitimacy.

illettré, ~e /iletre/ a. & n.m., f. illiterate.

illicite /ilisit/ a. illicit.

illimité /ilimite/ a. unlimited.

illisible /ilizibl/ a. illegible; (livre) unreadable.

illogique /ilɔʒik/ a. illogical.

illumin|er /ilymine/ v.t., **s'~er** v. pr. light up. **~ation** n.f. illumination. **~é a.** (monument) floodlit.

illusion /ilyzjɔ̃/ n.f. illusion. **se faire des ~s,** delude o.s. **~ner** /-jɔne/ v.t.

delude. ⁓**niste** /-jɔnist/ *n.m./f.* conjuror.

illusoire /ilyzwar/ *a.* illusory.

illustre /ilystr/ *a.* illustrious.

illustr|er /ilystre/ *v.t.* illustrate. **s'⁓er** *v. pr.* become famous. ⁓**ation** *n.f.* illustration. ⁓**é** *a.* illustrated; *n.m.* illustrated magazine.

îlot /ilo/ *n.m.* island; (*de maisons*) block.

ils /il/ *pron.* they.

imag|e /imaʒ/ *n.f.* picture; (*métaphore*) image; (*reflet*) reflection. ⁓**é** *a.* full of imagery.

imaginaire /imaʒinɛr/ *a.* imaginary.

imaginati|f, ⁓**ve** /imaʒinatif, -v/ *a.* imaginative.

imagin|er /imaʒine/ *v.t.* imagine; (*inventer*) think up. **s'⁓er** *v. pr.* imagine (**que**, that) ⁓**ation** *n.f.* imagination.

imbattable /ɛ̃batabl/ *a.* unbeatable.

imbécil|e /ɛ̃besil/ *a.* idiotic. —*n.m./f.* idiot. ⁓**lité** *n.f.* idiocy; (*action*) idiotic thing.

imbib|er /ɛ̃bibe/ *v.t.* soak (**de**, with). **être ⁓é**, (*fam.*) be sozzled. **s'⁓er** *v. pr.* become soaked.

imbriqué /ɛ̃brike/ *a.* (*lié*) linked.

imbroglio /ɛ̃brɔglio/ *n.m.* imbroglio.

imbu /ɛ̃by/ *a.* ⁓ **de**, full of.

imbuvable /ɛ̃byvabl/ *a.* undrinkable; (*personne: fam.*) insufferable.

imit|er /imite/ *v.t.* imitate; (*personnage*) impersonate; (*faire comme*) do the same as; (*document*) copy. ⁓**ateur**, ⁓**atrice** *n.m., f.* imitator; impersonator. ⁓**ation** *n.f.* imitation; impersonation.

immaculé /imakyle/ *a.* spotless.

immangeable /ɛ̃mɑ̃ʒabl/ *a.* inedible.

immatricul|er /imatrikyle/ *v.t.* register. (**se**) **faire ⁓er**, register. ⁓**ation** *n.f.* registration.

immature /imatyr/ *a.* immature.

immédiat, ⁓**e** /imedja, -t/ *a.* immediate. —*n.m.* **dans l'⁓**, for the moment. ⁓**ement** /-tmɑ̃/ *adv.* immediately.

immens|e /imɑ̃s/ *a.* immense. ⁓**ément** *adv.* immensely. ⁓**ité** *n.f.* immensity.

immer|ger /imɛrʒe/ *v.t.* immerse. **s'⁓ger** *v. pr.* submerge. ⁓**sion** *n.f.* immersion.

immeuble /imœbl/ *n.m.* block of flats, building. ⁓ (**de bureaux**), (office) building *ou* block.

immigr|er /imigre/ *v.i.* immigrate. ⁓**ant**, ⁓**ante** *a. & n.m., f.* immigrant. ⁓**ation** *n.f.* immigration. ⁓**é**, ⁓**ée** *a. & n.m., f.* immigrant.

imminen|t, ⁓**te** /iminɑ̃, -t/ *a.* imminent. ⁓**ce** *n.f.* imminence.

immiscer (s') /(s)imise/ *v. pr.* interfere (**dans**, in).

immobil|e /imɔbil/ *a.* still, motionless. ⁓**ité** *n.f.* stillness; (*inaction*) immobility.

immobil|ier, ⁓**ière** /imɔbilje, -jɛr/ *a.* property. **agence ⁓ière**, estate agent's office; (*Amer.*) real estate office. **agent ⁓ier**, estate agent; (*Amer.*) real estate agent. **l'⁓ier**, property; (*Amer.*) real estate.

immobilis|er /imɔbilizɛ/ *v.t.* immobilize; (*stopper*) stop. **s'⁓er** *v. pr.* stop. ⁓**ation** *n.f.* immobilization.

immodéré /imɔdere/ *a.* immoderate.

immoler /imɔle/ *v.t.* sacrifice.

immonde /imɔ̃d/ *a.* filthy.

immondices /imɔ̃dis/ *n.f. pl.* refuse.

immor|al (*m. pl.* ⁓**aux**) /imɔral, -o/ *a.* immoral. ⁓**alité** *n.f.* immorality.

immortaliser /imɔrtalize/ *v.t.* immortalize.

immort|el, ⁓**elle** /imɔrtɛl/ *a.* immortal. ⁓**alité** *n.f.* immortality.

immuable /imɥabl/ *a.* unchanging.

immunis|er /imynize/ *v.t.* immunize. ⁓**é contre**, (*à l'abri de*) immune to.

immunité /imynite/ *n.f.* immunity.

impact /ɛ̃pakt/ *n.m.* impact.

impair[1] /ɛ̃pɛr/ *a.* (*numéro*) odd.

impair[2] /ɛ̃pɛr/ *n.m.* blunder.

impardonnable /ɛ̃pardɔnabl/ *a.* unforgivable.

imparfait, ⁓**e** /ɛ̃parfɛ, -t/ *a. & n.m.* imperfect.

impart|ial (*m. pl.* ⁓**iaux**) /ɛ̃parsjal, -jo/ *a.* impartial. ⁓**ialité** *n.f.* impartiality.

impasse /ɛ̃pɑs/ *n.f.* (*rue*) dead end, (*situation*) deadlock.

impassible /ɛ̃pasibl/ *a.* impassive.

impat|ient, ⁓**iente** /ɛ̃pasjɑ̃, -t/ *a.* impatient. ⁓**iemment** /-jamɑ̃/ *adv.* impatiently. ⁓**ience** *n.f.* impatience.

impatienter /ɛ̃pasjɑ̃te/ *v.t.* annoy. **s'⁓** *v. pr.* lose patience (**contre**, with).

impayable /ɛ̃pɛjabl/ *a.* (killingly) funny, hilarious.

impayé /ɛ̃pɛje/ *a.* unpaid.

impeccable /ɛ̃pekabl/ *a.* impeccable.

impénétrable /ɛ̃penetrabl/ *a.* impenetrable.

impensable /ɛ̃pɑ̃sabl/ *a.* unthinkable.

impérati|f, ⁓**ve** /ɛ̃peratif, -v/ *a.* imperative. —*n.m.* requirement; (*gram.*) imperative.

impératrice /ɛ̃peratris/ *n.f.* empress.

imperceptible /ɛ̃pɛrsɛptibl/ *a.* imperceptible.

imperfection /ɛ̃pɛrfɛksjɔ̃/ *n.f.* imperfection.

impér|ial (*m. pl.* **~iaux**) /ɛ̃perjal, -jo/ *a.* imperial. **~ialisme** *n.m.* imperialism.

impériale /ɛ̃perjal/ *n.f.* upper deck.

impérieu|x, **~se** /ɛ̃perjø, -z/ *a.* imperious; (*pressant*) pressing.

impérissable /ɛ̃perisabl/ *a.* undying.

imperméable /ɛ̃pɛrmeabl/ *a.* impervious (**à**, to); (*manteau*, *tissu*) waterproof. —*n.m.* raincoat.

impersonnel, **~le** /ɛ̃pɛrsɔnɛl/ *a.* impersonal.

impertinen|t, **~te** /ɛ̃pɛrtinã, -t/ *a.* impertinent. **~ce** *n.f.* impertinence.

imperturbable /ɛ̃pɛrtyrbabl/ *a.* unshakeable.

impét|ueux, **~ueuse** /ɛ̃petɥø, -z/ *a.* impetuous. **~uosité** *n.f.* impetuosity.

impitoyable /ɛ̃pitwajabl/ *a.* merciless.

implacable /ɛ̃plakabl/ *a.* implacable.

implant /ɛ̃plã/ *n.m.* implant.

implant|er /ɛ̃plãte/ *v.t.* establish. **s'~er** *v. pr.* become established. **~ation** *n.f.* establishment.

implication /ɛ̃plikasjɔ̃/ *n.f.* implication.

implicite /ɛ̃plisit/ *a.* implicit.

impliquer /ɛ̃plike/ *v.t.* imply (**que**, that). **~ dans**, implicate in.

implorer /ɛ̃plɔre/ *v.t.* implore.

impoli /ɛ̃pɔli/ *a.* impolite. **~tesse** *n.f.* impoliteness; (*remarque*) impolite remark.

impondérable /ɛ̃pɔ̃derabl/ *a. & n.m.* imponderable.

impopulaire /ɛ̃pɔpylɛr/ *a.* unpopular.

importance /ɛ̃pɔrtãs/ *n.f.* importance; (*taille*) size; (*ampleur*) extent. **sans ~**, unimportant.

important, **~e** /ɛ̃pɔrtã, -t/ *a.* important; (*en quantité*) considerable, sizeable, big. —*n.m.* l'**~**, the important thing.

import|er[1] /ɛ̃pɔrte/ *v.t.* (*comm.*) import. **~ateur**, **~atrice** *n.m.. f.* importer; *a.* importing. **~ation** *n.f.* import.

import|er[2] /ɛ̃pɔrte/ *v.i.* matter, be important (**à**, to). **il ~e que**, it is important that. **n'~e**, **peu ~e**, it does not matter. **n'~e comment**, anyhow. **n'~e où**, anywhere. **n'~e qui**, anybody. **n'~e quoi**, anything.

importun, **~e** /ɛ̃pɔrtœ̃, -yn/ *a.* troublesome. —*n.m., f.* nuisance. **~er** /-yne/ *v.t.* trouble.

imposant, **~e** /ɛ̃pozã, -t/ *a.* imposing.

imposer /ɛ̃poze/ *v.t.* impose (**à**, on); (*taxer*) tax. **s'~** *v. pr.* (*action*) be essential; (*se faire reconnaître*) stand out. **en ~ à qn.**, impress s.o.

imposition /ɛ̃pozisjɔ̃/ *n.f.* taxation. **~ des mains**, laying-on of hands.

impossibilité /ɛ̃pɔsibilite/ *n.f.* impossibility. **dans l'~ de**, unable to.

impossible /ɛ̃pɔsibl/ *a. & n.m.* impossible. **faire l'~**, do the impossible.

impost|eur /ɛ̃pɔstœr/ *n.m.* impostor. **~ure** *n.f.* imposture.

impôt /ɛ̃po/ *n.m.* tax. **~s**, (*contributions*) tax(ation), taxes. **~ sur le revenu**, income tax.

impotent, **~e** /ɛ̃pɔtã, -t/ *a.* crippled. —*n.m., f.* cripple.

impraticable /ɛ̃pratikabl/ *a.* (*route*) impassable.

imprécis, **~e** /ɛ̃presi, -z/ *a.* imprecise. **~ion** /-zjɔ̃/ *n.f.* imprecision.

imprégner /ɛ̃preɲe/ *v.t.* fill (**de**, with); (*imbiber*) impregnate (**de**, with). **s' ~ de**, become filled with; (*s'imbiber*) become impregnated with.

imprenable /ɛ̃prənabl/ *a.* impregnable.

impresario /ɛ̃presarjo/ *n.m.* manager.

impression /ɛ̃presjɔ̃/ *n.f.* impression; (*de livre*) printing.

impressionn|er /ɛ̃presjone/ *v.t.* impress. **~able** *a.* impressionable. **~ant**, **~ante** *a.* impressive.

imprévisible /ɛ̃previzibl/ *a.* unpredictable.

imprévoyant, **~e** /ɛ̃prevwajã, -t/ *a.* improvident.

imprévu /ɛ̃prevy/ *a.* unexpected. —*n.m.* unexpected incident.

imprim|er /ɛ̃prime/ *v.t.* print; (*marquer*) imprint; (*transmettre*) impart. **~ante** *n.f.* (*d'un ordinateur*) printer. **~é** *a.* printed; *n.m.* (*formulaire*) printed form. **~erie** *n.f.* (*art*) printing; (*lieu*) printing works. **~eur** *n.m.* printer.

improbable /ɛ̃prɔbabl/ *a.* unlikely, improbable.

impromptu /ɛ̃prɔ̃pty/ *a. & adv.* impromptu.

impropr|e /ɛ̃prɔpr/ *a.* incorrect. **~e à**, unfit for. **~iété**, *n.f.* incorrectness; (*erreur*) error.

improvis|er /ɛ̃prɔvize/ *v.t./i.* improvise. **~ation** *n.f.* improvisation.

improviste (à l') /(al)ɛ̃prɔvist/ *adv.* unexpectedly.

imprud|ent, **~ente** /ɛ̃prydã, -t/ *a.* careless. **il est ~ent de**, it is unwise to. **~emment** /-amã/ *adv.* carelessly. **~ence** *n.f.* carelessness; (*acte*) careless action.

impuden|t, **~te** /ɛ̃pydɑ̃, -t/ *a.* impudent. **~ce** *n.f.* impudence.

impudique /ɛ̃pydik/ *a.* immodest.

impuissan|t, **~te** /ɛ̃pɥisɑ̃, -t/ *a.* helpless; (*méd.*) impotent. **~t à,** powerless to. **~ce** *n.f.* helplessness; (*méd.*) impotence.

impulsi|f, **~ve** /ɛ̃pylsif, -v/ *a.* impulsive.

Impulsion /ɛ̃pylsjɔ̃/ *n.f.* (*poussée, influence*) impetus; (*instinct, mouvement*) impulse.

impunément /ɛ̃pynemɑ̃/ *adv.* with impunity.

impuni /ɛ̃pyni/ *a.* unpunished.

impunité /ɛ̃pynite/ *n.f.* impunity.

impur /ɛ̃pyr/ *a.* impure. **~eté** *n.f.* impurity.

imput|er /ɛ̃pyte/ *v.t.* **~er à,** impute to. **~able** *a.* ascribable (à, to).

inabordable /inabɔrdabl/ *a.* (*prix*) prohibitive.

inacceptable /inaksɛptabl/ *a.* unacceptable; (*scandaleux*) outrageous.

inaccessible /inaksesibl/ *a.* inaccessible.

inaccoutumé /inakutyme/ *a.* unaccustomed.

inachevé /inaʃve/ *a.* unfinished.

inacti|f, **~ve** /inaktif, -v/ *a.* inactive.

inaction /inaksjɔ̃/ *n.f.* inactivity.

inadapté, **~e** /inadapte/ *n.m.*, *f.* (*psych.*) maladjusted person.

inadéquat, **~e** /inadekwa, -t/ *a.* inadequate.

inadmissible /inadmisibl/ *a.* unacceptable.

inadvertance /inadvɛrtɑ̃s/ *n.f.* **par ~,** by mistake.

inaltérable /inalterabl/ *a.* stable, that does not deteriorate; (*sentiment*) unfailing.

inanimé /inanime/ *a.* (*évanoui*) unconscious; (*mort*) lifeless; (*matière*) inanimate.

inaperçu /inapɛrsy/ *a.* unnoticed.

inappréciable /inapresjabl/ *a.* invaluable.

inapte /inapt/ *a.* unsuited (à, to). **~ à faire,** incapable of doing.

inarticulé /inartikyle/ *a.* inarticulate.

inassouvi /inasuvi/ *a.* unsatisfied.

inattendu /inatɑ̃dy/ *a.* unexpected.

inattenti|f, **~ve** /inatãtif, -v/ *a.* inattentive (à, to).

inattention /inatɑ̃sjɔ̃/ *n.f.* inattention.

inaugur|er /inɔgyre/ *v.t.* inaugurate. **~ation** *n.f.* inauguration.

inaugur|al (*m. pl.* **~aux**) /inɔgyral, -o/ *a.* inaugural.

incalculable /ɛ̃kalkylabl/ *a.* incalculable.

incapable /ɛ̃kapabl/ *a.* incapable (**de qch.,** of sth.). **~ de faire,** unable to do, incapable of doing. —*n.m./f.* incompetent.

incapacité /ɛ̃kapasite/ *n.f.* incapacity. **dans l'~ de,** unable to.

incarcérer /ɛ̃karsere/ *v.t.* incarcerate.

incarn|er /ɛ̃karne/ *v.t.* embody. **~ation** *n.f.* embodiment, incarnation. **~é** *a.* (*ongle*) ingrowing.

incartade /ɛ̃kartad/ *n.f.* indiscretion, misdeed, prank.

incassable /ɛ̃kasabl/ *a.* unbreakable.

incendiaire /ɛ̃sɑ̃djɛr/ *a.* incendiary; (*propos*) inflammatory. —*n.m./f.* arsonist.

incend|ie /ɛ̃sɑ̃di/ *n.m.* fire. **~ie criminel,** arson. **~ier** *v.t.* set fire to.

incert|ain, **~aine** /ɛ̃sɛrtɛ̃, -ɛn/ *a.* uncertain; (*contour*) vague. **~itude** *n.f.* uncertainty.

incessamment /ɛ̃sɛsamɑ̃/ *adv.* shortly.

incessant, **~e** /ɛ̃sɛsɑ̃, -t/ *a.* incessant.

incest|e /ɛ̃sɛst/ *n.m.* incest. **~ueux, ~ueuse** *a.* incestuous.

inchangé /ɛ̃ʃɑ̃ʒe/ *a.* unchanged.

incidence /ɛ̃sidɑ̃s/ *n.f.* effect.

incident /ɛ̃sidɑ̃/ *n.m.* incident. **~ technique,** technical hitch.

incinér|er /ɛ̃sinere/ *v.t.* incinerate; (*mort*) cremate. **~ateur** *n.m.* incinerator.

incis|er /ɛ̃size/ *v.t.* (*abcès etc.*) lance. **~ion** *n.f.* lancing; (*entaille*) incision.

incisi|f, **~ve** /ɛ̃sizif, -v/ *a.* incisive.

incit|er /ɛ̃site/ *v.t.* incite (à, to). **~ation** *n.f.* incitement.

inclinaison /ɛ̃klinɛzɔ̃/ *n.f.* incline; (*de la tête*) tilt.

inclination[1] /ɛ̃klinasjɔ̃/ *n.f.* (*penchant*) inclination.

inclin|er /ɛ̃kline/ *v.t.* tilt, lean; (*courber*) bend; (*inciter*) encourage (à, to). —*v.i.* **~er à,** be inclined to. **s'~er** *v. pr.* (*se courber*) bow down; (*céder*) give in; (*chemin*) slope. **~er la tête,** (*approuver*) nod; (*révérence*) bow. **~ation**[2] *n.f.* (*de la tête*) nod; (*du buste*) bow.

incl|ure /ɛ̃klyr/ *v.t.* include; (*enfermer*) enclose. **jusqu'au lundi ~us,** up to and including Monday. **~usion** *n.f.* inclusion.

incognito /ɛ̃kɔnito/ *adv.* incognito.

incohéren|t, **~te** /ɛ̃kɔerɑ̃, -t/ *a.* incoherent. **~ce** *n.f.* incoherence.

incollable /ɛ̃kɔlabl/ *a.* **il est** ∼, he can't be stumped.
incolore /ɛ̃kɔlɔr/ *a.* colourless; (*crème, verre*) clear.
incomber /ɛ̃kɔ̃be/ *v.i.* **il vous**/*etc.* **incombe de,** it is your/*etc.* responsibility to.
incombustible /ɛ̃kɔ̃bystibl/ *a.* incombustible.
incommode /ɛ̃kɔmɔd/ *a.* awkward.
incommoder /ɛ̃kɔmɔde/ *v.t.* inconvenience.
incomparable /ɛ̃kɔ̃parabl/ *a.* incomparable.
incompatib|le /ɛ̃kɔ̃patibl/ *a.* incompatible. ∼**ilité** *n.f.* incompatibility.
incompéten|t, ∼**te** /ɛ̃kɔ̃petɑ̃, -t/ *a.* incompetent. ∼**ce** *n.f.* incompetence.
incompl|et, ∼**ète** /ɛ̃kɔ̃plɛ, -t/ *a.* incomplete.
incompréhensible /ɛ̃kɔ̃preɑ̃sibl/ *a.* incomprehensible.
incompréhension /ɛ̃kɔ̃preɑ̃sjɔ̃/ *n.f.* lack of understanding.
incompris, ∼**e** /ɛ̃kɔ̃pri, -z/ *a.* misunderstood.
inconcevable /ɛ̃kɔ̃svabl/ *a.* inconceivable.
inconciliable /ɛ̃kɔ̃siljabl/ *a.* irreconcilable.
inconditionnel, ∼**le** /ɛ̃kɔ̃disjɔnɛl/ *a.* unconditional.
inconduite /ɛ̃kɔ̃dɥit/ *n.f.* loose behaviour.
inconfort /ɛ̃kɔ̃fɔr/ *n.m.* discomfort. ∼**able** /-tabl/ *a.* uncomfortable.
incongru /ɛ̃kɔ̃gry/ *a.* unseemly.
inconnu, ∼**e** /ɛ̃kɔny/ *a.* unknown (**à,** to). —*n.m.,* *f.* stranger. —*n.m.* **l'**∼, the unknown. —*n.f.* unknown (quantity).
inconsc|ient, ∼**iente** /ɛ̃kɔ̃sjɑ̃, -t/ *a.* unconscious (**de,** of); (*fou*) mad. —*n.m.* (*psych.*) subconscious. ∼**iemment** /-jamɑ̃/ *adv.* unconsciously. ∼**ience** *n.f.* unconsciousness; (*folie*) madness.
inconsidéré /ɛ̃kɔ̃sidere/ *a.* thoughtless.
inconsistant, ∼**e** /ɛ̃kɔ̃sistɑ̃, -t/ *a.* (*fig.*) flimsy.
inconsolable /ɛ̃kɔ̃sɔlabl/ *a.* inconsolable.
inconstan|t, ∼**te** /ɛ̃kɔ̃stɑ̃, -t/ *a.* fickle. ∼**ce** *n.f.* fickleness.
incontest|able /ɛ̃kɔ̃tɛstabl/ *a.* indisputable. ∼**é** *a.* undisputed.
incontinen|t, ∼**te** /ɛ̃kɔ̃tinɑ̃, -t/ *a.* incontinent. ∼**ce** *n.f.* incontinence.
incontrôlable /ɛ̃kɔ̃trolabl/ *a.* unverifiable.

inconvenan|t, ∼**te** /ɛ̃kɔ̃vnɑ̃, -t/ *a.* improper. ∼**ce** *n.f.* impropriety.
inconvénient /ɛ̃kɔ̃venjɑ̃/ *n.m.* disadvantage; (*risque*) risk; (*objection*) objection.
incorpor|er /ɛ̃kɔrpɔre/ *v.t.* incorporate; (*mil.*) enlist. ∼**ation** *n.f.* incorporation; (*mil.*) enlistment.
incorrect /ɛ̃kɔrɛkt/ *a.* (*faux*) incorrect; (*malséant*) improper; (*impoli*) impolite.
incorrigible /ɛ̃kɔriʒibl/ *a.* incorrigible.
incrédul|e /ɛ̃kredyl/ *a.* incredulous. ∼**ité** *n.f.* incredulity.
increvable /ɛ̃krəvabl/ *a.* (*fam.*) tireless.
incriminer /ɛ̃krimine/ *v.t.* incriminate.
incroyable /ɛ̃krwajabl/ *a.* incredible.
incroyant, ∼**e** /ɛ̃krwajɑ̃, -t/ *n.m., f.* non-believer.
incrust|er /ɛ̃kryste/ *v.t.* (*décorer*) inlay (**de,** with). **s'**∼**er** (*invité: péj.*) take root. ∼**ation** *n.f.* inlay.
incubateur /ɛ̃kybatœr/ *n.m.* incubator.
inculp|er /ɛ̃kylpe/ *v.t.* charge (**de,** with). ∼**ation** *n.f.* charge. ∼**é,** ∼**ée** *n.m., f.* accused.
inculquer /ɛ̃kylke/ *v.t.* instil (**à,** into).
inculte /ɛ̃kylt/ *a.* uncultivated; (*personne*) uneducated.
incurable /ɛ̃kyrabl/ *a.* incurable.
incursion /ɛ̃kyrsjɔ̃/ *n.f.* incursion.
incurver /ɛ̃kyrve/ *v.t.*, **s'**∼ *v. pr.* curve.
Inde /ɛ̃d/ *n.f.* India.
indécen|t, ∼**te** /ɛ̃desɑ̃, -t/ *a.* indecent. ∼**ce** *n.f.* indecency.
indéchiffrable /ɛ̃deʃifrabl/ *a.* indecipherable.
indécis, ∼**e** /ɛ̃desi, -z/ *a.* indecisive; (*qui n'a pas encore pris de décision*) undecided. ∼**ion** /-izjɔ̃/ *n.f.* indecision.
indéfendable /ɛ̃defɑ̃dabl/ *a.* indefensible.
indéfini /ɛ̃defini/ *a.* indefinite; (*vague*) undefined. ∼**ment** *adv.* indefinitely. ∼**ssable** *a.* indefinable.
indélébile /ɛ̃delebil/ *a.* indelible.
indélicat, ∼**e** /ɛ̃delika, -t/ *a.* (*malhonnête*) unscrupulous.
indemne /ɛ̃dɛmn/ *a.* unharmed.
indemniser /ɛ̃dɛmnize/ *v.t.* compensate (**de,** for).
indemnité /ɛ̃dɛmnite/ *n.f.* indemnity; (*allocation*) allowance. ∼**s de licenciement,** redundancy payment.
indéniable /ɛ̃denjabl/ *a.* undeniable.
indépend|ant, ∼**ante** /ɛ̃depɑ̃dɑ̃, -t/ *a.* independent. ∼**amment** *adv.* independently. ∼**amment de,** apart from. ∼**ance** *n.f.* independence.

indescriptible /ɛ̃dɛskriptibl/ *a.* indescribable.

indésirable /ɛ̃dezirabl/ *a.* & *n.m./f.* undesirable.

indestructible /ɛ̃dɛstryktibl/ *a.* indestructible.

indétermination /ɛ̃detɛrminasjɔ̃/ *n.f.* indecision.

indéterminé /ɛ̃detɛrmine/ *a.* unspecified.

index /ɛ̃dɛks/ *n.m.* forefinger; (*liste*) index. **~er** *v.t.* index.

indic /ɛ̃dik/ (*fam.*) grass.

indica|teur, ~trice /ɛ̃dikatœr, -tris/ *n.m., f.* (*police*) informer. —*n.m.* (*livre*) guide; (*techn.*) indicator. **~teur des chemins de fer,** railway timetable. **~teur des rues,** street directory.

indicati|f, ~ve /ɛ̃dikatif, -v/ *a.* indicative (**de,** of). —*n.m.* (*radio*) signature tune; (*téléphonique*) dialling code; (*gram.*) indicative.

indication /ɛ̃dikasjɔ̃/ *n.f.* indication; (*renseignement*) information; (*directive*) instruction.

indice /ɛ̃dis/ *n.m.* sign; (*dans une enquête*) clue; (*des prix*) index; (*de salaire*) rating.

indien, ~ne /ɛ̃djɛ̃, -jɛn/ *a.* & *n.m., f.* Indian.

indifféremment /ɛ̃diferamɑ̃/ *adv.* equally.

indifféren|t, ~te /ɛ̃diferɑ̃, -t/ *a.* indifferent (**à, to**). **ça m'est ~t,** it makes no difference to me. **~ce** *n.f.* indifference.

indigène /ɛ̃diʒɛn/ *a.* & *n.m./f.* native.

indigen|t, ~te /ɛ̃diʒɑ̃, -t/ *a.* poor **~ce** *n.f.* poverty.

indigest|e /ɛ̃diʒɛst/ *a.* indigestible. **~ion** *n.f.* indigestion.

indignation /ɛ̃diɲasjɔ̃/ *n.f.* indignation.

indign|e /ɛ̃diɲ/ *a.* unworthy (**de,** of); (*acte*) vile. **~ité** *n.f.* unworthiness; (*acte*) vile act.

indigner /ɛ̃diɲe/ **s'~** *v. pr.* become indignant (**de,** at).

indiqu|er /ɛ̃dike/ *v.t.* show, indicate; (*renseigner sur*) point out, tell; (*déterminer*) give, state, appoint. **~er du doigt,** point to *ou* out *ou* at. **~é** *a.* (*heure*) appointed; (*opportun*) appropriate; (*conseillé*) recommended.

indirect /ɛ̃dirɛkt/ *a.* indirect.

indiscipliné /ɛ̃disipline/ *a.* unruly.

indiscr|et, ~ète /ɛ̃diskrɛ, -t/ *a.* inquisitive. **~étion** *n.f.* indiscretion; inquisitiveness.

indiscutable /ɛ̃diskytabl/ *a.* unquestionable.

indispensable /ɛ̃dispɑ̃sabl/ *a.* indispensable. **il est ~ qu'il vienne,** it is essential that he comes.

indispos|er /ɛ̃dispoze/ *v.t.* make unwell. **~er** (*mécontenter*) antagonize. **~é** *a.* unwell. **~ition** *n.f.* indisposition.

indistinct, ~e /ɛ̃distɛ̃(kt), -ɛ̃kt/ *a.* indistinct. **~ement** /-ɛktəmɑ̃/ *adv.* indistinctly; (*également*) without distinction.

individ|u /ɛ̃dividy/ *n.m.* individual. **~ualiste** *n.m./f.* individualist.

individuel, ~le /ɛ̃dividɥɛl/ *a.* individual; (*opinion*) personal. **chambre ~le,** single room. **maison ~le,** private house. **~lement** *adv.* individually.

indivisible /ɛ̃divizibl/ *a.* indivisible.

indolen|t, ~te /ɛ̃dolɑ̃, -t/ *a.* indolent. **~ce** *n.f.* indolence.

indolore /ɛ̃dolɔr/ *a.* painless.

Indonésie /cdɔnezi/ *n.f.* Indonesia.

Indonésien, ~ne /ɛdɔnezjɛ, -jɛn/ *a.* & *n.m., f.* Indonesian.

indu, ~e /ɛ̃dy/ *a.* **à une heure ~e,** at some ungodly hour.

induire /ɛ̃dɥir/ *v.t.* infer (**de,** from). **~ en erreur,** mislead.

indulgen|t, ~te /ɛ̃dylʒɑ̃, -t/ *a.* indulgent; (*clément*) lenient. **~ce** *n.f.* indulgence; leniency.

industri|e /ɛ̃dystri/ *n.f.* industry. **~alisé** *a.* industrialized.

industriel, ~le /ɛ̃dystrijɛl/ *a.* industrial. —*n.m.* industrialist. **~lement** *adv.* industrially.

inébranlable /inebrɑ̃labl/ *a.* unshakeable.

inédit, ~e /inedi, -t/ *a.* unpublished; (*fig.*) original.

inefficace /inefikas/ *a.* ineffective.

inég|al (*m. pl.* **~aux**) /inegal, -o/ *a.* unequal; (*irrégulier*) uneven. **~alé** *a.* unequalled. **~alable** *a.* matchless. **~alité** *n.f.* (*injustice*) inequality; (*irrégularité*) unevenness; (*différence*) difference (**de,** between).

inéluctable /inelyktabl/ *a.* inescapable.

inept|e /inɛpt/ *a.* inept, absurd. **~ie** /inɛpsi/ *n.f.* ineptitude.

inépuisable /inepɥizabl/ *a.* inexhaustible.

inert|e /inɛrt/ *a.* inert; (*mort*) lifeless. **~ie** /inɛrsi/ *n.f.* inertia.

inespéré /inɛspere/ *a.* unhoped for.

inestimable /inɛstimabl/ *a.* priceless.

inévitable /inevitabl/ *a.* inevitable.

inexact, ~e /inɛgza(kt), -akt/ *a.*

(*imprécis*) inaccurate; (*incorrect*) incorrect.

inexcusable /inɛkskyzabl/ *a.* unforgivable.

inexistant, ~e /inɛgzistã, -t/ *a.* nonexistent.

inexorable /inɛgzɔrabl/ *a.* inexorable.

inexpérience /inɛksperjãs/ *n.f.* inexperience.

inexpli|cable /inɛksplikabl/ *a.* inexplicable. ~qué *a.* unexplained.

in extremis /inɛkstremis/ *adv. & a.* (*par nécessité*) (taken/done etc.) as a last resort; (*au dernier moment*) (at the) last minute.

inextricable /inɛkstrikabl/ *a.* inextricable.

infaillible /ɛ̃fajibl/ *a.* infallible.

infâme /ɛ̃fam/ *a.* vile.

infamie /ɛ̃fami/ *n.f.* infamy; (*action*) vile action.

infanterie /ɛ̃fãtri/ *n.f.* infantry.

infantile /ɛ̃fãtil/ *a.* infantile.

infantilisme /ɛ̃fãtilism/ *n.m.* infantilism. **faire de l'~,** be childish.

infarctus /ɛ̃farktys/ *n.m.* coronary (thrombosis).

infatigable /ɛ̃fatigabl/ *a.* tireless.

infatué /ɛ̃fatɥe/ *a.* ~ **de sa personne,** full of himself.

infect /ɛ̃fɛkt/ *a.* revolting.

infect|er /ɛ̃fɛkte/ *v.t.* infect. **s'~er** *v. pr.* become infected. ~**ion** /-ksjɔ̃/ *n.f.* infection.

infectieu|x, ~se /ɛ̃fɛksjø, -z/ *a.* infectious.

inférieur, ~e /ɛ̃ferjœr/ *a.* (*plus bas*) lower; (*moins bon*) inferior (**à,** to). —*n.m., f.* inferior. ~ **à,** (*plus petit que*) smaller than.

infériorité /ɛ̃ferjɔrite/ *n.f.* inferiority.

infern|al (*m. pl.* ~**aux**) /ɛ̃fɛrnal, -o/ *a.* infernal.

infester /ɛ̃fɛste/ *v.t.* infest.

infid|èle /ɛ̃fidɛl/ *a.* unfaithful. ~**élité** *n.f.* unfaithfulness; (*acte*) infidelity.

infiltr|er (s') /(s)ɛ̃filtre/ *v. pr.* **s'~er (dans),** (*personnes, idées, etc.*) infiltrate; (*liquide*) percolate. ~**ation** *n.f.* infiltration.

infime /ɛ̃fim/ *a.* tiny, minute.

infini /ɛ̃fini/ *a.* infinite. —*n.m.* infinity. **à l'~,** endlessly. ~**ment** *adv.* infinitely.

infinité /ɛ̃finite/ *n.f.* **une ~ de,** an infinite amount of.

infinitésimal /ɛ̃finitezimal/ *a.* infinitesimal.

infinitif /ɛ̃finitif/ *n.m.* infinitive.

infirm|e /ɛ̃firm/ *a. & n.m./f.* disabled (person). ~**ité** *n.f.* disability.

infirmer /ɛ̃firme/ *v.t.* invalidate.

infirm|erie /ɛ̃firmɔri/ *n.f.* sickbay, infirmary. ~**ier** *n.m.* (male) nurse. ~**ière** *n.f.* nurse. ~**ière-chef,** sister.

inflammable /ɛ̃flamabl/ *a.* (in)flammable.

inflammation /ɛ̃flamɑsjɔ̃/ *n.f.* inflammation.

inflation /ɛ̃flasjɔ̃/ *n.f.* inflation.

inflexible /ɛ̃flɛksibl/ *a.* inflexible.

inflexion /ɛ̃flɛksjɔ̃/ *n.f.* inflexion.

infliger /ɛ̃fliʒe/ *v.t.* inflict; (*sanction*) impose.

influen|ce /ɛ̃flyãs/ *n.f.* influence. ~**çable** *a.* easily influenced. ~**cer** *v.t.* influence.

influent, ~e /ɛ̃flyã, -t/ *a.* influential.

influer /ɛ̃flye/ *v.i.* ~ **sur,** influence.

info /ɛ̃fo/ *n.f.* (some) news. **les ~s,** the news.

informa|teur, ~**trice** /ɛ̃fɔrmatœr, -tris/ *n.m., f.* informant.

informaticien, ~**ne** /ɛ̃fɔrmatisjɛ̃, -jɛn/ *n.m., f.* computer scientist.

information /ɛ̃fɔrmasjɔ̃/ *n.f.* information; (*jurid.*) inquiry. **une ~,** (some) information; (*nouvelle*) (some) news. **les ~s,** the news.

informati|que /ɛ̃fɔrmatik/ *n.f.* computer science; (*techniques*) data processing. ~**ser** *v.t.* computerize.

informe /ɛ̃fɔrm/ *a.* shapeless.

informer /ɛ̃fɔrme/ *v.t.* inform (**de,** about, of). **s'~** *v. pr.* enquire (**de,** about).

infortune /ɛ̃fɔrtyn/ *n.f.* misfortune.

infraction /ɛ̃fraksjɔ̃/ *n.f.* offence. ~ **à,** breach of.

infranchissable /ɛ̃frãʃisabl/ *a.* impassable; (*fig.*) insuperable.

infrarouge /ɛ̃fraruʒ/ *a.* infra-red.

infrastructure /ɛ̃frastryktyr/ *n.f.* infrastructure.

infructueu|x, ~se /ɛ̃fryktɥø, -z/ *a.* fruitless.

infus|er /ɛ̃fyze/ *v.t./i.* infuse, brew. ~**ion** *n.f.* herb-tea, infusion.

ingénier (s') /(s)ɛ̃ʒenje/ *v. pr.* **s'~ à,** strive to.

ingénieur /ɛ̃ʒenjœr/ *n.m.* engineer.

ingén|ieux, ~**ieuse** /ɛ̃ʒenjø, -z/ *a.* ingenious. ~**iosité** *n.f.* ingenuity.

ingénu /ɛ̃ʒeny/ *a.* naïve.

ingér|er (s') /(s)ɛ̃ʒere/ *v. pr.* **s'~er dans,** interfere in. ~**ence** *n.f.* interference.

ingrat, ~e /ɛ̃gra, -t/ *a.* ungrateful; (*pénible*) thankless; (*disgracieux*) unattractive. ~**itude** /-tityd/ *n.f.* ingratitude.

ingrédient /ɛ̃gredjɑ̃/ *n.m.* ingredient.

ingurgiter /ɛ̃gyrʒite/ *v.t.* swallow.

inhabité /inabite/ *a.* uninhabited.

inhabituel, ~le /inabituɛl/ *a.* unusual.

inhalation /inalasjɔ̃/ *n.f.* inhaling.

inhérent, ~e /inerɑ̃, -t/ *a.* inherent (**à**, in).

inhibition /inibisjɔ̃/ *n.f.* inhibition.

inhospital|ier, ~ière /inɔspitalje, -jɛr/ *a.* inhospitable.

inhumain, ~e /inymɛ̃, -ɛn/ *a.* inhuman.

inhum|er /inyme/ *v.t.* bury. **~ation** *n.f.* burial.

inimaginable /inimaʒinabl/ *a.* unimaginable.

inimitié /inimitje/ *n.f.* enmity.

ininterrompu /inɛ̃tɛrɔ̃py/ *a.* continuous, uninterrupted.

iniqu|e /inik/ *a.* iniquitous. **~ité** *n.f.* iniquity.

init|ial (*m. pl.* **~iaux**) /inisjal, -jo/ *a.* initial. **~ialement** *adv.* initially.

initiale /inisjal/ *n.f.* initial.

initialis|er /inisjalize/ (*comput.*) format. **~ation** *n.f.* formatting.

initiative /inisjativ/ *n.f.* initiative.

init|ier /inisje/ *v.t.* initiate (**à**, into). **s'~ier** *v. pr.* become initiated (**à**, into). **~iateur, ~iatrice** *n.m.*, *f.* initiator. **~iation** *n.f.* initiation.

inject|er /ɛ̃ʒɛkte/ *v.t.* inject. **~é de sang**, bloodshot. **~ion** /-ksjɔ̃/ *n.f.* injection.

injur|e /ɛ̃ʒyr/ *n.f.* insult. **~ier** *v.t.* insult. **~ieux, ~ieuse** *a.* insulting.

injust|e /ɛ̃ʒyst/ *a.* unjust, unfair. **~ice** *n.f.* injustice.

inlassable /ɛ̃lɑsabl/ *a.* tireless.

inné /ine/ *a.* innate, inborn.

innocen|t, ~ e /inɔsɑ̃, -t/ *a. & n.m., f.* innocent. **~ce** *n.f.* innocence.

innocenter /inɔsɑ̃te/ *v.t.* (*disculper*) clear, prove innocent.

innombrable /inɔ̃brabl/ *a.* countless.

innov|er /inɔve/ *v.i.* innovate. **~ateur, ~atrice** *n.m.*, *f.* innovator. **~ation** *n.f.* innovation.

inoccupé /inɔkype/ *a.* unoccupied.

inoculer /inɔkyle/ *v.t.* inoculate.

inodore /inɔdɔr/ *a.* odourless.

inoffensi|f, ~ve /inɔfɑ̃sif, -v/ *a.* harmless.

inond|er /inɔ̃de/ *v.t.* flood; (*mouiller*) soak; (*envahir*) inundate (**de**, with). **~é de soleil**, bathed in sunlight. **~ation** *n.f.* flood; (*action*) flooding.

inopérant, ~e /inɔperɑ̃, -t/ *a.* inoperative.

inopiné /inɔpine/ *a.* unexpected.

inopportun, ~e /inɔpɔrtœ̃, -yn/ *a.* inopportune.

inoubliable /inublijabl/ *a.* unforgettable.

inouï /inwi/ *a.* incredible.

inox /inɔks/ *n.m.* (P.) stainless steel.

inoxydable /inɔksidabl/ *a.* **acier ~**, stainless steel.

inqualifiable /ɛ̃kalifjabl/ *a.* unspeakable.

inqu|iet, ~iète /ɛ̃kjɛ, -ɛkjɛt/ *a.* worried. —*n.m.*, *f.* worrier.

inquiét|er /ɛ̃kjete/ *v.t.* worry. **s'~er** worry (**de**, about). **~ant, ~ante** *a.* worrying.

inquiétude /ɛ̃kjetyd/ *n.f.* anxiety, worry.

inquisition /ɛ̃kizisjɔ̃/ *n.f.* inquisition.

insaisissable /ɛ̃sezisabl/ *a.* indefinable.

insalubre /ɛ̃salybr/ *a.* unhealthy.

insanité /ɛ̃sanite/ *n.f.* insanity.

insatiable /ɛ̃sasjabl/ *a.* insatiable.

insatisfaisant, ~e /ɛ̃satisfəzɑ̃, -t/ *a.* unsatisfactory.

insatisfait, ~e /ɛ̃satisfɛ, -t/ *a.* (*mécontent*) dissatisfied; (*frustré*) unfulfilled.

inscription /ɛ̃skripsjɔ̃/ *n.f.* inscription; (*immatriculation*) enrolment.

inscrire† /ɛ̃skrir/ *v.t.* write (down); (*graver, tracer*) inscribe; (*personne*) enrol; (*sur une liste*) put down. **s'~** *v. pr.* put one's name down. **s'~ à**, (*école*) enrol at; (*club, parti*) join; (*examen*) enter for. **s'~ dans le cadre de**, come within the framework of.

insecte /ɛ̃sɛkt/ *n.m.* insect.

insecticide /ɛ̃sɛktisid/ *n.m.* insecticide.

insécurité /ɛ̃sekyrite/ *n.f.* insecurity.

insensé /ɛ̃sɑ̃se/ *a.* mad.

insensib|le /ɛ̃sɑ̃sibl/ *a.* insensitive (**à**, to); (*graduel*) imperceptible. **~ilité** *n.f.* insensitivity.

inséparable /ɛ̃separabl/ *a.* inseparable.

insérer /ɛ̃sere/ *v.t.* insert. **s'~ dans**, be part of.

insidieu|x, ~se /ɛ̃sidjø, -z/ *a.* insidious.

insigne /ɛ̃siɲ/ *n.m.* badge. **~(s)**, (*d'une fonction*) insignia.

insignifian|t, ~te /ɛ̃siɲifjɑ̃, -t/ *a.* insignificant. **~ce** *n.f.* insignificance.

insinuation /ɛ̃sinɥasjɔ̃/ *n.f.* insinuation.

insinuer /ɛ̃sinɥe/ *v.t.* insinuate. **s'~ dans**, penetrate.

insipide /ɛ̃sipid/ *a.* insipid.

insistan|t, ~te /ɛ̃sistɑ̃, -t/ *a.* insistent. **~ce** *n.f.* insistence.

insister /ɛ̃siste/ *v.i.* insist (**pour faire,** on doing). **~ sur**, stress.

insolation /ɛsɔlasjɔ̃/ n.f. (méd.) sunstroke.

insolen|t, ~**te** /ɛsɔlã, -t/ a. insolent. ~**ce** n.f. insolence.

insolite /ɛsɔlit/ a. unusual.

insoluble /ɛsɔlybl/ a. insoluble.

insolvable /ɛsɔlvabl/ a. insolvent.

insomnie /ɛsɔmni/ n.f. insomnia.

insonoriser /ɛsɔnɔrize/ v.t. sound-proof.

insoucian|t, ~**te** /ɛsusjã, -t/ a. carefree. ~**ce** n.f. unconcern.

insoumission /ɛsumisjɔ̃/ n.f. rebelliousness.

insoupçonnable /ɛsupsɔnabl/ a. undetectable.

insoutenable /ɛsutnabl/ a. unbearable; (argument) untenable.

inspec|ter /ɛspɛkte/ v.t. inspect. ~**teur,** ~**trice** n.m., f. inspector. ~**tion** /-ksjɔ̃/ n.f. inspection.

inspir|er /ɛspire/ v.t. inspire. —v.i. breathe in. ~**er à qn.,** inspire s.o. with. **s'**~**er de,** be inspired by. ~**ation** n.f. inspiration; (respiration) breath.

instab|le /ɛstabl/ a. unstable; (temps) unsettled; (meuble, équilibre) unsteady. ~**ilité** n.f. instability; unsteadiness.

install|er /ɛstale/ v.t. install; (gaz, meuble) put in; (étagère) put up; (équiper) fit out. **s'**~**er** v. pr. settle (down); (emménager) settle in. **s'**~**er comme,** set o.s. up as. ~**ation** n.f. installation; (de local) fitting out; (de locataire) settling in. ~**ations** n.f. pl. (appareils) fittings.

instance /ɛstãs/ n.f. authority; (prière) entreaty. **avec** ~, with insistence. **en** ~, pending. **en** ~ **de,** in the course of, on the point of.

instant /ɛstã/ n.m. moment, instant. **à l'**~, this instant.

instantané /ɛstãtane/ a. instantaneous; (café) instant.

instar /ɛstar/ n.m. **à l'**~ **de,** like.

instaur|er /ɛstore/ v.t. institute. ~**ation** n.f. institution.

instiga|teur, ~**trice** /ɛstigatœr, -tris/ n.m., f. instigator. ~**tion** /-asjɔ̃/ n.f. instigation.

instinct /ɛstɛ̃/ n.m. instinct. **d'**~, instinctively.

instincti|f, ~**ve** /ɛstɛ̃ktif, -v/ a. instinctive. ~**vement** adv. instinctively.

instit /ɛstit/ n.m./f. (fam.) teacher.

instituer /ɛstitɥe/ v.t. establish.

institut /ɛstity/ n.m. institute. ~ **de beauté,** beauty parlour. ~ **univer-**

sitaire de technologie, polytechnic, technical college.

institu|teur, ~**trice** /ɛstitytœr, -tris/ n.m., f. primary-school teacher.

institution /ɛstitysjɔ̃/ n.f. institution; (école) private school.

instructi|f, ~**ve** /ɛstryktif, -v/ a. instructive.

instruction /ɛstryksjɔ̃/ n.f. education; (document) directive. ~**s,** (ordres, mode d'emploi) instructions.

instruire† /ɛstrɥir/ v.t. teach, educate. ~ **de,** inform of. **s'**~ v. pr. educate o.s. **s'**~ **de,** enquire about.

instruit, ~**e** /ɛstrɥi, -t/ a. educated.

instrument /ɛstrymã/ n.m. instrument; (outil) implement.

insu /ɛsy/ n.m. **à l'**~ **de,** without the knowledge of.

insubordination /ɛsybɔrdinasjɔ̃/ n.f. insubordination.

insuffisan|t, ~**te** /ɛsyfizã, -t/ a. inadequate; (en nombre) insufficient. ~**ce** n.f. inadequacy.

insulaire /ɛsylɛr/ a. island. —n.m./f. islander.

insuline /ɛsylin/ n.f. insulin.

insult|e /ɛsylt/ n.f. insult. ~**er** v.t. insult.

insupportable /ɛsypɔrtabl/ a. unbearable.

insurg|er (s') /(s)ɛsyrʒe/ v. pr. rebel. ~**é,** ~**ée** a. & n.m., f. rebel.

insurmontable /ɛsyrmɔ̃tabl/ a. insurmountable.

insurrection /ɛsyrɛksjɔ̃/ n.f. insurrection.

intact /ɛtakt/ a. intact.

intangible /ɛtãʒibl/ a. intangible.

intarissable /ɛtarisabl/ a. inexhaustible.

intégr|al (m. pl. ~**aux**) /ɛtegral, -o/ a. integral, -o/ a. complete; (édition) unabridged. ~**alement** adv. in full. ~**alité** n.f. whole. **dans son** ~**alité,** in full.

intégrant, ~**e** /ɛtegrã, -t/ a. **faire partie** ~**e de,** be part and parcel of.

intègre /ɛtɛgr/ a. upright.

intégr|er /ɛtegre/ v.t., **s'**~**er** v. pr. integrate. ~**ation** n.f. integration.

intégri|ste /ɛtegrist/ a. fundamentalist. ~**sme** /-sm/ n.m. fundamentalism.

intégrité /ɛtegrite/ n.f. integrity.

intellect /ɛtelɛkt/ n.m. intellect. ~**uel,** ~**uelle** a. & n.m., f. intellectual.

intelligence /ɛteliʒãs/ n.f. intelligence; (compréhension) understanding; (complicité) complicity.

intelligen|t, ~**ente** /ɛteliʒã, -t/ a. intelligent. ~**emment** /-amã/ adv. intelligently.

intelligible /ɛ̃teliʒibl/ *a.* intelligible.

intempéries /ɛ̃tɑ̃peri/ *n.f. pl.* severe weather.

intempesti|f, ∼**ve** /ɛ̃tɑ̃pɛstif, -v/ *a.* untimely.

intenable /ɛ̃tnabl/ *a.* unbearable; (*enfant*) impossible.

intendan|t, ∼**te** /ɛ̃tɑ̃dɑ̃, -t/ *n.m.* (*mil.*) quartermaster. —*n.m., f.* (*scol.*) bursar. ∼**ce** *n.f.* (*scol.*) bursar's office.

intens|e /ɛ̃tɑ̃s/ *a.* intense; (*circulation*) heavy. ∼**ément** *adv.* intensely. ∼**ifier** *v.t.*, s'∼**ifier** *v. pr.* intensify. ∼**ité** *n.f.* intensity.

intensi|f, ∼**ve** /ɛ̃tɑ̃sif, -v/ *a.* intensive.

intenter /ɛ̃tɑ̃te/ *v.t.* ∼ **un procès** *ou* **une action,** institute proceedings (**à, contre,** against).

intention /ɛ̃tɑ̃sjɔ̃/ *n.f.* intention (**de faire,** of doing). **à l'**∼ **de qn.,** for s.o. ∼**né** /-jɔne/ *a.* **bien/mal** ∼**né,** well-/ill-intentioned.

intentionnel, ∼**le** /ɛ̃tɑ̃sjɔnɛl/ *a.* intentional.

inter- /ɛ̃tɛr/ *préf.* inter-.

interaction /ɛ̃tɛraksjɔ̃/ *n.f.* interaction.

intercaler /ɛ̃tɛrkale/ *v.t.* insert.

intercéder /ɛ̃tɛrsede/ *v.i.* intercede (**en faveur de,** on behalf of).

intercept|er /ɛ̃tɛrsɛpte/ *v.t.* intercept. ∼**ion** /-psjɔ̃/ *n.f.* interception.

interchangeable /ɛ̃tɛrʃɑ̃ʒabl/ *a.* interchangeable.

interdiction /ɛ̃tɛrdiksjɔ̃/ *n.f.* ban. ∼ **de fumer,** no smoking.

interdire† /ɛ̃tɛrdir/ *v.t.* forbid; (*officiellement*) ban, prohibit. ∼ **à qn. de faire,** forbid s.o. to do.

interdit, ∼**e** /ɛ̃tɛrdi, -t/ *a.* (*étonné*) nonplussed.

intéressant, ∼**e** /ɛ̃teresɑ̃, -t/ *a.* interesting; (*avantageux*) attractive.

intéressé, ∼**e** /ɛ̃terese/ *a.* (*en cause*) concerned; (*pour profiter*) self-interested. —*n.m., f.* person concerned.

intéresser /ɛ̃terese/ *v.t.* interest; (*concerner*) concern. **s'**∼ **à,** be interested in.

intérêt /ɛ̃terɛ/ *n.m.* interest; (*égoïsme*) self-interest. ∼**(s),** (*comm.*) interest. **vous avez** ∼ **à,** it is in your interest to.

interférence /ɛ̃tɛrferɑ̃s/ *n.f.* interference.

intérieur /ɛ̃terjœr/ *a.* inner, inside; (*vol, politique*) domestic; (*vie, calme*) inner. —*n.m.* interior; (*de boîte, tiroir*) inside. **à l'**∼ **(de),** inside; (*fig.*) within. ∼**ement** *adv.* inwardly.

intérim /ɛ̃terim/ *n.m.* interim. **assurer**

l'∼**,** deputize (**de,** for). **par** ∼**,** acting. **faire de l'**∼**,** temp. ∼**aire** *a.* temporary, interim.

interjection /ɛ̃tɛrʒɛksjɔ̃/ *n.f.* interjection.

interlocu|teur, ∼**trice** /ɛ̃tɛrlɔkytœr, -tris/ *n.m., f.* **son** ∼**teur,** the person one is speaking to.

interloqué /ɛ̃tɛrlɔke/ *a.* **être** ∼**,** be taken aback.

intermède /ɛ̃tɛrmɛd/ *n.m.* interlude.

intermédiaire /ɛ̃tɛrmedjɛr/ *a.* intermediate. —*n.m./f.* intermediary.

interminable /ɛ̃tɛrminabl/ *a.* endless.

intermittence /ɛ̃tɛrmitɑ̃s/ *n.f.* **par** ∼**,** intermittently.

intermittent, ∼**e** /ɛ̃tɛrmitɑ̃, -t/ *a.* intermittent.

internat /ɛ̃tɛrna/ *n.m.* boarding-school.

internation|al (*m. pl.* ∼**aux**) /ɛ̃tɛrnasjɔnal, -o/ *a.* international.

interne /ɛ̃tɛrn/ *a.* internal. —*n.m./f.* (*scol.*) boarder.

intern|er /ɛ̃tɛrne/ *v.t.* (*pol.*) intern; (*méd.*) confine. ∼**ement** *n.m.* (*pol.*) internment.

interpell|er /ɛ̃tɛrpəle/ *v.t.* shout to; (*apostropher*) shout at; (*interroger*) question. ∼**ation** *n.f.* (*pol.*) questioning.

interphone /ɛ̃tɛrfɔn/ *n.m.* intercom.

interposer (s') /(s)ɛ̃tɛrpoze/ *v. pr.* intervene.

interpr|ète /ɛ̃tɛrprɛt/ *n.m./f.* interpreter; (*artiste*) performer. ∼**étariat** *n.m.* interpreting.

interprét|er /ɛ̃tɛrprete/ *v.t.* interpret; (*jouer*) play; (*chanter*) sing. ∼**ation** *n.f.* interpretation; (*d'artiste*) performance.

interroga|teur, ∼**trice** /ɛ̃tɛrɔgatœr, -tris/ *a.* questioning.

interrogati|f, ∼**ve** /ɛ̃tɛrɔgatif, -v/ *a.* interrogative.

interrogatoire /ɛ̃tɛrɔgatwar/ *n.m.* interrogation.

interro|ger /ɛ̃tɛrɔʒe/ *v.t.* question; (*élève*) test. ∼**gateur,** ∼**gatrice** *a.* questioning. ∼**gation** *n.f.* question; (*action*) questioning; (*épreuve*) test.

interr|ompre† /ɛ̃tɛrɔ̃pr/ *v.t.* break off, interrupt; (*personne*) interrupt. **s'**∼**ompre** *v. pr.* break off. ∼**upteur** *n.m.* switch. ∼**uption** *n.f.* interruption; (*arrêt*) break.

intersection /ɛ̃tɛrsɛksjɔ̃/ *n.f.* intersection.

interstice /ɛ̃tɛrstis/ *n.m.* crack.

interurbain /ɛ̃tɛryrbɛ̃/ *n.m.* long-distance telephone service.

intervalle /ɛ̃tɛrval/ *n.m.* space; (*temps*) interval. **dans l'~,** in the meantime.

interven|ir† /ɛ̃tɛrvənir/ *v.i.* intervene; (*survenir*) occur; (*méd.*) operate. **~tion** /-vɑ̃sjɔ̃/ *n.f.* intervention; (*méd.*) operation.

intervertir /ɛ̃tɛrvɛrtir/ *v.t.* invert.

interview /ɛ̃tɛrvju/ *n.f.* interview. **~er** /-ve/ *v.t.* interview.

intestin /ɛ̃tɛstɛ̃/ *n.m.* intestine.

intim|e /ɛ̃tim/ *a.* intimate; (*fête, vie*) private; (*dîner*) quiet. —*n.m./f.* intimate friend. **~ement** *adv.* intimately. **~ité** *n.f.* intimacy; (*vie privée*) privacy.

intimid|er /ɛ̃timide/ *v.t.* intimidate. **~ation** *n.f.* intimidation.

intituler /ɛ̃tityle/ *v.t.* entitle. **s'~** *v. pr.* be entitled.

intolérable /ɛ̃tɔlerabl/ *a.* intolerable.

intoléran|t, **~te** /ɛ̃tɔlerɑ̃, -t/ *a.* intolerant. **~ce** *n.f.* intolerance.

intonation /ɛ̃tɔnasjɔ̃/ *n.f.* intonation.

intox /ɛ̃tɔks/ *n.m.* (*fam.*) brainwashing.

intoxi|quer /ɛ̃tɔsike/ *v.t.* poison; (*pol.*) brainwash. **~cation** *n.f.* poisoning; (*pol.*) brainwashing.

intraduisible /ɛ̃tradu̞izibl/ *a.* untranslatable.

intraitable /ɛ̃trɛtabl/ *a.* inflexible.

intransigean|t, **~te** /ɛ̃trɑ̃siʒɑ̃, -t/ *a.* intransigent. **~ce** *n.f.* intransigence.

intransiti|f, **~ve** /ɛ̃trɑ̃zitif, -v/ *a.* intransitive.

intraveineu|x, **~se** /ɛ̃travɛnø, -z/ *a.* intravenous.

intrépide /ɛ̃trepid/ *a.* fearless.

intrigu|e /ɛ̃trig/ *n.f.* intrigue; (*théâtre*) plot. **~er** *v.t./i.* intrigue.

intrinsèque /ɛ̃trɛ̃sɛk/ *a.* intrinsic.

introduction /ɛ̃trɔdyksjɔ̃/ *n.f.* introduction.

introduire† /ɛ̃trɔdu̞ir/ *v.t.* introduce, bring in; (*insérer*) put in, insert. **~ qn.,** show s.o. in. **s'~ dans,** get into, enter.

introspecti|f, **~ve** /ɛ̃trɔspɛktif, -v/ *a.* introspective.

introuvable /ɛ̃truvabl/ *a.* that cannot be found.

introverti, **~e** /ɛ̃trɔvɛrti/ *n.m., f.* introvert. —*a.* introverted.

intrus, **~e** /ɛ̃try, -z/ *n.m., f.* intruder. **~ion** /-zjɔ̃/ *n.f.* intrusion.

intuiti|f, **~ve** /ɛ̃tu̞itif, -v/ *a.* intuitive.

intuition /ɛ̃tu̞isjɔ̃/ *n.f.* intuition.

inusable /inyzabl/ *a.* hard-wearing.

inusité /inyzite/ *a.* little used.

inutil|e /inytil/ *a.* useless; (*vain*) needless. **~ement** *adv.* needlessly. **~ité** *n.f.* uselessness.

inutilisable /inytilizabl/ *a.* unusable.

invalid|e /ɛ̃valid/ *a.* & *n.m./f.* disabled (person). **~ité** *n.f.* disablement.

invariable /ɛ̃varjabl/ *a.* invariable.

invasion /ɛ̃vazjɔ̃/ *n.f.* invasion.

invectiv|e /ɛ̃vɛktiv/ *n.f.* invective. **~er** *v.t.* abuse.

invend|able /ɛ̃vɑ̃dabl/ *a.* unsaleable. **~u** *a.* unsold.

inventaire /ɛ̃vɑ̃tɛr/ *n.m.* inventory. **faire l'~ de,** take stock of.

invent|er /ɛ̃vɑ̃te/ *v.t.* invent. **~eur** *n.m.* inventor. **~ion** /ɛ̃vɑ̃sjɔ̃/ *n.f.* invention.

inventi|f, **~ve** /ɛ̃vɑ̃tif, -v/ *a.* inventive.

inverse /ɛ̃vɛrs/ *a.* opposite; (*ordre*) reverse. —*n.m.* reverse. **~ment** /-əmɑ̃/ *adv.* conversely.

invers|er /ɛ̃vɛrse/ *v.t.* reverse, invert. **~ion** *n.f.* inversion.

investigation /ɛ̃vɛstigasjɔ̃/ *n.f.* investigation.

invest|ir /ɛ̃vɛstir/ *v.t.* invest. **~issement** *n.m.* (*comm.*) investment.

investiture /ɛ̃vɛstityr/ *n.f.* nomination.

invétéré /ɛ̃vetere/ *a.* inveterate.

invincible /ɛ̃vɛ̃sibl/ *a.* invincible.

invisible /ɛ̃vizibl/ *a.* invisible.

invit|er /ɛ̃vite/ *v.t.* invite (à, to). **~ation** *n.f.* invitation. **~é,** **~ée** *n.m., f.* guest.

invivable /ɛ̃vivabl/ *a.* unbearable.

involontaire /ɛ̃vɔlɔ̃tɛr/ *a.* involuntary.

invoquer /ɛ̃vɔke/ *v.t.* call upon, invoke; (*alléguer*) plead.

invraisembl|able /ɛ̃vrɛsɑ̃blabl/ *a.* improbable; (*incroyable*) incredible. **~ance** *n.f.* improbability.

invulnérable /ɛ̃vylnerabl/ *a.* invulnerable.

iode /jɔd/ *n.m.* iodine.

ion /jɔ̃/ *n.m.* ion.

ira, irait /ira, irɛ/ *voir* **aller**[1].

Irak /irak/ *n.m.* Iraq. **~ien,** **~ienne** *a.* & *n.m., f.* Iraqi.

Iran /irɑ̃/ *n.m.* Iran. **~ien,** **~ienne** /iranjɛ̃, -jɛn/ *a.* & *n.m., f.* Iranian.

irascible /irasibl/ *a.* irascible.

iris /iris/ *n.m.* iris.

irlandais, **~e** /irlɑ̃dɛ, -z/ *a.* Irish. —*n.m., f.* Irishman, Irishwoman.

Irlande /irlɑ̃d/ *n.f.* Ireland.

iron|ie /irɔni/ *n.f.* irony. **~ique** *a.* ironic(al).

irraisonné /irɛzɔne/ *a.* irrational.

irrationnel, **~le** /irasjɔnɛl/ *a.* irrational.

irréalisable /irealizabl/ *a.* (*projet*) unworkable.

irrécupérable /irekyperabl/ *a.* irretrievable, beyond recall.
irréel, **~le** /ireel/ *a.* unreal.
irréfléchi /irefleʃi/ *a.* thoughtless.
irréfutable /irefytabl/ *a.* irrefutable.
irrégul|ier, **~ière** /iregylje, -jɛr/ *a.* irregular. **~arité** *n.f.* irregularity.
irrémédiable /iremedjabl/ *a.* irreparable.
irremplaçable /irɑ̃plasabl/ *a.* irreplaceable.
irréparable /ireparabl/ *a.* beyond repair.
irréprochable /ireprɔʃabl/ *a.* flawless.
irrésistible /irezistibl/ *a.* irresistible; (*drôle*) hilarious.
irrésolu /irezɔly/ *a.* indecisive.
irrespirable /irɛspirabl/ *a.* stifling.
irresponsable /irɛspɔ̃sabl/ *a.* irresponsible.
irréversible /ireversibl/ *a.* irreversible.
irrévocable /irevɔkabl/ *a.* irrevocable.
Irrigation /irigasjɔ̃/ *n.f.* irrigation.
Irriguer /irige/ *v.t.* irrigate.
irrit|er /irite/ *v.t.* irritate. **s'~er de**, be annoyed at. **~able** *a.* irritable. **~ation** *n.f.* irritation.
irruption /irypsjɔ̃/ *n.f.* **faire ~ dans**, burst into.
Islam /islam/ *n.m.* Islam.
islamique /islamik/ *a.* Islamic.
islandais, **~e** /islɑ̃dɛ, -z/ *a.* Icelandic. *n.m.*, *f.* Icelander. *n.m.* (*lang.*) Icelandic.
Islande /islɑ̃d/ *n.f.* Iceland.
isolé /izɔle/ *a.* isolated. **~ment** *adv.* in isolation.
isol|er /izɔle/ *v.t.* isolate; (*électr.*) insulate. **s'~er** *v. pr.* isolate o.s. **~ant** *n.m.* insulating material, **~ation** *n.f.* insulation. **~ement** *n.m.* isolation.
isoloir /izɔlwar/ *n.m.* polling booth.
Isorel /izɔrɛl/ *n.m.* (P.) hardboard.
isotope /izɔtɔp/ *n.m.* isotope.
Israël /israɛl/ *n.m.* Israel.
israélien, **~ne** /israeljɛ̃, -jɛn/ *a.* & *n.m.*, *f.* Israeli.
israélite /israelit/ *a.* Jewish. *n.m./f.* Jew, Jewess.
issu /isy/ *a.* **être ~ de**, come from.
issue /isy/ *n.f.* exit; (*résultat*) outcome; (*fig.*) solution. **à l'~ de**, at the conclusion of. **rue** *ou* **voie sans ~**, dead end.
isthme /ism/ *n.m.* isthmus.
Italie /itali/ *n.f.* Italy.
italien, **~ne** /italjɛ̃, -jɛn/ *a.* & *n.m.*, *f.* Italian. *—n.m.* (*lang.*) Italian.
italique /italik/ *n.m.* italics.

itinéraire /itinerɛr/ *n.m.* itinerary, route.
itinérant, **~e** /itinerɑ̃, -t/ *a.* itinerant.
I.U.T. /iyte/ *n.m.* (*abrév.*) polytechnic.
I.V.G. /iveʒe/ *n.f.* (*abrév.*) abortion.
ivoire /ivwar/ *n.m.* ivory.
ivr|e /ivr/ *a.* drunk. **~esse** *n.f.* drunkenness. **~ogne** *n.m.* drunk(ard).

J

j' /ʒ/ *voir* **je**.
jacasser /ʒakase/ *v.i.* chatter.
jachère (en) /(ɑ̃)ʒaʃɛr/ *adv.* fallow.
jacinthe /ʒasɛ̃t/ *n.f.* hyacinth.
jade /ʒad/ *n.m.* jade.
jadis /ʒadis/ *adv.* long ago.
jaillir /ʒajir/ *v.i.* (*liquide*) spurt (out); (*lumière*) stream out; (*apparaître*, *fuser*) burst forth.
jais /ʒɛ/ *n.m.* (**noir**) **de ~**, jet-black.
jalon /ʒalɔ̃/ *n.m.* (*piquet*) marker. **~ner** /-ɔne/ *v.t.* mark (out).
jalou|x, **~se** /ʒalu, -z/ *a.* jealous. **~ser** *v.t.* be jealous of. **~sie** *n.f.* jealousy; (*store*) (venetian) blind.
jamais /ʒamɛ/ *adv.* ever. (**ne**) **~**, never. **il ne boit ~**, he never drinks. **à ~**, for ever. **si ~**, if ever.
jambe /ʒɑ̃b/ *n.f.* leg.
jambon /ʒɑ̃bɔ̃/ *n.m.* ham. **~neau** (*pl.* **~neaux**) /-ɔno/ *n.m.* knuckle of ham.
jante /ʒɑ̃t/ *n.f.* rim.
janvier /ʒɑ̃vje/ *n.m.* January.
Japon /ʒapɔ̃/ *n.m.* Japan.
japonais, **~e** /ʒapɔnɛ, -z/ *a.* & *n.m.*, *f.* Japanese, *—n.m.* (*lang.*) Japanese.
japper /ʒape/ *v.i.* yelp.
jaquette /ʒakɛt/ *n.f.* (*de livre*, *femme*) jacket; (*d'homme*) morning coat.
jardin /ʒardɛ̃/ *n.m.* garden. **~ d'enfants**, nursery (school). **~ public**, public park.
jardin|er /ʒardine/ *v.i.* garden. **~age** *n.m.* gardening. **~ier**, **~ière** *n.m.*, *f.* gardener; *n.f.* (*meuble*) plant-stand. **~ière de légumes**, mixed vegetables.
jargon /ʒargɔ̃/ *n.m.* jargon.
jarret /ʒarɛ/ *n.m.* back of the knee.
jarretelle /ʒartɛl/ *n.f.* suspender; (*Amer.*) garter.
jarretière /ʒartjɛr/ *n.f.* garter.
jaser /ʒaze/ *v.i.* jabber.
jasmin /ʒasmɛ̃/ *n.m.* jasmine.
jatte /ʒat/ *n.f.* bowl.

jauge /ʒoʒ/ *n.f.* capacity; (*de navire*) tonnage; (*compteur*) gauge. ~**er** *v.t.* gauge.

jaune /ʒon/ *a. & n.m.* yellow; (*péj.*) scab. ~**e d'œuf**, (egg) yolk. **rire** ~**e**, laugh on the other side of one's face. ~**ir** *v.t./i.* turn yellow.

jaunisse /ʒonis/ *n.f.* jaundice.

javelot /ʒavlo/ *n.m.* javelin.

jazz /dʒɑz/ *n.m.* jazz.

J.C. /ʒezykri/ *n.m.* (*abrév.*) **500 avant/après** ~, 500 B.C./A.D.

je, j'* /ʒə, ʒ/ *pron.* I.

jean /dʒin/ *n.m.* jeans.

jeep /(d)ʒip/ *n.f.* jeep.

jerrycan /(d)ʒerikan/ *n.m.* jerrycan.

jersey /ʒɛrzɛ/ *n.m.* jersey.

Jersey /ʒɛrzɛ/ *n.f.* Jersey.

Jésus /ʒezy/ *n.m.* Jesus.

jet¹ /ʒɛ/ *n.m.* throw; (*de liquide, vapeur*) jet. ~ **d'eau**, fountain.

jet² /dʒɛt/ *n.m.* (*avion*) jet.

jetable /ʒətabl/ *a.* disposable.

jetée /ʒte/ *n.f.* pier.

jeter /ʒte/ *v.t.* throw; (*au rebut*) throw away; (*regard, ancre, lumière*) cast; (*cri*) utter; (*bases*) lay. ~ **un coup d'œil**, have *ou* take a look (**à**, at). **se** ~ **contre**, (*heurter*) bash into. **se** ~ **dans**, (*fleuve*) flow into. **se** ~ **sur**, (*se ruer sur*) rush at.

jeton /ʒtɔ̃/ *n.m.* token; (*pour compter*) counter.

jeu (*pl.* ~**x**) /ʒø/ *n.m.* game; (*amusement*) play; (*au casino etc.*) gambling; (*théâtre*) acting; (*série*) set; (*de lumière, ressort*) play. **en** ~, (*honneur*) at stake; (*forces*) at work. ~ **de cartes**, (*paquet*) pack of cards. ~ **d'échecs**, (*boîte*) chess set. ~ **de mots**, pun. ~ **télévisé**, television quiz.

jeudi /ʒødi/ *n.m.* Thursday.

jeun (à) /(a)ʒœ̃/ *adv.* **être/rester à** ~, be/stay without food; **comprimé à prendre à** ~, tablet to be taken on an empty stomach.

jeune /ʒœn/ *a.* young. —*n.m./f.* young person. ~ **fille**, girl. ~**s mariés**, newlyweds. **les** ~**s**, young people.

jeûne /ʒøn/ *n.m.* fast. ~**er** *v.i.* fast.

jeunesse /ʒœnɛs/ *n.f.* youth; (*apparence*) youthfulness. **la** ~, (*jeunes*) the young.

joaillier, ~ière /ʒɔaje, -jɛr/ *n.m., f.* jeweller. ~**erie** *n.f.* jewellery; (*magasin*) jeweller's shop.

job /dʒɔb/ *n.m.* (*fam.*) job.

jockey /ʒɔkɛ/ *n.m.* jockey.

joie /ʒwa/ *n.f.* joy.

joindre† /ʒwɛ̃dr/ *v.t.* join (**à**, to);

(*contacter*) contact; (*mains, pieds*) put together; (*efforts*) combine; (*dans une enveloppe*) enclose. **se** ~ **à**, join.

joint, ~e /ʒwɛ̃, -t/ *a.* (*efforts*) joint; (*pieds*) together. —*n.m.* joint; (*ligne*) join; (*de robinet*) washer. ~**ure** /-tyr/ *n.f.* joint; (*ligne*) join.

joker /ʒɔkɛr/ *n.m.* (*carte*) joker.

joli /ʒɔli/ *a.* pretty, nice; (*somme, profit*) nice. **c'est du** ~!, (*ironique*) charming! **c'est bien** ~ **mais**, that is all very well but. ~**ment** *adv.* prettily; (*très: fam.*) awfully.

jonc /ʒɔ̃/ *n.m.* (bul)rush.

joncher /ʒɔ̃ʃe/ *v.t.*, ~**é de**, littered with.

jonction /ʒɔ̃ksjɔ̃/ *n.f.* junction.

jongler /ʒɔ̃gle/ *v.i.* juggle. ~**eur**, ~**euse** *n.m., f.* juggler.

jonquille /ʒɔ̃kij/ *n.f.* daffodil.

Jordanie /ʒɔrdani/ *n.f.* Jordan.

joue /ʒu/ *n.f.* cheek.

jouer /ʒwe/ *v.t./i.* play; (*théâtre*) act; (*au casino etc.*) gamble; (*fonctionner*) work; (*film, pièce*) put on; (*cheval*) back; (*être important*) count. ~**er à** *ou* **de**, play. ~**er la comédie**, put on an act. **bien** ~**é!**, well done!

jouet /ʒwɛ/ *n.m.* toy; (*personne, fig.*) plaything; (*victime*) victim.

joueu|r, ~se /ʒwœr, -øz/ *n.m., f.* player; (*parieur*) gambler.

joufflu /ʒufly/ *a.* chubby-cheeked; (*visage*) chubby.

joug /ʒu/ *n.m.* yoke.

jouir /ʒwir/ *v.i.* (*sexe*) come. ~ **de**, enjoy.

jouissance /ʒwisɑ̃s/ *n.f.* pleasure; (*usage*) use (**de qch.**, of sth.).

joujou (*pl.* ~**x**) /ʒuʒu/ *n.m.* (*fam.*) toy.

jour /ʒur/ *n.m.* day; (*opposé à nuit*) day(time); (*lumière*) daylight; (*aspect*) light; (*ouverture*) gap. **de nos** ~**s**, nowadays. **du** ~ **au lendemain**, overnight. **il fait** ~, it is (day)light. ~ **chômé** *ou* **férié**, public holiday. ~ **de fête**, holiday. ~ **ouvrable**, ~ **de travail**, working day. **mettre à** ~, update. **mettre au** ~, uncover. **au grand** ~, in the open. **donner le** ~, give birth. **voir le** ~, be born. **vivre au** ~ **le jour**, live from day to day.

journ|al (*pl.* ~**aux**) /ʒurnal, -o/ *n.m.* (news)paper; (*spécialisé*) journal; (*intime*) diary; (*radio*) news. ~**al de bord**, log-book.

journal|ier, ~ière /ʒurnalje, -jɛr/ *a.* daily.

journalis|te /ʒurnalist/ *n.m./f.* journalist. ~**me** *n.m.* journalism.

journée /ʒurne/ *n.f.* day.

journellement /ʒurnɛlmã/ *adv.* daily.

jov|ial (*m. pl.* ~**iaux**) /ʒɔvjal, -jo/ *a.* jovial.

joyau (*pl.* ~**x**) /ʒwajo/ *n.m.* gem.

joyeu|x, ~**se** /ʒwajø, -z/ *a.* merry, joyful. ~**x anniversaire,** happy birthday. ~**sement** *adv.* merrily.

jubilé /ʒybile/ *n.m.* jubilee.

jubil|er /ʒybile/ *v.i.* be jubilant. ~**ation** *n.f.* jubilation.

jucher /ʒyʃe/ *v.t.,* **se** ~ *v. pr.* perch.

juda|ïque /ʒydaik/ *a.* Jewish. ~**sme** *n.m.* Judaism.

judas /ʒyda/ *n.m.* peep-hole.

judiciaire /ʒydisjɛr/ *a.* judicial.

judicieu|x, ~**se** /ʒydisjø, -z/ *a.* judicious.

judo /ʒydo/ *n.m.* judo.

juge /ʒyʒ/ *n.m.* judge; (*arbitre*) referee. ~ **de paix,** Justice of the Peace. ~ **de touche,** linesman.

jugé (au) /(o)ʒyʒe/ *adv.* by guesswork.

jugement /ʒyʒmã/ *n.m.* judgement; (*criminel*) sentence.

jugeote /ʒyʒɔt/ *n.f.* (*fam.*) gumption, common sense.

juger /ʒyʒe/ *v.t./i.* judge; (*estimer*) consider (**que,** that). ~ **de,** judge.

juguler /ʒygyle/ *v.t.* stifle, check.

jui|f, ~**ve** /ʒɥif, -v/ *a.* Jewish. —*n.m.,* f. Jew, Jewess.

juillet /ʒɥijɛ/ *n.m.* July.

juin /ʒɥɛ̃/ *n.m.* June.

jules /ʒyl/ *n.m.* (*fam.*) guy.

jum|eau, ~**elle** (*m. pl.* ~**eaux**) /ʒymo, -ɛl/ *a. & n.m., f.* twin. ~**elage** *n.m.* twinning. ~**eler** *v.t.* (*villes*) twin.

jumelles /ʒymɛl/ *n.f. pl.* binoculars.

jument /ʒymã/ *n.f.* mare.

jungle /ʒœ̃gl/ *n.f.* jungle.

junior /ʒynjɔr/ *n.m./f. & a.* junior.

junte /ʒœ̃t/ *n.f.* junta.

jupe /ʒyp/ *n.f.* skirt.

jupon /ʒypɔ̃/ *n.m.* slip, petticoat.

juré, ~**e** /ʒyre/ *n.m.,* f. juror. —*a.* sworn.

jurer /ʒyre/ *v.t.* swear (**que,** that). —*v.i.* (*pester*) swear; (*contraster*) clash (**avec,** with). ~ **de qch./de faire,** swear to sth./to do.

juridiction /ʒyridiksjɔ̃/ *n.f.* jurisdiction; (*tribunal*) court of law.

juridique /ʒyridik/ *a.* legal.

juriste /ʒyrist/ *n.m./f.* legal expert.

juron /ʒyrɔ̃/ *n.m.* swear-word.

jury /ʒyri/ *n.m.* jury.

jus /ʒy/ *n.m.* juice; (*de viande*) gravy. ~ **de fruit,** fruit juice.

jusque /ʒysk(ə)/ *prép.* **jusqu'à,** (up) to, as far as; (*temps*) until, till; (*limite*) up to; (*y compris*) even. **jusqu'à ce que,** until. **jusqu'à présent,** until now. **jusqu'en,** until. **jusqu'où?,** how far? ~ **dans,** ~ **sur,** as far as.

juste /ʒyst/ *a.* fair, just; (*légitime*) just; (*correct, exact*) right; (*vrai*) true; (*vêtement*) tight; (*quantité*) on the short side. **le** ~ **milieu,** the happy medium. —*adv.* rightly, correctly; (*chanter*) in tune; (*seulement, exactement*) just. (**un peu**) ~, (*calculer, mesurer*) a bit fine *ou* close. **au** ~, exactly. **c'était** ~, (*presque raté*) it was a close thing.

justement /ʒystəmã/ *adv.* just; (*avec justice ou justesse*) justly.

justesse /ʒystɛs/ *n.f.* accuracy. **de** ~, just, narrowly.

justice /ʒystis/ *n.f.* justice; (*autorités*) law; (*tribunal*) court.

justif|ier /ʒystifje/ *v.t.* justify. —*v.i.* ~**ier de,** prove. **se** ~**ier** *v. pr.* justify o.s. ~**iable** *a.* justifiable. ~**ication** *n.f.* justification.

juteu|x, ~**se** /ʒytø, -z/ *a.* juicy.

juvénile /ʒyvenil/ *a.* youthful.

juxtaposer /ʒykstapoze/ *v.t.* juxtapose.

K

kaki /kaki/ *a. invar. & n.m.* khaki.

kaléidoscope /kaleidɔskɔp/ *n.m.* kaleidoscope.

kangourou /kãguru/ *n.m.* kangaroo.

karaté /karate/ *n.m.* karate.

kart /kart/ *n.m.* go-cart.

kascher /kaʃɛr/ *a. invar.* kosher.

képi /kepi/ *n.m.* kepi.

kermesse /kɛrmɛs/ *n.f.* fair; (*de charité*) fête.

kérosène /kerozɛn/ *n.m.* kerosene, aviation fuel.

kibboutz /kibuts/ *n.m.* kibbutz.

kidnapp|er /kidnape/ *v.t.* kidnap. ~**eur,** ~**euse** *n.m.,* f. kidnapper.

kilo /kilo/ *n.m.* kilo.

kilogramme /kilɔgram/ *n.m.* kilogram.

kilohertz /kilɔɛrts/ *n.m.* kilohertz.

kilom|ètre /kilɔmɛtr/ *n.m.* kilometre. ~**étrage** *n.m.* (*approx.*) mileage.

kilowatt /kilɔwat/ *n.m.* kilowatt.

kinésithérapie /kineziterapi/ *n.f.* physiotherapy.

kiosque /kjɔsk/ *n.m.* kiosk. ~ **à musique,** bandstand.

kit /kit/ *n.m.* **meubles en ～,** flat-pack furniture.

kiwi /kiwi/ *n.m.* kiwi (*fruit, bird*).

klaxon /klaksɔn/ *n.m.* (P.) (*auto.*) horn. **～ner** /-e/ *v.i.* sound one's horn.

knock-out /nɔkawt/ *n.m.* knock-out.

ko /kao/ *n.m.* (*comput.*) k.

K.O. /kao/ *a. invar.* (knocked) out.

k-way /kawe/ *n.m. invar.* (P.) cagoule.

kyste /kist/ *n.m.* cyst.

L

l', la /l, la/ *voir* **le.**

là /la/ *adv.* there; (*ici*) here; (*chez soi*) in; (*temps*) then. **c'est là que,** this is where. **là où,** where. **là-bas** *adv.* over there. **là-dedans** *adv.* inside, in there. **là-dessous** *adv.* underneath, under there. **là-dessus** *adv.* on there. **là-haut** *adv.* up there; (*à l'étage*) upstairs.

-là /la/ *adv.* (*après un nom précédé de ce, cette, etc.*) **cet homme-là,** that man. **ces maisons-là,** those houses.

label /label/ *n.m.* (*comm.*) seal.

labeur /labœr/ *n.m.* toil.

labo /labo/ *n.m.* (*fam.*) lab.

laboratoire /labɔratwar/ *n.m.* laboratory.

laborieu|x, ～se /labɔrjø, -z/ *a.* laborious; (*personne*) industrious; (*dur*) heavy going. **classes/masses ～ses,** working classes/masses.

labour /labur/ *n.m.* ploughing; (*Amer.*) plowing. **～er** *v.t./i.* plough; (*Amer.*) plow; (*déchirer*) rip at. **～eur** *n.m.* ploughman; (*Amer.*) plowman.

labyrinthe /labirɛ̃t/ *n.m.* maze.

lac /lak/ *n.m.* lake.

lacer /lase/ *v.t.* lace up.

lacérer /lasere/ *v.t.* tear (up).

lacet /lasɛ/ *n.m.* (shoe-)lace; (*de route*) sharp bend, zigzag.

lâche /lɑʃ/ *a.* cowardly; (*détendu*) loose. —*n.m./f.* coward. **～ment** *adv.* in a cowardly way.

lâcher /lɑʃe/ *v.t.* let go of; (*abandonner*) give up; (*laisser*) leave; (*libérer*) release; (*parole*) utter; (*desserrer*) loosen. —*v.i.* give way. **～ prise,** let go.

lâcheté /lɑʃte/ *n.f.* cowardice.

laconique /lakɔnik/ *a.* laconic.

lacrymogène /lakrimɔʒɛn/ *a.* **gaz ～,** tear gas. **grenade ～,** tear gas grenade.

lacté /lakte/ *a.* milk.

lacune /lakyn/ *n.f.* gap.

ladite /ladit/ *voir* **ledit.**

lagune /lagyn/ *n.f.* lagoon.

laïc /laik/ *n.m.* layman.

laid, ～e /lɛ, lɛd/ *a.* ugly; (*action*) vile. **～eur** /lɛdœr/ *n.f.* ugliness.

lain|e /lɛn/ *n.f.* wool. **de ～e,** woollen. **～age** *n.m.* woollen garment.

laïque /laik/ *a.* secular; (*habit, personne*) lay. —*n.m./f.* layman, laywoman.

laisse /lɛs/ *n.f.* lead, leash.

laisser /lese/ *v.t.* leave. **～ qn. faire,** let s.o. do. **～ qch. à qn.,** let s.o. have sth., leave s.o. sth. **～ tomber,** drop. **se ～ aller,** let o.s. go. **～-aller** *n.m. invar.* carelessness. **laissez-passer** *n.m. invar.* pass.

lait /lɛ/ *n.m.* milk. **frère/sœur de ～,** foster-brother/-sister. **～age** /lɛtaʒ/ *n.m.* milk product. **～eux, ～euse** /lɛtø, -z/ *a.* milky.

lait|ier, ～ière /letje, lɛtjɛr/ *a.* dairy. —*n.m.*, *f.* dairyman, dairywoman. —*n.m.* (*livreur*) milkman. **～erie** /lɛtri/ *n.f.* dairy.

laiton /lɛtɔ̃/ *n.m.* brass.

laitue /lety/ *n.f.* lettuce.

laïus /lajys/ *n.m.* (*péj.*) big speech.

lama /lama/ *n.m.* llama.

lambeau (*pl.* ～x) /lɑ̃bo/ *n.m.* shred. **en ～x,** in shreds.

lambris /lɑ̃bri/ *n.m.* panelling.

lame /lam/ *n.f.* blade; (*lamelle*) strip; (*vague*) wave. **～ de fond,** ground swell.

lamelle /lamɛl/ *n.f.* (thin) strip.

lamentable /lamɑ̃tabl/ *a.* deplorable.

lament|er (se) /(sə)lamɑ̃te/ *v. pr.* moan. **～ation(s)** *n.f.* (*pl.*) moaning.

laminé /lamine/ *a.* laminated.

lampadaire /lɑ̃padɛr/ *n.m.* standard lamp; (*de rue*) street lamp.

lampe /lɑ̃p/ *n.f.* lamp; (*de radio*) valve; (*Amer.*) vacuum tube. **～ (de poche),** torch; (*Amer.*) flashlight. **～ de chevet,** bedside lamp.

lampion /lɑ̃pjɔ̃/ *n.m.* (Chinese) lantern.

lance /lɑ̃s/ *n.f.* spear; (*de tournoi*) lance; (*tuyau*) hose. **～ d'incendie,** fire hose.

lancée /lɑ̃se/ *n.f.* **continuer sur sa ～,** keep going.

lanc|er /lɑ̃se/ *v.t.* throw; (*avec force*) hurl; (*navire, idée, personne*) launch; (*émettre*) give out; (*regard*) cast; (*moteur*) start. **se ～er** *v. pr.* (*sport*) gain momentum; (*se précipiter*) rush. **se ～er dans,** launch into. —*n.m.* throw; (*action*) throwing. **～ement** *n.m.* throwing; (*de navire*) launching. **～e-**

missiles *n.m. invar.* missile launcher. **~e-pierres** *n.m. invar.* catapult.

lancinant, ~e /lãsinã, -t/ *a.* haunting; (*douleur*) throbbing.

landau /lãdo/ *n.m.* pram; (*Amer.*) baby carriage.

lande /lãd/ *n.f.* heath, moor.

langage /lãgaʒ/ *n.m.* language.

langoureu|x, ~se /lãgurø, -z/ *a.* languid.

langoust|e /lãgust/ *n.f.* (spiny) lobster. **~ine** *n.f.* (Norway) lobster.

langue /lãg/ *n.f.* tongue; (*idiome*) language. **il m'a tiré la ~,** he stuck out his tongue out at me. **de ~ anglaise/française,** English-/French-speaking. **~ maternelle,** mother tongue.

languette /lãgɛt/ *n.f.* tongue.

langueur /lãgœr/ *n.f.* languor.

langu|ir /lãgir/ *v.i.* languish; (*conversation*) flag. **faire ~ir qn.,** keep s.o. waiting. **se ~ir de,** miss. **~issant, ~issante** *a.* languid.

lanière /lanjɛr/ *n.f.* strap.

lanterne /lãtɛrn/ *n.f.* lantern; (*électrique*) lamp; (*de voiture*) sidelight.

laper /lape/ *v.t./i.* lap.

lapider /lapide/ *v.t.* stone.

lapin /lapɛ̃/ *n.m.* rabbit. **poser un ~ à qn.,** stand s.o. up.

laps /laps/ *n.m.* **~ de temps,** lapse of time.

lapsus /lapsys/ *n.m.* slip (of the tongue).

laquais /lakɛ/ *n.m.* lackey.

laqu|e /lak/ *n.f.* lacquer. **~er** *v.t.* lacquer.

laquelle /lakɛl/ *voir* **lequel.**

larcin /larsɛ̃/ *n.m.* theft.

lard /lar/ *n.m.* (pig's) fat; (*viande*) bacon.

large /larʒ/ *a.* wide, broad; (*grand*) large; (*non borné*) broad; (*généreux*) generous. —*adv.* (*mesurer*) broadly; (*voir*) big. —*n.m.* **de ~,** (*mesure*) wide. **le ~,** (*mer*) the open sea. **au ~ de,** (*en face de: naut*) off **~. d'esprit,** broad-minded. **~ment** /-əmã/ *adv.* widely; (*ouvrir*) wide; (*amplement*) amply; (*généreusement*) generously; (*au moins*) easily.

largesse /larʒɛs/ *n.f.* generosity.

largeur /larʒœr/ *n.f.* width, breadth; (*fig.*) breadth.

larguer /large/ *v.t.* drop. **~ les amarres,** cast off.

larme /larm/ *n.f.* tear; (*goutte: fam.*) drop.

larmoyant, ~e /larmwajã, -t/ *a.* tearful.

larron /larɔ̃/ *n.m.* thief.

larve /larv/ *n.f.* larva.

larvé /larve/ *a.* latent.

laryngite /larɛ̃ʒit/ *n.f.* laryngitis.

larynx /larɛ̃ks/ *n.m.* larynx.

las, ~se /la, las/ *a.* weary.

lasagnes /lazaɲ/ *n.f. pl.* lasagne.

lasci|f, ~ve /lasif, -v/ *a.* lascivious.

laser /lazɛr/ *n.m.* laser.

lasse /las/ *voir* **las.**

lasser /lase/ *v.t.* weary. **se ~** *v. pr.* weary (**de,** of).

lassitude /lasityd/ *n.f.* weariness.

lasso /laso/ *n.m.* lasso.

latent, ~e /latã, -t/ *a.* latent.

latér|al (*m. pl.* **~aux**) /lateral, -o/ *a.* lateral.

latex /latɛks/ *n.m.* latex.

latin, ~e /latɛ̃, -in/ *a. & n.m., f.* Latin. —*n.m.* (*lang.*) Latin.

latitude /latityd/ *n.f.* latitude.

latrines /latrin/ *n.f. pl.* latrine(s).

latte /lat/ *n.f.* lath; (*de plancher*) board.

lauréat, ~e /lɔrea, -t/ *a.* prize-winning. —*n.m., f.* prize-winner.

laurier /lɔrje/ *n.m.* laurel; (*culin.*) bay-leaves.

lavable /lavabl/ *a.* washable.

lavabo /lavabo/ *n.m.* wash-basin. **~s,** toilet(s).

lavage /lavaʒ/ *n.m.* washing. **~ de cerveau,** brainwashing.

lavande /lavãd/ *n.f.* lavender.

lave /lav/ *n.f.* lava.

lav|er /lave/ *v.t.* wash; (*injure etc.*) avenge. **se ~er** *v. pr.* wash (o.s.). (**se**) **~er de,** clear (o.s.) of. **~e-glace** *n.m.* windscreen washer. **~eur de carreaux,** window-cleaner. **~e-vaisselle** *n.m. invar.* dishwasher.

laverie /lavri/ *n.f.* **~ (automatique),** launderette; (*Amer.*) laundromat.

lavette /lavɛt/ *n.f.* dishcloth; (*péj.*) wimp.

lavoir /lavwar/ *n.m.* wash-house.

laxati|f, ~ve /laksatif, v/ *a. & n.m.* laxative.

laxisme /laksism/ *n.m.* laxity.

layette /lejɛt/ *n.f.* baby clothes.

le *ou* **l'*, la** *ou* **l'*** (*pl.* **les**) /lə, l/, /la, lʒ/ *article* the; (*mesure*) a, per. —*pron.* (*homme*) him; (*femme*) her; (*chose, animal*) it. **les** *pron.* them. **aimer le thé/la France,** like tea/France. **le matin,** in the morning. **il sort le mardi,** he goes out on Tuesdays. **levez le bras,** raise your arm. **je le connais,** I know him. **je le sais,** I know (it).

lécher /leʃe/ *v.t.* lick.

lèche-vitrines /lɛʃvitrin/ *n.m.* **faire du** ～, go window-shopping.

leçon /ləsɔ̃/ *n.f.* lesson. **faire la** ～ **à,** lecture.

lec|teur, ～**trice** /lɛktœr, -tris/ *n.m.,* *f.* reader; (*univ.*) foreign language assistant. ～**teur de cassettes,** cassette player. ～**teur de disquettes,** (disk) drive.

lecture /lɛktyr/ *n.f.* reading.

ledit, ladite (*pl.* **lesdit(e)s**) /lədi, ladit, ledi(t)/ *a.* the aforesaid.

lég|al (*m. pl.* ～**aux**) /legal, -o/ *a.* legal. ～**alement** *adv.* legally. ～**aliser** *v.t.* legalize. ～**alité** *n.f.* legality; (*loi*) law.

légation /legɑsjɔ̃/ *n.f.* legation.

légend|e /leʒɑ̃d/ *n.f.* (*histoire, inscription*) legend. ～**aire** *a.* legendary.

lég|er, ～**ère** /leʒe, -ɛr/ *a.* light; (*bruit, faute, maladie*) slight; (*café, argument*) weak; (*imprudent*) thoughtless; (*frivole*) fickle. **à la** ～**ère,** thoughtlessly. ～**èrement** /-ɛrmɑ̃/ *adv.* lightly; (*agir*) thoughtlessly; (*un peu*) slightly. ～**èreté** /-ɛrte/ *n.f.* lightness; thoughtlessness.

légion /leʒjɔ̃/ *n.f.* legion. **une** ～ **de,** a crowd of. ～**naire** /-jɔnɛr/ *n.m.* (*mil.*) legionnaire.

législati|f, ～**ve** /leʒislatif, -v/ *a.* legislative.

législation /leʒislɑsjɔ̃/ *n.f.* legislation.

législature /leʒislatyr/ *n.f.* term of office.

légitim|e /leʒitim/ *a.* legitimate. **en état de** ～**e défense,** acting in self-defence. ～**ité** *n.f.* legitimacy.

legs /lɛg/ *n.m.* legacy.

léguer /lege/ *v.t.* bequeath.

légume /legym/ *n.m.* vegetable.

lendemain /lɑ̃dmɛ̃/ *n.m.* **le** ～**,** the next day, the day after; (*fig.*) the future. **le** ～ **de,** the day after. **le** ～ **matin/soir,** the next morning/evening.

lent, ～**e** /lɑ̃, lɑ̃t/ *a.* slow. ～**ement** /lɑ̃tmɑ̃/ *adv.* slowly. ～**eur** /lɑ̃tœr/ *n.f.* slowness.

lentille[1] /lɑ̃tij/ *n.f.* (*plante*) lentil.

lentille[2] /lɑ̃tij/ *n.f.* (*verre*) lens; ～**s de contact,** (contact) lenses.

léopard /leɔpar/ *n.m.* leopard.

lèpre /lɛpr/ *n.f.* leprosy.

lequel, laquelle (*pl.* **lesquel(le)s**) /ləkɛl, lakɛl, lekɛl/ *pron.* (*à + lequel = auquel,* *à + lesquel(le)s = auxquel(le)s; de + lequel = duquel, de + lesquel(le)s = desquel(le)s*) which; (*interrogatif*) which (one); (*personne*) who; (*complément indirect*) whom.

les /le/ *voir* **le.**

lesbienne /lɛsbjɛn/ *n.f.* lesbian.

léser /leze/ *v.t.* wrong.

lésiner /lezine/ *v.i.* **ne pas** ～ **sur,** not stint on.

lésion /lezjɔ̃/ *n.f.* lesion.

lesquels, lesquelles /lekɛl/ *voir* **lequel.**

lessive /lesiv/ *n.f.* washing-powder; (*linge, action*) washing.

lest /lɛst/ *n.m.* ballast. **jeter du** ～**,** (*fig.*) climb down. ～**er** *v.t.* ballast.

leste /lɛst/ *a.* nimble; (*grivois*) coarse.

léthar|gie /letarʒi/ *n.f.* lethargy. ～**ique** *a.* lethargic.

lettre /lɛtr/ *n.f.* letter. **à la** ～**,** literally. **en toutes** ～**s,** in full. ～ **exprès,** express letter. **les** ～**s,** (*univ.*) (the) arts.

lettré /letre/ *a.* well-read.

leucémie /løsemi/ *n.f.* leukaemia.

leur /lœr/ *a.* (*f. invar.*) their. —*pron.* (to) them. **le** ～**, la** ～**, les** ～**s,** theirs.

leurr|e /lœr/ *n.m.* illusion; (*duperie*) deception. ～**er** *v.t.* delude.

levain /ləvɛ̃/ *n.m.* leaven.

levé /ləve/ *a.* (*debout*) up.

levée /ləve/ *n.f.* lifting; (*de courrier*) collection; (*de troupes, d'impôts*) levying.

lever /ləve/ *v.t.* lift (up), raise; (*interdiction*) lift; (*séance*) close; (*armée, impôts*) levy. —*v.i.* (*pâte*) rise. **se** ～ *v. pr.* get up; (*soleil, rideau*) rise; (*jour*) break. —*n.m.* **au** ～**,** on getting up. ～ **du jour,** daybreak. ～ **du rideau,** (*théâtre*) curtain (up). ～ **du soleil,** sunrise.

levier /ləvje/ *n.m.* lever.

lèvre /lɛvr/ *n.f.* lip.

lévrier /levrije/ *n.m.* greyhound.

levure /ləvyr/ *n.f.* yeast. ～ **alsacienne** *ou* **chimique,** baking powder.

lexicographie /lɛksikɔgrafi/ *n.f.* lexicography.

lexique /lɛksik/ *n.m.* vocabulary; (*glossaire*) lexicon.

lézard /lezar/ *n.m.* lizard.

lézard|e /lezard/ *n.f.* crack. **se** ～**er** *v. pr.* crack.

liaison /ljɛzɔ̃/ *n.f.* connection; (*transport*) link; (*contact*) contact; (*gram., mil.*) liaison; (*amoureuse*) affair.

liane /ljan/ *n.f.* creeper.

liasse /ljas/ *n.f.* bundle, wad.

Liban /libɑ̃/ *n.m.* Lebanon.

libanais, ～**e** /libanɛ, -z/ *a. & n.m., f.* Lebanese.

libell|er /libele/ *v.t.* (*cheque*) write; (*lettre*) draw up. ～**é à l'ordre de,** made out to.

libellule /libelyl/ *n.f.* dragonfly.
libér|al (*m. pl.* ~**aux**) /liberal, -o/ *a.*
liberal. **les professions** ~**ales** the
professions. ~**alement** *adv.* liberally.
~**alisme** *n.m.* liberalism. ~**alité** *n.f.*
liberality.
libér|er /libere/ *v.t.* (*personne*) free,
release; (*pays*) liberate, free. **se** ~**er** *v.
pr.* free o.s. ~**ateur,** ~**atrice** *a.*
liberating; *n.m., f.* liberator. ~**ation** *n.f.*
release; (*de pays*) liberation.
liberté /liberte/ *n.f.* freedom, liberty;
(*loisir*) free time. **en** ~ **provisoire,** on
bail. **être/mettre en** ~, be/set free.
libertin, ~**e** /libertɛ̃, -in/ *a. & n.m., f.*
libertine.
librair|e /librer/ *n.m./f.* bookseller. ~**ie**
/-eri/ *n.f.* bookshop.
libre /libr/ *a.* free; (*place, pièce*) vacant,
free; (*passage*) clear; (*école*) private
(*usually religious*). ~ **de qch./de faire,**
free from sth./to do. ~**-échange** *n.m.*
free trade. ~**ment** /-əmã/ *adv.* freely.
~**-service** (*pl.* ~**s-services**) *n.m.* self-
service.
Libye /libi/ *n.f.* Libya.
libyen, ~**ne** /libjɛ̃, -jɛn/ *a. & n.m., f.*
Libyan.
licence /lisãs/ *n.f.* licence; (*univ.*)
degree.
licencié, ~**e** /lisãsje/ *n.m., f.* ~ **ès
lettres/sciences,** Bachelor of Arts/
Science.
licenc|ier /lisãsje/ *v.t.* make redundant,
(*pour faute*) dismiss. ~**iements** *n.m. pl.*
redundancies.
licencieu|x, ~**se** /lisãsjø, -z/ *a.*
licentious, lascivious.
lichen /liken/ *n.m.* lichen.
licite /lisit/ *a.* lawful.
licorne /likɔrn/ *n.f.* unicorn.
lie /li/ *n.f.* dregs.
liège /ljɛʒ/ *n.m.* cork.
lien /ljɛ̃/ *n.m.* (*rapport*) link; (*attache*)
bond, tie; (*corde*) rope.
lier /lje/ *v.t.* tie up, bind; (*relier*) link;
(*engager, unir*) bind. ~ **conversation,**
strike up a conversation. **se** ~ **avec,**
make friends with. **ils sont très liés,**
they are very close.
lierre /ljɛr/ *n.m.* ivy.
lieu (*pl.* ~**x**) /ljø/ *n.m.* place. ~**x,**
(*locaux*) premises; (*d'un accident*)
scene. **au** ~ **de,** instead of. **avoir** ~,
take place. **tenir** ~ **de,** serve as. **en
premier** ~, firstly. **en dernier** ~,
lastly. ~ **commun,** commonplace.
lieutenant /ljøtnã/ *n.m.* lieutenant.
lièvre /ljɛvr/ *n.m.* hare.

ligament /ligamã/ *n.m.* ligament.
ligne /liɲ/ *n.f.* line; (*trajet*) route;
(*formes*) lines; (*de femme*) figure. **en**
~, (*joueurs etc.*) lined up; (*personne au
téléphone*) on the phone.
lignée /liɲe/ *n.f.* ancestry, line.
ligoter /ligɔte/ *v.t.* tie up.
ligu|e /lig/ *n.f.* league. **se** ~**er** *v. pr.* form
a league (**contre,** against).
lilas /lila/ *n.m. & a. invar.* lilac.
limace /limas/ *n.f.* slug.
limande /limãd/ *n.f.* (*poisson*) dab.
lim|e /lim/ *n.f.* file. ~**e à ongles,** nail file.
~**er** *v.t.* file.
limier /limje/ *n.m.* bloodhound;
(*policier*) sleuth.
limitation /limitɑsjɔ̃/ *n.f.* limitation. ~
de vitesse, speed limit.
limit|e /limit/ *n.f.* limit; (*de jardin,
champ*) boundary. —*a.* (*vitesse, âge*)
maximum. **cas** ~**e,** borderline case.
date ~**e,** deadline. ~**er** *v.t.* limit;
(*délimiter*) form the border of.
limoger /limɔʒe/ *v.t.* dismiss.
limon /limɔ̃/ *n.m.* stilt.
limonade /limɔnad/ *n.f.* lemonade.
limpid|e /lɛ̃pid/ *a.* limpid, clear. ~**ité** *n.f.*
clearness.
lin /lɛ̃/ *n.m.* (*tissu*) linen.
linceul /lɛ̃sœl/ *n.m.* shroud.
linéaire /lineɛr/ *a.* linear.
linge /lɛ̃ʒ/ *n.m.* linen; (*lessive*) washing;
(*torchon*) cloth. ~ (**de corps**),
underwear. ~**rie** *n.f.* underwear.
lingot /lɛ̃go/ *n.m.* ingot.
linguiste /lɛ̃guist/ *n.m./f.* linguist.
linguistique /lɛ̃guistik/ *a.* linguistic.
—*n.f.* linguistics.
lino /lino/ *n.m.* lino.
linoléum /linɔleɔm/ *n.m.* linoleum.
lion, ~**ne** /ljɔ̃, ljɔn/ *n.m., f.* lion, lioness.
le L~, Leo.
lionceau (*pl.* ~**x**) /liɔ̃so/ *n.m.* lion cub.
liquéfier /likefje/ *v.t.,* **se** ~ *v. pr.* liquefy.
liqueur /likœr/ *n.f.* liqueur.
liquide /likid/ *a. & n.m.* liquid. (**argent**)
~, ready money. **payer en** ~, pay
cash.
liquid|er /likide/ *v.t.* liquidate; (*vendre*)
sell. ~**ation** *n.f.* liquidation; (*vente*)
(clearance) sale.
lire[1]† /lir/ *v.t./i.* read.
lire[2] /lir/ *n.f.* lira.
lis[1] /li/ *voir* **lire**[1].
lis[2] /lis/ *n.m.* (*fleur*) lily.
lisible /lizibl/ *a.* legible; (*roman etc.*)
readable.
lisière /lizjɛr/ *n.f.* edge.
liss|e /lis/ *a.* smooth. ~**er** *v.t.* smooth.

liste /list/ *n.f.* list. ∼ **électorale**, register of voters.

listing /listiŋ/ *n.m.* printout.

lit[1] /li/ *voir* **lire**[1].

lit[2] /li/ *n.m.* (*de personne, fleuve*) bed. **se mettre au** ∼, get into bed. ∼ **de camp**, camp-bed. ∼ **d'enfant**, cot. ∼ **d'une personne**, single bed.

litanie /litani/ *n.f.* litany.

litchi /litʃi/ *n.m.* litchi.

literie /litri/ *n.f.* bedding.

litière /litjɛr/ *n.f.* (*paille*) litter.

litige /litiʒ/ *n.m.* dispute.

litre /litr/ *n.m.* litre.

littéraire /literɛr/ *a.* literary.

littér|al (*m. pl.* ∼**aux**) /literal, -o/ *a.* literal. ∼**alement** *adv.* literally.

littérature /literatyr/ *n.f.* literature.

littor|al (*pl.* ∼**aux**) /litɔral, -o/ *n.m.* coast.

liturg|ie /lityrʒi/ *n.f.* liturgy. ∼**ique** *a.* liturgical.

livide /livid/ *a.* (*blême*) pallid.

livraison /livrɛzɔ̃/ *n.f.* delivery.

livre[1] /livr/ *n.m.* book. ∼ **de bord**, log-book. ∼ **de compte**, books. ∼ **de poche**, paperback.

livre[2] /livr/ *n.f.* (*monnaie, poids*) pound.

livrée /livre/ *n.f.* livery.

livr|er /livre/ *v.t.* deliver; (*abandonner*) give over (**à**, to); (*secret*) give away. ∼**é à soi-même**, left to o.s. **se** ∼**er à**, give o.s. over to; (*actes, boisson*) indulge in; (*se confier à*) confide in; (*effectuer*) carry out.

livret /livre/ *n.m.* book; (*mus.*) libretto. ∼ **scolaire**, school report (book).

livreu|r, ∼se /livrœr, -øz/ *n.m., f.* delivery boy *ou* girl.

lobe /lɔb/ *n.m.* lobe.

loc|al[1] (*m. pl.* ∼**aux**) /lɔkal, -o/ *a.* local. ∼**alement** *adv.* locally.

loc|al[2] (*pl.* ∼**aux**) /lɔkal, -o/ *n.m.* premises. ∼**aux**, premises.

localisé /lɔkalize/ *a.* localized.

localité /lɔkalite/ *n.f.* locality.

locataire /lɔkatɛr/ *n.m./f.* tenant; (*de chambre, d'hôtel*) lodger.

location /lɔkasjɔ̃/ *n.f.* (*de maison*) renting; (*de voiture*) hiring, renting; (*de place*) booking, reservation; (*guichet*) booking office; (*théâtre*) box office; (*par propriétaire*) renting out; hiring out. **en** ∼, (*voiture*) on hire, rented.

lock-out /lɔkawt/ *n.m. invar.* lockout.

locomotion /lɔkɔmosjɔ̃/ *n.f.* locomotion.

locomotive /lɔkɔmɔtiv/ *n.f.* engine, locomotive.

locution /lɔkysjɔ̃/ *n.f.* phrase.

logarithme /lɔgaritm/ *n.m.* logarithm.

loge /lɔʒ/ *n.f.* (*de concierge*) lodge; (*d'acteur*) dressing-room; (*de spectateur*) box.

logement /lɔʒmã/ *n.m.* accommodation; (*appartement*) flat; (*habitat*) housing.

log|er /lɔʒe/ *v.t.* accommodate. —*v.i.* ∼**er** *v. pr.* live. **trouver à se** ∼**er**, find accommodation. **être** ∼**é**, live. **se** ∼**er dans**, (*balle*) lodge itself in.

logeu|r, ∼se /lɔʒœr, -øz/ *n.m., f.* landlord, landlady.

logiciel /lɔʒisjɛl/ *n.m.* software.

logique /lɔʒik/ *a.* logical. —*n.f.* logic. ∼**ment** *adv.* logically.

logis /lɔʒi/ *n.m.* dwelling.

logistique /lɔʒistik/ *n.f.* logistics.

logo /lɔgo/ *n.m.* logo.

loi /lwa/ *n.f.* law.

loin /lwɛ̃/ *adv.* far (away). **au** ∼, far away. **de** ∼, from far away; (*de beaucoup*) by far. ∼ **de là**, far from it. **plus** ∼, further. **il revient de** ∼, (*fig.*) he had a close shave.

lointain, ∼e /lwɛ̃tɛ̃, -ɛn/ *a.* distant. —*n.m.* distance.

loir /lwar/ *n.m.* dormouse.

loisir /lwazir/ *n.m.* (*spare*) time. ∼**s**, spare time; (*distractions*) spare time activities. **à** ∼, at one's leisure.

londonien, ∼ne /lɔ̃dɔnjɛ̃, -jɛn/ *a.* London. —*n.m., f.* Londoner.

Londres /lɔ̃dr/ *n.m./f.* London.

long, ∼ue /lɔ̃, lɔ̃g/ *a.* long. —*n.m.* **de** ∼, (*mesure*) long. **à la** ∼**ue**, in the end. **à** ∼ **terme**, long-term. **de** ∼ **en large**, back and forth. ∼ **à faire**, a long time doing. (**tout**) **le** ∼ **de**, (all) along.

longer /lɔ̃ʒe/ *v.t.* go along; (*limiter*) border.

longévité /lɔ̃ʒevite/ *n.f.* longevity.

longiligne /lɔ̃ʒiliɲ/ *a.* tall and slender.

longitude /lɔ̃ʒityd/ *n.f.* longitude.

longtemps /lɔ̃tã/ *adv.* a long time. **avant** ∼, before long. **trop** ∼, too long. **ça prendra** ∼, it will take a long time.

longue /lɔ̃g/ *voir* **long**.

longuement /lɔ̃gmã/ *adv.* at length.

longueur /lɔ̃gœr/ *n.f.* length. ∼**s**, (*de texte etc.*) over-long parts. **à** ∼ **de journée**, all day long. ∼ **d'onde**, wavelength.

longue-vue /lɔ̃gvy/ *n.f.* telescope.

look /luk/ *n.m.* (*fam.*) look, image.

lopin /lɔpɛ̃/ *n.m.* ∼ **de terre,** patch of land.

loquace /lɔkas/ *a.* talkative.

loque /lɔk/ *n.f.* ∼**s**, rags. ∼ **(humaine)**, (human) wreck.

loquet /lɔkɛ/ *n.m.* latch.

lorgner /lɔrɲe/ *v.t.* eye.

lors de /lɔrdə/ *prép.* at the time of.

lorsque /lɔrsk(ə)/ *conj.* when.

losange /lɔzɑ̃ʒ/ *n.m.* diamond.

lot /lo/ *n.m.* prize; (*portion, destin*) lot.

loterie /lɔtri/ *n.f.* lottery.

lotion /losjɔ̃/ *n.f.* lotion.

lotissement /lɔtismɑ̃/ *n.m.* (*à construire*) building plot; (*construit*) (housing) development.

louable /lwabl/ *a.* praiseworthy.

louange /lwɑ̃ʒ/ *n.f.* praise.

louche[1] /luʃ/ *a.* shady, dubious.

louche[2] /luʃ/ *n.f.* ladle.

loucher /luʃe/ *v.i.* squint.

louer[1] /lwe/ *v.t.* (*maison*) rent; (*voiture*) hire, rent; (*place*) book, reserve; (*propriétaire*) rent out; hire out. **à ~,** to let, for rent (*Amer.*)

louer[2] /lwe/ *v.t.* (*approuver*) praise (**de,** for). **se ~ de,** congratulate o.s. on.

loufoque /lufɔk/ *a.* (*fam.*) crazy.

loup /lu/ *n.m.* wolf.

loupe /lup/ *n.f.* magnifying glass.

louper /lupe/ *v.t.* (*fam.*) miss.

lourd, ~e /lur, -d/ *a.* heavy; (*chaleur*) close; (*faute*) gross. **~ de conséquences,** with dire consequences. **~ement** /-dəmɑ̃/ *adv.* heavily. **~eur** /-dœr/ *n.f.* heaviness.

lourdaud, ~e /lurdo, -d/ *a.* loutish. —*n.m., f.* lout, oaf.

loutre /lutr/ *n.f.* otter.

louve /luv/ *n.f.* she-wolf.

louveteau (*pl.* **~x**) /luvto/ *n.m.* wolf cub; (*scout*) Cub (Scout).

louvoyer /luvwaje/ *v.i.* (*fig.*) sidestep the issue; (*naut.*) tack.

loy|al (*m. pl.* **~aux**) /lwajal, -o/ *a.* loyal; (*honnête*) fair. **~alement** *adv.* loyally; fairly. **~auté** *n.f.* loyalty, fairness.

loyer /lwaje/ *n.m.* rent.

lu /ly/ *voir* **lire**[1].

lubie /lybi/ *n.f.* whim.

lubrif|ier /lybrifje/ *v.t.* lubricate. **~iant** *n.m.* lubricant.

lubrique /lybrik/ *a.* lewd.

lucarne /lykarn/ *n.f.* skylight.

lucid|e /lysid/ *a.* lucid. **~ité** *n.f.* lucidity.

lucrati|f, ~ve /lykratif, -v/ *a.* lucrative. **à but non ~f,** non-profit-making.

lueur /lɥœr/ *n.f.* (faint) light, glimmer; (*fig.*) glimmer, gleam.

luge /lyʒ/ *n.f.* toboggan.

lugubre /lygybr/ *a.* gloomy.

lui /lɥi/ *pron.* him; (*sujet*) he; (*chose*) it; (*objet indirect*) (to) him; (*femme*) (to)

her; (*chose*) (to) it. **~-même** *pron.* himself; itself.

luire† /lɥir/ *v.i.* shine; (*reflet humide*) glisten; (*reflet chaud, faible*) glow.

lumbago /lɔ̃bago/ *n.m.* lumbago.

lumière /lymjɛr/ *n.f.* light. **~s,** (*connaissances*) knowledge. **faire (toute) la ~ sur,** clear up.

luminaire /lyminɛr/ *n.m.* lamp.

lumineu|x, ~se /lyminø, -z/ *a.* luminous; (*éclairé*) illuminated; (*source, rayon*) (of) light; (*vif*) bright.

lunaire /lynɛr/ *a.* lunar.

lunatique /lynatik/ *a.* temperamental.

lunch /lœntʃ/ *n.m.* buffet lunch.

lundi /lœdi/ *n.m.* Monday.

lune /lyn/ *n.f.* moon. **~ de miel,** honeymoon.

lunette /lynɛt/ *n.f.* **~s,** glasses; (*de protection*) goggles. **~ arrière,** (*auto.*) rear window. **~s de soleil,** sunglasses.

luron /lyrɔ̃/ *n.m.* **gai** *ou* **joyeux ~,** (*fam.*) quite a lad.

lustre /lystr/ *n.m.* (*éclat*) lustre; (*objet*) chandelier.

lustré /lystre/ *a.* shiny.

luth /lyt/ *n.m.* lute.

lutin /lytɛ̃/ *n.m.* goblin.

lutrin /lytrɛ̃/ *n.m.* lectern.

lutt|e /lyt/ *n.f.* fight, struggle; (*sport*) wrestling. **~er** *v.i.* fight, struggle; (*sport*) wrestle. **~eur, ~euse** *n.m., f.* fighter; (*sport*) wrestler.

luxe /lyks/ *n.m.* luxury. **de ~,** luxury; (*produit*) de luxe.

Luxembourg /lyksɑ̃bur/ *n.m.* Luxemburg.

lux|er /lykse/ *v.t.* **se ~er le genou,** dislocate one's knee. **~ation** *n.f.* dislocation.

luxueu|x, ~se /lyksɥø, -z/ *a.* luxurious.

luxure /lyksyr/ *n.f.* lust.

luxuriant, ~e /lyksyrjɑ̃, -t/ *a.* luxuriant.

luzerne /lyzɛrn/ *n.f.* (*plante*) lucerne, alfalfa.

lycée /lise/ *n.m.* (secondary) school. **~n, ~nne** /-ɛ̃, -ɛn/ *n.m., f.* pupil (at secondary school).

lynch|er /lɛ̃ʃe/ *v.t.* lynch. **~age** *n.m.* lynching.

lynx /lɛ̃ks/ *n.m.* lynx.

lyophilis|er /ljɔfilize/ *v.t.* freeze-dry. **~é** *a.* freeze-dried.

lyre /lir/ *n.f.* lyre.

lyri|que /lirik/ *a.* (*poésie*) lyric; (*passionné*) lyrical. **artiste/théâtre**

~**que,** opera singer/-house. ~**sme** *n.m.*
lyricism.
lys /lis/ *n.m.* lily.

M

m' /m/ *voir* me.
ma /ma/ *voir* mon.
maboul /mabul/ *a.* (*fam.*) mad.
macabre /makabr/ *a.* gruesome,
macabre.
macadam /makadam/ *n.m.* (*goudronné*)
Tarmac (P.).
macaron /makarɔ̃/ *n.m.* (*gâteau*)
macaroon; (*insigne*) badge.
macaronis /makarɔni/ *n.m.* *pl.*
macaroni.
macédoine /masedwan/ *n.f.* mixed
vegetables. ~ **de fruits,** fruit salad.
macérer /masere/ *v.t./i.* soak; (*dans du
vinaigre*) pickle.
mâchefer /maʃfɛr/ *n.m.* clinker.
mâcher /maʃe/ *v.t.* chew. **ne pas** ~ **ses
mots,** not mince one's words.
machiavélique /makjavelik/ *a.* machiavellian.
machin /maʃɛ̃/ *n.m.* (*chose: fam.*) thing;
(*personne: fam.*) what's-his-name.
machin|al (*m. pl.* ~**aux**) /maʃinal, -o/
a. automatic. ~**alement** *adv.* automatically.
machinations /maʃinɑsjɔ̃/ *n.f.* *pl.*
machinations.
machine /maʃin/ *n.f.* machine; (*d'un
train, navire*) engine. ~ **à écrire,**
typewriter. ~ **à laver/coudre,** wash-
ing-/sewing-machine. ~ **à sous,** fruit
machine; (*Amer.*) slot-machine. ~-
outil (*pl.* ~**s-outils**) *n.f.* machine tool.
~**rie** *n.f.* machinery.
machiner /maʃine/ *v.t.* plot.
machiniste /maʃinist/ *n.m.* (*théâtre*)
stage-hand; (*conducteur*) driver.
macho /ma(t)ʃo/ *n.m.* (*fam.*) macho.
mâchoire /mɑʃwar/ *n.f.* jaw.
mâchonner /maʃɔne/ *v.t.* chew at.
maçon /masɔ̃/ *n.m.* builder; (*poseur de
briques*) bricklayer. ~**nerie** /-ɔnri/
n.f. brickwork; (*pierres*) stonework,
masonry.
maçonnique /masɔnik/ *a.* Masonic.
macrobiotique /makrɔbjɔtik/ *a.* macrobiotic.
maculer /makyle/ *v.t.* stain.
Madagascar /madagaskar/ *n.f.* Madagascar.

madame (*pl.* **mesdames**) /madam,
medam/ *n.f.* madam. **M**~ *ou* **Mme
Dupont,** Mrs Dupont. **bonsoir, mesdames,** good evening, ladies.
madeleine /madlɛn/ *n.f.* madeleine
(*small shell-shaped sponge-cake*).
mademoiselle (*pl.* **mesdemoiselles**)
/madmwazɛl, medmwazɛl/ *n.f.* miss.
M~ *ou* **Mlle Dupont,** Miss Dupont.
bonsoir, mesdemoiselles, good evening, ladies.
madère /madɛr/ *n.m.* (*vin*) Madeira.
madone /madɔn/ *n.f.* madonna.
madrig|al (*pl.* ~**aux**) /madrigal, -o/
n.m. madrigal.
maestro /maɛstro/ *n.m.* maestro.
maf(f)ia /mafja/ *n.f.* Mafia.
magasin /magazɛ̃/ *n.m.* shop, store;
(*entrepôt*) warehouse; (*d'une arme
etc.*) magazine.
magazine /magazin/ *n.m.* magazine;
(*émission*) programme.
Maghreb /magrɛb/ *n.m.* North Africa.
~**in,** ~**ine** *a. & n.m., f.* North African.
magicien, ~**ne** /maʒisjɛ̃, -jɛn/ *n.m., f.*
magician.
magie /maʒi/ *n.f.* magic.
magique /maʒik/ *a.* magic; (*mystérieux*)
magical.
magistr|al (*m. pl.* ~**aux**) /maʒistral,
-o/ *a.* masterly; (*grand: hum.*) colossal.
~**alement** *adv.* in a masterly fashion.
magistrat /maʒistra/ *n.m.* magistrate.
magistrature /maʒistratyr/ *n.f.* judi-
ciary.
magnanim|e /maɲanim/ *a.* mag-
nanimous. ~**ité** *n.f.* magnanimity.
magnat /magna/ *n.m.* tycoon, magnate.
magner (se) /(sə)maɲe/ *v. pr.* (*argot*)
hurry.
magnésie /maɲezi/ *n.f.* magnesia.
magnéti|que /maɲetik/ *a.* magnetic.
~**ser** *v.t.* magnetize. ~**sme** *n.m.*
magnetism.
magnétophone /maɲetɔfɔn/ *n.m.* tape
recorder. ~ **à cassettes,** cassette
recorder.
magnétoscope /maɲetɔskɔp/ *n.m.*
video-recorder.
magnifi|que /maɲifik/ *a.* magnificent.
~**cence** *n.f.* magnificence.
magnolia /maɲɔlja/ *n.m.* magnolia.
magot /mago/ *n.m.* (*fam.*) hoard (of
money).
magouill|er /maguje/ *v.i.* (*fam.*) schem-
ing. ~**eur,** ~**euse** *n.m., f.* (*fam.*)
schemer. ~**e** *n.f.* (*fam.*) scheming.
magret /magrɛ/ *n.m.* ~ **de canard,**
steaklet of duck.

mai /mɛ/ *n.m.* May.

maigr|e /mɛgr/ *a.* thin; (*viande*) lean; (*yaourt*) low-fat; (*fig.*) poor, meagre. **faire ~e,** abstain from meat. **~ement** *adv.* poorly. **~eur** *n.f.* thinness; leanness; (*fig.*) meagreness.

maigrir /megrir/ *v.i.* get thin(ner); (*en suivant un régime*) slim. —*v.t.* make thin(ner).

maille /maj/ *n.f.* stitch; (*de filet*) mesh. **~ filée,** ladder, run.

maillet /majɛ/ *n.m.* mallet.

maillon /majɔ̃/ *n.m.* link.

maillot /majo/ *n.m.* (*de sport*) jersey. **~ (de corps),** vest. **~ (de bain),** (swimming) costume.

main /mɛ̃/ *n.f.* hand. **avoir la ~ heureuse,** be lucky. **donner la ~ à qn.,** hold s.o.'s hand. **en ~s propres,** in person. **en bonnes ~s,** in good hands. **~ courante,** handrail. **~-d'œuvre** (*pl.* **~s-d'œuvre**) *n.f.* labour; (*ensemble d'ouvriers*) labour force. **~-forte** *n.f. invar.* assistance. **se faire la ~,** get the hang of it. **perdre la ~,** lose one's touch. **sous la ~,** to hand. **vol/attaque à ~ armée,** armed robbery/attack.

mainmise /mɛ̃miz/ *n.f.* **~ sur,** complete hold on.

maint, ~e /mɛ̃, mɛ̃t/ *a.* many a. **~s,** many. **à ~es reprises,** on many occasions.

maintenant /mɛ̃tnɑ̃/ *adv.* now; (*de nos jours*) nowadays.

maintenir† /mɛ̃tnir/ *v.t.* keep, maintain; (*soutenir*) hold up; (*affirmer*) maintain. **se ~** *v. pr.* (*continuer*) persist; (*rester*) remain.

maintien /mɛ̃tjɛ̃/ *n.m.* (*attitude*) bearing; (*conservation*) maintenance.

maire /mɛr/ *n.m.* mayor.

mairie /meri/ *n.f.* town hall; (*administration*) town council.

mais /mɛ/ *conj.* but. **~ oui, ~ si,** of course. **~ non,** definitely not.

maïs /mais/ *n.m.* (*à cultiver*) maize; (*culin.*) sweet corn; (*Amer.*) corn.

maison /mɛzɔ̃/ *n.f.* house; (*foyer*) home; (*immeuble*) building. **~ (de commerce),** firm. —*a. invar.* (*culin.*) home-made. **à la ~,** at home. **rentrer** *ou* **aller à la ~,** go home. **~ des jeunes,** youth centre. **~ de repos, ~ de convalescence,** convalescent home. **~ de retraite,** old people's home. **~ mère,** parent company.

maisonnée /mɛzɔne/ *n.f.* household.

maisonnette /mɛzɔnɛt/ *n.f.* small house, cottage.

maître /mɛtr/ *n.m.* master. **~ (d'école),** schoolmaster. **~ de,** in control of. **se rendre ~ de,** gain control of; (*incendie*) bring under control. **~ assistant/de conférences,** junior/senior lecturer. **~ chanteur,** blackmailer. **~ d'hôtel,** head waiter; (*domestique*) butler. **~ nageur,** swimming instructor.

maîtresse /mɛtrɛs/ *n.f.* mistress. **~ (d'école),** schoolmistress. —*a.f.* (*idée, poutre, qualité*) main. **~ de,** in control of.

maîtris|e /mɛtriz/ *n.f.* mastery; (*univ.*) master's degree. **~e (de soi),** self control. **~er** *v.t.* master; (*incendie*) control; (*personne*) subdue. **se ~er** *v. pr.* control o.s.

maïzena /maizena/ *n.f.* (P.) cornflour.

majesté /maʒɛste/ *n.f.* majesty.

majestueu|x, ~se /maʒɛstɥø, -z/ *a.* majestic. **~sement** *adv.* majestically.

majeur /maʒœr/ *a.* major; (*jurid.*) of age. —*n.m.* middle finger. **en ~e partie,** mostly. **la ~e partie de,** most of.

major|er /maʒɔre/ *v.t.* increase. **~ation** *n.f.* increase (**de,** in).

majorit|é /maʒɔrite/ *n.f.* majority. **en ~é,** chiefly. **~aire** *a.* majority. **être ~aire,** be in the majority

Majorque /maʒɔrk/ *n.f.* Majorca.

majuscule /maʒyskyl/ *a.* capital. —*n.f.* capital letter.

mal¹ /mal/ *adv.* badly; (*incorrectement*) wrong(ly). **~ (à l'aise),** uncomfortable. **aller ~,** (*malade*) be bad. **c'est ~ de,** it is wrong *ou* bad to. **~ entendre/comprendre,** not hear/understand properly. **~ famé,** of ill repute. **~ fichu,** (*personne; fam.*) feeling lousy. **~ en point,** in a bad state. **pas ~,** not bad; quite a lot.

mal² (*pl.* **maux**) /mal, mo/ *n.m.* evil; (*douleur*) pain, ache; (*maladie*) disease; (*effort*) trouble; (*dommage*) harm; (*malheur*) misfortune. **avoir ~ à la tête/aux dents/à la gorge,** have a headache/a toothache/a sore throat. **avoir le ~ de mer/du pays,** be seasick/homesick. **faire du ~ à,** hurt, harm. **se donner du ~ pour faire qch.,** go to a lot of trouble to do sth.

malade /malad/ *a.* sick, ill; (*bras, gorge*) bad; (*plante*) diseased. **tu es complètement ~!,** (*fam.*) you're mad. —*n.m./f.* sick person; (*d'un médecin*) patient.

maladie /maladi/ *n.f.* illness, disease.

maladi|f, ~ve /maladif, -v/ *a.* sickly; (*peur*) morbid.

maladresse /maladrɛs/ n.f. clumsiness; (*erreur*) blunder.

maladroit, ∼e /maladrwa, -t/ a. & n.m., f. clumsy (person).

malais, ∼e¹ /malɛ, -z/ a. & n.m., f. Malay.

malaise² /malɛz/ n.m. feeling of faintness *ou* dizziness; (*fig.*) uneasiness, malaise.

malaisé /maleze/ a. difficult.

malaria /malarja/ n.f. malaria.

Malaysia /malɛzja/ n.f. Malaysia.

malaxer /malakse/ v.t. (*pétrir*) knead; (*mêler*) mix.

malchanc|e /malʃɑ̃s/ n.f. misfortune. **∼eux, ∼euse** a. unlucky.

malcommode /malkɔmɔd/ a. awkward.

mâle /mal/ a. male; (*viril*) manly. —n.m. male.

malédiction /malediksjɔ̃/ n.f. curse.

maléfice /malefis/ n.m. evil spell.

maléfique /malefik/ a. evil.

malencontreu|x, ∼se /malɑ̃kɔ̃trø, -z/ a. unfortunate.

malentendant, ∼e a. & n.m., f. hard of hearing.

malentendu /malɑ̃tɑ̃dy/ n.m. misunderstanding.

malfaçon /malfasɔ̃/ n.f. fault.

malfaisant, ∼e /malfəzɑ̃, -t/ a. harmful.

malfaiteur /malfɛtœr/ n.m. criminal.

malformation /malfɔrmɑsjɔ̃/ n.f. malformation.

malgache /malgaʃ/ a. & n.m./f. Malagasy.

malgré /malgre/ prép. in spite of, despite. **∼ tout,** after all.

malhabile /malabil/ a. clumsy.

malheur /malœr/ n.m. misfortune; (*accident*) accident. **faire un ∼,** be a big hit.

malheureu|x, ∼se /malœrø, -z/ a. unhappy; (*regrettable*) unfortunate; (*sans succès*) unlucky; (*insignifiant*) wretched. —n.m., f. (poor) wretch. **∼sement** adv. unfortunately.

malhonnête /malɔnɛt/ a. dishonest. **∼té** n.f. dishonesty; (*action*) dishonest action.

malic|e /malis/ n.f. mischievousness; (*méchanceté*) malice. **∼ieux, ∼ieuse** a. mischievous.

mal|in, ∼igne /malɛ̃, -iɲ/ a. clever, smart; (*méchant*) malicious; (*tumeur*) malignant; (*difficile: fam.*) difficult. **∼ignité** n.f. malignancy.

malingre /malɛ̃gr/ a. puny.

malintentionné /malɛ̃tɑ̃sjɔne/ a. malicious.

malle /mal/ n.f. (*valise*) trunk; (*auto.*) boot; (*auto., Amer.*) trunk.

malléable /maleabl/ a. malleable.

mallette /malɛt/ n.f. (small) suitcase.

malmener /malmɔne/ v.t. manhandle, handle roughly.

malnutrition /malnytrisjɔ̃/ n.f. malnutrition.

malodorant, ∼e /malɔdɔrɑ̃, -t/ a. smelly, foul-smelling.

malotru /malɔtry/ n.m. boor.

malpoli /malpɔli/ a. impolite.

malpropre /malprɔpr/ a. dirty. **∼té** /-əte/ n.f. dirtiness.

malsain, ∼e /malsɛ̃, -ɛn/ a. unhealthy.

malt /malt/ n.m. malt.

maltais, ∼e /maltɛ, -z/ a. & n.m., f. Maltese.

Malte /malt/ n.f. Malta.

maltraiter /maltrete/ v.t. ill-treat.

malveillan|t, ∼te /malvɛjɑ̃, -t/ a. malevolent. **∼ce** n.f. malevolence.

maman /mamɑ̃/ n.f. mum(my), mother.

mamelle /mamɛl/ n.f. teat.

mamelon /mamlɔ̃/ n.m. (*anat.*) nipple; (*colline*) hillock.

mamie /mami/ n.f. (*fam.*) granny.

mammifère /mamifɛr/ n.m. mammal.

mammouth /mamut/ n.m. mammoth.

manche¹ /mɑ̃ʃ/ n.f. sleeve; (*sport, pol.*) round. **la M∼,** the Channel.

manche² /mɑ̃ʃ/ n.m. (*d'un instrument*) handle. **∼ à balai,** broomstick.

manchette /mɑ̃ʃɛt/ n.f. cuff; (*de journal*) headline.

manchot¹, ∼e /mɑ̃ʃo, -ɔt/ a. & n.m., f. one-armed (person); (*sans bras*) armless (person).

manchot² /mɑ̃ʃo/ n.m. (*oiseau*) penguin.

mandarin /mɑ̃darɛ̃/ n.m. (*fonctionnaire*) mandarin.

mandarine /mɑ̃darin/ n.f. tangerine, mandarin (orange).

mandat /mɑ̃da/ n.m. (*postal*) money order; (*pol.*) mandate; (*procuration*) proxy; (*de police*) warrant. **∼aire** /-tɛr/ n.m. (*représentant*) representative. **∼er** /-te/ v.t. (*pol.*) delegate.

manège /manɛʒ/ n.m. riding-school; (*à la foire*) merry-go-round; (*manœuvre*) wiles, ploy.

manette /manɛt/ n.f. lever; (*comput.*) joystick.

mangeable /mɑ̃ʒabl/ a. edible.

mangeoire /mɑ̃ʒwar/ n.f. trough.

mang|er /mɑ̃ʒe/ v.t./i. eat; (*fortune*) go

through; (*ronger*) eat into. —*n.m.* food.
donner à ᴗer à, feed. **ᴗeur, ᴗeuse**
n.m., f. eater.
mangue /mãg/ *n.f.* mango.
maniable /manjabl/ *a.* easy to handle.
maniaque /manjak/ *a.* fussy. —*n.m./f.*
fuss-pot; (*fou*) maniac. **un ᴗ de,** a
maniac for.
manie /mani/ *n.f.* habit; obsession.
man|ier /manje/ *v.t.* handle. **ᴗiement**
n.m. handling.
manière /manjɛr/ *n.f.* way, manner. **ᴗs,**
(*politesse*) manners; (*chichis*) fuss. **de
cette ᴗ,** in this way. **de ᴗ à,** so as to. **de
toute ᴗ,** anyway, in any case.
maniéré /manjere/ *a.* affected.
manif /manif/ *n.f.* (*fam.*) demo.
manifestant, ᴗe /manifɛstã, -t/ *n.m.,
f.* demonstrator.
manifeste /manifɛst/ *a.* obvious. —*n.m.*
manifesto.
manifest|er[1] /manifɛste/ *v.t.* show,
manifest. **se ᴗer** *v. pr.* (*sentiment*)
show itself; (*apparaître*) appear.
ᴗation[1] *n.f.* expression, demonstration, manifestation; (*de maladie*) ap
pearance.
manifest|er[2] /manifɛste/ *v.i.* (*pol.*)
demonstrate. **ᴗation**[2] *n.f.* (*pol.*)
demonstration; (*événement*) event.
manigan|ce /manigãs/ *n.f.* little plot.
ᴗer *v.t.* plot.
manipul|er /manipyle/ *v.t.* handle;
(*péj.*) manipulate. **ᴗation** *n.f.* handling; (*péj.*) manipulation.
manivelle /manivɛl/ *n.f.* crank.
manne /man/ *n.f.* (*aubaine*) god-send.
mannequin /mankɛ̃/ *n.m.* (*personne*)
model; (*statue*) dummy.
manœuvr|e[1] /manœvr/ *n.f.* manœuvre.
ᴗer *v.t./i.* manœuvre; (*machine*)
operate.
manœuvre[2] /manœvr/ *n.m.* (*ouvrier*)
labourer.
manoir /manwar/ *n.m.* manor.
manque /mãk/ *n.m.* lack (**de,** of); (*vide*)
gap. **ᴗs,** (*défauts*) faults. **ᴗ à gagner,**
loss of profit. **en (état de) ᴗ,** having
withdrawal symptoms.
manqué /mãke/ *a.* (*écrivain etc.*) failed.
garçon ᴗ, tomboy.
manquement /mãkmã/ *n.m.* **ᴗ à,**
breach of.
manquer /mãke/ *v.t.* miss; (*gâcher*)
spoil; (*examen*) fail. —*v.i.* be short *ou*
lacking; (*absent*) be absent; (*en moins,
disparu*) be missing; (*échouer*) fail. **ᴗ
à,** (*devoir*) fail in. **ᴗ de,** be short of,
lack. **il/ça lui manque,** he misses

him/it. **ᴗ (de) faire,** (*faillir*) nearly do.
ne pas ᴗ de, not fail to.
mansarde /mãsard/ *n.f.* attic.
manteau (*pl.* **ᴗx**) /mãto/ *n.m.* coat.
manucur|e /manykyr/ *n.m./f.* manicurist.
ᴗer *v.t.* manicure.
manuel, ᴗle /manɥɛl/ *a.* manual.
—*n.m.* (*livre*) manual. **ᴗlement** *adv.*
manually.
manufactur|e /manyfaktyr/ *n.f.* factory.
ᴗé *a.* manufactured.
manuscrit, ᴗe /manyskri, -t/ *a.*
handwritten. —*n.m.* manuscript.
manutention /manytãsjõ/ *n.f.* handling.
mappemonde /mapmõd/ *n.f.* world
map; (*sphère*) globe.
maquereau (*pl.* **ᴗx**) /makro/ *n.m.*
(*poisson*) mackerel; (*fam.*) pimp.
maquette /makɛt/ *n.f.* (*scale*) model;
(*mise en page*) paste-up.
maquill|er /makije/ *v.t.* make up;
(*truquer*) fake. **se ᴗer** *v. pr.* make (o.s.)
up. **ᴗage** *n.m.* make-up.
maquis /maki/ *n.m.* (*paysage*) scrub;
(*mil.*) Maquis, underground.
maraîch|er, ᴗère /marɛʃe, -ɛʃɛr/
n.m., f. market gardener; (*Amer.*) truck
farmer. **cultures ᴗères,** market gar-
dening.
marais /marɛ/ *n.m.* marsh.
marasme /marasm/ *n.m.* slump.
marathon /maratõ/ *n.m.* marathon.
marbre /marbr/ *n.m.* marble.
marc /mar/ *n.m.* (*eau-de-vie*) marc. **ᴗ
de café,** coffee-grounds.
marchand, ᴗe /marʃã, -d/ *n.m., f.*
trader; (*de charbon, vins*) merchant.
—*a.* (*valeur*) market. **ᴗ de couleurs,**
ironmonger; (*Amer.*) hardware merchant. **ᴗ de journaux,** newsagent. **ᴗ
de légumes,** greengrocer. **ᴗ de
poissons,** fishmonger.
marchand|er /marʃãde/ *v.t.* haggle
over. —*v.i.* haggle. **ᴗage** *n.m.*
haggling.
marchandise /marʃãdiz/ *n.f.* goods.
marche /marʃ/ *n.f.* (*démarche, trajet*)
walk; (*rythme*) pace; (*mil., mus.*)
march; (*d'escalier*) step; (*sport*) walking; (*de machine*) working; (*de
véhicule*) running. **en ᴗ,** (*train etc.*)
moving. **faire ᴗ arrière,** (*véhicule*)
reverse. **mettre en ᴗ,** start (up). **se
mettre en ᴗ,** start moving.
marché /marʃe/ *n.m.* market; (*contrat*)
deal. **faire son ᴗ,** do one's shopping. **ᴗ
aux puces,** flea market. **Mᴗ commun,**
Common Market. **ᴗ noir,** black
market.

marchepied /marʃəpje/ n.m. (de train, camion) step.

march|er /marʃe/ v.i. walk; (aller) go; (fonctionner) work, run; (prospérer) go well; (consentir: fam.) agree. ∼er (au pas), (mil.) march. faire ∼er qn., pull s.o.'s leg. ∼eur, ∼euse n.m., f. walker.

mardi /mardi/ n.m. Tuesday. M∼ gras, Shrove Tuesday.

mare /mar/ n.f. (étang) pond; (flaque) pool.

marécag|e /marekaʒ/ n.m. marsh. ∼eux, ∼euse a. marshy.

maréch|al (pl. ∼aux) /mareʃal, -o/ n.m. marshal. ∼al-ferrant (pl. ∼aux-ferrants) blacksmith.

marée /mare/ n.f. tide; (poissons) fresh fish. ∼ haute/basse, high/low tide. ∼ noire, oil-slick.

marelle /marɛl/ n.f. hopscotch.

margarine /margarin/ n.f. margarine.

marge /marʒ/ n.f. margin. en ∼ de, (à l'écart de) on the fringe(s) of. ∼ bénéficiaire, profit margin.

margin|al, ∼ale (m. pl. ∼aux) /marʒinal, -o/ a. marginal. —n.m., f. drop-out.

marguerite /margərit/ n.f. daisy; (qui imprime) daisy-wheel.

mari /mari/ n.m. husband.

mariage /marjaʒ/ n.m. marriage; (cérémonie) wedding.

marié, ∼e /marje/ a. married. —n.m. (bride)groom. —n.f. bride. les ∼s, the bride and groom.

marier /marje/ v.t. marry. se ∼ v.pr. get married, marry. se ∼ avec, marry, get married to.

marin, ∼e /marɛ̃, -in/ a. sea. —n.m. sailor. —n.f. navy. ∼e marchande, merchant navy.

mariner /marine/ v.t./i. marinate. faire ∼, (fam.) keep hanging around.

marionnette /marjɔnɛt/ n.f. puppet; (à fils) marionette.

maritalement /maritalmɑ̃/ adv. as husband and wife.

maritime /maritim/ a. maritime, coastal; (droit, agent) shipping.

mark /mark/ n.m. mark.

marmaille /marmaj/ n.f. (enfants: fam.) brats.

marmelade /marməlad/ n.f. stewed fruit. ∼ (d'oranges), marmalade.

marmite /marmit/ n.f. (cooking-)pot.

marmonner /marmɔne/ v.t./i. mumble.

marmot /marmo/ n.m. (fam.) kid.

marmotter /marmɔte/ v.t./i. mumble.

Maroc /marɔk/ n.m. Morocco.

marocain, ∼e /marɔkɛ̃, -ɛn/ a. & n.m., f. Moroccan.

maroquinerie /marɔkinri/ n.f. (magasin) leather goods shop.

marotte /marɔt/ n.f. fad, craze.

marquant, ∼e /markɑ̃, -t/ a. (remarquable) outstanding; (qu'on n'oublie pas) significant.

marque /mark/ n.f. mark; (de produits) brand, make. à vos ∼s!, (sport) on your marks! de ∼, (comm.) brand-name; (fig.) important. ∼ de fabrique, trade mark. ∼ déposée, registered trade mark.

marqué /marke/ a. marked.

marquer /marke/ v.t. mark; (indiquer) show; (écrire) note down; (point, but) score; (joueur) mark; (animal) brand. —v.i. (trace) leave a mark; (événement) stand out.

marqueterie /markɛtri/ n.f. marquetry.

marquis, ∼e[1] /marki, -z/ n.m., f. marquis, marchioness.

marquise[2] /markiz/ n.f. (auvent) glass awning.

marraine /marɛn/ n.f. godmother.

marrant, ∼e /marɑ̃, -t/ a. (fam.) funny.

marre /mar/ adv. en avoir ∼, (fam.) be fed up (de, with).

marrer (se) /(sə)mare/ v. pr. (fam.) laugh, have a (good) laugh.

marron /marɔ̃/ n.m. chestnut; (couleur) brown; (coup: fam.) thump. —a. invar. brown. ∼ d'Inde, horse-chestnut.

mars /mars/ n.m. March.

marsouin /marswɛ̃/ n.m. porpoise.

marteau (pl. ∼x) /marto/ n.m. hammer. ∼ (de porte), (door) knocker. ∼ piqueur ou pneumatique, pneumatic drill. être ∼, (fam.)mad.

marteler /martəle/ v.t. hammer.

mart|ial (m. pl. ∼iaux) /marsjal, -jo/ a. martial.

martien, ∼ne /marsjɛ̃, -jɛn/ a. & n.m., f. Martian.

martyr, ∼e[1] /martir/ n.m., f. martyr. —a. martyred. ∼iser v.t. martyr; (fig.) batter.

martyre[2] /martir/ n.m. (souffrance) martyrdom.

marxis|te /marksist/ a. & n.m./f. Marxist. ∼me n.m. Marxism.

mascara /maskara/ n.m. mascara.

mascarade /maskarad/ n.f. masquerade.

mascotte /maskɔt/ n.f. mascot.

masculin, ∼e /maskylɛ̃, -in/ a. masculine; (sexe) male; (mode, équipe) men's. —*n.m.* masculine. ∿**ité** /-inite/ *n.f.* masculinity.

maso /mazo/ *n.m./f.* (*fam.*) masochist. —*a. invar.* masochistic.

masochis|te /mazɔʃist/ *n.m./f.* masochist. —*a.* masochistic. ∿**me** *n.m.* masochism.

masqu|e /mask/ *n.m.* mask. ∿**er** *v.t.* (*cacher*) hide, conceal (**à**, from); (*lumière*) block (off).

massacr|e /masakr/ *n.m.* massacre. ∿**er** *v.t.* massacre; (*abîmer: fam.*) spoil.

massage /masaʒ/ *n.m.* massage.

masse /mas/ *n.f.* (*volume*) mass; (*gros morceau*) lump, mass; (*outil*) sledge-hammer. **en** ∿, (*vendre*) in bulk; (*venir*) in force; (*production*) mass. **la** ∿, (*foule*) the masses. **une** ∿ **de**, (*fam.*) masses of.

masser[1] /mase/ *v.t.*, **se** ∿ *v. pr.* (*gens, foule*) mass.

mass|er[2] /mase/ *v.t.* (*pétrir*) massage. ∿**eur**, ∿**euse** *n.m., f.* masseur, masseuse.

massi|f, ∿ve /masif, -v/ *a.* massive; (*or, argent*) solid. —*n.m.* (*de fleurs*) clump; (*géog.*) massif. ∿**vement** *adv.* (*en masse*) in large numbers.

massue /masy/ *n.f.* club, bludgeon.

mastic /mastik/ *n.m.* putty.

mastiquer /mastike/ *v.t.* (*mâcher*) chew.

masturb|er (se) /(sə)mastyrbe/ *v. pr.* masturbate. ∿**ation** *n.f.* masturbation.

masure /mazyr/ *n.f.* hovel.

mat /mat/ *a.* (*couleur*) matt; (*bruit*) dull. **être** ∿, (*aux échecs*) be checkmate.

mât /mɑ/ *n.m.* mast; (*pylône*) pole.

match /matʃ/ *n.m.* match; (*Amer.*) game. (**faire**) ∿ **nul**, tie, draw. ∿ **aller**, first leg. ∿ **retour**, return match.

matelas /matla/ *n.m.* mattress. ∿ **pneumatique**, air mattress.

matelassé /matlase/ *a.* padded; (*tissu*) quilted.

matelot /matlo/ *n.m.* sailor.

mater /mate/ *v.t.* (*personne*) subdue; (*réprimer*) stifle.

matérialiser (se) /(sə)materjalize/ *v. pr.* materialize.

matérialiste /materjalist/ *a.* materialistic. —*n.m./f.* materialist.

matériaux /materjo/ *n.m. pl.* materials.

matériel, ∿le /materjɛl/ *a.* material. —*n.m.* equipment, materials; (*d'un ordinateur*) hardware.

maternel, ∿le /matɛrnɛl/ *a.* motherly, maternal; (*rapport de parenté*) maternal. —*n.f.* nursery school.

maternité /matɛrnite/ *n.f.* maternity hospital; (*état de mère*) motherhood.

mathémati|que /matematik/ *a.* mathematical. —*n.f. pl.* mathematics. ∿**cien**, ∿**cienne** *n.m., f.* mathematician.

maths /mat/ *n.f. pl.* (*fam.*) maths.

matière /matjɛr/ *n.f.* matter; (*produit*) material; (*sujet*) subject. **en** ∿ **de**, as regards. ∿ **plastique**, plastic. ∿**s grasses**, fat. **à 0% de** ∿**s grasses**, fat free. ∿**s premières**, raw materials.

matin /matɛ̃/ *n.m.* morning. **de bon** ∿, early in the morning.

matin|al (*m. pl.* ∿**aux**) /matinal, -o/ *a.* morning; (*de bonne heure*) early. **être** ∿, be up early.

matinée /matine/ *n.f.* morning; (*spectacle*) matinée.

matou /matu/ *n.m.* tom-cat.

matraqu|e /matrak/ *n.f.* (*de police*) truncheon; (*Amer.*) billy (club). ∿**er** *v.t.* club, beat; (*message*) plug.

matrice /matris/ *n.f.* (*techn.*) matrix.

matrimon|ial (*m. pl.* ∿**iaux**) /matrimɔnjal, jo/ *a.* matrimonial.

maturité /matyrite/ *n.f.* maturity.

maudire† /modir/ *v.t.* curse.

maudit, ∿e /modi, -t/ *a.* (*fam.*) damned.

maugréer /mogree/ *v.i.* grumble.

mausolée /mozole/ *n.m.* mausoleum.

maussade /mosad/ *a.* gloomy.

mauvais, ∿e /movɛ, z/ *a.* bad; (*erroné*) wrong; (*malveillant*) evil; (*désagréable*) nasty, bad; (*mer*) rough. —*n.m.* **il fait** ∿, the weather is bad. **le** ∿ **moment**, the wrong time. ∿**e herbe**, weed. ∿**e langue**, gossip. ∿**e passe**, tight spot. ∿ **traitements**, ill-treatment.

mauve /mov/ *a. & n.m.* mauve.

mauviette /movjɛt/ *n.f.* weakling.

maux /mo/ *voir* **mal**[2].

maxim|al (*m. pl.* ∿**aux**) /maksimal, -o/ *a.* maximum.

maxime /maksim/ *n.f.* maxim.

maximum /maksimɔm/ *a. & n.m.* maximum. **au** ∿, as much as possible; (*tout au plus*) at most.

mayonnaise /majɔnɛz/ *n.f.* mayonnaise.

mazout /mazut/ *n.m.* (fuel) oil.

me, m'* /mə, m/ *pron.* me; (*indirect*) (to) me; (*réfléchi*) myself.

méandre /meɑ̃dr/ *n.m.* meander.

mec /mɛk/ *n.m.* (*fam.*) bloke, guy.

mécanicien /mekanisjɛ̃/ *n.m.* mechanic; (*rail.*) train driver.

mécani|que /mekanik/ *a.* mechanical; (*jouet*) clockwork. **problème** ∿**que**, engine trouble. —*n.f.* mechanics;

(*mécanisme*) mechanism. ∼**ser** *v.t.* mechanize.

mécanisme /mekanism/ *n.m.* mechanism.

méch|ant, ∼ante /meʃɑ̃, -t/ *a.* (*cruel*) wicked; (*désagréable*) nasty; (*enfant*) naughty; (*chien*) vicious; (*sensationnel*: *fam.*) terrific. —*n.m.*, *f.* (*enfant*) naughty child. ∼**amment** *adv.* wickedly. ∼**anceté** *n.f.* wickedness; (*action*) wicked action.

mèche /mɛʃ/ *n.f.* (*de cheveux*) lock; (*de bougie*) wick; (*d'explosif*) fuse. **de ∼ avec,** in league with.

méconnaissable /mekɔnɛsabl/ *a.* unrecognizable.

méconn|aître /mekɔnɛtr/ *v.t.* be ignorant of; (*mésestimer*) underestimate. ∼**aissance** *n.f.* ignorance. ∼**u** *a.* unrecognized.

mécontent, ∼e /mekɔ̃tɑ̃, -t/ *a.* dissatisfied (**de,** with); (*irrité*) annoyed (**de,** at, with). ∼**ement** /-tmɑ̃/ *n.m.* dissatisfaction; annoyance. ∼**er** /-te/ *v.t.* dissatisfy; (*irriter*) annoy.

médaill|e /medaj/ *n.f.* medal; (*insigne*) badge; (*bijou*) medallion. ∼**é, ∼ée** *n.m.*, *f.* medal holder.

médaillon /medajɔ̃/ *n.m.* medallion; (*bijou*) locket.

médecin /mɛdsɛ̃/ *n.m.* doctor.

médecine /mɛdsin/ *n.f.* medicine.

média /medja/ *n.m.* medium. **les ∼s,** the media.

média|teur, ∼trice /medjatœr, -tris/ *n.m.*, *f.* mediator.

médiation /medjɑsjɔ̃/ *n.f.* mediation.

médiatique /medjatik/ *a.* **événement/personnalité ∼,** media event/personality.

médic|al (*m. pl.* ∼**aux**) /medikal, -o/ *a.* medical.

médicament /medikamɑ̃/ *n.m.* medicine.

médicin|al (*m. pl.* ∼**aux**) /medisinal, -o/ *a.* medicinal.

médico-lég|al (*m. pl.* ∼**aux**) /mediko-legal, -o/ *a.* forensic.

médiév|al (*m. pl.* ∼**aux**) /medjeval, -o/ *a.* medieval.

médiocr|e /medjɔkr/ *a.* mediocre, poor. ∼**ement** *adv.* (*peu*) not very; (*mal*) in a mediocre way. ∼**ité** *n.f.* mediocrity.

médire /medir/ *v.i.* ∼ **de,** speak ill of.

médisance /medizɑ̃s/ *n.f.* ∼(**s**), malicious gossip.

méditati|f, ∼ve /meditatif, -v/ *a.* (*pensif*) thoughtful.

médit|er /medite/ *v.t./i.* meditate. ∼**er de,** plan to. ∼**ation** *n.f.* meditation.

Méditerranée /mediterane/ *n.f.* **la ∼,** the Mediterranean.

méditerranéen, ∼ne /mediteraneɛ̃, -ɛn/ *a.* Mediterranean.

médium /medjɔm/ *n.m.* (*personne*) medium.

méduse /medyz/ *n.f.* jellyfish.

meeting /mitiŋ/ *n.m.* meeting.

méfait /mefɛ/ *n.m.* misdeed. **les ∼s de,** (*conséquences*) the ravages of.

méfian|t, ∼te /mefjɑ̃, -t/ *a.* distrustful. ∼**ce** *n.f.* distrust.

méfier (se) /(sə)mefje/ *v. pr.* be wary *ou* careful. **se ∼ de,** distrust, be wary of.

mégarde (par) /(par)megard/ *adv.* by accident, accidentally.

mégère /meʒɛr/ *n.f.* (*femme*) shrew.

mégot /mego/ *n.m.* (*fam.*) cigarette-end.

meilleur, ∼e /mejœr/ *a.* & *adv.* better (**que,** than). **le ∼ livre**/*etc.,* the best book/*etc.* **mon ∼ ami**/*etc.,* my best friend/*etc.* ∼ **marché,** cheaper. —*n.m.*, *f.* **le ∼/la ∼e,** the best (one).

mélancol|ie /melɑ̃kɔli/ *n.f.* melancholy. ∼**ique** *a.* melancholy.

mélang|e /melɑ̃ʒ/ *n.m.* mixture, blend. ∼**er** *v.t.*, **se ∼er** *v. pr.* mix, blend; (*embrouiller*) mix up.

mélasse /melas/ *n.f.* treacle; (*Amer.*) molasses.

mêlée /mele/ *n.f.* scuffle; (*rugby*) scrum.

mêler /mele/ *v.t.* mix (**à,** with); (*qualités*) combine; (*embrouiller*) mix up. ∼ **à,** (*impliquer dans*) involve in. **se ∼** *v. pr.* mix; combine. **se ∼ à,** (*se joindre à*) join. **se ∼ de,** meddle in. **mêle-toi de ce qui te regarde,** mind your own business.

méli-mélo /melimelo/ *n.m.* (*pl.* **mélis-mélos**) jumble.

mélo /melo/ (*fam.*) *n.m.* melodrama. —*a. invar.* melodramatic.

mélod|ie /melɔdi/ *n.f.* melody. ∼**ieux, ∼ieuse** *a.* melodious. ∼**ique** *a.* melodic.

mélodram|e /melɔdram/ *n.m.* melodrama. ∼**atique** *a.* melodramatic.

mélomane /melɔman/ *n.m.*/*f.* music lover.

melon /mlɔ̃/ *n.m.* melon. (**chapeau**) ∼, bowler (hat).

membrane /mɑ̃bran/ *n.f.* membrane.

membre[1] /mɑ̃br/ *n.m.* limb.

membre[2] /mɑ̃br/ *n.m.* (*adhérent*) member.

même /mɛm/ *a.* same. **ce livre**/*etc.* ∼, this very book/*etc.* **la bonté**/*etc.* ∼, kindness/*etc.* itself. —*pron.* **le ∼/la ∼,** the same (one). —*adv.* even. **à ∼,** (*sur*)

directly on. **à ~ de,** in a position to. **de
~,** (*aussi*) too; (*de la même façon*)
likewise. **de ~ que,** just as. **en ~
temps,** at the same time.
mémé /meme/ *n.f.* (*fam.*) granny.
mémo /memo/ *n.m.* memo.
mémoire /memwar/ *n.f.* memory.
—*n.m.* (*requête*) memorandum; (*univ.*)
dissertation. **~s,** (*souvenirs écrits*)
memoirs. **à la ~ de,** to the memory of.
de ~, from memory. **~ morte/vive,**
(*comput.*) ROM/RAM.
mémorable /memɔrabl/ *a.* memorable.
mémorandum /memɔrɑ̃dɔm/ *n.m.*
memorandum.
menac|e /mənas/ *n.f.* threat. **~er** *v.t.*
threaten (**de faire,** to do).
ménage /menaʒ/ *n.m.* (married) couple;
(*travail*) housework. **se mettre en ~,**
set up house. **scène de ~,** scene.
dépenses du ~, household expenditure.
ménagement /menaʒmɑ̃/ *n.m.* care and
consideration.
ménag|er[1], **~ère** /menaʒe, -ɛr/ *a.*
household, domestic. **travaux ~ers,**
housework. —*n.f.* housewife.
ménag|er[2] /menaʒe/ *v.t.* treat with tact;
(*utiliser*) be sparing in the use of;
(*organiser*) prepare (carefully).
ménagerie /menaʒri/ *n.f.* menagerie.
mendiant, ~e /mɑ̃djɑ̃, -t/ *n.m., f.*
beggar.
mendicité /mɑ̃disite/ *n.f.* begging.
mendier /mɑ̃dje/ *v.t.* beg for. —*v.i.* beg.
menées /məne/ *n.f. pl.* schemings.
mener /məne/ *v.t.* lead; (*entreprise,
pays*) run. —*v.i.* lead. **~ à,**
(*accompagner à*) take to. **~ à bien,** see
through.
meneur /mənœr/ *n.m.* (*chef*)
(ring)leader. **~ de jeu,** compère;
(*Amer.*) master of ceremonies.
méningite /menɛ̃ʒit/ *n.f.* meningitis.
ménopause /menɔpoz/ *n.f.* menopause.
menotte /mənɔt/ *n.f.* (*fam.*) hand. **~s,**
handcuffs.
mensong|e /mɑ̃sɔ̃ʒ/ *n.m.* lie; (*action*)
lying. **~er, ~ère** *a.* untrue.
menstruation /mɑ̃stryasjɔ̃/ *n.f.* menstruation.
mensualité /mɑ̃sɥalite/ *n.f.* monthly
payment.
mensuel, ~le /mɑ̃sɥɛl/ *a. & n.m.*
monthly. **~lement** *adv.* monthly.
mensurations /mɑ̃syrasjɔ̃/ *n.f. pl.*
measurements.
ment|al (*m. pl.* **~aux**) /mɑ̃tal, -o/ *a.*
mental.

mentalité /mɑ̃talite/ *n.f.* mentality.
menteu|r, ~se /mɑ̃tœr, -øz/ *n.m., f.*
liar. —*a.* untruthful.
menthe /mɑ̃t/ *n.f.* mint.
mention /mɑ̃sjɔ̃/ *n.f.* mention;
(*annotation*) note; (*scol.*) grade. **~
bien,** (*scol.*) distinction. **~ner** /-jɔne/
v.t. mention.
mentir† /mɑ̃tir/ *v.i.* lie.
menton /mɑ̃tɔ̃/ *n.m.* chin.
mentor /mɛ̃tɔr/ *n.m.* mentor.
menu[1] /məny/ *n.m.* (*carte*) menu;
(*repas*) meal.
menu[2] /məny/ *a.* (*petit*) tiny; (*fin*) fine;
(*insignifiant*) minor. —*adv.* (*couper*)
fine.
menuis|ier /mənɥizje/ *n.m.* carpenter,
joiner. **~erie** *n.f.* carpentry, joinery.
méprendre (se) /(sə)meprɑ̃dr/ *v. pr.* **se
~ sur,** be mistaken about.
mépris /mepri/ *n.m.* contempt, scorn
(**de,** for). **au ~ de,** in defiance of.
méprisable /meprizabl/ *a.* despicable.
méprise /mepriz/ *n.f.* mistake.
mépris|er /meprize/ *v.t.* scorn, despise.
~ant, ~ante *a.* scornful.
mer /mɛr/ *n.f.* sea; (*marée*) tide. **en
haute ~,** on the open sea.
mercenaire /mɛrsənɛr/ *n.m. & a.*
mercenary.
merci /mɛrsi/ *int.* thank you, thanks (**de,
pour,** for). —*n.f.* mercy. **~ beaucoup,
~ bien,** thank you very much.
merc|ier, ~ière /mɛrsje, -jɛr/ *n.m., f.*
haberdasher; (*Amer.*) notions merchant.
~erie *n.f.* haberdashery; (*Amer.*)
notions store.
mercredi /mɛrkrədi/ *n.m.* Wednesday.
~ des Cendres, Ash Wednesday.
mercure /mɛrkyr/ *n.m.* mercury.
merde /mɛrd/ *n.f.* (*fam.*) shit. **être dans
la ~,** be in a mess.
mère /mɛr/ *n.f.* mother. **~ de famille,**
mother.
méridien /meridjɛ̃/ *n.m.* meridian.
méridion|al, ~ale (*m. pl.* **~aux**)
/meridjɔnal, -o/ *a.* southern. —*n.m.,
f.* southerner.
meringue /mərɛ̃g/ *n.f.* meringue.
mérite /merit/ *n.m.* merit. **il n'a aucun
~,** that's as it should be. **il a du ~,** it's
very much to his credit.
mérit|er /merite/ *v.t.* deserve. **~ant,
~ante** *a.* deserving.
méritoire /meritwar/ *a.* commend-
able.
merlan /mɛrlɑ̃/ *n.m.* whiting.
merle /mɛrl/ *n.m.* blackbird.
merveille /mɛrvɛj/ *n.f.* wonder, marvel.

à ~, wonderfully. **faire des ~s,** work wonders.

merveilleu|x, ~se /mɛrvɛjø, -z/ *a.* wonderful, marvellous. **~sement** *adv.* wonderfully.

mes /me/ *voir* **mon**.

mésange /mezɑ̃ʒ/ *n.f.* tit(mouse).

mésaventure /mezavɑ̃tyr/ *n.f.* misadventure.

mesdames /medam/ *voir* **madame**.

mesdemoiselles /medmwazɛl/ *voir* **mademoiselle**.

mésentente /mezɑ̃tɑ̃t/ *n.f.* disagreement.

mesquin, ~e /mɛskɛ̃, -in/ *a.* mean. ~**erie** /-inri/ *n.f.* meanness.

mess /mɛs/ *n.m.* (*mil.*) mess.

messag|e /mesaʒ/ *n.m.* message. ~**er,** ~**ère** *n.m., f.* messenger.

messe /mɛs/ *n.f.* (*relig.*) mass.

Messie /mesi/ *n.m.* Messiah.

messieurs /mesjø/ *voir* **monsieur**.

mesure /məzyr/ *n.f.* measurement; (*quantité, étalon*) measure; (*disposition*) measure, step; (*cadence*) time; (*modération*) moderation. **à ~ que,** as. **dans la ~ où,** in so far as. **dans une certaine ~,** to some extent. **en ~ de,** in a position to.

mesuré /məzyre/ *a.* measured; (*personne*) moderate.

mesurer /məzyre/ *v.t.* measure; (*juger*) assess; (*argent, temps*) ration. **se ~ avec,** pit o.s. against.

met /mɛ/ *voir* **mettre**.

métabolisme /metabɔlism/ *n.m.* metabolism.

mét|al (*pl.* ~**aux**) /metal, -o/ *n.m.* metal. ~**allique** *a.* (*objet*) metal; (*éclat etc.*) metallic.

métallurg|ie /metalyrʒi/ *n.f.* (*industrie*) steel *ou* metal industry. ~**iste** *n.m.* steel *ou* metal worker.

métamorphos|e /metamɔrfoz/ *n.f.* metamorphosis. ~**er** *v.t.,* **se** ~**er** *v. pr.* transform.

métaphor|e /metafɔr/ *n.f.* metaphor. ~**ique** *a.* metaphorical.

météo /meteo/ *n.f.* (*bulletin*) weather forecast.

météore /meteɔr/ *n.m.* meteor.

météorolog|ie /meteɔrɔlɔʒi/ *n.f.* meteorology; (*service*) weather bureau. ~**ique** *a.* weather; (*études etc.*) meteorological.

méthod|e /metɔd/ *n.f.* method; (*ouvrage*) course, manual. ~**ique** *a.* methodical.

méticuleu|x, ~**se** /metikylø, -z/ *a.* meticulous.

métier /metje/ *n.m.* job; (*manuel*) trade; (*intellectuel*) profession; (*expérience*) skill. ~ **(à tisser),** loom. **remettre sur le ~,** keep going back to the drawing-board.

métis, ~**se** /metis/ *a. & n.m., f.* half-caste.

métrage /metraʒ/ *n.m.* length. **court ~,** short film. **long ~,** full-length film.

mètre /mɛtr/ *n.m.* metre; (*règle*) rule. ~ **ruban,** tape-measure.

métreur /metrœr/ *n.m.* quantity surveyor.

métrique /metrik/ *a.* metric.

métro /metro/ *n.m.* underground; (*à Paris*) Métro.

métropol|e /metrɔpɔl/ *n.f.* metropolis; (*pays*) mother country. ~**itain,** ~**itaine** *a.* metropolitan.

mets[1] /mɛ/ *n.m.* dish.

mets[2] /mɛ/ *voir* **mettre**.

mettable /mɛtabl/ *a.* wearable.

metteur /mɛtœr/ *n.m.* ~ **en scène,** (*théâtre*) producer; (*cinéma*) director.

mettre† /mɛtr/ *v.t.* put; (*vêtement*) put on; (*radio, chauffage, etc.*) put *ou* switch on; (*table*) lay; (*pendule*) set; (*temps*) take; (*installer*) put in; (*supposer*) suppose. **se ~** *v. pr.* put o.s.; (*objet*) go; (*porter*) wear. ~ **bas,** give birth. ~ **qn. en boîte,** pull s.o.'s leg. ~ **en cause** *ou* **en question,** question. ~ **en colère,** make angry. ~ **en valeur,** highlight. (*un bien*) exploit. **se ~ à,** (*entrer dans*) get *ou* go into. **se ~ à faire,** start doing. **se ~ à l'aise,** make o.s. comfortable. **se ~ à table,** sit down at the table. **se ~ au travail,** set to work. **(se) ~ en ligne,** line up. **se ~ dans tous ses états,** get into a state. **se ~ du sable dans les yeux,** get sand in one's eyes.

meuble /mœbl/ *n.m.* piece of furniture. ~**s,** furniture.

meublé /møble/ *n.m.* furnished flatlet.

meubler /møble/ *v.t.* furnish; (*fig.*) fill. **se ~** *v. pr.* buy furniture.

meugl|er /møgle/ *v.i.* moo. ~**ement(s)** *n.m.* (*pl.*) mooing.

meule /møl/ *n.f.* (*de foin*) haystack; (*à moudre*) millstone.

meun|ier, ~**ière** /mønje, -jɛr/ *n.m., f.* miller.

meurs, meurt /mœr/ *voir* **mourir**.

meurtr|e /mœrtr/ *n.m.* murder. ~**ier,** ~**ière** *a.* deadly; *n.m.* murderer; *n.f.* murderess.

meurtr|ir /mœrtrir/ *v.t.* bruise. ~**issure** *n.f.* bruise.

meute /møt/ *n.f.* (*troupe*) pack.

mexicain, ∼e /mɛksikɛ̃, -ɛn/ *a. & n.m., f.* Mexican.

Mexique /mɛksik/ *n.m.* Mexico.

mi- /mi/ *préf.* mid-, half-. **à mi-chemin,** half-way. **à mi-côte,** half-way up the hill. **la mi-juin**/*etc.*, mid-June/*etc.*

miaou /mjau/ *n.m.* mew.

miaul|er /mjole/ *v.i.* mew. ∼**ement** *n.m.* mew.

miche /miʃ/ *n.f.* round loaf.

micro /mikro/ *n.m.* microphone, mike; (*comput.*) micro.

micro- /mikro/ *préf.* micro-.

microbe /mikrɔb/ *n.m.* germ.

microfilm /mikrɔfilm/ *n.m.* microfilm.

micro-onde /mikrɔɔd/ *n.f.* microwave. **un (four à)** ∼**s,** microwave (oven).

microphone /mikrɔfɔn/ *n.m.* microphone.

microplaquette /mikrɔplakɛt/ *n.f.* (micro)chip.

microprocesseur /mikrɔprɔsɛsœr/ *n.m.* microprocess.

microscop|e /mikrɔskɔp/ *n.m.* microscope. ∼**ique** *a.* microscopic.

microsillon /mikrɔsijɔ̃/ *n.m.* longplaying record.

midi /midi/ *n.m.* twelve o'clock, midday; noon; (*déjeuner*) lunch-time; (*sud*) south. **le M∼,** the South of France.

mie /mi/ *n.f.* soft part (of the loaf). **un pain de** ∼, a sandwich loaf.

miel /mjɛl/ *n.m.* honey.

mielleu|x, ∼se /mjɛlø, -z/ *a.* unctuous.

mien, ∼ne /mjɛ̃, mjɛn/ *pron.* **le** ∼, **la** ∼**ne, les** ∼**(ne)s,** mine.

miette /mjɛt/ *n.f.* crumb; (*fig.*) scrap. **en** ∼**s,** in pieces.

mieux /mjø/ *adv. & a. invar.* better (**que,** than). **le** *ou* **la** *ou* **les** ∼, (the) best. —*n.m.* best; (*progrès*) improvement. **faire de son** ∼, do one's best. **tu ferais** ∼ **de faire,** you would be better off doing. **le** ∼ **serait de,** the best thing would be to.

mièvre /mjɛvr/ *a.* genteel and insipid.

mignon, ∼ne /miɲɔ̃, -ɔn/ *a.* pretty.

migraine /migrɛn/ *n.f.* headache.

migration /migrasjɔ̃/ *n.f.* migration.

mijoter /miʒɔte/ *v.t./i.* simmer; (*tramer*: *fam.*) cook up.

mil /mil/ *n.m.* a thousand.

milic|e /milis/ *n.f.* militia. ∼**ien** *n.m.* militiaman.

milieu (*pl.* ∼**x**) /miljø/ *n.m.* middle; (*environnement*) environment; (*groupe*) circle; (*voie*) middle way; (*criminel*) underworld. **au** ∼ **de,** in the middle of.

en plein *ou* **au beau** ∼ **de,** right in the middle (of).

militaire /militɛr/ *a.* military. —*n.m.* soldier.

milit|er /milite/ *v.i.* be a militant. ∼**er pour,** militate in favour of. ∼**ant,** ∼**ante** *n.m., f.* militant.

milk-shake /milkʃɛk/ *n.m.* milk shake.

mille[1] /mil/ *a. & n.m. invar.* a thousand. **deux** ∼, two thousand. **dans le** ∼, bang on target.

mille[2] /mil/ *n.m.* ∼ **(marin),** (nautical) mile.

millénaire /milenɛr/ *n.m.* millennium.

mille-pattes /milpat/ *n.m. invar.* centipede.

millésime /milezim/ *n.m.* year.

millésimé /milezime/ *a.* **vin** ∼, vintage wine.

millet /mijɛ/ *n.m.* millet.

milliard /miljar/ *n.m.* thousand million, billion. ∼**aire** /-dɛr/ *n.m./f.* multimillionaire.

millier /milje/ *n.m.* thousand. **un** ∼ **(de),** about a thousand.

millimètre /milimɛtr/ *n.m.* millimetre.

million /miljɔ̃/ *n.m.* million. **deux** ∼**s (de),** two million. ∼**naire** /-jɔnɛr/ *n.m./f.* millionaire.

mim|e /mim/ *n.m./f.* (*personne*) mime. —*n.m.* (*art*) mime. ∼**er** *v.t.* mime; (*singer*) mimic.

mimique /mimik/ *n.f.* (expressive) gestures.

mimosa /mimoza/ *n.m.* mimosa.

minable /minabl/ *a.* shabby.

minaret /minarɛ/ *n.m.* minaret.

minauder /minode/ *v.i.* simper.

minc|e /mɛ̃s/ *a.* thin; (*svelte, insignifiant*) slim. *int.* dash (it). ∼**ir** *v.i.* get slimmer. **ça te** ∼**it,** it makes you look slimmer. ∼**eur** *n.f.* thinness; slimness.

mine[1] /min/ *n.f.* expression; (*allure*) appearance. **avoir bonne** ∼, look well. **faire** ∼ **de,** make as if to.

mine[2] /min/ *n.f.* (*exploitation, explosif*) mine; (*de crayon*) lead. ∼ **de charbon,** coal-mine.

miner /mine/ *v.t.* (*saper*) undermine; (*garnir d'explosifs*) mine. **minerai** /minrɛ/ *n.m.* ore.

minér|al (*m. pl.* ∼**aux**) /mineral, -o/ *a.* mineral. —*n.m.* (*pl.* ∼**aux**) mineral.

minéralogique /mineralɔʒik/ *a.* **plaque** ∼, number/license (*Amer.*) plate.

minet, ∼te /minɛ, -t/ *n.m., f.* (*chat*: *fam.*) puss(y).

mineur[1], **~e** /minœr/ a. minor; (*jurid.*) under age. —*n.m.*, *f.* (*jurid.*) minor.

mineur[2] /minœr/ *n.m.* (*ouvrier*) miner.

mini- /mini/ *préf.* mini-.

miniature /minjatyr/ *n.f.* & *a.* miniature.

minibus /minibys/ *n.m.* minibus.

min|ier, **~ière** /minje, -jɛr/ a. mining.

minim|al (*m. pl.* **~aux**) /minimal, -o/ a. minimum.

minime /minim/ a. minor. —*n.m./f.* (*sport*) junior.

minimiser /minimize/ *v.t.* minimize.

minimum /minimɔm/ a. & *n.m.* minimum. **au ~**, (*pour le moins*) at the very least.

mini-ordinateur /miniɔrdinatœr/ *n.m.* minicomputer.

minist|ère /ministɛr/ *n.m.* ministry; (*gouvernement*) government. **~ère de l'Intérieur,** Home Office; (*Amer.*) Department of the Interior. **~ériel,** **~érielle** a. ministerial, government.

ministre /ministr/ *n.m.* minister. **~ de l'Intérieur,** Home Secretary; (*Amer.*) Secretary of the Interior.

Minitel /minitɛl/ *n.m.* (P.) Minitel (*telephone videotext system*).

minorer /minɔre/ *v.t.* reduce.

minorit|é /minɔrite/ *n.f.* minority. **~aire** a. minority. **être ~aire,** be in the minority.

minuit /minɥi/ *n.m.* midnight.

minuscule /minyskyl/ a. minute. —*n.f.* (*lettre*) **~**, small letter.

minut|e /minyt/ *n.f.* minute. **~er** *v.t.* time (to the minute).

minuterie /minytri/ *n.f.* time-switch.

minutie /minysi/ *n.f.* meticulousness.

minutieu|x, **~se** /minysjø, -z/ a. meticulous. **~sement** adv. meticulously.

mioche /mjɔʃ/ *n.m.*, *f.* (*fam.*) youngster, kid.

mirabelle /mirabɛl/ *n.f.* (mirabelle) plum.

miracle /mirɑkl/ *n.m.* miracle.

miraculeu|x, **~se** /mirakylø, -z/ a. miraculous. **~sement** adv. miraculously.

mirage /miraʒ/ *n.m.* mirage.

mire /mir/ *n.f.* (*fig.*) centre of attraction; (TV) test card.

miro /miro/ a. invar. (*fam.*) short-sighted.

mirobolant, ~e /mirɔbɔlɑ̃, -t/ a. (*fam.*) marvellous.

miroir /mirwar/ *n.m.* mirror.

miroiter /mirwate/ *v.i.* gleam, shimmer.

mis, ~e[1] /mi, miz/ *voir* **mettre.** —*a.* **bien ~,** well-dressed.

misanthrope /mizɑ̃trɔp/ *n.m.* misanthropist. —*a.* misanthropic.

mise[2] /miz/ *n.f.* (*argent*) stake; (*tenue*) attire. **~ à feu,** blast-off. **~ au point,** adjustment; (*fig.*) clarification. **~ de fonds,** capital outlay. **~ en garde,** warning. **~ en scène,** (*théâtre*) production; (*cinéma*) direction.

miser /mize/ *v.t.* (*argent*) bet, stake (**sur,** on). **~ sur,** (*compter sur*: *fam.*) bank on.

misérable /mizerabl/ a. miserable, wretched; (*indigent*) poverty-stricken; (*minable*) seedy. —*n.m./f.* wretch.

mis|ère /mizɛr/ *n.f.* (grinding) poverty; (*malheur*) misery. **~éreux, ~éreuse** *n.m.*, *f.* pauper.

miséricorde /mizerikɔrd/ *n.f.* mercy.

missel /misɛl/ *n.m.* missal.

missile /misil/ *n.m.* missile.

mission /misjɔ̃/ *n.m.* mission. **~naire** /-jɔnɛr/ *n.m./f.* missionary.

missive /misiv/ *n.f.* missive.

mistral /mistral/ *n.m.* invar. (*vent*) mistral.

mitaine /mitɛn/ *n.f.* mitten.

mit|e /mit/ *n.f.* (clothes-)moth. **~é** a. moth-eaten.

mi-temps /mitɑ̃/ *n.f.* invar. (*repos*: *sport*) half-time; (*période*: *sport*) half. **à ~,** part time.

miteu|x, ~se /mitø, -z/ a. shabby.

mitigé /mitiʒe/ a. (*modéré*) lukewarm.

mitonner /mitɔne/ *v.t.* cook slowly with care; (*fig.*) cook up.

mitoyen, ~ne /mitwajɛ̃, -ɛn/ a. **mur ~,** party wall.

mitrailler /mitraje/ *v.t.* machine-gun; (*fig.*) bombard.

mitraill|ette /mitrajɛt/ *n.f.* sub-machine-gun. **~euse** *n.f.* machine-gun.

mi-voix (à) /(a)mivwa/ adv. in an undertone.

mixeur /miksœr/ *n.m.* liquidizer, blender.

mixte /mikst/ a. mixed; (*usage*) dual; (*tribunal*) joint; (*école*) co-educational.

mixture /mikstyr/ *n.f.* (*péj.*) mixture.

mobile[1] /mɔbil/ a. mobile; (*pièce*) moving; (*feuillet*) loose. —*n.m.* (*art*) mobile.

mobile[2] /mɔbil/ *n.m.* (*raison*) motive.

mobilier /mɔbilje/ *n.m.* furniture.

mobilis|er /mɔbilize/ *v.t.* mobilize. **~ation** *n.f.* mobilization.

mobilité /mɔbilite/ *n.f.* mobility.

mobylette /mɔbilɛt/ *n.f.* (P.) moped.

mocassin /mɔkasɛ̃/ *n.m.* moccasin.

moche /mɔʃ/ *a.* (*laid*: *fam.*) ugly; (*mauvais*: *fam.*) lousy.

modalité /mɔdalite/ *n.f.* mode.

mode[1] /mɔd/ *n.f.* fashion; (*coutume*) custom. **à la ∼,** fashionable.

mode[2] /mɔd/ *n.m.* method, mode; (*genre*) way. **∼ d'emploi,** directions (for use).

modèle /mɔdɛl/ *n.m. & a.* model. **∼ réduit,** (small-scale) model.

modeler /mɔdle/ *v.t.* model (**sur,** on). **se ∼ sur,** model o.s. on.

modem /mɔdɛm/ *n.m.* modem.

modéré, ∼e /mɔdere/ *a. & n.m.,* f. moderate. **∼ment** *adv.* moderately.

modér|**er** /mɔdere/ *v.t.* moderate. **se ∼er** *v. pr.* restrain o.s. **∼ateur, ∼atrice** *a.* moderating. **∼ation** *n.f.* moderation.

modern|**e** /mɔdɛrn/ *a.* modern. —*n.m.* modern style. **∼iser** *v.t.* modernize.

modest|**e** /mɔdɛst/ *a.* modest. **∼ement** *adv.* modestly. **∼ie** *n.f.* modesty.

modif|**ier** /mɔdifje/ *v.t.* modify. **se ∼ier** *v. pr.* alter. **∼ication** *n.f.* modification.

modique /mɔdik/ *a.* low.

modiste /mɔdist/ *n.f.* milliner.

module /mɔdyl/ *n.m.* module.

modul|**er** /mɔdyle/ *v.t./i.* modulate. **∼ation** *n.f.* modulation.

moelle /mwal/ *n.f.* marrow. **∼ épinière,** spinal cord.

moelleu|**x, ∼se** /mwalø, ɛ/ *a.* soft; (*onctueux*) smooth.

mœurs /mœr(s)/ *n.f. pl.* (*morale*) morals; (*habitudes*) customs; (*manières*) ways.

moi /mwa/ *pron.* me; (*indirect*) (to) me; (*sujet*) I. —*n.m.* self. **∼-même** *pron.* myself.

moignon /mwaɲɔ̃/ *n.m.* stump.

moindre /mwɛ̃dr/ *a.* (*moins grand*) less(er). **le** *ou* **la ∼, les ∼s,** the slightest, the least.

moine /mwan/ *n.m.* monk.

moineau (*pl.* **∼x**) /mwano/ *n.m.* sparrow.

moins /mwɛ̃/ *adv.* less (**que,** than). —*prép.* (*soustraction*) minus. **∼ de,** (*quantité*) less, not so much (**que,** as); (*objets, personnes*) fewer, not so many (**que,** as). **∼ de dix francs/d'une livre/***etc.,* less than ten francs/one pound/*etc.* **le** *ou* **la** *ou* **les ∼,** the least. **le ∼ grand/haut,** the smallest/lowest. **au ∼, du ∼,** at least. **de ∼,** less. **en ∼,** less; (*manquant*) missing. **une heure ∼ dix,** ten to one. **à ∼ que,** unless. **de ∼ en moins,** less and less.

mois /mwa/ *n.m.* month.

moïse /mɔiz/ *n.m.* Moses basket.

mois|**i** /mwazi/ *a.* mouldy. —*n.m.* mould. **de ∼i,** (*odeur, goût*) musty. **∼ir** *v.i.* go mouldy. **∼issure** *n.f.* mould.

moisson /mwasɔ̃/ *n.f.* harvest.

moissonn|**er** /mwasɔne/ *v.t.* harvest, reap. **∼eur, ∼euse** *n.m.,* f. harvester. **∼euse-batteuse** (*pl.* **∼euses-batteuses**) *n.f.* combine harvester.

moit|**e** /mwat/ *a.* sticky, clammy. **∼eur** *n.f.* stickiness.

moitié /mwatje/ *n.f.* half; (*milieu*) half-way mark. **à ∼,** half way. **à ∼ vide/fermé/***etc.,* half empty/ closed/*etc.* **à ∼ prix,** (at) half-price. **la ∼ de,** half (of). **∼ moitié,** half-and-half.

moka /mɔka/ *n.m.* (*gâteau*) coffee cream cake.

mol /mɔl/ *voir* **mou.**

molaire /mɔlɛr/ *n.f.* molar.

molécule /mɔlekyl/ *n.f.* molecule.

molester /mɔlɛste/ *v.t.* manhandle, rough up.

molle /mɔl/ *voir* **mou.**

moll|**ement** /mɔlmɑ̃/ *adv.* softly; (*faiblement*) feebly. **∼esse** *n.f.* softness; (*faiblesse, indolence*) feebleness.

mollet /mɔlɛ/ *n.m.* (*de jambe*) calf.

molletonné /mɔltɔne/ *a.* (fleece-)lined.

mollir /mɔlir/ *v.i.* soften; (*céder*) yield.

mollusque /mɔlysk/ *n.m.* mollusc.

môme /mom/ *n.m./f.* (*fam.*) kid.

moment /mɔmɑ̃/ *n.m.* moment; (*période*) time. (**petit**) **∼,** short while. **au ∼ où,** when. **par ∼s,** now and then. **du ∼ où** *ou* **que,** seeing that. **en ce ∼,** at the moment.

momentané /mɔmɑ̃tane/ *a.* momentary. **∼ment** *adv.* momentarily; (*en ce moment*) at present.

momie /mɔmi/ *n.f.* mummy.

mon, ma *ou* **mon*** (*pl.* **mes**) /mɔ̃, ma, mɔ̃, me/ *a.* my.

Monaco /mɔnako/ *n.f.* Monaco.

monarchie /mɔnarʃi/ *n.f.* monarchy.

monarque /mɔnark/ *n.m.* monarch.

monastère /mɔnastɛr/ *n.m.* monastery.

monceau (*pl.* **∼x**) /mɔ̃so/ *n.m.* heap, pile.

mondain, ∼e /mɔ̃dɛ̃, -ɛn/ *a.* society, social.

monde /mɔ̃d/ *n.m.* world. **du ∼,** (a lot of) people; (*quelqu'un*) somebody. **le (grand) ∼,** (high) society. **se faire un ∼ de qch.,** make a great deal of fuss about sth.

mond|**ial** (*m. pl.* **∼iaux**) /mɔ̃djal, -jo/

a. world; (*influence*) worldwide. ～**ialement** *adv.* the world over.

monégasque /mɔnegask/ *a. & n.m./f.* Monegasque.

monétaire /mɔnetɛr/ *a.* monetary.

moni|teur, ～**trice** /mɔnitœr, -tris/ *n.m., f.* instructor, instructress; (*de colonie de vacances*) supervisor; (*Amer.*) (camp) counselor.

monnaie /mɔnɛ/ *n.f.* currency; (*pièce*) coin; (*appoint*) change. **faire la** ～ **de,** get change for. **faire à qn. la** ～ **de,** give s.o. change for. **menue** *ou* **petite** ～, small change.

monnayer /mɔneje/ *v.t.* convert into cash.

mono /mɔno/ *a. invar.* mono.

monocle /mɔnɔkl/ *n.m.* monocle.

monocorde /mɔnɔkɔrd/ *a.* monotonous.

monogramme /mɔnɔgram/ *n.m.* monogram.

monologue /mɔnɔlɔg/ *n.m.* monologue.

monopol|e /mɔnɔpɔl/ *n.m.* monopoly. ～**iser** *v.t.* monopolize.

monosyllabe /mɔnɔsilab/ *n.m.* monosyllable.

monoton|e /mɔnɔtɔn/ *a.* monotonous. ～**ie** *n.f.* monotony.

monseigneur /mɔ̃sɛɲœr/ *n.m.* Your *ou* His Grace.

monsieur (*pl.* **messieurs**) /məsjø, mesjø/ *n.m.* gentleman. **M**～ *ou* **M. Dupont,** Mr Dupont. **Messieurs** *ou* **MM. Dupont,** Messrs Dupont. **oui** ～, yes; (*avec déférence*) yes, sir.

monstre /mɔ̃str/ *n.m.* monster. —*a.* (*fam.*) colossal.

monstr|ueux, ～**ueuse** /mɔ̃stryø, -z/ *a.* monstrous. ～**uosité** *n.f.* monstrosity.

mont /mɔ̃/ *n.m.* mount. **par** ～**s et par vaux,** up hill and down dale.

montage /mɔ̃taʒ/ *n.m.* (*assemblage*) assembly; (*cinéma*) editing.

montagn|e /mɔ̃taɲ/ *n.f.* mountain; (*région*) mountains. ～**es russes,** roller-coaster. ～**ard,** ～**arde** *n.m., f.* mountain dweller. ～**eux,** ～**euse** *a.* mountainous.

montant[1], ～**e** /mɔ̃tɑ̃, -t/ *a.* rising; (*col*) high-necked.

montant[2] /mɔ̃tɑ̃/ *n.m.* amount; (*pièce de bois*) upright.

mont-de-piété (*pl.* **monts-de-piété**) /mɔ̃dpjete/ *n.m.* pawnshop.

monte-charge /mɔ̃tʃarʒ/ *n.m. invar.* service lift; (*Amer.*) dumb waiter.

montée /mɔ̃te/ *n.f.* ascent, climb; (*de prix*) rise; (*côte*) hill. **au milieu de la** ～, halfway up. **à la** ～ **de lait,** when the milk comes.

monter /mɔ̃te/ *v.i.* (*aux. être*) go *ou* come up; (*grimper*) climb; (*prix, mer*) rise. ～ **à,** (*cheval*) mount. ～ **dans,** (*train, avion*) get on to; (*voiture*) get into. ～ **sur,** (*colline*) climb up; (*trône*) ascend. —*v.t.* (*aux. avoir*) go *ou* come up; (*objet*) take *ou* bring up; (*cheval, garde*) mount; (*société*) start up. ～ **à cheval,** (*sport*) ride. ～ **en flèche,** soar. ～ **en graine,** go to seed.

monteu|r, ～**se** /mɔ̃tœr, -øz/ *n.m., f.* (*techn.*) fitter; (*cinéma*) editor.

monticule /mɔ̃tikyl/ *n.m.* mound.

montre /mɔ̃tr/ *n.f.* watch. ～**-bracelet** (*pl.* ～**s-bracelets**) *n.f.* wrist-watch. **faire** ～ **de,** show.

montrer /mɔ̃tre/ *v.t.* show (**à,** to). **se** ～ *v. pr.* show o.s.; (*être*) be; (*s'avérer*) prove to be. ～ **du doigt,** point to.

monture /mɔ̃tyr/ *n.f.* (*cheval*) mount; (*de lunettes*) frame; (*de bijou*) setting.

monument /mɔnymɑ̃/ *n.m.* monument. ～ **aux morts,** war memorial. ～**al** (*m. pl.* ～**aux**) /-tal, -to/ *a.* monumental.

moqu|er (se) /(sə)mɔke/ *v. pr.* **se** ～**er de,** make fun of. **je m'en** ～**e,** (*fam.*) I couldn't care less. ～**erie** *n.f.* mockery. ～**eur,** ～**euse** *a.* mocking.

moquette /mɔkɛt/ *n.f.* fitted carpet; (*Amer.*) wall-to-wall carpeting.

mor|al, ～**ale** (*m. pl.* ～**aux**) /mɔral, -o/ *a.* moral. —*n.m.* (*pl.* ～**aux**) morale. —*n.f.* moral code; (*mœurs*) morals; (*de fable*) moral. **avoir le** ～**al,** be on form. **ça m'a remonté le** ～**al,** it gave me a boost. **faire la** ～**ale à,** lecture. ～**alement** *adv.* morally. ～**alité** *n.f.* morality; (*de fable*) moral.

moralisa|teur, ～**trice** /mɔralizatœr, -tris/ *a.* moralizing.

morbide /mɔrbid/ *a.* morbid.

morceau (*pl.* ～**x**) /mɔrso/ *n.m.* piece, bit; (*de sucre*) lump; (*de viande*) cut; (*passage*) passage. **manger un** ～, have a bite to eat. **mettre en** ～**x,** smash *ou* tear *etc.* to bits.

morceler /mɔrsəle/ *v.t.* fragment.

mordant, ～**e** /mɔrdɑ̃, -t/ *a.* scathing; (*froid*) biting. —*n.m.* (*énergie*) vigour, punch.

mordiller /mɔrdije/ *v.t.* nibble at.

mord|re /mɔrdr/ *v.t./i.* bite. ～**re sur,** overlap into. ～**re à l'hameçon,** bite. ～**u,** ～**ue** *n.m., f.* (*fam.*) fan; *a.* bitten. ～**u de,** (*fam.*) crazy about.

morfondre (se) /(sə)mɔrfɔ̃dr/ *v. pr.* mope, wait anxiously.

morgue¹ /mɔrg/ n.f. morgue, mortuary.

morgue² /mɔrg/ n.f. (attitude) haughtiness.

moribond, ~e /mɔribɔ̃, -d/ a. dying.

morne /mɔrn/ a. dull.

morose /mɔroz/ a. morose.

morphine /mɔrfin/ n.f. morphine.

mors /mɔr/ n.m. (de cheval) bit.

morse¹ /mɔrs/ n.m. walrus.

morse² /mɔrs/ n.m. (code) Morse code.

morsure /mɔrsyr/ n.f. bite.

mort¹ /mɔr/ n.f. death.

mort², **~e** /mɔr, -t/ a. dead. —n.m., f. dead man, dead woman. **les ~s**, the dead. **~ de fatigue**, dead tired. **~-né** a. stillborn.

mortadelle /mɔrtadɛl/ n.f. mortadella.

mortalité /mɔrtalite/ n.f. death rate.

mortel, ~le /mɔrtɛl/ a. mortal; (accident) fatal; (poison, silence) deadly. —n.m., f. mortal. **~lement** adv. mortally.

mortier /mɔrtje/ n.m. mortar.

mortifié /mɔrtifje/ a. mortified.

mortuaire /mɔrtɥɛr/ a. (cérémonie) funeral; (avis) death.

morue /mɔry/ n.f. cod.

mosaïque /mɔzaik/ n.f. mosaic.

Moscou /mɔsku/ n.m./f. Moscow.

mosquée /mɔske/ n.f. mosque.

mot /mo/ n.m. word; (lettre, message) line, note. **~ d'ordre**, watchword. **~ de passe**, password. **~s croisés**, crossword (puzzle).

motard /mɔtar/ n.m. biker; (policier) police motorcyclist.

motel /mɔtɛl/ n.m. motel.

moteur¹ /mɔtœr/ n.m. engine, motor. **barque à ~**, motor launch.

mo|teur², **~trice** /mɔtœr, -tris/ a. (nerf) motor; (force) driving. **à 4 roues motrices**, 4-wheel drive.

motif /mɔtif/ n.m. reason; (jurid.) motive; (dessin) pattern.

motion /mosjɔ̃/ n.f. motion.

motiv|er /mɔtive/ v.t. motivate; (justifier) justify. **~ation** n.f. motivation.

moto /mɔto/ n.f. motor cycle. **~cycliste** n.m./f. motorcyclist.

motorisé /mɔtɔrize/ a. motorized.

motrice /mɔtris/ voir **moteur**².

motte /mɔt/ n.f. lump; (de beurre) slab; (de terre) clod. **~ de gazon**, turf.

mou ou **mol*, molle** /mu, mɔl/ a. soft; (péj.) flabby; (faible, indolent) feeble. —n.m. du **~**, slack. **avoir du ~**, be slack.

mouchard, ~e /muʃar, -d/ n.m., f. informer; (scol.) sneak. **~er** /-de/ v.t. (fam.) inform on.

mouche /muʃ/ n.f. fly.

moucher (se) /(sə)muʃe/ v. pr. blow one's nose.

moucheron /muʃrɔ̃/ n.m. midge.

moucheté /muʃte/ a. speckled.

mouchoir /muʃwar/ n.m. hanky; handkerchief; (en papier) tissue.

moudre /mudr/ v.t. grind.

moue /mu/ n.f. long face. **faire la ~**, pull a long face.

mouette /mwɛt/ n.f. (sea)gull.

moufle /mufl/ n.f. (gant) mitten.

mouill|er /muje/ v.t. wet, make wet. **se ~er** v. pr. get (o.s.) wet. **~er (l'ancre)**, anchor. **~é** a. wet.

moulage /mulaʒ/ n.m. cast.

moul|e¹ /mul/ n.m. mould. **~er** v.t. mould; (statue) cast. **~e à gâteau**, cake tin. **~e à tarte**, flan dish.

moule² /mul/ n.f. (coquillage) mussel.

moulin /mulɛ̃/ n.m. mill, (moteur. fam.) engine. **~ à vent**, windmill.

moulinet /mulinɛ/ n.m. (de canne à pêche) reel. **faire des ~s avec qch.**, twirl sth. around.

moulinette /mulinɛt/ n.f. (P.) purée maker.

moulu /muly/ a. ground; (fatigué: fam.) dead beat.

moulure /mulyr/ n.f. moulding.

mourant, ~e /murɑ̃, -t/ a. dying. —n.m., f. dying person.

mourir† /murir/ v.i. (aux. être) die. **~ d'envie de**, be dying to. **~ de faim**, be starving. **~ d'ennui**, be dead bored.

mousquetaire /muskətɛr/ n.m. musketeer.

mousse¹ /mus/ n.f. moss; (écume) froth, foam; (de savon) lather; (dessert) mousse. **~ à raser**, shaving cream.

mousse² /mus/ n.m. ship's boy.

mousseline /muslin/ n.f. muslin; (de soie) chiffon.

mousser /muse/ v.i. froth, foam; (savon) lather.

mousseu|x, ~se /musø, -z/ a. frothy. —n.m. sparkling wine.

mousson /musɔ̃/ n.f. monsoon.

moustach|e /mustaʃ/ n.f. moustache. **~es**, (d'animal) whiskers. **~u** a. wearing a moustache.

moustiquaire /mustikɛr/ n.f. mosquito-net.

moustique /mustik/ n.m. mosquito.

moutarde /mutard/ n.f. mustard.

mouton /mutɔ̃/ n.m. sheep; (peau) sheepskin; (viande) mutton.

mouvant, ∼e /muvã, -t/ a. changing; (*terrain*) shifting.

mouvement /muvmã/ n.m. movement; (*agitation*) bustle; (*en gymnastique*) exercise; (*impulsion*) impulse; (*tendance*) tendency. **en** ∼, in motion.

mouvementé /muvmãte/ a. eventful.

mouvoir† /muvwar/ v.t. (*membre*) move. **se** ∼ v. pr. move.

moyen[1], ∼**ne** /mwajɛ̃, -jɛn/ a. average; (*médiocre*) poor. —n.f. average; (*scol.*) pass-mark. **de taille** ∼**ne**, medium-sized. ∼ **âge**, Middle Ages. ∼**ne d'âge**, average age. **M**∼-**Orient** n.m. Middle East. ∼**nement** /-jɛnmã/ adv. moderately.

moyen[2] /mwajɛ̃/ n.m. means, way. ∼**s**, means; (*dons*) abilities. **au** ∼ **de**, by means of. **il n'y a pas** ∼ **de**, it is not possible to.

moyennant /mwajɛnã/ prép. (*pour*) for; (*grâce à*) with.

moyeu (pl. ∼**x**) /mwajø/ n.m. hub.

mû, mue[1] /my/ a. driven (**par**, by).

mucoviscidose /mykɔvisidoz/ n.f. cystic fibrosis.

mue[2] /my/ n.f. moulting; (*de voix*) breaking of the voice.

muer /mɥe/ v.i. moult; (*voix*) break. **se** ∼ **en**, change into.

muesli /mysli/ n.m. muesli.

muet, ∼**te** /mɥɛ, -t/ a. (*personne*) dumb; (*fig.*) speechless (**de**, with); (*silencieux*) silent. —n.m., f. dumb person.

mufle /myfl/ n.m. nose, muzzle; (*personne*: fam.) boor, lout.

mugir /myʒir/ v.i. (*vache*) moo; (*bœuf*) bellow; (*fig.*) howl.

muguet /mygɛ/ n.m. lily of the valley.

mule /myl/ n.f. (she-)mule; (*pantoufle*) mule.

mulet /mylɛ/ n.m. (he-)mule.

multi- /mylti/ préf. multi-.

multicolore /myltikɔlɔr/ a. multi-coloured.

multination|al, ∼**ale** (m. pl. ∼**aux**) /myltinasjɔnal, -o/ a. & n.f. multinational.

multiple /myltipl/ a. & n.m. multiple.

multiplicité /myltiplisite/ n.f. multiplicity, abundance.

multipl|ier /myltiplije/ v.t., **se** ∼**ier** v. pr. multiply. ∼**ication** n.f. multiplication.

multitude /myltityd/ n.f. multitude, mass.

municip|al (m. pl. ∼**aux**) /mynisipal,

-o/ a. municipal; (*conseil*) town. ∼**alité** n.f. (*ville*) municipality; (*conseil*) town council.

munir /mynir/ v.t. ∼ **de,** provide with. **se** ∼ **de,** provide o.s. with.

munitions /mynisjɔ̃/ n.f. pl. ammunition.

mur /myr/ n.m. wall. ∼ **du son,** sound barrier.

mûr /myr/ a. ripe; (*personne*) mature.

muraille /myrɑj/ n.f. (high) wall.

mur|al (m. pl. ∼**aux**) /myral, -o/ a. wall; (*tableau*) mural.

mûre /myr/ n.f. blackberry.

muret /myrɛ/ n.m. low wall.

mûrir /myrir/ v.t./i. ripen; (*abcès*) come to a head; (*personne, projet*) mature.

murmur|e /myrmyr/ n.m. murmur. ∼**er** v.t./i. murmur.

musc /mysk/ n.m. musk.

muscade /myskad/ n.f. **noix (de)** ∼, nutmeg.

muscl|e /myskl/ n.m. muscle. ∼**é** a. muscular, brawny.

muscul|aire /myskylɛr/ a. muscular. ∼**ature** n.f. muscles.

museau (pl. ∼**x**) /myzo/ n.m. muzzle; (*de porc*) snout.

musée /myze/ n.m. museum; (*de peinture*) art gallery.

museler /myzle/ v.t. muzzle.

muselière /myzəljɛr/ n.f. muzzle.

musette /myzɛt/ n.f. haversack.

muséum /myzeɔm/ n.m. (natural history) museum.

music|al (m. pl. ∼**aux**) /myzikal, -o/ a. musical.

music-hall /myzikol/ n.m. variety theatre.

musicien, ∼**ne** /myzisjɛ̃, -jɛn/ a. musical. —n.m., f. musician.

musique /myzik/ n.f. music; (*orchestre*) band.

musulman, ∼**e** /myzylmã, -an/ a. & n.m., f. Muslim.

mutation /mytasjɔ̃/ n.f. change; (*biologique*) mutation.

muter /myte/ v.t. transfer.

mutil|er /mytile/ v.t. mutilate. ∼**ation** n.f. mutilation. ∼**é**, ∼**ée** a. & n.m., f. disabled (person).

mutin, ∼**e** /mytɛ̃, -in/ a. saucy. —n.m., f. rebel.

mutin|er (se) /(sə)mytine/ v. pr. mutiny. ∼**é** a. mutinous. ∼**erie** n.f. mutiny.

mutisme /mytism/ n.f. silence.

mutuel, ∼**le** /mytɥɛl/ a. mutual. —n.f. Friendly Society; (*Amer.*) benefit society. ∼**lement** adv. mutually; (*l'un l'autre*) each other.

myop|e /mjɔp/ *a.* short-sighted. **~ie** *n.f.* short-sightedness.

myosotis /mjozɔtis/ *n.m.* forget-me-not.

myriade /mirjad/ *n.f.* myriad.

myrtille /mirtij/ *n.f.* bilberry; (*Amer.*) blueberry.

mystère /mistɛr/ *n.m.* mystery.

mystérieu|x, ~se /misterjø, -z/ *a.* mysterious.

mystif|ier /mistifje/ *v.t.* deceive, hoax. **~ication** *n.f.* hoax.

mysti|que /mistik/ *a.* mystic(al). **—**n.m./f. (*puissance*) mystique. **~cisme** *n.m.* mysticism.

myth|e /mit/ *n.m.* myth. **~ique** *a.* mythical.

mytholog|ie /mitolɔʒi/ *n.f.* mythology. **~ique** *a.* mythological.

mythomane /mitɔman/ *n.m./f.* compulsive liar (and fantasizer).

N

n' /n/ *voir* **ne**.

nacr|e /nakr/ *n.f.* mother-of-pearl. **~é** *a.* pearly.

nage /naʒ/ *n.f.* swimming; (*manière*) (swimming) stroke. **à la ~,** by swimming. **traverser à la ~,** swim across. **en ~,** sweating

nageoire /naʒwar/ *n.f.* fin.

nag|er /naʒe/ *v.t./i.* swim. **~eur, ~euse** *n.m., f.* swimmer.

naguère /nagɛr/ *adv.* some time ago.

naï|f, ~ve /naif, -v/ *a.* naïve.

nain, ~e /nɛ̃, nɛn/ *n.m., f. & a.* dwarf.

naissance /nesɑ̃s/ *n.f.* birth. **donner ~ à,** give birth to. (*fig.*) give rise to.

naître† /nɛtr/ *v.i.* be born; (*résulter*) arise (**de,** from). **faire ~,** (*susciter*) give rise to.

naïveté /naivte/ *n.f.* naïvety.

nana /nana/ *n.f.* (*fam.*) girl.

nanti /nɑ̃ti/ *n.m.* **les ~s,** the affluent.

nantir /nɑ̃tir/ *v.t.* **~ de,** provide with.

naphtaline /naftalin/ *n.f.* mothballs.

nappe /nap/ *n.f.* table-cloth; (*de pétrole, gaz*) layer. **~ phréatique,** ground water.

napperon /naprɔ̃/ *n.m.* (cloth) table-mat.

narcotique /narkɔtik/ *a. & n.m.* narcotic.

narguer /narge/ *v.t.* mock.

narine /narin/ *n.f.* nostril.

narquois, ~e /narkwa, -z/ *a.* derisive.

narr|er /nare/ *v.t.* narrate. **~ateur, ~atrice** *n.m., f.* narrator. **~ation** *n.f.* narrative; (*action*) narration; (*scol.*) composition.

nas|al (*m. pl.* **~aux**) /nazal, -o/ *a.* nasal.

naseau (*pl.* **~x**) /nazo/ *n.m.* nostril.

nasiller /nazije/ *v.i.* have a nasal twang.

nat|al (*m. pl.* **~als**) /natal/ *a.* native.

natalité /natalite/ *n.f.* birth rate.

natation /natasjɔ̃/ *n.f.* swimming.

nati|f, ~ve /natif, -v/ *a.* native.

nation /nɑsjɔ̃/ *n.f.* nation.

nation|al, ~ale (*m. pl.* **~aux**) /nasjonal, -o/ *a.* national. **—**n.f. A road; (*Amer.*) highway. **~aliser** *v.t.* nationalize. **~alisme** *n.m.* nationalism.

nationalité /nasjonalite/ *n.f.* nationality.

Nativité /nativite/ *n.f.* **la ~,** the Nativity.

natte /nat/ *n.f.* (*de cheveux*) plait; (*tapis de paille*) mat.

naturaliser /natyralize/ *v.t.* naturalize.

nature /natyr/ *n.f.* nature. **—**a. invar. (*eau, omelette, etc.*) plain. **de ~ à,** likely to. **payer en ~,** pay in kind. **~ morte,** still life.

naturel, ~le /natyrɛl/ *a.* natural. **—**n.m. nature; (*simplicité*) naturalness. **~lement** *adv.* naturally.

naufrag|e /nofraʒ/ *n.m.* (ship)-wreck. **faire ~e,** be shipwrecked; (*bateau*) be wrecked. **~é, ~ée** *a. & n.m., f.* shipwrecked (person).

nauséabond, ~e /nozeabɔ̃, -d/ *a.* nauseating.

nausée /noze/ *n.f.* nausea.

nautique /notik/ *a.* nautical; (*sports*) aquatic.

nav|al (*m. pl.* **~s**) /naval/ *a.* naval.

navet /navɛ/ *n.m.* turnip; (*film, tableau*) dud.

navette /navɛt/ *n.f.* shuttle (service). **faire la ~,** shuttle back and forth.

navigable /navigabl/ *a.* navigable.

navig|uer /navige/ *v.i.* sail; (*piloter*) navigate. **~ateur** *n.m.* seafarer; (*d'avion*) navigator. **~ation** *n.f.* navigation; (*trafic*) shipping.

navire /navir/ *n.m.* ship.

navré /navre/ *a.* sorry (**de,** to).

navrer /navre/ *v.t.* upset.

ne, n'* /nə, n/ *adv.* **ne pas,** not. **ne jamais,** never. **ne plus,** (*temps*) no longer, not any more. **ne que,** only. **je crains qu'il ne parte,** (*sans valeur négative*) I am afraid he will leave.

né, née /ne/ *voir* **naître**. **—**a. & n.m., f. born. **il est né,** he was born. **premier-/dernier-né,** first-/last-born. **née Martin,** née Martin.

néanmoins /neɑ̃mwɛ̃/ *adv.* nevertheless.

néant /neɑ̃/ *n.m.* nothingness; (*aucun*) none.

nébuleu|x, **~se** /nebylø, -z/ *a.* nebulous.

nécessaire /nesesɛr/ *a.* necessary. —*n.m.* (*sac*) bag; (*trousse*) kit. **le ~,** (*l'indispensable*) the necessities. **faire le ~,** do what is necessary. **~ment** *adv.* necessarily.

nécessité /nesesite/ *n.f.* necessity.

nécessiter /nesesite/ *v.t.* necessitate.

nécrologie /nekrɔlɔʒi/ *n.f.* obituary.

néerlandais, **~e** /neɛrlɑ̃dɛ, -z/ *a.* Dutch. —*n.m.*, *f.* Dutchman, Dutchwoman. —*n.m.* (*lang.*) Dutch.

nef /nɛf/ *n.f.* nave.

néfaste /nefast/ *a.* harmful (**à**, to); (*funeste*) ill-fated.

négati|f, **~ve** /negatif, -v/ *a.* & *n.m.*, *f.* negative.

négation /negɑsjɔ̃/ *n.f.* negation.

négligé /negliʒe/ *a.* (*tenue*, *travail*) slovenly. —*n.m.* (*tenue*) négligé.

négligeable /negliʒabl/ *a.* negligible, insignificant.

néglige|nt, **~te** /negliʒɑ̃, -t/ *a.* careless, negligent. **~ce** *n.f.* carelessness, negligence; (*erreur*) omission.

négliger /negliʒe/ *v.t.* neglect; (*ne pas tenir compte de*) disregard. **se ~** *v. pr.* neglect o.s.

négoc|e /negɔs/ *n.m.* business. **~iant**, **~iante** *n.m.*, *f.* merchant.

négoc|ier /negɔsje/ *v.t./i.* negotiate. **~iable** *a.* negotiable. **~iateur**, **~iatrice** *n.m.*, *f.* negotiator. **~iation** *n.f.* negotiation.

nègre[1] /nɛgr/ *a.* (*musique etc.*) Negro.

nègre[2] /nɛgr/ *n.m.* (*écrivain*) ghost writer.

neig|e /nɛʒ/ *n.f.* snow. **~eux**, **~euse** *a.* snowy.

neiger /neʒe/ *v.i.* snow.

nénuphar /nenyfar/ *n.m.* waterlily.

néologisme /neɔlɔʒism/ *n.m.* neologism.

néon /neɔ̃/ *n.m.* neon.

néo-zélandais, **~e** /neɔzelɑ̃dɛ, -z/ *a.* New Zealand. —*n.m.*, *f.* New Zealander.

nerf /nɛr/ *n.m.* nerve; (*vigueur*: *fam.*) stamina.

nerv|eux, **~euse** /nɛrvø, -z/ *a.* nervous; (*irritable*) nervy; (*centre*, *cellule*) nerve-; (*voiture*) responsive. **~eusement** *adv.* nervously. **~osité** *n.f.* nervousness; (*irritabilité*) touchiness.

nervure /nɛrvyr/ *n.f.* (*bot.*) vein.

net, **~te** /nɛt/ *a.* (*clair*, *distinct*) clear; (*propre*) clean; (*soigné*) neat; (*prix*, *poids*) net. —*adv.* (*s'arrêter*) dead; (*refuser*) flatly; (*parler*) plainly; (*se casser*) clean. **~tement** *adv.* clearly; (*certainement*) definitely.

netteté /nɛtte/ *n.f.* clearness.

nettoy|er /nɛtwaje/ *v.t.* clean. **~age** *n.m.* cleaning. **~age à sec,** dry-cleaning.

neuf[1] /nœf/ (/nœv/ *before heures, ans*) *a.* & *n.m.* nine.

neu|f[2], **~ve** /nœf, -v/ *a.* & *n.m.* new. **remettre à ~f,** brighten up. **du ~f,** (*fait nouveau*) some new development.

neutr|e /nøtr/ *a.* neutral; (*gram.*) neuter. —*n.m.* (*gram.*) neuter. **~alité** *n.f.* neutrality.

neutron /nøtrɔ̃/ *n.m.* neutron.

neuve /nœv/ *voir* **neuf**[2].

neuvième /nœvjɛm/ *a.* & *n.m./f.* ninth.

neveu (*pl.* **~x**) /nəvø/ *n.m.* nephew.

névros|e /nevroz/ *n.f.* neurosis. **~é**, **~ée** *a.* & *n.m.*, *f.* neurotic.

nez /ne/ *n.m.* nose. **~ à nez,** face to face. **~ épaté,** flat nose. **~ retroussé,** turned-up nose. **avoir du ~,** have flair.

ni /ni/ *conj.* neither, nor. **ni grand ni petit,** neither big nor small. **ni l'un ni l'autre ne fument,** neither (one nor the other) smokes.

niais, **~e** /njɛ, -z/ *a.* silly. —*n.m.*, *f.* simpleton. **~erie** /-zri/ *n.f.* silliness.

niche /niʃ/ *n.f.* (*de chien*) kennel; (*cavité*) niche; (*farce*) trick.

nichée /niʃe/ *n.f.* brood.

nicher /niʃe/ *v.i.* nest. **se ~** *v. pr.* nest; (*se cacher*) hide.

nickel /nikɛl/ *n.m.* nickel. **c'est ~!,** (*fam.*) it's spotless.

nicotine /nikɔtin/ *n.f.* nicotine.

nid /ni/ *n.m.* nest. **~ de poule,** pot-hole.

nièce /njɛs/ *n.f.* niece.

nier /nje/ *v.t.* deny.

nigaud, **~e** /nigo, -d/ *a.* silly. —*n.m.*, *f.* silly idiot.

nippon, **~e** /nipɔ̃, -ɔn/ *a.* & *n.m.*, *f.* Japanese.

niveau (*pl.* **~x**) /nivo/ *n.m.* level; (*compétence*) standard. **au ~,** up to standard. **~ à bulle,** spirit-level. **~ de vie,** standard of living.

nivel|er /nivle/ *v.t.* level. **~lement** /-ɛlmɑ̃/ *n.m.* levelling.

noble /nɔbl/ *a.* noble. —*n.m./f.* nobleman, noblewoman.

noblesse /nɔbles/ *n.f.* nobility.

noce /nɔs/ *n.f.* wedding; (*personnes*) wedding guests. **~s,** wedding. **faire la ~,** (*fam.*) make merry.

noci|f, **~ve** /nɔsif, -v/ *a.* harmful.

noctambule /nɔktãbyl/ *n.m./f.* night-owl, late-night reveller.

nocturne /nɔktyrn/ *a.* nocturnal.

Noël /nɔel/ *n.m.* Christmas.

nœud[1] /nø/ *n.m.* knot; (*ornemental*) bow. **~s**, (*fig.*) ties. **~ coulant**, noose. **~ papillon**, bow-tie.

nœud[2] /nø/ *n.m.* (*naut.*) knot.

noir, **~e** /nwar/ *a.* black; (*obscur, sombre*) dark; (*triste*) gloomy. —*n.m.* black; (*obscurité*) dark. **travail au ~**, moonlighting. —*n.m.*, *f.* (*personne*) Black. —*n f* (*mus.*) crotchet. **~ceur** *n.f.* blackness; (*indignité*) vileness.

noircir /nwarsir/ *v.t./i.*, **se ~** *v. pr.* blacken.

nois|ette /nwazɛt/ *n.f.* hazel-nut; (*de beurre*) knob. **~etier** *n.m.* hazel tree.

noix /nwa/ *n.f.* nut; (*du noyer*) walnut; (*de beurre*) knob. **~ de cajou**, cashew nut. **~ de coco**, coconut. **à la ~**, (*fam.*) useless.

nom /nɔ̃/ *n.m.* name; (*gram.*) noun. **au ~ de**, on behalf of. **~ de famille**, surname. **~ de jeune fille**, maiden name. **~ propre**, proper noun.

nomade /nɔmad/ *a.* nomadic. —*n.m./f.* nomad.

no man's land /nɔmanslãd/ *n.m. invar.* no man's land.

nombre /nɔ̃br/ *n.m.* number. **au ~ de**, (*parmi*) amongst (*l'un de*) one of. **en (grand) ~**, in large numbers.

nombreu|x, **~se** /nɔ̃brø, -z/ *a.* numerous; (*important*) large.

nombril /nɔ̃bri/ *n.m.* navel.

nomin|al (*m. pl.* **~aux**) /nɔminal, -o/ *a.* nominal.

nomination /nɔminasjɔ̃/ *n.f.* appointment.

nommément /nɔmemã/ *adv.* by name.

nommer /nɔme/ *v.t.* name; (*élire*) appoint. **se ~** *v. pr.* (*s'appeler*) be called.

non /nɔ̃/ *adv.* no; (*pas*) not. —*n.m. invar.* no. **~ (pas) que**, not that. **il vient, ~?**, he is coming, isn't he? **moi ~ plus**, neither am, do, can, *etc.* I.

non- /nɔ̃/ *préf.* non-. **~-fumeur**, non-smoker.

nonante /nɔnãt/ *a.* & *n.m.* ninety.

nonchalance /nɔ̃ʃalãs/ *n.f.* nonchalance.

non-sens /nɔ̃sãs/ *n.m.* absurdity.

non-stop /nɔnstɔp/ *a. invar.* non-stop.

nord /nɔr/ *n.m.* north. —*a. invar.* north; (*partie*) northern; (*direction*) northerly. **au ~ de**, to the north of. **~-africain**, **~-africaine** *a.* & *n.m.*, *f.* North

African. **~-est** *n.m.* north-east. **~-ouest** *n.m.* north-west.

nordique /nɔrdik/ *a.* & *n.m./f.* Scandinavian.

norm|al, **~ale** (*m. pl.* **~aux**) /nɔrmal, -o/ *a.* normal. —*n.f.* normality; (*norme*) norm; (*moyenne*) average. **~alement** *adv.* normally.

normand, **~e** /nɔrmã, -d/ *a.* & *n.m.*, *f.* Norman.

Normandie /nɔrmãdi/ *n f.* Normandy.

norme /nɔrm/ *n.f.* norm; (*de production*) standard.

Norvège /nɔrvɛʒ/ *n.f.* Norway.

norvégien, **~ne** /nɔrveʒjɛ̃, -jɛn/ *a.* & *n.m.*, *f.* Norwegian.

nos /no/ *voir* **notre**.

nostalg|ie /nɔstalʒi/ *n.f.* nostalgia. **~ique** *a.* nostalgic.

notable /nɔtabl/ *a.* & *n.m.* notable.

notaire /nɔtɛr/ *n.m.* notary.

notamment /nɔtamã/ *adv.* notably.

notation /nɔtasjɔ̃/ *n.f.* notation; (*remarque*) remark.

note /nɔt/ *n.f.* (*remarque*) note; (*chiffrée*) mark; (*facture*) bill; (*mus.*) note. **~ (de service)**, memorandum. **prendre ~ de**, take note of.

not|er /nɔte/ *v.t.* note, notice; (*écrire*) note (down); (*devoir*) mark. **bien/mal ~é**, (*employé etc.*) highly/poorly rated.

notice /nɔtis/ *n.f.* note; (*mode d'emploi*) directions.

notifi|er /nɔtifje/ *v.t.* notify (**à**, to). **~cation** *n.f.* notification.

notion /nosjɔ̃/ *n.f.* notion.

notoire /nɔtwar/ *a.* well-known; (*criminel*) notorious.

notre (*pl.* **nos**) /nɔtr, no/ *a.* our.

nôtre /notr/ *pron.* **le ou la ~**, **les ~s**, ours.

nouer /nwe/ *v.t.* tie, knot; (*relations*) strike up.

noueu|x, **~se** /nwø, -z/ *a.* gnarled.

nougat /nuga/ *n.m.* nougat.

nouille /nuj/ *n.f.* (*idiot: fam.*) idiot.

nouilles /nuj/ *n.f. pl.* noodles.

nounours /nunurs/ *n.m.* teddy bear.

nourri /nuri/ *a.* (*fig.*) intense. **logé ~**, bed and board. **~ au sein**, breastfed.

nourrice /nuris/ *n.f.* child-minder; (*qui allaite*) wet-nurse.

nourr|ir /nurir/ *v.t.* feed; (*faire vivre*) feed, provide for; (*sentiment: fig.*) nourish. —*v.i.* be nourishing. **se ~ir** *v. pr.* eat. **se ~ir de**, feed on. **~issant**, **~issante** *a.* nourishing.

nourrisson /nurisɔ̃/ *n.m.* infant.

nourriture /nurityr/ *n.f.* food.

nous /nu/ *pron.* we; (*complément*) us; (*indirect*) (to) us; (*réfléchi*) ourselves; (*l'un l'autre*) each other. ∼-**mêmes** *pron.* ourselves.

nouveau *ou* **nouvel***, **nouvelle**[1] (*m. pl.* ∼x) /nuvo, nuvɛl/ *a.* & *n.m.* new. —*n.m.*, *f.* (*élève*) new boy, new girl. **de** ∼, **à** ∼, again. **du** ∼, (*fait nouveau*) some new development. **nouvel an**, new year. ∼x **mariés**, newly-weds. ∼-**né**, ∼-**née** *a.* new-born; *n.m.*, *f.* newborn baby. ∼ **venu**, **nouvelle venue**, newcomer. **Nouvelle Zélande**, New Zealand.

nouveauté /nuvote/ *n.f.* novelty; (*chose*) new thing.

nouvelle[2] /nuvɛl/ *n.f.* (piece of) news; (*récit*) short story. ∼s, news.

nouvellement /nuvɛlmɑ̃/ *adv.* newly, recently.

novembre /nɔvɑ̃br/ *n.m.* November.

novice /nɔvis/ *a.* inexperienced. —*n.m./f.* novice.

noyade /nwajad/ *n.f.* drowning.

noyau (*pl.* ∼x) /nwajo/ *n.m.* (*de fruit*) stone; (*de cellule*) nucleus; (*groupe*) group; (*centre: fig.*) core.

noyauter /nwajote/ *v.t.* (*organisation*) infiltrate.

noyer[1] /nwaje/ *v.t.* drown; (*inonder*) flood. **se** ∼**er** *v. pr.* drown; (*volontairement*) drown o.s. **se** ∼**er dans un verre d'eau**, make a mountain out of a molehill. ∼**é**, ∼**ée** *n.m.*, *f.* drowning person; (*mort*) drowned person.

noyer[2] /nwaje/ *n.m.* (*arbre*) walnut-tree.

nu /ny/ *a.* naked; (*mains, mur, fil*) bare. —*n.m.* nude. **se mettre à nu**, (*fig.*) bare one's heart. **mettre à nu**, lay bare. **nu-pieds** *adv.* barefoot; *n.m. pl.* beach shoes. **nu- tête** *adv.* bareheaded. **à l'oeil nu**, to the naked eye.

nuage /nɥaʒ/ *n.m.* cloud. ∼**eux**, ∼**euse** *a.* cloudy.

nuance /nɥɑ̃s/ *n.f.* shade; (*de sens*) nuance; (*différence*) difference.

nuancer /nɥɑ̃se/ *v.t.* (*opinion*) qualify.

nucléaire /nykleɛr/ *a.* nuclear.

nudis|te /nydist/ *n.m./f.* nudist. ∼**me** *n.m.* nudism.

nudité /nydite/ *n.f.* (*de personne*) nudity; (*de chambre etc.*) bareness.

nuée /nɥe/ *n.f.* (*foule*) host.

nues /ny/ *n.f. pl.* **tomber des** ∼, be amazed. **porter aux** ∼, extol.

nuire† /nɥir/ *v.i.* ∼ **à**, harm.

nuisible /nɥizibl/ *a.* harmful.

nuit /nɥi/ *n.f.* night. **cette** ∼, tonight; (*hier*) last night. **il fait** ∼, it is dark. ∼ **blanche**, sleepless night. **la** ∼, **de** ∼, at night. ∼ **de noces**, wedding night.

nul, ∼**le** /nyl/ *a.* (*aucun*) no; (*zéro*) nil; (*qui ne vaut rien*) useless; (*non valable*) null. **match** ∼, draw. ∼ **en**, no good at. —*pron.* no one. ∼ **autre**, no one else. ∼**le part**, nowhere. ∼**lement** *adv.* not at all. ∼**lité** *n.f.* uselessness; (*personne*) useless person.

numéraire /nymerɛr/ *n.m.* cash.

numér|al (*pl.* ∼**aux**) /nymeral, -o/ *n.m.* numeral.

numérique /nymerik/ *a.* numerical; (*montre, horloge*) digital.

numéro /nymero/ *n.m.* number; (*de journal*) issue; (*spectacle*) act. ∼**ter** /-ɔte/ *v.t.* number.

nuque /nyk/ *n.f.* nape (of the neck).

nurse /nœrs/ *n.f.* (children's) nurse.

nutriti|f, ∼**ve** /nytritif, -v/ *a.* nutritious; (*valeur*) nutritional.

nutrition /nytrisjɔ̃/ *n.f.* nutrition.

nylon /nilɔ̃/ *n.m.* nylon.

nymphe /nɛ̃f/ *n.f.* nymph.

O

oasis /ɔazis/ *n.f.* oasis.

obéir /ɔbeir/ *v.i.* obey. ∼ **à**, obey. **être obéi**, be obeyed.

obéissan|t, ∼**te** /ɔbeisɑ̃, -t/ *a.* obedient. ∼**ce** *n.f.* obedience.

obèse /ɔbɛz/ *a.* obese.

obésité /ɔbezite/ *n.f.* obesity.

object|er /ɔbʒɛkte/ *v.t.* put forward (as an excuse). ∼**er que**, object that. ∼**ion** /-ksjɔ̃/ *n.f.* objection.

objecteur /ɔbʒɛktœr/ *n.m.* ∼ **de conscience**, conscientious objector.

objecti|f, ∼**ve** /ɔbʒɛktif, -v/ *a.* objective. —*n.m.* objective; (*photo.*) lens. ∼**vement** *adv.* objectively. ∼**vité** *n.f.* objectivity.

objet /ɔbʒɛ/ *n.m.* object; (*sujet*) subject. **être** *ou* **faire l'**∼ **de**, be the subject of; (*recevoir*) receive. ∼ **d'art**, objet d'art. ∼s **de toilette**, toilet requisites. ∼s **trouvés**, lost property; (*Amer.*) lost and found.

obligation /ɔbligɑsjɔ̃/ *n.f.* obligation; (*comm.*) bond. **être dans l'**∼ **de**, be under obligation to.

obligatoire /ɔbligatwar/ *a.* compulsory.

~ment adv. of necessity; (fam.) inevitably.

obligean|t, **~te** /ɔbliʒɑ̃, -t/ a. obliging, kind. **~ce** n.f. kindness.

oblig|er /ɔbliʒe/ v.t. compel, oblige (à **faire**, to do); (aider) oblige. **être ~é de**, have to. **~é à qn.**, obliged to s.o. (**de**, for).

oblique /ɔblik/ a. oblique. **regard ~**, sidelong glance. **en ~**, at an angle.

obliquer /ɔblike/ v.i. turn off (**vers**, towards).

oblitérer /ɔblitere/ v.t. (timbre) cancel.

oblong, **~ue** /ɔblɔ̃, -g/ a. oblong.

obnubilé, **~e** /ɔbnybile/ a. obsessed.

obsc|ène /ɔpsɛn/ a. obscene. **~énité** n.f. obscenity.

obscur /ɔpskyr/ a. dark; (confus, humble) obscure.

obscurantisme /ɔpskyrɑ̃tizm/ n.m. obscurantism.

obscurcir /ɔpskyrsir/ v.t. darken; (fig.) obscure. **s'~** v. pr. (ciel etc.) darken.

obscurité /ɔpskyrite/ n.f. dark(-ness); (passage, situation) obscurity.

obséd|er /ɔpsede/ v.t. obsess. **~ant**, **~ante** a. obsessive. **~é**, **~ée** n.m., f. maniac.

obsèques /ɔpsɛk/ n.f. pl. funeral.

observation /ɔpsɛrvasjɔ̃/ n.f. observation; (reproche) criticism; (obéissance) observance. **en ~**, under observation.

observatoire /ɔpsɛrvatwar/ n.m. observatory; (mil.) observation post.

observ|er /ɔpsɛrve/ v.t. observe; (surveiller) watch, observe. **faire ~er qch.**, point sth. out (à, to). **~ateur**, **~atrice** a. observant. n.m., f. observer.

obsession /ɔpsesjɔ̃/ n.f. obsession.

obstacle /ɔpstakl/ n.m. obstacle; (cheval) jump; (athlète) hurdle. **faire ~ à**, stand in the way of.

obstétrique /ɔpstetrik/ n.f. obstetrics.

obstin|é /ɔpstine/ a. obstinate. **~ation** n.f. obstinacy.

obstiner (s') /(s)ɔpstine/ v. pr. persist (à, in).

obstruction /ɔpstryksjɔ̃/ n.f. obstruction. **faire de l'~**, obstruct.

obstruer /ɔpstrye/ v.t. obstruct.

obten|ir† /ɔptnir/ v.t. get, obtain. **~tion** /-ɑ̃sjɔ̃/ n.f. obtaining.

obturateur /ɔptyratœr/ n.m. (photo.) shutter.

obtus, **~e** /ɔpty, -z/ a. obtuse.

obus /ɔby/ n.m. shell.

occasion /ɔkazjɔ̃/ n.f. opportunity (**de faire**, of doing); (circonstance) occasion; (achat) bargain; (article non neuf)

second-hand buy. **à l'~**, sometimes. **d'~**, second-hand. **~nel**, **~nelle** /-jɔnɛl/ a. occasional.

occasionner /ɔkazjɔne/ v.t. cause.

occident /ɔksidɑ̃/ n.m. west. **~al**, **~ale** (m. pl. **~aux**) /-tal, -to/ a. western. **—n.m., f.** westerner.

occulte /ɔkylt/ a. occult.

occupant, **~e** /ɔkypɑ̃, -t/ n.m., f. occupant. **—n.m.** (mil.) forces of occupation.

occupation /ɔkypasjɔ̃/ n.f. occupation.

occupé /ɔkype/ a. busy; (place, pays) occupied; (téléphone) engaged; (Amer.) busy.

occuper /ɔkype/ v.t. occupy; (poste) hold. **s'~** v. pr. (s'affairer) keep busy (à faire, doing). **s'~ de**, (personne, problème) take care of; (bureau, firme) be in charge of.

occurrence (en l') /(ɑ̃l)ɔkyrɑ̃s/ adv. in this case.

océan /ɔseɑ̃/ n.m. ocean.

ocre /ɔkr/ a. invar. ochre.

octane /ɔktan/ n.m. octane.

octante /ɔktɑ̃t/ a. (régional) eighty.

octave /ɔktav/ n.f. (mus.) octave.

octet /ɔktɛ/ n.m. byte.

octobre /ɔktɔbr/ n.m. October.

octogone /ɔktɔgɔn/ n.m. octagon.

octroyer /ɔktrwaje/ v.t. grant.

oculaire /ɔkylɛr/ a. ocular.

oculiste /ɔkylist/ n.m./f. eye-specialist.

ode /ɔd/ n.f. ode.

odeur /ɔdœr/ n.f. smell.

odieu|x, **~se** /ɔdjø, -z/ a. odious.

odorant, **~e** /ɔdɔrɑ̃, -t/ a. sweet-smelling.

odorat /ɔdɔra/ n.m. (sense of) smell.

œcuménique /ekymenik/ a. ecumenical.

œil (pl. **yeux**) /œj, jø/ n.m. eye. **à l'~**, (fam.) free. **à mes yeux**, in my view. **faire de l'~ à**, make eyes at. **faire les gros yeux à**, scowl at. **ouvrir l'~**, keep one's eye open. **fermer l'~**, shut one's eyes. **~ poché**, black eye. **yeux bridés**, slit eyes.

œillade /œjad/ n.f. wink.

œillères /œjɛr/ n.f. pl. blinkers.

œillet /œjɛ/ n.m. (plante) carnation; (trou) eyelet.

œuf (pl. **~s**) /œf, ø/ n.m. egg. **~ à la coque/dur/sur le plat**, boiled/hard-boiled/fried egg.

œuvre /œvr/ n.f. (ouvrage, travail) work. **~ d'art**, work of art. **~ (de bienfaisance)**, charity. **être à l'~**, be at work. **mettre en ~**, (moyens) implement.

œuvrer /œvre/ v.i. work.

off /ɔf/ a. invar. voix ∼, voice off.

offense /ɔfɑ̃s/ n.f. insult; (péché) offence.

offens|er /ɔfɑse/ v.t. offend. s'∼er de, take offence at. ∼ant, ∼ante a. offensive.

offensi|f, ∼ve /ɔfɑsif, -v/ a. & n.f. offensive.

offert, ∼e /ɔfɛr, -t/ voir offrir.

office /ɔfis/ n.m. office; (relig.) service; (de cuisine) pantry. d'∼, automatically.

officiel, ∼le /ɔfisjɛl/ a. & n.m., f. official. ∼lement adv. officially.

officier[1] /ɔfisje/ n.m. officer.

officier[2] /ɔfisje/ v.i. (relig.) officiate.

officieu|x, ∼se /ɔfisjø, -z/ a. unofficial. ∼sement adv. unofficially.

offrande /ɔfrɑ̃d/ n.f. offering.

offrant /ɔfrɑ̃/ n.m. au plus ∼, to the highest bidder.

offre /ɔfr/ n.f. offer; (aux enchères) bid. l'∼ et la demande, supply and demand. ∼s d'emploi, jobs advertised, (rubrique) situations vacant.

offrir† /ɔfrir/ v.t. offer (de faire, to do); (cadeau) give; (acheter) buy. s'∼ v. pr. offer o.s. (comme, as); (spectacle) present itself; (s'acheter) treat o.s. to. ∼ à boire à, (chez soi) give a drink to; (au café) buy a drink for.

offusquer /ɔfyske/ v.t. offend.

ogive /ɔʒiv/ n.f. (atomique etc.) warhead.

ogre /ɔgr/ n.m. ogre.

oh /o/ int. oh.

oie /wa/ n.f. goose.

oignon /ɔɲɔ̃/ n.m. (légume) onion; (de tulipe etc.) bulb.

oiseau (pl. ∼x) /wazo/ n.m. bird.

oisi|f, ∼ve /wazif, -v/ a. idle. ∼veté n.f. idleness.

O.K. /ɔke/ int. O.K.

oléoduc /ɔleɔdyk/ n.m. oil pipeline.

oliv|e /ɔliv/ n.f. & a. invar. olive. ∼ier n.m. olive-tree.

olympique /ɔlɛ̃pik/ a. Olympic.

ombrag|e /ɔ̃braʒ/ n.m. shade. prendre ∼e de, take offence at. ∼é a. shady. ∼eux, ∼euse a. easily offended.

ombre /ɔ̃br/ n.f. (pénombre) shade; (contour) shadow; (soupçon: fig.) hint, shadow. dans l'∼, (secret) in the dark. faire de l'∼ à qn., be in s.o.'s light.

ombrelle /ɔ̃brɛl/ n.f. parasol.

omelette /ɔmlɛt/ n.f. omelette.

omettre† /ɔmɛtr/ v.t. omit.

omission /ɔmisjɔ̃/ n.f. omission.

omnibus /ɔmnibys/ n.m. stopping train.

omoplate /ɔmɔplat/ n.f. shoulder-blade.

on /ɔ̃/ pron. we, you, one; (les gens) people, they; (quelqu'un) someone. on dit, people say, they say, it is said (que, that).

once /ɔ̃s/ n.f. ounce.

oncle /ɔ̃kl/ n.m. uncle.

onctueu|x, ∼se /ɔktɥø, -z/ a. smooth.

onde /ɔ̃d/ n.f. wave. ∼s courtes/longues, short/long wave. sur les ∼s, on the radio.

ondée /ɔ̃de/ n.f. shower.

on-dit /ɔ̃di/ n.m. invar. les ∼, rumour.

ondul|er /ɔ̃dyle/ v.i. undulate; (cheveux) be wavy. ∼ation n.f. wave, undulation. ∼é a. (chevelure) wavy.

onéreu|x, ∼se /ɔnerø, -z/ a. costly.

ongle /ɔ̃gl/ n.m. (finger-)nail. se faire les ∼s, do one's nails.

ont /ɔ̃/ voir avoir.

ONU /ɔny/ abrév. (Organisation des nations unies) UN.

onyx /ɔniks/ n.m. onyx.

onz|e /ɔ̃z/ a. & n.m. eleven. ∼ième a. & n.m./f. eleventh.

opale /ɔpal/ n.f. opal.

opa|que /ɔpak/ a. opaque. ∼cité n.f. opaqueness.

open /ɔpɛn/ n.m. open (champion-ship).

opéra /ɔpera/ n.m. opera; (édifice) opera-house. ∼-comique (pl. ∼s-comiques) n.m. light opera.

opérateur /ɔperatœr/ n.m. (caméra-man) cameraman.

opération /ɔperasjɔ̃/ n.f. operation; (comm.) deal.

opérationnel, ∼le /ɔperasjɔnɛl/ a. operational.

opératoire /ɔperatwar/ a. (méd.) surgical. bloc ∼, operating suite.

opérer /ɔpere/ v.t. (personne) operate on; (kyste etc.) remove; (exécuter) carry out, make. se faire ∼, have an operation. —v.i. (méd.) operate; (faire effet) work. s'∼ v. pr. (se produire) occur.

opérette /ɔperɛt/ n.f. operetta.

opiner /ɔpine/ v.i. nod.

opiniâtre /ɔpinjɑtr/ a. obstinate.

opinion /ɔpinjɔ̃/ n.f. opinion.

opium /ɔpjɔm/ n.m. opium.

opportun, ∼e /ɔpɔrtœ̃, -yn/ a. opportune. ∼ité n.f. opportune-ness.

opposant, ∼e /ɔpozɑ̃, -t/ n.m., f. opponent.

opposé /ɔpoze/ a. (sens, angle, etc.) opposite; (factions) opposing; (intérêts) conflicting. —n.m. opposite. à l'∼, (*opinion etc.*) contrary (**de**, to). **être ~ à**, be opposed to.

opposer /ɔpoze/ *v.t.* (*objets*) place opposite each other; (*personnes*) oppose; (*contraster*) contrast; (*résistance, argument*) put up. **s'~** *v. pr.* (*personnes*) confront each other; (*styles*) contrast. **s'~ à**, oppose.

opposition /ɔpozisjɔ̃/ *n.f.* opposition. **par ~ à**, in contrast with. **entrer en ~ avec**, come into conflict with. **faire ~ à un chèque**, stop a cheque.

oppress|er /ɔprese/ *v.t.* oppress. **~ant, ~ante** *a.* oppressive. **~eur** *n.m.* oppressor. **~ion** *n.f.* oppression.

opprimer /ɔprime/ *v.t.* oppress.

opter /ɔpte/ *v.i.* **~ pour**, opt for.

opticien, ~ne /ɔptisjɛ̃, -jɛn/ *n.m., f.* optician.

optimis|te /ɔptimist/ *n.m./f.* optimist. **—a.** optimistic. **~me** *n.m.* optimism.

optimum /ɔptimɔm/ *a. & n.m.* optimum.

option /ɔpsjɔ̃/ *n.f.* option.

optique /ɔptik/ *a.* (*verre*) optical. **—n.f.** (*perspective*) perspective.

opulen|t, ~te /ɔpylɑ̃, -t/ *a.* opulent. **~ce** *n.f.* opulence.

or[1] /ɔr/ *n.m.* gold. **d'~**, golden. **en or**, gold; (*occasion*) golden.

or[2] /ɔr/ *conj.* now, well.

oracle /ɔrakl/ *n.m.* oracle.

orag|e /ɔraʒ/ *n.m.* (thunder)storm. **~eux, ~euse** *a.* stormy.

oraison /ɔrɛzɔ̃/ *n.f.* prayer.

or|al (*m. pl.* **~aux**) /ɔral, -o/ *a.* oral. **—n.m.** (*pl.* **~aux**) oral.

orang|e /ɔrɑ̃ʒ/ *n.f. & a. invar.* orange. **~é** *a.* orange-coloured. **~er** *n.m.* orange-tree.

orangeade /ɔrɑ̃ʒad/ *n.f.* orangeade.

orateur /ɔratœr/ *n.m.* speaker.

oratorio /ɔratɔrjo/ *n.m.* oratorio.

orbite /ɔrbit/ *n.f.* orbit; (*d'œil*) socket.

orchestr|e /ɔrkɛstr/ *n.m.* orchestra; (*de jazz*) band; (*parterre*) stalls. **~er** *v.t.* orchestrate.

orchidée /ɔrkide/ *n.f.* orchid.

ordinaire /ɔrdinɛr/ *a.* ordinary; (*habituel*) usual; (*qualité*) standard. **—n.m. l'~**, the ordinary; (*nourriture*) the standard fare. **d'~**, **à l'~**, usually. **~ment** *adv.* usually.

ordinateur /ɔrdinatœr/ *n.m.* computer.

ordination /ɔrdinasjɔ̃/ *n.f.* (*relig.*) ordination.

ordonnance /ɔrdɔnɑ̃s/ *n.f.* (*ordre, décret*) order; (*de médecin*) prescription; (*soldat*) orderly.

ordonné /ɔrdɔne/ *a.* tidy.

ordonner /ɔrdɔne/ *v.t.* order (**à qn. de**, s.o. to); (*agencer*) arrange; (*méd.*) prescribe; (*prêtre*) ordain.

ordre /ɔrdr/ *n.m.* order; (*propreté*) tidiness. **aux ~s de qn.**, at s.o.'s disposal. **avoir de l'~**, be tidy. **de premier ~**, first-rate. **l'~ du jour**, (*programme*) agenda. **mettre en ~**, tidy (up). **de premier ~**, first rate. **jusqu'à nouvel ~**, until further notice. **un ~ de grandeur**, an approximate idea.

ordure /ɔrdyr/ *n.f.* filth. **~s**, (*détritus*) rubbish; (*Amer.*) garbage. **~s ménagères**, household refuse.

oreille /ɔrɛj/ *n.f.* ear.

oreiller /ɔreje/ *n.m.* pillow.

oreillons /ɔrɛjɔ̃/ *n.m. pl.* mumps.

orfèvr|e /ɔrfɛvr/ *n.m.* goldsmith, silversmith. **~erie** *n.f.* goldsmith's *ou* silversmith's trade.

organe /ɔrgan/ *n.m.* organ; (*porte-parole*) mouthpiece.

organigramme /ɔrganigram/ *n.m.* flow chart.

organique /ɔrganik/ *a.* organic.

organisation /ɔrganizasjɔ̃/ *n.f.* organization.

organis|er /ɔrganize/ *v.t.* organize. **s'~er** *v. pr.* organize o.s. **~ateur, ~atrice** *n m, f* organizer.

organisme /ɔrganism/ *n.m.* body, organism.

organiste /ɔrganist/ *n.m./f.* organist.

orgasme /ɔrgasm/ *n.m.* orgasm.

orge /ɔrʒ/ *n.f.* barley.

orgelet /ɔrʒɔlɛ/ *n.m.* (*furoncle*) sty.

orgie /ɔrʒi/ *n.f.* orgy.

orgue /ɔrg/ *n.m.* organ. **~s** *n.f. pl.* organ. **~ de Barbarie**, barrel-organ.

orgueil /ɔrgœj/ *n.m.* pride.

orgueilleu|x, ~se /ɔrgœjø, -z/ *a.* proud.

Orient /ɔrjɑ̃/ *n.m.* **l'~**, the Orient.

orientable /ɔrjɑ̃tabl/ *a.* adjustable.

orient|al, ~ale (*m. pl.* **~aux**) /ɔrjɑ̃tal, -o/ *a.* eastern; (*de l'Orient*) oriental. **—n.m., f.** Oriental.

orientation /ɔrjɑ̃tasjɔ̃/ *n.f.* direction; (*d'une politique*) course; (*de maison*) aspect. **~ professionnelle**, careers advisory service.

orienté /ɔrjɑ̃te/ *a.* (*partial*) slanted, tendentious.

orienter /ɔrjɑ̃te/ *v.t.* position; (*personne*) direct. **s'~** *v. pr.* (*se repérer*) find one's bearings. **s'~ vers**, turn towards.

orifice /ɔrifis/ *n.m.* orifice.

origan /ɔrigɑ̃/ *n.m.* oregano.

originaire /ɔriʒinɛr/ *a.* être ~ de, be a native of.

origin|al, ~ale (*m. pl.* ~aux) /ɔriʒinal, -o/ *a.* original; (*curieux*) eccentric. —*n.m.* original. —*n.m., f.* eccentric. ~**alité** *n.f.* originality; eccentricity.

origine /ɔriʒin/ *n.f.* origin. à l'~, originally. d'~, (*pièce, pneu*) original.

originel, ~le /ɔriʒinɛl/ *a.* original.

orme /ɔrm/ *n.m.* elm.

ornement /ɔrnəmɑ̃/ *n.m.* ornament. ~al (*m. pl.* ~aux) /-tal, -to/ *a.* ornamental.

orner /ɔrne/ *v.t.* decorate.

ornière /ɔrnjɛr/ *n.f.* rut.

ornithologie /ɔrnitɔlɔʒi/ *n.f.* ornithology.

orphelin, ~e /ɔrfəlɛ̃, -in/ *n.m., f.* orphan. —*a.* orphaned. ~**at** /-ina/ *n.m.* orphanage.

orteil /ɔrtɛj/ *n.m.* toe.

orthodox|e /ɔrtɔdɔks/ *a.* orthodox. ~**ie** *n.f.* orthodoxy.

orthograph|e /ɔrtɔgraf/ *n.f.* spelling. ~**ier** *v.t.* spell.

orthopédique /ɔrtɔpedik/ *a.* orthopaedic.

ortie /ɔrti/ *n.f.* nettle.

os (*pl.* **os**) /ɔs, o/ *n.m.* bone.

OS *abrév. voir* **ouvrier spécialisé**.

oscar /ɔskar/ *n.m.* award; (*au cinéma*) oscar.

oscill|er /ɔsile/ *v.i.* sway; (*techn.*) oscillate; (*hésiter*) waver, fluctuate. ~**ation** *n.f.* (*techn.*) oscillation; (*variation*) fluctuation.

oseille /ozɛj/ *n.f.* (*plante*) sorrel.

os|er /oze/ *v.t./i.* dare. ~**é** *a.* daring.

osier /ozje/ *n.m.* wicker.

ossature /ɔsatyr/ *n.f.* frame.

ossements /ɔsmɑ̃/ *n.m. pl.* bones.

osseu|x, ~se /ɔsø, -z/ *a.* bony; (*tissu*) bone.

ostensible /ɔstɑ̃sibl/ *a.* conspicuous, obvious.

ostentation /ɔstɑ̃tasjɔ̃/ *n.f.* ostentation.

ostéopathe /ɔsteɔpat/ *n.m./f.* osteopath.

otage /ɔtaʒ/ *n.m.* hostage.

otarie /ɔtari/ *n.f.* sea-lion.

ôter /ote/ *v.t.* remove (à qn., from s.o.); (*déduire*) take away.

otite /ɔtit/ *n.f.* ear infection.

ou /u/ *conj.* or. **ou bien**, or else. **vous ou moi**, either you or me.

où /u/ *adv. & pron.* where; (*dans lequel*) in which; (*sur lequel*) on which; (*auquel*) at which. **d'où**, from which; (*pour cette raison*) hence. **d'où?**, from where? **par où**, through which. **par où?**, which way? **où qu'il soit**, wherever he may be. **au prix où c'est**, at those prices. **le jour où**, the day when.

ouate /wat/ *n.f.* cotton wool; (*Amer.*) absorbent cotton.

oubli /ubli/ *n.m.* forgetfulness; (*trou de mémoire*) lapse of memory; (*négligence*) oversight. **l'~**, (*tomber dans, sauver de*) oblivion.

oublier /ublije/ *v.t.* forget. **s'~** *v. pr.* forget o.s.; (*chose*) be forgotten.

oublieu|x, ~se /ublijø, -z/ *a.* forgetful (**de**, of).

ouest /wɛst/ *n.m.* west. —*a. invar.* west; (*partie*) western; (*direction*) westerly.

ouf /uf/ *int.* phew.

oui /wi/ *adv.* yes.

oui-dire (**par**) /(par)widir/ *adv.* by hearsay.

ouïe /wi/ *n.f.* hearing.

ouïes /wi/ *n.f. pl.* gills.

ouille /uj/ *int.* ouch.

ouïr /wir/ *v.t.* hear.

ouragan /uragɑ̃/ *n.m.* hurricane.

ourler /urle/ *v.t.* hem.

ourlet /urlɛ/ *n.m.* hem.

ours /urs/ *n.m.* bear. ~ **blanc**, polar bear. ~ **en peluche**, teddy bear. ~ **mal léché**, boor.

ouste /ust/ *int.* (*fam.*) scram.

outil /uti/ *n.m.* tool.

outillage /utijaʒ/ *n.m.* tools; (*d'une usine*) equipment.

outiller /utije/ *v.t.* equip.

outrage /utraʒ/ *n.m.* (*grave*) insult.

outrag|er /utraʒe/ *v.t.* offend. ~**eant, ~eante** *a.* offensive.

outranc|e /utrɑ̃s/ *n.f.* excess. à ~**e**, to excess; (*guerre*) all-out. ~**ier, ~ière** *a.* excessive.

outre /utr/ *prép.* besides. **en ~**, besides. ~**-mer** *adv.* overseas. ~ **mesure**, excessively.

outrepasser /utrəpase/ *v.t.* exceed.

outrer /utre/ *v.t.* exaggerate; (*indigner*) incense.

outsider /awtsajdœr/ *n.m.* outsider.

ouvert, ~e /uvɛr, -t/ *voir* **ouvrir**. —*a.* open; (*gaz, radio, etc.*) on. ~**ement** /-təmɑ̃/ *adv.* openly.

ouverture /uvɛrtyr/ *n.f.* opening; (*mus.*) overture; (*photo.*) aperture. ~**s**, (*offres*) overtures. ~ **d'esprit**, open-mindedness.

ouvrable /uvrabl/ *a.* **jour ~**, working day.

ouvrag|e /uvraʒ/ *n.m.* (*travail, livre*)

work; (*couture*) needlework. ~é *a.* finely worked.

ouvreuse /uvrøz/ *n.f.* usherette.

ouvr|ier, ~**ière** /uvrije, -jɛr/ *n.m., f.* worker. —*a.* working-class; (*conflit*) industrial; (*syndicat*) workers'. ~**ier qualifié/spécialisé,** skilled/unskilled worker.

ouvr|ir† /uvrir/ *v.t.* open (up); (*gaz, robinet, etc.*) turn *ou* switch on. —*v.i.* open (up). s'~**ir** *v. pr.* open (up). s'~**ir à qn.,** open one's heart to s.o. ~**e-boîte(s)** *n.m.* tin-opener. ~**e-bouteille(s)** *n.m.* bottle-opener.

ovaire /ɔvɛr/ *n.m.* ovary.

ovale /ɔval/ *a. & n.m.* oval.

ovation /ɔvasjɔ̃/ *n.f.* ovation.

overdose /ɔvɛrdoz/ *n.f.* overdose.

ovni /ɔvni/ *n.m.* (*abrév.*) UFO.

ovule /ɔvyl/ *n.f.* (*à féconder*) egg; (*gynécologique*) pessary.

oxyder (s') /(s)ɔkside/ *v. pr.* become oxidized.

oxygène /ɔksiʒɛn/ *n.m.* oxygen.

oxygéner (s') /(s)ɔksiʒene/ *v. pr.* (*fam.*) get some fresh air.

ozone /ozon/ *n.f.* ozone. **la couche d'**~, the ozone layer.

P

pacemaker /pesmekœr/ *n.m.* pacemaker.

pachyderme /paʃidɛrm/ *n.m.* elephant.

pacifier /pasifje/ *v.t.* pacify.

pacifique /pasifik/ *a.* peaceful; (*personne*) peaceable; (*géog.*) Pacific. —*n.m.* **P**~, Pacific (Ocean).

pacifiste /pasifist/ *n.m./f.* pacifist.

pacotille /pakɔtij/ *n.f.* trash.

pacte /pakt/ *n.m.* pact.

pactiser /paktize/ *v.i.* ~ **avec,** be in league *ou* agreement with.

paddock /padɔk/ *n.m.* paddock.

pag|aie /pagɛ/ *n.f.* paddle. ~**ayer** *v.i.* paddle.

pagaille /pagaj/ *n.f.* mess, shambles.

page /paʒ/ *n.f.* page. **être à la** ~, be up to date.

pagode /pagɔd/ *n.f.* pagoda.

paie /pɛ/ *n.f.* pay.

paiement /pɛmã/ *n.m.* payment.

païen, ~**ne** /pajɛ̃, -jɛn/ *a. & n.m., f.* pagan.

paillasse /pajas/ *n.f.* straw mattress; (*dans un laboratoire*) draining-board.

paillasson /pajasɔ̃/ *n.m.* doormat.

paille /paj/ *n.f.* straw; (*défaut*) flaw.

paillette /pajɛt/ *n.f.* (*sur robe*) sequin; (*de savon*) flake. ~**s d'or,** gold-dust.

pain /pɛ̃/ *n.m.* bread: (*unité*) loaf (of bread); (*de savon etc.*) bar. ~ **d'épice,** gingerbread. ~ **grillé,** toast.

pair[1] /pɛr/ *a.* (*nombre*) even.

pair[2] /pɛr/ *n.m.* (*personne*) peer. **au** ~, (*jeune fille etc.*) au pair. **aller de** ~, go together (**avec,** with).

paire /pɛr/ *n.f.* pair.

paisible /pezibl/ *a.* peaceful.

paître /pɛtr/ *v.i.* (*brouter*) graze.

paix /pɛ/ *n.f.* peace; (*papier*) peace treaty.

Pakistan /pakistɑ̃/ *n.m.* Pakistan.

pakistanais, ~**e** /pakistanɛ, -z/ *a. & n.m., f.* Pakistani.

palace /palas/ *n.m.* luxury hotel.

palais[1] /palɛ/ *n.m.* palace. **P**~ **de Justice,** Law Courts. ~ **des sports,** sports stadium.

palais[2] /palɛ/ *n.m.* (*anat.*) palate.

palan /palɑ̃/ *n.m.* hoist.

pâle /pal/ *a.* pale.

Palestine /palɛstin/ *n.f.* Palestine.

palestinien, ~**ne** /palɛstinjɛ̃, -jɛn/ *a. & n.m., f.* Palestinian.

palet /palɛ/ *n.m.* (*hockey*) puck.

paletot /palto/ *n.m.* thick jacket.

palette /palɛt/ *n.f.* palette.

pâleur /palœr/ *n.f.* paleness.

palier /palje/ *n.m.* (*d'escalier*) landing; (*étape*) stage; (*de route*) level stretch.

pâlir /palir/ *v.t./i.* (turn) pale.

palissade /palisad/ *n.f.* fence.

pallier /palje/ *v.t.* alleviate.

palmarès /palmarɛs/ *n.m.* list of prize winners.

palm|e /palm/ *n.f.* palm leaf; (*symbole*) palm; (*de nageur*) flipper. ~**ier** *n.m.* palm(-tree).

palmé /palme/ *a.* (*patte*) webbed.

pâl|ot, ~**te** /palo, -ɔt/ *a.* pale.

palourde /palurd/ *n.f.* clam.

palper /palpe/ *v.t.* feel.

palpit|er /palpite/ *v.i.* (*battre*) pound, palpitate; (*frémir*) quiver. ~**ations** *n.f. pl.* palpitations. ~**ant,** ~**ante** *a.* thrilling.

paludisme /palydism/ *n.m.* malaria.

pâmer (se) /(sə)pame/ *v. pr.* swoon.

pamphlet /pãflɛ/ *n.m.* satirical pamphlet.

pamplemousse /pãpləmus/ *n.m.* grapefruit.

pan[1] /pã/ *n.m.* piece; (*de chemise*) tail.

pan² /pɑ̃/ *int.* bang.
panacée /panase/ *n.f.* panacea.
panache /panaʃ/ *n.m.* plume; (*bravoure*) gallantry; (*allure*) panache.
panaché /panaʃe/ *a.* (*bariolé, mélangé*) motley. **glace** ∼**e,** mixed-flavour ice cream. —*n.m.* shandy. **bière** ∼**e, demi** ∼**,** shandy.
pancarte /pɑ̃kart/ *n.f.* sign; (*de manifestant*) placard.
pancréas /pɑ̃kreas/ *n.m.* pancreas.
pané /pane/ *a.* breaded.
panier /panje/ *n.m.* basket. ∼ **à provisions,** shopping basket. ∼ **à salade,** (*fam.*) police van.
paniqu|e /panik/ *n.f.* panic. (*fam.*) ∼**er** *v.i.* panic.
panne /pan/ *n.f.* breakdown. **être en** ∼**,** have broken down. **être en** ∼ **sèche,** have run out of petrol *ou* gas (*Amer.*). ∼ **d'électricité** *ou* **de courant,** power failure.
panneau (*pl.* ∼**x**) /pano/ *n.m.* sign; (*publicitaire*) hoarding; (*de porte etc.*) panel. ∼ **(d'affichage),** notice-board. ∼ **(de signalisation),** road sign.
panoplie /panɔpli/ *n.f.* (*jouet*) outfit; (*gamme*) range.
panoram|a /panɔrama/ *n.m.* panorama. ∼**ique** *a.* panoramic.
panse /pɑ̃s/ *n.f.* paunch.
pans|er /pɑ̃se/ *v.t.* (*plaie*) dress; (*personne*) dress the wound(s) of; (*cheval*) groom. ∼**ement** *n.m.* dressing. ∼**ement adhésif,** sticking-plaster.
pantalon /pɑ̃talɔ̃/ *n.m.* (pair of) trousers. ∼**s,** trousers.
panthère /pɑ̃tɛr/ *n.f.* panther.
pantin /pɑ̃tɛ̃/ *n.m.* puppet.
pantomime /pɑ̃tɔmim/ *n.f.* mime; (*spectacle*) mime show.
pantoufle /pɑ̃tufl/ *n.f.* slipper.
paon /pɑ̃/ *n.m.* peacock.
papa /papa/ *n.m.* dad(dy). **de** ∼**,** (*fam.*) old-time.
papauté /papote/ *n.f.* papacy.
pape /pap/ *n.m.* pope.
paperass|e /papras/ *n.f.* ∼**e(s),** (*péj.*) papers. ∼**erie** *n.f.* (*péj.*) papers; (*tracasserie*) red tape.
papet|ier, -ière /paptje, -jɛr/ *n.m., f.* stationer. ∼**erie** /papetri/ *n.f.* (*magasin*) stationer's shop.
papier /papje/ *n.m.* paper; (*formulaire*) form. ∼**s (d'identité),** (identity) papers. ∼ **à lettres,** writing-paper. ∼ **aluminium,** tin foil. ∼ **buvard,** blotting-paper. ∼ **calque,** tracing-paper. ∼ **carbone,** carbon paper. ∼ **collant,** sticky paper. ∼ **de verre,** sandpaper. ∼ **hygiénique,** toilet-paper. ∼ **journal,** newspaper. ∼ **mâché,** papier mâché. ∼ **peint,** wallpaper.
papillon /papijɔ̃/ *n.m.* butterfly; (*contravention*) parking-ticket. ∼ **(de nuit),** moth.
papot|er /papote/ *v.i.* prattle. ∼**age** *n.m.* prattle.
paprika /paprika/ *n.m.* paprika.
Pâque /pɑk/ *n.f.* Passover.
paquebot /pakbo/ *n.m.* liner.
pâquerette /pakrɛt/ *n.f.* daisy.
Pâques /pak/ *n.f. pl.* & *n.m.* Easter.
paquet /pakɛ/ *n.m.* packet; (*de cartes*) pack; (*colis*) parcel. **un** ∼ **de,** (*tas*) a mass of.
par /par/ *prép.* by; (*à travers*) through; (*motif*) out of, from; (*provenance*) from. **commencer/finir** ∼ **qch.,** begin/end with sth. **commencer/finir** ∼ **faire,** begin by/end up (by) doing. ∼ **an/mois/***etc.***,** a *ou* per year/ month/*etc.* ∼ **avion,** (*lettre*) (by) airmail. ∼**-ci,** **par-là,** here and there. ∼ **contre,** on the other hand. ∼ **hasard,** by chance. ∼ **ici/là,** this/that way. ∼ **inadvertance,** inadvertently. ∼ **intermittence,** intermittently. ∼ **l'intermédiaire de,** through. ∼ **jour,** a day. ∼ **malheur** *ou* **malchance,** unfortunately. ∼ **miracle,** miraculously. ∼ **moments,** at times. ∼ **opposition à,** as opposed to. ∼ **personne,** each, per person.
parabole /parabɔl/ *n.f.* (*relig.*) parable; (*maths*) parabola.
paracétamol /parasetamɔl/ *n.m.* paracetamol.
parachever /paraʃve/ *v.t.* perfect.
parachut|e /paraʃyt/ *n.m.* parachute. ∼**er** *v.t.* parachute. ∼**iste** *n.m./f.* parachutist; (*mil.*) paratrooper.
parad|e /parad/ *n.f.* parade; (*sport*) parry; (*réplique*) reply. ∼**er** *v.i.* show off.
paradis /paradi/ *n.m.* paradise. ∼ **fiscal,** tax haven.
paradox|e /paradɔks/ *n.m.* paradox. ∼**al** (*m. pl.* ∼**aux**) *a.* paradoxical.
paraffine /parafin/ *n.f.* paraffin wax.
parages /paraʒ/ *n.m. pl.* area, vicinity.
paragraphe /paragraf/ *n.m.* paragraph.
paraître† /parɛtr/ *v.i.* appear; (*sembler*) seem, appear; (*ouvrage*) be published, come out. **faire** ∼**,** (*ouvrage*) bring out.
parallèle /paralɛl/ *a.* parallel; (*illégal*) unofficial. —*n.m.* parallel. **faire un** ∼ **entre,** draw a parallel between. **faire le**

~, make a connection. —*n.f.* parallel (line). ~**ment** *adv.* parallel (à, to).

paraly|ser /paralize/ *v.t.* paralyse. ~**sie** *n.f.* paralysis. ~**tique** *a.* & *n.m./f.* paralytic.

paramètre /parametr/ *n.m.* parameter.

paranoïa /paranɔja/ *n.f.* paranoia.

parapet /parapɛ/ *n.m.* parapet.

paraphe /paraf/ *n.m.* signature.

paraphrase /parafraz/ *n.f.* paraphrase.

parapluie /paraplɥi/ *n.m.* umbrella.

parasite /parazit/ *n.m.* parasite. ~**s**, (*radio*) interference.

parasol /parasɔl/ *n.m.* sunshade.

paratonnerre /paratɔnɛr/ *n.m.* lightning-conductor *ou* -rod.

paravent /paravã/ *n.m.* screen.

parc /park/ *n.m.* park; (*de bétail*) pen; (*de bébé*) play-pen; (*entrepôt*) depot. ~ **de stationnement,** car-park.

parcelle /parsɛl/ *n.f.* fragment; (*de terre*) plot.

parce que /parsk(ə)/ *conj.* because.

parchemin /parʃəmɛ̃/ *n.m.* parchment.

parcimon|ie /parsimɔni/ *n.f.* avec ~**ie**, parsimoniously. ~**ieux, ~ieuse** *a.* parsimonious.

parcmètre /parkmɛtr/ *n.m.* parking-meter.

parcourir† /parkurir/ *v.t.* travel *ou* go through; (*distance*) travel; (*des yeux*) glance at *ou* over.

parcours /parkur/ *n.m.* route; (*voyage*) journey.

par-delà /pardəla/ *prép.* & *adv.* beyond.

par-derrière /pardɛrjɛr/ *prép.* & *adv.* behind, at the back *ou* rear (of).

par-dessous /pardəsu/ *prép.* & *adv.* under(neath).

pardessus /pardəsy/ *n.m.* overcoat.

par-dessus /pardəsy/ *prép.* & *adv.* over. ~ **bord,** overboard. ~ **le marché,** into the bargain. ~ **tout,** above all.

par-devant /pardəvã/ *adv.* at *ou* from the front, in front.

pardon /pardɔ̃/ *n.m.* forgiveness. (**je vous demande**) ~**!,** (I am) sorry!; (*pour demander qch.*) excuse me!

pardonn|er /pardɔne/ *v.t.* forgive. ~**er qch. à qn.,** forgive s.o. for sth. ~**able** *a.* forgivable.

paré /pare/ *a.* ready.

pare-balles /parbal/ *a. invar.* bullet-proof.

pare-brise /parbriz/ *n.m. invar.* windscreen; (*Amer.*) windshield.

pare-chocs /parʃɔk/ *n.m. invar.* bumper.

pareil, ~le /parɛj/ *a.* similar (à to); (*tel*) such (a). —*n.m., f.* equal. —*adv.* (*fam.*) the same. **c'est** ~, it is the same. **vos** ~**s,** (*péj.*) those of your type, those like you. ~**lement** *adv.* the same.

parement /parmã/ *n.m.* facing.

parent, ~e /parã, -t/ *a.* related (**de,** to). —*n.m., f.* relative, relation. ~**s** (*père et mère*) *n.m. pl.* parents. ~ **seul,** single parent.

parenté /parãte/ *n.f.* relationship.

parenthèse /parãtɛz/ *n.f.* bracket, parenthesis; (*fig.*) digression.

parer¹ /pare/ *v.t.* (*coup*) parry. —*v.i.* ~ **à,** deal with. ~ **au plus pressé,** tackle the most urgent things first.

parer² /pare/ *v.t.* (*orner*) adorn.

paress|e /parɛs/ *n.f.* laziness. ~**er** /-ese/ *v.i.* laze (about). ~**eux, ~euse** *a.* lazy; *n.m., f.* lazybones.

parfaire /parfɛr/ *v.t.* perfect.

parfait, ~e /parfɛ, -t/ *a.* perfect. ~**ement** /-tmã/ *adv.* perfectly; (*bien sûr*) certainly.

parfois /parfwa/ *adv.* sometimes.

parfum /parfœ̃/ *n.m.* scent; (*substance*) perfume, scent; (*goût*) flavour.

parfum|er /parfyme/ *v.t.* perfume; (*gâteau*) flavour. se ~**er** *v. pr.* put on one's perfume. ~**é** *a.* fragrant; (*savon*) scented. ~**erie** *n.f.* (*produits*) perfumes; (*boutique*) perfume shop.

pari /pari/ *n.m.* bet.

par|ier /parje/ *v.t.* bet. ~**ieur, ~ieuse** *n.m., f.* punter, better.

Paris /pari/ *n.m./f.* Paris.

parisien, ~ne /parizjɛ̃, -jɛn/ *a.* Paris, Parisian. —*n.m., f.* Parisian.

parit|é /parite/ *n.f.* parity. ~**aire** *a.* (*commission*) joint.

parjur|e /parʒyr/ *n.m.* perjury. —*n.m./f.* perjurer. se ~**er** *v. pr.* perjure o.s.

parking /parkiŋ/ *n.m.* car-park; (*Amer.*) parking-lot; (*stationnement*) parking.

parlement /parləmã/ *n.m.* parliament. ~**aire** /-tɛr/ *a.* parliamentary; *n.m./f.* Member of Parliament; (*fig.*) negotiator. ~**er** /-te/ *v.i.* negotiate.

parl|er /parle/ *v.i.* talk, speak (à, to). —*v.t.* (*langue*) speak; (*politique, affaires, etc.*) talk. se ~**er** *v. pr.* (*langue*) be spoken. —*n.m.* speech; (*dialecte*) dialect. ~**ant, ~ante** *a.* (*film*) talking; (*fig.*) eloquent. ~**eur, ~euse** *n.m., f.* talker.

parloir /parlwar/ *n.m.* visiting room.

parmi /parmi/ *prép.* among(st).

parod|ie /parɔdi/ *n.f.* parody. ~**ier** *v.t.* parody.

paroi /parwa/ *n.f.* wall; (*cloison*) partition (wall). ~ **rocheuse,** rock face.

paroiss|e /parwas/ *n.f.* parish. ~**ial** (*m. pl.* ~**iaux**) *a.* parish. ~**ien**, ~**ienne** *n.m.*, *f.* parishioner.

parole /parɔl/ *n.f.* (*mot, promesse*) word; (*langage*) speech. **demander la** ~, ask to speak. **prendre la** ~, (begin to) speak. **tenir** ~, keep one's word. **croire qn. sur** ~, take s.o.'s word for it.

paroxysme /parɔksism/ *n.m.* height, highest point.

parquer /parke/ *v.t.*, **se** ~ *v. pr.* (*auto.*) park. ~ **des réfugiés**, pen up refugees.

parquet /parkɛ/ *n.m.* floor; (*jurid.*) public prosecutor's department.

parrain /parɛ̃/ *n.m.* godfather; (*fig.*) sponsor. ~**er** /-ene/ *v.t.* sponsor.

pars, part[1] /par/ *voir* **partir**.

parsemer /parsəme/ *v.t.* strew (**de**, with).

part[2] /par/ *n.f.* share, part. **à** ~, (*de côté*) aside; (*séparément*) apart; (*excepté*) apart from. **d'autre** ~, on the other hand; (*de plus*) moreover. **de la** ~ **de**, from. **de toutes** ~**s**, from all sides. **de** ~ **et d'autre**, on both sides. **d'une** ~, on the one hand. **faire** ~ **à qn.**, inform s.o. (**de**, of). **faire la** ~ **des choses**, make allowances. **prendre** ~ **à**, take part in; (*joie, douleur*) share. **pour ma** ~, as for me.

partag|e /partaʒ/ *n.m.* dividing; sharing out; (*part*) share. ~**er** *v.t.* divide; (*distribuer*) share out; (*avoir en commun*) share. **se** ~**er qch.**, share sth.

partance (en) /(ã)partãs/ *adv.* about to depart.

partant /partã/ *n.m.* (*sport*) starter.

partenaire /partənɛr/ *n.m./f.* partner.

parterre /partɛr/ *n.m.* flower-bed; (*théâtre*) stalls.

parti /parti/ *n.m.* (*pol.*) party; (*en mariage*) match; (*décision*) decision. ~ **pris**, prejudice. **prendre** ~ **pour**, side with. **j'en prends mon** ~, I've come to terms with that.

part|ial (*m. pl.* ~**iaux**) /parsjal, -jo/ *a.* biased. ~**ialité** *n.f.* bias.

participe /partisip/ *n.m.* (*gram.*) participle.

particip|er /partisipe/ *v.i.* ~**er à**, take part in, participate in; (*profits, frais*) share; (*spectacle*) appear in. ~**ant**, ~**ante** *n.m.*, *f.* participant (**à**, in); (*à un concours*) entrant. ~**ation** *n.f.* participation; sharing; (*comm.*) interest. (*d'un artiste*) appearance.

particularité /partikylarite/ *n.f.* particularity.

particule /partikyl/ *n.f.* particle.

particul|ier, ~**ière** /partikylje, -jɛr/ *a.* (*spécifique*) particular; (*bizarre*) peculiar; (*privé*) private. —*n.m.* private individual. **en** ~**ier**, in particular; (*en privé*) in private. ~**ier à**, peculiar to. ~**ièrement** *adv.* particularly.

partie /parti/ *n.f.* part; (*cartes, sport*) game; (*jurid.*) party; (*sortie*) outing, party. **une** ~ **de pêche**, a fishing trip. **en** ~, partly. ~ **faire** ~ **de**, be part of; (*adhérer à*) belong to. **en grande** ~, largely. ~ **intégrante**, integral part.

partiel, ~**le** /parsjɛl/ *a.* partial. —*n.m.* (*univ.*) class examination. ~**lement** *adv.* partially, partly.

partir† /partir/ *v.i.* (*aux. être*) go; (*quitter un lieu*) leave, go; (*tache*) come out; (*bouton*) come off; (*coup de feu*) go off; (*commencer*) start. **à** ~ **de**, from.

partisan, ~**e** /partizã, -an/ *n.m.*, *f.* supporter. —*n.m.* (*mil.*) partisan. **être** ~ **de**, be in favour of.

partition /partisjɔ̃/ *n.f.* (*mus.*) score.

partout /partu/ *adv.* everywhere. ~ **où**, wherever.

paru /pary/ *voir* **paraître**.

parure /paryr/ *n.f.* adornment; (*bijoux*) jewellery; (*de draps*) set.

parution /parysjɔ̃/ *n.f.* publication.

parvenir† /parvənir/ *v.i.* (*aux. être*) ~ **à**, reach; (*résultat*) achieve. ~ **à faire**, manage to do. **faire** ~, send.

parvenu, ~**e** /parvəny/ *n.m.*, *f.* upstart.

parvis /parvi/ *n.m.* (*place*) square.

pas[1] /pɑ/ *adv.* not. (**ne**) ~, not. **je ne sais** ~, I do not know. ~ **de sucre/livres/***etc.*, no sugar/books/*etc.* ~ **du tout**, not at all. ~ **encore**, not yet. ~ **mal**, not bad; (*beaucoup*) quite a lot (**de**, of). ~ **vrai?**, (*fam.*) isn't that so?

pas[2] /pɑ/ *n.m.* step; (*bruit*) footstep; (*trace*) footprint; (*vitesse*) pace; (*de vis*) thread. **à deux** ~ (**de**), close by. **au** ~, at a walking pace; (*véhicule*) very slowly. **au** ~ (**cadencé**), in step. **à** ~ **de loup**, stealthily. **faire les cent** ~, walk up and down. **faire les premiers** ~, take the first steps. **sur le** ~ **de la porte**, on the doorstep.

passable /pɑsabl/ *a.* tolerable. **mention** ~, pass mark.

passage /pɑsaʒ/ *n.m.* passing, passage; (*traversée*) crossing; (*visite*) visit; (*chemin*) way, passage; (*d'une œuvre*) passage. **de** ~, (*voyageur*) visiting; (*amant*) casual. ~ **à niveau**, level crossing. ~ **clouté**, pedestrian crossing. ~ **interdit**, (*panneau*) no thoroughfare. ⁓ **souterrain,** subway; (*Amer.*) underpass.

passag|er, ⁓**ère** /pɑsaʒe, -ɛr/ *a.* temporary. —*n.m., f.* passenger. ⁓**er clandestin,** stowaway.

passant, ⁓**e** /pɑsɑ̃, -t/ *a.* (*rue*) busy. —*n.m., f.* passer-by. —*n.m.* (*anneau*) loop.

passe /pɑs/ *n.f.* pass. **bonne/ mauvaise** ⁓, good/bad patch. **en** ⁓ **de,** on the road to. ⁓**-droit,** *n.m.* special privilege. ⁓**-montagne** *n.m.* Balaclava. ⁓**partout** *n.m. invar.* master-key; *a. invar.* for all occasions. ⁓**-temps** *n.m. invar.* pastime.

passé /pɑse/ *a.* (*révolu*) past; (*dernier*) last; (*fini*) over; (*fané*) faded. —*prép.* after. —*n.m.* past. ⁓ **de mode,** out of fashion.

passeport /pɑspɔr/ *n.m.* passport.

passer /pɑse/ *v.i.* (*aux. être ou avoir*) pass; (*aller*) go; (*venir*) come; (*temps*) pass (by), go by, (*film*) be shown; (*couleur*) fade. —*v.t.* (*aux. avoir*) pass, cross; (*donner*) pass, hand; (*mettre*) put; (*oublier*) overlook; (*enfiler*) slip on; (*dépasser*) go beyond; (*temps*) spend, pass; (*film*) show; (*examen*) take; (*commande*) place; (*soupe*) strain. **se** ⁓ *v. pr.* happen, take place. **laisser** ⁓, let through; (*occasion*) miss. ⁓ **à tabac,** (*fam.*) beat up. ⁓ **devant,** (*édifice*) go past. ⁓ **en fraude,** smuggle. ⁓ **outre,** take no notice (à, of). ⁓ **par,** go through. ⁓ **pour,** (*riche etc.*) be taken to be. ⁓ **sur,** (*détail*) pass over. ⁓ **l'aspirateur,** hoover, vacuum. ⁓ **un coup de fil à qn.,** give s.o. a ring. **je vous passe Mme X,** (*par le standard*) I'm putting you through to Mrs X; (*en donnant l'appareil*) I'll hand you over to Mrs X. **se** ⁓ **de,** go ou do without.

passerelle /pɑsrɛl/ *n.f.* footbridge; (*pour accéder à un avion, à un navire*) gangway.

pass|eur, ⁓**euse** /pɑsœr, œz/ *n.m., f.* smuggler.

passible /pɑsibl/ *a.* ⁓ **de,** liable to.

passi|f, ⁓**ve** /pɑsif, -v/ *a.* passive. —*n.m.* (*comm.*) liabilities. ⁓**vité** *n.f.* passiveness.

passion /pɑsjɔ̃/ *n.f.* passion.

passionn|er /pɑsjɔne/ *v.t.* fascinate. **se** ⁓**er pour,** have a passion for. ⁓**é** *a.* passionate. **être** ⁓**é de,** have a passion for. ⁓**ément** *adv.* passionately.

passoire /pɑswar/ *n.f.* (*à thé*) strainer; (*à légumes*) colander.

pastel /pɑstɛl/ *n.m. & a. invar.* pastel.

pastèque /pɑstɛk/ *n.f.* watermelon.

pasteur /pɑstœr/ *n.m.* (*relig.*) minister.

pasteurisé /pɑstœrize/ *a.* pasteurized.

pastiche /pɑstiʃ/ *n.m.* pastiche.

pastille /pɑstij/ *n.f.* (*bonbon*) pastille, lozenge.

pastis /pɑstis/ *n.m.* aniseed liqueur.

patate /pɑtat/ *n.f.* (*fam.*) potato. ⁓ **(douce),** sweet potato.

patauger /pɑtoʒe/ *v.i.* splash about.

pâte /pɑt/ *n.f.* paste; (*farine*) dough; (*à tarte*) pastry; (*à frire*) batter. ⁓**s (alimentaires),** pasta. ⁓ **à modeler,** Plasticine (P.). ⁓ **dentifrice,** toothpaste.

pâté /pɑte/ *n.m.* (*culin.*) pâté; (*d'encre*) ink-blot. ⁓ **de maisons,** block of houses; (*de sable*) sand-pie. ⁓ **en croûte,** meat pie.

pâtée /pɑte/ *n.f.* feed, mash.

patelin /pɑtlɛ̃/ *n.m.* (*fam.*) village.

patent, ⁓**e**[1] /pɑtɑ̃, -t/ *a.* patent.

patent|e[2] /pɑtɑ̃t/ *n.f.* trade licence. ⁓**é** *a.* licensed.

patère /pɑtɛr/ *n.f.* (*coat*) peg.

patern|el, ⁓**elle** /pɑtɛrnɛl/ *a.* paternal. ⁓**ité** *n.f.* paternity.

pâteu|x, ⁓**se** /pɑtø, -z/ *a.* pasty; (*langue*) coated.

pathétique /pɑtetik/ *a.* moving. —*n.m.* pathos.

patholog|ie /pɑtɔlɔʒi/ *n.f.* pathology. ⁓**ique** *a.* pathological.

pat|ient, ⁓**iente** /pɑsjɑ̃, -t/ *a. & n.m., f.* patient. ⁓**iemment** /-jamɑ̃/ *adv.* patiently. ⁓**ience** *n.f.* patience.

patienter /pɑsjɑ̃te/ *v.i.* wait.

patin /pɑtɛ̃/ *n.m.* skate. ⁓ **à roulettes,** roller-skate.

patin|er /pɑtine/ *v.i.* skate; (*voiture*) spin. ⁓**age** *n.m.* skating. ⁓**eur,** ⁓**euse** *n.m., f.* skater.

patinoire /pɑtinwar/ *n.f.* skating-rink.

pâtir /pɑtir/ *v.i.* suffer (**de,** from).

pâtiss|ier, ⁓**ière** /pɑtisje, -jɛr/ *n.m., f.* pastry-cook, cake-shop owner. ⁓**erie** *n.f.* cake shop; (*gâteau*) pastry; (*art*) cake making.

patois /pɑtwa/ *n.m.* patois.

patraque /pɑtrak/ *a.* (*fam.*) peaky, out of sorts.

patrie /pɑtri/ *n.f.* homeland.

patrimoine /pɑtrimwan/ *n.m.* heritage.

patriot|e /pɑtrijɔt/ *a.* patriotic. —*n.m./f.* patriot. ⁓**ique** *a.* patriotic. ⁓**isme** *n.m.* patriotism.

patron[1], ⁓**ne** /pɑtrɔ̃, -ɔn/ *n.m., f.*

employer, boss; (*propriétaire*) owner, boss; (*saint*) patron saint. ~**al** (*m. pl.* ~**aux**) /-ɔnal, -o/ *a.* employers'. ~**at** /-ɔna/ *n.m.* employers.

patron² /patrɔ̃/ *n.m.* (*couture*) pattern.

patronage /patrɔnaʒ/ *n.m.* patronage; (*foyer*) youth club.

patronner /patrɔne/ *v.t.* support.

patrouill|e /patruj/ *n.f.* patrol. ~**er** *v.i.* patrol.

patte /pat/ *n.f.* leg; (*pied*) foot; (*de chat*) paw. ~**s**, (*favoris*) sideburns.

pâturage /pɑtyraʒ/ *n.m.* pasture.

pâture /pɑtyr/ *n.f.* food.

paume /pom/ *n.f.* (*de main*) palm.

paumé, ~**e** /pome/ *n.m.*, *f.* (*fam.*) wretch, loser.

paumer /pome/ *v.t.* (*fam.*) lose.

paupière /popjɛr/ *n.f.* eyelid.

pause /poz/ *n.f.* pause; (*halte*) break.

pauvre /povr/ *a.* poor. —*n.m./f.* poor man, poor woman. ~**ment** /-əmɑ̃/ *adv.* poorly. ~**té** /-əte/ *n.f.* poverty.

pavaner (se) /(sə)pavane/ *v. pr.* strut.

pav|er /pave/ *v.t.* pave; (*chaussée*) cobble. ~**é** *n.m.* paving-stone; cobble(stone).

pavillon¹ /pavijɔ̃/ *n.m.* house; (*de gardien*) lodge.

pavillon² /pavijɔ̃/ *n.m.* (*drapeau*) flag.

pavoiser /pavwaze/ *v.t.* deck with flags. —*v.i.* put out the flags.

pavot /pavo/ *n.m.* poppy.

payant, ~**e** /pɛjɑ̃, -t/ *a.* (*billet*) for which a charge is made; (*spectateur*) (fee-)paying; (*rentable*) profitable.

payer /peje/ *v.t./i.* pay; (*service, travail, etc.*) pay for; (*acheter*) buy (à, for). se ~ *v. pr.* (*s'acheter*) buy o.s. **faire** ~ **à** qn., (*cent francs etc.*) charge s.o. (**pour**, for). **se** ~ **la tête de**, make fun of. **il me le paiera!**, he'll pay for this.

pays /pei/ *n.m.* country; (*région*) region; (*village*) village. **du** ~, local. **les P~-Bas**, the Netherlands. **le** ~ **de Galles**, Wales.

paysage /peizaʒ/ *n.m.* landscape.

paysan, ~**ne** /peizɑ̃, -an/ *n.m.*, *f.* farmer, country person; (*péj.*) peasant. —*a.* (*agricole*) farming; (*rural*) country.

PCV (en) /(ɑ̃)peseve/ *adv.* **appeler** *ou* **téléphoner en** ~, reverse the charges; (*Amer.*) call collect.

PDG *abrév. voir* **président directeur général**.

péage /peaʒ/ *n.m.* toll; (*lieu*) toll-gate.

peau (*pl.* ~**x**) /po/ *n.f.* skin; (*cuir*) hide. ~ **de chamois**, chamois(-leather). ~

de mouton, sheepskin. **être bien/mal dans sa** ~, be/not be at ease with oneself.

pêche¹ /pɛʃ/ *n.f.* peach.

pêche² /pɛʃ/ *n.f.* (*activité*) fishing; (*poissons*) catch. ~ **à la ligne**, angling.

péché /peʃe/ *n.m.* sin.

péch|er /peʃe/ *v.i.* sin. ~**er par timidité/etc.**, be too timid/*etc.* ~**eur**, ~**eresse** *n.m.*, *f.* sinner.

pêch|er /peʃe/ *v.t.* (*poisson*) catch; (*dénicher: fam.*) dig up. —*v.i.* fish. ~**eur** *n.m.* fisherman; (*à la ligne*) angler.

pécule /pekyl/ *n.m.* (*économies*) savings.

pécuniaire /pekynjɛr/ *a.* financial.

pédago|gie /pedagɔʒi/ *n.f.* education. ~**gique** *a.* educational. ~**gue** *n.m./f.* teacher.

pédal|e /pedal/ *n.f.* pedal. ~**er** *v.i.* pedal.

pédalo /pedalo/ *n.m.* pedal boat.

pédant, ~**e** /pedɑ̃, -t/ *a.* pedantic.

pédé /pede/ *n.m.* (*argot*) queer, fag (*Amer.*).

pédestre /pedɛstr/ *a.* **faire de la randonnée** ~, go walking *ou* hiking.

pédiatre /pedjatr/ *n.m./f.* paediatrician.

pédicure /pedikyr/ *n.m./f.* chiropodist.

pedigree /pedigri/ *n.m.* pedigree.

pègre /pɛgr/ *n.f.* underworld.

peign|e /pɛɲ/ *n.m.* comb. ~**er** /peɲe/ *v.t.* comb; (*personne*) comb the hair of. **se** ~**er** *v. pr.* comb one's hair.

peignoir /pɛɲwar/ *n.m.* dressing-gown.

peindre† /pɛ̃dr/ *v.t.* paint.

peine /pɛn/ *n.f.* sadness, sorrow; (*effort, difficulté*) trouble; (*punition*) punishment; (*jurid.*) sentence. **avoir de la** ~, feel sad. **faire de la** ~ **à**, hurt. **ce n'est pas la** ~ **de faire**, it is not worth (while) doing. **se donner** *ou* **prendre la** ~ **de faire**, go to the trouble of doing. ~ **de mort** death penalty.

peine (à) /(a)pɛn/ *adv.* hardly.

peiner /pene/ *v.i.* struggle. —*v.t.* sadden.

peintre /pɛ̃tr/ *n.m.* painter. ~ **en bâtiment**, house painter.

peinture /pɛ̃tyr/ *n.f.* painting; (*matière*) paint. ~ **à l'huile**, oil-painting.

péjorati|f, ~**ve** /peʒɔratif, -v/ *a.* pejorative.

pelage /pəlaʒ/ *n.m.* coat, fur.

pêle-mêle /pɛlmɛl/ *adv.* in a jumble.

peler /pəle/ *v.t./i.* peel.

pèlerin /pɛlrɛ̃/ *n.m.* pilgrim. ~**age** /-inaʒ/ *n.m.* pilgrimage.

pèlerine /pɛlrin/ *n.f.* cape.

pélican /pelikɑ̃/ *n.m.* pelican.

pelle /pɛl/ n.f. shovel; (d'enfant) spade. ~tée n.f. shovelful.

pellicule /pelikyl/ n.f. film. ~s, (cheveux) dandruff.

pelote /pəlɔt/ n.f. ball; (d'épingles) pincushion.

peloton /plɔtɔ̃/ n.m. troop, squad; (sport) pack. ~ d'exécution, firing-squad.

pelotonner (se) /(sə)plɔtɔne/ v. pr. curl up.

pelouse /pluz/ n.f. lawn.

peluche /plyʃ/ n.f. (tissu) plush; (jouet) cuddly toy. **en** ~, (lapin, chien) fluffy, furry.

pelure /plyr/ n.f. peeling.

pén|al (m. pl. ~aux) /penal, -o/ a. penal. ~aliser v.t. penalize. ~alité n.f. penalty.

penalt|y (pl. ~ies) /penalti/ n.m. penalty (kick).

penaud, ~e /pəno, -d/ a. sheepish.

penchant /pɑ̃ʃɑ̃/ n.m. inclination; (goût) liking (pour, for).

pench|er /pɑ̃ʃe/ v.t. tilt. —v.i. lean (over), tilt. **se** ~er v. pr. lean (forward). ~er pour, favour. **se** ~er sur, (problème etc.) examine.

pendaison /pɑ̃dɛzɔ̃/ n.f. hanging.

pendant¹ /pɑ̃dɑ̃/ prép. (au cours de) during; (durée) for. ~ que, while.

pendant², ~e /pɑ̃dɑ̃, -t/ a. hanging; (question etc.) pending. —n.m. (contrepartie) matching piece (de, to). **faire** ~ à, match. ~ d'oreille, drop earring.

pendentif /pɑ̃dɑ̃tif/ n.m. pendant.

penderie /pɑ̃dri/ n.f. wardrobe.

pend|re /pɑ̃dr/ v.t./i. hang. **se** ~re v. pr. hang (à, from); (se tuer) hang o.s. ~re la crémaillère, have a house-warming. ~u, ~ue a. hanging (à, from); n.m., f. hanged man, hanged woman.

pendul|e /pɑ̃dyl/ n.f. clock. —n.m. pendulum. ~ette n.f. (travelling) clock.

pénétr|er /penetre/ v.i. ~er (dans), enter. —v.t. penetrate. **se** ~er de, become convinced of. ~ant, ~ante a. penetrating.

pénible /penibl/ a. difficult; (douloureux) painful; (fatigant) tiresome. ~ment /-əmɑ̃/ adv. with difficulty; (cruellement) painfully.

péniche /peniʃ/ n.f. barge.

pénicilline /penisilin/ n.f. penicillin.

péninsule /penɛ̃syl/ n.f. peninsula.

pénis /penis/ n.m. penis.

pénitence /penitɑ̃s/ n.f. (peine) penance; (regret) penitence; (fig.) punishment. **faire** ~, repent.

péniten|cier /penitɑ̃sje/ n.m. penitentiary. ~tiaire /-sjɛr/ a. prison.

pénombre /penɔ̃br/ n.f. half-light.

pensée¹ /pɑ̃se/ n.f. thought.

pensée² /pɑ̃se/ n.f. (fleur) pansy.

pens|er /pɑ̃se/ v.t./i. think. ~er à, (réfléchir à) think about; (se souvenir de, prévoir) think of. ~er faire, think of doing. **faire** ~er à, remind one of. ~eur n.m. thinker.

pensi|f, ~ve /pɑ̃sif, -v/ a. pensive.

pension /pɑ̃sjɔ̃/ n.f. (scol.) boarding-school; (repas, somme) board; (allocation) pension. ~ (de famille), guest-house. ~ alimentaire, (jurid.) alimony. ~naire /-jɔnɛr/ n.m./f. boarder; (d'hôtel) guest. ~nat /-jɔna/ n.m. boarding-school.

pente /pɑ̃t/ n.f. slope. **en** ~, sloping.

Pentecôte /pɑ̃tkot/ n.f. **la** ~, Whitsun.

pénurie /penyri/ n.f. shortage.

pépé /pepe/ n.m. (fam.) grandad.

pépier /pepje/ v.i. chirp.

pépin /pepɛ̃/ n.m. (graine) pip; (ennui, fam.) hitch; (parapluie, fam.) brolly.

pépinière /pepinjɛr/ n.f. (tree) nursery.

perçant, ~e /pɛrsɑ̃, -t/ a. (froid) piercing; (regard) keen.

percée /pɛrse/ n.f. opening; (attaque) breakthrough.

perce-neige /pɛrsənɛʒ/ n.m./f. invar. snowdrop.

percepteur /pɛrsɛptœr/ n.m. tax-collector.

perceptible /pɛrsɛptibl/ a. perceptible.

perception /pɛrsɛpsjɔ̃/ n.f. perception; (d'impôts) collection.

percer /pɛrse/ v.t. pierce; (avec perceuse) drill; (mystère) penetrate. —v.i. break through; (dent) come through.

perceuse /pɛrsøz/ n.f. drill.

percevoir† /pɛrsəvwar/ v.t. perceive; (impôt) collect.

perche /pɛrʃ/ n.f. (bâton) pole.

perch|er /pɛrʃe/ v.t., **se** ~er v. pr. perch. ~oir n.m. perch.

percolateur /pɛrkɔlatœr/ n.m. percolator.

percussion /pɛrkysjɔ̃/ n.f. percussion.

percuter /pɛrkyte/ v.t. strike; (véhicule) crash into.

perd|re /pɛrdr/ v.t./i. lose; (gaspiller) waste; (ruiner) ruin. **se** ~re v. pr. get lost; (rester inutilisé) go to waste. ~ant, ~ante a. losing; n.m., f. loser. ~u a. (endroit) isolated; (moments) spare; (malade) finished.

perdreau (pl. ~x) /pɛrdro/ n.m. (young) partridge.

perdrix /pɛrdri/ *n.f.* partridge.

père /pɛr/ *n.m.* father. ∼ **de famille,** father, family man. ∼ **spirituel,** father figure. **le** ∼ **Noël,** Father Christmas, Santa Claus.

péremptoire /perãptwar/ *a.* peremptory.

perfection /pɛrfɛksjɔ̃/ *n.f.* perfection.

perfectionn|er /pɛrfɛksjɔne/ *v.t.* improve. **se** ∼**er en anglais**/*etc.*, improve one's English/*etc.* ∼**é** *a.* sophisticated. ∼**ement** *n.m.* improvement.

perfectionniste /pɛrfɛksjɔnist/ *n.m./f.* perfectionist.

perfid|e /pɛrfid/ *a.* perfidious, treacherous. ∼**ie** *n.f.* perfidy.

perfor|er /pɛrfɔre/ *v.t.* perforate; (*billet, bande*) punch. ∼**ateur** *n.m.* (*appareil*) punch. ∼**ation** *n.f.* perforation; (*trou*) hole.

performan|ce /pɛrfɔrmɑ̃s/ *n.f.* performance. ∼**t,** ∼**te** *a.* high-performance, successful.

perfusion /pɛrfyzjɔ̃/ *n.f.* drip. **mettre qn. sous** ∼, put s.o. on a drip.

péricliter /periklite/ *v.i.* decline, be in rapid decline.

péridural /peridyral/ *a.* (**anesthésie**) ∼**e,** epidural.

péril /peril/ *n.m.* peril.

périlleu|x, ∼**se** /perijø, -z/ *a.* perilous.

périmé /perime/ *a.* expired; (*désuet*) outdated.

périmètre /perimɛtr/ *n.m.* perimeter.

périod|e /perjɔd/ *n.f.* period. ∼**ique** *a.* periodic(al); *n.m.* (*journal*) periodical.

péripétie /peripesi/ *n.f.* (unexpected) event, adventure.

périphér|ie /periferi/ *n.f.* periphery; (*banlieue*) outskirts. ∼**ique** *a.* peripheral; *n.m.* (**boulevard**) ∼**ique,** ring road.

périple /peripl/ *n.m.* journey.

pér|ir /perir/ *v.i.* perish, die. ∼**issable** *a.* perishable.

périscope /periskɔp/ *n.m.* periscope.

perle /pɛrl/ *n.f.* (*bijou*) pearl; (*boule, de sueur*) bead.

permanence /pɛrmanɑ̃s/ *n.f.* permanence; (*bureau*) duty office; (*scol.*) study room. **de** ∼, on duty. **en** ∼, permanently. **assurer une** ∼, keep the office open.

permanent, ∼**e** /permanɑ̃, -t/ *a.* permanent; (*spectacle*) continuous; (*comité*) standing. —*n.f.* (*coiffure*) perm.

perméable /pɛrmeabl/ *a.* permeable; (*personne*) susceptible (**à,** to).

permettre† /pɛrmɛtr/ *v.t.* allow, permit. ∼ **à qn. de,** allow *ou* permit s.o. to. **se** ∼ **de,** take the liberty to.

permis, ∼**e** /pɛrmi, -z/ *a.* allowed. —*n.m.* licence, permit. ∼ (**de conduire**), driving-licence.

permission /pɛrmisjɔ̃/ *n.f.* permission. **en** ∼, (*mil.*) on leave.

permut|er /pɛrmyte/ *v.t.* change round. ∼**ation** *n.f.* permutation.

pernicieu|x, ∼**se** /pɛrnisjø, -z/ *a.* pernicious.

Pérou /peru/ *n.m.* Peru.

perpendiculaire /pɛrpɑ̃dikylɛr/ *a.* & *n.f.* perpendicular.

perpétrer /pɛrpetre/ *v.t.* perpetrate.

perpétuel, ∼**le** /pɛrpetɥɛl/ *a.* perpetual.

perpétuer /pɛrpetɥe/ *v.t.* perpetuate.

perpétuité (à) /(a)pɛrpetɥite/ *adv.* for life.

perplex|e /pɛrplɛks/ *a.* perplexed. ∼**ité** *n.f.* perplexity.

perquisition /pɛrkizisjɔ̃/ *n.f.* (police) search. ∼**ner** /-jɔne/ *v.t./i.* search.

perron /pɛrɔ̃/ *n.m.* (front) steps.

perroquet /pɛrɔkɛ/ *n.m.* parrot.

perruche /perʃ/ *n.f.* budgerigar.

perruque /peryk/ *n.f.* wig.

persan, ∼**e** /pɛrsɑ̃, -an/ *a.* & *n.m.* (*lang.*) Persian.

persécut|er /pɛrsekyte/ *v.t.* persecute. ∼**ion** /-ysjɔ̃/ *n.f.* persecution.

persévér|er /pɛrsevere/ *v.i.* persevere. ∼**ance** *n.f.* perseverance.

persienne /pɛrsjɛn/ *n.f.* (outside) shutter.

persil /pɛrsi/ *n.m.* parsley.

persistan|t, ∼**te** /pɛrsistɑ̃, -t/ *a.* persistent; (*feuillage*) evergreen. ∼**ce** *n.f.* persistence.

persister /pɛrsiste/ *v.i.* persist (**à faire,** in doing).

personnage /pɛrsɔnaʒ/ *n.m.* character; (*important*) personality.

personnalité /pɛrsɔnalite/ *n.f.* personality.

personne /pɛrsɔn/ *n.f.* person. ∼**s,** people. —*pron.* (*quelqu'un*) anybody. (**ne**) ∼, nobody.

personnel, ∼**le** /pɛrsɔnɛl/ *a.* personal; (*égoïste*) selfish. —*n.m.* staff. ∼**lement** *adv.* personally.

personnifier /pɛrsɔnifje/ *v.t.* personify.

perspective /pɛrspɛktiv/ *n.f.* (*art*) perspective; (*vue*) view; (*possibilité*) prospect; (*point de vue*) viewpoint, perspective.

perspicac|e /pɛrspikas/ *a.* shrewd. ∼**ité** *n.f.* shrewdness.

persua|der /pɛrsɥade/ *v.t.* persuade (**de**

faire, to do). ~**sion** /-ɥɑzjɔ̃/ *n.f.* persuasion.

persuasi|f, ~**ve** /pɛrsɥazif, -v/ *a.* persuasive.

perte /pɛrt/ *n.f.* loss; (*ruine*) ruin. **à** ~ **de vue,** as far as the eye can see. ~ **de,** (*temps, argent*) waste of. ~ **sèche,** total loss. ~**s,** (*méd.*) discharge.

pertinen|t, ~**te** /pɛrtinɑ̃, -t/ *a.* pertinent; (*esprit*) judicious. ~**ce** *n.f.* pertinence.

perturb|er /pɛrtyrbe/ *v.t.* disrupt; (*personne*) perturb. ~**ateur,** ~**atrice** *a.* disruptive; *n.m., f.* disruptive element. ~**ation** *n.f.* disruption.

pervenche /pɛrvɑ̃ʃ/ *n.f.* periwinkle; (*fam.*) traffic warden.

pervers, ~**e** /pɛrvɛr, -s/ *a.* perverse; (*dépravé*) perverted. ~**ion** /-sjɔ̃/ *n.f.* perversion.

pervert|ir /pɛrvɛrtir/ *v.t.* pervert. ~**i,** ~**ie** *n.m., f.* pervert.

pes|ant, ~**ante** /pəzɑ̃, t/ *a.* heavy. ~**amment** *adv.* heavily. ~**anteur** *n.f.* heaviness. **la** ~**anteur,** (*force*) gravity.

pèse-personne /pɛzpɛrsɔn/ *n.m.* (bath room) scales.

pes|er /pəze/ *v.t./i.* weigh. ~**er sur,** bear upon. ~**ée** *n.f.* weighing; (*effort*) pressure.

peseta /pezeta/ *n.f.* peseta.

pessimis|te /pesimist/ *a.* pessimistic. —*n.m.* pessimist. ~**me** *n.m.* pessimism.

peste /pɛst/ *n.f.* plague; (*personne*) pest.

pester /pɛste/ *v.i.* ~ (**contre**), curse.

pestilentiel, ~**le** /pɛstilɑ̃sjɛl/ *a.* fetid, stinking.

pet /pɛ/ *n.m.* fart.

pétale /petal/ *n.m.* petal.

pétanque /petɑ̃k/ *n.f.* bowls.

pétarader /petarade/ *v.i.* backfire.

pétard /petar/ *n.m.* banger.

péter /pete/ *v.i.* fart; (*fam.*) go bang; (*casser: fam.*) snap.

pétill|er /petije/ *v.i.* (*feu*) crackle; (*champagne, yeux*) sparkle. ~**er d'intelligence,** sparkle with intelligence. ~**ant,** ~**ante** *a.* (*gazeux*) fizzy.

petit, ~**e** /pti, -t/ *a.* small; (*avec nuance affective*) little; (*jeune*) young, small; (*faible*) slight; (*mesquin*) petty. —*n.m., f.* little child; (*scol.*) junior. ~**s,** (*de chat*) kittens; (*de chien*) pups. **en** ~, in miniature. ~ **ami,** boy-friend. ~**e amie,** girl-friend. ~ **à petit,** little by little. ~**es annonces,** small ads. ~**e cuiller,** teaspoon. ~ **déjeuner,** breakfast. **le** ~ **écran,** the small screen,

television. ~-**enfant** (*pl.* ~**s-enfants**) *n.m.* grandchild. ~**e-fille** (*pl.* ~**es-filles**) *n.f.* granddaughter. ~-**fils** (*pl.* ~**s-fils**) *n.m.* grandson. ~ **pain,** roll. ~-**pois** (*pl.* ~**s-pois**) *n.m.* garden pea.

petitesse /ptitɛs/ *n.f.* smallness; (*péj.*) meanness.

pétition /petisjɔ̃/ *n.f.* petition.

pétrifier /petrifje/ *v.t.* petrify.

pétrin /petrɛ̃/ *n.m.* (*situation: fam.*) **dans le** ~, in a fix.

pétrir /petrir/ *v.t.* knead.

pétrol|e /petrɔl/ *n.m.* (*brut*) oil; (*pour lampe etc.*) paraffin. **lampe à** ~**e,** oil lamp. ~**ier,** ~**ière** *a.* oil; *n.m.* (*navire*) oil-tanker.

pétulant, ~**e** /petylɑ̃, -t/ *a.* exuberant, full of high spirits.

peu /pø/ *adv.* ~ (**de**), (*quantité*) little, not much; (*nombre*) few, not many. ~ **intéressant**/*etc.*, not very interesting/*etc.* —*pron.* few. —*n.m.* little. **un** ~ (**de**), a little. **à** ~ **près,** more or less. **de** ~, only just. ~ **à peu,** gradually. ~ **après**/**avant,** shortly after/before. ~ **de chose,** not much. ~ **nombreux,** few. ~ **souvent,** seldom. **pour** ~ **que,** as long as.

peuplade /pœplad/ *n.f.* tribe.

peuple /pœpl/ *n.m.* people.

peupler /pœple/ *v.t.* populate.

peuplier /pøplije/ *n.m.* poplar.

peur /pœr/ *n.f.* fear. **avoir** ~, be afraid (**de, of**). **de** ~ **de,** for fear of. **faire** ~ **à,** frighten. ~**eux,** ~**euse** *a.* fearful, timid.

peut /pø/ *voir* **pouvoir**[1].

peut-être /pøtɛtr/ *adv.* perhaps, maybe. ~ **que,** perhaps, maybe.

peux /pø/ *voir* **pouvoir**[1].

pèze /pɛz/ *n.m.* (*fam.*) **du** ~, money, dough.

phallique /falik/ *a.* phallic.

phantasme /fɑ̃tasm/ *n.m.* fantasy.

phare /far/ *n.m.* (*tour*) lighthouse; (*de véhicule*) headlight. ~ **antibrouillard,** fog lamp.

pharmaceutique /farmasøtik/ *a.* pharmaceutical.

pharmac|ie /farmasi/ *n.f.* (*magasin*) chemist's (shop); (*Amer.*) pharmacy; (*science*) pharmacy; (*armoire*) medicine cabinet. ~**ien,** ~**ienne** *n.m., f.* chemist, pharmacist.

pharyngite /farɛ̃ʒit/ *n.f.* pharyngitis.

phase /faz/ *n.f.* phase.

phénomène /fenɔmɛn/ *n.m.* phenomenon; (*original: fam.*) eccentric.

philanthrop|e /filɑ̃trɔp/ *n.m./f.* philanthropist. ~**ique** *a.* philanthropic.

philatél|ie /filateli/ *n.f.* philately. **∼iste** *n.m./f.* philatelist.

philharmonique /filarmɔnik/ *a.* philharmonic.

Philippines /filipin/ *n.f. pl.* **les ∼**, the Philippines.

philosoph|e /filɔzɔf/ *n.m./f.* philosopher. —*a.* philosophical. **∼ie** *n.f.* philosophy. **∼ique** *a.* philosophical.

phobie /fɔbi/ *n.f.* phobia.

phonétique /fɔnetik/ *a.* phonetic.

phoque /fɔk/ *n.m.* (*animal*) seal.

phosphate /fɔsfat/ *n.m.* phosphate.

phosphore /fɔsfɔr/ *n.m.* phosphorus.

photo /fɔto/ *n.f.* photo; (*art*) photography. **prendre en ∼**, take a photo of. **∼ d'identité**, passport photograph.

photocop|ie /fɔtɔkɔpi/ *n.f.* photocopy. **∼ier** *v.t.* photocopy. **∼ieuse** *n.f.* photocopier.

photogénique /fɔtɔʒenik/ *a.* photogenic.

photograph|e /fɔtɔgraf/ *n.m./f.* photographer. **∼ie** *n.f.* photograph; (*art*) photography. **∼ier** *v.t.* take a photo of. **∼ique** *a.* photographic.

phrase /fraz/ *n.f.* sentence.

physicien, ∼ne /fizisjɛ̃, -jɛn/ *n.m., f.* physicist.

physiologie /fizjɔlɔʒi/ *n.f.* physiology.

physionomie /fizjɔnɔmi/ *n.f.* face.

physique[1] /fizik/ *a.* physical. —*n.m.* physique. **au ∼**, physically. **∼ment** *adv.* physically.

physique[2] /fizik/ *n.f.* physics.

piailler /pjɑje/ *v.i.* squeal, squawk.

pian|o /pjano/ *n.m.* piano. **∼iste** *n.m./f.* pianist.

pianoter /pjanɔte/ *v.t.* (*air*) tap out. —*v.i.* (**sur, on**) (*ordinateur*) tap away; (*table*) tap one's fingers.

pic /pik/ *n.m.* (*outil*) pickaxe; (*sommet*) peak; (*oiseau*) woodpecker. **à ∼**, (*verticalement*) sheer; (*couler*) straight to the bottom; (*arriver*) just at the right time.

pichenette /piʃnɛt/ *n.f.* flick.

pichet /piʃɛ/ *n.m.* jug.

pickpocket /pikpɔkɛt/ *n.m.* pickpocket.

pick-up /pikœp/ *n.m. invar.* record-player.

picorer /pikɔre/ *v.t./i.* peck.

picot|er /pikɔte/ *v.t.* prick; (*yeux*) make smart. **∼ement** *n.m.* pricking; smarting.

pie /pi/ *n.f.* magpie.

pièce /pjɛs/ *n.f.* piece; (*chambre*) room; (*pour raccommoder*) patch; (*écrit*) document. **∼ (de monnaie)**, coin. **∼ (de théâtre)**, play. **dix francs**/*etc.* (**la**

∼, ten francs/*etc.* each. **∼ de rechange**, spare part. **∼ détachée**, part. **∼ d'identité**, identity paper. **∼ montée**, tiered cake. **∼s justificatives**, supporting documents. **deux/trois** *etc.* **∼s**, two-/three-/*etc.* room flat *ou* apartment (*Amer.*).

pied /pje/ *n.m.* foot; (*de meuble*) leg; (*de lampe*) base; (*de salade*) plant. **à ∼**, on foot. **au ∼ de la lettre**, literally. **avoir ∼**, have a footing. **avoir les ∼s plats**, have flat feet. **comme un ∼**, (*fam.*) terribly. **mettre sur ∼**, set up. **∼ bot**, club-foot. **sur un ∼ d'égalité**, on an equal footing. **mettre les ∼s dans le plat**, put one's foot in it. **c'est le ∼!**, (*fam.*) it's great!

piédest|al (*pl.* **∼aux**) /pjedɛstal, -o/ *n.m.* pedestal.

piège /pjɛʒ/ *n.m.* trap.

piég|er /pjeʒe/ *v.t.* trap; (*avec explosifs*) booby-trap. **lettre/voiture ∼ée**, letter-/car-bomb.

pierr|e /pjɛr/ *n.f.* stone. **∼e d'achoppement**, stumbling-block. **∼e de touche**, touchstone. **∼e précieuse**, precious stone. **∼e tombale**, tombstone. **∼eux, ∼euse** *a.* stony.

piété /pjete/ *n.f.* piety.

piétiner /pjetine/ *v.i.* stamp one's feet; (*ne pas avancer: fig.*) mark time. —*v.t.* trample (on).

piéton /pjetɔ̃/ *n.m.* pedestrian. **∼nier, ∼nière** /-ɔnje, -jɛr/ *a.* pedestrian.

piètre /pjɛtr/ *a.* wretched.

pieu (*pl.* **∼x**) /pjø/ *n.m.* post, stake.

pieuvre /pjœvr/ *n.f.* octopus.

pieu|x, ∼se /pjø, -z/ *a.* pious.

pif /pif/ *n.m.* (*fam.*) nose.

pigeon /piʒɔ̃/ *n.m.* pigeon.

piger /piʒe/ *v.t./i.* (*fam.*) understand, get (it).

pigment /pigmɑ̃/ *n.m.* pigment.

pignon /piɲɔ̃/ *n.m.* (*de maison*) gable.

pile /pil/ *n.f.* (*tas, pilier*) pile; (*électr.*) battery; (*atomique*) pile. —*adv.* (*s'arrêter: fam.*) dead. **à dix heures ∼**, (*fam.*) at ten on the dot. **∼ ou face?**, heads or tails?

piler /pile/ *v.t.* pound.

pilier /pilje/ *n.m.* pillar.

pill|er /pije/ *v.t.* loot. **∼age** *n.m.* looting. **∼ard, ∼arde** *n.m., f.* looter.

pilonner /pilɔne/ *v.t.* pound.

pilori /pilɔri/ *n.m.* **mettre** *ou* **clouer au ∼**, pillory.

pilot|e /pilɔt/ *n.m.* pilot; (*auto.*) driver. —*a.* pilot. **∼er** *v.t.* (*aviat., naut.*) pilot; (*auto.*) drive; (*fig.*) guide.

pilule /pilyl/ *n.f.* pill. **la ~**, the pill.

piment /pimɑ̃/ *n.m.* pepper, pimento; (*fig.*) spice. **~é** /-te/ *a.* spicy.

pimpant, ~e /pɛ̃pɑ̃, -t/ *a.* spruce.

pin /pɛ̃/ *n.m.* pine.

pinard /pinar/ *n.m.* (*vin; fam.*) plonk, cheap wine.

pince /pɛ̃s/ *n.f.* (*outil*) pliers; (*levier*) crowbar; (*de crabe*) pincer; (*à sucre*) tongs. **~ (à épiler)**, tweezers. **~ (à linge)**, (clothes-)peg.

pinceau (*pl. ~x*) /pɛ̃so/ *n.m.* paintbrush.

pinc|er /pɛ̃se/ *v.t.* pinch; (*arrêter: fam.*) pinch. **se ~er le doigt**, catch one's finger. **~é** *a.* (*ton, air*) stiff. **~ée** *n.f.* pinch (**de**, of).

pince-sans-rire /pɛ̃sɑ̃rir/ *a. invar.* po-faced. **c'est un ~**, he's po-faced.

pincettes /pɛ̃sɛt/ *n.f. pl.* (fire) tongs.

pinède /pinɛd/ *n.f.* pine forest.

pingouin /pɛ̃gwɛ̃/ *n.m.* penguin.

ping-pong /piŋpɔ̃g/ *n.m.* table tennis, ping-pong.

pingre /pɛ̃gr/ *a.* miserly.

pinson /pɛ̃sɔ̃/ *n.m.* chaffinch.

pintade /pɛ̃tad/ *n.f.* guinea-fowl.

pioch|e /pjɔʃ/ *n.f.* pick(axe). **~er** *v.t./i.* dig; (*étudier: fam.*) study hard, slog away (at).

pion /pjɔ̃/ *n.m.* (*de jeu*) piece; (*échecs*) pawn; (*scol., fam.*) supervisor.

pionnier /pjɔnje/ *n.m.* pioneer.

pipe /pip/ *n.f.* pipe. **fumer la ~**, smoke a pipe.

pipe-line /piplin/ *n.m.* pipeline.

piquant, ~e /pikɑ̃, -t/ *a.* (*barbe etc.*) prickly; (*goût*) pungent; (*détail etc.*) spicy. **—n.m.** prickle; (*de hérisson*) spine, prickle; (*fig.*) piquancy.

pique¹ /pik/ *n.f.* (*arme*) pike.

pique² /pik/ *n.m.* (*cartes*) spades.

pique-niqu|e /piknik/ *n.m.* picnic. **~er** *v.i.* picnic.

piquer /pike/ *v.t.* prick; (*langue*) burn, sting; (*abeille etc.*) sting; (*serpent etc.*) bite; (*enfoncer*) stick; (*coudre*) (machine-)stitch; (*curiosité*) excite; (*crise*) have; (*voler: fam.*) pinch. **—v.i.** (*avion*) dive; (*goût*) be hot. **~ une tête**, plunge headlong. **se ~ de**, pride o.s. on.

piquet /pikɛ/ *n.m.* stake; (*de tente*) peg. **au ~**, (*scol.*) in the corner. **~ de grève**, (strike) picket.

piqûre /pikyr/ *n.f.* prick; (*d'abeille etc.*) sting; (*de serpent etc.*) bite; (*point*) stitch; (*méd.*) injection, shot (*Amer.*). **faire une ~ à qn.**, give s.o. an injection.

pirate /pirat/ *n.m.* pirate. **~ de l'air**, hijacker. **~rie** *n.f.* piracy.

pire /pir/ *a.* worse (**que**, than). **le ~ livre/*etc.***, the worst book/*etc.* **—n.m. le ~**, the worst (thing). **au ~**, at worst.

pirogue /pirɔg/ *n.f.* canoe, dug-out.

pirouette /pirwɛt/ *n.f.* pirouette.

pis¹ /pi/ *n.m.* (*de vache*) udder.

pis² /pi/ *a. invar. & adv.* worse. **aller de mal en ~**, go from bad to worse.

pis-aller /pizale/ *n.m. invar.* stopgap, temporary expedient.

piscine /pisin/ *n.f.* swimming-pool. **~ couverte**, indoor swimming-pool.

pissenlit /pisɑ̃li/ *n.m.* dandelion.

pistache /pistaʃ/ *n.f.* pistachio.

piste /pist/ *n.f.* track; (*de personne, d'animal*) track, trail; (*aviat.*) runway; (*de cirque*) ring; (*de ski*) run; (*de patinage*) rink; (*de danse*) floor; (*sport*) race-track. **~ cyclable**, cycle-track; (*Amer.*) bicycle path.

pistolet /pistɔlɛ/ *n.m.* gun, pistol; (*de peintre*) spray-gun.

piston /pistɔ̃/ *n.m.* (*techn.*) piston. **il a un ~**, (*fam.*) somebody is pulling strings for him.

pistonner /pistɔne/ *v.t.* (*fam.*) recommend, pull strings for.

piteu|x, ~se /pitø, -z/ *a.* pitiful.

pitié /pitje/ *n.f.* pity. **il me fait ~, j'ai ~ de lui**, I pity him

piton /pitɔ̃/ *n.m.* (*à crochet*) hook; (*sommet pointu*) peak.

pitoyable /pitwajabl/ *a.* pitiful.

pitre /pitr/ *n.m.* clown. **faire le ~**, clown around.

pittoresque /pitɔrɛsk/ *a.* picturesque.

pivot /pivo/ *n.m.* pivot. **~er** /-ɔte/ *v.i.* revolve; (*personne*) swing round.

pizza /pidza/ *n.f.* pizza.

placage /plakaʒ/ *n.m.* (*en bois*) veneer; (*sur un mur*) facing.

placard /plakar/ *n.m.* cupboard; (*affiche*) poster. **~er** /-de/ *v.t.* (*affiche*) post up; (*mur*) cover with posters.

place /plas/ *n.f.* place; (*espace libre*) room, space; (*siège*) seat, place; (*prix d'un trajet*) fare; (*esplanade*) square; (*emploi*) position; (*de parking*) space. **à la ~ de**, instead of. **en ~, à sa ~**, in its place. **faire ~ à**, give way to. **sur ~**, on the spot. **remettre qn. à sa ~**, put s.o. in his place. **ça prend de la ~**, it takes up a lot of room. **se mettre à la ~ de qn.** put oneself in s.o.'s shoes *ou* place.

placebo /plasebo/ *n.m.* placebo.

placenta /plasɛ̃ta/ *n.m.* placenta.

plac|er /plase/ *v.t.* place; (*invité, spectateur*) seat; (*argent*) invest. **se ~er** *v. pr.* (*personne*) take up a

position; (*troisième etc.: sport*) come
(in); (*à un endroit*) to go and stand (à,
in). **~é** *a.* (*sport*) placed. **bien ~é**
pour, in a position to. **~ement** *n.m.*
(*d'argent*) investment.

placide /plasid/ *a.* placid.

plafond /plafɔ̃/ *n.m.* ceiling.

plage /plaʒ/ *n.f.* beach; (*station*)
(seaside) resort; (*aire*) area.

plagiat /plaʒja/ *n.m.* plagiarism.

plaid /plɛd/ *n.m.* travelling-rug.

plaider /plede/ *v.t./i.* plead.

plaid|oirie /plɛdwari/ *n.f.* (defence)
speech. **~oyer** *n.m.* plea.

plaie /plɛ/ *n.f.* wound; (*personne: fam.*)
nuisance.

plaignant, **~e** /plɛɲɑ̃, -t/ *n.m.,* *f.*
plaintiff.

plaindre† /plɛ̃dr/ *v.t.* pity. **se ~** *v. pr.*
complain (**de,** about). **se ~ de,** (*souffrir
de*) complain of.

plaine /plɛn/ *n.f.* plain.

plaint|e /plɛ̃t/ *n.f.* complaint; (*gémisse-
ment*) groan. **~if,** **~ive** *a.* plaintive.

plaire† /plɛr/ *v.i.* **~ à,** please. **ça lui
plaît,** he likes it. **elle lui plaît,** he likes
her. **ça me plaît de faire,** I like *ou* enjoy
doing. **s'il vous plaît,** please. **se ~** *v. pr.*
(*à Londres etc.*) like *ou* enjoy it.

plaisance /plɛzɑ̃s/ *n.f.* **la (navigation
de) ~,** yachting.

plaisant, **~e** /plɛzɑ̃, -t/ *a.* pleasant;
(*drôle*) amusing.

plaisant|er /plɛzɑ̃te/ *v.i.* joke. **~erie** *n.f.*
joke. **~in** *n.m.* joker.

plaisir /plezir/ *n.m.* pleasure. **faire ~ à,**
please. **pour le ~,** for fun *ou* pleasure.

plan¹ /plɑ̃/ *n.m.* plan; (*de ville*) map;
(*surface, niveau*) plane. **~ d'eau,**
expanse of water. **premier ~,**
foreground. **dernier ~,** background.

plan², **~e** /plɑ̃, -an/ *a.* flat.

planche /plɑ̃ʃ/ *n.f.* board, plank;
(*gravure*) plate; (*de potager*) bed. **~ à
repasser,** ironing-board. **~ à voile,**
sailboard; (*sport*) windsurfing.

plancher /plɑ̃ʃe/ *n.m.* floor.

plancton /plɑ̃ktɔ̃/ *n.m.* plankton.

plan|er /plane/ *v.i.* glide. **~er sur,**
(*mystère, danger*) hang over. **~eur**
n.m. (*avion*) glider.

planète /planɛt/ *n.f.* planet.

planif|ier /planifje/ *v.t.* plan. **~ication**
n.f. planning.

planqu|e /plɑ̃k/ *n.f.* (*fam.*) hideout;
(*emploi: fam.*) cushy job. **~er** *v.t.,* **se
~er** *v. pr.* hide.

plant /plɑ̃/ *n.m.* seedling; (*de légumes*)
bed.

plante /plɑ̃t/ *n.f.* plant. **~ des pieds,** sole
(of the foot).

plant|er /plɑ̃te/ *v.t.* (*plante etc.*) plant;
(*enfoncer*) drive in; (*installer*) put up;
(*mettre*) put. **rester ~é,** stand still,
remain standing. **~ation** *n.f.* planting;
(*de tabac etc.*) plantation.

plantureu|x, **~se** /plɑ̃tyrø, -z/ *a.*
abundant; (*femme*) buxom.

plaque /plak/ *n.f.* plate; (*de marbre*)
slab; (*insigne*) badge; (*commémorative*)
plaque. **~ chauffante,** hotplate. **~ minéralogique,** number-plate.

plaqu|er /plake/ *v.t.* (*bois*) veneer;
(*aplatir*) flatten; (*rugby*) tackle;
(*abandonner: fam.*) ditch. **~er qch.
sur** *ou* **contre,** make sth. stick to. **~age**
n.m. (*rugby*) tackle.

plasma /plasma/ *n.m.* plasma.

plastic /plastik/ *n.m.* plastic explosive.

plastique /plastik/ *a. & n.m.* plastic. **en
~,** plastic.

plastiquer /plastike/ *v.t.* blow up.

plat¹, **~e** /pla, -t/ *a.* flat. **—***n.m.* (*de la
main*) flat. **à ~** *adv.* (*poser*) flat; *a.*
(*batterie, pneu*) flat. **à ~ ventre,** flat on
one's face.

plat² /pla/ *n.m.* (*culin.*) dish; (*partie de
repas*) course.

platane /platan/ *n.m.* plane(-tree).

plateau (*pl.* **~x**) /plato/ *n.m.* tray;
(*d'électrophone*) turntable, deck; (*de
balance*) pan; (*géog.*) plateau. **~ de
fromages,** cheeseboard.

plateau-repas (*pl.* **plateaux-repas**) *n.m.*
tray meal.

plate-bande (*pl.* **plates-bandes**) /plat-
bɑ̃d/ *n.f.* flower-bed.

plate-forme (*pl.* **plates-formes**) /plat-
fɔrm/ *n.f.* platform.

platine¹ /platin/ *n.m.* platinum.

platine² /platin/ *n.f.* (*de tourne-disque*)
turntable.

platitude /platityd/ *n.f.* platitude.

platonique /platɔnik/ *a.* platonic.

plâtr|e /platr/ *n.m.* plaster; (*méd.*)
(plaster) cast. **~er** *v.t.* plaster;
(*membre*) put in plaster.

plausible /plozibl/ *a.* plausible.

plébiscite /plebisit/ *n.m.* plebiscite.

plein, **~e** /plɛ̃, plɛn/ *a.* full (**de,** of);
(*total*) complete. **—***n.m.* **faire le ~**
(**d'essence**), fill up (the tank). **à ~,** to
the full. **à ~ temps,** full-time. **en ~ air,**
in the open air. **en ~ milieu/visage,**
right in the middle/the face. **en ~e
nuit/etc.,** in the middle of the night/etc.
~ les mains, all over one's hands.

pleinement /plɛnmã/ adv. fully.

pléthore /pletɔr/ n.f. over-abundance, plethora.

pleurer /plœre/ v.i. cry, weep (**sur**, over); (yeux) water. —v.t. mourn.

pleurésie /plœrezi/ n.f. pleurisy.

pleurnicher /plœrniʃe/ v.i. (fam.) snivel.

pleurs (en) /(ã)plœr/ adv. in tears.

pleuvoir† /plœvwar/ v.i. rain; (fig.) rain ou shower down. **il pleut**, it is raining. **il pleut à verse** ou **à torrents**, it is pouring.

pli /pli/ n.m. fold; (de jupe) pleat; (de pantalon) crease; (enveloppe) cover; (habitude) habit. **(faux)** ~, crease.

pliant, ~**e** /plijã, -t/ a. folding; (parapluie) telescopic. —n.m. folding stool, camp-stool.

plier /plije/ v.t. fold; (courber) bend; (personne) submit (**à**, to). —v.i. bend; (personne) submit. **se** ~ v. pr. fold. **se** ~ **à**, submit to.

plinthe /plɛ̃t/ n.f. skirting-board; (Amer.) baseboard.

plisser /plise/ v.t. crease; (yeux) screw up; (jupe) pleat.

plomb /plɔ̃/ n.m. lead; (fusible) fuse. ~**s**, (de chasse) lead shot. **de** ou **en** ~, lead. **de** ~, (ciel) leaden.

plomb|er /plɔ̃be/ v.t. (dent) fill. ~**age** n.m. filling.

plomb|ier /plɔ̃bje/ n.m. plumber. ~**erie** n.f. plumbing.

plongeant, ~**e** /plɔ̃ʒã, -t/ a. (vue) from above; (décolleté) plunging.

plongeoir /plɔ̃ʒwar/ n.m. diving-board.

plongeon /plɔ̃ʒɔ̃/ n.m. dive.

plong|er /plɔ̃ʒe/ v.i. dive; (route) plunge. —v.t. plunge. **se** ~**er** v. pr. plunge (**dans**, into). ~**é dans**, (lecture) immersed in. ~**ée** n.f. diving. **en** ~**ée** (sous-marin) submerged. ~**eur**, ~**euse** n.m., f. diver; (employé) dishwasher.

plouf /pluf/ n.m. & int. splash.

ployer /plwaje/ v.t./i. bend.

plu /ply/ voir **plaire**, **pleuvoir**.

pluie /plɥi/ n.f. rain; (averse) shower. ~ **battante/diluvienne**, driving/torrential rain.

plumage /plymaʒ/ n.m. plumage.

plume /plym/ n.f. feather; (stylo) pen; (pointe) nib.

plumeau (pl. ~**x**) /plymo/ n.m. feather duster.

plumer /plyme/ v.t. pluck.

plumier /plymje/ n.m. pencil box.

plupart /plypar/ n.f. most. **la** ~ **des**, (gens, cas, etc.) most. **la** ~ **du temps**, most of the time. **pour la** ~, for the most part.

pluriel, ~**le** /plyrjɛl/ a. & n.m. plural. **au** ~, (nom) plural.

plus¹ /ply/ adv. de négation. **(ne)** ~, (temps) no longer, not any more. **(ne)** ~ **de**, (quantité) no more. **je n'y vais** ~, I do not go there any longer ou any more. **(il n'y a)** ~ **de pain**, (there is) no more bread.

plus² /ply/ (/plyz/ before vowel, /plys/ in final position) adv. more (**que**, than). ~ **âgé/tard/etc.**, older/later/etc. ~ **beau/** etc., more beautiful/etc. **le** ~, the most. **le** ~ **beau/**etc., the most beautiful; (de deux) the more beautiful. **le** ~ **de**, (gens etc.) most. ~ **de**, (pain etc.) more; (dix jours etc.) more than. **il est** ~ **de huit heures/**etc. it is after eight/etc. o'clock. **de** ~, more (**que**, than); (en outre) moreover. **(âgés) de** ~ **de** (huit ans etc.) over, more than. **de** ~ **en plus**, more and more. **en** ~, extra. **en** ~ **de**, in addition to. ~ **ou moins**, more or less.

plus³ /plys/ conj. plus.

plusieurs /plyzjœr/ a. & pron. several.

plus-value /plyvaly/ n.f. (bénéfice) profit.

plutôt /plyto/ adv. rather (**que**, than).

pluvieu|x, ~**se** /plyvjø, -z/ a. rainy.

pneu (pl. ~**s**) /pnø/ n.m. tyre; (lettre) express letter. ~**matique** a. inflatable.

pneumonie /pnœmɔni/ n.f. pneumonia.

poche /pɔʃ/ n.f. pocket; (sac) bag. ~**s**, (sous les yeux) bags.

pocher /pɔʃe/ v.t. (œuf) poach.

pochette /pɔʃɛt/ n.f. pack(et), envelope; (sac) bag, pouch; (d'allumettes) book; (de disque) sleeve; (mouchoir) pocket handkerchief. ~ **surprise**, lucky bag.

podium /pɔdjɔm/ n.m. rostrum.

poêle¹ /pwal/ n.f. (**à frire**), frying-pan.

poêle² /pwal/ n.m. stove.

poème /pɔɛm/ n.m. poem.

poésie /pɔezi/ n.f. poetry; (poème) poem.

poète /pɔɛt/ n.m. poet.

poétique /pɔetik/ a. poetic.

poids /pwa/ n.m. weight. ~ **coq/ lourd/plume**, bantamweight/heavy-weight/featherweight. ~ **lourd**, (camion) lorry, juggernaut; (Amer.) truck.

poignant, ~**e** /pwaɲã, -t/ a. poignant.

poignard /pwaɲar/ n.m. dagger. ~**er** /-de/ v.t. stab.

poigne /pwaɲ/ n.f. grip. **avoir de la** ~, have an iron fist.

poignée /pwaɲe/ *n.f.* handle; (*quantité*) handful. **~ de main,** handshake.

poignet /pwaɲɛ/ *n.m.* wrist; (*de chemise*) cuff.

poil /pwal/ *n.m.* hair; (*pelage*) fur; (*de brosse*) bristle. **~s,** (*de tapis*) pile. **à ~,** (*fam.*) naked. **~u** *a.* hairy.

poinçon /pwɛ̃sɔ̃/ *n.m.* awl; (*marque*) hallmark. **~ner** /-ɔne/ *v.t.* (*billet*) punch. **~neuse** /-ɔnøz/ *n.f.* punch.

poing /pwɛ̃/ *n.m.* fist.

point¹ /pwɛ̃/ *n.m.* point; (*note: scol.*) mark; (*tache*) spot, dot; (*de couture*) stitch. **~ (final),** full stop, period. **à ~,** (*culin.*) medium; (*arriver*) at the right time. **faire le ~,** take stock. **mettre au ~,** (*photo.*) focus; (*technique*) perfect; (*fig.*) clear up. **deux ~s,** colon. **~ culminant,** peak. **~ de repère,** landmark. **~s de suspension,** suspension points. **~ de suture,** (*méd.*) stitch. **~ de vente,** retail outlet. **~ de vue,** point of view. **~ d'interrogation/ d'exclamation,** question/exclamation-mark. **~ du jour,** daybreak. **~ mort,** (*auto.*) neutral. **~ virgule,** semicolon. **sur le ~ de,** about to.

point² /pwɛ̃/ *adv.* **(ne) ~,** not.

pointe /pwɛ̃t/ *n.f.* point, tip; (*clou*) tack; (*de grille*) spike; (*fig.*) touch (**de,** of). **de ~,** (*industrie*) highly advanced. **en ~,** pointed. **heure de ~,** peak hour. **sur la ~ des pieds,** on tiptoe.

pointer¹ /pwɛ̃te/ *v.t.* (*cocher*) tick off. **—*v.i.*** (*employé*) clock in *ou* out. **se ~** *v. pr.* (*fam.*) turn up.

pointer² /pwɛ̃te/ *v.t.* (*diriger*) point, aim.

pointillé /pwɛ̃tije/ *n.m.* dotted line. **—*a.*** dotted.

pointilleu|x, **~se** /pwɛ̃tijø, -z/ *a.* fastidious, particular.

pointu /pwɛ̃ty/ *a.* pointed; (*aiguisé*) sharp.

pointure /pwɛ̃tyr/ *n.f.* size.

poire /pwar/ *n.f.* pear.

poireau (*pl.* **~x**) /pwaro/ *n.m.* leek.

poireauter /pwarote/ *v.i.* (*fam.*) hang about.

poirier /pwarje/ *n.m.* pear-tree.

pois /pwa/ *n.m.* pea; (*dessin*) dot.

poison /pwazɔ̃/ *n.m.* poison.

poisseu|x, **~se** /pwasø, -z/ *a.* sticky.

poisson /pwasɔ̃/ *n.m.* fish. **~ rouge,** goldfish. **~ d'avril,** April fool. **les P~s,** Pisces.

poissonn|ier, **~ière** /pwasɔnje, -jɛr/ *n.m.*, *f.* fishmonger. **~erie** *n.f.* fish shop.

poitrail /pwatraj/ *n.m.* breast.

poitrine /pwatrin/ *n.f.* chest; (*seins*) bosom; (*culin.*) breast.

poivr|e /pwavr/ *n.m.* pepper. **~é** *a.* peppery. **~ière** *n.f.* pepper-pot.

poivron /pwavrɔ̃/ *n.m.* pepper, capsicum.

poivrot, **~e** /pwavro, -ɔt/ *n.m.*, *f.* (*fam.*) drunkard.

poker /pɔkɛr/ *n.m.* poker.

polaire /pɔlɛr/ *a.* polar.

polariser /pɔlarize/ *v.t.* polarize.

polaroïd /pɔlarɔid/ *n.m.* (P.) Polaroid (P.).

pôle /pol/ *n.m.* pole.

polémique /pɔlemik/ *n.f.* argument. **—*a.*** controversial.

poli /pɔli/ *a.* (*personne*) polite. **~ment** *adv.* politely.

polic|e¹ /pɔlis/ *n.f.* police; (*discipline*) (law and) order. **~ier,** **~ière** *a.* police; (*roman*) detective; *n.m.* policeman.

police² /pɔlis/ *n.f.* (*d'assurance*) policy.

polio(myélite) /pɔljɔ(mjelit)/ *n.f.* polio(myelitis).

polir /pɔlir/ *v.t.* polish.

polisson, **~ne** /pɔlisɔ̃, -ɔn/ *a.* naughty. **—*n.m.*,** *f.* rascal.

politesse /pɔlitɛs/ *n.f.* politeness; (*parole*) polite remark.

politicien, **~ne** /pɔlitisjɛ̃, -jɛn/ *n.m.*, *f.* (*péj.*) politician.

politi|que /pɔlitik/ *a.* political. **—*n.f.*** politics; (*ligne de conduite*) policy. **~ser** *v.t.* politicize.

pollen /pɔlɛn/ *n.m.* pollen.

polluant, **~e** /pɔlɥɑ̃, -t/ *a.* polluting. **—*n.m.*** pollutant.

poll|uer /pɔlɥe/ *v.t.* pollute. **~ution** *n.f.* pollution.

polo /pɔlo/ *n.m.* polo; (*vêtement*) sports shirt, tennis shirt.

Pologne /pɔlɔɲ/ *n.f.* Poland.

polonais, **~e** /pɔlɔnɛ, -z/ *a.* Polish. **—*n.m.*,** *f.* Pole. **—*n.m.*** (*lang.*) Polish.

poltron, **~ne** /pɔltrɔ̃, -ɔn/ *a.* cowardly. **—*n.m.*,** *f.* coward.

polycopier /pɔlikɔpje/ *v.t.* duplicate, stencil.

polygamie /pɔligami/ *n.f.* polygamy.

polyglotte /pɔliglɔt/ *n.m.*/*f.* polyglot.

polyvalent, **~e** /pɔlivalɑ̃, -t/ *a.* varied; (*personne*) versatile.

pommade /pɔmad/ *n.f.* ointment.

pomme /pɔm/ *n.f.* apple; (*d'arrosoir*) rose. **~ d'Adam,** Adam's apple. **~ de pin,** pine cone. **~ de terre,** potato. **~s frites,** chips; (*Amer.*) French fries. **tomber dans les ~s,** (*fam.*) pass out.

pommeau (*pl.* ~x) /pɔmo/ *n.m.* (*de canne*) knob.

pommette /pɔmɛt/ *n.f.* cheek-bone.

pommier /pɔmje/ *n.m.* apple-tree.

pompe /pɔ̃p/ *n.f.* pump; (*splendeur*) pomp. ~ **à incendie**, fire-engine. ~**s funèbres**, undertaker's.

pomper /pɔ̃pe/ *v.t.* pump; (*copier*: *fam.*) copy, crib. ~ **l'air à qn.**, (*fam.*) get on s.o.'s nerves.

pompeu|x, ~**se** /pɔ̃pø, -z/ *a.* pompous.

pompier /pɔ̃pje/ *n.m.* fireman.

pompiste /pɔ̃pist/ *n.m./f.* petrol pump attendant; (*Amer.*) gas station attendant.

pompon /pɔ̃pɔ̃/ *n.m.* pompon.

pomponner /pɔ̃pɔne/ *v.t.* deck out.

poncer /pɔ̃se/ *v.t.* rub down.

ponctuation /pɔ̃ktɥasjɔ̃/ *n.f.* punctuation.

ponct|uel, ~**uelle** /pɔ̃ktɥɛl/ *a.* punctual. ~**ualité** *n.f.* punctuality.

ponctuer /pɔ̃ktɥe/ *v.t.* punctuate.

pondéré /pɔ̃dere/ *a.* level-headed.

pondre /pɔ̃dr/ *v.t./i.* lay.

poney /pɔnɛ/ *n.m.* pony.

pont /pɔ̃/ *n.m.* bridge; (*de navire*) deck; (*de graissage*) ramp. **faire le** ~, take the extra day(s) off (*between holidays*). ~ **aérien**, airlift. ~**levis** (*pl.* ~**s-levis**) *n.m.* drawbridge.

ponte /pɔ̃t/ *n.f.* laying (of eggs).

pontife /pɔ̃tif/ *n.m.* (*souverain*) ~, pope.

pontific|al (*m. pl.* ~**aux**) /pɔ̃tifikal, -o/ *a.* papal.

pop /pɔp/ *n.m. & a. invar.* (*mus.*) pop.

popote /pɔpɔt/ *n.f.* (*fam.*) cooking.

populace /pɔpylas/ *n.f.* (*péj.*) rabble.

popul|aire /pɔpylɛr/ *a.* popular; (*expression*) colloquial; (*quartier, origine*) working class. ~**arité** *n.f.* popularity.

population /pɔpylasjɔ̃/ *n.f.* population.

populeu|x, ~**se** /pɔpylø, -z/ *a.* populous.

porc /pɔr/ *n.m.* pig; (*viande*) pork.

porcelaine /pɔrsəlɛn/ *n.f.* china, porcelain.

porc-épic (*pl.* **porcs-épics**) /pɔrkepik/ *n.m.* porcupine.

porche /pɔrʃ/ *n.m.* porch.

porcherie /pɔrʃəri/ *n.f.* pigsty.

por|e /pɔr/ *n.m.* pore. ~**eux**, ~**euse** *a.* porous.

pornograph|ie /pɔrnɔgrafi/ *n.f.* pornography. ~**ique** *a.* pornographic.

port[1] /pɔr/ *n.m.* port, harbour. **à bon** ~, safely. ~ **maritime**, seaport.

port[2] /pɔr/ *n.m.* (*transport*) carriage; (*d'armes*) carrying; (*de barbe*) wearing.

portail /pɔrtaj/ *n.m.* portal.

portant, ~**e** /pɔrtɑ̃, -t/ *a.* **bien/mal** ~, in good/bad health.

portati|f, ~**ve** /pɔrtatif, -v/ *a.* portable.

porte /pɔrt/ *n.f.* door; (*passage*) doorway; (*de jardin, d'embarquement*) gate. **mettre à la** ~, throw out. ~ **d'entrée**, front door. ~**-fenêtre** (*pl.* ~**s-fenêtres**) *n.f.* French window.

porté /pɔrte/ *a.* ~ **à**, inclined to. ~ **sur**, fond of.

portée /pɔrte/ *n.f.* (*d'une arme*) range; (*de voûte*) span; (*d'animaux*) litter; (*impact*) significance; (*mus.*) stave. **à** ~ **de**, within reach of. **à** ~ **de (la) main**, within (arm's) reach. **hors de** ~ **(de)**, out of reach (of). **à la** ~ **de qn.** at s.o.'s level.

portefeuille /pɔrtəfœj/ *n.m.* wallet; (*de ministre*) portfolio.

portemanteau (*pl.* ~x) /pɔrtmɑ̃to/ *n.m.* coat *ou* hat stand.

port|er /pɔrte/ *v.t.* carry; (*vêtement, bague*) wear; (*fruits, responsabilité, nom*) bear; (*coup*) strike; (*amener*) bring; (*inscrire*) enter. —*v.i.* (*bruit*) carry; (*coup*) hit home. ~**er sur**, rest on; (*concerner*) bear on. **se** ~**er bien**, be *ou* feel well. **se** ~**er candidat**, stand as a candidate. ~**er aux nues**, praise to the skies. ~**é-avions** *n.m. invar.* aircraft-carrier. ~**e-bagages** *n.m. invar.* luggage rack. ~**e-bonheur** *n.m. invar.* (*objet*) charm. ~**e-clefs** *n.m. invar.* key-ring. ~**e-documents** *n.m. invar.* attaché case, document wallet. ~**e-monnaie** *n.m. invar.* purse. ~**e-parole** *n.m. invar.* spokesman. ~**e-voix** *n.m. invar.* megaphone.

porteu|r, ~**se** /pɔrtœr, -øz/ *n.m.*, *f.* (*de nouvelles*) bearer; (*méd.*) carrier. —*n.m.* (*rail.*) porter.

portier /pɔrtje/ *n.m.* door-man.

portière /pɔrtjɛr/ *n.f.* door.

portillon /pɔrtijɔ̃/ *n.m.* gate.

portion /pɔrsjɔ̃/ *n.f.* portion.

portique /pɔrtik/ *n.m.* portico; (*sport*) crossbar.

porto /pɔrto/ *n.m.* port (wine).

portrait /pɔrtrɛ/ *n.m.* portrait. ~**-robot** (*pl.* ~**s-robots**) *n.m.* identikit, photofit.

portuaire /pɔrtɥɛr/ *a.* port.

portugais, ~**e** /pɔrtygɛ, -z/ *a. & n.m.*, *f.* Portuguese. —*n.m.* (*lang.*) Portuguese.

Portugal /pɔrtygal/ *n.m.* Portugal.

pose /poz/ *n.f.* installation; (*attitude*) pose; (*photo.*) exposure.

posé /poze/ *a.* calm, serious.

poser /poze/ *v.t.* put (down); (*installer*) install, put in; (*fondations*) lay; (*question*) ask; (*problème*) pose. —*v.i.* (*modèle*) pose. **se** ~ *v. pr.* (*avion, oiseau*) land; (*regard*) alight; (*se présenter*) arise. ~ **sa candidature,** apply (à, for).

positi|f, ~**ve** /pozitif, -v/ *a.* positive.

position /pozisjɔ̃/ *n.f.* position; (*banque*) balance (of account). **prendre** ~, take a stand.

posologie /pozɔlɔʒi/ *n.f.* directions for use.

poss|éder /posede/ *v.t.* possess; (*propriété*) own, possess. ~**esseur** *n.m.* possessor; owner.

possessi|f, ~**ve** /posesif, -v/ *a.* possessive.

possession /posesjɔ̃/ *n.f.* possession. **prendre** ~ **de,** take possession of.

possibilité /posibilite/ *n.f.* possibility.

possible /posibl/ *a.* possible. —*n.m.* le ~, what is possible. **dès que** ~, as soon as possible. **faire son** ~, do one's utmost. **le plus tard**/*etc.* ~, as late/*etc.* as possible. **pas** ~, impossible; (*int.*) really!

post- /pɔst/ *préf.* post-.

post|al (*m. pl.* ~**aux**) /pɔstal, -o/ *a.* postal.

poste¹ /pɔst/ *n.f.* (*service*) post; (*bureau*) post office. ~ **aérienne,** airmail. **mettre à la** ~, post. ~ **restante,** poste restante.

poste² /pɔst/ *n.m.* (*lieu, emploi*) post; (*de radio, télévision*) set; (*téléphone*) extension (number). ~ **d'essence,** petrol *ou* gas (*Amer.*) station. ~ **d'incendie,** fire point. ~ **de pilotage,** cockpit. ~ **de police,** police station. ~ **de secours,** first-aid post.

poster¹ /pɔste/ *v.t.* (*lettre, personne*) post.

poster² /pɔstɛr/ *n.m.* poster.

postérieur /pɔsterjœr/ *a.* later; (*partie*) back. ~ **à,** after. —*n.m.* (*fam.*) posterior.

postérité /pɔsterite/ *n.f.* posterity.

posthume /pɔstym/ *a.* posthumous.

postiche /pɔstiʃ/ *a.* false.

post|ier, ~**ière** /pɔstje, -jɛr/ *n.m., f.* postal worker.

post-scriptum /pɔstskriptɔm/ *n.m. invar.* postscript.

postul|er /pɔstyle/ *v.t./i.* apply (à *ou* **pour,** for); (*principe*) postulate. ~**ant,** ~**ante** *n.m., f.* applicant.

posture /pɔstyr/ *n.f.* posture.

pot /po/ *n.m.* pot; (*en carton*) carton; (*en verre*) jar; (*chance: fam.*) luck; (*boisson: fam.*) drink. ~**-au-feu** /pɔtofø/ *n.m. invar.* (*plat*) stew. ~ **d'échappement,** exhaust-pipe. ~**-de-vin** (*pl.* ~**s-de-vin**) *n.m.* bribe. ~**-pourri,** (*pl.* ~**s-pourris**) *n.m.* pot pourri.

potable /pɔtabl/ *a.* drinkable. **eau** ~, drinking water.

potage /pɔtaʒ/ *n.m.* soup.

potag|er, ~**ère** /pɔtaʒe, -ɛr/ *a.* vegetable. —*n.m.* vegetable garden.

pote /pɔt/ *n.m.* (*fam.*) chum.

poteau (*pl.* ~**x**) /pɔto/ *n.m.* post; (*télégraphique*) pole. ~ **indicateur,** signpost.

potelé /pɔtle/ *a.* plump.

potence /pɔtɑ̃s/ *n.f.* gallows.

potentiel, ~**le** /pɔtɑ̃sjɛl/ *a. & n.m.* potential.

pot|erie /pɔtri/ *n.f.* pottery; (*objet*) piece of pottery. ~**ier** *n.m.* potter.

potins /pɔtɛ̃/ *n.m. pl.* gossip.

potion /posjɔ̃/ *n.f.* potion.

potiron /pɔtirɔ̃/ *n.m.* pumpkin.

pou (*pl.* ~**x**) /pu/ *n.m.* louse.

poubelle /pubɛl/ *n.f.* dustbin; (*Amer.*) garbage can.

pouce /pus/ *n.m.* thumb; (*de pied*) big toe; (*mesure*) inch.

poudr|e /pudr/ *n.f.* powder. ~**e (à canon),** gunpowder. **en** ~**e,** (*lait*) powdered; (*chocolat*) drinking. ~**er** *v.t.* powder. ~**eux,** ~**euse** *a.* powdery.

poudrier /pudrije/ *n.m.* (powder) compact.

poudrière /pudrijɛr/ *n.f.* (*région: fig.*) powder-keg.

pouf /puf/ *n.m.* pouffe.

pouffer /pufe/ *v.i.* guffaw.

pouilleu|x, ~**se** /pujø, -z/ *a.* filthy.

poulailler /pulaje/ *n.m.* (hen-)coop.

poulain /pulɛ̃/ *n.m.* foal; (*protégé*) protégé.

poule /pul/ *n.f.* hen; (*culin.*) fowl; (*femme: fam.*) tart; (*rugby*) group.

poulet /pulɛ/ *n.m.* chicken.

pouliche /puliʃ/ *n.f.* filly.

poulie /puli/ *n.f.* pulley.

pouls /pu/ *n.m.* pulse.

poumon /pumɔ̃/ *n.m.* lung.

poupe /pup/ *n.f.* stern.

poupée /pupe/ *n.f.* doll.

poupon /pupɔ̃/ *n.m.* baby. ~**nière** /-ɔnjɛr/ *n.f.* crèche, day nursery.

pour /pur/ *prép.* for; (*envers*) to; (*à la*

place de) on behalf of; (*comme*) as. ∼ **cela,** for that reason. ∼ **cent,** per cent. ∼ **de bon,** for good. ∼ **faire,** (in order) to do. ∼ **que,** so that. ∼ **moi,** as for me. ∼ **petit**/*etc.* **qu'il soit,** however small/*etc.* he may be. **trop poli**/*etc.* ∼, too polite/*etc.* to. **le** ∼ **et le contre,** the pros and cons. ∼ **ce qui est de,** as for.

pourboire /purbwar/ *n.m.* tip.

pourcentage /pursɑ̃taʒ/ *n.m.* percentage.

pourchasser /purʃase/ *v.t.* pursue.

pourparlers /purparle/ *n.m. pl.* talks.

pourpre /purpr/ *a. & n.m.* crimson, (*violet*) purple.

pourquoi /purkwa/ *conj. & adv.* why. —*n.m. invar.* reason.

pourra, pourrait /pura, purɛ/ *voir* **pouvoir**[1].

pourr|ir /purir/ *v.t./i.* rot. ∼**l** *a.* rotten. ∼**iture** *n.f.* rot.

poursuite /pursɥit/ *n.f.* pursuit (**de,** of). ∼**s,** (*jurid.*) legal action.

poursuiv|re† /pursɥivr/ *v.t.* pursue; (*continuer*) continue (**with**). ∼**re** (**en justice),** (*au criminel*) prosecute; (*au civil*) sue. —*v.i.,* **se** ∼**re** *v. pr.* continue. ∼**ant,** ∼**ante** *n.m., f.* pursuer.

pourtant /purtɑ̃/ *adv.* yet.

pourtour /purtur/ *n.m.* perimeter.

pourv|oir† /purvwar/ *v.t.* ∼**oir de,** provide with. —*v.i.* ∼**oir à,** provide for. ∼**u de,** supplied with. —*v. pr.* **se** ∼**oir de** (*argent*) provide o.s. with. ∼**oyeur,** ∼**oyeuse** *n.m., f.* supplier.

pourvu que /purvyk(ə)/ *conj.* (*condition*) provided (that); (*souhait*) let us hope (that). **pourvu qu'il ne soit rien arrivé,** I hope nothing's happened.

pousse /pus/ *n.f.* growth; (*bourgeon*) shoot.

poussé /puse/ *a.* (*études*) advanced.

poussée /puse/ *n.f.* pressure; (*coup*) push; (*de prix*) upsurge; (*méd.*) outbreak.

pousser /puse/ *v.t.* push; (*du coude*) nudge; (*cri*) let out; (*soupir*) heave; (*continuer*) continue; (*exhorter*) urge (à, to); (*forcer*) drive (à, to); (*amener*) bring (à, to). —*v.i.* push; (*grandir*) grow. **faire** ∼ (*cheveux*) let grow; (*plante*) grow. **se** ∼ *v. pr.* move over *ou* up.

poussette /pusɛt/ *n.f.* push-chair; (*Amer.*) (baby) stroller.

pouss|ière /pusjɛr/ *n.f.* dust. ∼**iéreux,** ∼**iéreuse** *a.* dusty.

poussi|f, ∼**ve** /pusif, -v/ *a.* short-winded, wheezing.

poussin /pusɛ̃/ *n.m.* chick.

poutre /putr/ *n.f.* beam: (*en métal*) girder.

pouvoir[1]† /puvwar/ *v. aux.* (*possibilité*) can, be able; (*permission, éventualité*) may, can. **il peut/pouvait/pourrait venir,** he can/could/might come. **je n'ai pas pu,** I could not. **j'ai pu faire,** (*réussi à*) I managed to do. **je n'en peux plus,** I am exhausted. **il se peut que,** it may be that.

pouvoir[2] /puvwar/ *n.m.* power; (*gouvernement*) government. **au** ∼, in power. ∼**s publics,** authorities.

prairie /preri/ *n.f.* meadow.

praline /pralin/ *n.f.* sugared almond.

praticable /pratikabl/ *a.* practicable.

praticien, ∼**ne** /pratisjɛ̃, -jɛn/ *n.m., f.* practitioner.

pratiquant, ∼**e** /pratikɑ̃, -t/ *a.* practising. —*n.m., f.* churchgoer.

pratique /pratik/ *a.* practical. —*n.f.* practice; (*expérience*) experience. **la** ∼ **du golf/du cheval,** golfing/riding. ∼**ment** *adv.* in practice; (*presque*) practically.

pratiquer /pratike/ *v.t./i.* practise; (*sport*) play; (*faire*) make.

pré /pre/ *n.m.* meadow.

pré- /pre/ *préf.* pre-.

préalable /prealabl/ *a.* preliminary, prior. —*n.m.* precondition. **au** ∼, first.

préambule /preɑ̃byl/ *n.m.* preamble.

préau (*pl.* ∼**x**) /preo/ *n.m.* (*scol.*) playground shelter.

préavis /preavi/ *n.m.* (advance) notice.

précaire /prekɛr/ *a.* precarious.

précaution /prekosjɔ̃/ *n.f.* (*mesure*) precaution; (*prudence*) caution.

précéd|ent, ∼**ente** /presedɑ̃, -t/ *a.* previous. —*n.m.* precedent. ∼**emment** /-amɑ̃/ *adv.* previously.

précéder /presede/ *v.t./i.* precede.

précepte /presɛpt/ *n.m.* precept.

précep|teur, ∼**trice** /preseptœr, -tris/ *n.m., f.* tutor.

prêcher /preʃe/ *v.t./i.* preach.

précieu|x, ∼**se** /presjø, -z/ *a.* precious.

précipice /presipis/ *n.m.* abyss, chasm.

précipit|é /presipite/ *a.* hasty. ∼**amment** *adv.* hastily. ∼**ation** *n.f.* haste.

précipiter /presipite/ *v.t.* throw, precipitate; (*hâter*) hasten. **se** ∼ *v. pr.* rush (**sur,** at, on to); (*se jeter*) throw o.s.; (*s'accélérer*) speed up.

précis, ∼**e** /presi, -z/ *a.* precise; (*mécanisme*) accurate. —*n.m.* summary. **dix heures**/*etc.* ∼**es,** ten o'clock/*etc.* sharp. **∼ément** /-zemɑ̃/ *adv.* precisely.

préciser /presize/ *v.t./i.* specify; (*pensée*) be more specific about. **se ∼** *v. pr.* become clear(er).

précision /presizjɔ̃/ *n.f.* precision; (*détail*) detail.

précoc|e /prekɔs/ *a.* early; (*enfant*) precocious. **∼ité** *n.f.* earliness; precociousness.

préconçu /prekɔ̃sy/ *a.* preconceived.

préconiser /prekɔnize/ *v.t.* advocate.

précurseur /prekyrsœr/ *n.m.* forerunner.

prédécesseur /predesesœr/ *n.m.* predecessor.

prédicateur /predikatœr/ *n.m.* preacher.

prédilection /predilɛksjɔ̃/ *n.f.* preference.

préd|ire† /predir/ *v.t.* predict. **∼iction** *n.f.* prediction.

prédisposer /predispoze/ *v.t.* predispose.

prédominant, ∼e /predɔminɑ̃, -t/ *a.* predominant.

prédominer /predɔmine/ *v.i.* predominate.

préfabriqué /prefabrike/ *a.* prefabricated.

préface /prefas/ *n.f.* preface.

préfecture /prefektyr/ *n.f.* prefecture. **∼ de police**, police headquarters.

préférence /preferɑ̃s/ *n.f.* preference. **de ∼**, preferably. **de ∼ à**, in preference to.

préférentiel, ∼le /preferɑ̃sjɛl/ *a.* preferential.

préfér|er /prefere/ *v.t.* prefer (à, to). **je ne préfère pas**, I'd rather not. **∼er faire**, prefer to do. **∼able** *a.* preferable. **∼é, ∼ée** *a. & n.m., f.* favourite.

préfet /prefɛ/ *n.m.* prefect. **∼ de police**, prefect *ou* chief of police.

préfixe /prefiks/ *n.m.* prefix.

préhistorique /preistɔrik/ *a.* prehistoric.

préjudic|e /preʒydis/ *n.m.* harm, prejudice. **porter ∼e à**, harm. **∼iable** *a.* harmful.

préjugé /preʒyʒe/ *n.m.* prejudice. **avoir un ∼ contre**, be prejudiced against. **sans ∼s**, without prejudices.

préjuger /preʒyʒe/ *v.i.* **∼ de**, prejudge.

prélasser (se) /(sə)prelase/ *v. pr.* loll (about).

prél|ever /prelve/ *v.t.* deduct (**sur**, from); (*sang*) take. **∼èvement** *n.m.* deduction. **∼èvement de sang**, blood sample.

préliminaire /preliminɛr/ *a. & n.m.* preliminary. **∼s**, (*sexuels*) foreplay.

prélude /prelyd/ *n.m.* prelude.

prématuré /prematyre/ *a.* premature. —*n.m.* premature baby.

prémédit|er /premedite/ *v.t.* premeditate. **∼ation** *n.f.* premeditation.

prem|ier, ∼ière /prəmje, -jɛr/ *a.* first; (*rang*) front, first; (*enfance*) early; (*nécessité, souci*) prime; (*qualité*) top, prime; (*état*) original. —*n.m., f.* first (one). —*n.m.* (*date*) first; (*étage*) first floor. —*n.f.* (*rail.*) first class; (*exploit jamais vu*) first; (*cinéma, théâtre*) première. **de ∼ier ordre**, first-rate. **en ∼ier**, first. **∼ier jet**, first draft. **∼ier ministre**, Prime Minister.

premièrement /prəmjɛrmɑ̃/ *adv.* firstly.

prémisse /premis/ *n.f.* premiss.

prémonition /premɔnisjɔ̃/ *n.f.* premonition.

prémunir /premynir/ *v.t.* protect (**contre**, against).

prenant, ∼e /prənɑ̃, -t/ *a.* (*activité*) engrossing; (*enfant*) demanding.

prénatal (*m. pl.* **∼s**) /prenatal/ *a.* antenatal; (*Amer.*) prenatal.

prendre† /prɑ̃dr/ *v.t.* take; (*attraper*) catch, get; (*acheter*) get; (*repas*) have; (*engager, adopter*) take on; (*poids*) put on; (*chercher*) pick up; (*panique, colère*) take hold of. —*v.i.* (*liquide*) set; (*feu*) catch; (*vaccin*) take. **se ∼ pour**, think one is. **s'en ∼ à**, attack; (*rendre responsable*) blame. **s'y ∼**, set about (it).

preneu|r, ∼se /prənœr, -øz/ *n.m., f.* buyer. **être ∼r**, be willing to buy. **trouver ∼r**, find a buyer.

prénom /prenɔ̃/ *n.m.* first name. **∼mer** /-ɔme/ *v.t.* call. **se ∼mer** *v. pr.* be called.

préoccup|er /preɔkype/ *v.t.* worry; (*absorber*) preoccupy. **se ∼er de**, be worried about; be preoccupied about. **∼ation** *n.f.* worry; (*idée fixe*) preoccupation.

préparatifs /preparatif/ *n.m. pl.* preparations.

préparatoire /preparatwar/ *a.* preparatory.

prépar|er /prepare/ *v.t.* prepare; (*repas, café*) make. **se ∼er** *v. pr.* prepare o.s.; (*être proche*) be brewing. **∼er à qn.**, (*surprise*) have (got) in store for s.o. **∼ation** *n.f.* preparation.

prépondéran|t, ∼te /prepɔ̃derɑ̃, -t/ *a.* dominant. **∼ce** *n.f.* dominance.

prépos|er /prepoze/ *v.t.* put in charge (**à**, of). **∼é, ∼ée** *n.m., f.* employee; (*des postes*) postman, postwoman.

préposition /prepozisjɔ̃/ n.f. preposition.

préretraite /preratrɛt/ n.f. early retirement.

prérogative /prerɔgativ/ n.f. prerogative.

près /prɛ/ adv. near, close. ~ **de**, near (to), close to; (presque) nearly. **à cela** ~, apart from that. **de** ~, closely.

présag|e /prezaʒ/ n.m. foreboding, omen. ~**er** v.t. forebode.

presbyte /prɛsbit/ a. long-sighted, farsighted.

presbytère /prɛsbitɛr/ n.m. presbytery.

prescr|ire† /prɛskrir/ v.t. prescribe. ~**iption** n.f. prescription.

préséance /preseãs/ n.f. precedence.

présence /prezãs/ n.f. presence; (scol.) attendance.

présent, ~e /prezã, -t/ a. present. —n.m. (temps, cadeau) present. **à** ~, now.

présent|er /prezãte/ v.t. present; (personne) introduce (**à**, to); (montrer) show. **se** ~**er** v. pr. introduce o.s. (**à**, to); (aller) go; (apparaître) appear; (candidat) come forward; (occasion etc.) arise. ~**er bien**, have a pleasing appearance. **se** ~**er à**, (examen) sit for; (élection) stand for. **se** ~**er bien**, look good. ~**able** a. presentable. ~**ateur**, ~**atrice** n.m., f. presenter. ~**ation** n.f. presentation; introduction.

préservatif /prezɛrvatif/ n.m. condom.

préserv|er /prezɛrve/ v.t. protect. ~**ation** n.f. protection, preservation.

présiden|t, ~te /prezidã, -t/ n.m., f. president; (de firme, comité) chairman, chairwoman. ~**t directeur général**, managing director. ~**ce** n.f. presidency; chairmanship.

présidentiel, ~le /prezidãsjɛl/ a. presidential.

présider /prezide/ v.t. preside over. —v.i. preside.

présomption /prezɔ̃psjɔ̃/ n.f. presumption.

présomptueu|x, ~se /prezɔ̃ptɥø, -z/ a. presumptuous.

presque /prɛsk(ə)/ adv. almost, nearly. ~ **jamais**, hardly ever. ~ **rien**, hardly anything. ~ **pas (de)**, hardly any.

presqu'île /prɛskil/ n.f. peninsula.

pressant, ~e /prɛsã, -t/ a. pressing, urgent.

presse /prɛs/ n.f. (journaux, appareil) press.

pressent|ir /prɛsãtir/ v.t. sense. ~**iment** n.m. presentiment.

press|er /prese/ v.t. squeeze, press; (appuyer sur, harceler) press; (hâter) hasten; (inciter) urge (**de**, to). —v.i. (temps) press; (affaire) be pressing. **se** ~**er** v. pr. (se hâter) hurry; (se grouper) crowd. ~**é** a. in a hurry; (orange, citron) freshly squeezed. ~**e-papiers** n.m. invar. paperweight.

pressing /presiŋ/ n.m. (magasin) drycleaner's.

pression /prɛsjɔ̃/ n.f. pressure. —n.m./f. (bouton) press-stud; (Amer.) snap.

pressoir /prɛswar/ n.m. press.

pressuriser /prɛsyrize/ v.t. pressurize.

prestance /prɛstãs/ n.f. (imposing) presence.

prestation /prɛstasjɔ̃/ n.f. allowance; (d'artiste etc.) performance.

prestidigita|teur, ~trice /prɛstidiʒitatœr, -tris/ n.m., f. conjuror. ~**tion** /-asjɔ̃/ n.f. conjuring.

prestig|e /prɛstiʒ/ n.m. prestige. ~**ieux, ~ieuse** a. prestigious.

présumer /prezyme/ v.t. presume. ~ **que**, assume that. ~ **de**, overrate.

prêt[1], ~**e** /prɛ, -t/ a. ready (**à qch.**, for sth., **à faire**, to do). ~**-à-porter** /prɛ(t)aporte/ n.m. invar. ready-to-wear clothes.

prêt[2] /prɛ/ n.m. loan.

prétendant /pretãdã/ n.m. (amoureux) suitor.

prétend|re /pretãdr/ v.t. claim (**que**, that); (vouloir) intend. ~**re qn. riche**/etc., claim that s.o. is rich/etc. ~**u** a. so-called. ~**ument** adv. supposedly, allegedly.

prétent|ieux, ~ieuse /pretãsjø, -z/ a. pretentious. ~**ion** n.f. pretentiousness; (exigence) claim.

prêt|er /prete/ v.t. lend (**à**, to); (attribuer) attribute. —v.i. ~**er à**, lead to. ~**er attention**, pay attention. ~**er serment**, take an oath. ~**eur**, ~**euse** /pretœr, -øz/ n.m., f. (money)lender. ~**eur sur gages**, pawnbroker.

prétext|e /pretɛkst/ n.m. pretext, excuse. ~**er** v.t. plead.

prêtre /prɛtr/ n.m. priest.

prêtrise /prɛtriz/ n.f. priesthood.

preuve /prœv/ n.f. proof. **faire** ~ **de**, show. **faire ses** ~**s**, prove one's ou its worth.

prévaloir /prevalwar/ v.i. prevail.

prévenan|t, ~te /prevnã, -t/ a. thoughtful. ~**ce(s)** n.f. (pl.) thoughtfulness.

prévenir† /prevnir/ v.t. (menacer)

warn; (*informer*) tell; (*éviter, anticiper*) forestall.

préventi|f, **~ve** /prevãtif, -v/ *a.* preventive.

prévention /prevãsjɔ̃/ *n.f.* prevention; (*préjuge*) prejudice. **~ routière**, road safety.

prévenu, **~e** /prɛvny/ *n.m.*, *f.* defendant.

prév|oir† /prevwar/ *v.t.* foresee; (*temps*) forecast; (*organiser*) plan (for), provide for; (*envisager*) allow (for). **~u pour**, (*jouet etc.*) designed for. **~isible** *a.* foreseeable. **~ision** *n.f.* prediction; (*météorologique*) forecast.

prévoyan|t, **~te** /prevwajã, -t/ *a.* showing foresight. **~ce** *n.f.* foresight.

prier /prije/ *v.i.* pray. —*v.t.* pray to; (*implorer*) beg (**de**, to); (*demander à*) ask (**de**, to). **je vous en prie**, please; (*il n'y a pas de quoi*) don't mention it.

prière /prijɛr/ *n.f.* prayer; (*demande*) request. **~ de**, (*vous êtes prié de*) will you please.

primaire /primɛr/ *a.* primary.

primauté /primote/ *n.f.* primacy.

prime /prim/ *n.f.* free gift; (*d'employé*) bonus; (*subvention*) subsidy; (*d'assurance*) premium.

primé /prime/ *a.* prize-winning.

primer /prime/ *v.t./i.* excel.

primeurs /primœr/ *n.f. pl.* early fruit and vegetables.

primevère /primvɛr/ *n.f.* primrose.

primiti|f, **~ve** /primitif, -v/ *a.* primitive; (*originel*) original. —*n.m.*, *f.* primitive.

primord|ial (*m. pl.* **~iaux**) /primɔrdjal, -jo/ *a.* essential.

princ|e /prɛ̃s/ *n.m.* prince. **~esse** *n.f.* princess. **~ier**, **~ière** *a.* princely.

princip|al (*m. pl.* **~aux**) /prɛ̃sipal, -o/ *a.* main, principal. —*n.m.* (*pl.* **~aux**) headmaster; (*chose*) main thing. **~alement** *adv.* mainly.

principauté /prɛ̃sipote/ *n.f.* principality.

principe /prɛ̃sip/ *n.m.* principle. **en ~**, theoretically; (*d'habitude*) as a rule.

printan|ier, **~ière** /prɛ̃tanje, -jɛr/ *a.* spring(-like).

printemps /prɛ̃tã/ *n.m.* spring.

priorit|é /prijɔrite/ *n.f.* priority; (*auto.*) right of way. **~aire** *a.* priority. **être ~aire**, have priority.

pris, **~e¹** /pri, -z/ *voir* **prendre**. —*a.* (*place*) taken; (*personne, journée*) busy; (*gorge*) infected. **~ de**, (*peur, fièvre, etc.*) stricken with. **~ de panique**, panic-stricken.

prise² /priz/ *n.f.* hold, grip; (*animal etc. attrapé*) catch; (*mil.*) capture. **~ (de courant)**, (*mâle*) plug; (*femelle*) socket. **aux ~s avec**, at grips with. **~ de conscience**, awareness. **~ de contact**, first contact, initial meeting. **~ de position**, stand. **~ de sang**, blood test.

priser /prize/ *v.t.* (*estimer*) prize.

prisme /prism/ *n.m.* prism.

prison /prizɔ̃/ *n.f.* prison, gaol, jail; (*réclusion*) imprisonment. **~nier**, **~nière** /-ɔnje, -jɛr/ *n.m.*, *f.* prisoner.

privé /prive/ *a.* private. —*n.m.* (*comm.*) private sector. **en ~**, **dans le ~**, in private.

priv|er /prive/ *v.t.* **~er de**, deprive of. **se ~er de**, go without. **~ation** *n.f.* deprivation; (*sacrifice*) hardship.

privil|ège /privilɛʒ/ *n.m.* privilege. **~égié**, **~égiée** *a.* & *n.m.*, *f.* privileged (person).

prix /pri/ *n.m.* price; (*récompense*) prize. **à tout ~**, at all costs. **au ~ de**, (*fig.*) at the expense of. **~ coûtant**, **~ de revient**, cost price. **à ~ fixe**, set price.

pro- /pro/ *préf.* pro-.

probab|le /prɔbabl/ *a.* probable, likely. **~ilité** *n.f.* probability. **~lement** *adv.* probably.

probant, **~e** /prɔbã, -t/ *a.* convincing, conclusive.

probité /prɔbite/ *n.f.* integrity.

problème /prɔblɛm/ *n.m.* problem.

procéd|er /prɔsede/ *v.i.* proceed. **~er à**, carry out. **~é** *n.m.* process; (*conduite*) behaviour.

procédure /prɔsedyr/ *n.f.* procedure.

procès /prɔsɛ/ *n.m.* (*criminel*) trial; (*civil*) lawsuit, proceedings. **~-verbal** (*pl.* **~-verbaux**) *n.m.* report; (*contravention*) ticket.

procession /prɔsesjɔ̃/ *n.f.* procession.

processus /prɔsesys/ *n.m.* process.

prochain, **~e** /prɔʃɛ̃, -ɛn/ *a.* (*suivant*) next; (*proche*) imminent; (*avenir*) near. **je descends à la ~e**, I'm getting off at the next stop. —*n.m.* fellow. **~ement** /-ɛnmã/ *adv.* soon.

proche /prɔʃ/ *a.* near, close; (*avoisinant*) neighbouring; (*parent, ami*) close. **~ de**, close *ou* near to. **de ~ en proche**, gradually. **dans un ~ avenir**, in the near future. **être ~**, (*imminent*) be approaching. **~s** *n.m. pl.* close relations. **P~-Orient** *n.m.* Near East.

proclam|er /prɔklame/ *v.t.* declare, proclaim. **~ation** *n.f.* declaration, proclamation.

procréation /prɔkreasjɔ̃/ n.f. procreation.

procuration /prɔkyrasjɔ̃/ n.f. proxy.

procurer /prɔkyre/ v.t. bring (à, to). se ∼ v. pr. obtain.

procureur /prɔkyrœr/ n.m. public prosecutor.

prodig|e /prɔdiʒ/ n.m. marvel; (personne) prodigy. **enfant/musicien** ∼**e**, child/musical prodigy. ∼**ieux**, ∼**ieuse** a. tremendous, prodigious.

prodigu|e /prɔdig/ a. wasteful. **fils** ∼**e**, prodigal son. ∼**er** v.t. ∼**er à**, lavish on.

producti|f, ∼**ve** /prɔdyktif, -v/ a. productive. ∼**vité** n.f. productivity.

prod|uire† /prɔdɥir/ v.t. produce. se ∼**uire** v. pr. (survenir) happen; (acteur) perform. ∼**ucteur**, ∼**uctrice** a. producing; n.m., f. producer. ∼**uction** n.f. production; (produit) product.

produit /prɔdɥi/ n.m. product. ∼**s**, (de la terre) produce. ∼ **chimique**, chemical. ∼**s alimentaires**, foodstuffs. ∼ **de consommation**, consumer goods. ∼ **national brut**, gross national product.

proéminent, ∼**e** /prɔeminã, -t/ a. prominent.

prof /prɔf/ n.m. (fam.) teacher.

profane /prɔfan/ a. secular. —n.m./f. lay person.

profaner /prɔfane/ v.t. desecrate.

proférer /prɔfere/ v.t. utter.

professer[1] /prɔfese/ v.t. (déclarer) profess.

professer[2] /prɔfese/ v.t./i. (enseigner) teach.

professeur /prɔfesœr/ n.m. teacher; (univ.) lecturer; (avec chaire) professor.

profession /prɔfesjɔ̃/ n.f. occupation; (intellectuelle) profession. ∼**nel**, ∼**nelle** /-jɔnɛl/ a. professional; (école) vocational; n.m., f. professional.

professorat /prɔfesɔra/ n.m. teaching.

profil /prɔfil/ n.m. profile.

profiler (se) /(sə)prɔfile/ v. pr. be outlined.

profit /prɔfi/ n.m. profit. **au** ∼ **de**, in aid of. ∼**able** /-tabl/ a. profitable.

profiter /prɔfite/ v.i. ∼ **à**, benefit. ∼ **de**, take advantage of.

profond, ∼**e** /prɔfɔ̃, -d/ a. deep; (sentiment, intérêt) profound; (causes) underlying. **au plus** ∼ **de**, in the depths of. ∼**ément** /-demã/ adv. deeply; (différent, triste) profoundly; (dormir) soundly. ∼**eur** /-dœr/ n.f. depth.

profusion /prɔfyzjɔ̃/ n.f. profusion.

progéniture /prɔʒenityr/ n.f. offspring.

programmation /prɔgramasjɔ̃/ n.f. programming.

programm|e /prɔgram/ n.m. programme; (matières: scol.) syllabus; (informatique) program. ∼**e (d'études)**, curriculum. ∼**er** v.t. (ordinateur, appareil) program; (émission) schedule. ∼**eur**, ∼**euse** n.m., f. computer programmer.

progrès /prɔgrɛ/ n.m. & n.m. pl. progress. **faire des** ∼, make progress.

progress|er /prɔgrese/ v.i. progress. ∼**ion** /-esjɔ̃/ n.f. progression.

progressi|f, ∼**ve** /prɔgresif, -v/ a. progressive. ∼**vement** adv. progressively.

progressiste /prɔgresist/ a. progressive.

prohib|er /prɔibe/ v.t. prohibit. ∼**ition** n.f. prohibition.

prohibiti|f, ∼**ve** /prɔibitif, -v/ a. prohibitive.

proie /prwa/ n.f. prey. **en** ∼ **à**, tormented by.

projecteur /prɔʒɛktœr/ n.m. floodlight; (mil.) searchlight; (cinéma) projector.

projectile /prɔʒɛktil/ n.m. missile.

projection /prɔʒɛksjɔ̃/ n.f. projection; (séance) show.

projet /prɔʒɛ/ n.m. plan; (ébauche) draft. ∼ **de loi**, bill.

projeter /prɔʒte/ v.t. plan (de, to); (film) project, show; (jeter) hurl, project.

prolét|aire /prɔletɛr/ n.m./f. proletarian. ∼**ariat** n.m. proletariat. ∼**arien**, ∼**arienne** a. proletarian.

prolifér|er /prɔlifere/ v.i. proliferate. ∼**ation** n.f. proliferation.

prolifique /prɔlifik/ a. prolific.

prologue /prɔlɔg/ n.m. prologue.

prolongation /prɔlɔ̃gasjɔ̃/ n.f. extension. ∼**s**, (football) extra time.

prolong|er /prɔlɔ̃ʒe/ v.t. prolong. se ∼**er** v. pr. continue, extend. ∼**é** a. prolonged. ∼**ement** n.m. extension.

promenade /prɔmnad/ n.f. walk; (à bicyclette, à cheval) ride; (en auto) drive, ride. **faire une** ∼, go for a walk.

promen|er /prɔmne/ v.t. take for a walk. ∼**er sur qch.**, (main, regard) run over sth. se ∼**er** v. pr. walk. **(aller) se** ∼**er**, go for a walk. ∼**eur**, ∼**euse** n.m., f. walker.

promesse /prɔmɛs/ n.f. promise.

promett|re† /prɔmɛtr/ v.t./i. promise. ∼**re (beaucoup)**, be promising. se ∼**re de**, resolve to. ∼**eur**, ∼**euse** a. promising.

promontoire /prɔmɔ̃twar/ *n.m.* headland.

promoteur /prɔmɔtœr/ *n.m.* (*immobilier*) property developer.

prom|ouvoir /prɔmuvwar/ *v.t.* promote. **être ~u**, be promoted. **~otion** *n.f.* promotion; (*univ.*) year; (*comm.*) special offer.

prompt, ~e /prɔ̃, -t/ *a.* swift.

prôner /prone/ *v.t.* extol; (*préconiser*) preach, advocate.

pronom /prɔnɔ̃/ *n.m.* pronoun. **~inal** (*m. pl.* **~inaux**) /-ɔminal, -o/ *a.* pronominal.

prononc|er /prɔnɔ̃se/ *v.t.* pronounce; (*discours*) make. **se ~er** *v. pr.* (*mot*) be pronounced; (*personne*) make a decision (**pour**, in favour of). **~é** *a.* pronounced. **~iation** *n.f.* pronunciation.

pronosti|c /prɔnɔstik/ *n.m.* forecast; (*méd.*) prognosis. **~quer** *v.t.* forecast.

propagande /prɔpagɑ̃d/ *n.f.* propaganda.

propag|er /prɔpaʒe/ *v.t.*, **se ~er** *v. pr.* spread. **~ation** /-gasjɔ̃/ *n.f.* spread(ing).

proph|ète /prɔfɛt/ *n.m.* prophet. **~étie** /-esi/ *n.f.* prophecy. **~étique** *a.* prophetic. **~étiser** *v.t./i.* prophesy.

propice /prɔpis/ *a.* favourable.

proportion /prɔpɔrsjɔ̃/ *n.f.* proportion; (*en mathématiques*) ratio. **toutes ~s gardées**, making appropriate allowances. **~né** /-jɔne/ *a.* proportionate (**à**, to). **~nel, ~nelle** /-jɔnɛl/ *a.* proportional. **~ner** /-jɔne/ *v.t.* proportion.

propos /prɔpo/ *n.m.* intention; (*sujet*) subject. —*n.m. pl.* (*paroles*) remarks. **à ~**, at the right time; (*dans un dialogue*) by the way. **à ~ de**, about. **à tout ~**, at every possible occasion.

propos|er /prɔpoze/ *v.t.* propose; (*offrir*) offer. **se ~er** *v. pr.* volunteer (**pour**, to); (*but*) set o.s. **se ~er de faire**, propose to do. **~ition** *n.f.* proposal; (*affirmation*) proposition; (*gram.*) clause.

propre[1] /prɔpr/ *a.* clean; (*soigné*) neat; (*honnête*) decent. **mettre au ~**, write out again neatly. **c'est du ~!** (*ironique*) well done! **~ment**[1] /-əmɑ̃/ *adv.* cleanly; neatly; decently.

propre[2] /prɔpr/ *a.* (*à soi*) own; (*sens*) literal. **~ à**, (*qui convient*) suited to; (*spécifique*) peculiar to. **~-à-rien** *n.m./f.* good-for-nothing. **~ment**[2] /-əmɑ̃/ *adv.* strictly. **le bureau/***etc.* **~ment dit**, the office/*etc.* itself.

propreté /prɔprəte/ *n.f.* cleanliness; (*netteté*) neatness.

propriétaire /prɔprijetɛr/ *n.m./f.* owner; (*comm.*) proprietor; (*qui loue*) landlord, landlady.

propriété /prɔprijete/ *n.f.* property; (*droit*) ownership.

propuls|er /prɔpylse/ *v.t.* propel. **~ion** *n.f.* propulsion.

prorata /prɔrata/ *n.m. invar.* **au ~ de**, in proportion to.

proroger /prɔrɔʒe/ *v.t.* (*contrat*) defer; (*passeport*) extend.

prosaïque /prozaik/ *a.* prosaic.

proscr|ire /prɔskrir/ *v.t.* proscribe. **~it, ~ite** *a.* proscribed; *n.m., f.* (*exilé*) exile.

prose /proz/ *n.f.* prose.

prospec|ter /prɔspɛkte/ *v.t.* prospect. **~teur, ~trice** *n.m., f.* prospector. **~tion** /-ksjɔ̃/ *n.f.* prospecting.

prospectus /prɔspɛktys/ *n.m.* leaflet.

prosp|ère /prɔspɛr/ *a.* flourishing, thriving. **~érer** *v.i.* thrive, prosper. **~érité** *n.f.* prosperity.

prostern|er (se) /(sə)prɔstɛrne/ *v. pr.* bow down. **~é** *a.* prostrate.

prostit|uée /prɔstitɥe/ *n.f.* prostitute. **~ution** *n.f.* prostitution.

prostré /prɔstre/ *a.* prostrate.

protagoniste /prɔtagɔnist/ *n.m.* protagonist.

protec|teur, ~trice /prɔtɛktœr, -tris/ *n.m., f.* protector. —*a.* protective.

protection /prɔtɛksjɔ̃/ *n.f.* protection; (*fig.*) patronage.

protég|er /prɔteʒe/ *v.t.* protect; (*fig.*) patronize. **se ~er** *v. pr.* protect o.s. **~é** *n.m.* protégé. **~ée** *n.f.* protégée.

protéine /prɔtein/ *n.f.* protein.

protestant, ~e /prɔtɛstɑ̃, -t/ *a. & n.m., f.* Protestant.

protest|er /prɔtɛste/ *v.t./i.* protest. **~ation** *n.f.* protest.

protocole /prɔtɔkɔl/ *n.m.* protocol.

prototype /prɔtɔtip/ *n.m.* prototype.

protubéran|t, ~te /prɔtyberɑ̃, -t/ *a.* bulging. **~ce,** *n.f.* protuberance.

proue /pru/ *n.f.* bow, prow.

prouesse /prues/ *n.f.* feat, exploit.

prouver /pruve/ *v.t.* prove.

provenance /prɔvnɑ̃s/ *n.f.* origin. **en ~ de**, from.

provenç|al, ~ale (*m. pl.* **~aux**) /prɔvɑ̃sal, -o/ *a. & n.m., f.* Provençal.

Provence /prɔvɑ̃s/ *n.f.* Provence.

provenir† /prɔvnir/ *v.i.* **~ de**, come from.

proverb|e /prɔvɛrb/ *n.m.* proverb. **~ial** (*m. pl.* **~iaux**) *a.* proverbial.

providence /prɔvidɑ̃s/ *n.f.* providence.
provinc|e /prɔvɛ̃s/ *n.f.* province. **de ~e**, provincial. **la ~e**, the provinces. **~ial**, **~iale** (*m. pl.* **~iaux**) *a. & n.m.*, *f.* provincial.
proviseur /prɔvizœr/ *n.m.* headmaster, principal.
provision /prɔvizjɔ̃/ *n.f.* supply, store; (*dans un compte*) funds; (*acompte*) deposit. **~s**, (*vivres*) provisions. **panier à ~s**, shopping basket.
provisoire /prɔvizwar/ *a.* temporary. **~ment** *adv.* temporarily.
provo|quer /prɔvɔke/ *v.t.* cause; (*exciter*) arouse; (*défier*) provoke. **~cant**, **~cante** *a.* provocative. **~cation** *n.f.* provocation.
proximité /prɔksimite/ *n.f.* proximity. **à ~ de**, close to.
prude /pryd/ *a.* prudish. —*n.f.* prude.
prud|ent, **~ente** /prydɑ̃, -t/ *a.* cautious; (*sage*) wise. **soyez ~ent**, be careful. **~emment** /-amɑ̃/ *adv.* cautiously; wisely. **~ence** *n.f.* caution; wisdom.
prune /pryn/ *n.f.* plum.
pruneau (*pl.* **~x**) /pryno/ *n.m.* prune.
prunelle[1] /prynɛl/ *n.f.* (*pupille*) pupil.
prunelle[2] /prynɛl/ *n.f.* (*fruit*) sloe.
psaume /psom/ *n.m.* psalm.
pseudo- /psødɔ/ *préf.* pseudo-.
pseudonyme /psødɔnim/ *n.m.* pseudonym.
psychanalys|e /psikanaliz/ *n.f.* psychoanalysis. **~er** *v.t.* psychoanalyse. **~te** /-st/ *n.m./f.* psychoanalyst.
psychiatr|e /psikjatr/ *n.m./f.* psychiatrist. **~ie** *n.f.* psychiatry. **~ique** *a.* psychiatric.
psychique /psiʃik/ *a.* mental, psychological.
psycholo|gie /psikɔlɔʒi/ *n.f.* psychology. **~gique** *a.* psychological. **~gue** *n.m./f.* psychologist.
psychosomatique /psikɔsɔmatik/ *a.* psychosomatic.
psychothérapie /psikɔterapi/ *n.f.* psychotherapy.
PTT *abrév.* (*Postes, Télécommunications et Télédiffusion*) Post Office.
pu /py/ *voir* **pouvoir**[1].
puant, **~e** /pɥɑ̃, -t/ *a.* stinking. **~eur** /-tœr/ *n.f.* stink.
pub /pyb/ *n.f.* **la ~**, advertising. **une ~**, an advert.
puberté /pybɛrte/ *n.f.* puberty.
publi|c, **~que** /pyblik/ *a.* public. —*n.m.* public; (*assistance*) audience. **en ~c**, in public.

publicit|é /pyblisite/ *n.f.* publicity, advertising; (*annonce*) advertisement. **~aire** *a.* publicity.
publ|ier /pyblije/ *v.t.* publish. **~ication** *n.f.* publication.
publiquement /pyblikmɑ̃/ *adv.* publicly.
puce[1] /pys/ *n.f.* flea. **marché aux ~s**, flea market.
puce[2] /pys/ *n.f.* (*électronique*) chip.
pud|eur /pydœr/ *n.f.* modesty. **~ique** *a.* modest.
pudibond, **~e** /pydibɔ̃, -d/ *a.* prudish.
puer /pɥe/ *v.i.* stink. —*v.t.* stink of.
puéricultrice /pɥerikyltris/ *n.f.* children's nurse.
puéril /pɥeril/ *a.* puerile.
pugilat /pyʒila/ *n.m.* fight.
puis /pɥi/ *adv.* then.
puiser /pɥize/ *v.t.* draw (**qch. dans**, sth. from). —*v.i.* **~ dans qch.**, dip into sth.
puisque /pɥisk(ə)/ *conj.* since, as.
puissance /pɥisɑ̃s/ *n.f.* power. **en ~** *a.* potential; *adv.* potentially.
puiss|ant, **~ante** /pɥisɑ̃, -t/ *a.* powerful. **~amment** *adv.* powerfully.
puits /pɥi/ *n.m.* well; (*de mine*) shaft.
pull(-over) /pyl(ɔvɛr)/ *n.m.* pullover, jumper.
pulpe /pylp/ *n.f.* pulp.
pulsation /pylsasjɔ̃/ *n.f.* (heart-)beat.
pulvéris|er /pylverize/ *v.t.* pulverize; (*liquide*) spray. **~ateur** *n.m.* spray.
punaise /pynɛz/ *n.f.* (*insecte*) bug; (*clou*) drawing-pin; (*Amer.*) thumbtack.
punch[1] /pɔ̃ʃ/ *n.m.* punch.
punch[2] /pœnʃ/ *n.m.* **avoir du ~**, have drive.
pun|ir /pynir/ *v.t.* punish. **~ition** *n.f.* punishment.
punk /pœnk/ *a. invar.* punk.
pupille[1] /pypij/ *n.f.* (*de l'œil*) pupil.
pupille[2] /pypij/ *n.m./f.* (*enfant*) ward.
pupitre /pypitr/ *n.m.* (*scol.*) desk. **~ à musique**, music stand.
pur /pyr/ *a.* pure; (*whisky*) neat. **~ement** *adv.* purely. **~eté** *n.f.* purity. **~-sang** *n.m. invar.* (*cheval*) thoroughbred.
purée /pyre/ *n.f.* purée; (*de pommes de terre*) mashed potatoes.
purgatoire /pyrgatwar/ *n.m.* purgatory.
purg|e /pyrʒ/ *n.f.* purge. **~er** *v.t.* (*pol., méd.*) purge; (*peine: jurid.*) serve.
purif|ier /pyrifje/ *v.t.* purify. **~ication** *n.f.* purification.
purin /pyrɛ̃/ *n.m.* (liquid) manure.

puritain, ~e /pyritɛ̃, -ɛn/ n.m., f. puritan. —a. puritanical.

pus /py/ n.m. pus.

pustule /pystyl/ n.f. pimple.

putain /pytɛ̃/ n.f. (fam.) whore.

putréfier (se) /(sə)pytrefje/ v. pr. putrefy.

putsch /putʃ/ n.m. putsch.

puzzle /pœzl/ n.m. jigsaw (puzzle).

P-V abrév. (procès-verbal) ticket, traffic fine.

pygmée /pigme/ n.m. pygmy.

pyjama /piʒama/ n.m. pyjamas. **un** ~, a pair of pyjamas.

pylône /pilon/ n.m. pylon.

pyramide /piramid/ n.f. pyramid.

Pyrénées /pirene/ n.f. pl. **les** ~, the Pyrenees.

pyromane /pirɔman/ n.m./f. arsonist.

Q

QG abrév. (quartier général) HQ.

QI abrév. (quotient intellectuel) IQ.

qu' /k/ voir **que**.

quadrill|er /kadrije/ v.t. (zone) comb, control. ~**age** n.m. (mil.) control. ~**é** a. (papier) squared.

quadrupède /kadrypɛd/ n.m. quadruped.

quadrupl|e /kadrypl/ a. & n.m. quadruple. ~**er** v.t./i. quadruple. ~**és**, ~**ées** n.m., f. pl. quadruplets.

quai /ke/ n.m. (de gare) platform; (de port) quay; (de rivière) embankment.

qualificatif /kalifikatif/ n.m. (épithète) term.

qualif|ier /kalifje/ v.t. qualify; (décrire) describe (de, as). **se** ~**ier** v. pr. qualify (pour, for). ~**ication** n.f. qualification; description. ~**ié** a. qualified; (main d'œuvre) skilled.

qualit|é /kalite/ n.f. quality; (titre) occupation. **en** ~**é de**, in one's capacity as. ~**atif**, ~**ative** a. qualitative.

quand /kɑ̃/ conj. & adv. when. ~ **même**, all the same. ~ **(bien) même**, even if.

quant (à) /kɑ̃t(a)/ prép. as for.

quant-à-soi /kɑ̃taswa/ n.m. **rester sur son** ~, stand aloof.

quantit|é /kɑ̃tite/ n.f. quantity. **une** ~**é de**, a lot of. **des** ~**és**, masses. ~**atif**, ~**ative** a. quantitative.

quarantaine /karɑ̃tɛn/ n.f. (méd.) quarantine. **une** ~ **(de)**, about forty.

quarant|e /karɑ̃t/ a. & n.m. forty. ~**ième** a. & n.m./f. fortieth.

quart /kar/ n.m. quarter; (naut.) watch. ~ **(de litre)**, quarter litre. ~ **de finale**, quarter-final. ~ **d'heure**, quarter of an hour.

quartier /kartje/ n.m. neighbourhood, district; (de lune, bœuf) quarter; (de fruit) segment. ~**s**, (mil.) quarters. **de** ~, **du** ~, local. ~ **général**, headquarters. **avoir** ~ **libre**, be free.

quartz /kwarts/ n.m. quartz.

quasi- /kazi/ préf. quasi-.

quasiment /kazimɑ̃/ adv. almost.

quatorz|e /katɔrz/ a. & n.m. fourteen. ~**ième** a. & n.m./f. fourteenth.

quatre /katr(ə)/ a. & n.m. four. ~**vingt(s)** a. & n.m. eighty. ~**vingt-dix** a. & n.m. ninety.

quatrième /katrijɛm/ a. & n.m./f. fourth. ~**ment** adv. fourthly.

quatuor /kwatyɔr/ n.m. quartet.

que, qu'* /kə, k/ conj. that; (comparaison) than. **qu'il vienne**, let him come. **qu'il vienne ou non**, whether he comes or not. **ne faire** ~ **demander**/etc., only ask/etc. —adv. **(ce)** ~ **tu es bête, qu'est-ce** ~ **tu es bête**, how silly you are. ~ **de**, what a lot of. —pron. rel. (personne) that, whom; (chose) that, which; (temps, moment) when; (interrogatif) what. **un jour**/etc. ~, one day/etc. when. ~ **faites-vous?**, **qu'est-ce** ~ **vous faites?**, what are you doing?

Québec /kebɛk/ n.m. Quebec.

quel, ~le /kɛl/ a. what; (interrogatif) which, what; (qui) who. —pron. which. ~ **dommage**, what a pity. ~ **qu'il soit**, (chose) whatever ou whichever it may be; (personne) whoever he may be.

quelconque /kɛlkɔ̃k/ a. any, some; (banal) ordinary; (médiocre) poor.

quelque /kɛlkə/ a. some. ~**s**, a few, some. —adv. (environ) some. **et** ~, (fam.) and a bit. ~ **chose**, something; (interrogation) anything. ~ **part**, somewhere. ~ **peu**, somewhat.

quelquefois /kɛlkəfwa/ adv. sometimes.

quelques|-uns, ~-unes /kɛlkəzœ̃, -yn/ pron. some, a few.

quelqu'un /kɛlkœ̃/ pron. someone, somebody; (interrogation) anyone, anybody.

quémander /kemɑ̃de/ v.t. beg for.

qu'en-dira-t-on /kɑ̃diratɔ̃/ n.m. invar. **le** ~, gossip.

querell|e /kɔrɛl/ *n.f.* quarrel. **~eur,**
~euse *a.* quarrelsome.
quereller (se) /(sə)kɑrele/ *v. pr.* quarrel.
question /kɛstjɔ̃/ *n.f.* question; (*affaire*)
matter, question. **en ~,** in question; (*en*
jeu) at stake. **il est ~ de,** (*cela*
concerne) it is about; (*on parle de*) there
is talk of. **il n'en est pas ~,** it is out of
the question. **~ner** /-jɔne/ *v.t.* question.
questionnaire /kɛstjɔnɛr/ *n.m.* questionnaire.
quêt|e /kɛt/ *n.f.* (*relig.*) collection. **en ~e**
de, in search of. **~er** /kete/ *v.i.* collect
money; *v.t.* seek.
quetsche /kwɛtʃ/ *n.f.* (sort of dark red)
plum.
queue /kø/ *n.f.* tail; (*de poêle*) handle;
(*de fruit*) stalk; (*de fleur*) stem; (*file*)
queue; (*file: Amer.*) line; (*de train*) rear.
faire la ~, queue (up); (*Amer.*) line up.
~ de cheval, pony-tail.
qui /ki/ *pron. rel.* (*personne*) who;
(*chose*) which, that; (*interrogatif*) who;
(*après prép.*) whom; (*quiconque*)
whoever. **à ~ est ce stylo/***etc.***?,** whose
pen/*etc.* is this? **qu'est-ce ~?,** what? **~**
est-ce qui?, who? **~ que ce soit,**
anyone.
quiche /kiʃ/ *n.f.* quiche.
quiconque /kikɔ̃k/ *pron.* whoever;
(*n'importe qui*) anyone.
quiétude /kjetyd/ *n.f.* quiet.
quignon /kiɲɔ̃/ *n.m.* **~ de pain,** chunk of
bread.
quille[1] /kij/ *n.f.* (*de bateau*) keel.
quille[2] /kij/ *n.f.* (*jouet*) skittle.
quincaill|ier, ~ière /kɛ̃kaje, -jɛr/
n.m., f. hardware dealer. **~erie** *n.f.*
hardware; (*magasin*) hardware shop.
quinine /kinin/ *n.f.* quinine.
quinquennal (*m. pl.* **~aux**) /kɛ̃kenal,
-o/ *a.* five-year.
quint|al (*pl.* **~aux**) /kɛ̃tal, -o/ *n.m.*
quintal (= *100 kg*).
quinte /kɛ̃t/ *n.f.* **~ de toux,** coughing fit.
quintette /kɛ̃tɛt/ *n.m.* quintet.
quintupl|e /kɛ̃typl/ *a.* fivefold. —*n.m.*
quintuple. **~er** *v.t./i.* increase fivefold.
~és, ~ées, *n.m., f. pl.* quintuplets.
quinzaine /kɛ̃zɛn/ *n.f.* **une ~ (de),** about
fifteen.
quinz|e /kɛ̃z/ *a. & n.m.* fifteen. **~e jours,**
two weeks. **~ième** *a. & n.m./f.*
fifteenth.
quiproquo /kiprɔko/ *n.m.* misunderstanding.
quittance /kitɑ̃s/ *n.f.* receipt.
quitte /kit/ *a.* quits (**envers,** with). **~ à**
faire, even if it means doing.

quitter /kite/ *v.t.* leave; (*vêtement*) take
off. **se ~** *v. pr.* part.
quoi /kwa/ *pron.* what; (*après prép.*)
which. **de ~ vivre/manger/***etc.***,**
(*assez*) enough to live on/to eat/*etc.* **de**
~ écrire, sth. to write with, what is
necessary to write with. **~ que,**
whatever. **~ que ce soit,** anything.
quoique /kwak(ə)/ *conj.* (al)though.
quolibet /kɔlibɛ/ *n.m.* gibe.
quorum /kɔrɔm/ *n.m.* quorum.
quota /kɔta/ *n.m.* quota.
quote-part (*pl.* **quotes-parts**) /kɔtpar/
n.f. share.
quotidien, ~ne /kɔtidjɛ̃, -jɛn/ *a.* daily;
(*banal*) everyday. —*n.m.* daily (paper).
~nement /-jɛnmɑ̃/ *adv.* daily.
quotient /kɔsjɑ̃/ *n.m.* quotient.

R

rab /rab/ *n.m.* (*fam.*) extra. **il y en a en**
~, there's some over.
rabâcher /rabaʃe/ *v.t.* keep repeating.
rabais /rabɛ/ *n.m.* (price) reduction.
rabaisser /rabese/ *v.t.* (*déprécier*)
belittle; (*réduire*) reduce.
rabat /raba/ *n.m.* flap. **~-joie** *n.m. invar.*
killjoy.
rabattre /rabatr/ *v.t.* pull *ou* put down;
(*diminuer*) reduce; (*déduire*) take off.
se ~ *v. pr.* (*se refermer*) close;
(*véhicule*) cut in, turn sharply. **se ~ sur,**
fall back on.
rabbin /rabɛ̃/ *n.m.* rabbi.
rabibocher /rabiboʃe/ *v.t.* (*fam.*) reconcile.
rablot /rablo/ *n.m.* (*fam.*) = **rab.**
râblé /rable/ *a.* stocky, sturdy.
rabot /rabo/ *n.m.* plane. **~er** /-ɔte/ *v.t.*
plane.
raboteu|x, ~se /rabotø, -z/ *a.* uneven.
rabougri /rabugri/ *a.* stunted.
rabrouer /rabrue/ *v.t.* snub.
racaille /rakaj/ *n.f.* rabble.
raccommoder /rakɔmɔde/ *v.t.* mend;
(*personnes: fam.*) reconcile.
raccompagner /rakɔ̃paɲe/ *v.t.* see *ou*
take back (home).
raccord /rakɔr/ *n.m.* link; (*de papier*
peint) join. **~ (de peinture),** touch-
up.
raccord|er /rakɔrde/ *v.t.* connect, join.
~ement *n.m.* connection.
raccourci /rakursi/ *n.m.* short cut. **en ~,**
in brief.

raccourcir /rakursir/ v.t. shorten. —v.i. get shorter.

raccrocher /rakrɔʃe/ v.t. hang back up; (personne) grab hold of; (relier) connect. ~ (le récepteur), hang up. se ~ à, cling to; (se relier à) be connected to ou with.

rac|e /ras/ n.f. race; (animale) breed. de ~e, pure-bred. ~ial (m. pl. ~iaux) a. racial.

rachat /raʃa/ n.m. buying (back); (de pécheur) redemption.

racheter /raʃte/ v.t. buy (back); (davantage) buy more; (nouvel objet) buy another; (pécheur) redeem. se ~ v. pr. make amends.

racine /rasin/ n.f. root. ~ carrée/cubique, square/cube root.

racis|te /rasist/ a. & n.m./f. racist. ~me n.m. racism.

racket /raket/ n.m. racketeering.

raclée /rakle/ n.f. (fam.) thrashing.

racler /rakle/ v.t. scrape. se ~ la gorge, clear one's throat.

racol|er /rakɔle/ v.t. solicit; (marchand, parti) drum up. ~age n.m. soliciting.

racontars /rakɔ̃tar/ n.m. pl. (fam.) gossip, stories.

raconter /rakɔ̃te/ v.t. (histoire) tell, relate; (vacances etc.) tell about. ~ à qn. que, tell s.o. that, say to s.o. that.

racorni /rakɔrni/ a. hard(ened).

radar /radar/ n.m. radar.

rade /rad/ n.f. harbour. en ~, (personne: fam.) stranded, behind.

radeau (pl. ~x) /rado/ n.m. raft.

radiateur /radjatœr/ n.m. radiator; (électrique) heater.

radiation /radjɑsjɔ̃/ n.f. (énergie) radiation.

radic|al (m. pl. ~aux) /radikal, -o/ a. radical. —n.m. (pl. ~aux) radical.

radier /radje/ v.t. cross off.

radieu|x, ~se /radjø, -z/ a. radiant.

radin, ~e /radɛ̃, -in/ a. (fam.) stingy.

radio /radjo/ n.f. radio; (radiographie) X-ray.

radioacti|f, ~ve /radjoaktif, -v/ a. radioactive. ~vité n.f. radioactivity.

radiocassette /radjokaset/ n.f. radio-cassette-player.

radiodiffus|er /radjodifyze/ v.t. broadcast. ~ion n.f. broadcasting.

radiograph|ie /radjografi/ n.f. (photographie) X-ray. ~ier v.t. X-ray. ~ique a. X-ray.

radiologue /radjɔlɔg/ n.m./f. radiographer.

radiophonique /radjofɔnik/ a. radio.

radis /radi/ n.m. radish. **ne pas avoir un ~**, be broke.

radoter /radɔte/ v.i. (fam.) talk drivel.

radoucir (se) /(sə)radusir/ v. pr. calm down; (temps) become milder.

rafale /rafal/ n.f. (de vent) gust; (tir) burst of gunfire.

raffermir /rafɛrmir/ v.t. strengthen. se ~ v. pr. become stronger.

raffin|é /rafine/ a. refined. ~ement n.m. refinement.

raffin|er /rafine/ v.t. refine. ~age n.m. refining. ~erie n.f. refinery.

raffoler /rafɔle/ v.i. ~ de, be extremely fond of.

raffut /rafy/ n.m. (fam.) din.

rafiot /rafjo/ n.m. (fam.) boat.

rafistoler /rafistɔle/ v.t. (fam.) patch up.

rafle /rafl/ n.f. (police) raid.

rafler /rafle/ v.t. grab, swipe.

rafraîch|ir /rafreʃir/ v.t. cool (down); (raviver) brighten up; (personne, mémoire) refresh. se ~ir v. pr. (se laver) freshen up; (boire) refresh o.s.; (temps) get cooler. ~issant, ~issante a. refreshing.

rafraîchissement /rafreʃismɑ̃/ n.m. (boisson) cold drink. ~s, (fruits etc.) refreshments.

ragaillardir /ragajardir/ v.t. (fam.) buck up. se ~ v. pr. buck up.

rag|e /raʒ/ n.f. rage; (maladie) rabies. **faire ~e**, rage. ~e de dents, raging toothache. ~er v.i. rage. ~eur, ~euse a. ill-tempered. ~eant, ~eante a. maddening.

ragot(s) /rago/ n.m. (pl.) (fam.) gossip.

ragoût /ragu/ n.m. stew.

raid /rɛd/ n.m. (mil.) raid; (sport) rally.

raid|e /rɛd/ a. stiff; (côte) steep; (corde) tight; (cheveux) straight. —adv. (en pente) steeply. ~eur n.f. stiffness; steepness.

raidir /redir/ v.t., se ~ v. pr. stiffen; (position) harden; (corde) tighten.

raie[1] /rɛ/ n.f. line; (bande) strip; (de cheveux) parting.

raie[2] /rɛ/ n.f. (poisson) skate.

raifort /refɔr/ n.m. horse-radish.

rail /raj/ n.m. (barre) rail. **le ~**, (transport) rail.

raill|er /raje/ v.t. mock (at). ~erie n.f. mocking remark. ~eur, ~euse a. mocking.

rainure /renyr/ n.f. groove.

raisin /rezɛ̃/ n.m. ~(s), grapes. ~ sec, raisin.

raison /rezɔ̃/ n.f. reason. **à ~ de**, at the

rate of. **avec ~,** rightly. **avoir ~,** be right (**de faire,** to do). **avoir ~ de qn.,** get the better of s.o. **donner ~ à,** prove right. **en ~ de,** (*cause*) because of. **~ de plus,** all the more reason. **perdre la ~,** lose one's mind.

raisonnable /rɛzɔnabl/ *a.* reasonable, sensible.

raisonn|er /rɛzɔne/ *v.i.* reason. —*v.t.* (*personne*) reason with. **~ement** *n.m.* reasoning; (*propositions*) argument.

rajeunir /raʒœnir/ *v.t.* make (look) younger; (*moderniser*) modernize; (*méd.*) rejuvenate. —*v.i.* look younger.

rajout /raʒu/ *n.m.* addition. **~er** /-te/ *v.t.* add.

rajust|er /raʒyste/ *v.t.* straighten; (*salaires*) (re)adjust. **~ement** *n.m.* (re)adjustment.

râl|e /rɑl/ *n.m.* (*de blessé*) groan. **~er** *v.i.* groan; (*protester: fam.*) moan.

ralent|ir /ralɑ̃tir/ *v.t./i.,* **se ~** *v. pr.* slow down. **~i** *a.* slow; *n.m.* (*cinéma*) slow motion. **être** *ou* **tourner au ~i,** tick over, idle.

rall|ier /ralje/ *v.t.* rally; (*rejoindre*) rejoin. **se ~ier** *v. pr.* rally. **se ~ier à,** (*avis*) come over to. **~iement** *n.m.* rallying.

rallonge /ralɔ̃ʒ/ *n.f.* (*de table*) extension. **~ de,** (*supplément de*) extra.

rallonger /ralɔ̃ʒe/ *v.t.* lengthen.

rallumer /ralyme/ *v.t.* light (up) again; (*lampe*) switch on again; (*ranimer: fig.*) revive.

rallye /rali/ *n.m.* rally.

ramadan /ramadɑ̃/ *n.m.* Ramadan.

ramassé /ramase/ *a.* squat; (*concis*) concise.

ramass|er /ramase/ *v.t.* pick up; (*récolter*) gather; (*recueillir*) collect. **se ~er** *v. pr.* draw o.s. together, curl up. **~age** *n.m.* (*cueillette*) gathering. **~age scolaire,** school bus service.

rambarde /rɑ̃bard/ *n.f.* guardrail.

rame /ram/ *n.f.* (*aviron*) oar; (*train*) train; (*perche*) stake.

rameau (*pl.* **~x**) /ramo/ *n.m.* branch.

ramener /ramne/ *v.t.* bring back. **~ à,** (*réduire à*) reduce to. **se ~** *v. pr.* (*fam.*) turn up. **se ~ à,** (*problème*) come down to.

ram|er /rame/ *v.i.* row. **~eur, ~euse** *n.m., f.* rower.

ramif|ier (se) /(sə)ramifje/ *v. pr.* ramify. **~ication** *n.f.* ramification.

ramollir /ramɔlir/ *v.t.,* **se ~** *v. pr.* soften.

ramon|er /ramɔne/ *v.t.* sweep. **~eur** *n.m.* (chimney-)sweep.

rampe /rɑ̃p/ *n.f.* banisters; (*pente*) ramp. **~ de lancement,** launching pad.

ramper /rɑ̃pe/ *v.i.* crawl.

rancard /rɑ̃kar/ *n.m.* (*fam.*) appointment.

rancart /rɑ̃kar/ *n.m.* **mettre** *ou* **jeter au ~,** (*fam.*) scrap.

ranc|e /rɑ̃s/ *a.* rancid. **~ir** *v.i.* go *ou* turn rancid.

rancœur /rɑ̃kœr/ *n.f.* resentment.

rançon /rɑ̃sɔ̃/ *n.f.* ransom. **~ner** /-ɔne/ *v.t.* hold to ransom.

rancun|e /rɑ̃kyn/ *n.f.* grudge. **sans ~!,** no hard feelings. **~ier, ~ière** *a.* vindictive.

randonnée /rɑ̃dɔne/ *n.f.* walk; (*en auto, vélo*) ride.

rang /rɑ̃/ *n.m.* row; (*hiérarchie, condition*) rank. **se mettre en ~,** line up. **au premier ~,** in the first row; (*fig.*) at the forefront. **de second ~,** (*péj.*) second-rate.

rangee /rɑ̃ʒe/ *n.f.* row.

rang|er /rɑ̃ʒe/ *v.t.* put away; (*chambre etc.*) tidy (up); (*disposer*) place; (*véhicule*) park. **se ~er** *v. pr.* (*véhicule*) park; (*s'écarter*) stand aside; (*s'assagir*) settle down. **se ~er à,** (*avis*) accept. **~ement** *n.m.* (*de chambre*) tidying (up); (*espace*) storage space.

ranimer /ranime/ *v.t.,* **se ~** *v. pr.* revive.

rapace[1] /rapas/ *n.m.* bird of prey.

rapace[2] /rapas/ *a.* grasping.

rapatr|ier /rapatrije/ *v.t.* repatriate. **~iement** *n.m.* repatriation.

râp|e /rap/ *n.f.* (*culin.*) grater; (*lime*) rasp. **~er** *v.t.* grate; (*bois*) rasp.

râpé /rape/ *a.* threadbare. **c'est ~!,** (*fam.*) that's right out!

rapetisser /raptise/ *v.t.* make smaller. —*v.i.* get smaller.

râpeu|x, ~se /rapø, -z/ *a.* rough.

rapid|e /rapid/ *a.* fast, rapid. —*n.m.* (*train*) express (train); (*cours d'eau*) rapids *pl.* **~ement** *adv.* fast, rapidly. **~ité** *n.f.* speed.

rapiécer /rapjese/ *v.t.* patch.

rappel /rapɛl/ *n.m.* recall; (*deuxième avis*) reminder; (*de salaire*) back pay; (*méd.*) booster.

rappeler /raple/ *v.t.* call back; (*diplomate, réserviste*) recall; (*évoquer*) remind, recall. **~ qch. à qn.,** (*redire*) remind s.o. of sth. **se ~** *v. pr.* remember, recall.

rapport /rapɔr/ *n.m.* connection; (*compte rendu*) report; (*profit*) yield.

~s, (*relations*) relations. **en ~ avec**, (*accord*) in keeping with. **mettre/se mettre en ~ avec**, put/get in touch with. **par ~ à**, in relation to. **~s (sexuels)**, intercourse.

rapport|er /raporte/ *v.t.* bring back; (*profit*) bring in; (*dire, répéter*) report. —*v.i.* (*comm.*) bring in a good return; (*mouchard: fam.*) tell. **se ~er à**, relate to. **s'en ~er à**, rely on. **~eur, ~euse** *n.m., f.* (*mouchard*) tell-tale; *n.m.* (*instrument*) protractor.

rapproch|er /raproʃe/ *v.t.* bring closer (**de**, to); (*réconcilier*) bring together; (*comparer*) compare. **se ~er** *v. pr.* get *ou* come closer (**de**, to); (*personnes, pays*) come together; (*s'apparenter*) be close (**de**, to). **~é** *a.* close. **~ement** *n.m.* reconciliation; (*rapport*) connection; (*comparaison*) parallel.

rapt /rapt/ *n.m.* abduction.

raquette /rakɛt/ *n.f.* (*de tennis*) racket; (*de ping-pong*) bat.

rare /rar/ *a.* rare; (*insuffisant*) scarce. **~ment** *adv.* rarely, seldom. **~té** *n.f.* rarity; scarcity; (*objet*) rarity.

raréfier (se) /(sə)rarefje/ *v. pr.* become scarce.

ras, ~e /ra, raz/ *a.* (*herbe, poil*) short. **à ~ de**, very close to. **en avoir ~ le bol**, (*fam.*) be really fed up. **~e campagne**, open country. **coupé à ~**, cut short. **à ~ bord**, to the brim. **pull ~ du cou**, round-neck pull-over. **~-le-bol** *n.m.* (*fam.*) anger. **en avoir ~ le bol**, be fed-up.

ras|er /raze/ *v.t.* shave; (*cheveux, barbe*) shave off; (*frôler*) skim; (*abattre*) raze; (*ennuyer: fam.*) bore. **se ~er** *v. pr.* shave. **~age** *n.m.* shaving. **~eur, ~euse** *n.m., f.* (*fam.*) bore.

rasoir /razwar/ *n.m.* razor.

rassas|ier /rasazje/ *v.t.* satisfy. **être ~ié de**, have had enough of.

rassembl|er /rasɑ̃ble/ *v.t.* gather; (*courage*) muster. **se ~er** *v. pr.* gather. **~ement** *n.m.* gathering.

rasseoir (se) /(sə)raswar/ *v. pr.* sit down again.

rass|is, ~ise *ou* **~ie** /rasi, -z/ *a.* (*pain*) stale.

rassurer /rasyre/ *v.t.* reassure.

rat /ra/ *n.m.* rat.

ratatiner (se) /(sə)ratatine/ *v. pr.* shrivel up.

rate /rat/ *n.f.* spleen.

râteau (*pl.* **~x**) /rato/ *n.m.* rake.

râtelier /ratəlje/ *n.m.*; (*fam.*) dentures.

rat|er /rate/ *v.t./i.* miss; (*gâcher*) spoil;

(*échouer*) fail. **c'est ~é**, that's right out. **~é, ~ée** *n.m., f.* (*personne*) failure. **avoir des ~és**, (*auto.*) backfire.

ratif|ier /ratifje/ *v.t.* ratify. **~ication** *n.f.* ratification.

ratio /rasjo/ *n.m.* ratio.

ration /rasjɔ̃/ *n.f.* ration.

rationaliser /rasjɔnalize/ *v.t.* rationalize.

rationnel, ~le /rasjɔnɛl/ *a.* rational.

rationn|er /rasjɔne/ *v.t.* ration. **~ement** *n.m.* rationing.

ratisser /ratise/ *v.t.* rake; (*fouiller*) comb.

rattacher /rataʃe/ *v.t.* tie up again; (*relier*) link; (*incorporer*) join.

rattrapage /ratrapaʒ/ *n.m.* **~ scolaire**, remedial classes.

rattraper /ratrape/ *v.t.* catch; (*rejoindre*) catch up with; (*retard, erreur*) make up for. **se ~** *v. pr.* catch up; (*se dédommager*) make up for it. **se ~ à**, catch hold of.

ratur|e /ratyr/ *n.f.* deletion. **~er** *v.t.* delete.

rauque /rok/ *a.* raucous, harsh.

ravager /ravaʒe/ *v.t.* devastate, ravage.

ravages /ravaʒ/ *n.m. pl.* **faire des ~**, wreak havoc.

raval|er /ravale/ *v.t.* (*façade etc.*) clean; (*humilier*) lower (**à**, down to). **~ement** *n.m.* cleaning.

ravi /ravi/ *a.* delighted (**que**, that).

ravier /ravje/ *n.m.* hors-d'œuvre dish.

ravigoter /ravigɔte/ *v.t.* (*fam.*) buck up.

ravin /ravɛ̃/ *n.m.* ravine.

ravioli /ravjɔli/ *n.m. pl.* ravioli.

ravir /ravir/ *v.t.* delight. **~ à qn.**, (*enlever*) rob s.o. of.

raviser (se) /(sə)ravize/ *v. pr.* change one's mind.

ravissant, ~e /ravisɑ̃, -t/ *a.* beautiful.

ravisseu|r, ~se /ravisœr, -øz/ *n.m., f.* kidnapper.

ravitaill|er /ravitaje/ *v.t.* provide with supplies; (*avion*) refuel. **se ~er** *v. pr.* stock up. **~ement** *n.m.* provision of supplies (**de**, to), refuelling; (*denrées*) supplies.

raviver /ravive/ *v.t.* revive.

rayé /reje/ *a.* striped.

rayer /reje/ *v.t.* scratch; (*biffer*) cross out.

rayon /rɛjɔ̃/ *n.m.* ray; (*planche*) shelf; (*de magasin*) department; (*de roue*) spoke; (*de cercle*) radius. **~ de miel**, honeycomb. **~ X**, X-ray. **en connaître un ~**, (*fam.*) know one's stuff.

rayonn|er /rɛjɔne/ *v.i.* radiate; (*de joie*)

beam; (*se déplacer*) tour around (*from a central point*). ~ement *n.m.* (*éclat*) radiance; (*influence*) influence; (*radiations*) radiation.

rayure /rejyr/ *n.f.* scratch; (*dessin*) stripe. **à ~s**, striped.

raz-de-marée /radmare/ *n.m. invar.* tidal wave. ~ **électoral**, landslide.

re- /rə/ *préf.* re-.

ré- /re/ *préf.* re-.

réacteur /reaktœr/ *n.m.* jet engine; (*nucléaire*) reactor.

réaction /reaksjɔ̃/ *n.f.* reaction. ~ **en chaîne**, chain reaction. ~**naire** /-jɔnɛr/ *a. & n.m./f.* reactionary.

réadapter /readapte/ *v.t.*, **se** ~ *v. pr.* readjust (**à**, to).

réaffirmer /reafirme/ *v.t.* reaffirm.

réagir /reaʒir/ *v.i.* react.

réalis|er /realize/ *v.t.* carry out; (*effort, bénéfice, achat*) make; (*rêve*) fulfil; (*film*) produce, direct; (*capital*) realize; (*se rendre compte de*) realize. **se ~er** *v. pr.* materialize. ~**ateur**, ~**atrice** *n.m., f.* (*cinéma*) director; (*TV*) producer. ~**ation** *n.f.* realization; (*œuvre*) achievement.

réalis|te /realist/ *a.* realistic. —*n.m./f.* realist. ~**me** *n.m.* realism.

réalité /realite/ *n.f.* reality.

réanim|er /reanime/ *v.t.* resuscitate. ~**ation** *n.f.* resuscitation. **service de ~ation**, intensive care.

réapparaître /reaparɛtr/ *v.i.* reappear.

réarm|er (se) /(sə)rearme/ *v. pr.* rearm. ~**ement** *n.m.* rearmament.

rébarbati|f, ~**ve** /rebarbatif, -v/ *a.* forbidding, off-putting.

rebâtir /rɑbɑtir/ *v.t.* rebuild.

rebelle /rəbɛl/ *a.* rebellious; (*soldat*) rebel. —*n.m./f.* rebel.

rebeller (se) /(sə)rəbele/ *v. pr.* rebel, hit back defiantly.

rébellion /rebeljɔ̃/ *n.f.* rebellion.

rebiffer (se) /(sə)rəbife/ *v. pr.* (*fam.*) rebel.

rebond /rəbɔ̃/ *n.m.* bounce; (*par ricochet*) rebound. ~**ir** /-dir/ *v.i.* bounce; rebound.

rebondi /rəbɔ̃di/ *a.* chubby.

rebondissement /rəbɔ̃dismɑ̃/ *n.m.* (new) development.

rebord /rəbɔr/ *n.m.* edge. ~ **de la fenêtre**, window-ledge.

rebours (à) /(a)rəbur/ *adv.* the wrong way.

rebrousse-poil (à) /(a)rəbruspwal/ *adv.* (*fig.*) **prendre qn.** ~, rub s.o. up the wrong way.

rebrousser /rəbruse/ *v.t.* ~ **chemin**, turn back.

rebuffade /rəbyfad/ *n.f.* rebuff.

rébus /rebys/ *n.m.* rebus.

rebut /rəby/ *n.m.* **mettre** *ou* **jeter au ~**, scrap.

rebut|er /rəbyte/ *v.t.* put off. ~**ant**, ~**ante** *a.* off-putting.

récalcitrant, ~**e** /rekalsitrɑ̃, -t/ *a.* stubborn.

recal|er /rəkale/ *v.t.* (*fam.*) fail. **se faire ~er** *ou* **être ~é**, fail.

récapitul|er /rekapityle/ *v.t./i.* recapitulate. ~**ation** *n.f.* recapitulation.

recel /rəsɛl/ *n.m.* receiving. ~**er** /rəs(ə)le/ *v.t.* (*objet volé*) receive; (*cacher*) conceal.

récemment /resamɑ̃/ *adv.* recently.

recens|er /rəsɑ̃se/ *v.t.* (*population*) take a census of; (*objets*) list. ~**ement** *n.m.* census; list.

récent, ~**e** /resɑ̃, -t/ *a.* recent.

récépissé /resepise/ *n.m.* receipt.

récepteur /reseptœr/ *n.m.* receiver.

récepti|f, ~**ve** /reseptif, -v/ *a.* receptive.

réception /resɛpsjɔ̃/ *n.f.* reception. ~ **de**, (*lettre etc.*) receipt of. ~**niste** /-jɔnist/ *n.m./f.* receptionist.

récession /resesjɔ̃/ *n.f.* recession.

recette /rəsɛt/ *n.f.* (*culin.*) recipe; (*argent*) takings. ~**s**, (*comm.*) receipts.

receveu|r, ~**se** /rəsəvœr, øz/ *n.m., f.* (*des impôts*) tax collector.

recevoir† /rəsvwar/ *v.t.* receive; (*client, malade*) see; (*obtenir*) get, receive. **être reçu (à)**, pass. —*v.i.* (*médecin*) receive patients. **se ~** *v. pr.* (*tomber*) land.

rechange (de) /(də)rəʃɑ̃ʒ/ *a.* (*roue, vêtements, etc.*) spare; (*solution etc.*) alternative.

réchapper /reʃape/ *v.i.* ~ **de** *ou* **à**, come through, survive.

recharg|e /rəʃarʒ/ *n.f.* (*de stylo*) refill. ~**er** *v.t.* refill; (*batterie*) recharge.

réchaud /reʃo/ *n.m.* stove.

réchauff|er /reʃofe/ *v.t.* warm up. **se ~er** *v. pr.* warm o.s. up; (*temps*) get warmer. ~**ement** *n.m.* (*de température*) rise (**de**, in).

rêche /rɛʃ/ *a.* rough.

recherche /rəʃɛrʃ/ *n.f.* search (**de**, for); (*raffinement*) elegance. ~(**s**), (*univ.*) research. ~**s**, (*enquête*) investigations.

recherch|er /rəʃɛrʃe/ *v.t.* search for. ~**é** *a.* in great demand; (*élégant*) elegant. ~**é pour meurtre**, wanted for murder.

rechigner /rəʃiɲe/ *v.i.* ~ **à**, balk at.

rechut|e /rəʃyt/ *n.f.* (*méd.*) relapse. ~**er** *v.i.* relapse.

récidiv|e /residiv/ *n.f.* second offence. ~**er** *v.i.* commit a second offence.

récif /resif/ *n.m.* reef.

récipient /resipjɑ̃/ *n.m.* container.

réciproque /resiprɔk/ *a.* mutual, reciprocal. ~**ment** *adv.* each other; (*inversement*) conversely.

récit /resi/ *n.m.* (*compte rendu*) account, story; (*histoire*) story.

récital (*pl.* ~s) /resital/ *n.m.* recital.

récit|er /resite/ *v.t.* recite. ~**ation** *n.f.* recitation.

réclame /reklam/ *n.f.* **faire de la** ~, advertise. **en** ~, on offer.

réclam|er /reklame/ *v.t.* call for, demand; (*revendiquer*) claim. —*v.i.* complain. ~**ation** *n.f.* complaint.

reclus, ~**e** /rəkly, -z/ *n.m.,* *f.* recluse. —*a.* cloistered.

réclusion /reklyzjɔ̃/ *n.f.* imprisonment.

recoin /rəkwɛ̃/ *n.m.* nook.

récolt|e /rekɔlt/ *n.f.* (*action*) harvest; (*produits*) crop, harvest; (*fig.*) crop. ~**er** *v.t.* harvest, gather; (*fig.*) collect.

recommand|er /rəkɔmɑ̃de/ *v.t.* recommend; (*lettre*) register. **envoyer en** ~**é,** send registered. ~**ation** *n.f.* recommendation.

recommence|r /rəkɔmɑ̃se/ *v.t./i.* (*reprendre*) begin *ou* start again; (*refaire*) repeat. **ne** ~ **pas,** don't do it again.

récompens|e /rekɔ̃pɑ̃s/ *n.f.* reward; (*prix*) award. ~**er** *v.t.* reward (**de,** for).

réconcil|ier /rekɔ̃silje/ *v.t.* reconcile. **se** ~**ier** *v. pr.* become reconciled (**avec,** with). ~**iation** *n.f.* reconciliation.

reconduire† /rəkɔ̃dɥir/ *v.t.* see home; (*à la porte*) show out; (*renouveler*) renew.

réconfort /rekɔ̃fɔr/ *n.m.* comfort. ~**er** /-te/ *v.t.* comfort.

reconnaissable /rəkɔnɛsabl/ *a.* recognizable.

reconnaissan|t, ~**te** /rəkɔnɛsɑ̃, -t/ *a.* grateful (**de,** for). ~**ce** *n.f.* gratitude; (*fait de reconnaître*) recognition; (*mil.*) reconnaissance.

reconnaître† /rəkɔnɛtr/ *v.t.* recognize; (*admettre*) admit (**que,** that); (*mil.*) reconnoitre; (*enfant, tort*) acknowledge.

reconstituant /rəkɔ̃stitɥɑ̃/ *n.m.* tonic.

reconstituer /rəkɔ̃stitɥe/ *v.t.* reconstitute; (*crime*) reconstruct.

reconstr|uire† /rəkɔ̃strɥir/ *v.t.* rebuild. ~**uction** *n.f.* rebuilding.

reconversion /rəkɔ̃vɛrsjɔ̃/ *n.f.* (*de main-d'œuvre*) redeployment.

recopier /rəkɔpje/ *v.t.* copy out.

record /rəkɔr/ *n.m. & a. invar.* record.

recoupe|r /rəkupe/ *v.t.* confirm. **se** ~ *v. pr.* check, tally, match up. **par** ~**ment,** by making connections.

recourbé /rəkurbe/ *a.* curved; (*nez*) hooked.

recourir /rəkurir/ *v.i.* ~ **à,** resort to.

recours /rəkur/ *n.m.* resort. **avoir** ~ **à,** have recourse to, resort to.

recouvrer /rəkuvre/ *v.t.* recover.

recouvrir† /rəkuvrir/ *v.t.* cover.

récréation /rekreasjɔ̃/ *n.f.* recreation; (*scol.*) playtime.

récrier (se) /(sə)rekrije/ *v. pr.* cry out.

récrimination /rekriminasjɔ̃/ *n.f.* recrimination.

recroqueviller (se) /(sə)rəkrɔkvije/ *v. pr.* curl up.

recrudescence /rəkrydesɑ̃s/ *n.f.* new outbreak.

recrue /rəkry/ *n.f.* recruit.

recrut|er /rəkryte/ *v.t.* recruit. ~**ement** *n.m.* recruitment.

rectang|le /rektɑ̃gl/ *n.m.* rectangle. ~**ulaire** *a.* rectangular.

rectif|ier /rektifje/ *v.t.* correct, rectify. ~**ication** *n.f.* correction.

recto /rɛkto/ *n.m.* front of the page.

reçu /rəsy/ *voir* **recevoir.** —*n.m.* receipt. —*a.* accepted; (*candidat*) successful.

recueil /rəkœj/ *n.m.* collection.

recueill|ir† /rəkœjir/ *v.t.* collect; (*prendre chez soi*) take in. **se** ~**ir** *v. pr.* meditate. ~**ement** *n.m.* meditation. ~**i** *a.* meditative.

recul /rəkyl/ *n.m.* retreat; (*éloignement*) distance; (*déclin*) decline. (**mouvement de**) ~, backward movement. ~**ade** *n.f.* retreat.

reculé /rəkyle/ *a.* (*région*) remote.

reculer /rəkyle/ *v.t./i.* move back; (*véhicule*) reverse; (*armée*) retreat; (*diminuer*) decline; (*différer*) postpone. ~ **devant,** (*fig.*) shrink from.

reculons (à) /(a)rəkylɔ̃/ *adv.* backwards.

récupér|er /rekypere/ *v.t./i.* recover; (*vieux objets*) salvage. ~**ation** *n.f.* recovery; salvage.

récurer /rekyre/ *v.t.* scour. **poudre à** ~, scouring powder.

récuser /rekyze/ *v.t.* challenge. **se** ~ *v. pr.* state that one is not qualified to judge.

recycl|er /rəsikle/ *v.t.* (*personne*) retrain; (*chose*) recycle. **se** ~**er** *v. pr.* retrain. ~**age** *n.m.* retraining; recycling.

rédac|teur, ~**trice** /redaktœr, -tris/

n.m., f. writer, editor. **le ⁓teur en chef,** the editor (in chief).

rédaction /redaksjɔ̃/ *n.f.* writing; (*scol.*) composition; (*personnel*) editorial staff.

reddition /redisjɔ̃/ *n.f.* surrender.

redemander /rədmɑ̃de/ *v.t.* ask again for; ask for more of.

redevable /rədvabl/ *a.* être ⁓ à qn. de, (*argent*) owe sb; (*fig.*) be indebted to s.o. for.

redevance /rədvɑ̃s/ *n.f.*⁓(*de télévision*) licence fee.

rédiger /rediʒe/ *v.t.* write; (*contrat*) draw up.

redire† /rədir/ *v.t.* repeat. **avoir** *ou* **trouver à ⁓ à,** find fault with.

redondant, ⁓**e** /rədɔ̃dɑ̃, -t/ *a.* superfluous.

redonner /rədɔne/ *v.t.* give back; (*davantage*) give more.

redoubl|er /rəduble/ *v.t./i.* increase; (*classe: scol.*) repeat. ⁓**er de prudence/***etc.*, be more careful/*etc.* ⁓**ement** *n.m.* (*accroissement*) increase (**de,** in).

redout|er /rədute/ *v.t.* dread. ⁓**able** *a.* formidable.

redoux /rədu/ *n.m.* milder weather.

redress|er /rədrese/ *v.t.* straighten (out *ou* up); (*situation*) right, redress. **se ⁓er** *v. pr.* (*personne*) straighten (o.s.) up; (*se remettre debout*) stand up; (*pays, économie*) recover. ⁓**ement** /rədresmɑ̃/ *n.m.* (*relèvement*) recovery.

réduction /redyksjɔ̃/ *n.f.* reduction.

réduire† /reduir/ *v.t.* reduce (**à,** to). **se ⁓ à,** (*revenir à*) come down to.

réduit¹, ⁓**e** /redui, -t/ *a.* (*objet*) small-scale; (*limité*) limited.

réduit² /redui/ *n.m.* recess.

réédu|quer /reedyke/ *v.t.* (*personne*) rehabilitate; (*membre*) re-educate. ⁓**cation** *n.f.* rehabilitation; re-education.

réel, ⁓**le** /reɛl/ *a.* real. —*n.m.* reality. ⁓**lement** *adv.* really.

réexpédier /reɛkspedje/ *v.t.* forward; (*retourner*) send back.

refaire† /rəfɛr/ *v.t.* do again; (*erreur, voyage*) make again; (*réparer*) do up, redo.

réfection /refɛksjɔ̃/ *n.f.* repair.

réfectoire /refɛktwar/ *n.m.* refectory.

référence /referɑ̃s/ *n.f.* reference.

référendum /referɛ̃dɔm/ *n.m.* referendum.

référer /refere/ *v.i.* **en ⁓ à,** refer the matter to. **se ⁓ à,** refer to.

refermer /rəfɛrme/ *v.t.*, **se ⁓,** *v. pr.* close (again).

refiler /rəfile/ *v.t.* (*fam.*) palm off (**à,** on).

réfléch|ir /refleʃir/ *v.i.* think (**à,** about). —*v.t.* reflect. **se ⁓ir** *v. pr.* be reflected. ⁓**i** *a.* (*personne*) thoughtful; (*verbe*) reflexive.

refl|et /rəflɛ/ *n.m.* reflection; (*lumière*) light. ⁓**éter** /-ete/ *v.t.* reflect. **se ⁓éter** *v. pr.* be reflected.

réflexe /reflɛks/ *a. & n.m.* reflex.

réflexion /reflɛksjɔ̃/ *n.f.* reflection; (*pensée*) thought, reflection. **à la ⁓,** on second thoughts.

refluer /rəflye/ *v.i.* flow back; (*foule*) retreat.

reflux /rəfly/ *n.m.* (*de marée*) ebb.

refondre /rəfɔ̃dr/ *v.t.* recast.

réform|e /reform/ *n.f.* reform. ⁓**ateur,** ⁓**atrice** *n.m., f.* reformer. ⁓**er** *v.t.* reform; (*soldat*) invalid (out of the army).

refoul|er /rəfule/ *v.t.* (*larmes*) force back; (*désir*) repress. ⁓**é** *a.* repressed. ⁓**ement** *n.m.* repression.

réfractaire /refraktɛr/ *a.* être ⁓ à, resist.

refrain /rəfrɛ̃/ *n.m.* chorus. **le même ⁓,** the same old story.

réfréner /refrene/ *v.t.* curb, check.

réfrigér|er /refriʒere/ *v.t.* refrigerate. ⁓**ateur** *n.m.* refrigerator.

refroid|ir /rəfrwadir/ *v.t./i.* cool (down). **se ⁓ir** *v. pr.* (*personne, temps*) get cold; (*ardeur*) cool (off). ⁓**issement** *n.m.* cooling; (*rhume*) chill.

refuge /rəfyʒ/ *n.m.* refuge; (*chalet*) mountain hut.

réfugi|er (se) /(sə)refyʒje/ *v. pr.* take refuge. ⁓**ié,** ⁓**iée** *n.m., f.* refugee.

refus /rəfy/ *n.m.* refusal. **ce n'est pas de ⁓,** I wouldn't say no. ⁓**er** /-ze/ *v.t.* refuse (**de,** to); (*recaler*) fail. **se ⁓er à,** (*évidence etc.*) reject.

réfuter /refyte/ *v.t.* refute.

regagner /rəgɑɲe/ *v.t.* regain; (*revenir à*) get back to.

regain /rəgɛ̃/ *n.m.* ⁓ **de,** renewal of.

régal (*pl.* ⁓**s**) /regal/ *n.m.* treat. ⁓**er** *v.t.* treat (**de,** to). **se ⁓er** *v. pr.* treat o.s. (**de,** to).

regard /rəgar/ *n.m.* (*expression, coup d'œil*) look; (*fixe*) stare; (*vue, œil*) eye. **au ⁓ de,** in regard to. **en ⁓ de,** compared with.

regardant, ⁓**e** /rəgardɑ̃, -t/ *a.* careful (with money). **peu ⁓ (sur),** not fussy (about).

regarder /rəgarde/ *v.t.* look at; (*observer*) watch; (*considérer*) consider; (*concerner*) concern. **~ (fixement)**, stare at. —*v.i.* look. **~ à**, (*qualité etc.*) pay attention to. **~ vers**, (*maison*) face. **se ~** *v. pr.* (*personnes*) look at each other.

régates /regat/ *n.f. pl.* regatta.

régénérer /reʒenere/ *v.t.* regenerate.

régen|t, ~te /reʒã, -t/ *n.m., f.* regent. **~ce** *n.f.* regency.

régenter /reʒãte/ *v.t.* rule.

reggae /rege/ *n.m.* reggae.

régie /reʒi/ *n.f.* (*entreprise*) public corporation; (*radio, TV*) control room; (*cinéma, théâtre*) production.

regimber /rəʒɛ̃be/ *v.i.* balk.

régime /reʒim/ *n.m.* (*organisation*) system; (*pol.*) regime; (*méd.*) diet; (*de moteur*) speed; (*de bananes*) bunch. **se mettre au ~**, go on a diet.

régiment /reʒimã/ *n.m.* regiment.

région /reʒjɔ̃/ *n.f.* region. **~al** (*m. pl.* **~aux**) /-jɔnal, -o/ *a.* regional.

régir /reʒir/ *v.t.* govern.

régisseur /reʒisœr/ *n.m.* (*théâtre*) stage-manager; (*cinéma, TV*) assistant director.

registre /rəʒistr/ *n.m.* register.

réglage /reglaʒ/ *n.m.* adjustment.

règle /rɛgl/ *n.f.* rule; (*instrument*) ruler. **~s**, (*de femme*) period. **en ~**, in order. **~ à calculer**, slide-rule.

réglé /regle/ *a.* (*vie*) ordered; (*arrangé*) settled.

règlement /rɛgləmã/ *n.m.* regulation; (*règles*) regulations; (*solution, paiement*) settlement. **~aire** /-tɛr/ *a.* (*uniforme*) regulation.

réglement|er /rɛgləmãte/ *v.t.* regulate. **~ation** *n.f.* regulation.

régler /regle/ *v.t.* settle; (*machine*) adjust; (*programmer*) set; (*facture*) settle; (*personne*) settle up with; (*papier*) rule. **~ son compte à**, settle a score with.

réglisse /reglis/ *n.f.* liquorice.

règne /rɛɲ/ *n.m.* reign; (*végétal, animal, minéral*) kingdom.

régner /reɲe/ *v.i.* reign.

regorger /rəgɔrʒe/ *v.i.* **~ de**, be overflowing with.

regret /rəgrɛ/ *n.m.* regret. **à ~**, with regret.

regrett|er /rəgrete/ *v.t.* regret; (*personne*) miss. **~able** *a.* regrettable.

regrouper /rəgrupe/ *v.t.*, group together. **se ~** *v. pr.* gather (together).

régulariser /regylarize/ *v.t.* regularize.

régulation /regylasjɔ̃/ *n.f.* regulation.

régul|ier, ~ière /regylje, -jɛr/ *a.* regular; (*qualité, vitesse*) steady, even; (*ligne, paysage*) even; (*légal*) legal; (*honnête*) honest. **~arité** *n.f.* regularity; steadiness; evenness. **~ièrement** *adv.* regularly; (*d'ordinaire*) normally.

réhabilit|er /reabilite/ *n.f.* rehabilitate. **~ation** *n.f.* rehabilitation.

rehausser /rəose/ *v.t.* raise; (*faire valoir*) enhance.

rein /rɛ̃/ *n.m.* kidney. **~s**, (*dos*) back.

réincarnation /reɛ̃karnasjɔ̃/ *n.f.* reincarnation.

reine /rɛn/ *n.f.* queen. **~-claude** *n.f.* greengage.

réinsertion /reɛ̃sɛrsjɔ̃/ *n.f.* reintegration, rehabilitation.

réintégrer /reɛ̃tegre/ *v.t.* (*lieu*) return to; (*jurid.*) reinstate.

réitérer /reitere/ *v.t.* repeat.

rejaillir /rəʒajir/ *v.i.* **~ sur**, rebound on.

rejet /rəʒɛ/ *n.m.* rejection.

rejeter /rəʒte/ *v.t.* throw back; (*refuser*) reject; (*vomir*) bring up; (*déverser*) discharge. **~ une faute/etc. sur qn.**, shift the blame for a mistake/etc. on to s.o.

rejeton(s) /rəʒtɔ̃/ *n.m.* (*pl.*) (*fam.*) offspring.

rejoindre† /rəʒwɛ̃dr/ *v.t.* go back to, rejoin; (*rattraper*) catch up with; (*rencontrer*) join, meet. **se ~** *v. pr.* (*personnes*) meet; (*routes*) join, meet.

réjoui /reʒwi/ *a.* joyful.

réjou|ir /reʒwir/ *v.t.* delight. **se ~ir** *v. pr.* be delighted (**de qch.**, at sth.). **~issances** *n.f. pl.* festivities. **~issant, ~issante** *a.* cheering.

relâche /rəlɑʃ/ *n.m.* (*repos*) respite. **faire ~**, (*théâtre*) close.

relâché /rəlɑʃe/ *a.* lax.

relâch|er /rəlɑʃe/ *v.t.* slacken; (*personne*) release; (*discipline*) relax. **se ~er** *v. pr.* slacken. **~ement** *n.m.* slackening.

relais /rəlɛ/ *n.m.* relay. **~ (routier)**, roadside café.

relanc|e /rəlɑ̃s/ *n.f.* boost. **~er** *v.t.* boost, revive; (*renvoyer*) throw back.

relati|f, ~ve /rəlatif/ *a.* relative.

relation /rəlasjɔ̃/ *n.f.* relation(ship); (*ami*) acquaintance; (*récit*) account. **~s**, relation. **en ~ avec qn.**, in touch with s.o.

relativement /rəlativmã/ *adv.* relatively. **~ à**, in relation to.

relativité /rəlativite/ *n.f.* relativity.

relax|er (se) /(sə)rəlakse/ *v. pr.* relax. **~ation** *n.f.* relaxation. **~e** *a.* (*fam.*) laid-back.

relayer /rəleje/ *v.t.* relieve; (*émission*) relay. **se ~** *v. pr.* take over from one another.

reléguer /rəlege/ *v.t.* relegate.

relent /rəlɑ̃/ *n.m.* stink.

relève /rəlɛv/ *n.f.* relief. **prendre** *ou* **assurer la ~,** take over (**de,** from).

relevé /rəlve/ *n.m.* list; (*de compte*) statement; (*de compteur*) reading. —*a.* spicy.

relever /rəlve/ *v.t.* pick up; (*personne tombée*) help up; (*remonter*) raise; (*col*) turn up; (*manches*) roll up; (*sauce*) season; (*goût*) bring out; (*compteur*) read; (*défi*) accept; (*relayer*) relieve; (*remarquer, noter*) note; (*rebâtir*) rebuild. —*v.i.* **~ de,** (*dépendre de*) be the concern of; (*méd.*) recover from. **se ~** *v. pr.* (*personne*) get up (again); (*pays, économie*) recover.

relief /rəljɛf/ *n.m.* relief. **mettre en ~,** highlight.

relier /rəlje/ *v.t.* link (**à,** to); (*ensemble*) link together; (*livre*) bind.

religieu|x, ~se /rəliʒjø, -z/ *a.* religious. —*n m* monk —*n f* nun; (*culin.*) choux bun.

religion /rəliʒjɔ̃/ *n.f.* religion.

reliquat /rəlika/ *n.m.* residue.

relique /rəlik/ *n.f.* relic.

reliure /rəljyr/ *n.f.* binding.

reluire /rəlɥir/ *v.i.* shine. **faire ~,** shine.

reluisant, ~e /rəlɥizɑ̃, -t/ *a.* **peu** *ou* **pas ~,** not brilliant.

reman|ier (se) /(sə)rəmanje/ *v.t.* revise; (*ministère*) reshuffle. **~iement** *n m* revision; reshuffle.

remar|ier (se) /(sə)rəmarje/ *v. pr.* remarry.

remarquable /rəmarkabl/ *a.* remarkable.

remarque /rəmark/ *n.f.* remark; (*par écrit*) note.

remarquer /rəmarke/ *v.t.* notice; (*dire*) say. **faire ~,** point out (**à,** to). **se faire ~,** attract attention. **remarque(z),** mind you.

remblai /rɑ̃blɛ/ *n.m.* embankment.

rembourrer /rɑ̃bure/ *v.t.* pad.

rembours|er /rɑ̃burse/ *v.t.* repay; (*billet, frais*) refund. **~ement** *n.m.* repayment; refund.

remède /rəmɛd/ *n.m.* remedy; (*médicament*) medicine.

remédier /rəmedje/ *v.i.* **~ à,** remedy.

remémorer (se) /(sə)rəmemɔre/ *v. pr.* recall.

remerc|ier /rəmɛrsje/ *v.t.* thank (**de,** for); (*licencier*) dismiss. **~iements** *n.m. pl.* thanks.

remettre† /rəmɛtr/ *v.t.* put back; (*vêtement*) put back on; (*donner*) hand (over); (*devoir, démission*) hand in; (*restituer*) give back; (*différer*) put off; (*ajouter*) add; (*se rappeler*) remember; (*peine*) remit. **se ~** *v. pr.* (*guérir*) recover. **se ~ à,** go back to. **se ~ à faire,** start doing again. **s'en ~ à,** leave it to. **~ en cause** *ou* **en question,** call into question.

réminiscence /reminisɑ̃s/ *n.f.* reminiscence.

remise¹ /rəmiz/ *n.f.* (*abri*) shed.

remise² /rəmiz/ *n.f.* (*rabais*) discount; (*livraison*) delivery; (*ajournement*) postponement. **~ en cause** *ou* **en question,** calling into question.

remiser /rəmize/ *v.t.* put away.

rémission /remisjɔ̃/ *n.f.* remission.

remontant /rəmɔ̃tɑ̃/ *n.m.* tonic.

remontée /rəmɔ̃te/ *n.f.* ascent; (*d'eau, de prix*) rise. **~ mécanique,** ski-lift.

remont|er /rəmɔ̃te/ *v.i.* go *ou* come (back) up; (*prix, niveau*) rise (again); (*revenir*) go back. —*v.t.* (*rue etc.*) go *ou* come (back) up; (*relever*) raise; (*montre*) wind up; (*objet démonté*) put together again; (*personne*) buck up. **~e-pente** *n.m.* ski-lift.

remontoir /rəmɔ̃twar/ *n.m.* winder.

remontrer /rəmɔ̃tre/ *v.t.* show again. **en ~ à qn.,** go one up on s.o.

remords /rəmɔr/ *n.m.* remorse. **avoir un** *ou* **des ~,** feel remorse.

remorqu|e /rəmɔrk/ *n f* (*véhicule*) trailer. **en ~e,** on tow. **~er** *v.t.* tow.

remorqueur /rəmɔrkœr/ *n.m.* tug.

remous /rəmu/ *n.m.* eddy; (*de bateau*) backwash; (*fig.*) turmoil.

rempart /rɑ̃par/ *n.m.* rampart.

remplaçant, ~e /rɑ̃plasɑ̃, -t/ *n.m., f.* replacement; (*joueur*) reserve.

remplac|er /rɑ̃plase/ *v.t.* replace. **~ement** *n.m.* replacement.

rempli /rɑ̃pli/ *a.* full (**de,** of).

rempl|ir /rɑ̃plir/ *v.t.* fill (up); (*formulaire*) fill (in *ou* out); (*tâche, condition*) fulfil. **se ~ir** *v. pr.* fill (up). **~issage** *n.m.* filling; (*de texte*) padding.

remporter /rɑ̃pɔrte/ *v.t.* take back; (*victoire*) win.

remuant, ~e /rəmɥɑ̃, -t/ *a.* restless.

remue-ménage /rəmymenaʒ/ *n.m. invar.* commotion, bustle.

remuer /rəmɥe/ v.t./i. move; (thé, café)
stir; (gigoter) fidget. **se ~** v. pr.
move.

rémunér|er /remynere/ v.t. pay. **~ation**
n.f. payment.

renâcler /rənɑkle/ v.i. snort. **~ à**, balk
at, jib at.

ren|aître /rənɛtr/ v.i. be reborn;
(sentiment) be revived. **~aissance** n.f.
rebirth.

renard /rənar/ n.m. fox.

renchérir /rɑ̃ʃerir/ v.i. become dearer.
~ sur, go one better than.

rencontr|e /rɑ̃kɔ̃tr/ n.f. meeting; (de
routes) junction; (mil.) encounter;
(match) match; (Amer.) game. **~er** v.t.
meet; (heurter) strike; (trouver) find. **se
~er** v. pr. meet.

rendement /rɑ̃dmɑ̃/ n.m. yield; (travail)
output.

rendez-vous /rɑ̃devu/ n.m. appointment; (d'amoureux) date; (lieu)
meeting-place. **prendre ~ (avec)**,
make an appointment (with).

rendormir (se) /(sə)rɑ̃dɔrmir/ v. pr. go
back to sleep.

rendre /rɑ̃dr/ v.t. give back, return;
(donner en retour) return; (monnaie)
give; (hommage) pay; (justice) dispense; (jugement) pronounce. **~
heureux/possible**/etc., make happy/
possible/etc. **—v.i.** (terres) yield;
(vomir) vomit. **se ~** v. pr. (capituler)
surrender; (aller) go (à, to); (ridicule,
utile, etc.) make o.s. **~ compte de,**
report on. **~ des comptes à,** be
accountable to. **~ justice à qn.,** do s.o.
justice. **~ service (à),** help. **~ visite à,**
visit. **se ~ compte de,** realize.

rendu /rɑ̃dy/ a. **être ~,** (arrivé) have
arrived.

rêne /rɛn/ n.f. rein.

renégat, ~e /rənega, -t/ n.m., f.
renegade.

renfermé /rɑ̃fɛrme/ n.m. stale smell.
sentir le ~, smell stale. **—a.**
withdrawn.

renfermer /rɑ̃fɛrme/ v.t. contain. **se ~
(en soi-même),** withdraw (into o.s.).

renfl|é /rɑ̃fle/ a. bulging. **~ement** n.m.
bulge.

renflouer /rɑ̃flue/ v.t. refloat.

renfoncement /rɑ̃fɔ̃smɑ̃/ n.m. recess.

renforcer /rɑ̃fɔrse/ v.t. reinforce.

renfort /rɑ̃fɔr/ n.m. reinforcement. **de
~,** (armée, personnel) back-up. **à
grand ~ de,** with a great deal of.

renfrogn|er (se) /(sə)rɑ̃frɔɲe/ v. pr.
scowl. **~é** a. surly, sullen.

rengaine /rɑ̃gɛn/ n.f. (péj.) **la même ~,**
the same old story.

renier /rənje/ v.t. (personne, pays)
disown, deny; (foi) renounce.

renifler /rənifle/ v.t./i. sniff.

renne /rɛn/ n.m. reindeer.

renom /rənɔ̃/ n.m. renown; (réputation)
reputation. **~mé** /-ɔme/ a. famous.
~mée /-ɔme/ n.f. fame; reputation.

renonc|er /rənɔ̃se/ v.i. **~er à,** (habitude,
ami, etc.) give up, renounce. **~er à
faire,** give up (all thought of) doing.
~ement n.m., **~iation** n.f. renunciation.

renouer /rənwe/ v.t. tie up (again);
(reprendre) renew. **—v.i. ~ avec,** start
up again with.

renouveau (pl. **~x**) /rənuvo/ n.m.
revival.

renouvel|er /rənuvle/ v.t. renew;
(réitérer) repeat. **se ~er** v. pr.
be renewed; be repeated. **~lement**
/-vɛlmɑ̃/ n.m. renewal.

rénov|er /renove/ v.t. (édifice) renovate;
(institution) reform. **~ation** n.f.
renovation; reform.

renseignement /rɑ̃sɛɲmɑ̃/ n.m. **~(s),**
information. **(bureau des) ~s,** information desk.

renseigner /rɑ̃seɲe/ v.t. inform, give
information to. **se ~** v. pr. enquire,
make enquiries, find out.

rentab|le /rɑ̃tabl/ a. profitable. **~ilité**
n.f. profitability.

rent|e /rɑ̃t/ n.f. (private) income;
(pension) pension, annuity. **~ier,
~ière** n.m., f. person of private
means.

rentrée /rɑ̃tre/ n.f. return; **la ~
parlementaire** the reopening of Parliament; (scol.) start of the new year.

rentrer /rɑ̃tre/ (aux. être) v.i. go ou
come back home, return home; (entrer)
go ou come in; (entrer à nouveau) go ou
come back in; (revenu) come in;
(élèves) go back. **~ dans,** (heurter)
smash into. **—v.t.** (aux. avoir) bring in;
(griffes) draw in; (vêtement) tuck in **~
dans l'ordre,** be back to normal. **~
dans ses frais,** break even.

renverse (à la) /(ala)rɑ̃vɛrs/ adv.
backwards.

renvers|er /rɑ̃vɛrse/ v.t. knock over ou
down; (piéton) knock down; (liquide)
upset, spill; (mettre à l'envers) turn
upside down; (gouvernement) overturn;
(inverser) reverse. **se ~er** v. pr.
(véhicule) overturn; (verre, vase) fall
over. **~ement** n.m. (pol.) overthrow.

renv|oi /rãvwa/ *n.m.* return; dismissal; expulsion; postponement; reference; (*rot*) belch. **~oyer†** *v.t.* send back, return; (*employé*) dismiss; (*élève*) expel; (*ajourner*) postpone; (*référer*) refer; (*réfléchir*) reflect.

réorganiser /reɔrganize/ *v.t.* reorganize.

réouverture /reuvɛrtyr/ *n.f.* reopening.

repaire /rəpɛr/ *n.m.* den.

répandre /repãdr/ *v.t.* (*liquide*) spill; (*étendre, diffuser*) spread; (*lumière, sang*) shed; (*odeur*) give off. **se ~** *v. pr.* spread; (*liquide*) spill. **se ~ en,** (*injures etc.*) pour forth, launch forth into.

répandu /repãdy/ *a.* (*courant*) widespread.

répar|er /repare/ *v.t.* repair, mend; (*faute*) make amends for; (*remédier à*) put right. **~ateur** *n.m.* repairer. **~ation** *n.f.* repair; (*compensation*) compensation.

repartie /rəparti/ *n.f.* retort. **avoir (le sens) de la ~,** be good at repartee.

repartir† /rəpartir/ *v.i.* start (up) again; (*voyageur*) set off again; (*s'en retourner*) go back.

répart|ir /repartir/ *v.t.* distribute; (*partager*) share out; (*étaler*) spread. **~ition** *n.f.* distribution.

repas /rəpɑ/ *n m* meal

repass|er /rəpase/ *v.i.* come *ou* go back. —*v.t.* (*linge*) iron; (*leçon*) go over; (*examen*) retake, (*film*) show again. **~age** *n.m.* ironing.

repêcher /rəpeʃe/ *v.t.* fish out; (*candidat*) allow to pass.

repentir /rəpãtir/ *n.m.* repentance. **se ~** *v. pr.* (*relig.*) repent (**de,** of). **se ~ de,** (*regretter*) regret.

répercu|ter /reperkyte/ *v.t.* (*bruit*) echo. **se ~ter** *v. pr.* echo. **se ~ter sur,** have repercussions on. **~ssion** *n.f.* repercussion.

repère /rəpɛr/ *n.m.* mark; (*jalon*) marker; (*fig.*) landmark.

repérer /rəpere/ *v.t.* locate, spot. **se ~** *v. pr.* find one's bearings.

répert|oire /repertwar/ *n.m.* index; (*artistique*) repertoire. **~orier** *v.t.* index.

répéter /repete/ *v.t.* repeat. —*v.t./i.* (*théâtre*) rehearse. **se ~** *v. pr.* be repeated; (*personne*) repeat o.s.

répétition /repetisjɔ̃/ *n.f.* repetition; (*théâtre*) rehearsal.

repiquer /rəpike/ *v.t.* (*plante*) plant out.

répit /repi/ *n.m.* rest, respite.

replacer /rəplase/ *v.t.* replace.

repl|i /rəpli/ *n.m.* fold; (*retrait*)

withdrawal. **~ier** *v.t.* fold (up); (*ailes, jambes*) tuck in. **se ~ier** *v. pr.* withdraw (**sur soi-même,** into o.s.).

répliqu|e /replik/ *n.f.* reply; (*riposte*) retort; (*discussion*) objection; (*théâtre*) line(s); (*copie*) replica. **~er** *v.t./i.* reply; (*riposter*) retort; (*objecter*) answer back.

répondant, ~e /repɔ̃dã, -t/ *n.m., f.* guarantor. **avoir du ~,** have money behind one.

répondeur /repɔ̃dœr/ *n.m.* answering machine.

répondre /repɔ̃dr/ *v.t.* (*remarque etc.*) reply with. **~ que,** answer *ou* reply that. —*v.i.* answer, reply; (*être insolent*) answer back; (*réagir*) respond (**à,** to). **~ à,** answer. **~ de,** answer for.

réponse /repɔ̃s/ *n.f.* answer, reply; (*fig.*) response.

report /rəpɔr/ *n.m.* (*transcription*) transfer; (*renvoi*) postponement.

reportage /rəpɔrtaʒ/ *n.m.* report; (*en direct*) commentary, (*par écrit*) article.

reporter[1] /rəpɔrte/ *v.t.* take back; (*ajourner*) put off; (*transcrire*) transfer. **se ~ à,** refer to.

reporter[2] /rəpɔrtɛr/ *n.m.* reporter.

repos /rəpo/ *n.m.* rest; (*paix*) peace; (*tranquillité*) peace and quiet; (*moral*) peace of mind.

repos|er /rəpoze/ *v.t.* put down again; (*délasser*) rest. —*v.i.* rest (**sur,** on). **se ~er** *v. pr.* rest. **se ~er sur,** rely on. **~ant, ~ante** *a.* restful. **laisser ~er,** (*pâte*) leave to stand.

repoussant, ~e /rəpusã, -t/ *a.* repulsive.

repousser /rəpuse/ *v.t.* push back; (*écarter*) push away; (*dégoûter*) repel; (*décliner*) reject; (*ajourner*) put back. —*v.i.* grow again.

répréhensible /repreãsibl/ *a.* blameworthy.

reprendre† /rəprãdr/ *v.t.* take back; (*retrouver*) regain; (*souffle*) get back; (*évadé*) recapture; (*recommencer*) resume; (*redire*) repeat; (*modifier*) alter; (*blâmer*) reprimand. **~ du pain**/*etc.*, take some more bread/*etc.* —*v.i.* (*recommencer*) resume; (*affaires*) pick up. **se ~** *v. pr.* (*se ressaisir*) pull o.s. together; (*se corriger*) correct o.s. **on ne m'y reprendra pas,** I won't be caught out again.

représailles /rəprezaj/ *n.f. pl.* reprisals.

représentati|f, ~ve /rəprezãtatif, -v/ *a.* representative.

représent|er /rəprezãte/ *v.t.* represent;

(*théâtre*) perform. **se** 〜**er** *v. pr.* (*s'imaginer*) imagine. 〜**ant**, 〜**ante** *n.m.*, *f.* representative. 〜**ation** *n.f.* representation; (*théâtre*) performance.

réprimand|e /reprimɑ̃d/ *n.f.* reprimand. 〜**er** *v.t.* reprimand.

répr|imer /reprime/ *v.t.* (*peuple*) repress (*sentiment*) suppress. 〜**ession** *n.f.* repression.

repris /rəpri/ *n.m.* 〜 **de justice**, ex-convict.

reprise /rəpriz/ *n.f.* resumption; (*théâtre*) revival; (*télévision*) repeat; (*de tissu*) darn, mend; (*essor*) recovery; (*comm.*) part-exchange, trade-in. **à plusieurs** 〜**s**, on several occasions.

repriser /rəprize/ *v.t.* darn, mend.

réprobation /reprɔbasjɔ̃/ *n.f.* condemnation.

reproch|e /rəprɔʃ/ *n.m.* reproach, blame. 〜**er** *v.t.* 〜**er qch. à qn.**, reproach *ou* blame s.o. for sth.

reprod|uire† /rəprɔdɥir/ *v.t.* reproduce. **se** 〜**uire** *v. pr.* reproduce; (*arriver*) recur. 〜**ucteur**, 〜**uctrice** *a.* reproductive. 〜**uction** *n.f.* reproduction.

réprouver /repruve/ *v.t.* condemn.

reptile /rɛptil/ *n.m.* reptile.

repu /rəpy/ *a.* satiated.

républi|que /repyblik/ *n.f.* republic. 〜**que populaire**, people's republic. 〜**cain**, 〜**caine** *a.* & *n.m.*, *f.* republican.

répudier /repydje/ *v.t.* repudiate.

répugnance /repyɲɑ̃s/ *n.f.* repugnance; (*hésitation*) reluctance.

répugn|er /repyɲe/ *v.i.* 〜**er à**, be repugnant to. 〜**er à faire**, be reluctant to do. 〜**ant**, 〜**ante** *a.* repulsive.

répulsion /repylsjɔ̃/ *n.f.* repulsion.

réputation /repytasjɔ̃/ *n.f.* reputation.

réputé /repyte/ *a.* renowned (**pour**, for). 〜 **pour être**, reputed to be.

requérir /rəkerir/ *v.t.* require, demand.

requête /rəkɛt/ *n.f.* request; (*jurid.*) petition.

requiem /rekɥijɛm/ *n.m. invar.* requiem.

requin /rəkɛ̃/ *n.m.* shark.

requis, 〜**e** /rəki, -z/ *a.* required.

réquisition /rekizisjɔ̃/ *n.f.* requisition. 〜**ner** /-jɔne/ *v.t.* requisition.

rescapé, 〜**e** /rɛskape/ *n.m.*, *f.* survivor. —*a.* surviving.

rescousse /rɛskus/ *n.f.* **à la** 〜, to the rescue.

réseau (*pl.* 〜**x**) /rezo/ *n.m.* network.

réservation /rezɛrvasjɔ̃/ *n.f.* reservation. **bureau de** 〜, booking office.

réserve /rezɛrv/ *n.f.* reserve; (*restriction*) reservation, reserve; (*indienne*) reser-

vation; (*entrepôt*) store-room. **en** 〜, in reserve. **les** 〜**s**, (*mil.*) the reserves.

réserv|er /rezɛrve/ *v.t.* reserve; (*place*) book, reserve. **se** 〜**er le droit de**, reserve the right to. 〜**é** *a.* (*personne*, *place*) reserved.

réserviste /rezɛrvist/ *n.m.* reservist.

réservoir /rezɛrvwar/ *n.m.* tank; (*lac*) reservoir.

résidence /rezidɑ̃s/ *n.f.* residence.

résident, 〜**e** /rezidɑ̃, -t/ *n.m.*, *f.* resident foreigner. 〜**iel**, 〜**ielle** /-sjɛl/ *a.* residential.

résider /rezide/ *v.i.* reside.

résidu /rezidy/ *n.m.* residue.

résign|er (se) /(sə)reziɲe/ *v. pr.* **se** 〜**er à faire**, resign o.s. to doing. 〜**ation** *n.f.* resignation.

résilier /rezilje/ *v.t.* terminate.

résille /rezij/ *n.f.* (hair)net.

résine /rezin/ *n.f.* resin.

résistance /rezistɑ̃s/ *n.f.* resistance; (*fil électrique*) element.

résistant, 〜**e** /rezistɑ̃, -t/ *a.* tough.

résister /reziste/ *v.i.* resist. 〜 **à**, resist; (*examen*, *chaleur*) stand up to.

résolu /rezɔly/ *voir* **résoudre**. —*a.* resolute. 〜 **à**, resolved to. 〜**ment** *adv.* resolutely.

résolution /rezɔlysjɔ̃/ *n.f.* (*fermeté*) resolution; (*d'un problème*) solving.

résonance /rezɔnɑ̃s/ *n.f.* resonance.

résonner /rezɔne/ *v.i.* resound.

résor|ber /rezɔrbe/ *v.t.* reduce. **se** 〜**ber** *v. pr.* be reduced. 〜**ption** *n.f.* reduction.

résoudre† /rezudr/ *v.t.* solve; (*décider*) decide on. **se** 〜 **à**, resolve to.

respect /rɛspɛ/ *n.m.* respect.

respectab|le /rɛspɛktabl/ *a.* respectable. 〜**ilité** *n.f.* respectability.

respecter /rɛspɛkte/ *v.t.* respect. **faire** 〜, (*loi*, *décision*) enforce.

respecti|f, 〜**ve** /rɛspɛktif, -v/ *a.* respective. 〜**vement** *adv.* respectively.

respectueu|x, 〜**se** /rɛspɛktɥø, -z/ *a.* respectful.

respir|er /rɛspire/ *v.i.* breathe; (*se reposer*) get one's breath. —*v.t.* breathe; (*exprimer*) radiate. 〜**ation** *n.f.* breathing; (*haleine*) breath. 〜**atoire** *a.* breathing.

resplend|ir /rɛsplɑ̃dir/ *v.i.* shine (**de**, with). 〜**issant**, 〜**issante** *a.* radiant.

responsabilité /rɛspɔ̃sabilite/ *n.f.* responsibility; (*légale*) liability.

responsable /rɛspɔ̃sabl/ *a.* responsible (**de**, for). 〜 **de**, (*chargé de*) in charge of. —*n.m./f.* person in charge; (*coupable*) person responsible.

resquiller /rɛskije/ v.i. (*fam.*) get in
without paying; (*dans la queue*) jump
the queue.

ressaisir (se) /(sə)rəsezir/ v. pr. pull o.s.
together.

ressasser /rəsase/ v.t. keep going over.

ressembl|er /rəsɑ̃ble/ v.i. ~**er à**,
resemble, look like. **se** ~**er** v. pr. look
alike. ~**ance** n.f. resemblance. ~**ant**,
~**ante** a. (*portrait*) true to life; (*pareil*)
alike.

ressemeler /rəsəmle/ v.t. sole.

ressentiment /rəsɑ̃timɑ̃/ n.m. resentment.

ressentir /rəsɑ̃tir/ v.t. feel. **se** ~ **de**, feel
the effects of.

resserre /rəsɛr/ n.f. shed.

resserrer /rəsere/ v.t. tighten;
(*contracter*) contract. **se** ~ v. pr.
tighten; contract; (*route etc.*) narrow.

resservir /rəsɛrvir/ v.i. come in useful
(again).

ressort /rəsɔr/ n.m. (*objet*) spring; (*fig.*)
energy. **du** ~ **de**, within the jurisdiction
ou scope of. **en dernier** ~, in the last
resort.

ressortir† /rəsɔrtir/ v.i. go *ou* come back
out; (*se voir*) stand out. **faire** ~, bring
out. ~ **de**, (*résulter*) result *ou* emerge
from.

ressortissant, ~**e** /rəsɔrtisɑ̃, -t/ n.m., f.
national.

ressource /rəsurs/ n.f. resource. ~**s**,
resources.

ressusciter /resysite/ v.i. come back to
life.

restant, ~**e** /rɛstɑ̃, -t/ a. remaining.
—n.m. remainder.

restaur|ant /rɛstɔrɑ̃/ n.m. restaurant.
~**ateur**, ~**atrice** n.m., f. restaurant
owner.

restaur|er /rɛstɔre/ v.t. restore. **se** ~**er** v.
pr. eat. ~**ation** n.f. restoration;
(*hôtellerie*) catering.

reste /rɛst/ n.m. rest; (*d'une soustraction*) remainder. ~**s**, remains (**de**, of);
(*nourriture*) leftovers. **un** ~ **de
pain**/*etc.*, some left-over bread/*etc.* **au**
~, **du** ~, moreover, besides.

rest|er /rɛste/ v.i. (*aux. être*) stay,
remain; (*subsister*) be left, remain. **il**
~**e du pain**/*etc.*, there is some
bread/*etc.* left (over). **il me** ~**e du pain,**
I have some bread left (over). **il me** ~**e**
à, it remains for me to. **en** ~**er à,** go no
further than. **en** ~**er là,** stop there.

restit|uer /rɛstitɥe/ v.t. (*rendre*) return,
restore; (*son*) reproduce. ~**ution** n.f.
return.

restreindre† /rɛstrɛ̃dr/ v.t. restrict. **se** ~
v. pr. (*dans les dépenses*) cut down.

restricti|f, ~**ve** /rɛstriktif, -v/ a.
restrictive.

restriction /rɛstriksjɔ̃/ n.f. restriction.

résultat /rezylta/ n.m. result.

résulter /rezylte/ v.i. ~ **de,** result from.

résum|er /rezyme/ v.t., **se** ~**er** v. pr.
summarize. ~**é** n.m. summary. **en** ~**é,**
in short.

résurrection /rezyrɛksjɔ̃/ n.f. resurrec-
tion; (*renouveau*) revival.

rétabl|ir /retablir/ v.t. restore;
(*personne*) restore to health. **se** ~**ir** v.
pr. be restored; (*guérir*) recover.
~**issement** n.m. restoring; (*méd.*)
recovery.

retaper /rətape/ v.t. (*maison etc.*) do up.
se ~ v. pr. (*guérir*) get back on one's
feet.

retard /rətar/ n.m. lateness; (*sur un
programme*) delay; (*infériorité*) back-
wardness. **avoir du** ~, be late;
(*montre*) be slow. **en** ~, late; (*retardé*)
backward. **en** ~ **sur,** behind. **rattraper**
ou **combler son** ~, catch up.

retardataire /rətardatɛr/ n.m./f. latecomer. —a. (*arrivant*) late.

retardé /rətarde/ a. backward.

retardement (à) /(a)rətardəmɑ̃/ a.
(*bombe etc.*) delayed-action.

retarder /rətarde/ v.t. delay; (*sur un
programme*) set back; (*montre*) put
back. —v.i. (*montre*) be slow; (*fam.*)
be out of touch.

retenir† /rətnir/ v.t. hold back; (*souffle,
attention, prisonnier*) hold; (*eau,
chaleur*) retain, hold; (*larmes*) hold
back; (*garder*) keep; (*retarder*) detain;
(*réserver*) book; (*se rappeler*) remember; (*déduire*) deduct; (*accepter*)
accept. **se** ~ v. pr. (*se contenir*) restrain
o.s. **se** ~ **à,** hold on to. **se** ~ **de,** stop o.s.
from.

rétention /retɑ̃sjɔ̃/ n.f. retention.

retent|ir /rətɑ̃tir/ v.i. ring out (**de,** with).
~**issant,** ~**issante** a. resounding.
~**issement** n.m. (*effet, répercussion*)
effect.

retenue /rətny/ n.f. restraint; (*somme*)
deduction; (*scol.*) detention.

réticen|t, ~**te** /retisɑ̃, -t/ a. (*hésitant*)
reluctant; (*réservé*) reticent. ~**ce** n.f.
reluctance; reticence.

rétif, ~**ve** /retif, -v/ a. restive,
recalcitrant.

rétine /retin/ n.f. retina.

retiré /rətire/ a. (*vie*) secluded; (*lieu*)
remote.

retirer /rətire/ v.t. (sortir) take out; (ôter) take off; (argent, candidature) withdraw; (avantage) derive. ∼ à qn., take away from s.o. se ∼ v. pr. withdraw, retire.

retombées /rətɔ̃be/ n.f. pl. fall-out.

retomber /rətɔ̃be/ v.i. fall; (à nouveau) fall again. ∼ dans, (erreur etc.) fall back into.

rétorquer /retɔrke/ v.t. retort.

rétorsion /retɔrsjɔ̃/ n.f. mesures de ∼, retaliation.

retouch|e /rətuʃ/ n.f. touch-up; alteration. ∼er v.t. touch up; (vêtement) alter.

retour /rətur/ n.m. return. être de ∼, be back (de, from). ∼ en arrière, flashback. par ∼ du courrier, by return of post. en ∼, in return.

retourner /rəturne/ v.t. (aux. avoir) turn over; (vêtement) turn inside out; (lettre, compliment) return; (émouvoir: fam.) upset. —v.i. (aux. être) go back, return. se ∼ v. pr. turn round; (dans son lit) twist and turn. s'en ∼, go back. se ∼ contre, turn against.

retracer /rətrase/ v.t. retrace.

rétracter /retrakte/ v.t., se ∼ v. pr. retract.

retrait /rətrɛ/ n.m. withdrawal; (des eaux) ebb, receding. être (situé) en ∼, be set back.

retraite /rətrɛt/ n.f. retirement; (pension) (retirement) pension; (fuite, refuge) retreat. mettre à la ∼, pension off. prendre sa ∼, retire.

retraité, ∼e /rətrete/ a. retired. —n.m., f. (old-age) pensioner, senior citizen.

retrancher /rətrɑ̃ʃe/ v.t. remove; (soustraire) deduct. se ∼ v. pr. (mil.) entrench o.s. se ∼ derrière/dans, take refuge behind/in.

retransm|ettre /rətrɑ̃smɛtr/ v.t. broadcast. ∼ission n.f. broadcast.

rétrécir /retresir/ v.t. narrow; (vêtement) take in. —v.i. (tissu) shrink. se ∼, (rue) narrow.

rétrib|uer /retribɥe/ v.t. pay. ∼ution n.f. payment.

rétroacti|f, ∼ve /retrɔaktif, -v/ a. retrospective. augmentation à effet ∼f, backdated pay rise.

rétrograd|e /retrɔgrad/ a. retrograde. ∼er v.i. (reculer) fall back, recede; v.t. demote.

rétrospectivement /retrɔspɛktivmɑ̃/ adv. in retrospect.

retrousser /rətruse/ v.t. pull up.

retrouvailles /rətruvɑj/ n.f. pl. reunion.

retrouver /rətruve/ v.t. find (again); (rejoindre) meet (again); (forces, calme) regain; (se rappeler) remember. se ∼ v. pr. find o.s. (back); (se réunir) meet (again). s'y ∼, (s'orienter) comprendre) find one's way; (rentrer dans ses frais) break even.

rétroviseur /retrɔvizœr/ n.m. (auto.) (rear-view) mirror.

réunion /reynjɔ̃/ n.f. meeting; (d'objets) collection.

réunir /reynir/ v.t. gather, collect; (rapprocher) bring together; (convoquer) call together; (raccorder) join; (qualités) combine. se ∼ v. pr. meet.

réussi /reysi/ a. successful.

réussir /reysir/ v.i. succeed, be successful (à faire, in doing). ∼ à qn., work well for s.o.; (climat etc.) agree with s.o. —v.t. make a success of.

réussite /reysit/ n.f. success; (jeu) patience.

revaloir /rəvalwar/ v.t. je vous revaudrai cela, (en mal) I'll pay you back for this; (en bien) I'll repay you some day.

revaloriser /rəvalɔrize/ v.t. (monnaie) revalue; (salaires) raise.

revanche /rəvɑ̃ʃ/ n.f. revenge; (sport) return ou revenge match. en ∼, on the other hand.

rêvasser /rɛvase/ v.i. day-dream.

rêve /rɛv/ n.m. dream. faire un ∼, have a dream.

revêche /rəvɛʃ/ a. ill-tempered.

réveil /revɛj/ n.m. waking up, (fig.) awakening; (pendule) alarm-clock.

réveill|er /reveje/ v.t., se ∼er v. pr. wake (up); (fig.) awaken. ∼é a. awake. ∼e-matin n.m. invar. alarm-clock.

réveillon /revɛjɔ̃/ n.m. (Noël) Christmas Eve; (nouvel an) New Year's Eve. ∼ner /-jɔne/ v.i. celebrate the réveillon.

révél|er /revele/ v.t. reveal. se ∼er v. pr. be revealed. se ∼er facile/etc., prove easy/etc. ∼ateur a. revealing. —n.m. (photo) developer. ∼ation n.f. revelation.

revenant /rəvnɑ̃/ n.m. ghost.

revendi|quer /rəvɑ̃dike/ v.t. claim. ∼catif, ∼cative a. (mouvement etc.) in support of one's claims. ∼cation n.f. claim; (action) claiming.

revend|re /rəvɑ̃dr/ v.t. sell (again). ∼eur, ∼euse n.m., f. dealer.

revenir† /rəvnir/ v.i. (aux. être) come back, return (à, to). ∼ à, (activité) go back to; (se résumer à) come down to;

(*échoir à*) fall to; (*coûter*) cost. ~ **de**, (*maladie, surprise*) get over. ~ **sur ses pas**, retrace one's steps. **faire** ~, (*culin.*) brown. **ça me revient**, it comes back to me.

revente /rəvɑ̃t/ *n.f.* resale.

revenu /rəvny/ *n.m.* income; (*d'un état*) revenue.

rêver /reve/ *v.t./i.* dream (**à** *ou* **de**, of).

réverbération /reverberɑsjɔ̃/ *n.f.* reflection, reverberation.

réverbère /reverbɛr/ *n.m.* street lamp.

révérenc|e /reverɑ̃s/ *n.f.* reverence; (*salut d'homme*) bow; (*salut de femme*) curtsy. ~**ieux**, ~**ieuse** *a.* reverent.

révérend, ~**e** /reverɑ̃, -d/ *a. & n.m.* reverend.

rêverie /revri/ *n.f.* day-dream; (*activité*) day-dreaming.

revers /rəver/ *n.m.* reverse; (*de main*) back; (*d'étoffe*) wrong side; (*de veste*) lapel; (*tennis*) backhand; (*fig.*) set-back.

réversible /reversibl/ *a.* reversible.

revêt|ir /rəvetir/ *v.t.* cover; (*habit*) put on; (*prendre, avoir*) assume. ~**ement** /-vɛtmɑ̃/ *n.m.* covering; (*de route*) surface.

rêveu|r, ~**se** /revœr, -øz/ *a.* dreamy. *n.m., f.* dreamer.

revigorer /rəvigore/ *v.t.* revive.

revirement /rəvirmɑ̃/ *n.m.* sudden change.

révis|er /revize/ *v.t.* revise; (*véhicule*) overhaul. ~**ion** *n.f.* revision; overhaul.

revivre† /rəvivr/ *v.i.* live again. —*v.t.* relive. **faire** ~, revive.

révocation /revokɑsjɔ̃/ *n.f.* repeal; (*d'un fonctionnaire*) dismissal.

revoir† /rəvwar/ *v.t.* see (again); (*réviser*) revise. **au** ~, goodbye.

révolte /revolt/ *n.f.* revolt.

révolt|er /revolte/ *v.t., se* ~**er** *v. pr.* revolt. ~**ant**, ~**ante** *a.* revolting. ~**é**, ~**ée** *n.m., f.* rebel.

révolu /revoly/ *a.* past.

révolution /revolysjɔ̃/ *n.f.* revolution. ~**naire** /-jɔnɛr/ *a. & n.m./f.* revolutionary. ~**ner** /- jɔne/ *v.t.* revolutionize.

revolver /revolver/ *n.m.* revolver, gun.

révoquer /revoke/ *v.t.* repeal; (*fonctionnaire*) dismiss.

revue /rəvy/ *n.f.* (*examen, défilé*) review; (*magazine*) magazine; (*spectacle*) variety show.

rez-de-chaussée /redʃose/ *n.m. invar.* ground floor; (*Amer.*) first floor.

RF *abrév.* (*République Française*) French Republic.

rhabiller (se) /(sə)rabije/ *v. pr.* get dressed (again), dress (again).

rhapsodie /rapsodi/ *n.f.* rhapsody.

rhétorique /retorik/ *n.f.* rhetoric. —*a.* rhetorical.

rhinocéros /rinoseros/ *n.m.* rhinoceros.

rhubarbe /rybarb/ *n.f.* rhubarb.

rhum /rɔm/ *n.m.* rum.

rhumatis|me /rymatism/ *n.m.* rheumatism. ~**ant**, ~**ante** /-zɑ̃, -t/ *a.* rheumatic.

rhume /rym/ *n.m.* cold. ~ **des foins**, hay fever.

ri /ri/ *voir* **rire**.

riant, ~**e** /rjɑ̃, -t/ *a.* cheerful.

ricaner /rikane/ *v.i.* snigger, giggle.

riche /riʃ/ *a.* rich (**en**, in). —*n.m./f.* rich person. ~**ment** *adv.* richly.

richesse /riʃɛs/ *n.f.* wealth; (*de sol, décor*) richness. ~**s**, wealth.

ricoch|er /rikoʃe/ *v.i.* rebound, ricochet. ~**et** *n.m.* rebound, ricochet. **par** ~**er**, indirectly.

rictus /riktys/ *n.m.* grin, grimace.

rid|e /rid/ *n.f.* wrinkle; (*sur l'eau*) ripple. ~**er** *v.t.* wrinkle; (*eau*) ripple.

rideau (*pl.* ~**x**) /rido/ *n.m.* curtain; (*métallique*) shutter; (*fig.*) screen. ~ **de fer**, (*pol.*) Iron Curtain.

ridicul|e /ridikyl/ *a.* ridiculous. —*n.m.* absurdity. **le** ~**e**, ridicule. ~**iser** *v.t.* ridicule.

rien /rjɛ̃/ *pron.* (**ne**) ~, nothing. —*n.m.* trifle. **de** ~**!**, don't mention it! ~ **d'autre/de plus**, nothing else/more. ~ **du tout**, nothing at all. ~ **que**, just, only. **trois fois** ~, next to nothing. **il n'y est pour** ~, he has nothing to do with it. **en un** ~ **de temps**, in next to no time. ~ **à faire**, it's no good!

rieu|r, ~**se** /rjœr, rjøz/ *a.* merry.

rigid|e /riʒid/ *a.* rigid; (*muscle*) stiff. ~**ité** *n.f.* rigidity; stiffness.

rigole /rigol/ *n.f.* channel.

rigol|er /rigole/ *v.i.* laugh; (*s'amuser*) have some fun; (*plaisanter*) joke. ~**ade** *n.f.* fun.

rigolo, ~**te** /rigolo, -ot/ *a.* (*fam.*) funny. —*n.m., f.* (*fam.*) joker.

rigoureu|x, ~**se** /rigurø, -z/ *a.* rigorous; (*hiver*) harsh. ~**sement** *adv.* rigorously.

rigueur /rigœr/ *n.f.* rigour. **à la** ~, at a pinch. **être de** ~, be the rule. **tenir** ~ **à qn. de qch.**, hold sth. against s.o.

rim|e /rim/ *n.f.* rhyme. ~**er** *v.i.* rhyme (**avec**, with). **cela ne** ~**e à rien**, it makes no sense.

rin|cer /rɛ̃se/ v.t. rinse. ~**çage** n.m. rinse; (action) rinsing. ~**ce-doigts** n.m. invar. finger-bowl.

ring /riŋ/ n.m. boxing ring.

ripost|e /ripɔst/ n.f. retort; (mil.) reprisal. ~**er** v.i. retaliate; v.t. retort (**que**, that). ~**er à**, (attaque) counter; (insulte etc.) reply to.

rire† /rir/ v.i. laugh (**de**, at); (plaisanter) joke; (s'amuser) have fun. **c'était pour** ~, it was a joke. —n.m. laugh. ~**s, le** ~, laughter.

risée /rize/ n.f. **la** ~ **de,** the laughing-stock of.

risible /rizibl/ a. laughable.

risqu|e /risk/ n.m. risk. ~**é** a. risky; (osé) daring. ~**er** v.t. risk. ~**er de faire,** stand a good chance of doing. **se** ~**er à/dans,** venture to/into.

rissoler /risɔle/ v.t./i. brown. (**faire**) ~, brown.

ristourne /risturn/ n.f. discount.

rite /rit/ n.m. rite; (habitude) ritual.

rituel, ~**le** /rituɛl/ a. & n.m. ritual.

rivage /rivaʒ/ n.m. shore.

riv|al, ~**ale** (m. pl. ~**aux**) /rival, -o/ n.m., f. rival. —a. rival. ~**aliser** v.i. compete (**avec**, with). ~**alité** n.f. rivalry.

rive /riv/ n.f. (de fleuve) bank; (de lac) shore.

riv|er /rive/ v.t. rivet. ~**er son clou à qn.,** shut s.o. up. ~**et** n.m. rivet.

riverain, ~**e** /rivrɛ̃, -ɛn/ a. riverside. —n.m., f. riverside resident; (d'une rue) resident.

rivière /rivjɛr/ n.f. river.

rixe /riks/ n.f. brawl.

riz /ri/ n.m. rice. ~**ière** /rizjɛr/ n.f. paddy(-field), rice field.

robe /rɔb/ n.f. (de femme) dress; (de juge) robe; (de cheval) coat. ~ **de chambre,** dressing-gown.

robinet /rɔbinɛ/ n.m. tap; (Amer.) faucet.

robot /rɔbo/ n.m. robot.

robuste /rɔbyst/ a. robust. ~**sse** /-ɛs/ n.f. robustness.

roc /rɔk/ n.m. rock.

rocaill|e /rɔkɑj/ n.f. rocky ground; (de jardin) rockery. ~**eux,** ~**euse** a. (terrain) rocky.

roch|e /rɔʃ/ n.f. rock. ~**eux,** ~**euse** a. rocky.

rocher /rɔʃe/ n.m. rock.

rock /rɔk/ n.m. (mus.) rock.

rod|er /rɔde/ v.t. (auto.) run in; (auto., Amer.) break in. **être** ~**é,** (personne) be broken in. ~**age** n.m. running in; breaking in.

rôd|er /rode/ v.i. roam; (suspect) prowl. ~**eur,** ~**euse** n.m., f. prowler.

rogne /rɔɲ/ n.f. (fam.) anger.

rogner /rɔɲe/ v.t. trim; (réduire) cut. ~ **sur,** cut down on.

rognon /rɔɲɔ̃/ n.m. (culin.) kidney.

rognures /rɔɲyr/ n.f. pl. scraps.

roi /rwa/ n.m. king. **les Rois mages,** the Magi. **la fête des Rois,** Twelfth Night.

roitelet /rwatlɛ/ n.m. wren.

rôle /rol/ n.m. role, part.

romain, ~**e** /rɔmɛ̃, -ɛn/ a. & n.m., f. Roman. —n.f. (laitue) cos.

roman /rɔmɑ̃/ n.m. novel; (fig.) story; (genre) fiction.

romance /rɔmɑ̃s/ n.f. sentimental ballad.

romanc|ier, ~**ière** /rɔmɑ̃sje/, /-jɛr/ n.m., f. novelist.

romanesque /rɔmanɛsk/ a. romantic; (fantastique) fantastic. **œuvres** ~**s,** novels, fiction.

romanichel, ~**le** /rɔmaniʃɛl/ n.m., f. gypsy.

romanti|que /rɔmɑ̃tik/ a. & n.m./f. romantic. ~**sme** n.m. romanticism.

rompre† /rɔ̃pr/ v.t./i. break; (relations) break off; (fiancés) break it off. **se** ~ v. pr. break.

rompu /rɔ̃py/ a. (exténué) exhausted.

ronces /rɔ̃s/ n.f. pl. brambles.

ronchonner /rɔ̃ʃɔne/ v.i. (fam.) grumble.

rond, ~**e¹** /rɔ̃, rɔ̃d/ a. round; (gras) plump; (ivre: fam.) tight. —n.m. (cercle) ring; (tranche) slice. **il n'a pas un** ~, (fam.) he hasn't got a penny. **en** ~, in a circle. ~**ement** /rɔ̃dmɑ̃/ adv. briskly; (franchement) straight. ~**eur** /rɔ̃dœr/ n.f. roundness; (franchise) frankness; (embonpoint) plumpness. ~**-point** (pl. ~**s-points**) n.m. round-about; (Amer.) traffic circle.

ronde² /rɔ̃d/ n.f. round(s); (de policier) beat; (mus.) semibreve.

rondelet, ~**te** /rɔ̃dlɛ, -t/ a. chubby.

rondelle /rɔ̃dɛl/ n.f. (techn.) washer; (tranche) slice.

rondin /rɔ̃dɛ̃/ n.m. log.

ronfl|er /rɔ̃fle/ v.i. snore; (moteur) hum. ~**ement(s)** n.m. (pl.) snoring; humming.

rong|er /rɔ̃ʒe/ v.t. gnaw (at); (vers, acide) eat into; (personne: fig.) consume. **se** ~**er les ongles,** bite one's nails. ~**eur** n.m. rodent.

ronronn|er /rɔ̃rɔne/ v.i. purr. ~**ement** n.m. purr(ing).

roquette /rɔkɛt/ n.f. rocket.

rosace /rɔzas/ n.f. (d'église) rose window.

rosaire /rozɛr/ n.m. rosary.

rosbif /rɔsbif/ n.m. roast beef.

rose /roz/ n.f. rose. —a. pink; (situation, teint) rosy. —n.m. pink.

rosé /roze/ a. pinkish; (vin) rosé. —n.m. rosé.

roseau (pl. ∿x) /rozo/ n.m. reed.

rosée /roze/ n.f. dew.

roseraie /rozrɛ/ n.f. rose garden.

rosette /rozɛt/ n.f. rosette.

rosier /rozje/ n.m. rose-bush, rose tree.

rosse /rɔs/ a. (fam.) nasty.

rosser /rose/ v.t. thrash.

rossignol /rɔsiɲɔl/ n.m. nightingale.

rot /ro/ n.m. (fam.) burp.

rotati|f, ∿ve /rɔtatif, -v/ a. rotary.

rotation /rɔtasjɔ̃/ n.f. rotation.

roter /rɔte/ v.i. (fam.) burp.

rotin /rɔtɛ̃/ n.m. (rattan) cane.

rôt|ir /rotir/ v.t./i., **se ∿ir** v. pr. roast. **∿i** n.m. roasting meat; (cuit) roast. **∿i de porc,** roast pork.

rôtisserie /rotisri/ n.f. grill-room.

rôtissoire /rotiswar/ n.f. (roasting) spit.

rotule /rɔtyl/ n.f. kneecap.

roturi|er, ère /rɔtyrje, -ɛr/ n.m., f. commoner.

rouage /rwaʒ/ n.m. (techn.) (working) part. **∿s,** (d'une organisation: fig.) wheels.

roucouler /rukule/ v.i. coo.

roue /ru/ n.f. wheel. **∿ (dentée),** cog (-wheel). **∿ de secours,** spare wheel.

roué /rwe/ a. wily, calculating.

rouer /rwe/ v.t. **∿ de coups,** thrash.

rouet /rwe/ n.m. spinning-wheel.

rouge /ruʒ/ a. red; (fer) red-hot. —n.m. red; (vin) red wine; (fard) rouge. **∿ (à lèvres),** lipstick. —n.m./f. (pol.) red. **∿-gorge** (pl. **∿s-gorges**) n.m. robin.

rougeole /ruʒɔl/ n.f. measles.

rougeoyer /ruʒwaje/ v.i. glow (red).

rouget /ruʒɛ/ n.m. red mullet.

rougeur /ruʒœr/ n.f. redness; (tache) red blotch; (gêne, honte) red face.

rougir /ruʒir/ v.t./i. turn red; (de honte) blush.

rouill|e /ruj/ n.f. rust. **∿é a.** rusty. **∿er** v.i., **se ∿er** v. pr. get rusty, rust.

roulant, ∿e /rulɑ̃, -t/ a. (meuble) on wheels; (escalier) moving.

rouleau (pl. **∿x**) /rulo/ n.m. roll; (outil, vague) roller. **∿ à pâtisserie,** rolling-pin. **∿ compresseur,** steamroller.

roulement /rulmɑ̃/ n.m. rotation; (bruit) rumble; (succession de personnes) turnover; (de tambour) roll. **∿ à billes,** ball-bearing. **par ∿,** in rotation.

rouler /rule/ v.t./i. roll; (ficelle, manches) roll up; (duper: fam.) cheat; (véhicule, train) go, travel; (conducteur) drive. **se ∿ dans** v. pr. roll (over) in.

roulette /rulɛt/ n.f. (de meuble) castor; (de dentiste) drill; (jeu) roulette. **comme sur des ∿s,** very smoothly.

roulis /ruli/ n.m. rolling.

roulotte /rulɔt/ n.f. caravan.

roumain, ∿e /rumɛ̃, -ɛn/ a. & n.m., f. Romanian.

Roumanie /rumani/ n.f. Romania.

roupiller /rupije/ v.i. (fam.) sleep.

rouquin, ∿e /rukɛ̃, -in/ a. (fam.) red-haired. —n.m., f. (fam.) redhead.

rouspéter /ruspete/ v.i. (fam.) grumble, moan, complain.

rousse /rus/ voir **roux.**

roussir /rusir/ v.t. scorch. —v.i. turn brown.

route /rut/ n.f. road; (naut., aviat.) route; (direction) way; (voyage) journey; (chemin: fig.) path. **en ∿,** on the way. **en ∿!,** let's go! **mettre en ∿,** start. **∿ nationale,** trunk road, main road. **se mettre en ∿,** set out.

rout|ier, ∿ière /rutje, -jɛr/ a. road. —n.m. long-distance lorry driver ou truck driver (Amer.); (restaurant) roadside café.

routine /rutin/ n.f. routine.

rouvrir /ruvrir/ v.t., **se ∿ir** v. pr. reopen, open again.

rou|x, ∿sse /ru, rus/ a. red, reddish-brown; (personne) red-haired. —n.m., f. redhead.

roy|al (m. pl. **∿aux**) /rwajal, -jo/ a. royal; (total: fam.) thorough. **∿alement** adv. royally.

royaume /rwajom/ n.m. kingdom. **R∿-Uni** n.m. United Kingdom.

royauté /rwajote/ n.f. royalty.

ruade /ryad, rɥad/ n.f. kick.

ruban /rybɑ̃/ n.m. ribbon; (de magnétophone) tape; (de chapeau) band. **∿ adhésif,** sticky tape.

rubéole /rybeɔl/ n.f. German measles.

rubis /rybi/ n.m. ruby; (de montre) jewel.

rubrique /rybrik/ n.f. heading; (article) column.

ruche /ryʃ/ n.f. beehive.

rude /ryd/ a. rough; (pénible) tough; (grossier) crude; (fameux: fam.) tremendous. **∿ment** adv. (frapper etc.) hard; (traiter) harshly; (très: fam.) awfully.

rudiment|s /rydimã/ *n.m. pl.* rudiments. **∼aire** /-tɛr/ *a.* rudimentary.
rudoyer /rydwaje/ *v.t.* treat harshly.
rue /ry/ *n.f.* street.
ruée /rɥe/ *n.f.* rush.
ruelle /rɥɛl/ *n.f.* alley.
ruer /rɥe/ *v.i.* (*cheval*) kick. **se ∼ dans/vers,** rush into/towards. **se ∼ sur,** pounce on.
rugby /rygbi/ *n.m.* Rugby.
rugby|man (*pl.* **∼men**) /rygbiman, -mɛn/ *n.m.* Rugby player.
rug|ir /ryʒir/ *v.i.* roar. **∼issement** *n.m.* roar.
rugueu|x, **∼se** /rygø, -z/ *a.* rough.
ruin|e /rɥin/ *n.f.* ruin. **en ∼e(s),** in ruins. **∼er** *v.t.* ruin.
ruineu|x, **∼se** /rɥinø, -z/ *a.* ruinous.
ruisseau (*pl.* **∼x**) /rɥiso/ *n.m.* stream; (*rigole*) gutter.
ruisseler /rɥisle/ *v.i.* stream.
rumeur /rymœr/ *n.f.* (*nouvelle*) rumour; (*son*) murmur, hum; (*protestation*) rumblings.
ruminer /rymine/ *v.t./i.* (*herbe*) ruminate; (*méditer*) meditate.
rupture /ryptyr/ *n.f.* break; (*action*) breaking; (*de contrat*) breach; (*de pourparlers*) breakdown.
rur|al (*m. pl.* **∼aux**) /ryral, -o/ *a.* rural.
rus|e /ryz/ *n.f.* cunning; (*perfidie*) trickery. **une ∼e,** a trick, a ruse. **∼é** *a.* cunning.
russe /rys/ *a. & n.m./f.* Russian. —*n.m.* (*lang.*) Russian.
Russie /rysi/ *n.f.* Russia.
rustique /rystik/ *a.* rustic.
rustre /rystr/ *n.m.* lout, boor.
rutilant, **∼e** /rytilã, -t/ *a.* sparkling, gleaming.
rythm|e /ritm/ *n.m.* rhythm; (*vitesse*) rate; (*de la vie*) pace. **∼é,** **∼ique** *adjs.* rhythmical.

S

s' /s/ *voir* **se.**
sa /sa/ *voir* **son**[1].
SA *abrév.* (*société anonyme*) PLC.
sabbat /saba/ *n.m.* sabbath. **∼ique** *a.* **année ∼ique,** sabbatical year.
sabl|e /sabl/ *n.m.* sand. **∼es mouvants,** quicksands. **∼er** *v.t.* sand. **∼er le champagne,** drink champagne. **∼eux,** **∼euse,** **∼onneux,** **∼onneuse** *adjs.* sandy.

sablier /sablije/ *n.m.* (*culin.*) egg-timer.
saborder /saborde/ *v.t.* (*navire, projet*) scuttle.
sabot /sabo/ *n.m.* (*de cheval etc.*) hoof; (*chaussure*) clog; (*de frein*) shoe. **∼ de Denver,** (wheel) clamp.
sabot|er /sabote/ *v.t.* sabotage; (*bâcler*) botch. **∼age** *n.m.* sabotage; (*acte*) act of sabotage. **∼eur,** **∼euse** *n.m.,* f. saboteur.
sabre /sabr/ *n.m.* sabre.
sac /sak/ *n.m.* bag; (*grand, en toile*) sack. **mettre à ∼,** (*maison*) ransack; (*ville*) sack. **∼ à dos,** rucksack. **∼ à main,** handbag. **∼ de couchage,** sleeping-bag. **mettre dans le même ∼,** lump together.
saccad|e /sakad/ *n.f.* jerk. **∼é** *a.* jerky.
saccager /sakaʒe/ *v.t.* (*ville, pays*) sack; (*maison*) ransack; (*ravager*) wreck.
saccharine /sakarin/ *n.f.* saccharin.
sacerdoce /saserdɔs/ *n.m.* priesthood; (*fig.*) vocation.
sachet /saʃɛ/ *n.m.* (small) bag; (*de médicament etc.*) sachet. **∼ de thé,** tea-bag.
sacoche /sakɔʃ/ *n.f.* bag; (*d'élève*) satchel; (*de moto*) saddle-bag.
sacquer /sake/ *v.t.* (*fam.*) sack. **je ne peux pas le ∼,** I can't stand him.
sacr|e /sakr/ *n.m.* (*de roi*) coronation; (*d'évêque*) consecration. **∼er** *v.t.* crown; consecrate.
sacré /sakre/ *a.* sacred; (*maudit: fam.*) damned.
sacrement /sakrəmã/ *n.m.* sacrament.
sacrifice /sakrifis/ *n.m.* sacrifice.
sacrifier /sakrifje/ *v.t.* sacrifice. **∼ à,** conform to. **se ∼** *v. pr.* sacrifice o.s.
sacrilège /sakrilɛʒ/ *n.m.* sacrilege. —*a.* sacrilegious.
sacristain /sakristɛ̃/ *n.m.* sexton.
sacristie /sakristi/ *n.f.* (*protestante*) vestry; (*catholique*) sacristy.
sacro-saint, **∼e** /sakrɔsɛ̃, -t/ *a.* sacrosanct.
sadi|que /sadik/ *a.* sadistic. —*n.m./f.* sadist. **∼sme** *n.m.* sadism.
safari /safari/ *n.m.* safari.
sagace /sagas/ *a.* shrewd.
sage /saʒ/ *a.* wise; (*docile*) good. —*n.m.* wise man. **∼-femme** (*pl.* **∼s-femmes**) *n.f.* midwife. **∼ment** *adv.* wisely; (*docilement*) quietly. **∼sse** /-ɛs/ *n.f.* wisdom.
Sagittaire /saʒitɛr/ *n.m.* **le ∼,** Sagittarius.
Sahara /saara/ *n.m.* **le ∼,** the Sahara (desert).

saignant, ∼e /sɛɲɑ̃, -t/ a. (*culin.*) rare.

saign|er /seɲe/ v.t./i. bleed. ∼**er du nez,** have a nosebleed. ∼**ée** n.f. bleeding. ∼**ement** n.m. bleeding. ∼**ement de nez,** nosebleed.

saill|ie /saji/ n.f. projection. **faire** ∼**ie,** project. ∼**ant,** ∼**ante** a. projecting; (*remarquable*) salient.

sain, ∼e /sɛ̃, sɛn/ a. healthy; (*moralement*) sane. ∼ **et sauf,** safe and sound. ∼**ement** /sɛnmɑ̃/ adv. healthily; (*juger*) sanely.

saindoux /sɛ̃du/ n.m. lard.

saint, ∼e /sɛ̃, sɛ̃t/ a. holy; (*bon, juste*) saintly. —n.m., f. saint. **S**∼**e-Esprit** n.m. Holy Spirit. **S**∼**-Siège** n.m. Holy See. **S**∼**-Sylvestre** n.f. New Year's Eve. **S**∼**e Vierge,** Blessed Virgin.

sainteté /sɛ̃tte/ n.f. holiness; (*d'un lieu*) sanctity.

sais /sɛ/ voir **savoir.**

saisie /sezi/ n.f. (*jurid.*) seizure; (*comput.*) keyboarding. ∼ **de données,** data capture.

sais|ir /sezir/ v.t. grab (hold of), seize; (*occasion, biens*) seize; (*comprendre*) grasp; (*frapper*) strike; (*comput.*) keyboard, capture. ∼**i de,** (*peur*) stricken by, overcome by. **se** ∼**ir de,** seize. ∼**issant,** ∼**issante** a. (*spectacle*) gripping.

saison /sɛzɔ̃/ n.f. season. **la morte** ∼**,** the off season. ∼**nier,** ∼**nière** /-ɔɲe, -jɛr/ a. seasonal.

sait /sɛ/ voir **savoir.**

salad|e /salad/ n.f. salad; (*laitue*) lettuce; (*désordre: fam.*) mess. ∼**ier** n.m. salad bowl.

salaire /salɛr/ n.m. wages, salary.

salami /salami/ n.m. salami.

salarié, ∼e /salarje/ a. wage-earning. —n.m., f. wage-earner.

salaud /salo/ n.m. (*argot*) bastard.

sale /sal/ a. dirty, filthy; (*mauvais*) nasty.

sal|er /sale/ v.t. salt. ∼**é** a. (*goût*) salty; (*plat*) salted; (*viande, poisson*) salt; (*grivois: fam.*) spicy; (*excessif: fam.*) steep.

saleté /salte/ n.f. dirtiness; (*crasse*) dirt, (*action*) dirty trick; (*obscénité*) obscenity. ∼(**s**), (*camelote*) rubbish. ∼**s,** (*détritus*) mess.

salière /saljɛr/ n.f. salt-cellar.

salin, ∼e /salɛ̃, -in/ a. saline.

sal|ir /salir/ v.t. (make) dirty; (*réputation*) tarnish. **se** ∼**ir** v. pr. get dirty. ∼**issant,** ∼**issante** a. dirty; (*étoffe*) easily dirtied.

salive /saliv/ n.f. saliva.

salle /sal/ n.f. room; (*grande, publique*) hall; (*d'hôpital*) ward; (*théâtre, cinéma*) auditorium. ∼ **à manger,** dining-room. ∼ **d'attente,** waiting-room. ∼ **de bains,** bathroom. ∼ **de séjour,** living-room. ∼ **de classe,** class-room. ∼ **d'embarquement,** departure lounge. ∼ **d'opération,** operating theatre. ∼ **des ventes,** saleroom.

salon /salɔ̃/ n.m. lounge; (*de coiffure, beauté*) salon; (*exposition*) show. ∼ **de thé,** tea-room.

salope /salɔp/ n.f. (*argot*) bitch.

saloperie /salɔpri/ n.f. (*fam.*) (*action*) dirty trick; (*chose de mauvaise qualité*) rubbish.

salopette /salɔpɛt/ n.f. dungarees; (*d'ouvrier*) overalls.

salsifis /salsifi/ n.m. salsify.

saltimbanque /saltɛ̃bɑ̃k/ n.m./f. (street ou fairground) acrobat.

salubre /salybr/ a. healthy.

saluer /salɥe/ v.t. greet; (*en partant*) take one's leave of; (*de la tête*) nod to; (*de la main*) wave to; (*mil.*) salute.

salut /saly/ n.m. greeting; (*de la tête*) nod; (*de la main*) wave; (*mil.*) salute; (*sauvegarde, rachat*) salvation. —int. (*bonjour: fam.*) hallo; (*au revoir: fam.*) bye-bye.

salutaire /salytɛr/ a. salutary.

salutation /salytɑsjɔ̃/ n.f. greeting. **veuillez agréer, Monsieur, mes** ∼**s distingués,** yours faithfully.

salve /salv/ n.f. salvo.

samedi /samdi/ n.m. Saturday.

sanatorium /sanatɔrjɔm/ n.m. sanatorium

sanctifier /sɑ̃ktifje/ v.t. sanctify.

sanction /sɑ̃ksjɔ̃/ n.f. sanction. ∼**ner** /-jɔne/ v.t. sanction; (*punir*) punish.

sanctuaire /sɑ̃ktɥɛr/ n.m. sanctuary.

sandale /sɑ̃dal/ n.f. sandal.

sandwich /sɑ̃dwitʃ/ n.m. sandwich.

sang /sɑ̃/ n.m. blood. ∼**-froid** n.m. invar. calm, self-control. **se faire du mauvais** ∼ ou **un** ∼ **d'encre** be worried stiff.

sanglant, ∼e /sɑ̃glɑ̃, -t/ a. bloody.

sangl|e /sɑ̃gl/ n.f. strap. ∼**er** v.t. strap.

sanglier /sɑ̃glije/ n.m. wild boar.

sanglot /sɑ̃glo/ n.m. sob. ∼**er** /-ɔte/ v.i. sob.

sangsue /sɑ̃sy/ n.f. leech.

sanguin, ∼e /sɑ̃gɛ̃, -in/ a. (*groupe etc.*) blood; (*caractère*) fiery.

sanguinaire /sɑ̃giner/ a. bloodthirsty.

sanitaire /sanitɛr/ a. health; (*conditions*)

sanitary; (*appareils, installations*) bathroom, sanitary. **~s** *n.m. pl.* bathroom.

sans /sɑ̃/ *prép.* without. **~ que vous le sachiez,** without your knowing. **~-abri** /sɑ̃zabri/ *n.m.|f. invar.* homeless person. **~ ça, ~ quoi,** otherwise. **~ arrêt,** nonstop. **~ encombre/faute/tarder,** without incident/fail/delay. **~fin/goût/ limite,** endless/tasteless/limitless. **~- gêne** *a. invar.* inconsiderate, thoughtless; *n.m. invar.* thoughtlessness. **~ importance / pareil / précédent / travail,** unimportant/unparalleled/un-precedented/unemployed. **~ plus,** but no more than that, but nothing more.

santé /sɑ̃te/ *n.f.* health. **à ta** *ou* **votre ~,** cheers!

saoul, ~e /su, sul/ *voir* **soûl.**

saper /sape/ *v.t.* undermine.

sapeur /sapœr/ *n.m.* (*mil.*) sapper. **~- pompier** (*pl.* **~s-pompiers**) *n.m.* fireman.

saphir /safir/ *n.m.* sapphire.

sapin /sapɛ̃/ *n.m.* fir(-tree). **~ de Noël,** Christmas tree.

sarbacane /sarbakan/ *n.f.* (*jouet*) pea-shooter.

sarcas|me /sarkasm/ *n.m.* sarcasm. **~tique** *a.* sarcastic.

sarcler /sarkle/ *v.t.* weed.

sardine /sardin/ *n.f.* sardine.

sardonique /sardɔnik/ *a.* sardonic.

sarment /sarmɑ̃/ *n.m.* vine shoot.

sas /sɑ(s)/ *n.m.* (*naut., aviat.*) airlock.

satané /satane/ *a.* (*fam.*) blasted.

satanique /satanik/ *a.* satanic.

satellite /satelit/ *n.m.* satellite.

satin /satɛ̃/ *n.m.* satin.

satir|e /satir/ *n.f.* satire. **~ique** *a.* satirical.

satisfaction /satisfaksjɔ̃/ *n.f.* satisfaction.

satis|faire† /satisfɛr/ *v.t.* satisfy. —*v.i.* **~faire à,** satisfy. **~faisant, ~faisante** *a.* (*acceptable*) satisfactory. **~fait, ~faite** *a.* satisfied (**de,** with).

satur|er /satyre/ *v.t.* saturate. **~ation** *n.f.* saturation.

sauc|e /sos/ *n.f.* sauce; (*jus de viande*) gravy. **~er** *v.t.* (*plat*) wipe. **se faire ~er** (*fam.*) get soaked. **~e tartare,** tartar sauce. **~ière** *n.f.* sauce-boat.

saucisse /sosis/ *n.f.* sausage.

saucisson /sosisɔ̃/ *n.m.* (slicing) sausage.

sauf[1] /sof/ *prép.* except. **~ er-reur/imprévu,** barring error/the un-foreseen. **~ avis contraire,** unless you hear otherwise.

sau|f[2], ~ve /sof, sov/ *a.* safe, unharmed. **~f-conduit** *n.m.* safe conduct.

sauge /soʒ/ *n.f.* (*culin.*) sage.

saugrenu /sogrəny/ *a.* preposterous, ludicrous.

saule /sol/ *n.m.* willow. **~ pleureur,** weeping willow.

saumon /somɔ̃/ *n.m.* salmon. —*a. invar.* salmon-pink.

saumure /somyr/ *n.f.* brine.

sauna /sona/ *n.m.* sauna.

saupoudrer /sopudre/ *v.t.* sprinkle (**de,** with).

saut /so/ *n.m.* jump, leap. **faire un ~ chez qn.,** pop round to s.o.'s (place). **le ~,** (*sport*) jumping. **~ en hauteur/longueur,** high/long jump. **~ périlleux,** somersault. **au ~ du lit,** on getting up.

sauté /sote/ *a. & n.m.* (*culin.*) sauté.

saut|er /sote/ *v.i.* jump, leap; (*exploser*) blow up; (*fusible*) blow; (*se détacher*) come off. —*v.t.* jump (over); (*page, classe*) skip. **faire ~er,** (*détruire*) blow up; (*fusible*) blow; (*casser*) break; (*culin.*) sauté; (*renvoyer: fam.*) kick out. **~er à la corde,** skip. **~er aux yeux,** be obvious. **~e-mouton** *n.m.* leap-frog. **~er au cou de qn.,** fling one's arms round s.o. **~er sur une occasion,** jump at an opportunity.

sauterelle /sotrɛl/ *n.f.* grasshopper.

sautiller /sotije/ *v.i.* hop.

sauvage /sovaʒ/ *a.* wild; (*primitif, cruel*) savage; (*farouche*) unsociable; (*illégal*) unauthorized. —*n.m.|f.* unsociable person; (*brute*) savage. **~rie** *n.f.* savagery.

sauve /sov/ *voir* **sauf[2].**

sauvegard|e /sovgard/ *n.f.* safeguard; (*comput.*) backup. **~er** *v.t.* safeguard; (*comput.*) save.

sauv|er /sove/ *v.t.* save; (*d'un danger*) rescue, save; (*matériel*) salvage. **se ~er** *v. pr.* (*fuir*) run away; (*partir: fam.*) be off. **~e-qui-peut** *n.m. invar.* stampede. **~etage** *n.m.* rescue; salvage. **~eteur** *n.m.* rescuer. **~eur** *n.m.* saviour.

sauvette (à la) /(ala)sovɛt/ *adv.* hastily; (*vendre*) illicitly.

savamment /savamɑ̃/ *adv.* learnedly; (*avec habileté*) skilfully.

savan|t, ~e /savɑ̃, -t/ *a.* learned; (*habile*) skilful. —*n.m.* scientist.

saveur /savœr/ *n.f.* flavour; (*fig.*) savour.

savoir† /savwar/ *v.t.* know; (*apprendre*) hear. **elle sait conduire/nager,** she can drive/swim. —*n.m.* learning. **à ~,** namely. **faire ~ à qn. que,** inform s.o.

that. **je ne saurais pas,** I could not, I cannot. **(pas) que je sache,** (not) as far as I know.

savon /savɔ̃/ *n.m.* soap. **passer un ~ à qn.,** (*fam.*) give s.o. a dressing down. **~ner** /-ɔne/ *v.t.* soap. **~nette** /-ɔnɛt/ *n.f.* bar of soap. **~neux, ~neuse** /-ɔnø, -z/ *a.* soapy.

savour|er /savure/ *v.t.* savour. **~eux, ~euse** *a.* tasty; (*fig.*) spicy.

saxo(phone) /saksɔ(fɔn)/ *n.m.* sax-(ophone).

scabreu|x, ~se /skabrø, -z/ *a.* risky; (*indécent*) obscene.

scandal|e /skɑ̃dal/ *n.m.* scandal; (*tapage*) uproar; (*en public*) noisy scene. **faire ~e,** shock people. **faire un ~e,** make a scene. **~eux, ~euse** *a.* scandalous. **~iser** *v.t.* scandalize, shock.

scander /skɑ̃de/ *v.t.* (*vers*) scan; (*slogan*) chant.

scandinave /skɑ̃dinav/ *a.* & *n.m./f.* Scandinavian.

Scandinavie /skɑ̃dinavi/ *n.f.* Scandinavia.

scarabée /skarabe/ *n.m.* beetle.

scarlatine /skarlatin/ *n.f.* scarlet fever.

scarole /skarɔl/ *n.f.* endive.

sceau (*pl.* **~x**) /so/ *n.m.* seal.

scélérat /selera/ *n.m.* scoundrel.

scell|er /sele/ *v.t.* seal; (*fixer*) cement. **~és** *n.m. pl.* seals.

scénario /senarjo/ *n.m.* scenario.

scène /sɛn/ *n.f.* scene; (*estrade, art dramatique*) stage. **mettre en ~,** (*pièce*) stage. **~ de ménage,** domestic scene.

scepti|que /sɛptik/ *a.* sceptical. —*n.m./f.* sceptic. **~cisme** *n.m.* scepticism.

sceptre /sɛptr/ *n.m.* sceptre.

schéma /ʃema/ *n.m.* diagram. **~tique** *a.* diagrammatic; (*sommaire*) sketchy.

schisme /ʃism/ *n.m.* schism.

schizophrène /skizɔfrɛn/ *a.* & *n.m./f.* schizophrenic.

sciatique /sjatik/ *n.f.* sciatica.

scie /si/ *n.f.* saw.

sciemment /sjamɑ̃/ *adv.* knowingly.

scien|ce /sjɑ̃s/ *n.f.* science; (*savoir*) knowledge. **~ce-fiction** *n.f.* science fiction. **~tifique** *a.* scientific; *n.m./f.* scientist.

scier /sje/ *v.t.* saw.

scinder /sɛ̃de/ *v.t.,* **se ~** *v. pr.* split.

scintill|er /sɛ̃tije/ *v.i.* glitter; (*étoile*) twinkle. **~ement** *n.m.* glittering; twinkling.

scission /sisjɔ̃/ *n.f.* split.

sciure /sjyr/ *n.f.* sawdust.

sclérose /skleroz/ *n.f.* sclerosis. **~ en plaques,** multiple sclerosis.

scol|aire /skɔlɛr/ *a.* school. **~arisation** *n.f.,* **~arité** *n.f.* schooling. **~arisé** *a.* provided with schooling.

scorbut /skɔrbyt/ *n.m.* scurvy.

score /skɔr/ *n.m.* score.

scories /skɔri/ *n.f. pl.* slag.

scorpion /skɔrpjɔ̃/ *n.m.* scorpion. **le S~,** Scorpio.

scotch[1] /skɔtʃ/ *n.m.* (*boisson*) Scotch (whisky).

scotch[2] /skɔtʃ/ *n.m.* (P.) Sellotape (P.); (*Amer.*) Scotch (tape) (P.).

scout, ~e /skut/ *n.m.* & *a.* scout.

script /skript/ *n.m.* (*cinéma*) script; (*écriture*) printing. **~-girl,** continuity girl.

scrupul|e /skrypyl/ *n.m.* scruple. **~eusement** *adv.* scrupulously. **~eux, ~euse** *a.* scrupulous.

scruter /skryte/ *v.t.* examine, scrutinize.

scrutin /skrytɛ̃/ *n.m.* (*vote*) ballot; (*opération électorale*) poll.

sculpt|er /skylte/ *v.t.* sculpture; (*bois*) carve (**dans,** out of). **~eur** *n.m.* sculptor. **~ure** *n.f.* sculpture.

se, s'* /sə, s/ *pron.* himself; (*femelle*) herself; (*indéfini*) oneself; (*non humain*) itself; (*pl.*) themselves; (*réciproque*) each other, one another. **se parler,** (*à soi-même*) talk to o.s.; (*réciproque*) talk to each other. **se faire,** (*passif*) be done. **se laver les mains,** (*possessif*) wash one's hands.

séance /seɑ̃s/ *n.f.* session; (*cinéma, théâtre*) show. **~ de pose,** sitting. **~ tenante,** forthwith.

seau (*pl.* **~x**) /so/ *n.m.* bucket, pail.

sec, sèche /sɛk, sɛʃ/ *a.* dry; (*fruits*) dried; (*coup, bruit*) sharp; (*cœur*) hard; (*whisky*) neat; (*Amer.*) straight. —*n.m.* **à ~,** (*sans eau*) dry; (*sans argent*) broke. **au ~,** in a dry place. —*n.f.* (*fam.*) (*cigarette*) fag.

sécateur /sekatœr/ *n.m.* (*pour les haies*) shears; (*petit*) secateurs.

sécession /sesesjɔ̃/ *n.f.* secession. **faire ~,** secede.

sèche /sɛʃ/ *voir* **sec. ~ment** *adv.* drily.

sèche-cheveux /sɛʃʃəvø/ *n.m. invar.* hair-drier.

sécher /seʃe/ *v.t./i.* dry; (*cours: fam.*) skip; (*ne pas savoir: fam.*) be stumped. **se ~** *v. pr.* dry o.s.

sécheresse /seʃrɛs/ *n.f.* dryness; (*temps sec*) drought.

séchoir /seʃwar/ *n.m.* drier.

second, **~e¹** /sgɔ̃, -d/ *a. & n.m., f.*
second. —*n.m.* (*adjoint*) second in
command; (*étage*) second floor,
(*Amer.*) third floor. —*n.f.* (*transport*)
second class.

secondaire /sgɔ̃dɛr/ *a.* secondary.

seconde² /sgɔ̃d/ *n.f.* (*instant*) second.

seconder /sgɔ̃de/ *v.t.* assist.

secouer /skwe/ *v.t.* shake; (*poussière,
torpeur*) shake off. **se ~**, (*fam.*) (*se
dépêcher*) get a move on; (*réagir*)
shake o.s. up.

secour|ir /skurir/ *v.t.* assist, help. **~able**
a. helpful. **~iste** *n.m./f.* first-aid worker.

secours /skur/ *n.m.* assistance, help.
—*n.m. pl.* (*méd.*) first aid. **au ~!**, help!
de ~, emergency; (*équipe, opération*)
rescue.

secousse /skus/ *n.f.* jolt, jerk;
(*électrique*) shock; (*séisme*) tremor.

secr|et, **~ète** /səkrɛ, -t/ *a.* secret.
—*n.m.* secret; (*discrétion*) secrecy. **le
~et professionnel**, professional
secrecy. **~et de Polichinelle**, open
secret. **en ~et**, in secret, secretly.

secrétaire /skreter/ *n.m./f.* secretary. **~
de direction**, executive secretary.
—*n.m.* (*meuble*) writing-desk. **~
d'État**, junior minister.

secrétariat /skretarja/ *n.m.* secretarial
work; (*bureau*) secretary's office; (*d'un
organisme*) secretariat.

sécrét|er /sekrete/ *v.t.* secrete. **~ion**
/-sjɔ̃/ *n.f.* secretion.

sect|e /sɛkt/ *n.f.* sect. **~aire** *a.* sectar-
ian.

secteur /sɛktœr/ *n.m.* area; (*mil., comm.*)
sector; (*circuit: électr.*) mains. **~
primaire/secondaire/tertiaire**, pri-
mary/secondary/tertiary industry.

section /sɛksjɔ̃/ *n.f.* section; (*transports
publics*) fare stage; (*mil.*) platoon.
~ner /-jɔne/ *v.t.* sever.

sécu /seky/ *n.f.* (*fam.*) **la ~**, the social
security services.

séculaire /sekylɛr/ *a.* age-old.

sécul|ier, **~ière** /sekylje, -jɛr/ *a.*
secular.

sécuriser /sekyrize/ *v.t.* reassure.

sécurité /sekyrite/ *n.f.* security;
(*absence de danger*) safety. **en ~**, safe,
secure. **S~ sociale**, social services,
social security services.

sédatif /sedatif/ *n.m.* sedative.

sédentaire /sedɑ̃ter/ *a.* sedentary.

sédiment /sedimɑ̃/ *n.m.* sediment.

séditieu|x, **~se** /sedisjø, -z/ *a.*
seditious.

sédition /sedisjɔ̃/ *n.f.* sedition.

séd|uire† /sedɥir/ *v.t.* charm; (*plaire à*)
appeal to; (*abuser de*) seduce.
~ucteur, **~uctrice** *a.* seductive; *n.m.,
f.* seducer. **~uction** *n.f.* seduction;
(*charme*) charm. **~uisant**, **~uisante** *a.*
attractive.

segment /sɛgmɑ̃/ *n.m.* segment.

ségrégation /segregɑsjɔ̃/ *n.f.* segrega-
tion.

seigle /sɛgl/ *n.m.* rye.

seigneur /sɛɲœr/ *n.m.* lord. **le S~**, the
Lord.

sein /sɛ̃/ *n.m.* breast; (*fig.*) bosom. **au ~
de,** in the midst of.

Seine /sɛn/ *n.f.* Seine.

séisme /seism/ *n.m.* earthquake.

seiz|e /sɛz/ *a. & n.m.* sixteen. **~ième** *a. &
n.m./f.* sixteenth.

séjour /seʒur/ *n.m.* stay; (*pièce*) living-
room. **~ner** *v.i.* stay.

sel /sɛl/ *n.m.* salt; (*piquant*) spice.

sélect /selɛkt/ *a.* select.

sélecti|f, **~ve** /selɛktif, -v/ *a.* selective.

sélection /selɛksjɔ̃/ *n.f.* selection. **~ner**
/-jɔne/ *v.t.* select.

self(-service) /sɛlf(sɛrvis)/ *n.m.* self-
service.

selle /sɛl/ *n.f.* saddle.

seller /sele/ *v.t.* saddle.

sellette /selɛt/ *n.f.* **sur la ~**, (*question*)
under examination; (*personne*) in the
hot seat.

selon /slɔ̃/ *prép.* according to (**que,**
whether).

semaine /smɛn/ *n.f.* week. **en ~**, in the
week.

sémantique /semɑ̃tik/ *a.* semantic.
—*n.f.* semantics.

sémaphore /semafɔr/ *n.m.* (*appareil*)
semaphore.

semblable /sɑ̃blabl/ *a.* similar (**à,** to). **de
~s propos**/*etc.,* (*tels*) such remarks/
etc. —*n.m.* fellow (creature).

semblant /sɑ̃blɑ̃/ *n.m.* **faire ~ de,**
pretend to. **un ~ de,** a semblance of.

sembl|er /sɑ̃ble/ *v.i.* seem (**à,** to; **que,**
that). **il me ~e que,** it seems to me that.

semelle /smɛl/ *n.f.* sole.

semence /smɑ̃s/ *n.f.* seed; (*clou*) tack.
~s, (*graines*) seed.

sem|er /sme/ *v.t.* sow; (*jeter, parsemer*)
strew; (*répandre*) spread; (*personne:
fam.*) lose. **~eur**, **~euse** *n.m., f.*
sower.

semestr|e /smɛstr/ *n.m.* half-year;
(*univ.*) semester. **~iel**, **~ielle** *a.* half-
yearly.

semi- /səmi/ *préf.* semi-.

séminaire /seminɛr/ *n.m.* (*relig.*) seminary; (*univ.*) seminar.

semi-remorque /səmirəmɔrk/ *n.m.* articulated lorry; (*Amer.*) semi(-trailer).

semis /smi/ *n.m.* (*terrain*) seed-bed; (*plant*) seedling.

sémit|e /semit/ *a.* Semitic. —*n.m./f.* Semite. ∼**ique** *a.* Semitic.

semonce /səmɔ̃s/ *n.f.* reprimand. **coup de** ∼, warning shot.

semoule /smul/ *n.f.* semolina.

sénat /sena/ *n.m.* senate. ∼**eur** /-tœr/ *n.m.* senator.

sénil|e /senil/ *a.* senile. ∼**ité** *n.f.* senility.

sens /sɑ̃s/ *n.m.* sense; (*signification*) meaning, sense; (*direction*) direction. **à mon** ∼, to my mind. **à** ∼ **unique,** (*rue etc.*) one-way. **ça n'a pas de** ∼, that does not make sense. ∼ **commun,** common sense. ∼ **giratoire,** roundabout; (*Amer.*) rotary. ∼ **interdit,** no entry; (*rue*) one-way street. **dans le** ∼ **des aiguilles d'une montre,** clockwise. ∼ **dessus dessous,** upside down.

sensation /sɑ̃sasjɔ̃/ *n.f.* feeling, sensation. **faire** ∼, create a sensation. ∼**nel,** ∼**nelle** /-jɔnɛl/ *a.* sensational.

sensé /sɑ̃se/ *a.* sensible.

sensibiliser /sɑ̃sibilize/ *v.t.* ∼ **à,** make sensitive to.

sensib|le /sɑ̃sibl/ *a.* sensitive (**à,** to); (*appréciable*) noticeable. ∼**ilité** *n.f.* sensitivity. ∼**lement** *adv.* noticeably; (*à peu près*) more or less.

sensoriel, ∼**le** /sɑ̃sɔrjɛl/ *a.* sensory.

sens|uel, ∼**uelle** /sɑ̃sɥɛl/ *a.* sensuous; (*sexuel*) sensual. ∼**ualité** *n.f.* sensuousness; sensuality.

sentenc|e /sɑ̃tɑ̃s/ *n.f.* sentence. ∼**ieux,** ∼**ieuse** *a.* sententious.

senteur /sɑ̃tœr/ *n.f.* scent.

sentier /sɑ̃tje/ *n.m.* path.

sentiment /sɑ̃timɑ̃/ *n.m.* feeling. **avoir le** ∼ **de,** be aware of.

sentiment|al (*m. pl.* ∼**aux**) /sɑ̃timɑ̃tal, -o/ *a.* sentimental. ∼**alité** *n.f.* sentimentality.

sentinelle /sɑ̃tinɛl/ *n.f.* sentry.

sentir† /sɑ̃tir/ *v.t.* feel; (*odeur*) smell; (*goût*) taste; (*pressentir*) sense. ∼ **la lavande**/*etc.*, smell of lavender/*etc.* —*v.i.* smell. **je ne peux pas le** ∼, (*fam.*) I can't stand him. **se** ∼ **fier/mieux**/*etc.*, feel proud/better/*etc.*

séparatiste /separatist/ *a. & n.m./f.* separatist.

séparé /separe/ *a.* separate; (*conjoints*) separated. ∼**ment** *adv.* separately.

sépar|er /separe/ *v.t.* separate; (*en deux*) split. **se** ∼**er** *v. pr.* separate, part (**de,** from); (*se détacher*) split. **se** ∼**er de,** (*se défaire de*) part with. ∼**ation** *n.f.* separation.

sept /sɛt/ *a. & n.m.* seven.

septante /sɛptɑ̃t/ *a. & n.m.* (*en Belgique, Suisse*) seventy.

septembre /sɛptɑ̃br/ *n.m.* September.

septentrion|al (*m. pl.* ∼**aux**) /sɛptɑ̃tri-jɔnal, -o/ *a.* northern.

septième /sɛtjɛm/ *a. & n.m./f.* seventh.

sépulcre /sepylkr/ *n.m.* (*relig.*) sepulchre.

sépulture /sepyltyr/ *n.f.* burial; (*lieu*) burial place.

séquelles /sekɛl/ *n.f. pl.* (*maladie*) after-effects; (*fig.*) aftermath.

séquence /sekɑ̃s/ *n.f.* sequence.

séquestrer /sekɛstre/ *v.t.* confine (illegally); (*biens*) impound.

sera, serait /sra, srɛ/ *voir* **être.**

serein, ∼**e** /sarɛ̃, -ɛn/ *a.* serene.

sérénade /serenad/ *n.f.* serenade.

sérénité /serenite/ *n.f.* serenity.

sergent /sɛrʒɑ̃/ *n.m.* sergeant.

série /seri/ *n.f.* series; (*d'objets*) set. **de** ∼, (*véhicule etc.*) standard. **fabrication ou production en** ∼, mass production.

sérieu|x, ∼**se** /serjø, -z/ *a.* serious; (*digne de foi*) reliable; (*chances, raison*) good. —*n.m.* seriousness. **garder/perdre son** ∼**x,** keep/be unable to keep a straight face. **prendre au** ∼**x,** take seriously. ∼**sement** *adv.* seriously.

serin /srɛ̃/ *n.m.* canary.

seringue /srɛ̃g/ *n.f.* syringe.

serment /sɛrmɑ̃/ *n.m.* oath; (*promesse*) pledge.

sermon /sɛrmɔ̃/ *n.m.* sermon. ∼**ner** /-ɔne/ *v.t.* (*fam.*) lecture.

séropositi|f, ∼**ve** /serɔpozitif, -v/ *a.* HIV-positive.

serpe /sɛrp/ *n.f.* bill(hook).

serpent /sɛrpɑ̃/ *n.m.* snake. ∼ **à sonnettes,** rattlesnake.

serpenter /sɛrpɑ̃te/ *v.i.* meander.

serpentin /sɛrpɑ̃tɛ̃/ *n.m.* streamer.

serpillière /sɛrpijɛr/ *n.f.* floor-cloth.

serre¹ /sɛr/ *n.f.* (*local*) greenhouse.

serre² /sɛr/ *n.f.* (*griffe*) claw.

serré /sere/ *a.* (*habit, nœud, programme*) tight; (*personnes*) packed, crowded; (*lutte, mailles*) close; (*cœur*) heavy.

serrer /sere/ *v.t.* (*saisir*) grip; (*presser*) squeeze; (*vis, corde, ceinture*) tighten; (*poing, dents*) clench; (*pieds*) pinch. ∼ **qn. dans ses bras,** hug. ∼ **les rangs,**

close ranks. ～ **qn.**, (*vêtement*) be tight on s.o. —*v.i.* ～ **à droite,** keep over to the right. **se** ～ *v. pr.* (*se rapprocher*) squeeze (up) (**contre,** against). ～ **de près,** follow closely. ～ **la main à,** shake hands with.

serrur|e /seryr/ *n.f.* lock. ～**ier** *n.m.* locksmith.

sertir /sɛrtir/ *v.t.* (*bijou*) set.

sérum /serɔm/ *n.m.* serum.

servante /sɛrvãt/ *n.f.* (maid)servant.

serveu|r, ～**se** /sɛrvœr, -øz/ *n.m., f.* waiter, waitress; (*au bar*) barman, barmaid.

serviable /sɛrvjabl/ *a.* helpful.

service /sɛrvis/ *n.m.* service; (*fonction, temps de travail*) duty; (*pourboire*) service (charge). ～ (**non**) **compris,** service (not) included. **être de** ～, be on duty. **pendant le** ～, (when) on duty. **rendre un** ～**/mauvais** ～ **à qn.,** do s.o. a favour/disservice. ～ **d'ordre,** (*policiers*) police. ～ **après-vente,** after-sales service. ～ **militaire,** military service.

serviette /sɛrvjɛt/ *n.f.* (*de toilette*) towel; (*sac*) briefcase. ～ (**de table**), serviette; (*Amer.*) napkin. ～ **hygiénique,** sanitary towel.

servile /sɛrvil/ *a.* servile.

servir† /sɛrvir/ *v.t./i.* serve; (*être utile*) be of use, serve. ～ **qn.** (**à table**), wait on s.o. **ça sert à,** (*outil, récipient, etc.*) it is used for. **ça me sert à/de,** I use it for/as. ～ **de,** serve as, be used as. ～ **à qn. de guide/***etc.,* act as a guide/*etc.* for s.o. **se** ～ *v. pr.* (*à table*) help o.s. (**de,** to). **se** ～ **de,** use.

serviteur /sɛrvitœr/ *n.m.* servant.

servitude /sɛrvityd/ *n.f.* servitude.

ses /se/ *voir* **son**¹.

session /sesjɔ̃/ *n.f.* session.

seuil /sœj/ *n.m.* doorstep; (*entrée*) doorway; (*fig.*) threshold.

seul, ～**e** /sœl/ *a.* alone, on one's own; (*unique*) only. **un** ～ **travail/***etc.,* only one job/*etc.* **pas un** ～ **ami/***etc.,* not a single friend/*etc.* **parler tout** ～, talk to o.s. **faire qch. tout** ～, do sth. on one's own. —*n.m., f.* **le** ～, **la** ～**e,** the only one. **un** ～, **une** ～**e,** only one. **pas un** ～, not (a single) one.

seulement /sœlmã/ *adv.* only.

sève /sɛv/ *n.f.* sap.

sév|ère /sevɛr/ *a.* severe. ～**èrement** *adv.* severely. ～**érité** /-erite/ *n.f.* severity.

sévices /sevis/ *n.m. pl.* cruelty.

sévir /sevir/ *v.i.* (*fléau*) rage. ～ **contre,** punish.

sevrer /səvre/ *v.t.* wean.

sex|e /sɛks/ *n.m.* sex; (*organes*) sex organs. ～**isme** *n.m.* sexism. ～**iste** *a.* sexist.

sex|uel, ～**uelle** /sɛksɥɛl/ *a.* sexual. ～**ualité** *n.f.* sexuality.

seyant, ～**e** /sɛjã, -t/ *a.* becoming.

shampooing /ʃãpwɛ̃/ *n.m.* shampoo.

shérif /ʃerif/ *n.m.* sheriff.

short /ʃɔrt/ *n.m.* (pair of) shorts.

si¹ (**s'** *before* **il, ils**) /si, s/ *conj.* if; (*interrogation indirecte*) if, whether. **si on partait?,** (*suggestion*) what about going? **s'il vous** *ou* **te plaît,** please. **si oui,** if so. **si seulement,** if only.

si² /si/ *adv.* (*tellement*) so; (*oui*) yes. **un si bon repas,** such a good meal. **pas si riche que,** not as rich as. **si habile qu'il soit,** however skilful he may be. **si bien que,** with the result that.

siamois, ～**e** /sjamwa, -z/ *a.* Siamese.

Sicile /sisil/ *n.f.* Sicily.

sida /sida/ *n.m.* (*méd.*) AIDS.

sidéré /sidere/ *a.* staggered.

sidérurgie /sideryrʒi/ *n.f.* iron and steel industry.

siècle /sjɛkl/ *n.m.* century; (*époque*) age.

siège /sjɛʒ/ *n.m.* seat; (*mil.*) siege. ～ **éjectable,** ejector seat. ～ **social,** head office, headquarters.

siéger /sjeʒe/ *v.i.* (*assemblée*) sit.

sien, ～**ne** /sjɛ̃, sjɛn/ *pron.* **le** ～, **la** ～**ne, les** ～**(ne)s,** his; (*femme*) hers; (*chose*) its. **les** ～**s,** (*famille*) one's family.

sieste /sjɛst/ *n.f.* nap; (*en Espagne*) siesta. **faire la** ～, have an afternoon nap.

siffl|er /sifle/ *v.i.* whistle; (*avec un sifflet*) blow one's whistle; (*serpent, gaz*) hiss. —*v.t.* (*air*) whistle; (*chien*) whistle to *ou* for; (*acteur*) hiss; (*signaler*) blow one's whistle for. ～**ement** *n.m.* whistling. **un** ～**ement,** a whistle.

sifflet /siflɛ/ *n.m.* whistle. ～**s,** (*huées*) boos.

siffloter /siflɔte/ *v.t./i.* whistle.

sigle /sigl/ *n.m.* abbreviation, acronym.

sign|al (*pl.* ～**aux**) /siɲal, -o/ *n.m.* signal. ～**aux lumineux,** (*auto.*) traffic signals.

signal|er /siɲale/ *v.t.* indicate; (*par une sonnerie, un écriteau*) signal; (*dénoncer, mentionner*) report; (*faire remarquer*) point out. **se** ～**er par,** distinguish o.s. by. ～**ement** *n.m.* description.

signalisation /siɲalizasjɔ̃/ *n.f.* signalling, signposting; (*signaux*) signals.

signataire /siɲatɛr/ *n.m./f.* signatory.

signature /siɲatyr/ *n.f.* signature; (*action*) signing.

signe /siɲ/ *n.m.* sign; (*de ponctuation*) mark. **faire ∼ à**, beckon (**de**, to); (*contacter*) contact. **faire ∼ que non**, shake one's head. **faire ∼ que oui**, nod.

signer /siɲe/ *v.t.* sign. **se ∼** *v. pr.* (*relig.*) cross o.s.

signet /siɲɛ/ *m.* bookmark.

significati|f, **∼ve** /siɲifikatif, -v/ *a.* significant.

signification /siɲifikasjɔ̃/ *n.f.* meaning.

signifier /siɲifje/ *v.t.* mean, signify; (*faire connaître*) make known (**à**, to).

silenc|e /silɑ̃s/ *n.m.* silence; (*mus.*) rest. **garder le ∼e**, keep silent. **∼ieux**, **∼ieuse** *a.* silent; *n.m.* (*auto.*) silencer; (*auto., Amer.*) muffler.

silex /silɛks/ *n.m.* flint.

silhouette /silwɛt/ *n.f.* outline, silhouette.

silicium /silisjɔm/ *n.m.* silicon.

sillage /sijaʒ/ *n.m.* (*trace d'eau*) wake.

sillon /sijɔ̃/ *n.m.* furrow; (*de disque*) groove.

sillonner /sijɔne/ *v.t.* criss-cross.

silo /silo/ *n.m.* silo.

simagrées /simagre/ *n.f. pl.* fuss, pretence.

simil|aire /similɛr/ *a.* similar. **∼itude** *n.f.* similarity.

simple /sɛ̃pl/ *a.* simple; (*non double*) single. —*n.m.* (*tennis*) singles. **∼ d'esprit** *n.m./f.* simpleton. **∼ soldat**, private. **∼ment** /-əmɑ̃/ *adv.* simply.

simplicité /sɛ̃plisite/ *n.f.* simplicity; (*naïveté*) simpleness.

simplif|ier /sɛ̃plifje/ *v.t.* simplify. **∼ication** *n.f.* simplification.

simpliste /sɛ̃plist/ *a.* simplistic.

simulacre /simylakr/ *n.m.* pretence, sham.

simul|er /simyle/ *v.t.* simulate. **∼ateur** *m.* (*appareil*) simulator. **∼ation** *n.f.* simulation.

simultané /simyltane/ *a.* simultaneous. **∼ment** *adv.* simultaneously.

sinc|ère /sɛ̃sɛr/ *a.* sincere. **∼èrement** *adv.* sincerely. **∼érité** *n.f.* sincerity.

singe /sɛ̃ʒ/ *n.m.* monkey, ape.

singer /sɛ̃ʒe/ *v.t.* mimic, ape.

singeries /sɛ̃ʒri/ *n.f. pl.* antics.

singulariser (se) /(sə)sɛ̃gylarize/ *v. pr.* make o.s. conspicuous.

singul|ier, **∼ière** /sɛ̃gylje, -jɛr/ *a.* peculiar, remarkable; (*gram.*) singular. —*n.m.* (*gram.*) singular. **∼arité** *n.f.*

peculiarity. **∼ièrement** *adv.* peculiarly; (*beaucoup*) remarkably.

sinistre[1] /sinistr/ *a.* sinister.

sinistr|e[2] /sinistr/ *n.m.* disaster; (*incendie*) blaze; (*dommages*) damage. **∼é** *a.* disaster-stricken; *n.m., f.* disaster victim.

sinon /sinɔ̃/ *conj.* (*autrement*) otherwise; (*sauf*) except (**que**, that); (*si ce n'est*) if not.

sinueu|x, **∼se** /sinɥø, -z/ *a.* winding; (*fig.*) tortuous.

sinus /sinys/ *n.m.* (*anat.*) sinus.

sionisme /sjɔnism/ *n.m.* Zionism.

siphon /sifɔ̃/ *n.m.* siphon; (*de WC*) U-bend.

sirène[1] /sirɛn/ *n.f.* (*appareil*) siren.

sirène[2] /sirɛn/ *n.f.* (*femme*) mermaid.

sirop /siro/ *n.m.* syrup; (*boisson*) cordial.

siroter /sirɔte/ *v.t.* sip.

sirupeu|x, **∼se** /sirypø, -z/ *a.* syrupy.

sis, **∼e** /si, siz/ *a.* situated.

sismique /sismik/ *a.* seismic.

site /sit/ *n.m.* setting; (*pittoresque*) beauty spot; (*emplacement*) site; (*monument etc.*) place of interest.

sitôt /sito/ *adv.* **∼ entré/***etc.*, immediately after coming in/*etc*. **∼ que**, as soon as. **pas de ∼**, not for a while.

situation /sitɥasjɔ̃/ *n.f.* situation, position. **∼ de famille**, marital status.

situ|er /sitɥe/ *v.t.* situate, locate. **se ∼er** *v. pr.* (*se trouver*) be situated. **∼é** *a.* situated.

six /sis/ (/si/ *before consonant*, /siz/ *before vowel*) *a. & n.m.* six. **∼ième** /sizjɛm/ *a. & n.m./f.* sixth.

sketch (*pl.* **∼es**) /skɛtʃ/ *n.m.* (*théâtre*) sketch.

ski /ski/ *n.m.* (*patin*) ski; (*sport*) skiing. **faire du ∼**, ski. **∼ de fond**, cross-country skiing. **∼ nautique**, water-skiing.

sk|ier /skje/ *v.i.* ski. **∼leur**, **∼leuse** *n.m., f.* skier.

slalom /slalɔm/ *n.m.* slalom.

slave /slav/ *a.* Slav; (*lang.*) Slavonic. —*n.m./f.* Slav.

slip /slip/ *n.m.* (*d'homme*) (under)pants; (*de femme*) knickers; (*Amer.*) panties. **∼ de bain**, (swimming) trunks; (*du bikini*) briefs.

slogan /slɔgɑ̃/ *n.m.* slogan.

smoking /smɔkiŋ/ *n.m.* evening *ou* dinner suit, dinner-jacket.

snack(-bar) /snak(bar)/ *n.m.* snack-bar.

snob /snɔb/ *n.m./f.* snob. —*a.* snobbish. **∼isme** *n.m.* snobbery.

sobr|e /sɔbr/ a. sober. ∼iété n.f. sobriety.

sobriquet /sɔbrikɛ/ n.m. nickname.

sociable /sɔsjabl/ a. sociable.

soc|ial (m. pl. ∼iaux) /sɔsjal, -jo/ a. social.

socialis|te /sɔsjalist/ n.m./f. socialist. ∼me n.m. socialism.

société /sɔsjete/ n.f. society; (compagnie, firme) company.

sociolo|gie /sɔsjɔlɔʒi/ n.f. sociology. ∼gique a. sociological. ∼gue n.m./f. sociologist.

socle /sɔkl/ n.m. (de colonne, statue) plinth; (de lampe) base.

socquette /sɔkɛt/ n.f. ankle sock.

soda /sɔda/ n.m. (fizzy) drink.

sodium /sɔdjɔm/ n.m. sodium.

sœur /sœr/ n.f. sister.

sofa /sɔfa/ n.m. sofa.

soi /swa/ pron. oneself. **en** ∼, in itself. ∼-**disant** a. invar. so-called; (qui se veut tel) self-styled; adv. supposedly.

soie /swa/ n.f. silk.

soif /swaf/ n.f. thirst. **avoir** ∼, be thirsty. **donner** ∼ **à**, make thirsty.

soigné /swaɲe/ a. tidy, neat; (bien fait) careful.

soigner /swaɲe/ v.t. look after, take care of; (tenue, style) take care over; (maladie) treat. **se** ∼ v. pr. look after o.s.

soigneu|x , ∼**se** /swaɲø, -z/ a. careful (**de**, about); (ordonné) tidy. ∼**sement** adv. carefully.

soi-même /swamɛm/ pron. oneself.

soin /swɛ̃/ n.m. care; (ordre) tidiness. ∼**s**, care; (méd.) treatment. **avoir** ou **prendre** ∼ **de qn./de faire**, take care of s.o./to do. **premiers** ∼**s**, first aid.

soir /swar/ n.m. evening.

soirée /sware/ n.f. evening; (réception) party. ∼ **dansante**, dance.

soit /swa/ voir **être**. —conj. (à savoir) that is to say. ∼ . . . **soit**, either . . . or.

soixantaine /swasɑ̃tɛn/ n.f. **une** ∼ (**de**), about sixty.

soixant|e /swasɑ̃t/ a. & n.m. sixty. ∼**e-dix** a. & n.m. seventy. ∼**e-dixième** a. & n.m./f. seventieth. ∼**ième** a. & n.m./f. sixtieth.

soja /sɔʒa/ n.m. (graines) soya beans; (plante) soya.

sol /sɔl/ n.m. ground; (de maison) floor; (terrain agricole) soil.

solaire /sɔlɛr/ a. solar; (huile, filtre) sun. **les rayons** ∼**s**, the sun's rays.

soldat /sɔlda/ n.m. soldier.

solde¹ /sɔld/ n.f. (salaire) pay.

solde² /sɔld/ n.m. (comm.) balance. ∼**s**, (articles) sale goods. **en** ∼, (acheter etc.) at sale price. **les** ∼**s**, the sales.

solder /sɔlde/ v.t. reduce; (liquider) sell off at sale price; (compte) settle. **se** ∼ **par**, (aboutir à) end in.

sole /sɔl/ n.f. (poisson) sole.

soleil /sɔlɛj/ n.m. sun; (chaleur) sunshine; (fleur) sunflower. **il y a du** ∼, it is sunny.

solennel, ∼**le** /sɔlanɛl/ a. solemn.

solennité /sɔlanite/ n.f. solemnity.

solex /sɔlɛks/ n.m. (P.) moped.

solfège /sɔlfɛʒ/ n.m. elementary musical theory.

solid|aire /sɔlidɛr/ a. (mécanismes) interdependent; (couple) (mutually) supportive; (ouvriers) who show solidarity. ∼**arité** n.f. solidarity.

solidariser (**se**) /(sə)sɔlidarize/ v. pr. show solidarity (**avec**, with).

solid|e /sɔlid/ a. solid. —n.m. (objet) solid; (corps) sturdy. ∼**ement** adv. solidly. ∼**ité** n.f. solidity.

solidifier /sɔlidifje/ v.t., **se** ∼ v. pr. solidify.

soliste /sɔlist/ n.m./f. soloist.

solitaire /sɔlitɛr/ a. solitary. —n.m./f. (ermite) hermit; (personne insociable) loner.

solitude /sɔlityd/ n.f. solitude.

solive /sɔliv/ n.f. joist.

sollicit|er /sɔlisite/ v.t. request; (attirer, pousser) prompt; (tenter) tempt; (faire travailler) make demands on. ∼**ation** n.f. earnest request.

sollicitude /sɔlisityd/ n.f. concern.

solo /sɔlo/ n.m. & a. invar. (mus.) solo.

solstice /sɔlstis/ n.m. solstice.

soluble /sɔlybl/ a. soluble.

solution /sɔlysjɔ̃/ n.f. solution.

solvable /sɔlvabl/ a. solvent.

solvant /sɔlvɑ̃/ n.m. solvent.

sombre /sɔ̃br/ a. dark; (triste) sombre.

sombrer /sɔ̃bre/ v.i. sink (**dans**, into).

sommaire /sɔmɛr/ a. summary; (tenue, repas) scant. —n.m. summary.

sommation /sɔmasjɔ̃/ n.f. (mil.) warning; (jurid.) summons.

somme¹ /sɔm/ n.f. sum. **en** ∼, ∼ **toute**, in short. **faire la** ∼ **de**, add (up), total (up).

somme² /sɔm/ n.m. (sommeil) nap.

sommeil /sɔmɛj/ n.m. sleep; (besoin de dormir) drowsiness. **avoir** ∼, be ou feel sleepy. ∼**ler** /-meje/ v.i. doze; (fig.) lie dormant.

sommelier /sɔməlje/ n.m. wine waiter.

sommer /sɔme/ v.t. summon.

sommes /sɔm/ *voir* **être**.

sommet /sɔmɛ/ *n.m.* top; (*de montagne*) summit; (*de triangle*) apex; (*gloire*) height.

sommier /sɔmje/ *n.m.* base (of bed).

somnambule /sɔmnɑ̃byl/ *n.m.* sleep-walker.

somnifère /sɔmnifɛr/ *n.m.* sleeping-pill.

somnolen|t, ~te /sɔmnɔlɑ̃, -t/ *a.* drowsy. **~ce** *n.f.* drowsiness.

somnoler /sɔmnɔle/ *v.i.* doze.

sompt|ueux, ~ueuse /sɔ̃ptɥø, -z/ *a.* sumptuous. **~uosité** *n.f.* sumptuousness.

son[1], **sa** *ou* **son*** (*pl.* **ses**) /sɔ̃, sa, sɔ̃, se/ *a.* his; (*femme*) her; (*chose*) its; (*indéfini*) one's.

son[2] /sɔ̃/ *n.m.* (*bruit*) sound.

son[3] /sɔ̃/ *n.m.* (*de blé*) bran.

sonar /sɔnar/ *n.* Sonar.

sonate /sɔnat/ *n.f.* sonata.

sonde /sɔ̃d/ *n.f.* (*pour les forages*) drill; (*méd.*) probe.

sond|er /sɔ̃de/ *v.t.* sound, (*terrain*) drill; (*personne*) sound out. **~age** *n.m.* sounding; drilling. **~age (d'opinion),** (opinion) poll.

song|e /sɔ̃ʒ/ *n.m.* dream. **~er** *v.i.* dream; *v.t.* **~er que,** think that. **~er à,** think about. **~eur, ~euse** *a.* pensive.

sonnantes /sɔnɑ̃t/ *a.f. pl.* **à six**/*etc.* **heures ~,** on the stroke of six/*etc.*

sonné /sɔne/ *a.* (*fam.*) crazy; (*fatigué*) knocked out.

sonn|er /sɔne/ *v.t./i.* ring; (*clairon, glas*) sound; (*heure*) strike; (*domestique*) ring for. **midi ~é,** will past noon. **~er de,** (*clairon etc.*) sound, blow.

sonnerie /sɔnri/ *n.f.* ringing; (*de clairon*) sound; (*mécanisme*) bell.

sonnet /sɔnɛ/ *n.m.* sonnet.

sonnette /sɔnɛt/ *n.f.* bell.

sonor|e /sɔnɔr/ *a.* resonant; (*onde, effets, etc.*) sound. **~ité** *n.f.* resonance; (*d'un instrument*) tone.

sonoris|er /sɔnɔrize/ *v.t.* (*salle*) wire for sound. **~ation** *n.f.* (*matériel*) sound equipment.

sont /sɔ̃/ *voir* **être**.

sophistiqué /sɔfistike/ *a.* sophisticated.

soporifique /sɔpɔrifik/ *a.* soporific.

sorbet /sɔrbɛ/ *n.m.* sorbet.

sorcellerie /sɔrsɛlri/ *n.f.* witchcraft.

sorc|ier /sɔrsje/ *n.m.* sorcerer. **~ière** *n.f.* witch.

sordide /sɔrdid/ *a.* sordid; (*lieu*) squalid.

sort /sɔr/ *n.m.* (*destin, hasard*) fate; (*condition*) lot; (*maléfice*) spell. **tirer (qch.) au ~,** draw lots (for sth.).

sortant, ~e /sɔrtɑ̃, -t/ *a.* (*président etc.*) outgoing.

sorte /sɔrt/ *n.f.* sort, kind. **de ~ que,** so that. **en quelque ~,** in a way. **faire en ~ que,** see to it that.

sortie /sɔrti/ *n.f.* departure, exit; (*porte*) exit; (*promenade, dîner*) outing; (*invective*) outburst; (*parution*) appearance; (*de disque, gaz*) release; (*d'un ordinateur*) output. **~s,** (*argent*) outgoings.

sortilège /sɔrtilɛʒ/ *n.m.* (magic) spell.

sortir[†] /sɔrtir/ *v.i.* (*aux. être*) go out, leave; (*venir*) come out; (*aller au spectacle etc.*) go out; (*livre, film*) come out; (*plante*) come up. **~ de,** (*pièce*) leave; (*milieu social*) come from; (*limites*) go beyond. —*v.t.* (*aux. avoir*) take out; (*dire: fam.*) come out with. **~ d'affaire, (s')en ~,** get out of an awkward situation. **~ du commun** *ou* **de l'ordinaire,** be out of the ordinary.

sosie /sɔzi/ *n.m.* double.

sot, ~te /so, sɔt/ *a.* foolish.

sottise /sɔtiz/ *n.f.* foolishness; (*action, remarque*) foolish thing.

sou /su/ *n.m.* **~s,** money. **pas un ~,** not a penny. **sans le ~,** without a penny. **près de ses ~s,** tight-fisted.

soubresaut /subrəso/ *n.m.* (sudden) start.

souche /suʃ/ *n.f.* (*d'arbre*) stump, (*de famille, vigne*) stock, (*de carnet*) counterfoil. **planté comme une ~,** standing like an idiot.

souci[1] /susi/ *n.m.* (*inquiétude*) worry; (*préoccupation*) concern. **se faire du ~,** worry.

souci[2] /susi/ *n.m.* (*plante*) marigold.

soucier (se) /(sə)susje/ *v. pr.* **se ~ de,** be concerned about.

soucieu|x, ~se /susjø, -z/ *a.* concerned (**de,** about).

soucoupe /sukup/ *n.f.* saucer. **~ volante,** flying saucer.

soudain, ~e /sudɛ̃, -ɛn/ *a.* sudden. —*adv.* suddenly. **~ement** /-ɛnmɑ̃/ *adv.* suddenly. **~eté** /-ɛnte/ *n.f.* suddenness.

soude /sud/ *n.f.* soda.

soud|er /sude/ *v.t.* solder, (*à la flamme*) weld. **se ~er** *v. pr.* (*os*) knit (together). **~ure** *n.f.* soldering, welding; (*substance*) solder.

soudoyer /sudwaje/ *v.t.* bribe.

souffle /sufl/ *n.m.* blow, puff; (*haleine*) breath; (*respiration*) breathing; (*explosion*) blast; (*vent*) breath of air.

soufflé /sufle/ *n.m.* (*culin.*) soufflé.
souffl|er /sufle/ *v.i.* blow; (*haleter*) puff.
—*v.t.* (*bougie*) blow out; (*poussière, fumée*) blow; (*par explosion*) destroy; (*chuchoter*) whisper. **~er son rôle à,** prompt. **~eur, ~euse** *n.m., f.* (*théâtre*) prompter.
soufflet /sufle/ *n.m.* (*instrument*) bellows.
souffrance /sufrɑ̃s/ *n.f.* suffering. **en ~,** (*affaire*) pending.
souffr|ir† /sufrir/ *v.i.* suffer (*de,* from). —*v.t.* (*endurer*) suffer; (*admettre*) admit of. **il ne peut pas le ~ir,** he cannot stand *ou* bear him. **~ant, ~ante** *a.* unwell.
soufre /sufr/ *n.m.* sulphur.
souhait /swɛ/ *n.m.* wish. **nos ~s de,** (*vœux*) good wishes for. **à vos ~s!,** bless you!
souhait|er /swete/ *v.t.* (*bonheur etc.*) wish for. (*question, poussière*) wish s.o. sth. **~er que/faire,** hope that/to do. **~able** /swɛtabl/ *a.* desirable.
souiller /suje/ *v.t.* soil.
soûl, ~e /su, sul/ *a.* drunk. —*n.m.* **tout son ~,** as much as one can.
soulag|er /sulaʒe/ *v.t.* relieve. **~ement** *n.m.* relief.
soûler /sule/ *v.t.* make drunk. **se ~** *v. pr.* get drunk.
soulèvement /sulɛvmɑ̃/ *n.m.* uprising.
soulever /sulve/ *v.t.* lift, raise; (*exciter*) stir; (*question, poussière*) raise. **se ~** *v. pr.* lift *ou* raise o.s. up; (*se révolter*) rise up.
soulier /sulje/ *n.m.* shoe.
souligner /suliɲe/ *v.t.* underline; (*taille, yeux*) emphasize.
soum|ettre† /sumetr/ *v.t.* (*dompter, assujettir*) subject (**à,** to); (*présenter*) submit (**à,** to). **se ~ettre** *v. pr.* submit (**à,** to). **~is, ~ise** *a.* submissive. **~ission** *n.f.* submission.
soupape /supap/ *n.f.* valve.
soupçon /supsɔ̃/ *n.m.* suspicion. **un ~ de,** (*fig.*) a touch of. **~ner** /-ɔne/ *v.t.* suspect. **~neux, ~neuse** /-ɔnø, -z/ *a.* suspicious.
soupe /sup/ *n.f.* soup.
souper /supe/ *n.m.* supper. —*v.i.* have supper.
soupeser /supəze/ *v.t.* judge the weight of; (*fig.*) weigh up.
soupière /supjɛr/ *n.f.* (soup) tureen.
soupir /supir/ *n.m.* sigh. **pousser un ~,** heave a sigh. **~er** *v.i.* sigh.
soupir|ail (*pl.* **~aux**) /supiraj, -o/ *n.m.* small basement window.

soupirant /supirɑ̃/ *n.m.* suitor.
souple /supl/ *a.* supple; (*règlement, caractère*) flexible. **~sse** /-ɛs/ *n.f.* suppleness; flexibility.
source /surs/ *n.f.* source; (*eau*) spring. **de ~ sûre,** from a reliable source. **~ thermale,** hot springs.
sourcil /sursi/ *n.m.* eyebrow.
sourciller /sursije/ *v.i.* **sans ~,** without batting an eyelid.
sourd, ~e /sur, -d/ *a.* deaf; (*bruit, douleur*) dull; (*inquiétude, conflit*) silent, hidden. —*n.m., f.* deaf person. **faire la ~e oreille,** turn a deaf ear. **~-muet** (*pl.* **~s-muets**), **~e-muette** (*pl.* **~es-muettes**) *a.* deaf and dumb; *n.m., f.* deaf mute.
sourdine /surdin/ *n.f.* (*mus.*) mute. **en ~,** quietly.
souricière /surisjɛr/ *n.f.* mousetrap; (*fig.*) trap.
sourire /surir/ *n.m.* smile. **garder le ~,** keep smiling. —*v.i.* smile (**à,** at). **~ à,** (*fortune*) smile on.
souris /suri/ *n.f.* mouse.
sournois, ~e /surnwa, -z/ *a.* sly, underhand. **~ement** /-zmɑ̃/ *adv.* slyly.
sous /su/ *prép.* under, beneath. **~ la main,** handy. **~ la pluie,** in the rain. **~ peu,** shortly. **~ terre,** underground.
sous- /su/ *préf.* (*subordination*) sub-; (*insuffisance*) under-.
sous-alimenté /suzalimɑ̃te/ *a.* undernourished.
sous-bois /subwa/ *n.m. invar.* undergrowth.
souscr|ire /suskrir/ *v.i.* **~ire à,** subscribe to. **~iption** *n.f.* subscription.
sous-direct|eur, ~rice /sudirɛktœr, -ris/ *n.m., f.* assistant manager.
sous-entend|re /suzɑ̃tɑ̃dr/ *v.t.* imply. **~u** *n.m.* insinuation.
sous-estimer /suzɛstime/ *v.t.* underestimate.
sous-jacent, ~e /suʒasɑ̃, -t/ *a.* underlying.
sous-marin, ~e /sumarɛ̃, -in/ *a.* underwater. —*n.m.* submarine.
sous-officier /suzɔfisje/ *n.m.* noncommissioned officer.
sous-préfecture /suprefɛktyr/ *n.f.* subprefecture.
sous-produit /suprɔdɥi/ *n.m.* byproduct.
sous-programme /suprɔgram/ *n.m.* subroutine.
soussigné, ~e /susiɲe/ *a. & n.m., f.* undersigned.

sous-sol /susɔl/ *n.m.* (*cave*) basement.

sous-titr|e /sutitr/ *n.m.* subtitle. **~er** *v.t.* subtitle.

soustr|aire† /sustrɛr/ *v.t.* remove; (*déduire*) subtract. **se ~aire à**, escape from. **~action** *n.f.* (*déduction*) subtraction.

sous-trait|er /sutrete/ *v.t.* subcontract. **~ant** *n.m.* subcontractor.

sous-verre /suvɛr/ *n.m. invar.* picture frame, glass mount.

sous-vêtement /suvɛtmɑ̃/ *n.m.* undergarment. **~s,** underwear.

soutane /sutan/ *n.f.* cassock.

soute /sut/ *n.f.* (*de bateau*) hold. **~ à charbon,** coal-bunker.

soutenir† /sutnir/ *v.t.* support; (*fortifier*, *faire durer*) sustain; (*résister à*) withstand. **~ que,** maintain that. **se ~** *v. pr.* (*se tenir debout*) support o.s.

soutenu /sutny/ *a.* (*constant*) sustained; (*style*) lofty.

souterrain, **~e** /sutɛrɛ̃, -ɛn/ *a.* underground. —*n.m.* underground passage, subway.

soutien /sutjɛ̃/ *n.m.* support. **~-gorge** (*pl.* **~s-gorge**) *n.m.* bra.

soutirer /sutire/ *v.t.* **~ à qn.,** extract from s.o.

souvenir[1] /suvnir/ *n.m.* memory, recollection; (*objet*) memento; (*cadeau*) souvenir. **en ~ de,** in memory of.

souvenir[2]† (**se**) /(sə)suvnir/ *v. pr.* **se ~ de,** remember. **se ~ que,** remember that.

souvent /suvɑ̃/ *adv.* often.

souverain, **~e** /suvrɛ̃, -ɛn/ *a.* sovereign; (*extrême*; *péj.*) supreme. —*n.m.*, *f.* sovereign. **~eté** /-ɛnte/ *n.f.* sovereignty.

soviétique /sɔvjetik/ *a.* Soviet. —*n.m./f.* Soviet citizen.

soyeu|x, **~se** /swajø, -z/ *a.* silky.

spacieu|x, **~se** /spasjø, -z/ *a.* spacious.

spaghetti /spageti/ *n.m. pl.* spaghetti.

sparadrap /sparadra/ *n.m.* sticking plaster; (*Amer.*) adhesive tape *ou* bandage.

spasm|e /spasm/ *n.m.* spasm. **~odique** *a.* spasmodic.

spat|ial (*m. pl.* **~iaux**) /spasjal, -jo/ *a.* space.

spatule /spatyl/ *n.f.* spatula.

speaker, **~ine** /spikœr, -rin/ *n.m.*, *f.* announcer.

spéc|ial (*m. pl.* **~iaux**) /spesjal, -jo/ *a.* special; (*singulier*) peculiar. **~ialement** *adv.* especially; (*exprès*) specially.

spécialis|er (**se**) /(sə)spesjalize/ *v. pr.* specialize (**dans,** in). **~ation** *n.f.* specialization.

spécialiste /spesjalist/ *n.m./f.* specialist.

spécialité /spesjalite/ *n.f.* speciality; (*Amer.*) specialty.

spécif|ier /spesifje/ *v.t.* specify. **~ication** *n.f.* specification.

spécifique /spesifik/ *a.* specific.

spécimen /spesimɛn/ *n.m.* specimen.

spectacle /spɛktakl/ *n.m.* sight, spectacle; (*représentation*) show.

spectaculaire /spɛktakylɛr/ *a.* spectacular.

specta|teur, **~trice** /spɛktatœr, -tris/ *n.m.*, *f.* onlooker; (*sport*) spectator. **les ~teurs,** (*théâtre*) the audience.

spectre /spɛktr/ *n.m.* (*revenant*) spectre; (*images*) spectrum.

spécul|er /spekyle/ *v.i.* speculate. **~ateur,** **~atrice** *n.m.*, *f.* speculator. **~ation** *n.f.* speculation.

spéléologie /speleɔlɔʒi/ *n.f.* cave exploration, pot-holing; (*Amer.*) spelunking.

sperme /spɛrm/ *n.m.* sperm.

sph|ère /sfɛr/ *n.f.* sphere. **~érique** *a.* spherical.

sphinx /sfɛ̃ks/ *n.m.* sphinx.

spirale /spiral/ *n.f.* spiral.

spirite /spirit/ *n.m./f.* spiritualist.

spirituel, **~le** /spiritɥɛl/ *a.* spiritual; (*amusant*) witty.

spiritueux /spiritɥø/ *n.m.* (*alcool*) spirit.

splend|ide /splɑ̃did/ *a.* splendid. **~eur** *n.f.* splendour.

spongieu|x, **~se** /spɔ̃ʒjø, -z/ *a.* spongy.

sponsor /spɔ̃sɔr/ *n.m.* sponsor. **~iser** *v.t.* sponsor.

spontané /spɔ̃tane/ *a.* spontaneous. **~ité** *n.f.* spontaneity. **~ment** *adv.* spontaneously.

sporadique /spɔradik/ *a.* sporadic.

sport /spɔr/ *n.m.* sport. —*a. invar.* (*vêtements*) casual. **veste/voiture de ~,** sports jacket/car.

sport|if, **~ve** /spɔrtif, -v/ *a.* sporting; (*physique*) athletic; (*résultats*) sports. —*n.m.* sportsman. —*n.f.* sportswoman.

spot /spɔt/ *n.m.* spotlight; (*publicitaire*) ad.

spray /sprε/ *n.m.* spray; (*méd.*) inhaler.

sprint /sprint/ *n.m.* sprint. **~er** *v.i.* sprint; *n.m.* /-œr/ sprinter.

square /skwar/ *n.m.* (public) garden.

squash /skwaʃ/ *n.m.* squash.

squatter /skwatœr/ *n.m.* squatter. **~iser** *v.t.* squat in.

squelett|e /skəlɛt/ *n.m.* skeleton. **~ique**

/-etik/ *a.* skeletal; (*maigre*) all skin and bone.

stabiliser /stabilize/ *v.t.* stabilize.

stab|le /stabl/ *a.* stable. **~ilité** *n.f.* stability.

stade[1] /stad/ *n.m.* (*sport*) stadium.

stade[2] /stad/ *n.m.* (*phase*) stage.

stag|e /staʒ/ *n.m.* course. **~iaire** *a.* & *n.m./f.* course member; (*apprenti*) trainee.

stagn|er /stagne/ *v.i.* stagnate. **~ant, ~ante** *a.* stagnant. **~ation** *n.f.* stagnation.

stand /stãd/ *n.m.* stand, stall. **~ de tir,** (shooting-)range.

standard[1] /stãdar/ *n.m.* switchboard. **~iste** /-dist/ *n.m./f.* switchboard operator.

standard[2] /stãdar/ *a. invar.* standard. **~iser** /-dize/ *v.t.* standardize.

standing /stãdiŋ/ *n.m.* status, standing. **de ~,** (*hôtel etc.*) luxury.

star /star/ *n.f.* (*actrice*) star.

starter /startɛr/ *n.m.* (*auto.*) choke.

station /stasjõ/ *n.f.* station; (*halte*) stop. **~ balnéaire,** seaside resort. **~ debout,** standing position. **~ de taxis,** taxi rank; (*Amer.*) taxi stand. **~-service** (*pl.* **~s-service**) *n.f.* service station. **~ thermale,** spa.

stationnaire /stasjɔnɛr/ *a.* stationary.

stationn|er /stasjɔne/ *v.i.* park. **~ement** *n.m.* parking.

statique /statik/ *a.* static.

statistique /statistik/ *n.f.* statistic; (*science*) statistics. **—**a. statistical.

statue /staty/ *n.f.* statue.

statuer /statɥe/ *v.i.* **~ sur,** rule on.

statu quo /statykwo/ *n.m.* status quo.

stature /statyr/ *n.f.* stature.

statut /staty/ *n.m.* status. **~s,** (*règles*) statutes. **~aire** /-tɛr/ *a.* statutory.

steak /stɛk/ *n.m.* steak.

stencil /stensil/ *n.m.* stencil.

sténo /steno/ *n.f.* (*personne*) stenographer; (*sténographie*) shorthand.

sténodactylo /stenɔdaktilo/ *n.f.* shorthand typist; (*Amer.*) stenographer.

sténographie /stenɔgrafi/ *n.f.* shorthand.

stéréo /stereo/ *n.f.* & *a. invar.* stereo. **~phonique** /-eɔfɔnik/ *a.* stereophonic.

stéréotype /stereɔtip/ *n.m.* stereotype. **~é** *a.* stereotyped.

stéril|e /steril/ *a.* sterile. **~ité** *n.f.* sterility.

stérilet /sterilɛ/ *n.m.* coil, IUD.

stérilis|er /sterilize/ *v.t.* sterilize. **~ation** *n.f.* sterilization.

stéroïde /sterɔid/ *a.* & *n.m.* steroid.

stéthoscope /stetɔskɔp/ *n.m.* stethoscope.

stigmat|e /stigmat/ *n.m.* mark, stigma. **~iser** *v.t.* stigmatize.

stimul|er /stimyle/ *v.t.* stimulate. **~ant** *n.m.* stimulus; (*médicament*) stimulant. **~ateur cardiaque,** pacemaker. **~ation** *n.f.* stimulation.

stipul|er /stipyle/ *v.t.* stipulate. **~ation** *n.f.* stipulation.

stock /stɔk/ *n.m.* stock. **~er** *v.t.* stock. **~iste** *n.m.* stockist; (*Amer.*) dealer.

stoïque /stɔik/ *a.* stoical. **—**n.m./f. stoic.

stop /stɔp/ *int.* stop. **—**n.m. stop sign; (*feu arrière*) brake light. **faire du ~,** (*fam.*) hitch-hike.

stopper /stɔpe/ *v.t./i.* stop; (*vêtement*) mend, reweave.

store /stɔr/ *n.m.* blind; (*Amer.*) shade; (*de magasin*) awning.

strabisme /strabism/ *n.m.* squint.

strapontin /strapõtɛ̃/ *n.m.* folding seat, jump seat.

stratagème /strataʒɛm/ *n.m.* stratagem.

stratég|ie /strateʒi/ *n.f.* strategy. **~ique** *a.* strategic.

stress /strɛs/ *n.* stress, **~ant** *a.* stressful. **~er** *v.t.* put under stress.

strict /strikt/ *a.* strict; (*tenue, vérité*) plain. **le ~ minimum,** the absolute minimum. **~ement** *adv.* strictly.

strident, ~e /stridã, -t/ *a.* shrill.

str|ie /stri/ *n.f.* streak. **~ier** *v.t.* streak.

strip-tease /striptiz/ *n.m.* strip-tease.

strophe /strɔf/ *n.f.* stanza, verse.

structur|e /stryktyr/ *n.f.* structure. **~al** (*m. pl.* **~aux**) *a.* structural. **~er** *v.t.* structure.

studieu|x, ~se /stydjø, -z/ *a.* studious; (*période*) devoted to study.

studio /stydjo/ *n.m.* (*d'artiste, de télévision, etc.*) studio; (*logement*) studio flat, bed-sitter.

stupéf|ait, ~aite /stypefɛ, -t/ *a.* amazed. **~action** *n.f.* amazement.

stupéf|ier /stypefje/ *v.t.* amaze. **~iant, ~iante** *a.* amazing; *n.m.* drug, narcotic.

stupeur /stypœr/ *n.f.* amazement; (*méd.*) stupor.

stupid|e /stypid/ *a.* stupid. **~ité** *n.f.* stupidity.

styl|e /stil/ *n.m.* style. **~isé** *a.* stylized.

stylé /stile/ *a.* well-trained.

styliste /stilist/ *n.m./f.* fashion designer.

stylo /stilo/ *n.m.* pen. **~ (à) bille,** ball-point pen. **~ (à) encre,** fountain-pen.

su /sy/ *voir* **savoir.**

suave /sɥav/ *a.* sweet.

subalterne /sybaltɛrn/ a. & n.m./f. subordinate.

subconscient, ~e /sypkɔ̃sjã, -t/ a. & n.m. subconscious.

subdiviser /sybdivize/ v.t. subdivide.

subir /sybir/ v.t. suffer; (*traitement, expériences*) undergo.

subit, ~e /sybi, -t/ a. sudden. **~ement** /-tmã/ adv. suddenly.

subjecti|f, ~ve /sybʒɛktif, -v/ a. subjective. **~vité** n.f. subjectivity.

subjonctif /sybʒɔ̃ktif/ a. & n.m. subjunctive.

subjuguer /sybʒyge/ v.t. (*charmer*) captivate.

sublime /syblim/ a. sublime.

submer|ger /sybmɛrʒe/ v.t. submerge; (*fig.*) overwhelm. **~sion** n.f. submersion.

subordonné, ~e /sybɔrdɔne/ a. & n.m., f. subordinate.

subord|onner /sybɔrdɔne/ v.t. subordinate (**à,** to). **~ination** n.f. subordination.

subreptice /sybrɛptis/ a. surreptitious.

subside /sybzid/ n.m. grant.

subsidiare /sypsidjɛr/ a. subsidiary.

subsist|er /sybziste/ v.i. subsist; (*durer, persister*) exist. **~ance** n.f. subsistence.

substance /sypstãs/ n.f. substance.

substantiel, ~le /sypstãsjɛl/ a. substantial.

substantif /sypstãtif/ n.m. noun.

substit|uer /sypstitɥe/ v.t. substitute (**à,** for). **se ~uer à,** (*remplacer*) substitute for; (*évincer*) take over from. **~ut** n.m. substitute; (*jurid.*) deputy public prosecutor. **~ution** n.f. substitution.

subterfuge /sybtɛrfyʒ/ n.m. subterfuge.

subtil /sybtil/ a. subtle. **~ité** n.f. subtlety.

subtiliser /syptilize/ v.t. **~ qch. (à qn.),** spirit sth. away (from s.o.).

subvenir /sybvənir/ v.i. **~ à,** provide for.

subvention /sybvãsjɔ̃/ n.f. subsidy. **~ner** /-jɔne/ v.t. subsidize.

subversi|f, ~ve /sybvɛrsif, -v/ a. subversive.

subversion /sybvɛrsjɔ̃/ n.f. subversion.

suc /syk/ n.m. juice.

succédané /syksedane/ n.m. substitute (**de,** for).

succéder /syksede/ v.i. **~ à,** succeed. **se ~ v. pr.** succeed one another.

succès /syksɛ/ n.m. success. **à ~,** (*film, livre, etc.*) successful. **avoir du ~,** be a success.

successeur /syksesœr/ n.m. successor.

successi|f, ~ve /syksesif, -v/ a. successive. **~vement** adv. successively.

succession /syksesjɔ̃/ n.f. succession; (*jurid.*) inheritance.

succinct, ~e /syksɛ̃, -t/ a. succinct.

succomber /sykɔ̃be/ v.i. die. **~ à,** succumb to.

succulent, ~e /sykylã, -t/ a. succulent.

succursale /sykyrsal/ n.f. (*comm.*) branch.

sucer /syse/ v.t. suck.

sucette /sysɛt/ n.f. (*bonbon*) lollipop; (*tétine*) dummy; (*Amer.*) pacifier.

sucr|e /sykr/ n.m. sugar. **~e d'orge,** barley sugar. **~e en poudre,** caster sugar; (*Amer.*) finely ground sugar. **~e glace,** icing sugar. **~e roux,** brown sugar. **~ier, ~ière** a. sugar; n.m. (*récipient*) sugar-bowl.

sucr|er /sykre/ v.t. sugar, sweeten. **~é** a. sweet; (*additionné de sucre*) sweetened.

sucreries /sykrəri/ n.f. pl. sweets.

sud /syd/ n.m. south. —a. invar. south; (*partie*) southern; (*direction*) southerly. **~-africain, ~-africaine** a. & n.m., f. South African. **~-est** n.m. south-east. **~-ouest** n.m. south-west.

Suède /sɥɛd/ n.f. Sweden.

suédois, ~e /sɥedwa, -z/ a. Swedish. —n.m., f. Suède, —n.m. (*lang.*) Swedish.

suer /sɥe/ v.t./i. sweat. **faire ~ qn.,** (*fam.*) get on s.o.'s nerves.

sueur /sɥœr/ n.f. sweat. **en ~,** sweating.

suff|ire† /syfir/ v.i. be enough (**à qn.,** for s.o.). **il ~it de faire,** one only has to do. **il ~it d'une goutte pour,** a drop is enough to. **~ire à,** (*besoin*) satisfy. **se ~ire à soi-même,** be self-sufficient.

suffis|ant, ~ante /syfizã, -t/ a. sufficient; (*vaniteux*) conceited. **~amment** adv. sufficiently. **~amment de,** sufficient. **~ance** n.f. (*vanité*) conceit.

suffixe /syfiks/ n.m. suffix.

suffoquer /syfɔke/ v.t./i. choke, suffocate.

suffrage /syfraʒ/ n.m. (*voix: pol.*) vote; (*modalité*) suffrage.

sugg|érer /sygʒere/ v.t. suggest. **~estion** /-ʒɛstjɔ̃/ n.f. suggestion.

suggesti|f, ~ve /sygʒɛstif, -v/ a. suggestive.

suicid|e /sɥisid/ n.m. suicide. **~aire** a. suicidal.

suicid|er (se) /(sə)sɥiside/ v. pr. commit suicide. **~é, ~ée** n.m., f. suicide.

suie /sɥi/ *n.f.* soot.

suint|er /sɥɛ̃te/ *v.i.* ooze. **~ement** *n.m.* oozing.

suis /sɥi/ *voir* être, suivre.

Suisse /sɥis/ *n.f.* Switzerland.

suisse /sɥis/ *a. & n.m.* Swiss. **~sse** /-ɛs/ *n.f.* Swiss (woman).

suite /sɥit/ *n.f.* continuation, rest; (*d'un film*) sequel; (*série*) series; (*appartement, escorte*) suite; (*résultat*) consequence; (*cohérence*) order. **~s**, (*de maladie*) after-effects. **à la ~, de ~,** (*successivement*) in succession. **à la ~ de,** (*derrière*) behind. **à la ~ de, par ~ de,** as a result of. **faire ~ (à),** follow. **par la ~,** afterwards. **~ à votre lettre du,** further to your letter of the.

suivant[1], **~e** /sɥivɑ̃, -t/ *a.* following, next. —*n.m.*, *f.* following *ou* next person.

suivant[2] /sɥivɑ̃/ *prép.* (*selon*) according to.

suivi /sɥivi/ *a.* steady, sustained; (*cohérent*) consistent. **peu/très ~,** (*cours*) poorly-/well-attended.

suivre† /sɥivr/ *v.t./i.* follow; (*comprendre*) keep up (with), follow. **se ~** *v. pr.* follow each other. **faire ~,** (*courrier etc.*) forward.

sujet[1], **~te** /syʒɛ, -t/ *a.* **~ à,** liable *ou* subject to. —*n.m.*, *f.* (*gouverné*) subject.

sujet[2] /syʒɛ/ *n.m.* (*matière, individu*) subject; (*motif*) cause; (*gram.*) subject. **au ~ de,** about.

sulfurique /sylfyrik/ *a.* sulphuric.

sultan /syltɑ̃/ *n.m.* sultan.

summum /sɔmɔm/ *n.m.* height.

super /sypɛr/ *n.m.* (*essence*) four-star, premium (*Amer.*). —*a. invar.* (*fam.*) great. —*adv.* (*fam.*) ultra, fantastically.

superbe /sypɛrb/ *a.* superb.

supercherie /sypɛrʃəri/ *n.f.* trickery.

supérette /sypɛrɛt/ *n.f.* minimarket.

superficie /sypɛrfisi/ *n.f.* area.

superficiel, ~le /sypɛrfisjɛl/ *a.* superficial.

superflu /sypɛrfly/ *a.* superfluous. —*n.m.* (*excédent*) surplus.

supérieur, ~e /sypɛrjœr/ *a.* (*plus haut*) upper; (*quantité, nombre*) greater (à, than); (*études, principe*) higher (à, than); (*meilleur, hautain*) superior (à, to). —*n.m.*, *f.* superior.

supériorité /sypɛrjɔrite/ *n.f.* superiority.

superlati|f, ~ve /sypɛrlatif, -v/ *a. & n.m.* superlative.

supermarché /sypɛrmarʃe/ *n.m.* supermarket.

superposer /sypɛrpoze/ *v.t.* superimpose.

superproduction /sypɛrprɔdyksjɔ̃/ *n.f.* (*film*) spectacular.

superpuissance /sypɛrpɥisɑ̃s/ *n.f.* superpower.

supersonique /sypɛrsɔnik/ *a.* supersonic.

superstit|ion /sypɛrstisjɔ̃/ *n.f.* superstition. **~ieux, ~ieuse** *a.* superstitious.

superviser /sypɛrvize/ *v.t.* supervise.

supplanter /syplɑ̃te/ *v.t.* supplant.

suppléan|t, ~te /sypleɑ̃, -t/ *n.m., f. & a.* (*professeur*) **~t,** supply teacher; (*juge*) **~t,** deputy (judge). **~ce** *n.f.* (*fonction*) temporary appointment.

suppléer /syplee/ *v.t.* (*remplacer*) replace; (*ajouter*) supply. —*v.i.* **~ à,** (*compenser*) make up for.

supplément /syplemɑ̃/ *n.m.* (*argent*) extra charge; (*de frites, légumes*) extra portion. **en ~,** extra. **un ~ de,** (*travail etc.*) extra. **payer pour un ~ de bagages,** pay extra for excess luggage. **~aire** /-tɛr/ *a.* extra, additional.

supplic|e /syplis/ *n.m.* torture. **~ier** *v.t.* torture.

supplier /syplije/ *v.t.* beg, beseech (de, to).

support /sypɔr/ *n.m.* support; (*publicitaire: fig.*) medium.

support|er[1] /sypɔrte/ *v.t.* (*endurer*) bear; (*subir*) suffer; (*soutenir*) support; (*résister à*) withstand. **~able** *a.* bearable.

supporter[2] /sypɔrtɛr/ *n.m.* (*sport*) supporter.

suppos|er /sypoze/ *v.t.* suppose; (*impliquer*) imply. **à ~er que,** supposing that. **~ition** *n.f.* supposition.

suppositoire /sypozitwar/ *n.m.* suppository.

suppr|imer /syprime/ *v.t.* get rid of, remove; (*annuler*) cancel; (*mot*) delete. **~imer à qn.,** (*enlever*) take away from s.o. **~ession** *n.f.* removal; cancellation; deletion.

suprématie /sypremasi/ *n.f.* supremacy.

suprême /syprɛm/ *a.* supreme.

sur /syr/ *prép.* on, upon; (*par-dessus*) over; (*au sujet de*) about, on; (*proportion*) out of; (*mesure*) by. **aller/tourner**/etc. **~,** go/turn/etc. towards. **mettre/jeter**/etc. **~,** put/throw/etc. on to. **~-le-champ** *adv.* immediately. **~ le qui-vive,** on the alert. **~ mesure,** made to measure. **~ place,** on the spot. **~ ce,** hereupon.

sur- /syr/ *préf.* over-.

sûr /syr/ *a.* certain, sure; (*sans danger*) safe; (*digne de confiance*) reliable; (*main*) steady; (*jugement*) sound.

surabondance /syrabɔ̃dãs/ *n.f.* super-abundance.

suranné /syrane/ *a.* outmoded.

surcharg|e /syrʃarʒ/ *n.f.* overloading; (*poids*) extra load. **~er** *v.t.* overload; (*texte*) alter.

surchauffer /syrʃofe/ *v.t.* overheat.

surchoix /syrʃwa/ *a. invar.* of finest quality.

surclasser /syrklɑse/ *v.t.* outclass.

surcroît /syrkrwa/ *n.m.* increase (**de**, in), additional amount (**de**, of). **de ~**, in addition.

surdité /syrdite/ *n.f.* deafness.

sureau (*pl.* **~x**) /syro/ *n.m.* (*arbre*) elder.

surélever /syrɛlve/ *v.t.* raise.

sûrement /syrmã/ *adv.* certainly; (*sans danger*) safely.

surench|ère /syrãʃɛr/ *n.f.* higher bid. **~érir** *v.t.* bid higher (**sur**, than).

surestimer /syrɛstime/ *v.t.* overestimate.

sûreté /syrte/ *n.f.* safety; (*garantie*) surety; (*d'un geste*) steadiness. **être en ~**, be safe. **S~** (**nationale**), *division of French Ministère de l'Intérieur in charge of police.*

surexcité /syrɛksite/ *a.* very excited.

surf /syrf/ *n.m.* surfing.

surface /syrfas/ *n.f.* surface. **faire ~**, (*sous-marin etc.*) surface. **en ~**, (*fig.*) superficially.

surfait, **~e** /syrfɛ, -t/ *a.* overrated.

surgelé /syrʒəle/ *a.* (deep-)frozen **(aliments)** **~s**, frozen food.

surgir /syrʒir/ *v.i.* appear (suddenly); (*difficulté*) arise.

surhomme /syrɔm/ *n.m.* superman.

surhumain, **~e** /syrymɛ̃, -ɛn/ *a.* superhuman.

surlendemain /syrlãdmɛ̃/ *n.m.* **le ~**, two days later. **le ~ de**, two days after.

surligneur /syrliɲœr/ *n.m.* highlighter (pen).

surmen|er /syrməne/ *v.t.*, **se ~er** *v. pr.* overwork. **~age** *n.m.* overworking; (*méd.*) overwork.

surmonter /syrmɔ̃te/ *v.t.* (*vaincre*) overcome, surmount; (*être au-dessus de*) surmount, top.

surnager /syrnaʒe/ *v.i.* float.

surnaturel, **~le** /syrnatyrɛl/ *a.* supernatural.

surnom /syrnɔ̃/ *n.m.* nickname. **~mer** /-ɔme/ *v.t.* nickname.

surnombre (**en**) /(ã)syrnɔ̃br/ *adv.* too many. **il est en ~**, he is one too many.

surpasser /syrpase/ *v.t.* surpass.

surpeuplé /syrpœple/ *a.* overpopulated.

surplomb /syrplɔ̃/ *n.m.* **en ~**, overhanging. **~er** /-be/ *v.t./i.* overhang.

surplus /syrply/ *n.m.* surplus.

surpr|endre† /syrprãdr/ *v.t.* (*étonner*) surprise; (*prendre au dépourvu*) catch, surprise; (*entendre*) overhear. **~enant**, **~enante** *a.* surprising. **~is**, **~ise** *a.* surprised (**de**, at).

surprise /syrpriz/ *n.f.* surprise. **~-partie** (*pl.* **~s-parties**) *n.f.* party.

surréalisme /syrrealism/ *n.m.* surrealism.

sursaut /syrso/ *n.m.* start, jump. **en ~**, with a start. **~ de**, (*regain*) burst of. **~er** /-te/ *v.i.* start, jump.

sursis /syrsi/ *n.m.* reprieve; (*mil.*) deferment. **deux ans (de prison) avec ~**, a two-year suspended sentence.

surtaxe /syrtaks/ *n.f.* surcharge.

surtout /syrtu/ *adv.* especially, mainly; (*avant tout*) above all. **~ pas**, certainly not.

surveillant, **~e** /syrvɛjã, -t/ *n.m., f.* (*de prison*) warder; (*au lycée*) supervisor (in charge of discipline).

surveill|er /syrveje/ *v.t.* watch; (*travaux, élèves*) supervise. **~ance** *n.f.* watch; supervision; (*de la police*) surveillance.

survêtement /syrvɛtmã/ *n.m.* (*sport*) track suit.

survie /syrvi/ *n.f.* survival.

survivance /syrvivãs/ *n.f.* survival.

surviv|re† /syrvivr/ *v.i.* survive. **~re à**, (*conflit etc.*) survive; (*personne*) outlive. **~ant**, **~ante** *a.* surviving; *n.m., f.* survivor.

survol /syrvɔl/ *n.m.* **le ~ de**, flying over. **~er** *v.t.* fly over; (*livre*) skim through.

survolté /syrvɔlte/ *a.* (*surexcité*) worked up.

susceptib|le /sysɛptibl/ *a.* touchy. **~le de faire**, (*possibilité*) liable to do; (*capacité*) able to do. **~ilité** *n.f.* susceptibility.

susciter /sysite/ *v.t.* (*éveiller*) arouse; (*occasionner*) create.

suspect, **~e** /syspɛ, -ɛkt/ *a.* (*témoignage*) suspect; (*individu*) suspicious. **~ de**, suspected of. —*n.m., f.* suspect. **~er** /-ɛkte/ *v.t.* suspect.

suspend|re /syspãdr/ *v.t.* (*arrêter, différer, destituer*) suspend; (*accrocher*) hang (up). **se ~re à,** hang from. **~u à,** hanging from.

suspens (en) /(ɑ̃)syspɑ̃/ *adv.* (*affaire*) in abeyance; (*dans l'indécision*) in suspense.

suspense /syspɑ̃s/ *n.m.* suspense.

suspension /syspɑ̃sjɔ̃/ *n.f.* suspension; (*lustre*) chandelier.

suspicion /syspisjɔ̃/ *n.f.* suspicion.

susurrer /sysyre/ *v.t./i.* murmur.

suture /sytyr/ *n.f.* **point de ~,** stitch.

svelte /svɛlt/ *a.* slender.

S.V.P. *abrév. voir* **s'il vous plaît.**

sweat-shirt /switʃœrt/ *n.m.* sweat-shirt.

syllabe /silab/ *n.f.* syllable.

symbol|e /sɛ̃bɔl/ *n.m.* symbol. **~ique** *a.* symbolic(al). **~iser** *v.t.* symbolize.

symétr|ie /simetri/ *n.f.* symmetry. **~ique** *a.* symmetrical.

sympa /sɛ̃pa/ *a. invar.* (*fam.*) nice. **sois ~,** be a pal.

sympath|ie /sɛ̃pati/ *n.f.* (*goût*) liking; (*affinité*) affinity; (*condoléances*) sympathy. **~ique** *a.* nice, pleasant.

sympathis|er /sɛ̃patize/ *v.i.* get on well (**avec,** with). **~ant, ~ante** *n.m., f.* sympathizer.

symphon|ie /sɛ̃fɔni/ *n.f.* symphony. **~ique** *a.* symphonic; (*orchestre*) symphony.

symposium /sɛ̃pozjɔm/ *n.m.* symposium.

sympt|ôme /sɛ̃ptom/ *n.m.* symptom. **~omatique** /-ɔmatik/ *a.* symptomatic.

synagogue /sinagɔg/ *n.f.* synagogue.

synchroniser /sɛ̃krɔnize/ *v.t.* synchronize.

syncope /sɛ̃kɔp/ *n.f.* (*méd.*) black-out.

syncoper /sɛ̃kɔpe/ *v.t.* syncopate.

syndic /sɛ̃dik/ *n.m.* **~ (d'immeuble),** managing agent.

syndic|at /sɛ̃dika/ *n.m.* (trade) union. **~at d'initiative,** tourist office. **~al** (*m. pl.* **~aux**) *a.* (trade-)union. **~aliste** *n.m./f.* trade-unionist; *a.* (trade-)union.

syndiqué, ~e /sɛ̃dike/ *n.m., f.* (trade-) union member.

syndrome /sɛ̃drom/ *n.m.* syndrome.

synonyme /sinɔnim/ *a.* synonymous. **—***n.m.* synonym.

syntaxe /sɛ̃taks/ *n.f.* syntax.

synthèse /sɛ̃tɛz/ *n.f.* synthesis.

synthétique /sɛ̃tetik/ *a.* synthetic.

synthé(tiseur) /sɛ̃te(tizœr)/ *n.m.* synthesizer.

syphilis /sifilis/ *n.f.* syphilis.

Syrie /siri/ *n.f.* Syria.

syrien, ~ne /sirjɛ̃, -jɛn/ *a. & n.m., f.* Syrian.

systématique /sistematik/ *a.* systematic. **~ment** *adv.* systematically.

système /sistɛm/ *n.m.* system. **le ~ D,** coping with problems.

T

t' /t/ *voir* **te.**

ta /ta/ *voir* **ton**[1].

tabac /taba/ *n.m.* tobacco; (*magasin*) tobacconist's shop. **—***a. invar.* buff. **~ à priser,** snuff.

tabasser /tabase/ *v.t.* (*fam.*) beat up.

table /tabl/ *n.f.* table. **à ~!,** come and eat! **faire ~ rase,** make a clean sweep (**de,** of). **~ de nuit,** bedside table. **~ des matières,** table of contents. **~ roulante,** (tea-)trolley; (*Amer.*) (serving) cart.

tableau (*pl.* **~x**) /tablo/ *n.m.* picture; (*peinture*) painting; (*panneau*) board; (*graphique*) chart; (*liste*) list. **~ (noir),** blackboard. **~ d'affichage,** notice-board. **~ de bord,** dashboard.

tabler /table/ *v.i.* **~ sur,** count on.

tablette /tablɛt/ *n.f.* shelf. **~ de chocolat,** bar of chocolate.

tablier /tablije/ *n.m.* apron; (*de pont*) platform; (*de magasin*) shutter.

tabloïd(e) /tablɔid/ *a. & n.m.* tabloïd.

tabou /tabu/ *n.m. & a.* taboo.

tabouret /taburɛ/ *n.m.* stool.

tabulateur /tabylatœr/ *n.m.* tabulator.

tac /tak/ *n.m.* **du ~ au tac,** tit for tat.

tache /taʃ/ *n.f.* mark, spot; (*salissure*) stain. **faire ~ d'huile,** spread. **~ de rousseur,** freckle.

tâche /taʃ/ *n.f.* task, job.

tacher /taʃe/ *v.t.* stain. **se ~** *v. pr.* (*personne*) get stains on one's clothes.

tâcher /taʃe/ *v.i.* **~ de faire,** try to do.

tacheté /taʃte/ *a.* spotted.

tacite /tasit/ *a.* tacit.

taciturne /tasityrn/ *a.* taciturn.

tact /takt/ *n.m.* tact.

tactile /taktil/ *a.* tactile.

tactique /taktik/ *a.* tactical. **—***n.f.* tactics. **une ~,** a tactic.

taie /tɛ/ *n.f.* **~ d'oreiller,** pillowcase.

taillader /tajade/ *v.t.* gash, slash.

taille[1] /taj/ *n.f.* (*milieu du corps*) waist; (*hauteur*) height; (*grandeur*) size. **de ~,** sizeable. **être de ~ à faire,** be up to doing.

taill|e[2] /taj/ *n.f.* cutting; pruning;

(*forme*) cut. **~er** *v.t.* cut; (*arbre*) prune; (*crayon*) sharpen; (*vêtement*) cut out. **se ~er** *v. pr.* (*argot*) clear off. **~e-crayon(s)** *n.m. invar.* pencil-sharpener.

tailleur /tɑjœr/ *n.m.* tailor; (*costume*) lady's suit. **en ~**, cross-legged.

taillis /taji/ *n.m.* copse.

taire† /tɛr/ *v.t.* say nothing about. **se ~** *v. pr.* be silent *ou* quiet; (*devenir silencieux*) fall silent. **faire ~**, silence.

talc /talk/ *n.m.* talcum powder.

talent /talɑ̃/ *n.m.* talent. **~ueux, ~ueuse** /-tɥø, -z/ *a.* talented.

taloche /talɔʃ/ *n.f.* (*fam.*) slap.

talon /talɔ̃/ *n.m.* heel; (*de chèque*) stub.

talonner /talɔne/ *v.t.* follow hard on the heels of.

talus /taly/ *n.m.* embankment.

tambour /tɑ̃bur/ *n.m.* drum; (*personne*) drummer; (*porte*) revolving door.

tambourin /tɑ̃burɛ̃/ *n.m.* tambourine.

tambouriner /tɑ̃burine/ *v.t./i.* drum (**sur, on**).

tamis /tami/ *n.m.* sieve. **~er** /-ze/ *v.t.* sieve.

Tamise /tamiz/ *n.f.* Thames.

tamisé /tamize/ *a.* (*lumière*) subdued.

tampon /tɑ̃pɔ̃/ *n.m.* (*pour boucher*) plug; (*ouate*) wad, pad; (*timbre*) stamp; (*de train*) buffer. **~ (hygiénique)**, tampon.

tamponner /tɑ̃pɔne/ *v.t.* crash into; (*timbrer*) stamp; (*plaie*) dab; (*mur*) plug. **se ~** *v. pr.* (*véhicules*) crash into each other.

tandem /tɑ̃dem/ *n.m.* (*bicyclette*) tandem; (*personnes*: *fig.*) duo.

tandis que /tɑ̃dik(ə)/ *conj.* while.

tangage /tɑ̃gaʒ/ *n.m.* pitching.

tangente /tɑ̃ʒɑ̃t/ *n.f.* tangent.

tangible /tɑ̃ʒibl/ *a.* tangible.

tango /tɑ̃go/ *n.m.* tango.

tanguer /tɑ̃ge/ *v.i.* pitch.

tanière /tanjɛr/ *n.f.* den.

tank /tɑ̃k/ *n.m.* tank.

tann|er /tane/ *v.t.* tan. **~é** *a.* (*visage*) tanned, weather-beaten.

tant /tɑ̃/ *adv.* (*travailler, manger, etc.*) so much. **~ (de)**, (*quantité*) so much; (*nombre*) so many. **~ que**, as long as; (*autant que*) as much as. **en ~ que**, (*comme*) as. **~ mieux!**, fine!, all the better! **~ pis!**, too bad!

tante /tɑ̃t/ *n.f.* aunt.

tantôt /tɑ̃to/ *adv.* sometimes; (*cet après-midi*) this afternoon.

tapag|e /tapaʒ/ *n.m.* din. **~eur, ~euse** *a.* rowdy; (*tape-à-l'œil*) flashy.

tapant, ~e /tapɑ̃, -t/ *a.* à deux/trois/*etc.* heures **~es** at exactly two/three/*etc.* o'clock.

tape /tap/ *n.f.* slap. **~-à-l'œil** *a. invar.* flashy, tawdry.

taper /tape/ *v.t.* bang; (*enfant*) slap; (*emprunter*: *fam.*) touch for money. **~ (à la machine)**, type. —*v.i.* (*cogner*) bang; (*soleil*) beat down. **~ dans**, (*puiser dans*) dig into. **~ sur**, thump; (*critiquer*: *fam*) knock. **se ~** *v. pr.* (*repas*: *fam.*) put away; (*corvée*: *fam.*) do.

tap|ir (se) /(sə)tapir/ *v. pr.* crouch. **~i** *a.* crouching.

tapis /tapi/ *n.m.* carpet; (*petit*) rug; (*aux cartes*) baize. **~ de bain**, bath mat. **~-brosse** *n.m.* doormat. **~ de sol**, groundsheet. **~ roulant**, (*pour objets*) conveyor belt.

tapiss|er /tapise/ *v.t.* (wall)paper; (*fig.*) cover (**de**, with). **~erie** *n.f.* tapestry; (*papier peint*) wallpaper. **~ier, ~ière** *n.m., f.* (*décorateur*) interior decorator; (*qui recouvre un siège*) upholsterer.

tapoter /tapote/ *v.t.* tap, pat.

taquin, ~e /takɛ̃, -in/ *a.* fond of teasing. —*n.m., f.* tease(r). **~er** /-ine/ *v.t.* tease. **~erie(s)** /-inri/ *n.f.* (*pl.*) teasing.

tarabiscoté /tarabiskote/ *a.* over-elaborate.

tard /tar/ *adv.* late. **au plus ~**, at the latest. **plus ~**, later. **sur le ~**, late in life.

tard|er /tarde/ *v.i.* (*être lent à venir*) be a long time coming. **~er (à faire)**, take a long time (doing), delay (doing). **sans (plus) ~er**, without (further) delay. **il me ~er de**, I long to.

tardi|f, ~ve /tardif, -v/ *a.* late; (*regrets*) belated.

tare /tar/ *n.f.* (*défaut*) defect.

taré /tare/ *a.* cretin.

targette /tarʒɛt/ *n.f.* bolt.

targuer (se) /(sə)targe/ *v. pr.* **se ~ de**, boast about.

tarif /tarif/ *n.m.* tariff; (*de train, taxi*) fare. **~s postaux**, postage *ou* postal rates. **~aire** *a.* tariff.

tarir /tarir/ *v.t./i.*, **se ~** *v. pr.* dry up.

tartare /tartar/ *a.* (*culin.*) tartar.

tarte /tart/ *n.f.* tart; (*Amer.*) (open) pie. —*a. invar.* (*sot*: *fam.*) stupid; (*laid*: *fam.*) ugly.

tartin|e /tartin/ *n.f.* slice of bread. **~e beurrée**, slice of bread and butter. **~er** *v.t.* spread.

tartre /tartr/ *n.m.* (*bouilloire*) fur, calcium deposit; (*dents*) tartar.

tas /tɑ/ *n.m.* pile, heap. **un** *ou* **des ∼ de,** (*fam.*) lots of.

tasse /tɑs/ *n.f.* cup. **∼ à thé,** tea-cup.

tasser /tɑse/ *v.t.* pack, squeeze; (*terre*) pack (down). **se ∼** *v. pr.* (*terrain*) sink; (*se serrer*) squeeze up.

tâter /tɑte/ *v.t.* feel; (*fig.*) sound out. **—***v.i.* **∼ de,** try out.

tatillon, **∼ne** /tatijɔ̃, -jɔn/ *a.* finicky.

tâtonn|er /tɑtɔne/ *v.i.* grope about. **∼ements** *n.m. pl.* (*essais*) trial and error.

tâtons (à) /(a)tatɔ̃/ *adv.* **avancer** *ou* **marcher à ∼,** grope one's way along.

tatou|er /tatwe/ *v.t.* tattoo. **∼age** *n.m.* (*dessin*) tattoo.

taudis /todi/ *n.m.* hovel.

taule /tol/ *n.f.* (*fam.*) prison.

taup|e /top/ *n.f.* mole. **∼inière** *n.f.* molehill.

taureau (*pl.* **∼x**) /tɔro/ *n.m.* bull. **le T∼,** Taurus.

taux /to/ *n.m.* rate.

taverne /tavɛrn/ *n.f.* tavern.

tax|e /taks/ *n.f.* tax. **∼e sur la valeur ajoutée,** value added tax. **∼er** *v.t.* tax; (*produit*) fix the price of. **∼er qn. de,** accuse s.o. of.

taxi /taksi/ *n.m.* taxi(-cab); (*personne*: *fam.*) taxi-driver.

taxiphone /taksifɔn/ *n.m.* pay phone.

Tchécoslovaquie /tʃekɔslɔvaki/ *n.f.* Czechoslovakia.

tchèque /tʃɛk/ *a. & n.m./f.* Czech.

te, t'* /tə, t/ *pron.* you; (*indirect*) (to) you; (*réfléchi*) yourself.

technicien, **∼ne** /tɛknisjɛ̃, -jɛn/ *n.m., f.* technician.

technique /tɛknik/ *a.* technical. **—***n.f.* technique. **∼ment** *adv.* technically.

technolog|ie /tɛknɔlɔʒi/ *n.f.* technology. **∼ique** *a.* technological.

teck /tɛk/ *n.m.* teak.

tee-shirt /tiʃœrt/ *n.m.* tee-shirt.

teindre† /tɛ̃dr/ *v.t.* dye. **se ∼ les cheveux** *v. pr.* dye one's hair.

teint /tɛ̃/ *n.m.* complexion.

teint|e /tɛ̃t/ *n.f.* shade, tint. **une ∼e de,** (*fig.*) a tinge of. **∼er** *v.t.* (*papier, verre, etc.*) tint; (*bois*) stain.

teintur|e /tɛ̃tyr/ *n.f.* dyeing; (*produit*) dye. **∼erie** *n.f.* (*boutique*) dry-cleaner's. **∼ier,** **∼ière** *n.m., f.* dry-cleaner.

tel, **∼le** /tɛl/ *a.* such. **un ∼ livre/***etc.*, such a book/*etc.* **un ∼ chagrin/***etc.*,

such sorrow/*etc.* **∼ que,** such as, like; (*ainsi que*) (just) as. **∼ ou tel,** such-and-such. **∼ quel,** (just) as it is.

télé /tele/ *n.f.* (*fam.*) TV.

télécommande /telekɔmɑ̃d/ *n.f.* remote control.

télécommunications /telekɔmynikasjɔ̃/ *n.f. pl.* telecommunications.

télécopi|e /telekɔpi/ *n.f.* tele(fax). **∼eur** *n.m.* fax machine.

téléfilm /telefilm/ *n.m.* (tele)film.

télégramme /telegram/ *n.m.* telegram.

télégraph|e /telegraf/ *n.m.* telegraph. **∼ier** *v.t./i.* **∼ier (à),** cable. **∼ique** *a.* telegraphic; (*fil, poteau*) telegraph.

téléguid|er /telegide/ *v.t.* control by radio. **∼é** *a.* radio-controlled.

télématique /telematik/ *n.f.* computer communications.

télépathe /telepat/ *a. & n.m., f.* psychic.

télépathie /telepati/ *n.f.* telepathy.

téléphérique /teleferik/ *n.m.* cable-car.

téléphon|e /telefɔn/ *n.m.* (tele)phone. **∼e rouge,** (*pol.*) hot line. **∼er** *v.t./i.* **∼er (à),** (tele)phone. **∼ique** *a.* (tele)phone. **∼iste** *n.m./f.* operator.

télescop|e /teleskɔp/ *n.m.* telescope. **∼ique** *a.* telescopic.

télescoper /teleskɔpe/ *v.t.* smash into. **se ∼** *v. pr.* (*véhicules*) smash into each other.

télésiège /telesjɛʒ/ *n.m.* chair-lift.

téléski /teleski/ *n.m.* ski tow.

téléspecta|teur, **∼trice** /telespɛktatœr, -tris/ *n.m., f.* (television) viewer.

télévente /televɑ̃t/ *n.f.* telesales.

télévis|é /televize/ *a.* **émission ∼ée,** television programme. **∼eur** *n.m.* television set.

télévision /televizjɔ̃/ *n.f.* television.

télex /telɛks/ *n.m.* telex.

télexer /telɛkse/ *v.t.* telex.

telle /tɛl/ *voir* **tel.**

tellement /tɛlmɑ̃/ *adv.* (*tant*) so much; (*si*) so. **∼ de,** (*quantité*) so much; (*nombre*) so many.

témér|aire /temerɛr/ *a.* rash. **∼ité** *n.f.* rashness.

témoignage /temwaɲaʒ/ *n.m.* testimony, evidence; (*récit*) account. **∼ de,** (*sentiment*) token of.

témoigner /temwaɲe/ *v.i.* testify (**de,** to). **—***v.t.* show. **∼ que,** testify that.

témoin /temwɛ̃/ *n.m.* witness; (*sport*) baton. **être ∼ de,** witness. **∼ oculaire,** eyewitness.

tempe /tɑ̃p/ *n.f.* (*anat.*) temple.

tempérament /tɑ̃peramɑ̃/ *n.m.* temperament; (*physique*) constitution. **à ~,** (*acheter*) on hire-purchase; (*Amer.*) on the instalment plan.

température /tɑ̃peratyr/ *n.f.* temperature.

tempér|er /tɑ̃pere/ *v.t.* temper. **~é** *a.* (*climat*) temperate.

tempête /tɑ̃pɛt/ *n.f.* storm. **~ de neige,** snowstorm.

tempêter /tɑ̃pete/ *v.i.* (*crier*) rage.

temple /tɑ̃pl/ *n.m.* temple; (*protestant*) church.

temporaire /tɑ̃pɔrɛr/ *a.* temporary. **~ment** *adv.* temporarily.

temporel, ~le /tɑ̃pɔrɛl/ *a.* temporal.

temporiser /tɑ̃pɔrize/ *v.i.* play for time.

temps[1] /tɑ̃/ *n.m.* time; (*gram.*) tense; (*étape*) stage. **à ~ partiel/plein,** part-/full-time. **ces derniers ~,** lately. **dans le ~,** at one time. **dans quelque ~,** in a while. **de ~ en temps,** from time to time. **~ d'arrêt,** pause. **avoir tout son ~,** have plenty of time.

temps[2] /tɑ̃/ *n.m.* (*atmosphère*) weather. **~ de chien,** filthy weather. **quel ~ fait-il?,** what's the weather like?

tenace /tɔnas/ *a.* stubborn.

ténacité /tenasite/ *n.f.* stubbornness.

tenaille(s) /tɔnaj/ *n.f.* (*pl.*) pincers.

tenanc|ier, ~ière /tɔnɑ̃sje, -jɛr/ *n.m., f.* keeper (**de,** of).

tenant /tɔnɑ̃/ *n.m.* (*partisan*) supporter; (*d'un titre*) holder.

tendance /tɑ̃dɑ̃s/ *n.f.* tendency; (*opinions*) leanings; (*évolution*) trend. **avoir ~ à,** have a tendency to, tend to.

tendon /tɑ̃dɔ̃/ *n.m.* tendon.

tendre[1] /tɑ̃dr/ *v.t.* stretch; (*piège*) set; (*bras*) stretch out; (*main*) hold out; (*cou*) crane; (*tapisserie*) hang. **~ à qn.,** hold out to s.o. —*v.i.* **~ à,** tend to. **~ l'oreille,** prick up one's ears.

tendre[2] /tɑ̃dr/ *a.* tender; (*couleur, bois*) soft. **~ment** /-ɔmɑ̃/ *adv.* tenderly. **~sse** /-ɛs/ *n.f.* tenderness.

tendu /tɑ̃dy/ *a.* (*corde*) tight; (*personne, situation*) tense; (*main*) outstretched.

tén|èbres /tenɛbr/ *n.f. pl.* darkness. **~ébreux, ~ébreuse** *a.* dark.

teneur /tɔnœr/ *n.f.* content.

tenir† /tɔnir/ *v.t.* hold; (*pari, promesse, hôtel*) keep; (*place*) take up; (*propos*) utter; (*rôle*) play. **~ de,** (*avoir reçu de*) have got from. **~ pour,** regard as. **~ propre/chaud/***etc.*, keep clean/warm/*etc.* —*v.i.* hold. **~ à,** be attached to. **~ à faire,** be anxious to do. **~ dans,** fit into. **~ de qn.,** take after s.o. **se ~** *v. pr.*

(*rester*) remain; (*debout*) stand; (*avoir lieu*) be held. **se ~ à,** hold on to. **se ~ bien,** behave o.s. **s'en ~ à,** (*se limiter à*) confine o.s. to. **~ bon,** stand firm. **~ compte de,** take into account. **~ le coup,** hold out. **~ tête à,** stand up to. **tiens!,** (*surprise*) hey!

tennis /tenis/ *n.m.* tennis; (*terrain*) tennis-court. —*n.m. pl.* (*chaussures*) sneakers. **~ de table,** table tennis.

ténor /tenɔr/ *n.m.* tenor.

tension /tɑ̃sjɔ̃/ *n.f.* tension. **avoir de la ~,** have high blood-pressure.

tentacule /tɑ̃takyl/ *n.m.* tentacle.

tentative /tɑ̃tativ/ *n.f.* attempt.

tente /tɑ̃t/ *n.f.* tent.

tenter[1] /tɑ̃te/ *v.t.* try (**de faire,** to do).

tent|er[2] /tɑ̃te/ *v.t.* (*allécher*) tempt. **~é de,** tempted to. **~ation** *n.f.* temptation.

tenture /tɑ̃tyr/ *n.f.* (wall) hanging. **~s,** drapery.

tenu /tɔny/ *voir* **tenir.** —*a.* **bien ~,** well kept. **~ de,** obliged to.

ténu /teny/ *a.* (*fil etc.*) fine; (*cause, nuance*) tenuous.

tenue /tɔny/ *n.f.* (*habillement*) dress; (*de sport*) clothes; (*de maison*) upkeep; (*conduite*) (good) behaviour; (*maintien*) posture. **~ de soirée,** evening dress.

ter /tɛr/ *a. invar.* (*numéro*) B, b.

térébenthine /terebɑ̃tin/ *n.f.* turpentine.

tergiverser /tɛrʒivɛrse/ *v.i.* procrastinate.

terme /tɛrm/ *n.m.* (*mot*) term; (*date limite*) time-limit; (*fin*) end; (*date de loyer*) term. **à long/court ~,** long-/short-term. **en bons ~s,** on good terms (**avec,** with).

termin|al, ~ale (*m. pl.* **~aux**) /tɛrminal, -o/ *a.* terminal. (**classe**) **~ale,** sixth form; (*Amer.*) twelfth grade. —*n.m.* (*pl.* **~aux**) terminal.

termin|er /tɛrmine/ *v.t./i.* finish; (*soirée, débat*) end, finish. **se ~er** *v. pr.* end (**par,** with). **~aison** *n.f.* (*gram.*) ending.

terminologie /tɛrminɔlɔʒi/ *n.f.* terminology.

terminus /tɛrminys/ *n.m.* terminus.

terne /tɛrn/ *a.* dull, drab.

ternir /tɛrnir/ *v.t./i.,* **se ~** *v. pr.* tarnish.

terrain /tɛrɛ̃/ *n.m.* ground; (*parcelle*) piece of land; (*à bâtir*) plot. **~ d'aviation,** airfield. **~ de camping,** campsite. **~ de golf,** golf-course. **~ de jeu,** playground. **~ vague,** waste ground; (*Amer.*) vacant lot.

terrasse /tɛras/ *n.f.* terrace; (*de café*) pavement area.

terrassement /tɛrasmɑ̃/ *n.m.* excavation.

terrasser /tɛrase/ *v.t.* (*adversaire*) floor; (*maladie*) strike down.

terrassier /tɛrasje/ *n.m.* navvy, labourer, ditch-digger.

terre /tɛr/ *n.f.* (*planète, matière*) earth; (*étendue, pays*) land; (*sol*) ground; (*domaine*) estate. **à ∼,** (*naut.*) ashore. **par ∼,** (*tomber, jeter*) to the ground; (*s'asseoir, poser*) on the ground. **∼ (cuite),** terracotta. **∼-à-terre** *a. invar.* matter-of-fact, down-to-earth. **∼-plein** *n.m.* platform, (*auto.*) central reservation. **la ∼ ferme,** dry land. **∼ glaise,** clay.

terreau /tɛro/ *n.m. invar.* compost.

terrer (se) /(sə)tɛre/ *v. pr.* hide o.s., dig o.s. in.

terrestre /tɛrɛstr/ *a.* land; (*de notre planète*) earth's; (*fig.*) earthly.

terreur /tɛrœr/ *n.f.* terror.

terreu|x, **∼se** /tɛrø, -z/ *a.* earthy; (*sale*) grubby.

terrible /tɛribl/ *a.* terrible; (*formidable*: *fam.*) terrific.

terrien, **∼ne** /tɛrjɛ̃, -jɛn/ *n.m.*, *f.* earth-dweller.

terrier /tɛrje/ *n.m.* (*trou de lapin etc.*) burrow; (*chien*) terrier.

terrifier /tɛrifje/ *v.t.* terrify.

terrine /tɛrin/ *n.f.* (*culin.*) terrine.

territ|oire /tɛritwar/ *n.m.* territory. **∼orial** (*m. pl.* **∼oriaux**) *a.* territorial.

terroir /tɛrwar/ *n.m.* (*sol*) soil; (*région*) region. **du ∼,** country.

terroriser /tɛrɔrize/ *v.t.* terrorize.

terroris|te /tɛrɔrist/ *n.m./f.* terrorist. **∼me** *n.m.* terrorism.

tertre /tɛrtr/ *n.m.* mound.

tes /te/ *voir* **ton**[1].

tesson /tesɔ̃/ *n.m.* **∼ de bouteille,** piece of broken bottle.

test /tɛst/ *n.m.* test. **∼er** *v.t.* test.

testament /tɛstamɑ̃/ *n.m.* (*jurid.*) will; (*politique, artistique*) testament. **Ancien/Nouveau T∼,** Old/New Testament.

testicule /tɛstikyl/ *n.m.* testicle.

tétanos /tetanos/ *n.m.* tetanus.

têtard /tɛtar/ *n.m.* tadpole.

tête /tɛt/ *n.f.* head; (*figure*) face; (*cheveux*) hair; (*cerveau*) brain. **à la ∼ de,** at the head of. **à ∼ reposée,** in a leisurely moment. **de ∼,** (*calculer*) in one's head. **en ∼,** (*sport*) in the lead. **faire la ∼,** sulk. **faire une ∼,** (*football*) head the ball. **tenir ∼ à qn.,**

stand up to s.o. **une forte ∼,** a rebel. **la ∼ la première,** head first. **il n'en fait qu'à sa ∼,** he does just as he pleases. **de la ∼ aux pieds,** from head to toe. **∼-à-queue** *n.m. invar.* (*auto.*) spin. **∼-à-tête** *n.m. invar.* tête-à-tête. **en ∼-à-tête,** in private.

tétée /tete/ *n.f.* feed.

téter /tete/ *v.t./i.* suck.

tétine /tetin/ *n.f.* (*de biberon*) teat; (*sucette*) dummy; (*Amer.*) pacifier.

têtu /tety/ *a.* stubborn.

texte /tɛkst/ *n.m.* text; (*de leçon*) subject; (*morceau choisi*) passage.

textile /tɛkstil/ *n.m. & a.* textile.

textuel, **∼le** /tɛkstɥɛl/ *a.* literal.

texture /tɛkstyr/ *n.f.* texture.

thaïlandais, **∼e** /tailɑ̃dɛ, -z/ *a. & n.m.*, *f.* Thai.

Thaïlande /tailɑ̃d/ *n.f.* Thailand.

thé /te/ *n.m.* tea.

théâtr|al (*m. pl.* **∼aux**) /teatral, -o/ *a.* theatrical.

théâtre /teatr/ *n.m.* theatre; (*jeu forcé*) play-acting; (*d'un crime*) scene. **faire du ∼,** act.

théière /tejɛr/ *n.f.* teapot.

thème /tɛm/ *n.m.* theme; (*traduction*: *scol.*) prose.

théolog|ie /teɔlɔʒi/ *n.f.* theology. **∼ien** *n.m.* theologian. **∼ique** *a.* theological.

théorème /teɔrɛm/ *n.m.* theorem.

théor|ie /teɔri/ *n.f.* theory. **∼icien,** **∼icienne** *n.m.*, *f.* theorist. **∼ique** *a.* theoretical. **∼iquement,** *adv.* theoretically.

thérap|ie /terapi/ *n.f.* therapy. **∼eutique** *a.* therapeutic.

thermique /tɛrmik/ *a.* thermal.

thermomètre /tɛrmɔmɛtr/ *n.m.* thermometer.

thermonucléaire /tɛrmɔnykleɛr/ *a.* thermonuclear.

thermos /tɛrmos/ *n.m./f.* (P.) Thermos (P.) (flask).

thermostat /tɛrmɔsta/ *n.m.* thermostat.

thésauriser /tezɔrize/ *v.t./i.* hoard.

thèse /tɛz/ *n.f.* thesis.

thon /tɔ̃/ *n.m.* (*poisson*) tuna.

thrombose /trɔ̃boz/ *n.f.* thrombosis.

thym /tɛ̃/ *n.m.* thyme.

thyroïde /tirɔid/ *n.f.* thyroid.

tibia /tibja/ *n.m.* shin-bone.

tic /tik/ *n.m.* (*contraction*) twitch; (*manie*) mannerism.

ticket /tikɛ/ *n.m.* ticket.

tic-tac /tiktak/ *n.m. invar.* (*de pendule*) ticking. **faire ∼,** go tick tock.

tiède /tjɛd/ *a.* lukewarm; (*atmosphère*)

mild. **tiédeur** /tjedœr/ *n.f.* lukewarm-
ness; mildness.

tiédir /tjedir/ *v.t./i.* **(faire)** ~, warm
slightly.

tien, ~ne /tjɛ̃, tjɛn/ *pron.* le ~, la ~ne,
les ~(ne)s, yours. **à la ~ ne!**, cheers!

tiens, tient /tjɛ̃/ *voir* **tenir**.

tiercé /tjɛrse/ *n.m.* place-betting.

tier|s, ~**ce** /tjɛr, -s/ *a.* third. —*n.m.*
(*fraction*) third; (*personne*) third party.
T~s-Monde *n.m.* Third World.

tifs /tif/ *n.m. pl.* (*fam.*) hair.

tige /tiʒ/ *n.f.* (*bot.*) stem, stalk; (*en métal*)
shaft.

tignasse /tiɲas/ *n.f.* mop of hair.

tigre /tigr/ *n.m.* tiger. ~**sse** /-ɛs/ *n.f.*
tigress.

tigré /tigre/ *a.* (*rayé*) striped; (*chat*)
tabby.

tilleul /tijœl/ *n.m.* lime(-tree), linden
(-tree); (*infusion*) lime tea.

timbale /tɛ̃bal/ *n.f.* (*gobelet*) (metal)
tumbler.

timbr|e /tɛ̃br/ *n.m.* stamp; (*sonnette*)
bell; (*de voix*) tone. ~**e- poste** (*pl.* ~**es-
poste**) *n.m.* postage stamp. ~**er** *v.t.*
stamp.

timbré /tɛ̃bre/ *a.* (*fam.*) crazy.

timid|e /timid/ *a.* timid. ~**ité** *n.f.*
timidity.

timoré /timɔre/ *a.* timorous.

tintamarre /tɛ̃tamar/ *n.m.* din.

tint|er /tɛ̃te/ *v.i.* ring; (*clefs*) jingle.
~**ement** *n.m.* ringing; jingling.

tique /tik/ *n.f.* (*insecte*) tick.

tir /tir/ *n.m.* (*sport*) shooting; (*action de
tirer*) firing; (*feu, rafale*) fire. ~ **à l'arc**,
archery. ~ **forain**, shooting-gallery.

tirade /tirad/ *n.f.* soliloquy.

tirage /tiraʒ/ *n.m.* (*de photo*) printing;
(*de journal*) circulation; (*de livre*)
edition, (*de loterie*) draw; (*de
cheminée*) draught. ~ **au sort**, drawing
lots.

tiraill|er /tiraje/ *v.t.* pull (away) at;
(*harceler*) plague. ~**é entre**,
(*possibilités etc.*) torn between.
~**ement** *n.m.* (*douleur*) gnawing pain;
(*conflit*) conflict.

tiré /tire/ *a.* (*traits*) drawn.

tire-bouchon /tirbuʃɔ̃/ *n.m.* cork-screw.

tire-lait /tirlɛ/ *n.m.* breastpump.

tirelire /tirlir/ *n.f.* money-box; (*Amer.*)
coin-bank.

tirer /tire/ *v.t.* pull; (*navire*) tow, tug;
(*langue*) stick out; (*conclusion, trait,
rideaux*) draw; (*coup de feu*) fire;
(*gibier*) shoot; (*photo*) print. ~ **de**,
(*sortir*) take *ou* get out of; (*extraire*)

extract from; (*plaisir, nom*) derive
from. —*v.i.* shoot, fire (**sur**, at). ~ **sur**,
(*couleur*) verge on; (*corde*) pull at. **se
~ v. pr.** (*fam.*) clear off. **se ~ de**, get
out of. **s'en ~**, (*en réchapper*) pull
through; (*réussir: fam.*) cope. ~ **à sa
fin**, be drawing to a close. ~ **au clair**,
clarify. ~ **au sort**, draw lots (for). ~
parti de, take advantage of. ~ **profit
de**, profit from.

tiret /tirɛ/ *n.m.* dash.

tireur /tirœr/ *n.m.* gunman. ~ **d'élite**,
marksman. ~ **isolé**, sniper.

tiroir /tirwar/ *n.m.* drawer. ~**-caisse** (*pl.*
~**s-caisses**) *n.m.* till.

tisane /tizan/ *n.f.* herb-tea.

tison /tizɔ̃/ *n.m.* ember.

tisonnier /tizɔnje/ *n.m.* poker.

tiss|er /tise/ *v.t.* weave. ~**age** *n.m.*
weaving. ~**erand** /tisrɑ̃/ *n.m.* weaver.

tissu /tisy/ *n.m.* fabric, material;
(*biologique*) tissue. **un ~ de**, (*fig.*) a
web of. ~**-éponge** (*pl.* ~**s-éponge**)
n.m. towelling.

titre /titr/ *n.m.* title; (*diplôme*)
qualification; (*comm.*) bond. ~**s**,
(*droits*) claims. (**gros**) ~**s**, headlines. **à
ce ~**, (*pour cette qualité*) as such. **à ~
d'exemple**, as an example. **à juste ~**,
rightly. **à ~ privé**, in a private capacity.
~ **de propriété**, title-deed.

titré /titre/ *a.* titled.

titrer /titre/ *v.t.* (*journal*) give as a
headline.

tituber /titybe/ *v.i.* stagger.

titul|aire /titylɛr/ *a.* **être ~aire**, have
tenure. **être ~aire de**, hold. —*n.m./f.*
(*de permis etc.*) holder. ~**ariser** *v.t.*
give tenure to.

toast /tost/ *n.m.* piece of toast;
(*allocution*) toast.

toboggan /tɔbɔga/ *n.m.* (*traîneau*)
toboggan; (*glissière*) slide; (*auto.*)
flyover; (*auto., Amer.*) overpass.

toc /tɔk/ *int.* ~ **toc!** knock knock!

tocsin /tɔksɛ̃/ *n.m.* alarm (bell).

toge /tɔʒ/ *n.f.* (*de juge etc.*) gown.

tohu-bohu /tɔybɔy/ *n.m.* hubbub.

toi /twa/ *pron.* you; (*réfléchi*) yourself.
lève-~, stand up.

toile /twal/ *n.f.* cloth; (*sac, tableau*)
canvas; (*coton*) cotton. ~ **d'araignée**,
(spider's) web; (*délabrée*) cobweb. ~
de fond, backdrop, backcloth.

toilette /twalɛt/ *n.f.* washing; (*habillement*) clothes, dress. ~**s**, (*cabinets*)
toilet(s). **de ~**, (*articles, savon, etc.*)
toilet. **faire sa ~**, wash (and get ready).

toi-même /twamɛm/ *pron.* yourself.

toiser /twaze/ *v.t.* ~ **qn.,** look s.o. up and down.

toison /twazɔ̃/ *n.f.* (*laine*) fleece.

toit /twa/ *n.m.* roof. ~ **ouvrant,** (*auto.*) sun-roof.

toiture /twatyr/ *n.f.* roof.

tôle /tol/ *n.f.* (*plaque*) iron sheet. ~ **ondulée,** corrugated iron.

tolérable /tolerabl/ *a.* tolerable.

toléran|t, ~**te** /tolerã, -t/ *a.* tolerant. ~**ce** *n.f.* tolerance; (*importations: comm.*) allowance.

tolérer /tolere/ *v.t.* tolerate; (*importations: comm.*) allow.

tollé /tole/ *n.m.* hue and cry.

tomate /tomat/ *n.f.* tomato.

tombe /tɔ̃b/ *n.f.* grave; (*avec monument*) tomb.

tombeau (*pl.* ~**x**) /tɔ̃bo/ *n.m.* tomb.

tombée /tɔ̃be/ *n.f.* ~ **de la nuit,** nightfall.

tomber /tɔ̃be/ *v.i.* (*aux. être*) fall; (*fièvre, vent*) drop; (*enthousiasme*) die down. **faire** ~, knock over; (*gouvernement*) bring down. **laisser** ~, drop; (*abandonner*) let down. **laisse** ~**!,** forget it! ~ **à l'eau,** (*projet*) fall through. ~ **bien** *ou* **à point,** come at the right time. ~ **en panne,** break down. ~ **en syncope,** faint. ~ **sur,** (*trouver*) run across.

tombola /tɔ̃bola/ *n.f.* tombola; (*Amer.*) lottery.

tome /tom/ *n.m.* volume.

ton[1]**, ta** *ou* **ton*** (*pl.* **tes**) /tɔ̃, ta, tɔ̃n, te/ *a.* your.

ton[2] /tɔ̃/ *n.m.* tone; (*gamme: mus.*) key; (*hauteur de la voix*) pitch. **de bon** ~**,** in good taste.

tonalité /tonalite/ *n.f.* tone; (*téléphone*) dialling tone; (*téléphone: Amer.*) dial tone.

tond|re /tɔ̃dr/ *v.t.* (*herbe*) mow; (*mouton*) shear; (*cheveux*) clip. ~**euse** *n.f.* shears; clippers. ~**euse (à gazon),** (lawn-)mower.

tongs /tɔ̃g/ *n.f. pl.* flip-flops.

tonifier /tonifje/ *v.t.* tone up.

tonique /tonik/ *a. & n.m.* tonic.

tonne /ton/ *n.f.* ton(ne).

tonneau (*pl.* ~**x**) /tono/ *n.m.* (*récipient*) barrel; (*naut.*) ton; (*culbute*) somersault.

tonnelle /tonɛl/ *n.f.* bower.

tonner /tone/ *v.i.* thunder.

tonnerre /tonɛr/ *n.m.* thunder.

tonte /tɔ̃t/ *n.f.* (*de gazon*) mowing; (*de moutons*) shearing.

tonton /tɔ̃tɔ̃/ *n.m.* (*fam.*) uncle.

tonus /tonys/ *n.m.* energy.

top /top/ *n.m.* (*signal pour marquer un instant précis*) stroke.

topo /topo/ *n.m.* (*fam.*) talk, oral report.

toquade /tokad/ *n.f.* craze; (*pour une personne*) infatuation.

toque /tok/ *n.f.* (fur) hat; (*de jockey*) cap; (*de cuisinier*) hat.

toqué /toke/ *a.* (*fam.*) crazy.

torche /torʃ/ *n.f.* torch.

torcher /torʃe/ *v.t.* (*fam.*) wipe.

torchon /torʃɔ̃/ *n.m.* cloth, duster; (*pour la vaisselle*) tea-towel; (*Amer.*) dishtowel.

tordre /tordr/ *v.t.* twist; (*linge*) wring. **se** ~ *v. pr.* twist, bend; (*de douleur*) writhe. **se** ~ **(de rire),** split one's sides.

tordu /tordy/ *a.* twisted, bent; (*esprit*) warped.

tornade /tornad/ *n.f.* tornado.

torpeur /torpœr/ *n.f.* lethargy.

torpill|e /torpij/ *n.f.* torpedo. ~**er** *v.t.* torpedo.

torréfier /torefje/ *v.t.* roast.

torrent /torã/ *n.m.* torrent. ~**iel,** ~**ielle** /-sjɛl/ *a.* torrential.

torride /torid/ *a.* torrid.

torsade /torsad/ *n.f.* twist.

torse /tors/ *n.m.* chest; (*sculpture*) torso.

tort /tor/ *n.m.* wrong. **à** ~ **,** wrongly. **à** ~ **et à travers,** without thinking. **avoir** ~**,** be wrong (**de faire,** to do). **donner** ~ **à,** prove wrong. **être dans son** ~**,** be in the wrong. **faire (du)** ~ **à,** harm.

torticolis /tortikoli/ *n.m.* stiff neck.

tortiller /tortije/ *v.t.* twist, twirl. **se** ~ *v. pr.* wriggle, wiggle.

tortionnaire /torsjonɛr/ *n.m.* torturer.

tortue /torty/ *n.f.* tortoise; (*de mer*) turtle.

tortueu|x, ~**se** /tortɥø, -z/ *a.* (*explication*) tortuous; (*chemin*) twisting.

tortur|e(s) /tortyr/ *n.f.* (*pl.*) torture. ~**er** *v.t.* torture.

tôt /to/ *adv.* early. **plus** ~**,** earlier. **au plus** ~**,** at the earliest. **le plus** ~ **possible,** as soon as possible. ~ **ou tard,** sooner or later.

tot|al (*m. pl.* ~**aux**) /total, -o/ *a.* total. —*n.m.* (*pl.* ~**aux**) total. —*adv.* (*fam.*) to conclude, in short. **au** ~**al,** all in all. ~**alement** *adv.* totally. ~**aliser** *v.t.* total.

totalitaire /totalitɛr/ *a.* totalitarian.

totalité /totalite/ *n.f.* entirety. **la** ~ **de,** all of.

toubib /tubib/ *n.m.* (*fam.*) doctor.

touchant, ~**e** /tuʃã, -t/ *a.* (*émouvant*) touching.

touche /tuʃ/ *n.f.* (*de piano*) key; (*de*

peintre) touch. **(ligne de)** ～, touch-line.
une ～ de, a touch of.

toucher[1] /tuʃe/ *v.t.* touch; (*émouvoir*)
move, touch; (*contacter*) get in touch
with; (*cible*) hit; (*argent*) draw;
(*chèque*) cash; (*concerner*) affect.
—*v.i.* ～ **à,** touch; (*question*) touch on;
(*fin, but*) approach. **je vais lui en ～ un
mot,** I'll talk to him about it. **se ～** *v. pr.*
(*lignes*) touch.

toucher[2] /tuʃe/ *n.m.* (*sens*) touch.

touffe /tuf/ *n.f.* (*de poils, d'herbe*) tuft;
(*de plantes*) clump.

touffu /tufy/ *a.* thick, bushy; (*fig.*)
complex.

toujours /tuʒur/ *adv.* always; (*encore*)
still; (*en tout cas*) anyhow. **pour ～,** for
ever.

toupet /tupɛ/ *n.m.* (*culot: fam.*) cheek,
nerve.

toupie /tupi/ *n.f.* (*jouet*) top.

tour[1] /tur/ *n.f.* tower; (*immeuble*) tower
block; (*échecs*) rook.

tour[2] /tur/ *n.m.* (*mouvement, succession,
tournure*) turn; (*excursion*) trip; (*à
pied*) walk; (*en auto*) drive; (*artifice*)
trick; (*circonférence*) circumference;
(*techn.*) lathe. ～ **(de piste),** lap. **à ～ de
rôle,** in turn. **à mon**/*etc.* ～, when it is
my/*etc.* turn. **c'est mon**/*etc.* ～ **de,** it is
my/*etc.* turn to. **faire le ～ de,** go round;
(*question*) survey. ～ **de contrôle,**
control tower. ～ **d'horizon,** survey. ～
de passe-passe, sleight of hand. ～ **de
taille,** waist measurement; (*ligne*)
waistline.

tourbe /turb/ *n.f.* peat.

tourbillon /turbijɔ̃/ *n.m.* whirlwind;
(*d'eau*) whirlpool; (*fig.*) whirl, swirl.
～**ner** /-jɔne/ *v.i.* whirl, swirl.

tourelle /turɛl/ *n.f.* turret.

tourisme /turism/ *n.m.* tourism. **faire du
～,** do some sightseeing.

tourist|e /turist/ *n.m./f.* tourist. ～**ique** *a.*
tourist; (*route*) scenic.

tourment /turmã/ *n.m.* torment. ～**er**
/-te/ *v.t.* torment. **se ～er** *v. pr.* worry.

tournage /turnaʒ/ *n.m.* (*cinéma*) shooting.

tournant[1] /turnã, -t/ *a.* (*qui
pivote*) revolving.

tournant[2] /turnã/ *n.m.* bend; (*fig.*)
turning-point.

tourne-disque /turnədisk/ *n.m.* record-
player.

tournée /turne/ *n.f.* (*voyage, consom-
mations*) round; (*théâtre*) tour. **faire la
～,** make the rounds (**de,** of). **je paye** *ou*
j'offre la ～, I'll buy this round.

tourner /turne/ *v.t.* turn; (*film*) shoot,
make. —*v.i.* turn; (*toupie, tête*) spin;
(*moteur, usine*) run. **se ～** *v. pr.* turn. ～
au froid, turn cold. ～ **autour de,** go
round; (*personne, maison*) hang
around; (*terre*) revolve round;
(*question*) centre on. ～ **de l'œil,** (*fam.*)
faint. ～ **en dérision,** mock. ～ **en
ridicule,** ridicule. ～ **le dos à,** turn
one's back on. ～ **mal,** turn out
badly.

tournesol /turnəsɔl/ *n.m.* sunflower.

tournevis /turnəvis/ *n.m.* screwdriver.

tourniquet /turnikɛ/ *n.m.* (*barrière*)
turnstile.

tournoi /turnwa/ *n.m.* tournament.

tournoyer /turnwaje/ *v.i.* whirl.

tournure /turnyr/ *n.f.* turn; (*locution*)
turn of phrase.

tourte /turt/ *n.f.* pie.

tourterelle /turtərɛl/ *n.f.* turtle-dove.

Toussaint /tusɛ̃/ *n.f.* **la ～,** All Saints'
Day.

tousser /tuse/ *v.i.* cough.

tout[1], ～**e** (*pl.* **tous, toutes** /tu, tut/ *a.* all;
(*n'importe quel*) any; (*tout à fait*)
entirely. ～ **le pays**/*etc.*, the whole
country/*etc.*, all the country/*etc.* ～**e la
nuit/journée,** the whole night/day. ～
un paquet, a whole pack. **tous les
jours/mois**/*etc.*, every day/month/*etc.*
—*pron.* everything, all. **tous** /tus/,
toutes, all. **prendre ～,** take everything,
take it all. ～ **ce que,** all that. ～ **le
monde,** everyone. **tous les deux, toutes
les deux,** both of them. **tous les trois,** all
three (of them). —*adv.* (*très*) very;
(*tout à fait*) quite. ～ **au
bout/début**/*etc.*, right at the end/begin-
ning/*etc.* **le ～ premier,** the very first. ～
en chantant/marchant/*etc.*, while
singing/walking/*etc.* ～ **à coup,** all of a
sudden. ～ **à fait,** quite, completely. ～ **à
l'heure,** in a moment; (*passé*) a
moment ago. ～ **au** *ou* **le long de,**
throughout. ～ **au plus/moins,** at
most/least. ～ **de même,** all the same. ～
de suite, straight away. ～ **entier,**
whole. ～ **le contraire,** quite the
opposite. ～ **neuf,** brand-new. ～ **nu,**
stark naked. ～ **près,** nearby. ～**-
puissant,** ～**e-puissante** *a.* omnipotent.
～ **seul,** alone. ～ **terrain** *a. invar.* all
terrain.

tout[2] /tu/ *n.m.* (*ensemble*) whole. **en ～,**
in all. **pas du ～!,** not at all!

tout-à-l'égout /tutalegu/ *n.m.* main
drainage.

toutefois /tutfwa/ *adv.* however.

toux /tu/ *n.f.* cough.

toxicomane /tɔksikɔman/ *n.m./f.* drug addict.

toxine /tɔksin/ *n.f.* toxin.

toxique /tɔksik/ *a.* toxic.

trac /trak/ *n.m.* le ∼, nerves; (*théâtre*) stage fright.

tracas /traka/ *n.m.* worry. ∼ser /-se/ *v.t.,* se ∼ser *v. pr.* worry.

trace /tras/ *n.f.* trace, mark; (*d'animal, de pneu*) tracks; (*vestige*) trace. **sur la ∼ de,** on the track of. ∼s de pas, footprints.

tracé /trase/ *n.m.* (*ligne*) line; (*plan*) layout.

tracer /trase/ *v.t.* draw, trace; (*écrire*) write; (*route*) mark out.

trachée(-artère) /traʃe(artɛr)/ *n.f.* windpipe.

tract /trakt/ *n.m.* leaflet.

tractations /traktɑsjɔ̃/ *n.f. pl.* dealings.

tracteur /traktœr/ *n.m.* tractor.

traction /traksjɔ̃/ *n.f.* (*sport*) press-up, push-up.

tradition /tradisjɔ̃/ *n.f.* tradition. ∼nel, ∼nelle /-jɔnɛl/ *a.* traditional.

trad|uire† /traduir/ *v.t.* translate; (*sentiment*) express. ∼uire en justice, take to court. ∼ucteur, ∼uctrice *n.m.,* *f.* translator. ∼uction *n.f.* translation.

trafic /trafik/ *n.m.* (*commerce, circulation*) traffic.

trafiqu|er /trafike/ *v.i.* traffic. —*v.t.* (*fam.*) (*vin*) doctor; (*moteur*) fiddle with. ∼ant, ∼ante *n.m.,* *f.* trafficker; (*d'armes, de drogues*) dealer.

tragédie /traʒedi/ *n.f.* tragedy.

tragique /traʒik/ *a.* tragic. ∼ment *adv.* tragically.

trah|ir /trair/ *v.t.* betray. ∼ison *n.f.* betrayal; (*crime*) treason.

train /trɛ̃/ *n.m.* (*rail.*) train; (*allure*) pace. **en ∼,** (*en forme*) in shape. **en ∼ de faire,** (busy) doing. **mettre en ∼,** start up. ∼ **d'atterrissage,** undercarriage. ∼ **électrique,** (*jouet*) electric train set. ∼ **de vie,** lifestyle.

traînard, ∼e /trɛnar, -d/ *n.m.,* *f.* slowcoach; (*Amer.*) slowpoke; (*en marchant*) straggler.

traîne /trɛn/ *n.f.* (*de robe*) train. **à la ∼,** lagging behind; (*en remorque*) in tow.

traîneau (*pl.* ∼x) /trɛno/ *n.m.* sledge.

traînée /trene/ *n.f.* (*trace*) trail; (*bande*) streak; (*femme: péj.*) slut.

traîner /trene/ *v.t.* drag (along); (*véhicule*) pull. —*v.i.* (*pendre*) trail; (*rester en arrière*) trail behind; (*flâner*) hang about; (*papiers, affaires*) lie around. ∼ (**en longueur**), drag on. **se ∼** *v. pr.* (*par terre*) crawl. (**faire**) ∼ **en longueur,** drag out. ∼ **les pieds,** drag one's feet. **ça n'a pas traîné!,** that didn't take long.

train-train /trɛ̃trɛ̃/ *n.m.* routine.

traire† /trɛr/ *v.t.* milk.

trait /trɛ/ *n.m.* line; (*en dessinant*) stroke; (*caractéristique*) feature, trait; (*acte*) act. ∼s, (*du visage*) features. **avoir ∼ à,** relate to. **d'un ∼,** (*boire*) in one gulp. ∼ **d'union,** hyphen; (*fig.*) link.

traite /trɛt/ *n.f.* (*de vache*) milking; (*comm.*) draft. **d'une (seule) ∼,** in one go, at a stretch.

traité /trete/ *n.m.* (*pacte*) treaty; (*ouvrage*) treatise.

traitement /trɛtmɑ̃/ *n.m.* treatment; (*salaire*) salary. ∼ **de données,** data processing. ∼ **de texte,** word processing.

traiter /trete/ *v.t.* treat; (*affaire*) deal with; (*données, produit*) process. ∼ **qn. de lâche/*etc.*,** call s.o. a coward/*etc.* —*v.i.* deal (**avec,** with). ∼ **de,** (*sujet*) deal with.

traiteur /trɛtœr/ *n.m.* caterer; (*boutique*) delicatessen.

traître, ∼sse /trɛtr, -ɛs/ *a.* treacherous. —*n.m./f.* traitor.

trajectoire /traʒɛktwar/ *n.f.* path.

trajet /traʒɛ/ *n.m.* (*à parcourir*) distance; (*voyage*) journey; (*itinéraire*) route.

trame /tram/ *n.f.* (*de tissu*) weft; (*de récit etc.*) framework. **usé jusqu'à la ∼,** threadbare.

trame|r /trame/ *v.t.* plot; (*complot*) hatch. **qu'est ce qui se ∼?,** what's brewing?

tramway /tramwɛ/ *n.m.* tram; (*Amer.*) streetcar.

tranchant, ∼e /trɑ̃ʃɑ̃, -t/ *a.* sharp; (*fig.*) cutting. —*n.m.* cutting edge. **à double ∼,** two-edged.

tranche /trɑ̃ʃ/ *n.f.* (*rondelle*) slice; (*bord*) edge; (*partie*) portion.

tranchée /trɑ̃ʃe/ *n.f.* trench.

tranch|er¹ /trɑ̃ʃe/ *v.t.* cut; (*question*) decide. —*v.i.* (*décider*) decide. ∼é *a.* (*net*) clear-cut.

trancher² /trɑ̃ʃe/ *v.i.* (*contraster*) contrast (**sur,** with).

tranquill|e /trɑ̃kil/ *a.* quiet; (*esprit*) at rest; (*conscience*) clear. **être/laisser ∼e,** be/leave in peace. ∼ement *adv.* quietly. ∼ité *n.f.* (peace and) quiet; (*d'esprit*) peace of mind.

tranquillisant /trãkilizã/ *n.m.* tranquillizer.

tranquilliser /trãkilize/ *v.t.* reassure.

transaction /trãzaksjõ/ *n.f.* transaction.

transat /trãzat/ *n.m.* (*fam.*) deckchair.

transatlantique /trãzatlãtik/ *n.m.* transatlantic liner. —*a.* transatlantic.

transborder /trãsbɔrde/ *v.t.* transfer, transship.

transcend|er /trãsãde/ *v.t.* transcend. ∼**ant**, ∼**ante** *a.* transcendent.

transcr|ire /trãskrir/ *v.t.* transcribe. ∼**iption** *n.f.* transcription; (*copie*) transcript.

transe /trãs/ *n.f.* **en** ∼, in a trance; (*fig.*) very excited.

transférer /trãsfere/ *v.t.* transfer.

transfert /trãsfɛr/ *n.m.* transfer.

transform|er /trãsfɔrme/ *v.t.* change; (*radicalement*) transform; (*vêtement*) alter. **se** ∼**er** *v. pr.* change; be transformed. **(se)** ∼**er en**, turn into. ∼**ateur** *n.m.* transformer. ∼**ation** *n.f.* change; transformation.

transfuge /trãsfyʒ/ *n.m.* renegade.

transfusion /trãsfyzjõ/ *n.f.* transfusion.

transgresser /trãsgrese/ *v.t.* disobey.

transiger /trãsiʒe/ *v.i.* compromise. **ne pas** ∼ **sur**, not compromise on.

transi /trãzi/ *a.* chilled to the bone.

transistor /trãzistɔr/ *n.m.* (*dispositif, poste de radio*) transistor.

transit /trãzit/ *n.m.* transit. ∼**er** *v.t./i.* pass in transit.

transiti|f, ∼**ve** /trãzitif, -v/ *a.* transitive.

transi|tion /trãzisjõ/ *n.f.* transition. ∼**toire** *a.* (*provisoire*) transitional.

translucide /trãslysid/ *a.* translucent.

transm|ettre† /trãsmetr/ *v.t.* pass on; (*techn.*) transmit; (*radio*) broadcast. ∼**ission** *n.f.* transmission; (*radio*) broadcasting.

transparaître /trãsparɛtr/ *v.i.* show (through).

transparen|t, ∼**te** /trãsparã, -t/ *a.* transparent. ∼**ce** *n.f.* transparency.

transpercer /trãsperse/ *v.t.* pierce.

transpir|er /trãspire/ *v.i.* perspire. ∼**ation** *n.f.* perspiration.

transplant|er /trãsplãte/ *v.t.* (*bot., méd.*) transplant. ∼**ation** *n.f.* (*bot.*) transplantation; (*méd.*) transplant.

transport /trãspɔr/ *n.m.* transport(ation); (*sentiment*) rapture. **les** ∼**s**, transport. **les** ∼**s en commun**, public transport.

transport|er /trãspɔrte/ *v.t.* transport; (*à*

la main) carry. **se** ∼**er** *v. pr.* take o.s. (**à**, to). ∼**eur** *n.m.* haulier; (*Amer.*) trucker.

transposer /trãspoze/ *v.t.* transpose.

transvaser /trãsvaze/ *v.t.* decant.

transvers|al (*m. pl.* ∼**aux**) /trãvɛrsal, -o/ *a.* cross, transverse.

trap|èze /trapɛz/ *n.m.* (*sport*) trapeze. ∼**éziste** /-ezist/ *n.m./f.* trapeze artist.

trappe /trap/ *n.f.* trapdoor.

trappeur /trapœr/ *n.m.* trapper.

trapu /trapy/ *a.* stocky.

traquenard /traknar/ *n.m.* trap.

traquer /trake/ *v.t.* track down.

traumatis|me /tromatism/ *n.m.* trauma. ∼**ant**, ∼**ante** /-zã, -t/ *a.* traumatic. ∼**er** /-ze/ *v.t.* traumatize.

trav|ail (*pl.* ∼**aux**) /travaj, -o/ *n.m.* work; (*emploi, poste*) job; (*façonnage*) working. ∼**aux**, work. **en** ∼**ail**, (*femme*) in labour. ∼**ail à la chaîne**, production line work. ∼**ail à la pièce** *ou* **à la tâche**, piece-work. ∼**ail au noir**, (*fam.*) moonlighting. ∼**aux forcés**, hard labour. ∼**aux manuels**, handicrafts. ∼**aux ménagers**, housework.

travaill|er /travaje/ *v.i.* work; (*se déformer*) warp. ∼**er à**, (*livre etc.*) work on. —*v.t.* (*façonner*) work; (*étudier*) work at *ou* on; (*tourmenter*) worry. ∼**eur**, ∼**euse** *n.m.*, *f.* worker; *a.* hardworking.

travailliste /travajist/ *a.* Labour. —*n.m./f.* Labour party member.

travers /travɛr/ *n.m.* (*défaut*) failing. **à** ∼, through. **au** ∼ **(de)**, through. **de** ∼, (*chapeau, nez*) crooked; (*mal*) badly, the wrong way; (*regarder*) askance. **en** ∼ **(de)**, across.

traverse /travɛrs/ *n.f.* (*rail*) sleeper; (*rail, Amer.*) tie.

traversée /travɛrse/ *n.f.* crossing.

traverser /travɛrse/ *v.t.* cross; (*transpercer*) go (right) through; (*période, forêt*) *ou* pass through.

traversin /travɛrsɛ̃/ *n.m.* bolster.

travesti /travɛsti/ *n.m.* transvestite.

travestir /travɛstir/ *v.t.* disguise; (*vérité*) misrepresent.

trébucher /trebyʃe/ *v.i.* stumble, trip (over). **faire** ∼, trip (up).

trèfle /trefl/ *n.m.* (*plante*) clover; (*cartes*) clubs.

treillage /trejaʒ/ *n.m.* trellis.

treillis[1] /treji/ *n.m.* trellis; (*en métal*) wire mesh.

treillis[2] /treji/ *n.m.* (*tenue militaire*) combat uniform.

treiz|e /trɛz/ *a. & n.m.* thirteen. ∼**ième** *a. & n.m./f.* thirteenth.

tréma /trema/ *n.m.* diaeresis.

trembl|er /trãble/ *v.i.* shake, tremble; (*lumière*, *voix*) quiver. **~ement** *n.m.* shaking; (*frisson*) shiver. **~ement de terre,** earthquake.

trembloter /trãblɔte/ *v.i.* quiver.

trémousser (se) /(sə)tremuse/ *v. pr.* wriggle, wiggle.

trempe /trãp/ *n.f.* (*caractère*) calibre.

tremper /trãpe/ *v.t./i.* soak; (*plonger*) dip; (*acier*) temper. **mettre à ~ ou faire ~,** soak. **~ dans,** (*fig.*) be involved in. **se ~** *v. pr.* (*se baigner*) have a dip.

trempette /trãpɛt/ *n.f.* **faire ~,** have a little dip.

tremplin /trãplɛ̃/ *n.m.* springboard.

trentaine /trãtɛn/ *n.f.* **une ~ (de),** about thirty. **il a la ~,** he's about thirty.

trent|e /trãt/ *a. & n.m.* thirty. **~ième** *a. & n.m./f.* thirtieth. **se mettre sur son ~e et un,** put on one's Sunday best. **tous les ~e-six du mois,** once in a blue moon.

trépider /trepide/ *v.i.* vibrate.

trépied /trepje/ *n.m.* tripod.

trépigner /trepiɲe/ *v.i.* stamp one's feet.

très /trɛ/ (/trɛz/ *before vowel*) *adv.* very. **~ aimé/estimé,** much liked/esteemed.

trésor /trezɔr/ *n.m.* treasure; (*ressources*: *comm.*) finances. **le T~,** the revenue department.

trésorerie /trezɔrri/ *n.f.* (*bureaux*) accounts department; (*du Trésor*) revenue office; (*argent*) finances; (*gestion*) accounts.

trésor|ier, ~ière /trezɔrje, -jɛr/ *n.m.*, *f.* treasurer.

tressaill|ir /tresajir/ *v.i.* shake, quiver; (*sursauter*) start. **~ement** *n.m.* quiver; start.

tressauter /tresote/ *v.i.* (*sursauter*) start, jump.

tresse /trɛs/ *n.f.* braid, plait.

tresser /trese/ *v.t.* braid, plait.

tréteau (*pl.* **~x**) /treto/ *n.m.* trestle. **~x,** (*théâtre*) stage.

treuil /trœj/ *n.m.* winch.

trêve /trɛv/ *n.f.* truce; (*fig.*) respite. **~ de plaisanteries,** enough of this joking.

tri /tri/ *n.m.* (*classement*) sorting; (*sélection*) selection. **faire le ~ de,** sort; select. **~age** /-jaʒ/ *n.m.* sorting.

triang|le /trijãgl/ *n.m.* triangle. **~ulaire** *a.* triangular.

trib|al (*m. pl.* **~aux**) /tribal, -o/ *a.* tribal.

tribord /tribɔr/ *n.m.* starboard.

tribu /triby/ *n.f.* tribe.

tribulations /tribylɑsjɔ̃/ *n.f. pl.* tribulations.

tribun|al (*m. pl.* **~aux**) /tribynal, -o/ *n.m.* court. **~al d'instance,** magistrates' court.

tribune /tribyn/ *n.f.* (public) gallery; (*dans un stade*) grandstand; (*d'orateur*) rostrum; (*débat*) forum.

tribut /triby/ *n.m.* tribute.

tributaire /tribytɛr/ *a.* **~ de,** dependent on.

trich|er /triʃe/ *v.i.* cheat. **~erie** *n.f.* cheating. **une ~erie,** piece of trickery. **~eur, ~euse** *n.m.*, *f.* cheat.

tricolore /trikɔlɔr/ *a.* three-coloured; (*français*) red, white and blue; (*français*: *fig.*) French.

tricot /triko/ *n.m.* knitting; (*pull*) sweater. **en ~,** knitted. **~ de corps,** vest; (*Amer.*) undershirt. **~er** /-ɔte/ *v.t./i.* knit.

trictrac /triktrak/ *n.m.* backgammon.

tricycle /trisikl/ *n.m.* tricycle.

trier /trije/ *v.t.* (*classer*) sort; (*choisir*) select.

trilogie /trilɔʒi/ *n.f.* trilogy.

trimbaler /trɛ̃bale/ *v.t.*, **se ~** *v. pr.* (*fam.*) trail around.

trimer /trime/ *v.i.* (*fam.*) slave.

trimestr|e /trimɛstr/ *n.m.* quarter; (*scol.*) term. **~iel, ~ielle** *a.* quarterly; (*bulletin*) end-of-term.

tringle /trɛ̃gl/ *n.f.* rod.

Trinité /trinite/ *n.f.* **la ~,** (*dogme*) the Trinity; (*fête*) Trinity.

trinquer /trɛ̃ke/ *v.i.* clink glasses.

trio /trijo/ *n.m.* trio.

triomph|e /trijɔ̃f/ *n.m.* triumph. **~al** (*m. pl.* **~aux**) *a.* triumphant.

triomph|er /trijɔ̃fe/ *v.i.* triumph (**de,** over); (*jubiler*) be triumphant. **~ant, ~ante** *a.* triumphant.

trip|es /trip/ *n.f. pl.* (*mets*) tripe; (*entrailles*: *fam.*) guts.

triple /tripl/ *a.* triple, treble. —*n.m.* **le ~,** three times as much (**de,** as). **~ment** /-əmã/ *adv.* trebly.

tripl|er /triple/ *v.t./i.* triple, treble. **~és, ~ées** *n.m.*, *f. pl.* triplets.

tripot /tripo/ *n.m.* gambling den.

tripoter /tripɔte/ *v.t.* (*fam.*) fiddle with. —*v.i.* (*fam.*) fiddle about.

trique /trik/ *n.f.* cudgel.

trisomique /trizɔmik/ *a.* **enfant ~,** Down's (syndrome) child.

triste /trist/ *a.* sad; (*rue, temps, couleur*) gloomy; (*lamentable*) wretched, dreadful. **~ment** /- əmã/ *adv.* sadly. **~sse** /-ɛs/ *n.f.* sadness; gloominess.

triv|ial (*m. pl.* ～**iaux**) /trivjal, -jo/ *a.* coarse. ～**ialité** *n.f.* coarseness.

troc /trɔk/ *n.m.* exchange; (*comm.*) barter.

troène /trɔɛn/ *n.m.* (*bot.*) privet.

trognon /trɔɲɔ̃/ *n.m.* (*de pomme*) core.

trois /trwa/ *a.* & *n.m.* three. **hôtel** ～**étoiles**, three-star hotel. ～**ième** /-zjɛm/ *a.* & *n.m./f.* third. ～**ièmement** /-zjɛmmɑ̃/ *adv.* thirdly.

trombe /trɔ̃b/ *n.f.* ～ **d'eau,** downpour.

trombone /trɔ̃bɔn/ *n.m.* (*mus.*) trombone; (*agrafe*) paper-clip.

trompe /trɔ̃p/ *n.f.* (*d'éléphant*) trunk; (*mus.*) horn.

tromp|er /trɔ̃pe/ *v.t.* deceive, mislead; (*déjouer*) elude. **se** ～**er** *v. pr.* be mistaken. **se** ～**er de route/train/***etc.*, take the wrong road/train/*etc.* ～**erie** *n.f.* deception. ～**eur,** ～**euse** *a.* (*personne*) deceitful; (*chose*) deceptive.

trompette /trɔ̃pɛt/ *n.f.* trumpet.

tronc /trɔ̃/ *n.m.* trunk; (*boîte*) collection box.

tronçon /trɔ̃sɔ̃/ *n.m.* section. ～**ner** /-ɔne/ *v.t.* cut into sections.

trôn|e /tron/ *n.m.* throne. ～**er** *v.i.* occupy the place of honour.

tronquer /trɔ̃ke/ *v.t.* truncate.

trop /tro/ *adv.* (*grand, loin, etc*) too; (*boire, marcher,* etc.) too much. ～ **(de),** (*quantité*) too much; (*nombre*) too many. **c'est** ～ **chauffé,** it's overheated. **de** ～**, en** ～ too much; too many. **il a bu un verre de** ～**,** he's had one too many. **de** ～**,** (*intrus*) in the way. ～**-plein** *n.m.* excess; (*dispositif*) overflow.

trophée /trɔfe/ *n.m.* trophy.

tropic|al (*m. pl.* ～**aux**) /trɔpikal, -o/ *a.* tropical.

tropique /trɔpik/ *n.m.* tropic. ～**s,** tropics.

troquer /trɔke/ *v.t.* exchange; (*comm.*) barter (**contre,** for).

trot /tro/ *n.m.* trot. **aller au** ～**,** trot. **au** ～**,** (*fam.*) on the double.

trotter /trɔte/ *v.i.* trot.

trotteuse /trɔtøz/ *n.f.* (*aiguille de montre*) second hand.

trottiner /trɔtine/ *v.i.* patter along.

trottinette /trɔtinɛt/ *n.f.* (*jouet*) scooter.

trottoir /trɔtwar/ *n.m.* pavement; (*Amer.*) sidewalk. ～ **roulant,** moving walkway.

trou /tru/ *n.m.* hole; (*moment*) gap; (*lieu: péj.*) dump. ～ **(de mémoire),** lapse (of memory). ～ **de la serrure,** keyhole. **faire son** ～**,** carve one's niche.

trouble /trubl/ *a.* (*eau, image*) unclear; (*louche*) shady. —*n.m.* agitation. ～**s,** (*pol.*) disturbances; (*méd.*) trouble.

troubl|er /truble/ *v.t.* disturb; (*eau*) make cloudy; (*inquiéter*) trouble. ～**ant,** ～**ante** *a.* disturbing. **se** ～**er** *v. pr.* (*personne*) become flustered. ～**e-fête** *n.m./ f. invar.* killjoy.

trouée /true/ *n.f.* gap, open space; (*mil.*) breach (**dans,** in).

trouer /true/ *v.t.* make a hole *ou* holes in. **mes chaussures se sont trouées,** my shoes have got holes in them.

trouille /truj/ *n.f.* **avoir la** ～**,** (*fam.*) be scared.

troupe /trup/ *n.f.* troop; (*d'acteurs*) troupe. ～**s,** (*mil.*) troops.

troupeau (*pl.* ～**x**) /trupo/ *n.m.* herd; (*de moutons*) flock.

trousse /trus/ *n.f.* case, bag; (*de réparations*) kit. **aux** ～**s de,** on the tail of. ～ **de toilette,** toilet bag.

trousseau (*pl.* ～**x**) /truso/ *n.m.* (*de clefs*) bunch; (*de mariée*) trousseau.

trouvaille /truvaj/ *n.f.* find.

trouver /truve/ *v.t.* find; (*penser*) think. **aller/venir** ～**,** (*rendre visite à*) go/come and see. **se** ～ *v. pr.* find o.s.; (*être*) be; (*se sentir*) feel. **il se trouve que,** it happens that. **se** ～ **mal,** faint.

truand /tryɑ̃/ *n m* gangster.

truc /tryk/ *n.m.* (*moyen*) way; (*artifice*) trick, (*chose. fam.*) thing. ～**age** *n.m.* = **truquage.**

truchement /tryʃmɑ̃/ *n.m.* **par le** ～ **de,** through.

truculent, ～**e** /trykylɑ̃, -t/ *a.* colourful.

truelle /tryɛl/ *n.f.* trowel.

truffe /tryf/ *n f* (*champignon, chocolat*) truffle; (*nez*) nose.

truffer /tryfe/ *v.t.* (*fam.*) fill, pack (**de,** with).

truie /trɥi/ *n.f.* (*animal*) sow.

truite /trɥit/ *n.f.* trout.

truqu|er /tryke/ *v.t.* fix, rig; (*photo, texte*) fake. ～**age** *n.m.* fixing; faking; (*cinéma*) special effect.

trust /trœst/ *n.m.* (*comm.*) trust.

tsar /tsar/ *n.m.* tsar, czar.

tsigane /tsigan/ *a.* & *n.m./f.* (Hungarian) gypsy.

tu[1] /ty/ *pron.* (*parent, ami, enfant, etc.*) you.

tu[2] /ty/ *voir* **taire.**

tuba /tyba/ *n.m.* (*mus.*) tuba; (*sport*) snorkel.

tube /tyb/ *n.m.* tube.

tubercul|eux, ～**euse** /tybɛrkylø, -z/ *a.*

être ∼eux, have tuberculosis. **∼ose** *n.f.* tuberculosis.

tubulaire /tybylɛr/ *a.* tubular.

tubulure /tybylyr/ *n.f.* tubing.

tu|er /tɥe/ *v.t.* kill; (*d'une balle*) shoot, kill; (*épuiser*) exhaust. **se ∼er** *v. pr.* kill o.s.; (*accident*) be killed. **∼ant, ∼ante,** *a.* exhausting. **∼é, ∼ée** *n.m., f.* person killed. **∼eur, ∼euse** *n.m., f.* killer.

tuerie /tyri/ *n.f.* slaughter.

tue-tête (à) /(a)tytɛt/ *adv.* at the top of one's voice.

tuile /tɥil/ *n.f.* tile; (*malchance*: *fam.*) (stroke of) bad luck.

tulipe /tylip/ *n.f.* tulip.

tuméfié /tymefje/ *a.* swollen.

tumeur /tymœr/ *n.f.* tumour.

tumult|e /tymylt/ *n.m.* commotion; (*désordre*) turmoil. **∼ueux, ∼ueuse** *a.* turbulent.

tunique /tynik/ *n.f.* tunic.

Tunisie /tynizi/ *n.f.* Tunisia.

tunisien, ∼ne /tynizjɛ̃, -jɛn/ *a. & n.m., f.* Tunisian.

tunnel /tynɛl/ *n.m.* tunnel.

turban /tyrbɑ̃/ *n.m.* turban.

turbine /tyrbin/ *n.f.* turbine.

turbo /tyrbɔ/ *a.* turbo. *n.f.* (*voiture*) turbo.

turbulen|t, ∼te /tyrbylɑ̃, -t/ *a.* boisterous, turbulent. **∼ce** *n.f.* turbulence.

tur|c, ∼que /tyrk/ *a.* Turkish. —*n.m., f.* Turk. —*n.m.* (*lang.*) Turkish.

turf /tyrf/ *n.m.* **le ∼,** the turf. **∼iste** *n.m./f.* racegoer.

Turquie /tyrki/ *n.f.* Turkey.

turquoise /tyrkwaz/ *a. invar.* turquoise.

tutelle /tytɛl/ *n.f.* (*jurid.*) guardianship; (*fig.*) protection.

tu|teur, ∼trice /tytœr, -tris/ *n.m., f.* (*jurid.*) guardian. —*n.m.* (*bâton*) stake.

tut|oyer /tytwaje/ *v.t.* address familiarly (using *tu*). **∼oiement** *n.m.* use of (familiar) *tu*.

tuyau (*pl.* **∼x**) /tɥijo/ *n.m.* pipe; (*conseil*: *fam.*) tip. **∼ d'arrosage,** hose-pipe. **∼ter** *v.t.* (*fam.*) give a tip to. **∼terie** *n.f.* piping.

TVA *abrév.* (*taxe sur la valeur ajoutée*) VAT.

tympan /tɛ̃pɑ̃/ *n.m.* ear-drum.

type /tip/ *n.m.* (*modèle*) type; (*traits*) features; (*individu*: *fam.*) bloke, guy. —*a. invar.* typical. **le ∼ même de,** a classic example of.

typhoïde /tifɔid/ *n.f.* typhoid (fever).

typhon /tifɔ̃/ *n.m.* typhoon.

typhus /tifys/ *n.m.* typhus.

typique /tipik/ *a.* typical. **∼ment** *adv.* typically.

tyran /tirɑ̃/ *n.m.* tyrant.

tyrann|ie /tirani/ *n.f.* tyranny. **∼ique** *a.* tyrannical. **∼iser** *v.t.* oppress, tyrannize.

U

ulcère /ylsɛr/ *n.m.* ulcer.

ulcérer /ylsere/ *v.t.* (*vexer*) embitter, gall.

ULM *abrév. m.* (*ultraléger motorisé*) microlight.

ultérieur /ylterjœr/ *a.,* **∼ement** *adv.* later.

ultimatum /yltimatɔm/ *n.m.* ultimatum.

ultime /yltim/ *a.* final.

ultra /yltra/ *n.m./f.* hardliner.

ultra- /yltra/ *préf.* ultra-.

un, une /œ̃, yn/ *a.* one; (*indéfini*) a, an. **un enfant,** /œ̃nɑ̃fɑ̃/ a child. —*pron. & n.m., f.* one. **l'un,** one. **les uns,** some. **l'un et l'autre,** both. **l'un l'autre, les uns les autres,** each other. **l'un ou l'autre,** either. **la une,** (*de journal*) front page. **un autre,** another. **un par un,** one by one.

unanim|e /ynanim/ *a.* unanimous. **∼ité** *n.f.* unanimity. **à l'∼ité,** unanimously.

uni /yni/ *a.* united; (*couple*) close; (*surface*) smooth; (*sans dessins*) plain.

unième /ynjɛm/ *a.* -first. **vingt et ∼,** twenty-first. **cent ∼,** one hundred and first.

unif|ier /ynifje/ *v.t.* unify. **∼ication** *n.f.* unification.

uniform|e /ynifɔrm/ *n.m.* uniform. —*a.* uniform. **∼ément** *adv.* uniformly. **∼iser** *v.t.* standardize. **∼ité** *n.f.* uniformity.

unilatér|al (*m. pl.* **∼aux**) /ynilateral, -o/ *a.* unilateral.

union /ynjɔ̃/ *n.f.* union. **l'U∼ soviétique,** the Soviet Union.

unique /ynik/ *a.* (*seul*) only; (*prix, voie*) one; (*incomparable*) unique. **enfant ∼,** only child. **sens ∼,** one-way street. **∼ment** *adv.* only, solely.

unir /ynir/ *v.t.,* **s'∼** *v. pr.* unite, join.

unisson (à l') /(al)ynisɔ̃/ *adv.* in unisson.

unité /ynite/ *n.f.* unit; (*harmonie*) unity.

univers /ynivɛr/ *n.m.* universe.

universel, ∼le /ynivɛrsɛl/ *a.* universal.

universit|é /ynivɛrsite/ *n.f.* university. **~aire** *a.* university; *n.m./f.* academic.

uranium /yranjɔm/ *n.m.* uranium.

urbain, ~e /yrbɛ̃, -ɛn/ *a.* urban.

urbanisme /yrbanism/ *n.m.* town planning; (*Amer.*) city planning.

urgence /yrʒɑ̃s/ *n.f.* (*cas*) emergency; (*de situation, tâche, etc.*) urgency. **d'~** *a.* emergency; *adv.* urgently.

urgent, ~e /yrʒɑ̃, -t/ *a.* urgent.

urger /yrʒe/ *v.i.* **ça urge!,** (*fam.*) it's getting urgent.

urin|e /yrin/ *n.f.* urine. **~er** *v.i.* urinate.

urinoir /yrinwar/ *n.m.* urinal.

urne /yrn/ *n.f.* (*électorale*) ballot-box; (*vase*) urn. **aller aux ~s,** go to the polls.

URSS *abrév.* (*Union des Républiques Socialistes Soviétiques*) USSR.

urticaire /yrtikɛr/ *n.f.* **une crise d'~,** nettle rash.

us /ys/ *n.m. pl.* **les us et coutumes,** habits and customs.

usage /yzaʒ/ *n.m.* use; (*coutume*) custom; (*de langage*) usage. **à l'~ de,** for. **d'~,** (*habituel*) customary. **faire ~ de,** make use of.

usagé /yzaʒe/ *a.* worn.

usager /yzaʒe/ *n.m.* user.

usé /yze/ *a.* worn (out); (*banal*) trite.

user /yze/ *v.t.* wear (out); (*consommer*) use (up). —*v.i.* **~ de,** use. **s'~** *v. pr.* (*tissu etc.*) wear (out).

usine /yzin/ *n.f.* factory; (*de métallurgie*) works.

usité /yzite/ *a.* common.

ustensile /ystɑ̃sil/ *n.m.* utensil.

usuel, ~le /yzɥɛl/ *a.* ordinary, everyday.

usufruit /yzyfrɥi/ *n.m.* usufruct.

usure /yzyr/ *n.f.* (*détérioration*) wear (and tear).

usurper /yzyrpe/ *v.t.* usurp.

utérus /yterys/ *n.m.* womb, uterus.

utile /ytil/ *a.* useful. **~ment** *adv.* usefully.

utilis|er /ytilize/ *v.t.* use. **~able** *a.* usable. **~ation** *n.f.* use.

utilitaire /ytiliter/ *a.* utilitarian.

utilité /ytilite/ *n.f.* use(fulness).

utop|ie /ytɔpi/ *n.f.* Utopia; (*idée*) Utopian idea. **~ique** *a.* Utopian.

UV *abrév. f.* (*unité de valeur*) (*scol.*) credit.

V

va /va/ *voir* **aller**[1].

vacanc|e /vakɑ̃s/ *n.f.* (*poste*) vacancy. **~es,** holiday(s); (*Amer.*) vacation. **en ~es,** on holiday. **~ier, ~ière** *n.m., f.* holiday-maker; (*Amer.*) vacationer.

vacant, ~e /vakɑ̃, -t/ *a.* vacant.

vacarme /vakarm/ *n.m.* uproar.

vaccin /vaksɛ̃/ *n.m.* vaccine; (*inoculation*) vaccination.

vaccin|er /vaksine/ *v.t.* vaccinate. **~ation** *n.f.* vaccination.

vache /vaʃ/ *n.f.* cow. —*a.* (*méchant: fam.*) nasty. **~ment** *adv.* (*très: fam.*) damned; (*pleuvoir, manger, etc.: fam.*) a hell of a lot. **~rie** *n.f.* (*fam.*) nastiness; (*chose: fam.*) nasty thing.

vacill|er /vasije/ *v.i.* sway, wobble; (*lumière*) flicker; (*fig.*) falter. **~ant, ~ante** *a.* (*mémoire, démarche*) shaky.

vadrouiller /vadruje/ *v.i.* (*fam.*) wander about.

va-et-vient /vaevjɛ̃/ *n.m. invar.* to and fro (*motion*); (*de personnes*) comings and goings.

vagabond, ~e /vagabɔ̃, -d/ *n.m., f.* (*péj.*) vagrant, vagabond. **~er** /-de/ *v.i.* wander.

vagin /vaʒɛ̃/ *n.m.* vagina.

vagir /vaʒir/ *v.i.* cry.

vague[1] /vag/ *a.* vague. —*n.m.* vagueness. **il est resté dans le ~,** he was vague about it. **~ment** *adv.* vaguely.

vague[2] /vag/ *n.f.* wave. **~ de fond,** ground swell. **~ de froid,** cold spell. **~ de chaleur,** hot spell.

vaill|ant, ~ante /vajɑ̃, -t/ *a.* brave; (*vigoureux*) healthy. **~amment** /-amɑ̃/ *adv.* bravely.

vaille /vaj/ *voir* **valoir**.

vain, ~e /vɛ̃, vɛn/ *a.* vain. **en ~,** in vain. **~ement** /vɛnmɑ̃/ *adv.* vainly.

vain|cre[†] /vɛ̃kr/ *v.t.* defeat; (*surmonter*) overcome. **~cu, ~cue** *n.m., f.* (*sport*) loser. **~queur** *n.m.* victor; (*sport*) winner.

vais /vɛ/ *voir* **aller**[1].

vaisseau (*pl.* **~x**) /vɛso/ *n.m.* ship; (*veine*) vessel. **~ spatial,** space-ship.

vaisselle /vɛsɛl/ *n.f.* crockery; (*à laver*) dishes. **faire la ~,** do the washing-up, wash the dishes. **produit pour la ~,** washing-up liquid.

val (*pl.* **~s** *ou* **vaux**) /val, vo/ *n.m.* valley.

valable /valabl/ *a.* valid; (*de qualité*) worthwhile.

valet /valɛ/ *n.m.* (*cartes*) jack. **~ (de chambre),** manservant. **~ de ferme,** farm-hand.

valeur /valœr/ *n.f.* value; (*mérite*) worth, value. **~s,** (*comm.*) stocks and shares. **avoir de la ~,** be valuable.

valid|e /valid/ *a.* (*personne*) fit; (*billet*) valid. **~er** *v.t.* validate. **~ité** *n.f.* validity.

valise /valiz/ *n.f.* (suit)case. **faire ses ~s,** pack (one's bags).

vallée /vale/ *n.f.* valley.

vallon /valɔ̃/ *n.m.* (small) valley. **~né** /-ɔne/ *a.* undulating.

valoir† /valwar/ *v.i.* be worth; (*s'appliquer*) apply. **~ qch.,** be worth sth.; (*être aussi bon que*) be as good as sth. —*v.t.* **~ qch. à qn.,** bring s.o. sth. **se ~** *v. pr.* (*être équivalents*) be as good as each other. **faire ~,** put forward to advantage; (*droit*) assert. **~ la peine, ~ le coup,** be worth it. **ça ne vaut rien,** it is no good. **il vaudrait mieux faire,** we'd better do. **ça ne me dit rien qui vaille,** I don't think much of it.

valoriser /valɔrize/ *v.t.* add value to. **se sentir valorisé,** feel valued.

vals|e /vals/ *n.f.* waltz. **~er** *v.i.* waltz.

valve /valv/ *n.f.* valve.

vampire /vɑ̃pir/ *n.m.* vampire.

van /vɑ̃/ *n.m.* van.

vandal|e /vɑ̃dal/ *n.m./f.* vandal. **~isme** *n.m.* vandalism.

vanille /vanij/ *n.f.* vanilla.

vanit|é /vanite/ *n.f.* vanity. **~eux, ~euse** *a.* vain, conceited.

vanne /van/ *n.f.* (*d'écluse*) sluice(-gate); (*fam.*) joke.

vant|ail (*pl.* **~aux**) /vɑ̃taj, -o/ *n.m.* door, flap.

vantard, ~e /vɑ̃tar, -d/ *a.* boastful; *n.m., f.* boaster. **~ise** /-diz/ *n.f.* boastfulness; (*acte*) boast.

vanter /vɑ̃te/ *v.t.* praise. **se ~** *v. pr.* boast (**de,** about).

va-nu-pieds /vanypje/ *n.m./f. invar.* vagabond, beggar.

vapeur¹ /vapœr/ *n.f.* (*eau*) steam; (*brume, émanation*) vapour.

vapeur² /vapœr/ *n.m.* (*bateau*) steamer.

vaporeu|x, ~se /vapɔrø, -z/ *a.* hazy; (*léger*) filmy, flimsy.

vaporis|er /vapɔrize/ *v.t.* spray. **~ateur** *n.m.* spray.

vaquer /vake/ *v.i.* **~ à,** attend to.

varappe /varap/ *n.f.* rock climbing.

vareuse /varøz/ *n.f.* (*d'uniforme*) tunic.

variable /varjabl/ *a.* variable; (*temps*) changeable.

variante /varjɑ̃t/ *n.f.* variant.

varicelle /varisɛl/ *n.f.* chicken-pox.

varices /varis/ *n.f. pl.* varicose veins.

var|ier /varje/ *v.t./i.* vary. **~iation** *n.f.* variation. **~ié** *a.* (*non monotone, étendu*) varied; (*divers*) various.

variété /varjete/ *n.f.* variety. **~s,** (*spectacle*) variety.

variole /varjɔl/ *n.f.* smallpox.

vase¹ /vɑz/ *n.m.* vase.

vase² /vɑz/ *n.f.* (*boue*) silt, mud.

vaseu|x, ~se /vɑzø, -z/ *a.* (*confus*: *fam.*) woolly, hazy.

vasistas /vazistɑs/ *n.m.* fanlight, hinged panel (*in door or window*).

vaste /vast/ *a.* vast, huge.

vaudeville /vodvil/ *n.m.* vaudeville, light comedy.

vau-l'eau (à) /(a)volo/ *adv.* downhill.

vaurien, ~ne /vorjɛ̃, -jɛn/ *n.m., f.* good-for-nothing.

vautour /votur/ *n.m.* vulture.

vautrer (se) /(sə)votre/ *v. pr.* sprawl. **se ~ dans,** (*vice, boue*) wallow in.

va-vite (à la) /(ala)vavit/ *adv.* (*fam.*) in a hurry.

veau (*pl.* **~x**) /vo/ *n.m.* calf; (*viande*) veal; (*cuir*) calfskin.

vécu /veky/ *voir* **vivre.** —*a.* (*réel*) true, real.

vedette¹ /vədɛt/ *n.f.* (*artiste*) star. **en ~,** (*objet*) in a prominent position; (*personne*) in the limelight.

vedette² /vədɛt/ *n.f.* (*bateau*) launch.

végét|al (*m. pl.* **~aux**) /veʒetal, -o/ *a.* plant. —*n.m.* (*pl.* **~aux**) plant.

végétalien, ~ne /veʒetaljɛ̃, -jɛn/ *n.m., f. & a.* vegan.

végétarien, ~ne /veʒetarjɛ̃, -jɛn/ *a. & n.m., f.* vegetarian.

végétation /veʒetɑsjɔ̃/ *n.f.* vegetation. **~s,** (*méd.*) adenoids.

végéter /veʒete/ *v.i.* vegetate.

véhémen|t, ~te /veemɑ̃, -t/ *a.* vehement. **~ce** *n.f.* vehemence.

véhicul|e /veikyl/ *n.m.* vehicle. **~er** *v.t.* convey.

veille¹ /vɛj/ *n.f.* **la ~ (de),** the day before. **la ~ de Noël,** Christmas Eve. **à la ~ de,** on the eve of.

veille² /vɛj/ *n.f.* (*état*) wakefulness.

veillée /veje/ *n.f.* evening (gathering); (*mortuaire*) vigil, wake.

veiller /veje/ *v.i.* stay up *ou* awake. **~ à,** attend to. **~ sur,** watch over. —*v.t.* (*malade*) watch over.

veilleur /vɛjœr/ *n.m.* **~ de nuit,** night-watchman.

veilleuse /vɛjøz/ *n.f.* night-light; (*de véhicule*) sidelight; (*de réchaud*) pilot-light. **mettre qch. en ~,** put sth. on the back burner.

veinard, ~e /vɛnar, -d/ n.m., f. (fam.)
lucky devil.

veine¹ /vɛn/ n.f. (anat.) vein; (nervure,
filon) vein.

veine² /vɛn/ n.f. (chance: fam.) luck.
avoir de la ~, (fam.) be lucky.

velcro /vɛlkrɔ/ n.m. (P.) velcro.

véliplanchiste /veliplɑ̃ʃist/ n.m./f.
windsurfer.

vélo /velo/ n.m. bicycle, bike; (activité)
cycling.

vélodrome /velɔdrɔm/ n.m. velodrome,
cycle-racing track.

vélomoteur /velɔmɔtœr/ n.m. moped.

velours /vlur/ n.m. velvet. ~ **côtelé**, ~ **à
côtes**, corduroy.

velouté /velute/ a. smooth. —n.m.
smoothness.

velu /vəly/ a. hairy.

venaison /vənɛzɔ̃/ n.f. venison.

vendange|s /vɑ̃dɑ̃ʒ/ n.f. pl. grape
harvest. ~**er** v.i. pick the grapes. ~**eur**,
~**euse** n.m., f. grape-picker.

vendetta /vɑ̃deta/ n.f. vendetta.

vendeu|r, ~**se** /vɑ̃dœr, -øz/ n.m., f.
shop assistant; (marchand) salesman,
saleswoman; (jurid.) vendor, seller.

vendre /vɑ̃dr/ v.t., **se** ~ v. pr. sell. **à** ~,
for sale.

vendredi /vɑ̃drədi/ n.m. Friday. **V~
saint**, Good Friday.

vénéneu|x, ~**se** /venenø, -z/ a.
poisonous.

vénérable /venerabl/ a. venerable.

vénérer /venere/ v.t. revere.

vénérien, ~**ne** /venerjɛ̃, -jɛn/ a.
venereal.

vengeance /vɑ̃ʒɑ̃s/ n.f. revenge, vengeance.

veng|er /vɑ̃ʒe/ v.t. avenge. **se** ~**er** v. pr.
take (one's) revenge (**de**, for). ~**eur**,
~**eresse** a. vengeful; n.m., f. avenger.

ven|in /vənɛ̃/ n.m. venom. ~**imeux**,
~**imeuse** a. poisonous, venomous.

venir† /vənir/ v.i. (aux. être) come (**de**,
from). ~ **faire**, come to do. **venez faire**,
come and do. ~ **de faire**, to have just
done. **il vient/venait d'arriver**, he
has/had just arrived. **en** ~ **à**, (question,
conclusion, etc.) come to. **en** ~ **aux
mains**, come to blows. **faire** ~, send
for. **il m'est venu à l'esprit** ou **à l'idée
que**, it occurred to me that.

vent /vɑ̃/ n.m. wind. **être dans le** ~,
(fam.) be with it. **il fait du** ~, it is
windy.

vente /vɑ̃t/ n.f. sale. ~ **(aux enchères)**,
auction. **en** ~, on ou for sale. ~ **de
charité**, (charity) bazaar.

ventil|er /vɑ̃tile/ v.t. ventilate. ~**ateur**
n.m. fan, ventilator. ~**ation** n.f.
ventilation.

ventouse /vɑ̃tuz/ n.f. (dispositif) suction
pad; (pour déboucher l'évier etc.)
plunger.

ventre /vɑ̃tr/ n.m. belly, stomach;
(utérus) womb. **avoir/prendre du** ~,
have/develop a paunch.

ventriloque /vɑ̃trilɔk/ n.m./f. ventriloquist.

ventru /vɑ̃try/ a. pot-bellied.

venu /vəny/ voir **venir**. —a. **bien** ~, (à
propos) timely. **mal** ~, untimely. **être
mal** ~ **de faire**, have no grounds for
doing.

venue /vəny/ n.f. coming.

vêpres /vɛpr/ n.f. pl. vespers.

ver /vɛr/ n.m. worm; (des fruits, de la
viande) maggot; (du bois) woodworm.
~ **luisant**, glow-worm. ~ **à soie**,
silkworm. ~ **solitaire**, tapeworm. ~ **de
terre**, earthworm.

véranda /verɑ̃da/ n.f. veranda.

verb|e /vɛrb/ n.m. (gram.) verb. ~**al** (m.
pl. ~**aux**) a. verbal.

verdâtre /vɛrdɑtr/ a. greenish.

verdict /vɛrdikt/ n.m. verdict.

verdir /vɛrdir/ v.i. turn green.

verdoyant, ~**e** /vɛrdwajɑ̃, -t/ a. green,
verdant.

verdure /vɛrdyr/ n.f. greenery.

véreu|x, ~**se** /verø, -z/ a. maggoty,
wormy; (malhonnête: fig.) shady.

verger /vɛrʒe/ n.m. orchard.

vergla|s /vɛrɡla/ n.m. (black) ice;
(Amer.) sleet. ~**cé** a. icy.

vergogne (sans) /(sɑ̃)vɛrɡɔɲ/ a. shameless. —adv. shamelessly.

véridique /veridik/ a. truthful.

vérif|ier /verifje/ v.t. check, verify;
(compte) audit; (confirmer) confirm.
~**ication** n.f. check(ing), verification.

véritable /veritabl/ a. true, real;
(authentique) real. ~**ment** /-əmɑ̃/ adv.
really.

vérité /verite/ n.f. truth; (de tableau,
roman) trueness to life. **en** ~, in fact.

vermeil, ~**le** /vɛrmɛj/ a. bright red.

vermicelle(s) /vɛrmisɛl/ n.m. (pl.)
vermicelli.

vermine /vɛrmin/ n.f. vermin.

vermoulu /vɛrmuly/ a. wormeaten.

vermouth /vɛrmut/ n.m. (apéritif)
vermouth.

verni /vɛrni/ a. (fam.) lucky.
chaussures ~**es**, patent (leather) shoes.

vernir /vɛrnir/ v.t. varnish.

vernis /vɛrni/ n.m. varnish; (de poterie)

glaze. ~ **à ongles,** nail polish *ou* varnish.

vernissage /vɛrnisaʒ/ *n.m.* (*exposition*) preview.

vernisser /vɛrnise/ *v.t.* glaze.

verra, verrait /vɛra, vɛrɛ/ *voir* **voir.**

verre /vɛr/ *n.m.* glass. **prendre** *ou* **boire un** ~, have a drink. ~ **de contact,** contact lens. ~ **dépoli/grossissant,** frosted/magnifying glass. ~**rie** *n.f.* (*objets*) glassware.

verrière /vɛrjɛr/ *n.f.* (*toit*) glass roof; (*paroi*) glass wall.

verrou /vɛru/ *n.m.* bolt. **sous les** ~**s,** behind bars.

verrouiller /vɛruje/ *v.t.* bolt.

verrue /vɛry/ *n.f.* wart.

vers[1] /vɛr/ *prép.* towards; (*temps*) about.

vers[2] /vɛr/ *n.m.* (*ligne*) line. **les** ~, (*poésie*) verse.

versant /vɛrsã/ *n.m.* slope, side.

versatile /vɛrsatil/ *a.* fickle.

verse (à) /(a)vɛrs/ *adv.* in torrents.

versé /vɛrse/ *a.* ~ **dans,** versed in.

Verseau /vɛrso/ *n.m.* **le** ~, Aquarius.

vers|er /vɛrse/ *v.t./i.* pour; (*larmes, sang*) shed; (*basculer*) overturn; (*payer*) pay. ~**ement** *n.m.* payment.

verset /vɛrsɛ/ *n.m.* (*relig.*) verse.

version /vɛrsjõ/ *n.f.* version; (*traduction*) translation.

verso /vɛrso/ *n.m.* back (of the page).

vert, ~**e** /vɛr, -t/ *a.* green; (*vieillard*) sprightly. —*n.m.* green.

vertèbre /vɛrtɛbr/ *n.f.* vertebra.

vertement /vɛrtəmã/ *adv.* sharply.

vertic|al, ~**ale** (*m. pl.* ~**aux**) /vɛrtikal, -o/ *a. & n.f.* vertical. **à la** ~**ale,** ~**alement** *adv.* vertically.

vertig|e /vɛrtiʒ/ *n.m.* dizziness. ~**es,** dizzy spells. **avoir le** *ou* **un** ~**e,** feel dizzy. ~**ineux,** ~**ineuse** *a.* dizzy; (*très grand*) staggering.

vertu /vɛrty/ *n.f.* virtue. **en** ~ **de,** by virtue of. ~**eux,** ~**euse** /-tɥø, -z/ *a.* virtuous.

verve /vɛrv/ *n.f.* spirit, wit.

verveine /vɛrvɛn/ *n.f.* verbena.

vésicule /vezikyl/ *n.f.* ~ **biliaire,** gall-bladder.

vessie /vesi/ *n.f.* bladder.

veste /vɛst/ *n.f.* jacket.

vestiaire /vɛstjɛr/ *n.m.* cloakroom; (*sport*) changing-room.

vestibule /vɛstibyl/ *n.m.* hall.

vestige /vɛstiʒ/ *n.m.* (*objet*) relic; (*trace*) vestige.

veston /vɛstõ/ *n.m.* jacket.

vêtement /vɛtmã/ *n.m.* article of clothing. ~**s,** clothes.

vétéran /veterã/ *n.m.* veteran.

vétérinaire /veterinɛr/ *n.m./f.* vet, veterinary surgeon, (*Amer.*) veterinarian.

vétille /vetij/ *n.f.* trifle.

vêt|ir /vetir/ *v.t.,* **se** ~**ir** *v. pr.* dress. ~**u** *a.* dressed (**de,** in).

veto /veto/ *n.m. invar.* veto.

vétuste /vetyst/ *a.* dilapidated.

veu|f, ~**ve** /vœf, -v/ *a.* widowed. —*n.m.* widower. —*n.f.* widow.

veuille /vœj/ *voir* **vouloir.**

veule /vøl/ *a.* feeble.

veut, veux /vø/ *voir* **vouloir.**

vexation /vɛksasjõ/ *n.f.* humiliation.

vex|er /vɛkse/ *v.t.* upset, hurt. **se** ~**er** *v. pr.* be upset, be hurt. ~**ant,** ~**ante** *a.* upsetting.

via /vja/ *prép.* via.

viable /vjabl/ *a.* viable.

viaduc /vjadyk/ *n.m.* viaduct.

viande /vjãd/ *n.f.* meat.

vibr|er /vibre/ *v.i.* vibrate; (*être ému*) thrill. ~**ant,** ~**ante** *a.* (*émouvant*) vibrant. ~**ation** *n.f.* vibration.

vicaire /vikɛr/ *n.m.* curate.

vice /vis/ *n.m.* (*moral*) vice; (*défectuosité*) defect.

vice- /vis/ *préf.* vice-.

vice versa /vis(e)vɛrsa/ *adv.* vice versa.

vicier /visje/ *v.t.* taint.

vicieu|x, ~**se** /visjø, -z/ *a.* depraved. —*n.m., f.* pervert.

vicin|al (*pl.* ~**aux**) /visinal, -o/ *a.m.* **chemin** ~**al,** by-road, minor road.

vicomte /vikõt/ *n.m.* viscount.

victime /viktim/ *n.f.* victim; (*d'un accident*) casualty.

vict|oire /viktwar/ *n.f.* victory; (*sport*) win. ~**orieux,** ~**orieuse** *a.* victorious; (*équipe*) winning.

victuailles /viktɥaj/ *n.f. pl.* provisions.

vidang|e /vidãʒ/ *n.f.* emptying; (*auto.*) oil change; (*dispositif*) waste pipe. ~**er** *v.t.* empty.

vide /vid/ *a.* empty. —*n.m.* emptiness, void; (*trou, manque*) gap; (*espace sans air*) vacuum. **à** ~, empty.

vidéo /video/ *a. invar.* video. **jeu** ~, video game. ~**cassette** *n.f.* video(tape). ~**thèque** *n.f.* video library.

vide-ordures /vidɔrdyr/ *n.m. invar.* (rubbish) chute.

vider /vide/ *v.t.* empty; (*poisson*) gut; (*expulser: fam.*) throw out. ~ **les lieux,** vacate the premises. **se** ~ *v. pr.* empty.

videur /vidœr/ *n.m.* bouncer.

vie /vi/ *n.f.* life; (*durée*) lifetime. **à ~, pour la ~,** for life. **donner la ~ à,** give birth to. **en ~,** alive. **~ chère,** high cost of living.

vieil /vjɛj/ *voir* **vieux.**

vieillard /vjejar/ *n.m.* old man.

vieille /vjɛj/ *voir* **vieux.**

vieillesse /vjejɛs/ *n.f.* old age.

vieill|ir /vjejir/ *v.i.* grow old, age; (*mot, idée*) become old-fashioned. —*v.t.* age. **~issement** *n.m.* ageing.

viens, vient /vjɛ̃/ *voir* **venir.**

vierge /vjɛrʒ/ *n.f.* virgin. **la V~,** Virgo. —*a.* virgin; (*feuille, film*) blank.

vieux *ou* **vieil*, vieille** (*m. pl.* **vieux**) /vjø, vjɛj/ *a.* old. —*n.m. &* **vieux** /vjø/ *n.m.* old woman. **les ~,** old people. **mon ~,** (*fam.*) old man *ou* boy. **ma vieille,** (*fam.*) old girl, dear. **vieille fille,** (*péj.*) spinster. **~ garçon,** bachelor. **~ jeu** *a. invar.* old-fashioned.

vif, vive /vif, viv/ *a.* lively; (*émotion, vent*) keen; (*froid*) biting; (*lumière*) bright; (*douleur, parole*) sharp; (*souvenir, style, teint*) vivid; (*succès, impatience*) great. **brûler/enterrer ~,** burn/bury alive. **de vive voix,** personally. **avoir les nerfs à ~,** be on edge.

vigie /viʒi/ *n.f.* look-out.

vigilan|t, ~te /viʒilɑ̃, -t/ *a.* vigilant. **~ce** *n.f.* vigilance.

vigne /viɲ/ *n.f.* (*plante*) vine; (*vignoble*) vineyard.

vigneron, ~ne /viɲrɔ̃, -ɔn/ *n.m., f.* wine-grower.

vignette /viɲɛt/ *n.f.* (*étiquette*) label; (*auto*) road tax sticker.

vignoble /viɲɔbl/ *n.m.* vineyard.

vigoureu|x, ~se /vigurø, -z/ *a.* vigorous, sturdy.

vigueur /vigœr/ *n.f.* vigour. **être/entrer en ~,** (*loi*) be/come into force. **en ~,** (*terme*) in use.

VIH *abrév.* (*virus d'immunodéficience humaine*) HIV.

vil /vil/ *a.* vile, base.

vilain, ~e /vilɛ̃, -ɛn/ *a.* (*mauvais*) nasty; (*laid*) ugly.

villa /villa/ *n.f.* (detached) house.

village /vilaʒ/ *n.m.* village.

villageois, ~e /vilaʒwa, -z/ *a.* village. —*n.m., f.* villager.

ville /vil/ *n.f.* town; (*importante*) city. **~ d'eaux,** spa.

vin /vɛ̃/ *n.m.* wine. **~ d'honneur,** reception. **~ ordinaire,** table wine.

vinaigre /vinɛgr/ *n.m.* vinegar.

vinaigrette /vinɛgrɛt/ *n.f.* oil and vinegar dressing, vinaigrette.

vindicati|f, ~ve /vɛ̃dikatif, -v/ *a.* vindictive.

vingt /vɛ̃/ (/vɛ̃t/ *before vowel and in numbers 22–29*) *a. & n.m.* twenty. **~ième** *a. & n.m./f.* twentieth.

vingtaine /vɛ̃tɛn/ *n.f.* **une ~ (de),** about twenty.

vinicole /vinikɔl/ *a.* wine(-growing).

vinyle /vinil/ *n.m.* vinyl.

viol /vjɔl/ *n.m.* (*de femme*) rape; (*de lieu, loi*) violation.

violacé /vjɔlase/ *a.* purplish.

viol|ent, ~ente /vjɔlɑ̃, -t/ *a.* violent. **~emment** /ama/ *adv.* violently. **~ence** *n.f.* violence; (*acte*) act of violence.

viol|er /vjɔle/ *v.t.* rape; (*lieu, loi*) violate. **~ation** *n.f.* violation.

violet, ~te /vjɔlɛ, -t/ *a. & n.m.* purple. —*n.f.* violet.

violon /vjɔlɔ̃/ *n.m.* violin. **~iste** /-ɔnist/ *n.m./f.* violinist. **~ d'Ingres,** hobby.

violoncell|e /vjɔlɔ̃sɛl/ *n.m.* cello. **~iste** /-elist/ *n.m./f.* cellist.

vipère /vipɛr/ *n.f.* viper, adder.

virage /viraʒ/ *n.m.* bend; (*de véhicule*) turn; (*changement d'attitude:* *fig.*) change of course.

virée /vire/ *n.f.* (*fam.*) trip, outing.

vir|er /vire/ *v.i.* turn. **~er de bord,** tack. **~er au rouge/***etc.***,** turn red/*etc.* —*v.t.* (*argent*) transfer; (*expulser:* *fam.*) throw out. **~ement** *n.m.* (*comm.*) (credit) transfer.

virevolter /virvɔlte/ *v.i.* spin round, swing round.

virginité /virʒinite/ *n.f.* virginity.

virgule /virgyl/ *n.f.* comma; (*dans un nombre*) (decimal) point.

viril /viril/ *a.* manly, virile. **~ité** *n.f.* manliness, virility.

virtuel, ~le /virtɥɛl/ *a.* virtual. **~lement** *adv.* virtually.

virtuos|e /virtɥoz/ *n.m./f.* virtuoso. **~ité** *n.f.* virtuosity.

virulen|t, ~te /virylɑ̃, -t/ *a.* virulent. **~ce** *n.f.* virulence.

virus /virys/ *n.m.* virus.

vis¹ /vi/ *voir* **vivre, voir.**

vis² /vis/ *n.f.* screw.

visa /viza/ *n.m.* visa.

visage /vizaʒ/ *n.m.* face.

vis-à-vis /vizavi/ *adv.* face to face, opposite. **~ de,** opposite; (*à l'égard de*) with respect to. —*n.m. invar.* (*personne*) person opposite.

viscères /visɛr/ *n.m. pl.* intestines.

visées /vize/ *n.f. pl.* aim. **avoir des ~ sur,** have designs on.

viser /vize/ *v.t.* aim at; (*concerner*) be aimed at; (*timbrer*) stamp. —*v.i.* aim. **~ à**, aim at; (*mesure, propos*) be aimed at.

visib|le /vizibl/ *a.* visible. **~ilité** *n.f.* visibility. **~lement** *adv.* visibly.

visière /vizjɛr/ *n.f.* (*de casquette*) peak; (*de casque*) visor.

vision /vizjɔ̃/ *n.f.* vision.

visionnaire /vizjɔnɛr/ *a.* & *n.m./f.* visionary.

visionn|er /vizjɔne/ *v.t.* view. **~euse** *n.f.* (*appareil*) viewer.

visite /vizit/ *n.f.* visit; (*examen*) examination; (*personne*) visitor. **heures de ~,** visiting hours. **~ guidée,** guided tour. **rendre ~ à,** visit. **être en ~ (chez qn.),** be visiting (s.o.).

visit|er /vizite/ *v.t.* visit; (*examiner*) examine. **~eur, ~euse** *n.m., f.* visitor.

vison /vizɔ̃/ *n.m.* mink.

visqueu|x, ~se /viskø, -z/ *a.* viscous.

visser /vise/ *v.t.* screw (on).

visuel, ~le /vizɥɛl/ *a.* visual.

vit /vi/ *voir* **vivre, voir.**

vit|al (*m. pl.* **~aux**) /vital, -o/ *a.* vital. **~alité** *n.f.* vitality.

vitamine /vitamin/ *n.f.* vitamin.

vite /vit/ *adv.* fast, quickly; (*tôt*) soon. **~!,** quick! **faire ~,** be quick.

vitesse /vitɛs/ *n.f.* speed; (*régime: auto.*) gear. **à toute ~,** at top speed. **en ~,** in a hurry, quickly.

vitic|ole /vitikɔl/ *a.* wine. **~ulteur** *n.m.* wine-grower. **~ulture** *n.f.* wine-growing.

vitrage /vitraʒ/ *n.m.* (*vitres*) windows. **double-~,** double glazing.

vitr|ail (*pl.* **~aux**) /vitraj, -o/ *n.m.* stained-glass window.

vitr|e /vitr/ *n.f.* (window) pane; (*de véhicule*) window. **~é a.** glass, glazed. **~er** *v.t.* glaze.

vitrine /vitrin/ *n.f.* (shop) window; (*meuble*) display cabinet.

vivable /vivabl/ *a.* **ce n'est pas ~,** it's unbearable.

vivace /vivas/ *a.* (*plante, sentiment*) perennial.

vivacité /vivasite/ *n.f.* liveliness; (*agilité*) quickness; (*d'émotion, de l'air*) keenness; (*de souvenir, style, teint*) vividness.

vivant, ~e /vivɑ̃, -t/ *a.* (*doué de vie, en usage*) living; (*en vie*) alive, living; (*actif, vif*) lively. —*n.m.* **un bon ~,** a bon viveur. **de son ~,** in one's lifetime. **les ~s,** the living.

vivats /viva/ *n.m. pl.* cheers.

vive¹ /viv/ *voir* **vif.**

vive² /viv/ *int.* **~ le roi/président/***etc.***!,** long live the king/president/*etc.*!

vivement /vivmɑ̃/ *adv.* (*vite, sèchement*) sharply; (*avec éclat*) vividly; (*beaucoup*) greatly. **~ la fin!,** roll on the end, I'll be glad when it's the end!

vivier /vivje/ *n.m.* fish-pond.

vivifier /vivifje/ *v.t.* invigorate.

vivisection /vivisɛksjɔ̃/ *n.f.* vivisection.

vivoter /vivɔte/ *v.i.* plod on, get by.

vivre† /vivr/ *v.i.* live. **~ de,** (*nourriture*) live on. —*v.t.* (*vie*) live; (*période, aventure*) live through. **~s** *n.m. pl.* supplies. **faire ~,** (*famille etc.*) support. **~ encore,** be still alive.

vlan /vlɑ̃/ *int.* bang.

vocabulaire /vɔkabylɛr/ *n.m.* vocabulary.

voc|al (*m. pl.* **~aux**) /vɔkal, -o/ *a.* vocal.

vocalise /vɔkaliz/ *n.f.* voice exercise.

vocation /vɔkasjɔ̃/ *n.f.* vocation.

vociférer /vɔsifere/ *v.t./i.* scream.

vodka /vɔdka/ *n.f.* vodka.

vœu (*pl.* **~x**) /vø/ *n.m.* (*souhait*) wish; (*promesse*) vow.

vogue /vɔg/ *n.f.* fashion, vogue.

voguer /vɔge/ *v.i.* sail.

voici /vwasi/ *prép.* here is, this is; (*au pluriel*) here are, these are. **me ~,** here I am. **~ un an,** (*temps passé*) a year ago. **~ un an que,** it is a year since.

voie /vwa/ *n.f.* (*route*) road; (*chemin*) way; (*moyen*) means, way; (*partie de route*) lane; (*rails*) track; (*quai*) platform. **en ~ de,** in the process of. **en ~ de développement,** (*pays*) developing. **par la ~ des airs,** by air. **~ de dégagement,** slip-road. **~ ferrée,** railway; (*Amer.*) railroad. **~ lactée,** Milky Way. **~ navigable,** waterway. **~ publique,** public highway. **~ sans issue,** cul-de-sac, dead end. **sur la bonne ~,** (*fig.*) well under way. **mettre sur une ~ de garage,** (*fig.*) sideline.

voilà /vwala/ *prép.* there is, that is; (*au pluriel*) there are, those are; (*voici*) here is; here are. **le ~,** there he is. **~!,** right!; (*en offrant qch.*) there you are! **~ un an,** (*temps passé*) a year ago. **~ un an que,** it is a year since.

voilage /vwalaʒ/ *n.m.* net curtain.

voile¹ /vwal/ *n.f.* (*de bateau*) sail; (*sport*) sailing.

voile² /vwal/ *n.m.* veil; (*tissu léger et fin*) net.

voil|er[1] /vwale/ v.t. veil. **se ~er** v. pr. (*devenir flou*) become hazy. **~é** a. (*terme, femme*) veiled; (*flou*) hazy.

voiler[2] /vwale/ v.t., **se ~** v. pr. (*roue etc.*) buckle.

voilier /vwalje/ n.m. sailing-ship.

voilure /vwalyr/ n.f. sails.

voir† /vwar/ v.t./i. see. **se ~** v. pr. (*être visible*) show; (*se produire*) be seen; (*se trouver*) find o.s.; (*se fréquenter*) see each other. **ça n'a rien à ~ avec**, that has nothing to do with. **faire ~, laisser ~**, show. **je ne peux pas le ~**, (*fam.*) I cannot stand him. **~ trouble**, have blurred vision. **voyons!**, (*irritation*) come on!

voire /vwar/ adv. indeed.

voirie /vwari/ n.f. (*service*) highway maintenance. **travaux de ~**, roadworks.

voisin, ~e /vwazɛ̃, -in/ a. (*proche*) neighbouring; (*adjacent*) next (**de**, to); (*semblable*) similar (**de**, to). —n.m., f. neighbour. **le ~**, the man next door.

voisinage /vwazinaʒ/ n.m. neighbourhood; (*proximité*) proximity.

voiture /vwatyr/ n.f. (*motor*) car; (*wagon*) coach, carriage. **en ~!**, all aboard! **~ à cheval**, horse-drawn carriage. **~ de course**, racing-car. **~ d'enfant**, pram; (*Amer.*) baby carriage. **~ de tourisme**, private car.

voix /vwa/ n.f. voice; (*suffrage*) vote. **à ~ basse**, in a whisper.

vol[1] /vɔl/ n.m. (*d'avion, d'oiseau*) flight; (*groupe d'oiseaux etc.*) flock, flight. **à ~ d'oiseau**, as the crow flies. **~ libre**, hang-gliding. **~ plané**, gliding.

vol[2] /vɔl/ n.m. (*délit*) theft; (*hold-up*) robbery. **~ à la tire**, pickpocketing.

volage /vɔlaʒ/ a. fickle.

volaille /vɔlɑj/ n.f. **la ~**, (*poules etc.*) poultry. **une ~**, a fowl.

volant /vɔlɑ̃/ n.m. (steering-)wheel; (*de jupe*) flounce.

volcan /vɔlkɑ̃/ n.m. volcano. **~ique** /-anik/ a. volcanic.

volée /vɔle/ n.f. flight; (*oiseaux*) flight, flock; (*de coups, d'obus*) volley. **à toute ~**, with full force. **de ~, à la ~**, in flight.

voler[1] /vɔle/ v.i. (*oiseau etc.*) fly.

vol|er[2] /vɔle/ v.t./i. steal (**à**, from). **il ne l'a pas ~é**, he deserved it. **~er qn.**, rob s.o. **~eur, ~euse** n.m., f. thief; a. thieving.

volet /vɔlɛ/ n.m. (*de fenêtre*) shutter; (*de document*) (folded ou tear-off) section. **trié sur le ~**, hand-picked.

voleter /vɔlte/ v.i. flutter.

volière /vɔljɛr/ n.f. aviary.

volontaire /vɔlɔ̃tɛr/ a. voluntary; (*personne*) determined. —n.m./f. volunteer. **~ment** adv. voluntarily; (*exprès*) intentionally.

volonté /vɔlɔ̃te/ n.f. (*faculté, intention*) will; (*souhait*) wish; (*énergie*) will-power. **à ~**, (*à son gré*) at will. **bonne ~**, goodwill. **mauvaise ~**, ill will. **faire ses quatre ~s**, do exactly as one pleases.

volontiers /vɔlɔ̃tje/ adv. (*de bon gré*) with pleasure, willingly, gladly; (*ordinairement*) readily.

volt /vɔlt/ n.m. volt. **~age** n.m. voltage.

volte-face /vɔltəfas/ n.f. invar. about-face. **faire ~**, turn round.

voltige /vɔltiʒ/ n.f. acrobatics.

voltiger /vɔltiʒe/ v.i. flutter.

volubile /vɔlybil/ a. voluble.

volume /vɔlym/ n.m. volume.

volumineu|x, ~se /vɔlyminø, -z/ a. bulky.

volupt|é /vɔlypte/ n.f. sensual pleasure. **~ueux, ~ueuse** a. voluptuous.

vom|ir /vɔmir/ v.t./i. vomit. **~i** n.m. vomit. **~issement(s)** n.m. (*pl.*) vomiting.

vont /vɔ̃/ voir **aller**[1].

vorace /vɔras/ a. voracious.

vos /vo/ voir **votre**.

vote /vɔt/ n.m. (*action*) voting; (*d'une loi*) passing; (*suffrage*) vote.

vot|er /vɔte/ v.i. vote. —v.t. vote for; (*adopter*) pass; (*crédits*) vote. **~ant, ~ante** n.m., f. voter.

votre (*pl.* **vos**) /vɔtr, vo/ a. your.

vôtre /votr/ pron. **le** ou **la ~, les ~s**, yours.

vou|er /vwe/ v.t. dedicate (**à**, to); (*promettre*) vow. **~é à l'échec**, doomed to failure.

vouloir† /vulwar/ v.t. want (**faire**, to do). **ça ne veut pas bouger**/etc., it will not move/etc. **je voudrais/voudrais bien venir**/etc., I should ou would like/really like to come/etc. **je veux bien venir**/etc., I am happy to come/etc. **voulez-vous attendre**/etc.?, will you wait/etc.? **veuillez attendre**/etc., kindly wait/etc. **~ absolument faire**, insist on doing. **comme** ou **si vous voulez**, if you like ou wish. **en ~ à qn.**, have a grudge against s.o.; (*être en colère contre*) be annoyed with s.o. **qu'est ce qu'il me veut?**, what does he want with me? **ne pas ~ de qch./qn.**, not want sth./s.o. **~ dire**, mean. **~ du bien à**, wish well.

voulu /vuly/ *a.* (*délibéré*) intentional; (*requis*) required.

vous /vu/ *pron.* (*sujet, complément*) you; (*indirect*) (to) you; (*réfléchi*) yourself; (*pl.*) yourselves; (*l'un l'autre*) each other. ~**-même** *pron.* yourself. ~**-mêmes** *pron.* yourselves.

voûte /vut/ *n.f.* (*plafond*) vault; (*porche*) archway.

voûté /vute/ *a.* bent, stooped. **il a le dos** ~, he's stooped.

vouv|oyer /vuvwaje/ *v.t.* address politely (using *vous*). ~**oiement** *n.m.* use of (polite) *vous*.

voyage /vwajaʒ/ *n.m.* journey, trip; (*par mer*) voyage. ~**(s)**, (*action*) travelling. ~ **d'affaires**, business trip. ~ **de noces,** honeymoon. ~ **organisé**, (package) tour.

voyag|er /vwajaʒe/ *v.i.* travel. ~**eur**, ~**euse** *n.m., f.* traveller.

voyant¹, ~**e** /vwajã, -t/ *a.* gaudy. —*n.f.* (*femme*) clairvoyant.

voyant² /vwajã/ *n.m.* (*signal*) (*warning*) light.

voyelle /vwajɛl/ *n.f.* vowel.

voyeur /vwajœr/ *n.m.* voyeur.

voyou /vwaju/ *n.m.* hooligan.

vrac (en) /(ã)vrak/ *adv.* in disorder; (*sans emballage, au poids*) loose, in bulk.

vrai /vrɛ/ *a.* true; (*réel*) real. —*n.m.* truth. **à** ~ **dire,** to tell the truth.

vraiment /vrɛmã/ *adv.* really.

vraisembl|able /vrɛsãblabl/ *a.* likely. ~**ablement** *adv.* very likely. ~**ance** *n.f.* likelihood, plausibility.

vrille /vrij/ *n.f.* (*aviat.*) spin.

vromb|ir /vrɔ̃bir/ *v.i.* hum. ~**issement** *n.m.* humming.

VRP *abrév. m.* (*voyageur représentant placier*) rep.

vu /vy/ *voir* **voir**. —*a.* **bien/mal** ~, well/not well thought of. —*prép.* in view of. ~ **que,** seeing that.

vue /vy/ *n.f.* (*spectacle*) sight; (*sens*) (eye)sight; (*panorama, idée*) view. **avoir en** ~, have in mind. **à** ~, (*tirer, payable*) at sight. **de** ~, by sight. **perdre de** ~, lose sight of. **en** ~, (*proche*) in sight; (*célèbre*) in the public eye. **en** ~ **de faire,** with a view to doing.

vulg|aire /vylgɛr/ *a.* (*grossier*) vulgar; (*ordinaire*) common. ~**arité** *n.f.* vulgarity.

vulgariser /vylgarize/ *v.t.* popularize.

vulnérab|le /vylnerabl/ *a.* vulnerable. ~**ilité** *n.f.* vulnerability.

vulve /vylv/ *n.f.* vulva.

W

wagon /vagɔ̃/ *n.m.* (*de voyageurs*) carriage; (*Amer.*) car; (*de marchandises*) wagon; (*Amer.*) freight car. ~**-lit** (*pl.* ~**s-lits**) *n.m.* sleeping-car, sleeper. ~**-restaurant** (*pl.* ~**s-restaurants**) *n.m.* dining-car.

walkman /wɔkman/ *n.m.* (P.) walkman.

wallon, ~**ne** /walɔ̃, -ɔn/ *a. & n.m., f.* Walloon.

waters /watɛr/ *n.m. pl.* toilet.

watt /wat/ *n.m.* watt.

w.-c. /(dublə)vese/ *n.m. pl.* toilet.

week-end /wikɛnd/ *n.m.* weekend.

western /wɛstɛrn/ *n.m.* western.

whisk|y (*pl.* ~**ies**) /wiski/ *n.m.* whisky.

X

xénophob|e /ksenɔfɔb/ *a.* xenophobic. —*n.m./f.* xenophobe. ~**ie** *n.f.* xenophobia.

xérès /kserɛs/ *n.m.* sherry.

xylophone /ksilɔfɔn/ *n.m.* xylophone.

Y

y /i/ *adv. & pron.* there; (*dessus*) on it; (*pl.*) on them; (*dedans*) in it; (*pl.*) in them. **s'y habituer,** (*à cela*) get used to it. **s'y attendre,** expect it. **y penser,** think of it. **il y entra,** (*dans cela*) he entered it. **j'y vais,** I'm on my way. **ça y est,** that is it. **y être pour qch.,** have sth. to do with it.

yacht /jɔt/ *n.m.* yacht.

yaourt /jaur(t)/ *n.m.* yoghurt. ~**ière** /-tjɛr/ *n.f.* yoghurt maker.

yeux /jø/ *voir* **œil**.

yiddish /(j)idiʃ/ *n.m.* Yiddish.

yoga /jɔga/ *n.m.* yoga.

yougoslave /jugɔslav/ *a. & n.m./f.* Yugoslav.

Yougoslavie /jugɔslavi/ *n.f.* Yugoslavia.

yo-yo /jojo/ *n.m. invar.* (P.) yo-yo (P.).

yuppie /jøpi/ *n.m./f.* yuppie.

Z

zèbre /zɛbr/ *n.m.* zebra.

zébré /zebre/ *a.* striped.

zèle /zɛl/ *n.m.* zeal.

zélé /zele/ *a.* zealous.

zénith /zenit/ *n.m.* zenith.

zéro /zero/ *n.m.* nought, zero; (*température*) zero; (*dans un numéro*) 0; (*football*) nil; (*football*: *Amer.*) zero; (*personne*) nonentity. **(re)partir de ~,** start from scratch.

zeste /zɛst/ *n.m.* peel. **un ~ de,** (*fig.*) a pinch of.

zézayer /zezeje/ *v.i.* lisp.

zigzag /zigzag/ *n.m.* zigzag. **en ~,** zigzag. **~uer** /-e/ *v.i.* zigzag.

zinc /zɛ̃g/ *n.m.* (*métal*) zinc; (*comptoir*: *fam.*) bar.

zizanie /zizani/ *n.f.* **semer la ~,** put the cat among the pigeons.

zizi /zizi/ *n.m.* (*fam.*) willy.

zodiaque /zɔdjak/ *n.m.* zodiac.

zona /zona/ *n.m.* (*méd.*) shingles.

zone /zon/ *n.f.* zone, area; (*faubourgs*) shanty town. **~ bleue,** restricted parking zone.

zoo /zo(o)/ *n.m.* zoo.

zoolog|ie /zɔɔlɔʒi/ *n.f.* zoology. **~ique** *a.* zoological. **~iste** *n.m./f.* zoologist.

zoom /zum/ *n.m.* zoom lens.

zut /zyt/ *int.* blast (it), (oh) hell.

ANGLAIS–FRANÇAIS
ENGLISH–FRENCH

A

a /eɪ, *unstressed* ə/ *a.* (*before vowel* **an** /æn, ən/) un(e). **I'm a painter,** je suis peintre. **ten pence a kilo,** dix pence le kilo. **once a year,** une fois par an.

aback /ə'bæk/ *adv.* **taken ~,** déconcerté, interdit.

abandon /ə'bændən/ *v.t.* abandonner. —*n.* désinvolture *f.* **~ed** *a.* (*behaviour*) débauché. **~ment** *n.* abandon *m*

abashed /ə'bæʃt/ *a.* confus.

abate /ə'beɪt/ *v.i.* se calmer. —*v.t.* diminuer. **~ment** *n.* diminution *f.*

abattoir /'æbətwɑ:(r)/ *n.* abattoir *m.*

abbey /'æbɪ/ *n.* abbaye *f.*

abb|ot /'æbət/ *n.* abbé *m.* **~ess** *n.* abbesse *f.*

abbreviat|e /ə'bri:vɪeɪt/ *v.t.* abréger. **~ion** /-'eɪʃn/ *n.* abréviation *f.*

abdicat|e /'æbdɪkeɪt/ *v.t./i.* abdiquer. **~ion** /-'keɪʃn/ *n.* abdication *f.*

abdom|en /'æbdəmən/ *n.* abdomen *m.* **~inal** /-'dɒmɪnl/ *a.* abdominal.

abduct /æb'dʌkt/ *v.t.* enlever. **~ion** /-kʃn/ *n.* rapt *m.* **~or** *n.* ravisseur|r, -se *m., f.*

aberration /æbə'reɪʃn/ *n.* aberration *f.*

abet /ə'bet/ *v.t.* (*p.t.* **abetted**) (*jurid.*) encourager.

abeyance /ə'beɪəns/ *n.* **in ~,** (*matter*) en suspens; (*custom*) en désuétude.

abhor /əb'hɔ:(r)/ *v.t.* (*p.t.* **abhorred**) exécrer. **~rence** /-'hɒrəns/ *n.* horreur *f.* **~rent** /-'hɒrənt/ *a.* exécrable.

abide /ə'baɪd/ *v.t.* supporter. **~ by,** respecter.

abiding /ə'baɪdɪŋ/ *a.* éternel.

ability /ə'bɪlətɪ/ *n.* aptitude *f.* (**to do,** à faire); (*talent*) talent *m.*

abject /'æbdʒekt/ *a.* abject.

ablaze /ə'bleɪz/ *a.* en feu. **~ with,** (*anger etc.: fig.*) enflammé de.

abl|e /'eɪbl/ *a.* (**-er, -est**) capable (**to,** de). **be ~e,** pouvoir; (*know how to*) savoir. **~y** *adv.* habilement.

ablutions /ə'blu:ʃnz/ *n. pl.* ablutions *f. pl.*

abnormal /æb'nɔ:ml/ *a.* anormal. **~ity** /-'mælətɪ/ *n.* anomalie *f.* **~ly** *adv.* (*unusually*) exceptionnellement.

aboard /ə'bɔ:d/ *adv.* à bord. —*prep.* à bord de.

abode /ə'bəʊd/ (*old use*) demeure *f.* **of no fixed ~,** sans domicile fixe.

aboli|sh /ə'bɒlɪʃ/ *v.t.* supprimer, abolir. **~tion** /æbə'lɪʃn/ *n.* suppression *f.*, abolition *f*

abominable /ə'bɒmɪnəbl/ *a.* abominable.

abominat|e /ə'bɒmɪneɪt/ *v.t.* exécrer. **~ion** /-'neɪʃn/ *n.* abomination *f.*

aboriginal /æbə'rɪdʒənl/ *a. & n.* aborigène (*m.*).

aborigines /æbə'rɪdʒəni:z/ *n. pl.* aborigènes *m. pl.*

abort /ə'bɔ:t/ *v.t.* faire avorter. —*v.i.* avorter. **~ive** *a.* (*attempt etc.*) manqué.

abortion /ə'bɔ:ʃn/ *n.* avortement *m.* **have an ~,** se faire avorter.

abound /ə'baʊnd/ *v.i.* abonder (**in,** en).

about /ə'baʊt/ *adv.* (*approximately*) environ; (*here and there*) çà et là; (*all round*) partout, autour; (*nearby*) dans les parages; (*of rumour*) en circulation. —*prep.* au sujet de; (*round*) autour de; (*somewhere in*) dans. **~-face, ~-turn** *ns.* (*fig.*) volte-face *f. invar.* **~ here,** par ici. **be ~ to do,** être sur le point de faire. **how** *or* **what ~ leaving,** si on partait. **what's the film ~?,** quel est le sujet du film? **talk ~,** parler de.

above /ə'bʌv/ *adv.* au-dessus; (*on page*) ci-dessus. —*prep.* au-dessus de. **he is not ~ lying,** il n'est pas incapable de mentir. **~ all,** par-dessus tout. **~-board** *a.* honnête. **~-mentioned** *a.* mentionné ci-dessus.

abrasion /ə'breɪʒn/ *n.* frottement *m.*; (*injury*) écorchure *f.*

abrasive /ə'breɪsɪv/ *a.* abrasif; (*manner*) brusque. —*n.* abrasif *m.*

abreast /ə'brest/ *adv.* de front. **keep ~ of,** se tenir au courant de.

abridge /ə'brɪdʒ/ v.t. abréger. ~**ment** n. abrégement m., réduction f.; (*abridged text*) abrégé m.

abroad /ə'brɔːd/ adv. à l'étranger; (*far and wide*) de tous côtés.

abrupt /ə'brʌpt/ a. (*sudden, curt*) brusque; (*steep*) abrupt. ~**ly** adv. (*suddenly*) brusquement; (*curtly, rudely*) avec brusquerie. ~**ness** n. brusquerie f.

abscess /'æbses/ n. abcès m.

abscond /əb'skɒnd/ v.i. s'enfuir.

abseil /'æbseɪl/ v.i. descendre en rappel.

absen|t[1] /'æbsənt/ a. absent; (*look etc.*) distrait. ~**ce** n. absence f.; (*lack*) manque m. **in the** ~**ce of**, à défaut de. ~**tly** adv. distraitement. ~**t-minded** a. distrait. ~**t-mindedness** n. distraction f.

absent[2] /əb'sent/ v. pr. ~ **o.s.**, s'absenter.

absentee /æbsən'tiː/ n. absent(e) m. (f.). ~**ism** n. absentéisme m.

absolute /'æbsəluːt/ a. absolu; (*coward etc.: fam.*) véritable. ~**ly** adv. absolument.

absolution /æbsə'luːʃn/ n. absolution f.

absolve /əb'zɒlv/ v.t. (*from sin*) absoudre (**from**, de); (*from vow etc.*) délier (**from**, de).

absor|b /əb'sɔːb/ v.t. absorber. ~**ption** n. absorption f.

absorbent /əb'sɔːbənt/ a. absorbant. ~ **cotton**, (*Amer.*) coton hydrophile m.

abst|ain /əb'steɪn/ v.i. s'abstenir (**from**, de). ~**ention** /-'stenʃn/ n. abstention f.; (*from drink*) abstinence f.

abstemious /əb'stiːmɪəs/ a. sobre.

abstinen|ce /'æbstɪnəns/ n. abstinence f. ~**t** a. sobre.

abstract[1] /'æbstrækt/ a. abstrait. —n. (*quality*) abstrait m.; (*summary*) résumé m.

abstract[2] /əb'strækt/ v.t. retirer, extraire. ~**ion** /-kʃn/ n. extraction f.; (*idea*) abstraction f.

abstruse /əb'struːs/ a. obscur.

absurd /əb'sɜːd/ a. absurde. ~**ity** n. absurdité f.

abundan|t /ə'bʌndənt/ a. abondant. ~**ce** n. abondance f. ~**tly** adv. (*entirely*) tout à fait.

abuse[1] /ə'bjuːz/ v.t. (*misuse*) abuser de; (*ill-treat*) maltraiter; (*insult*) injurier.

abus|e[2] /ə'bjuːs/ n. (*misuse*) abus m. (**of**, de); (*insults*) injures f. pl. ~**ive** a. injurieux. **get** ~**ive**, devenir grossier.

abut /ə'bʌt/ v.i. (p.t. **abutted**) être contigu (**on**, à).

abysmal /ə'bɪzməl/ a. (*great*) profond; (*bad: fam.*) exécrable.

abyss /ə'bɪs/ n. abîme m.

academic /ækə'demɪk/ a. universitaire; (*scholarly*) intellectuel; (*pej.*) théorique. —n. universitaire m./f. ~**ally** /-lɪ/ adv. intellectuellement.

academ|y /ə'kædəmɪ/ n. (*school*) école f. **A**~**y**, (*society*) Académie f. ~**ician** /-'mɪʃn/ n. académicien(ne) m. (f.).

accede /ək'siːd/ v.i. ~ **to**, (*request, post, throne*) accéder à.

accelerat|e /ək'seləreɪt/ v.t. accélérer. —v.i. (*speed up*) s'accélérer; (*auto.*) accélérer. ~**ion** /-'reɪʃn/ n. accélération f.

accelerator /ək'seləreɪtə(r)/ n. (*auto.*) accélérateur m.

accent[1] /'æksənt/ n. accent m.

accent[2] /æk'sent/ v.t. accentuer.

accentuat|e /ək'sentʃʊeɪt/ v.t. accentuer. ~**ion** /-'eɪʃn/ n. accentuation f.

accept /ək'sept/ v.t. accepter. ~**able** a. acceptable. ~**ance** n. acceptation f.; (*approval, favour*) approbation f.

access /'ækses/ n. accès m. (**to sth.**, à qch.; **to s.o.**, auprès de qn.). ~**ible** /ək'sesəbl/ a. accessible. ~ **road**, route d'accès f.

accession /æk'seʃn/ n. accession f.; (*thing added*) nouvelle acquisition f.

accessory /ək'sesərɪ/ a. accessoire. —n. accessoire m.; (*person: jurid.*) complice m./f.

accident /'æksɪdənt/ n. accident m.; (*chance*) hasard m. ~**al** /-'dentl/ a. accidentel, fortuit. ~**ally** /-'dentəlɪ/ adv. involontairement. ~**-prone**, qui attire les accidents.

acclaim /ə'kleɪm/ v.t. acclamer. —n. acclamation(s) f. (pl.).

acclimat|e /'æklɪmeɪt/ v.t./i. (*Amer.*) (s')acclimater. ~**ion** /-'meɪʃn/ n. (*Amer.*) acclimatation f.

acclimatiz|e /ə'klaɪmətaɪz/ v.t./i. (s')acclimater. ~**ation** /-'zeɪʃn/ n. acclimatation f.

accommodat|e /ə'kɒmədeɪt/ v.t. loger, avoir de la place pour; (*adapt*) adapter; (*supply*) fournir; (*oblige*) obliger. ~**ing** a. obligeant. ~**ion** /-'deɪʃn/ n. (*living premises*) logement m.; (*rented rooms*) chambres f. pl.

accompan|y /ə'kʌmpənɪ/ v.t. accompagner. ~**iment** n. accompagnement m. ~**ist** n. accompagnateur, -trice m., f.

accomplice /ə'kʌmplɪs/ n. complice m./f.

accomplish /əˈkʌmplɪʃ/ *v.t.* (*perform*) accomplir; (*achieve*) réaliser. ~ed *a.* accompli. ~ment *n.* accomplissement *m.* ~ments *n. pl.* (*abilities*) talents *m. pl.*

accord /əˈkɔːd/ *v.i.* concorder. —*v.t.* accorder. —*n.* accord *m.* **of one's own** ~, de sa propre initiative. ~ance *n.* **in** ~ance **with**, conformément à.

according /əˈkɔːdɪŋ/ *adv.* ~ **to**, selon, suivant. ~ly *adv.* en conséquence.

accordion /əˈkɔːdɪən/ *n.* accordéon *m.*

accost /əˈkɒst/ *v.t.* aborder.

account /əˈkaʊnt/ *n.* (*comm.*) compte *m.*; (*description*) compte rendu *m.*; (*importance*) importance *f.* —*v.t.* considérer. ~ **for**, rendre compte de, expliquer. **on** ~ **of**, à cause de. **on no** ~, en aucun cas. **take into** ~, tenir compte de. ~**able** *a.* responsable (**for**, de; **to**, envers). ~**ability** /-əˈbɪlətɪ/ *n.* responsabilité *f.*

accountan|t /əˈkaʊntənt/ *n.* comptable *m./f.*, expert-comptable *m.* ~**cy** *n.* comptabilité *f.*

accredited /əˈkredɪtɪd/ *a.* accrédité.

accrue /əˈkruː/ *v.i.* s'accumuler. ~ **to**, (*come to*) revenir à.

accumulat|e /əˈkjuːmjʊleɪt/ *v.t./i.* (s')accumuler. ~**ion** /ˈleɪʃn/ *n.* accumulation *f.*

accumulator /əˈkjuːmjʊleɪtə(r)/ *n.* (*battery*) accumulateur *m.*

accura|te /ˈækjərət/ *a.* exact, précis. ~**cy** *n.* exactitude *f.*, précision *f.* ~**tely** *adv.* exactement, avec précision.

accus|e /əˈkjuːz/ *v.t.* accuser. **the** ~**ed**, l'accusé(e) *m (f.)* ~**ation** /ækjuːˈzeɪʃn/ *n.* accusation *f.*

accustom /əˈkʌstəm/ *v.t.* accoutumer. ~**ed** *a.* accoutumé. **become** ~**ed to**, s'accoutumer à.

ace /eɪs/ *n.* (*card, person*) as *m.*

ache /eɪk/ *n.* douleur *f.*, mal *m.* —*v.i.* faire mal. **my leg** ~**s**, ma jambe me fait mal, j'ai mal à la jambe.

achieve /əˈtʃiːv/ *v.t.* réaliser, accomplir; (*success*) obtenir. ~**ment** *n.* réalisation *f.* (**of**, de); (*feat*) exploit *m.*, réussite *f.*

acid /ˈæsɪd/ *a. & n.* acide (*m.*). ~**ity** /əˈsɪdətɪ/ *n.* acidité *f.* ~ **rain**, pluies acides *f. pl.*

acknowledge /əkˈnɒlɪdʒ/ *v.t.* reconnaître. ~ (**receipt of**), accuser réception de. ~**ment** *n.* reconnaissance *f.*; accusé de réception *m.*

acme /ˈækmɪ/ *n.* sommet *m.*

acne /ˈæknɪ/ *n.* acné *f.*

acorn /ˈeɪkɔːn/ *n.* (*bot.*) gland *m.*

acoustic /əˈkuːstɪk/ *a.* acoustique. ~**s** *n. pl.* acoustique *f.*

acquaint /əˈkweɪnt/ *v.t.* ~ **s.o. with sth.**, mettre qn. au courant de qch. **be** ~**ed with**, (*person*) connaître; (*fact*) savoir. ~**ance** *n.* (*knowledge, person*) connaissance *f.*

acquiesce /ækwɪˈes/ *v.i.* consentir. ~**nce** *n.* consentement *m.*

acqui|re /əˈkwaɪə(r)/ *v.t.* acquérir; (*habit*) prendre. ~**sition** /ækwɪˈzɪʃn/ *n.* acquisition *f.* ~**sitive** /əˈkwɪzətɪv/ *a.* avide, âpre au gain.

acquit /əˈkwɪt/ *v.t.* (*p.t.* **acquitted**) acquitter. ~ **o.s. well**, bien s'en tirer. ~**tal** *n.* acquittement *m.*

acre /ˈeɪkə(r)/ *n.* (*approx.*) demi-hectare *m.* ~**age** *n.* superficie *f.*

acrid /ˈækrɪd/ *a.* âcre.

acrimon|ious /ækrɪˈməʊnɪəs/ *a.* acerbe, acrimonieux. ~**y** /ˈækrɪmənɪ/ *n.* acrimonie *f.*

acrobat /ˈækrəbæt/ *n.* acrobate *m./f.* ~**ic** /-ˈbætɪk/ *a.* acrobatique. ~**ics** /-ˈbætɪks/ *n. pl.* acrobatie *f.*

acronym /ˈækrənɪm/ *n.* sigle *m.*

across /əˈkrɒs/ *adv. & prep.* (*side to side*) d'un côté à l'autre (**de**); (*on other side*) de l'autre côté (**from**, **de**); (*crosswise*) en travers (de), à travers. **go** *or* **walk** ~, traverser.

acrylic /əˈkrɪlɪk/ *a. & n.* acrylique (*m.*).

act /ækt/ *n.* (*deed, theatre*) acte *m.*; (*in variety show*) numéro *m.*; (*decree*) loi *f.* —*v.i.* agir; (*theatre*) jouer; (*function*) marcher; (*pretend*) jouer la comédie. —*v.t.* (*part, role*) jouer. ~ **as**, servir de. ~**ing** *a.* (*temporary*) intérimaire; *n.* (*theatre*) jeu *m.*

action /ˈækʃn/ *n.* action *f.*; (*mil.*) combat *m.* **out of** ~, hors de service. **take** ~, agir.

activate /ˈæktɪveɪt/ *v.t.* (*machine*) actionner; (*reaction*) activer.

activ|e /ˈæktɪv/ *a.* actif; (*interest*) vif; (*volcano*) en activité. ~**ism** *n.* activisme *m.* ~**ist** *n.* activiste *m./f.* ~**ity** /-ˈtɪvətɪ/ *n.* activité *f.*

ac|tor /ˈæktə(r)/ *n.* acteur *m.* ~**tress** *n.* actrice *f.*

actual /ˈæktʃʊəl/ *a.* réel; (*example*) concret. **the** ~ **pen which**, le stylo même que. **in the** ~ **house**, (*the house itself*) dans la maison elle-même. **no** ~ **promise**, pas de promesse en tant que telle. ~**ity** /-ˈælətɪ/ *n.* réalité *f.* ~**ly** *adv.* (*in fact*) en réalité, réellement.

actuary /'æktʃuərɪ/ *n.* actuaire *m./f.*

acumen /'ækjumen, *Amer.* ə'kju:mən/ *n.* perspicacité *f.*

acupunctur|e /'ækjupʌŋktʃə(r)/ *n.* acupuncture *f.* **~ist** *n.* acupuncteur *m.*

acute /ə'kju:t/ *a.* aigu; (*mind*) pénétrant; (*emotion*) intense, vif; (*shortage*) grave. **~ly** *adv.* vivement. **~ness** *n.* intensité *f.*

ad /æd/ *n.* (*fam.*) annonce *f.*

AD *abbr.* après J.-C.

adamant /'ædəmənt/ *a.* inflexible.

Adam's apple /'ædəmz'æpl/ *n.* pomme d'Adam *f.*

adapt /ə'dæpt/ *v.t./i.* (s')adapter. **~ation** /-'teɪʃn/ *n.* adaptation *f.* **~or** *n.* (*electr.*) adaptateur *m.*; (*for two plugs*) prise multiple *f.*

adaptab|le /ə'dæptəbl/ *a.* souple; (*techn.*) adaptable. **~ility** /-'bɪlətɪ/ *n.* souplesse *f.*

add /æd/ *v.t./i.* ajouter. **~** (**up**), (*total*) additionner. **~ up to,** (*total*) s'élever à. **~ing machine,** machine à calculer *f.*

adder /'ædə(r)/ *n.* vipère *f.*

addict /'ædɪkt/ *n.* intoxiqué(e) *m.* (*f.*); (*fig.*) fanatique *m./f.*

addict|ed /ə'dɪktɪd/ *a.* **~ed to,** (*drink*) adonné à. **be ~ed to,** (*fig.*) être un fanatique de. **~ion** /-kʃn/ *n.* (*med.*) dépendance *f.*; (*fig.*) manie *f.* **~ive** *a.* (*drug etc.*) qui crée une dépendance.

addition /ə'dɪʃn/ *n.* addition *f.* **in ~,** en outre. **~al** /-ʃənl/ *a.* supplémentaire.

additive /'ædɪtɪv/ *n.* additif *m.*

address /ə'dres/ *n.* adresse *f.*; (*speech*) allocution *f.* —*v.t.* adresser; (*speak to*) s'adresser à. **~ee** /ædre'si:/ *n.* destinataire *m./f.*

adenoids /'ædɪnɔɪdz/ *n. pl.* végétations (adénoïdes) *f. pl.*

adept /'ædept, *Amer.* ə'dept/ *a. & n.* expert (**at, en**) (*m.*).

adequa|te /'ædɪkwət/ *a.* suffisant; (*satisfactory*) satisfaisant. **~cy** *n.* quantité suffisante *f.*; (*of person*) compétence *f.* **~tely** *adv.* suffisamment.

adhere /əd'hɪə(r)/ *v.i.* adhérer (**to,** à). **~ to,** (*fig.*) respecter. **~nce** /-rəns/ *n.* adhésion *f.*

adhesion /əd'hi:ʒn/ *n.* (*grip*) adhérence *f.*; (*support: fig.*) adhésion *f.*

adhesive /əd'hi:sɪv/ *a. & n.* adhésif (*m.*).

ad infinitum /ædɪnfɪ'naɪtəm/ *adv.* à l'infini.

adjacent /ə'dʒeɪsnt/ *a.* contigu (**to,** à).

adjective /'ædʒɪktɪv/ *n.* adjectif *m.*

adjoin /ə'dʒɔɪn/ *v.t.* être contigu à.

adjourn /ə'dʒɜ:n/ *v.t.* ajourner. —*v.t./i.* **~** (**the meeting**), suspendre la séance. **~ to,** (*go*) se retirer à.

adjudicate /ə'dʒu:dɪkeɪt/ *v.t./i.* juger.

adjust /ə'dʒʌst/ *v.t.* (*machine*) régler; (*prices*) (r)ajuster; (*arrange*) rajuster, arranger. —*v.t./i.* **~** (**o.s.**) **to,** s'adapter à. **~able** *a.* réglable. **~ment** *n.* (*techn.*) réglage *m.*; (*of person*) adaptation *f.*

ad lib /æd'lɪb/ *v.i.* (*p.t.* **ad libbed**) (*fam.*) improviser.

administer /ad'mɪnɪstə(r)/ *v.t.* administrer.

administration /ədmɪnɪ'streɪʃn/ *n.* administration *f.*

administrative /əd'mɪnɪstrətɪv/ *a.* administratif.

administrator /əd'mɪnɪstreɪtə(r)/ *n.* administra|teur, -trice *m.*, *f.*

admirable /'ædmərəbl/ *a.* admirable.

admiral /'ædmərəl/ *n.* amiral *m.*

admir|e /əd'maɪə(r)/ *v.t.* admirer. **~ation** /ædmə'reɪʃn/ *n.* admiration *f.* **~er** *n.* admira|teur, -trice *m.*, *f.*

admissible /əd'mɪsəbl/ *a.* admissible.

admission /əd'mɪʃn/ *n.* admission *f.*; (*to museum, theatre, etc.*) entrée *f.*; (*confession*) aveu *m.*

admit /əd'mɪt/ *v.t.* (*p.t.* **admitted**) laisser entrer; (*acknowledge*) reconnaître, admettre. **~ to,** avouer. **~tance** *n.* entrée *f.* **~tedly** *adv.* il est vrai (que).

admonish /əd'mɒnɪʃ/ *v.t.* réprimander.

ado /ə'du:/ *n.* **without more ~,** sans plus de cérémonies.

adolescen|t /ædə'lesnt/ *n. & a.* adolescent(e) (*m.* (*f.*)). **~ce** *n.* adolescence *f.*

adopt /ə'dɒpt/ *v.t.* adopter. **~ed** *a.* (*child*) adoptif. **~ion** /-pʃn/ *n.* adoption *f.*

adoptive /ə'dɒptɪv/ *a.* adoptif.

ador|e /ə'dɔ:(r)/ *v.t.* adorer. **~able** *a.* adorable. **~ation** /ædə'reɪʃn/ *n.* adoration *f.*

adorn /ə'dɔ:n/ *v.t.* orner. **~ment** *n.* ornement *m.*

adrift /ə'drɪft/ *a. & adv.* à la dérive.

adroit /ə'drɔɪt/ *a.* adroit.

adulation /ædjʊ'leɪʃn/ *n.* adulation *f.*

adult /'ædʌlt/ *a. & n.* adulte (*m./f.*). **~hood** *n.* condition d'adulte *f.*

adulterate /ə'dʌltəreɪt/ *v.t.* falsifier, frelater, altérer.

adulter|y /ə'dʌltərɪ/ *n.* adultère *m.* **~er,** **~ess** *ns.* époux|x, -se adultère *m.*, *f.* **~ous** *a.* adultère.

advance /əd'vɑ:ns/ *v.t.* avancer. —*v.i.* (s')avancer; (*progress*) avancer. —*n.*

avance *f.* —*a.* (*payment*) anticipé. **in ~**, à l'avance. **~d** *a.* avancé; (*studies*) supérieur. **~ment** *n.* avancement *m.*

advantage /əd'vɑːntɪdʒ/ *n.* avantage *m.* **take ~ of**, profiter de; (*person*) exploiter. **~ous** /ædvən'teɪdʒəs/ *a.* avantageux.

advent /'ædvənt/ *n.* arrivée *f.*

Advent /'ædvənt/ *n.* Avent *m.*

adventur|e /əd'ventʃə(r)/ *n.* aventure *f.* **~er** *n.* explora|teur, -trice *m.*, *f.*; (*pej.*) aventur|ier, -ière *m.*, *f.* **~ous** *a.* aventureux.

adverb /'ædvɜːb/ *n.* adverbe *m.*

adversary /'ædvəsərɪ/ *n.* adversaire *m./f.*

advers|e /'ædvɜːs/ *a.* défavorable. **~ity** /əd'vɜːsətɪ/ *n.* adversité *f.*

advert /'ædvɜːt/ *n.* (*fam.*) annonce *f.*; (*TV*) pub *f.*, publicité *f.* **~isement** /əd'vɜːtɪsmənt/ *n.* publicité *f.*; (*in paper etc.*) annonce *f.*

advertis|e /'ædvətaɪz/ *v.t./i.* faire de la publicité (pour); (*sell*) mettre une annonce (pour vendre). **~ for**, (*seek*) chercher (par voie d'annonce). **~ing** *n.* publicité *f.* **~er** /-ə(r)/ *n.* annonceur *m.*

advice /əd'vaɪs/ *n.* conseil(s) *m.* (*pl.*); (*comm.*) avis *m.* **some ~, a piece of ~**, un conseil.

advis|e /əd'vaɪz/ *v.t.* conseiller; (*inform*) aviser. **~e against**, déconseiller. **~able** *a.* conseillé, prudent (**to**, de). **~er** *n.* conse|iller, -ère *m.*, *f.* **~ory** *a.* consultatif.

advocate[1] /'ædvəkət/ *n.* (*jurid.*) avocat *m.* **~s of**, les défenseurs de.

advocate[2] /'ædvəkeɪt/ *v.t.* recommander.

aegis /'iːdʒɪs/ *n.* **under the ~ of**, sous l'égide de *f.*

aeon /'iːən/ *n.* éternité *f.*

aerial /'eərɪəl/ *a.* aérien. —*n.* antenne *f.*

aerobatics /eərə'bætɪks/ *n. pl.* acrobatie aérienne *f.*

aerobics /eə'rəʊbɪks/ *n.* aérobic *m.*

aerodrome /'eərədrəʊm/ *n.* aérodrome *m.*

aerodynamic /eərəʊdaɪ'næmɪk/ *a.* aérodynamique.

aeroplane /'eərəpleɪn/ *n.* avion *m.*

aerosol /'eərəsɒl/ *n.* atomiseur *m.*

aesthetic /iːs'θetɪk, *Amer.* es'θetɪk/ *a.* esthétique.

afar /ə'fɑː(r)/ *adv.* **from ~**, de loin.

affable /'æfəbl/ *a.* affable.

affair /ə'feə(r)/ *n.* (*matter*) affaire *f.*; (*romance*) liaison *f.*

affect /ə'fekt/ *v.t.* affecter. **~ation** /æfek'teɪʃn/ *n.* affectation *f.* **~ed** *a.* affecté.

affection /ə'fekʃn/ *n.* affection *f.*

affectionate /ə'fekʃənət/ *a.* affectueux.

affiliat|e /ə'filieɪt/ *v.t.* affilier. **~ed company**, filiale *f.* **~ion** /-'eɪʃn/ *n.* affiliation *f.*

affinity /ə'finətɪ/ *n.* affinité *f.*

affirm /ə'fɜːm/ *v.t.* affirmer. **~ation** /æfə'meɪʃn/ *n.* affirmation *f.*

affirmative /ə'fɜːmətɪv/ *a.* affirmatif. —*n.* affirmative *f.*

affix /ə'fiks/ *v.t.* apposer.

afflict /ə'flɪkt/ *v.t.* affliger. **~ion** /-kʃn/ *n.* affliction *f.*, détresse *f.*

affluen|t /'æfluənt/ *a.* riche. **~ce** *n.* richesse *f.*

afford /ə'fɔːd/ *v.t.* avoir les moyens d'acheter; (*provide*) fournir. **~ to do**, avoir les moyens de faire; (*be able*) se permettre de faire. **can you ~ the time?**, avez-vous le temps?

affray /ə'freɪ/ *n.* rixe *f.*

affront /ə'frʌnt/ *n.* affront *m.* —*v.t.* insulter.

afield /ə'fiːld/ *adv.* **far ~**, loin.

afloat /ə'fləʊt/ *adv.* à flot.

afoot /ə'fʊt/ *adv.* **sth. is ~**, il se trame *or* se prépare qch.

aforesaid /ə'fɔːsed/ *a.* susdit.

afraid /ə'freɪd/ *a.* **be ~**, avoir peur (**of**, **to**, de; **that**, que); (*be sorry*) regretter. **I am ~ that**, (*regret to say*) je regrette de dire que.

afresh /ə'freʃ/ *adv.* de nouveau.

Afric|a /'æfrɪkə/ *n.* Afrique *f.* **~an** *a.* & *n.* africain(e) (*m.* (*f.*)).

after /'ɑːftə(r)/ *adv.* & *prep.* après. —*conj.* après que. **~ doing**, après avoir fait. **~ all** après tout. **~-effect** *n.* suite *f.* **~-sales service**, service après-vente *m.* **~ the manner of**, d'après. **be ~**, (*seek*) chercher.

aftermath /'ɑːftəmɑːθ/ *n.* suites *f. pl.*

afternoon /ɑːftə'nuːn/ *n.* après-midi *m./f. invar.*

afters /'ɑːftəz/ *n. pl.* (*fam.*) dessert *m.*

aftershave /'ɑːftəʃeɪv/ *n.* lotion après-rasage *f.*

afterthought /'ɑːftəθɔːt/ *n.* réflexion après coup *f.* **as an ~**, en y repensant.

afterwards /'ɑːftəwədz/ *adv.* après, par la suite.

again /ə'gen/ *adv.* de nouveau, encore une fois; (*besides*) en outre. **do ~**, **see ~***/etc.*, refaire, revoir/*etc.*

against /ə'genst/ *prep.* contre. **~ the law**, illégal.

age /eɪdʒ/ *n.* âge *m.* —*v.t./i.* (*pres. p.* **ageing**) vieillir. **~ group**, tranche d'âge *f.* **~ limit**, limite d'âge. **for ~s,**

(*fam.*) une éternité. **of** ~, (*jurid.*) majeur. **ten years of** ~, âgé de dix ans. ~**less** *a.* toujours jeune.

aged[1] /'eɪdʒd/ *a.* ~ **six**, âgé de six ans.

aged[2] /'eɪdʒɪd/ *a.* âgé, vieux.

agen|cy /'eɪdʒənsɪ/ *n.* agence *f.*; (*means*) entremise *f.* ~**t** *n.* agent *m.*

agenda /ə'dʒendə/ *n.* ordre du jour *m.*

agglomeration /əglɒmə'reɪʃn/ *n.* agglomération *f.*

aggravat|e /'ægrəveɪt/ *v.t.* (*make worse*) aggraver; (*annoy: fam.*) exaspérer. ~**ion** /-'veɪʃn/ *n.* aggravation *f.*; exaspération *f.*; (*trouble: fam.*) ennuis *m. pl.*

aggregate /'ægrɪgət/ *a. & n.* total (*m.*).

aggress|ive /ə'gresɪv/ *a.* agressif. ~**ion** /-ʃn/ *n.* agression *f.* ~**iveness** *n.* agressivité *f.* ~**or** *n.* agresseur *m.*

aggrieved /ə'gri:vd/ *a.* peiné.

aghast /ə'gɑ:st/ *a.* horrifié.

agil|e /'ædʒaɪl, *Amer.* 'ædʒl/ *a.* agile. ~**ity** /ə'dʒɪlətɪ/ *n.* agilité *f.*

agitat|e /'ædʒɪteɪt/ *v.t.* agiter. ~**ion** /-'teɪʃn/ *n.* agitation *f.* ~**or** *n.* agitalteur, -trice *m., f.*

agnostic /æg'nɒstɪk/ *a. & n.* agnostique (*m./f.*).

ago /ə'gəʊ/ *adv.* il y a. **a month** ~, il y a un mois. **long** ~, il y a long-temps. **how long** ~?, il y a combien de temps?

agog /ə'gɒg/ *a.* impatient, en émoi.

agon|y /'ægənɪ/ *n.* grande souffrance *f.*; (*mental*) angoisse *f.* ~**ize** *v.i.* souffrir. ~**ize over**, se torturer l'esprit pour. ~**ized** *a.* angoissé. ~**izing** *a.* angoissant.

agree /ə'gri:/ *v.i.* être *or* se mettre d'accord (**on**, sur); (*of figures*) concorder. —*v.t.* (*date*) convenir de. ~ **that**, reconnaître que. ~ **to do**, accepter de faire. ~ **to sth.**, accepter qch. **onions don't** ~ **with me**, je ne digère pas les oignons. ~**d** *a.* (*time, place*) convenu. **be** ~**d**, être d'accord.

agreeable /ə'gri:əbl/ *a.* agréable. **be** ~, (*willing*) être d'accord.

agreement /ə'gri:mənt/ *n.* accord *m.* **in** ~, d'accord.

agricultur|e /'ægrɪkʌltʃə(r)/ *n.* agriculture *f.* ~**al** /-'kʌltʃərəl/ *a.* agricole.

aground /ə'graʊnd/ *adv.* **run** ~, (*of ship*) (s')échouer.

ahead /ə'hed/ *adv.* (*in front*) en avant, devant; (*in advance*) à l'avance. ~ **of** s.o., devant qn.; en avance sur qn. ~ **of time**, en avance. **straight** ~, tout droit.

aid /eɪd/ *v.t.* aider. —*n.* aide *f.* **in** ~ **of**, au profit de.

aide /eɪd/ *n.* aide *m./f.*

AIDS /eɪdz/ *n.* (*med.*) sida *m.*

ail /eɪl/ *v.t.* **what** ~**s you?**, qu'avez-vous? ~**ing** *a.* souffrant. ~**ment** *n.* maladie *f.*

aim /eɪm/ *v.t.* diriger; (*gun*) braquer (**at**, sur); (*remark*) destiner. —*v.i.* viser. —*n.* but *m.* ~ **at**, viser. ~ **to**, avoir l'intention de. **take** ~, viser. ~**less** *a.*, ~**lessly** *adv.* sans but.

air /eə(r)/ *n.* air *m.* —*v.t.* aérer; (*views*) exposer librement. —*a.* (*base etc.*) aérien. ~**-bed** *n.* matelas pneumatique *m.* ~**-conditioned** *a.* climatisé. ~**-conditioning** *n.* climatisation *f.* ~ **force/hostess**, armée/hôtesse de l'air *f.* ~ **letter**, aérogramme *m.* ~**mail**, poste aérienne *f.* **by** ~**mail**, par avion. ~ **raid**, attaque aérienne *f.* ~ **terminal**, aérogare *f.* ~ **traffic controller**, aiguilleur du ciel *m.* **by** ~, par avion. **in the** ~, (*rumour*) répandu; (*plan*) incertain. **on the** ~, sur l'antenne.

airborne /'eəbɔːn/ *a.* en (cours de) vol; (*troops*) aéroporté.

aircraft /'eəkrɑːft/ *n. invar.* avion *m.* ~**-carrier** *n.* porte-avions *m. invar.*

airfield /'eəfiːld/ *n.* terrain d'aviation *m.*

airgun /'eəgʌn/ *n.* carabine à air comprimé *f.*

airlift /'eəlɪft/ *n.* pont aérien *m.* —*v.t.* transporter par pont aérien.

airline /'eəlaɪn/ *n.* ligne aérienne *f.* ~**r** /-ə(r)/ *n.* avion de ligne *m.*

airlock /'eəlɒk/ *n.* (*in pipe*) bulle d'air *f.*; (*chamber: techn.*) sas *m.*

airman /'eəmən/ *n.* (*pl.* -**men**) aviateur *m.*

airplane /'eəpleɪn/ *n.* (*Amer.*) avion *m.*

airport /'eəpɔːt/ *n.* aéroport *m.*

airsickness /'eəsɪknɪs/ *n.* mal de l'air *m.*

airtight /'eətaɪt/ *a.* hermétique.

airways /'eəweɪz/ *n. pl.* compagnie d'aviation *f.*

airworthy /'eəwɜːðɪ/ *a.* en état de navigation.

airy /'eərɪ/ *a.* (**-ier, -iest**) bien aéré; (*manner*) désinvolte.

aisle /aɪl/ *n.* (*of church*) nef latérale *f.*; (*gangway*) couloir *m.*

ajar /ə'dʒɑː(r)/ *adv. & a.* entr'ouvert.

akin /ə'kɪn/ *a.* ~ **to**, apparenté à.

alabaster /'æləbɑːstə(r)/ *n.* albâtre *m.*

à la carte /ɑːlɑː'kɑːt/ *adv. & a.* (*culin.*) à la carte.

alacrity /ə'lækrətɪ/ *n.* empressement *m.*

alarm /ə'lɑːm/ *n.* alarme *f.*; (*clock*) réveil *m.* —*v.t.* alarmer. ~**-clock** *n.*

réveil *m.*, réveille-matin *m. invar.* ~**ist**
n. alarmiste *m./f.*

alas /ə'læs/ *int.* hélas.

albatross /'ælbətrɒs/ *n.* albatros *m.*

album /'ælbəm/ *n.* album *m.*

alcohol /'ælkəhɒl/ *n.* alcool *m.* ~**ic**
/-'hɒlɪk/ *a.* alcoolique; (*drink*) al-
coolisé; *n.* alcoolique *m./f.* ~**ism**
n. alcoolisme *m.*

alcove /'ælkəʊv/ *n.* alcôve *f.*

ale /eɪl/ *n.* bière *f.*

alert /ə'lɜːt/ *a.* (*lively*) vif; (*watchful*)
vigilant. —*n.* alerte *f.* —*v.t.* alerter. ~
s.o. to, prévenir qn. de. **on the** ~, sur le
qui-vive. ~**ness** *n.* vivacité *f.*; vigilance
f.

A-level /'eɪlevl/ *n.* baccalauréat *m.*

algebra /'ældʒɪbrə/ *n.* algèbre *f.* ~**ic**
/-'breɪk/ *a.* algébrique.

Algeria /æl'dʒɪərɪə/ *n.* Algérie *f.* ~**n** *a.*
& *n.* algérien(ne) (*m.* (*f.*)).

algorithm /'ælgərɪðm/ *n.* algorithme *m.*

alias /'eɪlɪəs/ *n.* (*pl.* -**ases**) faux nom *m.*
—*adv.* alias.

alibi /'ælɪbaɪ/ *n.* (*pl.* -**is**) alibi *m.*

alien /'eɪlɪən/ *n.* & *a.* étrangler, -ère (*m.*,
f.) (**to**, à).

alienat|e /'eɪlɪəneɪt/ *v.t.* aliéner. ~**e
one's friends/***etc.*, s'aliéner ses
amis/*etc.* ~**ion** /-'neɪʃn/ *n.* aliénation *f.*

alight[1] /ə'laɪt/ *v.i.* (*person*) descendre;
(*bird*) se poser.

alight[2] /ə'laɪt/ *a.* en feu, allumé.

align /ə'laɪn/ *v.t.* aligner. ~**ment** *n.*
alignement *m.*

alike /ə'laɪk/ *a.* semblable. —*adv.* de la
même façon. **look** *or* **be** ~, se
ressembler.

alimony /'ælɪmənɪ, *Amer.* -məʊnɪ/ *n.*
pension alimentaire *f.*

alive /ə'laɪv/ *a.* vivant. ~ **to**, sensible à,
sensibilisé à. ~ **with**, grouillant de.

alkali /'ælkəlaɪ/ *n.* (*pl.* -**is**) alcali *m.*

all /ɔːl/ *a.* tout(e), tous, toutes. —*pron.*
tous, toutes; (*everything*) tout. —*adv.*
tout. ~ **(the) men**, tous les hommes. ~
of it, (le) tout. ~ **of us**, nous tous. ~
but, presque. ~ **for sth.**, à fond pour
qch. ~ **in**, (*exhausted*) épuisé. ~**-in** *a.*
tout compris. ~**-in wrestling**, catch *m.*
~ **out**, à fond. ~**-out** *a.* (*effort*)
maximum. ~ **over**, partout (sur *or*
dans); (*finished*) fini. ~ **right**, bien;
(*agreeing*) bon! ~ **round**, dans tous les
domaines; (*for all*) pour tous. ~**-round**
a. général. ~ **there**, (*alert*) éveillé. ~
the better, tant mieux. ~ **the same,**
tout de même. **the best of** ~, le
meilleur.

allay /ə'leɪ/ *v.t.* calmer.

allegation /ælɪ'geɪʃn/ *n.* allégation *f.*

allege /ə'ledʒ/ *v.t.* prétendre. ~**dly** /-ɪdlɪ/
adv. d'après ce qu'on dit.

allegiance /ə'liːdʒəns/ *n.* fidélité *f.*

allerg|y /'ælədʒɪ/ *n.* allergie *f.* ~**ic**
/ə'lɜːdʒɪk/ *a.* allergique (**to**, à).

alleviate /ə'liːvɪeɪt/ *v.t.* alléger.

alley /'ælɪ/ *n.* (*street*) ruelle *f.*

alliance /ə'laɪəns/ *n.* alliance *f.*

allied /'ælaɪd/ *a.* allié.

alligator /'ælɪgeɪtə(r)/ *n.* alligator *m.*

allocat|e /'æləkeɪt/ *v.t.* (*assign*) attribuer;
(*share out*) distribuer. ~**ion** /-'keɪʃn/ *n.*
allocation *f.*

allot /ə'lɒt/ *v.t.* (*p.t.* **allotted**) attribuer.
~**ment** *n.* attribution *f.*; (*share*) partage
m.; (*land*) parcelle de terre *f.* (*louée
pour la culture*).

allow /ə'laʊ/ *v.t.* permettre; (*grant*)
accorder; (*reckon on*) prévoir; (*agree*)
reconnaître. ~ **s.o. to**, permettre à qn.
de. ~ **for**, tenir compte de.

allowance /ə'laʊəns/ *n.* allocation *f.*,
indemnité *f.* **make** ~**s for**, être
indulgent envers; (*take into account*)
tenir compte de.

alloy /'ælɔɪ/ *n.* alliage *m.*

allude /ə'luːd/ *v.i.* ~ **to**, faire allusion à.

allure /ə'lʊə(r)/ *v.t.* attirer.

allusion /ə'luːʒn/ *n.* allusion *f.*

ally[1] /'ælaɪ/ *n.* allié(e) *m.* (*f.*).

ally[2] /ə'laɪ/ *v.t.* allier. ~ **o.s. with**, s'allier
à *or* avec.

almanac /'ɔːlmənæk/ *n.* almanach *m.*

almighty /ɔːl'maɪtɪ/ *a.* tout-puissant;
(*very great: fam.*) sacré, formidable.

almond /'ɑːmənd/ *n.* amande *f.*

almost /'ɔːlməʊst/ *adv.* presque.

alms /ɑːmz/ *n.* aumône *f.*

alone /ə'ləʊn/ *a.* & *adv.* seul.

along /ə'lɒŋ/ *prep.* le long de. —*adv.*
come ~, venir. **go** *or* **walk** ~, passer.
all ~, (*time*) tout le temps, depuis le
début. ~ **with**, avec.

alongside /əlɒŋ'saɪd/ *adv.* (*naut.*) bord à
bord. **come** ~, accoster. —*prep.* le long
de.

aloof /ə'luːf/ *adv.* à l'écart. —*a.* distant.
~**ness** *n.* réserve *f.*

aloud /ə'laʊd/ *adv.* à haute voix.

alphabet /'ælfəbet/ *n.* alphabet *m.* ~**ical**
/-'betɪkl/ *a.* alphabétique.

alpine /'ælpaɪn/ *a.* (*landscape*) alpestre;
(*climate*) alpin.

Alpine /'ælpaɪn/ *a.* des Alpes.

Alps /ælps/ *n. pl.* **the** ~, les Alpes *f. pl.*

already /ɔːl'redɪ/ *adv.* déjà.

alright /ɔːl'raɪt/ *a.* & *adv.* = **all right.**

Alsatian /æl'seɪʃn/ n. (dog) berger allemand m.

also /'ɔːlsəʊ/ adv. aussi.

altar /'ɔːltə(r)/ n. autel m.

alter /'ɔːltə(r)/ v.t./i. changer. ∼**ation** /-'reɪʃn/ n. changement m.; (to garment) retouche f.

alternate[1] /ɔːl'tɜːnət/ a. alterné, alternatif; (Amer.) = **alternative**. **on ∼ days**/etc., (first one then the other) tous les deux jours/etc. ∼**ly** adv. tour à tour.

alternate[2] /'ɔːltəneɪt/ v.i. alterner. —v.t. faire alterner.

alternative /ɔːl'tɜːnətɪv/ a. autre; (policy) de rechange. —n. alternative f., choix m. ∼**ly** adv. comme alternative. **or ∼ly**, ou alors.

alternator /'ɔːltəneɪtə(r)/ n. alternateur m.

although /ɔːl'ðəʊ/ conj. bien que.

altitude /'æltɪtjuːd/ n. altitude f.

altogether /ɔːltə'geðə(r)/ adv. (completely) tout à fait; (on the whole) à tout prendre.

aluminium /æljʊ'mɪnɪəm/ (Amer. **aluminum** /ə'luːmɪnəm/) n. aluminium m.

always /'ɔːlweɪz/ adv. toujours.

am /æm/ see be.

a.m. /eɪ'em/ adv. du matin.

amalgamate /ə'mælgəmeɪt/ v.t./i. (s')amalgamer; (comm.) fusionner.

amass /ə'mæs/ v.t. amasser.

amateur /'æmətə(r)/ n. amateur m. —a. (musician etc.) amateur invar. ∼**ish** a. (pej.) d'amateur. ∼**ishly** adv. en amateur.

amaz|e /ə'meɪz/ v.t. étonner. ∼**ed** a. étonné. ∼**ement** n. étonnement m. ∼**ingly** adv. étonnamment.

ambassador /æm'bæsədə(r)/ n. ambassadeur m.

amber /'æmbə(r)/ n. ambre m.; (auto.) feu orange m.

ambigu|ous /æm'bɪgjʊəs/ a. ambigu. ∼**ity** /-'gjuːətɪ/ n. ambiguïté f.

ambiti|on /æm'bɪʃn/ n. ambition f. ∼**ous** a. ambitieux.

ambivalent /æm'bɪvələnt/ a. ambigu, ambivalent.

amble /'æmbl/ v.i. marcher sans se presser, s'avancer lentement.

ambulance /'æmbjʊləns/ n. ambulance f.

ambush /'æmbʊʃ/ n. embuscade f. —v.t. tendre une embuscade à.

amenable /ə'miːnəbl/ a. obligeant. ∼ **to**, (responsive) sensible à.

amend /ə'mend/ v.t. modifier, corriger. ∼**ment** n. (to rule) amendement m.

amends /ə'mendz/ n. pl. **make ∼**, réparer son erreur.

amenities /ə'miːnətɪz/ n. pl. (pleasant features) attraits m. pl.; (facilities) aménagements m. pl.

America /ə'merɪkə/ n. Amérique f. ∼**n** a. & n. américain(e) (m. (f.)).

amiable /'eɪmɪəbl/ a. aimable.

amicable /'æmɪkəbl/ a. amical.

amid(st) /ə'mɪd(st)/ prep. au milieu de.

amiss /ə'mɪs/ a. & adv. mal. **sth. ∼**, qch. qui ne va pas. **take sth. ∼**, être offensé par qch.

ammonia /ə'məʊnɪə/ n. (gas) ammoniac m.; (water) ammoniaque f.

ammunition /æmjʊ'nɪʃn/ n. munitions f. pl.

amnesia /æm'niːzɪə/ n. amnésie f.

amnesty /'æmnəstɪ/ n. amnistie f.

amok /ə'mɒk/ adv. **run ∼**, devenir fou furieux; (crowd) se déchaîner.

among(st) /ə'mʌŋ(st)/ prep. parmi, entre. ∼ **the crowd**, (in the middle of) parmi la foule. ∼ **the English**/etc., (race, group) chez les Anglais/etc. ∼ **ourselves**/etc., entre nous/etc.

amoral /eɪ'mɒrəl/ a. amoral.

amorous /'æmərəs/ a. amoureux.

amorphous /ə'mɔːfəs/ a. amorphe.

amount /ə'maʊnt/ n. quantité f.; (total) montant m.; (sum of money) somme f. —v.i. ∼ **to**, (add up to) s'élever à; (be equivalent to) revenir à.

amp /æmp/ n. (fam.) ampère m.

ampere /'æmpeə(r)/ n. ampère m.

amphibi|an /æm'fɪbɪən/ n. amphibie m. ∼**ous** a. amphibie.

ampl|e /'æmpl/ a. (-er, -est) (enough) (bien) assez de; (large, roomy) ample. ∼**y** adv. amplement.

amplif|y /'æmplɪfaɪ/ v.t. amplifier. ∼**ier** n. amplificateur m.

amputat|e /'æmpjʊteɪt/ v.t. amputer. ∼**ion** /-'teɪʃn/ n. amputation f.

amuck /ə'mʌk/ see **amok**.

amuse /ə'mjuːz/ v.t. amuser. ∼**ment** n. amusement m., divertissement m. ∼**ment arcade**, salle de jeux f.

an /æn, unstressed ən/ see **a**.

anachronism /ə'nækrənɪzəm/ n. anachronisme m.

anaem|ia /ə'niːmɪə/ n. anémie f. ∼**ic** a. anémique.

anaesthetic /ænɪs'θetɪk/ n. anesthésique m. **give an ∼**, faire une anesthésie (**to**, à).

analogue, analog /'ænəlɒg/ a. analogique.

analogy /ə'nælədʒɪ/ n. analogie f.

analys|e (*Amer.* **analyze**) /'ænəlaɪz/ v.t. analyser. **~t** /-ɪst/ n. analyste m./f.

analysis /ə'næləsɪs/ n. (pl. **-yses** /-əsiːz/) analyse f.

analytic(al) /ænə'lɪtɪk(l)/ a. analytique.

anarch|y /'ænəkɪ/ n. anarchie f. **~ist** n. anarchiste m./f.

anathema /ə'næθəmə/ n. **that is ~ to me**, j'ai cela en abomination.

anatom|y /ə'nætəmɪ/ n. anatomie f. **~ical** /ænə'tɒmɪkl/ a. anatomique.

ancest|or /'ænsestə(r)/ n. ancêtre m. **~ral** /-'sestrəl/ a. ancestral.

anchor /'æŋkə(r)/ n. ancre f. —v.t. mettre à l'ancre. —v.i. jeter l'ancre.

anchovy /'æntʃəvɪ/ n. anchois m.

ancient /'eɪnʃənt/ a. ancien.

ancillary /æn'sɪlərɪ/ a. auxiliaire.

and /ænd, *unstressed* ən(d)/ conj. et. **go ~ see him**, allez le voir. **richer ~ richer**, de plus en plus riche.

anecdote /'ænɪkdəʊt/ n. anecdote f.

anemia /ə'niːmɪə/ n. (*Amer.*) = **anaemia**.

anesthetic /ænɪs'θetɪk/ (*Amer.*) = **anaesthetic**.

anew /ə'njuː/ adv. de or à nouveau.

angel /'eɪndʒl/ n. ange m. **~ic** /æn'dʒelɪk/ a. angélique.

anger /'æŋgə(r)/ n. colère f. —v.t. mettre en colère, fâcher.

angle[1] /'æŋgl/ n. angle m.

angle[2] /'æŋgl/ v.i. pêcher (à la ligne). **~ for**, (*fig.*) quêter. **~r** /-ə(r)/ n. pêcheu|r, -se m., f.

Anglican /'æŋglɪkən/ a. & n. anglican(e) (m. (f.)).

Anglo- /'æŋgləʊ/ pref. anglo-.

Anglo-Saxon /'æŋgləʊ'sæksn/ a. & n. anglo-saxon(ne) (m. (f.)).

angr|y /'æŋgrɪ/ a. (**-ier, -iest**) fâché, en colère. **get ~y**, se fâcher, se mettre en colère (**with**, contre). **make s.o. ~y**, mettre qn. en colère. **~ily** adv. en colère.

anguish /'æŋgwɪʃ/ n. angoisse f.

angular /'æŋgjʊlə(r)/ a. (*features*) anguleux.

animal /'ænɪml/ n. & a. animal (m.).

animate[1] /'ænɪmət/ a. animé.

animat|e[2] /'ænɪmeɪt/ v.t. animer. **~ion** /-'meɪʃn/ n. animation f.

animosity /ænɪ'mɒsətɪ/ n. animosité f.

aniseed /'ænɪsiːd/ n. anis m.

ankle /'æŋkl/ n. cheville f. **~ sock**, socquette f.

annex /ə'neks/ v.t. annexer. **~ation** /ænek'seɪʃn/ n. annexion f.

annexe /'æneks/ n. annexe f.

annihilate /ə'naɪəleɪt/ v.t. anéantir.

anniversary /ænɪ'vɜːsərɪ/ n. anniversaire m.

announce /ə'naʊns/ v.t. annoncer. **~ment** n. annonce f. **~r** /-ə(r)/ n. (*radio, TV*) speaker(ine) m. (f.).

annoy /ə'nɔɪ/ v.t. agacer, ennuyer. **~ance** n. contrariété f. **~ed** a. fâché (**with**, contre). **get ~ed**, se fâcher. **~ing** a. ennuyeux.

annual /'ænjʊəl/ a. annuel. —n. publication annuelle f. **~ly** adv. annuellement.

annuity /ə'njuːɪtɪ/ n. rente (viagère) f.

annul /ə'nʌl/ v.t. (p.t. **annulled**) annuler. **~ment** n. annulation f.

anomal|y /ə'nɒməlɪ/ n. anomalie f. **~ous** a. abnormal.

anonym|ous /ə'nɒnɪməs/ a. anonyme. **~ity** /ænə'nɪmətɪ/ n. anonymat m.

anorak /'ænəræk/ n. anorak m.

another /ə'nʌðə(r)/ a. & pron. un(e) autre. **~ coffee**, (*one more*) encore un café. **~ ten minutes**, encore dix minutes, dix minutes de plus.

answer /'ɑːnsə(r)/ n. réponse f.; (*solution*) solution f. —v.t. répondre à; (*prayer*) exaucer. —v.i. répondre. **~ the door**, ouvrir la porte. **~ back**, répondre. **~ for**, répondre de. **~ to**, (*superior*) dépendre de; (*description*) répondre à. **~able** a. responsable (**for**, de; **to**, devant). **~ing machine**, répondeur m.

ant /ænt/ n. fourmi f.

antagonis|m /æn'tægənɪzəm/ n. antagonisme m. **~tic** /-'nɪstɪk/ a. antagoniste.

antagonize /æn'tægənaɪz/ v.t. provoquer l'hostilité de.

Antarctic /æn'tɑːktɪk/ a. & n. antarctique (m.).

ante- /'æntɪ/ pref. anti-, anté-.

antelope /'æntɪləʊp/ n. antilope f.

antenatal /'æntɪneɪtl/ a. prénatal.

antenna /æn'tenə/ n. (pl. **-ae** /-iː/) (*of insect*) antenne f.; (pl. **-as**; *aerial*: *Amer.*) antenne f.

anthem /'ænθəm/ n. (*relig.*) motet m.; (*of country*) hymne national m.

anthology /æn'θɒlədʒɪ/ n. anthologie f.

anthropolog|y /ænθrə'pɒlədʒɪ/ n. anthropologie f. **~ist** n. anthropologue m./f.

anti- /'æntɪ/ pref. anti-. **~-aircraft** a. antiaérien.

antibiotic /æntɪbaɪ'ɒtɪk/ n. antibiotique m.

antibody /'æntɪbɒdɪ/ n. anticorps m.

antic /'æntɪk/ n. bouffonnerie f.

anticipat|e /æn'tɪsɪpeɪt/ v.t. (foresee, expect) prévoir, ‹attendre à; (forestall) devancer. ~ion /-'peɪʃn/ n. attente f. **in ~ion of**, en prévision or attente de.

anticlimax /æntɪ'klaɪmæks/ n. (letdown) déception f. **it was an ~**, ça n'a pas répondu à l'attente.

anticlockwise /æntɪ'klɒkwaɪz/ adv. & a. dans le sens inverse des aiguilles d'une montre.

anticyclone /æntɪ'saɪkləʊn/ n. anticyclone m.

antidote /'æntɪdəʊt/ n. antidote m.

antifreeze /'æntɪfriːz/ n. antigel m.

antihistamine /æntɪ'hɪstəmiːn/ n. antihistaminique m.

antipathy /æn'tɪpəθɪ/ n. antipathie f.

antiquated /'æntɪkweɪtɪd/ a. vieillot, suranné.

antique /æn'tiːk/ a. (old) ancien; (from antiquity) antique. —n. objet ancien m., antiquité f. **~ dealer**, antiquaire m./f. **~ shop**, magasin d'antiquités m.

antiquity /æn'tɪkwətɪ/ n. antiquité f.

anti-Semiti|c /æntɪsɪ'mɪtɪk/ a. antisémite. **~sm** /-'semɪtɪzəm/ n. antisémitisme m.

antiseptic /æntɪ'septɪk/ a. & n. antiseptique (m.).

antisocial /æntɪ'səʊʃl/ a. asocial, antisocial; (unsociable) insociable.

antithesis /æn'tɪθəsɪs/ n. (pl. -eses /-əsiːz/) antithèse f.

antlers /'æntləz/ n. pl. bois m. pl.

anus /'eɪnəs/ n. anus m.

anvil /'ænvɪl/ n. enclume f.

anxiety /æŋ'zaɪətɪ/ n. (worry) anxiété f.; (eagerness) impatience f.

anxious /'æŋkʃəs/ a. (troubled) anxieux; (eager) impatient (**to**, de). **~ly** adv. anxieusement; impatiemment.

any /'enɪ/ a. (some) du, de l', de la, des; (after negative) de, d'; (every) tout; (no matter which) n'importe quel. **at ~ moment**, à tout moment. **have you ~ water?**, avez-vous de l'eau? —pron. (no matter which one) n'importe lequel; (someone) quelqu'un; (any amount of it or them) en. **I do not have ~**, je n'en ai pas. **did you see ~ of them?**, en avez-vous vu? —adv. (a little) un peu. **do you have ~ more?**, en avez-vous encore? **do you have ~ more tea?**, avez-vous encore du thé? **not ~**, nullement. **I don't do it ~ more**, je ne le fais plus.

anybody /'enɪbɒdɪ/ pron. n'importe qui;

(somebody) quelqu'un; (after negative) personne. **he did not see ~**, il n'a vu personne.

anyhow /'enɪhaʊ/ adv. de toute façon; (badly) n'importe comment.

anyone /'enɪwʌn/ pron. = **anybody**.

anything /'enɪθɪŋ/ pron. n'importe quoi; (something) quelque chose; (after negative) rien. **he did not see ~**, il n'a rien vu. **~ but**, (cheap etc.) nullement. **~ you do**, tout ce que tu fais.

anyway /'enɪweɪ/ adv. de toute façon.

anywhere /'enɪweə(r)/ adv. n'importe où; (somewhere) quelque part; (after negative) nulle part. **he does not go ~**, il ne va nulle part. **~ you go**, partout où tu vas, où que tu ailles. **~ else**, partout ailleurs.

apart /ə'pɑːt/ adv. (on or to one side) à part; (separated) séparé; (into pieces) en pièces. **~ from**, à part, excepté. **ten metres ~**, (distant) à dix mètres l'un de l'autre. **come ~**, (break) tomber en morceaux; (machine) se démonter. **legs ~**, les jambes écartées. **keep ~**, séparer. **take ~**, démonter.

apartment /ə'pɑːtmənt/ n. (Amer.) appartement m. **~s**, logement m.

apath|y /'æpəθɪ/ n. apathie f. **~etic** /-'θetɪk/ a. apathique.

ape /eɪp/ n. singe m. —v.t. singer.

aperitif /ə'perətɪf/ n. apéritif m.

aperture /'æpətʃə(r)/ n. ouverture f.

apex /'eɪpeks/ n. sommet m.

apiece /ə'piːs/ adv. chacun.

apologetic /əpɒlə'dʒetɪk/ a. (tone etc.) d'excuse. **be ~**, s'excuser. **~ally** /-lɪ/ adv. en s'excusant.

apologize /ə'pɒlədʒaɪz/ v.i. s'excuser (**for**, de; **to**, auprès de).

apology /ə'pɒlədʒɪ/ n. excuses f. pl.; (defence of belief) apologie f.

Apostle /ə'pɒsl/ n. apôtre m.

apostrophe /ə'pɒstrəfɪ/ n. apostrophe f.

appal /ə'pɔːl/ v.t. (p.t. **appalled**) épouvanter. **~ling** a. épouvantable.

apparatus /æpə'reɪtəs/ n. (machine & anat.) appareil m.

apparel /ə'pærəl/ n. habillement m.

apparent /ə'pærənt/ a. apparent. **~ly** adv. apparemment.

appeal /ə'piːl/ n. appel m.; (attractiveness) attrait m., charme m. —v.i. (jurid.) faire appel. **~ to s.o.**, (beg) faire appel à qn.; (attract) plaire à qn. **~ to s.o. for sth.**, demander qch. à qn. **~ing** a. (attractive) attirant.

appear /ə'pɪə(r)/ v.i. apparaître; (arrive) se présenter; (seem, be published) paraître; (*theatre*) jouer. ~ **on TV**, passer à la télé. ~**ance** *n.* apparition *f.*; (*aspect*) apparence *f.*

appease /ə'piːz/ *v.t.* apaiser.

appendicitis /əpendɪ'saɪtɪs/ *n.* appendicite *f.*

appendix /ə'pendɪks/ *n.* (*pl.* **-ices** /-ɪsiːz/) appendice *m.*

appetite /'æpɪtaɪt/ *n.* appétit *m.*

appetizer /'æpɪtaɪzə(r)/ *n.* (*snack*) amuse-gueule *m. invar.*; (*drink*) apéritif *m.*

appetizing /'æpɪtaɪzɪŋ/ *a.* appétissant.

applaud /ə'plɔːd/ *v.t./i.* applaudir; (*decision*) applaudir à. ~**se** *n.* applaudissements *m. pl.*

apple /'æpl/ *n.* pomme *f.* ~**-tree** *n.* pommier *m.*

appliance /ə'plaɪəns/ *n.* appareil *m.*

applicable /'æplɪkəbl/ *a.* applicable.

applicant /'æplɪkənt/ *n.* candidat(e) *m.* (*f.*) (**for**, à).

application /æplɪ'keɪʃn/ *n.* application *f.*; (*request, form*) demande *f.*; (*for job*) candidature *f.*

apply /ə'plaɪ/ *v.t.* appliquer. —*v.i.* ~ **to**, (*refer*) s'appliquer à; (*ask*) s'adresser à. ~ **for**, (*job*) postuler pour; (*grant*) demander. ~ **o.s. to**, s'appliquer à. **applied** *a.* appliqué

appoint /ə'pɔɪnt/ *v.t.* (*to post*) nommer; (*fix*) désigner. **well-~ed** *a.* bien équipé. ~**ment** *n.* nomination *f.*; (*meeting*) rendez-vous *m. invar.*; (*job*) poste *m.* **make an ~ment**, prendre rendez-vous (**with**, avec).

apportion /ə'pɔːʃn/ *v.t.* répartir.

apprais|e /ə'preɪz/ *v.t.* évaluer. ~**al** *n.* évaluation *f.*

appreciable /ə'priːʃəbl/ *a.* appréciable.

appreciat|e /ə'priːʃɪeɪt/ *v.t.* (*like*) apprécier; (*understand*) comprendre; (*be grateful for*). être reconnaissant de. —*v.i.* prendre de la valeur. ~**ion** /-'eɪʃn/ *n.* appréciation *f.*; (*gratitude*) reconnaissance *f.*; (*rise*) augmentation *f.* ~**ive** /ə'priːʃɪətɪv/ *a.* reconnaissant; (*audience*) enthousiaste.

apprehen|d /æprɪ'hend/ *v.t.* (*arrest, fear*) appréhender; (*understand*) comprendre. ~**sion** *n.* appréhension *f.*

apprehensive /æprɪ'hensɪv/ *a.* inquiet. **be ~ of**, craindre.

apprentice /ə'prentɪs/ *n.* apprenti *m.* —*v.t.* mettre en apprentissage. ~**ship** *n.* apprentissage *m.*

approach /ə'prəʊtʃ/ *v.t.* (s')approcher de; (*accost*) aborder; (*with request*) s'adresser à. —*v.i.* (s')approcher. —*n.*

approche *f.* **an ~ to**, (*problem*) une façon d'aborder; (*person*) une démarche auprès de. ~**able** *a.* accessible; (*person*) abordable.

appropriate¹ /ə'prəʊprɪət/ *a.* approprié, propre. ~**ly** *adv.* à propos.

appropriate² /ə'prəʊprɪeɪt/ *v.t.* s'approprier.

approval /ə'pruːvl/ *n.* approbation *f.* **on ~**, à *or* sous condition.

approv|e /ə'pruːv/ *v.t./i.* approuver. ~**e of**, approuver. ~**ingly** *adv.* d'un air *or* d'un ton approbateur.

approximate¹ /ə'prɒksɪmət/ *a.* approximatif. ~**ly** *adv.* approximativement.

approximat|e² /ə'prɒksɪmeɪt/ *v.i.* ~**e to**, se rapprocher de. ~**ion** /-'meɪʃn/ *n.* approximation *f.*

apricot /'eɪprɪkɒt/ *n.* abricot *m.*

April /'eɪprəl/ *n.* avril *m.* **make an ~ fool of**, faire un poisson d'avril à.

apron /'eɪprən/ *n.* tablier *m.*

apse /æps/ *n.* (*of church*) abside *f.*

apt /æpt/ *a.* (*suitable*) approprié; (*pupil*) doué. **be ~ to**, avoir tendance à. ~**ly** *adv.* à propos.

aptitude /'æptɪtjuːd/ *n.* aptitude *f.*

aqualung /'ækwəlʌŋ/ *n.* scaphandre autonome *m.*

aquarium /ə'kweərɪəm/ *n.* (*pl.* **-ums**) aquarium *m.*

Aquarius /ə'kweərɪəs/ *n.* le Verseau.

aquatic /ə'kwætɪk/ *a.* aquatique; (*sport*) nautique.

aqueduct /'ækwɪdʌkt/ *n.* aqueduc *m.*

Arab /'ærəb/ *n. & a.* arabe (*m./f.*). ~**ic** *a. & n.* (*lang.*) arabe (*m.*). ~**ic numerals**, chiffres arabes *m. pl.*

Arabian /ə'reɪbɪən/ *a.* arabe.

arable /'ærəbl/ *a.* arable.

arbiter /'ɑːbɪtə(r)/ *n.* arbitre *m.*

arbitrary /'ɑːbɪtrərɪ/ *a.* arbitraire.

arbitrat|e /'ɑːbɪtreɪt/ *v.i.* arbitrer. ~**ion** /-'treɪʃn/ *n.* arbitrage *m.* ~**or** *n.* arbitre *m.*

arc /ɑːk/ *n.* arc *m.*

arcade /ɑː'keɪd/ *n.* (*shops*) galerie *f.*; (*arches*) arcades *f. pl.*

arch¹ /ɑːtʃ/ *n.* arche *f.*; (*in church etc.*) arc *m.*; (*of foot*) voûte plantaire *f.* —*v.t./i.* (s')arquer.

arch² /ɑːtʃ/ *a.* (*playful*) malicieux.

arch- /ɑːtʃ/ *pref.* (*hypocrite etc.*) grand, achevé.

archaeolog|y /ɑːkɪ'ɒlədʒɪ/ *n.* archéologie *f.* ~**ical** /-ə'lɒdʒɪkl/ *a.* archéologique. ~**ist** *n.* archéologue *m./f.*

archaic /ɑːˈkeɪɪk/ a. archaïque.
archbishop /ɑːtʃˈbɪʃəp/ n. archevêque m.
archeology /ɑːkɪˈɒlədʒɪ/ n. (Amer.) = **archaeology**.
archer /ˈɑːtʃə(r)/ n. archer m. ∼**y** n. tir à l'arc m.
archetype /ˈɑːkɪtaɪp/ n. archétype m., modèle m.
archipelago /ɑːkɪˈpeləgəʊ/ n. (pl. -os) archipel m.
architect /ˈɑːkɪtekt/ n. architecte m.
architectur|e /ˈɑːkɪtektʃə(r)/ n. architecture f. ∼**al** /-ˈtektʃərəl/ a. architectural.
archiv|es /ˈɑːkaɪvz/ n. pl. archives f. pl. ∼**ist** /-ɪvɪst/ n. archiviste m./f.
archway /ˈɑːtʃweɪ/ n. voûte f.
Arctic /ˈɑːktɪk/ a. & n. arctique (m.). **arctic** a. glacial.
ardent /ˈɑːdnt/ a. ardent. ∼**ly** adv. ardemment.
ardour /ˈɑːdə(r)/ n. ardeur f.
arduous /ˈɑːdjʊəs/ a. ardu.
are /ɑː(r)/ see **be**.
area /ˈeərɪə/ n. (surface) superficie f.; (region) région f.; (district) quartier m.; (fig.) domaine m. **parking/picnic** ∼, aire de parking/de pique-nique f.
arena /əˈriːnə/ n. arène f.
aren't /ɑːnt/ = **are not**.
Argentin|a /ɑːdʒənˈtiːnə/ n. Argentine f. ∼**e** /ˈɑːdʒəntaɪn/, ∼**ian** /-ˈtɪnɪən/ a. & n. argentin(e) (m. (f.)).
argu|e /ˈɑːgjuː/ v.i. (quarrel) se disputer; (reason) argumenter. —v.t. (debate) discuter. ∼**e that**, alléguer que. ∼**able** /-ʊəbl/ a. le cas selon certains. ∼**ably** adv. selon certains.
argument /ˈɑːgjʊmənt/ n. dispute f.; (reasoning) argument m.; (discussion) débat m. ∼**ative** /-ˈmentətɪv/ a. raisonneur, contrariant.
arid /ˈærɪd/ a. aride.
Aries /ˈeəriːz/ n. le Bélier.
arise /əˈraɪz/ v.i. (p.t. arose, p.p. arisen) se présenter; (old use) se lever. ∼ **from**, résulter de.
aristocracy /ærɪˈstɒkrəsɪ/ n. aristocratie f.
aristocrat /ˈærɪstəkræt, Amer. əˈrɪstəkræt/ n. aristocrate m./f. ∼**ic** /-ˈkrætɪk/ a. aristocratique.
arithmetic /əˈrɪθmətɪk/ n. arithmétique f.
ark /ɑːk/ n. (relig.) arche f.
arm[1] /ɑːm/ n. bras m. ∼ **in arm**, bras dessus bras dessous. ∼**band** n. brassard m.

arm[2] /ɑːm/ v.t. armer. ∼**ed robbery**, vol à main armée m.
armament /ˈɑːməmənt/ n. armement m.
armchair /ˈɑːmtʃeə(r)/ n. fauteuil m.
armistice /ˈɑːmɪstɪs/ n. armistice m.
armour /ˈɑːmə(r)/ n. armure f.; (on tanks etc.) blindage m. ∼**-clad**, ∼**ed** adjs. blindé.
armoury /ˈɑːmərɪ/ n. arsenal m.
armpit /ˈɑːmpɪt/ n. aisselle f.
arms /ɑːmz/ n. pl. (weapons) armes f. pl. ∼ **dealer**, trafiquant d'armes m.
army /ˈɑːmɪ/ n. armée f.
aroma /əˈrəʊmə/ n. arôme m. ∼**tic** /ærəˈmætɪk/ a. aromatique.
arose /əˈrəʊz/ see **arise**.
around /əˈraʊnd/ adv. (tout) autour; (here and there) çà et là. —prep. autour de. ∼ **here**, par ici.
arouse /əˈraʊz/ v.t. (awaken, cause) éveiller; (excite) exciter.
arrange /əˈreɪndʒ/ v.t. arranger; (time, date) fixer. ∼ **to**, s'arranger pour. ∼**ment** n. arrangement m. **make** ∼**ments**, prendre des dispositions.
array /əˈreɪ/ v.t. (mil.) déployer; (dress) vêtir. —n. **an** ∼ **of**, (display) un étalage impressionnant de.
arrears /əˈrɪəz/ n. pl. arriéré m. **in** ∼, (rent) arriéré. **he is in** ∼, il a des paiements en retard.
arrest /əˈrest/ v.t. arrêter; (attention) retenir. —n. arrestation f. **under** ∼, en état d'arrestation.
arrival /əˈraɪvl/ n. arrivée f. **new** ∼, nouveau venu m., nouvelle venue f.
arrive /əˈraɪv/ v.i. arriver.
arrogan|t /ˈærəgənt/ a. arrogant. ∼**ce** n. arrogance f. ∼**tly** adv. avec arrogance.
arrow /ˈærəʊ/ n. flèche f.
arse /ɑːs/ n. (sl.) cul m. (sl.)
arsenal /ˈɑːsənl/ n. arsenal m.
arsenic /ˈɑːsnɪk/ n. arsenic m.
arson /ˈɑːsn/ n. incendie criminel m. ∼**ist** n. incendiaire m./f.
art /ɑːt/ n. art m.; (fine arts) beaux-arts m. pl. ∼**s**, (univ.) lettres f. pl. ∼ **gallery**, (public) musée (d'art) m.; (private) galerie (d'art) f. ∼ **school**, école des beaux-arts f.
artefact /ˈɑːtɪfækt/ n. objet fabriqué m.
arter|y /ˈɑːtərɪ/ n. artère f. ∼**ial** /-ˈtɪərɪəl/ a. artériel. ∼**ial road**, route principale f.
artful /ˈɑːtfl/ a. astucieux, rusé. ∼**ness** n. astuce f.
arthriti|s /ɑːˈθraɪtɪs/ n. arthrite f. ∼**c** /-ɪtɪk/ a. arthritique.
artichoke /ˈɑːtɪtʃəʊk/ n. artichaut m.

article /'ɑːtɪkl/ n. article m. ~ **of clothing**, vêtement m. ~**d** a. (jurid.) en stage.

articulate[1] /ɑːˈtɪkjʊlət/ a. (person) capable de s'exprimer clairement; (speech) distinct.

articulat|**e**[2] /ɑːˈtɪkjʊleɪt/ v.t./i. articuler. ~**ed lorry**, semi-remorque m. ~**ion** /-ˈleɪʃn/ n. articulation f.

artifice /'ɑːtɪfɪs/ n. artifice m.

artificial /ɑːtɪˈfɪʃl/ a. artificiel. ~**ity** /-ʃɪˈælətɪ/ n. manque de naturel m.

artillery /ɑːˈtɪlərɪ/ n. artillerie f.

artisan /ɑːtɪˈzæn/ n. artisan m.

artist /'ɑːtɪst/ n. artiste m./f. ~**ic** /-ˈtɪstɪk/ a. artistique. ~**ry** n. art m.

artiste /ɑːˈtiːst/ n. (entertainer) artiste m./f.

artless /'ɑːtlɪs/ a. ingénu, naïf.

artwork /'ɑːtwɜːk/ n. (of book) illustrations f. pl.

as /æz, unstressed əz/ adv. & conj. comme; (while) pendant que. **as you get older**, en vieillissant. **as she came in**, en entrant. **as a mother**, en tant que mère. **as a gift**, en cadeau. **as from Monday**, à partir de lundi. **as tall as**, aussi grand que. ~ **for, as to**, quant à ~ **if**, comme si. **you look as if you're tired**, vous avez l'air (d'être) fatigué. **as much, as many**, autant (as, que). **as soon as**, aussitôt que. **as well**, aussi (as, bien que). **as wide as possible**, aussi large que possible.

asbestos /æzˈbestɒs/ n. amiante f.

ascend /əˈsend/ v.t. gravir; (throne) monter sur. —v.i. monter. ~**ant** n. **be in the ~ant**, monter.

ascent /əˈsent/ n. (climbing) ascension f.; (slope) côte f.

ascertain /æsəˈteɪn/ v.t. s'assurer de. ~ **that**, s'assurer que.

ascetic /əˈsetɪk/ a. ascétique. —n. ascète m./f.

ascribe /əˈskraɪb/ v.t. attribuer.

ash[1] /æʃ/ n. ~ **(tree)**, frêne m.

ash[2] /æʃ/ n. cendre f. **Ash Wednesday**, Mercredi des Cendres m. ~**en** a. cendreux.

ashamed /əˈʃeɪmd/ a. **be ~**, avoir honte (of, de).

ashore /əˈʃɔː(r)/ adv. à terre.

ashtray /'æʃtreɪ/ n. cendrier m.

Asia /'eɪʃə, Amer. 'eɪʒə/ n. Asie f. ~**n** a. & n. asiatique (m./f.). **the ~n community**, la communauté indo-pakistanaise. ~**tic** /-ɪˈætɪk/ a. asiatique.

aside /əˈsaɪd/ adv. de côté. —n. aparté m. ~ **from**, à part.

ask /ɑːsk/ v.t./i. demander; (a question) poser; (invite) inviter. ~ **s.o. sth.**, demander qch. à qn. ~ **s.o. to do**, demander à qn. de faire. ~ **about**, (thing) se renseigner sur; (person) demander des nouvelles de. ~ **for**, demander.

askance /əˈskæns/ adv. **look ~ at**, regarder avec méfiance.

askew /əˈskjuː/ adv. & a. de travers.

asleep /əˈsliːp/ a. endormi; (numb) engourdi. —adv. **fall ~**, s'endormir.

asparagus /əˈspærəgəs/ n. (plant) asperge f., (culin.) asperges f. pl.

aspect /'æspekt/ n. aspect m.; (direction) orientation f.

aspersions /əˈspɜːʃnz/ n. pl. **cast ~ on**, calomnier.

asphalt /'æsfælt, Amer. 'æsfɔːlt/ n. asphalte m. —v.t. asphalter.

asphyxiat|**e** /əsˈfɪksɪeɪt/ v.t./i. (s')asphyxier. ~**ion** /-ˈeɪʃn/ n. asphyxie f.

aspir|**e** /əsˈpaɪə(r)/ v.i. ~**e to**, aspirer à. ~**ation** /æspəˈreɪʃn/ n. aspiration f.

aspirin /'æsprɪn/ n. aspirine f.

ass /æs/ n. âne m.; (person: fam.) idiot(e) m. (f.).

assail /əˈseɪl/ v.t. assaillir. ~**ant** n. agresseur m.

assassin /əˈsæsɪn/ n. assassin m.

assassinat|**e** /əˈsæsɪneɪt/ v.t. assassiner. ~**ion** /-ˈneɪʃn/ n. assassinat m.

assault /əˈsɔːlt/ n. (mil.) assaut m.; (jurid.) agression f. —v.t. (person: jurid.) agresser.

assembl|**e** /əˈsembl/ v.t. (things) assembler; (people) rassembler. —v.i. s'assembler, se rassembler. ~**age** n. assemblage m.

assembly /əˈsemblɪ/ n. assemblée f. ~ **line**, chaîne de montage f.

assent /əˈsent/ n. assentiment m. —v.i. consentir.

assert /əˈsɜːt/ v.t. affirmer; (one's rights) revendiquer. ~**ion** /-ʃn/ n. affirmation f. ~**ive** a. affirmatif, péremptoire.

assess /əˈses/ v.t. évaluer; (payment) déterminer le montant de. ~**ment** n. évaluation f. ~**or** n. (valuer) expert m.

asset /'æset/ n. (advantage) atout m. ~**s**, (comm.) actif m.

assiduous /əˈsɪdjʊəs/ a. assidu.

assign /əˈsaɪn/ v.t. (allot) assigner. ~ **s.o. to**, (appoint) affecter qn. à.

assignment /əˈsaɪnmənt/ n. (task) mission f., tâche f.; (schol.) rapport m.

assimilat|**e** /əˈsɪmɪleɪt/ v.t./i. (s')assimiler. ~**ion** /-ˈleɪʃn/ n. assimilation f.

assist /ə'sɪst/ v.t./i. aider. ～ance n. aide f.

assistant /ə'sɪstənt/ n. aide m./f.; (in shop) vendeulr, -se m., f. —a. (manager etc.) adjoint.

associat|e¹ /ə'səʊʃɪeɪt/ v.t. associer. —v.i. ～e with, fréquenter. ～ion /-'eɪʃn/ n. association f.

associate² /ə'səʊʃɪət/ n. & a. associé(e) (m. (f.)).

assort|ed /ə'sɔːtɪd/ a. divers; (foods) assortis. ～ment n. assortiment m. an ～ment of guests/etc., des invités/etc. divers.

assume /ə'sjuːm/ v.t. supposer, présumer; (power, attitude) prendre; (role, burden) assumer.

assumption /ə'sʌmpʃn/ n. (sth. supposed) supposition f.

assurance /ə'ʃʊərəns/ n. assurance f.

assure /ə'ʃʊə(r)/ v.t. assurer. ～d a. assuré. ～dly /-rɪdlɪ/ adv. assurément.

asterisk /'æstərɪsk/ n. astérisque m.

astern /ə'stɜːn/ adv. à l'arrière.

asthma /'æsmə/ n. asthme m. ～tic /-'mætɪk/ a. & n. asthmatique (m./f.).

astonish /ə'stɒnɪʃ/ v.t. étonner. ～ingly adv. étonnamment. ～ment n. étonnement m.

astound /ə'staʊnd/ v.t. stupéfier.

astray /ə'streɪ/ adv. & a. go ～, s'égarer. lead ～, égarer.

astride /ə'straɪd/ adv. & prep. à califourchon (sur).

astrolog|y /ə'strɒlədʒɪ/ n. astrologie f. ～er n. astrologue m.

astronaut /'æstrənɔːt/ n. astronaute m./f.

astronom|y /ə'strɒnəmɪ/ n. astronomie f. ～er n. astronome m. ～ical /æstrə'nɒmɪkl/ a. astronomique.

astute /ə'stjuːt/ a. astucieux. ～ness n. astuce f.

asylum /ə'saɪləm/ n. asile m.

at /æt, unstressed ət/ prep. à. **at the doctor's/**etc., chez le médecin/etc. **surprised at,** (cause) étonné de. **angry at,** fâché contre. **not at all,** pas du tout. **no wind/**etc. **at all,** (of any kind) pas le moindre vent/etc. **at night,** la nuit. **at once,** tout de suite; (simultaneously) à la fois. **～ sea,** en mer. **at times,** parfois.

ate /et/ see eat.

atheis|t /'eɪθɪɪst/ n. athée m./f. ～m /-zəm/ n. athéisme m.

athlet|e /'æθliːt/ n. athlète m./f. ～ic /-'letɪk/ a. athlétique. ～ics /-'letɪks/ n. pl. athlétisme m.

Atlantic /ət'læntɪk/ a. atlantique. —n. ～ **(Ocean),** Atlantique m.

atlas /'ætləs/ n. atlas m.

atmospher|e /'ætməsfɪə(r)/ n. atmosphère f. ～ic /-'ferɪk/ a. atmosphérique.

atoll /'ætɒl/ n. atoll m.

atom /'ætəm/ n. atome m. ～ic /ə'tɒmɪk/ a. atomique. ～(ic) **bomb,** bombe atomique f.

atomize /'ætəmaɪz/ v.t. atomiser. ～r /-ə(r)/ n. atomiseur m.

atone /ə'təʊn/ v.i. ～ **for,** expier. ～ment n. expiation f.

atrocious /ə'trəʊʃəs/ a. atroce.

atrocity /ə'trɒsətɪ/ n. atrocité f.

atrophy /'ætrəfɪ/ n. atrophie f. —v.t./i. (s')atrophier.

attach /ə'tætʃ/ v.t./i. (s')attacher; (letter) joindre (to, à). ～ed a. **be ～ed to,** (like) être attaché à. **the ～ed letter,** la lettre ci-jointe. ～ment n. (accessory) accessoire m.; (affection) attachement m.

attaché /ə'tæʃeɪ/ n. (pol.) attaché(e) m. (f.). ～ **case,** mallette f.

attack /ə'tæk/ n. attaque f.; (med.) crise f. —v.t. attaquer. ～er n. agresseur m., attaquant(e) m. (f.).

attain /ə'teɪn/ v.t. atteindre (à); (gain) acquérir. ～able a. accessible. ～ment n. acquisition f. (of, de). ～ments, réussites f. pl.

attempt /ə'tempt/ v.t. tenter. —n. tentative f. **an ～ on s.o.'s life,** un attentat contre qn.

attend /ə'tend/ v.t. assister à; (class) suivre; (school, church) aller à; (escort) accompagner. —v.i. assister. ～ **(to),** (look after) s'occuper de. ～ance n. présence f.; (people) assistance f.

attendant /ə'tendənt/ n. employé(e) m. (f.); (servant) serviteur m. —a. concomitant.

attention /ə'tenʃn/ n. attention f.; ～!, (mil.) garde-à-vous! **pay ～,** faire or prêter attention (to, à).

attentive /ə'tentɪv/ a. attentif; (considerate) attentionné. ～ly adv. attentivement. ～ness n. attention f.

attenuate /ə'tenjʊeɪt/ v.t. atténuer.

attest /ə'test/ v.t./i. ～ **(to),** attester. ～ation /æte'steɪʃn/ n. attestation f.

attic /'ætɪk/ n. grenier m.

attitude /'ætɪtjuːd/ n. attitude f.

attorney /ə'tɜːnɪ/ n. mandataire m.; (Amer.) avocat m.

attract /ə'trækt/ v.t. attirer. ～ion /-kʃn/ n. attraction f.; (charm) attrait m.

attractive /ə'træktɪv/ a. attrayant, séduisant. ～ly adv. agréablement. ～ness n. attrait m., beauté f.

attribute[1] /ə'trɪbju:t/ v.t. ~ **to,** attribuer à.

attribute[2] /'ætrɪbju:t/ n. attribut m.

attrition /ə'trɪʃn/ n. **war of** ~, guerre d'usure f.

aubergine /'əʊbəʒi:n/ n. aubergine f.

auburn /'ɔ:bən/ a. châtain roux invar.

auction /'ɔ:kʃn/ n. vente aux enchères f.—v.t. vendre aux enchères. ~**eer** /ɔ:ʃə'nɪə(r)/ n. commissaire-priseur m.

audaci|ous /ɔ:'deɪʃəs/ a. audacieux. ~**ty** /-æsətɪ/ n. audace f.

audible /'ɔ:dəbl/ a. audible.

audience /'ɔ:dɪəns/ n. auditoire m.; (theatre, radio) public m.; (interview) audience f.

audio typist /'ɔ:dɪəʊ'taɪpɪst/ n. audiotypiste m./f.

audio-visual /ɔ:dɪəʊ'vɪʒʊəl/ a. audio-visuel.

audit /'ɔ:dɪt/ n. vérification des comptes f. —v.t. vérifier.

audition /ɔ:'dɪʃn/ n. audition f. —v.t./i. auditionner.

auditor /'ɔ:dɪtə(r)/ n. commissaire aux comptes m.

auditorium /ɔ:dɪ'tɔ:rɪəm/ n. (of theatre etc.) salle f.

augur /'ɔ:gə(r)/ v.i. ~ **well/ill,** être de bon/mauvais augure.

August /'ɔ:gəst/ n. août m.

aunt /ɑ:nt/ n. tante f.

au pair /əʊ'peə(r)/ n. jeune fille au pair f.

aura /'ɔ:rə/ n. atmosphère f.

auspices /'ɔ:spɪsɪz/ n. pl. auspices m. pl., égide f.

auspicious /ɔ:'spɪʃəs/ a. favorable.

auster|e /ɔ:'stɪə(r)/ a. austère. ~**ity** /-erətɪ/ n. austérité f.

Australia /ɒ'streɪlɪə/ n. Australie f. ~**n** a. & n. australien(ne) (m. (f.)).

Austria /'ɒstrɪə/ n. Autriche f. ~**n** a. & n. autrichien(ne) (m. (f.)).

authentic /ɔ:'θentɪk/ a. authentique. ~**ity** /-ən'tɪsətɪ/ n. authenticité f.

authenticate /ɔ:'θentɪkeɪt/ v.t. authentifier.

author /'ɔ:θə(r)/ n. auteur m. ~**ship** n. (origin) paternité f.

authoritarian /ɔ:θɒrɪ'teərɪən/ a. autoritaire.

authorit|y /ɔ:'θɒrətɪ/ n. autorité f.; (permission) autorisation f. ~**ative** /-ɪtətɪv/ a. (credible) qui fait autorité; (trusted) autorisé; (manner) autoritaire.

authoriz|e /'ɔ:θəraɪz/ v.t. autoriser. ~**ation** /-'zeɪʃn/ n. autorisation f.

autistic /ɔ:'tɪstɪk/ a. autistique.

autobiography /ɔ:təbaɪ'ɒgrəfɪ/ n. autobiographie f.

autocrat /'ɔ:təkræt/ n. autocrate m. ~**ic** /-'krætɪk/ a. autocratique.

autograph /'ɔ:təgrɑ:f/ n. autographe m. —v.t. signer, dédicacer.

auto-immune /ɔ:təʊɪ'mju:n/ a. auto-immune.

automat|e /'ɔ:təmeɪt/ v.t. automatiser. ~**ion** /-'meɪʃn/ n. automatisation f.

automatic /ɔ:tə'mætɪk/ a. automatique. —n. (auto.) voiture automatique f. ~**ally** /-klɪ/ adv. automatiquement.

automobile /'ɔ:təməbi:l/ n. (Amer.) auto(mobile) f.

autonom|y /ɔ:'tɒnəmɪ/ n. autonomie f. ~**ous** a. autonome.

autopsy /'ɔ:tɒpsɪ/ n. autopsie f.

autumn /'ɔ:təm/ n. automne m. ~**al** /-'tʌmnəl/ a. automnal.

auxiliary /ɔ:g'zɪlɪərɪ/ a. & n. auxiliaire (m./f.) ~ **(verb),** auxiliaire m.

avail /ə'veɪl/ v.t. ~ **o.s. of,** profiter de. —n. **of no** ~, inutile. **to no** ~, sans résultat.

availab|le /ə'veɪləbl/ a. disponible. ~**ility** /-'bɪlətɪ/ n. disponibilité f.

avalanche /'ævəlɑ:nʃ/ n. avalanche f.

avant-garde /ævɑ̃'gɑ:d/ a. d'avant-garde.

avaric|e /'ævərɪs/ n. avarice f. ~**ious** /-'rɪʃəs/ a. avare.

avenge /ə'vendʒ/ v.t. venger ~ **o.s.,** se venger (**on,** de).

avenue /'ævənju:/ n. avenue f.; (line of approach: fig.) voie f.

average /'ævərɪdʒ/ n. moyenne f. —a. moyen. —v.t./i. faire la moyenne de; (produce, do) faire en moyenne. **on** ~, en moyenne.

avers|e /ə'vɜ:s/ a. **be** ~**e to,** répugner à. ~**ion** /-ʃn/ n. aversion f.

avert /ə'vɜ:t/ v.t. (turn away) détourner; (ward off) éviter.

aviary /'eɪvɪərɪ/ n. volière f.

aviation /eɪvɪ'eɪʃn/ n. aviation f.

avid /'ævɪd/ a. avide.

avocado /ævə'kɑ:dəʊ/ n. (pl. -os) avocat m.

avoid /ə'vɔɪd/ v.t. éviter. ~**able** a. évitable. ~**ance** n. **the** ~**ance of** s.o./sth. is . . ., éviter qn./qch., c'est . . .

await /ə'weɪt/ v.t. attendre.

awake /ə'weɪk/ v.t./i. (p.t. awoke, p.p. awoken) (s')éveiller. —a. **be** ~, ne pas dormir, être (r)éveillé.

awaken /ə'weɪkən/ v.t./i. (s')éveiller.

award /ə'wɔ:d/ v.t. attribuer. —n. récompense f., prix m.; (scholarship) bourse *f.* **pay ~,** augmentation (salariale) *f.*

aware /ə'weə(r)/ *a.* averti. **be ~ of,** (*danger*) être conscient de; (*fact*) savoir. **become ~ of,** prendre conscience de. **~ness** *n.* conscience *f.*

awash /ə'wɒʃ/ *a.* inondé (**with,** de).

away /ə'weɪ/ *adv.* (*far*) (au) loin; (*absent*) absent, parti; (*persistently*) sans arrêt; (*entirely*) complètement. **~ from,** loin de. **move ~,** s'écarter; (*to new home*) déménager. **six kilometres ~,** à six kilomètres (de distance). **take ~,** emporter. —*a. & n.* **~ (match),** match à l'extérieur *m.*

awe /ɔː/ *n.* crainte (révérencielle) *f.* **~-inspiring, ~some** *adjs.* terrifiant; (*sight*) imposant. **~struck** *a.* terrifié.

awful /'ɔːfl/ *a.* affreux. **~ly** /'ɔːflɪ/ *adv.* (*badly*) affreusement; (*very: fam.*) rudement.

awhile /ə'waɪl/ *adv.* quelque temps.

awkward /'ɔːkwəd/ *a.* difficile; (*inconvenient*) inopportun; (*clumsy*) maladroit; (*embarrassing*) gênant; (*embarrassed*) gêné. **~ly** *adv.* maladroitement; avec gêne. **~ness** *n.* maladresse *f.*; (*discomfort*) gêne *f.*

awning /'ɔːnɪŋ/ *n.* auvent *m.*; (*of shop*) store *m.*

awoke, awoken /ə'wəʊk, ə'wəʊkən/ *see* **awake.**

awry /ə'raɪ/ *adv.* **go ~,** mal tourner. **sth. is ~,** qch. ne va pas.

axe, (*Amer.*) **ax** /æks/ *n.* hache *f.* —*v.t.* (*pres. p.* **axing**) réduire; (*eliminate*) supprimer; (*employee*) renvoyer.

axiom /'æksɪəm/ *n.* axiome *m.*

axis /'æksɪs/ *n.* (*pl.* **axes** /-siːz/) axe *m.*

axle /'æksl/ *n.* essieu *m.*

ay(e) /aɪ/ *adv. & n.* oui (*m. invar.*).

B

BA *abbr. see* **Bachelor of Arts.**

babble /'bæbl/ *v.i.* babiller; (*stream*) gazouiller. —*n.* babillage *m.*

baboon /bə'buːn/ *n.* babouin *m.*

baby /'beɪbɪ/ *n.* bébé *m.* **~ carriage,** (*Amer.*) voiture d'enfant *f.* **~-sit** *v.i.* garder les enfants. **~-sitter** *n.* babysitter *m./f.*

babyish /'beɪbɪʃ/ *a.* enfantin.

bachelor /'bætʃələ(r)/ *n.* célibataire *m.* **B~ of Arts/Science,** licencié(e) ès lettres/sciences *m.* (*f.*).

back /bæk/ *n.* (*of person, hand, page, etc.*) dos *m.*; (*of house*) derrière *m.*; (*of vehicle*) arrière *m.*; (*of room*) fond *m.*; (*of chair*) dossier *m.*; (*football*) arrière *m.* —*a.* de derrière, arrière *invar.*; (*taxes*) arriéré. —*adv.* en arrière; (*returned*) de retour, rentré. —*v.t.* (*support*) appuyer; (*bet on*) miser sur; (*vehicle*) faire reculer. —*v.i.* (*of person, vehicle*) reculer. **at the ~ of beyond,** au diable. **at the ~ of the book,** à la fin du livre. **come ~,** revenir. **give ~,** rendre. **take ~,** reprendre. **I want it ~,** je veux le récupérer. **in ~ of,** (*Amer.*) derrière. **~-bencher** *n.* (*pol.*) membre sans portefeuille *m.* **~ down,** abandonner, se dégonfler. **~ number,** vieux numéro *m.* **~ out,** se dégager, se dégonfler; (*auto.*) sortir en reculant. **~ pedal** *v.i.* pédaler en arrière; (*fig.*) faire machine arrière (**on,** à propos de). **~ up,** (*support*) appuyer. **~-up** *n.* appui *m.*; (*Amer.,* *jam*) embouteillage *m.*; (*comput.*) sauvegarde *f.*; *a.* de réserve; (*comput.*) de sauvegarde.

backache /'bækeɪk/ *n.* mal de reins *m.*, mal aux reins *m.*

backbiting /'bækbaɪtɪŋ/ *n.* médisance *f.*

backbone /'bækbəʊn/ *n.* colonne vertébrale *f.*

backdate /bæk'deɪt/ *v.t.* antidater; (*arrangement*) rendre rétroactif.

backer /'bækə(r)/ *n.* partisan *m.*; (*comm.*) bailleur de fonds *m.*

backfire /bæk'faɪə(r)/ *v.i.* (*auto.*) pétarader; (*fig.*) mal tourner.

backgammon /bæk'gæmən/ *n.* trictrac *m.*

background /'bækgraʊnd/ *n.* fond *m.*, arrière-plan *m.*; (*context*) contexte *m.*; (*environment*) milieu *m.*; (*experience*) formation *f.* —*a.* (*music, noise*) de fond.

backhand /'bækhænd/ *n.* revers *m.* **~ed** *a.* équivoque. **~ed stroke,** revers *m.* **~er** *n.* revers *m.*; (*bribe: sl.*) pot de vin *m.*

backing /'bækɪŋ/ *n.* appui *m.*

backlash /'bæklæʃ/ *n.* choc en retour *m.*, répercussions *f. pl.*

backlog /'bæklɒg/ *n.* accumulation (de travail) *f.*

backpack /'bækpæk/ *n.* sac à dos *m.*

backside /'bæksaɪd/ *n.* (*buttocks: fam.*) derrière *m.*

backstage /bæk'steɪdʒ/ *a. & adv.* dans les coulisses.

backstroke /'bækstrəʊk/ *n.* dos crawlé *m.*

backtrack /'bæktræk/ v.i. rebrousser chemin; (change one's opinion) faire marche arrière.

backward /'bækwəd/ a. (step etc.) en arrière; (retarded) arriéré.

backwards /'bækwədz/ adv. en arrière; (walk) à reculons; (read) à l'envers; (fall) à la renverse. **go ∼ and forwards,** aller et venir.

backwater /'bækwɔ:tə(r)/ n. (pej.) trou perdu m.

bacon /'beɪkən/ n. lard m.; (in rashers) bacon m.

bacteria /bæk'tɪərɪə/ n. pl. bactéries f. pl. ∼l a. bactérien.

bad /bæd/ a. (**worse, worst**) mauvais; (wicked) méchant; (ill) malade; (accident) grave; (food) gâté. **feel ∼,** se sentir mal. **go ∼,** se gâter. **∼ language,** gros mots m. pl. **∼-mannered** a. mal élevé. **∼-tempered** a. grincheux **∼ly** adv mal; (hurt) grièvement. **too ∼!,** tant pis; (I'm sorry) dommage! **want ∼ly,** avoir grande envie de.

badge /bædʒ/ n. insigne m.; (of identity) plaque f.

badger /'bædʒə(r)/ n. blaireau m. —v.t. harceler.

badminton /'bædmɪntən/ n. badminton m.

baffle /'bæfl/ v.t. déconcerter.

bag /bæg/ n. sac m. **∼s,** (luggage) bagages m.pl.; (under eyes) poches f. pl. —v.t. (p.t. **bagged**) mettre en sac; (take: fam.) s'adjuger. **∼s of,** (fam.) beaucoup de.

baggage /'bægɪdʒ/ n. bagages m. pl. **∼ reclaim,** livraison des bagages f.

baggy /'bægɪ/ a. trop grand.

bagpipes /'bægpaɪps/ n. pl. cornemuse f.

Bahamas /bə'hɑ:məz/ n. pl. **the ∼,** les Bahamas f.pl.

bail[1] /beɪl/ n. caution f. **on ∼,** sous caution. —v.t. mettre en liberté (provisoire) sous caution. **∼ out,** (fig.) sortir d'affaire.

bail[2] /beɪl/ n. (cricket) bâtonnet m.

bail[3] /beɪl/ v.t. (naut.) écoper.

bailiff /'beɪlɪf/ n. huissier m.

bait /beɪt/ n. appât m. —v.t. appâter; (fig.) tourmenter.

bake /beɪk/ v.t. (faire) cuire (au four). —v.i. cuire (au four); (person) faire du pain or des gâteaux. **∼ed beans,** haricots blancs à la tomate m.pl. **∼ed potato,** pomme de terre en robe des champs f. **∼er** n. boulanger, -ère m., f.

∼ing n. cuisson f. **∼ing-powder** n. levure f.

bakery /'beɪkərɪ/ n. boulangerie f.

Balaclava /bælə'klɑ:və/ n. **∼ (helmet),** passe-montagne m.

balance /'bæləns/ n. équilibre m.; (scales) balance f.; (outstanding sum: comm.) solde m.; (of payments, of trade) balance f.; (remainder) reste m.; (money in account) position f. —v.t. tenir en équilibre; (weigh up & comm.) balancer; (budget) équilibrer; (to compensate) contrebalancer. —v i. être en équilibre. **∼d** a. équilibré.

balcony /'bælkənɪ/ n. balcon m.

bald /bɔ:ld/ a. (**-er, -est**) chauve; (tyre) lisse; (fig.) simple. **∼ing** a. **be ∼ing,** perdre ses cheveux. **∼ness** n. calvitie f.

bale[1] /beɪl/ n. (of cotton) balle f.; (of straw) botte f.

bale[2] /beɪl/ v.i. **∼ out,** sauter en parachute.

baleful /'beɪlful/ a. sinistre.

balk /bɔ:k/ v.t. contrecarrer. —v.i. **∼ at,** reculer devant.

ball[1] /bɔ:l/ n. (golf, tennis, etc.) balle f.; (football) ballon m.; (croquet, billiards, etc.) boule f.; (of wool) pelote f.; (sphere) boule f. **∼-bearing** n. roulement à billes m. **∼-cock** n. robinet à flotteur m. **∼-point** n. stylo à bille m.

ball[2] /bɔ:l/ n. (dance) bal m.

ballad /'bæləd/ n. ballade f.

ballast /'bæləst/ n. lest m.

ballerina /bælə'ri:nə/ n. ballerine f.

ballet /'bæleɪ/ n. ballet m.

ballistic /bə'lɪstɪk/ a. **∼ missile,** engin balistique m.

balloon /bə'lu:n/ n. ballon m.

ballot /'bælət/ n. scrutin m. **∼-(paper),** bulletin de vote m. **∼-box** n. urne f. —v.i. (p.t. **balloted**) (pol.) voter. —v.t. (members) consulter par voie de scrutin.

ballroom /'bɔ:lrʊm/ n. salle de bal f.

ballyhoo /bælɪ'hu:/ n. (publicity) battage m.; (uproar) tapage m.

balm /bɑ:m/ n. baume m. **∼y** a. (fragrant) embaumé; (mild) doux; (crazy: sl.) dingue.

baloney /bə'ləʊnɪ/ n. (sl.) idioties f. pl., calembredaines f. pl.

balustrade /bælə'streɪd/ n. balustrade f.

bamboo /bæm'bu:/ n. bambou m.

ban /bæn/ v.t. (p.t. **banned**) interdire. **∼ from,** exclure de. —n. interdiction f.

banal /bə'nɑ:l, Amer. 'beɪnl/ a. banal. **∼ity** /-ælətɪ/ n. banalité f.

banana /bə'nɑːnə/ n. banane f.

band /bænd/ n. (*strip*, *group of people*) bande f.; (*mus.*) orchestre m.; (*pop group*) groupe m. (*mil.*) fanfare f. —v.i. ~ **together**, se liguer.

bandage /'bændɪdʒ/ n. pansement m. —v.t. bander, panser.

bandit /'bændɪt/ n. bandit m.

bandstand /'bændstænd/ n. kiosque à musique m.

bandwagon /'bændwægən/ n. **climb on the** ~, prendre le train en marche.

bandy[1] /'bændɪ/ v.t. ~ **about**, (*rumours*, *ideas*, etc.) faire circuler.

bandy[2] /'bændɪ/ a. (-ier, -iest) qui a les jambes arquées.

bang /bæŋ/ n. (*blow*, *noise*) coup (violent) m.; (*explosion*) détonation f.; (*of door*) claquement m. —v.t./i. frapper; (*door*) claquer. —int. vlan. —adv. (*fam.*) exactement. ~ **in the middle**, en plein milieu. ~ **one's head**, se cogner la tête. ~**s**, frange f.

banger /'bæŋə(r)/ n. (*firework*) pétard m.; (*culin.*, *sl.*) saucisse f. (**old**) ~, (*car*: *sl.*) guimbarde f.

bangle /'bæŋgl/ n. bracelet m.

banish /'bænɪʃ/ v.t. bannir.

banisters /'bænɪstəz/ n. pl. rampe (d'escalier) f.

banjo /'bændʒəʊ/ (pl. -os) banjo m.

bank[1] /bæŋk/ n. (*of river*) rive f.; (*of earth*) talus m.; (*of sand*) banc m. —v.t. (*earth*) amonceler; (*fire*) couvrir. —v.i. (*aviat.*) virer.

bank[2] /bæŋk/ n. banque f. —v.t. mettre en banque. —v.i. ~ **with**, avoir un compte à. ~ **account**, compte en banque m. ~ **card**, carte bancaire f. ~ **holiday**, jour férié m. ~ **on**, compter sur. ~ **statement**, relevé de compte m.

bank|ing /'bæŋkɪŋ/ n. opérations bancaires f. pl.; (*as career*) la banque. ~**er** n. banquier m.

banknote /'bæŋknəʊt/ n. billet de banque m.

bankrupt /'bæŋkrʌpt/ a. **be** ~, être en faillite. **go** ~, faire faillite. —n. failli(e) m. (f.). —v.t. mettre en faillite. ~**cy** n. faillite f.

banner /'bænə(r)/ n. bannière f.

banns /bænz/ n. pl. bans m. pl.

banquet /'bæŋkwɪt/ n. banquet m.

banter /'bæntə(r)/ n. plaisanterie f. —v.i. plaisanter.

bap /bæp/ n. petit pain m.

baptism /'bæptɪzəm/ n. baptême m.

Baptist /'bæptɪst/ n. baptiste m./f.

baptize /bæp'taɪz/ v.t. baptiser.

bar /bɑː(r)/ n. (*of metal*) barre f.; (*on window & jurid.*) barreau m.; (*of chocolate*) tablette f.; (*pub*) bar m.; (*counter*) comptoir m., bar m.; (*division*: *mus.*) mesure f.; (*fig.*) obstacle m. —v.t. (p.t. **barred**) (*obstruct*) barrer; (*prohibit*) interdire; (*exclude*) exclure. —prep. sauf. ~ **code**, code-barres m. invar. ~ **of soap**, savonnette f.

Barbados /bɑː'beɪdɒs/ n. Barbade f.

barbarian /bɑː'beərɪən/ n. barbare m./f.

barbari|c /bɑː'bærɪk/ a. barbare. ~**ty** /-ətɪ/ n. barbarie f.

barbarous /'bɑːbərəs/ a. barbare.

barbecue /'bɑːbɪkjuː/ n. barbecue m. —v.t. griller, rôtir (au barbecue).

barbed /bɑːbd/ a. ~ **wire**, fil de fer barbelé m.

barber /'bɑːbə(r)/ n. coiffeur m. (*pour hommes*).

barbiturate /bɑː'bɪtjʊrət/ n. barbiturique m.

bare /beə(r)/ a. (-er, -est) (*not covered or adorned*) nu; (*cupboard*) vide; (*mere*) simple. —v.t. mettre à nu.

barefaced /'beəfeɪst/ a. éhonté.

barefoot /'beəfʊt/ a. nu-pieds invar., pieds nus.

barely /'beəlɪ/ adv. à peine.

bargain /'bɑːgɪn/ n. (*deal*) marché m.; (*cheap thing*) occasion f. —v.i. négocier; (*haggle*) marchander. **not** ~ **for**, ne pas s'attendre à.

barge /bɑːdʒ/ n. chaland m. —v.i. ~ **in**, interrompre; (*into room*) faire irruption.

baritone /'bærɪtəʊn/ n. baryton m.

bark[1] /bɑːk/ n. (*of tree*) écorce f.

bark[2] /bɑːk/ n. (*of dog*) aboiement m. —v.i. aboyer.

barley /'bɑːlɪ/ n. orge f. ~ **sugar**, sucre d'orge m.

barmaid /'bɑːmeɪd/ n. serveuse f.

barman /'bɑːmən/ n. (pl. -men) barman m.

barmy /'bɑːmɪ/ a. (*sl.*) dingue.

barn /bɑːn/ n. grange f.

barometer /bə'rɒmɪtə(r)/ n. baromètre m.

baron /'bærən/ n. baron m. ~**ess** n. baronne f.

baroque /bə'rɒk, Amer. bə'rəʊk/ a. & n. baroque (m.).

barracks /'bærəks/ n. pl. caserne f.

barrage /'bærɑːʒ, Amer. bə'rɑːʒ/ n. (*barrier*) barrage m.; (*mil.*) tir de barrage m.; (*of complaints*) série f.

barrel /'bærəl/ n. tonneau m.; (of oil) baril m.; (of gun) canon m. **~-organ** n. orgue de Barbarie m.

barren /'bærən/ a. stérile.

barricade /bærɪ'keɪd/ n. barricade f. —v.t. barricader.

barrier /'bærɪə(r)/ n. barrière f.

barring /'bɑːrɪŋ/ prep. sauf.

barrister /'bærɪstə(r)/ n. avocat m.

barrow /'bærəʊ/ n. charrette à bras f.; (wheelbarrow) brouette f.

bartender /'bɑːtendə(r)/ n. (Amer.) barman m.

barter /'bɑːtə(r)/ n. troc m., échange m. —v.t. troquer, échanger (**for**, contre).

base /beɪs/ n. base f. —v.t. baser (**on**, sur; **in**, à). —a. bas, ignoble. **~less** a. sans fondement.

baseball /'beɪsbɔːl/ n. base-ball m.

baseboard /'beɪsbɔːd/ n. (Amer.) plinthe f.

basement /'beɪsmənt/ n. sous-sol m.

bash /bæʃ/ v.t. cogner. —n. coup (violent) m. **have a ~ at**, (sl.) s'essayer à. **~ed in**, enfoncé.

bashful /'bæʃfl/ a. timide.

basic /'beɪsɪk/ a. fondamental, élémentaire. **the ~s**, les éléments de base m. pl. **~ally** /-klɪ/ adv. au fond.

basil /'bæzɪl, Amer. 'beɪzl/ n. basilic m.

basin /'beɪsn/ n. (for liquids) cuvette f.; (for food) bol m.; (for washing) lavabo m.; (of river) bassin m.

basis /'beɪsɪs/ n. (pl. bases /-siːz/) base f.

bask /bɑːsk/ v.i. se chauffer.

basket /'bɑːskɪt/ n. corbeille f.; (with handle) panier m.

basketball /'bɑːskɪtbɔːl/ n. basket(ball) m.

Basque /bɑːsk/ a. & n. basque (m./f.).

bass[1] /beɪs/ a. (mus.) bas, grave. —n. (pl. **basses**) basse f.

bass[2] /bæs/ n. invar. (freshwater fish) perche f.; (sea) bar m.

bassoon /bə'suːn/ n. basson m.

bastard /'bɑːstəd/ n. bâtard(e) m. (f.); (sl.) salaud, -ope m., f.

baste[1] /beɪst/ v.t. (sew) bâtir.

baste[2] /beɪst/ v.t. (culin.) arroser.

bastion /'bæstɪən/ n. bastion m.

bat[1] /bæt/ n. (cricket etc.) batte f.; (table tennis) raquette f. —v.t. (p.t. **batted**) (ball) frapper. **not ~ an eyelid**, ne pas sourciller.

bat[2] /bæt/ n. (animal) chauve-souris f.

batch /bætʃ/ n. (of people) fournée f.; (of papers) paquet m.; (of goods) lot m.

bated /'beɪtɪd/ a. **with ~ breath**, en retenant son souffle.

bath /bɑːθ/ n. (pl. **-s** /bɑːðz/) bain m.; (tub) baignoire f. (swimming) **~s**, piscine f. —v.t. donner un bain à —a. de bain. **have a ~**, prendre un bain. **~ mat**, tapis de bain m.

bathe /beɪð/ v.t. baigner. —v.i. se baigner; (Amer.) prendre un bain. —n. bain (de mer) m. **~r** /-ə(r)/ n. baigneur, -se m., f.

bathing /'beɪðɪŋ/ n. baignade f. **~-costume** n. maillot de bain m.

bathrobe /'bæθrəʊb/ m. (Amer.) robe de chambre f.

bathroom /'bɑːθrʊm/ n. salle de bains f.

baton /'bætən/ n. (mil.) bâton m.; (mus.) baguette f.

battalion /bə'tæljən/ n. bataillon m.

batter /'bætə(r)/ v.t. (strike) battre; (ill-treat) maltraiter. —n. (culin.) pâte (à frire) f. **~ed** a. (pan, car) cabossé; (face) meurtri. **~ing** n. **take a ~ing**, subir des coups.

battery /'bætərɪ/ n. (mil., auto.) batterie f.; (of torch, radio) pile f.

battle /'bætl/ n. bataille f.; (fig.) lutte f. —v.i. se battre.

battlefield /'bætlfiːld/ n. champ de bataille m.

battlements /'bætlmənts/ n. pl. (crenellations) créneaux m. pl.; (wall) remparts m. pl.

battleship /'bætlʃɪp/ n. cuirassé m.

baulk /bɔːk/ v.t./i. = **balk**.

bawd|y /'bɔːdɪ/ a. (-ier, -iest) paillard. **~iness** n. paillardise f.

bawl /bɔːl/ v.t./i. brailler.

bay[1] /beɪ/ n. (bot.) laurier m. **~-leaf** n. feuille de laurier f.

bay[2] /beɪ/ n. (geog., archit.) baie f.; (area) aire f. **~ window**, fenêtre en saillie f.

bay[3] /beɪ/ n. (bark) aboiement m. —v.i. aboyer. **at ~**, aux abois. **keep** or **hold at ~**, tenir à distance.

bayonet /'beɪənɪt/ n. baïonnette f.

bazaar /bə'zɑː(r)/ n. (shop, market) bazar m.; (sale) vente f.

BC abbr. (before Christ) avant J.-C.

be /biː/ v.i. (present tense **am, are, is**; p.t. **was, were**; p.p. **been**) être. **be hot/right**/etc., avoir chaud/raison/etc. **he is 30**, (age) il a 30 ans. **it is fine/cold**/etc., (weather) il fait beau/froid/etc. **I'm a painter—are you?**, je suis peintre—ah oui?, **how are you?**, (health) comment allez-vous? **he is to leave**, (must) il doit partir; (will) il va partir, il est prévu qu'il parte. **how much is it?**, (cost) ça fait or c'est combien? **be reading/walking**/*etc.*, (*aux.*) lire/marcher/*etc.* **the child was found**, l'enfant a été retrouvé, on a retrouvé l'enfant. **have been to**, avoir été à, être allé à.

beach /biːtʃ/ *n.* plage *f.*

beacon /'biːkən/ *n.* (*lighthouse*) phare *m.*; (*marker*) balise *f.*

bead /biːd/ *n.* perle *f.*

beak /biːk/ *n.* bec *m.*

beaker /'biːkə(r)/ *n.* gobelet *m.*

beam /biːm/ *n.* (*timber*) poutre *f.*; (*of light*) rayon *m.*; (*of torch*) faisceau *m.* —*v.i.* (*radiate*) rayonner. —*v.t.* (*broadcast*) diffuser. ∼**ing** *a.* radieux.

bean /biːn/ *n.* haricot *m.*; (*of coffee*) grain *m.*

bear[1] /beə(r)/ *n.* ours *m.*

bear[2] /beə(r)/ *v.t.* (*p.t.* **bore**, *p.p.* **borne**) (*carry, show, feel*) porter; (*endure, sustain*) supporter; (*child*) mettre au monde. —*v.i.* ∼ **left**/*etc.*, (*go*) prendre à gauche/*etc.* ∼ **in mind**, tenir compte de. ∼ **on**, se rapporter à. ∼ **out**, corroborer. ∼ **up!**, courage! ∼**able** *a.* supportable. ∼**er** *n.* porteur, -se *m., f.*

beard /biəd/ *n.* barbe *f.* ∼**ed** *a.* barbu.

bearing /'beərɪŋ/ *n.* (*behaviour*) maintien *m.*; (*relevance*) rapport *m.* **get one's** ∼**s**, s'orienter.

beast /biːst/ *n.* bête *f.*; (*person*) brute *f.*

beastly /'biːstlɪ/ *a.* (-ier, -iest) (*fam.*) détestable.

beat /biːt/ *v.t./i.* (*p.t.* **beat**, *p.p.* **beaten**) battre. —*n.* (*of drum, heart*) battement *m.*; (*mus.*) mesure *f.*; (*of policeman*) ronde *f.* ∼ **a retreat**, battre en retraite. ∼ **it!**, dégage! ∼ **s.o. down**, faire baisser son prix à qn. ∼ **off the competition**, éliminer la concurrence. ∼ **up**, tabasser. **it** ∼**s me**, (*fam.*) ça me dépasse. ∼**er** *n.* batteur *m.* ∼**ing** *n.* raclée *f.*

beautician /bjuː'tɪʃn/ *n.* esthéticien(ne) *m.* (*f.*).

beautiful /'bjuːtɪfl/ *a.* beau. ∼**ly** /-flɪ/ *adv.* merveilleusement.

beautify /'bjuːtɪfaɪ/ *v.t.* embellir.

beauty /'bjuːtɪ/ *n.* beauté *f.* ∼ **parlour**, institut de beauté *m.* ∼ **spot**, grain de beauté *m.*; (*fig.*) site pittoresque *m.*

beaver /'biːvə(r)/ *n.* castor *m.*

became /bɪ'keɪm/ *see* **become**.

because /bɪ'kɒz/ *conj.* parce que. ∼ **of**, à cause de.

beck /bek/ *n.* **at the** ∼ **and call of**, aux ordres de.

beckon /'bekən/ *v.t./i.* ∼ **(to)**, faire signe à.

become /bɪ'kʌm/ *v.t./i.* (*p.t.* **became**, *p.p.* **become**) devenir; (*befit*) convenir à. **what has** ∼ **of her?**, qu'est-elle devenue?

becoming /bɪ'kʌmɪŋ/ *a.* (*seemly*) bienséant; (*clothes*) seyant.

bed /bed/ *n.* lit *m.*; (*layer*) couche *f.*; (*of sea*) fond *m.*; (*of flowers*) parterre *m.* **go to** ∼, (aller) se coucher. —*v.i.* (*p.t.* **bedded**). ∼ **down**, se coucher. ∼**ding** *n.* literie *f.*

bedbug /'bedbʌg/ *n.* punaise *f.*

bedclothes /'bedkləʊðz/ *n. pl.* couvertures *f. pl.* et draps *m. pl.*

bedevil /bɪ'devl/ *v.t.* (*p.t.* **bedevilled**) (*confuse*) embrouiller; (*plague*) tourmenter.

bedlam /'bedləm/ *n.* chahut *m.*

bedraggled /bɪ'drægld/ *a.* (*untidy*) débraillé.

bedridden /'bedrɪdn/ *a.* cloué au lit.

bedroom /'bedrʊm/ *n.* chambre (à coucher) *f.*

bedside /'bedsaɪd/ *n.* chevet *m.* ∼ **book**, livre de chevet *m.*

bedsit, bedsitter /'bedsɪt, -'sɪtə(r)/ *ns.* (*fam.*) *n.* chambre meublée *f.*, studio *m.*

bedspread /'bedspred/ *n.* dessus-de-lit *m. invar.*

bedtime /'bedtaɪm/ *n.* heure du coucher *f.*

bee /biː/ *n.* abeille *f.* **make a** ∼**-line for**, aller tout droit vers.

beech /biːtʃ/ *n.* hêtre *m.*

beef /biːf/ *n.* bœuf *m.* —*v.i.* (*grumble*: *sl.*) rouspéter.

beefburger /'biːfbɜːgə(r)/ *n.* hamburger *m.*

beefeater /'biːfiːtə(r)/ *n.* hallebardier *m.*

beefy /'biːfɪ/ *a.* (-ier, -iest) musclé.

beehive /'biːhaɪv/ *n.* ruche *f.*

been /biːn/ *see* **be**.

beer /bɪə(r)/ *n.* bière *f.*

beet /biːt/ *n.* (*plant*) betterave *f.*

beetle /'biːtl/ *n.* scarabée *m.*

beetroot /'biːtruːt/ *n. invar.* (*culin.*) betterave *f.*

befall /bɪ'fɔːl/ *v.t.* (*p.t.* **befell**, *p.p.* **befallen**) arriver à.

befit /bɪ'fɪt/ *v.t.* (*p.t.* **befitted**) convenir à, seoir à.

before /bɪ'fɔː(r)/ *prep.* (*time*) avant; (*place*) devant. —*adv.* avant; (*already*) déjà. —*conj.* ∼ **leaving**, avant de partir. ∼ **he leaves**, avant qu'il (ne) parte. **the day** ∼, la veille. **two days** ∼, deux jours avant.

beforehand /bɪ'fɔːhænd/ *adv.* à l'avance, avant.

befriend /bɪ'frend/ *v.t.* offrir son amitié
à, aider.

beg /beg/ *v.t.* (*p.t.* **begged**) (*entreat*)
supplier (**to do**, de faire). ~ (**for**),
(*money, food*) mendier; (*request*)
solliciter, demander. —*v.i.* ~ (**for
alms**), mendier. **it is going** ~**ging**,
personne n'en veut.

began /bɪ'gæn/ *see* begin.

beggar /'begə(r)/ *n.* mendiant(e) *m.* (*f.*);
(*sl.*) individu *m.*

begin /bɪ'gɪn/ *v.t./i.* (*p.t.* **began**, *p.p.*
begun, *pres. p.* **beginning**) commencer
(**to do**, à faire). ~**ner** *n.* débutant(e) *m.*
(*f.*). ~**ning** *n.* commencement *m.*,
début *m.*

begrudge /bɪ'grʌdʒ/ *v.t.* (*envy*) envier;
(*give unwillingly*) donner à contrecœur.
~ **doing**, faire à contrecœur.

beguile /bɪ'gaɪl/ *v.t.* tromper.

begun /bɪ'gʌn/ *see* begin.

behalf /bɪ'hɑːf/ *n.* **on** ~ **of**, pour; (*as
representative*) au nom de, pour (le
compte de).

behave /bɪ'heɪv/ *v.i.* se conduire. ~
(**o.s.**), se conduire bien.

behaviour, (*Amer.*) **behavior** /bɪ'heɪv-
jə(r)/ *n.* conduite *f.*, comportement *m.*

behead /bɪ'hed/ *v.t.* décapiter.

behind /bɪ'haɪnd/ *prep.* derrière; (*in
time*) en retard sur. —*adv.* derrière;
(*late*) en retard. —*n.* (*buttocks*) derrière
m. **leave** ~, oublier.

behold /bɪ'həʊld/ *v.t.* (*p.t.* **beheld**) (*old
use*) voir.

beige /beɪʒ/ *a. & n.* beige (*m.*).

being /'biːɪŋ/ *n.* (*person*) être *m.* **bring
into** ~, créer. **come into** ~, prendre
naissance.

belated /bɪ'leɪtɪd/ *a.* tardif.

belch /beltʃ/ *v.i.* faire un renvoi. —*v.t.* ~
out, (*smoke*) vomir. —*n.* renvoi *m.*

belfry /'belfrɪ/ *n.* beffroi *m.*

Belgi|um /'beldʒəm/ *n.* Belgique *f.* ~**an**
a. & n. belge (*m./f.*).

belie /bɪ'laɪ/ *v.t.* démontir.

belief /bɪ'liːf/ *n.* croyance *f.*; (*trust*)
confiance *f.*; (*faith: relig.*) foi *f.*

believ|e /bɪ'liːv/ *v.t./i.* croire. ~**e in**,
croire à; (*deity*) croire en. ~**able** *a.*
croyable. ~**er** *n.* croyant(e) *m.* (*f.*).

belittle /bɪ'lɪtl/ *v.t.* déprécier.

bell /bel/ *n.* cloche *f.*; (*small*) clochette
f.; (*on door*) sonnette *f.*; (*of phone*)
sonnerie *f.*

belligerent /bɪ'lɪdʒərənt/ *a. & n.*
belligérant(e) (*m.* (*f.*)).

bellow /'beləʊ/ *v.t./i.* beugler.

bellows /'beləʊz/ *n. pl.* soufflet *m.*

belly /'belɪ/ *n.* ventre *m.* ~**-ache** *n.* mal
au ventre *m.*

bellyful /'belɪfʊl/ *n.* **have a** ~, en avoir
plein le dos.

belong /bɪ'lɒŋ/ *v.i.* ~ **to**, appartenir à;
(*club*) être membre de.

belongings /bɪ'lɒŋɪŋz/ *n. pl.* affaires *f.
pl.*

beloved /bɪ'lʌvɪd/ *a. & n.* bien-aimé(e)
(*m.* (*f.*)).

below /bɪ'ləʊ/ *prep.* au-dessous de; (*fig.*)
indigne de. —*adv.* en dessous; (*on
page*) ci-dessous.

belt /belt/ *n.* ceinture *f.*; (*techn.*) courroie
f.; (*fig.*) région *f.* —*v.t.* (*hit: sl.*) rosser.
—*v.i.* (*rush: sl.*) filer à toute allure.

beltway /'beltweɪ/ *n.* (*Amer.*)
périphérique *m.*

bemused /bɪ'mjuːzd/ *a.* (*confused*)
stupéfié; (*thoughtful*) pensif.

bench /bentʃ/ *n.* banc *m.*; (*working-
table*) établi *m.* **the** ~, (*jurid.*) la
magistrature (*assise*). ~**-mark** *n.*
repère *m.*

bend /bend/ *v.t./i.* (*p.t.* **bent**) (*se*)
courber; (*arm, leg*) plier. —*n.* courbe
f.; (*in road*) virage *m.*; (*of arm, knee*)
pli *m.* ~ **down** *or* **over**, se pencher.

beneath /bɪ'niːθ/ *prep.* sous, au-dessous
de; (*fig.*) indigne de. —*adv.* (*au-*)
dessous.

benefactor /'benɪfæktə(r)/ *n.* bien-
faiteur, -trice *m.*, *f.*

beneficial /benɪ'fɪʃl/ *a.* avantageux,
favorable.

benefit /'benɪfɪt/ *n.* avantage *m.*;
(*allowance*) allocation *f.* —*v.t.* (*p.t.*
benefited, *pres. p.* **benefiting**) (*be
useful to*) profiter à; (*do good to*) faire
du bien à. ~ **from**, tirer profit de.

benevolen|t /bɪ'nevələnt/ *a.* bienveil-
lant. ~**ce** *n.* bienveillance *f.*

benign /bɪ'naɪn/ *a.* (*kindly*) bienveillant;
(*med.*) bénin.

bent /bent/ *see* bend. —*n.* (*talent*)
aptitude *f.*, (*inclination*) penchant *m.*
—*a.* tordu; (*sl.*) corrompu. ~ **on doing**,
décidé à faire.

bequeath /bɪ'kwiːð/ *v.t.* léguer.

bequest /bɪ'kwest/ *n.* legs *m.*

bereave|d /bɪ'riːvd/ *a.* **the** ~**d wife**/*etc.*,
la femme/*etc.* du disparu. ~**ment** *n.*
deuil *m.*

beret /'bereɪ/ *n.* béret *m.*

Bermuda /bə'mjuːdə/ *n.* Bermudes *f. pl.*

berry /'berɪ/ *n.* baie *f.*

berserk /bə'sɜːk/ *a.* **go** ~, devenir fou
furieux.

berth /bɜːθ/ *n.* (*in train, ship*) couchette

f.; (*anchorage*) mouillage *m.* —*v.i.* mouiller. **give a wide ~ to,** éviter.

beseech /bɪ'siːtʃ/ *v.t.* (*p.t.* besought) implorer, supplier.

beset /bɪ'set/ *v.t.* (*p.t.* beset, *pres. p.* **besetting**) (*attack*) assaillir; (*surround*) entourer.

beside /bɪ'saɪd/ *prep.* à côté de. ~ o.s., hors de soi. ~ the point, sans rapport.

besides /bɪ'saɪdz/ *prep.* en plus de; (*except*) excepté. —*adv.* en plus.

besiege /bɪ'siːdʒ/ *v.t.* assiéger.

best /best/ *a.* meilleur. the ~ book/*etc.*, le meilleur livre/*etc.* —*adv.* (the) ~, (*sing etc.*) le mieux. —*n.* the ~ (one), le meilleur, la meilleure. ~ man, garçon d'honneur *m.* the ~ part of, la plus grande partie de. the ~ thing is to . . . , le mieux est de . . . do one's ~, faire de son mieux. make the ~ of, s'accommoder de.

bestow /bɪ'stəʊ/ *v.t.* accorder.

best-seller /best'selə(r)/ *n.* best-seller *m.*, succès de librairie *m.*

bet /bet/ *n.* pari *m.* —*v.t.i.* (*p.t.* bet or **betted**, *pres. p.* **betting**) parier.

betray /bɪ'treɪ/ *v.t.* trahir. ~al *n.* trahison *f.*

better /'betə(r)/ *a.* meilleur. —*adv.* mieux. —*v.t.* (*improve*) améliorer; (*do better than*) surpasser. —*n.* one's ~s, ses supérieurs *m. pl.* be ~ off, (*financially*) avoir plus d'argent. he's ~ off at home, il est mieux chez lui. I had ~ go, je ferais mieux de partir. the ~ part of, la plus grande partie de. get ~, s'améliorer; (*recover*) se remettre. get the ~ of, l'emporter sur. so much the ~, tant mieux.

betting-shop /'betɪŋʃɒp/ *n.* bureau de P.M.U. *m.*

between /bɪ'twiːn/ *prep.* entre. —*adv.* in ~, au milieu.

beverage /'bevərɪdʒ/ *n.* boisson *f.*

bevy /'bevɪ/ *n.* essaim *m.*

beware /bɪ'weə(r)/ *v.i.* prendre garde (of, à).

bewilder /bɪ'wɪldə(r)/ *v.t.* désorienter, embarrasser. ~ment *n.* désorientation *f.*

bewitch /bɪ'wɪtʃ/ *v.t.* enchanter.

beyond /bɪ'jɒnd/ *prep.* au-delà de; (*doubt, reach*) hors de; (*besides*) excepté. —*adv.* au-delà. it is ~ me, ça me dépasse.

bias /'baɪəs/ *n.* (*inclination*) penchant *m.*; (*prejudice*) préjugé *m.* —*v.t.* (*p.t.* **biased**) influencer. ~ed *a.* partial.

bib /bɪb/ *n.* bavoir *m.*

Bible /'baɪbl/ *n.* Bible *f.*

biblical /'bɪblɪkl/ *a.* biblique.

bicarbonate /baɪ'kɑːbənət/ *n.* bicarbonate *m.*

biceps /'baɪseps/ *n.* biceps *m.*

bicker /'bɪkə(r)/ *v.i.* se chamailler.

bicycle /'baɪsɪkl/ *n.* bicyclette *f.* —*v.i.* faire de la bicyclette.

bid[1] /bɪd/ *n.* (*at auction*) offre *f.*, enchère *f.*; (*attempt*) tentative *f.* —*v.t.i.* (*p.t.* & *p.p.* **bid**, *pres. p.* **bidding**) (*offer*) faire une offre *or* une enchère (de). the highest ~der, le plus offrant.

bid[2] /bɪd/ *v.t.* (*p.t.* bade /bæd/, *p.p.* bidden *or* bid, *pres. p.* bidding) ordonner; (*say*) dire. ~ding *n.* ordre *m.*

bide /baɪd/ *v.t.* ~ one's time, attendre le bon moment.

biennial /baɪ'enɪəl/ *a.* biennal.

bifocals /baɪ'fəʊklz/ *n. pl.* lunettes bifocales *f. pl.*

big /bɪg/ *a.* (**bigger, biggest**) grand; (*in bulk*) gros; (*generous: sl.*) généreux: —*adv.* (*fam.*) en grand; (*earn: fam.*) gros. ~ business, les grandes affaires. ~-headed *a.* prétentieux. ~ shot, (*sl.*) huile *f.* think ~, (*fam.*) voir grand.

bigam|y /'bɪgəmɪ/ *n.* bigamie *f.* ~ist *n.* bigame *m./f.* ~ous *a.* bigame.

bigot /'bɪgət/ *n.* fanatique *m./f.* ~ed *a.* fanatique. ~ry *n.* fanatisme *m.*

bike /baɪk/ *n.* (*fam.*) vélo *m.*

bikini /bɪ'kiːnɪ/ *n.* (*pl.* -is) bikini *m.*

bilberry /'bɪlbərɪ/ *n.* myrtille *f.*

bile /baɪl/ *n.* bile *f.*

bilingual /baɪ'lɪŋgwəl/ *a.* bilingue.

bilious /'bɪlɪəs/ *a.* bilieux.

bill[1] /bɪl/ *n.* (*invoice*) facture *f.*; (*in hotel, for gas, etc.*) note *f.*; (*in restaurant*) addition *f.*; (*of sale*) acte *m.*; (*pol.*) projet de loi *m.*; (*banknote: Amer.*) billet de banque *m.* —*v.t.* (*person: comm.*) envoyer la facture à; (*theatre*) on the ~, à l'affiche.

bill[2] /bɪl/ *n.* (*of bird*) bec *m.*

billboard /'bɪlbɔːd/ *n.* panneau d'affichage *m.*

billet /'bɪlɪt/ *n.* cantonnement *m.* —*v.t.* (*p.t.* **billeted**) cantonner (on, chez).

billfold /'bɪlfəʊld/ *n.* (*Amer.*) porte-feuille *m.*

billiards /'bɪljədz/ *n.* billard *m.*

billion /'bɪljən/ *n.* billion *m.*; (*Amer.*) milliard *m.*

billy-goat /'bɪlɪgəʊt/ *n.* bouc *m.*

bin /bɪn/ *n.* (*for rubbish, litter*) boîte (à ordures), poubelle *f.*; (*for bread*) huche *f.*, coffre *m.*

binary /'baɪnərɪ/ *a.* binaire.

bind /baɪnd/ v.t. (p.t. **bound**) lier; (*book*) relier; (*jurid.*) obliger. —n. (*bore: sl.*) plaie f. **be ~ing on,** être obligatoire pour.

binding /'baɪndɪŋ/ n. reliure f.

binge /bɪndʒ/ n. **go on a ~,** (*spree: sl.*) faire la bringue.

bingo /'bɪŋgəʊ/ n. loto m.

binoculars /bɪ'nɒkjʊləz/ n. pl. jumelles f. pl.

biochemistry /baɪəʊ'kemɪstrɪ/ n. biochimie f.

biodegradable /baɪəʊdɪ'greɪdəbl/ a. biodégradable.

biograph|y /baɪ'ɒɡrəfɪ/ n. biographie f. **~er** n. biographe m./f.

biolog|y /baɪ'ɒlədʒɪ/ n. biologie f. **~ical** /-ə'lɒdʒɪkl/ a. biologique. **~ist** n. biologiste m./f.

biorhythm /'baɪəʊrɪðəm/ n. biorythme m.

birch /bɜːtʃ/ n. (*tree*) bouleau m.; (*whip*) verge f., fouet m.

bird /bɜːd/ n. oiseau m.; (*fam.*) individu m.; (*girl: sl.*) poule f.

Biro /'baɪərəʊ/ n. (pl. **-os**) (P.) stylo à bille m., Bic m. (P.).

birth /bɜːθ/ n. naissance f. **give ~,** accoucher. **~ certificate,** acte de naissance m. **~-control** n. contrôle des naissances m. **~-rate** n. natalité f.

birthday /'bɜːθdeɪ/ n. anniversaire m.

birthmark /'bɜːθmɑːk/ n. tache de vin f., envie f.

biscuit /'bɪskɪt/ n. biscuit m.; (*Amer.*) petit pain (au lait) m.

bisect /baɪ'sekt/ v.t. couper en deux.

bishop /'bɪʃəp/ n. évêque m.

bit¹ /bɪt/ n. morceau m.; (*of horse*) mors m.; (*of tool*) mèche f. **a ~,** (*a little*) un peu.

bit² /bɪt/ see **bite**.

bit³ /bɪt/ n. (*comput.*) bit m., élement binaire m.

bitch /bɪtʃ/ n. chienne f.; (*woman: fam.*) garce f. —v.i. (*grumble: fam.*) râler. **~y** a. (*fam.*) vache.

bite /baɪt/ v.t./i. (p.t. **bit**, p.p. **bitten**) mordre. —n. morsure f.; (*by insect*) piqûre f.; (*mouthful*) bouchée f. **~ one's nails,** se ronger les ongles. **have a ~,** manger un morceau.

biting /'baɪtɪŋ/ a. mordant.

bitter /'bɪtə(r)/ a. amer; (*weather*) glacial, âpre. —n. bière anglaise f. **~ly** adv. amèrement. **it is ~ly cold,** il fait un temps glacial. **~ness** n. amertume f.

bitty /'bɪtɪ/ a. décousu.

bizarre /bɪ'zɑː(r)/ a. bizarre.

blab /blæb/ v.i. (p.t. **blabbed**) jaser.

black /blæk/ a. (**-er, -est**) noir. —n. (*colour*) noir m. **B~,** (*person*) Noir(e) m. (f.). —v.t. noircir; (*goods*) boycotter. **~ and blue,** couvert de bleus. **~ eye,** œil poché m. **~ ice,** verglas m. **~ list,** liste noire f. **~ market,** marché noir m. **~ sheep,** brebis galeuse f. **~ spot,** point noir m.

blackberry /'blækbərɪ/ n. mûre f.

blackbird /'blækbɜːd/ n. merle m.

blackboard /'blækbɔːd/ n. tableau noir m.

blackcurrant /'blækkʌrənt/ n. cassis m.

blacken /'blækən/ v.t./i. noircir.

blackhead /'blækhed/ n. point noir m.

blackleg /'blækleg/ n. jaune m.

blacklist /'blæklɪst/ v.t. mettre sur la liste noire *or* à l'index.

blackmail /'blækmeɪl/ n. chantage m. —v.t. faire chanter. **~er** n. maître-chanteur m.

blackout /'blækaʊt/ n. panne d'électricité f.; (*med.*) syncope f.

blacksmith /'blæksmɪθ/ n. forgeron m.

bladder /'blædə(r)/ n. vessie f.

blade /bleɪd/ n. (*of knife etc.*) lame f.; (*of propeller, oar*) pale f. **~ of grass,** brin d'herbe m.

blame /bleɪm/ v.t. accuser. —n. faute f. **~ s.o. for sth.,** reprocher qch. à qn. **he is to ~,** il est responsable (**for,** de). **~less** a. irréprochable.

bland /blænd/ a. (**-er, -est**) (*gentle*) doux; (*insipid*) fade.

blank /blæŋk/ a. blanc; (*look*) vide; (*cheque*) en blanc. —n. blanc m. **~ (cartridge),** cartouche à blanc f.

blanket /'blæŋkɪt/ n. couverture f.; (*layer: fig.*) couche f. —v.t. (p.t. **blanketed**) recouvrir.

blare /bleə(r)/ v.t./i. beugler. —n. vacarme m., beuglement m.

blarney /'blɑːnɪ/ n. boniment m.

blasé /'blɑːzeɪ/ a. blasé.

blasphem|y /'blæsfəmɪ/ n. blasphème m. **~ous** a. blasphématoire; (*person*) blasphémateur.

blast /blɑːst/ n. explosion f.; (*wave of air*) souffle m.; (*of wind*) rafale f.; (*noise from siren etc.*) coup m. —v.t. (*blow up*) faire sauter. **~ed** a. (*fam.*) maudit, fichu. **~-furnace** n. haut fourneau m. **~ off,** être mis à feu. **~-off** n. mise à feu f.

blatant /'bleɪtnt/ a. (*obvious*) flagrant; (*shameless*) éhonté.

blaze¹ /bleɪz/ n. flamme f.; (*conflagration*) incendie m.; (*fig.*) éclat *m.* —*v.i.* (*fire*) flamber; (*sky, eyes, etc.*) flamboyer.

blaze² /bleɪz/ *v.t.* ～ **a trail**, montrer *or* marquer la voie.

blazer /'bleɪzə(r)/ *n.* blazer *m.*

bleach /bliːtʃ/ *n.* décolorant *m.*; (*for domestic use*) eau de Javel *f.* —*v.t./i.* blanchir; (*hair*) décolorer.

bleak /bliːk/ *a.* (**-er, -est**) morne.

bleary /'blɪəri/ *a.* (*eyes*) voilé.

bleat /bliːt/ *n.* bêlement *m.* —*v.i.* bêler.

bleed /bliːd/ *v.t./i.* (*p.t.* **bled**) saigner.

bleep /bliːp/ *n.* bip *m.* ～**er** *n.* bip *m.*

blemish /'blemɪʃ/ *n.* tare *f.*, défaut *m.*; (*on reputation*) tache *f.* —*v.t.* entacher.

blend /blend/ *v.t./i.* (se) mélanger. —*n.* mélange *m.* ～**er** *n.* mixer *n.*

bless /bles/ *v.t.* bénir. **be ～ed with**, avoir le bonheur de posséder. ～**ing** *n.* bénédiction *f.*; (*benefit*) avantage *m.*; (*stroke of luck*) chance *f.*

blessed /'blesɪd/ *a.* (*holy*) saint; (*damned: fam.*) sacré.

blew /bluː/ *see* **blow**¹.

blight /blaɪt/ *n.* (*disease: bot.*) rouille *f.*; (*fig.*) fléau *m.*

blind /blaɪnd/ *a.* aveugle. —*v.t.* aveugler. —*n.* (*on window*) store *m.*; (*deception*) feinte *f.* **be ～ to**, ne pas voir. ～ **alley**, impasse *f.* ～ **corner**, virage sans visibilité *m.* ～ **man**, aveugle *m.* ～ **spot**, (*auto.*) angle mort *m.* ～**ers** *n. pl.* (*Amer.*) œillères *f. pl.* ～**ly** *adv.* aveuglément. ～**ness** *n.* cécité *f.*

blindfold /'blaɪndfəʊld/ *a. & adv.* les yeux bandés. —*n.* bandeau *m.* —*v.t.* bander les yeux à.

blink /blɪŋk/ *v.i.* cligner des yeux; (*of light*) clignoter.

blinkers /'blɪŋkəz/ *n. pl.* œillères *f. pl.*

bliss /blɪs/ *n.* félicité *f.* ～**ful** *a.* bienheureux. ～**fully** *adv.* joyeusement, merveilleusement.

blister /'blɪstə(r)/ *n.* ampoule *f.* (*on paint*) cloque *f.* —*v.i.* se couvrir d'ampoules; cloquer.

blithe /blaɪð/ *a.* joyeux.

blitz /blɪts/ *n.* (*aviat.*) raid éclair *m.* —*v.t.* bombarder.

blizzard /'blɪzəd/ *n.* tempête de neige *f.*

bloated /'bləʊtɪd/ *a.* gonflé.

bloater /'bləʊtə(r)/ *n.* hareng saur *m.*

blob /blɒb/ *n.* (*drop*) (grosse) goutte *f.*; (*stain*) tache *f.*

bloc /blɒk/ *n.* bloc *m.*

block /blɒk/ *n.* bloc *m.*; (*buildings*) pâté de maisons *m.*; (*in pipe*) obstruction *f.* ～ (**of flats**), immeuble *m.* —*v.t.* bloquer. ～ **letters**, majuscules *f. pl.*

～**age** *n.* obstruction *f.* ～**-buster** *n.* gros succès *m.*

blockade /blɒ'keɪd/ *n.* blocus *m.* —*v.t.* bloquer.

bloke /bləʊk/ *n.* (*fam.*) type *m.*

blond /blɒnd/ *a. & n.* blond (*m.*).

blonde /blɒnd/ *a. & n.* blonde (*f.*).

blood /blʌd/ *n.* sang. —*a.* (*donor, bath, etc.*) de sang; (*bank, poisoning, etc.*) du sang; (*group, vessel*) sanguin. ～**curdling** *a.* à tourner le sang. ～**less** *a.* (*fig.*) pacifique. ～**-pressure** *n.* tension artérielle *f.* ～ **test**, prise de sang *f.*

bloodhound /'blʌdhaʊnd/ *n.* limier *m.*

bloodshed /'blʌdʃed/ *n.* effusion de sang *f.*

bloodshot /'blʌdʃɒt/ *a.* injecté de sang.

bloodstream /'blʌdstriːm/ *n.* sang *m.*

bloodthirsty /'blʌdθɜːsti/ *a.* sanguinaire.

bloody /'blʌdi/ *a.* (**-ier, -iest**) sanglant; (*sl.*) sacré. —*adv.* (*sl.*) vachement. ～**minded** *a.* (*fam.*) hargneux, obstiné.

bloom /bluːm/ *n.* fleur *f.* —*v.i.* fleurir; (*fig.*) s'épanouir.

bloomer /'bluːmə(r)/ *n.* (*sl.*) gaffe *f.*

blossom /'blɒsəm/ *n.* fleur(s) *f.* (*pl.*). —*v.i.* fleurir; (*person: fig.*) s'épanouir.

blot /blɒt/ *n.* tache *f.* —*v.t.* (*p.t.* **blotted**) tacher; (*dry*) sécher. ～ **out**, effacer. ～**ter**, ～**ting-paper** *ns.* buvard *m.*

blotch /blɒtʃ/ *n.* tache *f.* ～**y** *a.* couvert de taches.

blouse /blaʊz/ *n.* chemisier *m.*

blow¹ /bləʊ/ *v.t./i.* (*p.t.* **blew**, *p.p.* **blown**) souffler; (*fuse*) (faire) sauter; (*squander: sl.*) claquer; (*opportunity*) rater. ～ **one's nose**, se moucher. ～ **a whistle**, siffler. ～ **away** *or* **off**, emporter. ～**-dry** *v.t.* sécher; *n.* brushing *m.* ～ **out**, (*candle*) souffler. ～**-out** *n.* (*of tyre*) éclatement *m.* ～ **over**, passer. ～ **up**, (faire) sauter; (*tyre*) gonfler; (*photo.*) aggrandir.

blow² /bləʊ/ *n.* coup *m.*

blowlamp /'bləʊlæmp/ *n.* chalumeau *m.*

blown /bləʊn/ *see* **blow**¹.

blowtorch /'bləʊtɔːtʃ/ *n.* (*Amer.*) chalumeau *m.*

blowy /'bləʊi/ *a.* **it is ～**, il y a du vent.

bludgeon /'blʌdʒən/ *n.* gourdin *m.* —*v.t.* matraquer.

blue /bluː/ *a.* (**-er, -est**) bleu; (*film*) porno. —*n.* bleu *m.* **come out of the ～**, être inattendu. **have the ～s**, avoir le cafard.

bluebell /'bluːbel/ *n.* jacinthe des bois *f.*

bluebottle /'bluːbɒtl/ *n.* mouche à viande *f.*

blueprint /'bluːprɪnt/ n. plan m.

bluff[1] /blʌf/ v.t./i. bluffer. —n. bluff m. **call. s.o.'s ~**, dire chiche à qn.

bluff[2] /blʌf/ a. (person) brusque.

blunder /'blʌndə(r)/ v.i. faire une gaffe; (move) avancer à tâtons. —n. gaffe f.

blunt /blʌnt/ a. (knife) émoussé; (person) brusque. —v.t. émousser. **~ly** adv. carrément. **~ness** n. brusquerie f.

blur /blɜː(r)/ n. tache floue f. —v.t. (p.t. **blurred**) rendre flou.

blurb /blɜːb/ n. résumé publicitaire m.

blurt /blɜːt/ v.t. **~ out**, lâcher, dire.

blush /blʌʃ/ v.i. rougir. —n. rougeur f. **~er** n. blush m.

bluster /'blʌstə(r)/ v.i. (wind) faire rage; (swagger) fanfaronner. **~y** a. à bourrasques.

boar /bɔː(r)/ n. sanglier m.

board /bɔːd/ n. planche f.; (for notices) tableau m; (food) pension f; (committee) conseil m. —v.t./i. (bus, train) monter dans; (naut.) monter à bord (de). **~ of directors**, conseil d'administration m. **go by the ~**, passer à l'as. **full ~**, pension complète f. **half ~**, demi-pension f. **on ~**, à bord. **~ up**, boucher. **~ with**, être en pension chez. **~er** n. pensionnaire m./f. **~ing-house** n. pension de famille) f. **~ing-school** n. pensionnat m., pension f.

boast /bəʊst/ v.i. se vanter (**about**, de). —v.t. s'enorgueillir de. —n. vantardise f. **~er** n. vantard(e) m. (f.). **~ful** a. vantard. **~fully** adv. en se vantant.

boat /bəʊt/ n. bateau m.; (small) canot m. **in the same ~**, logé à la même enseigne. **~ing** n. canotage m.

boatswain /'bəʊsn/ n. maître d'équipage m.

bob[1] /bɒb/ v.i. (p.t. **bobbed**). **~ up and down**, monter et descendre.

bob[2] /bɒb/ n. invar. (sl.) shilling m.

bobby /'bɒbɪ/ n. (fam.) flic m.

bobsleigh /'bɒbsleɪ/ n. bob(-sleigh) m.

bode /bəʊd/ v.i. **~ well/ill**, être de bon/mauvais augure.

bodily /'bɒdɪlɪ/ a. physique, corporel. —adv. physiquement; (in person) en personne.

body /'bɒdɪ/ n. corps m.; (mass) masse f.; (organization) organisme m. **~(work)**, (auto.) carrosserie f. **the main ~ of**, le gros de. **~-builder** n. culturiste m./f. **~-building** n. culturisme m.

bodyguard /'bɒdɪgɑːd/ n. garde du corps m.

bog /bɒg/ n. marécage m. —v.t. (p.t. **bogged**). **get ~ged down**, s'embourber.

boggle /'bɒgl/ v.i. **the mind ~s**, on est stupéfait.

bogus /'bəʊgəs/ a. faux.

bogy /'bəʊgɪ/ n. (annoyance) embêtement m. **~(man)**, croquemitaine m.

boil[1] /bɔɪl/ n. furoncle m.

boil[2] /bɔɪl/ v.t./i. (faire) bouillir. **bring to the ~**, porter à ébullition. **~ down to**, se ramener à. **~ over**, déborder. **~ing hot**, bouillant. **~ing point**, point d'ébullition m. **~ed** a. (egg) à la coque; (potatoes) à l'eau.

boiler /'bɔɪlə(r)/ n. chaudière f. **~ suit**, bleu (de travail) m.

boisterous /'bɔɪstərəs/ a. tapageur.

bold /bəʊld/ a. (-er, -est) hardi; (cheeky) effronté; (type) gras. **~ness** n. hardiesse f.

Bolivia /bə'lɪvɪə/ n. Bolivie f. **~n** a. & n. bolivien(ne) (m. (f.)).

bollard /'bɒləd/ n. (on road) borne f.

bolster /'bəʊlstə(r)/ n. traversin m. —v.t. soutenir.

bolt /bəʊlt/ n. verrou m.; (for nut) boulon m.; (lightning) éclair m. —v.t. (door etc.) verrouiller; (food) engouffrer. —v.i. se sauver. **~ upright**, tout droit.

bomb /bɒm/ n. bombe f. —v.t. bombarder. **~ scare**, alerte à la bombe f. **~er** n. (aircraft) bombardier m.; (person) plastiqueur m.

bombard /bɒm'bɑːd/ v.t. bombarder.

bombastic /bɒm'bæstɪk/ a. grandiloquent.

bombshell /'bɒmʃel/ n. **be a ~**, tomber comme une bombe.

bona fide /bəʊnə'faɪdɪ/ a. de bonne foi.

bond /bɒnd/ n. (agreement) engagement m.; (link) lien m.; (comm.) obligation f., bon m. **in ~**, (entreposé) en douane.

bondage /'bɒndɪdʒ/ n. esclavage m.

bone /bəʊn/ n. os m.; (of fish) arête f. —v.t. désosser. **~-dry** a. tout à fait sec. **~ idle**, paresseux comme une couleuvre.

bonfire /'bɒnfaɪə(r)/ n. feu m.; (for celebration) feu de joie m.

bonnet /'bɒnɪt/ n. (hat) bonnet m.; (of vehicle) capot m.

bonus /'bəʊnəs/ n. prime f.

bony /'bəʊnɪ/ a. (-ier, -iest) (thin) osseux; (meat) plein d'os; (fish) plein d'arêtes.

boo /buː/ int. hou. —v.t./i. huer. —n. huée f.

boob /buːb/ n. (*blunder*: *sl.*) gaffe f.
—v.i. (*sl.*) gaffer.

booby-trap /'buːbɪtræp/ n. engin piégé
m. —v.t. (*p.t.* **-trapped**) piéger.

book /bʊk/ n. livre m.; (*of tickets etc.*)
carnet m. **~s**, (*comm.*) comptes m. pl.
—v.t. (*reserve*) réserver; (*driver*) faire
un P.V. à; (*player*) prendre le nom de;
(*write down*) inscrire. —v.i. retenir des
places. **~able** a. qu'on peut retenir.
(fully) ~ed, complet. **~ing office**,
guichet m.

bookcase /'bʊkkeɪs/ n. bibliothèque f.

bookkeeping /'bʊkiːpɪŋ/ n. comptabilité f.

booklet /'bʊklɪt/ n. brochure f.

bookmaker /'bʊkmeɪkə(r)/ n. bookmaker m.

bookseller /'bʊkselə(r)/ n. libraire m./f.

bookshop /'bʊkʃɒp/ n. librairie f.

bookstall /'bʊkstɔːl/ n. kiosque (à
journaux) m.

boom /buːm/ v.i. (*gun, wind, etc.*)
gronder; (*trade*) prospérer. —n.
grondement m.; (*comm.*) boom m.,
prospérité f.

boon /buːn/ n. (*benefit*) aubaine f.

boost /buːst/ v.t. stimuler; (*morale*)
remonter; (*price*) augmenter; (*publicize*)
faire de la réclame pour. —n. **give a ~
to**, = **boost**.

boot /buːt/ n. (*knee-length*); botte f.;
(*ankle-length*) chaussure (montante) f.;
(*for walking*) chaussure de marche
f.; (*sport*) chaussure de sport f.;
(*of vehicle*) coffre m. —v.t./i. **~
up**, (*comput.*) démarrer, lancer (le
programme). **get the ~**, (*sl.*) être mis à
la porte.

booth /buːð/ n. (*for telephone*) cabine f.;
(*at fair*) baraque f.

booty /'buːtɪ/ n. butin m.

booze /buːz/ v.i. (*fam.*) boire
(beaucoup). —n. (*fam.*) alcool m.;
(*spree*) beuverie f.

border /'bɔːdə(r)/ n. (*edge*) bord m.;
(*frontier*) frontière f.; (*in garden*)
bordure f. —v.i. **~ on**, (*be next to*,
come close to) être voisin de, avoisiner.

borderline /'bɔːdəlaɪn/ n. ligne de
démarcation f. **~ case**, cas limite m.

bore[1] /bɔː(r)/ see **bear**[2].

bore[2] /bɔː(r)/ v.t./i. (*techn.*) forer.

bore[3] /bɔː(r)/ v.t. ennuyer. —n. raseulr,
-se m., f.; (*thing*) ennui m. **be ~d**,
s'ennuyer. **~dom** n. ennui m. **boring** a.
ennuyeux.

born /bɔːn/ a. né. **be ~**, naître.

borne /bɔːn/ see **bear**[2].

borough /'bʌrə/ n. municipalité f.

borrow /'bɒrəʊ/ v.t. emprunter (**from**,
à). **~ing** n. emprunt m.

bosom /'bʊzəm/ n. sein m. **~ friend**,
ami(e) intime m. (f.).

boss /bɒs/ n. (*fam.*) patron(ne) m. (f.)
—v.t. **~ (about)**, (*fam.*) donner des
ordres à, régenter.

bossy /'bɒsɪ/ a. autoritaire.

botan|y /'bɒtənɪ/ n. botanique f. **~ical**
/bə'tænɪkl/ a. botanique. **~ist** n.
botaniste m./f.

botch /bɒtʃ/ v.t. bâcler, saboter.

both /bəʊθ/ a. les deux. —pron. tous or
toutes (les) deux, l'un(e) et l'autre.
—adv. à la fois. **~ the books**, les deux
livres. **we ~ agree**, nous sommes tous
les deux d'accord. **I bought ~ (of
them)**, j'ai acheté les deux. **I saw ~ of
you**, je vous ai vus tous les deux.
~ Paul and Anne, (et) Paul et
Anne.

bother /'bɒðə(r)/ v.t. (*annoy, worry*)
ennuyer; (*disturb*) déranger. —v.i. se
déranger. —n. ennui m.; (*effort*) peine
f. **don't ~ (calling)**, ce n'est pas la
peine (d'appeler). **don't ~ about us**, ne
t'inquiète pas pour nous. **I can't be
~ed**, j'ai la flemme. **it's no ~**, ce n'est
rien.

bottle /'bɒtl/ n. bouteille f.; (*for baby*)
biberon m. —v.t. mettre en bouteille(s).
~ bank, collecteur (de verre usagé) m.
~-opener n. ouvre-bouteille(s) m. **~
up**, contenir.

bottleneck /'bɒtlnek/ n. (*traffic jam*)
bouchon m.

bottom /'bɒtəm/ n. fond m.; (*of hill,
page, etc.*) bas m.; (*buttocks*) derrière
m. —a. inférieur, du bas. **~less** a.
insondable.

bough /baʊ/ n. rameau m.

bought /bɔːt/ see **buy**.

boulder /'bəʊldə(r)/ n. rocher m.

boulevard /'buːləvɑːd/ n. boulevard m.

bounce /baʊns/ v.i. rebondir; (*person*)
faire des bonds, bondir; (*cheques*: *sl.*)
être refusé. —v.t. faire rebondir. —n.
rebond m.

bouncer /'baʊnsə(r)/ n. videur m.

bound[1] /baʊnd/ v.i. (*leap*) bondir. —n.
bond m.

bound[2] /baʊnd/ see **bind**. —a. **be ~
for**, être en route pour, aller. vers. **~ to**,
(*obliged*) obligé de; (*certain*) sûr de.

boundary /'baʊndrɪ/ n. limite f.

bound|s /baʊndz/ n. pl. limites f. pl. **out
of ~s**, interdit. **~ed by**, limité par.
~less a. sans bornes.

bouquet /buˈkeɪ/ n. bouquet m.

bout /baʊt/ n. période f.; (med.) accès m.; (boxing) combat m.

boutique /buːˈtiːk/ n. boutique (de mode) f.

bow[1] /baʊ/ n. (weapon) arc m.; (mus.) archet m.; (knot) nœud m. ~-**legged** a. aux jambes arquées. ~-**tie** n. nœud papillon m.

bow[2] /baʊ/ n. (with head) salut m.; (with body) révérence f. —v.t./i. (s')incliner.

bow[3] /baʊ/ n. (naut.) proue f.

bowels /ˈbaʊəlz/ n. pl. intestins m. pl.; (fig.) entrailles f. pl.

bowl[1] /bəʊl/ n. cuvette f.; (for food) bol m.; (for soup etc.) assiette creuse f.

bowl[2] /bəʊl/ n. (ball) boule f. —v.t./i. (cricket) lancer. ~ **over**, bouleverser. ~**ing** n. jeu de boules m. ~**ing-alley** n. bowling m.

bowler[1] /ˈbəʊlə(r)/ n. (cricket) lanceur m.

bowler[2] /ˈbəʊlə(r)/ n. ~ (**hat**), (chapeau) melon m.

box[1] /bɒks/ n. boîte f.; (cardboard) carton m. (theatre) loge f. —v.t. mettre en boîte. **the** ~, (fam.) la télé. ~ **in**, enfermer. ~-**office** n. bureau de location m. **Boxing Day**, le lendemain de Noël.

box[2] /bɒks/ v.t./i. (sport) boxer. ~ **s.o.'s ears**, gifler qn. ~**ing** n. boxe f.; a. de boxe.

boy /bɔɪ/ n. garçon m. ~-**friend** n. (petit) ami m. ~**hood** n. enfance f. ~**ish** a. enfantin, de garçon.

boycott /ˈbɔɪkɒt/ v.t. boycotter. —n. boycottage m.

bra /brɑː/ n. soutien-gorge m.

brace /breɪs/ n. (fastener) attache f.; (dental) appareil m.; (for bit) vilbrequin m. ~**s**, (for trousers) bretelles f. pl. —v.t. soutenir. ~ **o.s.**, rassembler ses forces.

bracelet /ˈbreɪslɪt/ n. bracelet m.

bracing /ˈbreɪsɪŋ/ a. vivifiant.

bracken /ˈbrækən/ n. fougère f.

bracket /ˈbrækɪt/ n. (for shelf etc.) tasseau m., support m.; (group) tranche f. (**round**) ~, (printing sign) parenthèse f. (**square**) ~, crochet m. —v.t. (p.t. **bracketed**) mettre entre parenthèses or crochets.

brag /bræg/ v.i. (p.t. **bragged**) se vanter.

braid /breɪd/ n. (trimming) galon m.; (of hair) tresse f.

Braille /breɪl/ n. braille m.

brain /breɪn/ n. cerveau m. ~**s**, (fig.) intelligence f. —v.t. assommer. ~-

child n. invention personnelle f. ~-**drain** n. exode des cerveaux m. ~**less** a. stupide.

brainwash /ˈbreɪnwɒʃ/ v.t. faire un lavage de cerveau à.

brainwave /ˈbreɪnweɪv/ n. idée géniale f., trouvaille f.

brainy /ˈbreɪnɪ/ a. (-**ier**, -**iest**) intelligent.

braise /breɪz/ v.t. braiser.

brake /breɪk/ n. (auto & fig.) frein m. —v.t./i. freiner. ~ **fluid**, liquide de frein m. ~ **light**, feu de stop m. ~ **lining**, garniture de frein f.

bramble /ˈbræmbl/ n. ronce f.

bran /bræn/ n. (husks) son m.

branch /brɑːntʃ/ n. branche f.; (of road) embranchement m.; (comm.) succursale f.; (of bank) agence f. —v.i. ~ (**off**), bifurquer.

brand /brænd/ n. marque f. —v.t. ~ **s.o. as**, donner à qn. la réputation de. ~-**new** a. tout neuf.

brandish /ˈbrændɪʃ/ v.t. brandir.

brandy /ˈbrændɪ/ n. cognac m.

brash /bræʃ/ a. effronté.

brass /brɑːs/ n. cuivre m. **get down to** ~ **tacks**, en venir aux choses sérieuses. **the** ~, (mus.) les cuivres m. pl. **top** ~, (sl.) gros bonnets m. pl.

brassière /ˈbræsɪə(r), Amer. brəˈzɪər/ n. soutien-gorge m.

brat /bræt/ n. (child: pej.) môme m./f.; (ill-behaved) garnement m.

bravado /brəˈvɑːdəʊ/ n. bravade f.

brave /breɪv/ a. (-**er**, -**est**) courageux, brave. —n. (American Indian) brave m. v.t. braver. ~**ry** /-ərɪ/ n. courage m.

bravo /ˈbrɑːvəʊ/ int. bravo.

brawl /brɔːl/ n. bagarre f. —v.i. se bagarrer.

brawn /brɔːn/ n. muscles m. pl. ~**y** a. musclé.

bray /breɪ/ n. braiment m. —v.i. braire.

brazen /ˈbreɪzn/ a. effronté.

brazier /ˈbreɪzɪə(r)/ n. brasero m.

Brazil /brəˈzɪl/ n. Brésil m. ~**ian** a. & n. brésilien(ne) (m. (f.)).

breach /briːtʃ/ n. violation f.; (of contract) rupture f.; (gap) brèche f. —v.t. ouvrir une brèche dans.

bread /bred/ n. pain m. ~ **and butter**, tartine f. ~-**bin**, (Amer.) ~-**box** ns. boîte à pain f. ~-**winner** n. soutien de famille m.

breadcrumbs /ˈbredkrʌmz/ n. pl. (culin.) chapelure f.

breadline /ˈbredlaɪn/ n. **on the** ~, dans l'indigence.

breadth /bretθ/ n. largeur f.
break /breɪk/ v.t. (p.t. **broke**, p.p.
  broken) casser; (smash into pieces)
  briser; (vow, silence, rank, etc.) rompre;
  (law) violer; (a record) battre; (news)
  révéler; (journey) interrompre; (heart,
  strike, ice) briser. —v.i. (se) casser; se
  briser. —n. cassure f., rupture f.; (in
  relationship, continuity) rupture f.;
  (interval) interruption f.; (at school)
  récréation f., récré f.; (for coffee) pause
  f.; (luck: fam.) chance f. ∼ one's arm,
  se casser le bras. ∼ away from, quitter.
  ∼ down v.i. (collapse) s'effondrer;
  (fail) échouer; (machine) tomber en
  panne; v.t. (door) enfoncer; (analyse)
  analyser. ∼ even, rentrer dans ses frais.
  ∼-in n. cambriolage m. ∼ into, cambrioler. ∼ off, (se) détacher; (suspend)
  rompre; (stop talking) s'interrompre. ∼
  out, (fire, war, etc.) éclater. ∼ up,
  (end) (faire) cesser; (couple) rompre;
  (marriage) (se) briser; (crowd) (se)
  disperser; (schools) entrer en vacances.
  ∼able a. cassable. ∼age n. casse f.
breakdown /'breɪkdaʊn/ n. (techn.)
  panne f.; (med.) dépression f.; (of
  figures) analyse f. —a. (auto.) de
  dépannage.
breaker /'breɪkə(r)/ n. (wave) brisant m.
breakfast /'brekfəst/ n. petit déjeuner
  m.
breakthrough /'breɪkθru:/ n. percée f.
breakwater /'breɪkwɔːtə(r)/ n. brise-
  lames m. invar.
breast /brest/ n. sein m.; (chest) poitrine
  f. ∼-feed v.t. (p.t. -fed) allaiter. ∼-
  stroke n. brasse f.
breath /breθ/ n. souffle m., haleine f. out
  of ∼, essoufflé. under one's ∼, tout
  bas. ∼less a. essoufflé.
breathalyser /'breθəlaɪzə(r)/ n. alcootest m.
breath|e /briːð/ v.t./i. respirer. ∼ in,
  inspirer. ∼ out, expirer. ∼ing n.
  respiration f.
breather /'briːðə(r)/ n. moment de repos
  m.
breathtaking /'breθteɪkɪŋ/ a. à vous
  couper le souffle.
bred /bred/ see breed.
breeches /'brɪtʃɪz/ n. pl. culotte f.
breed /briːd/ v.t. (p.t. bred) élever; (give
  rise to) engendrer. —v.i. se reproduire.
  —n. race f. ∼er n. éleveur m. ∼ing n.
  élevage m.; (fig.) éducation f.
breez|e /briːz/ n. brise f. ∼y a. (weather)
  frais; (cheerful) jovial; (casual) désinvolte.

Breton /'bretn/ a. & n. breton(ne) (m.
  (f.)).
brevity /'brevətɪ/ n. brièveté f.
brew /bruː/ v.t. (beer) brasser; (tea)
  faire infuser. —v.i. fermenter; infuser;
  (fig.) se préparer. —n. décoction f.
  ∼er n. brasseur m. ∼ery n. brasserie f.
bribe /braɪb/ n. pot-de-vin m. —v.t.
  soudoyer, acheter. ∼ry /-ərɪ/ n.
  corruption f.
brick /brɪk/ n. brique f.
bricklayer /'brɪkleɪə(r)/ n. maçon m.
bridal /'braɪdl/ a. nuptial.
bride /braɪd/ n. mariée f.
bridegroom /'braɪdɡrʊm/ n. marié m.
bridesmaid /'braɪdzmeɪd/ n. demoiselle
  d'honneur f.
bridge[1] /brɪdʒ/ n. pont m.; (naut.)
  passerelle f.; (of nose) arête f. —v.t. ∼
  a gap, combler une lacune.
bridge[2] /brɪdʒ/ n. (cards) bridge m.
bridle /'braɪdl/ n. bride f. —v.t. brider.
  ∼-path n. allée cavalière f.
brief[1] /briːf/ a. (-er, -est) bref. ∼ly adv.
  brièvement. ∼ness n. brièveté f.
brief[2] /briːf/ n. instructions f. pl.; (jurid.)
  dossier m. —v.t. donner des instruc-
  tions à. ∼ing n. briefing m.
briefcase /'briːfkeɪs/ n. serviette f.
briefs /briːfs/ n. pl. slip m.
brigad|e /brɪ'ɡeɪd/ n. brigade f. ∼ier
  /-ə'dɪə(r)/ n. général de brigade m.
bright /braɪt/ a. (-er, -est) brillant, vif;
  (day, room) clair; (cheerful) gai;
  (clever) intelligent. ∼ly adv. brillam-
  ment. ∼ness n. éclat m.
brighten /'braɪtn/ v.t. égayer. —v.i.
  (weather) s'éclaircir; (of face)
  s'éclairer.
brillian|t /'brɪljənt/ a. brillant; (light)
  éclatant; (very good: fam.) super. ∼ce
  n. éclat m.
brim /brɪm/ n. bord m. —v.i. (p.t.
  brimmed). ∼ over, déborder.
brine /braɪn/ n. saumure f.
bring /brɪŋ/ v.t. (p.t. brought) (thing)
  apporter; (person, vehicle) amener. ∼
  about, provoquer. ∼ back, rapporter;
  ramener. ∼ down, faire tomber; (shoot
  down, knock down) abattre. ∼ forward, avancer. ∼ off, réussir. ∼ out,
  (take out) sortir; (show) faire ressortir;
  (book) publier. ∼ round or to, ranimer.
  ∼ to bear, (pressure etc.) exercer. ∼
  up, élever; (med.) vomir; (question)
  soulever.
brink /brɪŋk/ n. bord m.
brisk /brɪsk/ a. (-er, -est) vif. ∼ness n.
  vivacité f.

bristl|e /'brɪsl/ n. poil m. —v.i. se hérisser. **∼ing with,** hérissé de.

Britain /'brɪtn/ n. Grande-Bretagne f.

British /'brɪtɪʃ/ a. britannique. **the ∼,** les Britanniques m. pl.

Briton /'brɪtn/ n. Britannique m./f.

Brittany /'brɪtənɪ/ n. Bretagne f.

brittle /'brɪtl/ a. fragile.

broach /brəʊtʃ/ v.t. entamer.

broad /brɔːd/ a. (-er, -est) large; (daylight, outline) grand. **∼ bean,** fève f. **∼-minded** a. large d'esprit. **∼ly** adv. en gros.

broadcast /'brɔːdkɑːst/ v.t./i. (p.t. broadcast) diffuser; (person) parler à la télévision or à la radio. —n. émission f.

broaden /'brɔːdn/ v.t./i. (s')élargir.

broccoli /'brɒkəlɪ/ n. invar. brocoli m.

brochure /'brəʊʃə(r)/ n. brochure f.

broke /brəʊk/ see **break.** —a. (penniless: sl.) fauché.

broken /'brəʊkən/ see **break.** —a. **∼ English,** mauvais anglais m. **∼-hearted** a. au cœur brisé.

broker /'brəʊkə(r)/ n. courtier m.

brolly /'brɒlɪ/ n. (fam.) pépin m.

bronchitis /brɒŋ'kaɪtɪs/ n. bronchite f.

bronze /brɒnz/ n. bronze m. —v.t./i. (se) bronzer.

brooch /brəʊtʃ/ n. broche f.

brood /bruːd/ n. nichée f., couvée f. —v.i. couver; (fig.) méditer tristement. **∼y** a. mélancolique.

brook[1] /brʊk/ n. ruisseau m.

brook[2] /brʊk/ v.t. souffrir.

broom /bruːm/ n. balai m.

broomstick /'bruːmstɪk/ n. manche à balai m.

broth /brɒθ/ n. bouillon m.

brothel /'brɒθl/ n. maison close f.

brother /'brʌðə(r)/ n. frère m. **∼hood** n. fraternité f. **∼-in-law** n. (pl. **∼s-in-law**) beau-frère m. **∼ly** a. fraternel.

brought /brɔːt/ see **bring.**

brow /braʊ/ n. front m.; (of hill) sommet m.

browbeat /'braʊbiːt/ v.t. (p.t. **-beat,** p.p. **-beaten**) intimider.

brown /braʊn/ a. (-er, -est) marron (invar.); (cheveux) brun. —n. marron m.; brun m. —v.t./i. brunir; (culin.) (faire) dorer. **be ∼ed off,** (sl.) en avoir ras le bol. **∼ bread,** pain bis m. **∼ sugar,** cassonade f.

Brownie /'braʊnɪ/ n. jeannette f.

browse /braʊz/ v.i. feuilleter; (animal) brouter.

bruise /bruːz/ n. bleu m. —v.t. (hurt)

faire un bleu à; (fruit) abîmer. **∼d** a. couvert de bleus.

brunch /brʌntʃ/ n. petit déjeuner copieux m. (pris comme déjeuner).

brunette /bruː'net/ n. brunette f.

brunt /brʌnt/ n. **the ∼ of,** le plus fort de.

brush /brʌʃ/ n. brosse f.; (skirmish) accrochage m.; (bushes) broussailles f. pl. —v.t. brosser. **∼ against,** effleurer. **∼ aside,** écarter. **give s.o. the ∼-off,** (reject: fam.) envoyer promener qn. **∼ up (on),** se remettre à.

Brussels /'brʌslz/ n. Bruxelles m./f. **∼ sprouts,** choux de Bruxelles m. pl.

brutal /'bruːtl/ a. brutal. **∼ity** /-'tælətɪ/ n. brutalité f.

brute /bruːt/ n. brute f. **by ∼ force,** par la force.

B.Sc. abbr. see **Bachelor of Science.**

bubble /'bʌbl/ n. bulle f. —v.i. bouillonner. **∼ bath,** bain moussant m. **∼ over,** déborder.

buck[1] /bʌk/ n. mâle m. —v.i. ruer. **∼ up,** (sl.) prendre courage; (hurry: sl.) se grouiller.

buck[2] /bʌk/ n. (Amer., sl.) dollar m.

buck[3] /bʌk/ n. **pass the ∼,** rejeter la responsabilité (**to,** sur).

bucket /'bʌkɪt/ n. seau m. **∼ shop,** agence de charters f.

buckle /'bʌkl/ n. boucle f. —v.t./i. (fasten) (se) boucler; (bend) voiler. **∼ down to,** s'atteler à.

bud /bʌd/ n. bourgeon m. —v.i. (p.t. budded) bourgeonner.

Buddhis|t /'bʊdɪst/ a. & n. bouddhiste (m./f.) **∼m** /-ɪzəm/ n. bouddhisme m.

budding /'bʌdɪŋ/ a. (talent etc.) naissant; (film star etc.) en herbe.

buddy /'bʌdɪ/ n. (fam.) copain m.

budge /bʌdʒ/ v.t./i. (faire) bouger.

budgerigar /'bʌdʒərɪgɑː(r)/ n. perruche f.

budget /'bʌdʒɪt/ n. budget m. —v.i. (p.t. budgeted). **∼ for,** prévoir (dans son budget).

buff /bʌf/ n. (colour) chamois m.; (fam.) fanatique m./f.

buffalo /'bʌfələʊ/ n. (pl. -oes or -o) buffle m.; (Amer.) bison m.

buffer /'bʌfə(r)/ n. tampon m. **∼ zone,** zone tampon f.

buffet[1] /'bʊfeɪ/ n. (meal, counter) buffet m. **∼ car,** buffet m.

buffet[2] /'bʌfɪt/ n. (blow) soufflet m. —v.t. (p.t. buffeted) souffleter.

buffoon /bə'fuːn/ n. bouffon m.

bug /bʌg/ n. (insect) punaise f.; (any small insect) bestiole f.; (germ: sl.)

microbe *m.*; (*device*: *sl.*) micro *m.*; (*defect*: *sl.*) défaut *m.* —*v.t.* (*p.t.* **bugged**) mettre des micros dans; (*Amer.*, *sl.*) embêter.

buggy /'bʌgɪ/ *n.* (*child's*) poussette *f.*

bugle /'bju:gl/ *n.* clairon *m.*

build /bɪld/ *v.t./i.* (*p.t.* **built**) bâtir, construire. —*n.* carrure *f.* ∼ **up**, (*increase*) augmenter, monter; (*accumulate*) (s')accumuler. ∼**-up** *n.* accumulation *f.*; (*fig.*) publicité *f.* ∼**er** *n.* entrepreneur *m.*; (*workman*) ouvrier *m.*

building /'bɪldɪŋ/ *n.* bâtiment *m.*; (*dwelling*) immeuble *m.* ∼ **society**, caisse d'épargne-logement *f.*

built /bɪlt/ *see* **build**. ∼**-in** *a.* encastré. ∼**-up area**, agglomération *f.*, zone urbanisée *f.*

bulb /bʌlb/ *n.* oignon *m.*; (*electr.*) ampoule *f.* ∼**ous** *a.* bulbeux.

Bulgaria /bʌl'geərɪə/ *n.* Bulgarie *f.* ∼**n** *a.* & *n.* bulgare (*m./f.*).

bulge /bʌldʒ/ *n.* renflement *m.* —*v.i.* se renfler, être renflé. **be** ∼**ing with**, être gonflé *or* bourré de.

bulimia /bju:'lɪmɪə/ *n.* boulimie *f.*

bulk /bʌlk/ *n.* grosseur *f.* **in** ∼, en gros; (*loose*) en vrac. **the** ∼ **of**, la majeure partie de. ∼**y** *a.* gros.

bull /bʊl/ *n.* taureau *m.* ∼**'s-eye** *n.* centre (de la cible) *m.*

bulldog /'bʊldɒg/ *n.* bouledogue *m.*

bulldoze /'bʊldəʊz/ *v.t.* raser au bulldozer. ∼**r** /-ə(r)/ *n.* bulldozer *m.*

bullet /'bʊlɪt/ *n.* balle *f.* ∼**-proof** *a.* pare-balles *invar.*; (*vehicle*) blindé.

bulletin /'bʊlətɪn/ *n.* bulletin *m.*

bullfight /'bʊlfaɪt/ *n.* corrida *f.* ∼**er** *n.* torero *m.*

bullion /'bʊljən/ *n.* or *or* argent en lingots *m.*

bullring /'bʊlrɪŋ/ *n.* arène *f.*

bully /'bʊlɪ/ *n.* brute *f.*; tyran *m.* —*v.t.* (*treat badly*) brutaliser; (*persecute*) tyranniser; (*coerce*) forcer (**into**, à).

bum¹ /bʌm/ *n.* (*sl.*) derrière *m.*

bum² /bʌm/ *n.* (*Amer.*, *sl.*) vagabond(e) *m.* (*f.*).

bumble-bee /'bʌmblbi:/ *n.* bourdon *m.*

bump /bʌmp/ *n.* choc *m.*; (*swelling*) bosse *f.* —*v.t./i.* cogner, heurter. ∼ **along**, cahoter. ∼ **into**, (*hit*) rentrer dans; (*meet*) tomber sur. ∼**y** *a.* cahoteux.

bumper /'bʌmpə(r)/ *n.* pare-chocs *m.* *invar.* —*a.* exceptionnel.

bumptious /'bʌmpʃəs/ *a.* prétentieux.

bun /bʌn/ *n.* (*cake*) petit pain au lait *m.*; (*hair*) chignon *m.*

bunch /bʌntʃ/ *n.* (*of flowers*) bouquet *m.*; (*of keys*) trousseau *m.*; (*of people*) groupe *m.*; (*of bananas*) régime *m.* ∼ **of grapes**, grappe de raisin *f.*

bundle /'bʌndl/ *n.* paquet *m.* —*v.t.* mettre en paquet; (*push*) pousser.

bung /bʌŋ/ *n.* bonde *f.* —*v.t.* boucher; (*throw*: *sl.*) flanquer.

bungalow /'bʌŋgələʊ/ *n.* bungalow *m.*

bungle /'bʌŋgl/ *v.t.* gâcher.

bunion /'bʌnjən/ *n.* (*med.*) oignon *m.*

bunk¹ /bʌŋk/ *n.* couchette *f.* ∼**-beds** *n. pl.* lits superposés *m. pl.*

bunk² /bʌŋk/ *n.* (*nonsense*: *sl.*) foutaise(s) *f.* (*pl.*).

bunker /'bʌŋkə(r)/ *n.* (*mil.*) bunker *m.*

bunny /'bʌnɪ/ *n.* (*children's use*) (Jeannot) lapin *m.*

buoy /bɔɪ/ *n.* bouée *f.* —*v.t.* ∼ **up**, (*hearten*) soutenir, encourager.

buoyan|t /'bɔɪənt/ *a.* (*cheerful*) gai. ∼**cy** *n.* gaieté *f.*

burden /'bɜ:dn/ *n.* fardeau *m.* —*v.t.* accabler. ∼**some** *a.* lourd.

bureau /'bjʊərəʊ/ *n.* (*pl.* **-eaux** /-əʊz/) bureau *m.*

bureaucracy /bjʊə'rɒkrəsɪ/ *n.* bureaucratie *f.*

bureaucrat /'bjʊərəkræt/ *n.* bureaucrate *m./f.* ∼**ic** /-'krætɪk/ *a.* bureaucratique.

burglar /'bɜːglə(r)/ *n.* cambrioleur *m.* ∼**ize** *v.t.* (*Amer.*) cambrioler. ∼ **alarm**, alarme *f.* ∼**y** *n.* cambriolage *m.*

burgle /'bɜːgl/ *v.t.* cambrioler.

Burgundy /'bɜːgəndɪ/ *n.* (*wine*) bourgogne *m.*

burial /'berɪəl/ *n.* enterrement *m.*

burlesque /bɜː'lesk/ *n.* (*imitation*) parodie *f.*

burly /'bɜːlɪ/ *a.* (**-ier, -iest**) costaud, solidement charpenté.

Burm|a /'bɜːmə/ *n.* Birmanie *f.* ∼**ese** /-'miːz/ *a.* & *n.* birman(e) (*m.* (*f.*)).

burn /bɜːn/ *v.t./i.* (*p.t.* **burned** *or* **burnt**) brûler. —*n.* brûlure *f.* ∼ **down** *or* **be** ∼**ed down**, être réduit en cendres. ∼**er** *n.* brûleur *m.* ∼**ing** *a.* (*fig.*) brûlant.

burnish /'bɜːnɪʃ/ *v.t.* polir.

burnt /bɜːnt/ *see* **burn**.

burp /bɜːp/ *n.* (*fam.*) rot *m.* —*v.i.* (*fam.*) roter.

burrow /'bʌrəʊ/ *n.* terrier *m.* —*v.t.* creuser.

bursar /'bɜːsə(r)/ *n.* économe *m./f.*

bursary /'bɜːsərɪ/ *n.* bourse *f.*

burst /bɜːst/ *v.t./i.* (*p.t.* **burst**) crever, (faire) éclater. —*n.* explosion *f.*; (*of laughter*) éclat *m.*; (*surge*) élan *m.* **be** ∼**ing with**, déborder de. ∼ **into**, faire irruption dans. ~ **into tears,** fondre en larmes. ~ **out laughing,** éclater de rire. ~ **pipe,** conduite qui a éclaté *f.*

bury /'berɪ/ *v.t.* (*person etc.*) enterrer; (*hide, cover*) enfouir; (*engross, thrust*) plonger.

bus /bʌs/ *n.* (*pl.* **buses**) (auto)bus *m.* —*v.t.* transporter en bus. —*v.i.* (*p.t.* **bussed**) prendre l'autobus. ~**-stop** *n.* arrêt d'autobus *m.*

hush /bʊʃ/ *n.* buisson *m.*; (*land*) brousse *f.* ~**y** *a.* broussailleux.

business /'bɪznɪs/ *n.* (*task, concern*) affaire *f.*; (*commerce*) affaires *f. pl.*; (*line of work*) métier *m.*; (*shop*) commerce *m.* **he has no** ~ **to,** il n'a pas le droit de. **mean** ~**,** être sérieux. **that's none of your** ~**!,** ça ne vous regarde pas! ~**man,** homme d'affaires *m.*

businesslike /'bɪznɪslaɪk/ *a.* sérieux.

busker /'bʌskə(r)/ *n.* musicien(ne) des rues *m. (f.).*

hust[1] /bʌst/ *n.* buste *m.*; (*bosom*) poitrine *f.*

bust[2] /bʌst/ *v.t./i.* (*p.t.* **busted** or **bust**) (*burst: sl.*) crever; (*break: sl.*) (se) casser. —*a.* (*broken, finished: sl.*) fichu. ~**-up** *n.* (*sl.*) engueulade *f.* **go** ~**,** (*sl.*) faire faillite.

bustl|e /'bʌsl/ *v.i.* s'affairer. —*n* affairement *m.*, remue-ménage *m.* ~**ing** *a.* (*place*) bruyant, animé.

bus|y /'bɪzɪ/ *a.* (**-ier, -iest**) occupé; (*street*) animé; (*day*) chargé. —*v.t.* ~**y o.s. with,** s'occuper à. ~**ily** *adv.* activement.

busybody /'bɪzɪbɒdɪ/ *n.* **be a** ~**,** faire la mouche du coche.

but /bʌt, *unstressed* bət/ *conj.* mais. —*prep.* sauf. —*adv.* (*only*) seulement. ~ **for,** sans. **nobody** ~**,** personne d'autre que. **nothing** ~**,** rien que.

butane /'bjuːteɪn/ *n.* butane *m.*

butcher /'bʊtʃə(r)/ *n.* boucher *m.* —*v.t.* massacrer. ~**y** *n.* boucherie *f.*, massacre *m.*

butler /'bʌtlə(r)/ *n.* maître d'hôtel *m.*

butt /bʌt/ *n.* (*of gun*) crosse *f.*; (*of cigarette*) mégot *m.*; (*target*) cible *f.*; (*barrel*) tonneau; (*Amer., fam.*) derrière *m.* —*v.i.* ~ **in,** interrompre.

butter /'bʌtə(r)/ *n.* beurre *m.* —*v.t.* beurrer. ~**-bean** *n.* haricot blanc *m.* ~**-fingers** *n.* maladroit(e) *m. (f.).*

buttercup /'bʌtəkʌp/ *n.* bouton-d'or *m.*

butterfly /'bʌtəflaɪ/ *n.* papillon *m.*

buttock /'bʌtək/ *n.* fesse *f.*

button /'bʌtn/ *n.* bouton *m.* —*v.t./i.* ~ **(up),** (se) boutonner.

buttonhole /'bʌtnhəʊl/ *n.* boutonnière *f.* —*v.t.* accrocher.

buttress /'bʌtrɪs/ *n.* contrefort *m.* —*v.t.* soutenir.

buxom /'bʌksəm/ *a.* bien en chair.

buy /baɪ/ *v.t.* (*p.t.* **bought**) acheter (**from,** à); (*believe: sl.*) croire, avaler. —*n.* achat *m.* ~ **sth for s.o.** acheter qch. à qn., prendre qch. pour qn. ~**er** *n.* acheteulr, -se *m., f.*

buzz /bʌz/ *n.* bourdonnement *m.* —*v.i.* bourdonner. ~ **off,** (*sl.*) ficher le camp. ~**er** *n.* sonnerie *f.*

by /baɪ/ *prep.* par, de; (*near*) à côté de; (*before*) avant; (*means*) en, à, par. **by bike,** à vélo. **by car,** en auto. **by day,** de jour. **by the kilo,** au kilo. **by running**/*etc.*, en courant/*etc.* **by sea,** par mer. **by that time,** à ce moment-là. **by the way,** à propos. —*adv.* (*near*) tout près. **by and large,** dans l'ensemble. **by-election** *n.* élection partielle *f.* ~**law** *n.* arrêté *m.*; (*of club etc.*) statut *m.* **by o.s.,** tout seul. **by-product** *n.* sous-produit *m.*; (*fig.*) conséquence. **by-road** *n.* chemin de traverse *m.*

bye(-bye) /baɪ('baɪ)/ *int.* (*fam.*) au revoir, salut.

hypass /'baɪpɑːs/ *n.* (*auto.*) route qui contourne *f.*; (*med.*) pontage *m.* —*v.t.* contourner.

bystander /'baɪstændə(r)/ *n.* spectateur, -trice *m., f.*

byte /baɪt/ *n.* octet *m.*

byword /'baɪwɜːd/ *n.* **be a** ~ **for,** être connu pour.

C

cab /kæb/ *n.* taxi *m.*; (*of lorry, train*) cabine *f.*

cabaret /'kæbəreɪ/ *n.* spectacle (de cabaret) *m.*

cabbage /'kæbɪdʒ/ *n.* chou *m.*

cabin /'kæbɪn/ *n.* (*hut*) cabane *f.*; (*in ship, aircraft*) cabine *f.*

cabinet /'kæbɪnɪt/ *n.* (petite) armoire *f.*, meuble de rangement *m.*; (*for filing*) classeur *m.* **C**~**,** (*pol.*) cabinet *m.* ~**maker** *n.* ébéniste *m.*

cable /'keɪbl/ *n.* câble *m.* —*v.t.* câbler. ~**-car** *n.* téléphérique *m.* ~ **railway,** funiculaire *m.*

caboose /kə'buːs/ *n.* (*rail., Amer.*) fourgon *m.*

cache /kæʃ/ *n.* (*place*) cachette *f.* **a ~ of arms**, des armes cachées.

cackle /'kækl/ *n.* caquet *m.* —*v.i.* caqueter.

cactus /'kæktəs/ *n.* (*pl.* **-ti** /-taɪ/ *or* **-tuses**) cactus *m.*

caddie /'kædɪ/ *n.* (*golf*) caddie *m.*

caddy /'kædɪ/ *n.* boîte à thé *f.*

cadence /'keɪdns/ *n.* cadence *f.*

cadet /kə'det/ *n.* élève officier *m.*

cadge /kædʒ/ *v.t.* se fairer payer, écornifler. —*v.i.* quémander. **~ money from**, taper. **~r** /-ə(r)/ *n.* écornifleulr, -se *m.*, *f.*

Caesarean /sɪ'zeərɪən/ *a.* **~ (section)**, césarienne *f.*

café /'kæfeɪ/ *n.* café(-restaurant) *m.*

cafeteria /kæfɪ'tɪərɪə/ *n.* cafétéria *f.*

caffeine /'kæfiːn/ *n.* caféine *f.*

cage /keɪdʒ/ *n.* cage *f.* —*v.t.* mettre en cage.

cagey /'keɪdʒɪ/ *a.* (*secretive*: *fam.*) peu communicatif.

cagoule /kə'guːl/ *n.* K-way *n.* (P.).

Cairo /'kaɪərəʊ/ *n.* le Caire *m.*

cajole /kə'dʒəʊl/ *v.t.* **~ s.o. into doing**, faire l'enjoleur pour que qn. fasse.

cake /keɪk/ *n.* gâteau *m.* **~d** *a.* durci. **~d with**, raidi par.

calamit|y /kə'læmətɪ/ *n.* calamité *f.* **~ous** *a.* désastreux.

calcium /'kælsɪəm/ *n.* calcium *m.*

calculat|e /'kælkjʊleɪt/ *v.t./i.* calculer; (*Amer.*) supposer. **~ed** *a.* (*action*) délibéré. **~ing** *a.* calculateur. **~ion** /-'leɪʃn/ *n.* calcul *m.* **~or** *n.* calculatrice *f.*

calculus /'kælkjʊləs/ *n.* (*pl.* **-li** /-laɪ/ *or* **-luses**) calcul *m.*

calendar /'kælɪndə(r)/ *n.* calendrier *m.*

calf[1] /kɑːf/ *n.* (*pl.* **calves**) (*young cow or bull*) veau *m.*

calf[2] /kɑːf/ *n.* (*pl.* **calves**) (*of leg*) mollet *m.*

calibre /'kælɪbə(r)/ *n.* calibre *m.*

calico /'kælɪkəʊ/ *n.* calicot *m.*

call /kɔːl/ *v.t./i.* appeler. **~ (in** *or* **round)**, (*visit*) passer. —*n.* appel *m.*; (*of bird*) cri *m.*; visite *f.* **be ~ed**, (*named*) s'appeler. **be on ~**, être de garde. **~ back**, rappeler; (*visit*) repasser. **~-box** *n.* cabine téléphonique *f.* **~ for**, (*require*) demander; (*fetch*) passer prendre. **~-girl** *n.* call-girl *f.* **~ off**, annuler. **~ out (to)**, appeler. **~ on**, (*visit*) passer chez; (*appeal to*) faire appel à. **~ up**, appeler (au téléphone); (*mil.*) mobiliser, appeler. **~er** *n.* visiteulr, -se *m.*, *f.*; (*on phone*) personne qui appelle *f.* **~ing** *n.* vocation *f.*

callous /'kæləs/ *a.*, **~ly** *adv.* sans pitié. **~ness** *n.* manque de pitié *m.*

callow /'kæləʊ/ *a.* (**-er**, **-est**) inexpérimenté.

calm /kɑːm/ *a.* (**-er**, **-est**) calme. —*n.* calme *m.* —*v.t./i.* **~ (down)**, (se) calmer. **~ness** *n.* calme *m.*

calorie /'kælərɪ/ *n.* calorie *f.*

camber /'kæmbə(r)/ *n.* (*of road*) bombement *m.*

camcorder /'kæmkɔːdə(r)/ *n.* caméscope *m.*

came /keɪm/ *see* **come**.

camel /'kæml/ *n.* chameau *m.*

cameo /'kæmɪəʊ/ *n.* (*pl.* **-os**) camée *m.*

camera /'kæmərə/ *n.* appareil (-photo) *m.*; (*for moving pictures*) caméra *f.* **in ~**, à huis clos. **~man** *n.* (*pl.* **-men**) caméraman *m.*

camouflage /'kæməflɑːʒ/ *n.* camouflage *m.* —*v.t.* camoufler.

camp[1] /kæmp/ *n.* camp *m.* —*v.i.* camper. **~-bed** *n.* lit de camp *m.* **~er** *n.* campeulr, -se *m.*, *f.* **~er(-van)**, camping-car *m.* **~ing** *n.* camping *m.*

camp[2] /kæmp/ *a.* (*mannered*) affecté; (*vulgar*) de mauvais goût.

campaign /kæm'peɪn/ *n.* campagne *f.* —*v.i.* faire campagne.

campsite /'kæmpsaɪt/ *n.* (*for holidaymakers*) camping *m.*

campus /'kæmpəs/ *n.* (*pl.* **-puses**) campus *m.*

can[1] /kæn/ *n.* bidon *m.*; (*sealed container for food*) boîte *f.* —*v.t.* (*p.t.* **canned**) mettre en boîte. **~ it!**, (*Amer.*, *sl.*) ferme-la! **~ned music**, musique de fond enregistrée *f.* **~-opener** *n.* ouvre-boîte(s) *m.*

can[2] /kæn, *unstressed* kən/ *v. aux.* (*be able to*) pouvoir; (*know how to*) savoir.

Canad|a /'kænədə/ *n.* Canada *m.* **~ian** /kə'neɪdɪən/ *a.* & *n.* canadien(ne) (*m.* (*f.*)).

canal /kə'næl/ *n.* canal *m.*

canary /kə'neərɪ/ *n.* canari *m.*

cancel /'kænsl/ *v.t./i.* (*p.t.* **cancelled**) (*call off, revoke*) annuler; (*cross out*) barrer; (*a stamp*) oblitérer. **~ out**, (se) neutraliser. **~lation** /-ə'leɪʃn/ *n.* annulation *f.*; oblitération *f.*

cancer /'kænsə(r)/ *n.* cancer *m.* **~ous** *a.* cancéreux.

Cancer /'kænsə(r)/ *n.* le Cancer.

candid /'kændɪd/ *a.* franc. **~ness** *n.* franchise *f.*

candida|te /'kændɪdeɪt/ *n.* candidat(e) *m.* (*f.*). **~cy** /-əsɪ/ *n.* candidature *f.*

candle /'kændl/ *n.* bougie *f.*, chandelle *f.*; (*in church*) cierge *m.*

candlestick /'kændlstɪk/ *n.* bougeoir *m.*, chandelier *m.*

candour, (*Amer.*) **candor** /'kændə(r)/ *n.* franchise *f.*

candy /'kændɪ/ *n.* (*Amer.*) bonbon(s) *m.* (*pl.*) ~**-floss** *n.* barbe à papa *f.*

cane /keɪn/ *n.* canne *f.*; (*for baskets*) rotin *m.*; (*for punishment*: *schol.*) baguette *f.*, bâton *m.* —*v.t.* donner des coups de baguette *or* de bâton à, fustiger.

canine /'keɪnaɪn/ *a.* canin.

canister /'kænɪstə(r)/ *n.* boîte *f.*

cannabis /'kænəbɪs/ *n.* cannabis *m.*

cannibal /'kænɪbl/ *n.* cannibale *m./f.* ~**ism** *n.* cannibalisme *m.*

cannon /'kænən/ *n.* (*pl.* ~ *or* ~**s**) canon *m.* ~**-ball** *n.* boulet de canon *m.*

cannot /'kænɒt/ = **can not**.

canny /'kænɪ/ *a.* rusé, madré.

canoe /kə'nuː/ *n.* (*sport*) canoë *m.*, kayak *m.* —*v.i.* faire du canoë *or* du kayak. ~**ist** *n.* canoéiste *m./f.*

canon /'kænən/ *n.* (*clergyman*) chanoine *m.*; (*rule*) canon *m.*

canonize /'kænənaɪz/ *v.t.* canoniser.

canopy /'kænəpɪ/ *n.* dais *m.*; (*over doorway*) marquise *f.*

can't /kɑːnt/ = **can not**.

cantankerous /kæn'tæŋkərəs/ *a.* acariâtre, grincheux.

canteen /kæn'tiːn/ *n.* (*restaurant*) cantine *f.*; (*flask*) bidon *m.*

canter /'kæntə(r)/ *n.* petit galop *m.* —*v.i.* aller au petit galop.

canvas /'kænvəs/ *n.* toile *f.*

canvass /'kænvəs/ *v.t./i.* (*comm.*, *pol.*) solliciter des commandes *or* des voix (de). ~**ing** *n.* (*comm.*) démarchage *m.*; (*pol.*) démarchage électoral *m.* ~ **opinion**, sonder l'opinion.

canyon /'kænjən/ *n.* cañon *m.*

cap /kæp/ *n.* (*hat*) casquette *f.*; (*of bottle*, *tube*) bouchon *m.*; (*of beer or milk bottle*) capsule *f.*; (*of pen*) capuchon *m.*; (*for toy gun*) amorce *f.* —*v.t.* (*p.t.* **capped**) (*bottle*) capsuler; (*outdo*) surpasser. ~**ped with**, coiffé de.

capab|le /'keɪpəbl/ *a.* (*person*) capable (**of**, de), compétent. **be ~le of**, (*of situation*, *text*, *etc.*) être susceptible de. ~**ility** /-'bɪlətɪ/ *n.* capacité *f.* ~**ly** *adv.* avec compétence.

capacity /kə'pæsətɪ/ *n.* capacité *f.* **in one's ~ as**, en sa qualité de.

cape[1] /keɪp/ *n.* (*cloak*) cape *f.*

cape[2] /keɪp/ *n.* (*geog.*) cap *m.*

caper[1] /'keɪpə(r)/ *v.i.* gambader. —*n.* (*prank*) farce *f.*; (*activity*: *sl.*) affaire *f.*

caper[2] /'keɪpə(r)/ *n.* (*culin.*) câpre *f.*

capital /'kæpɪtl/ *a.* capital. —*n.* (*town*) capitale *f.*; (*money*) capital *m.* ~ (**letter**), majuscule *f.*

capitalis|t /'kæpɪtəlɪst/ *a. & n.* capitaliste (*m./f.*). ~**m** /-zəm/ *n.* capitalisme *m.*

capitalize /'kæpɪtəlaɪz/ *v.i.* ~ **on**, tirer profit de.

capitulat|e /kə'pɪtʃʊleɪt/ *v.i.* capituler. ~**ion** /-'leɪʃn/ *n.* capitulation *f.*

capricious /kə'prɪʃəs/ *a.* capricieux.

Capricorn /'kæprɪkɔːn/ *n.* le Capricorne.

capsize /kæp'saɪz/ *v.t./i.* (faire) chavirer.

capsule /'kæpsjuːl/ *n.* capsule *f.*

captain /'kæptɪn/ *n.* capitaine *m.*

caption /'kæpʃn/ *n.* (*for illustration*) légende *f.*; (*heading*) sous-titre *m.*

captivate /'kæptɪveɪt/ *v.t.* captiver.

captiv|e /'kæptɪv/ *a. & n.* captif, -ve (*m.*, *f.*). ~**ity** /-'tɪvətɪ/ *n.* captivité *f.*

capture /'kæptʃə(r)/ *v.t.* (*person*, *animal*) prendre, capturer; (*attention*) retenir. —*n.* capture *f.*

car /kɑː(r)/ *n.* voiture *f.* ~ **ferry**, ferry *m.* ~**-park** *n.* parking *m.* ~ **phone**, téléphone de voiture *m.* ~**-wash** *n.* station de lavage *f.*, lave-auto *m.*

carafe /kə'ræf/ *n.* carafe *f.*

caramel /'kærəmel/ *n.* caramel *m.*

carat /'kærət/ *n.* carat *m.*

caravan /'kærəvæn/ *n.* caravane *f.*

carbohydrate /kɑːbəʊ'haɪdreɪt/ *n.* hydrate de carbone *m.*

carbon /'kɑːbən/ *n.* carbone *m.* ~ **copy**, ~ **paper**, carbone *m.*

carburettor, (*Amer.*) **carburetor** /kɑːbjʊ'retə(r)/ *n.* carburateur *m.*

carcass /'kɑːkəs/ *n.* carcasse *f.*

card /kɑːd/ *n.* carte *f.* ~**-index** *n.* fichier *m.*

cardboard /'kɑːdbɔːd/ *n.* carton *m.*

cardiac /'kɑːdɪæk/ *a.* cardiaque.

cardigan /'kɑːdɪgən/ *n.* cardigan *m.*

cardinal /'kɑːdɪnl/ *a.* cardinal. —*n.* (*relig.*) cardinal *m.*

care /keə(r)/ *n.* (*attention*) soin *m.*, attention *f.*; (*worry*) souci *m.*; (*protection*) garde *f.* —*v.i.* ~ **about**, s'intéresser à. ~ **for**, s'occuper de; (*invalid*) soigner. ~ **to** *or* **for**, aimer, vouloir. **I don't** ~, ça m'est égal. **take** ~ **of**, s'occuper de. **take** ~ (**of yourself**), prends soin de toi. **take** ~ **to do sth.**, faire bien attention à faire qch.

career /kə'rɪə(r)/ *n.* carrière *f.* —*v.i.* aller à toute vitesse.

carefree /'keəfriː/ *a.* insouciant.
careful /'keəfl/ *a.* soigneux; (*cautious*) prudent. (**be**) ∼!, (fais) attention! ∼**ly** *adv.* avec soin.
careless /'keəlɪs/ *a.* négligent; (*work*) peu soigné. ∼ **about,** peu soucieux de. ∼**ly** *adv.* négligemment. ∼**ness** *n.* négligence *f.*
caress /kə'res/ *n.* caresse. —*v.t.* caresser.
caretaker /'keəteɪkə(r)/ *n.* gardien(ne) *m.* (*f.*). —*a.* (*president*) par intérim.
cargo /'kɑːgəʊ/ *n.* (*pl.* **-oes**) cargaison *f.* ∼ **boat,** cargo *m.*
Caribbean /kærɪ'biːən/ *a.* caraïbe. —*n.* the ∼, (*sea*) la mer des Caraïbes; (*islands*) les Antilles *f. pl.*
caricature /'kærɪkətjʊə(r)/ *n.* caricature *f.* —*v.t.* caricaturer.
caring /'keərɪŋ/ *a.* (*mother, son, etc.*) aimant. —*n.* affection *f.*
carnage /'kɑːnɪdʒ/ *n.* carnage *m.*
carnal /'kɑːnl/ *a.* charnel.
carnation /kɑː'neɪʃn/ *n.* œillet *m.*
carnival /'kɑːnɪvl/ *n.* carnaval *m.*
carol /'kærəl/ *n.* chant (de Noël) *m.*
carp[1] /kɑːp/ *n. invar.* carpe *f.*
carp[2] /kɑːp/ *v.i.* ∼ (**at**), critiquer.
carpent|er /'kɑːpɪntə(r)/ *n.* charpentier *m.*; (*for light woodwork, furniture*) menuisier *m.* ∼**ry** *n.* charpenterie *f.*; menuiserie *f.*
carpet /'kɑːpɪt/ *n.* tapis *m.* —*v.t.* (*p.t.* **carpeted**) recouvrir d'un tapis. ∼**-sweeper** *n.* balai mécanique *m.* **on the** ∼, (*fam.*) sur la sellette.
carriage /'kærɪdʒ/ *n.* (*rail & horse-drawn*) voiture *f.*; (*of goods*) transport *m.*; (*cost*) port *m.*
carriageway /'kærɪdʒweɪ/ *n.* chaussée *f.*
carrier /'kærɪə(r)/ *n.* transporteur *m.*; (*med.*) porteu|r, -se *m.*, *f.* ∼ (**bag**), sac en plastique *m.*
carrot /'kærət/ *n.* carotte *f.*
carry /'kærɪ/ *v.t./i.* porter; (*goods*) transporter; (*involve*) comporter; (*motion*) voter. **be carried away,** s'emballer. ∼**-cot** *n.* porte-bébé *m.* ∼ **off,** enlever; (*prize*) remporter. ∼ **on,** continuer; (*behave: fam.*) se conduire (mal). ∼ **out,** (*an order, plan*) exécuter; (*duty*) accomplir; (*task*) effectuer.
cart /kɑːt/ *n.* charrette *f.* —*v.t.* transporter; (*heavy object*: *sl.*) trimballer.
cartilage /'kɑːtɪlɪdʒ/ *n.* cartilage *m.*
carton /'kɑːtn/ *n.* (*box*) carton *m.*; (*of yoghurt, cream*) pot *m.*; (*of cigarettes*) cartouche *f.*

cartoon /kɑː'tuːn/ *n.* dessin (humoristique) *m.*; (*cinema*) dessin animé *m.* ∼**ist** *n.* dessinalteur, -trice *m.*, *f.*
cartridge /'kɑːtrɪdʒ/ *n.* cartouche *f.*
carve /kɑːv/ *v.t.* tailler; (*meat*) découper.
cascade /kæs'keɪd/ *n.* cascade *f.* —*v.i.* tomber en cascade.
case[1] /keɪs/ *n.* cas *m.*; (*jurid.*) affaire *f.*; (*phil.*) arguments *m. pl.* **in** ∼ **he comes,** au cas où il viendrait. **in** ∼ **of fire,** en cas d'incendie. **in** ∼ **of any problems,** au cas où il y aurait un problème. **in that** ∼, à ce moment-là.
case[2] /keɪs/ *n.* (*crate*) caisse *f.*; (*for camera, cigarettes, spectacles, etc.*) étui *m.*; (*suitcase*) valise *f.*
cash /kæʃ/ *n.* argent *m.* —*a.* (*price etc.*) (au) comptant. —*v.t.* encaisser. ∼ **a cheque,** (*person*) encaisser un chèque; (*bank*) payer un chèque. **pay** ∼, payer comptant. **in** ∼, en espèces. ∼ **desk,** caisse *f.* ∼ **dispenser,** distributeur de billets *m.* ∼**-flow** *n.* cash-flow *m.* ∼ **in** (**on**), profiter (de). ∼ **register,** caisse enregistreuse *f.*
cashew /'kæʃuː/ *n.* noix de cajou *f.*
cashier /kæ'ʃɪə(r)/ *n.* caisslier, -ière *m.*, *f.*
cashmere /'kæʃmɪə(r)/ *n.* cachemire *m.*
casino /kə'siːnəʊ/ *n.* (*pl.* **-os**) casino *m.*
cask /kɑːsk/ *n.* tonneau *m.*
casket /'kɑːskɪt/ *n.* (*box*) coffret *m.*; (*coffin: Amer.*) cercueil *m.*
casserole /'kæsərəʊl/ *n.* (*utensil*) cocotte *f.*; (*stew*) daube *f.*
cassette /kə'set/ *n.* cassette *f.*
cast /kɑːst/ *v.t.* (*p.t.* **cast**) (*throw*) jeter; (*glance, look*) jeter; (*shadow*) projeter; (*vote*) donner; (*metal*) couler. ∼ (**off**), (*shed*) se dépouiller de. —*n.* (*theatre*) distribution *f.*; (*of dice*) coup *m.*; (*mould*) moule *m.*; (*med.*) plâtre *m.* ∼ **iron,** fonte *f.* ∼**-iron** *a.* de fonte; (*fig.*) solide. ∼**-offs** *n. pl.* vieux vêtements *m. pl.*
castanets /kæstə'nets/ *n. pl.* castagnettes *f. pl.*
castaway /'kɑːstəweɪ/ *n.* naufragé(e) *m.* (*f.*).
caste /kɑːst/ *n.* caste *f.*
castle /'kɑːsl/ *n.* château *m.*; (*chess*) tour *f.*
castor /'kɑːstə(r)/ *n.* (*wheel*) roulette *f.* ∼ **sugar,** sucre en poudre *m.*
castrat|e /kæ'streɪt/ *v.t.* châtrer. ∼**ion** /-ʃn/ *n.* castration *f.*
casual /'kæʒʊəl/ *a.* (*remark*) fait au hasard; (*meeting*) fortuit; (*attitude*) désinvolte; (*work*) temporaire;

(*clothes*) sport *invar.* **~ly** *adv.* par hasard; (*carelessly*) avec désinvolture.
casualty /'kæʒʊəltɪ/ *n.* (*dead*) mort(e) *m.* (*f.*); (*injured*) blessé(e) *m.* (*f.*); (*accident victim*) accidenté(e) *m.* (*f.*).
cat /kæt/ *n.* chat *m.* **C~'s-eyes** *n. pl.* (P.) catadioptres *m. pl.*
catalogue /'kætəlɒg/ *n.* catalogue *m.* —*v.t.* cataloguer.
catalyst /'kætəlɪst/ *n.* catalyseur *m.*
catapult /'kætəpʌlt/ *n.* lance-pierres *m. invar.* —*v.t.* catapulter.
cataract /'kætərækt/ *n.* (*waterfall & med.*) cataracte *f.*
catarrh /kə'tɑː(r)/ *n.* rhume *m.*, catarrhe *m.*
catastroph|e /kə'tæstrəfɪ/ *n.* catastrophe *f.* **~ic** /kætə'strɒfɪk/ *a.* catastrophique.
catch /kætʃ/ *v.t.* (*p.t.* **caught**) attraper; (*grab*) prendre, saisir; (*catch unawares*) surprendre; (*jam, trap*) prendre; (*understand*) saisir. —*v.i.* prendre; (*get stuck*) se prendre (**in,** dans). —*n.* capture *f.*, prise *f.*; (*on door*) loquet *m.*; (*fig.*) piège *m.* **~ fire,** prendre feu. **~ on,** (*fam.*) prendre, devenir populaire. **~ out,** prendre en faute. **~-phrase** *n.* slogan *m.* **~ sight of,** apercevoir. **~ s.o.'s eye,** attirer l'attention de qn. **~ up,** se rattraper. **~ up (with),** rattraper.
catching /'kætʃɪŋ/ *a.* contagieux.
catchment /'kætʃmənt/ *n.* **~ area,** région desservie *f.*
catchy /'kætʃɪ/ *a.* facile à retenir.
categorical /kætɪ'gɒrɪkl/ *a.* catégorique.
category /'kætɪgərɪ/ *n.* catégorie *f.*
cater /'keɪtə(r)/ *v.i.* s'occuper de la nourriture. **~ for,** (*pander to*) satisfaire; (*of magazine etc.*) s'adresser à. **~er** *n.* traiteur *m.*
caterpillar /'kætəpɪlə(r)/ *n.* chenille *f.*
cathedral /kə'θiːdrəl/ *n.* cathédrale *f.*
catholic /'kæθəlɪk/ *a.* universel. **C~** *a. & n.* catholique (*m./f.*). **C~ism** /kə'θɒlɪsɪzəm/ *n.* catholicisme *m.*
cattle /'kætl/ *n. pl.* bétail *m.*
catty /'kætɪ/ *a.* méchant.
caucus /'kɔːkəs/ *n.* comité électoral *m.*
caught /kɔːt/ *see* **catch.**
cauliflower /'kɒlɪflaʊə(r)/ *n.* chou-fleur *m.*
cause /kɔːz/ *n.* cause *f.*; (*reason*) raison *f.*, motif *m.* —*v.t.* causer. **~ sth. to grow/move/etc.,** faire pousser/bouger/ *etc.* qch.
causeway /'kɔːzweɪ/ *n.* chaussée *f.*
cauti|on /'kɔːʃn/ *n.* prudence *f.*; (*warning*) avertissement *m.* —*v.t.*

avertir. **~ous** *a.* prudent. **~ously** *adv.* prudemment.
cavalier /kævə'lɪə(r)/ *a.* cavalier.
cavalry /'kævəlrɪ/ *n.* cavalerie *f.*
cave /keɪv/ *n.* caverne *f.*, grotte *f.* —*v.i.* **~ in,** s'effondrer; (*agree*) céder.
caveman /'keɪvmæn/ *n.* (*pl.* **-men**) homme des cavernes *m.*
cavern /'kævən/ *n.* caverne *f.*
caviare, *Amer.* caviar /'kævɪɑː(r)/ *n.* caviar *m.*
caving /'keɪvɪŋ/ *n.* spéléologie *f.*
cavity /'kævətɪ/ *n.* cavité *f.*
cavort /kə'vɔːt/ *v.i.* gambader.
CD /siː'diː/ *n.* compact disc *m.*
cease /siːs/ *v.t./i.* cesser. **~-fire** *n.* cessez-le-feu *m. invar.* **~less** *a.* incessant.
cedar /'siːdə(r)/ *n.* cèdre *m.*
cede /siːd/ *v.t.* céder.
cedilla /sɪ'dɪlə/ *n.* cédille *f.*
ceiling /'siːlɪŋ/ *n.* plafond *m.*
celebrat|e /'selɪbreɪt/ *v.t.* (*perform, glorify*) célébrer; (*event*) fêter, célébrer. —*v.i.* **we shall ~e,** on va fêter ça. **~ion** /-'breɪʃn/ *n.* fête *f.*
celebrated /'selɪbreɪtɪd/ *a.* célèbre.
celebrity /sɪ'lebrətɪ/ *n.* célébrité *f.*
celery /'selərɪ/ *n.* céleri *m.*
cell /sel/ *n.* cellule *f.*; (*electr.*) élément *m.*
cellar /'selə(r)/ *n.* cave *f.*
cell|o /'tʃeləʊ/ *n.* (*pl.* -os) violoncelle *m.* **~ist** *n.* violoncelliste *m./f.*
Cellophane /'seləfeɪn/ *n.* (P.) cellophane *f.* (P.).
Celt /kelt/ *n.* Celte *m./f.* **~ic** *a.* celtique, celte.
cement /sɪ'ment/ *n.* ciment *m.* —*v.t.* cimenter. **~-mixer** *n.* bétonnière *f.*
cemetery /'semətrɪ/ *n.* cimetière *m.*
censor /'sensə(r)/ *n.* censeur *m.* —*v.t.* censurer. **the ~,** la censure. **~ship** *n.* censure *f.*
censure /'senʃə(r)/ *n.* blâme *m.* —*v.t.* blâmer.
census /'sensəs/ *n.* recensement *m.*
cent /sent/ *n.* (*coin*) cent *m.*
centenary /sen'tiːnərɪ, *Amer.* 'sentənərɪ/ *n.* centenaire *m.*
centigrade /'sentɪgreɪd/ *a.* centigrade.
centilitre, *Amer.* centiliter /'sentɪliːtə(r)/ *n.* centilitre *m.*
centimetre, *Amer.* centimeter /'sentɪmiːtə(r)/ *n.* centimètre *m.*
centipede /'sentɪpiːd/ *n.* millepattes *m. invar.*
central /'sentrəl/ *a.* central. **~ heating,** chauffage central *m.* **~ize** *v.t.* centraliser. **~ly** *adv.* (*situated*) au centre.

centre /'sentə(r)/ *n.* centre *m.* —*v.t.* (*p.t.* **centred**) centrer. —*v.i.* **~ on**, tourner autour de.

centrifugal /sen'trɪfjʊgl/ *a.* centrifuge.

century /'sentʃərɪ/ *n.* siècle *m.*

ceramic /sɪ'ræmɪk/ *a.* (*art*) céramique; (*object*) en céramique.

cereal /'sɪərɪəl/ *n.* céréale *f.*

cerebral /'serɪbrəl, *Amer.* sə'ri:brəl/ *a.* cérébral.

ceremonial /serɪ'məʊnɪəl/ *a.* de cérémonie. —*n.* cérémonial *m.*

ceremon|y /'serɪmənɪ/ *n.* cérémonie *f.* **~ious** /-'məʊnɪəs/ *a.* solennel.

certain /'sɜːtn/ *a.* certain. **for ~**, avec certitude. **make ~ of**, s'assurer de. **~ly** *adv.* certainement. **~ty** *n.* certitude *f.*

certificate /sə'tɪfɪkət/ *n.* certificat *m.*

certify /'sɜːtɪfaɪ/ *v.t.* certifier.

cervical /sɜː'vaɪkl/ *a.* cervical.

cessation /se'seɪʃn/ *n.* cessation *f.*

cesspit, cesspool /'sespɪt, 'sespuːl/ *ns.* fosse d'aisances *f.*

chafe /tʃeɪf/ *v.t.* frotter (contre).

chaff /tʃɑːf/ *v.t.* taquiner.

chaffinch /'tʃæfɪntʃ/ *n.* pinson *m.*

chagrin /'ʃægrɪn/ *n.* vif dépit *m.*

chain /tʃeɪn/ *n.* chaîne *f.* —*v.t.* enchaîner. **~ reaction**, réaction en chaîne *f.* **~-smoke** *v.i.* fumer de manière ininterrompue. **~ store**, magasin à succursales multiples *m.*

chair /tʃeə(r)/ *n.* chaise *f.*; (*armchair*) fauteuil *m.*; (*univ.*) chaire *f.* —*v.t.* (*preside over*) présider.

chairman /'tʃeəmən/ *n.* (*pl.* **-men**) président(e) *m.* (*f.*).

chalet /'ʃæleɪ/ *n.* chalet *m.*

chalk /tʃɔːk/ *n.* craie *f.* **~y** *a.* crayeux.

challeng|e /'tʃælɪndʒ/ *n.* défi *m.*; (*task*) gageure *f.* —*v.t.* (*summon*) défier (**to do**, de faire); (*question truth of*) contester. **~er** *n.* (*sport*) challenger *m.* **~ing** *a.* stimulant.

chamber /'tʃeɪmbə(r)/ *n.* (*old use*) chambre *f.* **~ music**, musique de chambre *f.* **~-pot** *n.* pot de chambre *m.*

chambermaid /'tʃeɪmbəmeɪd/ *n.* femme de chambre *f.*

chamois /'ʃæmɪ/ *n.* **~(-leather)**, peau de chamois *f.*

champagne /ʃæm'peɪn/ *n.* champagne *m.*

champion /'tʃæmpɪən/ *n.* champion(ne) *m.* (*f.*). —*v.t.* défendre. **~ship** *n.* championnat *m.*

chance /tʃɑːns/ *n.* (*luck*) hasard *m.*; (*opportunity*) occasion *f.*; (*likelihood*) chances *f. pl.*; (*risk*) risque *m.* —*a.*

fortuit. —*v.t.* **~ doing**, prendre le risque de faire. **~ it**, risquer le coup. **by ~**, par hasard. **by any ~**, par hasard. **~s are that**, il est probable que.

chancellor /'tʃɑːnsələ(r)/ *n.* chancelier *m.* **C~ of the Exchequer**, Chancelier de l'Échiquier.

chancy /'tʃɑːnsɪ/ *a.* risqué.

chandelier /ʃændə'lɪə(r)/ *n.* lustre *m.*

change /tʃeɪndʒ/ *v.t.* (*alter*) changer; (*exchange*) échanger (**for**, contre); (*money*) changer. **~ trains/one's dress**/*etc.*, (*by substitution*) changer de train/de robe/*etc.* —*v.i.* changer; (*change clothes*) se changer. —*n.* changement *m.*; (*money*) monnaie *f.* **a ~ for the better**, une amélioration. **a ~ for the worse**, un changement en pire. **~ into**, se transformer en; (*clothes*) mettre. **a ~ of clothes**, des vêtements de rechange. **~ one's mind**, changer d'avis. **~ over**, passer (**to**, à). **for a ~**, pour changer. **~-over** *n.* passage *m.* **~able** *a.* changeant; (*weather*) variable. **~ing** *a.* changeant. **~-ing room**, (*in shop*) cabine d'essayage; (*sport.*) vestiaire *m.*

channel /'tʃænl/ *n.* chenal *m.*; (*TV*) chaîne *f.*; (*medium, agency*) canal *m.*; (*groove*) rainure *f.* —*v.t.* (*p.t.* **channelled**) (*direct*) canaliser. **the (English) C~**, la Manche. **the C~ Islands**, les îles anglo-normandes *f. pl.*

chant /tʃɑːnt/ *n.* (*relig.*) psalmodie *f.*; (*of demonstrators*) chant (scandé) *m.* —*v.t./i.* psalmodier; scander (des slogans).

chao|s /'keɪɒs/ *n.* chaos *m.* **~tic** /-'ɒtɪk/ *a.* chaotique.

chap /tʃæp/ *n.* (*man: fam.*) type *m.*

chapel /'tʃæpl/ *n.* chapelle *f.*; (*Nonconformist*) église (nonconformiste) *f.*

chaperon /'ʃæpərəʊn/ *n.* chaperon *m.* —*v.t.* chaperonner.

chaplain /'tʃæplɪn/ *n.* aumônier *m.*

chapped /tʃæpt/ *a.* gercé.

chapter /'tʃæptə(r)/ *n.* chapitre *m.*

char¹ /tʃɑː(r)/ *n.* (*fam.*) femme de ménage *f.*

char² /tʃɑː(r)/ *v.t.* (*p.t.* **charred**) carboniser.

character /'kærəktə(r)/ *n.* caractère *m.*; (*in novel, play*) personnage *m.* **of good ~**, de bonne réputation. **~ize** *v.t.* caractériser.

characteristic /kærəktə'rɪstɪk/ *a. & n.* caractéristique (*f.*). **~ally** *adv.* typiquement.

charade /ʃəˈrɑːd/ n. charade f.
charcoal /ˈtʃɑːkəʊl/ n. charbon (de bois) m.
charge /tʃɑːdʒ/ n. prix m.; (mil.) charge f.; (jurid.) inculpation f., accusation f.; (task, custody) charge f. **~s**, frais m. pl. —v.t. faire payer, (ask) demander (**for**, pour); (enemy, gun) charger; (jurid.) inculper, accuser (**with**, de). —v.i. foncer, se précipiter. **~ card**, carte d'achat f. **~ it to my account**, mettez-le sur mon compte. **in ~ of**, responsable de. **take ~ of**, prendre en charge, se charger de. **~able to**, (comm.) aux frais de.
charisma /kəˈrɪzmə/ n. magnétisme m. **~tic** /kærɪzˈmætɪk/ a. charismatique.
charit|y /ˈtʃærətɪ/ n. charité f.; (society) fondation charitable f. **~able** a. charitable.
charlatan /ˈʃɑːlətən/ n. charlatan m.
charm /tʃɑːm/ n. charme m.; (trinket) amulette f. v.t. charmer. **~ing** a. charmant.
chart /tʃɑːt/ n. (naut.) carte (marine) f.; (table) tableau m., graphique m. —v.t. (route) porter sur la carte.
charter /ˈtʃɑːtə(r)/ n. charte f. **~ (flight)**, charter m. —v.t. affréter. **~ed accountant**, expert-comptable m.
charwoman /ˈtʃɑːwʊmən/ n. (pl. -women) femme de ménage f.
chase /tʃeɪs/ v.t. poursuivre. —v.i. courir (**after**, après). —n. chasse f. **~ away** or **off**, chasser.
chasm /ˈkæzəm/ n. abîme m.
chassis /ˈʃæsɪ/ n. châssis m.
chaste /tʃeɪst/ a. chaste.
chastise /tʃæˈstaɪz/ v.t. châtier.
chastity /ˈtʃæstətɪ/ n. chasteté f.
chat /tʃæt/ n. causette f. —v.i. (p.t. chatted) bavarder. **have a ~**, bavarder. **~ show**, talk-show m. **~ up**, (fam.) draguer. **~ty** a. bavard.
chatter /ˈtʃætə(r)/ n. bavardage m. —v.i. bavarder. **his teeth are ~ing**, il claque des dents.
chatterbox /ˈtʃætəbɒks/ n. bavard(e) m. (f.).
chauffeur /ˈʃəʊfə(r)/ n. chauffeur (de particulier) m.
chauvinis|t /ˈʃəʊvɪnɪst/ n. chauvin(e) m. (f.). **male ~t**, (pej.) phallocrate m. **~m** /-zəm/ n. chauvinisme m.
cheap /tʃiːp/ a. (-er, -est) bon marché invar.; (fare, rate) réduit; (worthless) sans valeur. **~er**, meilleur marché invar. **~(ly)** adv. à bon marché. **~ness** n. bas prix m.

cheapen /ˈtʃiːpən/ v.t. déprécier.
cheat /tʃiːt/ v.i. tricher; (by fraud) frauder. v.t. (defraud) frauder; (deceive) tromper. —n. escroc m.
check[1] /tʃek/ v.t./i. vérifier; (tickets) contrôler; (stop) enrayer, arrêter; (restrain) contenir; (rebuke) réprimander; (tick off: Amer.) cocher. —n. vérification f.; contrôle m.; (curb) frein m.; (chess) échec m.; (bill: Amer.) addition f.; (cheque: Amer.) chèque m. **~ in**, signer le registre; (at airport) passer à l'enregistrement. **~-in** n. en registrement m. **~-list** n. liste récapitulative f. **~ out**, régler sa note. **~-out** n. caisse f. **~-point** n. contrôle m. **~ up**, vérifier. **~ up on**, (detail) vérifier; (situation) s'informer sur. **~-up** n. examen médical m.
check[2] /tʃek/ n. (pattern) carreaux m. pl. **~ed** a. à carreaux.
checking /ˈtʃekɪŋ/ a. **~ account**, (Amer.) compte courant m.
checkmate /ˈtʃekmeɪt/ n. échec et mat m.
checkroom /ˈtʃekrʊm/ n. (Amer.) vestiaire m.
cheek /tʃiːk/ n. joue f.; (impudence) culot m. **~y** a. effronté.
cheer /tʃɪə(r)/ n. gaieté f. **~s**, acclamations f. pl.; (when drinking) à votre santé. —v.t. acclamer, applaudir. **~ (up)**, (gladden) remonter le moral à. **~ up**, prendre courage. **~ful** à gai. **~fulness** n. gaieté f.
cheerio /tʃɪərɪˈəʊ/ int. (fam.) salut.
cheese /tʃiːz/ n. fromage m.
cheetah /ˈtʃiːtə/ n. guépard m.
chef /ʃef/ n. (cook) chef m.
chemical /ˈkemɪkl/ a. chimique. —n. produit chimique m.
chemist /ˈkemɪst/ n. pharmacien(ne) m. (f.); (scientist) chimiste m./f. **~'s shop**, pharmacie f. **~ry** n. chimie f.
cheque /tʃek/ n. chèque m. **~-book** n. chéquier m. **~ card**, carte bancaire f.
chequered /ˈtʃekəd/ a. (pattern) à carreaux; (fig.) mouvementé.
cherish /ˈtʃerɪʃ/ v.t. chérir; (hope) nourrir, caresser.
cherry /ˈtʃerɪ/ n. cerise f.
chess /tʃes/ n. échecs m. pl. **~-board** n. échiquier m.
chest /tʃest/ n. (anat.) poitrine f.; (box) coffre m. **~ of drawers**, commode f.
chestnut /ˈtʃesnʌt/ n. châtaigne f.; (edible) marron m., châtaigne f.
chew /tʃuː/ v.t. mâcher. **~ing-gum** n. chewing-gum m.
chic /ʃiːk/ a. chic invar.

chick /tʃɪk/ n. poussin m.
chicken /'tʃɪkɪn/ n. poulet m. —a. (sl.) froussard. —v.i. ~ out, (sl.) se dégonfler. ~-pox n. varicelle f.
chick-pea /'tʃɪkpiː/ n. pois chiche m.
chicory /'tʃɪkərɪ/ n. (for salad) endive f.; (in coffee) chicorée f.
chief /tʃiːf/ n. chef m. —a. principal. ~ly adv. principalement.
chilblain /'tʃɪlbleɪn/ n. engelure f.
child /tʃaɪld/ n. (pl. children /'tʃɪldrən/) enfant m./f. ~hood n. enfance f. ~ish a. enfantin. ~less a. sans enfants. ~like a. innocent, candide. ~-minder n. nourrice f.
childbirth /'tʃaɪldbɜːθ/ n. accouchement m.
Chile /'tʃɪlɪ/ n. Chili m. ~an a. & n. chilien(ne) (m. (f.)).
chill /tʃɪl/ n. froid m.; (med.) refroidissement m. —a. froid. —v.t. (person) donner froid à; (wine) rafraîchir; (food) mettre au frais. ~y a. froid; (sensitive to cold) frileux. be or feel ~y, avoir froid.
chilli /'tʃɪlɪ/ n. (pl. -ies) piment m.
chime /tʃaɪm/ n. carillon m. —v.t./i. carillonner.
chimney /'tʃɪmnɪ/ n. cheminée f. ~-sweep n. ramoneur m.
chimpanzee /tʃɪmpæn'ziː/ n. chimpanzé m.
chin /tʃɪn/ n. menton m.
china /'tʃaɪnə/ n. porcelaine f.
Chin|a /'tʃaɪnə/ n. Chine f. ~ese /-'niːz/ a. & n. chinois(e) (m. (f.)).
chink¹ /tʃɪŋk/ n. (slit) fente f.
chink² /tʃɪŋk/ n. tintement m. —v.t./i. (faire) tinter.
chip /tʃɪp/ n. (on plate etc.) ébréchure f.; (piece) éclat m.; (of wood) copeau m.; (culin.) frite f.; (microchip) microplaquette f., puce f. —v.t./i. (p.t. chipped) (s')ébrécher. ~ in, (fam.) dire son mot; (with money: fam.) contribuer. (potato) ~s, (Amer.) chips m. pl.
chipboard /'tʃɪpbɔːd/ n. aggloméré m.
chiropodist /kɪ'rɒpədɪst/ n. pédicure m./f.
chirp /tʃɜːp/ n. pépiement m. —v.i. pépier.
chirpy /'tʃɜːpɪ/ a. gai.
chisel /'tʃɪzl/ n. ciseau m. —v.t. (p.t. chiselled) ciseler.
chit /tʃɪt/ n. note f., mot m.
chit-chat /'tʃɪttʃæt/ n. bavardage m.
chivalr|y /'ʃɪvlrɪ/ n. galanterie f. ~ous a. chevaleresque.
chives /tʃaɪvz/ n. pl. ciboulette f.
chlorine /'klɔːriːn/ n. chlore m.

choc-ice /'tʃɒkaɪs/ n. esquimau m.
chock /tʃɒk/ n. cale f. ~-a-block, ~-full adjs. archiplein.
chocolate /'tʃɒklət/ n. chocolat m.
choice /tʃɔɪs/ n. choix m. —a. de choix.
choir /'kwaɪə(r)/ n. chœur m.
choirboy /'kwaɪəbɔɪ/ n. jeune choriste m.
choke /tʃəʊk/ v.t./i. (s')étrangler. —n. starter m. ~ (up), boucher.
cholera /'kɒlərə/ n. choléra m.
cholesterol /kə'lestərɒl/ n. cholestérol m.
choose /tʃuːz/ v.t./i. (p.t. chose, p.p. chosen) choisir. ~ to do, décider de faire.
choosy /'tʃuːzɪ/ a. (fam.) exigeant.
chop /tʃɒp/ v.t./i. (p.t. chopped) (wood) couper (à la hache); (food) hacher. —n. (meat) côtelette f. ~ down, abattre. ~per n. hachoir m.; (sl.) hélicoptère m. ~ping-board n. planche à découper f.
choppy /'tʃɒpɪ/ a. (sea) agité.
chopstick /'tʃɒpstɪk/ n. baguette f.
choral /'kɔːrəl/ a. choral.
chord /kɔːd/ n. (mus.) accord m.
chore /tʃɔː(r)/ n. travail (routinier) m.; (unpleasant task) corvée f.
choreography /kɒrɪ'ɒgrəfɪ/ n. chorégraphie f.
chortle /'tʃɔːtl/ n. gloussement m. —v.i. glousser.
chorus /'kɔːrəs/ n. chœur m.; (of song) refrain m.
chose, chosen /tʃəʊz, 'tʃəʊzn/ see choose.
Christ /kraɪst/ n. le Christ m.
christen /'krɪsn/ v.t. baptiser. ~ing n. baptême m.
Christian /'krɪstʃən/ a. & n. chrétien(ne) (m. (f.)). ~ name, prénom m. ~ity /-stɪ'ænətɪ/ n. christianisme m.
Christmas /'krɪsməs/ n. Noël m. —a. (card, tree, etc.) de Noël. ~-box n. étrennes f. pl. ~ Day/Eve, le jour/la veille de Noël.
chrome /krəʊm/ n. chrome m.
chromium /'krəʊmɪəm/ n. chrome m.
chromosome /'krəʊməsəʊm/ n. chromosome m.
chronic /'krɒnɪk/ a. (situation, disease) chronique; (bad: fam.) affreux.
chronicle /'krɒnɪkl/ n. chronique f.
chronolog|y /krə'nɒlədʒɪ/ n. chronologie f. ~ical /krɒnə'lɒdʒɪkl/ a. chronologique.
chrysanthemum /krɪ'sænθəməm/ n. chrysanthème m.
chubby /'tʃʌbɪ/ a. (-ier, -iest) dodu, potelé.

chuck /tʃʌk/ v.t. (fam.) lancer. **~ away** or **out**, (fam.) balancer.

chuckle /'tʃʌkl/ n. gloussement m. —v.i. glousser, rire.

chuffed /tʃʌft/ a. (sl.) bien content.

chum /tʃʌm/ n. copIain, -ine m., f. **~my** a. amical. **~my with**, copain avec.

chunk /tʃʌŋk/ n. (gros) morceau m.

chunky /'tʃʌŋkɪ/ a. trapu.

church /tʃɜːtʃ/ n. église f.

churchyard /'tʃɜːtʃjɑːd/ n. cimetière m.

churlish /'tʃɜːlɪʃ/ a. grossier.

churn /'tʃɜːn/ n. baratte f.; (milk-can) bidon m. —v.t. baratter. **~ out**, produire (en série).

chute /ʃuːt/ n. glissière f.; (for rubbish) vide-ordures m. invar.

chutney /'tʃʌtnɪ/ n. condiment (de fruits) m.

cider /'saɪdə(r)/ n. cidre m.

cigar /sɪ'gɑː(r)/ n. cigare m.

cigarette /sɪgə'ret/ n. cigarette f. **~ end**, mégot m. **~-holder** n. fume cigarette m. invar.

cinder /'sɪndə(r)/ n. cendre f.

cine-camera /'sɪnɪkæmərə/ n. caméra f.

cinema /'sɪnəmə/ n. cinéma m.

cinnamon /'sɪnəmən/ n. cannelle f.

cipher /'saɪfə(r)/ n. (numeral, code) chiffre m.; (person) nullité f.

circle /'sɜːkl/ n. cercle m.; (theatre) balcon m. —v.t. (go round) faire le tour de; (word, error, etc.) entourer d'un cercle. —v.i. décrire des cercles.

circuit /'sɜːkɪt/ n. circuit m. **~-breaker** n. disjoncteur m.

circuitous /sɜː'kjuːɪtəs/ a. indirect.

circular /'sɜːkjʊlə(r)/ a. & n. circulaire (f.).

circulate /'sɜːkjʊleɪt/ v.t./i. (faire) circuler. **~ion** /-'leɪʃn/ n. circulation f.; (of newspaper) tirage m.

circumcise /'sɜːkəmsaɪz/ v.t. circoncire. **~ion** /-'sɪʒn/ n. circoncision f.

circumference /sɜː'kʌmfərəns/ n. circonférence f.

circumflex /'sɜːkəmfleks/ n. circonflexe m.

circumspect /'sɜːkəmspekt/ a. circonspect.

circumstance /'sɜːkəmstəns/ n. circonstance f. **~s**, (financial) situation financière f.

circus /'sɜːkəs/ n. cirque m.

cistern /'sɪstən/ n. réservoir m.

citadel /'sɪtədel/ n. citadelle f.

cite /saɪt/ v.t. citer. **~ation** /-'teɪʃn/ n. citation f.

citizen /'sɪtɪzn/ n. citoyen(ne) m. (f.); (of

town) habitant(e) m. (f.). **~ship** n. citoyenneté f.

citrus /'sɪtrəs/ a. **~ fruit(s)**, agrumes m. pl.

city /'sɪtɪ/ n. (grande) ville f. **the C~**, la Cité de Londres.

civic /'sɪvɪk/ a. civique. **~ centre**, centre administratif m. **~s** n. pl. instruction civique f.

civil /'sɪvl/ a. civil; (rights) civique; (defence) passif. **~ engineer**, ingénieur civil m. **C~ Servant**, fonctionnaire m./f. **C~ Service**, fonction publique f. **~ war**, guerre civile f. **~ity** /sɪ'vɪlətɪ/ n. civilité f.

civilian /sɪ'vɪlɪən/ a. & n. civil(e) (m. (f.)).

civilize /'sɪvəlaɪz/ v.t. civiliser. **~ation** /-'zeɪʃn/ n. civilisation f.

civvies /'sɪvɪz/ n. pl. **in ~**, (sl.) en civil.

clad /klæd/ a. **~ in**, vêtu de.

claim /kleɪm/ v.t. revendiquer, réclamer; (assert) prétendre. n. revendication f., prétention f.; (assertion) affirmation f.; (for insurance) réclamation f.; (right) droit m.

claimant /'kleɪmənt/ n. (of social benefits) demandeur m.

clairvoyant /kleə'vɔɪənt/ n. voyant(e) m. (f.).

clam /klæm/ n. palourde f.

clamber /'klæmbə(r)/ v.i. grimper.

clammy /'klæmɪ/ a. (-ier, -iest) moite.

clamour /'klæmə(r)/ n. clameur f., cris m. pl. —v.i. **~ for**, demander à grands cris.

clamp /klæmp/ n. agrafe f.; (large) crampon m.; (for carpentry) serre-joint(s) m.; (for car) sabot de Denver m. —v.t. serrer; (car) mettre un sabot de Denver à. **~ down on**, sévir contre.

clan /klæn/ n. clan m.

clandestine /klæn'destɪn/ a. clandestin.

clang /klæŋ/ n. son métallique m.

clanger /'klæŋə(r)/ n. (sl.) bévue f.

clap /klæp/ v.t./i. (p.t. **clapped**) applaudir; (put forcibly) mettre. —n. applaudissement m.; (of thunder) coup m. **~ one's hands**, battre des mains.

claptrap /'klæptræp/ n. baratin m.

claret /'klærət/ n. bordeaux rouge m.

clarify /'klærɪfaɪ/ v.t./i. (se) clarifier. **~ication** /-ɪ'keɪʃn/ n. clarification f.

clarinet /klærɪ'net/ n. clarinette f.

clarity /'klærətɪ/ n. clarté f.

clash /klæʃ/ n. choc m.; (fig.) conflit m. —v.i. (metal objects) s'entrechoquer; (fig.) se heurter.

clasp /klɑːsp/ n. (fastener) fermoir m., agrafe f. —v.t. serrer.

class /klɑːs/ n. classe f. —v.t. classer.
classic /'klæsɪk/ a. & n. classique (m.).
~**s**, (univ.) les humanités f. pl. ~**al** a.
classique.
classif|y /'klæsɪfaɪ/ v.t. classifier.
~**ication** /-ɪ'keɪʃn/ n. classification f.
~**ied** a. (information etc.) secret. ~**ied
advertisement,** petite annonce f.
classroom /'klɑːsrʊm/ n. salle de classe
f.
classy /'klɑːsɪ/ a. (sl.) chic invar.
clatter /'klætə(r)/ n. cliquetis m. —v.i.
cliqueter.
clause /klɔːz/ n. clause f.; (gram.)
proposition f.
claustrophob|ia /klɔːstrə'fəʊbɪə/ n.
claustrophobie f. ~**ic** a. & n.
claustrophobe (m./f.).
claw /klɔː/ n. (of animal, small bird)
griffe f.; (of bird of prey) serre f.; (of
lobster) pince f. —v.t. griffer.
clay /kleɪ/ n. argile f.
clean /kliːn/ a. (-er, -est) propre; (shape,
stroke, etc.) net. —adv. complètement.
—v.t. nettoyer. —v.i. ~ **up,** faire le
nettoyage. ~ **one's teeth,** se brosser les
dents. ~**-shaven** a. glabre. ~**er** n. (at
home) femme de ménage f.;
(industrial) agent de nettoyage m./f.;
(of clothes) teinturlier, -ière m., f. ~**ly**
adv. proprement; (sharply) nettement.
cleanliness /'klenlɪnɪs/ n. propreté f.
cleans|e /klenz/ v.t. nettoyer; (fig.)
purifier. ~**ing cream,** crème démaquill-
lante f.
clear /klɪə(r)/ a. (-er, -est) clair; (glass)
transparent; (profit) net; (road) dégagé.
—adv. complètement. —v.t. (free)
dégager (**of,** de); (table) débarrasser;
(building) évacuer; (cheque) encaisser;
(jump over) franchir; (debt) liquider;
(jurid.) disculper. ~ (**away** or **off**),
(remove) enlever. —v.i. (fog) se dissiper.
~ **of,** (away from) à l'écart de. ~ **off** or
out, (sl.) décamper. ~ **out,** (clean)
nettoyer. ~ **up,** (tidy) ranger; (mystery)
éclaircir; (of weather) s'éclaircir. **make
sth. ~,** être très clair sur qch. ~**-cut** a. net.
~**ly** adv. clairement.
clearance /'klɪərəns/ n. (permission)
autorisation f.; (space) dégagement m.
~ **sale,** liquidation f.
clearing /'klɪərɪŋ/ n. clairière f.
clearway /'klɪəweɪ/ n. route à stationnement interdit f.
cleavage /'kliːvɪdʒ/ n. clivage m.;
(breasts) décolleté m.
clef /klef/ n. (mus.) clé f.
cleft /kleft/ n. fissure f.

clemen|t /'klemənt/ a. clément. ~**cy** n.
clémence f.
clench /klentʃ/ v.t. serrer.
clergy /'klɜːdʒɪ/ n. clergé m. ~**man** n.
(pl. -men) ecclésiastique m.
cleric /'klerɪk/ n. clerc m. ~**al** a. (relig.)
clérical; (of clerks) de bureau,
d'employé.
clerk /klɑːk, Amer. klɜːk/ n. employé(e)
de bureau m. (f.). (Amer.) (**sales**) ~,
vendeur|r, -se m., f.
clever /'klevə(r)/ a. (-er, -est) intelligent; (skilful) habile. ~**ly** adv.
intelligemment; habilement. ~**ness** n.
intelligence f.
cliché /'kliːʃeɪ/ n. cliché m.
click /klɪk/ n. déclic m. —v.i. faire un
déclic; (people: sl.) s'entendre. se
plaire. —v.t. (heels, tongue) faire
claquer.
client /'klaɪənt/ n. client(e) m. (f.).
clientele /kliːən'tel/ n. clientèle f.
cliff /klɪf/ n. falaise f.
climat|e /'klaɪmɪt/ n. climat m. ~**ic**
/-'mætɪk/ a. climatique.
climax /'klaɪmæks/ n. point culminant
m.; (sexual) orgasme m.
climb /klaɪm/ v.t. (stairs) monter,
grimper; (tree, ladder) monter or
grimper à; (mountain) faire l'ascension
de. —v.i. monter, grimper. —n. montée
f. ~ **down,** (fig.) reculer. ~**-down,** n.
recul m. ~**er** n. (sport) alpiniste m./f.
clinch /klɪntʃ/ v.t. (a deal) conclure.
cling /klɪŋ/ v.i. (p.t. **clung**) se
cramponner (**to,** à); (stick) coller. ~**-
film** n. (P.) film adhésif.
clinic /'klɪnɪk/ n. centre médical m.;
(private) clinique f.
clinical /'klɪnɪkl/ a. clinique.
clink /klɪŋk/ n. tintement m. —v.t./i.
(faire) tinter.
clinker /'klɪŋkə(r)/ n. mâchefer m.
clip[1] /klɪp/ n. (for paper) trombone m.;
(for hair) barrette f.; (for tube) collier
m. —v.t. (p.t. **clipped**) attacher (**to,** à).
clip[2] /klɪp/ v.t. (p.t. **clipped**) (cut)
couper. —n. coupe f.; (of film) extrait
m.; (blow: fam.) taloche f. ~**ping** n.
coupure f.
clippers /'klɪpəz/ n. pl. tondeuse f.; (for
nails) coupe-ongles m.
clique /kliːk/ n. clique f.
cloak /kləʊk/ n. (grande) cape f.,
manteau ample m.
cloakroom /'kləʊkrʊm/ n. vestiaire m.;
(toilet) toilettes f. pl.
clobber /'klɒbə(r)/ n. (sl.) affaires f. pl.
—v.t. (hit: sl.) rosser.

clock /klɒk/ *n.* pendule *f.*; (*large*) horloge *f.* —*v.i.* ~ **in** *or* **out**, pointer. ~ **up**, (*miles etc.*: *fam.*) faire. ~-**tower** *n.* clocher *m.*

clockwise /'klɒkwaɪz/ *a.* & *adv.* dans le sens des aiguilles d'une montre.

clockwork /'klɒkwɜːk/ *n.* mécanisme *m.* —*a.* mécanique.

clog /klɒg/ *n.* sabot *m.* —*v.t./i.* (*p.t.* **clogged**) (se) boucher.

cloister /'klɔɪstə(r)/ *n.* cloître *m.*

close[1] /kləʊs/ *a.* (**-er**, **-est**) (*near*) proche (**to**, de); (*link*, *collaboration*) étroit; (*examination*) attentif; (*friend*) intime; (*order*, *match*) serré; (*weather*) lourd. ~ **together**, (*crowded*) serrés. —*adv.* (tout) près. —*n.* (*street*) impasse *f.* ~ **by**, ~ **at hand**, tout près. ~-**up** *n.* gros plan *m.* **have a ~ shave**, l'échapper belle. **keep a ~ watch on**, surveiller de près. ~**ly** *adv.* (*follow*) de près. ~**ness** *n.* proximité *f.*

close[2] /kləʊz/ *v.t.* fermer. —*v.i.* se fermer; (*of shop etc.*) fermer; (*end*) (se) terminer. —*n.* fin *f.* ~**d shop**, organisation qui exclut les travailleurs non syndiqués *f.*

closet /'klɒzɪt/ *n.* (*Amer.*) placard *m.*

closure /'kləʊʒə(r)/ *n.* fermeture *f.*

clot /klɒt/ *n.* (*of blood*) caillot *m.*; (*in sauce*) grumeau *m.* —*v.t./i.* (*p.t.* **clotted**) (se) coaguler.

cloth /klɒθ/ *n.* tissu *m.*; (*duster*) linge *m.*; (*table-cloth*) nappe *f.*

cloth|e /kləʊð/ *v.t.* vêtir. ~**ing** *n.* vêtements *m. pl.*

clothes /kləʊðz/ *n. pl.* vêtements *m. pl.*, habits *m. pl.* ~-**brush** *n.* brosse à habits *f.* ~-**hanger** *n.* cintre *m.* ~-**line** *n.* corde à linge *f.* ~-**peg**, (*Amer.*) ~-**pin** *ns.* pince à linge *f.*

cloud /klaʊd/ *n.* nuage *m.* —*v.i.* se couvrir (de nuages); (*become gloomy*) s'assombrir. ~**y** *a.* (*sky*) couvert; (*liquid*) trouble.

cloudburst /'klaʊdbɜːst/ *n.* trombe d'eau *f.*

clout /klaʊt/ *n.* (*blow*) coup de poing *m.*; (*power*: *fam.*) pouvoir effectif *m.* —*v.t.* frapper.

clove /kləʊv/ *n.* clou de girofle *m.* ~ **of garlic**, gousse d'ail *f.*

clover /'kləʊvə(r)/ *n.* trèfle *m.*

clown /klaʊn/ *n.* clown *m.* —*v.i.* faire le clown.

cloy /klɔɪ/ *v.t.* écœurer.

club /klʌb/ *n.* (*group*) club *m.*; (*weapon*) massue *f.* ~**s**, (*cards*) trèfle *m.* —*v.t./i.* (*p.t.* **clubbed**) matraquer. (**golf**) ~, club

(de golf) *m.* ~ **together**, (*share costs*) se cotiser.

cluck /klʌk/ *v.i.* glousser.

clue /kluː/ *n.* indice *m.*; (*in crossword*) définition *f.* **I haven't a ~**, (*fam.*) je n'en ai pas la moindre idée.

clump /klʌmp/ *n.* massif *m.*

clums|y /'klʌmzɪ/ *a.* (**-ier**, **-iest**) maladroit; (*tool*) peu commode. ~**iness** *n.* maladresse *f.*

clung /klʌŋ/ *see* **cling**.

cluster /'klʌstə(r)/ *n.* (petit) groupe *m.* —*v.i.* se grouper.

clutch /klʌtʃ/ *v.t.* (*hold*) serrer fort; (*grasp*) saisir. —*v.i.* ~ **at**, (*try to grasp*) essayer de saisir. —*n.* étreinte *f.*; (*auto.*) embrayage *m.*

clutter /'klʌtə(r)/ *n.* désordre *m.*, fouillis *m.* —*v.t.* encombrer.

coach /kəʊtʃ/ *n.* autocar *m.*; (*of train*) wagon *m.*; (*horse-drawn*) carrosse *m.*; (*sport*) entraîneur, -se *m.*, *f.* —*v.t.* donner des leçons (particulières) à; (*sport*) entraîner.

coagulate /kəʊ'ægjʊleɪt/ *v.t./i.* (se) coaguler.

coal /kəʊl/ *n.* charbon *m.* ~-**mine** *n.* mine de charbon *f.*

coalfield /'kəʊlfiːld/ *n.* bassin houiller *m.*

coalition /kəʊə'lɪʃn/ *n.* coalition *f.*

coarse /kɔːs/ *a.* (**-er**, **-est**) grossier. ~**ness** *n.* caractère grossier *m.*

coast /kəʊst/ *n.* côte *f.* —*v.i.* (*car*, *bicycle*) descendre en roue libre. ~**al** *a.* côtier.

coaster /'kəʊstə(r)/ *n.* (*ship*) caboteur *m.*; (*mat*) dessous de verre *m.*

coastguard /'kəʊstɡɑːd/ *n.* gardecôte *m.*

coastline /'kəʊstlaɪn/ *n.* littoral *m.*

coat /kəʊt/ *n.* manteau *m.*; (*of animal*) pelage *m.*; (*of paint*) couche *f.* —*v.t.* enduire, couvrir; (*with chocolate*) enrober (**with**, de). ~-**hanger** *n.* cintre *m.* ~ **of arms**, armoiries *f. pl.* ~**ing** *n.* couche *f.*

coax /kəʊks/ *v.t.* amadouer.

cob /kɒb/ *n.* (*of corn*) épi *m.*

cobble[1] /'kɒbl/ *n.* pavé *m.* ~-**stone** *n.* pavé *m.*

cobble[2] /'kɒbl/ *v.t.* rapetasser.

cobbler /'kɒblə(r)/ *n.* (*old use*) cordonnier *m.*

cobweb /'kɒbweb/ *n.* toile d'araignée *f.*

cocaine /kəʊ'keɪn/ *n.* cocaïne *f.*

cock /kɒk/ *n.* (*oiseau*) mâle *m.*; (*rooster*) coq *m.* —*v.t.* (*gun*) armer; (*ears*) dresser. ~-**and-bull story**, histoire à dormir debout *f.* ~-**eyed** *a.* (*askew*: *sl.*) de travers. ~-**up** *n.* (*sl.*) pagaille *f.*

cockerel /'kɒkərəl/ n. jeune coq m.
cockle /'kɒkl/ n. (culin.) coque f.
cockney /'kɒknɪ/ n. Cockney m./f.
cockpit /'kɒkpɪt/ n. poste de pilotage m.
cockroach /'kɒkrəʊtʃ/ n. cafard m.
cocksure /kɒk'ʃʊə(r)/ a. sûr de soi.
cocktail /'kɒkteɪl/ n. cocktail m. ~ **party**, cocktail m. **fruit** ~, macédoine (de fruits) f.
cocky /'kɒkɪ/ a. (-ier, -iest) trop sûr de soi, arrogant.
cocoa /'kəʊkəʊ/ n. cacao m.
coconut /'kəʊkənʌt/ n. noix de coco m.
cocoon /kə'kuːn/ n. cocon m.
COD abbr. (cash on delivery) paiement à la livraison m.
cod /kɒd/ n. invar. morue f. ~**-liver oil**, huile de foie de morue f.
coddle /'kɒdl/ v.t. dorloter.
code /kəʊd/ n. code m. —v.t. coder.
codify /'kəʊdɪfaɪ/ v.t. codifier.
coeducational /kəʊedʒʊ'keɪʃənl/ a. (school, teaching) mixte.
coerce /kəʊ'ɜːs/ v.t. contraindre. ~**ion** /-ʃn/ n. contrainte f.
coexist /kəʊɪg'zɪst/ v.i. coexister. ~**ence** n. coexistence f.
coffee /'kɒfɪ/ n. café m. ~ **bar**, café m., cafétéria f. ~**-pot** n. cafetière f. ~**table** n. table basse f.
coffer /'kɒfə(r)/ n. coffre m.
coffin /'kɒfɪn/ n. cercueil m.
cog /kɒg/ n. dent f.; (fig.) rouage m.
cogent /'kəʊdʒənt/ a. convaincant; (relevant) pertinent.
cognac /'kɒnjæk/ n. cognac m.
cohabit /kəʊ'hæbɪt/ v.i. vivre en concubinage.
coherent /kəʊ'hɪərənt/ a. cohérent.
coil /kɔɪl/ v.t./i. (s')enrouler. —n. rouleau m.; (one ring) spire f.; (contraceptive) stérilet m.
coin /kɔɪn/ n. pièce (de monnaie) f. —v.t. (word) inventer. ~**age** n. monnaie f.; (fig.) invention ~**-box** n. téléphone public m.
coincide /kəʊɪn'saɪd/ v.i. coïncider.
coinciden|ce /kəʊ'ɪnsɪdəns/ n. coïncidence f. ~**tal** /-'dentl/ a. dû à une coïncidence.
coke /kəʊk/ n. coke m.
colander /'kʌləndə(r)/ n. passoire f.
cold /kəʊld/ a. (-er, -est) froid. **be** or **feel** ~, avoir froid. **it is** ~, il fait froid. —n. froid m.; (med.) rhume m. ~**-blooded** a. sans pitié. ~ **cream**, crème de beauté f. **get** ~ **feet**, se dégonfler. ~**-shoulder** v.t. snober. ~ **sore**, bouton de fièvre m. ~**ness** n. froideur f.

coleslaw /'kəʊlslɔː/ n. salade de chou cru f.
colic /'kɒlɪk/ n. coliques f. pl.
collaborat|e /kə'læbəreɪt/ v.i. collaborer. ~**ion** /-'reɪʃn/ n. collaboration f. ~**or** n. collaborateur, -trice m., f.
collage /'kɒlɑːʒ/ n. collage m.
collapse /kə'læps/ v.i. s'effondrer; (med.) avoir un malaise. —n. effondrement m.
collapsible /kə'læpsəbl/ a. pliant.
collar /'kɒlə(r)/ n. col m.; (of dog) collier m. —v.t. (take: sl.) piquer. ~**-bone** n. clavicule f.
collateral /kə'lætərəl/ n. nantissement m.
colleague /'kɒliːg/ n. collègue m./f.
collect /kə'lekt/ v.t. rassembler; (pick up) ramasser; (call for) passer prendre; (money, rent) encaisser; (taxes) percevoir; (as hobby) collectionner. —v.i. se rassembler; (dust) s'amasser. —adv. **call** ~, (Amer.) téléphoner en PCV. ~**ion** /-kʃn/ n. collection f.; (in church) quête f.; (of mail) levée f. ~**or** n. (as hobby) collectionneur, -se m., f.
collective /kə'lektɪv/ a. collectif.
college /'kɒlɪdʒ/ n. (for higher education) institut m., école f.; (within university) collège m. **be at** ~, être en faculté.
collide /kə'laɪd/ v.i. entrer en collision (**with**, avec).
colliery /'kɒlɪərɪ/ n. houillère f.
collision /kə'lɪʒn/ n. collision f.
colloquial /kə'ləʊkwɪəl/ a. familier. ~**ism** n. expression familière f.
collusion /kə'luːʒn/ n. collusion f.
colon /'kəʊlən/ n. (gram.) deux-points m. invar.; (anat.) côlon m.
colonel /'kɜːnl/ n. colonel m.
colonize /'kɒlənaɪz/ v.t. coloniser.
colon|y /'kɒlənɪ/ n. colonie f. ~**ial** /kə'ləʊnɪəl/ a. & n. colonial(e) (m. (f.)).
colossal /kə'lɒsl/ a. colossal.
colour /'kʌlə(r)/ n. couleur f. —a. (photo etc.) en couleur; (TV set) couleur invar. —v.t. colorer; (with crayon) colorier. ~**-blind** a. daltonien. ~**-fast** a. grand teint. invar. ~**ful** a. coloré; (person) haut en couleur. ~**ing** n. (of skin) teint m.; (in food) colorant m.
coloured /'kʌləd/ a. (person, pencil) de couleur. —n. personne de couleur f.
colt /kəʊlt/ n. poulain m.
column /'kɒləm/ n. colonne f.

columnist /'kɒləmnɪst/ *n.* journaliste chroniqueur *m.*

coma /'kəʊmə/ *n.* coma *m.*

comb /kəʊm/ *n.* peigne *m.* —*v.t.* peigner; (*search*) ratisser. ~ **one's hair,** se peigner.

combat /'kɒmbæt/ *n.* combat *m.* —*v.t.* (*p.t.* **combated**) combattre. ~**ant** /-ətənt/ *n.* combattant(e) *m.* (*f.*).

combination /kɒmbɪ'neɪʃn/ *n.* combinaison *f.*

combine[1] /kəm'baɪn/ *v.t./i.* (se) combiner, (s')unir.

combine[2] /'kɒmbaɪn/ *n.* (*comm.*) trust *m.*, cartel *m.* ~ **harvester,** moissonneuse-batteuse *f.*

combustion /kəm'bʌstʃən/ *n.* combustion *f.*

come /kʌm/ *v.i.* (*p.t.* **came,** *p.p.* **come**) venir; (*occur*) arriver; (*sexually*) jouir. ~ **about,** arriver. ~ **across,** rencontrer *or* trouver par hasard. ~ **away** *or* **off,** se détacher, partir. ~ **back,** revenir. ~-**back** *n.* rentrée *f.*; (*retort*) réplique *f.* ~ **by,** obtenir. ~ **down,** descendre; (*price*) baisser. ~-**down** *n.* humiliation *f.* ~ **forward,** se présenter. ~ **from,** être de. ~ **in,** entrer. ~ **in for,** recevoir. ~ **into,** (*money*) hériter de. ~ **off,** (*succeed*) réussir; (*fare*) s'en tirer. ~ **on,** (*actor*) entrer en scène; (*light*) s'allumer; (*improve*) faire des progrès. ~ **on!,** allez! ~ **out,** sortir. ~ **round** *or* **to,** revenir à soi. ~ **through,** s'en tirer (indemne de). ~ **to,** (*amount*) revenir à; (*decision, conclusion*) arriver à. ~ **up,** monter; (*fig.*) se présenter. ~ **up against,** rencontrer. **get one's** ~-**uppance** *n.* (*fam.*) finir par recevoir ce qu'on mérite. ~ **up with,** (*find*) trouver; (*produce*) produire.

comedian /kə'miːdɪən/ *n.* comique *m.*

comedy /'kɒmədɪ/ *n.* comédie *f.*

comely /'kʌmlɪ/ *a.* (**-ier, -iest**) (*old use*) avenant, beau.

comet /'kɒmɪt/ *n.* comète *f.*

comfort /'kʌmfət/ *n.* confort *m.*; (*consolation*) réconfort *m.* —*v.t.* consoler. ~ **s,** ses aises. ~**able** *a.* (*chair, car, etc.*) confortable; (*person*) à l'aise, bien; (*wealthy*) aisé.

comforter /'kʌmfətə(r)/ *n.* (*baby's dummy*) sucette *f.*; (*quilt*: *Amer.*) édredon *m.*

comfy /'kʌmfɪ/ *a.* (*fam.*) = **comfortable.**

comic /'kɒmɪk/ *a.* comique. —*n.* (*person*) comique *m.*; (*periodical*) comic *m.* ~ **strip,** bande dessinée *f.* ~**al** *a.* comique.

coming /'kʌmɪŋ/ *n.* arrivée *f.* —*a.* à venir. ~**s and goings,** allées et venues *f. pl.*

comma /'kɒmə/ *n.* virgule *f.*

command /kə'mɑːnd/ *n.* (*authority*) commandement *m.*; (*order*) ordre *m.*; (*mastery*) maîtrise *f.* —*v.t.* commander (**s.o. to,** à qn. de); (*be able to use*) disposer de; (*require*) nécessiter; (*respect*) inspirer. ~**er** *n.* commandant *m.* ~**ing** *a.* imposant.

commandeer /kɒmən'dɪə(r)/ *v.t.* réquisitionner.

commandment /kə'mɑːndmənt/ *n.* commandement *m.*

commando /kə'mɑːndəʊ/ *n.* (*pl.* **-os**) commando *m.*

commemorat|e /kə'meməreɪt/ *v.t.* commémorer. ~**ion** /-'reɪʃn/ *n.* commémoration *f.* ~**ive** /-ətɪv/ *a.* commémoratif.

commence /kə'mens/ *v.t./i.* commencer. ~**ment** *n.* commencement *m.*; (*univ.*, *Amer.*) cérémonie de distribution des diplômes *f.*

commend /kə'mend/ *v.t.* (*praise*) louer; (*entrust*) confier. ~**able** *a.* louable. ~**ation** /kɒmen'deɪʃn/ *n.* éloge *m.*

commensurate /kə'menʃərət/ *a.* proportionné.

comment /'kɒment/ *n.* commentaire *m.* —*v.i.* faire des commentaires. ~ **on,** commenter.

commentary /'kɒməntrɪ/ *n.* commentaire *m.*; (*radio, TV*) reportage *m.*

commentat|e /'kɒmənteɪt/ *v.i.* faire un reportage. ~**or** *n.* commentateur, -trice *m., f.*

commerce /'kɒmɜːs/ *n.* commerce *m.*

commercial /kə'mɜːʃl/ *a.* commercial; (*traveller*) de commerce. —*n.* publicité *f.* ~**ize** *v.t.* commercialiser.

commiserat|e /kə'mɪzəreɪt/ *v.i.* compatir (**with,** avec). ~**ion** /-'reɪʃn/ *n.* commisération *f.*

commission /kə'mɪʃn/ *n.* commission *f.*; (*order for work*) commande *f.* —*v.t.* (*order*) commander; (*mil.*) nommer officier. ~ **to do,** charger de faire. **out of** ~, hors service. ~**er** *n.* préfet (de police) *m.*; (*in E.C.*) commissaire *m.*

commissionaire /kəmɪʃə'neə(r)/ *n.* commissionnaire *m.*

commit /kə'mɪt/ *v.t.* (*p.t.* **committed**) commettre; (*entrust*) confier. ~ **o.s.,** s'engager. ~ **perjury,** se parjurer. ~ **suicide,** se suicider. ~ **to memory,** apprendre par cœur. ~**ment** *n.* engagement *m.*

committee /kə'mɪtɪ/ n. comité m.

commodity /kə'mɒdətɪ/ n. produit m., article m.

common /'kɒmən/ a. (-er, -est) (shared by all) commun; (usual) courant, commun; (vulgar) vulgaire, commun. —n. terrain communal m. ~ law, droit coutumier m. C~ Market, Marché Commun m. ~-room n. (schol.) salle commune f. ~ sense, bon sens m. House of C~s, Chambre des Communes f. in ~, en commun. ~ly adv. communément.

commoner /'kɒmənə(r)/ n. roturier, -ière m., f.

commonplace /'kɒmənpleɪs/ a. banal. —n. banalité f.

Commonwealth /'kɒmənwelθ/ n. the ~, le Commonwealth m.

commotion /kə'məʊʃn/ n. agitation f., remue-ménage m. invar.

communal /'kɒmjʊnl/ a. (shared) commun; (life) collectif.

commune /'kɒmju:n/ n. (group) communauté f.

communicat|e /kə'mju:nɪkeɪt/ v.t./i. communiquer. ~ion/-'keɪʃn/ n. communication f. ~ive /-ətɪv/ a. communicatif.

communion /kə'mju:nɪən/ n. communion f.

communiqué /kə'mju:nɪkeɪ/ n. communiqué m.

Communis|t /'kɒmjʊnɪst/ a. & n. communiste (m./f.) ~m /-zəm/ n. communisme m.

community /kə'mju:nətɪ/ n. communauté f.

commutation /kɒmju:'teɪʃn/ n. ~ ticket, carte d'abonnement f.

commute /kə'mju:t/ v.i. faire la navette. —v.t. (jurid.) commuer. ~r /-ə(r)/ n. banlieusard(e) m. (f.).

compact[1] /kəm'pækt/ a. compact. ~ /'kɒmpækt/ disc, (disque) compact m.

compact[2] /'kɒmpækt/ n. (lady's case) poudrier m.

companion /kəm'pænjən/ n. compagnon, -agne m., f. ~ship n. camaraderie f.

company /'kʌmpənɪ/ n. (companionship, firm) compagnie f.; (guests) invité(e)s m. (f.) pl.

comparable /'kɒmpərəbl/ a. comparable.

compar|e /kəm'peə(r)/ v.t. comparer (with, to, à). ~ed with or to, en comparaison de. —v.i. être comparable.

~ative /-'pærətɪv/ a. (study, form) comparatif; (comfort etc.) relatif. **~atively** /-'pærətɪvlɪ/ adv. relativement.

comparison /kəm'pærɪsn/ n. comparaison f.

compartment /kəm'pɑ:tmənt/ n. compartiment m.

compass /'kʌmpəs/ n. (for direction) boussole f.; (scope) portée f. ~(es), (for drawing) compas m.

compassion /kəm'pæʃn/ n. compassion f. ~ate a. compatissant.

compatib|le /kəm'pætəbl/ a. compatible. ~ility /-'bɪlətɪ/ n. compatibilité f.

compatriot /kəm'pætrɪət/ n. compatriote m./f.

compel /kəm'pel/ v.t. (p.t. compelled) contraindre. ~ling a. irrésistible.

compendium /kəm'pendɪəm/ n. abrégé m., résumé m.

compensat|e /'kɒmpənseɪt/ v.t./i. (financially) dédommager (for, de). ~e for sth., compenser qch. ~ion /-'seɪʃn/ n. compensation f.; (financial) dédommagement m.

compete /kəm'pi:t/ v.i. concourir. ~ with, rivaliser avec.

competen|t /'kɒmpɪtənt/ a. compétent. ~ce n. compétence f.

competition /kɒmpɪ'tɪʃn/ n. (contest) concours m.; (sport) compétition f.; (comm.) concurrence f.

competitive /kəm'petətɪv/ a. (prices) concurrentiel, compétitif. ~ examination, concours m.

competitor /kəm'petɪtə(r)/ n. concurrent(e) m. (f.).

compile /kəm'paɪl/ v.t. (list) dresser; (book) rédiger. ~r /-ə(r)/ n. rédacteur, -trice m., f.

complacen|t /kəm'pleɪsnt/ a. content de soi. ~cy contentement de soi m.

complain /kəm'pleɪn/ v.i. se plaindre (about, of, de).

complaint /kəm'pleɪnt/ n. plainte f.; (in shop etc.) réclamation f.; (illness) maladie f.

complement /'kɒmplɪmənt/ n. complément m. —v.t. compléter. ~ary /-'mentrɪ/ a. complémentaire.

complet|e /kəm'pli:t/ a. complet; (finished) achevé; (downright) parfait. —v.t. achever; (a form) remplir. ~ely adv. complètement. ~ion /-ʃn/ n. achèvement m.

complex /'kɒmpleks/ a. complexe. —n. (psych., archit.) complexe m. ~ity /kəm'pleksətɪ/ n. complexité f.

complexion /kəm'plekʃn/ n. (of face) teint m.; (fig.) caractère m.

compliance /kəm'plaɪəns/ n. (agreement) conformité f.

complicat|e /'kɒmplɪkeɪt/ v.t. compliquer. **~ed** a. compliqué. **~ion** /-'keɪʃn/ n. complication f.

complicity /kəm'plɪsətɪ/ n. complicité f.

compliment /'kɒmplɪmənt/ n. compliment m. —v.t. /'kɒmplɪment/ complimenter.

complimentary /kɒmplɪ'mentrɪ/ a. (offert) à titre gracieux; (praising) flatteur.

comply /kəm'plaɪ/ v.i. **~ with**, se conformer à, obéir à.

component /kəm'pəʊnənt/ n. (of machine etc.) pièce f.; (chemical substance) composant m.; (element: fig.) composante f. —a. constituant.

compose /kəm'pəʊz/ v.t. composer. **~ o.s.**, se calmer. **~d** a. calme. **~r** /-ə(r)/ n. (mus.) compositeur m.

composition /kɒmpə'zɪʃn/ n. composition f.

compost /'kɒmpɒst, Amer. 'kɒmpəʊst/ n. compost m.

composure /kəm'pəʊʒə(r)/ n. calme m.

compound¹ /'kɒmpaʊnd/ n. (substance, word) composé m.; (enclosure) enclos m. —a. composé.

compound² /kəm'paʊnd/ v.t. (problem etc.) aggraver.

comprehen|d /kɒmprɪ'hend/ v.t. comprendre. **~sion** n. compréhension f.

comprehensive /kɒmprɪ'hensɪv/ a. étendu, complet; (insurance) tous-risques invar. **~ school**, collège d'enseignement secondaire m.

compress /kəm'pres/ v.t. comprimer. **~ion** /-ʃn/ n. compression f.

comprise /kəm'praɪz/ v.t. comprendre, inclure.

compromise /'kɒmprəmaɪz/ n. compromis m. —v.t. compromettre. —v.i. transiger, trouver un compromis. **not ~ on**, ne pas transiger sur.

compulsion /kəm'pʌlʃn/ n. contrainte f.

compulsive /kəm'pʌlsɪv/ a. (psych.) compulsif; (liar, smoker) invétéré.

compulsory /kəm'pʌlsərɪ/ a. obligatoire.

compunction /kəm'pʌŋkʃn/ n. scrupule m.

computer /kəm'pjuːtə(r)/ n. ordinateur m. **~ science**, informatique f. **~ize** v.t. informatiser.

comrade /'kɒmr(e)ɪd/ n. camarade m./f. **~ship** n. camaraderie f.

con¹ /kɒn/ v.t. (p.t. **conned**) (sl.) rouler,

escroquer (**out of**, de). —n. (sl.) escroquerie f. **~ s.o. into doing**, arnaquer qn. en lui faisant faire. **~ man**, (sl.) escroc m.

con² /kɒn/ see **pro**.

concave /'kɒŋkeɪv/ a. concave.

conceal /kən'siːl/ v.t. dissimuler. **~ment** n. dissimulation f.

concede /kən'siːd/ v.t. concéder. —v.i. céder.

conceit /kən'siːt/ n. suffisance f. **~ed** a. suffisant.

conceivab|le /kən'siːvəbl/ a. concevable. **~y** adv. this may **~**y be done, il est concevable que cela puisse se faire.

conceive /kən'siːv/ v.t./i. concevoir. **~ of**, concevoir.

concentrat|e /'kɒnsntreɪt/ v.t./i. (se) concentrer. **~ion** /-'treɪʃn/ n. concentration f.

concept /'kɒnsept/ n. concept m. **~ual** /kən'septʃʊəl/ a. notionnel.

conception /kən'sepʃn/ n. conception f.

concern /kən'sɜːn/ n. (interest, business) affaire f.; (worry) inquiétude f.; (firm: comm.) entreprise f., affaire f. —v.i. concerner. **~ o.s. with, be ~ed with**, s'occuper de. **~ing** prep. en ce qui concerne.

concerned /kən'sɜːnd/ a. inquiet.

concert /'kɒnsət/ n. concert m. **in ~**, ensemble.

concerted /kən'sɜːtɪd/ a. concerté.

concertina /kɒnsə'tiːnə/ n. concertina m.

concerto /kən'tʃeətəʊ/ n. (pl. **-os**) concerto m.

concession /kən'seʃn/ n. concession f.

conciliation /kənsɪlɪ'eɪʃn/ n. conciliation f.

concise /kən'saɪs/ a. concis. **~ly** adv. avec concision. **~ness** n. concision f.

conclu|de /kən'kluːd/ v.t. conclure. —v.i. se terminer. **~ding** a. final. **~sion** n. conclusion f.

conclusive /kən'kluːsɪv/ a. concluant. **~ly** adv. de manière concluante.

concoct /kən'kɒkt/ v.t. confectionner; (invent: fig.) fabriquer. **~ion** /-kʃn/ n. mélange m.

concourse /'kɒŋkɔːs/ n. (rail.) hall m.

concrete /'kɒŋkriːt/ n. béton m. —a. concret. —v.t. bétonner. **~-mixer** n. bétonnière f.

concur /kən'kɜː(r)/ v.i. (p.t. **concurred**) être d'accord.

concurrently /kən'kʌrəntlɪ/ adv. simultanément.

concussion /kən'kʌʃn/ n. commotion (cérébrale) f.

condemn /kən'dem/ v.t. condamner. ∼**ation** /kɒndem'neɪʃn/ n. condamnation f.

condens|e /kən'dens/ v.t./i. (se) condenser. ∼**ation** /kɒnden'seɪʃn/ n. condensation f.; (mist) buée f.

condescend /kɒndɪ'send/ v.i. condescendre.

condiment /'kɒndɪmənt/ n. condiment m.

condition /kən'dɪʃn/ n. condition f. —v.t. conditionner. **on** ∼ **that,** à condition que. ∼**al** a. conditionnel. **be** ∼**al upon,** dépendre de. ∼**er** n. après-shampooing m.

condolences /kən'dəʊlənsɪz/ n. pl. condoléances f. pl.

condom /'kɒndɒm/ n. préservatif m.

condominium /kɒndə'mɪnɪəm/ n. (Amer.) copropriété f.

condone /kən'dəʊn/ v.t. pardonner, fermer les yeux sur.

conducive /kən'dju:sɪv/ a. ∼ **to,** favorable à.

conduct[1] /kən'dʌkt/ v.t. conduire; (orchestra) diriger.

conduct[2] /'kɒndʌkt/ n. conduite f.

conduct|or /kən'dʌktə(r)/ n. chef d'orchestre m.; (of bus) receveur m.; (on train: Amer.) chef de train m.; (electr.) conducteur m. ∼**ress** n. receveuse f.

cone /kəʊn/ n. cône m.; (of ice-cream) cornet m.

confectioner /kən'fekʃənə(r)/ n. confiseur, -se m., f. ∼**y** n. confiserie f.

confederation /kɒnfedə'reɪʃn/ n. confédération f.

confer /kən'fɜ:(r)/ v.t./i. (p.t. conferred) conférer.

conference /'kɒnfərəns/ n. conférence f.

confess /kən'fes/ v.t./i. avouer; (relig.) (se) confesser. ∼**ion** /-ʃn/ n. confession f.; (of crime) aveu m.

confessional /kən'feʃənl/ n. confessionnal m.

confetti /kən'fetɪ/ n. confettis m. pl.

confide /kən'faɪd/ v.t. confier. —v.i. ∼ **in,** se confier à.

confiden|t /'kɒnfɪdənt/ a. sûr. ∼**ce** n. (trust) confiance f.; (boldness) confiance en soi f.; (secret) confidence f. ∼**ce trick,** escroquerie f. **in** ∼**ce,** en confidence.

confidential /kɒnfɪ'denʃl/ a. confidentiel.

configure /kən'fɪgə(r)/ v.t. (comput.) configurer.

confine /kən'faɪn/ v.t. enfermer; (limit)

limiter. ∼**d space,** espace réduit. ∼**d to,** limité à. ∼**ment** n. détention f.; (med.) couches f. pl.

confines /'kɒnfaɪnz/ n. pl. confins m. pl.

confirm /kən'fɜ:m/ v.t. confirmer. ∼**ation** /kɒnfə'meɪʃn/ n. confirmation f. ∼**ed** a. (bachelor) endurci; (smoker) invétéré.

confiscat|e /'kɒnfɪskeɪt/ v.t. confisquer. ∼**ion** /-'keɪʃn/ n. confiscation f.

conflagration /kɒnflə'greɪʃn/ n. incendie m.

conflict[1] /'kɒnflɪkt/ n. conflit m.

conflict[2] /kən'flɪkt/ v.i. (statements, views) être en contradiction (with, avec); (appointments) tomber en même temps (with, que). ∼**ing** a. contradictoire.

conform /kən'fɔ:m/ v.t./i. (se) conformer. ∼**ist** n. conformiste m./f.

confound /kən'faʊnd/ v.t. confondre. ∼**ed** a. (fam.) sacré.

confront /kən'frʌnt/ v.t. affronter. ∼ **with,** confronter avec. ∼**ation** /kɒnfrʌn'teɪʃn/ n. confrontation f.

confus|e /kən'fju:z/ v.t. embrouiller; (mistake, confound) confondre. **become** ∼**ed,** s'embrouiller. **I am** ∼**ed,** je m'y perds. ∼**ing** a. déroutant. ∼**ion** /-ʒn/ n. confusion f.

congeal /kən'dʒi:l/ v.t./i. (se) figer.

congenial /kən'dʒi:nɪəl/ a. sympathique.

congenital /kən'dʒenɪtl/ a. congénital.

congest|ed /kən'dʒestɪd/ a. encombré; (med.) congestionné. ∼**ion** /-stʃən/ n. (traffic) encombrement(s) m. (pl.); (med.) congestion f.

conglomerate /kən'glɒmərət/ n. (comm.) conglomérat m.

congratulat|e /kən'grætjʊleɪt/ v.t. féliciter (on, de). ∼**ions** /-'leɪʃnz/ n. pl. félicitations f. pl.

congregat|e /'kɒngrɪgeɪt/ v.i. se rassembler. ∼**ion** /-'geɪʃn/ n. assemblée f.

congress /'kɒngres/ n. congrès m. **C**∼, (Amer.) le Congrès.

conic(al) /'kɒnɪk(l)/ a. conique.

conifer /'kɒnɪfə(r)/ n. conifère m.

conjecture /kən'dʒektʃə(r)/ n. conjecture f. —v.t./i. conjecturer.

conjugal /'kɒndʒʊgl/ a. conjugal.

conjugat|e /'kɒndʒʊgeɪt/ v.t. conjuguer. ∼**ion** /-'geɪʃn/ n. conjugaison f.

conjunction /kən'dʒʌŋkʃn/ n. conjonction f. **in** ∼ **with,** conjointement avec.

conjunctivitis /kɒndʒʌŋktɪ'vaɪtɪs/ n. conjonctivite f.

conjur|e /'kʌndʒə(r)/ v.i. faire des tours de passe-passe. —v.t. ∼**e up,** faire apparaître. **~or** *n*. prestidigitateur, -trice *m.*, *f.*

conk /kɒŋk/ *v.i.* **~ out,** (*sl.*) tomber en panne.

conker /'kɒŋkə(r)/ *n*. (*horse-chestnut fruit*: *fam.*) marron *m.*

connect /kə'nekt/ *v.t./i.* (se) relier; (*in mind*) faire le rapport entre; (*install*, *wire up to mains*) brancher. **~ with,** (*of train*) assurer la correspondance avec. **~ed** *a*. lié. **be ~ed with,** avoir rapport à; (*deal with*) avoir des rapports avec.

connection /kə'nekʃn/ *n*. rapport *m.*; (*rail*) correspondance *f.*; (*phone call*) communication *f.*; (*electr.*) contact *m.*; (*joining piece*) raccord *m.* **~s,** (*comm.*) relations *f. pl.*

conniv|e /kə'naɪv/ *v.i.* **~e at,** se faire le complice de. **~ance** *n*. connivence *f.*

connoisseur /kɒnə'sɜː(r)/ *n*. connaisseur *m.*

connot|e /kə'nəʊt/ *v.t.* connoter. **~ation** /kɒnə'teɪʃn/ *n*. connotation *f.*

conquer /'kɒŋkə(r)/ *v.t.* vaincre; (*country*) conquérir. **~or** *n*. conquérant *m.*

conquest /'kɒŋkwest/ *n*. conquête *f.*

conscience /'kɒnʃəns/ *n*. conscience *f.*

conscientious /kɒnʃɪ'enʃəs/ *a*. consciencieux.

conscious /'kɒnʃəs/ *a*. conscient; (*deliberate*) voulu. **~ly** *adv.* consciemment. **~ness** *n*. conscience *f.*; (*med.*) connaissance *f.*

conscript[1] /kən'skrɪpt/ *v.t.* recruter par conscription. **~ion** /-pʃn/ *n*. conscription *f.*

conscript[2] /'kɒnskrɪpt/ *n*. conscrit *m.*

consecrate /'kɒnsɪkreɪt/ *v.t.* consacrer.

consecutive /kən'sekjʊtɪv/ *a*. consécutif. **~ly** *adv.* consécutivement.

consensus /kən'sensəs/ *n*. consensus *m.*

consent /kən'sent/ *v.i.* consentir (**to,** à). —*n.* consentement *m.*

consequence /'kɒnsɪkwəns/ *n*. conséquence *f.*

consequent /'kɒnsɪkwənt/ *a*. résultant. **~ly** *adv.* par conséquent.

conservation /kɒnsə'veɪʃn/ *n*. préservation *f.* **~ area,** zone classée *f.*

conservationist /kɒnsə'veɪʃənɪst/ *n*. défenseur de l'environnement *m.*

conservative /kən'sɜːvətɪv/ *a*. conservateur; (*estimate*) modeste. **C~** *a.* & *n.* conservateur, -trice (*m.* (*f.*)).

conservatory /kən'sɜːvətrɪ/ *n*. (*greenhouse*) serre *f.*; (*room*) véranda *f.*

conserve /kən'sɜːv/ *v.t.* conserver; (*energy*) économiser.

consider /kən'sɪdə(r)/ *v.t.* considérer; (*allow for*) tenir compte de; (*possibility*) envisager (**doing,** de faire). **~ation** /-'reɪʃn/ *n*. considération *f.*; (*respect*) égard(s) *m.* (*pl.*). **~ing** *prep.* compte tenu de.

considerabl|e /kən'sɪdərəbl/ *a*. considérable; (*much*) beaucoup de. **~y** *adv.* beaucoup, considérablement.

considerate /kən'sɪdərət/ *a*. prévenant, attentionné.

consign /kən'saɪn/ *v.t.* (*entrust*) confier; (*send*) expédier. **~ment** *n*. envoi *m.*

consist /kən'sɪst/ *v.i.* consister (**of,** en; **in doing,** à faire).

consisten|t /kən'sɪstənt/ *a*. cohérent. **~t with,** conforme à. **~cy** *n*. (*of liquids*) consistance *f.*; (*of argument*) cohérence *f.* **~tly** *adv.* régulièrement.

consol|e /kən'səʊl/ *v.t.* consoler. **~ation** /kɒnsə'leɪʃn/ *n*. consolation *f.*

consolidat|e /kən'sɒlɪdeɪt/ *v.t./i.* (se) consolider. **~ion** /-'deɪʃn/ *n*. consolidation *f.*

consonant /'kɒnsənənt/ *n*. consonne *f.*

consort[1] /'kɒnsɔːt/ *n*. époux *m.*, épouse *f.*

consort[2] /kən'sɔːt/ *v.i.* **~ with,** fréquenter.

consortium /kən'sɔːtɪəm/ *n*. (*pl.* **-tia**) consortium *m.*

conspicuous /kən'spɪkjʊəs/ *a*. (*easily seen*) en évidence; (*showy*) voyant; (*noteworthy*) remarquable.

conspiracy /kən'spɪrəsɪ/ *n*. conspiration *f.*

conspire /kən'spaɪə(r)/ *v.i.* (*person*) comploter (**to do, de** faire), conspirer; (*events*) conspirer (**to do,** à faire).

constable /'kʌnstəbl/ *n*. agent de police *m.*, gendarme *m.*

constant /'kɒnstənt/ *a*. incessant; (*unchanging*) constant; (*friend*) fidèle. —*n.* constante *f.* **~ly** *adv.* constamment.

constellation /kɒnstə'leɪʃn/ *n*. constellation *f.*

consternation /kɒnstə'neɪʃn/ *n*. consternation *f.*

constipat|e /'kɒnstɪpeɪt/ *v.t.* constiper. **~ion** /-'peɪʃn/ *n*. constipation *f.*

constituency /kən'stɪtjʊənsɪ/ *n*. circonscription électorale *f.*

constituent /kən'stɪtjʊənt/ *a*. constitutif. —*n.* élément constitutif *m.*; (*pol.*) électeur, -trice *m.*, *f.*

constitut|e /'kɒnstɪtjuːt/ *v.t.* constituer. **~ion** /-'tjuːʃn/ *n*. constitution *f.*

~**ional** /-'tju:ʃənl/ a. constitutionnel; n. promenade f.

constrain /kən'streɪn/ v.t. contraindre.

constraint /kən'streɪnt/ n. contrainte f.

constrict /kən'strɪkt/ v.t. resserrer; (movement) gêner. ~**ion** /-kʃn/ n. resserrement m.

construct /kən'strʌkt/ v.t. construire. ~**ion** /-kʃn/ n. construction f. ~**ion worker,** ouvrier de bâtiment m.

constructive /kən'strʌktɪv/ a. constructif.

construe /kən'stru:/ v.t. interpréter.

consul /'kɒnsl/ n. consul m. ~**ar** /-jʊlə(r)/ a. consulaire.

consulate /'kɒnsjʊlət/ n. consulat m.

consult /kən'sʌlt/ v.t. consulter. —v.i. ~ **with,** conférer avec. ~**ation** /kɒnsl'teɪʃn/ n. consultation f.

consultant /kən'sʌltənt/ n. conseiller, -ère m., f.; (med.) spécialiste m./f.

consume /kən'sju:m/ v.t. consommer; (destroy) consumer. ~**r** /-ə(r)/ n. consomma|teur, -trice m., f. a. (society) de consommation.

consumerism /kən'sju:mərɪzəm/ n. protection des consommateurs f.

consummate /'kɒnsəmeɪt/ v.t. consommer.

consumption /kən'sʌmpʃn/ n. consommation f.; (med.) phtisie f.

contact /'kɒntækt/ n. contact m.; (person) relation f. —v.t. contacter. ~ **lenses,** lentilles (de contact) f. pl.

contagious /kən'teɪdʒəs/ a. contagieux.

contain /kən'teɪn/ v.t. contenir. ~ **o.s.,** se contenir. ~**er** n. récipient m.; (for transport) container m.

contaminat|e /kən'tæmɪneɪt/ v.t. contaminer. ~**ion** /-'neɪʃn/ n. contamination f.

contemplat|e /'kɒntəmpleɪt/ v.t. (gaze at) contempler; (think about) envisager. ~**ion** /-'pleɪʃn/ n. contemplation f.

contemporary /kən'temprərɪ/ a. & n. contemporain(e) (m. (f.)).

contempt /kən'tempt/ n. mépris m. ~**ible** a. méprisable. ~**uous** /-tʃʊəs/ a. méprisant.

contend /kən'tend/ v.t. soutenir. —v.i. ~ **with,** (compete) rivaliser avec; (face) faire face à. ~**er** n. adversaire m./f.

content[1] /kən'tent/ a. satisfait. —v.t. contenter. ~**ed** a. satisfait. ~**ment** n. contentement m.

content[2] /'kɒntent/ n. (of letter) contenu m.; (amount) teneur f. ~**s,** contenu m.

contention /kən'tenʃn/ n. dispute f.; (claim) affirmation f.

contest[1] /'kɒntest/ n. (competition) concours m.; (fight) combat m.

contest[2] /kən'test/ v.t. contester; (compete for or in) disputer. ~**ant** n. concurrent(e) m. (f.).

context /'kɒntekst/ n. contexte m.

continent /'kɒntɪnənt/ n. continent m. **the C~,** l'Europe (continentale) f. ~**al** /-'nentl/ a. continental; européen. ~**al quilt,** couette f.

contingen|t /kən'tɪndʒənt/ a. **be ~t upon,** dépendre de. —n. (mil.) contingent m. ~**cy** n. éventualité f. ~**cy plan,** plan d'urgence m.

continual /kən'tɪnjʊəl/ a. continuel. ~**ly** adv. continuellement.

continu|e /kən'tɪnju:/ v.t./i. continuer; (resume) reprendre. ~**ance** n. continuation f. ~**ation** /-ʊ'eɪʃn/ n. continuation f.; (after interruption) reprise f.; (new episode) suite f. ~**ed** a. continu.

continuity /kɒntɪ'nju:ətɪ/ n. continuité f.

continuous /kən'tɪnjʊəs/ a. continu. ~ **stationery,** papier continu m. ~**ly** adv. sans interruption, continûment.

contort /kən'tɔ:t/ v.t. tordre. ~ **o.s.,** se contorsionner. ~**ion** /-ʃn/ n. torsion f.; contorsion f. ~**ionist** /-ʃənɪst/ n. contorsionniste m./f.

contour /'kɒntʊə(r)/ n. contour m.

contraband /'kɒntrəbænd/ n. contrebande f.

contraception /kɒntrə'sepʃn/ n. contraception f.

contraceptive /kɒntrə'septɪv/ a. & n. contraceptif (m.).

contract[1] /'kɒntrækt/ n. contrat m.

contract[2] /kən'trækt/ v.t./i. (se) contracter. ~**ion** /-kʃn/ n. contraction f.

contractor /kən'træktə(r)/ n. entrepreneur m.

contradict /kɒntrə'dɪkt/ v.t. contredire. ~**ion** /-kʃn/ n. contradiction f. ~**ory** a. contradictoire.

contralto /kən'træltəʊ/ n. (pl. **-os**) contralto m.

contraption /kən'træpʃn/ n. (fam.) engin m., truc m.

contrary[1] /'kɒntrərɪ/ a. contraire (**to,** à). —n. contraire m. —adv. ~ **to,** contrairement à. **on the ~,** au contraire.

contrary[2] /kən'treərɪ/ a. entêté.

contrast[1] /'kɒntrɑ:st/ n. contraste m.

contrast[2] /kən'trɑ:st/ v.t./i. contraster. ~**ing** a. contrasté.

contraven|e /kɒntrə'vi:n/ v.t. enfreindre. ~**tion** /-'venʃn/ n. infraction f.

contribut|e /kən'trɪbjuːt/ v.t. donner. —v.i. **~e to,** contribuer à; (take part) participer à; (newspaper) collaborer à. **~ion** /kɒntrɪ'bjuːʃn/ n. contribution f. **~or** n. collaborateur, -trice m., f.

contrivance /kən'traɪvəns/ n. (device) appareil m., truc m.

contrive /kən'traɪv/ v.t. imaginer. **~ to do,** trouver moyen de faire. **~d** a. tortueux.

control /kən'trəʊl/ v.t. (p.t. controlled) (a firm etc.) diriger; (check) contrôler; (restrain) maîtriser. —n. contrôle m.; (mastery) maîtrise f. **~s,** commandes f. pl.; (knobs) boutons m. pl. **~ tower,** tour de contrôle f. **have under ~,** (event) avoir en main. **in ~ of,** maître de.

controversial /kɒntrə'vɜːʃl/ a. discutable, discuté.

controversy /'kɒntrəvɜːsɪ/ n. controverse f.

conurbation /kɒnɜː'beɪʃn/ n. agglomération f., conurbation f.

convalesce /kɒnvə'les/ v.i. être en convalescence. **~nce** n. convalescence f. **~nt** a. & n. convalescent(e) (m. (f.)). **~nt home,** maison de convalescence f.

convector /kən'vektə(r)/ n. radiateur à convection m.

convene /kən'viːn/ v.t. convoquer. —v.i. se réunir.

convenience /kən'viːnɪəns/ n. commodité f. **~s,** toilettes f. pl. **all modern ~s,** tout le confort moderne. **at your ~,** quand cela vous conviendra, à votre convenance. **~ foods,** plats tout préparés m. pl.

convenient /kən'viːnɪənt/ a. commode, pratique; (time) bien choisi. **be ~ for,** convenir à. **~ly** adv. (arrive) à propos. **~ly situated,** bien situé.

convent /'kɒnvənt/ n. couvent m.

convention /kən'venʃn/ n. (assembly, agreement) convention f; (custom) usage m. **~al** a. conventionnel.

converge /kən'vɜːdʒ/ v.i. converger.

conversant /kən'vɜːsnt/ a. **be ~ with,** connaître; (fact) savoir; (machinery) s'y connaître en.

conversation /kɒnvə'seɪʃn/ n. conversation f. **~al** a. (tone etc.) de la conversation; (French etc.) de tous les jours. **~alist** n. causeur, -se m., f.

converse¹ /kən'vɜːs/ v.i. s'entretenir, converser (**with,** avec).

converse² /'kɒnvɜːs/ a. & n. inverse (m.). **~ly** adv. inversement.

conver|t¹ /kən'vɜːt/ v.t. convertir; (house) aménager. —v.i. **~t into,** se transformer en. **~sion** /-ʃn/ n. conversion f. **~tible** a. convertible. —n. (car) décapotable f.

convert² /'kɒnvɜːt/ n. converti(e) m. (f.).

convex /'kɒnveks/ a. convexe.

convey /kən'veɪ/ v.t. (wishes, order) transmettre; (goods, people) transporter; (idea, feeling) communiquer. **~ance** n. transport m. **~or belt,** tapis roulant m.

convict¹ /kən'vɪkt/ v.t. déclarer coupable. **~ion** /-kʃn/ n. condamnation f; (opinion) conviction f.

convict² /'kɒnvɪkt/ n. prisonnier, ère m., f.

convinc|e /kən'vɪns/ v.t. convaincre. **~ing** a. convaincant.

convivial /kən'vɪvɪəl/ a. joyeux.

convoke /kən'vəʊk/ v.t. convoquer.

convoluted /'kɒnvəluːtɪd/ a. (argument etc.) compliqué.

convoy /'kɒnvɔɪ/ n. convoi m.

convuls|e /kən'vʌls/ v.t. convulser; (fig.) bouleverser. **be ~ed with laughter,** se tordre de rire. **~ion** /-ʃn/ n. convulsion f.

coo /kuː/ v.i. roucouler.

cook /kʊk/ v.t./i. (faire) cuire; (of person) faire la cuisine. —n. cuisinier, -ière m., f. **~ up,** (fam.) fabriquer. **~ing** n. cuisine f.; a. de cuisine.

cooker /'kʊkə(r)/ n. (stove) cuisinière f.; (apple) pomme à cuire f.

cookery /'kʊkərɪ/ n. cuisine f. **~ book,** livre de cuisine m.

cookie /'kʊkɪ/ n. (Amer.) biscuit m.

cool /kuːl/ a. (-er, -est) frais; (calm) calme; (unfriendly) froid. —n. fraîcheur f.; (calmness; sl.) sang-froid m. —v.t./i. rafraîchir. **in the ~,** au frais. **~ box,** glacière f. **~er** n. (for food) glacière f.; **~ly** adv. calmement; froidement. **~ness** n. fraîcheur f.; froideur f.

coop /kuːp/ n. poulailler m. —v.t. **~ up,** enfermer.

co-operat|e /kəʊ'ɒpəreɪt/ v.i. coopérer. **~ion** /-'reɪʃn/ n. coopération f.

co-operative /kəʊ'ɒpərətɪv/ a. coopératif. —n. coopérative f.

co-opt /kəʊ'ɒpt/ v.t. coopter.

co-ordinat|e /kəʊ'ɔːdɪneɪt/ v.t. coordonner. **~ion** /-'neɪʃn/ n. coordination f.

cop /kɒp/ v.t. (p.t. copped) (sl.) piquer. —n. (policeman; sl.) flic m. **~ out,** (sl.) se dérober. **~-out** n. (sl.) dérobade f.

cope /kəʊp/ v.i. assurer. ~ with, s'en sortir avec.

copious /'kəʊpɪəs/ a. copieux.

copper¹ /'kɒpə(r)/ n. cuivre m.; (coin) sou m. —a. de cuivre.

copper² /'kɒpə(r)/ n. (sl.) flic m.

coppice, copse /'kɒpɪs, kɒps/ ns. taillis m.

copulat|e /'kɒpjʊleɪt/ v.i. s'accoupler. ~ion /-'leɪʃn/ n. copulation f.

copy /'kɒpɪ/ n. copie f.; (of book, newspaper) exemplaire m.; (print: photo.) épreuve f. —v.t./i. copier. ~-writer n. rédacteur-concepteur m., rédactrice-conceptrice f.

copyright /'kɒpɪraɪt/ n. droit d'auteur m., copyright m.

coral /'kɒrəl/ n. corail m.

cord /kɔːd/ n. (petite) corde f.; (of curtain, pyjamas, etc.) cordon m.; (electr.) cordon électrique m.; (fabric) velours côtelé m.

cordial /'kɔːdɪəl/ a. cordial. —n. (fruit-flavoured drink) sirop m.

cordon /'kɔːdɒn/ n. cordon m. —v.t. ~ off, mettre un cordon autour de.

corduroy /'kɔːdərɔɪ/ n. velours côtelé m., velours à côtes m.

core /kɔː(r)/ n. (of apple) trognon m.; (of problem) cœur m.; (techn.) noyau m. —v.t. vider.

cork /kɔːk/ n. liège m.; (for bottle) bouchon m. —v.t. boucher.

corkscrew /'kɔːkskruː/ n. tire-bouchon m.

corn¹ /kɔːn/ n. blé m.; (maize: Amer.) maïs m.; (seed) grain m. ~-cob n. épi de maïs m.

corn² /kɔːn/ n. (hard skin) cor m.

cornea /'kɔːnɪə/ n. cornée f.

corned /kɔːnd/ a. ~ beef, corned-beef m.

corner /'kɔːnə(r)/ n. coin m.; (bend in road) virage m.; (football) corner m. —v.t. coincer, acculer; (market) accaparer. —v.i. prendre un virage. ~-stone n. pierre angulaire f.

cornet /'kɔːnɪt/ n. cornet m.

cornflakes /'kɔːnfleɪks/ n. pl. corn flakes m. pl.

cornflour /'kɔːnflaʊə(r)/ n. farine de maïs f.

cornice /'kɔːnɪs/ n. corniche f.

cornstarch /kɔːnstɑːtʃ/ n. Amer. = cornflour.

cornucopia /kɔːnjʊ'kəʊpɪə/ n. corne d'abondance f.

Corn|wall /'kɔːnwəl/ n. Cornouailles f. ~ish a. de Cornouailles.

corny /'kɔːnɪ/ a. (-ier, -iest) (trite: fam.) rebattu; (mawkish: fam.) à l'eau de rose.

corollary /kə'rɒlərɪ, Amer. 'kɒrələrɪ/ n. corollaire m.

coronary /'kɒrənərɪ/ n. infarctus m.

coronation /kɒrə'neɪʃn/ n. couronnement m.

coroner /'kɒrənə(r)/ n. coroner m.

corporal¹ /'kɔːpərəl/ n. caporal m.

corporal² /'kɔːpərəl/ a. ~ punishment, châtiment corporel m.

corporate /'kɔːpərət/ a. en commun; (body) constitué.

corporation /kɔːpə'reɪʃn/ n. (comm.) société f.; (of town) municipalité f.

corps /kɔː(r)/ n. (pl. corps /kɔːz/) corps m.

corpse /kɔːps/ n. cadavre m.

corpulent /'kɔːpjʊlənt/ a. corpulent.

corpuscle /'kɔːpʌsl/ n. globule m.

corral /kə'rɑːl/ n. (Amer.) corral m.

correct /kə'rekt/ a. (right) exact, juste, correct; (proper) correct. you are ~, vous avez raison. —v.t. corriger. ~ion /-kʃn/ n. correction f.

correlat|e /'kɒrəleɪt/ v.t./i. (faire) correspondre. ~ion /-'leɪʃn/ n. corrélation f.

correspond /kɒrɪ'spɒnd/ v.i. correspondre. ~ence n. correspondance f. ~ence course, cours par correspondance m. ~ent n. correspondant(e) m.(f.).

corridor /'kɒrɪdɔː(r)/ n. couloir m.

corroborate /kə'rɒbəreɪt/ v.t. corroborer.

corro|de /kə'rəʊd/ v.t./i. (se) corroder. ~sion n. corrosion f.

corrosive /kə'rəʊsɪv/ a. corrosif.

corrugated /'kɒrəgeɪtɪd/ a. ondulé. ~ iron, tôle ondulée f.

corrupt /kə'rʌpt/ a. corrompu. —v.t. corrompre. ~ion /-pʃn/ n. corruption f.

corset /'kɔːsɪt/ n. (boned) corset m.; (elasticated) gaine f.

Corsica /'kɔːsɪkə/ n. Corse f.

cortisone /'kɔːtɪzəʊn/ n. cortisone f.

cos /kɒs/ n. laitue romaine f.

cosh /kɒʃ/ n. matraque f. —v.t. matraquer.

cosmetic /kɒz'metɪk/ n. produit de beauté m. —a. cosmétique; (fig., pej.) superficiel.

cosmic /'kɒzmɪk/ a. cosmique.

cosmonaut /'kɒzmənɔːt/ n. cosmonaute m./f.

cosmopolitan /kɒzmə'pɒlɪt(ə)n/ a. & n. cosmopolite (m./f.).

cosmos /'kɒzmɒs/ n. cosmos m.

Cossack /'kɒsæk/ n. cosaque m.

cosset /'kɒsɪt/ v.t. (p.t. **cosseted**) dorloter.

cost /kɒst/ v.t. (p.t. **cost**) coûter; (p.t. **costed**) établir le prix de. —n. coût m. **~s**, (jurid.) dépens m. pl. **at all ~s**, à tout prix. **to one's ~**, à ses dépens. **~-effective** a. rentable. **~-effectiveness** n. rentabilité f. **~ price**, prix de revient m. **~ of living**, coût de la vie.

co-star /'kəʊstɑː(r)/ n. partenaire m./f.

costly /'kɒstlɪ/ a. (**-ier, -iest**) coûteux; (valuable) précieux.

costume /'kɒstjuːm/ n. costume m.; (for swimming) maillot m. **~ jewellery**, bijoux de fantaisie m. pl.

cosy /'kəʊzɪ/ a. (**-ier, -iest**) confortable, intime. —n. couvrethéière m. **~iness** n. confort m.

cot /kɒt/ n. lit d'enfant m.; (camp-bed: Amer.) lit de camp m.

cottage /'kɒtɪdʒ/ n. petite maison de campagne f., (thatched) chaumière f. **~ cheese**, fromage blanc (maigre) m. **~ industry**, activité artisanale f. **~ pie**, hachis Parmentier m.

cotton /'kɒtn/ n. coton m.; (for sewing) fil (à coudre) m. —v.i. **~ on**, (sl.) piger. **~ candy**, (Amer.) barbe à papa f. **~ wool**, coton hydrophile m.

couch /kaʊtʃ/ n. divan m. —v.t. (express) formuler.

couchette /kuːˈʃet/ n. couchette f.

cough /kɒf/ v.i. tousser. —n. toux f. **~ up**, (sl.) cracher, payer.

could /kʊd, unstressed kəd/ p.t. of **can²**.

couldn't /'kʊdnt/ = **could not**.

council /'kaʊnsl/ n. conseil m. **~ house**, maison construite par la municipalité f., (approx.) H.L.M. m./f.

councillor /'kaʊnsələ(r)/ n. conseiller, -ère municipal(e) m., f.

counsel /'kaʊnsl/ n. conseil m. —n. invar. (jurid.) avocat(e) m. (f.). **~lor** n. conseiller, -ère m., f.

count¹ /kaʊnt/ v.t./i. compter. —n. compte m. **~ on**, compter sur.

count² /kaʊnt/ n. (nobleman) comte m.

countdown /'kaʊntdaʊn/ n. compte à rebours m.

countenance /'kaʊntɪnəns/ n. mine f. —v.t. admettre, approuver.

counter¹ /'kaʊntə(r)/ n. comptoir m.; (in bank etc.) guichet m.; (token) jeton m.

counter² /'kaʊntə(r)/ adv. **~ to**, à l'encontre de. —a. opposé. —v.t. opposer; (blow) parer. —v.i. riposter.

counter- /'kaʊntə(r)/ pref. contre-.

counteract /kaʊntər'ækt/ v.t. neutraliser.

counter-attack /'kaʊntərətæk/ n. contre-attaque f. —v.t./i. contre-attaquer.

counterbalance /'kaʊntəbæləns/ n. contrepoids m. —v.t. contre-balancer.

counter-clockwise /kaʊntə'klɒkwaɪz/ a. & adv. (Amer.) dans le sens inverse des aiguilles d'une montre.

counterfeit /'kaʊntəfɪt/ a. & n. faux (m.). —v.t. contrefaire.

counterfoil /'kaʊntəfɔɪl/ n. souche f.

countermand /kaʊntə'mɑːnd/ v.t. annuler.

counterpart /'kaʊntəpɑːt/ n. équivalent m.; (person) homologue m./f.

counter-productive /kaʊntəprə'dʌktɪv/ a. (measure) qui produit l'effet contraire.

countersign /'kaʊntəsaɪn/ v.t. contresigner.

counter-tenor /'kaʊntətenə(r)/ n. haute-contre m.

countess /'kaʊntɪs/ n. comtesse f.

countless /'kaʊntlɪs/ a. innombrable.

countrified /'kʌntrɪfaɪd/ a. rustique.

country /'kʌntrɪ/ n. (land, region) pays m.; (homeland) patrie f.; (countryside) campagne f. **~ dance**, danse folklorique f.

countryman /'kʌntrɪmən/ n. (pl. **-men**) campagnard m.; (fellow citizen) compatriote m.

countryside /'kʌntrɪsaɪd/ n. campagne f.

county /'kaʊntɪ/ n. comté m.

coup /kuː/ n. (achievement) joli coup m.; (pol.) coup d'état m.

coupé /'kuːpeɪ/ n. (car) coupé m.

couple /'kʌpl/ n. (people, animals) couple m. —v.t./i. (s')accoupler. **a ~ (of)**, (two or three) deux ou trois.

coupon /'kuːpɒn/ n. coupon m.; (for shopping) bon or coupon de réduction m.

courage /'kʌrɪdʒ/ n. courage m. **~ous** /kə'reɪdʒəs/ a. courageux.

courgette /kʊə'ʒet/ n. courgette f.

courier /'kʊrɪə(r)/ n. messager, -ère m., f.; (for tourists) guide m.

course /kɔːs/ n. cours m.; (for training) stage m.; (series) série f.; (culin.) plat m.; (for golf) terrain m.; (at sea) itinéraire m. **change ~**, changer de cap. **~ (of action)**, façon de faire f. **during the ~ of**, pendant. **in due ~**, en temps utile. **of ~**, bien sûr.

court /kɔːt/ *n.* cour *f.*; (*tennis*) court *m.* —*v.t.* faire la cour à; (*danger*) rechercher. **~ martial,** (*pl.* **courts martial**) conseil de guerre *m.* **~-martial** *v.t.* (*p.t.* **-martialled**) faire passer en conseil de guerre. **~-house** *n.* (*Amer.*) palais de justice *m.* **~ shoe,** escarpin *m.* **go to ~,** aller devant les tribunaux.

courteous /ˈkɜːtɪəs/ *a.* courtois.

courtesy /ˈkɜːtəsɪ/ *n.* courtoisie *f.* **by ~ of,** avec la permission de.

courtier /ˈkɔːtɪə(r)/ *n.* (*old use*) courtisan *m.*

courtroom /ˈkɔːtrʊm/ *n.* salle de tribunal *f.*

courtyard /ˈkɔːtjɑːd/ *n.* cour *f.*

cousin /ˈkʌzn/ *n.* cousin(e) *m.* (*f.*). **first ~,** cousin(e) germain(e) *m.* (*f.*).

cove /kəʊv/ *n.* anse *f.*, crique *f.*

covenant /ˈkʌvənənt/ *n.* convention *f.*

Coventry /ˈkɒvntrɪ/ *n.* **send to ~,** mettre en quarantaine.

cover /ˈkʌvə(r)/ *v.t.* couvrir. —*n.* (*for bed, book, etc.*) couverture *f.*; (*lid*) couvercle *m.*; (*for furniture*) housse *f.*; (*shelter*) abri *m.* **~ charge,** couvert *m.* **~ up,** cacher; (*crime*) couvrir. **~ up for,** couvrir. **~-up** *n.* tentative pour cacher la vérité *f.* **take ~,** se mettre à l'abri. **~ing** *n.* enveloppe *f.* **~ing letter,** lettre *f.* (*jointe à un document*).

coverage /ˈkʌvərɪdʒ/ *n.* reportage *m.*

coveralls /ˈkʌvərɔːlz/ (*Amer.*) bleu de travail *m.*

covert /ˈkʌvət, Amer.* /ˈkəʊvɜːrt/ *a.* (*activity*) secret; (*threat*) voilé (*look*) dérobé.

covet /ˈkʌvɪt/ *v.t.* convoiter.

cow /kaʊ/ *n.* vache *f.*

coward /ˈkaʊəd/ *n.* lâche *m./f.* **~ly** *a.* lâche.

cowardice /ˈkaʊədɪs/ *n.* lâcheté *f.*

cowboy /ˈkaʊbɔɪ/ *n.* cow-boy *m.*

cower /ˈkaʊə(r)/ *v.i.* se recroqueviller (sous l'effet de la peur).

cowshed /ˈkaʊʃed/ *n.* étable *f.*

cox /kɒks/ *n.* barreur *m.* —*v.t.* barrer.

coxswain /ˈkɒksn/ *n.* barreur *m.*

coy /kɔɪ/ *a.* (**-er, -est**) (faussement) timide, qui fait le *or* la timide.

cozy /ˈkəʊzɪ/ *Amer.* = **cosy.**

crab /kræb/ *n.* crabe *m.* —*v.i.* (*p.t.* **crabbed**) rouspéter. **~-apple** *n.* pomme sauvage *f.*

crack /kræk/ *n.* fente *f.*; (*in glass*) fêlure *f.*; (*noise*) craquement *m.*; (*joke: sl.*) plaisanterie *f.* —*a.* (*fam.*) d'élite, —*v.t./i.* (*break partially*) (se) fêler;

(*split*) (se) fendre; (*nut*) casser; (*joke*) raconter; (*problem*) résoudre. **~ down on,** (*fam.*) sévir contre. **~ up,** (*fam.*) craquer. **get ~ing,** (*fam.*) s'y mettre.

cracked /krækt/ *a.* (*sl.*) cinglé.

cracker /ˈkrækə(r)/ *n.* pétard *m.*; (*culin.*) biscuit (salé) *m.*

crackers /ˈkrækəz/ *a.* (*sl.*) cinglé.

crackle /ˈkrækl/ *v.i.* crépiter. —*n.* crépitement *m.*

crackpot /ˈkrækpɒt/ *n.* (*sl.*) cinglé(e) *m.* (*f.*).

cradle /ˈkreɪdl/ *n.* berceau *m.* —*v.t.* bercer.

craft[1] /krɑːft/ *n.* métier artisanal *m.*; (*technique*) art *m.*; (*cunning*) ruse *f.*

craft[2] /krɑːft/ *n. invar.* (*boat*) bateau *m.*

craftsman /ˈkrɑːftsmən/ *n.* (*pl.* **-men**) artisan *m.* **~ship** *n.* art *m.*

crafty /ˈkrɑːftɪ/ *a.* (**-ier, -iest**) rusé.

crag /kræg/ *n.* rocher à pic *m.* **~gy** *a.* à pic; (*face*) rude.

cram /kræm/ *v.t./i.* (*p.t.* **crammed**). **~ (for an exam),** bachoter. **~ into,** (*pack*) (s')entasser dans. **~ with,** (*fill*) bourrer de.

cramp /kræmp/ *n.* crampe *f.*

cramped /kræmpt/ *a.* à l'étroit.

cranberry /ˈkrænbərɪ/ *n.* canneberge *f.*

crane /kreɪn/ *n.* grue *f.* —*v.t.* (*neck*) tendre.

crank[1] /kræŋk/ *n.* (*techn.*) manivelle *f.*

crank[2] /kræŋk/ *n.* excentrique *m./f.* **~y** *a.* excentrique; (*Amer.*) grincheux.

cranny /ˈkrænɪ/ *n.* fissure *f.*

craps /kræps/ *n.* **shoot ~,** (*Amer.*) jouer aux dés.

crash /kræʃ/ *n.* accident *m.*; (*noise*) fracas *m.*; (*of thunder*) coup *m.*; (*of firm*) faillite *f.* —*v.t./i.* avoir un accident (avec); (*of plane*) s'écraser; (*two vehicles*) se percuter. —*a.* (*course*) intensif. **~-helmet** *n.* casque (anti-choc) *m.* **~ into,** rentrer dans. **~ land** *v.i.* atterrir en catastrophe.

crass /kræs/ *a.* grossier.

crate /kreɪt/ *n.* cageot *m.*

crater /ˈkreɪtə(r)/ *n.* cratère *m.*

cravat /krəˈvæt/ *n.* foulard *m.*

crav|e /kreɪv/ *v.t./i.* **~e (for),** désirer ardemment. **~ing** *n.* envie irrésistible *f.*

crawl /krɔːl/ *v.i.* ramper; (*vehicle*) se traîner. —*n.* (*pace*) pas *m.*; (*swimming*) crawl *m.* **be ~ing with,** grouiller de.

crayfish /ˈkreɪfɪʃ/ *n. invar.* écrevisse *f.*

crayon /ˈkreɪən/ *n.* crayon *m.*

craze /kreɪz/ *n.* engouement *m.*

crazed /kreɪzd/ *a.* affolé.

craz|y /ˈkreɪzɪ/ *a.* (**-ier, -iest**) fou. **~y**

about, (*person*) fou de; (*thing*) fana *or* fou de. **~iness** *n.* folie *f.* **~y paving,** dallage irrégulier *m.*

creak /kriːk/ *n.* grincement *m.* —*v.i.* grincer. **~y** *a.* grinçant.

cream /kriːm/ *n.* crème *f.* —*a.* crème *invar.* —*v.t.* écrémer. **~ cheese,** fromage frais *m.* **~ off,** se servir en prenant. **~y** *a.* crémeux.

crease /kriːs/ *n.* pli *m.* —*v.t./i.* (se) froisser.

creat|e /kriː'eit/ *v.t.* créer. **~ion** /-ʃn/ *n.* création *f.* **~ive** *a.* créateur. **~or** *n.* créateur, trice *m.*, *f.*

creature /'kriːtʃə(r)/ *n.* créature *f.*

crèche /kreʃ/ *n.* garderie *f.*

credence /'kriːdns/ *n.* **give ~ to,** ajouter foi à.

credentials /krɪ'denʃlz/ *n. pl.* (*identity*) pièces d'identité *f. pl.*; (*competence*) références *f. pl.*

credib|le /'kredəbl/ *a.* (*excuse etc.*) croyable, plausible. **~ility** /-'bɪləti/ *n.* crédibilité *f.*

credit /'kredɪt/ *n.* crédit *m.*; (*honour*) honneur *m.* **in ~,** créditeur. **~s,** (*cinema*) générique *m.* —*a.* (*balance*) créditeur. —*v.t.* (*p.t.* **credited**) croire; (*comm.*) créditer. **~ card,** carte de crédit *f.* **~ note,** avoir *m* **~ s.o. with,** attribuer à qn. **~-worthy** *a.* solvable. **~or** *n.* créancier, -ière *m.*, *f.*

creditable /'kredɪtəbl/ *a.* méritoire, honorable.

credulous /'kredjʊləs/ *a.* crédule.

creed /kriːd/ *n.* credo *m.*

creek /kriːk/ *n.* crique *f.*; (*Amer.*) ruisseau *m.* **up the ~,** (*sl.*) dans le pétrin.

creep /kriːp/ *v.i* (*p.t.* **crept**) ramper; (*fig.*) se glisser. —*n.* (*person:* sl.) pauvre type *m.* **give s.o. the ~s,** faire frissonner qn. **~er** *n.* liane *f.* **~y** *a.* qui fait frissonner.

cremat|e /krɪ'meit/ *v.t.* incinérer. **~ion** /-ʃn/ *n.* incinération *f.*

crematorium /kremə'tɔːriəm/ *n.* (*pl.* **-ia**) crématorium *m.*

Creole /'kriːəʊl/ *n.* créole *m./f.*

crêpe /kreɪp/ *n.* crêpe *m.* **~ paper,** papier crépon *m.*

crept /krept/ *see* **creep.**

crescendo /krɪ'ʃendəʊ/ *n.* (*pl.* **-os**) crescendo *m.*

crescent /'kresnt/ *n.* croissant *m.*; (*fig.*) rue en demi-lune *f.*

cress /kres/ *n.* cresson *m.*

crest /krest/ *n.* crête *f.*; (*coat of arms*) armoiries *f. pl.*

Crete /kriːt/ *n.* Crète *f.*

cretin /'kretɪn, *Amer.* 'kriːtn/ *n.* crétin(e) *m.* (*f.*). **~ous** *a.* crétin.

crevasse /krɪ'væs/ *n.* crevasse *f.*

crevice /'krevɪs/ *n.* fente *f.*

crew /kruː/ *n.* équipage *m.*; (*gang*) équipe *f.* **~ cut,** coupe en brosse *f.* **~ neck,** (col) ras du cou *m.*

crib¹ /krɪb/ *n.* lit d'enfant *m.*

crib² /krɪb/ *v.t./i.* (*p.t.* **cribbed**) copier. —*n.* (*schol.*, *fam.*) traduction *f.*, aide-mémoire *m. invar.*

crick /krɪk/ *n.* (*in neck*) torticolis *m.*

cricket¹ /'krɪkɪt/ *n.* (*sport*) cricket *m* **~er** *n.* joueur de cricket *m.*

cricket² /'krɪkɪt/ *n.* (*insect*) grillon *m.*

crime /kraɪm/ *n.* crime *m.*; (*minor*) délit *m.*; (*acts*) criminalité *f.*

criminal /'krɪmɪnl/ *a.* & *n.* criminel(le) (*m.* (*f.*)).

crimp /krɪmp/ *v.t.* (*hair*) friser.

crimson /'krɪmzn/ *a.* & *n.* cramoisi (*m.*).

cring|e /krɪndʒ/ *v.i.* reculer; (*fig.*) s'humilier. **~ing** *a.* servile.

crinkle /'krɪŋkl/ *v.t./i.* (se) froisser. —*n.* pli *m.*

cripple /'krɪpl/ *n.* infirme *m./f.* —*v.t.* estropier; (*fig.*) paralyser.

crisis /'kraɪsɪs/ *n.* (*pl.* **crises** /-siːz/) crise *f*

crisp /krɪsp/ *a.* (**-er, -est**) (*culin.*) croquant; (*air*, *reply*) vif. **~s** *n. pl.* chips *m. pl.*

criss-cross /'krɪskrɒs/ *a.* entrecroisé. —*v.t./i.* (s')entrecroiser.

criterion /kraɪ'tɪəriən/ *n.* (*pl.* **-ia**) critère *m.*

critic /'krɪtɪk/ *n.* critique *m.* **~al** *a.* critique. **~ally** *adv.* d'une manière critique; (*ill*) gravement.

criticism /'krɪtɪsɪzəm/ *n.* critique *f.*

criticize /'krɪtɪsaɪz/ *v.t./i.* critiquer.

croak /krəʊk/ *n.* (*bird*) croassement; (*frog*) coassement *m.* —*v.i.* croasser; coasser.

crochet /'krəʊʃeɪ/ *n.* crochet *m.* —*v.t.* faire au crochet.

crockery /'krɒkərɪ/ *n.* vaisselle *f.*

crocodile /'krɒkədaɪl/ *n.* crocodile *m.*

crocus /'krəʊkəs/ *n.* (*pl.* **-uses**) crocus *m.*

crony /'krəʊnɪ/ *n.* copain, -ine *m.*, *f.*

crook /krʊk/ *n.* (*criminal:* fam.) escroc *m.*; (*stick*) houlette *f.*

crooked /'krʊkɪd/ *a.* tordu; (*winding*) tortueux; (*askew*) de travers; (*dishonest:* fig.) malhonnête. **~ly** *adv.* de travers.

croon /kruːn/ *v.t./i.* chantonner.

crop /krɒp/ n. récolte f.; (fig.) quantité f. —v.t. (p.t. **cropped**) couper. —v.i. ~ **up**, se présenter.

croquet /'krəʊkeɪ/ n. croquet m.

croquette /krəʊ'ket/ n. croquette f.

cross /krɒs/ n. croix f.; (hybrid) hybride m. —v.t./i. traverser; (legs, animals) croiser; (cheque) barrer; (paths) se croiser. —a. en colère, fâché (**with**, contre). ~-**check** v.t. vérifier (pour confirmer). ~-**country** (**running**), cross m. ~ **off** or **out**, rayer. ~ **s.o.'s mind**, venir à l'esprit de qn. **talk at** ~ **purposes**, parler sans se comprendre. ~**ly** adv. avec colère.

crossbar /'krɒsbɑː(r)/ n. barre transversale f.

cross-examine /krɒsɪg'zæmɪn/ v.t. faire subir un examen contradictoire à.

cross-eyed /'krɒsaɪd/ a. **be** ~, loucher.

crossfire /'krɒsfaɪə(r)/ n. feux croisés m. pl.

crossing /'krɒsɪŋ/ n. (by boat) traversée f.; (on road) passage clouté m.

cross-reference /krɒs'refrəns/ n. renvoi m.

crossroads /'krɒsrəʊdz/ n. carrefour m.

cross-section /krɒs'sekʃn/ n. coupe transversale f.; (sample: fig.) échantillon m.

cross-wind /'krɒswɪnd/ n. vent de travers m.

crosswise /'krɒswaɪz/ adv. en travers.

crossword /'krɒswɜːd/ n. mots croisés m. pl.

crotch /krɒtʃ/ n. (of garment) entre-jambes m. invar.

crotchet /'krɒtʃɪt/ n. (mus.) noire f.

crotchety /'krɒtʃɪtɪ/ a. grincheux.

crouch /kraʊtʃ/ v.i. s'accroupir.

crow /krəʊ/ n. corbeau m. —v.i. (of cock) (p.t. **crew**) chanter; (fig.) jubiler. **as the** ~ **flies**, à vol d'oiseau. ~'**s feet**, pattes d'oie f. pl.

crowbar /'krəʊbɑː(r)/ n. pied-de-biche m.

crowd /kraʊd/ n. foule f. —v.i. affluer. —v.t. remplir. ~ **into**, (s')entasser dans. ~**ed** a. plein.

crown /kraʊn/ n. couronne f.; (top part) sommet m. —v.t. couronner. **C**~ **Court**, Cour d'assises f. **C**~ **prince**, prince héritier m.

crucial /'kruːʃl/ a. crucial.

crucifix /'kruːsɪfɪks/ n. crucifix m.

crucif|y /'kruːsɪfaɪ/ v.t. crucifier. ~**ixion** /-'fɪkʃn/ n. crucifixion f.

crude /kruːd/ a. (-**er**, -**est**) (raw) brut; (rough, vulgar) grossier.

cruel /krʊəl/ a. (**crueller**, **cruellest**) cruel. ~**ty** n. cruauté f.

cruet /'kruːɪt/ n. huilier m.

cruis|e /kɪuːz/ n. croisière f. —v.i. (ship) croiser; (tourists) faire une croisière; (vehicle) rouler. ~**er** n. croiseur m. ~**ing speed**, vitesse de croisière f.

crumb /krʌm/ n. miette f.

crumble /'krʌmbl/ v.t./i. (s')effriter; (bread) (s')émietter; (collapse) s'écrouler.

crummy /'krʌmɪ/ a. (-**ier**, -**iest**) (sl.) moche, minable.

crumpet /'krʌmpɪt/ n. (culin.) petite crêpe (grillée) f.

crumple /'krʌmpl/ v.t./i. (se) froisser.

crunch /krʌntʃ/ v.t. croquer. —n. (event) moment critique m. **when it comes to the** ~, quand ça devient sérieux.

crusade /kruː'seɪd/ n. croisade f. ~**r** /-ə(r)/ n. (knight) croisé m.; (fig.) militant(e) m. (f.).

crush /krʌʃ/ v.t. écraser; (clothes) froisser. —n. (crowd) presse f. **a** ~ **on**, (sl.) le béguin pour.

crust /krʌst/ n. croûte f. ~**y** a. croustillant.

crutch /krʌtʃ/ n. béquille f.; (crotch) entre-jambes m. invar.

crux /krʌks/ n. **the** ~ **of**, (problem etc.) le nœud de.

cry /kraɪ/ n. cri m. —v.i. (weep) pleurer; (call out) crier. ~-**baby** n. pleurnicheur, -se m., f. ~ **off**, abandonner.

crying /'kraɪɪŋ/ a. (evil etc.) flagrant. **a** ~ **shame**, une vraie honte.

crypt /krɪpt/ n. crypte f.

cryptic /'krɪptɪk/ a. énigmatique.

crystal /'krɪstl/ n. cristal m. ~-**clear** a. parfaitement clair. ~**lize** v.t./i. (se) cristalliser.

cub /kʌb/ n. petit m. **Cub** (**Scout**), louveteau m.

Cuba /'kjuːbə/ n. Cuba m. ~**n** a. & n. cubain(e) (m. (f.)).

cubby-hole /'kʌbɪhəʊl/ n. cagibi m.

cub|e /kjuːb/ n. cube m. ~**ic** a. cubique; (metre etc.) cube.

cubicle /'kjuːbɪkl/ n. (in room, hospital, etc.) box m.; (at swimming-pool) cabine f.

cuckoo /'kʊkuː/ n. coucou m.

cucumber /'kjuːkʌmbə(r)/ n. concombre m.

cuddl|e /'kʌdl/ v.t. câliner. —v.i. (**kiss and**) ~**e**, s'embrasser. —n. caresse f. ~**y** a. câlin, caressant.

cudgel /'kʌdʒl/ n. gourdin m.

cue¹ /kjuː/ n. signal m.; (theatre) réplique f.

cue² /kjuː/ n. (billiards) queue f.

cuff /kʌf/ n. manchette f.; (Amer.) revers m. —v.t. gifler. **∼-link** n. bouton de manchette m. **off the ∼**, impromptu.

cul-de-sac /'kʌldəsæk/ n. (pl. **culs-de-sac**) impasse f.

culinary /'kʌlɪnərɪ/ a. culinaire.

cull /kʌl/ v.t. (select) choisir; (kill) abattre sélectivement.

culminat|e /'kʌlmɪneɪt/ v.i. **∼e in**, se terminer par. **∼ion** /-'neɪʃn/ n. point culminant m.

culprit /'kʌlprɪt/ n. coupable m./f.

cult /kʌlt/ n. culte m. **∼ movie**, film culte.

cultivat|e /'kʌltɪveɪt/ v.t. cultiver. **∼ion** /-'veɪʃn/ n. culture f.

cultural /'kʌltʃərəl/ a. culturel.

culture /'kʌltʃə(r)/ n. culture f. **∼d** a. cultivé.

cumbersome /'kʌmbəsəm/ a. encombrant.

cumulative /'kjuːmjʊlətɪv/ a. cumulatif.

cunning /'kʌnɪŋ/ a. rusé. —n. astuce f., ruse f.

cup /kʌp/ n. tasse f.; (prize) coupe f. **Cup final**, finale de la coupe f. **∼ size**, profondeur de bonnet f. **∼-tie** n. match de coupe m.

cupboard /'kʌbəd/ n. placard m., armoire f.

cupful /'kʌpfʊl/ n. tasse f.

Cupid /'kjuːpɪd/ n. Cupidon m.

curable /'kjʊərəbl/ a. guérissable.

curate /'kjʊərət/ n. vicaire m.

curator /kjʊə'reɪtə(r)/ n. (of museum) conservateur m.

curb¹ /kɜːb/ n. (restraint) frein m. —v.t. (desires etc.) refréner; (price increase etc.) freiner.

curb², (Amer.) **kerb**:/kɜːb/ n. bord du trottoir m.

curdle /'kɜːdl/ v.t./i. (se) cailler.

curds /kɜːdz/ n. pl. lait caillé m.

cure¹ /kjʊə(r)/ v.t. guérir; (fig.) éliminer —n. (recovery) guérison f.; (remedy) remède m.

cure² /kjʊə(r)/ v.t. (culin.) fumer; (in brine) saler.

curfew /'kɜːfjuː/ n. couvre-feu m.

curio /'kjʊərɪəʊ/ n. (pl. **-os**) curiosité f., bibelot m.

curi|ous /'kjʊərɪəs/ a. curieux. **∼osity** /-'ɒsɪtɪ/ n. curiosité f.

curl /kɜːl/ v.t./i. (hair) boucler. —n. boucle f. **∼ up**, se pelotonner; (shrivel) se racornir.

curler /'kɜːlə(r)/ n. bigoudi m.

curly /'kɜːlɪ/ a. (-ier, -iest) bouclé.

currant /'kʌrənt/ n. raisin de Corinthe m.; (berry) groseille f.

currency /'kʌrənsɪ/ n. (money) monnaie f.; (acceptance) cours m. **foreign ∼**, devises étrangères f. pl.

current /'kʌrənt/ a. (common) courant; (topical) actuel; (year etc.) en cours. —n. courant m. **∼ account**, compte courant m. **∼ events**, l'actualité f. **∼ly** adv. actuellement.

curriculum /kə'rɪkjʊləm/ n. (pl. **-la**) programme scolaire m. **∼ vitae**, curriculum vitae m.

curry¹ /'kʌrɪ/ n. curry m., cari m.

curry² /'kʌrɪ/ v.t. **∼ favour with**, chercher les bonnes grâces de.

curse /kɜːs/ n. malédiction f.; (oath) juron m. —v.t. maudire. —v.i. (swear) jurer.

cursor /'kɜːsə(r)/ n. curseur m.

cursory /'kɜːsərɪ/ a. (trop) rapide.

curt /kɜːt/ a. brusque.

curtail /kɜː'teɪl/ v.t. écourter, raccourcir; (expenses etc.) réduire.

curtain /'kɜːtn/ n. rideau m.

curtsy /'kɜːtsɪ/ n. révérence f. —v.i. faire une révérence.

curve /kɜːv/ n. courbe f. —v.t./i. (se) courber; (of road) tourner.

cushion /'kʊʃn/ n. coussin m. —v.t. (a blow) amortir; (fig.) protéger.

cushy /'kʊʃɪ/ a. (-ier, -iest) (job etc.: fam.) pépère.

custard /'kʌstəd/ n. crème anglaise f.; (set) crème renversée f.

custodian /kʌ'stəʊdɪən/ n. gardien(ne) m. (f.).

custody /'kʌstədɪ/ n. garde f.; (jurid.) détention préventive f.

custom /'kʌstəm/ n. coutume f.; (patronage: comm.) clientèle f. **∼-built**, **∼-made** adjs. fait etc. sur commande. **∼ary** a. d'usage.

customer /'kʌstəmə(r)/ n. client(e) m. (f.); (fam.) **an odd/a difficult ∼**, un individu curieux/difficile.

customize /'kʌstəmaɪz/ v.t. personnaliser.

customs /'kʌstəmz/ n. pl. douane f. —a. douanier. **∼ officer**, douanier m.

cut /kʌt/ v.t./i. (p.t. **cut**, pres. p. **cutting**) couper; (hedge, jewel) tailler; (prices etc.) réduire. —n. coupure f.; (of clothes) coupe f.; (piece) morceau m.; réduction f. **∼ back or down (on)**, réduire. **∼-back** n. réduction f. **∼ in**, (auto.) se rabattre. **∼ off**, couper; (fig.)

isoler. **~ out,** découper; (*leave out*)
supprimer. **~-price** *a.* à prix réduit. **~
short,** (*visit*) écourter. **~ up,** couper;
(*carve*) découper. **~ up about,**
démoralisé par.

cute /kju:t/ *a.* (**-er, -est**) (*fam.*)
astucieux; (*Amer.*) mignon.

cuticle /'kju:tıkl/ *n.* petites peaux *f. pl.*
(*de l'ongle*).

cutlery /'kʌtlərı/ *n.* couverts *m. pl.*

cutlet /'kʌtlıt/ *n.* côtelette *f.*

cutting /'kʌtıŋ/ *a.* cinglant. —*n.* (*from
newspaper*) coupure *f.*; (*plant*) bouture
f. **~ edge,** tranchant *m.*

CV *abbr. see* **curriculum vitae.**

cyanide /'saıənaıd/ *n.* cyanure *m.*

cybernetics /saıbə'netıks/ *n.* cybernétique *f.*

cycl|e /'saıkl/ *n.* cycle *m.*; (*bicycle*) vélo
m. —*v.i.* aller à vélo. **~ing** *n.* cyclisme
m. **~ist** *n.* cycliste *m./f.*

cyclic(al) /'saıklık(l)/ *a.* cyclique.

cyclone /'saıkləʊn/ *n.* cyclone *m.*

cylind|er /'sılındə(r)/ *n.* cylindre *m.*
~rical /-'lındrıkl/ *a.* cylindrique.

cymbal /'sımbl/ *n.* cymbale *f.*

cynic /'sınık/ *n.* cynique *m./f.* **~al** *a.*
cynique. **~ism** /-sızəm/ *n.* cynisme
m.

cypress /'saıprəs/ *n.* cyprès *m.*

Cypr|us /'saıprəs/ *n.* Chypre *f.* **~iot**
/'sıprıət/ *a.* & *n.* cypriote (*m./f.*).

cyst /sıst/ *n.* kyste *m.* **~ic fibrosis,**
mucoviscidose *f.*

cystitis /sıst'aıtıs/ *n.* cystite *f.*

czar /zɑ:(r)/ *n.* tsar *m.*

Czech /tʃek/ *a.* & *n.* tchèque (*m./f.*).

Czechoslovak /tʃekə'sləʊvæk/ *a.* & *n.*
tchécoslovaque (*m./f.*). **~ia** /-slə
'vækıə/ *n.* Tchécoslovaquie *f.*

D

dab /dæb/ *v.t.* (*p.t.* **dabbed**) tamponner.
—*n.* **a ~ of,** un petit coup de; (*fam.*) **be
a ~ hand at,** avoir le coup de main
pour. **~ sth. on,** appliquer qch. à petits
coups sur.

dabble /'dæbl/ *v.i.* **~ in,** se mêler un peu
de. **~r** /-ə(r)/ *n.* amateur *m.*

dad /dæd/ *n.* (*fam.*) papa *m.* **~dy** *n.*
(*children's use*) papa *m.*

daffodil /'dæfədıl/ *n.* jonquille *f.*

daft /dɑ:ft/ *a.* (**-er, -est**) idiot.

dagger /'dægə(r)/ *n.* poignard *m.*

dahlia /'deılıə/ *n.* dahlia *m.*

daily /'deılı/ *a.* quotidien. —*adv.* tous les
jours. —*n.* (*newspaper*) quotidien *m.*;
(*charwoman*: *fam.*) femme de ménage
f.

dainty /'deıntı/ *a.* (**-ier, -iest**) délicat.

dairy /'deərı/ *n.* (*on farm*) laiterie *f.*;
(*shop*) crémerie *f.* **—a.** laitier.

daisy /'deızı/ *n.* pâquerette *f.* **~ wheel,**
marguerite *f.*

dale /deıl/ *n.* vallée *f.*

dam /dæm/ *n.* barrage *m.* —*v.t.* (*p.t.*
dammed) endiguer.

damag|e /'dæmıdʒ/ *n.* dégâts *m. pl.*,
dommages *m. pl.*; (*harm*: *fig.*) préjudice
m. **~es,** (*jurid.*) dommages et intérêts
m. pl. —*v.t.* abîmer; (*fig.*) nuire à. **~ing**
a. nuisible.

dame /deım/ *n.* (*old use*) dame *f.*;
(*Amer., sl.*) fille *f.*

damn /dæm/ *v.t.* (*relig.*) damner; (*swear
at*) maudire; (*condemn*: *fig.*) condamner. —*int.* zut, merde. —*n.* **not care a
~,** s'en foutre. —*a.* sacré. —*adv.* rudement. **~ation** /-'neıʃn/ *n.* damnation *f.*

damp /dæmp/ *n.* humidité *f.* —*a.* (**-er,
-est**) humide. —*v.t.* humecter; (*fig.*)
refroidir. **~en** *v.t.* = **damp. ~ness** *n.*
humidité *f.*

dance /dɑ:ns/ *v.t./i.* danser. —*n.* danse
f.; (*gathering*) bal *m.* **~ hall,** dancing
m., salle de danse *f.* **~r** /-ə(r)/ *n.*
danseur, -se *m.*, *f.*

dandelion /'dændılaıən/ *n.* pissenlit *m.*

dandruff /'dændrʌf/ *n.* pellicules *f. pl.*

dandy /'dændı/ *n.* dandy *m.*

Dane /deın/ *n.* Danois(e) *m.* (*f.*).

danger /'deındʒə(r)/ *n.* danger *m.*; (*risk*)
risque *m.* **be in ~ of,** risquer de. **~ous**
a. dangereux.

dangle /'dæŋgl/ *v.t./i.* (se) balancer,
(laisser) pendre. **~ sth. in front of s.o.,**
(*fig.*) faire miroiter qch. à qn.

Danish /'deınıʃ/ *a.* danois. —*n.* (*lang.*)
danois *m.*

dank /dæŋk/ *a.* (**-er, -est**) humide et
froid.

dapper /'dæpə(r)/ *a.* élégant.

dare /deə(r)/ *v.t.* **~ (to) do,** oser faire. **~
s.o. to do,** défier qn. de faire. —*n.* défi
m. **I ~ say,** je suppose (**that,** que).

daredevil /'deədevl/ *n.* casse-cou *m.
invar.*

daring /'deərıŋ/ *a.* audacieux.

dark /dɑ:k/ *a.* (**-er, -est**) obscur, sombre,
noir; (*colour*) foncé, sombre; (*skin*)
brun, foncé; (*gloomy*) sombre. —*n.*
noir *m.*; (*nightfall*) tombée de la nuit *f.*
~ horse, individu aux talents inconnus
m. **~-room** *n.* chambre noire *f.* **in the**

~, (*fig.*) dans l'ignorance (**about**, de).
~**ness** *n.* obscurité *f.*

darken /'dɑːkən/ *v.t./i.* (s')assombrir.

darling /'dɑːlɪŋ/ *a.* & *n.* chéri(e) (*m.* (*f.*)).

darn /dɑːn/ *v.t.* repriser.

dart /dɑːt/ *n.* fléchette *f.* ~**s**, (*game*) fléchettes *f. pl.* —*v.i.* s'élancer.

dartboard /'dɑːtbɔːd/ *n.* cible *f.*

dash /dæʃ/ *v.i.* (*hurry*) se dépêcher, (*forward etc.*) se précipiter. —*v.t.* jeter (avec violence); (*hopes*) briser. —*n.* ruée *f.*; (*stroke*) tiret *m.* **a** ~ **of**, un peu de. ~ **off**, (*leave*) partir en vitesse.

dashboard /'dæʃbɔːd/ *n.* tableau de bord *m.*

dashing /'dæʃɪŋ/ *a.* fringant.

data /'deɪtə/ *n. pl.* données *f. pl.* ~ **processing**, traitement des données *m.*

database /'deɪtəbeɪs/ *n.* base de données *f.*

date[1] /deɪt/ *n.* date *f.*; (*meeting: fam.*) rendez-vous *m.* —*v.t./i.* dater; (*go out with: fam.*) sortir avec. ~ **from**, dater de. **out of** ~, (*old-fashioned*) démodé, (*passport*) périmé. **to** ~, à ce jour. **up to** ~, (*modern*) moderne; (*list*) à jour. ~**d** /-ɪd/ *a.* démodé.

date[2] /deɪt/ *n.* (*fruit*) datte *f.*

daub /dɔːb/ *v.t.* barbouiller.

daughter /'dɔːtə(r)/ *n.* fille *f.* ~**-in-law** *n.* (*pl.* ~**s-in-law**) belle-fille *f.*

daunt /dɔːnt/ *v.t.* décourager.

dauntless /'dɔːntlɪs/ *a.* intrépide.

dawdle /'dɔːdl/ *v.i.* lambiner. ~**r** /-ə(r)/ *n.* lambin(e) *m.* (*f.*).

dawn /dɔːn/ *n.* aube *f.* —*v.i.* poindre; (*fig.*) naître. **it** ~**ed on me**, je m'en suis rendu compte.

day /deɪ/ *n.* jour *m.*; (*whole day*) journée *f.*; (*period*) époque *f.* ~**-break** *n.* point du jour *m.* ~**-dream** *n.* rêverie *f.*; *v.i.* rêvasser. **the** ~ **before**, la veille. **the following** *or* **next** ~, le lendemain.

daylight /'deɪlaɪt/ *n.* jour *m.*

daytime /'deɪtaɪm/ *n.* jour *m.*, journée *f.*

daze /deɪz/ *v.t.* étourdir; (*with drugs*) hébéter. —*n.* **in a** ~, étourdi; hébété.

dazzle /'dæzl/ *v.t.* éblouir.

deacon /'diːkən/ *n.* diacre *m.*

dead /ded/ *a.* mort; (*numb*) engourdi. —*adv.* complètement. —*n.* **in the** ~ **of**, au cœur de. **the** ~, les morts. ~ **beat**, éreinté. ~ **end**, impasse *f.* ~**-end job**, travail sans avenir *m.* **a** ~ **loss**, (*thing*) une perte de temps; (*person*) une catastrophe. ~**-pan** *a.* impassible. **in** ~ **centre**, au beau milieu. **stop** ~, s'arrêter net. **the race was a** ~ **heat**, ils ont été classés ex aequo.

deaden /'dedn/ *v.t.* (*sound, blow*) amortir; (*pain*) calmer.

deadline /'dedlaɪn/ *n.* date limite *f.*

deadlock /'dedlɒk/ *n.* impasse *f.*

deadly /'dedlɪ/ *a.* (**-ier, -iest**) mortel; (*weapon*) meurtrier.

deaf /def/ *a.* (**-er, -est**) sourd. **the** ~ **and dumb**, les sourds-muets. ~**-aid** *n.* appareil acoustique *m.* ~**ness** *n.* surdité *f.*

deafen /'defn/ *v.t.* assourdir.

deal /diːl/ *v.t.* (*p.t.* **dealt**) donner; (*a blow*) porter. —*v.i.* (*trade*) commercer. —*n.* affaire *f.*; (*cards*) donne *f.* **a great** *or* **good** ~, beaucoup (**of**, de). ~ **in**, faire le commerce de. ~ **with**, (*handle, manage*) s'occuper de; (*be about*) traiter de. ~**er** *n.* marchand(e) *m.* (*f.*); (*agent*) concessionnaire *m./f.*

dealings /'diːlɪŋz/ *n. pl.* relations *f. pl.*

dean /diːn/ *n.* doyen *m.*

dear /dɪə(r)/ *a.* (**-er, -est**) cher. —*n.* (*my*) ~, mon cher, ma chère; (*darling*) (mon) chéri, (ma) chérie. *adv.* cher. —*int.* **oh** ~!, oh mon Dieu! ~**ly** *adv.* tendrement; (*pay*) cher.

dearth /dɜːθ/ *n.* pénurie *f.*

death /deθ/ *n.* mort *f.* ~ **certificate**, acte de décès *m.* ~ **duty**, droits de succession *m. pl.* ~ **penalty**, peine de mort *f.* **it is a** ~**-trap**, (*place, vehicle*) il y a danger de mort. ~**ly** *a.* de mort, mortel.

debar /dɪ'bɑː(r)/ *v.t.* (*p.t.* **debarred**) exclure.

debase /dɪ'beɪs/ *v.t.* avilir.

debat|e /dɪ'beɪt/ *n.* discussion *f.*, débat *m.* —*v.t.* discuter. ~**e whether**, se demander si. ~**able** *a.* discutable.

debauch /dɪ'bɔːtʃ/ *v.t.* débaucher. ~**ery** *n.* débauche *f.*

debilitate /dɪ'bɪlɪteɪt/ *v.t.* débiliter.

debility /dɪ'bɪlətɪ/ *n.* débilité *f.*

debit /'debɪt/ *n.* débit *m.* **in** ~, débiteur. —*a.* (*balance*) débiteur. —*v.t.* (*p.t.* **debited**) débiter.

debris /'deɪbriː/ *n.* débris *m. pl.*

debt /det/ *n.* dette *f.* **in** ~, endetté. ~**or** *n.* débiteur, -trice *m., f.*

debunk /diː'bʌŋk/ *v.t.* (*fam.*) démythifier.

decade /'dekeɪd/ *n.* décennie *f.*

decaden|t /'dekədənt/ *a.* décadent. ~**ce** *n.* décadence *f.*

decaffeinated /diː'kæfɪneɪtɪd/ *a.* décaféiné.

decanter /dɪ'kæntə(r)/ *n.* carafe *f.*

decathlon /dɪ'kæθlən/ *n.* décathlon *m.*

decay /dɪ'keɪ/ *v.i.* se gâter, pourrir; (*fig.*)

décliner. —*n.* pourriture *f.*; (*of tooth*) carie *f.*; (*fig.*) déclin *m.*

deceased /dɪ'siːst/ *a.* décédé. —*n.* défunt(e) *m.* (*f.*).

deceit /dɪ'siːt/ *n.* tromperie *f.* **~ful** *a.* trompeur. **~fully** *adv.* d'une manière trompeuse.

deceive /dɪ'siːv/ *v.t.* tromper.

December /dɪ'sembə(r)/ *n.* décembre *m.*

decen|t /'diːsnt/ *a.* décent, convenable; (*good*: *fam.*) (assez) bon; (*kind*: *fam.*) gentil. **~cy** *n.* décence *f.* **~tly** *adv.* décemment.

decentralize /diː'sentrəlaɪz/ *v.t.* décentraliser.

decept|ive /dɪ'septɪv/ *a.* trompeur. **~ion** /-pʃn/ *n.* tromperie *f.*

decibel /'desɪbel/ *n.* décibel *m.*

decide /dɪ'saɪd/ *v.t./i.* décider; (*question*) régler. **~ on**, se décider pour. **~ to do**, décider de faire. **~d** /-ɪd/ *a.* (*firm*) résolu; (*clear*) net. **~dly** /-ɪdlɪ/ *adv.* résolument; nettement.

deciduous /dɪ'sɪdjʊəs/ *a.* à feuillage caduc.

decimal /'desɪml/ *a.* décimal. —*n.* décimale *f.* **~ point**, virgule *f.*

decimate /'desɪmeɪt/ *v.t.* décimer.

decipher /dɪ'saɪfə(r)/ *v.t.* déchiffrer.

decision /dɪ'sɪʒn/ *n.* décision *f.*

decisive /dɪ'saɪsɪv/ *a.* (*conclusive*) décisif; (*firm*) décidé. **~ly** *adv.* d'une façon décidée.

deck /dek/ *n.* pont *m.*; (*of cards*: *Amer.*) jeu *m.* **~-chair** *n.* chaise longue *f.* **top ~**, (*of bus*) impériale *f.*

declar|e /dɪ'kleə(r)/ *v.t.* déclarer. **~ation** /deklə'reɪʃn/ *n.* déclaration *f.*

decline /dɪ'klaɪn/ *v.t./i.* refuser (poliment); (*deteriorate*) décliner; (*fall*) baisser. —*n.* déclin *m.*; baisse *f.*

decode /diː'kəʊd/ *v.t.* décoder.

decompos|e /diːkəm'pəʊz/ *v.t./i.* (se) décomposer. **~ition** /-ɒmpə'zɪʃn/ *n.* décomposition *f.*

décor /'deɪkɔː/ *n.* décor *m.*

decorat|e /'dekəreɪt/ *v.t.* décorer; (*room*) peindre *or* tapisser. **~ion** /-'reɪʃn/ *n.* décoration *f.* **~ive** /-ətɪv/ *a.* décoratif.

decorator /'dekəreɪtə(r)/ *n.* peintre en bâtiment *m.* (**interior**) **~**, décoralteur, -trice d'appartements *m.*, *f.*

decorum /dɪ'kɔːrəm/ *n.* décorum *m.*

decoy[1] /'diːkɔɪ/ *n.* (*bird*) appeau *m.*; (*trap*) piège *m.*, leurre *m.*

decoy[2] /dɪ'kɔɪ/ *v.t.* attirer, appâter.

decrease /dɪ'kriːs/ *v.t./i.* diminuer. —*n.* /'diːkriːs/ diminution *f.*

decree /dɪ'kriː/ *n.* (*pol.*, *relig.*) décret *m.*;

(*jurid.*) jugement *m.* —*v.t.* (*p.t.* **decreed**) décréter.

decrepit /dɪ'krepɪt/ *a.* (*building*) délabré; (*person*) décrépit.

decry /dɪ'kraɪ/ *v.t.* dénigrer.

dedicat|e /'dedɪkeɪt/ *v.t.* dédier. **~e o.s. to**, se consacrer à. **~ed** *a.* dévoué. **~ion** /-'keɪʃn/ *n.* dévouement *m.*; (*in book*) dédicace *f.*

deduce /dɪ'djuːs/ *v.t.* déduire.

deduct /dɪ'dʌkt/ *v.t.* déduire; (*from wages*) retenir. **~ion** /-kʃn/ *n.* déduction *f.*; retenue *f.*

deed /diːd/ *n.* acte *m.*

deem /diːm/ *v.t.* juger.

deep /diːp/ *a.* (**-er**, **-est**) profond. —*adv.* profondément. **~ in thought**, absorbé dans ses pensées. **~ into the night**, tard dans la nuit. **~-freeze** *n.* congélateur *m.*; *v.t.* congeler. **~-fry**, frire. **~ly** *adv.* profondément.

deepen /'diːpən/ *v.t.* approfondir. —*v.i.* devenir plus profond; (*mystery*, *night*) s'épaissir.

deer /dɪə(r)/ *n. invar.* cerf *m.*; (*doe*) biche *f.*

deface /dɪ'feɪs/ *v.t.* dégrader.

defamation /defə'meɪʃn/ *n.* diffamation *f.*

default /dɪ'fɔːlt/ *v.i.* (*jurid.*) faire défaut. —*n.* **by ~**, (*jurid.*) par défaut. **win by ~**, gagner par forfait. —*a.* (*comput.*) par défaut.

defeat /dɪ'fiːt/ *v.t.* vaincre; (*thwart*) faire échouer. —*n.* défaite *f.*; (*of plan etc.*) échec *m.*

defect[1] /'diːfekt/ *n.* défaut *m.* **~ive** /dɪ'fektɪv/ *a.* défectueux.

defect[2] /dɪ'fekt/ *v.i.* faire défection. **~ to**, passer à. **~or** *n.* transfuge *m./f.*

defence /dɪ'fens/ *n.* défense *f.* **~less** *a.* sans défense.

defend /dɪ'fend/ *v.t.* défendre. **~ant** *n.* (*jurid.*) accusé(e) *m.* (*f.*). **~er**, défenseur *m.*

defense /dɪ'fens/ *n. Amer.* = **defence**.

defensive /dɪ'fensɪv/ *a.* défensif. —*n.* défensive *f.*

defer /dɪ'fɜː(r)/ *v.t.* (*p.t.* **deferred**) (*postpone*) différer, remettre.

deferen|ce /'defərəns/ *n.* déférence *f.* **~tial** /-'renʃl/ *a.* déférent.

defian|ce /dɪ'faɪəns/ *n.* défi *m.* **in ~ce of**, au mépris de. **~t** *a.* de défi. **~tly** *adv.* d'un air de défi.

deficien|t /dɪ'fɪʃnt/ *a.* insuffisant. **be ~t in**, manquer de. **~cy** *n.* insuffisance *f.*; (*fault*) défaut *m.*

deficit /'defɪsɪt/ *n.* déficit *m.*

defile /dɪ'faɪl/ v.t. souiller.
define /dɪ'faɪn/ v.t. définir.
definite /'defɪnɪt/ a. précis; (obvious) net; (firm) catégorique; (certain) certain. **~ly** adv. certainement; (clearly) nettement.
definition /defɪ'nɪʃn/ n. définition f.
definitive /dɪ'fɪnɪtɪv/ a. définitif.
deflat|e /dɪ'fleɪt/ v.t. dégonfler. **~ion** /-ʃn/ n. dégonflement m.; (comm.) déflation f.
deflect /dɪ'flekt/ v.t./i. (faire) dévier.
deforestation /di:fɒrɪ'steɪʃn/ n. déforestation.
deform /dɪ'fɔ:m/ v.t. déformer. **~ed** a. difforme. **~ity** n. difformité f.
defraud /dɪ'frɔ:d/ v.t. (state, customs) frauder. **~ s.o. of sth.,** escroquer qch. à qn.
defray /dɪ'freɪ/ v.t. payer.
defrost /di:'frɒst/ v.t. dégivrer.
deft /deft/ a. (-er, -est) adroit. **~ness** n. adresse f.
defunct /dɪ'fʌŋkt/ a. défunt.
defuse /di:'fju:z/ v.t. désamorcer.
defy /dɪ'faɪ/ v.t. défier; (attempts) résister à.
degenerate¹ /dɪ'dʒenəreɪt/ v.i. dégénérer (**into,** en).
degenerate² /dɪ'dʒenərət/ a. & n. dégénéré(e) (m. (f.)).
degrad|e /dɪ'greɪd/ v.t. dégrader. **~ation** /degrɪ'deɪʃn/ n. dégradation f.; (state) déchéance f.
degree /dɪ'gri:/ n. degré m.; (univ.) diplôme universitaire m.; (Bachelor's degree) licence f. **higher ~,** (univ.) maîtrise f. or doctorat m. **to such a ~ that,** à tel point que.
dehydrate /di:'haɪdreɪt/ v.t./i. (se) déshydrater.
de-ice /di:'aɪs/ v.t. dégivrer.
deign /deɪn/ v.t. **~ to do,** daigner faire.
deity /'di:ɪtɪ/ n. divinité f.
deject|ed /dɪ'dʒektɪd/ a. abattu. **~ion** /-kʃn/ n. abattement m.
delay /dɪ'leɪ/ v.t. retarder. —v.i. tarder. —n. (lateness, time overdue) retard m.; (waiting) délai m. **~ doing,** attendre pour faire.
delectable /dɪ'lektəbl/ a. délectable, très agréable.
delegate¹ /'delɪgət/ n. délégué(e) m. (f.).
delegat|e² /'delɪgeɪt/ v.t. déléguer. **~ion** /-'geɪʃn/ n. délégation f.
delet|e /dɪ'li:t/ v.t. effacer; (with line) barrer. **~ion** /-ʃn/ n. suppression f.; (with line) rature f.
deliberate¹ /dɪ'lɪbərət/ a. délibéré;

(steps, manner) mesuré. **~ly** adv. exprès, délibérément.
deliberat|e² /dɪ'lɪbəreɪt/ v.i. délibérer. —v.t. considérer. **~ion** /-'reɪʃn/ n. délibération f.
delica|te /'delɪkət/ a. délicat. **~cy** n. délicatesse f.; (food) mets délicat or raffiné m.
delicatessen /delɪkə'tesn/ n. épicerie fine f., charcuterie f.
delicious /dɪ'lɪʃəs/ a. délicieux.
delight /dɪ'laɪt/ n. grand plaisir m., joie f., délice m. (f. in pl.); (thing) délice m. (f. in pl.). v.t. réjouir. —v.i. **~ in,** prendre plaisir à. **~ed** a. ravi. **~ful** a. charmant, très agréable.
delinquen|t /dɪ'lɪŋkwənt/ a. & n. délinquant(e) (m. (f.)) **~cy** n. délinquance f.
deliri|ous /dɪ'lɪrɪəs/ a. **be ~ous,** délirer. **~um** n. délire m.
deliver /dɪ'lɪvə(r)/ v.t. (message) remettre; (goods) livrer; (letters) distribuer; (free) délivrer; (utter) prononcer; (med.) accoucher; (a blow) porter. **~ance** n. délivrance f. **~y** n. livraison f.; distribution f.; accouchement m.
delta /'deltə/ n. delta m.
delu|de /dɪ'lu:d/ v.t. tromper. **~de o.s.,** se faire des illusions. **~sion** /-ʒn/ n. illusion f.
deluge /'delju:dʒ/ n. déluge m. —v.t. inonder (**with,** de).
de luxe /də'lʌks/ a. de luxe.
delve /delv/ v.i. fouiller.
demagogue /'deməgɒg/ n. démagogue m./f.
demand /dɪ'mɑ:nd/ v.t. exiger; (in negotiations) réclamer. —n. exigence f.; (claim) revendication f.; (comm.) demande f. **In ~,** recherché. **on ~,** à la demande. **~ing** a. exigeant.
demarcation /di:mɑ:'keɪʃn/ n. démarcation f.
demean /dɪ'mi:n/ v.t. **~ o.s.,** s'abaisser, s'avilir.
demeanour, (Amer.) **demeanor** /dɪ'mi:nə(r)/ n. comportement m.
demented /dɪ'mentɪd/ a. dément.
demerara /demə'reərə/ n. (brown sugar) cassonade f.
demise /dɪ'maɪz/ n. décès m.
demo /'deməʊ/ n. (pl. **-os**) (demonstration: fam.) manif f.
demobilize /di:'məʊbəlaɪz/ v.t. démobiliser.
democracy /dɪ'mɒkrəsɪ/ n. démocratie f.

democrat /'deməkræt/ n. démocrate m./f. ∼**ic** /-'krætɪk/ a. démocratique.

demoli|sh /dɪ'mɒlɪʃ/ v.t. démolir. ∼**tion** /demə'lɪʃn/ n. démolition f.

demon /'di:mən/ n. démon m.

demonstrat|e /'demənstreɪt/ v.t. démontrer. —v.i. (pol.) manifester. ∼**ion** /-'streɪʃn/ n. démonstration f.; (pol.) manifestation f. ∼**or** n. manifestant(e) m. (f.).

demonstrative /dɪ'mɒnstrətɪv/ a. démonstratif.

demoralize /dɪ'mɒrəlaɪz/ v.t. démoraliser.

demote /dɪ'məʊt/ v.t. rétrograder.

demure /dɪ'mjʊə(r)/ a. modeste.

den /den/ n. antre m.

denial /dɪ'naɪəl/ n. dénégation f.; (statement) démenti m.

denigrate /'denɪgreɪt/ v.t. dénigrer.

denim /'denɪm/ n. toile de coton f. ∼**s**, (jeans) blue-jeans m. pl.

Denmark /'denmɑːk/ n. Danemark m.

denomination /dɪnɒmɪ'neɪʃn/ n. (relig.) confession f.; (money) valeur f.

denote /dɪ'nəʊt/ v.t. dénoter.

denounce /dɪ'naʊns/ v.t. dénoncer.

dens|e /dens/ a. (**-er, -est**) dense; (person) obtus. ∼**ely** adv. (packed etc.) très. ∼**ity** n. densité f.

dent /dent/ n. bosse f. —v.t. cabosser. **there is a** ∼ **in the car door,** la portière est cabossée.

dental /'dentl/ a. dentaire. ∼ **floss,** fil dentaire m. ∼ **surgeon,** dentiste m./f.

dentist /'dentɪst/ n. dentiste m./f. ∼**ry** n. art dentaire m.

dentures /'dentʃəz/ n. pl. dentier m.

denude /dɪ'nju:d/ v.t. dénuder.

denunciation /dɪnʌnsɪ'eɪʃn/ n. dénonciation f.

deny /dɪ'naɪ/ v.t. nier (**that,** que); (rumour) démentir; (disown) renier; (refuse) refuser.

deodorant /di:'əʊdərənt/ n. & a. déodorant m.

depart /dɪ'pɑːt/ v.i. partir. ∼ **from,** (deviate) s'écarter de.

department /dɪ'pɑːtmənt/ n. département m.; (in shop) rayon m.; (in office) service m. **D∼ of Health,** ministère de la santé m. ∼ **store,** grand magasin m.

departure /dɪ'pɑːtʃə(r)/ n. départ m. **a** ∼ **from,** (custom, diet, etc.) une entorse à.

depend /dɪ'pend/ v.i. dépendre (**on,** de). **it (all)** ∼**s,** ça dépend. ∼ **on,** (rely on) compter sur. ∼**ing on the weather,** selon le temps qu'il fera. ∼**able** a. sûr.

∼**ence** n. dépendance f. ∼**ent** a. dépendant. **be** ∼**ent on,** dépendre de.

dependant /dɪ'pendənt/ n. personne à charge f.

depict /dɪ'pɪkt/ v.t. (describe) dépeindre; (in picture) représenter.

deplete /dɪ'pli:t/ v.t. (reduce) réduire; (use up) épuiser.

deplor|e /dɪ'plɔː(r)/ v.t. déplorer. ∼**able** a. déplorable.

deploy /dɪ'plɔɪ/ v.t. déployer.

depopulate /di:'pɒpjʊleɪt/ v.t. dépeupler.

deport /dɪ'pɔːt/ v.t. expulser. ∼**ation** /di:pɔː'teɪʃn/ n. expulsion f.

depose /dɪ'pəʊz/ v.t. déposer.

deposit /dɪ'pɒzɪt/ v.t. (p.t. **deposited**) déposer. —n. dépôt m.; (of payment) acompte m.; (to reserve) arrhes f. pl.; (against damage) caution f.; (on bottle etc.) consigne f.; (of mineral) gisement m. ∼ **account,** compte dépôt m. ∼**or** n. (comm.) déposant(e) m. (f.), épargnant(e) m. (f.).

depot /'depəʊ, Amer. 'di:pəʊ/ n. dépôt m.; (Amer.) gare (routière) f.

deprav|e /dɪ'preɪv/ v.t. dépraver. ∼**ity** /-'prævətɪ/ n. dépravation f.

deprecate /'deprəkeɪt/ v.t. désapprouver.

depreciat|e /dɪ'pri:ʃɪeɪt/ v.t./i. (se) déprécier. ∼**ion** /-'eɪʃn/ n. dépréciation f.

depress /dɪ'pres/ v.t. (sadden) déprimer; (push down) appuyer sur. **become** ∼**ed,** déprimer. ∼**ing** a. déprimant. ∼**ion** /-ʃn/ n. dépression f.

deprivation /deprɪ'veɪʃn/ n. privation f.

deprive /dɪ'praɪv/ v.t. ∼ **of,** priver de. ∼**d** a. (child etc.) déshérité.

depth /depθ/ n. profondeur f. **be out of one's** ∼, perdre pied; (fig.) être perdu. **in the** ∼**s of,** au plus profond de.

deputation /depjʊ'teɪʃn/ n. députation f.

deputize /'depjʊtaɪz/ v.i. assurer l'intérim (**for,** de). —v.t. (Amer.) déléguer, nommer.

deputy /'depjʊtɪ/ n. suppléant(e) m. (f.) —a. adjoint. ∼ **chairman,** vice-président m.

derail /dɪ'reɪl/ v.t. faire dérailler. **be** ∼**ed,** dérailler. ∼**ment** n. déraillement m.

deranged /dɪ'reɪndʒd/ a. (mind) dérangé.

derelict /'derəlɪkt/ a. abandonné.

deri|de /dɪ'raɪd/ v.t. railler. ∼**sion** /-'rɪʒn/ n. dérision f. ∼**sive** a. (laughter, person) railleur.

derisory /dɪ'raɪsərɪ/ a. (scoffing) railleur; (offer etc.) dérisoire.

derivative /dɪ'rɪvətɪv/ a. & n. dérivé (m.).

deriv|e /dɪ'raɪv/ v.t. ~e from, tirer de. —v.i. ~e from, dériver de. ~ation /derɪ'veɪʃn/ n. dérivation f.

derogatory /dɪ'rɒgətrɪ/ a. (word) péjoratif; (remark) désobligeant.

derv /dɜːv/ n. gas-oil m., gazole m.

descend /dɪ'send/ v.t./i. descendre. **be ~ed from,** descendre de. ~ant n. descendant(e) m. (f.).

descent /dɪ'sent/ n. descente f.; (lineage) origine f.

descri|be /dɪ'skraɪb/ v.t. décrire. ~ption /-'skrɪpʃn/ n. description f. ~ptive /-'skrɪptɪv/ a. descriptif.

desecrat|e /'desɪkreɪt/ v.t. profaner. ~ion /-'kreɪʃn/ n. profanation f.

desert[1] /'dezət/ n. désert m. —a. désertique. ~ **island,** île déserte f.

desert[2] /dɪ'zɜːt/ v.t./i. déserter. ~ed a désert. ~er n. déserteur m. ~ion /-ʃn/ n. désertion f.

deserts /dɪ'zɜːts/ n. pl. one's ~, ce qu'on mérite.

deserv|e /dɪ'zɜːv/ v.t. mériter (to, de). ~edly /-ɪdlɪ/ adv. à juste titre. ~ing a. (person) méritant; (action) méritoire.

design /dɪ'zaɪn/ n. (sketch) dessin m., plan m.; (construction) conception f.; (pattern) motif m.; (style of dress) modèle m.; (aim) dessein m. —v.t. (sketch) dessiner; (devise, intend) concevoir. ~er n. dessinateur, -trice m., f.; (of fashion) styliste m./f.

designat|e /'dezɪgneɪt/ v.t. désigner. ~ion /-'neɪʃn/ n. désignation f.

desir|e /dɪ'zaɪə(r)/ n. désir m. —v.t. désirer. ~able a. désirable. ~ability /-ə'bɪlətɪ/ n. attrait m.

desk /desk/ n. bureau m.; (of pupil) pupitre m.; (in hotel) réception f.; (in bank) caisse f.

desolat|e /'desələt/ a. (place) désolé; (bleak, fig.) morne. ~ion /-'leɪʃn/ n. désolation f.

despair /dɪ'speə(r)/ n. désespoir m. —v.i. désespérer (of, de).

despatch /dɪ'spætʃ/ v.t. = dispatch.

desperate /'despərət/ a. désespéré; (criminal) prêt à tout. be ~ for, avoir une envie folle de. ~ly adv. désespérément; (worried) terriblement; (ill) gravement.

desperation /despə'reɪʃn/ n. désespoir m. **in** or **out of ~,** en désespoir de cause.

despicable /dɪ'spɪkəbl/ a. méprisable, infâme.

despise /dɪ'spaɪz/ v.t. mépriser.

despite /dɪ'spaɪt/ prep. malgré.

desponden|t /dɪ'spɒndənt/ a. découragé. ~cy n. découragement m.

despot /'despɒt/ n. despote m.

dessert /dɪ'zɜːt/ n. dessert m. ~spoon n. cuiller à dessert f. ~spoonful n. cuillerée à soupe f.

destination /destɪ'neɪʃn/ n. destination f.

destine /'destɪn/ v.t. destiner.

destiny /'destɪnɪ/ n. destin m.

destitute /'destɪtjuːt/ a. indigent. ~ of, dénué de.

destr|oy /dɪ'strɔɪ/ v.t. détruire; (animal) abattre. ~uction n. destruction f. ~uctive a. destructeur.

destroyer /dɪ'strɔɪə(r)/ n. (warship) contre-torpilleur m.

detach /dɪ'tætʃ/ v.t. détacher. ~able a. détachable. ~ed a. détaché. ~ed house, maison individuelle f.

detachment /dɪ'tætʃmənt/ n. détachement m.

detail /'diːteɪl/ n. détail m. —v.t. exposer en détail; (troops) détacher. go into ~, entrer dans le détail. ~ed a. détaillé.

detain /dɪ'teɪn/ v.t. retenir; (in prison) détenir. ~ee /diːteɪ'niː/ n détenu(e) m. (f.).

detect /dɪ'tekt/ v.t. découvrir; (perceive) distinguer; (tumour) dépister; (mine) détecter. ~ion /-kʃn/ n. découverte f.; dépistage m.; détection f. ~or n. détecteur m.

detective /dɪ'tektɪv/ n policier m.; (private) détective m.

detention /dɪ'tenʃn/ n. détention f.; (schol.) retenue f.

deter /dɪ'tɜː(r)/ v.t. (p.t. **deterred**) dissuader (from, de).

detergent /dɪ'tɜːdʒənt/ a. & n. détergent (m.).

deteriorat|e /dɪ'tɪərɪəreɪt/ v.i. se détériorer. ~ion /-'reɪʃn/ n. détérioration f.

determin|e /dɪ'tɜːmɪn/ v.t. déterminer. ~e to do, décider de faire. ~ation /-'neɪʃn/ n. détermination f. ~ed a. déterminé. ~ed to do, décidé à faire.

deterrent /dɪ'terənt, Amer. dɪ'tɜːrənt/ n. force de dissuasion f.

detest /dɪ'test/ v.t. détester. ~able a. détestable.

detonat|e /'detəneɪt/ v.t./i. (faire) détoner. ~ion /-'neɪʃn/ n. détonation f. ~or n. détonateur m.

detour /'diːtʊə(r)/ n. détour m.

detract /dɪ'trækt/ v.i. ~ **from,** (lessen) diminuer.

detriment /'detrɪmənt/ n. détriment m. ~**al** /-'mentl/ a. préjudiciable (**to, à**).

devalu|e /diː'væljuː/ v.t. dévaluer. ~**ation** /-jʊ'eɪʃn/ n. dévaluation f.

devastat|e /'devəsteɪt/ v.t. dévaster; (overwhelm: fig.) accabler. ~**ing** a. accablant.

develop /dɪ'veləp/ v.t./i. (p.t. **developed**) (se) développer; (contract) contracter; (build on, transform) exploiter, aménager; (change) évoluer; (appear) se manifester. ~ **into,** devenir. ~**ing country,** pays en voie de développement m. ~**ment** n. développement m. (**housing**) ~, lotissement m. (**new**) ~**ment,** fait nouveau m.

deviant /'diːvɪənt/ a. anormal. —n. (psych.) déviant m.

deviat|e /'diːvɪeɪt/ v.i. dévier. ~**e from,** (norm) s'écarter de. ~**ion** /-'eɪʃn/ n. déviation f.

device /dɪ'vaɪs/ n. appareil m.; (scheme) procédé m.

devil /'devl/ n. diable m. ~**ish** a. diabolique.

devious /'diːvɪəs/ a. tortueux. **he is** ~, il a l'esprit tortueux.

devise /dɪ'vaɪz/ v.t. inventer; (plan, means) combiner, imaginer.

devoid /dɪ'vɔɪd/ a. ~ **of,** dénué de.

devolution /diːvə'luːʃn/ n. décentralisation f.; (of authority, power) délégation f. (**to, à**).

devot|e /dɪ'vəʊt/ v.t. consacrer. ~**ed** a. dévoué. ~**edly** adv. avec dévouement. ~**ion** /-ʃn/ n. dévouement m.; (relig.) dévotion f. ~**ions,** (relig.) dévotions f. pl.

devotee /devə'tiː/ n. ~ **of,** passionné(e) de m. (f.).

devour /dɪ'vaʊə(r)/ v.t. dévorer.

devout /dɪ'vaʊt/ a. fervent.

dew /djuː/ n. rosée f.

dexterity /dek'sterətɪ/ n. dextérité f.

diabet|es /daɪə'biːtiːz/ n. diabète m. ~**ic** /-'betɪk/ a. & n. diabétique (m./f.).

diabolical /daɪə'bɒlɪkl/ a. diabolique; (bad: fam.) atroce.

diagnose /'daɪəgnəʊz/ v.t. diagnostiquer.

diagnosis /daɪəg'nəʊsɪs/ n. (pl. -oses) /-siːz/) diagnostic m.

diagonal /daɪ'ægənl/ a. diagonal. —n. diagonale f. ~**ly** adv. en diagonale.

diagram /'daɪəgræm/ n. schéma m.

dial /'daɪəl/ n. cadran m. —v.t. (p.t. **dialled**) (number) faire; (person)

appeler. ~**ling code,** (Amer.) ~ **code,** indicatif m. ~**ling tone,** (Amer.) ~ **tone,** tonalité f.

dialect /'daɪəlekt/ n. dialecte m.

dialogue /'daɪəlɒg/ n. dialogue m.

diameter /daɪ'æmɪtə(r)/ n. diamètre m.

diamond /'daɪəmənd/ n. diamant m.; (shape) losange m.; (baseball) terrain m. ~**s,** (cards) carreau m.

diaper /'daɪəpə(r)/ n. (baby's nappy: Amer.) couche f.

diaphragm /'daɪəfræm/ n. diaphragme m.

diarrhoea, (Amer.) **diarrhea** /daɪə'rɪə/ n. diarrhée f.

diary /'daɪərɪ/ n. (for appointments etc.) agenda m.; (appointments) emploi du temps m. (for private thoughts) journal intime m.

dice /daɪs/ n. invar. dé m. —v.t. (food) couper en dés.

dicey /'daɪsɪ/ a. (fam.) risqué.

dictat|e /dɪk'teɪt/ v.t./i. dicter. ~**ion** /-ʃn/ n. dictée f.

dictates /'dɪkteɪts/ n. pl. préceptes m. pl.

dictator /dɪk'teɪtə(r)/ n. dictateur m. ~**ship** n. dictature f.

dictatorial /dɪktə'tɔːrɪəl/ a. dictatorial.

diction /'dɪkʃn/ n. diction f.

dictionary /'dɪkʃənrɪ/ n. dictionnaire m.

did /dɪd/ see **do.**

diddle /'dɪdl/ v.t. (sl.) escroquer.

didn't /'dɪdnt/ = **did not.**

die¹ /daɪ/ v.i. (pres. p. **dying**) mourir. ~ **down,** diminuer. ~ **out,** disparaître. **be dying to do/for,** mourir d'envie de faire/de.

die² /daɪ/ n. (metal mould) matrice f., étampe f.

die-hard /'daɪhɑːd/ n. réactionnaire m./f.

diesel /'diːzl/ n. diesel m. ~ **engine,** moteur diesel m.

diet /'daɪət/ n. (habitual food) alimentation f.; (restricted) régime m. —v.i. suivre un régime.

diet|etic /daɪə'tetɪk/ a. diététique. ~**ician** n. diététicien(ne) m. (f.).

differ /'dɪfə(r)/ v.i. différer (**from,** de); (disagree) ne pas être d'accord.

differen|t /'dɪfrənt/ a. différent. ~**ce** n. différence f.; (disagreement) différend m. ~**tly** adv. différemment (**from,** de).

differential /dɪfə'renʃl/ a. & n. différentiel (m.).

differentiate /dɪfə'renʃɪeɪt/ v.t. différencier. —v.i. faire la différence (**between,** entre).

difficult /'dɪfɪkəlt/ a. difficile. ~**y** n. difficulté f.

diffiden|t /'dɪfɪdənt/ a. qui manque d'assurance. **~ce** n. manque d'assurance m.

diffuse¹ /dɪ'fju:s/ a. diffus.

diffus|e² /dɪ'fju:z/ v.t. diffuser. **~ion** /-ʒn/ n. diffusion f.

dig /dɪg/ v.t./i. (p.t. dug, pres. p. digging) creuser; (thrust) enfoncer. —n. (poke) coup de coude m.; (remark) coup de patte m.; (archaeol.) fouilles f. pl. **~s**, (lodgings: fam.) chambre meublée f. **~** (over), bêcher. **~** up, déterrer.

digest¹ /dɪ'dʒest/ v.t./i. digérer. **~ible** a. digestible. **~ion** /-stʃən/ n. digestion f.

digest² /'daɪdʒest/ n. sommaire m.

digestive /dɪ'dʒestɪv/ a. digestif.

digger /'dɪgə(r)/ n. (techn.) pelleteuse f., excavateur m.

digit /'dɪdʒɪt/ n. chiffre m.

digital /'dɪdʒɪtl/ a. (clock) numérique, à affichage numérique; (recording) numérique.

dignif|y /'dɪgnɪfaɪ/ v.t. donner de la dignité à. **~ied** a. digne.

dignitary /'dɪgnɪtərɪ/ n. dignitaire m.

dignity /'dɪgnɪtɪ/ n. dignité f.

digress /daɪ'gres/ v.i. faire une digression. **~ from**, s'écarter de. **~ion** /-ʃn/ n. digression f.

dike /daɪk/ n. digue f.

dilapidated /dɪ'læpɪdeɪtɪd/ a. délabré.

dilat|e /daɪ'leɪt/ v.t./i. (se) dilater. **~ion** /-ʃn/ n. dilatation f.

dilatory /'dɪlətərɪ/ a. dilatoire.

dilemma /dɪ'lemə/ n. dilemme m.

dilettante /dɪlɪ'tæntɪ/ n. dilettante m./f.

diligen|t /'dɪlɪdʒənt/ a. assidu. **~ce** n. assiduité f.

dilly-dally /'dɪlɪdælɪ/ v.i. (fam.) lanterner.

dilute /daɪ'lju:t/ v.t. diluer.

dim /dɪm/ a. (dimmer, dimmest) (weak) faible; (dark) sombre; (indistinct) vague; (fam.) stupide. v.t./i. (p.t. dimmed) (light) (s')atténuer. **~ly** adv. (shine) faiblement; (remember) vaguement. **~mer** n. **~** (switch), variateur d'intensité m. **~ness** n. faiblesse f.; (of room etc.) obscurité f.

dime /daɪm/ n. (in USA, Canada) pièce de dix cents f.

dimension /daɪ'menʃn/ n. dimension f.

diminish /dɪ'mɪnɪʃ/ v.t./i. diminuer.

diminutive /dɪ'mɪnjʊtɪv/ a. minuscule. —n. diminutif m.

dimple /'dɪmpl/ n. fossette f.

din /dɪn/ n. vacarme m.

dine /daɪn/ v.i. dîner. **~r** /-ə(r)/ n. dîneu|r, -se m., f.; (rail.) wagon-restaurant m.; (Amer.) restaurant à service rapide m.

dinghy /'dɪŋgɪ/ n. canot m.; (inflatable) canot pneumatique m.

dingy /'dɪndʒɪ/ a. (-ier, -iest) miteux, minable. **~iness** n. aspect miteux or minable m.

dining-room /'daɪnɪŋrʊm/ n. salle à manger f.

dinner /'dɪnə(r)/ n. (evening meal) dîner m.; (lunch) déjeuner m. **~-jacket** n. smoking m. **~ party**, dîner m.

dinosaur /'daɪnəsɔ:(r)/ n. dinosaure m.

dint /dɪnt/ n. by **~ of**, à force de.

diocese /'daɪəsɪs/ n. diocèse m.

dip /dɪp/ v.t./i. (p.t. dipped) plonger. —n. (slope) déclivité f.; (in sea) bain rapide m. **~ into**, (book) feuilleter; (savings) puiser dans. **~ one's headlights**, se mettre en code.

diphtheria /dɪf'θɪərɪə/ n. diphtérie f.

diphthong /'dɪfθɒŋ/ n. diphtongue f.

diploma /dɪ'pləʊmə/ n. diplôme m.

diplomacy /dɪ'pləʊməsɪ/ n. diplomatie f.

diplomat /'dɪpləmæt/ n. diplomate m./f. **~ic** /-'mætɪk/ a. (pol.) diplomatique; (tactful) diplomate.

dire /daɪə(r)/ a. (-er, -est) affreux; (need, poverty) extrême.

direct /dɪ'rekt/ a. direct. —adv. directement. —v.t. diriger; (letter, remark) adresser; (a play) mettre en scène. **~** s.o. to, indiquer à qn. le chemin de; (order) signifier à qn. de. **~ness** n. franchise f.

direction /dɪ'rekʃn/ n. direction f.; (theatre) mise en scène f. **~s**, indications f pl ask **~s**, demander le chemin. **~s for use**, mode d'emploi m.

directly /dɪ'rektlɪ/ adv. directement; (at once) tout de suite. —conj. dès que.

director /dɪ'rektə(r)/ n. directeur, -trice m., f., (theatre) metteur en scène m.

directory /dɪ'rektərɪ/ n. (phone book) annuaire m.

dirt /dɜ:t/ n. saleté f.; (earth) terre f. **~ cheap**, (sl.) très bon marché invar. **~-track** n. (sport) cendrée f.

dirty /'dɜ:tɪ/ a. (-ier, -iest) sale; (word) grossier. get **~**, se salir. —v.t./i. (se) salir.

disability /dɪsə'bɪlətɪ/ n. handicap m.

disable /dɪs'eɪbl/ v.t. rendre infirme. **~d** a. handicapé.

disadvantage /dɪsəd'vɑ:ntɪdʒ/ n. désavantage m. **~d** a. déshérité.

disagree /dɪsə'griː/ *v.i.* ne pas être d'accord (**with**, avec). ∼ **with s.o.**, (*food, climate*) ne pas convenir à qn. ∼**ment** *n.* désaccord *m.*; (*quarrel*) différend *m.*

disagreeable /dɪsə'griːəbl/ *a.* désagréable.

disappear /dɪsə'pɪə(r)/ *v.i.* disparaître. ∼**ance** *n.* disparition *f.*

disappoint /dɪsə'pɔɪnt/ *v.t.* décevoir. ∼**ing** *a.* décevant. ∼**ed** *a.* déçu. ∼**ment** *n.* déception *f.*

disapprov|e /dɪsə'pruːv/ *v.i.* ∼**e** (**of**), désapprouver. ∼**al** *n.* désapprobation *f.*

disarm /dɪs'ɑːm/ *v.t./i.* désarmer. ∼**ament** *n.* désarmement *m.*

disarray /dɪsə'reɪ/ *n.* désordre *m.*

disassociate /dɪsə'səʊʃɪeɪt/ *v.t.* = **dissociate.**

disast|er /dɪ'zɑːstə(r)/ *n.* désastre *m.* ∼**rous** *a.* désastreux.

disband /dɪs'bænd/ *v.t./i.* (se) disperser.

disbelief /dɪsbɪ'liːf/ *n.* incrédulité *f.*

disc /dɪsk/ *n.* disque *m.*; (*comput.*) = **disk.** ∼ **brake,** frein à disque *m.* ∼ **jockey,** disc-jockey *m.*, animateur *m.*

discard /dɪ'skɑːd/ *v.t.* se débarrasser de; (*beliefs etc.*) abandonner.

discern /dɪ'sɜːn/ *v.t.* discerner. ∼**ible** *a.* perceptible. ∼**ing** *a.* perspicace.

discharge[1] /dɪs'tʃɑːdʒ/ *v.t.* (*unload*) décharger; (*liquid*) déverser; (*duty*) remplir; (*dismiss*) renvoyer; (*prisoner*) libérer. —*v.i.* (*of pus*) s'écouler.

discharge[2] /'dɪstʃɑːdʒ/ *n.* (*med.*) écoulement *m.*; (*dismissal*) renvoi *m.*; (*electr.*) décharge *m.*

disciple /dɪ'saɪpl/ *n.* disciple *m.*

disciplin|e /'dɪsɪplɪn/ *n.* discipline *f.* —*v.t.* discipliner; (*punish*) punir. ∼**ary** *a.* disciplinaire.

disclaim /dɪs'kleɪm/ *v.t.* désavouer. ∼**er** *n.* correctif *m.*, précision *f.*

disclos|e /dɪs'kləʊz/ *v.t.* révéler. ∼**ure** /-ʒə(r)/ *n.* révélation *f.*

disco /'dɪskəʊ/ *n.* (*pl.* **-os**) (*club*: *fam.*) discothèque *f.*, disco *m.*

discol|our /dɪs'kʌlə(r)/ *v.t./i.* (se) décolorer. ∼**oration** /-'reɪʃn/ *n.* décoloration *f.*

discomfort /dɪs'kʌmfət/ *n.* gêne *f.*

disconcert /dɪskən'sɜːt/ *v.t.* déconcerter.

disconnect /dɪskə'nekt/ *v.t.* détacher; (*unplug*) débrancher; (*cut off*) couper.

discontent /dɪskən'tent/ *n.* mécontentement *m.* ∼**ed** *a.* mécontent.

discontinue /dɪskən'tɪnjuː/ *v.t.* interrompre, cesser.

discord /'dɪskɔːd/ *n.* discorde *f.*; (*mus.*) dissonance *f.* ∼**ant** /-'skɔːdənt/ *a.* discordant.

discothèque /'dɪskətek/ *n.* discothèque *f.*

discount[1] /'dɪskaʊnt/ *n.* rabais *m.*

discount[2] /dɪs'kaʊnt/ *v.t.* ne pas tenir compte de.

discourage /dɪ'skʌrɪdʒ/ *v.t.* décourager.

discourse /'dɪskɔːs/ *n.* discours *m.*

discourteous /dɪs'kɜːtɪəs/ *a.* impoli, peu courtois.

discover /dɪ'skʌvə(r)/ *v.t.* découvrir. ∼**y** *n.* découverte *f.*

discredit /dɪs'kredɪt/ *v.t.* (*p.t.* **discredited**) discréditer. —*n.* discrédit *m.*

discreet /dɪ'skriːt/ *a.* discret. ∼**ly** *adv.* discrètement.

discrepancy /dɪ'skrepənsɪ/ *n.* contradiction *f.*, incohérence *f.*

discretion /dɪ'skreʃn/ *n.* discrétion *f.*

discriminat|e /dɪ'skrɪmɪneɪt/ *v.t./i.* distinguer. ∼**e against,** faire de la discrimination contre. ∼**ing** *a.* (*person*) qui a du discernement. ∼**ion** /-'neɪʃn/ *n.* discernement *m.*; (*bias*) discrimination *f.*

discus /'dɪskəs/ *n.* disque *m.*

discuss /dɪ'skʌs/ *v.t.* (*talk about*) discuter de; (*argue about, examine critically*) discuter. ∼**ion** /-ʃn/ *n.* discussion *f.*

disdain /dɪs'deɪn/ *n.* dédain *m.* ∼**ful** *a.* dédaigneux.

disease /dɪ'ziːz/ *n.* maladie *f.* ∼**d** *a.* malade.

disembark /dɪsɪm'bɑːk/ *v.t./i.* débarquer.

disembodied /dɪsɪm'bɒdɪd/ *a.* désincarné.

disenchant /dɪsɪn'tʃɑːnt/ *v.t.* désenchanter. ∼**ment** *n.* désenchantement *m.*

disengage /dɪsɪn'geɪdʒ/ *v.t.* dégager; (*mil.*) retirer. —*v.i.* (*mil.*) retirer; (*auto.*) débrayer. ∼**ment** *n.* dégagement *m.*

disentangle /dɪsɪn'tæŋgl/ *v.t.* démêler.

disfavour, (*Amer.*) **disfavor** /dɪs'feɪvə(r)/ *n.* défaveur *f.*

disfigure /dɪs'fɪgə(r)/ *v.t.* défigurer.

disgrace /dɪs'greɪs/ *n.* (*shame*) honte *f.*; (*disfavour*) disgrâce *f.* —*v.t.* déshonorer. ∼**d** *a.* (*in disfavour*) disgracié. ∼**ful** *a.* honteux.

disgruntled /dɪs'grʌntld/ *a.* mécontent.

disguise /dɪs'gaɪz/ *v.t.* déguiser. —*n.* déguisement *m.* **in** ∼, déguisé.

disgust /dɪs'gʌst/ *n.* dégoût *m.* —*v.t.* dégoûter. ∼**ing** *a.* dégoûtant.

dish /dɪʃ/ n. plat m. —v.t. ∼ out, (fam.) distribuer. ∼ up, servir. the ∼es, (crockery) la vaisselle.

dishcloth /'dɪʃklɒθ/ n. lavette f.; (for drying) torchon m.

dishearten /dɪs'hɑːtn/ v.t. décourager.

dishevelled /dɪ'ʃevld/ a. échevelé.

dishonest /dɪs'ɒnɪst/ a. malhonnête. ∼y n. malhonnêteté f.

dishonour, (Amer.) **dishonor** /dɪs'ɒnə(r)/ n. déshonneur m. —v.t. déshonorer. ∼able a. déshonorant. ∼ably adv. avec déshonneur.

dishwasher /'dɪʃwɒʃə(r)/ n. lave-vaisselle m. invar.

disillusion /dɪsɪ'luːʒn/ v.t. désillusionner. ∼ment n. désillusion f.

disincentive /dɪsɪn'sentɪv/ n. be a ∼ to, décourager.

disinclined /dɪsɪn'klaɪnd/ a. ∼ to, peu disposé à.

disinfect /dɪsɪn'fekt/ v.t. désinfecter. ∼ant n. désinfectant m.

disinherit /dɪsɪn'herɪt/ v.t. déshériter.

disintegrate /dɪs'ɪntɪgreɪt/ v.t./i. (se) désintégrer.

disinterested /dɪs'ɪntrəstɪd/ a. désintéressé.

disjointed /dɪs'dʒɔɪntɪd/ a. (talk) décousu.

disk /dɪsk/ n. (Amer.) = disc; (comput.) disque m. ∼ drive, drive m., lecteur de disquettes m.

diskette /dɪs'ket/ n. disquette f.

dislike /dɪs'laɪk/ n. aversion f. —v.t. ne pas aimer.

dislocat|e /'dɪsləkeɪt/ v.t. (limb) disloquer. ∼ion /-'keɪʃn/ n. dislocation f.

dislodge /dɪs'lɒdʒ/ v.t. (move) déplacer; (drive out) déloger.

disloyal /dɪs'lɔɪəl/ a. déloyal. ∼ty n. déloyauté f.

dismal /'dɪzməl/ a. morne, triste.

dismantle /dɪs'mæntl/ v.t. démonter, défaire.

dismay /dɪs'meɪ/ n. consternation f. —v.t. consterner.

dismiss /dɪs'mɪs/ v.t. renvoyer; (appeal) rejeter; (from mind) écarter. ∼al n. renvoi m.

dismount /dɪs'maʊnt/ v.i. descendre, mettre pied à terre.

disobedien|t /dɪsə'biːdɪənt/ a. désobéissant. ∼ce n. désobéissance f.

disobey /dɪsə'beɪ/ v.t. désobéir à —v.i. désobéir.

disorder /dɪs'ɔːdə(r)/ n. désordre m.; (ailment) trouble(s) m. (pl.). ∼ly a. désordonné.

disorganize /dɪs'ɔːgənaɪz/ v.t. désorganiser.

disorientate /dɪs'ɔːrɪənteɪt/ v.t. désorienter.

disown /dɪs'əʊn/ v.t. renier.

disparaging /dɪ'spærɪdʒɪŋ/ a. désobligeant. ∼ly adv. de façon désobligeante.

disparity /dɪ'spærətɪ/ n. disparité f., écart m.

dispassionate /dɪ'spæʃənət/ a. impartial; (unemotional) calme.

dispatch /dɪ'spætʃ/ v.t. (send, complete) expédier, (troops) envoyer. —n. expédition f.; envoi m.; (report) dépêche f. ∼-rider n. estafette f.

dispel /dɪ'spel/ v.t. (p.t. dispelled) dissiper.

dispensary /dɪ'spensərɪ/ n. pharmacie f., officine f.

dispense /dɪ'spens/ v.t. distribuer; (medicine) préparer. —v.i. ∼ with, se passer de. ∼r /-ə(r)/ n. (container) distributeur m.

dispers|e /dɪ'spɜːs/ v.t./i. (se) disperser. ∼al n. dispersion f.

dispirited /dɪ'spɪrɪtɪd/ a. découragé, abattu.

displace /dɪs'pleɪs/ v.t. déplacer.

display /dɪ'spleɪ/ v.t. montrer, exposer; (feelings) manifester. —n. exposition f.; manifestation f.; (comm.) étalage m.; (of computer) visuel m.

displeas|e /dɪs'pliːz/ v.t. déplaire à. ∼ed with, mécontent de. ∼ure /-'pleʒə(r)/ n. mecontentement m.

disposable /dɪ'spəʊzəbl/ a. à jeter.

dispos|e /dɪ'spəʊz/ v.t. disposer. —v.i. ∼e of, se débarrasser de. well ∼ed to, bien disposé envers. ∼al n. (of waste) évacuation f. at s.o.'s ∼al, à la disposition de qn.

disposition /dɪspə'zɪʃn/ n. disposition f.; (character) naturel m.

disproportionate /dɪsprə'pɔːʃənət/ a. disproportionné.

disprove /dɪs'pruːv/ v.t. réfuter.

dispute /dɪ'spjuːt/ v.t. contester. —n. discussion f.; (pol.) conflit m. in ∼, contesté.

disqualif|y /dɪs'kwɒlɪfaɪ/ v.t. rendre inapte; (sport) disqualifier. ∼y from driving, retirer le permis à. ∼ication /-ɪ'keɪʃn/ n. disqualification f.

disquiet /dɪs'kwaɪət/ n. inquiétude f. ∼ing a. inquiétant.

disregard /dɪsrɪ'gɑːd/ v.t. ne pas tenir compte de. —n. indifférence f. (for, à).

disrepair /dɪsrɪ'peə(r)/ *n.* mauvais état *m.*, délabrement *m.*

disreputable /dɪs'repjʊtəbl/ *a.* peu recommendable.

disrepute /dɪsrɪ'pjuːt/ *n.* discrédit *m.*

disrespect /dɪsrɪ'spekt/ *n.* manque de respect *m.* ∼**ful** *a.* irrespectueux.

disrupt /dɪs'rʌpt/ *v.t.* (*disturb, break up*) perturber; (*plans*) déranger. ∼**ion** /-pʃn/ *n.* perturbation *f.* ∼**ive** *a.* perturbateur.

dissatisf|ied /dɪs'sætɪsfaɪd/ *a.* mécontent. ∼**action** /dɪsætɪs'fækʃn/ *n.* mécontentement *m.*

dissect /dɪ'sekt/ *v.t.* disséquer. ∼**ion** /-kʃn/ *n.* dissection *f.*

disseminate /dɪ'semɪneɪt/ *v.t.* disséminer.

dissent /dɪ'sent/ *v.i.* différer (**from**, de). —*n.* dissentiment *m.*

dissertation /dɪsə'teɪʃn/ *n.* (*univ.*) mémoire *m.*

disservice /dɪs'sɜːvɪs/ *n.* mauvais service *m.*

dissident /'dɪsɪdənt/ *a. & n.* dissident(e) (*m.* (*f.*)).

dissimilar /dɪ'sɪmɪlə(r)/ *a.* dissemblable, différent.

dissipate /'dɪsɪpeɪt/ *v.t./i.* (se) dissiper; (*efforts*) gaspiller. ∼**d** /-ɪd/ *a.* (*person*) débauché.

dissociate /dɪ'səʊʃɪeɪt/ *v.t.* dissocier. ∼ **o.s. from**, se désolidariser de.

dissolute /'dɪsəljuːt/ *a.* dissolu.

dissolution /dɪsə'luːʃn/ *n.* dissolution *f.*

dissolve /dɪ'zɒlv/ *v.t./i.* (se) dissoudre.

dissuade /dɪ'sweɪd/ *v.t.* dissuader.

distance /'dɪstəns/ *n.* distance *f.* **from a** ∼, de loin. **in the** ∼, au loin.

distant /'dɪstənt/ *a.* éloigné, lointain; (*relative*) éloigné; (*aloof*) distant.

distaste /dɪs'teɪst/ *n.* dégoût *m.* ∼**ful** *a.* désagréable.

distemper /dɪ'stempə(r)/ *n.* (*paint*) badigeon *m.*; (*animal disease*) maladie *f.* —*v.t.* badigeonner.

distend /dɪ'stend/ *v.t./i.* (se) distendre.

distil /dɪ'stɪl/ *v.t.* (*p.t.* **distilled**) distiller. ∼**lation** /-'leɪʃn/ *n.* distillation *f.*

distillery /dɪ'stɪlərɪ/ *n.* distillerie *f.*

distinct /dɪ'stɪŋkt/ *a.* distinct; (*marked*) net. **as** ∼ **from**, par opposition à. ∼**ion** /-kʃn/ *n.* distinction *f.*; (*in exam*) mention très bien *f.* ∼**ive** *a.* distinctif. ∼**ly** *adv.* (*see*) distinctement; (*forbid*) expressément; (*markedly*) nettement.

distinguish /dɪ'stɪŋgwɪʃ/ *v.t./i.* distinguer. ∼**ed** *a.* distingué.

distort /dɪ'stɔːt/ *v.t.* déformer. ∼**ion** /-ʃn/ *n.* distorsion *f.*; (*of facts*) déformation *f.*

distract /dɪ'strækt/ *v.t.* distraire. ∼**ed** *a.* (*distraught*) éperdu. ∼**ing** *a.* gênant. ∼**ion** /-kʃn/ *n.* (*lack of attention, entertainment*) distraction *f.*

distraught /dɪ'strɔːt/ *a.* éperdu.

distress /dɪ'stres/ *n.* douleur *f.*; (*poverty, danger*) détresse *f.* —*v.t.* peiner. ∼**ing** *a.* pénible.

distribut|e /dɪ'strɪbjuːt/ *v.t.* distribuer. ∼**ion** /-'bjuːʃn/ *n.* distribution *f.* ∼**or** *n.* distributeur *m.*

district /'dɪstrɪkt/ *n.* région *f.*; (*of town*) quartier *m.*

distrust /dɪs'trʌst/ *n.* méfiance *f.* —*v.t.* se méfier de.

disturb /dɪ'stɜːb/ *v.t.* déranger; (*alarm, worry*) troubler. ∼**ance** *n.* dérangement *m.* (**of**, de); (*noise*) tapage *m.* ∼**ances** *n. pl.* (*pol.*) troubles *m. pl.* ∼**ed** *a.* troublé; (*psychologically*) perturbé. ∼**ing** *a.* troublant.

disused /dɪs'juːzd/ *a.* désaffecté.

ditch /dɪtʃ/ *n.* fossé *m.* —*v.t.* (*sl.*) abandonner.

dither /'dɪðə(r)/ *v.i.* hésiter.

ditto /'dɪtəʊ/ *adv.* idem.

divan /dɪ'væn/ *n.* divan *m.*

div|e /daɪv/ *v.i.* plonger; (*rush*) se précipiter. —*n.* plongeon *m.*; (*of plane*) piqué *m.*; (*place: sl.*) bouge *m.* ∼**er** *n.* plongeur, -se *m.*, *f.* ∼**ing-board** *n.* plongeoir *m.* ∼**ing-suit** *n.* tenue de plongée *f.*

diverge /daɪ'vɜːdʒ/ *v.i.* diverger.

divergent /daɪ'vɜːdʒənt/ *a.* divergent.

diverse /daɪ'vɜːs/ *a.* divers.

diversify /daɪ'vɜːsɪfaɪ/ *v.t.* diversifier.

diversity /daɪ'vɜːsətɪ/ *n.* diversité *f.*

diver|t /daɪ'vɜːt/ *v.t.* détourner; (*traffic*) dévier. ∼**sion** /-ʃn/ *n.* détournement *m.*; (*distraction*) diversion *f.*; (*of traffic*) déviation *f.*

divest /daɪ'vest/ *v.t.* ∼ **of**, (*strip of*) priver de, déposséder de.

divide /dɪ'vaɪd/ *v.t./i.* (se) diviser.

dividend /'dɪvɪdend/ *n.* dividende *m.*

divine /dɪ'vaɪn/ *a.* divin.

divinity /dɪ'vɪnətɪ/ *n.* divinité *f.*

division /dɪ'vɪʒn/ *n.* division *f.*

divorce /dɪ'vɔːs/ *n.* divorce *m.* (**from**, d'avec). —*v.t./i.* divorcer (d'avec). ∼**d** *a.* divorcé.

divorcee /dɪvɔː'siː, *Amer.* dɪvɔː'seɪ/ *n.* divorcé(e) *m.* (*f.*).

divulge /daɪ'vʌldʒ/ *v.t.* divulguer.

DIY *abbr. see* **do-it-yourself.**

dizzy /'dɪzɪ/ a. (-ier, -iest) vertigineux. **be** or **feel** ～**y**, avoir le vertige. ～**iness** n. vertige m.

do /duː/ v.t./i. (3 sing. present tense **does**; p.t. **did**; p.p., **done**) faire; (progress, be suitable) aller; (be enough) suffire; (swindle: sl.) avoir. **do well/badly**, se débrouiller bien/mal. **do the house**, peindre ou nettoyer etc. la maison. **well done!**, bravo! **well done**, (culin.) bien cuit. **done for**, (fam.) fichu. —v. aux. **do you see?**, voyez-vous? **do you live here?**—**I do**, est-ce que vous habitez ici?—oui. **I do live here**, si, j'habite ici. **I do not smoke**, je ne fume pas. **don't you?**, **doesn't he?**, etc., n'est-ce pas? —n. (pl. **dos** or **do's**) soirée f., fête f. **dos and don'ts**, choses à faire et à ne pas faire. **do away with**, supprimer. **do in**, (sl.) tuer. **do-it-yourself** n. bricolage m.; a. (shop, book) de bricolage. **do out**, (clean) nettoyer. **do up**, (fasten) fermer; (house) refaire. **it's to** ～ **with the house**, c'est à propos de la maison. **it's nothing to do with me**, ça n'a rien à voir avec moi. **I could do with a holiday**, j'aurais bien besoin de vacances. ～ **without**, se passer de.

docile /'dəʊsaɪl/ a. docile.

dock[1] /dɒk/ n. dock m. —v.t./i. (sc) mettre à quai. ～**er** n. docker m.

dock[2] /dɒk/ n. (jurid.) banc des accusés m.

dock[3] /dɒk/ v.t. (money) retrancher.

dockyard /'dɒkjɑːd/ n. chantier naval m.

doctor /'dɒktə(r)/ n. médecin m., docteur m.; (univ.) docteur m. —v.t. (cat) châtrer; (fig.) altérer.

doctorate /'dɒktərət/ n. doctorat m.

doctrine /'dɒktrɪn/ n. doctrine f.

document /'dɒkjʊmənt/ n. document m. ～**ary** /-'mentrɪ/ a. & n. documentaire (m.). ～**ation** /-'eɪʃn/ n. documentation f.

doddering /'dɒdərɪŋ/ a. gâteux.

dodge /dɒdʒ/ v.t. esquiver. —v.i. faire un saut de côté —n. (fam.) truc m.

dodgems /'dɒdʒəmz/ n. pl. autos tamponneuses f. pl.

dodgy /'dɒdʒɪ/ a. (-ier, -iest) (fam.: difficult) épineux, délicat; (dangerous) douteux.

doe /dəʊ/ n. (deer) biche f.

does /dʌz/ see **do**.

doesn't /'dʌznt/ = **does not**.

dog /dɒg/ n. chien m. —v.t. (p.t. **dogged**) poursuivre. ～**-collar** n. (fam.) (faux) col d'ecclésiastique m. ～**-eared** a. écorné.

dogged /'dɒgɪd/ a. obstiné.

dogma /'dɒgmə/ n. dogme m. ～**tic** /-'mætɪk/ a. dogmatique.

dogsbody /'dɒgzbɒdɪ/ n. factotum m., bonne à tout faire f.

doily /'dɔɪlɪ/ n. napperon m.

doings /'duːɪŋz/ n. pl. (fam.) activités f. pl., occupations f. pl.

doldrums /'dɒldrəmz/ n. pl. **be in the** ～, (person) avoir le cafard.

dole /dəʊl/ v.t. ～ **out**, distribuer. —n. (fam.) indemnité de chômage f. **on the** ～, (fam.) au chômage.

doleful /'dəʊlfl/ a. triste, morne.

doll /dɒl/ n. poupée f. —v.t. ～ **up**, (fam.) bichonner.

dollar /'dɒlə(r)/ n. dollar m.

dollop /'dɒləp/ n. (of food etc.: fam.) gros morceau m.

dolphin /'dɒlfɪn/ n. dauphin m.

domain /də'meɪn/ n. domaine m.

dome /dəʊm/ n. dôme m.

domestic /də'mestɪk/ a. familial; (trade, flights, etc.) intérieur; (animal) domestique. ～ **science**, arts ménagers m. pl. ～**ated** a. (animal) domestiqué.

domesticity /dɒme'stɪsətɪ/ n. vie de famille f.

dominant /'dɒmɪnənt/ a. dominant.

dominat|e /'dɒmɪneɪt/ v.t./i. dominer. ～**ion** /-'neɪʃn/ n. domination f.

domineering /dɒmɪ'nɪərɪŋ/ a. dominateur, autoritaire.

dominion /də'mɪnjən/ n. (British pol.) dominion m.

domino /'dɒmɪnəʊ/ n. (pl. -oes) domino m. ～**es**, (game) dominos m. pl.

don[1] /dɒn/ v.t. (p.t. **donned**) revêtir, endosser.

don[2] /dɒn/ n. professeur d'université m.

donat|e /dəʊ'neɪt/ v.t. faire don de. ～**ion** /-ʃn/ n. don m.

done /dʌn/ see **do**.

donkey /'dɒŋkɪ/ n. âne m. **the** ～**-work** le sale boulot.

donor /'dəʊnə(r)/ n. donateur, -trice m., f.; (of blood) donneur, -se m., f.

don't /dəʊnt/ = **do not**.

doodle /'duːdl/ v.i. griffonner.

doom /duːm/ n. (ruin) ruine f.; (fate) destin m. —v.t. **be** ～**ed to**, être destiné or condamné à. ～**ed (to failure)**, voué à l'échec.

door /dɔː(r)/ n. porte f.; (of vehicle) portière f., porte f.

doorbell /'dɔːbel/ n. sonnette f.

doorman /'dɔːmən/ n. (pl. -men) portier m.

doormat /'dɔːmæt/ n. paillasson m.

doorstep /'dɔ:step/ n. pas de (la) porte m., seuil m.

doorway /'dɔ:weɪ/ n. porte f.

dope /dəʊp/ n. (fam.) drogue f.; (idiot: sl.) imbécile m./f. —v.t. doper. **~y** a. (foolish: sl.) imbécile.

dormant /'dɔ:mənt/ a. en sommeil.

dormitory /'dɔ:mɪtrɪ, Amer. 'dɔ:mɪtɔ:rɪ/ n. dortoir m.; (univ., Amer.) résidence f.

dormouse /'dɔ:maʊs/ n. (pl. -mice) loir m.

dos|e /dəʊs/ n. dose f. **~age** n. dose f.; (on label) posologie f.

doss /dɒs/ v.i. (sl.) roupiller. **~-house** n. asile de nuit m.

dossier /'dɒsɪə(r)/ n. dossier m.

dot /dɒt/ n. point m. on the **~**, (fam.) à l'heure pile. **~-matrix** a. (printer) matriciel.

dote /dəʊt/ v.i. **~ on**, être gaga de.

dotted /dɒtɪd/ a. (fabric) à pois. **~ line**, ligne en pointillés f. **~ with**, parsemé de.

dotty /'dɒtɪ/ a. (-ier, -iest) (fam.) cinglé, dingue.

double /'dʌbl/ a. double; (room, bed) pour deux personnes. —adv. deux fois. —n. double m.; (stuntman) doublure f. **~s**, (tennis) double m. —v.t./i. doubler; (fold) plier en deux. **at** or **on the ~**, au pas de course. **~ the size**, deux fois plus grand: **pay ~**, payer le double. **~-bass** n. (mus.) contrebasse f. **~-breasted** a. croisé. **~-check** v.t. revérifier. **~ chin**, double menton m. **~-cross** v.t. tromper. **~-dealing** n. double jeu m. **~-decker** n. autobus à impériale m. **~ Dutch**, de l'hébreu m.

doubly /'dʌblɪ/ adv. doublement.

doubt /daʊt/ n. doute m. —v.t. douter de. **~ if** or **that**, douter que. **~ful** a. incertain, douteux; (person) qui a des doutes. **~less** adv. sans doute.

dough /dəʊ/ n. pâte f.; (money: sl.) fric m.

doughnut /'dəʊnʌt/ n. beignet m.

douse /daʊs/ v.t. arroser; (light, fire) éteindre.

dove /dʌv/ n. colombe f.

Dover /'dəʊvə(r)/ n. Douvres m./f.

dovetail /'dʌvteɪl/ v.t./i. (s')ajuster.

dowdy /'daʊdɪ/ a. (-ier, -iest) (clothes) sans chic, monotone.

down[1] /daʊn/ n. (fluff) duvet m.

down[2] /daʊn/ adv. en bas; (of sun) couché; (lower) plus bas. —prep. en bas de; (along) le long de. —v.t. (knock down, shoot down) abattre; (drink) vider. **come** or **go ~**, descendre. **go ~**

to the post office, aller à la poste. **~-and-out** n. clochard(e) m. (f.). **~-hearted** a. découragé. **~-market** a. bas de gamme. **~ payment,** acompte m. **~-to-earth** a. terre-à-terre invar. **~ under,** aux antipodes. **~ with,** à bas.

downcast /'daʊnkɑ:st/ a. démoralisé.

downfall /'daʊnfɔ:l/ n. chute f.

downgrade /daʊn'greɪd/ v.t. déclasser.

downhill /daʊn'hɪl/ adv. **go ~**, descendre; (pej.) baisser.

downpour /'daʊnpɔ:(r)/ n. grosse averse f.

downright /'daʊnraɪt/ a. (utter) véritable; (honest) franc. —adv. carrément.

downs /daʊnz/ n. pl. région de collines f.

downstairs /daʊn'steəz/ adv. en bas. —a. d'en bas.

downstream /'daʊnstri:m/ adv. en aval.

downtown /'daʊntaʊn/ a. (Amer.) du centre de la ville. **~ Boston/**etc., le centre de Boston/etc.

downtrodden /'daʊntrɒdn/ a. opprimé.

downward /'daʊnwəd/ a. & adv., **~s** adv. vers le bas.

dowry /'daʊərɪ/ n. dot f.

doze /dəʊz/ v.i. sommeiller. **~ off,** s'assoupir. —n. somme m.

dozen /'dʌzn/ n. douzaine f. **a ~ eggs,** une douzaine d'œufs. **~s of,** (fam.) des dizaines de.

Dr abbr. (Doctor) Docteur.

drab /dræb/ a. terne.

draft[1] /drɑːft/ n. (outline) brouillon m.; (comm.) traite f. —v.t. faire le brouillon de; (draw up) rédiger. **the ~,** (mil., Amer.) la conscription. **a ~ treaty,** un projet de traité.

draft[2] /drɑːft/ n. (Amer.) = **draught**.

drag /dræg/ v.t./i. (p.t. **dragged**) traîner; (river) draguer; (pull away) arracher. —n. (task: fam.) corvée f.; (person: fam.) raseur, -se m., f. **in ~,** en travesti. **~ on,** s'éterniser.

dragon /'drægən/ n. dragon m.

dragon-fly /'drægənflaɪ/ n. libellule f.

drain /dreɪn/ v.t. (land) drainer; (vegetables) égoutter; (tank, glass) vider; (use up) épuiser. **~ (off),** (liquid) faire écouler. —v.i. **~ (off),** (of liquid) s'écouler. —n. (sewer) égout m. **~(-pipe),** tuyau d'écoulement m. **be a ~ on,** pomper. **~ing-board** n. égouttoir m.

drama /'drɑːmə/ n. art dramatique m., théâtre m.; (play, event) drame m. **~tic** /drə'mætɪk/ a. (situation) dramatique; (increase) spectaculaire. **~tist**

/'dræmətist/ n. dramaturge m. ~tize /'dræmətaɪz/ v.t. adapter pour la scène; (fig.) dramatiser.

drank /dræŋk/ see drink.

drape /dreɪp/ v.t. draper. ~s n. pl. (Amer.) rideaux m. pl.

drastic /'dræstɪk/ a. sévère.

draught /drɑːft/ n. courant d'air m. ~s, (game) dames f. pl. ~ beer, bière (à la) pression f. ~y a. plein de courants d'air.

draughtsman /'drɑːftsmən/ n. (pl. -men) dessinateur, -trice industriel(le) m., f.

draw /drɔː/ v.t. (p.t. drew, p.p. drawn) (pull) tirer; (attract) attirer; (pass) passer; (picture) dessiner; (line) tracer. —v.i. dessiner; (sport) faire match nul; (come, move) venir. —n. (sport) match nul m.; (in lottery) tirage au sort m. ~ back, (recoil) reculer. ~ near, (s')approcher (to, de). ~ out, (money) retirer. ~ up v.i. (stop) s'arrêter; v.t. (document) dresser; (chair) approcher.

drawback /'drɔːbæk/ n. inconvénient m.

drawbridge /'drɔːbrɪdʒ/ n. pont-levis m.

drawer /drɔː(r)/ n. tiroir m.

drawers /drɔːz/ n. pl. culotte f.

drawing /'drɔːɪŋ/ n. dessin m. ~-board n. planche à dessin f. ~-pin n. punaise f. ~-room n. salon m.

drawl /drɔːl/ n. voix traînante f.

drawn /drɔːn/ see draw. —a. (features) tiré; (match) nul.

dread /dred/ n. terreur f., crainte f. —v.t. redouter.

dreadful /'dredfl/ a. épouvantable, affreux. ~ly adv. terriblement.

dream /driːm/ n. rêve m. —v.t./i. (p.t. dreamed or dreamt) rêver. —a. (ideal) de ses rêves. ~ up, imaginer. ~er n. rêveur, -se m., f. ~y a. rêveur.

dreary /'drɪərɪ/ a. (-ier, -iest) triste; (boring) monotone. ~iness n. tristesse f.; monotonie f.

dredge /dredʒ/ n. drague f. —v.t./i. draguer. ~r /-ə(r)/ n. dragueur m.

dregs /dregz/ n. pl. lie f.

drench /drentʃ/ v.t. tremper.

dress /dres/ n. robe f.; (clothing) tenue f. —v.t./i. (s')habiller; (food) assaisonner; (wound) panser. ~ circle, premier balcon m. ~ rehearsal, répétition générale f. ~ up as, se déguiser en. get ~ed, s'habiller.

dresser /'dresə(r)/ n. buffet m.; (actor's) habilleur, -se m., f.

dressing /'dresɪŋ/ n. (sauce) assaisonne-

ment m.; (bandage) pansement m. ~-gown n. robe de chambre f. ~-room n. (sport) vestiaire m.; (theatre) loge f. ~-table n. coiffeuse f.

dressmak|er /'dresmeɪkə(r)/ n. couturière f. ~ing n. couture f.

dressy /'dresɪ/ a. (-ier, -iest) chic invar.

drew /druː/ see draw.

dribble /'drɪbl/ v.i. couler goutte à goutte; (person) baver; (football) dribbler.

dribs and drabs /drɪbzn'dræbz/ n. pl. petites quantités f. pl.

dried /draɪd/ a. (fruit etc.) sec.

drier /'draɪə(r)/ n. séchoir m.

drift /drɪft/ v.i. aller à la dérive; (pile up) s'amonceler. —n. dérive f.; amoncellement m.; (of events) tournure f.; (meaning) sens m. ~ towards, glisser vers. (snow) ~, congère f. ~er n. personne sans but dans la vie f.

driftwood /'drɪftwʊd/ n. bois flotté m.

drill /drɪl/ n. (tool) perceuse f.; (for teeth) roulette f.; (training) exercice m.; (procedure: fam.) marche à suivre f. (pneumatic) ~, marteau piqueur m. —v.t. percer; (train) entraîner. —v.i. être à l'exercice.

drily /'draɪlɪ/ adv. sèchement.

drink /drɪŋk/ v.t./i. (p.t. drank, p.p. drunk) boire. —n. (liquid) boisson f.; (glass of alcohol) verre m. a ~ of water, un verre d'eau. ~able a. (not unhealthy) potable; (palatable) buvable. ~er n. buveur, -se m., f. ~ing water, eau potable f.

drip /drɪp/ v.i. (p.t. dripped) (dé)goutter; (washing) s'égoutter. —n. goutte f.; (person: sl.) lavette f. ~-dry v.t. laisser égoutter; a. sans repassage.

dripping /'drɪpɪŋ/ n. (Amer. ~s) graisse de rôti f.

drive /draɪv/ v.t. (p.t. drove, p.p. driven) chasser, pousser; (vehicle) conduire; (machine) actionner. —v.i. conduire. —n. promenade en voiture f.; (private road) allée f.; (fig.) énergie f.; (psych.) instinct m.; (pol.) campagne f.; (auto.) traction; (golf, comput.) drive m. it's a two-hour ~, c'est deux heures en voiture. ~ at, en venir à. ~ away, (of car) partir. ~ in, (force in) enfoncer. ~ mad, rendre fou. left-hand ~, conduite à gauche f.

drivel /'drɪvl/ n. radotage m.

driver /'draɪvə(r)/ n. conducteur, -trice m., f., chauffeur m. ~'s license (Amer.), permis de conduire m.

driving /'draɪvɪŋ/ n. conduite f. ~

licence, permis de conduire *m*. ～ **rain,** pluie battante *f*. ～ **school,** auto-école *f*. **take one's** ～ **test,** passer son permis.

drizzle /'drɪzl/ *n*. bruine *f*. —*v.i.* bruiner.

dromedary /'drɒmədərɪ, (*Amer.*) 'drɒmədərɪ/ *n*. dromadaire *m*.

drone /drəʊn/ *n*. (*noise*) bourdonnement *m*.; (*bee*) faux bourdon *m*. —*v.i.* bourdonner; (*fig.*) parler d'une voix monotone.

drool /druːl/ *v.i.* baver (**over,** sur).

droop /druːp/ *v.i.* pencher, tomber.

drop /drɒp/ *n*. goutte *f*.; (*fall, lowering*) chute *f*. —*v.t./i.* (*p.t.* **dropped**) (*laisser*) tomber; (*decrease, lower*) baisser. ～ **(off),** (*person from car*) déposer. ～ **a line,** écrire un mot (**to,** à). ～ **in,** passer (**on, chez**). ～ **off,** (*doze*) s'assoupir. ～ **out,** se retirer (**of,** de); (*of student*) abandonner. ～**out** *n*. marginal(e) *m*. (*f.*), raté(e) *m*. (*f.*).

droppings /'drɒpɪŋz/ *n. pl.* crottes *f. pl.*

dross /drɒs/ *n*. déchets *m. pl.*

drought /draʊt/ *n*. sécheresse *f*.

drove /drəʊv/ *see* **drive.**

droves /drəʊvz/ *n. pl.* foule(s) *f*. (*pl.*).

drown /draʊn/ *v.t./i.* (se) noyer.

drowsy /'draʊzɪ/ *a*. somnolent. **be** *or* **feel** ～, avoir envie de dormir.

drudge /drʌdʒ/ *n*. esclave du travail *m*. ～**ry** /-ərɪ/ *n*. travail pénible et ingrat *m*.

drug /drʌg/ *n*. drogue *f*.; (*med.*) médicament *m*. —*v.t.* (*p.t.* **drugged**) droguer. ～ **addict,** drogué(e) *m*. (*f.*). ～**gist** *n*. pharmacien, -ne *m*., *f*.

drugstore /'drʌgstɔː(r)/ *n*. (*Amer.*) drugstore(ne) *m.(f.).*

drum /drʌm/ *n*. tambour *m*.; (*for oil*) bidon *m*. ～**s,** batterie *f*. —*v.i.* (*p.t.* **drummed**) tambouriner. —*v.t.* ～ **into s.o.,** répéter sans cesse à qn. ～ **up,** (*support*) susciter; (*business*) créer. ～**mer** *n*. tambour *m*.; (*in pop group*) batteur *m*.

drumstick /'drʌmstɪk/ *n*. baguette de tambour *f*.; (*of chicken*) pilon *m*.

drunk /drʌŋk/ *see* **drink.** —*a*. ivre. **get** ～, s'enivrer. —*n*., ～**ard** *n*. ivrogne(sse) *m*. (*f.*). ～**en** *a*. ivre; (*habitually*) ivrogne. ～**enness** *n*. ivresse *f*.

dry /draɪ/ *a*. (**drier, driest**) sec; (*day*) sans pluie. —*v.t./i.* (faire) sécher. **be** *or* **feel** ～, avoir soif. ～**-clean** *v.t.* nettoyer à sec. ～**-cleaner** *n*. teinturier *m*. ～ **run,** galop d'essai *m*. ～ **up,** (*dry dishes*) essuyer la vaisselle; (*of supplies*) (se) tarir; (*be silent: fam.*) se taire. ～**ness** *n*. sécheresse *f*.

dual /'djuːəl/ *a*. double. ～ **carriageway,** route à quatre voies *f*. ～**-purpose** *a*. qui fait double emploi.

dub /dʌb/ *v.t.* (*p.t.* **dubbed**) (*film*) doubler; (*nickname*) surnommer.

dubious /'djuːbɪəs/ *a*. (*pej.*) douteux. **be** ～ **about sth.,** (*person*) avoir des doutes sur qch.

duchess /'dʌtʃɪs/ *n*. duchesse *f*.

duck /dʌk/ *n*. canard *m*. —*v.i.* se baisser subitement. —*v.t.* (*head*) baisser; (*person*) plonger dans l'eau. ～**ling** *n*. caneton *m*.

duct /dʌkt/ *n*. conduit *m*.

dud /dʌd/ *a*. (*tool etc.: sl.*) mal fichu; (*coin: sl.*) faux; (*cheque: sl.*) sans provision. —*n*. **be a** ～, (*not work: sl.*) ne pas marcher.

dude /duːd/ *n*. (*Amer.*) dandy *m*.

due /djuː/ *a*. (*owing*) dû; (*expected*) attendu; (*proper*) qui convient. —*adv.* ～ **east**/*etc.*, droit vers l'est/*etc.* —*n*. dû *m*. ～**s,** droits *m. pl.*; (*of club*) cotisation *f*. ～ **to,** à cause de; (*caused by*) dû à. **she's** ～ **to leave now,** c'est prévu qu'elle parte maintenant. **in** ～ **course,** (*eventually*) avec le temps; (*at the right time*) en temps et lieu.

duel /'djuːəl/ *n*. duel *m*.

duet /djuː'et/ *n*. duo *m*.

duffle /'dʌfl/ *a*. ～ **bag,** sac de marin *m*. ～ **coat,** duffel-coat *m*.

dug /dʌg/ *see* **dig.**

duke /djuːk/ *n*. duc *m*.

dull /dʌl/ *a*. (**-er, -est**) ennuyeux; (*colour*) terne; (*weather*) morne; (*sound*) sourd; (*stupid*) bête; (*blunt*) émoussé. —*v.t.* (*pain*) amortir; (*mind*) engourdir.

duly /'djuːlɪ/ *adv.* comme il convient; (*in due time*) en temps voulu.

dumb /dʌm/ *a*. (**-er, -est**) muet; (*stupid: fam.*) bête.

dumbfound /dʌm'faʊnd/ *v.t.* sidérer, ahurir.

dummy /'dʌmɪ/ *n*. (*comm.*) article factice *m*.; (*of tailor*) mannequin *m*.; (*of baby*) sucette *f*. —*a*. factice. ～ **run,** galop d'essai *m*.

dump /dʌmp/ *v.t.* déposer; (*abandon: fam.*) se débarrasser de; (*comm.*) dumper. —*n*. tas d'ordures *m*.; (*refuse tip*) décharge *f*.; (*mil.*) dépôt *m*.; (*dull place: fam.*) trou *m*. **be in the** ～**s,** (*fam.*) avoir le cafard.

dumpling /'dʌmplɪŋ/ *n*. boulette de pâte *f*.

dumpy /'dʌmpɪ/ *a*. (**-ier, -iest**) boulot, rondelet.

dunce /dʌns/ n. cancre m., âne m.
dune /djuːn/ n. dune f.
dung /dʌŋ/ n. (*excrement*) bouse f., crotte f.; (*manure*) fumier m.
dungarees /dʌŋɡə'riːz/ n. pl. (*overalls*) salopette f.; (*jeans*: *Amer.*) jean m.
dungeon /'dʌndʒən/ n. cachot m.
dunk /dʌŋk/ v.t. tremper.
dupe /djuːp/ v.t. duper. —n. dupe f.
duplex /'djuːpleks/ n. duplex m.
duplicate[1] /'djuːplɪkət/ n. double m. —a. identique.
duplicat|e[2] /'djuːplɪkeɪt/ v.t. faire un double de; (*on machine*) polycopier. ~or n. duplicateur m.
duplicity /djuː'plɪsətɪ/ n. duplicité f.
durable /'djʊərəbl/ a. (*tough*) résistant; (*enduring*) durable.
duration /djʊ'reɪʃn/ n. durée f.
duress /djʊ'res/ n. contrainte f.
during /'djʊərɪŋ/ prep. pendant.
dusk /dʌsk/ n. crépuscule m.
dusky /'dʌskɪ/ a. (**-ier, -iest**) foncé.
dust /dʌst/ n. poussière f. —v.t. épousseter; (*sprinkle*) saupoudrer (**with,** de). ~-**jacket** n. jaquette f.
dustbin /'dʌstbɪn/ n. poubelle f.
duster /'dʌstə(r)/ n. chiffon m.
dustman /'dʌstmən/ n. (pl. **-men**) éboueur m.
dustpan /'dʌstpæn/ n. pelle à poussière f.
dusty /'dʌstɪ/ a. (**-ier, -iest**) poussiéreux.
Dutch /dʌtʃ/ a. hollandais. —n. (*lang.*) hollandais m. **go** ~, partager les frais. ~**man** n. Hollandais m. ~**woman** n. Hollandaise f.
dutiful /'djuːtɪfl/ a. obéissant.
dut|y /'djuːtɪ/ n. devoir m.; (*tax*) droit m. ~**ies,** (*of official etc.*) fonctions f. pl. ~**y-free** a. hors-taxe. **on** ~**y,** de service.
duvet /'duːveɪ/ n. couette f.
dwarf /dwɔːf/ n. (pl. **-fs**) nain(e) m. (f.). —v.t. rapetisser.
dwell /dwel/ v.i. (p.t. **dwelt**) demeurer. ~ **on,** s'étendre sur. ~**er** n. habitant(e) m. (f.). ~**ing** n. habitation f.
dwindle /'dwɪndl/ v.i. diminuer.
dye /daɪ/ v.t. (pres. p. **dyeing**) teindre. —n. teinture f.
dying /'daɪɪŋ/ a. mourant; (*art*) qui se perd.
dynamic /daɪ'næmɪk/ a. dynamique.
dynamism /'daɪnəmɪzəm/ n. dynamisme m.
dynamite /'daɪnəmaɪt/ n. dynamite f. —v.t. dynamiter.

dynamo /'daɪnəməʊ/ n. (pl. **-os**) dynamo f.
dynasty /'dɪnəstɪ, *Amer.* 'daɪnəstɪ/ n. dynastie f.
dysentery /'dɪsəntrɪ/ n. dysenterie f.
dyslexi|a /dɪs'leksɪə/ n. dyslexie f. ~**c** a. & n. dyslexique (m./f.)

E

each /iːtʃ/ a. chaque. —pron. chacun(e). ~ **one,** chacun(e). ~ **other,** l'un(e) l'autre, les un(e)s les autres. **know** ~ **other,** se connaître. **love** ~ **other,** s'aimer. **a pound** ~, (*get*) une livre chacun; (*cost*) une livre chaque.
eager /'iːɡə(r)/ a. impatient (**to,** de); (*supporter, desire*) ardent. **be** ~ **to,** (*want*) avoir envie de. ~ **for,** avide de. ~**ly** adv. avec impatience or ardeur. ~**ness** n. impatience f., désir m., ardeur f.
eagle /'iːɡl/ n. aigle m.
ear[1] /ɪə(r)/ n. oreille f. ~-**drum** n. tympan m. ~-**ring** n. boucle d'oreille f.
ear[2] /ɪə(r)/ n. (*of corn*) épi m.
earache /'ɪəreɪk/ n. mal à l'oreille m., mal d'oreille m.
earl /ɜːl/ n. comte m.
earlier /'ɜːlɪə(r)/ a. (*in series*) précédent; (*in history*) plus ancien, antérieur; (*in future*) plus avancé. —adv. précédemment; antérieurement; avant.
early /'ɜːlɪ/ (**-ier, -iest**) adv. tôt, de bonne heure; (*ahead of time*) en avance. —a. premier; (*hour*) matinal; (*fruit*) précoce; (*retirement*) anticipé. **have an** ~ **dinner,** dîner tôt. **in** ~ **summer,** au début de l'été.
earmark /'ɪəmɑːk/ v.t. destiner, réserver (**for,** à).
earn /ɜːn/ v.t. gagner; (*interest: comm.*) rapporter. ~ **s.o. sth.,** (*bring*) valoir qch. à qn.
earnest /'ɜːnɪst/ a. sérieux. **in** ~, sérieusement.
earnings /'ɜːnɪŋz/ n. pl. salaire m.; (*profits*) bénéfices m. pl.
earphone /'ɪəfəʊn/ n. écouteur m.
earshot /'ɪəʃɒt/ n. **within** ~, à portée de voix.
earth /ɜːθ/ n. terre f. —v.t. (*electr.*) mettre à la terre. **why/how/where on** ~ ... ?, pourquoi/comment/où diable ... ? ~**ly** a. terrestre.
earthenware /'ɜːθnweə(r)/ n. faïence f.

earthquake /'ɜ:θkweɪk/ n. tremblement de terre m.

earthy /'ɜ:θɪ/ a. (of earth) terreux; (coarse) grossier.

earwig /'ɪəwɪg/ n. perce-oreille m.

ease /iːz/ n. aisance f., facilité f.; (comfort) bien-être m. —v.t./i. (se) calmer; (relax) (se) détendre; (slow down) ralentir; (slide) glisser. **at ~**, à l'aise; (mil.) au repos. **with ~**, aisément.

easel /'iːzl/ n. chevalet m.

east /iːst/ n. est m. —a. d'est. —adv. vers l'est. **the E~**, (Orient) l'Orient m. **~erly** a. d'est. **~ern** a. de l'est, oriental. **~ward** a. à l'est. **~wards** adv. vers l'est.

Easter /'iːstə(r)/ n. Pâques f. pl. (or m. sing.). **~ egg**, œuf de Pâques m.

easy /'iːzɪ/ a. (-ier, -iest) facile; (relaxed) aisé. **~ chair**, fauteuil m. **go ~ with**, (fam.) y aller doucement avec. **take it ~**, ne pas se fatiguer. **easily** adv. facilement.

easygoing /iːzɪ'gəʊɪŋ/ a. (with people) accommodant; (relaxed) décontracté.

eat /iːt/ v.t./i. (p.t. **ate**, p.p. **eaten**) manger. **~ into**, ronger. **~able** a. mangeable. **~er** n. mangeur, -se m., f.

eau-de-Cologne /əʊdəkə'ləʊn/ n. eau de Cologne f.

eaves /iːvz/ n. pl. avant-toit m.

eavesdrop /'iːvzdrɒp/ v.i. (p.t. **-dropped**). **~ (on)**, écouter en cachette.

ebb /eb/ n. reflux m. —v.i. refluer; (fig.) décliner.

ebony /'ebənɪ/ n. ébène f.

ebullient /ɪ'bʌlɪənt/ a. exubérant.

EC abbr. (European Community) CE.

eccentric /ɪk'sentrɪk/ a. & n. excentrique (m./f.). **~ity** /eksen'trɪsətɪ/ n. excentricité f.

ecclesiastical /ɪkliːzɪ'æstɪkl/ a. ecclésiastique.

echo /'ekəʊ/ n. (pl. **-oes**) écho m. —v.t./i. (p.t. **echoed**, pres. p. **echoing**) (se) répercuter; (fig.) répéter.

eclipse /ɪ'klɪps/ n. éclipse f. —v.t. éclipser.

ecolog|y /iː'kɒlədʒɪ/ n. écologie f. **~ical** /iːkə'lɒdʒɪkl/ a. écologique.

economic /iːkə'nɒmɪk/ a. économique; (profitable) rentable. **~al** a. économique; (person) économe. **~s** n. économie politique f.

economist /ɪ'kɒnəmɪst/ n. économiste m./f.

econom|y /ɪ'kɒnəmɪ/ n. économie f. **~ize** v.i. **~ (on)**, économiser.

ecosystem /'iːkəʊsɪstəm/ n. écosystème m.

ecstasy /'ekstəsɪ/ n. extase f.

ECU /'eɪkjuː/ n. ÉCU m.

eczema /'eksɪmə/ n. eczéma m.

eddy /'edɪ/ n. tourbillon m.

edge /edʒ/ n. bord m.; (of town) abords m. pl.; (of knife) tranchant m. —v.t. border. —v.i. (move) se glisser. **have the ~ on**, (fam.) l'emporter sur. **on ~**, énervé.

edgeways /'edʒweɪz/ adv. de côte. **I can't get a word in ~**, je ne peux pas placer un mot.

edging /'edʒɪŋ/ n. bordure f.

edgy /'edʒɪ/ a. énervé.

edible /'edɪbl/ a. mangeable; (not poisonous) comestible.

edict /'iːdɪkt/ n. décret m.

edifice /'edɪfɪs/ n. édifice m.

edify /'edɪfaɪ/ v.t. édifier.

edit /'edɪt/ v.t. (p.t. **edited**) (newspaper) diriger; (prepare text of) mettre au point, préparer; (write) rédiger; (cut) couper.

edition /ɪ'dɪʃn/ n. édition f.

editor /'edɪtə(r)/ n. (writer) rédacteur, -trice m., f.; (annotator) éditeur, -trice m., f. **the ~ (in chief)**, le rédacteur en chef. **~ial** /-'tɔːrɪəl/ a. de la rédaction; n. éditorial m.

educat|e /'edʒʊkeɪt/ v.t. instruire; (mind, public) éduquer. **~ed** a. instruit. **~ion** /-'keɪʃn/ n. éducation f.; (schooling) enseignement m. **~ional** /-'keɪʃənl/ a. pédagogique, éducatif.

EEC abbr. (European Economic Community) CEE f.

eel /iːl/ n. anguille f.

eerie /'ɪərɪ/ a. (-ier, -iest) sinistre.

effect /ɪ'fekt/ n. effet m. —v.t. effectuer. **come into ~**, entrer en vigueur. **in ~**, effectivement. **take ~**, agir.

effective /ɪ'fektɪv/ a. efficace; (striking) frappant; (actual) effectif. **~ly** adv. efficacement; de manière frappante; effectivement. **~ness** n. efficacité f.

effeminate /ɪ'femɪnət/ a. efféminé.

effervescent /efə'vesnt/ a. effervescent.

efficien|t /ɪ'fɪʃnt/ a. efficace; (person) compétent. **~cy** n. efficacité f.; compétence f. **~tly** adv. efficacement.

effigy /'efɪdʒɪ/ n. effigie f.

effort /'efət/ n. effort m. **~less** a. facile.

effrontery /ɪ'frʌntərɪ/ n. effronterie f.

effusive /ɪ'fjuːsɪv/ a. expansif.

e.g. /iː'dʒiː/ abbr. par exemple.

egalitarian /ɪgælɪ'teərɪən/ a. égalitaire. —n. égalitariste m./f.

egg[1] /eg/ *n.* œuf *m.* **~-cup** *n.* coquetier *m.* **~-plant** *n.* aubergine *f.*

egg[2] /eg/ *v.t.* **~ on,** (*fam.*) inciter.

eggshell /'egʃel/ *n.* coquille d'œuf *f.*

ego /'i:gəʊ/ *n.* (*pl.* -os) moi *m.* **~(t)ism** *n.* égoïsme *m.* **~(t)ist** *n.* égoïste *m./f.*

Egypt /'i:dʒɪpt/ *n.* Égypte *f.* **~ian** /ɪ'dʒɪpʃn/ *a.* & *n.* égyptien(ne) (*m.* (*f.*)).

eh /eɪ/ *int.* (*fam.*) hein.

eiderdown /'aɪdədaʊn/ *n.* édredon *m.*

eight /eɪt/ *a.* & *n.* huit (*m.*). **eighth** /eɪtθ/ *a.* & *n.* huitième (*m./f.*).

eighteen /eɪ'ti:n/ *a.* & *n.* dix-huit (*m.*). **~th** *a.* & *n.* dix-huitième (*m./f.*).

eight|y /'eɪtɪ/ *a.* & *n.* quatre-vingts (*m.*) **~ieth** *a.* & *n.* quatre-vingtième (*m./f.*).

either /'aɪðə(r)/ *a.* & *pron.* l'un(e) ou l'autre; (*with negative*) ni l'un(e) ni l'autre; (*each*) chaque. —*adv.* non plus. —*conj.* **~ . . . or,** ou (bien) . . . ou (bien); (*with negative*) ni . . . ni.

eject /ɪ'dʒekt/ *v.t.* éjecter. **~or seat,** siège éjectable *m.*

eke /i:k/ *v.t.* **~ out,** faire durer; (*living*) gagner difficilement.

elaborate[1] /ɪ'læbərət/ *a.* compliqué, recherché.

elaborate[2] /ɪ'læbəreɪt/ *v.t.* élaborer. —*v.i.* préciser. **~ on,** s'étendre sur.

clapse /ɪ'læps/ *v.i.* s'écouler.

elastic /ɪ'læstɪk/ *a.* & *n.* élastique (*m.*). **~ band,** élastique *m.* **~ity** /elæ'stɪsətɪ/ *n.* élasticité *f.*

elated /ɪ'leɪtɪd/ *a.* fou de joie.

elbow /'elbəʊ/ *n.* coude *m.* **~ room,** possibilité de manœuvrer *f.*

elder[1] /'eldə(r)/ *a.* & *n.* aîné(e) (*m.* (*f.*)).

elder[2] /'eldə(r)/ *n.* (*tree*) sureau *m.*

elderly /'eldəlɪ/ *a.* (assez) âgé.

eldest /'eldɪst/ *a.* & *n.* aîné(e) (*m.* (*f.*))

elect /ɪ'lekt/ *v.t.* élire. —*a.* (*president etc.*) futur. **~ to do,** choisir de faire. **~ion** /-kʃn/ *n.* élection *f.*

elector /ɪ'lektə(r)/ *n.* électeur, -trice *m.*, *f.* **~al** *a.* électoral. **~ate** *n.* électorat *m.*

electric /ɪ'lektrɪk/ *a.* électrique. **~ blanket,** couverture chauffante *f.* **~al** *a.* électrique.

electrician /ɪlek'trɪʃn/ *n.* électricien *m.*

electricity /ɪlek'trɪsətɪ/ *n.* électricité *f.*

electrify /ɪ'lektrɪfaɪ/ *v.t.* électrifier; (*excite*) électriser.

electrocute /ɪ'lektrəkju:t/ *v.t.* électrocuter.

electron /ɪ'lektrɒn/ *n.* électron *m.*

electronic /ɪlek'trɒnɪk/ *a.* électronique. **~s** *n.* électronique *f.*

elegan|t /'elɪgənt/ *a.* élégant. **~ce** *n.* élégance *f.* **~tly** *adv.* élégamment.

element /'elɪmənt/ *n.* élément *m.*; (*of heater etc.*) résistance *f.* **~ary** /-'mentrɪ/ *a.* élémentaire.

elephant /'elɪfənt/ *n.* éléphant *m.*

elevat|e /'elɪveɪt/ *v.t.* élever. **~ion** /-'veɪʃn/ *n.* élévation *f.*

elevator /'elɪveɪtə(r)/ *n.* (*Amer.*) ascenseur *m.*

eleven /ɪ'levn/ *a.* & *n.* onze (*m.*). **~th** *a.* & *n.* onzième (*m./f.*).

elf /elf/ (*pl.* **elves**) lutin *m.*

elicit /ɪ'lɪsɪt/ *v.t.* obtenir (**from,** de).

eligible /'elɪdʒəbl/ *a.* admissible (**for,** à). **be ~ for,** (*entitled to*) avoir droit à.

eliminat|e /ɪ'lɪmɪneɪt/ *v.t.* éliminer. **~ion** /-'neɪʃn/ *n.* élimination *f.*

élit|e /eɪ'li:t/ *n.* élite *f.* **~ist** *a.* & *n.* élitiste (*m./f.*).

ellip|se /ɪ'lɪps/ *n.* ellipse *f.* **~tical** *a.* elliptique.

elm /elm/ *n.* orme *m.*

elocution /elə'kju:ʃn/ *n.* élocution *f.*

elongate /'i:lɒŋgeɪt/ *v.t.* allonger.

elope /ɪ'ləʊp/ *v.i.* s'enfuir. **~ment** *n.* fugue (amoureuse) *f.*

eloquen|t /'eləkwənt/ *a.* éloquent. **~ce** *n.* éloquence *f.* **~tly** *adv.* avec éloquence.

else /els/ *adv.* d'autre. **everybody ~,** tous les autres **nobody ~,** personne d'autre. **nothing ~,** rien d'autre. **or ~,** ou bien. **somewhere ~,** autre part. **~ where** *adv.* ailleurs.

elucidate /ɪ'lu:sɪdeɪt/ *v.t.* élucider.

elude /ɪ'lu:d/ *v.t.* échapper à; (*question*) éluder.

elusive /ɪ'lu:sɪv/ *a.* insaisissable.

emaciated /ɪ'meɪʃɪeɪtɪd/ *a.* émacié.

emanate /'eməneɪt/ *v.i.* émaner.

emancipat|e /ɪ'mænsɪpeɪt/ *v.t.* émanciper. **~ion** /-'peɪʃn/ *n.* émancipation *f.*

embalm /ɪm'bɑ:m/ *v.t.* embaumer.

embankment /ɪm'bæŋkmənt/ *n.* (*of river*) quai *m.*; (*of railway*) remblai *m.*, talus *m.*

embargo /ɪm'bɑ:gəʊ/ *n.* (*pl.* -oes) embargo *m.*

embark /ɪm'bɑ:k/ *v.t./i.* (s')embarquer. **~ on,** (*business etc.*) se lancer dans; (*journey*) commencer. **~ation** /embɑ:'keɪʃn/ *n.* embarquement *m.*

embarrass /ɪm'bærəs/ *v.t.* embarrasser, gêner. **~ment** *n.* embarras *m.*, gêne *f.*

embassy /'embəsɪ/ *n.* ambassade *f.*

embed /ɪm'bed/ *v.t.* (*p.t.* **embedded**) encastrer.

embellish /ɪm'belɪʃ/ *v.t.* embellir. **~ment** *n.* enjolivement *m.*

embers /'embəz/ *n. pl.* braise *f.*

embezzle /ɪmˈbezl/ v.t. détourner. ~ment n. détournement de fonds m. ~r /-ə(r)/ n. escroc m.

embitter /ɪmˈbɪtə(r)/ v.t. (person) aigrir; (situation) envenimer.

emblem /ˈembləm/ n. emblème m.

embod|y /ɪmˈbɒdɪ/ v.t. incarner, exprimer; (include) contenir. ~iment n. incarnation f.

emboss /ɪmˈbɒs/ v.t. (metal) repousser; (paper) gaufrer.

embrace /ɪmˈbreɪs/ v.t./i. (s')embrasser. —n. étreinte f.

embroider /ɪmˈbrɔɪdə(r)/ v.t. broder. ~y n. broderie f.

embroil /ɪmˈbrɔɪl/ v.t. mêler (in, à).

embryo /ˈembrɪəʊ/ n. (pl. -os) embryon m. ~nic /-ˈɒnɪk/ a. embryonnaire.

emend /ɪˈmend/ v.t. corriger.

emerald /ˈemərəld/ n. émeraude f.

emerge /ɪˈmɜːdʒ/ v.i. apparaître. ~nce /-əns/ n. apparition f.

emergency /ɪˈmɜːdʒənsɪ/ n. (crisis) crise f.; (urgent case: med.) urgence f. —a. d'urgence. ~ exit, sortie de secours f. ~ landing, atterrissage forcé. in an ~, en cas d'urgence.

emery /ˈemərɪ/ n. émeri m.

emigrant /ˈemɪɡrənt/ n. émigrant(e) m. (f.).

emigrat|e /ˈemɪɡreɪt/ v.i. émigrer. ~ion /-ˈɡreɪʃn/ n. émigration f.

eminen|t /ˈemɪnənt/ a. éminent. ~ce n. éminence f. ~tly adv. éminemment, parfaitement.

emissary /ˈemɪsərɪ/ n. émissaire m.

emi|t /ɪˈmɪt/ v.t. (p.t. emitted) émettre. ~ssion n. émission f.

emotion /ɪˈməʊʃn/ n. émotion f. ~al a. (person, shock) émotif; (speech, scene) émouvant.

emotive /ɪˈməʊtɪv/ a. émotif.

emperor /ˈempərə(r)/ n. empereur m.

emphasis /ˈemfəsɪs/ n. (on word) accent m. lay ~ on, mettre l'accent sur.

emphasize /ˈemfəsaɪz/ v.t. souligner; (syllable) insister sur.

emphatic /ɪmˈfætɪk/ a. catégorique; (manner) énergique.

empire /ˈempaɪə(r)/ n. empire m.

employ /ɪmˈplɔɪ/ v.t. employer. ~er n. employeu|r, -se m., f. ~ment n. emploi m. ~ment agency, agence de placement f.

employee /emplɔɪˈiː/ n. employé(e) m. (f.).

empower /ɪmˈpaʊə(r)/ v.t. autoriser (to do, à faire).

empress /ˈemprɪs/ n. impératrice f.

empt|y /ˈemptɪ/ a. (-ier, -est) vide; (promise) vain. —v.t./i. (se) vider. ~y-handed a. les mains vides. on an ~y stomach, à jeun. ~ies n. pl. bouteilles vides f. pl. ~iness n. vide m.

emulat|e /ˈemjʊleɪt/ v.t. imiter. ~ion /-ˈleɪʃn/ n. (comput.) émulation f.

emulsion /ɪˈmʌlʃn/ n. émulsion f. ~ (paint), peinture-émulsion f.

enable /ɪˈneɪbl/ v.t. ~ s.o. to, permettre à qn. de.

enact /ɪˈnækt/ v.t. (law) promulguer; (scene) représenter.

enamel /ɪˈnæml/ n. émail m. —v.t. (p.t. enamelled) émailler.

enamoured /ɪˈnæməd/ a. be ~ of, aimer beaucoup, être épris de.

encampment /ɪnˈkæmpmənt/ n. campement m.

encase /ɪnˈkeɪs/ v.t. (cover) recouvrir (in, de); (enclose) enfermer (in, dans).

enchant /ɪnˈtʃɑːnt/ v.t. enchanter. ~ing a. enchanteur. ~ment n. enchantement m.

encircle /ɪnˈsɜːkl/ v.t. encercler.

enclave /ˈenkleɪv/ n. enclave f.

enclose /ɪnˈkləʊz/ v.t. (land) clôturer; (with letter) joindre. ~d a. (space) clos; (market) couvert; (with letter) ci-joint.

enclosure /ɪnˈkləʊʒə(r)/ n. enceinte f.; (comm.) pièce jointe f.

encompass /ɪnˈkʌmpəs/ v.t. (include) inclure.

encore /ˈɒŋkɔː(r)/ int. & n. bis (m.).

encounter /ɪnˈkaʊntə(r)/ v.t. rencontrer. —n. rencontre f.

encourage /ɪnˈkʌrɪdʒ/ v.t. encourager. ~ment n. encouragement m.

encroach /ɪnˈkrəʊtʃ/ v.i. ~ upon, empiéter sur.

encumber /ɪnˈkʌmbə(r)/ v.t. encombrer.

encyclical /ɪnˈsɪklɪkl/ n. encyclique f.

encyclopaed|ia, encycloped|ia /ɪnsaɪkləˈpiːdɪə/ n. encyclopédie f. ~ic a. encyclopédique.

end /end/ n. fin f.; (farthest part) bout m. —v.t./i. (se) terminer. ~ up doing, finir par faire. come to an ~, prendre fin. ~-product, produit fini m. in the ~, finalement. no ~ of, (fam.) énormément de. on ~, (upright) debout; (in a row) de suite. put an ~ to, mettre fin à.

endanger /ɪnˈdeɪndʒə(r)/ v.t. mettre en danger.

endear|ing /ɪnˈdɪərɪŋ/ a. attachant. ~ment n. parole tendre f.

endeavour, (Amer.) **endeavor** /ɪnˈdevə(r)/ n. effort m. —v.i. s'efforcer (to, de).

ending /'endɪŋ/ n. fin f.

endive /'endɪv/ n. chicorée f.

endless /'endlɪs/ a. interminable; (*times*) innombrable; (*patience*) infini.

endorse /ɪn'dɔːs/ v.t. (*document*) endosser; (*action*) approuver. ∼ment n. (*auto.*) contravention f.

endow /ɪn'daʊ/ v.t. doter. ∼ed with, doté de. ∼ment n. dotation f. (of, de).

endur|e /ɪn'djʊə(r)/ v.t. supporter. —v.i. durer. ∼able a. supportable. ∼ance n. endurance f. ∼ing a. durable.

enemy /'enəmɪ/ n. & a. ennemi(e) (*m. (f.)*).

energetic /enə'dʒetɪk/ a. énergique.

energy /'enədʒɪ/ n. énergie f.

enforce /ɪn'fɔːs/ v.t. appliquer, faire respecter; (*impose*) imposer (on, à). ∼d a. forcé.

engage /ɪn'geɪdʒ/ v.t. engager. —v.i. ∼ in, prendre part à. ∼d a. fiancé; (*busy*) occupé. get ∼d, se fiancer. ∼ment n. fiançailles f. pl.; (*meeting*) rendez-vous m.; (*undertaking*) engagement m.

engaging /ɪn'geɪdʒɪŋ/ a. engageant, séduisant.

engender /ɪn'dʒendə(r)/ v.t. engendrer.

engine /'endʒɪn/ n. moteur m.; (*of train*) locomotive f.; (*of ship*) machine f. ∼driver n. mécanicien m.

engineer /endʒɪ'nɪə(r)/ n. ingénieur m.; (*appliance repairman*) dépanneur m. —v.t. (*contrive: fam.*) machiner. ∼ing n. (*mechanical*) mécanique f.; (*roadbuilding etc.*) génie m.

England /'ɪŋglənd/ n. Angleterre f.

English /'ɪŋglɪʃ/ a. anglais. —n. (*lang.*) anglais m. ∼-speaking a. anglophone. the ∼, les Anglais m. pl. ∼man n. Anglais m. ∼woman n. Anglaise f.

engrav|e /ɪn'greɪv/ v.t. graver. ∼ing n. gravure f.

engrossed /ɪn'grəʊst/ a. absorbé (in, par).

engulf /ɪn'gʌlf/ v.t. engouffrer.

enhance /ɪn'hɑːns/ v.t. rehausser; (*price, value*) augmenter.

enigma /ɪ'nɪgmə/ n. énigme f. ∼tic /enɪg'mætɪk/ a. énigmatique.

enjoy /ɪn'dʒɔɪ/ v.t. aimer (*doing*, faire); (*benefit from*) jouir de. ∼ o.s., s'amuser. ∼ your meal, bon appétit! ∼able a. agréable. ∼ment n. plaisir m.

enlarge /ɪn'lɑːdʒ/ v.t./i. (s')agrandir. ∼ upon, s'étendre sur. ∼ment n. agrandissement m.

enlighten /ɪn'laɪtn/ v.t. éclairer. ∼ment n. édification f.; (*information*) éclaircissements m. pl.

enlist /ɪn'lɪst/ v.t. (*person*) recruter; (*fig.*) obtenir. —v.i. s'engager.

enliven /ɪn'laɪvn/ v.t. animer.

enmity /'enmətɪ/ n. inimitié f.

enormity /ɪ'nɔːmətɪ/ n. énormité f.

enormous /ɪ'nɔːməs/ a. énorme. ∼ly adv. énormément.

enough /ɪ'nʌf/ adv. & n. assez. —a. assez de. ∼ glasses/time/etc., assez de verres/de temps/etc. have ∼ of, en avoir assez de.

enquir|e /ɪn'kwaɪə(r)/ v.t./i. demander. ∼e about, se renseigner sur. ∼y n. demande de renseignements f.

enrage /ɪn'reɪdʒ/ v.t. mettre en rage, rendre furieux.

enrich /ɪn'rɪtʃ/ v.t. enrichir.

enrol, (*Amer.*) enroll /ɪn'rəʊl/ v.t./i. (p.t. enrolled) (s')inscrire. ∼ment n. inscription f.

ensconce /ɪn'skɒns/ v.t. ∼ o.s., bien s'installer.

ensemble /ɒn'sɒmbl/ n. (*clothing & mus.*) ensemble m.

ensign /'ensən, 'ensaɪn/ n. (*flag*) pavillon m.

enslave /ɪn'sleɪv/ v.t. asservir.

ensue /ɪn'sjuː/ v.i. s'ensuivre.

ensure /ɪn'ʃʊə(r)/ v.t. assurer. ∼ that, (*ascertain*) s'assurer que.

entail /ɪn'teɪl/ v.t. entraîner.

entangle /ɪn'tæŋgl/ v.t. emmêler.

enter /'entə(r)/ v.t. (*room, club, race, etc.*) entrer dans; (*note down, register*) inscrire; (*data*) entrer, saisir. —v.i. entrer (into, dans). ∼ for, s'inscrire à.

enterprise /'entəpraɪz/ n. entreprise f.; (*boldness*) initiative f.

enterprising /'entəpraɪzɪŋ/ a. entreprenant.

entertain /entə'teɪn/ v.t. amuser, divertir; (*guests*) recevoir; (*ideas*) considérer. ∼er n. artiste m./f. ∼ing a. divertissant. ∼ment n. amusement m., divertissement m.; (*performance*) spectacle m.

enthral, (*Amer.*) enthrall /ɪn'θrɔːl/ v.t. (p.t. enthralled) captiver.

enthuse /ɪn'θjuːz/ v.i. ∼ over, s'enthousiasmer pour.

enthusiasm /ɪn'θjuːzɪæzəm/ n. enthousiasme m.

enthusiast /ɪn'θjuːzɪæst/ n. fervent(e) m. (f.), passionné(e) m. (f.) (for, de). ∼ic /-'æstɪk/ a. (*supporter*) enthousiaste. be ∼ic about, être enthousiasmé par. ∼ically /-'æstɪklɪ/ adv. avec enthousiasme.

entice /ɪn'taɪs/ v.t. attirer. ∼ to do,

entraîner à faire. **∿ment** n. (*attraction*) attrait m.

entire /ɪn'taɪə(r)/ a. entier. **∿ly** adv. entièrement.

entirety /ɪn'taɪərətɪ/ n. **in its ∿**, en entier.

entitle /ɪn'taɪtl/ v.t. donner droit à (**to sth.**, à qch.; **to do**, de faire). **∿d** a. (*book*) intitulé. **be ∿d to sth.**, avoir droit à qch. **∿ment** n. droit m.

entity /'entətɪ/ n. entité f.

entrails /'entreɪlz/ n. pl. entrailles f. pl.

entrance¹ /'entrəns/ n. (*entering, way in*) entrée f. (**to**, de); (*right to enter*) admission f. —a. (*charge, exam*) d'entrée.

entrance² /ɪn'trɑ:ns/ v.t. transporter.

entrant /'entrənt/ n. (*sport*) concurrent(e) m. (f.); (*in exam*) candidat(e) m. (f.).

entreat /ɪn'tri:t/ v.t. supplier.

entrenched /ɪn'trentʃt/ a. ancré.

entrepreneur /ɒntrəprə'nɜ:(r)/ n. entrepreneur m.

entrust /ɪn'trʌst/ v.t. conflier.

entry /'entrɪ/ n. (*entrance*) entrée f.; (*word on list*) mot inscrit m. **∿ form**, feuille d'inscription f.

enumerate /ɪ'nju:məreɪt/ v.t. énumérer.

enunciate /ɪ'nʌnsɪeɪt/ v.t. (*word*) articuler; (*ideas*) énoncer.

envelop /ɪn'veləp/ v.t. (*p.t.* **enveloped**) envelopper.

envelope /'envələup/ n. enveloppe f.

enviable /'envɪəbl/ a. enviable.

envious /'envɪəs/ a. envieux (**of sth.**, de qch.). **∿ of s.o.**, jaloux de qn. **∿ly** adv. avec envie.

environment /ɪn'vaɪərənmənt/ n. milieu m.; (*ecological*) environnement m. **∿al** /-'mentl/ a. du milieu; de l'environnement. **∿alist** n. spécialiste de l'environnement m./f.

envisage /ɪn'vɪzɪdʒ/ v.t. envisager.

envoy /'envɔɪ/ n. envoyé(e) m. (f.).

envy /'envɪ/ n. envie f. —v.t. envier.

enzyme /'enzaɪm/ n. enzyme m.

ephemeral /ɪ'femərəl/ a. éphémère.

epic /'epɪk/ n. épopée f. —a. épique.

epidemic /epɪ'demɪk/ n. épidémie f.

epilep|sy /'epɪlepsɪ/ n. épilepsie f. **∿tic** /-'leptɪk/ a. & n. épileptique (m./f.).

episode /'epɪsəud/ n. épisode m.

epistle /ɪ'pɪsl/ n. épître f.

epitaph /'epɪtɑ:f/ n. épitaphe f.

epithet /'epɪθet/ n. épithète f.

epitom|e /ɪ'pɪtəmɪ/ n. (*embodiment*) modèle m.; (*summary*) résumé m. **∿ize** v.t. incarner.

epoch /'i:pɒk/ n. époque f. **∿-making** a. qui fait époque.

equal /'i:kwəl/ a. & n. égal(e) (m.f.). —v.t. (*p.t.* **equalled**) égaler. **∿ opportunities/rights**, égalité des chances/ droits f. **∿ to**, (*task*) à la hauteur de. **∿ity** /ɪ'kwɒlətɪ/ n. égalité f. **∿ly** adv. également; (*just as*) tout aussi.

equalize /'i:kwəlaɪz/ v.t./i. égaliser. **∿r** /-ə(r)/ n. (*goal*) but égalisateur m.

equanimity /ekwə'nɪmətɪ/ n. égalité d'humeur f., calme m.

equate /ɪ'kweɪt/ v.t. assimiler, égaler (**with**, à).

equation /ɪ'kweɪʒn/ n. équation f.

equator /ɪ'kweɪtə(r)/ n. équateur m. **∿ial** /ekwə'tɔ:rɪəl/ a. équatorial.

equilibrium /i:kwɪ'lɪbrɪəm/ n. équilibre m.

equinox /'i:kwɪnɒks/ n. équinoxe m.

equip /ɪ'kwɪp/ v.t. (*p.t.* **equipped**) équiper (**with**, de). **∿ment** n. équipement m.

equitable /'ekwɪtəbl/ a. équitable.

equity /'ekwətɪ/ n. équité f.

equivalen|t /ɪ'kwɪvələnt/ a. & n. équivalent (m.). **∿ce** n. équivalence f.

equivocal /ɪ'kwɪvəkl/ a. équivoque.

era /'ɪərə/ n. ère f., époque f.

eradicate /ɪ'rædɪkeɪt/ v.t. supprimer, éliminer.

erase /ɪ'reɪz/ v.t. effacer. **∿r**/-ə(r)/ n. (*rubber*) gomme f.

erect /ɪ'rekt/ a. droit. —v.t. ériger. **∿ion** /-kʃn/ n. érection f.

ermine /'ɜ:mɪn/ n. hermine f.

ero|de /ɪ'rəud/ v.t. ronger. **∿sion** n. érosion f.

erotic /ɪ'rɒtɪk/ a. érotique. **∿ism** /-sɪzəm/ n. érotisme m.

err /ɜ:(r)/ v.i. (*be mistaken*) se tromper; (*sin*) pécher.

errand /'erənd/ n. course f.

erratic /ɪ'rætɪk/ a. (*uneven*) irrégulier; (*person*) capricieux.

erroneous /ɪ'rəunɪəs/ a. erroné.

error /'erə(r)/ n. erreur f.

erudit|e /'eru:daɪt, *Amer.* 'erjʊdaɪt/ a. érudit. **∿ion** /-'dɪʃn/ n. érudition f.

erupt /ɪ'rʌpt/ v.i. (*volcano*) entrer en éruption; (*fig.*) éclater. **∿ion** /-pʃn/ n. éruption f.

escalat|e /'eskəleɪt/ v.t./i. (s')intensifier; (*of prices*) monter en flèche. **∿ion** /-'leɪʃn/ n. escalade f.

escalator /'eskəleɪtə(r)/ n. escalier mécanique m., escalator m.

escapade /eskə'peɪd/ n. fredaine f.

escape /ɪ'skeɪp/ v.i. s'échapper (**from a**

place, d'un lieu); (*prisoner*) s'évader. —*v.t.* échapper à. —*n.* fuite *f.*, évasion *f.*; (*of gas etc.*) fuite *f.* ~ **from s.o.,** échapper à qn. ~ **to,** s'enfuir dans. **have a lucky** *or* **narrow** ~, l'échapper belle.

escapism /ɪ'skeɪpɪzəm/ *n.* évasion (de la réalité) *f.*

escort[1] /'eskɔːt/ *n.* (*guard*) escorte *f.*; (*of lady*) cavalier *m.*

escort[2] /ɪ'skɔːt/ *v.t.* escorter.

Eskimo /'eskɪməʊ/ *n.* (*pl.* -os) Esquimau(de) *m.* (*f.*).

especial /ɪ'speʃl/ *a.* particulier. ~**ly** *adv.* particulièrement.

espionage /'espɪənɑːʒ/ *n.* espionnage *m.*

esplanade /esplə'neɪd/ *n.* esplanade *f.*

espresso /e'spresəʊ/ *n.* (*pl.* -os) (café) express *m.*

essay /'eseɪ/ *n.* essai *m.*; (*schol.*) rédacton *f.*; (*univ.*) dissertation *f.*

essence /'esns/ *n.* essence *f.*; (*main point*) essentiel *m.*

essential /ɪ'senʃl/ *a.* essentiel. —*n. pl.* **the** ~**s,** l'essentiel *m.* ~**ly** *adv* essentiellement.

establish /ɪ'stæblɪʃ/ *v.t.* établir; (*business, state*) fonder. ~**ment** *n.* établissement *m.*; fondation *f.* **the E**~**ment,** les pouvoirs établis.

estate /ɪ'steɪt/ *n.* (*land*) propriété *f.*; (*possessions*) biens *m. pl.*; (*inheritance*) succession *f.*; (*district*) cité *f.*, complexe *m.* ~ **agent,** agent immobilier *m.* ~ **car,** break *m.*

esteem /ɪ'stiːm/ *v.t.* estimer. —*n.* estime *f.*

esthetic /es'θetɪk/ *a.* (*Amer.*) = **aesthetic.**

estimate[1] /'estɪmət/ *n.* (*calculation*) estimation *f.*; (*comm.*) devis *m.*

estimate[2] /'estɪmeɪt/ *v.t.* estimer. ~**ion** /-'meɪʃn/ *n.* jugement *m.*; (*high regard*) estime *f.*

estuary /'estʃʊərɪ/ *n.* estuaire *m.*

etc. /et'setərə/ *adv.* etc.

etching /'etʃɪŋ/ *n.* eau-forte *f.*

eternal /ɪ'tɜːnl/ *a.* éternel.

eternity /ɪ'tɜːnətɪ/ *n.* éternité *f.*

ether /'iːθə(r)/ *n.* éther *m.*

ethic /'eθɪk/ *n.* éthique *f.* ~**s,** moralité *f.* ~**al** *a.* éthique.

ethnic /'eθnɪk/ *a.* ethnique.

ethos /'iːθɒs/ *n.* génie *m.*

etiquette /'etɪket/ *n.* étiquette *f.*

etymology /etɪ'mɒlədʒɪ/ *n.* étymologie *f.*

eucalyptus /juːkə'lɪptəs/ *n.* (*pl.* -tuses) eucalyptus *m.*

eulogy /'juːlədʒɪ/ *n.* éloge *m.*

euphemism /'juːfəmɪzəm/ *n.* euphémisme *m.*

euphoria /juː'fɔːrɪə/ *n.* euphorie *f.*

eurocheque /'jʊərəʊtʃek/ *n.* eurochèque *m.*

Europe /'jʊərəp/ *n.* Europe *f.* ~**an** /-'pɪən/ *a.* & *n.* européen(ne) (*m.* (*f.*)). **E**~**an Community,** Communauté Européenne *f.*

euthanasia /juːθə'neɪzɪə/ *n.* euthanasie *f.*

evacuate /ɪ'vækjʊeɪt/ *v.t.* évacuer. ~**ion** /-'eɪʃn/ *n.* évacuation *f.*

evade /ɪ'veɪd/ *v.t.* esquiver. ~ **tax,** frauder le fisc.

evaluate /ɪ'væljʊeɪt/ *v.t.* évaluer.

evangelical /iːvæn'dʒelɪkl/ *a.* évangélique.

evangelist /ɪ'vændʒəlɪst/ *n.* évangéliste *m.*

evaporate /ɪ'væpəreɪt/ *v.i.* s'évaporer. ~**ed milk,** lait concentré *m.* ~**ion** /-'reɪʃn/ *n.* évaporation *f.*

evasion /ɪ'veɪʒn/ *n.* fuite *f.* (**of,** devant); (*excuse*) subterfuge *m.* **tax** ~, fraude fiscale.

evasive /ɪ'veɪsɪv/ *a.* évasif.

eve /iːv/ *n.* veille *f* (**of,** de).

even /'iːvn/ *a.* régulier; (*surface*) uni; (*equal, unvarying*) égal; (*number*) pair. —*v.t./i.* ~ (**out** *or* **up**), (s')égaliser. —*adv.* même. ~ **better**/*etc.*, (*still*) encore mieux/*etc.* **get** ~ **with,** se venger de. ~**ly** *adv.* régulièrement; (*equally*) de manière égale.

evening /'iːvnɪŋ/ *n.* soir *m.*; (*whole evening, event*) soirée *f.*

event /ɪ'vent/ *n.* événement *m.*; (*sport*) épreuve *f.* **in the** ~ **of,** en cas de. ~**ful** *a.* mouvementé.

eventual /ɪ'ventʃʊəl/ *a.* final, définitif. ~**ity** /-'ælətɪ/ *n.* éventualité *f.* ~**ly** *adv.* en fin de compte, (*in future*) un jour ou l'autre.

ever /'evə(r)/ *adv.* jamais; (*at all times*) toujours. ~ **since** *prep.* & *adv.* depuis (ce moment-là); *conj.* depuis que. ~ **so,** (*fam.*) vraiment.

evergreen /'evəgriːn/ *n.* arbre à feuilles persistantes *m.*

everlasting /evə'lɑːstɪŋ/ *a.* éternel.

every /'evrɪ/ *a.* chaque. ~ **one,** chacun(e). ~ **other day,** un jour sur deux, tous les deux jours.

everybody /'evrɪbɒdɪ/ *pron.* tout le monde.

everyday /'evrɪdeɪ/ *a.* quotidien.

everyone /'evrɪwʌn/ *pron.* tout le monde.

everything /'evrɪθɪŋ/ *pron.* tout.

everywhere /'evrɪweə(r)/ *adv.* partout. ~ **he goes,** partout où il va.

evict /ɪ'vɪkt/ v.t. expulser. ∼ion /-kʃn/ n. expulsion f.

evidence /'evɪdəns/ n. (proof) preuve(s) f. (pl.); (certainty) évidence f.; (signs) signes m. pl.; (testimony) témoignage m. **give** ∼, témoigner. **in** ∼, en vue.

evident /'evɪdənt/ a. évident. ∼ly adv. de toute évidence.

evil /'iːvl/ a. mauvais. —n. mal m.

evo|ke /ɪ'vəʊk/ v.t. évoquer. ∼cative /ɪ'vɒkətɪv/ a. évocateur.

evolution /iːvə'luːʃn/ n. évolution f.

evolve /ɪ'vɒlv/ v.i. se développer, évoluer. —v.t. développer.

ewe /juː/ n. brebis f.

ex- /eks/ pref. ex-, ancien.

exacerbate /ɪg'zæsəbeɪt/ v.t. exacerber.

exact[1] /ɪg'zækt/ a. exact. ∼ly adv. exactement. ∼ness n. exactitude f.

exact[2] /ɪg'zækt/ v.t. exiger (**from,** de). ∼ing a. exigeant.

exaggerat|e /ɪg'zædʒəreɪt/ v.t./i. exagérer. ∼ion /-'reɪʃn/ n. exagération f.

exalted /ɪg'zɔːltɪd/ a. (in rank) de haut rang; (ideal) élevé.

exam /ɪg'zæm/ n. (fam.) examen m.

examination /ɪgzæmɪ'neɪʃn/ n. examen m.

examine /ɪg'zæmɪn/ v.t. examiner; (witness etc.) interroger. ∼r /-ə(r)/ n. examinalteur, -trice m., f.

example /ɪg'zɑːmpl/ n. exemple m. **for** ∼, par exemple. **make an** ∼ **of,** punir pour l'exemple.

exasperat|e /ɪg'zæspəreɪt/ v.t. exaspérer. ∼ion /-'reɪʃn/ n. exaspération f.

excavat|e /'ekskəveɪt/ v.t. creuser; (uncover) déterrer. ∼ions /-'veɪʃnz/ n. pl. (archaeol.) fouilles f. pl.

exceed /ɪk'siːd/ v.t. dépasser. ∼ingly adv. extrêmement.

excel /ɪk'sel/ v.i. (p.t. **excelled**) exceller. —v.t. surpasser.

excellen|t /'eksələnt/ a. excellent. ∼ce n. excellence f. ∼tly adv. admirablement, parfaitement.

except /ɪk'sept/ prep. sauf, excepté. —v.t. excepter. ∼ **for,** à part. ∼ing prep. sauf, excepté.

exception /ɪk'sepʃn/ n. exception f. **take** ∼ **to,** s'offenser de.

exceptional /ɪk'sepʃənl/ a. exceptionnel. ∼ly adv. exceptionnellement.

excerpt /'eksɜːpt/ n. extrait m.

excess[1] /ɪk'ses/ n. excès m.

excess[2] /'ekses/ a. excédentaire. ∼ **fare,** supplément m. ∼ **luggage,** excédent de bagages m.

excessive /ɪk'sesɪv/ a. excessif. ∼ly adv. excessivement.

exchange /ɪks'tʃeɪndʒ/ v.t. échanger. —n. échange m.; (between currencies) change m. ∼ **rate,** taux d'échange m. (**telephone**) ∼, central (téléphonique) m.

exchequer /ɪks'tʃekə(r)/ n. (British pol.) Échiquier m.

excise /'eksaɪz/ n. impôt (indirect) m.

excit|e /ɪk'saɪt/ v.t. exciter; (enthuse) enthousiasmer. ∼able a. excitable. ∼ed a. excité. **get** ∼ed, s'exciter. ∼ement n. excitation f. ∼ing a. passionnant.

exclaim /ɪk'skleɪm/ v.t./i. exclamer, s'écrier.

exclamation /eksklə'meɪʃn/ n. exclamation f. ∼ **mark** or **point** (Amer.), point d'exclamation m.

exclu|de /ɪk'skluːd/ v.t. exclure. ∼sion n. exclusion f.

exclusive /ɪk'skluːsɪv/ a. (rights etc.) exclusif; (club etc.) sélect; (news item) en exclusivité. ∼ **of service**/etc., service/etc. non compris. ∼ly adv. exclusivement.

excrement /'ekskrəmənt/ n. excrément(s) m. (pl.).

excruciating /ɪk'skruːʃieɪtɪŋ/ a. atroce, insupportable.

excursion /ɪk'skɜːʃn/ n. excursion f.

excus|e[1] /ɪk'skjuːz/ v.t. excuser. ∼e **from,** (exempt) dispenser de. ∼e **me!,** excusez-moi!, pardon! ∼able a. excusable.

excuse[2] /ɪk'skjuːs/ n. excuse f.

ex-directory /eksdɪ'rektərɪ/ a. qui n'est pas dans l'annuaire.

execute /'eksɪkjuːt/ v.t. exécuter.

execution /eksɪ'kjuːʃn/ n. exécution f. ∼er n. bourreau m.

executive /ɪg'zekjʊtɪv/ n. (pouvoir) exécutif m.; (person) cadre m. —a. exécutif.

exemplary /ɪg'zemplərɪ/ a. exemplaire.

exemplify /ɪg'zemplɪfaɪ/ v.t. illustrer.

exempt /ɪg'zempt/ a. exempt (**from,** de). —v.t. exempter. ∼ion /-pʃn/ n. exemption f.

exercise /'eksəsaɪz/ n. exercice m. —v.t. exercer; (restraint, patience) faire preuve de. —v.i. prendre de l'exercice. ∼ **book,** cahier m.

exert /ɪg'zɜːt/ v.t. exercer. ∼ **o.s.,** se dépenser, faire des efforts. ∼ion /-ʃn/ n. effort m.

exhaust /ɪg'zɔːst/ v.t. épuiser. —n. (auto.) (pot d')échappement m. ∼ed a. épuisé. ∼ion /-stʃən/ n. épuisement m.

exhaustive /ɪgˈzɔːstɪv/ *a.* complet.
exhibit /ɪgˈzɪbɪt/ *v.t.* exposer; (*fig.*) faire preuve de. —*n.* objet exposé *m.* **∿or** *n.* exposant(e) *m.* (*f.*).
exhibition /eksɪˈbɪʃn/ *n.* exposition *f.*; (*act of showing*) démonstration *f.* **∿ist** *n.* exhibitionniste *m./f.*
exhilarat|e /ɪgˈzɪləreɪt/ *v.t.* transporter de joie; (*invigorate*) stimuler. **∿ing** *a.* euphorisant. **∿ion** /-ˈreɪʃn/ *n.* joie *f.*
exhort /ɪgˈzɔːt/ *v.t.* exhorter (**to**, à).
exhume /eksˈhjuːm/ *v.t.* exhumer.
exile /ˈeksaɪl/ *n.* exil *m.*; (*person*) exilé(e) *m.* (*f.*). —*v.t.* exiler.
exist /ɪgˈzɪst/ *v.i.* exister. **∿ence** *n.* existence *f.* **be in ∿ence**, exister. **∿ing** *a.* actuel.
exit /ˈeksɪt/ *n.* sortie *f.* —*v.t./i.* (*comput.*) sortir (de).
exodus /ˈeksədəs/ *n.* exode *m.*
exonerate /ɪgˈzɒnəreɪt/ *v.t.* disculper, innocenter.
exorbitant /ɪgˈzɔːbɪtənt/ *a.* exorbitant.
exorcize /ˈeksɔːsaɪz/ *v.t.* exorciser.
exotic /ɪgˈzɒtɪk/ *a.* exotique.
expan|d /ɪkˈspænd/ *v.t./i.* (*develop*) (se) développer; (*extend*) (s')étendre; (*metal, liquid*) (se) dilater. **∿sion** *n.* développement *m.*; dilatation *f.*; (*pol., comm.*) expansion *f.*
expanse /ɪkˈspæns/ *n.* étendue *f.*
expatriate /eksˈpætrɪət, *Amer.* eksˈpeɪt-rɪət/ *a. & n.* expatrié(e) (*m.* (*f.*)).
expect /ɪkˈspekt/ *v.t.* attendre, s'attendre à; (*suppose*) supposer; (*demand*) exiger; (*baby*) attendre. **∿ to do**, compter faire. **∿ation** /ekspekˈteɪʃn/ *n.* attente *f.*
expectan|t /ɪkˈspektənt/ *a.* **∿t look**, air d'attente *m.* **∿t mother**, future maman *f.* **∿cy** *n.* attente *f.*
expedient /ɪkˈspiːdɪənt/ *a.* opportun. —*n.* expédient *m.*
expedite /ˈekspɪdaɪt/ *v.t.* hâter.
expedition /ekspɪˈdɪʃn/ *n.* expédition *f.*
expel /ɪkˈspel/ *v.t.* (*p.t.* **expelled**) expulser; (*from school*) renvoyer.
expend /ɪkˈspend/ *v.t.* dépenser. **∿able** *a.* remplaçable.
expenditure /ɪkˈspendɪtʃə(r)/ *n.* dépense(s) *f.* (*pl.*).
expense /ɪkˈspens/ *n.* dépense *f.*; frais *m. pl.* **at s.o.'s ∿**, aux dépens de qn. **∿ account**, note de frais *f.*
expensive /ɪkˈspensɪv/ *a.* cher, coûteux; (*tastes, habits*) de luxe. **∿ly** *adv.* coûteusement.
experience /ɪkˈspɪərɪəns/ *n.* expérience *f.*; (*adventure*) aventure *f.* —*v.t.*

(*undergo*) connaître; (*feel*) éprouver. **∿d** *a.* expérimenté.
experiment /ɪkˈsperɪmənt/ *n.* expérience *f.* —*v.i.* faire une expérience. **∿al** /-ˈmentl/ *a.* expérimental.
expert /ˈekspɜːt/ *n.* expert(e) *m.* (*f.*). —*a.* expert. **∿ly** *adv.* habilement.
expertise /ekspɜːˈtiːz/ *n.* compétence *f.* (**in**, en).
expir|e /ɪkˈspaɪə(r)/ *v.i.* expirer. **∿ed** *a.* périmé. **∿y** *n.* expiration *f.*
expl|ain /ɪkˈspleɪn/ *v.t.* expliquer. **∿anation** /ekspləˈneɪʃn/ *n.* explication *f.* **∿anatory** /-ˈænətərɪ/ *a.* explicatif.
expletive /ɪkˈspliːtɪv, *Amer.* ˈeksplətɪv/ *n.* juron *m.*
explicit /ɪkˈsplɪsɪt/ *a.* explicite.
explo|de /ɪkˈspləʊd/ *v.t./i.* (faire) exploser. **∿sion** *n.* explosion *f.* **∿sive** *a. & n.* explosif (*m.*).
exploit¹ /ˈeksplɔɪt/ *n.* exploit *m.*
exploit² /ɪkˈsplɔɪt/ *v.t.* exploiter **∿ation** /eksplɔɪˈteɪʃn/ *n.* exploitation *f.*
exploratory /ɪkˈsplɒrətrɪ/ *a.* (*talks: pol.*) exploratoire.
explor|e /ɪkˈsplɔː(r)/ *v.t.* explorer; (*fig.*) examiner. **∿ation** /ekspləˈreɪʃn/ *n.* exploration *f.* **∿er** *n.* exploralteur, -trice *m., f.*
exponent /ɪkˈspəʊnənt/ *n.* interprète *m.* (**of**, de).
export¹ /ɪkˈspɔːt/ *v.t.* exporter. **∿er** *n.* exportateur *m.*
export² /ˈekspɔːt/ *n.* exportation *f.*
expos|e /ɪkˈspəʊz/ *v.t.* exposer; (*disclose*) dévoiler. **∿ure** /-ʒə(r)/ *n.* exposition *f.*; (*photo.*) pose *f.* **die of ∿ure**, mourir de froid.
expound /ɪkˈspaʊnd/ *v.t.* exposer.
express¹ /ɪkˈspres/ *a.* formel, exprès, (*letter*) exprès *invar.* —*adv.* (*by express post*) (par) exprès. —*n.* (*train*) rapide *m.*; (*less fast*) express *m.* **∿ly** *adv.* expressément.
express² /ɪkˈspres/ *v.t.* exprimer. **∿ion** /-ʃn/ *n.* expression *f.* **∿ive** *a.* expressif.
expressway /ɪkˈspresweɪ/ *n.* voie express *f.*
expulsion /ɪkˈspʌlʃn/ *n.* expulsion *f.*; (*from school*) renvoi *m.*
expurgate /ˈekspəgeɪt/ *v.t.* expurger.
exquisite /ˈekskwɪzɪt/ *a.* exquis. **∿ly** *adv.* d'une façon exquise.
ex-serviceman /eksˈsɜːvɪsmən/ *n.* (*pl.* **-men**) ancien combattant *m.*
extant /ekˈstænt/ *a.* existant.
extempore /ekˈstempərɪ/ *a. & adv.* impromptu.
exten|d /ɪkˈstend/ *v.t.* (*increase*)

étendre, agrandir; (*arm*, *leg*) étendre; (*prolong*) prolonger; (*house*) agrandir; (*grant*) offrir. —*v.i.* (*stretch*) s'étendre; (*in time*) se prolonger. ~**sion** *n.* (*of line*, *road*) prolongement *m.*; (*in time*) prolongation *f.*; (*building*) annexe *f.*; (*of phone*) appareil supplémentaire *m.*; (*phone number*) poste *m.*; (*cable*, *hose*, *etc.*) rallonge *f.*

extensive /ɪk'stensɪv/ *a.* vaste; (*study*) profond; (*damage etc.*) important. ~**ly** *adv.* (*much*) beaucoup; (*very*) très.

extent /ɪk'stent/ *n.* (*size*, *scope*) étendue *f.*; (*degree*) mesure *f.* **to some** ~, dans une certaine mesure. **to such an** ~ **that**, à tel point que.

extenuating /ɪk'stenjʊeɪtɪŋ/ *a.* ~ **circumstances**, circonstances atténuantes.

exterior /ɪk'stɪərɪə(r)/ *a. & n.* extérieur (*m.*).

exterminat|e /ɪk'stɜːmɪneɪt/ *v.t.* exterminer. ~**ion** /-'neɪʃn/ *n.* extermination *f.*

external /ɪk'stɜːnl/ *a.* extérieur; (*cause*, *medical use*) externe. ~**ly** *adv.* extérieurement.

extinct /ɪk'stɪŋkt/ *a.* (*species*) disparu; (*volcano*, *passion*) éteint. ~**ion** /-kʃn/ *n.* extinction *f.*

extinguish /ɪk'stɪŋgwɪʃ/ *v.t.* éteindre. ~**er** *n.* extincteur *m.*

extol /ɪk'stəʊl/ *v.t.* (*p.t.* **extolled**) exalter, chanter les louanges de.

extort /ɪk'stɔːt/ *v.t.* extorquer (**from**, à). ~**ion** /-ʃn/ *n.* (*jurid.*) extorsion (de fonds) *f.*

extortionate /ɪk'stɔːʃənət/ *a.* exorbitant.

extra /'ekstrə/ *a.* de plus, supplémentaire. —*adv.* plus (que d'habitude). ~ **strong**, extra-fort. —*n.* (*additional thing*) supplément *m.*; (*cinema*) figurant(e) *m.* (*f.*). ~ **charge**, supplément *m.* ~ **time**, (*football*) prolongation *f.*

extra- /'ekstrə/ *pref.* extra- .

extract[1] /ɪk'strækt/ *v.t.* extraire; (*promise*, *tooth*) arracher; (*fig.*) obtenir. ~**ion** /-kʃn/ *n.* extraction *f.*

extract[2] /'ekstrækt/ *n.* extrait *m.*

extra-curricular /ekstrəkə'rɪkjʊlə(r)/ *a.* parascolaire.

extradit|e /'ekstrədaɪt/ *v.t.* extrader. ~**ion** /-'dɪʃn/ *n.* extradition *f.*

extramarital /ekstrə'mærɪtl/ *a.* extra-conjugal.

extramural /ekstrə'mjʊərəl/ *a.* (*univ.*) hors faculté.

extraordinary /ɪk'strɔːdnrɪ/ *a.* extraordinaire.

extravagan|t /ɪk'strævəgənt/ *a.* extravagant; (*wasteful*) prodigue. ~**ce** *n.* extravagance *f.*; prodigalité *f.*

extrem|e /ɪk'striːm/ *a. & n.* extrême (*m.*). ~**ely** *adv.* extrêmement. ~**ist** *n.* extrémiste *m./f.*

extremity /ɪk'stremətɪ/ *n.* extrémité *f.*

extricate /'ekstrɪkeɪt/ *v.t.* dégager.

extrovert /'ekstrəvɜːt/ *n.* extraverti(e) *m.* (*f.*).

exuberan|t /ɪg'zjuːbərənt/ *a.* exubérant. ~**ce** *n.* exubérance *f.*

exude /ɪg'zjuːd/ *v.t.* (*charm etc.*) dégager.

exult /ɪg'zʌlt/ *v.i.* exulter.

eye /aɪ/ *n.* œil *m.* (*pl.* yeux). —*v.t.* (*p.t.* **eyed**, *pres. p.* **eyeing**) regarder. **keep an** ~ **on**, surveiller. ~**-catching** *a.* qui attire l'attention. ~**-opener** *n.* révélation *f.* ~**-shadow** *n.* ombre à paupières *f.*

eyeball /'aɪbɔːl/ *n.* globe oculaire *m.*

eyebrow /'aɪbraʊ/ *n.* sourcil *m.*

eyeful /'aɪfʊl/ *n.* **get an** ~, (*fam.*) se rincer l'œil.

eyelash /'aɪlæʃ/ *n.* cil *m.*

eyelet /'aɪlɪt/ *n.* œillet *m.*

eyelid /'aɪlɪd/ *n.* paupière *f.*

eyesight /'aɪsaɪt/ *n.* vue *f.*

eyesore /'aɪsɔː(r)/ *n.* horreur *f.*

eyewitness /'aɪwɪtnɪs/ *n.* témoin oculaire *m.*

F

fable /'feɪbl/ *n.* fable *f.*

fabric /'fæbrɪk/ *n.* (*cloth*) tissu *m.*

fabrication /fæbrɪ'keɪʃn/ *n.* (*invention*) invention *f.*

fabulous /'fæbjʊləs/ *a.* fabuleux; (*marvellous*: *fam.*) formidable.

façade /fə'sɑːd/ *n.* façade *f.*

face /feɪs/ *n.* visage *m.*, figure *f.*; (*aspect*) face *f.*; (*of clock*) cadran *m.* —*v.t.* être en face de; (*risk*) devoir affronter; (*confront*) faire face à, affronter. —*v.i.* se tourner; (*of house*) être exposé. ~**-flannel** *n.* gant de toilette *m.* ~**-lift** *n.* lifting *m.* **give a** ~**-lift to**, donner un coup de neuf à. ~ **value**, (*comm.*) valeur nominale. **take sth. at** ~ **value**, prendre qch. au premier degré. ~ **to face**, face à face. ~ **up/down**, tourné vers le haut/bas; (*risk*) devoir faire à. **in the** ~ **of**, ~**d with**, face à. **make a** (**funny**) ~, faire une grimace.

faceless /'feɪslɪs/ *a.* anonyme.

facet /'fæsɪt/ n. facette f.

facetious /fə'siːʃəs/ a. facétieux.

facial /'feɪʃl/ a. de la face, facial. —n. soin du visage m.

facile /'fæsaɪl, Amer. 'fæsl/ a. facile, superficiel.

facilitate /fə'sɪlɪteɪt/ v.t. faciliter.

facilit|y /fə'sɪlətɪ/ n. facilité f. ~ies, (equipment) équipements m. pl.

facing /'feɪsɪŋ/ n. parement m. —prep. en face de. —a. en face.

facsimile /fæk'sɪməlɪ/ n. facsimilé m. ~ transmission, télécopiage m.

fact /fækt/ n. fait m. as a matter of ~, in ~, en fait.

faction /'fækʃn/ n. faction f.

factor /'fæktə(r)/ n. facteur m.

factory /'fæktərɪ/ n. usine f.

factual /'fæktʃʊəl/ a. basé sur les faits.

faculty /'fækltɪ/ n. faculté f.

fad /fæd/ n. manie f., folie f.

fade /feɪd/ v.i. (sound) s'affaiblir; (memory) s'évanouir; (flower) se faner; (material) déteindre; (colour) passer.

fag /fæg/ n. (chore: fam.) corvée f.; (cigarette: sl.) sèche f.; (homosexual: Amer., sl.) pédé m.

fagged /fægd/ a. (tired) éreinté.

fail /feɪl/ v.i. échouer; (grow weak) (s'af)faiblir; (run short) manquer; (engine etc.) tomber en panne. —v.t. (exam) échouer à; (candidate) refuser, recaler; (disappoint) décevoir. ~ s.o., (of words etc.) manquer à qn. ~ to do, (not do) ne pas faire; (not be able) ne pas réussir à faire. without ~, à coup sûr.

failing /'feɪlɪŋ/ n. défaut m. —prep. à défaut de.

failure /'feɪljə(r)/ n. échec m.; (person) raté(e) m. (f.); (breakdown) panne f. ~ to do, (inability) incapacité de faire f.

faint /feɪnt/ a. (-er, -est) léger, faible. —v.i. s'évanouir. —n. évanouissement m. feel ~, (ill) se trouver mal. I haven't the ~est idea, je n'en ai pas la moindre idée. ~-hearted a. timide. ~ly adv. (weakly) faiblement; (slightly) légèrement. ~ness n. faiblesse f.

fair[1] /feə(r)/ n. foire f. ~-ground n. champ de foire m.

fair[2] /feə(r)/ a. (-er, -est) (hair, person) blond; (skin etc.) clair; (just) juste, équitable; (weather) beau; (amount, quality) raisonnable. —adv. (play) loyalement. ~ play, le fair-play. ~ly adv. (justly) équitablement; (rather) assez. ~ness n. justice f.

fairy /'feərɪ/ n. fée f. ~ story, ~-tale n. conte de fées m.

faith /feɪθ/ n. foi. f. ~-healer n. guérisseur, -se m., f.

faithful /'feɪθfl/ a. fidèle. ~ly adv. fidèlement. ~ness n. fidélité f.

fake /feɪk/ n. (forgery) faux m.; (person) imposteur m. it is a ~, c'est faux. —a. faux. —v.t. (copy) faire un faux de; (alter) falsifier, truquer; (illness) simuler.

falcon /'fɔːlkən/ n. faucon m.

fall /fɔːl/ v.i. (p.t. fell, p.p. fallen) tomber. —n. chute f.; (autumn: Amer.) automne m. Niagara F~s, chutes de Niagara. ~ back on, se rabattre sur. ~ behind, prendre du retard. ~ down or off, tomber. ~ for, (person: fam.) tomber amoureux de; (a trick: fam.) se laisser prendre à. ~ in, (mil.) se mettre en rangs. ~ off, (decrease) diminuer. ~ out, se brouiller (with, avec). ~-out n. retombées f. pl. ~ over, tomber (par terre.) ~ short, être insuffisant. ~ through, (plans) tomber à l'eau.

fallacy /'fæləsɪ/ n. erreur f.

fallible /'fæləbl/ a. faillible.

fallow /'fæləʊ/ a. en jachère.

false /fɔːls/ a. faux. ~hood n. mensonge m. ~ly adv. faussement. ~ness n. fausseté f.

falsetto /fɔːl'setəʊ/ n. (pl. -os) fausset m.

falsify /'fɔːlsɪfaɪ/ v.t. falsifier.

falter /'fɔːltə(r)/ v.i. vaciller; (nerve) faire défaut.

fame /feɪm/ n. renommée f.

famed /feɪmd/ a. renommé.

familiar /fə'mɪlɪə(r)/ a. familier. be ~ with, connaître. ~ity /-'ærətɪ/ n. familiarité f. ~ize v.t. familiariser.

family /'fæməlɪ/ n. famille f. —a. de famille, familial.

famine /'fæmɪn/ n. famine f.

famished /'fæmɪʃt/ a. affamé.

famous /'feɪməs/ a. célèbre. ~ly adv. (very well: fam.) à merveille.

fan[1] /fæn/ n. ventilateur m.; (hand-held) éventail m. —v.t. (p.t. fanned) éventer; (fig.) attiser. —v.i. ~ out, se déployer en éventail. ~ belt, courroie de ventilateur f.

fan[2] /fæn/ n. (of person) fan m./f., admirateur, -trice m., f.; (enthusiast) fervent(e) m. (f.), passionné(e) m. (f.).

fanatic /fə'nætɪk/ n. fanatique m./f. ~al a. fanatique. ~ism /-sɪzəm/ n. fanatisme m.

fancier /'fænsɪə(r)/ n. (dog/etc.) ~, amateur (de chiens/etc.) m.

fanciful /'fænsɪfl/ a. fantaisiste.

fancy /'fænsɪ/ n. (whim, fantasy)

fantaisie *f.*; (*liking*) goût *m.* —*a.* (*buttons etc.*) fantaisie *invar.*; (*prices*) extravagant; (*impressive*) impressionnant. —*v.t.* s'imaginer; (*want: fam.*) avoir envie de; (*like: fam.*) aimer. **take a ~ to s.o.,** se prendre d'affection pour qn. **it took my ~,** ça m'a plu. **~ dress,** déguisement *m.*

fanfare /'fænfeə(r)/ *n.* fanfare *f.*

fang /fæŋ/ *n.* (*of dog etc.*) croc *m.*; (*of snake*) crochet *m.*

fanlight /'fænlaɪt/ *n.* imposte *f.*

fantastic /fæn'tæstɪk/ *a.* fantastique.

fantas|y /'fæntəsɪ/ *n.* fantaisie *f.*; (*daydream*) fantasme *m.* **~ize** *v.i.* faire des fantasmes.

far /fɑː(r)/ *adv.* loin; (*much*) beaucoup; (*very*) très. —*a.* lointain; (*end, side*) autre. **~ away, ~ off,** au loin. **as ~ as,** (*up to*) jusqu'à. **as ~ as I know,** autant que je sache. **~-away** *a.* lointain. **by ~,** de loin. **~ from,** loin de. **the Far East,** l'Extrême-Orient *m.* **~-fetched** *a.* bizarre, exagéré. **~-reaching** *a.* de grande portée.

farc|e /fɑːs/ *n.* farce *f.* **~ical** *a.* ridicule, grotesque.

fare /feə(r)/ *n.* (*prix du*) billet *m.*; (*food*) nourriture *f.* —*v.i.* (*progress*) aller; (*manage*) se débrouiller.

farewell /feə'wel/ *int. & n.* adieu (*m.*).

farm /fɑːm/ *n.* ferme *f.* —*v.t.* cultiver. —*v.i.* être fermier. **~ out,** céder en sous-traitance. **~ worker,** ouvrier, -ère agricole *m., f.* **~er** *n.* fermier *m.* **~ing** *n.* agriculture *f.*

farmhouse /'fɑːmhaʊs/ *n.* ferme *f.*

farmyard /'fɑːmjɑːd/ *n.* basse-cour *f.*

fart /fɑːt/ *v.i.* péter. —*n.* pet *m.*

farth|er /'fɑːðə(r)/ *adv.* plus loin. —*a.* plus éloigné. **~est** *adv.* le plus loin; *a.* le plus éloigné.

fascinat|e /'fæsɪneɪt/ *v.t.* fasciner. **~ion** /-'neɪʃn/ *n.* fascination *f.*

Fascis|t /'fæʃɪst/ *n.* fasciste *m./f.* **~m** /-zəm/ *n.* fascisme *m.*

fashion /'fæʃn/ *n.* (*current style*) mode *f.*; (*manner*) façon *f.* —*v.t.* façonner. **~ designer,** styliste *m./f.* **in ~,** à la mode. **out of ~,** démodé. **~able** *a.,* **~ably** *adv.* à la mode.

fast[1] /fɑːst/ *a.* (**-er, -est**) rapide; (*colour*) grand teint *invar.*, fixe; (*firm*) fixe, solide. —*adv.* vite; (*firmly*) ferme. **be ~,** (*clock etc.*) avancer. **~ asleep,** profondément endormi. **~ food,** fast food *m.* restauration rapide *f.*

fast[2] /fɑːst/ *v.i.* (*go without food*) jeûner. —*n.* jeûne *m.*

fasten /'fɑːsn/ *v.t./i.* (s')attacher. **~er, ~ing** *ns.* attache *f.*, fermeture *f.*

fastidious /fə'stɪdɪəs/ *a.* difficile.

fat /fæt/ *n.* graisse *f.*; (*on meat*) gras *m.* —*a.* (**fatter, fattest**) gros, gras; (*meat*) gras; (*sum, volume: fig.*) gros. **a ~ lot,** (*sl.*) bien peu (**of,** de). **~-head** *n.* (*fam.*) imbécile *m./f.* **~ness** *n.* corpulence *f.*

fatal /'feɪtl/ *a.* mortel; (*fateful, disastrous*) fatal. **~ity** /fə'tælətɪ/ *n.* mort *m.* **~ly** *adv.* mortellement.

fatalist /'feɪtəlɪst/ *n.* fataliste *m./f.*

fate /feɪt/ *n.* (*controlling power*) destin *m.*, sort *m.*; (*one's lot*) sort *m.* **~ful** *a.* fatidique.

fated /'feɪtɪd/ *a.* destiné (**to,** à).

father /'fɑːðə(r)/ *n.* père *m.* **~-in-law** *n.* (*pl.* **~s-in-law**) beau-père *m.* **~hood** *n.* paternité *f.* **~ly** *a.* paternel.

fathom /'fæðəm/ *n.* brasse *f.* (*= 1,8 m.*). —*v.t.* **~ (out),** comprendre.

fatigue /fə'tiːg/ *n.* fatigue *f.* —*v.t.* fatiguer.

fatten /'fætn/ *v.t./i.* engraisser. **~ing** *a.* qui fait grossir.

fatty /'fætɪ/ *a.* gras; (*tissue*) adipeux. —*n.* (*person: fam.*) gros(se) *m.* (*f.*).

fatuous /'fætʃʊəs/ *a.* stupide.

faucet /'fɔːsɪt/ *n.* (*Amer.*) robinet *m.*

fault /fɔːlt/ *n.* (*defect, failing*) défaut *m.*; (*blame*) faute *f.*; (*geol.*) faille *f.* —*v.t.* **~ sth./s.o.,** trouver des défauts à qch./chez qn. **at ~,** fautif. **find ~ with,** critiquer. **~less** *a.* irréprochable. **~y** *a.* défectueux.

fauna /'fɔːnə/ *n.* faune *f.*

favour, (*Amer.*) **favor** /'feɪvə(r)/ *n.* faveur *f.* —*v.t.* favoriser; (*support*) être en faveur de; (*prefer*) préférer. **do s.o. a ~,** rendre service à qn. **in ~ of,** pour. **~able** *a.* favorable. **~ably** *adv.* favorablement.

favourit|e /'feɪvərɪt/ *a. & n.* favori(te) (*m.* (*f.*)). **~ism** *n.* favoritisme *m.*

fawn[1] /fɔːn/ *n.* faon *m.* —*a.* fauve.

fawn[2] /fɔːn/ *v.i.* **~ on,** flatter bassement, flagorner.

fax /fæks/ *n.* fax *m.*, télécopie *f.* —*v.t.* faxer, envoyer par télécopie. **~ machine,** télécopieur *m.*

FBI *abbr.* (*Federal Bureau of Investigation*) (*Amer.*) service d'enquêtes du Ministère de la Justice *m.*

fear /fɪə(r)/ *n.* crainte *f.*, peur *f.*; (*fig.*) risque *m.* —*v.t.* craindre. **for ~ of/that,** de peur de/que. **~ful** *a.* (*terrible*) affreux; (*timid*) craintif. **~less** *a.* intrépide. **~lessness** *n.* intrépidité *f.*

fearsome /'fɪəsəm/ a. redoutable.

feasib|le /'fi:zəbl/ a. faisable; (*likely*) plausible. **~ility** /-'bɪlətɪ/ n. possibilité f.; plausibilité f.

feast /fi:st/ n. festin m.; (*relig.*) fête f. —v.i. festoyer. —v.t. régaler. **~ on**, se régaler de.

feat /fi:t/ n. exploit m.

feather /'feðə(r)/ n. plume f. —v.t. **~ one's nest**, s'enrichir. **~ duster**, plumeau m.

featherweight /'feðəweɪt/ n. poids plume m. invar.

feature /'fi:tʃə(r)/ n. caractéristique f.; (*of person, face*) trait m.; (*film*) long métrage m.; (*article*) article vedette m. —v.t. représenter; (*give prominence to*) mettre en vedette. —v.i. figurer (**in**, dans).

February /'februərɪ/ n. février m.

feckless /'feklɪs/ a. inepte.

fed /fed/ see **feed**. —a. **be ~ up**, (*fam.*) en avoir marre (**with**, de).

federa|l /'fedərəl/ a. fédéral. **~tion** /-'reɪʃn/ n. fédération f.

fee /fi:/ n. (*for entrance*) prix m. **~(s)**, (*of doctor etc.*) honoraires m. pl.; (*of actor, artist*) cachet m.; (*for tuition*) frais m. pl.; (*for enrolment*) droits m. pl.

feeble /fi:bl/ a. (**-er, -est**) faible. **~-minded** a. faible d'esprit.

feed /fi:d/ v.t. (*p.t.* **fed**) nourrir, donner à manger à; (*suckle*) allaiter; (*supply*) alimenter. —v.i. se nourrir (**on**, de). —n. nourriture f.; (*of baby*) tétée f. **~ in information**, rentrer des données. **~er** n. alimentation f.

feedback /'fi:dbæk/ n. réaction(s) f. (pl.); (*med., techn.*) feed-back m.

feel /fi:l/ v.t. (*p.t.* **felt**) (*touch*) tâter; (*be conscious of*) sentir; (*emotion*) ressentir; (*experience*) éprouver, (*think*) estimer. —v.i. (*tired, lonely, etc.*) se sentir. **~ hot/thirsty/etc.**, avoir chaud/ soif/etc. **~ as if**, avoir l'impression de. **~ awful**, (*ill*) se sentir malade. **~ like**, (*want: fam.*) avoir envie de.

feeler /'fi:lə(r)/ n. antenne f. **put out a ~**, lancer un ballon d'essai.

feeling /'fi:lɪŋ/ n. sentiment m.; (*physical*) sensation f.

feet /fi:t/ see **foot**.

feign /feɪn/ v.t. feindre.

feint /feɪnt/ n. feinte f.

felicitous /fə'lɪsɪtəs/ a. heureux.

feline /'fi:laɪn/ a. félin.

fell¹ /fel/ v.t. (*cut down*) abattre.

fell² /fel/ see **fall**.

fellow /'feləʊ/ n. compagnon m.,

camarade m.; (*of society*) membre m.; (*man: fam.*) type m. **~-countryman** n. compatriote m. **~-passenger, ~-traveller** n. compagnon de voyage m. **~ship** n. camaraderie f.; (*group*) association f.

felony /'felənɪ/ n. crime m.

felt¹ /felt/ n. feutre m. **~-tip** n. feutre m.

felt² /felt/ see **feel**.

female /'fi:meɪl/ a. (*animal etc.*) femelle; (*voice, sex, etc.*) féminin. —n. femme f.; (*animal*) femelle f.

feminin|e /'femənɪn/ a. & n. féminin (m.). **~ity** /-'nɪnətɪ/ n. féminité f.

feminist /'femɪnɪst/ n. féministe m./f.

fenc|e /fens/ n. barrière f.; (*person: jurid.*) receleur, -se m., f. —v.t. **~e (in)**, clôturer. —v.i. (*sport*) faire de l'escrime. **~er** n. escrimeur, -se m., f. **~ing** n. escrime f.

fend /fend/ v.i. **~ for o.s.**, se débrouiller tout seul. —v.t. **~ off**, (*blow, attack*) parer.

fender /'fendə(r)/ n. (*for fireplace*) garde-feu m. invar.; (*mudguard: Amer.*) garde-boue m. invar.

fennel /'fenl/ n. (*culin.*) fenouil m.

ferment¹ /fə'ment/ v.t./i. (faire) fermenter. **~ation** /fɜ:men'teɪʃn/ n. fermentation f.

ferment² /'fɜ:ment/ n. ferment m.; (*excitement: fig.*) agitation f.

fern /fɜ:n/ n. fougère f.

feroc|ious /fə'rəʊʃəs/ a. féroce. **~ity** /-'rɒsətɪ/ n. férocité f.

ferret /'ferɪt/ n. (*animal*) furet m. —v.i. (*p.t.* **ferreted**) fureter. —v.t. **~ out**, dénicher.

ferry /'ferɪ/ n. ferry m., bac m. —v.t. transporter.

fertil|e /'fɜ:taɪl, Amer. 'fɜ:tl/ a. fertile; (*person, animal*) fécond. **~ity** /fə'tɪlətɪ/ n. fertilité f.; fécondité f. **~ize** /-əlaɪz/ v.t. fertiliser; féconder.

fertilizer /'fɜ:təlaɪzə(r)/ n. engrais m.

fervent /'fɜ:vənt/ a. fervent.

fervour /'fɜ:və(r)/ n. ferveur f.

fester /'festə(r)/ v.i. (*wound*) suppurer; (*fig.*) rester sur le cœur.

festival /'festɪvl/ n. festival m.; (*relig.*) fête f.

festiv|e /'festɪv/ a. de fête, gai. **~e season**, période des fêtes f. **~ity** /fe'stɪvətɪ/ n. réjouissances f. pl.

festoon /fe'stu:n/ v.i. **~ with**, orner de.

fetch /fetʃ/ v.t. (*go for*) aller chercher; (*bring person*) amener; (*bring thing*) apporter; (*be sold for*) rapporter.

fête /feɪt/ n. fête f. —v.t. fêter.

fetid /'fetɪd/ a. fétide.

fetish /'fetɪʃ/ n. (object) fétiche m.; (psych.) obsession f.

fetter /'fetə(r)/ v.t. enchaîner. ∼s n. pl. chaînes f. pl.

feud /fjuːd/ n. querelle f.

feudal /'fjuːdl/ a. féodal.

fever /'fiːvə(r)/ n. fièvre f. ∼ish a. fiévreux.

few /fjuː/ a. & n. peu (de). ∼ books, peu de livres. **they are** ∼, ils sont peu nombreux. **a** ∼ a. quelques; n. quelques-un(e)s. **a good** ∼, **quite a** ∼, (fam.) bon nombre (de). ∼er a. & n. moins (de). **be** ∼er, être moins nombreux (**than**, que). ∼est a. & n. le moins (de).

fiancé /fɪ'ɒnseɪ/ n. fiancé m.

fiancée /fɪ'ɒnseɪ/ n. fiancée f.

fiasco /fɪ'æskəʊ/ n. (pl. -os) fiasco m.

fib /fɪb/ n. mensonge m. ∼ber n. menteuɪr, -se m., f.

fibre, Amer. **fiber** /'faɪbə(r)/ n. fibre f. ∼ **optics**, fibres optiques.

fibreglass, Amer. **fiberglass** /'faɪbəɡlɑːs/ n. fibre de verre f.

fickle /'fɪkl/ a. inconstant.

fiction /'fɪkʃn/ n. fiction f. **(works of)** ∼, romans m. pl. ∼**al** a. fictif.

fictitious /fɪk'tɪʃəs/ a. fictif.

fiddle /'fɪdl/ n. (fam.) violon m.; (swindle: sl.) combine f. —v.i. (sl.) frauder. —v.t. (sl.) falsifier. ∼ **with**, (fam.) tripoter. ∼r /-ə(r)/ n. (fam.) violoniste m./f.

fidelity /fɪ'delətɪ/ n. fidélité f.

fidget /'fɪdʒɪt/ v.i. (p.t. **fidgeted**) remuer sans cesse. —n. **be a** ∼, être remuant. ∼ **with**, tripoter. ∼y a. remuant.

field /fiːld/ n. champ m.; (sport) terrain m.; (fig.) domaine m. —v.t./i. (ball: cricket) bloquer. ∼-**day** n. grande occasion f. ∼-**glasses** n. pl. jumelles f. pl. **F**∼ **Marshal**, maréchal m.

fieldwork /'fiːldwɜːk/ n. travaux pratiques m. pl.

fiend /fiːnd/ n. démon m. ∼ish a. diabolique.

fierce /fɪəs/ a. (-er, -est) féroce; (storm, attack) violent. ∼ness n. férocité f.; violence f.

fiery /'faɪərɪ/ a. (-ier, -iest) (hot) ardent; (spirited) fougueux.

fiesta /fɪ'estə/ n. fiesta f.

fifteen /fɪf'tiːn/ a. & n. quinze (m.). ∼th a. & n. quinzième (m./f.).

fifth /fɪfθ/ a. & n. cinquième (m./f.). ∼ **column**, cinquième colonne f.

fift|y /'fɪftɪ/ a. & n. cinquante (m.). ∼**ieth**

a. & n. cinquantième (m./f.). **a** ∼**y-fifty chance,** (equal) une chance sur deux.

fig /fɪɡ/ n. figue f.

fight /faɪt/ v.i. (p.t. **fought**) se battre; (struggle: fig.) lutter; (quarrel) se disputer. —v.t. se battre avec; (evil etc.: fig.) lutter contre. —n. (struggle) lutte f.; (quarrel) dispute f.; (brawl) bagarre f.; (mil.) combat m. ∼ **back**, se défendre. ∼ **off**, surmonter. ∼ **over sth.**, se disputer qch. ∼ **shy of**, fuir devant. ∼**er** n. (brawler, soldier) combattant m.; (fig.) battant m.; (aircraft) chasseur m. ∼**ing** n. combats m. pl.

figment /'fɪɡmənt/ n. invention f.

figurative /'fɪɡjərətɪv/ a. figuré.

figure /'fɪɡə(r)/ n. (number) chiffre m.; (diagram) figure f.; (shape) forme f.; (body) ligne f. ∼**s**, arithmétique f. —v.t. s'imaginer. —v.i. (appear) figurer. ∼ **out**, comprendre. ∼-**head** n. (person with no real power) prête-nom m. ∼ **of speech**, façon de parler f. **that** ∼**s**, (Amer., fam.) c'est logique.

filament /'fɪləmənt/ n. filament m.

filch /fɪltʃ/ v.t. voler, piquer.

fil|e¹ /faɪl/ n. (tool) lime f. —v.t. limer. ∼**ings** n. pl. limaille f.

fil|e² /faɪl/ n. dossier m., classeur m.; (comput.) fichier m.; (row) file f. —v.t. (papers) classer; (jurid.) déposer. —v.i. ∼e **in**, entrer en file. ∼e **past**, défiler devant. ∼**ing cabinet**, classeur m.

fill /fɪl/ v.t./i. (se) remplir. —n. **eat one's** ∼, manger à sa faim. **have had one's** ∼, en avoir assez. ∼ **in or up**, (form) remplir. ∼ **out**, (get fat) grossir. ∼ **up**, (auto.) faire le plein (d'essence).

fillet /'fɪlɪt, Amer. fɪ'leɪ/ n. filet m. —v.t. (p.t. **filleted**) découper en filets.

filling /'fɪlɪŋ/ n. (of tooth) plombage m.; (of sandwich) garniture f. ∼ **station**, station-service f.

filly /'fɪlɪ/ n. pouliche f.

film /fɪlm/ n. film m.; (photo.) pellicule f. —v.t. filmer. ∼-**goer** n. cinéphile m./f. ∼ **star**, vedette de cinéma f.

filter /'fɪltə(r)/ n. filtre m.; (traffic signal) flèche f. —v.t./i. filtrer; (of traffic) suivre la flèche. ∼ **coffee**, café-filtre m. ∼-**tip** n. bout filtre m.

filth ,∼**iness** /fɪlθ, fɪlθɪnəs/ n. saleté f. ∼y a. sale.

fin /fɪn/ n. (of fish, seal) nageoire f.; (of shark) aileron m.

final /'faɪnl/ a. dernier; (conclusive) définitif. —n. (sport) finale f. ∼**ist** n.

finaliste *m./f.* ∿**ly** *adv.* (*lastly, at last*) enfin, finalement; (*once and for all*) définitivement.

finale /fɪ'nɑːlɪ/ *n.* (*mus.*) final(e) *m.*

finalize /'faɪnəlaɪz/ *v.t.* mettre au point, fixer.

financ|e /'faɪnæns/ *n.* finance *f.* —*a.* financier. —*v.t.* financer. ∿**ier** /-'næn-sɪə(r)/ *n.* financier *m.*

financial /faɪ'nænʃl/ *a.* financier. ∿**ly** *adv.* financièrement.

find /faɪnd/ *v.t.* (*p.t.* **found**) trouver; (*sth. lost*) retrouver. —*n.* trouvaille *f.* ∿ **out** *v.t.* découvrir, *v.i.* se renseigner (*about,* sur). ∿**ings** *n. pl.* conclusions *f. pl.*

fine¹ /faɪn/ *n.* amende *f.* —*v.t.* condamner à une amende.

fine² /faɪn/ *a.* (**-er, -est**) fin; (*excellent*) beau. —*adv.* (très) bien; (*small*) fin. ∿ **arts,** beaux-arts *m. pl.* ∿**ly** *adv.* (*admirably*) magnifiquement; (*cut*) fin.

finery /'faɪnərɪ/ *n.* atours *m. pl.*

finesse /fɪ'nes/ *n.* finesse *f.*

finger /'fɪŋɡə(r)/ *n.* doigt *m.* —*v.t.* palper. ∿-**nail** *n.* ongle *m.* ∿-**stall** *n.* doigtier *m.*

fingerprint /'fɪŋɡəprɪnt/ *n.* empreinte digitale *f.*

fingertip /'fɪŋɡətɪp/ *n.* bout du doigt *m.*

finicking, finicky /'fɪnɪkɪŋ, 'fɪnɪkɪ/ *adjs.* méticuleux.

finish /'fɪnɪʃ/ *v.t./i.* finir. —*n.* fin *f.*; (*of race*) arrivée *f.*; (*appearance*) finition *f.* ∿ **doing,** finir de faire. ∿ **up doing,** finir par faire. ∿ **up in,** (*land up in*) se retrouver à.

finite /'faɪnaɪt/ *a.* fini.

Fin|land /'fɪnlənd/ *n.* finlande *f.* ∿**n** *n.* finlandais(e) *m.* (*f.*). ∿**nish** *a.* finlandais; *n.* (*lang.*) finnois *m.*

fir /fɜː(r)/ *n.* sapin *m.*

fire /'faɪə(r)/ *n.* feu *m.*; (*conflagration*) incendie *m.*; (*heater*) radiateur *m.* —*v.t.* (*bullet etc.*) tirer; (*dismiss*) renvoyer; (*fig.*) enflammer. —*v.i.* tirer (**at,** sur). ∿ **a gun,** tirer un coup de revolver *or* de fusil. **set** ∿ **to,** mettre le feu à. ∿ **alarm,** avertisseur d'incendie *m.* ∿ **brigade,** pompiers *m. pl.* ∿-**engine** *n.* voiture de pompiers *f.* ∿-**escape** *n.* escalier de secours *m.* ∿ **extinguisher,** extincteur d'incendie *m.* ∿ **station,** caserne de pompiers *f.*

firearm /'faɪərɑːm/ *n.* arme à feu *f.*

firecracker /'faɪəkrækə(r)/ *n.* (*Amer.*) pétard *m.*

firelight /'faɪəlaɪt/ *n.* lueur du feu *f.*

fireman /'faɪəmən/ *n.* (*pl.* **-men**) pompier *m.*

fireplace /'faɪəpleɪs/ *n.* cheminée *f.*

fireside /'faɪəsaɪd/ *n.* coin du feu *m.*

firewood /'faɪəwʊd/ *n.* bois de chauffage *m.*

firework /'faɪəwɜːk/ *n.* feu d'artifice *m.*

firing-squad /'faɪərɪŋskwɒd/ *n.* peloton d'exécution *m.*

firm¹ /fɜːm/ *n.* firme *f.*, société *f.*

firm² /fɜːm/ *a.* (**-er, -est**) ferme; (*belief*) solide. ∿**ly** *adv.* fermement. ∿**ness** *n.* fermeté *f.*

first /fɜːst/ *a.* premier. —*n.* premier, -ière *m.*, *f.* —*adv.* d'abord, première-ment; (*arrive etc.*) le premier, la première. **at** ∿, d'abord. **at** ∿ **hand,** de première main. **at** ∿ **sight,** à première vue. ∿ **aid,** premiers soins *m. pl.* ∿-**class** *a.* de première classe. ∿ **floor,** (*Amer.*) rez-de-chaussée *m. invar.* ∿ (**gear**), première (vitesse) *f.* **F**∿ **Lady,** (*Amer.*) épouse du Président *f.* ∿ **name,** prénom *m.* ∿ **of all,** tout d'abord. ∿-**rate** *a.* de premier ordre. ∿**ly** *adv.* premièrement.

fiscal /'fɪskl/ *a.* fiscal.

fish /fɪʃ/ *n.* (*usually invar.*) poisson *m.* —*v.i.* pêcher. ∿ **for,** (*cod etc.*) pêcher. ∿ **out,** (*from water*) repêcher; (*take out: fam.*) sortir. ∿**ing** *n.* pêche *f.* **go** ∿**ing,** aller à la pêche. ∿**ing rod,** canne à pêche *f.* ∿**y** *a.* de poisson; (*fig.*) louche.

fisherman /'fɪʃəmən/ *n.* (*pl.* **-men**) *n.* pêcheur *m.*

fishmonger /'fɪʃmʌŋɡə(r)/ *n.* pois-sonnier, -ière *m.*, *f.*

fission /'fɪʃn/ *n.* fission *f.*

fist /fɪst/ *n.* poing *m.*

fit¹ /fɪt/ *n.* (*bout*) accès *m.*, crise *f.*

fit² /fɪt/ *a.* (**fitter, fittest**) en bonne santé; (*proper*) convenable; (*good enough*) bon; (*able*) capable. —*v.t./i.* (*p.t.* **fitted**) (*clothes*) aller (à); (*match*) s'accorder (avec); (*put or go in or on*) (s')adapter (**to,** à); (*into space*) aller; (*install*) poser. —*n.* **be a good** ∿, (*dress*) être à la bonne taille. **in no** ∿ **state to do,** pas en état de faire. ∿ **in,** *v.t.* caser; *v.i.* (*newcomer*) s'intégrer. ∿ **out,** ∿ **up,** équiper. ∿**ness** *n.* santé *f.*; (*of remark*) justesse *f.*

fitful /'fɪtfl/ *a.* irrégulier.

fitment /'fɪtmənt/ *n.* meuble fixe *m.*

fitted /'fɪtɪd/ *a.* (*wardrobe*) encastré. ∿ **carpet,** moquette *f.*

fitting /'fɪtɪŋ/ *a.* approprié. —*n.* essayage *m.* ∿ **room,** cabine d'essayage *f.*

fittings /'fɪtɪŋz/ *n. pl.* (*in house*) installations *f. pl.*

five /faɪv/ *a. & n.* cinq (*m.*).

fiver /ˈfaɪvə(r)/ *n.* (*fam.*) billet de cinq livres *m.*

fix /fɪks/ *v.t.* (*make firm, attach, decide*) fixer; (*mend*) réparer; (*deal with*) arranger. —*n.* **in a ~,** dans le pétrin. **~ s.o. up with sth.,** trouver qch. à qn. **~ed** *a.* fixe.

fixation /fɪkˈseɪʃn/ *n.* fixation *f.*

fixture /ˈfɪkstʃə(r)/ *n.* (*sport*) match *m.* **~s,** (*in house*) installations *f. pl.*

fizz /fɪz/ *v.i.* pétiller. —*n.* pétillement *m.* **~y** *a.* gazeux.

fizzle /ˈfɪzl/ *v.i.* pétiller. **~ out,** (*plan etc.*) finir en queue de poisson.

flab /flæb/ *n.* (*fam.*) corpulence *f.* **~by** /ˈflæbɪ/ *a.* flasque.

flabbergast /ˈflæbəgɑːst/ *v.t.* sidérer, ahurir.

flag¹ /flæg/ *n.* drapeau *m.*; (*naut.*) pavillon *m.* —*v.t.* (*p.t.* **flagged**). **~ (down),** faire signe de s'arrêter à. **~-pole** *n.* mât *m.*

flag² /flæg/ *v.i.* (*p.t.* **flagged**) (*weaken*) faiblir; (*sick person*) s'affaiblir; (*droop*) dépérir.

flagon /ˈflægən/ *n.* bouteille *f.*

flagrant /ˈfleɪgrənt/ *a.* flagrant.

flagstone /ˈflægstəʊn/ *n.* dalle *f.*

flair /fleə(r)/ *n.* flair *m.*

flak /flæk/ *n.* (*fam.*) critiques *f. pl.*

flak|e /fleɪk/ *n.* flocon *m.*; (*of paint, metal*) écaille *f.* —*v.i.* s'écailler. **~y** *a.* (*paint*) écailleux.

flamboyant /flæmˈbɔɪənt/ *a.* (*colour*) éclatant; (*manner*) extravagant.

flame /fleɪm/ *n.* flamme *f.* —*v.i.* flamber. **burst into ~s,** exploser. **go up in ~s,** brûler.

flamingo /fləˈmɪŋgəʊ/ *n.* (*pl.* **-os**) flamant (rose) *m.*

flammable /ˈflæməbl/ *a.* inflammable.

flan /flæn/ *n.* tarte *f.*; (*custard tart*) flan *m.*

flank /flæŋk/ *n.* flanc *m.* —*v.t.* flanquer.

flannel /ˈflænl/ *n.* flannelle *f.*; (*for face*) gant de toilette *m.*

flannelette /flænəˈlet/ *n.* pilou *m.*

flap /flæp/ *v.i.* (*p.t.* **flapped**) battre. —*v.t.* **~ its wings,** battre des ailes. —*n.* (*of pocket*) rabat *m.*; (*of table*) abattant *m.* **get into a ~,** (*fam.*) s'affoler.

flare /fleə(r)/ *v.i.* **~ up,** s'enflammer, flamber; (*fighting*) éclater; (*person*) s'emporter. —*n.* flamboiement *m.*; (*mil.*) fusée éclairante *f.*; (*in skirt*) évasement *m.* **~d** *a.* (*skirt*) évasé.

flash /flæʃ/ *v.i.* briller; (*on and off*)

clignoter. —*v.t.* faire briller; (*aim torch*) diriger (**at,** sur); (*flaunt*) étaler. —*n.* éclair *m.*, éclat *m.*; (*of news, camera*) flash *m.* **in a ~,** en un éclair. **~ one's headlights,** faire un appel de phares. **~ past,** passer à toute vitesse.

flashback /ˈflæʃbæk/ *n.* retour en arrière *m.*

flashlight /ˈflæʃlaɪt/ *n.* (*torch*) lampe électrique *f.*

flashy /ˈflæʃɪ/ *a.* voyant.

flask /flɑːsk/ *n.* flacon *m.*; (*vacuum flask*) thermos *m./f. invar.* (P.).

flat /flæt/ *a.* (**flatter, flattest**) plat; (*tyre*) à plat; (*refusal*) catégorique; (*fare, rate*) fixe. —*adv.* (*say*) carrément. —*n.* (*rooms*) appartement *m.*; (*tyre: fam.*) crevaison *f.*; (*mus.*) bémol *m.* **~ out,** (*drive*) à toute vitesse; (*work*) d'arrache-pied. **~-pack** *a.* en kit. **~ly** *adv.* catégoriquement. **~ness** *n.* égalité *f.*

flatten /ˈflætn/ *v.t./i.* (s')aplatir.

flatter /ˈflætə(r)/ *v.t.* flatter. **~er** *n.* flatteur, -se *m., f.* **~ing** *a.* flatteur. **~y** *n.* flatterie *f.*

flatulence /ˈflætjʊləns/ *n.* flatulence *f.*

flaunt /flɔːnt/ *v.t.* étaler, afficher.

flautist /ˈflɔːtɪst/ *n.* flûtiste *m./f.*

flavour (*Amer.*) **flavor** /ˈfleɪvə(r)/ *n.* goût *m.*; (*of ice-cream etc.*) parfum *m.* —*v.t.* parfumer, assaisonner. **~ing** *n.* arôme synthétique *m.*

flaw /flɔː/ *n.* défaut *m.* **~ed** *a.* imparfait. **~less** *a.* parfait.

flax /flæks/ *n.* lin *m.* **~en** *a.* de lin.

flea /fliː/ *n.* puce *f.* **~ market,** marché aux puces *m.*

fleck /flek/ *n.* petite tache *f.*

fled /fled/ *see* **flee.**

fledged /fledʒd/ *a.* **fully-~,** (*doctor etc.*) diplômé; (*member, citizen*) à part entière.

flee /fliː/ *v.i.* (*p.t.* **fled**) s'enfuir. —*v.t.* s'enfuir de; (*danger*) fuir.

fleece /fliːs/ *n.* toison *f.* —*v.t.* voler.

fleet /fliːt/ *n.* (*naut., aviat.*) flotte *f.* **a ~ of vehicles,** un parc automobile.

fleeting /ˈfliːtɪŋ/ *a.* très bref.

Flemish /ˈflemɪʃ/ *a.* flamand. —*n.* (*lang.*) flamand *m.*

flesh /fleʃ/ *n.* chair *f.* **one's (own) ~ and blood,** les siens *m. pl.* **~y** *a.* charnu.

flew /fluː/ *see* **fly**².

flex¹ /fleks/ *v.t.* (*knee etc.*) fléchir; (*muscle*) faire jouer.

flex² /fleks/ *n.* (*electr.*) fil souple *m.*

flexib|le /ˈfleksəbl/ *a.* flexible. **~ility** /-ˈbɪlətɪ/ *n.* flexibilité *f.*

flexitime /'fleksɪtaɪm/ n. horaire variable m.

flick /flɪk/ n. petit coup m. —v.t. donner un petit coup à. ∼-knife n. couteau à cran d'arrêt m. ∼ through, feuilleter.

flicker /'flɪkə(r)/ v.i. vaciller. —n. vacillement m.; (light) lueur f.

flier /'flaɪə(r)/ n. = flyer.

flies /flaɪz/ n. pl. (on trousers: fam.) braguette f.

flight[1] /flaɪt/ n. (of bird, plane, etc.) vol m. ∼-deck n. poste de pilotage m. ∼ of stairs, escalier m.

flight[2] /flaɪt/ n. (fleeing) fuite f. put to ∼, mettre en fuite. take ∼, prendre la fuite.

flimsy /'flɪmzɪ/ a. (-ier, -iest) (pej.) mince, peu solide.

flinch /flɪntʃ/ v.i. (wince) broncher; (draw back) reculer.

fling /flɪŋ/ v.t. (p.t. flung) jeter. —n. have a ∼, faire la fête.

flint /flɪnt/ n. silex m.; (for lighter) pierre f.

flip /flɪp/ v.t. (p.t. flipped) donner un petit coup à. —n. chiquenaude f. ∼ through, feuilleter. ∼-flops n. pl. tongs f. pl.

flippant /'flɪpənt/ a. désinvolte.

flipper /'flɪpə(r)/ n. (of seal etc.) nageoire f.; (of swimmer) palme f.

flirt /flɜːt/ v.i. flirter. —n. flirteur, -se m., f. ∼ation /-'eɪʃn/ n. flirt m.

flit /flɪt/ v.i. (p.t. flitted) voltiger.

float /fləʊt/ v.t./i. (faire) flotter. —n. flotteur m.; (cart) char m.

flock /flɒk/ n. (of sheep etc.) troupeau m.; (of people) foule f. —v.i. venir en foule.

flog /flɒg/ v.t. (p.t. flogged) (beat) fouetter; (sell: sl.) vendre.

flood /flʌd/ n. inondation f.; (fig.) flot m. —v.t. inonder. —v.i. (building etc.) être inondé; (river) déborder; (people: fig.) affluer.

floodlight /'flʌdlaɪt/ n. projecteur m. —v.t. (p.t. floodlit) illuminer.

floor /flɔː(r)/ n. sol m., plancher m.; (for dancing) piste f.; (storey) étage m. —v.t. (knock down) terrasser; (baffle) stupéfier. ∼-board n. planche f.

flop /flɒp/ v.i. (p.t. flopped) s'agiter faiblement; (drop) s'affaler; (fail: sl.) échouer. —n. (sl.) échec m., fiasco m. ∼py a. lâche, flasque. ∼py (disk), disquette f.

flora /'flɔːrə/ n. flore f.

floral /'flɔːrəl/ a. floral.

florid /'flɒrɪd/ a. fleuri.

florist /'flɒrɪst/ n. fleuriste m./f.

flounce /flaʊns/ n. volant m.

flounder[1] /'flaʊndə(r)/ v.i. patauger (avec difficulté).

flounder[2] /'flaʊndə(r)/ n. (fish: Amer.) flet m., plie f.

flour /'flaʊə(r)/ n. farine f. ∼y a. farineux.

flourish /'flʌrɪʃ/ v.i. prospérer. —v.t. brandir. —n. geste élégant m.; (curve) floriture f.

flout /flaʊt/ v.t. faire fi de.

flow /fləʊ/ v.i. couler; (circulate) circuler; (traffic) s'écouler; (hang loosely) flotter. —n. (of liquid, traffic) écoulement m.; (of tide) flux m.; (of orders, words: fig.) flot m. ∼ chart, organigramme m. ∼ in, affluer. ∼ into, (of river) se jeter dans.

flower /'flaʊə(r)/ n. fleur f. —v.i. fleurir. ∼-bed n. plate-bande f. ∼ed a. à fleurs. ∼y a. fleuri.

flown /fləʊn/ see fly[2].

flu /fluː/ n (fam) grippe f

fluctuat|e /'flʌktʃʊeɪt/ v.i. varier. ∼ion /-'eɪʃn/ n variation f

flue /fluː/ n. (duct) tuyau m.

fluen|t /'fluːənt/ a. (style) aisé. be ∼t (in a language), parler (une langue) couramment. ∼cy n. facilité f. ∼tly adv. avec facilité; (lang.) couramment.

fluff /flʌf/ n. peluche(s) f. (pl.); (down) duvet m. ∼y a. pelucheux.

fluid /'fluːɪd/ a. & n. fluide (m.).

fluke /fluːk/ n. coup de chance m.

flung /flʌŋ/ see fling.

flunk /flʌŋk/ v.t./i. (Amer., fam.) être collé (à).

fluorescent /flʊə'resnt/ a. fluorescent.

fluoride /'flʊəraɪd/ n. (in toothpaste, water) fluor m.

flurry /'flʌrɪ/ n. (squall) rafale f.; (fig.) agitation f.

flush[1] /flʌʃ/ v.i. rougir. —v.t. nettoyer à grande eau. —n. (blush) rougeur f.; (fig.) excitation f. —a. ∼ with, (level with) au ras de. ∼ the toilet, tirer la chasse d'eau.

flush[2] /flʌʃ/ v.t. ∼ out, chasser.

fluster /'flʌstə(r)/ v.t. énerver.

flute /fluːt/ n. flûte f.

flutter /'flʌtə(r)/ v.i. voleter; (of wings) battre. —n. (of wings) battement m.; (fig.) agitation f.; (bet: fam.) pari m.

flux /flʌks/ n. changement continuel m.

fly[1] /flaɪ/ n. mouche f.

fly[2] /flaɪ/ v.i. (p.t. flew, p.p. flown) voler; (of passengers) voyager en avion; (of flag) flotter; (rush) filer. —v.t. (aircraft) piloter; (passengers, goods)

transporter par avion; (*flag*), arborer.
—*n.* (*of trousers*) braguette *f.* **~ off**,
s'envoler.

flyer /'flaɪə(r)/ *n.* aviateur *m.*; (*circular*:
Amer.) prospectus *m.*

flying /'flaɪɪŋ/ *a.* (*saucer etc.*) volant.
—*n.* (*activity*) aviation *f.* **~ buttress**,
arc-boutant *m.* **with ~ colours**, haut la
main. **~ start**, excellent départ *m.* **~
visit**, visite éclair *f.* (*a. invar.*).

flyover /'flaɪəʊvə(r)/ *n.* (*road*) toboggan
m., saut-de-mouton *m.*

flyweight /'flaɪweɪt/ *n.* poids mouche *m.*

foal /fəʊl/ *n.* poulain *m.*

foam /fəʊm/ *n.* écume *f.*, mousse *f.*
—*v.i.* écumer, mousser. **~ (rubber)** *n.*
caoutchouc mousse *m.*

fob /fɒb/ *v.t.* (*p.t.* **fobbed**) **~ off on (to)
s.o.**, (*palm off*) refiler à qn. **~ s.o. off
with**, forcer qn. à se contenter de.

focal /'fəʊkl/ *a.* focal.

focus /'fəʊkəs/ *n.* (*pl.* **-cuses** *or* **-ci** /-saɪ/)
foyer *m.*; (*fig.*) centre *m.* —*v.t./i.* (*p.t.*
focused) (*faire*) converger; (*instrument*) mettre au point; (*with camera*)
faire la mise au point (**on**, sur); (*fig.*)
(se) concentrer. **be in/out of ~**, être/ne
pas être au point.

fodder /'fɒdə(r)/ *n.* fourrage *m.*

foe /fəʊ/ *n.* ennemi(e) *m.*(*f.*).

foetus /'fiːtəs/ *n.* (*pl.* **-tuses**) fœtus *m.*

fog /fɒg/ *n.* brouillard *m.* —*v.t./i.* (*p.t.*
fogged) (*window etc.*) (s')embuer. **~-
horn** *n.* (*naut.*) corne de brume *f.* **~gy**
a. brumeux. **it is ~gy**, il fait du
brouillard.

fog(e)y /'fəʊgɪ/ *n.* (**old**) **~**, vieille
baderne *f.*

foible /'fɔɪbl/ *n.* faiblesse *f.*

foil[1] /fɔɪl/ *n.* (*tin foil*) papier
d'aluminium *m.*; (*fig.*) repoussoir *m.*

foil[2] /fɔɪl/ *v.t.* (*thwart*) déjouer.

foist /fɔɪst/ *v.t.* imposer (**on**, à).

fold[1] /fəʊld/ *v.t./i.* (se) plier; (*arms*)
croiser; (*fail*) s'effondrer. —*n.* pli *m.*
~er *n.* (*file*) chemise *f.*; (*leaflet*)
dépliant *m.* **~ing** *a.* pliant.

fold[2] /fəʊld/ *n.* (*for sheep*) parc à
moutons *m.*; (*relig.*) bercail *m.*

foliage /'fəʊlɪɪdʒ/ *n.* feuillage *m.*

folk /fəʊk/ *n.* gens *m. pl.* **~s**, parents *m.
pl.* —*a.* folklorique.

folklore /'fəʊklɔː(r)/ *n.* folklore *m.*

follow /'fɒləʊ/ *v.t./i.* suivre. **it ~s that**, il
s'ensuit que. **~ suit**, en faire autant. **~
up**, (*letter etc.*) donner suite à. **~er** *n.*
partisan *m.* **~ing** *n.* partisans *m. pl.*; *a.*
suivant; *prep.* à la suite de.

folly /'fɒlɪ/ *n.* sottise *f.*

foment /fəʊ'ment/ *v.t.* fomenter.

fond /fɒnd/ *a.* (**-er**, **-est**) (*loving*)
affectueux; (*hope*) cher. **be ~ of**, aimer.
~ness *n.* affection *f.*; (*for things*)
attachement *m.*

fondle /'fɒndl/ *v.t.* caresser.

food /fuːd/ *n.* nourriture *f.* —*a.*
alimentaire. **French ~**, la cuisine
française. **~ processor**, robot
(ménager) *m.*

fool /fuːl/ *n.* idiot(e) *m.* (*f.*). —*v.t.* duper.
—*v.i.* **~ around**, faire l'idiot.

foolhardy /'fuːlhɑːdɪ/ *a.* téméraire.

foolish /'fuːlɪʃ/ *a.* idiot. **~ly** *adv.*
sottement. **~ness** *n.* sottise *f.*

foolproof /'fuːlpruːf/ *a.* infaillible.

foot /fʊt/ *n.* (*pl.* **feet**) pied *m.*; (*measure*)
pied *m.* (= *30.48 cm.*); (*of stairs, page*)
bas *m.* —*v.t.* (*bill*) payer. **~-bridge** *n.*
passerelle *f.* **on ~**, à pied. **on** *or* **to one's
feet**, debout. **under s.o.'s feet**, dans les
jambes de qn.

footage /'fʊtɪdʒ/ *n.* (*of film*) métrage *m.*

football /'fʊtbɔːl/ *n.* (*ball*) ballon *m.*;
(*game*) football *m.* **~ pools**, paris sur
les matchs de football *m. pl.* **~er** *n.*
footballeur *m.*

foothills /'fʊthɪlz/ *n. pl.* contreforts *m.
pl.*

foothold /'fʊthəʊld/ *n.* prise *f.*

footing /'fʊtɪŋ/ *n.* prise (de pied) *f.*,
équilibre *m.*; (*fig.*) situation *f.* **on an
equal ~**, sur un pied d'égalité.

footlights /'fʊtlaɪts/ *n. pl.* rampe *f.*

footman /'fʊtmən/ *n.* (*pl.* **-men**) valet de
pied *m.*

footnote /'fʊtnəʊt/ *n.* note (en bas de la
page) *f.*

footpath /'fʊtpɑːθ/ *n.* sentier *m.*; (*at the
side of the road*) chemin *m.*

footprint /'fʊtprɪnt/ *n.* empreinte (de
pied) *f.*

footsore /'fʊtsɔː(r)/ *a.* **be ~**, avoir les
pieds douloureux.

footstep /'fʊtstep/ *n.* pas *m.*

footwear /'fʊtweə(r)/ *n.* chaussures *f. pl.*

for /fɔː(r), *unstressed* fə(r)/ *prep.* pour;
(*during*) pendant; (*before*) avant.
—*conj.* car. **a liking ~**, le goût de. **look
~**, chercher. **pay ~**, payer. **he has been
away ~**, il est absent depuis. **he
stopped ~ ten minutes**, il s'est arrêté
(pendant) dix minutes. **it continues ~
ten kilometres**, ça continue pendant dix
kilomètres. **~ ever**, pour toujours. **~
good**, pour de bon. **~ all my work**,
malgré mon travail.

forage /'fɒrɪdʒ/ *v.i.* fourrager. —*n.*
fourrage *m.*

foray /'fɒreɪ/ n. incursion f.

forbade /fə'bæd/ see **forbid**.

forbear /fɔː'beə(r)/ v.t./i. (p.t. **forbore**, p.p. **forborne**) s'abstenir. ~**ance** n. patience f.

forbid /fə'bɪd/ v.t. (p.t. **forbade**, p.p. **forbidden**) interdire, défendre (**s.o. to do**, à qn. de faire). ~ **s.o. sth.**, interdire or défendre qch. à qn. **you are** ~**den to leave**, il vous est interdit de partir.

forbidding /fə'bɪdɪŋ/ a. menaçant.

force /fɔːs/ n. force f. —v.t. forcer. ~ **into**, faire entrer de force. ~ **on**, imposer à. **come into** ~, entrer en vigueur. **the** ~**s**, les forces armées f. pl. ~**d** a. forcé. ~**ful** a. énergique.

force-feed /'fɔːsfiːd/ v.t. (p.t. **-fed**) nourrir de force.

forceps /'fɔːseps/ n. invar. forceps m.

forcibl|e /'fɔːsəbl/ ~**y** adv. de force.

ford /fɔːd/ n. gué m. —v.t. passer à gué.

fore /fɔː(r)/ a. antérieur. —n. **to the** ~, en évidence.

forearm /'fɔːrɑːm/ n. avant-bras m. invar.

foreboding /fɔː'bəʊdɪŋ/ n. pressentiment m.

forecast /'fɔːkɑːst/ v.t. (p.t. **forecast**) prévoir. —n. prévision f.

forecourt /'fɔːkɔːt/ n. (of garage) devant m.; (of station) cour f.

forefathers /'fɔːfɑːðəz/ n. pl. aïeux m. pl.

forefinger /'fɔːfɪŋgə(r)/ n. index m.

forefront /'fɔːfrʌnt/ n. premier rang m.

foregone /fɔː'gɒn/ a. ~ **conclusion**, résultat à prévoir m.

foreground /'fɔːgraʊnd/ n. premier plan m.

forehead /'fɒrɪd/ n. front m.

foreign /'fɒrən/ a. étranger; (trade) extérieur; (travel) à l'étranger. ~**er** n. étranger, -ère m., f.

foreman /'fɔːmən/ n. (pl. **-men**) contremaître m.

foremost /'fɔːməʊst/ a. le plus éminent. —adv. **first and** ~, tout d'abord.

forename /'fɔːneɪm/ n. prénom m.

forensic /fə'rensɪk/ a. médicolégal. ~ **medicine**, médecine légale f.

foreplay /'fɔːpleɪ/ n. préliminaires m. pl.

forerunner /'fɔːrʌnə(r)/ n. précurseur m.

foresee /fɔː'siː/ v.t. (p.t. **-saw**, p.p. **-seen**) prévoir. ~**able** a. prévisible.

foreshadow /fɔː'ʃædəʊ/ v.t. présager, laisser prévoir.

foresight /'fɔːsaɪt/ n. prévoyance f.

forest /'fɒrɪst/ n. forêt f.

forestall /fɔː'stɔːl/ v.t. devancer.

forestry /'fɒrɪstrɪ/ n. sylviculture f.

foretaste /'fɔːteɪst/ n. avant-goût m.

foretell /fɔː'tel/ v.t. (p.t. **foretold**) prédire.

forever /fə'revə(r)/ adv. toujours.

forewarn /fɔː'wɔːn/ v.t. avertir.

foreword /'fɔːwɜːd/ n. avant-propos m. invar.

forfeit /'fɔːfɪt/ n. (penalty) peine f.; (in game) gage m. —v.t. perdre.

forgave /fə'geɪv/ see **forgive**.

forge[1] /fɔːdʒ/ v.i. ~ **ahead**, aller de l'avant, avancer.

forge[2] /fɔːdʒ/ n. forge f. —v.t. (metal, friendship) forger; (copy) contrefaire, falsifier. ~**r** /-ə(r)/ n. faussaire m. ~**ry** /-ərɪ/ n. faux m., contrefaçon f.

forget /fə'get/ v.t./i. (p.t. **forgot**, p.p. **forgotten**) oublier. ~**-me-not** n. myosotis m. ~ **o.s.**, s'oublier. ~**ful** a. distrait. ~**ful of**, oublieux de.

forgive /fə'gɪv/ v.t. (p.t. **forgave**, p.p. **forgiven**) pardonner (**s.o. for sth.**, qch. à qn.). ~**ness** n. pardon m.

forgo /fɔː'gəʊ/ v.t. (p.t. **forwent**, p.p. **forgone**) renoncer à.

fork /fɔːk/ n. fourchette f.; (for digging etc.) fourche f.; (in road) bifurcation f. —v.i. (road) bifurquer. ~**-lift truck**, chariot élévateur m. ~ **out**, (sl.) payer. ~**ed** a. fourchu.

forlorn /fə'lɔːn/ a. triste, abandonné. ~ **hope**, mince espoir m.

form /fɔːm/ n. forme f.; (document) formulaire m.; (schol.) classe f. —v.t./i. (se) former. **on** ~, en forme.

formal /'fɔːml/ a. officiel, en bonne et due forme; (person) compassé, cérémonieux; (dress) de cérémonie; (denial, grammar) formel; (language) soutenu. ~**ity** /-'mælətɪ/ n. cérémonial m.; (requirement) formalité f. ~**ly** adv. officiellement.

format /'fɔːmæt/ n. format m. —v.t. (p.t. **formatted**) (disk) initialiser, formater.

formation /fɔː'meɪʃn/ n. formation f.

formative /'fɔːmətɪv/ a. formateur.

former /'fɔːmə(r)/ a. ancien; (first of two) premier. —n. **the** ~, celui-là, celle-là. ~**ly** adv. autrefois.

formidable /'fɔːmɪdəbl/ a. redoutable, terrible.

formula /'fɔːmjʊlə/ n. (pl. **-ae** /-iː/ or **-as**) formule f.

formulate /'fɔːmjʊleɪt/ v.t. formuler.

forsake /fə'seɪk/ v.t. (p.t. **forsook**, p.p. **forsaken**) abandonner.

fort /fɔːt/ n. (mil.) fort m.

forte /'fɔːteɪ/ n. (talent) fort m.

forth /fɔːθ/ *adv.* en avant. **and so ∼,** et ainsi de suite. **go back and ∼,** aller et venir.

forthcoming /fɔːθ'kʌmɪŋ/ *a.* à venir, prochain; (*sociable*: *fam.*) communicatif.

forthright /'fɔːθraɪt/ *a.* direct.

forthwith /fɔːθ'wɪθ/ *adv.* sur-le-champ.

fortif|y /'fɔːtɪfaɪ/ *v.t.* fortifier. **∼ication** /-ɪ'keɪʃn/ *n.* fortification *f.*

fortitude /'fɔːtɪtjuːd/ *n.* courage *m.*

fortnight /'fɔːtnaɪt/ *n.* quinze jours *m. pl.*, quinzaine *f.* **∼ly** *a.* bimensuel; *adv.* tous les quinze jours.

fortress /'fɔːtrɪs/ *n.* forteresse *f.*

fortuitous /fɔː'tjuːɪtəs/ *a.* fortuit.

fortunate /'fɔːtʃənət/ *a.* heureux. **be ∼,** avoir de la chance. **∼ly** *adv.* heureusement.

fortune /'fɔːtʃuːn/ *n.* fortune *f.* **∼-teller** *n.* diseuse de bonne aventure *f.* **have the good ∼ to,** avoir la chance de.

fort|y /'fɔːtɪ/ *a. & n.* quarante (*m.*). **∼y winks,** un petit somme. **∼ieth** *a. & n.* quarantième (*m./f.*).

forum /'fɔːrəm/ *n.* forum *m.*

forward /'fɔːwəd/ *a.* en avant; (*advanced*) précoce; (*pert*) effronté. —*n.* (*sport*) avant *m.* —*adv.* en avant. —*v.t.* (*letter*) faire suivre; (*goods*) expédier; (*fig.*) favoriser. **come ∼,** se présenter. **go ∼,** avancer. **∼ness** *n.* précocité *f.*

forwards /'fɔːwədz/ *adv.* en avant.

fossil /'fɒsl/ *n. & a.* fossile (*m.*).

foster /'fɒstə(r)/ *v.t.* (*promote*) encourager; (*child*) élever. **∼-child** *n.* enfant adoptif *m.* **∼-mother** *n.* mère adoptive *f.*

fought /fɔːt/ *see* **fight**.

foul /faʊl/ *a.* (**-er, -est**) (*smell, weather, etc.*) infect; (*place, action*) immonde; (*language*) ordurier. —*n.* (*football*) faute *f.* —*v.t.* souiller, encrasser. **∼-mouthed** *a.* au langage ordurier. **∼ play,** jeu irrégulier *m.*; (*crime*) acte criminel *m.* **∼ up,** (*sl.*) gâcher.

found¹ /faʊnd/ *see* **find**.

found² /faʊnd/ *v.t.* fonder. **∼ation** /-'deɪʃn/ *n.* fondation *f.*; (*basis*) fondement *m.*; (*make-up*) fond de teint *m.* **∼er¹** *n.* fondateur, -trice *m., f.*

founder² /'faʊndə(r)/ *v.i.* sombrer.

foundry /'faʊndrɪ/ *n.* fonderie *f.*

fountain /'faʊntɪn/ *n.* fontaine *f.* **∼-pen** *n.* stylo à encre *m.*

four /fɔː(r)/ *a. & n.* quatre (*m.*). **∼fold** *a.* quadruple; *adv.* au quadruple. **∼th** *a. & n.* quatrième (*m./f.*). **∼-wheel drive,**

quatre roues motrices; (*car*) quatre-quatre *f.*

foursome /'fɔːsəm/ *n.* partie à quatre *f.*

fourteen /fɔː'tiːn/ *a. & n.* quatorze (*m.*). **∼th** *a. & n.* quatorzième (*m./f.*).

fowl /faʊl/ *n.* volaille *f.*

fox /fɒks/ *n.* renard *m.* —*v.t.* (*baffle*) mystifier; (*deceive*) tromper.

foyer /'fɔɪeɪ/ *n.* (*hall*) foyer *m.*

fraction /'frækʃn/ *n.* fraction *f.*

fracture /'fræktʃə(r)/ *n.* fracture *f.* —*v.t./i.* (se) fracturer.

fragile /'frædʒaɪl, *Amer.* 'frædʒəl/ *a.* fragile.

fragment /'frægmənt/ *n.* fragment *m.* **∼ary** *a.* fragmentaire.

fragran|t /'freɪɡrənt/ *a.* parfumé. **∼ce** *n.* parfum *m.*

frail /freɪl/ *a.* (**-er, -est**) frêle.

frame /freɪm/ *n.* charpente *f.*; (*of picture*) cadre *m.*; (*of window*) châssis *m.*; (*of spectacles*) monture *f.* —*v.t.* encadrer; (*fig.*) formuler; (*jurid., sl.*) monter un coup contre. **∼ of mind,** humeur *f.*

framework /'freɪmwɜːk/ *n.* structure *f.*; (*context*) cadre *m.*

franc /fræŋk/ *n.* franc *m.*

France /frɑːns/ *n.* France *f.*

franchise /'fræntʃaɪz/ *n.* (*pol.*) droit de vote *m.*; (*comm.*) franchise *f.*

Franco- /'fræŋkəʊ/ *pref.* franco-.

frank¹ /fræŋk/ *a.* franc. **∼ly** *adv.* franchement. **∼ness** *n.* franchise *f.*

frank² /fræŋk/ *v.t.* affranchir.

frantic /'fræntɪk/ *a.* frénétique. **∼ with,** fou de.

fratern|al /frə'tɜːnl/ *a.* fraternel. **∼ity** *n.* (*bond*) fraternité *f.*; (*group, club*) confrérie *f.*

fraternize /'frætənaɪz/ *v.i.* fraterniser (**with,** avec).

fraud /frɔːd/ *n.* (*deception*) fraude *f.*; (*person*) imposteur *m.* **∼ulent** *a.* frauduleux.

fraught /frɔːt/ *a.* (*tense*) tendu. **∼ with,** chargé de.

fray¹ /freɪ/ *n.* rixe *f.*

fray² /freɪ/ *v.t./i.* (s')effilocher.

freak /friːk/ *n.* phénomène *m.* —*a.* anormal. **∼ish** *a.* anormal.

freckle /'frekl/ *n.* tache de rousseur *f.* **∼d** *a.* couvert de taches de rousseur.

free /friː/ *a.* (**freer** /'friːə(r)/, **freest** /'friːɪst/) libre; (*gratis*) gratuit; (*lavish*) généreux. —*v.t.* (*p.t.* **freed**) libérer; (*clear*) dégager. **∼ enterprise,** la libre entreprise. **a ∼ hand,** carte blanche *f.* **∼ kick,** coup franc *m.* **∼lance** *a. & n.*

free-lance (*m./f.*), indépendant(e) *m.*, *f.* ~ **(of charge)**, gratuit(ement). ~-**range** *a.* (*eggs*) de ferme. ~-**wheel** *v.i.* descendre en roue libre. ~-**wheeling** *a.* sans contraintes. ~**ly** *adv.* librement.

freedom /'fri:dəm/ *n.* liberté *f.*

Freemason /'fri:meɪsn/ *n.* franc-maçon *m.* ~**ry** *n.* francmaçonnerie *f.*

freeway /'fri:weɪ/ *n.* (*Amer.*) autoroute *f.*

freez|e /fri:z/ *v.t./i.* (*p.t.* **froze**, *p.p.* **frozen**) geler; (*culin.*) (se) congeler; (*wages etc.*) bloquer. —*n.* gel *m.*; blocage *m.* ~**e-dried** *a.* lyophilisé. ~**er** *n.* congélateur *m.* ~**ing** *a.* glacial. **below** ~**ing**, au-dessous de zéro.

freight /freɪt/ *n.* fret *m.* ~**er** *n.* (*ship*) cargo *m.*

French /frentʃ/ *a.* français. —*n.* (*lang.*) français *m.* ~ **bean,** haricot vert *m.* ~ **fries,** frites *f. pl.* ~-**speaking** *a.* francophone. ~ **window** *n.* porte-fenêtre *f.* **the** ~, les Français *m. pl.* ~**man** *n.* Français *m.* ~**woman** *n.* Française *f.*

frenz|y /'frenzɪ/ *n.* frénésie *f.* ~**ied** *a.* frénétique.

frequen|t¹ /'fri:kwənt/ *a.* fréquent. ~**cy** *n.* fréquence *f.* ~**tly** *adv.* fréquemment.

frequent² /frɪ'kwent/ *v.t.* fréquenter.

fresco /'freskəʊ/ *n.* (*pl.* -**os**) fresque *f.*

fresh /freʃ/ *a.* (-**er**, -**est**) frais; (*different, additional*) nouveau; (*cheeky: fam.*) culotté. ~**ly** *adv.* nouvellement. ~**ness** *n.* fraîcheur *f.*

freshen /'freʃn/ *v.i.* (*weather*) fraîchir. ~ **up,** (*person*) se rafraîchir.

fresher /'freʃə(r)/ *n.,* **freshman** /'freʃmən/ *n.* (*pl.* -**men**) bizuth *m./f.*

freshwater /'freʃwɔːtə(r)/ *a.* d'eau douce.

fret /fret/ *v.i.* (*p.t.* **fretted**) se tracasser. ~**ful** *a.* ronchon, insatisfait.

friar /'fraɪə(r)/ *n.* moine *m.*, frère *m.*

friction /'frɪkʃn/ *n.* friction *f.*

Friday /'fraɪdɪ/ *n.* vendredi *m.*

fridge /frɪdʒ/ *n.* frigo *m.*

fried /fraɪd/ *see* **fry.** —*a.* frit. ~ **eggs,** œufs sur le plat *m. pl.*

friend /frend/ *n.* ami(e) *m.* (*f.*). ~**ship** *n.* amitié *f.*

friend|ly /'frendlɪ/ *a.* (-**ier**, -**iest**) amical, gentil. **F**~**y Society,** mutuelle *f.*, société de prévoyance *f.* ~**iness** *n.* gentillesse *f.*

frieze /fri:z/ *n.* frise *f.*

frigate /'frɪgət/ *n.* frégate *f.*

fright /fraɪt/ *n.* peur *f.*; (*person, thing*) horreur *f.* ~**ful** *a.* affreux. ~**fully** *adv.* affreusement.

frighten /'fraɪtn/ *v.t.* effrayer. ~ **off,** faire fuir. ~**ed** *a.* effrayé. **be** ~**ed,** avoir peur (**of,** de). ~**ing** *a.* effrayant.

frigid /'frɪdʒɪd/ *a.* froid, glacial; (*psych.*) frigide. ~**ity** /-'dʒɪdətɪ/ *n.* frigidité *f.*

frill /frɪl/ *n.* (*trimming*) fanfreluche *f.* **with no** ~**s,** très simple.

fringe /frɪndʒ/ *n.* (*edging, hair*) frange *f.*; (*of area*) bordure *f.*; (*of society*) marge *f.* ~ **benefits,** avantages sociaux *m. pl.*

frisk /frɪsk/ *v.t.* (*search*) fouiller.

frisky /'frɪskɪ/ *a.* (-**ier**, -**iest**) fringant, frétillant.

fritter¹ /'frɪtə(r)/ *n.* beignet *m.*

fritter² /'frɪtə(r)/ *v.t.* ~ **away,** gaspiller.

frivol|ous /'frɪvələs/ *a.* frivole. ~**ity** /-'vɒlətɪ/ *n.* frivolité *f.*

frizzy /'frɪzɪ/ *a.* crépu, crêpelé.

fro /frəʊ/ *see* **to and fro.**

frock /frɒk/ *n.* robe *f.*

frog /frɒg/ *n.* grenouille *f.* **a** ~ **in one's throat,** un chat dans la gorge.

frogman /'frɒgmən/ *n.* (*pl.* -**men**) homme-grenouille *m.*

frolic /'frɒlɪk/ *v.i.* (*p.t.* **frolicked**) s'ébattre. —*n.* ébats *m. pl.*

from /frɒm, *unstressed* frəm/ *prep.* de; (*with time, prices, etc.*) à partir de, de; (*habit, conviction, etc.*) par; (*according to*) d'après. **take** ~ **s.o.,** prendre à qn. **take** ~ **one's pocket,** prendre dans sa poche.

front /frʌnt/ *n.* (*of car, train, etc.*) avant *m.*; (*of garment, building*) devant *m.*; (*mil., pol.*) front *m.*; (*of book, pamphlet, etc.*) début *m.*; (*appearance: fig.*) façade *f.* —*a.* de devant, avant *invar.*; (*first*) premier. ~ **door,** porte d'entrée *f.* ~-**wheel drive,** traction avant *f.* **in** ~ (**of**), devant. ~**age** *n.* façade *f.* ~**al** *a.* frontal; (*attack*) de front.

frontier /'frʌntɪə(r)/ *n.* frontière *f.*

frost /frɒst/ *n.* gel *m.*, gelée *f.*; (*on glass etc.*) givre *m.* —*v.t./i.* (se) givrer. ~-**bite** *n.* gelure *f.* ~-**bitten** *a.* gelé. ~**ed** *a.* (*glass*) dépoli. ~**ing** *n.* (*icing: Amer.*) glace *f.* ~**y** *a.* (*weather, welcome*) glacial; (*window*) givré.

froth /frɒθ/ *n.* mousse *f.*, écume *f.* —*v.i.* mousser, écumer. ~**y** *a.* mousseux.

frown /fraʊn/ *v.i.* froncer les sourcils. —*n.* froncement de sourcils *m.* ~ **on,** désapprouver.

froze /frəʊz/ *see* **freeze.**

frozen /'frəʊzn/ *see* **freeze.** —*a.* congelé.

frugal /'fru:gl/ *a.* (*person*) économe;

(*meal, life*) frugal. **~ly** *adv.* (*live*) simplement.

fruit /fruːt/ *n.* fruit *m.*; (*collectively*) fruits *m. pl.* **~ machine,** machine à sous *f.* **~ salad,** salade de fruits *f.* **~erer** *n.* fruitlier, -ière *m., f.* **~y** *a.* (*taste*) fruité.

fruit|ful /ˈfruːtfl/ *a.* (*discussions*) fructueux. **~less** *a.* stérile.

fruition /fruːˈɪʃn/ *n.* **come to ~,** se réaliser.

frustrat|e /frʌˈstreɪt/ *v.t.* (*plan*) faire échouer; (*person: psych.*) frustrer; (*upset: fam.*) exaspérer. **~ion** /-ʃn/ *n.* (*psych.*) frustration *f.*; (*disappointment*) déception *f.*

fry[1] /fraɪ/ *v.t./i.* (*p.t.* **fried**) (faire) frire. **~ing-pan** *n.* poêle (à frire) *f.*

fry[2] /fraɪ/ *n.* **the small ~,** le menu fretin.

fuddy-duddy /ˈfʌdɪdʌdɪ/ *n.* **be a ~,** (*sl.*) être vieux jeu *invar.*

fudge /fʌdʒ/ *n.* (sorte de) caramel mou *m.* —*v.t.* se dérober à.

fuel /ˈfjuːəl/ *n.* combustible *m.*; (*for car engine*) carburant *m.* —*v.t.* (*p.t.* **fuelled**) alimenter en combustible.

fugitive /ˈfjuːdʒətɪv/ *n. & a.* fugitif, -ve (*m., f.*).

fugue /fjuːg/ *n.* (*mus.*) fugue *f.*

fulfil /fʊlˈfɪl/ *v.t.* (*p.t.* **fulfilled**) accomplir, réaliser; (*condition*) remplier. **~ o.s.,** s'épanouir. **~ling** *a.* satisfaisant. **~ment** *n.* réalisation *f.*; épanouissement *m.*

full /fʊl/ *a.* (**-er, -est**) plein (**of,** de); (*bus, hotel*) complet; (*programme*) chargé; (*name*) complet; (*skirt*) ample. —*n.* **in ~,** intégral(ement). **to the ~,** complètement. **be ~** (**up**), n'avoir plus faim. **~ back,** (*sport*) arrière *m.* **~ moon,** pleine lune *f.* **~-scale** *a.* (*drawing etc.*) grandeur nature *invar.*; (*fig.*) de grande envergure. **at ~ speed,** à toute vitesse. **~ stop,** point *m.* **~-time** *a. & adv.* à plein temps. **~y** *adv.* complètement.

fulsome /ˈfʊlsəm/ *a.* excessif.

fumble /ˈfʌmbl/ *v.i.* tâtonner, fouiller. **~ with,** tripoter.

fume /fjuːm/ *v.i.* rager. **~s** *n. pl.* exhalaisons *f. pl.*, vapeurs *f. pl.*

fumigate /ˈfjuːmɪgeɪt/ *v.t.* désinfecter.

fun /fʌn/ *n.* amusement *m.* **be ~,** être chouette. **for ~,** pour rire. **~-fair** *n.* fête foraine *f.* **make ~ of,** se moquer de.

function /ˈfʌŋkʃn/ *n.* (*purpose, duty*) fonction *f.*; (*event*) réception *f.* —*v.i.* fonctionner. **~al** *a.* fonctionnel.

fund /fʌnd/ *n.* fonds *m.* —*v.t.* fournir les fonds pour.

fundamental /fʌndəˈmentl/ *a.* fondamental. **~ist** *n.* intégriste *m./f.* **~ism** *n.* intégrisme *m.*

funeral /ˈfjuːnərəl/ *n.* enterrement *m.*, funérailles *f. pl.* —*a.* funèbre.

fungus /ˈfʌŋgəs/ *n.* (*pl.* **-gi** /-gaɪ/) (*plant*) champignon *m.*; (*mould*) moisissure *f.*

funicular /fjuːˈnɪkjʊlə(r)/ *n.* funiculaire *m.*

funk /fʌŋk/ *m.* **be in a ~,** (*afraid: sl.*) avoir la frousse; (*depressed: Amer., sl.*) être déprimé.

funnel /ˈfʌnl/ *n.* (*for pouring*) entonnoir *m.*; (*of ship*) cheminée *f.*

funn|y /ˈfʌnɪ/ *a.* (**-ier, -iest**) drôle; (*odd*) bizarre. **~y business,** quelque chose de louche. **~ily** *adv.* drôlement; bizarrement.

fur /fɜː(r)/ *n.* fourrure *f.*; (*in kettle*) tartre *m.*

furious /ˈfjʊərɪəs/ *a.* furieux. **~ly** *adv.* furieusement.

furnace /ˈfɜːnɪs/ *n.* fourneau *m.*

furnish /ˈfɜːnɪʃ/ *v.t.* (*with furniture*) meubler; (*supply*) fournir. **~ings** *n. pl.* ameublement *m.*

furniture /ˈfɜːnɪtʃə(r)/ *n.* meubles *m. pl.*, mobilier *m.*

furrow /ˈfʌrəʊ/ *n.* sillon *m.*

furry /ˈfɜːrɪ/ *a.* (*animal*) à fourrure; (*toy*) en peluche.

furth|er /ˈfɜːðə(r)/ *a.* plus éloigné; (*additional*) supplémentaire. —*adv.* plus loin; (*more*) davantage. —*v.t.* avancer. **~er education,** formation continue *f.* **~est** *a.* le plus éloigné; *adv.* le plus loin.

furthermore /ˈfɜːðəmɔː(r)/ *adv.* en outre, de plus.

furtive /ˈfɜːtɪv/ *a.* furtif.

fury /ˈfjʊərɪ/ *n.* fureur *f.*

fuse[1] /fjuːz/ *v.t./i.* (*melt*) fondre; (*unite: fig.*) fusionner. —*n.* fusible *m.*, plomb *m.* **~ the lights** *etc.*, faire sauter les plombs.

fuse[2] /fjuːz/ *n.* (*of bomb*) amorce *f.*

fuselage /ˈfjuːzəlɑːʒ/ *n.* fuselage *m.*

fusion /ˈfjuːʒn/ *n.* fusion *f.*

fuss /fʌs/ *n.* (*when upset*) histoire(s) *f.* (*pl.*); (*when excited*) agitation *f.* —*v.i.* s'agiter. **make a ~,** faire des histoires; s'agiter; (*about food*) faire des chichis. **make a ~ of,** faire grand cas de. **~y** *a.* (*finicky*) tatillon; (*hard to please*) difficile.

futile /ˈfjuːtaɪl/ *a.* futile, vain.

future /ˈfjuːtʃə(r)/ *a.* futur. —*n.* avenir *m.*; (*gram.*) futur *m.* **in ~,** à l'avenir.

fuzz /fʌz/ n. (*fluff, growth*) duvet m.; (*police*: sl.) flics m. pl.

fuzzy /'fʌzɪ/ a. (*hair*) crépu; (*photograph*) flou; (*person*: fam.) à l'esprit confus.

G

gabardine /gæbə'diːn/ n. gabardine f.

gabble /'gæbl/ v.t./i. bredouiller. —n. baragouin m.

gable /'geɪbl/ n. pignon m.

gad /gæd/ v.i. (p.t. **gadded**). ~ about, se promener, aller çà et là.

gadget /'gædʒɪt/ n. gadget m.

Gaelic /'geɪlɪk/ n. gaélique m.

gaffe /gæf/ n. (*blunder*) gaffe f.

gag /gæg/ n. bâillon m.; (*joke*) gag m. —v.t. (p.t. **gagged**) bâillonner.

gaiety /'geɪətɪ/ n. gaieté f.

gaily /'geɪlɪ/ adv. gaiement.

gain /geɪn/ v.t. gagner; (*speed, weight*) prendre. —v.i. (*of clock*) avancer. —n. acquisition f.; (*profit*) gain m. ~ful a. profitable.

gait /geɪt/ n. démarche f.

gala /'gɑːlə/ n. (*festive occasion*) gala m.; (*sport*) concours m.

galaxy /'gæləksɪ/ n. galaxie f.

gale /geɪl/ n. tempête f.

gall /gɔːl/ n. bile f.; (*fig.*) fiel m.; (*impudence*: sl.) culot m. ~-bladder n. vésicule biliaire f.

gallant /'gælənt/ a. (*brave*) courageux; (*chivalrous*) galant. ~ry n. courage m.

galleon /'gælɪən/ n. galion m.

gallery /'gælərɪ/ n. galerie f. (art) ~, (*public*) musée m.

galley /'gælɪ/ n. (*ship*) galère f.; (*kitchen*) cambuse f.

Gallic /'gælɪk/ a. français. ~ism /-sɪzəm/ n. gallicisme m.

gallivant /gælɪ'vænt/ v.i. (*fam.*) se promener, aller çà et là.

gallon /'gælən/ n. gallon m. (*imperial* = 4.546 *litres*; Amer. = 3.785 *litres*).

gallop /'gæləp/ n. galop m. —v.i. (p.t. **galloped**) galoper.

gallows /'gæləʊz/ n. potence f.

galore /gə'lɔː(r)/ adv. en abondance, à gogo.

galosh /gə'lɒʃ/ n. (*overshoe*) caoutchouc m.

galvanize /'gælvənaɪz/ v.t. galvaniser.

gambit /'gæmbɪt/ n. (**opening**) ~,

(*move*) première démarche f.; (*ploy*) stratagème m.

gamble /'gæmbl/ v.t./i. jouer. —n. (*venture*) entreprise risquée f.; (*bet*) pari m.; (*risk*) risque m. ~e on, miser sur. ~er n. joueulr, se m., f. ~ing n. le jeu.

game[1] /geɪm/ n. jeu m.; (*football*) match m.; (*tennis*) partie f.; (*animals, birds*) gibier m. —a. (*brave*) brave. ~ for, prêt à.

game[2] /geɪm/ a. (*lame*) estropié.

gamekeeper /'geɪmkiːpə(r)/ n. garde-chasse m.

gammon /'gæmən/ n. jambon fumé m.

gamut /'gæmət/ n. gamme f.

gamy /'geɪmɪ/ a. faisandé.

gang /gæŋ/ n. bande f.; (*of workmen*) équipe f. —v.i. ~ up, se liguer (**on, against**, contre).

gangling /'gæŋglɪŋ/ a. dégingandé, grand et maigre.

gangrene /'gæŋgriːn/ n. gangrène f.

gangster /'gæŋstə(r)/ n. gangster m.

gangway /'gæŋweɪ/ n. passage m.; (*aisle*) allée f.; (*of ship*) passerelle f.

gaol /dʒeɪl/ n. & v.t. = **jail**.

gap /gæp/ n. trou m., vide m.; (*in time*) intervalle m.; (*in education*) lacune f.; (*difference*) écart m.

gape /geɪp/ v.i. rester bouche bée. ~ing a. béant.

garage /'gærɑːʒ, Amer. gə'rɑːʒ/ n. garage m. —v.t. mettre au garage.

garb /gɑːb/ n. costume m.

garbage /'gɑːbɪdʒ/ n. ordures f. pl.

garble /'gɑːbl/ v.t. déformer.

garden /'gɑːdn/ n. jardin m. —v.i. jardiner. ~er n. jardinlier, -ière m., f. ~ing n. jardinage m.

gargle /'gɑːgl/ v.i. se gargariser. —n. gargarisme m.

gargoyle /'gɑːgɔɪl/ n. gargouille f.

garish /'geərɪʃ/ a. voyant, criard.

garland /'gɑːlənd/ n. guirlande f.

garlic /'gɑːlɪk/ n. ail m.

garment /'gɑːmənt/ n. vêtement m.

garnish /'gɑːnɪʃ/ v.t. garnir (**with**, de). —n. garniture f.

garret /'gærət/ n. mansarde f.

garrison /'gærɪsn/ n. garnison f.

garrulous /'gærələs/ a. loquace.

garter /'gɑːtə(r)/ n. jarretière f. ~-belt n. porte-jarretelles n.m. invar.

gas /gæs/ n. (pl. **gases**) gaz m.; (*med.*) anesthésique m.; (*petrol*: Amer., *fam.*) essence f. —a. (*mask, pipe*) à gaz. —v.t. asphyxier; (*mil.*) gazer. —v.i. (*fam.*) bavarder.

gash /gæʃ/ n. entaille f. —v.t. entailler.

gasket /'gæskɪt/ n. (auto.) joint de culasse m.; (for pressure cooker) rondelle f.

gasoline /'gæsəli:n/ n. (petrol: Amer.) essence f.

gasp /gɑːsp/ v.i. haleter; (in surprise: fig.) avoir le souffle coupé. —n. halètement m.

gassy /'gæsɪ/ a. gazeux.

gastric /'gæstrɪk/ a. gastrique.

gastronomy /gæ'strɒnəmɪ/ n. gastronomie f.

gate /geɪt/ n. porte f.; (of metal) grille f.; (barrier) barrière f.

gatecrash /'geɪtkræʃ/ v.t./i. venir sans invitation (à). **~er** n. intrus(e) m.(f).

gateway /'geɪtweɪ/ n. porte f.

gather /'gæðə(r)/ v.t. (people, objects) rassembler; (pick up) ramasser; (flowers) cueillir; (fig.) comprendre; (sewing) froncer. —v.i. (people) se rassembler; (crowd) se former; (pile up) s'accumuler. **~ speed**, prendre de la vitesse. **~ing** n. rassemblement m.

gaudy /'gɔːdɪ/ a. (-ier, -iest) voyant, criard.

gauge /geɪdʒ/ n. jauge f., indicateur m. —v.t. jauger, évaluer.

gaunt /gɔːnt/ a. (lean) émacié; (grim) lugubre.

gauntlet /'gɔːntlɪt/ n. **run the ~ of,** subir (l'assaut de).

gauze /gɔːz/ n. gaze f.

gave /geɪv/ see **give**.

gawky /'gɔːkɪ/ a. (-ier, -iest) gauche, maladroit.

gawp (or **gawk**) /gɔːp, gɔːk/ v.i. **~ (at),** regarder bouche bée.

gay /geɪ/ a. (-er, -est) (joyful) gai; (fam.) gay invar. —n. gay m./f.

gaze /geɪz/ v.i. **~ (at),** regarder (fixement). —n. regard (fixe) m.

gazelle /gə'zel/ n. gazelle f.

gazette /gə'zet/ n. journal (officiel) m.

GB abbr. see **Great Britain**.

gear /gɪə(r)/ n. équipement m.; (techn.) engrenage m.; (auto.) vitesse f. —v.t. adapter. **~-lever,** (Amer.) **~-shift** ns. levier de vitesse m. **in ~,** en prise. **out of ~,** au point mort.

gearbox /'gɪəbɒks/ n. (auto.) boîte de vitesses f.

geese /giːs/ see **goose**.

gel /dʒel/ n. gelée f.; (for hair) gel m.

gelatine /'dʒelətiːn/ n. gélatine f.

gelignite /'dʒelɪgnaɪt/ n. nitroglycérine f.

gem /dʒem/ n. pierre précieuse f.

Gemini /'dʒemɪnaɪ/ n. les Gémeaux m. pl.

gender /'dʒendə(r)/ n. genre m.

gene /dʒiːn/ n. gène m.

genealogy /dʒiːnɪ'ælədʒɪ/ n. généalogie f.

general /'dʒenrəl/ a. général. —n. général m. **~ election,** élections législatives f. pl. **~ practitioner,** (med.) généraliste m. **in ~,** en général. **~ly** adv. généralement.

generaliz|e /'dʒenrəlaɪz/ v.t./i. généraliser. **~ation** /-'zeɪʃn/ n. généralisation f.

generate /'dʒenəreɪt/ v.t. produire.

generation /dʒenə'reɪʃn/ n. génération f.

generator /'dʒenəreɪtə(r)/ n. (electr.) groupe électrogène m.

gener|ous /'dʒenərəs/ a. généreux; (plentiful) copieux. **~osity** /-'rɒsətɪ/ n. générosité f.

genetic /dʒɪ'netɪk/ a. génétique. **~s** n. génétique f.

Geneva /dʒɪ'niːvə/ n. Genève m./f.

genial /'dʒiːnɪəl/ a. affable, sympathique; (climate) doux.

genital /'dʒenɪtl/ a. génital. **~s** n. pl. organes génitaux m. pl.

genius /'dʒiːnɪəs/ n. (pl. -uses) génie m.

genocide /'dʒenəsaɪd/ n. génocide m.

gent /dʒent/ n. (sl.) monsieur m.

genteel /dʒen'tiːl/ a. distingué.

gentl|e /'dʒentl/ a. (-er, -est) (mild, kind) doux; (slight) léger; (hint) discret. **~eness** n. douceur f. **~y** adv. doucement.

gentleman /'dʒentlmən/ n. (pl. -men) (man) monsieur m.; (well-bred) gentleman m.

genuine /'dʒenjuɪn/ a. (true) véritable; (person, belief) sincère.

geograph|y /dʒɪ'ɒgrəfɪ/ n. géographie f. **~er** n. géographe m./f. **~ical** /dʒɪə'græfɪkl/ a. géographique.

geolog|y /dʒɪ'ɒlədʒɪ/ n. géologie f. **~ical** /dʒɪə'lɒdʒɪkl/ a. géologique. **~ist** n. géologue m./f.

geometr|y /dʒɪ'ɒmətrɪ/ n. géométrie f. **~ic(al)** /dʒɪə'metrɪk(l)/ a. géométrique.

geranium /dʒə'reɪnɪəm/ n. géranium m.

geriatric /dʒerɪ'ætrɪk/ a. gériatrique.

germ /dʒɜːm/ n. (rudiment, seed) germe m.; (med.) microbe m.

German /'dʒɜːmən/ a. & n. allemand(e) (m. (f.)); (lang.) allemand m. **~ measles,** rubéole f. **~ shepherd,** (dog: Amer.) berger allemand m. **~ic** /dʒə'mænɪk/ a. germanique. **~y** n. Allemagne f.

germinate /'dʒɜ:mɪneɪt/ v.t./i. (faire) germer.

gestation /dʒe'steɪʃn/ n. gestation f.

gesticulate /dʒe'stɪkjʊleɪt/ v.i. gesticuler.

gesture /'dʒestʃə(r)/ n. geste m.

get /get/ v.t. (p.t. & p.p. **got**, p.p. Amer. **gotten**, pres. p. **getting**) avoir, obtenir, recevoir; (catch) prendre; (buy) acheter, prendre; (find) trouver; (fetch) aller chercher; (understand: sl.) comprendre. ~ s.o. to do sth., faire faire qch. à qn. ~ sth. done, faire faire qch. **did you ~ that number?**, tu as relevé le numéro? —v.i. aller, arriver (**to**, à); (become) devenir; (start) se mettre (**to**, à); (manage) parvenir (**to**, à). ~ **married/ready**/etc., se marier/se préparer/etc. ~ **promoted/hurt**/etc., être .promu/blessé/etc. ~ **arrested/ robbed**/etc., se faire arrêter/ voler/etc. **you ~ to use the computer**, vous utilisez l'ordinateur. **it's ~ting to be annoying**, ça commence à être agaçant. ~ **about,** (person) se déplacer. ~ **across,** (cross) traverser. ~ **along** or **by,** (manage) se débrouiller. ~ **along** or **on,** (progress) avancer. ~ **along** or **on with,** s'entendre avec. ~ **at,** (reach) parvenir à. **what are you ~ting at?**, où veux-tu en venir? ~ **away,** partir; (escape) s'échapper. ~ **back** v.i. revenir; v.t. (recover) récupérer. ~ **by** or **through,** (pass) passer. ~ **down** v.t./i. descendre; (depress) déprimer. ~ **in,** entrer, arriver. ~ **into,** (car) monter dans; (dress) mettre. ~ **into trouble,** avoir des ennuis. ~ **off** v.i. (from bus etc.) descendre; (leave) partir; (jurid.) être acquitté; v.t. (remove) enlever. ~ **on,** (on train etc.) monter; (succeed) réussir. ~ **on with,** (job) attaquer; (person) s'entendre avec. ~ **out,** sortir. ~ **out of,** (fig.) se soustraire à. ~ **over,** (illness) se remettre de. ~ **round,** (rule) contourner; (person) entortiller. ~ **through,** (finish) finir. ~ **up** v.i. se lever; v.t. (climb, bring) monter. ~-**up** n. (clothes: fam.) mise f.

getaway /'getəweɪ/ n. fuite f.

geyser /'gi:zə(r)/ n. chauffe-eau m. invar.; (geol.) geyser m.

Ghana /'gɑ:nə/ n. Ghana m.

ghastly /'gɑ:stlɪ/ a. (-ier, -iest) affreux; (pale) blême.

gherkin /'gɜ:kɪn/ n. cornichon m.

ghetto /'getəʊ/ n. (pl. -os) ghetto m.

ghost /gəʊst/ n. fantôme m. ~ly a. spectral.

giant /'dʒaɪənt/ n. & a. géant (m.).

gibberish /'dʒɪbərɪʃ/ n. baragouin m., charabia m.

gibe /dʒaɪb/ n. raillerie f. —v.i. ~ (**at**), railler.

giblets /'dʒɪblɪts/ n. pl. abattis m. pl., abats m. pl.

giddy /'gɪdɪ/ a. (-ier, -iest) vertigineux. **be** or **feel** ~y, avoir le vertige. ~iness n. vertige m.

gift /gɪft/ n. cadeau m.; (ability) don m. ~-**wrap** v.t. (p.t. -**wrapped**) faire un paquet-cadeau de.

gifted /'gɪftɪd/ a. doué.

gig /gɪg/ n. (fam.) concert m.

gigantic /dʒaɪ'gæntɪk/ a. gigantesque.

giggle /'gɪgl/ v.i. ricaner (sottement), glousser. —n. ricanement m. **the** ~s, le fou rire.

gild /gɪld/ v.t. dorer.

gill /dʒɪl/ n. (approx.) décilitre (imperial = 0.15 litre; Amer = 0.12 litre).

gills /gɪlz/ n. pl. ouïes f. pl.

gilt /gɪlt/ a. doré —n. dorure f. ~-**edged** a. (comm.) de tout repos.

gimmick /'gɪmɪk/ n. truc m.

gin /dʒɪn/ n. gin m.

ginger /'dʒɪndʒə(r)/ n. gingembre m. —a. roux. ~ **ale,** ~ **beer,** boisson gazeuse au gingembre f.

gingerbread /'dʒɪndʒəbred/ n. pain d'épice m.

gingerly /'dʒɪndʒəlɪ/ adv. avec précaution.

gipsy /'dʒɪpsɪ/ n. = **gypsy**.

giraffe /dʒɪ'rɑ:f/ n. girafe f.

girder /'gɜ:də(r)/ n. poutre f.

girdle /'gɜ:dl/ n. (belt) ceinture f.; (corset) gaine f.

girl /gɜ:l/ n. (petite) fille f.; (young woman) (jeune) fille f. ~-**friend** n. amie f.; (of boy) petite amie f. ~**hood** n. enfance f., jeunesse f. ~**ish** a. de (jeune) fille.

giro /'dʒaɪərəʊ/ n. (pl. -os) virement bancaire m.; (cheque: fam.) mandat m.

girth /gɜ:θ/ n. circonférence f.

gist /dʒɪst/ n. essentiel m.

give /gɪv/ v.t. (p.t. **gave**, p.p. **given**) donner; (gesture) faire; (laugh, sigh, etc.) pousser. ~ **s.o. sth.,** donner qch. à qn. —v.i. donner; (yield) céder; (stretch) se détendre. —n. élasticité f. ~ **away,** donner; (secret) trahir. ~ **back,** rendre. ~ **in,** (yield) se rendre. ~ **off,** dégager. ~ **out** v.t. distribuer; v.i. (become used up) s'épuiser. ~ **over,** (devote) consacrer; (stop: fam.) cesser. ~ **up** v.t./i. (renounce) renoncer (à);

(*yield*) céder. ~ **o.s. up**, se rendre. ~ **way**, céder; (*collapse*) s'effondrer.

given /'gɪvn/ *see* give. —*a.* donné. ~ **name**, prénom *m.*

glacier /'glæsɪə(r), *Amer.* 'gleɪʃər/ *n.* glacier *m.*

glad /glæd/ *a.* content. ~**ly** *adv.* avec plaisir.

gladden /'glædn/ *v.t.* réjouir.

gladiolus /glædɪ'əʊləs/ *n.* (*pl.* **-li** /-laɪ/) glaïeul *m.*

glam|our /'glæmə(r)/ *n.* enchantement *m.*, séduction *f.* ~**orize** *v.t.* rendre séduisant. ~**orous** *a.* séduisant, ensorcelant.

glance /glɑːns/ *n.* coup d'œil *m.* —*v.i.* ~ **at**, jeter un coup d'œil à.

gland /glænd/ *n.* glande *f.*

glar|e /gleə(r)/ *v.i.* briller très fort. —*n.* éclat (aveuglant) *m.*; (*stare: fig.*) regard furieux *m.* ~**e at**, regarder d'un air furieux. ~**ing** *a.* éblouissant; (*obvious*) flagrant.

glass /glɑːs/ *n.* verre *m.*; (*mirror*) miroir *m.* ~**es**, (*spectacles*) lunettes *f. pl.* ~**y** *a.* vitreux.

glaze /gleɪz/ *v.t.* (*door etc.*) vitrer; (*pottery*) vernisser. —*n.* vernis *m.*

gleam /gliːm/ *n.* lueur *f.* —*v.i.* luire.

glean /gliːn/ *v.t.* glaner.

glee /gliː/ *n.* joie *f.* ~ **club**, chorale *f.* ~**ful** *a.* joyeux.

glen /glen/ *n.* vallon *m.*

glib /glɪb/ *a.* (*person: pej.*) qui a la parole facile *or* du bagou; (*reply, excuse*) désinvolte, spécieux. ~**ly** *adv.* avec désinvolture.

glide /glaɪd/ *v.i.* glisser; (*of plane*) planer. ~**r** /-ə(r)/ *n.* planeur *m.*

glimmer /'glɪmə(r)/ *n.* lueur *f.* —*v.i.* luire.

glimpse /glɪmps/ *n.* aperçu *m.* **catch a** ~ **of**, entrevoir.

glint /glɪnt/ *n.* éclair *m.* —*v.i.* étinceler.

glisten /'glɪsn/ *v.i.* briller, luire.

glitter /'glɪtə(r)/ *v.i.* scintiller. —*n.* scintillement *m.*

gloat /gləʊt/ *v.i.* jubiler (**over**, à l'idée de).

global /'gləʊbl/ *a.* (*world-wide*) mondial; (*all-embracing*) global.

globe /gləʊb/ *n.* globe *m.*

gloom /gluːm/ *n.* obscurité *f.*; (*sadness: fig.*) tristesse *f.* ~**y** *a.* triste; (*pessimistic*) pessimiste.

glorif|y /'glɔːrɪfaɪ/ *v.t.* glorifier. **a** ~**ied waitress**/*etc.*, à peine plus qu'une serveuse/*etc.*

glorious /'glɔːrɪəs/ *a.* splendide; (*deed, hero, etc.*) glorieux.

glory /'glɔːrɪ/ *n.* gloire *f.*; (*beauty*) splendeur *f.* —*v.i.* ~ **in**, s'enorgueillir de.

gloss /glɒs/ *n.* lustre *m.*, brillant *m.* —*a.* brillant. —*v.i.* ~ **over**, (*make light of*) glisser sur; (*cover up*) dissimuler. ~**y** *a.* brillant.

glossary /'glɒsərɪ/ *n.* glossaire *m.*

glove /glʌv/ *n.* gant *m.* ~ **compartment**, (*auto.*) vide-poches *m. invar.* ~**d** *a.* ganté.

glow /gləʊ/ *v.i.* rougeoyer; (*person, eyes*) rayonner. —*n.* rougeoiement *m.*, éclat *m.* ~**ing** *a.* (*account etc.*) enthousiaste.

glucose /'gluːkəʊs/ *n.* glucose *m.*

glue /gluː/ *n.* colle *f.* —*v.t.* (*pres. p.* **gluing**) coller.

glum /glʌm/ *a.* (**glummer, glummest**) triste, morne.

glut /glʌt/ *n.* surabondance *f.*

glutton /'glʌtn/ *n.* glouton(ne) *m.* (*f.*). ~**ous** *a.* glouton. ~**y** *n.* gloutonnerie *f.*

glycerine /'glɪsəriːn/ *n.* glycérine *f.*

gnarled /nɑːld/ *a.* noueux.

gnash /næʃ/ *v.t.* ~ **one's teeth**, grincer des dents.

gnat /næt/ *n.* (*fly*) cousin *m.*

gnaw /nɔː/ *v.t./i.* ronger.

gnome /nəʊm/ *n.* gnome *m.*

go /gəʊ/ *v.i.* (*p.t.* **went**, *p.p.* **gone**) aller; (*leave*) partir; (*work*) marcher; (*become*) devenir; (*be sold*) se vendre; (*vanish*) disparaître. **my coat's gone**, mon manteau n'est plus là. ~ **via Paris**, passer par Paris. ~ **by car/on foot**, aller en voiture/à pied. ~ **for a walk/ride**, aller se promener/ faire un tour en voiture. **go red/dry**/*etc.*, rougir/tarir/ *etc.* **don't** ~ **telling him**, ne va pas lui dire. ~ **riding/shopping**/*etc.*, faire du cheval/les courses/*etc.* —*n.* (*pl.* **goes**) (*try*) coup *m.*; (*success*) réussite *f.*; (*turn*) tour *m.*; (*energy*) dynamisme *m.* **have a** ~, essayer. **be** ~**ing to do**, aller faire. ~ **across**, traverser. ~ **ahead!**, allez-y! ~**-ahead** *n.* feu vert *m.*; *a.* dynamique. ~ **away**, s'en aller. ~ **back**, retourner; (*go home*) rentrer. ~ **back on**, (*promise etc.*) revenir sur. ~ **bad** *or* **off**, se gâter. ~**-between** *n.* intermédiaire *m./f.* ~ **by**, (*pass*) passer. ~ **down**, descendre; (*sun*) se coucher. ~ **for**, aller chercher; (*like*) aimer; (*attack: sl.*) attaquer. ~ **in**, (r)entrer. ~ **in for**, (*exam*) se présenter à. ~ **into**, entrer dans; (*subject*) examiner. ~**kart** *n.* kart *m.* ~ **off**, partir; (*explode*) sauter; (*ring*) sonner; (*take place*) se

dérouler; (*dislike*) revenir de. ~ **on,**
continuer; (*happen*) se passer. ~ **out,**
sortir; (*light, fire*) s'éteindre. ~ **over,**
(*cross*) traverser; (*pass*) passer. ~ **over**
or **through,** (*check*) vérifier; (*search*)
fouiller. ~ **round,** (*be enough*) suffire.
~**-slow** *n.* grève perlée *f.* ~ **through,**
(*suffer*) subir. ~ **under,** (*sink*) couler;
(*fail*) échouer. ~ **up,** monter. ~
without, se passer de. **on the ~,** actif.

goad /gəʊd/ *v.t.* aiguillonner.

goal /gəʊl/ *n.* but *m.* ~**-post** *n.* poteau de
but *m.*

goalkeeper /ˈgəʊlkiːpə(r)/ *n.* gardien de
but *m.*

goat /gəʊt/ *n.* chèvre *f.*

goatee /gəʊˈtiː/ *n.* barbiche *f.*

gobble /ˈgɒbl/ *v.t.* engouffrer.

goblet /ˈgɒblɪt/ *n.* verre à pied *m.*

goblin /ˈgɒblɪn/ *n.* lutin *m.*

God /gɒd/ *n.* Dieu *m.* ~**-forsaken** *a.*
perdu.

god /gɒd/ *n.* dieu *m.* ~**dess** *n.* déesse *f.*
~**ly** *a.* dévot.

god|child /ˈgɒdtʃaɪld/ *n.* (*pl.* **-children**)
filleul(e) *m.* (*f.*). ~**daughter** *n.* filleule
f. ~**father** *n.* parrain *m.* ~**mother** *n.*
marraine *f.* ~**son** *n.* filleul *m.*

godsend /ˈgɒdsend/ *n.* aubaine *f.*

goggle /ˈgɒgl/ *v.i.* ~ (**at**), regarder avec
de gros yeux.

goggles /ˈgɒglz/ *n. pl.* lunettes
(protectrices) *f. pl.*

going /ˈgəʊɪŋ/ *n.* **it is slow/hard ~,** c'est
lent/difficile. —*a.* (*price, rate*) actuel.
~**s-on** *n. pl.* activités (bizarres) *f. pl.*

gold /gəʊld/ *n.* or *m.* —*a.* en or, d'or. ~-
mine *n.* mine d'or *f.*

golden /ˈgəʊldən/ *a.* d'or; (*in colour*)
doré, (*opportunity*) unique. ~ **wedding,** noces d'or *f. pl.*

goldfish /ˈgəʊldfɪʃ/ *n. invar.* poisson
rouge *m.*

gold-plated /gəʊldˈpleɪtɪd/ *a.* plaqué or.

goldsmith /ˈgəʊldsmɪθ/ *n.* orfèvre *m.*

golf /gɒlf/ *n.* golf *m.* ~**-ball,** balle de golf
f.; (*on typewriter*) boule *f.* ~**-course** *n.*
terrain de golf *m.* ~**er** *n.* joueur, -se de
golf *m., f.*

gondol|a /ˈgɒndələ/ *n.* gondole *f.* ~**ier**
/-ˈlɪə(r)/ *n.* gondolier *m.*

gone /gɒn/ *see* **go.** —*a.* parti. ~ **six
o'clock,** six heures passées. **the
butter's all ~,** il n'y a plus de beurre.

gong /gɒŋ/ *n.* gong *m.*

good /gʊd/ *a.* (**better, best**) bon;
(*weather*) beau; (*well-behaved*) sage.
—*n.* bien *m.* **as ~ as,** (*almost*)
pratiquement. **that's ~ of you,** c'est

gentil (de ta part). **be ~ with,** savoir s'y
prendre avec. **do ~,** faire du bien. **feel
~,** se sentir bien. ~**-for-nothing** *a.* &
n. propre à rien (*m./f.*). **G~ Friday,**
Vendredi saint *m.* ~**-afternoon,** ~
morning *ints.* bonjour. ~**-evening** *int.*
bonsoir. ~**-looking** *a.* beau. ~
natured *a.* gentil. ~ **name,** réputation
f. ~**-night** *int.* bonsoir, bonne nuit. **it is
~ for you,** ça vous fait du bien. **is it any
~?,** est-ce que c'est bien? **it's no ~,** ça
ne vaut rien. **it is no ~ shouting**/*etc.*, ça
ne sert à rien de crier/*etc.* **for ~,** pour
toujours. ~**ness** *n.* bonté *f.* **my ~ness!,**
mon Dieu!

goodbye /gʊdˈbaɪ/ *int.* & *n.* au revoir (*m.
invar.*).

goods /gʊdz/ *n. pl.* marchandises *f. pl.*

goodwill /gʊdˈwɪl/ *n.* bonne volonté *f.*

goody /ˈgʊdɪ/ *n.* (*fam.*) bonne chose *f.*
~**-goody** *n.* petit(e) saint(e) *m.* (*f.*).

gooey /ˈguːɪ/ *a.* (*sl.*) poisseux.

goof /guːf/ *v.i.* (*Amer.*) gaffer.

goose /guːs/ *n.* (*pl.* **geese**) oie *f.* ~**-flesh,**
~**-pimples** *ns.* chair de poule *f.*

gooseberry /ˈgʊzbərɪ/ *n.* groseille à
maquereau *f.*

gore¹ /gɔː(r)/ *n.* (*blood*) sang *m.*

gore² /gɔː(r)/ *v.t.* encorner.

gorge /gɔːdʒ/ *n.* (*geog.*) gorge *f.* —*v.t.*
~ **o.s.,** se gorger.

gorgeous /ˈgɔːdʒəs/ *a.* magnifique,
splendide, formidable.

gorilla /gəˈrɪlə/ *n.* gorille *m.*

gormless /ˈgɔːmlɪs/ *a.* (*sl.*) stupide.

gorse /gɔːs/ *n. invar.* ajonc(s) *m.* (*pl.*).

gory /ˈgɔːrɪ/ *a.* (**-ier, -iest**) sanglant;
(*horrific: fig.*) horrible.

gosh /gɒʃ/ *int.* mince (alors).

gospel /ˈgɒspl/ *n.* évangile *m.* **the G~,**
l'Évangile *m.*

gossip /ˈgɒsɪp/ *n.* bavardage(s) *m.* (*pl.*),
commérage(s) *m.* (*pl.*); (*person*)
bavard(e) *m.* (*f.*). —*v.i.* (*p.t.* **gossiped**)
bavarder. ~**y** *a.* bavard.

got /gɒt/ *see* **get.** —**have ~,** avoir. **have
~ to do,** devoir faire.

Gothic /ˈgɒθɪk/ *a.* gothique.

gouge /gaʊdʒ/ *v.t.* ~ **out,** arracher.

gourmet /ˈgʊəmeɪ/ *n.* gourmet *m.*

gout /gaʊt/ *n.* (*med.*) goutte *f.*

govern /ˈgʌvn/ *v.t./i.* gouverner. ~**ess**
/-ənɪs/ *n.* gouvernante *f.* ~**or** /-ənə(r)/
n. gouverneur *m.*

government /ˈgʌvənmənt/ *n.* gouvernement *m.* ~**al** /-ˈmentl/ *a.* gouvernemen-
tal.

gown /gaʊn/ *n.* robe *f.*; (*of judge,
teacher*) toge *f.*

GP *abbr. see* **general practitioner**.
grab /græb/ *v.t. (p.t.* **grabbed**) saisir.
grace /greɪs/ *n.* grâce *f.* —*v.t. (honour)*
honorer; *(adorn)* orner. **~ful** *a.*
gracieux.
gracious /'greɪʃəs/ *a. (kind)* bienveil-
lant; *(elegant)* élégant.
gradation /grə'deɪʃn/ *n.* gradation *f.*
grade /greɪd/ *n.* catégorie *f.; (of goods)*
qualité *f.; (on scale)* grade *m.; (school
mark)* note *f.; (class: Amer.)* classe *f.*
—*v.t.* classer; *(school work)* noter. **~
crossing,** *(Amer.)* passage à niveau *m.*
~ school, *(Amer.)* école primaire *f.*
gradient /'greɪdɪənt/ *n. (slope)* inclinaison *f.*
gradual /'grædʒʊəl/ *a.* progressif,
graduel. **~ly** *adv.* progressivement, peu
à peu.
graduate[1] /'grædʒʊət/ *n. (univ.)*
diplômé(e) *m. (f.).*
graduat|e[2] /'grædʒʊeɪt/ *v.i.* obtenir son
diplôme. —*v.t.* graduer. **~ion** /-'eɪʃn/
n. remise de diplômes *f.*
graffiti /grə'fiːtiː/ *n. pl.* graffiti *m. pl.*
graft[1] /grɑːft/ *n. (med., bot.)* greffe *f.*
(work) boulot. —*v.t.* greffer; *(work)*
trimer.
graft[2] /grɑːft/ *n. (bribery: fam.)*
corruption *f.*
grain /greɪn/ *n. (seed, quantity, texture)*
grain *m.; (in wood)* fibre *f.*
gram /græm/ *n.* gramme *m.*
gramm|ar /'græmə(r)/ *n.* grammaire *f.*
~atical /grə'mætɪkl/ *a.* grammatical.
grand /grænd/ *a.* (**-er, -est**) magnifique;
(duke, chorus) grand. **~ piano,** piano à
queue *m.*
grandad /'grændæd/ *n. (fam.)* papy
m.
grand|child /'græn(d)tʃaɪld/ *n. (pl.
-children)* petit(e)-enfant *m. (f.).*
~daughter *n.* petite-fille *f.* **~father** *n.*
grand-père *m.* **~mother** *n.* grand-
mère *f.* **~parents** *n. pl.* grands-
parents *m. pl.* **~son** *n.* petit-fils *m.*
grandeur /'grændʒə(r)/ *n.* grandeur *f.*
grandiose /'grændɪəʊs/ *a.* grandiose.
grandma /'grændmɑː/ *n.* = **granny**.
grandstand /'græn(d)stænd/ *n.* tribune
f.
granite /'grænɪt/ *n.* granit *m.*
granny /'grænɪ/ *n. (fam.)* grandmaman
f., mémé *f.,* mamie *f.*
grant /grɑːnt/ *v.t. (give)* accorder;
(request) accéder à; *(admit)* admettre
(that, que). —*n.* subvention *f.; (univ.)*
bourse *f.* **take sth. for ~ed,** considérer
qch. comme une chose acquise.

granulated /'grænjʊleɪtɪd/ *a.* **~ sugar,**
sucre semoule *m.*
granule /'grænjuːl/ *n.* granule *m.*
grape /greɪp/ *n.* grain de raisin *m.* **~s,**
raisin(s) *m. (pl.).*
grapefruit /'greɪpfruːt/ *n. invar.*
pamplemousse *m.*
graph /grɑːf/ *n.* graphique *m.*
graphic /'græfɪk/ *a. (arts etc.)*
graphique; *(fig.)* vivant, explicite. **~s**
n. pl. (comput.) graphiques *m. pl.*
grapple /græpl/ *v.i.* **~ with,** affronter,
être aux prises avec.
grasp /grɑːsp/ *v.t.* saisir. —*n. (hold)*
prise *f.; (strength of hand)* poigne *f.;
(reach)* portée *f.; (fig.)* compréhension
f.
grasping /'grɑːspɪŋ/ *a.* rapace.
grass /grɑːs/ *n.* herbe *f.* **~ roots,** peuple
m.; (pol.) base *f.* **~-roots** *a.* populaire.
~y *a.* herbeux.
grasshopper /'grɑːshɒpə(r)/ *n.* sauterelle *f.*
grassland /'grɑːslænd/ *n.* prairie *f.*
grate[1] /greɪt/ *n. (fireplace)* foyer *m.;
(frame)* grille *f.*
grate[2] /greɪt/ *v.t.* râper. —*v.i.* grincer.
~r /-ə(r)/ *n.* râpe *f.*
grateful /'greɪtfl/ *a.* reconnaissant. **~ly**
adv. avec reconnaissance.
gratif|y /'grætɪfaɪ/ *v.t.* satisfaire;
(please) faire plaisir à **~ied** *a.* très
heureux. **~ying** *a.* agréable.
grating /'greɪtɪŋ/ *n.* grille *f.*
gratis /'greɪtɪs, 'grætɪs/ *a. & adv.* gratis
(a. invar.).
gratitude /'grætɪtjuːd/ *n.* gratitude *f.*
gratuitous /grə'tjuːɪtəs/ *a.* gratuit.
gratuity /grə'tjuːətɪ/ *n. (tip)* pourboire
m.; (bounty: mil.) prime *f.*
grave[1] /greɪv/ *n.* tombe *f.* **~-digger** *n.*
fossoyeur *m.*
grave[2] /greɪv/ *a.* (**-er, -est**) *(serious)*
grave. **~ly** *adv.* gravement.
grave[3] /grɑːv/ *a.* **~ accent,** accent grave
m.
gravel /'grævl/ *n.* gravier *m.*
gravestone /'greɪvstəʊn/ *n.* pierre
tombale *f.*
graveyard /'greɪvjɑːd/ *n.* cimetière *m.*
gravitat|e /'grævɪteɪt/ *v.i.* graviter. **~ion**
/-'teɪʃn/ *n.* gravitation *f.*
gravity /'grævətɪ/ *n. (seriousness)*
gravité *f.; (force)* pesanteur *f.*
gravy /'greɪvɪ/ *n.* jus (de viande) *m.*
gray /greɪ/ *a. & n.* = **grey**.
graze[1] /greɪz/ *v.t./i. (eat)* paître.
graze[2] /greɪz/ *v.t. (touch)* frôler;
(scrape) écorcher. —*n.* écorchure *f.*

greas|e /gri:s/ n. graisse f. —v.t. graisser. ∼e-proof **paper,** papier sulfurisé m. ∼y a. graisseux.

great /greɪt/ a. (**-er, -est**) grand; (*very good*: *fam.*) magnifique. ∼ **Britain,** Grande-Bretagne f. ∼**grandfather** n. arrière-grandpère m. ∼**grandmother** n. arrière-grand-mère f. ∼**ly** adv. (*very*) très; (*much*) beaucoup. ∼**ness** n. grandeur f.

Greece /gri:s/ n. Grèce f.

greed /gri:d/ n. avidité f.; (*for food*) gourmandise f. ∼y a. avide; gourmand.

Greek /gri:k/ a. & n. grec(que) (m. (f.)); (*lang.*) grec m.

green /gri:n/ a. (**-er, -est**) vert; (*fig.*) naïf. —n. vert m.; (*grass*) pelouse f.; (*golf*) green m. ∼**s,** légumes verts m. pl. ∼ **belt,** ceinture verte f. ∼ **light,** feu vert m. ∼**ery** n. verdure f.

greengage /'gri:ngeɪdʒ/ n. (*plum*) reine-claude f.

greengrocer /'gri:nɡrəʊsə(r)/ n. marchand(e) de fruits et légumes m. (f.).

greenhouse /'gri:nhaʊs/ n. serre f.

greet /gri:t/ v.t. (*receive*) accueillir; (*address politely*) saluer. ∼**ing** n. accueil m. ∼**ings** n. pl. compliments m. pl.; (*wishes*) vœux m. pl. ∼**ings card,** carte de vœux f.

gregarious /grɪ'ɡeərɪəs/ a. (*instinct*) grégaire; (*person*) sociable.

grenade /grɪ'neɪd/ n. grenade f.

grew /gru:/ see **grow.**

grey /greɪ/ a. (**-er, -est**) gris; (*fig.*) triste. —n. gris m. **go** ∼, (*hair, person*) grisonner.

greyhound /'greɪhaʊnd/ n. lévrier m.

grid /grɪd/ n. grille f.; (*network: electr.*) réseau m.; (*culin.*) gril m.

grief /gri:f/ n. chagrin m. **come to** ∼, (*person*) avoir un malheur; (*fail*) tourner mal.

grievance /'gri:vns/ n. grief m.

grieve /gri:v/ v.t./i. (s')affliger. ∼ **for,** pleurer.

grill /grɪl/ n. (*cooking device*) gril m.; (*food*) grillade f.; (*auto.*) calandre f. —v.t./i. griller; (*interrogate*) cuisiner.

grille /grɪl/ n. grille f.

grim /grɪm/ a. (**grimmer, grimmest**) sinistre.

grimace /grɪ'meɪs/ n. grimace f. —v.i. grimacer.

grim|e /graɪm/ n. crasse f. ∼y a. crasseux.

grin /grɪn/ v.i. (*p.t.* **grinned**) sourire. —n. (*large*) sourire m.

grind /graɪnd/ v.t. (*p.t.* **ground**) écraser;

(*coffee*) moudre; (*sharpen*) aiguiser. —n. corvée f. ∼ **one's teeth,** grincer des dents. ∼ **to a halt,** devenir paralysé.

grip /grɪp/ v.t. (*p.t.* **gripped**) saisir; (*interest*) passionner. —n. prise f.; (*strength of hand*) poigne f.; (*bag*) sac de voyage m. **come to** ∼**s,** en venir aux prises.

gripe /graɪp/ n. ∼**s,** (*med.*) coliques f. pl. —v.i. (*grumble*: *sl.*) râler.

grisly /'grɪzlɪ/ a. (**-ier, -iest**) macabre, horrible.

gristle /'grɪsl/ n. cartilage m.

grit /ɡrɪt/ n. gravillon m., sable m.; (*fig.*) courage m. —v.t. (*p.t.* **gritted**) (*road*) sabler; (*teeth*) serrer.

grizzle /'grɪzl/ v.i. (*cry*) pleurnicher.

groan /ɡrəʊn/ v.i. gémir. —n. gémissement m.

grocer /'ɡrəʊsə(r)/ n. épicier, -ière m., f. ∼**ies** n. pl. (*goods*) épicerie f. ∼**y** n. (*shop*) épicerie f.

grog /ɡrɒɡ/ n. grog m.

groggy /'ɡrɒɡɪ/ a. (*weak*) faible; (*unsteady*) chancelant; (*ill*) mal fichu.

groin /ɡrɔɪn/ n. aine f.

groom /ɡru:m/ n. marié m.; (*for horses*) valet d'écurie m. —v.t. (*horse*) panser; (*fig.*) préparer.

groove /ɡru:v/ n. (*for door etc.*) rainure f.; (*in record*) sillon m.

grope /ɡrəʊp/ v.i. tâtonner. ∼ **for,** chercher à tâtons.

gross /ɡrəʊs/ a. (**-er, -est**) (*coarse*) grossier; (*comm.*) brut. —n. invar. grosse f. ∼**ly** adv. grossièrement; (*very*) extrêmement.

grotesque /ɡrəʊ'tesk/ a. grotesque, horrible.

grotto /'ɡrɒtəʊ/ n. (*pl.* **oos**) grotte f.

grotty /'ɡrɒtɪ/ a. (*sl.*) moche.

grouch /ɡraʊtʃ/ v.i. (*grumble*: *fam.*) rouspéter, râler.

ground[1] /ɡraʊnd/ n. terre f., sol m.; (*area*) terrain m.; (*reason*) raison f.; (*electr., Amer.*) masse f. ∼**s,** terres f. pl., parc m.; (*of coffee*) marc m. —v.t./i. (*naut.*) échouer; (*aircraft*) retenir au sol. **on the** ∼, par terre. **lose** ∼, perdre du terrain. ∼ **floor,** rez-de-chaussée m. invar. ∼ **rule,** règle de base f. ∼**less** a. sans fondement. ∼ **swell,** lame de fond f.

ground[2] /ɡraʊnd/ see **grind.** —a. ∼ **beef,** (*Amer.*) bifteck haché m.

grounding /'ɡraʊndɪŋ/ n. connaissances (de base) f. pl.

groundsheet /'ɡraʊndʃi:t/ n. tapis de sol m.

groundwork /'graʊndwɜ:k/ n. travail préparatoire m.

group /gru:p/ n. groupe m. —v.t./i. (se) grouper.

grouse[1] /graʊs/ n. invar. (bird) coq de bruyère m., grouse f.

grouse[2] /graʊs/ v.i. (grumble: fam.) rouspéter, râler.

grove /grəʊv/ n. bocage m.

grovel /'grɒvl/ v.i. (p.t. **grovelled**) ramper. ∿**ling** a. rampant.

grow /grəʊ/ v.i. (p.t. **grew**, p.p. **grown**) grandir; (of plant) pousser; (become) devenir. —v.t. cultiver. ∿ **up**, devenir adulte, grandir. ∿**er** n. cultivateur, -trice m., f. ∿**ing** a. grandissant.

growl /graʊl/ v.i. grogner. —n. grognement m.

grown /grəʊn/ see **grow**. —a. adulte. ∿**-up** a. & n. adulte (m./f.).

growth /grəʊθ/ n. croissance f.; (in numbers) accroissement m.; (of hair, tooth) (med.) tumeur f.

grub /grʌb/ n. (larva) larve f.; (food: sl.) bouffe f.

grubby /'grʌbɪ/ a. (-ier, -iest) sale.

grudge /grʌdʒ/ v.t. ∿ **doing**, faire à contrecœur. ∿ **s.o. sth.**, (success, wealth) en vouloir à qn. de qch. —n. rancune f. **have a** ∿ **against**, en vouloir à. **grudgingly** adv. à contrecœur.

gruelling /'gru:əlɪŋ/ a. exténuant.

gruesome /'gru:səm/ a. macabre.

gruff /grʌf/ a. (-er, -est) bourru.

grumble /'grʌmbl/ v.i. ronchonner, grogner (**at**, après).

grumpy /'grʌmpɪ/ a. (-ier, -iest) grincheux, grognon.

grunt /grʌnt/ v.i. grogner. —n. grognement m.

guarant|ee /gærən'ti:/ n. garantie f. —v.t. garantir. ∿**or** n. garant(e) m. (f.).

guard /gɑ:d/ v.t. protéger; (watch) surveiller. —v.i. ∿ **against**, se protéger contre. —n. (vigilance, mil., group) garde f.; (person) garde m.; (on train) chef de train m. ∿**ian** n. gardien(ne) m. (f.); (of orphan) tuteur, -trice m., f.

guarded /gɑ:dɪd/ a. prudent.

guerrilla /gə'rɪlə/ n. guérillero m. ∿ **warfare**, guérilla f.

guess /ges/ v.t./i. deviner; (suppose) penser. —n. conjecture f.

guesswork /'gesw3:k/ n. conjectures f. pl.

guest /gest/ n. invité(e) m. (f.); (in hotel) client(e) m. (f.). ∿**-house** n. pension f. ∿**-room** n. chambre d'ami f.

guffaw /gə'fɔ:/ n. gros rire m. —v.i. s'esclaffer, rire bruyamment.

guidance /'gaɪdns/ n. (advice) conseils m. pl.; (information) information f.

guide /gaɪd/ n. (person, book) guide m. —v.t. guider. ∿**d** /-ɪd/ a. ∿**d missile**, missile téléguidé m. ∿**-dog** n. chien d'aveugle m. ∿**-lines** n. pl. grandes lignes f. pl.

Guide /gaɪd/ n. (girl) guide f.

guidebook /'gaɪdbʊk/ n. guide m.

guild /gɪld/ n. corporation f.

guile /gaɪl/ n. ruse f.

guillotine /'gɪləti:n/ n. guillotine f.; (for paper) massicot m.

guilt /gɪlt/ n. culpabilité f. ∿**y** a. coupable.

guinea-pig /'gɪnɪpɪg/ n. cobaye m.

guinea-fowl /'gɪnɪfaʊl/ n. pintade f.

guise /gaɪz/ n. apparence f.

guitar /gɪ'tɑ:(r)/ n. guitare f. ∿**ist** n. guitariste m./f.

gulf /gʌlf/ n. (part of sea) golfe m.; (hollow) gouffre m.

gull /gʌl/ n. mouette f., goéland m.

gullet /'gʌlɪt/ n. gosier m.

gullible /'gʌləbl/ a. crédule.

gully /'gʌlɪ/ n. (ravine) ravine f.; (drain) rigole f.

gulp /gʌlp/ v.t. ∿ (**down**), avaler en vitesse. —v.i. (from fear etc.) avoir un serrement de gorge. —n. gorgée f.

gum[1] /gʌm/ n. (anat.) gencive f.

gum[2] /gʌm/ n. (from tree) gomme f.; (glue) colle f.; (for chewing) chewing-gum m. —v.t. (p.t. **gummed**) gommer.

gumboil /'gʌmbɔɪl/ n. abcès dentaire m.

gumboot /'gʌmbu:t/ n. botte de caoutchouc f.

gumption /'gʌmpʃn/ n. (fam.) initiative f., courage m., audace f.

gun /gʌn/ n. (pistol) revolver m.; (rifle) fusil m.; (large) canon m. —v.t. (p.t. **gunned**). ∿ **down**, abattre. ∿**ner** n. artilleur m.

gunfire /'gʌnfaɪə(r)/ n. fusillade f.

gunge /gʌndʒ/ n. (sl.) crasse f.

gunman /'gʌnmən/ n. (pl. **-men**) bandit armé m.

gunpowder /'gʌnpaʊdə(r)/ n. poudre à canon f.

gunshot /'gʌnʃɒt/ n. coup de feu m.

gurgle /'gɜ:gl/ n. glouglou m. —v.i. glouglouter.

guru /'gʊru:/ n. (pl. **-us**) gourou m.

gush /gʌʃ/ v.i. ∿ (**out**), jaillir. —n. jaillissement m.

gust /gʌst/ n. rafale f.; (of smoke) bouffée f. ∿**y** a. venteux.

gusto /'gʌstəʊ/ *n.* enthousiasme *m.*

gut /gʌt/ *n.* boyau *m.* ~s, boyaux *m. pl.*; ventre *m.*; (*courage: fam.*) cran *m.* —*v.t.* (*p.t.* **gutted**) (*fish*) vider; (*of fire*) dévaster.

gutter /'gʌtə(r)/ *n.* (*on roof*) gouttière *f.*; (*in street*) caniveau *m.*

guttural /'gʌtərəl/ *a.* guttural.

guy /gaɪ/ *n.* (*man: fam.*) type *m.*

guzzle /'gʌzl/ *v.t./i.* (*eat*) bâfrer; (*drink: Amer.*) boire d'un trait.

gym /dʒɪm/ *n.* (*fam.*) gymnase *m.*; (*fam.*) gym(nastique) *f.* ~-**slip** *n.* tunique *f.* ~-**nasium** *n.* gymnase *m.*

gymnast /'dʒɪmnæst/ *n.* gymnaste *m./f.* ~**ics** /-'næstɪks/ *n. pl.* gymnastique *f.*

gynaecology /gaɪnɪ'kɒlədʒɪ/ *n.* gynécologie *f.* ~**ist** *n.* gynécologue *m./f.*

gypsy /'dʒɪpsɪ/ *n.* bohémicn(nc) *m.* (*f.*).

gyrate /dʒaɪ'reɪt/ *v.i.* tournoyer.

H

haberdashery /hæbə'dæʃərɪ/ *n.* mercerie *f.*

habit /'hæbɪt/ *n.* habitude *f.*; (*costume: relig.*) habit *m.* **be in/get into the** ~ **of**, avoir/prendre l'habitude de.

habitable /'hæbɪtəbl/ *a.* habitable. ~**ation** /-'teɪʃn/ *n.* habitation *f.*

habitat /'hæbɪtæt/ *n.* habitat *m.*

habitual /hə'bɪtʃʊəl/ *a.* (*usual*) habituel; (*smoker, liar*) invétéré. ~**ly** *adv.* habituellement.

hack[1] /hæk/ *n.* (*old horse*) haridelle *f.*; (*writer*) nègre *m.*, écrivailleulr, -se *m.*, *f.*

hack[2] /hæk/ *v.t.* hacher, tailler.

hackneyed /'hæknɪd/ *a.* rebattu.

had /hæd/ *see* **have**.

haddock /'hædək/ *n. invar.* églefin *m.* **smoked** ~, haddock *m.*

haemorrhage /'heməriddʒ/ *n.* hémorragie *f.*

haemorrhoids /'heməroidz/ *n. pl.* hémorroïdes *f. pl.*

hag /hæg/ *n.* (vieille) sorcière *f.*

haggard /'hægəd/ *a.* (*person*) qui a le visage défait; (*face, look*) défait, hagard.

haggle /'hægl/ *v.i.* marchander. ~ **over**, (*object*) marchander; (*price*) discuter.

Hague (The) /(ðə)'heɪg/ *n.* La Haye.

hail[1] /heɪl/ *v.t.* (*greet*) saluer; (*taxi*) héler. —*v.i.* ~ **from**, venir de.

hail[2] /heɪl/ *n.* grêle *f.* —*v.i.* grêler.

hailstone /'heɪlstəʊn/ *n.* grêlon *m.*

hair /heə(r)/ *n.* (*on head*) cheveux *m. pl.*; (*on body, of animal*) poils *m. pl.*; (*single strand on head*) cheveu *m.*; (*on body*) poil *m.* ~-**do** *n.* (*fam.*) coiffure *f.* ~-**drier** *n.* séchoir (à cheveux) *m.* ~-**grip** *n.* pince à cheveux *f.* ~-**raising** *a.* horrifique. ~ **remover**, dépilatoire *m.* ~-**style** *n.* coiffure *f.*

hairbrush /'heəbrʌʃ/ *n.* brosse à cheveux *f.*

haircut /'heəkʌt/ *n.* coupe de cheveux *f.* **have a** ~, se faire couper les cheveux.

hairdresser /'heədresə(r)/ *n.* coiffeulr, -se *m.*, *f.*

hairpin /'heəpɪn/ *n.* épingle à cheveux *f.*

hairy /'heərɪ/ *a.* (-**ier**, -**iest**) poilu; (*terrifying: sl.*) horrifique.

hake /heɪk/ *n. invar.* colin *m.*

hale /heɪl/ *a.* vigoureux.

half /hɑːf/ *n.* (*pl.* **halves**) moitié *f.*, dcmi(e) *m.* (*f.*). *a.* demi. *adv.* à moitié. ~ **a dozen**, une demi-douzaine. ~ **an hour**, une demi-heure. **four and a** ~, quatre et demi(e). ~ **and half**, moitié moitié. **in** ~, en deux. ~-**back** *n.* (*sport*) demi *m.* ~-**caste** *n.* métis(se) *m.* (*f.*). ~-**hearted** *a.* tiède. **at** ~-**mast** *adv.* en berne. ~ **measure**, demi-mesure *f.* ~ **price**, moitié prix. ~-**term** *n.* congé de (de)mi-trimestre *m.* ~-**time** *n.* mi-temps *f.* ~-**way** *adv.* à mi-chcmin. ~-**wit** *n.* imbécile *m./f.*

halibut /'hælɪbət/ *n. invar.* (*fish*) flétan *m.*

hall /hɔːl/ *n.* (*room*) salle *f.*; (*entrance*) vestibule *m.*; (*mansion*) manoir *m.*; (*corridor*) couloir *m.* ~ **of residence**, foyer d'étudiants *m.*

hallelujah /hælɪ'luːjə/ *int. & n.* = **alleluia**

hallmark /'hɔːlmɑːk/ *n.* (*on gold etc.*) poinçon *m.*; (*fig.*) sceau *m.*

hallo /hə'ləʊ/ *int. & n.* bonjour (*m.*). ~!, (*on telephone*) allô!; (*in surprise*) tiens!

hallow /'hæləʊ/ *v.t.* sanctifier.

Hallowe'en /hæləʊ'iːn/ *n.* la veille de la Toussaint.

hallucination /həluːsɪ'neɪʃn/ *n.* hallucination *f.*

halo /'heɪləʊ/ *n.* (*pl.* -**oes**) auréole *f.*

halt /hɔːlt/ *n.* halte *f.* —*v.t./i.* (s')arrêter.

halve /hɑːv/ *v.t.* diviser en deux; (*time etc.*) réduire de moitié.

ham /hæm/ *n.* jambon *m.*; (*theatre: sl.*) cabotin(e) *m.* (*f.*). ~-**fisted** *a.* maladroit.

hamburger /'hæmbɜːgə(r)/ *n.* hamburger *m.*

hamlet /'hæmlɪt/ n. hameau m.

hammer /'hæmə(r)/ n. marteau m.
—v.t./i. marteler, frapper; (defeat)
battre à plate couture. ~ out,
(differences) arranger; (agreement)
arriver à.

hammock /'hæmək/ n. hamac m.

hamper[1] /'hæmpə(r)/ n. panier m.

hamper[2] /'hæmpə(r)/ v.t. gêner.

hamster /'hæmstə(r)/ n. hamster m.

hand /hænd/ n. main f.; (of clock)
aiguille f.; (writing) écriture f.;
(worker) ouvrlier, -ière m., f.; (cards)
jeu m. —v.t. donner. **at ~,** proche. ~-
baggage n. bagages à main m. pl. **give
s.o. a ~,** donner un coup de main à qn.
~ in or **over,** remettre. **~ out,** distribuer. **~-out** n. prospectus m.;
(money) aumône f. **on ~,** disponible.
on one's ~s, (fig.) sur les bras. **on the
one ~ . . . on the other ~,** d'une
part . . . d'autre part. **to ~,** à portée
de la main.

handbag /'hændbæg/ n. sac à main m.

handbook /'hændbʊk/ n. manuel m.

handbrake /'hændbreɪk/ n. frein à main
m.

handcuffs /'hændkʌfs/ n. pl. menottes f.
pl.

handful /'hændfʊl/ n. poignée f. **he's a
~!,** c'est du boulot!

handicap /'hændɪkæp/ n. handicap m.
—v.t. (p.t. **handicapped**) handicaper.

handicraft /'hændɪkrɑːft/ n. travaux
manuels m. pl., artisanat m.

handiwork /'hændɪwɜːk/ n. ouvrage m.

handkerchief /'hæŋkətʃɪf/ n. (pl. **-fs**)
mouchoir m.

handle /'hændl/ n. (of door etc.) poignée
f.; (of implement) manche m.; (of cup
etc.) anse f.; (of pan etc.) queue f.; (for
turning) manivelle f. —v.t. manier;
(deal with) s'occuper de; (touch)
toucher à.

handlebar /'hændlbɑː(r)/ n. guidon m.

handshake /'hændʃeɪk/ n. poignée de
main f.

handsome /'hænsəm/ a. (good-looking)
beau; (generous) généreux; (large)
considérable.

handwriting /'hændraɪtɪŋ/ n. écriture f.

handy /'hændɪ/ a. (-ier, -iest) (useful)
commode, utile; (person) adroit; (near)
accessible.

handyman /'hændɪmæn/ n. (pl. **-men**)
bricoleur m.; (servant) homme à tout
faire m.

hang /hæŋ/ v.t. (p.t. **hung**) suspendre,
accrocher; (p.t. **hanged**) (criminal)

pendre. —v.i. pendre. —n. **get the ~ of
doing,** trouver le truc pour faire. ~
about, traîner. **~-gliding** n. vol libre m.
~ on, (hold out) tenir bon; (wait: sl.)
attendre. **~ out** v.i. pendre; (live: sl.)
crécher; (spend time: sl.) passer son
temps; v.t. (washing) étendre. **~ up,**
(telephone) raccrocher. **~-up** n. (sl.)
complexe m.

hangar /'hæŋə(r)/ n. hangar m.

hanger /'hæŋə(r)/ n. (for clothes) cintre
m. **~-on** n. parasite m.

hangover /'hæŋəʊvə(r)/ n. (after drinking) gueule de bois f.

hanker /'hæŋkə(r)/ v.i. **~ after,** avoir
envie de. **~ing** n. envie f.

hanky-panky /'hæŋkɪpæŋkɪ/ n. (trickery: sl.) manigances f. pl.

haphazard /hæp'hæzəd/ a., **~ly** adv. au
petit bonheur, au hasard.

hapless /'hæplɪs/ a. infortuné.

happen /'hæpən/ v.i. arriver, se passer. **it
so ~s that,** il se trouve que. **he ~s to
know that,** il se trouve qu'il sait que.
~ing n. événement m.

happ|y /'hæpɪ/ a. (-ier, -iest) heureux.
I'm not ~y about the idea, je n'aime
pas trop l'idée. **~y with sth.,** satisfait de
qch. **~y medium** or **mean,** juste milieu
m. **~ily** adv. joyeusement; (fortunately) heureusement. **~iness** n. bonheur m. **~y-go-lucky** a. insouciant.

harass /'hærəs/ v.t. harceler. **~ment** n.
harcèlement m.

harbour, (Amer.) **harbor** /'hɑːbə(r)/ n.
port m. —v.t. (shelter) héberger.

hard /hɑːd/ a. (-er, -est) dur; (difficult)
difficile, dur. —adv. dur; (think)
sérieusement; (pull) fort. **~ and fast,**
concret. **~-boiled egg,** œuf dur m. **~
by,** tout près. **~ disk,** disque dur m. **~
done by,** mal traité. **~-headed** a.
réaliste. **~ of hearing,** dur d'oreille. **the
~ of hearing,** les malentendants m. pl.
~-line a. pur et dur. **~ shoulder,**
accotement stabilisé m. **~ up,** (fam.)
fauché. **~-wearing** a. solide. **~-
working** a. travailleur. **~ness** n. dureté
f.

hardboard /'hɑːdbɔːd/ n. Isorel m. (P.).

harden /'hɑːdn/ v.t./i. durcir.

hardly /'hɑːdlɪ/ adv. à peine. **~ ever,**
presque jamais.

hardship /'hɑːdʃɪp/ n. **~(s),** épreuves f.
pl., souffrance f.

hardware /'hɑːdweə(r)/ n. (metal
goods) quincaillerie f.; (machinery, of
computer) matériel m.

hardy /'hɑːdɪ/ a. (-ier, iest) résistant.

hare /heə(r)/ *n.* lièvre *m.* ~ **around,** courir partout. ~**-brained** *a.* écervelé.

hark /hɑːk/ *v.i.* écouter. ~ **back to,** revenir sur.

harm /hɑːm/ *n.* (*hurt*) mal *m.*; (*wrong*) tort *m.* —*v.t.* (*hurt*) faire du mal à; (*wrong*) faire du tort à; (*object*) endommager. **there is no** ~ **in,** il n'y a pas de mal à. ~**ful** *a.* nuisible. ~**less** *a.* inoffensif.

harmonica /hɑːˈmɒnɪkə/ *n.* harmonica *m.*

harmon|y /ˈhɑːmənɪ/ *n.* harmonie *f.* ~**ious** /-ˈməʊnɪəs/ *a.* harmonieux. ~**ize** *v.t./i.* (s')harmoniser.

harness /ˈhɑːnɪs/ *n.* harnais *m.* —*v.t.* (*horse*) harnacher; (*control*) maîtriser; (*use*) exploiter.

harp /hɑːp/ *n.* harpe *f.* —*v.i.* ~ **on** (*about*), rabâcher. ~**ist** *n.* harpiste *m./f.*

harpoon /hɑːˈpuːn/ *n.* harpon *m.*

harpsichord /ˈhɑːpsɪkɔːd/ *n.* clavecin *m.*

harrowing /ˈhærəʊɪŋ/ *a.* déchirant, qui déchire le cœur.

harsh /hɑːʃ/ *a.* (**-er, -est**) dur, rude; (*taste*) âpre; (*sound*) rude, âpre. ~**ly** *adv.* durement. ~**ness** *n.* dureté *f.*

harvest /ˈhɑːvɪst/ *n.* moisson *f.*, récolte *f.* **the wine** ~, les vendanges *f. pl.* —*v.t.* moissonner, récolter. ~**er** *n.* moissonneuse *f.*

has /hæz/ *see* **have.**

hash /hæʃ/ *n.* (*culin.*) hachis *m.*; (*fig.*) gâchis *m.* **make a** ~ **of,** (*bungle: sl.*) saboter.

hashish /ˈhæʃiːʃ/ *n.* ha(s)chisch *m.*

hassle /ˈhæsl/ *n.* (*fam.*) difficulté(s) *f.* (*pl.*); (*bother, effort: fam.*) mal *m.*, peine *f.*; (*quarrel: fam.*) chamaillerie *f.* —*v.t.* (*harass: fam.*) harceler.

haste /heɪst/ *n.* hâte *f.* **in** ~, à la hâte. **make** ~, se hâter.

hasten /ˈheɪsn/ *v.t./i.* (se) hâter.

hast|y /ˈheɪstɪ/ *a.* (**-ier, -iest**) précipité. ~**ily** *adv.* à la hâte.

hat /hæt/ *n.* chapeau *m.* **a** ~ **trick,** trois succès consécutifs.

hatch[1] /hætʃ/ *n.* (*for food*) passeplat *m.*; (*naut.*) écoutille *f.*

hatch[2] /hætʃ/ *v.t./i.* (faire) éclore.

hatchback /ˈhætʃbæk/ *n.* voiture avec hayon arrière *f.*

hatchet /ˈhætʃɪt/ *n.* hachette *f.*

hate /heɪt/ *n.* haine *f.* —*v.t.* haïr. ~**ful** *a.* haïssable.

hatred /ˈheɪtrɪd/ *n.* haine *f.*

haughty /ˈhɔːtɪ/ *a.* (**-ier, -iest**) hautain.

haul /hɔːl/ *v.t.* traîner, tirer. —*n.* (*of thieves*) butin *m.*; (*catch*) prise *f.*;

(*journey*) voyage *m.* ~**age** *n.* camionnage *m.* ~**ier** *n.* camionneur *m.*

haunch /hɔːntʃ/ *n.* **on one's** ~**es,** accroupi.

haunt /hɔːnt/ *v.t.* hanter. —*n.* endroit favori *m.*

have /hæv/ *v.t.* (*3 sing. present tense* **has;** *p.t.* **had**) avoir; (*meal, bath, etc.*) prendre; (*walk, dream, etc.*) faire. —*v. aux.* avoir; (*with aller, partir, etc. & pronominal verbs*) être. ~ **it out with,** s'expliquer avec. ~ **just done,** venir de faire. ~ **sth. done,** faire faire qch. ~ **to do,** devoir faire. **the** ~**s and have-nots,** les riches et les pauvres *m. pl.*

haven /ˈheɪvn/ *n.* havre *m.*, abri *m.*

haversack /ˈhævəsæk/ *n.* musette *f.*

havoc /ˈhævək/ *n.* ravages *m. pl.*

haw /hɔː/ *see* **hum.**

hawk[1] /hɔːk/ *n.* faucon *m.*

hawk[2] /hɔːk/ *v.t.* colporter. ~**er** *n.* colporteur, -se *m., f.*

hawthorn /ˈhɔːθɔːn/ *n.* aubépine *f.*

hay /heɪ/ *n.* foin *m.* ~ **fever,** rhume des foins *m.*

haystack /ˈheɪstæk/ *n.* meule de foin *f.*

haywire /ˈheɪwaɪə(r)/ *a.* **go** ~, (*plans*) se désorganiser; (*machine*) se détraquer.

hazard /ˈhæzəd/ *n.* risque *m.* —*v.t.* risquer, hasarder. ~ **warning lights,** feux de détresse *m. pl.* ~**ous** *a.* hasardeux, risqué.

haze /heɪz/ *n.* brume *f.*

hazel /ˈheɪzl/ *n.* (*bush*) noisetier *m.* ~**nut** *n.* noisette *f.*

hazy /ˈheɪzɪ/ *a.* (**-ier, -iest**) (*misty*) brumeux; (*fig.*) flou, vague.

he /hiː/ *pron.* il; (*emphatic*) lui. —*n.* mâle *m.*

head /hed/ *n.* tête *f.*; (*leader*) chef *m.*; (*of beer*) mousse *f.* —*a.* principal. —*v.t.* être à la tête de. —*v.i.* ~ **for,** se diriger vers. ~**-dress** *n.* coiffure *f.*; (*lady's*) coiffe *f.* ~**-on** *a. & adv.* de plein fouet. ~ **first,** la tête la première. ~**s or tails?,** pile ou face? ~ **office,** siège *m.* ~ **rest,** appui-tête *m.* ~ **the ball,** faire une tête. ~ **waiter,** maître d'hôtel *m.* ~**er** *n.* (*football*) tête *f.*

headache /ˈhedeɪk/ *n.* mal de tête *m.*

heading /ˈhedɪŋ/ *n.* titre *m.*; (*subject category*) rubrique *f.*

headlamp /ˈhedlæmp/ *n.* phare *m.*

headland /ˈhedlənd/ *n.* cap *m.*

headlight /ˈhedlaɪt/ *n.* phare *m.*

headline /ˈhedlaɪn/ *n.* titre *m.*

headlong /ˈhedlɒŋ/ *adv.* (*in a rush*) à toute allure.

head|master /hed'mɑ:stə(r)/ n. (of school) directeur m. **∼mistress** n. directrice f.

headphone /'hedfəʊn/ n. écouteur m. **∼s**, casque (à écouteurs) m.

headquarters /'hedkwɔ:təz/ n. pl. siège m., bureau central m.; (mil.) quartier général m.

headstrong /'hedstrɒŋ/ a. têtu.

headway /'hedweɪ/ n. progrès m. (pl.) **make ∼**, faire des progrès.

heady /'hedɪ/ a. (-ier, -iest) (wine) capiteux; (exciting) grisant.

heal /hi:l/ v.t./i. guérir.

health /helθ/ n. santé f. **∼ centre**, dispensaire m. **∼ foods**, aliments diététiques m. pl. **∼ insurance**, assurance médicale f. **∼y** a. sain; (person) en bonne santé.

heap /hi:p/ n. tas m. —v.t. entasser. **∼s of**, (fam.) des tas de.

hear /hɪə(r)/ v.t./i. (p.t. **heard** /hɜ:d/) entendre. **hear, hear!**, bravo! **∼ from**, recevoir des nouvelles de. **∼ of** or **about**, entendre parler de. **not ∼ of**, (refuse to allow) ne pas entendre parler de. **∼ing** n. ouïe f.; (of witness) audition f.; (of case) audience f. **∼ing-aid** n. appareil acoustique m.

hearsay /'hɪəseɪ/ n. ouï-dire m. invar. **from ∼**, par ouï-dire.

hearse /hɜ:s/ n. corbillard m.

heart /hɑ:t/ n. cœur m. **∼s**, (cards) cœur m. **at ∼**, au fond. **by ∼**, par cœur. **∼ attack**, crise cardiaque f. **∼-break** n. chagrin m. **∼-breaking** a. navrant. **be ∼-broken**, avoir le cœur brisé. **∼-to-heart** a. à cœur ouvert. **lose ∼**, perdre courage.

heartache /'hɑ:teɪk/ n. chagrin m.

heartburn /'hɑ:tbɜ:n/ n. brûlures d'estomac f. pl.

hearten /'hɑ:tn/ v.t. encourager.

heartfelt /'hɑ:tfelt/ a. sincère.

hearth /hɑ:θ/ n. foyer m.

heartless /'hɑ:tlɪs/ a. cruel.

heart|y /'hɑ:tɪ/ a. (-ier, -iest) (sincere) chaleureux; (meal) gros. **∼ily** adv. (eat) avec appétit.

heat /hi:t/ n. chaleur f.; (excitement: fig.) feu m.; (contest) éliminatoire f. —v.t./i. chauffer. **∼ stroke**, insolation f. **∼ up**, (food) réchauffer. **∼ wave**, vague de chaleur f. **∼er** n. radiateur m. **∼ing** n. chauffage m.

heated /'hi:tɪd/ a. (fig.) passionné.

heath /hi:θ/ n. (area) lande f.

heathen /'hi:ðn/ n. païen(ne) m. (f.).

heather /'heðə(r)/ n. bruyère f.

heave /hi:v/ v.t./i. (lift) (se) soulever; (a sigh) pousser; (throw: fam.) lancer; (retch) avoir des nausées.

heaven /'hevn/ n. ciel m. **∼ly** a. céleste; (pleasing: fam.) divin.

heav|y /'hevɪ/ a. (-ier, -iest) lourd; (cold, work, etc.) gros; (traffic) dense. **∼y goods vehicle**, poids lourd m. **∼y-handed** a. maladroit. **∼ily** adv. lourdement; (smoke, drink) beaucoup.

heavyweight /'hevɪweɪt/ n. poids lourd m.

Hebrew /'hi:bru:/ a. hébreu (m. only), hébraïque. —n. (lang.) hébreu m.

heckle /'hekl/ v.t. (speaker) interrompre, interpeller.

hectic /'hektɪk/ a. très bousculé, trépidant, agité.

hedge /hedʒ/ n. haie f. —v.t. entourer. —v.i. (in answering) répondre évasivement. **∼ one's bets**, protéger ses arrières.

hedgehog /'hedʒhɒg/ n. hérisson m.

heed /hi:d/ v.t. faire attention à. —n. **pay ∼ to**, faire attention à. **∼less** a. **∼less of**, inattentif à.

heel /hi:l/ n. talon m.; (man: sl.) salaud m. **down at ∼**, (Amer.) **down at the ∼s**, miteux.

hefty /'heftɪ/ a. (-ier, -iest) gros, lourd.

heifer /'hefə(r)/ n. génisse f.

height /haɪt/ n. hauteur f.; (of person) taille f.; (of plane, mountain) altitude f.; (of fame, glory) apogée m.; (of joy, folly, pain) comble m.

heighten /'haɪtn/ v.t. (raise) rehausser; (fig.) augmenter.

heinous /'heɪnəs/ a. atroce.

heir /eə(r)/ n. héritier m. **∼ess** n. héritière f.

heirloom /'eəlu:m/ n. bijou (meuble, tableau, etc.) de famille m.

held /held/ see **hold**[1].

helicopter /'helɪkɒptə(r)/ n. hélicoptère m.

heliport /'helɪpɔ:t/ n. héliport m.

hell /hel/ n. enfer m. **∼-bent** a. acharné (**on**, à). **∼ish** a. infernal.

hello /hə'ləʊ/ int. & n. = **hallo**.

helm /helm/ n. (of ship) barre f.

helmet /'helmɪt/ n. casque m.

help /help/ v.t./i. aider. —n. aide f.; (employees) personnel m.; (charwoman) femme de ménage f. **∼ o.s. to**, se servir de. **he cannot ∼ laughing**, il ne peut pas s'empêcher de rire. **∼er** n. aide m./f. **∼ful** a. utile; (person) serviable. **∼less** a. impuissant.

helping /'helpɪŋ/ n. portion f.

helter-skelter /heltə'skeltə(r)/ n. toboggan m. —adv. pêle-mêle.

hem /hem/ n. ourlet m. —v.t. (p.t. **hemmed**) ourler. ~ **in**, enfermer.

hemisphere /'hemɪsfɪə(r)/ n. hémisphère m.

hemorrhage /'hemərɪdʒ/ n. (Amer.) = **haemorrhage**.

hemorrhoids /'hemərɔɪdz/ n. pl. (Amer.) = **haemorrhoids**.

hen /hen/ n. poule f.

hence /hens/ adv. (for this reason) d'où; (from now) d'ici. ~**forth** adv. désormais.

henchman /'hentʃmən/ n. (pl. -men) acolyte m., homme de main m.

henpecked /'henpekt/ a. dominé or harcelé par sa femme.

hepatitis /hepə'taɪtɪs/ n. hépatite f.

her /hɜː(r)/ pron. la, l'*; (after prep.) elle. (**to**) ~, lui. **I know** ~, je la connais. —a. son, sa, pl. ses.

herald /'herəld/ v.t. annoncer.

herb /hɜːb, Amer. ɜːb/ n. herbe f. ~**s**, (culin.) fines herbes f. pl.

herd /hɜːd/ n. troupeau m. —v.t./i. ~ **together**, (s')entasser.

here /hɪə(r)/ adv. ici. ~!, (take this) tenez! ~ **is**, ~ **are**, voici. **I'm** ~, je suis là. ~**abouts** adv. par ici.

hereafter /hɪər'ɑːftə(r)/ adv. après; (in book) ci-après.

hereby /hɪə'baɪ/ adv. par le présent acte; (in letter) par la présente.

hereditary /hə'redɪtərɪ/ a. héréditaire.

heredity /hə'redɪtɪ/ n. hérédité f.

here|sy /'herəsɪ/ n. hérésie f. ~**tic** n. hérétique m./f.

herewith /hɪə'wɪð/ adv. (comm.) avec ceci, ci-joint.

heritage /'herɪtɪdʒ/ n. patrimoine m., héritage m.

hermit /'hɜːmɪt/ n. ermite m.

hernia /'hɜːnɪə/ n. hernie f.

hero /'hɪərəʊ/ n. (pl. -oes) héros m. ~**ine** /'herəʊɪn/ n. héroïne f. ~**ism** /'herəʊɪzəm/ n. héroisme m.

heroic /hɪ'rəʊɪk/ a. héroïque.

heroin /'herəʊɪn/ n. héroïne f.

heron /'herən/ n. héron m.

herpes /'hɜːpiːz/ n. herpès m.

herring /'herɪŋ/ n. hareng m.

hers /hɜːz/ poss. pron. le sien, la sienne, les sien(ne)s. **it is** ~, c'est à elle or le sien.

herself /hɜː'self/ pron. elle-même; (reflexive) se; (after prep.) elle.

hesitant /'hezɪtənt/ a. hésitant.

hesitat|e /'hezɪteɪt/ v.i. hésiter. ~**ion** /-'teɪʃn/ n. hésitation f.

het /het/ a. ~ **up**, (sl.) énervé.

heterosexual /hetərəʊ'seksjʊəl/ a. & n. hétérosexuel(le) (m. (f.)).

hexagon /'heksəgən/ n. hexagone m. ~**al** /-'ægənl/ a. hexagonal.

hey /heɪ/ int. dites donc.

heyday /'heɪdeɪ/ n. apogée m.

HGV abbr. see **heavy goods vehicle**.

hi /haɪ/ int. (greeting: Amer.) salut.

hibernat|e /'haɪbəneɪt/ v.i. hiberner. ~**ion** /-'neɪʃn/ n. hibernation f.

hiccup /'hɪkʌp/ n. hoquet m. —v.t. hoqueter. (**the**) ~**s**, le hoquet.

hide¹ /haɪd/ v.t. (p.t. **hid**, p.p. **hidden**) cacher (**from**, à). —v.i. se cacher (**from**, de). **go into hiding**, se cacher. ~**-out** n. (fam.) cachette f.

hide² /haɪd/ n. (skin) peau f.

hideous /'hɪdɪəs/ a. (dreadful) atroce; (ugly) hideux.

hiding /'haɪdɪŋ/ n. (thrashing: fam.) correction f.

hierarchy /'haɪərɑːkɪ/ n. hiérarchie f.

hi-fi /'haɪ'faɪ/ a. & n. hi-fi a. & f. invar.; (machine) chaîne hi-fi f.

high /haɪ/ a. (-er, -est) haut; (price, number) élevé; (priest, speed) grand; (voice) aigu. —n. a (**new**) ~, (recorded level) un record. —adv. haut. ~ **chair**, chaise haute f. ~**-handed** a. autoritaire. ~**-jump**, saut en hauteur m. ~**-level** a. de haut niveau. ~**-rise building**, tour f. ~ **road**, grand-route f. ~ **school**, lycée m. **in the** ~ **season**, en pleine saison. ~**-speed** a. ultra-rapide. ~ **spot**, (fam.) point culminant m. ~ **street**, grand-rue f. ~**-strung** a. (Amer.) nerveux. ~ **tea**, goûter-dîner m. ~**er education**, enseignement supérieur m.

highbrow /'haɪbraʊ/ a. & n. intellectuel(le) (m. (f.)).

highlight /'haɪlaɪt/ n. (vivid moment) moment fort m. ~**s**, (in hair) balayage m. **recorded** ~**s**, extraits enregistrés m. pl. —v.t. (emphasize) souligner.

highly /'haɪlɪ/ adv. extrêmement; (paid) très bien. ~**-strung** a. nerveux. **speak/think** ~ **of**, dire/penser du bien de.

Highness /'haɪnɪs/ n. Altesse f.

highway /'haɪweɪ/ n. route nationale f. ~ **code**, code de la route m.

hijack /'haɪdʒæk/ v.t. détourner. —n. détournement m. ~**er** n. pirate (de l'air) m.

hike /haɪk/ n. randonnée f. —v.i. faire de

la randonnée. **price** ~, hausse de prix *f.*
~**r** /-ə(r)/ *n.* randonneulr, -se *m., f.*

hilarious /hɪ'leərɪəs/ *a.* (*funny*)
désopilant.

hill /hɪl/ *n.* colline *f.*; (*slope*) côte *f.* ~**y**
a. accidenté.

hillside /'hɪlsaɪd/ *n.* coteau *m.*

hilt /hɪlt/ *n.* (*of sword*) garde *f.* **to the** ~,
tout à fait, au maximum.

him /hɪm/ *pron.* le, l'*; (*after prep.*) lui.
(**to**) ~, lui. **I know** ~, je le connais.

himself /hɪm'self/ *pron.* lui-même;
(*reflexive*) se; (*after prep.*) lui.

hind /haɪnd/ *a.* de derrière.

hind|er /'hɪndə(r)/ *v.t.* (*hamper*) gêner;
(*prevent*) empêcher. ~**rance** *n.*
obstacle *m.*, gêne *f.*

hindsight /'haɪndsaɪt/ *n.* **with** ~,
rétrospectivement.

Hindu /hɪn'du:/ *a. & n.* hindou(e) (*m.*
(*f.*)). ~**ism** /'hɪndu:ɪzəm/ *n.* hin-
douisme *m.*

hinge /hɪndʒ/ *n.* charnière *f.* —*v.i.* ~ **on**,
(*depend on*) dépendre de.

hint /hɪnt/ *n.* allusion *f.*; (*advice*) conseil
m. —*v.t.* laisser entendre. —*v.i.* ~ **at**,
faire allusion à.

hip /hɪp/ *n.* hanche *f.*

hippie /'hɪpɪ/ *n.* hippie *m./f.*

hippopotamus /hɪpə'pɒtəməs/ *n.* (*pl.*
-**muses**) hippopotame *m.*

hire /haɪə(r)/ *v.t.* (*thing*) louer; (*person*)
engager. —*n.* location *f.* ~**-car** *n.*
voiture de location *f.* ~**-purchase** *n.*
achat à crédit *m.*, vente à crédit *f.*

his /hɪz/ *a.* son, sa, *pl.* ses. —*poss. pron.*
le sien, la sienne, les sien(ne)s. **it is** ~,
c'est à lui *or* le sien.

hiss /hɪs/ *n.* sifflement *m.* —*v.t./i.* siffler.

historian /hɪ'stɔːrɪən/ *n.* historien(ne) *m.*
(*f.*).

histor|y /'hɪstərɪ/ *n.* histoire *f.* **make** ~**y**,
entrer dans l'histoire. ~**ic(al)**
/hɪ'stɒrɪk(l)/ *a.* historique.

hit /hɪt/ *v.t.* (*p.t.* **hit**, *pres. p.* **hitting**)
frapper; (*knock against, collide with*)
heurter; (*find*) trouver; (*affect, reach*)
toucher. —*v.i.* ~ **on**, (*find*) tomber sur.
—*n.* (*blow*) coup *m.*; (*fig.*) succès *m.*;
(*song*) tube *m.* ~ **it off**, s'entendre bien
(**with**, avec). ~**-or-miss** *a.* fait au petit
bonheur.

hitch /hɪtʃ/ *v.t.* (*fasten*) accrocher. —*n.*
(*snag*) anicroche *f.* ~ **a lift**, ~**-hike** *v.i.*
faire de l'auto-stop. ~**-hiker** *n.* auto-
stoppeulr, -se *m., f.* ~ **up**, (*pull up*)
remonter.

hi-tech /haɪ'tek/ *a. & n.* high-tech (*m.*)
invar.

hitherto /hɪðə'tu:/ *adv.* jusqu'ici.

HIV *abbr.* HIV. ~**-positive** *a.*
séropositif.

hive /haɪv/ *n.* ruche *f.* —*v.t.* ~ **off**,
séparer; (*industry*) vendre.

hoard /hɔːd/ *v.t.* amasser. —*n.*
réserve(s) *f.* (*pl.*); (*of money*) magot *m.*,
trésor *m.*

hoarding /'hɔːdɪŋ/ *n.* panneau
d'affichage *m.*

hoar-frost /'hɔːfrɒst/ *n.* givre *m.*

hoarse /hɔːs/ *a.* (-**er**, -**est**) enroué. ~**ness**
n. enrouement *m.*

hoax /həʊks/ *n.* canular *m.* —*v.t.* faire un
canular à.

hob /hɒb/ *n.* plaque chauffante *f.*

hobble /'hɒbl/ *v.i.* clopiner.

hobby /'hɒbɪ/ *n.* passe-temps *m. invar.*
~**-horse** *n.* (*fig.*) dada *m.*

hob-nob /'hɒbnɒb/ *v.i.* (*p.t.* **hob-
nobbed**) ~ **with**, frayer avec.

hock[1] /hɒk/ *n.* vin du Rhin *m.*

hock[2] /hɒk/ *v.t.* (*pawn: sl.*) mettre au
clou.

hockey /'hɒkɪ/ *n.* hockey *m.*

hoe /həʊ/ *n.* binette *f.* —*v.t.* (*pres. p.*
hoeing) biner.

hog /hɒg/ *n.* cochon *m.* —*v.t.* (*p.t.*
hogged) (*fam.*) accaparer.

hoist /hɔɪst/ *v.t.* hisser. —*n.* palan *m.*

hold[1] /həʊld/ *v.t.* (*p.t.* **held**) tenir;
(*contain*) contenir; (*interest, breath,
etc.*) retenir; (*possess*) avoir; (*believe*)
maintenir. —*v.i.* (*of rope, weather,
etc.*) tenir. —*n.* prise *f.* **get** ~ **of**, saisir;
(*fig.*) trouver. **on** ~, en suspens. ~
back, (*contain*) retenir; (*hide*) cacher.
~ **down**, (*person*) maîtriser; (*in struggle*)
retenir. ~ **on**, (*stand firm*) tenir bon;
(*wait*) attendre. ~ **on to**, (*keep*) garder;
(*cling to*) se cramponner à. ~ **one's
tongue**, se taire. ~ **out** *v.t.* (*offer*)
offrir; *v.i.* (*resist*) tenir le coup. ~ (**the
line**), **please**, ne quittez pas. ~ **up**,
(*support*) soutenir; (*delay*) retarder;
(*rob*) attaquer. ~**-up** *n.* retard *m.*; (*of
traffic*) bouchon *m.*; (*robbery*) hold-up
m. invar. **not** ~ **with**, désapprouver.
~**er** *n.* détenlteur, -trice *m., f.*; (*of post*)
titulaire *m./f.*; (*for object*) support
m.

hold[2] /həʊld/ *n.* (*of ship*) cale *f.*

holdall /'həʊldɔːl/ *n.* (*bag*) fourre-tout
m. invar.

holding /'həʊldɪŋ/ *n.* (*possession, land*)
possession *f.* ~ **company**, holding *m.*

hole /həʊl/ *n.* trou *m.* —*v.t.* trouer.

holiday /'hɒlədeɪ/ *n.* vacances *f. pl.*;
(*public*) jour férié *m.*; (*day off*) congé

m. —*v.i.* passer ses vacances. —*a.* de vacances. ∼**-maker** *n.* vacancier, -ière *m., f.*

holiness /'həʊlɪnɪs/ *n.* sainteté *f.*

holistic /həʊ'lɪstɪk/ *a.* holistique.

Holland /'hɒlənd/ *n.* Hollande *f.*

hollow /'hɒləʊ/ *a.* creux; (*fig.*) faux. —*n.* creux *m.* —*v.t.* creuser.

holly /'hɒlɪ/ *n.* houx *m.*

holster /'həʊlstə(r)/ *n.* étui de revolver *m.*

holy /'həʊlɪ/ *a.* (**-ier, -iest**) saint, sacré; (*water*) bénit. **H**∼ **Ghost, H**∼ **Spirit,** Saint-Esprit *m.*

homage /'hɒmɪdʒ/ *n.* hommage *m.*

home /həʊm/ *n.* maison *f.*, foyer *m.*; (*institution*) maison *f.*; (*for soldiers, workers*) foyer *m.*; (*country*) pays natal *m.* —*a.* de la maison, du foyer; (*of family*) de famille; (*pol.*) national, intérieur; (*match, visit*) à domicile. —*adv.* (**at**) ∼, à la maison, chez soi. **come** *or* **go** ∼, rentrer; (*from abroad*) rentrer dans son pays. **feel at** ∼ **with,** être à l'aise avec. **H**∼ **Counties,** région autour de Londres *f.* ∼**-made** *a.* (*food*) fait maison; (*clothes*) fait à la maison. **H**∼ **Office,** ministère de l'Intérieur *m.* **H**∼ **Secretary,** ministre de l'Intérieur *m.* ∼ **town,** ville natale *f.* ∼ **truth,** vérité bien sentie *f.* ∼**less** *a.* sans abri.

homeland /'həʊmlænd/ *n.* patrie *f.*

homely /'həʊmlɪ/ *a.* (**-ier, -iest**) simple; (*person: Amer.*) assez laid.

homesick /'həʊmsɪk/ *a.* **be** ∼, avoir le mal du pays.

homeward /'həʊmwəd/ *a.* (*journey*) de retour.

homework /'həʊmwɜːk/ *n.* devoirs *m. pl.*

homicide /'hɒmɪsaɪd/ *n.* homicide *m.*

homœopath|**y** /həʊmɪ'ɒpəθɪ/ *n.* homéopathie *f.* ∼**ic** *a.* homéopathique.

homogeneous /hɒmə'dʒiːnɪəs/ *a.* homogène.

homosexual /hɒmə'sekʃʊəl/ *a. & n.* homosexuel(le) (*m.* (*f.*)).

honest /'ɒnɪst/ *a.* honnête; (*frank*) franc. ∼**ly** *adv.* honnêtement; franchement. ∼**y** *n.* honnêteté *f.*

honey /'hʌnɪ/ *n.* miel *m.*; (*person: fam.*) chéri(e) *m.* (*f.*).

honeycomb /'hʌnɪkəʊm/ *n.* rayon de miel *m.*

honeymoon /'hʌnɪmuːn/ *n.* lune de miel *f.*

honk /hɒŋk/ *v.i.* klaxonner.

honorary /'ɒnərərɪ/ *a.* (*person*) honoraire; (*duties*) honorifique.

honour, (*Amer.*) **honor** /'ɒnə(r)/ *n.* honneur *m.* —*v.t.* honorer. ∼**able** *a.* honorable.

hood /hʊd/ *n.* capuchon *m.*; (*car roof*) capote *f.*; (*car engine cover: Amer.*) capot *m.*

hoodlum /'huːdləm/ *n.* voyou *m.*

hoodwink /'hʊdwɪŋk/ *v.t.* tromper.

hoof /huːf/ *n.* (*pl.* **-fs**) sabot *m.*

hook /hʊk/ *n.* crochet *m.*; (*on garment*) agrafe *f.*; (*for fishing*) hameçon *m.* —*v.t./i.* (s')accrocher; (*garment*) (s')agrafer. **off the** ∼, tiré d'affaire; (*phone*) décroché.

hooked /hʊkt/ *a.* crochu. ∼ **on,** (*sl.*) adonné à.

hooker /'hʊkə(r)/ *n.* (*rugby*) talonneur *m.*; (*Amer., sl.*) prostituée *f.*

hookey /'hʊkɪ/ *n.* **play** ∼, (*Amer., sl.*) faire l'école buissonnière.

hooligan /'huːlɪɡən/ *n.* houligan *m.*

hoop /huːp/ *n.* (*toy etc.*) cerceau *m.*

hooray /hʊ'reɪ/ *int. & n.* = **hurrah**.

hoot /huːt/ *n.* (h)ululement *m.*; coup de klaxon *m.*; huée *f.* —*v.i.* (*owl*) (h)ululer; (*of car*) klaxonner; (*jeer*) huer. ∼**er** *n.* klaxon *m.* (P.); (*of factory*) sirène *f.*

Hoover /'huːvə(r)/ *n.* (P.) aspirateur *m.* —*v.t.* passer à l'aspirateur.

hop¹ /hɒp/ *v.i.* (*p.t.* **hopped**) sauter (à cloche-pied). —*n.* saut *m.*; (*flight*) étape *f.* ∼ **in,** (*fam.*) monter. ∼ **it,** (*sl.*) décamper. ∼ **out,** (*fam.*) descendre.

hop² /hɒp/ *n.* ∼(**s**), houblon *m.*

hope /həʊp/ *n.* espoir *m.* —*v.t./i.* espérer. ∼ **for,** espérer (avoir). **I** ∼ **so,** je l'espère. ∼**ful** *a.* encourageant. **be** ∼**ful** (**that**), avoir bon espoir (que). ∼**fully** *adv.* avec espoir; (*it is hoped*) on l'espère. ∼**less** *a.* sans espoir; (*useless: fig.*) nul. ∼**lessly** *adv.* sans espoir *m.*

hopscotch /'hɒpskɒtʃ/ *n.* marelle *f.*

horde /hɔːd/ *n.* horde *f.*, foule *f.*

horizon /hə'raɪzn/ *n.* horizon *m.*

horizontal /hɒrɪ'zɒntl/ *a.* horizontal.

hormone /'hɔːməʊn/ *n.* hormone *f.*

horn /hɔːn/ *n.* corne *f.*; (*of car*) klaxon *m.* (P.); (*mus.*) cor *m.* —*v.i.* ∼ **in,** (*sl.*) interrompre. ∼**y** *a.* (*hands*) calleux.

hornet /'hɔːnɪt/ *n.* frelon *m.*

horoscope /'hɒrəskəʊp/ *n.* horoscope *m.*

horrible /'hɒrəbl/ *a.* horrible.

horrid /'hɒrɪd/ *a.* horrible.

horrific /hə'rɪfɪk/ *a.* horrifiant.

horr|**or** /'hɒrə(r)/ *n.* horreur *f.* —*a.* (*film etc.*) d'épouvante. ∼**ify** *v.t.* horrifier.

hors-d'œuvre /ɔː'dɜːvrə/ *n.* hors d'œuvre *m. invar.*

horse /hɔːs/ n. cheval m. ～-**chestnut** n. marron (d'Inde) m. ～-**race** n. course de chevaux f. ～-**radish** n. raifort m. ～ **sense,** (fam.) bon sens m.

horseback /'hɔːsbæk/ n. **on ～,** à cheval.

horseman /'hɔːsmən/ n. (pl. -**men**) cavalier m.

horsepower /'hɔːspaʊə(r)/ n. (unit) cheval (vapeur) m.

horseshoe /'hɔːsʃuː/ n. fer à cheval m.

horsy /'hɔːsɪ/ a. (face etc.) chevalin.

horticultur|e /'hɔːtɪkʌltʃə(r)/ n. horticulture f. ～**al** /-'kʌltʃərəl/ a. horticole.

hose /həʊz/ n. (tube) tuyau m. —v.t. arroser. ～-**pipe** n. tuyau m.

hosiery /'həʊzɪərɪ/ n. bonneterie f.

hospice /'hɒspɪs/ n. hospice m.

hospit|able /hɒ'spɪtəbl/ a. hospitalier. ～**ably** adv. avec hospitalité. ～**ality** /-'tælətɪ/ n. hospitalité f.

hospital /'hɒspɪtl/ n. hôpital m.

host[1] /həʊst/ n. (to guests) hôte m.; (on TV) animateur m. ～**ess** n. hôtesse f.

host[2] /həʊst/ n. **a ～ of,** une foule de.

host[3] /həʊst/ n. (relig.) hostie f.

hostage /'hɒstɪdʒ/ n. otage m.

hostel /'hɒstl/ n. foyer m. (**youth**) ～, auberge (de jeunesse) f.

hostil|e /'hɒstaɪl, Amer. 'hɒstl/a. hostile. ～**ity** /hɒ'stɪlətɪ/ n. hostilité f.

hot /hɒt/ a. (**hotter, hottest**) chaud; (culin.) épicé; (news) récent. **be** or **feel ～,** avoir chaud. **it is ～,** il fait chaud. —v.t./i. (p.t. **hotted**) ～ **up,** (fam.) chauffer. ～ **dog,** hot-dog m. ～ **line,** téléphone rouge m. ～ **shot,** (Amer., sl.) crack m. ～-**water bottle,** bouillotte f. **in ～ water,** (fam.) dans le pétrin. ～**ly** adv. vivement.

hotbed /'hɒtbed/ n. foyer m.

hotchpotch /'hɒtʃpɒtʃ/ n. fatras m.

hotel /həʊ'tel/ n. hôtel m. ～**ier** /-ɪeɪ/ n. hôtelier, -ière m., f.

hothead /'hɒthed/ n. tête brûlée f. ～**ed** a. impétueux.

hotplate /'hɒtpleɪt/ n. plaque chauffante f.

hound /haʊnd/ n. chien courant m. —v.t. poursuivre.

hour /'aʊə(r)/ n. heure f. ～**ly** a. & adv. toutes les heures. ～**ly rate,** tarif horaire m. **paid ～ly,** payé à l'heure.

house[1] /haʊs/ n. (pl. -**s** /'haʊzɪz/) n. maison f.; (theatre) salle f.; (pol.) chambre f. ～-**proud** a. méticuleux. ～-**warming** n. pendaison de la crémaillère f.

house[2] /haʊz/ v.t. loger; (of building) abriter; (keep) garder.

housebreaking /'haʊsbreɪkɪŋ/ n. cambriolage m.

housecoat /'haʊskəʊt/ n. blouse f., tablier m.

household /'haʊshəʊld/ n. (house, family) ménage m. —a. ménager. ～**er** n. occupant(e) m. (f.); (owner) propriétaire m./f.

housekeep|er /'haʊskiːpə(r)/ n. gouvernante f. ～**ing** n. ménage m.

housewife /'haʊswaɪf/ n. (pl. -**wives**) ménagère f.

housework /'haʊswɜːk/ n. ménage m. travaux de ménage m. pl.

housing /'haʊzɪŋ/ n. logement m. ～ **association,** service de logement m. ～ **development,** cité f.

hovel /'hɒvl/ n. taudis m.

hover /'hɒvə(r)/ v.i. (bird, threat, etc.) planer; (loiter) rôder.

hovercraft /'hɒvəkrɑːft/ n. aéroglisseur m.

how /haʊ/ adv. comment. ～ **long/tall is . . .?,** quelle est la longueur/hauteur de . . .? ～ **pretty!,** comme or que c'est joli! ～ **about a walk?,** si on faisait une promenade? ～ **are you?,** comment allez-vous? ～ **do you do?,** (introduction) enchanté. ～ **many?,** ～ **much?,** combien?

however /haʊ'evə(r)/ adv. de quelque manière que; (nevertheless) cependant. ～ **small/delicate/etc. it may be,** quelque petit/délicat/etc. que ce soit.

howl /haʊl/ n. hurlement m. —v.i. hurler.

howler /'haʊlə(r)/ n. (fam.) bévue f.

HP abbr. see **hire-purchase.**

hp abbr. see **horsepower.**

HQ abbr. see **headquarters.**

hub /hʌb/ n. moyeu m.; (fig.) centre m. ～-**cap** n. enjoliveur m.

hubbub /'hʌbʌb/ n. vacarme m.

huddle /'hʌdl/ v.i. se blottir.

hue[1] /hjuː/ n. (colour) teinte f.

hue[2] /hjuː/ n. ～ **and cry,** clameur f.

huff /hʌf/ n. **in a ～,** fâché, vexé.

hug /hʌg/ v.t. (p.t. **hugged**) serrer dans ses bras; (keep close to) serrer. —n. étreinte f.

huge /hjuːdʒ/ a. énorme. ～**ly** adv. énormément.

hulk /hʌlk/ n. (of ship) épave f.; (person) mastodonte m.

hull /hʌl/ n. (of ship) coque f.

hullo /hə'ləʊ/ int. & n. = **hallo.**

hum /hʌm/ v.t./i. (p.t. **hummed**)

(*person*) fredonner; (*insect*) bourdonner; (*engine*) vrombir. —*n.* bourdonnement *m.*; vrombissement *m.* ∿ **and haw,** hésiter.

human /'hju:mən/ *a.* humain. —*n.* être humain *m.* ∿**itarian** /-mænɪ'teərɪən/ *a.* humanitaire.

humane /hju:'meɪn/ *a.* humain, plein d'humanité.

humanity /hju:'mænətɪ/ *n.* humanité *f.*

humbl|e /'hʌmbl/ *a.* (**-er, -est**) humble. —*v.t.* humilier. ∿**y** *adv.* humblement.

humbug /'hʌmbʌg/ *n.* (*false talk*) hypocrisie *f.*

humdrum /'hʌmdrʌm/ *a.* monotone.

humid /'hju:mɪd/ *a.* humide. ∿**ity** /-'mɪdətɪ/ *n.* humidité *f.*

humiliat|e /hju:'mɪlɪeɪt/ *v.t.* humilier. ∿**ion** /-'eɪʃn/ *n.* humiliation *f.*

humility /hju:'mɪlətɪ/ *n.* humilité *f.*

humorist /'hju:mərɪst/ *n.* humoriste *m./f.*

hum|our, (*Amer.*) **hum|or** /'hju:mə(r)/ *n.* humour *m.*; (*mood*) humeur *f.* —*v.t.* ménager. ∿**orous** *a.* humoristique; (*person*) plein d'humour. ∿**orously** *adv.* avec humour.

hump /hʌmp/ *n.* bosse *f.* —*v.t.* voûter. **the** ∿, (*sl.*) le cafard.

hunch[1] /hʌntʃ/ *v.t.* voûter.

hunch[2] /hʌntʃ/ *n.* petite idée *f.*

hunchback /'hʌntʃbæk/ *n.* bossu(e) *m.* (*f.*).

hundred /'hʌndrəd/ *a. & n.* cent (*m.*). ∿**s of,** des centaines de. ∿**fold** *a.* centuple; *adv.* au centuple. ∿**th** *a. & n.* centième (*m./f.*).

hundredweight /'hʌndrədweɪt/ *n.* 50.8 kg.; (*Amer.*) 45.36 kg.

hung /hʌŋ/ *see* **hang.**

Hungar|y /'hʌŋgərɪ/ *n.* Hongrie *f.* ∿**ian** /-'geərɪən/ *a. & n.* hongrois(e) (*m.* (*f.*)).

hunger /'hʌŋgə(r)/ *n.* faim *f.* —*v.i.* ∿ **for,** avoir faim de. ∿**-strike** *n.* grève de la faim *f.*

hungr|y /'hʌŋgrɪ/ *a.* (**-ier, -iest**) affamé. **be** ∿**y,** avoir faim. ∿**ily** *adv.* avidement.

hunk /hʌŋk/ *n.* gros morceau *m.*

hunt /hʌnt/ *v.t./i.* chasser. —*n.* chasse *f.* ∿ **for,** chercher. ∿**er** *n.* chasseur *m.* ∿**ing** *n.* chasse *f.*

hurdle /'hɜ:dl/ *n.* (*sport*) haie *f.*; (*fig.*) obstacle *m.*

hurl /hɜ:l/ *v.t.* lancer.

hurrah, hurray /hʊ'rɑ:, hʊ'reɪ/ *int. & n.* hourra (*m.*).

hurricane /'hʌrɪkən, *Amer.* 'hʌrɪkeɪn/ *n.* ouragan *m.*

hurried /'hʌrɪd/ *a.* précipité. ∿**ly** *adv.* précipitamment.

hurry /'hʌrɪ/ *v.i.* se dépêcher, se presser. —*v.t.* presser, activer. —*n.* hâte *f.* **in a** ∿, pressé.

hurt /hɜ:t/ *v.t./i.* (*p.t.* **hurt**) faire mal (à); (*injure, offend*) blesser. —*a.* blessé. —*n.* mal *m.* ∿**ful** *a.* blessant.

hurtle /'hɜ:tl/ *v.t.* lancer. —*v.i.* ∿ **along,** avancer à toute vitesse.

husband /'hʌzbənd/ *n.* mari *m.*

hush /hʌʃ/ *v.t.* faire taire. —*n.* silence *m.* ∿**-hush** *a.* (*fam.*) ultra-secret. ∿ **up,** (*news etc.*) étouffer.

husk /hʌsk/ *n.* (*of grain*) enveloppe *f.*

husky /'hʌskɪ/ *a.* (**-ier, -iest**) (*hoarse*) rauque; (*burly*) costaud. —*n.* chien de traîneau *m.*

hustle /'hʌsl/ *v.t.* (*push, rush*) bousculer. —*v.i.* (*work busily: Amer.*) se démener. —*n.* bousculade *f.* ∿ **and bustle,** agitation *f.*

hut /hʌt/ *n.* cabane *f.*

hutch /hʌtʃ/ *n.* clapier *m.*

hyacinth /'haɪəsɪnθ/ *n.* jacinthe *f.*

hybrid /'haɪbrɪd/ *a. & n.* hybride (*m.*).

hydrangea /haɪ'dreɪndʒə/ *n.* hortensia *m.*

hydrant /'haɪdrənt/ *n.* (**fire**) ∿, bouche d'incendie *f.*

hydraulic /haɪ'drɔ:lɪk/ *a.* hydraulique.

hydroelectric /haɪdrəʊɪ'lektrɪk/ *a.* hydro-électrique.

hydrofoil /'haɪdrəʊfɔɪl/ *n.* hydroptère *m.*

hydrogen /'haɪdrədʒən/ *n.* hydrogène *m.* ∿ **bomb,** bombe à hydrogène *f.*

hyena /haɪ'i:nə/ *n.* hyène *f.*

hygiene /'haɪdʒi:n/ *n.* hygiène *f.*

hygienic /haɪ'dʒi:nɪk/ *a.* hygiénique.

hymn /hɪm/ *n.* cantique *m.*, hymne *m.*

hype /haɪp/ *n.* tapage publicitaire *m.* —*v.t.* faire du tapage autour de.

hyper- /'haɪpə(r)/ *pref.* hyper-.

hypermarket /'haɪpəmɑ:kɪt/ *n.* hypermarché *m.*

hyphen /'haɪfn/ *n.* trait d'union *m.* ∿**ate** *v.t.* mettre un trait d'union à.

hypno|sis /hɪp'nəʊsɪs/ *n.* hypnose *f.* ∿**tic** /-'nɒtɪk/ *a.* hypnotique.

hypnot|ize /'hɪpnətaɪz/ *v.t.* hypnotiser. ∿**ism** *n.* hypnotisme *m.*

hypochondriac /haɪpə'kɒndrɪæk/ *n.* malade imaginaire *m./f.*

hypocrisy /hɪ'pɒkrəsɪ/ *n.* hypocrisie *f.*

hypocrit|e /'hɪpəkrɪt/ *n.* hypocrite *m./f.* ∿**ical** /-'krɪtɪkl/ *a.* hypocrite.

hypodermic /haɪpə'dɜ:mɪk/ *a.* hypodermique. —*n.* seringue hypodermique *f.*

hypothermia /haɪpə'θɜːmɪə/ n. hypothermie f.

hypothe|sis /haɪ'pɒθəsɪs/ n. (pl. **-theses** /-siːz/) hypothèse f. ~**tical** /-ə'θetɪkl/ a. hypothétique.

hyster|ia /hɪ'stɪərɪə/ n. hystérie f. ~**ical** /-erɪkl/ a. hystérique; (person) surexcité.

hysterics /hɪ'sterɪks/ n. pl. crise de nerfs or de rire f.

I

I /aɪ/ pron. je, j'*; (stressed) moi.

ice /aɪs/ n. glace f.; (on road) verglas m. —v.t. (cake) glacer. —v.i. ~ (up), (window) se givrer; (river) geler. ~**cream** n. glace f. ~**-cube** n. glaçon m. ~ **hockey,** hockey sur glace m. ~ **lolly,** glace (sur bâtonnet) f. ~ **rink,** patinoire f. ~ **skate,** patin à glace m.

iceberg /'aɪsbɜːg/ n. iceberg m.

icebox /'aɪsbɒks/ n. (Amer.) réfrigérateur m.

Iceland /'aɪslənd/ n. Islande f. ~**er** n. Islandais(e) m. (f.). ~**ic** /-'lændɪk/ a. islandais; n. (lang.) islandais m.

icicle /'aɪsɪkl/ n. glaçon m.

icing /'aɪsɪŋ/ n. (sugar) glace f.

icon /'aɪkɒn/ n. icône f.

icy /'aɪsɪ/ a. (**-ier, -iest**) (hands, wind) glacé; (road) verglacé; (manner, welcome) glacial.

idea /aɪ'dɪə/ n. idée f.

ideal /aɪ'dɪəl/ a. idéal. —n. idéal m. ~**ize** v.t. idéaliser. ~**ly** adv. idéalement.

idealis|t /aɪ'dɪəlɪst/ n. idéaliste m./f. ~**m** /-zəm/ n. idéalisme m. ~**tic** /-'lɪstɪk/ a. idéaliste.

identical /aɪ'dentɪkl/ a. identique.

identif|y /aɪ'dentɪfaɪ/ v.t. identifier. —v.i. ~**y with,** s'identifier à. ~**ication** /-ɪ'keɪʃn/ n. identification f.; (papers) une pièce d'identité.

identikit /aɪ'dentɪkɪt/ n. ~ **picture,** portrait-robot m.

identity /aɪ'dentətɪ/ n. identité f.

ideolog|y /aɪdɪ'ɒlədʒɪ/ n. idéologie f. ~**ical** /-ə'lɒdʒɪkl/ a. idéologique.

idiocy /'ɪdɪəsɪ/ n. idiotie f.

idiom /'ɪdɪəm/ n. expression idiomatique f.; (language) idiome m. ~**atic** /-'mætɪk/ a. idiomatique.

idiosyncrasy /ɪdɪə'sɪŋkrəsɪ/ n. particularité f.

idiot /'ɪdɪət/ n. idiot(e) m. (f.). ~**ic** /-'ɒtɪk/ a. idiot.

idle /'aɪdl/ a. (**-er, -est**) désœuvré, oisif; (lazy) paresseux; (unemployed) sans travail; (machine) au repos; (fig.) vain. —v.i. (engine) tourner au ralenti. —v.t. ~ **away,** gaspiller. ~**ness** n. oisiveté f. ~**r** /-ə(r)/ n. oisif, -ve m., f.

idol /'aɪdl/ n. idole f. ~**ize** v.t. idolâtrer.

idyllic /ɪ'dɪlɪk, Amer. aɪ'dɪlɪk/ a. idyllique.

i.e. abbr. c'est-à-dire.

if /ɪf/ conj. si.

igloo /'ɪgluː/ n. igloo m.

ignite /ɪg'naɪt/ v.t./i. (s')enflammer.

ignition /ɪg'nɪʃn/ n. (auto.) allumage m. ~ **key,** clé de contact. ~ (**switch**), contact m.

ignoran|t /'ɪgnərənt/ a. ignorant (of, de). ~**ce** n. ignorance f. ~**tly** adv. par ignorance.

ignore /ɪg'nɔː(r)/ v.t. ne faire or prêter aucune attention à; (person in street etc.) faire semblant de ne pas voir; (facts) ne pas tenir compte de.

ilk /ɪlk/ n. (kind: fam.) acabit m.

ill /ɪl/ a. malade; (bad) mauvais. —adv. mal. —n. mal m. ~**-advised** a. peu judicieux. ~ **at ease,** mal à l'aise. ~**bred** a. mal élevé. ~**-fated** a. malheureux. ~ **feeling,** ressentiment m. ~**-gotten** a. mal acquis. ~**-natured** a. désagréable. ~**-treat** v.t. maltraiter. ~ **will,** malveillance f.

illegal /ɪ'liːgl/ a. illégal.

illegible /ɪ'ledʒəbl/ a. illisible.

illegitima|te /ɪlɪ'dʒɪtɪmət/ a. illégitime. ~**cy** n. illégitimité f.

illitera|te /ɪ'lɪtərət/ a. & n. illettré(e) (m. (f.)), analphabète m./f. ~**cy** n. analphabétisme m.

illness /'ɪlnɪs/ n. maladie f.

illogical /ɪ'lɒdʒɪkl/ a. illogique.

illuminat|e /ɪ'luːmɪneɪt/ v.t. éclairer; (decorate with lights) illuminer. ~**ion** /-'neɪʃn/ n. éclairage m.; illumination f.

illusion /ɪ'luːʒn/ n. illusion f.

illusory /ɪ'luːsərɪ/ a. illusoire.

illustrat|e /'ɪləstreɪt/ v.t. illustrer. ~**ion** /-'streɪʃn/ n. illustration f. ~**ive** /-ətɪv/ a. qui illustre.

illustrious /ɪ'lʌstrɪəs/ a. illustre.

image /'ɪmɪdʒ/ n. image f. (**public**) ~, (of firm, person) image de marque f. ~**ry** /-ərɪ/ n. images f. pl.

imaginary /ɪ'mædʒɪnərɪ/ a. imaginaire.

imaginat|ion /ɪmædʒɪ'neɪʃn/ n. imagination f. ~**ive** /ɪ'mædʒɪnətɪv/ a. plein d'imagination.

imagine /ɪˈmædʒɪn/ v.t. (*picture to o.s.*) (s')imaginer; (*suppose*) imaginer. ~**able** a. imaginable.

imbalance /ɪmˈbæləns/ n. déséquilibre m.

imbecile /ˈɪmbəsiːl/ n. & a. imbécile (m./f.).

imbue /ɪmˈbjuː/ v.t. imprégner.

imitat|e /ˈɪmɪteɪt/ v.t. imiter. ~**ion** /-ˈteɪʃn/ n. imitation f. ~**or** n. imitateur, -trice m., f.

immaculate /ɪˈmækjʊlət/ a. (*room, dress, etc.*) impeccable.

immaterial /ɪməˈtɪərɪəl/ a. sans importance (to, pour; that, que).

immature /ɪməˈtjʊə(r)/ a. pas mûr; (*person*) immature.

immediate /ɪˈmiːdɪət/ a. immédiat. ~**ly** adv. immédiatement; conj. dès que.

immens|e /ɪˈmens/ a. immense. ~**ely** adv. extrêmement, immensément. ~**ity** n. immensité f.

immers|e /ɪˈmɜːs/ v.t. plonger, immerger. ~**ion** /-ɜːʃn/ n. immersion f. ~**ion heater,** chauffe-eau (électrique) m. invar.

immigr|ate /ˈɪmɪɡreɪt/ v.i. immigrer. ~**ant** n. & a. immigré(e) (m. (f.)); (*newly-arrived*) immigrant(e) (m. (f.)). ~**ation** /-ˈɡreɪʃn/ n. immigration f. **go through ~ation,** passer le contrôle des passeports.

imminen|t /ˈɪmɪnənt/ a. imminent. ~**ce** n. imminence f.

immobil|e /ɪˈməʊbaɪl, Amer. ɪˈməʊbl/ a. immobile. ~**ize** /-əlaɪz/ v.t. immobiliser.

immoderate /ɪˈmɒdərət/ a. immodéré.

immor|al /ɪˈmɒrəl/ a. immoral. ~**ity** /ɪməˈrælətɪ/ n. immoralité f.

immortal /ɪˈmɔːtl/ a. immortel. ~**ity** /-ˈtælətɪ/ n. immortalité f. ~**ize** v.t. immortaliser.

immun|e /ɪˈmjuːn/ a. immunisé (**from, to,** contre). ~**ity** n. immunité f.

immuniz|e /ˈɪmjʊnaɪz/ v.t. immuniser. ~**ation** /-ˈzeɪʃn/ n. immunisation f.

imp /ɪmp/ n. lutin m.

impact /ˈɪmpækt/ n. impact m.

impair /ɪmˈpeə(r)/ v.t. détériorer.

impart /ɪmˈpɑːt/ v.t. communiquer, transmettre.

impartial /ɪmˈpɑːʃl/ a. impartial. ~**ity** /-ɪˈælətɪ/ n. impartialité f.

impassable /ɪmˈpɑːsəbl/ a. (*barrier etc.*) infranchissable; (*road*) impraticable.

impasse /ˈæmpɑːs, Amer. ˈɪmpæs/ n. impasse f.

impassioned /ɪmˈpæʃnd/ n. passionné.

impassive /ɪmˈpæsɪv/ a. impassible.

impatien|t /ɪmˈpeɪʃnt/ a. impatient. **get ~t,** s'impatienter. ~**ce** n. impatience f. ~**tly** adv. impatiemment.

impeccable /ɪmˈpekəbl/ a. impeccable.

impede /ɪmˈpiːd/ v.t. gêner.

impediment /ɪmˈpedɪmənt/ n. obstacle m. (**speech**) ~, défaut d'élocution m.

impel /ɪmˈpel/ v.t. (*p.t.* **impelled**) pousser, forcer (**to do,** à faire).

impending /ɪmˈpendɪŋ/ a. imminent.

impenetrable /ɪmˈpenɪtrəbl/ a. impénétrable.

imperative /ɪmˈperətɪv/ a. nécessaire; (*need etc.*) impérieux. —n. (*gram.*) impératif m.

imperceptible /ɪmpəˈseptəbl/ a. imperceptible.

imperfect /ɪmˈpɜːfɪkt/ a. imparfait; (*faulty*) défectueux. ~**ion** /-əˈfekʃn/ n. imperfection f.

imperial /ɪmˈpɪərɪəl/ a. impérial; (*measure*) légal (au Royaume-Uni). ~**ism** n. impérialisme m.

imperil /ɪmˈperəl/ v.t. (*p.t.* **imperilled**) mettre en péril.

imperious /ɪmˈpɪərɪəs/ a. impérieux.

impersonal /ɪmˈpɜːsənl/ a. impersonnel.

impersonat|e /ɪmˈpɜːsəneɪt/ v.t. se faire passer pour; (*mimic*) imiter. ~**ion** /-ˈneɪʃn/ n. imitation f. ~**or** n. imitateur, -trice m., f.

impertinen|t /ɪmˈpɜːtɪnənt/ a. impertinent. ~**ce** n. impertinence f. ~**tly** adv. avec impertinence.

impervious /ɪmˈpɜːvɪəs/ a. ~ **to,** imperméable à.

impetuous /ɪmˈpetʃʊəs/ a. impétueux.

impetus /ˈɪmpɪtəs/ n. impulsion f.

impinge /ɪmˈpɪndʒ/ v.i. ~ **on,** affecter; (*encroach*) empiéter sur.

impish /ˈɪmpɪʃ/ a. espiègle.

implacable /ɪmˈplækəbl/ a. implacable.

implant /ɪmˈplɑːnt/ v.t. implanter. —n. implant m.

implement[1] /ˈɪmplɪmənt/ n. (*tool*) outil m.; (*utensil*) ustensile m.

implement[2] /ˈɪmplɪment/ v.t. exécuter, mettre en pratique.

implicat|e /ˈɪmplɪkeɪt/ v.t. impliquer. ~**ion** /-ˈkeɪʃn/ n. implication f.

implicit /ɪmˈplɪsɪt/ a. (*implied*) implicite; (*unquestioning*) absolu.

implore /ɪmˈplɔː(r)/ v.t. implorer.

impl|y /ɪmˈplaɪ/ v.t. (*assume, mean*) impliquer; (*insinuate*) laisser entendre. ~**ied** a. implicite.

impolite /ɪmpəˈlaɪt/ a. impoli.

imponderable /ɪm'pɒndərəbl/ a. & n. impondérable (m.).

import[1] /ɪm'pɔːt/ v.t. importer. ~ation /-'teɪʃn/ n. importation f. ~er n. importalteur, -trice m., f.

import[2] /'ɪmpɔːt/ n. (article) importation f.; (meaning) sens m.

importan|t /ɪm'pɔːtnt/ a. important. ~ce n. importance f.

impos|e /ɪm'pəʊz/ v.t. imposer. —v.i. ~e on, abuser de l'amabilité de. ~ition /-ə'zɪʃn/ n. imposition f.; (fig.) dérangement m.

imposing /ɪm'pəʊzɪŋ/ a. imposant.

impossib|le /ɪm'pɒsəbl/ a. impossible. ~ility /-'bɪlətɪ/ n. impossibilité f.

impostor /ɪm'pɒstə(r)/ n. imposteur m.

impoten|t /'ɪmpətənt/ a. impuissant. ~ce n. impuissance f.

impound /ɪm'paʊnd/ v.t. confisquer, saisir.

impoverish /ɪm'pɒvərɪʃ/ v.t. appauvrir.

impracticable /ɪm'præktɪkəbl/ a. impraticable.

impractical /ɪm'præktɪkl/ a. peu pratique.

imprecise /ɪmprɪ'saɪs/ a. imprécis.

impregnable /ɪm'pregnəbl/ a. imprenable; (fig.) inattaquable.

impregnate /'ɪmpregneɪt/ v.t. imprégner (with, de).

impresario /ɪmprɪ'sɑːrɪəʊ/ n. (pl. -os) impresario m.

impress /ɪm'pres/ v.t. impressionner; (imprint) imprimer. ~ on s.o., faire comprendre à qn.

impression /ɪm'preʃn/ n. impression f. ~able a. impressionnable.

impressive /ɪm'presɪv/ a. impressionnant.

imprint[1] /'ɪmprɪnt/ n. empreinte f.

imprint[2] /ɪm'prɪnt/ v.t. imprimer.

imprison /ɪm'prɪzn/ v.t. emprisonner. ~ment n. emprisonnement m., prison f.

improbab|le /ɪm'prɒbəbl/ a. (not likely) improbable; (incredible) invraisemblable. ~ility /-'bɪlətɪ/ n. improbabilité f.

impromptu /ɪm'prɒmptjuː/ a. & adv. impromptu.

improp|er /ɪm'prɒpə(r)/ a. inconvenant, indécent; (wrong) incorrect. ~riety /-ə'praɪətɪ/ n. inconvenance f.

improve /ɪm'pruːv/ v.t./i. (s')améliorer. ~ment n. amélioration f.

improvis|e /'ɪmprəvaɪz/ v.t./i. improviser. ~ation /-'zeɪʃn/ n. improvisation f.

imprudent /ɪm'pruːdnt/ a. imprudent.

impuden|t /'ɪmpjʊdənt/ a. impudent. ~ce n. impudence f.

impulse /'ɪmpʌls/ n. impulsion f. on ~, sur un coup de tête.

impulsive /ɪm'pʌlsɪv/ a. impulsif. ~ly adv. par impulsion.

impunity /ɪm'pjuːnətɪ/ n. impunité f. with ~, impunément.

impur|e /ɪm'pjʊə(r)/ a. impur. ~ity n. impureté f.

impute /ɪm'pjuːt/ v.t. imputer.

in /ɪn/ prep. dans, à, en. —adv. (inside) dedans; (at home) là, à la maison; (in fashion) à la mode. **in the box/garden,** dans la boîte/le jardin. **in Paris/school,** à Paris/l'école. **in town,** en ville. **in the country,** à la campagne. **in winter/English,** en hiver/anglais. **in India,** en Inde. **in Japan,** au Japon. **in a firm manner/voice,** d'une manière/voix ferme. **in blue,** en bleu. **in ink,** à l'encre. **in uniform,** en uniforme. **in a skirt,** en jupe. **in a whisper,** en chuchotant. **in a loud voice,** d'une voix forte. **in winter,** en hiver. **in spring,** au printemps. **in an hour,** (at end of) au bout d'une heure. **in an hour('s time),** dans une heure. **in (the space of) an hour,** en une heure. **in doing,** en faisant. **in the evening,** le soir. **one in ten,** un sur dix. **in between,** entre les deux; (time) entretemps. **the best in,** le meilleur de. **we are in for,** on va avoir. **in-laws** n. pl. (fam.) beaux-parents m. pl. **~-patient** n. malade hospitalisé(e) m.(f.). **the ins and outs of,** les tenants et aboutissants de. **in so far as,** dans la mesure où.

inability /ɪnə'bɪlətɪ/ n. incapacité f. (to do, de faire).

inaccessible /ɪnæk'sesəbl/ a. inaccessible.

inaccurate /ɪn'ækjərət/ a. inexact.

inaction /ɪn'ækʃn/ n. inaction f.

inactiv|e /ɪn'æktɪv/ a. inactif. ~ity /-'tɪvətɪ/ n. inaction f.

inadequa|te /ɪn'ædɪkwət/ a. insuffisant. ~cy n. insuffisance f.

inadmissible /ɪnəd'mɪsəbl/ a. inadmissible.

inadvertently /ɪnəd'vɜːtəntlɪ/ adv. par mégarde.

inadvisable /ɪnəd'vaɪzəbl/ a. déconseillé, pas recommandé.

inane /ɪ'neɪn/ a. inepte.

inanimate /ɪn'ænɪmət/ a. inanimé.

inappropriate /ɪnə'prəʊprɪət/ a. inopportun; (term) inapproprié.

inarticulate /ɪnɑː'tɪkjʊlət/ a. qui a du mal à s'exprimer.

inasmuch as /ɪnəz'mʌtʃəz/ adv. en ce sens que; (because) vu que.

inattentive /ɪnə'tentɪv/ a. inattentif.

inaudible /ɪn'ɔːdɪbl/ a. inaudible.

inaugural /ɪ'nɔːgjʊrəl/ a. inaugural.

inaugurat|e /ɪ'nɔːgjʊreɪt/ v.t. (open, begin) inaugurer; (person) investir. **~ion** /-'reɪʃn/ n. inauguration f.; investiture f.

inauspicious /ɪnɔː'spɪʃəs/ a. peu propice.

inborn /ɪn'bɔːn/ a. inné.

inbred /ɪn'bred/ a. (inborn) inné.

inc. abbr. (incorporated) S.A.

incalculable /ɪn'kælkjʊləbl/ a. incalculable.

incapable /ɪn'keɪpəbl/ a. incapable.

incapacit|y /ɪnkə'pæsətɪ/ n. incapacité f. **~ate** v.t. rendre incapable (de travailler etc.).

incarcerate /ɪn'kɑːsəreɪt/ v.t. incarcérer.

incarnat|e /ɪn'kɑːneɪt/ a. incarné. **~ion** /-'neɪʃn/ n. incarnation f.

incendiary /ɪn'sendɪərɪ/ a. incendiaire. —n. (bomb) bombe incendiaire f.

incense[1] /'ɪnsens/ n. encens m.

incense[2] /ɪn'sens/ v.t. mettre en fureur.

incentive /ɪn'sentɪv/ n. motivation f.; (payment) prime (d'encouragement) f.

inception /ɪn'sepʃn/ n. début m.

incessant /ɪn'sesnt/ a. incessant. **~ly** adv. sans cesse.

incest /'ɪnsest/ n. inceste m. **~uous** /ɪn'sestjʊəs/ a. incestueux.

inch /ɪntʃ/ n. pouce m. (= 2.54 cm.). —v.i. avancer doucement.

incidence /'ɪnsɪdəns/ n. fréquence f.

incident /'ɪnsɪdənt/ n. incident m.; (in play, film, etc.) épisode m.

incidental /ɪnsɪ'dentl/ a. accessoire. **~ly** adv. accessoirement; (by the way) à propos.

incinerat|e /ɪn'sɪnəreɪt/ v.t. incinérer. **~or** n. incinérateur m.

incipient /ɪn'sɪpɪənt/ a. naissant.

incision /ɪn'sɪʒn/ n. incision f.

incisive /ɪn'saɪsɪv/ a. incisif.

incite /ɪn'saɪt/ v.t. inciter, pousser. **~ment** n. incitation f.

inclement /ɪn'klemənt/ a. inclément, rigoureux.

inclination /ɪnklɪ'neɪʃn/ n. (propensity, bowing) inclination f.

incline[1] /ɪn'klaɪn/ v.t./i. incliner. **be ~d to**, avoir tendance à.

incline[2] /'ɪnklaɪn/ n. pente f.

inclu|de /ɪn'kluːd/ v.t. comprendre, inclure. **~ding** prep. (y) compris. **~sion** n. inclusion f.

inclusive /ɪn'kluːsɪv/ a. & adv. inclus, compris. **be ~ of**, comprendre, inclure.

incognito /ɪnkɒg'niːtəʊ/ adv. incognito.

incoherent /ɪnkəʊ'hɪərənt/ a. incohérent.

income /'ɪnkʌm/ n. revenu m. **~ tax**, impôt sur le revenu m.

incoming /'ɪnkʌmɪŋ/ a. (tide) montant; (tenant etc.) nouveau.

incomparable /ɪn'kɒmprəbl/ a. incomparable.

incompatible /ɪnkəm'pætəbl/ a. incompatible.

incompeten|t /ɪn'kɒmpɪtənt/ a. incompétent. **~ce** n. incompétence f.

incomplete /ɪnkəm'pliːt/ a. incomplet.

incomprehensible /ɪnkɒmprɪ'hensəbl/ a. incompréhensible.

inconceivable /ɪnkən'siːvəbl/ a. inconcevable.

inconclusive /ɪnkən'kluːsɪv/ a. peu concluant.

incongruous /ɪn'kɒŋgrʊəs/ a. déplacé, incongru.

inconsequential /ɪnkɒnsɪ'kwenʃl/ a. sans importance.

inconsiderate /ɪnkən'sɪdərət/ a. (person) qui ne se soucie pas des autres; (act) irréfléchi.

inconsisten|t /ɪnkən'sɪstənt/ a. (treatment) sans cohérence, inconséquent; (argument) contradictoire; (performance) irrégulier. **~t with**, incompatible avec. **~cy** n. inconséquence f. contradiction f.; irrégularité f.

inconspicuous /ɪnkən'spɪkjʊəs/ a. peu en évidence.

incontinen|t /ɪn'kɒntɪnənt/ a. incontinent. **~ce** n. incontinence f.

inconvenien|t /ɪnkən'viːnɪənt/ a. incommode, peu pratique; (time) mal choisi. **be ~t for**, ne pas convenir à. **~ce** n. dérangement m.; (drawback) inconvénient m.; v.t. déranger.

incorporate /ɪn'kɔːpəreɪt/ v.t. incorporer; (include) contenir.

incorrect /ɪnkə'rekt/ a. inexact.

incorrigible /ɪn'kɒrɪdʒəbl/ a. incorrigible.

incorruptible /ɪnkə'rʌptəbl/ a. incorruptible.

increas|e[1] /ɪn'kriːs/ v.t./i. augmenter. **~ing** a. croissant. **~ingly** adv. de plus en plus.

increase[2] /'ɪnkriːs/ n. augmentation f. (in, of, de). **be on the ~**, augmenter.

incredible /ɪn'kredəbl/ a. incroyable.

incredulous /ɪn'kredjʊləs/ a. incrédule.

increment /'ɪnkrəmənt/ n. augmentation f.

incriminat|e /ɪn'krɪmɪneɪt/ v.t. incriminer. **~ing** a. compromettant.

incubat|e /'ɪnkjʊbeɪt/ v.t. (eggs) couver. ~**ion** /-'beɪʃn/ n. incubation f. ~**or** n. couveuse f.

inculcate /'ɪnkʌlkeɪt/ v.t. inculquer.

incumbent /ɪn'kʌmbənt/ n. (pol., relig.) titulaire m./f.

incur /ɪn'kɜ:(r)/ v.t. (p.t. **incurred**) encourir; (debts) contracter; (anger) s'exposer à.

incurable /ɪn'kjʊərəbl/ a. incurable.

incursion /ɪn'kɜ:ʃn/ n. incursion f.

indebted /ɪn'detɪd/ a. ~ **to s.o.**, redevable à qn. (**for**, de).

indecen|t /ɪn'di:snt/ a. indécent. ~**cy** n. indécence f.

indecision /ɪndɪ'sɪʒn/ n. indécision f.

indecisive /ɪndɪ'saɪsɪv/ a. indécis; (ending) peu concluant.

indeed /ɪn'di:d/ adv. en effet, vraiment.

indefensible /ɪndɪ'fensɪbl/ a. indéfendable.

indefinable /ɪndɪ'faɪnəbl/ a. indéfinissable.

indefinite /ɪn'defɪnɪt/ a. indéfini; (time) indéterminé. ~**ly** adv. indéfiniment.

indelible /ɪn'deləbl/ a. indélébile.

indemni|fy /ɪn'demnɪfaɪ/ v.t. (compensate) indemniser (**for**, de); (safeguard) garantir. ~**ty** /-nətɪ/ n. indemnité f.; garantie f.

indent /ɪn'dent/ v.t. (text) renfoncer. ~**ation** /-'teɪʃn/ n. (outline) découpure f.

independen|t /ɪndɪ'pendənt/ a. indépendant. ~**ce** n. indépendance f. ~**tly** adv. de façon indépendante. ~**tly of**, indépendamment de.

indescribable /ɪndɪ'skraɪbəbl/ a. indescriptible.

indestructible /ɪndɪ'strʌktəbl/ a. indestructible.

indeterminate /ɪndɪ'tɜ:mɪnət/ a. indéterminé.

index /'ɪndeks/ n. (pl. **indexes**) (figure) indice m.; (in book) index m.; (in library) catalogue m. —v.t. classer. ~ **card**, fiche f. ~ **finger** index m. ~**linked** a. indexé.

India /'ɪndɪə/ n. Inde f. ~**n** a. & n. indien(ne) (m. (f.)). ~**n summer**, été de la Saint-Martin m.

indicat|e /'ɪndɪkeɪt/ v.t. indiquer. ~**ion** /-'keɪʃn/ n. indication f. ~**or** n. (device) indicateur m.; (on vehicle) clignotant m.; (board) tableau m.

indicative /ɪn'dɪkətɪv/ a. indicatif. —n. (gram.) indicatif m.

indict /ɪn'daɪt/ v.t. accuser. ~**ment** n. accusation f.

indifferen|t /ɪn'dɪfrənt/ a. indifférent; (not good) médiocre. ~**ce** n. indifférence f.

indigenous /ɪn'dɪdʒɪnəs/ a. indigène.

indigest|ion /ɪndɪ'dʒestʃən/ n. indigestion f. ~**ible** /-təbl/ a. indigeste.

indign|ant /ɪn'dɪgnənt/ a. indigné. ~**ation** /-'neɪʃn/ n. indignation f.

indigo /'ɪndɪgəʊ/ n. indigo m.

indirect /ɪndɪ'rekt/ a. indirect. ~**ly** adv. indirectement.

indiscr|eet /ɪndɪ'skri:t/ a. indiscret; (not wary) imprudent. ~**etion** /-eʃn/ n. indiscrétion f.

indiscriminate /ɪndɪ'skrɪmɪnət/ a. qui manque de discernement; (random) fait au hasard. ~**ly** adv. sans discernement; au hasard.

indispensable /ɪndɪ'spensəbl/ a. indispensable.

indispos|ed /ɪndɪ'spəʊzd/ a. indisposé, souffrant. ~**ition** /-ə'zɪʃn/ n. indisposition f.

indisputable /ɪndɪ'spju:təbl/ a. incontestable.

indistinct /ɪndɪ'stɪŋkt/ a. indistinct.

indistinguishable /ɪndɪ'stɪŋgwɪʃəbl/ a. indifférenciable.

individual /ɪndɪ'vɪdʒʊəl/ a. individuel. —n. individu m. ~**ist** n. individualiste m./f. ~**ity** /-'ælətɪ/ n. individualité f. ~**ly** adv. individuellement.

indivisible /ɪndɪ'vɪzəbl/ a. indivisible.

indoctrinat|e /ɪn'dɒktrɪneɪt/ v.t. endoctriner. ~**ion** /-'neɪʃn/ n. endoctrinement m.

indolen|t /'ɪndələnt/ a. indolent. ~**ce** n. indolence f.

indomitable /ɪn'dɒmɪtəbl/ a. indomptable.

Indonesia /ɪndəʊ'ni:zɪə/ n. Indonésie f. ~**n** a. & n. indonésien(ne) (m. (f.)).

indoor /'ɪndɔ:(r)/ a. (clothes etc.) d'intérieur; (under cover) couvert. ~**s** /ɪn'dɔ:z/ adv. à l'intérieur.

induce /ɪn'dju:s/ v.t. (influence) persuader; (cause) provoquer. ~**ment** n. encouragement m.

induct /ɪn'dʌkt/ v.t. investir, installer; (mil., Amer.) incorporer.

indulge /ɪn'dʌldʒ/ v.t. (desires) satisfaire; (person) se montrer indulgent pour, gâter. —v.i. ~ **in**, se livrer à, s'offrir.

indulgen|t /ɪn'dʌldʒənt/ a. indulgent. ~**ce** n. indulgence f.; (treat) gâterie f.

industrial /ɪn'dʌstrɪəl/ a. industriel; (unrest etc.) ouvrier; (action) revendicatif; (accident) du travail. ~**ist** n.

industriel(le) _m.(f.)._ ~**ized** _a._ industrialisé.
industrious /ɪn'dʌstrɪəs/ _a._ travailleur, appliqué.
industry /'ɪndəstrɪ/ _n._ industrie _f._; (_zeal_) application _f._
inebriated /ɪ'niːbrɪeɪtɪd/ _a._ ivre.
inedible /ɪn'edɪbl/ _a._ (_food_) immangeable.
ineffective /ɪnɪ'fektɪv/ _a._ inefficace; (_person_) incapable.
ineffectual /ɪnɪ'fektʃʊəl/ _a._ inefficace; (_person_) incapable.
inefficien|t /ɪnɪ'fɪʃnt/ _a._ inefficace; (_person_) incompétent. ~**cy** _n._ inefficacité _f._; incompétence _f._
ineligible /ɪn'elɪdʒəbl/ _a._ inéligible. be ~ **for**, ne pas avoir droit à.
inept /ɪ'nept/ _a._ (_absurd_) inepte; (_out of place_) mal à propos.
inequality /ɪnɪ'kwɒlətɪ/ _n._ inégalité _f._
inert /ɪ'nɜːt/ _a._ inerte.
inertia /ɪ'nɜːʃə/ _n._ inertie _f._
inescapable /ɪnɪ'skeɪpəbl/ _a._ inéluctable.
inevitabl|e /ɪn'evɪtəbl/ _a._ inévitable. ~**y** _adv._ inévitablement.
inexact /ɪnɪg'zækt/ _a._ inexact.
inexcusable /ɪnɪk'skjuːzəbl/ _a._ inexcusable.
inexhaustible /ɪnɪg'zɔːstəbl/ _a._ inépuisable.
inexorable /ɪn'eksərəbl/ _a._ inexorable.
inexpensive /ɪnɪk'spensɪv/ _a._ bon marché _invar._, pas cher.
inexperience /ɪnɪk'spɪərɪəns/ _n._ inexpérience _f._ ~**d** _a._ inexpérimenté.
inexplicable /ɪnɪk'splɪkəbl/ _a._ inexplicable.
inextricable /ɪnɪk'strɪkəbl/ _a._ inextricable.
infallibl|e /ɪn'fæləbl/ _a._ infaillible. ~**ility** /-'bɪlətɪ/ _n._ infaillibilité _f._
infam|ous /'ɪnfəməs/ _a._ infâme. ~**y** _n._ infamie _f._
infan|t /'ɪnfənt/ _n._ (_baby_) nourrisson _m._; (_at school_) petit(e) enfant _m.(f.)_. ~**cy** _n._ petite enfance _f._; (_fig._) enfance _f._
infantile /'ɪnfəntaɪl/ _a._ infantile.
infantry /'ɪnfəntrɪ/ _n._ infanterie _f._
infatuat|ed /ɪn'fætʃʊeɪtɪd/ _a._ ~**ed with**, engoué de. ~**ion** /-'eɪʃn/ _n._ engouement _m._, béguin _m._
infect /ɪn'fekt/ _v.t._ infecter. ~ **s.o. with**, communiquer à qn. ~**ion** /-kʃn/ _n._ infection _f._
infectious /ɪn'fekʃəs/ _a._ (_med._) infectieux; (_fig._) contagieux.
infer /ɪn'fɜː(r)/ _v.t._ (_p.t._ **inferred**)

déduire. ~**ence** /'ɪnfərəns/ _n._ déduction _f._
inferior /ɪn'fɪərɪə(r)/ _a._ inférieur (**to**, à); (_work_, _product_) de qualité inférieure. —_n._ inférieur(e) _m._ (_f._). ~**ity** /-'ɒrətɪ/ _n._ infériorité _f._
infernal /ɪn'fɜːnl/ _a._ infernal. ~**ly** _adv._ (_fam._) atrocement.
inferno /ɪn'fɜːnəʊ/ _n._ (_pl._ -**os**) (_hell_) enfer _m._; (_blaze_) incendie _m._
infertil|e /ɪn'fɜːtaɪl, _Amer._ ɪn'fɜːtl/ _a._ infertile. ~**ity** /-ə'tɪlətɪ/ _n._ infertilité _f._
infest /ɪn'fest/ _v.t._ infester.
infidelity /ɪnfɪ'delətɪ/ _n._ infidélité _f._
infighting /'ɪnfaɪtɪŋ/ _n._ querelles internes _f. pl._
infiltrat|e /'ɪnfɪltreɪt/ _v.t./i._ s'infiltrer (dans). ~**ion** /-'treɪʃn/ _n._ infiltration _f._
infinite /'ɪnfɪnɪt/ _a._ infini. ~**ly** _adv._ infiniment.
infinitesimal /ɪnfɪnɪ'tesɪml/ _a._ infinitésimal.
infinitive /ɪn'fɪnətɪv/ _n._ infinitif _m._
infinity /ɪn'fɪnətɪ/ _n._ infinité _f._
infirm /ɪn'fɜːm/ _a._ infirme. ~**ity** _n._ infirmité _f._
infirmary /ɪn'fɜːmərɪ/ _n._ hôpital _m._; (_sick-bay_) infirmerie _f._
inflam|e /ɪn'fleɪm/ _v.t._ enflammer. ~**mable** /-'æməbl/ _a._ inflammable. ~**mation** /-ə'meɪʃn/ _n._ inflammation _f._
inflammatory /ɪn'flæmətrɪ/ _a._ incendiaire.
inflat|e /ɪn'fleɪt/ _v.t._ (_balloon_, _prices_, _etc._) gonfler. ~**able** _a._ gonflable.
inflation /ɪn'fleɪʃn/ _n._ inflation _f._ ~**ary** _a._ inflationniste.
inflection /ɪn'flekʃn/ _n._ inflexion _f._; (_suffix. gram._) désinence _f._
inflexible /ɪn'fleksəbl/ _a._ inflexible.
inflict /ɪn'flɪkt/ _v.t._ infliger (**on**, à).
influence /'ɪnflʊəns/ _n._ influence _f._ —_v.t._ influencer. **under the** ~, (_drunk_: _fam._) en état d'ivresse.
influential /ɪnflʊ'enʃl/ _a._ influent.
influenza /ɪnflʊ'enzə/ _n._ grippe _f._
influx /'ɪnflʌks/ _n._ afflux _m._
inform /ɪn'fɔːm/ _v.t._ informer (**of**, de). **keep** ~**ed**, tenir au courant. ~**ant** _n._ informateur, -trice _m._, _f._ ~**er** _n._ indicateur, -trice _m._, _f._
informal /ɪn'fɔːml/ _a._ (_simple_) simple, sans cérémonie; (_unofficial_) officieux; (_colloquial_) familier. ~**ity** /-'mælətɪ/ _n._ simplicité _f._ ~**ly** _adv._ sans cérémonie.
information /ɪnfə'meɪʃn/ _n._ renseignement(s) _m._ (_pl._), information(s) _f._ (_pl._).

some ∼, un renseignement. ∼ **technology,** informatique f.

informative /ɪnˈfɔːmətɪv/ a. instructif.

infra-red /ɪnfrəˈred/ a. infrarouge m.

infrastructure /ˈɪnfrəstrʌktʃə(r)/ n. infrastructure f.

infrequent /ɪnˈfriːkwənt/ a. peu fréquent. ∼**ly** adv. rarement.

infringe /ɪnˈfrɪndʒ/ v.t. contrevenir à. ∼ **on,** empiéter sur. ∼**ment** n. infraction f.

infuriate /ɪnˈfjʊərɪeɪt/ v.t. exaspérer, rendre furieux.

infus|e /ɪnˈfjuːz/ v.t. infuser. ∼**ion** /-ʒn/ n. infusion f.

ingen|ious /ɪnˈdʒiːnɪəs/ a. ingénieux. ∼**uity** /-ɪˈnjuːɪtɪ/ n. ingéniosité f.

ingenuous /ɪnˈdʒenjʊəs/ a. ingénu.

ingot /ˈɪŋgət/ n. lingot m.

ingrained /ɪnˈgreɪnd/ a. enraciné.

ingratiate /ɪnˈgreɪsɪeɪt/ v.t. ∼ **o.s. with,** gagner les bonnes grâces de.

ingratitude /ɪnˈgrætɪtjuːd/ n. ingratitude f.

ingredient /ɪnˈgriːdɪənt/ n. ingrédient m.

inhabit /ɪnˈhæbɪt/ v.t. habiter. ∼**able** a. habitable. ∼**ant** n. habitant(e) m. (f.).

inhale /ɪnˈheɪl/ v.t. inhaler; (tobacco smoke) avaler. ∼**r** n. spray m.

inherent /ɪnˈhɪərənt/ a. inhérent. ∼**ly** adv. en soi, intrinsèquement.

inherit /ɪnˈherɪt/ v.t. hériter (de). ∼**ance** n. héritage m.

inhibit /ɪnˈhɪbɪt/ v.t. (hinder) gêner; (prevent) empêcher. **be** ∼**ed,** avoir des inhibitions. ∼**ion** /-ˈbɪʃn/ n. inhibition f.

inhospitable /ɪnhɒˈspɪtəbl/ a. inhospitalier.

inhuman /ɪnˈhjuːmən/ a. (brutal, not human) inhumain. ∼**ity** /-ˈmænətɪ/ n. inhumanité f.

inhumane /ɪnhjuːˈmeɪn/ a. (unkind) inhumain.

inimitable /ɪˈnɪmɪtəbl/ a. inimitable.

iniquit|ous /ɪˈnɪkwɪtəs/ a. inique. ∼**y** /-ətɪ/ n. iniquité f.

initial /ɪˈnɪʃl/ n. initiale f. —v.t. (p.t. **initialled**) parapher. —a. initial. ∼**ly** adv. initialement.

initiat|e /ɪˈnɪʃɪeɪt/ v.t. (begin) amorcer; (scheme) lancer; (person) initier (**into,** à). ∼**ion** /-ˈeɪʃn/ n. initiation f.; (start) amorce f.

initiative /ɪˈnɪʃətɪv/ n. initiative f.

inject /ɪnˈdʒekt/ v.t. injecter; (new element: fig.) insuffler. ∼**ion** /-kʃn/ n. injection f., piqûre f.

injunction /ɪnˈdʒʌŋkʃn/ n. (court order) ordonnance f.

injure /ˈɪndʒə(r)/ v.t. blesser; (do wrong to) nuire à.

injury /ˈɪndʒərɪ/ n. (physical) blessure f.; (wrong) préjudice m.

injustice /ɪnˈdʒʌstɪs/ n. injustice f.

ink /ɪŋk/ n. encre f. ∼**-well** n. encrier m. ∼**y** a. taché d'encre.

inkling /ˈɪŋklɪŋ/ n. petite idée f.

inland /ˈɪnlənd/ a. l'intérieur. —adv. /ɪnˈlænd/ à l'intérieur. **I**∼ **Revenue,** fisc m.

in-laws /ˈɪnlɔːz/ n. pl. (parents) beaux-parents; (family) belle-famille f.

inlay¹ /ɪnˈleɪ/ v.t. (p.t. **inlaid**) incruster.

inlay² /ˈɪnleɪ/ n. incrustation f.

inlet /ˈɪnlet/ n. bras de mer m.; (techn.) arrivée f.

inmate /ˈɪnmeɪt/ n. (of asylum) interné(e) m. (f.); (of prison) détenu(e) m. (f.).

inn /ɪn/ n. auberge f.

innards /ˈɪnədz/ n. pl. (fam.) entrailles f. pl.

innate /ɪˈneɪt/ a. inné.

inner /ˈɪnə(r)/ a. intérieur, interne; (fig.) profond, intime. ∼ **city,** quartiers défavorisés m. pl. ∼**most** a. le plus profond. ∼ **tube,** chambre à air f.

innings /ˈɪnɪŋz/ n. invar. tour de batte m.; (fig.) tour m.

innkeeper /ˈɪnkiːpə(r)/ n. aubergiste m./f.

innocen|t /ˈɪnəsnt/ a. & n. innocent(e) (m. (f.)). ∼**ce** n. innocence f.

innocuous /ɪˈnɒkjʊəs/ a. inoffensif.

innovat|e /ˈɪnəveɪt/ v.i. innover. ∼**ion** /-ˈveɪʃn/ n. innovation f. ∼**or** n. innovateur, -trice m., f.

innuendo /ɪnjuːˈendəʊ/ n. (pl. -oes) insinuation f.

innumerable /ɪˈnjuːmərəbl/ a. innombrable.

inoculat|e /ɪˈnɒkjʊleɪt/ v.t. inoculer. ∼**ion** /-ˈleɪʃn/ n. inoculation f.

inoffensive /ɪnəˈfensɪv/ a. inoffensif.

inoperative /ɪnˈɒpərətɪv/ a. inopérant.

inopportune /ɪnˈɒpətjuːn/ a. inopportun.

inordinate /ɪˈnɔːdɪnət/ a. excessif. ∼**ly** adv. excessivement.

input /ˈɪnpʊt/ n. (data) données f. pl.; (computer process) entrée f.; (power: electr.) énergie f.

inquest /ˈɪnkwest/ n. enquête f.

inquire /ɪnˈkwaɪə(r)/ v.t./i. = **enquire.**

inquiry /ɪnˈkwaɪərɪ/ n. enquête f.

inquisition /ɪnkwɪˈzɪʃn/ n. inquisition f.

inquisitive /ɪnˈkwɪzətɪv/ a. curieux; (prying) indiscret.

inroad /'ɪnrəʊd/ n. incursion f.

insan|e /ɪn'seɪn/ a. fou. ~**ity** /ɪn'sænətɪ/ n. folie f., démence f.

insanitary /ɪn'sænɪtrɪ/ a. insalubre, malsain.

insatiable /ɪn'seɪʃəbl/ a. insatiable.

inscri|be /ɪn'skraɪb/ v.t. inscrire; (book) dédicacer. ~**ption** /-ɪpʃn/ n. inscription f.; dédicace f.

inscrutable /ɪn'skruːtəbl/ a. impénétrable.

insect /'ɪnsekt/ n. insecte m.

insecticide /ɪn'sektɪsaɪd/ n. insecticide m.

insecur|e /ɪnsɪ'kjʊə(r)/ a. (not firm) peu solide; (unsafe) peu sûr; (worried) anxieux. ~**ity** n. insécurité f.

insemination /ɪnsemɪ'neɪʃn/ n. insémination f.

insensible /ɪn'sensəbl/ a. insensible; (unconscious) inconscient.

insensitive /ɪn'sensətɪv/ a. insensible.

inseparable /ɪn'seprəbl/ a. inséparable.

insert[1] /ɪn'sɜːt/ v.t. insérer. ~**ion** /-ʃn/ n. insertion f.

insert[2] /'ɪnsɜːt/ n. insertion f.; (advertising) encart m.

in-service /'ɪnsɜːvɪs/ a. (training) continu.

inshore /ɪn'ʃɔː(r)/ a. côtier.

inside /ɪn'saɪd/ n. intérieur m. ~**(s)**, (fam.) entrailles f. pl. —a. intérieur. —adv. à l'intérieur, dedans. —prep. à l'intérieur de; (of time) en moins de. ~ **out**, à l'envers; (thoroughly) à fond.

insidious /ɪn'sɪdɪəs/ a. insidieux.

insight /'ɪnsaɪt/ n. (perception) perspicacité f.; (idea) aperçu m.

insignia /ɪn'sɪgnɪə/ n. pl. insignes m. pl.

insignificant /ɪnsɪg'nɪfɪkənt/ a. insignifiant.

insincer|e /ɪnsɪn'sɪə(r)/ a. peu sincère. ~**ity** /-'serətɪ/ n. manque de sincérité m.

insinuat|e /ɪn'sɪnjʊeɪt/ v.t. insinuer. ~**ion** /-'eɪʃn/ n. insinuation f.

insipid /ɪn'sɪpɪd/ a. insipide.

insist /ɪn'sɪst/ v.t./i. insister. ~ **on**, affirmer; (demand) exiger. ~ **on doing**, insister pour faire.

insisten|t /ɪn'sɪstənt/ a. insistant. ~**ce** n. insistance f. ~**tly** adv. avec insistance.

insole /'ɪnsəʊl/ n. (separate) semelle f.

insolen|t /'ɪnsələnt/ a. insolent. ~**ce** n. insolence f.

insoluble /ɪn'sɒljʊbl/ a. insoluble.

insolvent /ɪn'sɒlvənt/ a. insolvable.

insomnia /ɪn'sɒmnɪə/ n. insomnie f. ~**c** /-ɪæk/ n. insomniaque m./f.

inspect /ɪn'spekt/ v.t. inspecter; (tickets) contrôler. ~**ion** /-kʃn/ n. inspection f.; contrôle m. ~**or** n. inspecteur, -trice m., f.; (on train, bus) contrôleur, -se m., f.

inspir|e /ɪn'spaɪə(r)/ v.t. inspirer. ~**ation** /-ə'reɪʃn/ n. inspiration f.

instability /ɪnstə'bɪlətɪ/ n. instabilité f.

install /ɪn'stɔːl/ v.t. installer. ~**ation** /-ə'leɪʃn/ n. installation f.

instalment /ɪn'stɔːlmənt/ n. (payment) acompte m., versement m.; (of serial) épisode m.

instance /'ɪnstəns/ n. exemple m.; (case) cas m. **for** ~, par exemple. **in the first** ~, en premier lieu.

instant /'ɪnstənt/ a. immédiat; (food) instantané. —n. instant m. ~**ly** adv. immédiatement.

instantaneous /ɪnstən'teɪnɪəs/ a. instantané.

instead /ɪn'sted/ adv. plutôt. ~ **of doing**, au lieu de faire. ~ **of s.o.**, à la place de qn.

instep /'ɪnstep/ n. cou-de-pied m.

instigat|e /'ɪnstɪgeɪt/ v.t. provoquer. ~**ion** /-'geɪʃn/ n. instigation f. ~**or** n. instigateur, -trice m., f.

instil /ɪn'stɪl/ v.t. (p.t. **instilled**) inculquer; (inspire) insuffler.

instinct /'ɪnstɪŋkt/ n. instinct m. ~**ive** /ɪn'stɪŋktɪv/ a. instinctif.

institut|e /'ɪnstɪtjuːt/ n. institut m. —v.t. instituer; (inquiry etc.) entamer. ~**ion** /-'tjuːʃn/ n. institution f.; (school, hospital) établissement m.

instruct /ɪn'strʌkt/ v.t. instruire; (order) ordonner. ~ **s.o. in sth.**, enseigner qch. à qn. ~ **s.o. to do**, ordonner à qn. de faire. ~**ion** /-kʃn/ n. instruction f. ~**ions** /-kʃnz/ n. pl. (for use) mode d'emploi m. ~**ive** a. instructif. ~**or** n. professeur m.; (skiing, driving) moniteur, -trice m., f.

instrument /'ɪnstrəmənt/ n. instrument m. ~ **panel**, tableau de bord m.

instrumental /ɪnstrə'mentl/ a. instrumental. **be** ~ **in**, contribuer à. ~**ist** n. instrumentaliste m./f.

insubordinat|e /ɪnsə'bɔːdɪnət/ a. insubordonné. ~**ion** /-'neɪʃn/ n. insubordination f.

insufferable /ɪn'sʌfrəbl/ a. intolérable, insupportable.

insufficient /ɪnsə'fɪʃnt/ a. insuffisant. ~**ly** adv. insuffisamment.

insular /'ɪnsjʊlə(r)/ a. insulaire; (mind, person: fig.) borné.

insulat|e /'ɪnsjʊleɪt/ v.t. (room, wire,

etc.) isoler. **~ing tape,** chatterton *m.*
~ion /-ˈleɪʃn/ *n.* isolation *f.*
insulin /ˈɪnsjʊlɪn/ *n.* insuline *f.*
insult¹ /ɪnˈsʌlt/ *v.t.* insulter.
insult² /ˈɪnsʌlt/ *n.* insulte *f.*
insuperable /ɪnˈsjuːprəbl/ *a.* insurmontable.
insur|e /ɪnˈʃʊə(r)/ *v.t.* assurer. **~e that,**
(*ensure: Amer.*) s'assurer que. **~ance**
n. assurance *f.*
insurmountable /ɪnsəˈmaʊntəbl/ *a.*
insurmontable.
insurrection /ɪnsəˈrekʃn/ *n.* insurrection
f.
intact /ɪnˈtækt/ *a.* intact.
intake /ˈɪnteɪk/ *n.* admission(s) *f.* (*pl.*);
(*techn.*) prise *f.*
intangible /ɪnˈtændʒəbl/ *a.* intangible.
integral /ˈɪntɪɡrəl/ *a.* intégral. **be an ~
part of,** faire partie intégrante de.
integrat|e /ˈɪntɪɡreɪt/ *v.t./i.* (s')intégrer.
~ion /-ˈɡreɪʃn/ *n.* intégration *f.*;
(*racial*) déségrégation *f.*
integrity /ɪnˈteɡrətɪ/ *n.* intégrité *f.*
intellect /ˈɪntəlekt/ *n.* intelligence *f.*
~ual /-ˈlektʃʊəl/ *a. & n.* intellec-
tuel(le) (*m.* (*f.*)).
intelligen|t /ɪnˈtelɪdʒənt/ *a.* intelligent.
~ce *n.* intelligence *f.*; (*mil.*) renseignements *m. pl.* **~tly** *adv.* intelligemment.
intelligentsia /ɪntelɪˈdʒentsɪə/ *n.* intelligentsia *f.*
intelligible /ɪnˈtelɪdʒəbl/ *a.* intelligible.
intemperance /ɪnˈtempərəns/ *n.*
(*drunkenness*) ivrognerie *f.*
intend /ɪnˈtend/ *v.t.* destiner. **~ to do,**
avoir l'intention de faire. **~ed** *a.*
(*deliberate*) intentionnel; (*planned*)
prévu; *n.* (*future spouse: fam.*)
promis(e) *m.* (*f.*).
intens|e /ɪnˈtens/ *a.* intense; (*person*)
passionné. **~ely** *adv.* (*to live etc.*)
intensément; (*very*) extrêmement. **~ity**
n. intensité *f.*
intensif|y /ɪnˈtensɪfaɪ/ *v.t.* intensifier.
~ication /-ɪˈkeɪʃn/ *n.* intensification *f.*
intensive /ɪnˈtensɪv/ *a.* intensif. **in ~
care,** en réanimation.
intent /ɪnˈtent/ *n.* intention *f.* —*a.*
attentif. **~ on,** absorbé par. **~ on doing,**
résolu à faire. **~ly** *adv.* attentivement.
intention /ɪnˈtenʃn/ *n.* intention *f.* **~al** *a.*
intentionnel.
inter /ɪnˈtɜː(r)/ *v.t.* (*p.t.* **interred**)
enterrer.
inter- /ɪntə(r)/ *pref.* inter-.
interact /ɪntəˈrækt/ *v.i.* avoir une action
réciproque. **~ion** /-kʃn/ *n.* interaction
f.

intercede /ɪntəˈsiːd/ *v.i.* intercéder.
intercept /ɪntəˈsept/ *v.t.* intercepter.
~ion /-pʃn/ *n.* interception *f.*
interchange /ˈɪntətʃeɪndʒ/ *n.* (*road
junction*) échangeur *m.*
interchangeable /ɪntəˈtʃeɪndʒəbl/ *a.*
interchangeable.
intercom /ˈɪntəkɒm/ *n.* interphone *m.*
interconnected /ɪntəkəˈnektɪd/ *a.*
(*facts, events, etc.*) lié.
intercourse /ˈɪntəkɔːs/ *n.* (*sexual,
social*) rapports *m. pl.*
interest /ˈɪntrəst/ *n.* intérêt *m.*; (*stake*)
intérêts *m. pl.* —*v.t.* intéresser. **~ rates,**
taux d'intérêt *m. pl.* **~ed** *a.* intéressé. **be
~ed in,** s'intéresser à. **~ing** *a.*
intéressant.
interface /ˈɪntəfeɪs/ *n.* (*comput.*) interface *f.*; (*fig.*) zone de rencontre *f.*
interfer|e /ɪntəˈfɪə(r)/ *v.i.* se mêler des
affaires des autres. **~e in,** s'ingérer
dans. **~e with,** (*plans*) créer un
contretemps avec; (*work*) s'immiscer
dans; (*radio*) faire des interférences
avec; (*lock*) toucher à. **~ence**
n. ingérence *f.*; (*radio*) parasites
m. pl.
interim /ˈɪntərɪm/ *n.* intérim *m.* —*a.*
intérimaire.
interior /ɪnˈtɪərɪə(r)/ *n.* intérieur *m.* —*a.*
intérieur.
interjection /ɪntəˈdʒekʃn/ *n.* interjection
f.
interlinked /ɪntəˈlɪŋkt/ *a.* lié.
interlock /ɪntəˈlɒk/ *v.t./i.* (*techn.*)
(s')emboîter, (s')enclencher.
interloper /ˈɪntələʊpə(r)/ *n.* intrus(e) *m.*
(*f.*).
interlude /ˈɪntəluːd/ *n.* intervalle *m.*;
(*theatre, mus.*) intermède *m.*
intermarr|iage /ɪntəˈmærɪdʒ/ *n.* mari-
age entre membres de races différentes
m. **~y** *v.i.* se marier (entre eux).
intermediary /ɪntəˈmiːdɪərɪ/ *a. & n.*
intermédiaire (*m./f.*).
intermediate /ɪntəˈmiːdɪət/ *a.* intermédiaire; (*exam etc.*) moyen.
interminable /ɪnˈtɜːmɪnəbl/ *a.* interminable.
intermission /ɪntəˈmɪʃn/ *n.* pause *f.*;
(*theatre etc.*) entracte *m.*
intermittent /ɪntəˈmɪtnt/ *a.* intermittent.
~ly *adv.* par intermittence.
intern¹ /ɪnˈtɜːn/ *v.t.* interner. **~ee** /-ˈniː/
n. interné(e) *m.* (*f.*). **~ment** *n.*
internement *m.*
intern² /ˈɪntɜːn/ *n.* (*doctor: Amer.*)
interne *m./f.*
internal /ɪnˈtɜːnl/ *a.* interne; (*domestic:*

pol.) intérieur. **I~ Revenue,** (*Amer.*) fisc *m.* **~ly** *adv.* intérieurement.

international /ɪntə'næʃnəl/ *a.* & *n.* international (*m.*).

interplay /'ɪntəpleɪ/ *n.* jeu *m.*, interaction *f.*

interpolate /ɪn'tɜːpəleɪt/ *v.t.* interpoler.

interpret /ɪn'tɜːprɪt/ *v.t.* interpréter. —*v.i.* faire l'interprète. **~ation** /-'teɪʃn/ *n.* interprétation *f.* **~er** *n.* interprète *m./f.*

interrelated /ɪntərɪ'leɪtɪd/ *a.* en corrélation, lié.

interrogat|e /ɪn'terəgeɪt/ *v.t.* interroger. **~ion** /-'geɪʃn/ *n.* interrogation *f.* (**of,** de); (*session of questions*) interrogatoire *m.*

interrogative /ɪntə'rɒgətɪv/ *a.* & *n.* interrogatif (*m.*).

interrupt /ɪntə'rʌpt/ *v.t.* interrompre. **~ion** /-pʃn/ *n.* interruption *f.*

intersect /ɪntə'sekt/ *v.t./i.* (*lines, roads*) (se) couper. **~ion** /-kʃn/ *n.* intersection *f.*; (*crossroads*) croisement *m.*

interspersed /ɪntə'spɜːst/ *a.* (*scattered*) dispersé. **~ with,** parsemé de.

intertwine /ɪntə'twaɪn/ *v.t./i.* (s')entrelacer.

interval /'ɪntəvl/ *n.* intervalle *m.*; (*theatre*) entracte *m.* **at ~s,** par intervalles.

interven|e /ɪntə'viːn/ *v.i.* intervenir; (*of time*) s'écouler (**between,** entre); (*happen*) survenir. **~tion** /-'venʃn/ *n.* intervention *f.*

interview /'ɪntəvjuː/ *n.* (*with reporter*) interview *f.*; (*for job etc.*) entrevue *f.* —*v.t.* interviewer. **~er** *n.* interviewer *m.*

intestin|e /ɪn'testɪn/ *n.* intestin *m.* **~al** *a.* intestinal.

intima|te[1] /'ɪntɪmət/ *a.* intime; (*detailed*) profond. **~cy** *n.* intimité *f.* **~tely** *adv.* intimement.

intimate[2] /'ɪntɪmeɪt/ *v.t.* (*state*) annoncer; (*imply*) suggérer.

intimidat|e /ɪn'tɪmɪdeɪt/ *v.t.* intimider. **~ion** /-'deɪʃn/ *n.* intimidation *f.*

into /'ɪntuː, *unstressed* 'ɪntə/ *prep.* (*put, go, fall, etc.*) dans; (*divide, translate, etc.*) en.

intolerable /ɪn'tɒlərəbl/ *a.* intolérable.

intoleran|t /ɪn'tɒlərənt/ *a.* intolérant. **~ce** *n.* intolérance *f.*

intonation /ɪntə'neɪʃn/ *n.* intonation *f.*

intoxicat|e /ɪn'tɒksɪkeɪt/ *v.t.* enivrer. **~ed** *a.* ivre. **~ion** /-'keɪʃn/ *n.* ivresse *f.*

intra- /'ɪntrə/ *pref.* intra-.

intractable /ɪn'træktəbl/ *a.* très difficile.

intransigent /ɪn'trænsɪdʒənt/ *a.* intransigeant.

intransitive /ɪn'trænsətɪv/ *a.* (*verb*) intransitif.

intravenous /ɪntrə'viːnəs/ *a.* (*med.*) intraveineux.

intrepid /ɪn'trepɪd/ *a.* intrépide.

intrica|te /'ɪntrɪkət/ *a.* complexe. **~cy** *n.* complexité *f.*

intrigu|e /ɪn'triːg/ *v.t./i.* intriguer. —*n.* intrigue *f.* **~ing** *a.* très intéressant; (*curious*) curieux.

intrinsic /ɪn'trɪnsɪk/ *a.* intrinsèque. **~ally** /-klɪ/ *adv.* intrinsèquement.

introduce /ɪntrə'djuːs/ *v.t.* (*bring in, insert*) introduire; (*programme, question*) présenter. **~ s.o. to,** (*person*) présenter qn. à; (*subject*) faire connaître à qn.

introduct|ion /ɪntrə'dʌkʃn/ *n.* introduction *f.*; (*to person*) présentation *f.* **~ory** /-tərɪ/ *a.* (*letter, words*) d'introduction.

introspective /ɪntrə'spektɪv/ *a.* introspectif.

introvert /'ɪntrəvɜːt/ *n.* introverti(e) *m.* (*f.*).

intru|de /ɪn'truːd/ *v.i.* (*person*) s'imposer (**on s.o.,** à qn.), déranger. **~der** *n.* intrus(e) *m.* (*f.*). **~sion** *n.* intrusion *f.*

intuit|ion /ɪntjuː'ɪʃn/ *n.* intuition *f.* **~ive** /ɪn'tjuːɪtɪv/ *a.* intuitif.

inundat|e /'ɪnʌndeɪt/ *v.t.* inonder (**with,** de). **~ion** /-'deɪʃn/ *n.* inondation *f.*

invade /ɪn'veɪd/ *v.t.* envahir. **~r** /-ə(r)/ *n.* envahisseur, -se *m.*, *f.*

invalid[1] /'ɪnvəlɪd/ *n.* malade *m./f.*; (*disabled*) infirme *m./f.*

invalid[2] /ɪn'vælɪd/ *a.* non valable. **~ate** *v.t.* invalider.

invaluable /ɪn'væljʊəbl/ *a.* inestimable.

invariab|le /ɪn'veərɪəbl/ *a.* invariable. **~y** *adv.* invariablement.

invasion /ɪn'veɪʒn/ *n.* invasion *f.*

invective /ɪn'vektɪv/ *n.* invective *f.*

inveigh /ɪn'veɪ/ *v.i.* invectiver.

inveigle /ɪn'veɪgl/ *v.t.* persuader.

invent /ɪn'vent/ *v.t.* inventer. **~ion** /-enʃn/ *n.* invention *f.* **~ive** *a.* inventif. **~or** *n.* inven|teur, -trice *m.*, *f.*

inventory /'ɪnvəntrɪ/ *n.* inventaire *m.*

inverse /ɪn'vɜːs/ *a.* & *n.* inverse (*m.*). **~ly** *adv.* inversement.

inver|t /ɪn'vɜːt/ *v.t.* intervertir. **~ted commas,** guillemets *m. pl.* **~sion** *n.* inversion *f.*

invest /ɪn'vest/ *v.t.* investir; (*time, effort, fig.*) consacrer. —*v.i.* faire un investissement. **~ in,** (*buy: fam.*) se payer.

~ment *n.* investissement *m.* ~or *n.* actionnaire *m./f.*; (*saver*) épargnant(e) *m.* (*f.*).

investigat|e /ɪn'vestɪgeɪt/ *v.t.* étudier; (*crime etc.*) enquêter sur. ~ion /-'geɪʃn/ *n.* investigation *f.* **under ~ion**, à l'étude. ~or *n.* (*police*) enquêteur, -se *m.*, *f.*

inveterate /ɪn'vetərət/ *a.* invétéré.

invidious /ɪn'vɪdɪəs/ *a.* (*hateful*) odieux; (*unfair*) injuste.

invigilat|e /ɪn'vɪdʒɪleɪt/ *v.i.* (*schol.*) être de surveillance. ~or *n.* surveillant(e) *m.* (*f.*).

invigorate /ɪn'vɪgəreɪt/ *v.t.* vivifier; (*encourage*) stimuler.

invincible /ɪn'vɪnsəbl/ *a.* invincible.

invisible /ɪn'vɪzəbl/ *a.* invisible.

invit|e /ɪn'vaɪt/ *v.t.* inviter; (*ask for*) demander. ~ation /ɪnvɪ'teɪʃn/ *n.* invitation *f.* ~ing *a.* (*meal, smile, etc.*) engageant.

invoice /'ɪnvɔɪs/ *n.* facture *f.* —*v.t.* facturer.

invoke /ɪn'vəʊk/ *v.t.* invoquer.

involuntary /ɪn'vɒləntrɪ/ *a.* involontaire.

involve /ɪn'vɒlv/ *v.t.* entraîner; (*people*) faire participer. ~d *a.* (*complex*) compliqué; (*at stake*) en jeu. **be ~d in**, (*work*) participer à; (*crime*) être mêlé à. ~ment *n.* participation *f.* (**in**, à).

invulnerable /ɪn'vʌlnərəbl/ *a.* invulnérable.

inward /'ɪnwəd/ *a.* & *adv.* vers l'intérieur; (*feeling etc.*) intérieur. ~ly *adv.* intérieurement. ~s *adv.* vers l'intérieur.

iodine /'aɪədiːn/ *n.* iode *m.*; (*antiseptic*) teinture d'iode *f.*

iota /aɪ'əʊtə/ *n.* (*amount*) brin *m.*

IOU /aɪəʊ'juː/ *abbr.* (*I owe you*) reconnaissance de dette *f.*

IQ /aɪ'kjuː/ *abbr.* (*intelligence quotient*) QI *m.*

Iran /ɪ'rɑːn/ *n.* Iran *m.* ~**ian** /ɪ'reɪnɪən/ *a.* & *n.* iranien(ne) (*m.* (*f.*)).

Iraq /ɪ'rɑːk/ *n.* Irak *m.* ~**i** *a.* & *n.* irakien(ne) (*m.* (*f.*)).

irascible /ɪ'ræsəbl/ *a.* irascible.

irate /aɪ'reɪt/ *a.* en colère, furieux.

ire /'aɪə(r)/ *n.* courroux *m.*

Ireland /'aɪələnd/ *n.* Irlande *f.*

iris /'aɪərɪs/ *n.* (*anat.*, *bot.*) iris *m.*

Irish /'aɪərɪʃ/ *a.* irlandais. —*n.* (*lang.*) irlandais *m.* ~**man** *n.* Irlandais *m.* ~**woman** *n.* Irlandaise *f.*

irk /ɜːk/ *v.t.* ennuyer. ~**some** *a.* ennuyeux.

iron /'aɪən/ *n.* fer *m.*; (*appliance*) fer (à repasser) *m.* —*a.* de fer. —*v.t.* repasser. **I~ Curtain**, rideau de fer *m.* ~ **out**, faire disparaître. ~**ing-board** *n.* planche à repasser *f.*

ironic(al) /aɪ'rɒnɪk(l)/ *a.* ironique.

ironmonger /'aɪənmʌŋgə(r)/ *n.* quincaillier *m.* ~**y** *n.* quincaillerie *f.*

ironwork /'aɪənwɜːk/ *n.* ferronnerie *f.*

irony /'aɪərənɪ/ *n.* ironie *f.*

irrational /ɪ'ræʃənl/ *a.* irrationnel; (*person*) pas rationnel.

irreconcilable /ɪrekən'saɪləbl/ *a.* irréconciliable; (*incompatible*) inconciliable.

irrefutable /ɪ'refjʊtəbl/ *a.* irréfutable.

irregular /ɪ'regjʊlə(r)/ *a.* irrégulier. ~**ity** /-'lærətɪ/ *n.* irrégularité *f.*

irrelevan|t /ɪ'reləvənt/ *a.* sans rapport (**to**, avec). ~**ce** *n.* manque de rapport *m.*

irreparable /ɪ'repərəbl/ *a.* irréparable, irrémédiable.

irreplaceable /ɪrɪ'pleɪsəbl/ *a.* irremplaçable.

irrepressible /ɪrɪ'presəbl/ *a.* irrépressible.

irresistible /ɪrɪ'zɪstəbl/ *a.* irrésistible.

irresolute /ɪ'rezəluːt/ *a.* irrésolu.

irrespective /ɪrɪ'spektɪv/ *a.* ~ **of**, sans tenir compte de.

irresponsible /ɪrɪ'spɒnsəbl/ *a.* irresponsable.

irretrievable /ɪrɪ'triːvəbl/ *a.* irréparable.

irreverent /ɪ'revərənt/ *a.* irrévérencieux.

irreversible /ɪrɪ'vɜːsəbl/ *a.* irréversible; (*decision*) irrévocable.

irrevocable /ɪ'revəkəbl/ *a.* irrévocable.

irrigat|e /'ɪrɪgeɪt/ *v.t.* irriguer. ~**ion** /-'geɪʃn/ *n.* irrigation *f.*

irritable /'ɪrɪtəbl/ *a.* irritable.

irritat|e /'ɪrɪteɪt/ *v.t.* irriter. **be ~ed by**, être énervé par. ~**ing** *a.* énervant. ~**ion** /-'teɪʃn/ *n.* irritation *f.*

is /ɪz/ *see* **be**.

Islam /'ɪzlɑːm/ *n.* Islam *m.* ~**ic** /ɪz'læmɪk/ *a.* islamique.

island /'aɪlənd/ *n.* île *f.* **traffic ~**, refuge *m.* ~**er** *n.* insulaire *m./f.*

isle /aɪl/ *n.* île *f.*

isolat|e /'aɪsəleɪt/ *v.t.* isoler. ~**ion** /-'leɪʃn/ *n.* isolement *m.*

isotope /'aɪsətəʊp/ *n.* isotope *m.*

Israel /'ɪzreɪl/ *n.* Israël *m.* ~**i** /ɪz'reɪlɪ/ *a.* & *n.* israélien(ne) (*m.* (*f.*)).

issue /'ɪʃuː/ *n.* question *f.*; (*outcome*) résultat *m.*; (*of magazine etc.*) numéro *m.*; (*of stamps etc.*) émission *f.*; (*off-spring*) descendance *f.* —*v.t.* distribuer, donner; (*stamps etc.*) émettre; (*book*) publier; (*order*) donner. —*v.i.* ~ **from**, sortir de. **at** ~, en cause. **take** ~, engager une controverse.

isthmus /'ɪsməs/ *n.* isthme *m.*

it /ɪt/ *pron.* (*subject*) il, elle; (*object*) le, la, l'*; (*impersonal subject*) il; (*non-specific*) ce, c'*, cela, ça. **it is**, (*quiet, my book, etc.*) c'est. **it is/cold/warm/late/** *etc.*, il fait froid/chaud/tard/*etc.* **that's it**, c'est ça. **who is it?**, qui est-ce? **of it, from it**, en. **in it, at it, to it**, y.

IT *abbr. see* **information technology**.

italic /ɪ'tælɪk/ *a.* italique. —**s** *n. pl.* italique *m.*

Ital|y /'ɪtəlɪ/ *n.* Italie *f.* ~**ian** /ɪ'tælɪən/ *a. & n.* italien(ne) (*m.* (*f.*)); (*lang.*) italien *m.*

itch /ɪtʃ/ *n.* démangeaison *f.* —*v.i.* démanger. **my arm** ~**es**, mon bras me démange. **I am** ~**ing to**, ça me démange de. ~**y** *a.* qui démange.

item /'aɪtəm/ *n.* article *m.*, chose *f.*; (*on agenda*) question *f.* **news** ~, nouvelle *f.* ~**ize** *v.t.* détailler.

itinerant /aɪ'tɪnərənt/ *a.* itinérant; (*musician, actor*) ambulant.

itinerary /aɪ'tɪnərərɪ/ *n.* itinéraire *m.*

its /ɪts/ *a.* son, sa, *pl.* ses.

it's /ɪts/ – **it is, it has**.

itself /ɪt'self/ *pron.* lui-même, elle-même; (*reflexive*) se.

IUD *abbr.* (*intrauterine device*) stérilet *m.*

ivory /'aɪvərɪ/ *n.* ivoire *m.* ~ **tower**, tour d'ivoire *f.*

ivy /'aɪvɪ/ *n.* lierre *m.*

J

jab /dʒæb/ *v.t.* (*p.t.* **jabbed**) (*thrust*) enfoncer; (*prick*) piquer. —*n.* coup *m.*; (*injection*) piqûre *f.*

jabber /'dʒæbə(r)/ *v.i.* jacasser, bavarder; (*indistinctly*) bredouiller. —*n.* bavardage *m.*

jack /dʒæk/ *n.* (*techn.*) cric *m.*; (*cards*) valet *m.*; (*plug*) fiche *f.* —*v.t.* ~ **up**, soulever (avec un cric).

jackal /'dʒækɔːl/ *n.* chacal *m.*

jackass /'dʒækæs/ *n.* âne *m.*

jackdaw /'dʒækdɔː/ *n.* choucas *m.*

jacket /'dʒækɪt/ *n.* veste *f.*, veston *m.*; (*of book*) jaquette *f.*

jack-knife /'dʒæknaɪf/ *n.* couteau pliant *m.* —*v.i.* (*lorry*) faire un tête-à-queue.

jackpot /'dʒækpɒt/ *n.* gros lot *m.* **hit the** ~, gagner le gros lot.

Jacuzzi /dʒə'kuːzɪ/ *n.* (P.) bain à remous *m.*

jade /dʒeɪd/ *n.* (*stone*) jade *m.*

jaded /'dʒeɪdɪd/ *a.* las; (*appetite*) blasé.

jagged /'dʒægɪd/ *a.* dentelé.

jail /dʒeɪl/ *n.* prison *f.* —*v.t.* mettre en prison. ~**er** *n.* geôlier *m.*

jalopy /dʒə'lɒpɪ/ *n.* vieux tacot *m.*

jam¹ /dʒæm/ *n.* confiture *f.*

jam² /dʒæm/ *v.t./i.* (*p.t.* **jammed**) (*wedge, become wedged*) (se) coincer; (*cram*) (s')entasser; (*street etc.*) encombrer; (*thrust*) enfoncer; (*radio*) brouiller. —*n.* foule *f.*; (*of traffic*) embouteillage *m.*; (*situation: fam.*) pétrin *m.* ~**-packed** *a.* (*fam.*) bourré.

Jamaica /dʒə'meɪkə/ *n.* Jamaïque *f.*

jangle /'dʒæŋgl/ *n.* cliquetis *m.* —*v.t./i.* (faire) cliqueter.

janitor /'dʒænɪtə(r)/ *n.* concierge *m.*

January /'dʒænjʊərɪ/ *n.* janvier *m.*

Japan /dʒə'pæn/ *n.* Japon *m.* ~**ese** /dʒæpə'niːz/ *a. & n.* japonais(e) (*m.* (*f.*)); (*lang.*) japonais *m.*

jar¹ /dʒɑː(r)/ *n.* pot *m.*, bocal *m.*

jar² /dʒɑː(r)/ *v.i.* (*p.t.* **jarred**) grincer; (*of colours etc.*) détonner. —*v.t.* ébranler. —*n.* son discordant *m.* ~**ring** *a.* discordant.

jargon /'dʒɑːgən/ *n.* jargon *m.*

jasmine /'dʒæsmɪn/ *n.* jasmin *m.*

jaundice /'dʒɔːndɪs/ *n.* jaunisse *f.*

jaundiced /'dʒɔːndɪst/ *a.* (*envious*) envieux; (*bitter*) aigri.

jaunt /dʒɔːnt/ *n.* (*trip*) balade *f.*

jaunty /'dʒɔːntɪ/ *a.* (**-ier, -iest**) (*cheerful, sprightly*) allègre.

javelin /'dʒævlɪn/ *n.* javelot *m.*

jaw /dʒɔː/ *n.* mâchoire *f.* —*v.i.* (*talk: sl.*) jacasser.

jay /dʒeɪ/ *n.* geai *m.* ~**-walk** *v.i.* traverser la chaussée imprudemment.

jazz /dʒæz/ *n.* jazz *m.* —*v.t.* ~ **up**, animer. ~**y** *a.* tape-à-l'œil *invar.*

jealous /'dʒeləs/ *a.* jaloux. ~**y** *n.* jalousie *f.*

jeans /dʒiːnz/ *n. pl.* (blue-)jean *m.*

jeep /dʒiːp/ *n.* jeep *f.*

jeer /dʒɪə(r)/ *v.t./i.* ~ (**at**), railler; (*boo*) huer. —*n.* raillerie *f.*; huée *f.*

jell /dʒel/ *v.i.* (*set: fam.*) prendre. ~**ied** *a.* en gelée.

jelly /'dʒelɪ/ *n.* gelée *f.*

jellyfish /'dʒelɪfɪʃ/ *n.* méduse *f.*

jeopard|y /'dʒepədɪ/ *n.* péril *m.* ~**ize** *v.t.* mettre en péril.

jerk /dʒɜːk/ *n.* secousse *f.*; (*fool: sl.*)

idiot *m.*; (*creep*: *sl.*) salaud *m.* —*v.t.* donner une secousse à. ∼**ily** *adv.* par saccades. ∼**y** *a.* saccadé.

jersey /'dʒɜːzɪ/ *n.* (*garment*) chandail *m.*, tricot *m.*; (*fabric*) jersey *m.*

jest /dʒest/ *n.* plaisanterie *f.* —*v.i.* plaisanter. ∼**er** *n.* bouffon *m.*

Jesus /'dʒiːzəs/ *n.* Jésus *m.*

jet¹ /dʒet/ *n.* (*mineral*) jais *m.* ∼**-black** *a.* de jais.

jet² /dʒet/ *n.* (*stream*) jet *m.*; (*plane*) avion à réaction *m.*, jet *m.* ∼ **lag**, fatigue due au décalage horaire *f.* ∼**-propelled** *a.* à réaction.

jettison /'dʒetɪsn/ *v.t.* jeter à la mer; (*aviat.*) larguer; (*fig.*) abandonner.

jetty /'dʒetɪ/ *n.* (*breakwater*) jetée *f.*

Jew /dʒuː/ *n.* Juif *m.* ∼**ess** *n.* Juive *f.*

jewel /'dʒuːəl/ *n.* bijou *m.* ∼**led** *a.* orné de bijoux. ∼**ler** *n.* bijoutier, -ière *m.*, *f.* ∼**lery** *n.* bijoux *m. pl.*

Jewish /'dʒuːɪʃ/ *a.* juif.

Jewry /'dʒʊərɪ/ *n.* les Juifs *m. pl.*

jib /dʒɪb/ *v.i.* (*p.t.* **jibbed**) regimber (**at**, devant). —*n.* (*sail*) foc *m.*

jibe /dʒaɪb/ *n.* = **gibe**.

jiffy /'dʒɪfɪ/ *n.* (*fam.*) instant *m.*

jig /dʒɪg/ *n.* (*dance*) gigue *f.*

jiggle /'dʒɪgl/ *v.t.* secouer légèrement.

jigsaw /'dʒɪgsɔː/ *n.* puzzle *m.*

jilt /dʒɪlt/ *v.t.* laisser tomber.

jingle /'dʒɪŋgl/ *v.t./i.* (faire) tinter. —*n.* tintement *m.*; (*advertising*) jingle *m.*, sonal *m.*

jinx /dʒɪŋks/ *n.* (*person*: *fam.*) porte-malheur *m. invar.*; (*spell*: *fig.*) mauvais sort *m.*

jitter|s /'dʒɪtəz/ *n. pl.* the ∼**s**, (*fam.*) la frousse *f.* ∼**y** /-ərɪ/ *a.* be ∼**y**, (*fam.*) avoir la frousse.

job /dʒɒb/ *n.* travail *m.*; (*post*) poste *m.* have a ∼ doing, avoir du mal à faire. it is a good ∼ that, heureusement que. ∼**less** *a.* sans travail, au chômage.

jobcentre /'dʒɒbsentə(r)/ *n.* agence (nationale) pour l'emploi *f.*

jockey /'dʒɒkɪ/ *n.* jockey *m.* —*v.i.* (*manœuvre*) manœuvrer.

jocular /'dʒɒkjʊlə(r)/ *a.* jovial.

jog /dʒɒg/ *v.t.* (*p.t.* **jogged**) pousser; (*memory*) rafraîchir. —*v.i.* faire du jogging. ∼**ging** *n.* jogging *m.*

join /dʒɔɪn/ *v.t.* joindre, unir; (*club*) devenir membre de; (*political group*) adhérer à; (*army*) s'engager dans. ∼ **s.o.**, (*in activity*) se joindre à qn.; (*meet*) rejoindre qn. —*v.i.* (*roads etc.*) se rejoindre. —*n.* joint *m.* ∼ **in**, participer (à). ∼ **up**, (*mil.*) s'engager.

joiner /'dʒɔɪnə(r)/ *n.* menuisier *m.*

joint /dʒɔɪnt/ *a.* (*account, venture*) commun. —*n.* (*join*) joint *m.*; (*anat.*) articulation *f.*; (*culin.*) rôti *m.*; (*place*: *sl.*) boîte *f.* ∼ **author**, coauteur *m.* **out of** ∼, déboîté. ∼**ly** *adv.* conjointement.

joist /dʒɔɪst/ *n.* solive *f.*

jok|e /dʒəʊk/ *n.* plaisanterie *f.*; (*trick*) farce *f.* —*v.i.* plaisanter. **it's no** ∼**e**, ce n'est pas drôle. ∼**er** *n.* blagueur, -se *m.*, *f.*; (*pej.*) petit malin *m.*; (*cards*) joker *m.* ∼**ingly** *adv.* pour rire.

jolly /'dʒɒlɪ/ *a.* (-**ier**, -**iest**) gai. —*adv.* (*fam.*) rudement. ∼**ification** /-fɪ'keɪʃn/, ∼**ity** *ns.* réjouissances *f. pl.*

jolt /dʒəʊlt/ *v.t./i.* (*vehicle*, *passenger*) cahoter; (*shake*) secouer. —*n.* cahot *m.*; secousse *f.*

Jordan /'dʒɔːdn/ *n.* Jordanie *f.*

jostle /'dʒɒsl/ *v.t./i.* (*push*) bousculer; (*push each other*) se bousculer.

jot /dʒɒt/ *n.* brin *m.* —*v.t.* (*p.t.* **jotted**) ∼ **down**, noter. ∼**ter** *n.* (*pad*) bloc-notes *m.*

journal /'dʒɜːnl/ *n.* journal *m.* ∼**ism** *n.* journalisme *m.* ∼**ist** *n.* journaliste *m./f.* ∼**ese** /-'liːz/ *n.* jargon des journalistes *m.*

journey /'dʒɜːnɪ/ *n.* voyage *m.*; (*distance*) trajet *m.* —*v.i.* voyager.

jovial /'dʒəʊvɪəl/ *a.* jovial.

joy /dʒɔɪ/ *n.* joie *f.* ∼**-riding** *n.* courses en voitures volées *f. pl.* ∼**ful**, ∼**ous** *adjs.* joyeux.

joystick /'dʒɔɪstɪk/ *n.* (*comput.*) manette *f.*

jubil|ant /'dʒuːbɪlənt/ *a.* débordant de joie. **be** ∼**ant**, jubiler. ∼**ation** /-'leɪʃn/ *n.* jubilation *f.*

jubilee /'dʒuːbɪliː/ *n.* jubilé *m.*

Judaism /'dʒuːdeɪɪzəm/ *n.* judaïsme *m.*

judder /'dʒʌdə(r)/ *v.i.* vibrer. —*n.* vibration *f.*

judge /dʒʌdʒ/ *n.* juge *m.* —*v.t.* juger. **judging by**, à juger de. ∼**ment** *n.* jugement *m.*

judic|iary /dʒuː'dɪʃərɪ/ *n.* magistrature *f.* ∼**ial** *a.* judiciaire.

judicious /dʒuː'dɪʃəs/ *a.* judicieux.

judo /'dʒuːdəʊ/ *n.* judo *m.*

jug /dʒʌg/ *n.* cruche *f.*, pichet *m.*

juggernaut /'dʒʌgənɔːt/ *n.* (*lorry*) poids lourd *m.*, mastodonte *m.*

juggle /'dʒʌgl/ *v.t./i.* jongler (avec). ∼**r** /-ə(r)/ *n.* jongleur, -se *m.*, *f.*

juic|e /dʒuːs/ *n.* jus *m.* ∼**y** *a.* juteux; (*details etc.*: *fam.*) croustillant.

juke-box /'dʒuːkbɒks/ *n.* juke-box *m.*

July /dʒuː'laɪ/ *n.* juillet *m.*

jumble /'dʒʌmbl/ v.t. mélanger. —n. (*muddle*) fouillis m. ∼ **sale,** vente (de charité) f.

jumbo /'dʒʌmbəʊ/ a. ∼ **jet,** avion géant m., jumbo-jet m.

jump /dʒʌmp/ v.t./i. sauter; (*start*) sursauter; (*of price etc.*) faire un bond. —n. saut m.; sursaut m.; (*increase*) hausse f. ∼ **at,** sauter sur. ∼**-leads** n. pl. câbles de démarrage m. pl. ∼ **the gun,** agir prématurément. ∼ **the queue,** resquiller.

jumper /'dʒʌmpə(r)/ n. pull(-over) m.; (*dress. Amer.*) robe chasuble f.

jumpy /'dʒʌmpɪ/ a. nerveux.

junction /'dʒʌŋkʃn/ n. jonction f.; (*of roads etc.*) embranchement m.

juncture /'dʒʌŋktʃə(r)/ n. moment m ; (*state of affairs*) conjoncture f.

June /dʒuːn/ n. juin m.

jungle /'dʒʌŋgl/ n. jungle f.

junior /'dʒuːnɪə(r)/ a. (*in age*) plus jeune (**to,** que); (*in rank*) subalterne; (*school*) élémentaire; (*executive, doctor*) jeune. —n. cadet(te) m. (f.); (*schol.*) petit(e) élève m.(f.; (*sport*) junior m./f.

junk /dʒʌŋk/ n. bric-à-brac m. invar.; (*poor material*) camelote f. —v.t. (*Amer., sl.*) balancer. ∼ **food,** saloperies f. pl. ∼**-shop** n. boutique de brocanteur f.

junkie /'dʒʌŋkɪ/ n. (*sl.*) drogué(e) m (f.).

junta /'dʒʌntə/ n. junte f.

jurisdiction /dʒʊərɪs'dɪkʃn/ n. juridiction f.

jurisprudence /dʒʊərɪs'pruːdəns/ n. jurisprudence f.

juror /'dʒʊərə(r)/ n. juré m.

jury /'dʒʊərɪ/ n. jury m.

just /dʒʌst/ a. (*fair*) juste. —adv. juste, exactement; (*only, slightly*) juste; (*simply*) tout simplement. **he has/had** ∼ **left**/*etc.*, il vient/venait de partir/*etc.* **have** ∼ **missed,** avoir manqué de peu. **it's** ∼ **a cold,** ce n'est qu'un rhume. ∼ **as tall**/*etc.*, tout aussi grand/*etc.* (**as,** que). ∼ **as well,** heureusement (que). ∼ **listen!,** écoutez donc! ∼**ly** adv. avec justice.

justice /'dʒʌstɪs/ n. justice f. **J**∼ **of the Peace,** juge de paix m.

justifiab|le /dʒʌstɪ'faɪəbl/ a. justifiable. ∼**y** adv. avec raison.

justif|y /'dʒʌstɪfaɪ/ v.t. justifier. ∼**ication** /-ɪ'keɪʃn/ n. justification f.

jut /dʒʌt/ v.i. (p.t. **jutted**). ∼ **out,** faire saillie, dépasser.

juvenile /'dʒuːvənaɪl/ a. (*youthful*) juvénile; (*childish*) puéril; (*delinquent*) jeune; (*court*) pour enfants. —n. jeune m./f.

juxtapose /dʒʌkstə'pəʊz/ v.t. juxtaposer.

K

kaleidoscope /kə'laɪdəskəʊp/ n. kaléidoscope.

kangaroo /kæŋgə'ruː/ n. kangourou m.

karate /kə'rɑːtɪ/ n. karaté m.

kebab /kə'bæb/ n. brochette f.

keel /kiːl/ n. (*of ship*) quille f. —v.i. ∼ **over,** chavirer.

keen /kiːn/ a. (**-er, -est**) (*interest, wind, feeling, etc*) vif; (*mind, analysis*) pénétrant; (*edge, appetite*) aiguisé; (*eager*) enthousiaste. **be** ∼ **on,** (*person, thing: fam.*) aimer beaucoup. **be** ∼ **to do** *or* **on doing,** tenir beaucoup à faire. ∼**ly** adv. vivement; avec enthousiasme. ∼**ness** n. vivacité f.; enthousiasme m.

keep /kiːp/ v.t. (p.t. **kept**) garder; (*promise, shop, diary, etc.*) tenir; (*family*) entretenir; (*animals*) élever; (*rule etc.*) respecter; (*celebrate*) célébrer; (*delay*) retenir; (*prevent*) empêcher; (*conceal*) cacher. —v.i. (*food*) se garder; (*remain*) rester. ∼ (**on**), continuer (**doing,** à faire). —n. subsistance f.; (*of castle*) donjon m. **for** ∼**s,** (*fam.*) pour toujours. ∼ **back** v.t. retenir; v.i. ne pas s'approcher. ∼ **s.o. from doing,** empêcher qn. de faire. ∼ **in/out,** empêcher d'entrer/de sortir. ∼ **up,** (se) maintenir. ∼ **up (with),** suivre. ∼**er** n. gardien(ne) m. (f.). ∼**-fit** n. exercices physiques m. pl.

keeping /'kiːpɪŋ/ n. garde f. **in** ∼ **with,** en accord avec.

keepsake /'kiːpseɪk/ n. (*thing*) souvenir m.

keg /keg/ n. tonnelet m.

kennel /'kenl/ n. niche f.

Kenya /'kenjə/ n. Kenya m.

kept /kept/ see **keep.**

kerb /kɜːb/ n. bord du trottoir m.

kerfuffle /kə'fʌfl/ n. (*fuss: fam.*) histoire(s) f. (pl.).

kernel /'kɜːnl/ n. amande f.

kerosene /'kerəsiːn/ n. (*aviation fuel*) kérosène m.; (*paraffin*) pétrole (lampant) m.

ketchup /'ketʃəp/ n. ketchup m.

kettle /'ketl/ n. bouilloire f.

key /kiː/ n. clef f.; (of piano etc.) touche f. —a. clef (f. invar.). **~-ring** n. porte-clefs m. invar. —v.t. **~ in**, (comput.) saisir. **~ up**, surexciter.

keyboard /'kiːbɔːd/ n. clavier m.

keyhole /'kiːhəʊl/ n. trou de la serrure m.

keynote /'kiːnəʊt/ n. (of speech etc.) note dominante f.

keystone /'kiːstəʊn/ n. (archit., fig.) clef de voûte f.

khaki /'kɑːkɪ/ a. kaki invar.

kibbutz /kɪ'bʊts/ n. (pl. **-im** /-iːm/) n. kibboutz m.

kick /kɪk/ v.t./i. donner un coup de pied (à); (of horse) ruer. —n. coup de pied m.; ruade f.; (of gun) recul m.; (thrill: fam.) (malin) plaisir m. **~-off** n. coup d'envoi m. **~ out**, (fam.) flanquer dehors. **~ up**, (fuss, racket: fam.) faire.

kid /kɪd/ n. (goat, leather) chevreau m.; (child: sl.) gosse m./f. —v.t./i. (p.t. **kidded**) blaguer.

kidnap /'kɪdnæp/ v.t. (p.t. **kidnapped**) enlever, kidnapper. **~ping** n. enlève-ment m.

kidney /'kɪdnɪ/ n. rein m.; (culin.) rognon m.

kill /kɪl/ v.t. tuer; (fig.) mettre fin à. —n. mise à mort f. **~er** n. tueur, -se m., f. **~ing** n. massacre m., meurtre m.; a. (funny: fam.) tordant; (tiring: fam.) tuant.

killjoy /'kɪldʒɔɪ/ n. rabat-joie m. invar., trouble-fête m./f. invar.

kiln /kɪln/ n. four m.

kilo /'kiːləʊ/ n. (pl. **-os**) kilo m.

kilobyte /'kɪləbaɪt/ n. kilo-octet m.

kilogram /'kɪləgræm/ n. kilogramme m.

kilohertz /'kɪləhɜːts/ n. kilohertz m.

kilometre /'kɪləmiːtə(r)/ n. kilomètre m.

kilowatt /'kɪləwɒt/ n. kilowatt m.

kilt /kɪlt/ n. kilt m.

kin /kɪn/ n. parents m. pl.

kind[1] /kaɪnd/ n. genre m., sorte f., espèce f. **in ~ of**, (somewhat: fam.) un peu. **be two of a ~**, se rassembler.

kind[2] /kaɪnd/ a. (**-er, -est**) gentil, bon. **~-hearted** a. bon. **~ness** n. bonté f.

kindergarten /'kɪndəgɑːtn/ n. jardin d'enfants m.

kindle /'kɪndl/ v.t./i. (s')allumer.

kindly /'kaɪndlɪ/ a. (**-ier, -iest**) bienveil-lant. —adv. avec bonté. **~ wait**/etc., voulez-vous avoir la bonté d'attendre/ etc.

kindred /'kɪndrɪd/ a. apparenté. **~ spirit,** personne qui a les mêmes goûts f., âme sœur f.

kinetic /kɪ'netɪk/ a. cinétique.

king /kɪŋ/ n. roi m. **~-size(d)** a. géant.

kingdom /'kɪŋdəm/ n. royaume m.; (bot.) règne m.

kingfisher /'kɪŋfɪʃə(r)/ n. martin-pêcheur m.

kink /kɪŋk/ n. (in rope) entortillement m., déformation f.; (fig.) perversion f. **~y** a. (fam.) perverti.

kiosk /'kiːɒsk/ n. kiosque m. **telephone ~,** cabine téléphonique f.

kip /kɪp/ n. (sl.) roupillon m. —v.i. (p.t. **kipped**) (sl.) roupiller.

kipper /'kɪpə(r)/ n. hareng fumé m.

kirby-grip /'kɜːbɪgrɪp/ n. pince à cheveux f.

kiss /kɪs/ n. baiser m. —v.t./i. (s')embrasser.

kit /kɪt/ n. équipement m.; (clothing) affaires f. pl.; (set of tools etc.) trousse f.; (for assembly) kit m. —v.t. (p.t. **kitted**). **~ out**, équiper.

kitbag /'kɪtbæg/ n. sac m. (de marin etc.).

kitchen /'kɪtʃɪn/ n. cuisine f. **~ garden,** jardin potager m.

kitchenette /kɪtʃɪ'net/ n. kitchenette f.

kite /kaɪt/ n. (toy) cerf-volant m.

kith /kɪθ/ n. **~ and kin,** parents et amis m. pl.

kitten /'kɪtn/ n. chaton m.

kitty /'kɪtɪ/ n. (fund) cagnotte f.

knack /næk/ n. truc m., chic m.

knapsack /'næpsæk/ n. sac à dos m.

knave /neɪv/ n. (cards) valet m.

knead /niːd/ v.t. pétrir.

knee /niː/ n. genou m.

kneecap /'niːkæp/ n. rotule f.

kneel /niːl/ v.i. (p.t. **knelt**). **~ (down),** s'agenouiller.

knell /nel/ n. glas m.

knew /njuː/ see **know**.

knickers /'nɪkəz/ n. pl. (woman's undergarment) culotte f., slip m.

knife /naɪf/ n. (pl. **knives**) couteau m. —v.t. poignarder.

knight /naɪt/ n. chevalier m.; (chess) cavalier m. —v.t. faire or armer chevalier. **~hood** n. titre de chevalier m.

knit /nɪt/ v.t./i. (p.t. **knitted** or **knit**) tricoter; (bones etc.) (se) souder. **~ one's brow,** froncer les sourcils. **~ting** n. tricot m.

knitwear /'nɪtweə(r)/ n. tricots m. pl.

knob /nɒb/ n. bouton m.

knock /nɒk/ v.t./i. frapper, cogner; (*criticize*: *sl.*) critiquer. —*n.* coup *m.* ~ **about** *v.t.* malmener; *v.i.* vadrouiller. ~ **down**, (*chair, pedestrian*) renverser; (*demolish*) abattre; (*reduce*) baisser. ~**-down** *a.* (*price*) très bas. ~**-kneed** *a.* cagneux. ~ **off** *v.t.* faire tomber; (*fam.*) expédier; *v.i.* (*fam.*) s'arrêter de travailler. ~ **out**, (*by blow*) assommer; (*tire*) épuiser. ~**-out** *n.* (*boxing*) knock-out *m.* ~ **over**, renverser. ~ **up**, (*meal etc.*) préparer en vitesse. ~**er** *n.* heurtoir *m.*

knot /nɒt/ *n.* nœud *m.* —*v.t.* (*p.t.* **knotted**) nouer. ~**ty** /'nɒtɪ/ *a.* noueux; (*problem*) épineux.

know /nəʊ/ v.t./i. (*p.t.* **knew**, *p.p.* **known**) savoir (**that**, que); (*person, place*) connaître. ~ **how to do**, savoir comment faire. —*n.* **in the** ~, (*fam.*) dans le secret, au courant. ~ **about**, (*cars etc.*) s'y connaître en. ~**-all**, (*Amer.*) ~**-it-all** *n.* je-sais-tout *m.* /f. ~**-how** *n.* technique *f.* ~ **of**, connaître, avoir entendu parler de. ~**ingly** *adv.* (*consciously*) sciemment.

knowledge /'nɒlɪdʒ/ *n.* connaissance *f.*; (*learning*) connaissances *f. pl.* ~**able** *a.* bien informé.

known /nəʊn/ *see* **know.** —*a.* connu (*recognized*) reconnu.

knuckle /'nʌkl/ *n.* articulation du doigt *f.* —*v.i.* ~ **under**, se soumettre.

Koran /kə'rɑːn/ *n.* Coran *m.*

Korea /kə'rɪə/ *n.* Corée *f.*

kosher /'kəʊʃə(r)/ *a.* kascher *invar.*

kowtow /kaʊ'taʊ/ *v.i.* se prosterner (**to**, devant).

kudos /'kjuːdɒs/ *n.* (*fam.*) gloire *f.*

Kurd /kɜːd/ *a. & n.* kurde *m* /f.

L

lab /læb/ *n.* (*fam.*) labo *m.*

label /'leɪbl/ *n.* étiquette *f.* —*v.t.* (*p.t.* **labelled**) étiqueter.

laboratory /lə'bɒrətrɪ, *Amer.* 'læbrətɔːrɪ/ *n.* laboratoire *m.*

laborious /lə'bɔːrɪəs/ *a.* laborieux.

labour /'leɪbə(r)/ *n.* travail *m.*; (*workers*) main-d'œuvre *f.* —*v.i.* peiner. —*v.t.* trop insister sur. **in** ~, en train d'accoucher, en couches. ~**ed** *a.* laborieux.

Labour /'leɪbə(r)/ *n.* le parti travailliste *m.* —*a.* travailliste.

labourer /'leɪbərə(r)/ *n.* manœuvre *m.*; (*on farm*) ouvrier agricole *m.*

labyrinth /'læbərɪnθ/ *n.* labyrinthe *m.*

lace /leɪs/ *n.* dentelle *f.*; (*of shoe*) lacet *m.* —*v.t.* (*fasten*) lacer; (*drink*) arroser. ~**-ups** *n. pl.* chaussures à lacets *f. pl.*

lacerate /'læsəreɪt/ *v.t.* lacérer.

lack /læk/ *n.* manque *m.* —*v.t.* manquer de. **be** ~**ing**, manquer (**in**, de). **for** ~ **of**, faute de.

lackadaisical /lækə'deɪzɪkl/ *a.* indolent, apathique.

lackey /'lækɪ/ *n.* laquais *m.*

laconic /lə'kɒnɪk/ *a.* laconique.

lacquer /'lækə(r)/ *n.* laque *f.*

lad /læd/ *n.* garçon *m.*, gars *m.*

ladder /'lædə(r)/ *n.* échelle *f.*; (*in stocking*) maille filée *f.* —*v.t./i.* (*stocking*) filer.

laden /'leɪdn/ *a.* chargé (**with**, de).

ladle /'leɪdl/ *n.* louche *f.*

lady /'leɪdɪ/ *n.* dame *f.* ~ **friend**, amie *f.* ~**-in-waiting** *n.* dame d'honneur *f.* **young** ~, jeune femme *or* fille *f.* ~**like** *a.* distingué.

lady|bird /'leɪdɪbɜːd/ *n.* coccinelle *f.* ~**bug** *n.* (*Amer.*) coccinelle *f.*

lag[1] /læg/ *v.i.* (*p.t.* **lagged**) traîner. —*n.* (*interval*) décalage *m.*

lag[2] /læg/ *v.t.* (*p.t.* **lagged**) (*pipes*) calorifuger.

lager /'lɑːɡə(r)/ *n.* bière blonde *f.*

lagoon /lə'ɡuːn/ *n.* lagune *f.*

laid /leɪd/ *see* **lay**[2]. ~**-back** *a.* (*fam.*) cool.

lain /leɪn/ *see* **lie**[2].

lair /leə(r)/ *n.* tanière *f.*

laity /'leɪətɪ/ *n.* laïques *m. pl.*

lake /leɪk/ *n.* lac *m.*

lamb /læm/ *n.* agneau *m.*

lambswool /'læmzwʊl/ *n.* laine d'agneau *f.*

lame /leɪm/ *a.* (**-er, -est**) boiteux; (*excuse*) faible. ~**ly** *adv.* (*argue*) sans conviction. ~ **duck**, canard boiteux *m.*

lament /lə'ment/ *n.* lamentation *f.* —*v.t./i.* se lamenter (sur). ~**able** *a.* lamentable.

laminated /'læmɪneɪtɪd/ *a.* laminé.

lamp /læmp/ *n.* lampe *f.*

lamppost /'læmppəʊst/ *n.* réverbère *m.*

lampshade /'læmpʃeɪd/ *n.* abat-jour *m.* *invar.*

lance /lɑːns/ *n.* lance *f.* —*v.t.* (*med.*) inciser.

lancet /'lɑːnsɪt/ *n.* bistouri *m.*

land /lænd/ *n.* terre *f.*; (*plot*) terrain *m.*; (*country*) pays *m.* —*a.* terrestre;

(*policy, reform*) agraire. —*v.t./i.* débarquer; (*aircraft*) (se) poser, (faire) atterrir; (*fall*) tomber; (*obtain*) décrocher; (*put*) mettre; (*a blow*) porter. ∼**-locked** *a.* sans accès à la mer. ∼ **up,** se retrouver.

landed /'lændɪd/ *a.* foncier.

landing /'lændɪŋ/ *n.* débarquement *m.*; (*aviat.*) atterrissage *m.*; (*top of stairs*) palier *m.* ∼**-stage** *n.* débarcadère *m.* ∼**-strip** *n.* piste d'atterrissage *f.*

land|lady /'lændleɪdɪ/ *n.* propriétaire *f.*; (*of inn*) patronne *f.* ∼**lord** *n.* propriétaire *m.*; patron *m.*

landmark /'lændmɑːk/ *n.* (point de) repère *m.*

landscape /'læn(d)skeɪp/ *n.* paysage *m.* —*v.t.* aménager.

landslide /'lændslaɪd/ *n.* glissement de terrain *m.*; (*pol.*) raz-de-marée (électoral) *m. invar.*

lane /leɪn/ *n.* (*path, road*) chemin *m.*; (*strip of road*) voie *f.*; (*of traffic*) file *f.*; (*aviat.*) couloir *m.*

language /'læŋgwɪdʒ/ *n.* langue *f.*; (*speech, style*) langage *m.* ∼ **laboratory,** laboratoire de langue *m.*

languid /'læŋgwɪd/ *a.* languissant.

languish /'læŋgwɪʃ/ *v.i.* languir.

lank /læŋk/ *a.* grand et maigre.

lanky /'læŋkɪ/ *a.* (**-ier, -iest**) dégingandé, grand et maigre.

lanolin /'lænəʊlɪn/ *n.* lanoline *f.*

lantern /'læntən/ *n.* lanterne *f.*

lap[1] /læp/ *n.* genoux *m. pl.*; (*sport*) tour (de piste) *m.* —*v.t./i.* (*p.t.* **lapped**) ∼ **over,** (se) chevaucher.

lap[2] /læp/ *v.t.* (*p.t.* **lapped**). ∼ **up,** laper. —*v.i.* (*waves*) clapoter.

lapel /lə'pel/ *n.* revers *m.*

lapse /læps/ *v.i.* (*decline*) se dégrader; (*expire*) se périmer. —*n.* défaillance *f.*, erreur *f.*; (*of time*) intervalle *m.* ∼ **into,** retomber dans.

larceny /'lɑːsənɪ/ *n.* vol simple *m.*

lard /lɑːd/ *n.* saindoux *m.*

larder /'lɑːdə(r)/ *n.* garde-manger *m. invar.*

large /lɑːdʒ/ *a.* (**-er, -est**) grand, gros. **at** ∼, en liberté. **by and** ∼, en général. ∼**ly** *adv.* en grande mesure. ∼**ness** *n.* grandeur *f.*

lark[1] /lɑːk/ *n.* (*bird*) alouette *f.*

lark[2] /lɑːk/ *n.* (*bit of fun*: *fam.*) rigolade *f.* —*v.i.* (*fam.*) rigoler.

larva /'lɑːvə/ *n.* (*pl.* **-vae** /-viː/) larve *f.*

laryngitis /lærɪn'dʒaɪtɪs/ *n.* laryngite *f.*

larynx /'lærɪŋks/ *n.* larynx *m.*

lasagne /lə'zænjə/ *n.* lasagne *f.*

lascivious /lə'sɪvɪəs/ *a.* lascif.

laser /'leɪzə(r)/ *n.* laser *m.* ∼ **printer,** imprimante laser *f.*

lash /læʃ/ *v.t.* fouetter. —*n.* coup de fouet *m.*; (*eyelash*) cil *m.* ∼ **out,** (*spend*) dépenser follement. ∼ **out against,** attaquer.

lashings /'læʃɪŋz/ *n. pl.* ∼ **of,** (*cream etc.*: *sl.*) des masses de.

lass /læs/ *n.* jeune fille *f.*

lasso /læ'suː/ *n.* (*pl.* **-os**) lasso *m.*

last[1] /lɑːst/ *a.* dernier. —*adv.* en dernier; (*most recently*) la dernière fois. —*n.* dernier, -ière *m., f.*; (*remainder*) reste *m.* **at** (**long**) ∼, enfin. ∼**-ditch** *a.* ultime. ∼**-minute** *a.* de dernière minute. ∼ **night,** hier soir. **the** ∼ **straw,** le comble. **the** ∼ **word,** le mot de la fin. **on its** ∼ **legs,** sur le point de rendre l'âme. ∼**ly** *adv.* en dernier lieu.

last[2] /lɑːst/ *v.i.* durer. ∼**ing** *a.* durable.

latch /lætʃ/ *n.* loquet *m.*

late /leɪt/ *a.* (**-er, -est**) (*not on time*) en retard; (*recent*) récent; (*former*) ancien; (*hour, fruit, etc.*) tardif; (*deceased*) défunt. **the late Mrs X,** feu Mme X. ∼**st** /-ɪst/, (*last*) dernier. —*adv.* (*not early*) tard; (*not on time*) en retard. **in** ∼ **July,** fin juillet. **of** ∼, dernièrement. ∼**ness** *n.* retard *m.*; (*of event*) heure tardive *f.*

latecomer /'leɪtkʌmə(r)/ *n.* retardataire *m./f.*

lately /'leɪtlɪ/ *adv.* dernièrement.

latent /'leɪtnt/ *a.* latent.

lateral /'lætərəl/ *a.* latéral.

lathe /leɪð/ *n.* tour *m.*

lather /'lɑːðə(r)/ *n.* mousse *f.* —*v.t.* savonner. —*v.i.* mousser.

Latin /'lætɪn/ *n.* (*lang.*) latin *m.* —*a.* latin. ∼ **America,** Amérique latine *f.*

latitude /'lætɪtjuːd/ *n.* latitude *f.*

latrine /lə'triːn/ *n.* latrines *f. pl.*

latter /'lætə(r)/ *a.* dernier. —*n.* **the** ∼, celui-ci, celle-ci. ∼**-day** *a.* moderne. ∼**ly** *adv.* dernièrement.

lattice /'lætɪs/ *n.* treillage *m.*

laudable /'lɔːdəbl/ *a.* louable.

laugh /lɑːf/ *v.i.* rire (**at,** de). —*n.* rire *m.* ∼**able** *a.* ridicule. ∼**ing-stock** *n.* objet de risée *m.*

laughter /'lɑːftə(r)/ *n.* (*act*) rire *m.*; (*sound of laughs*) rires *m. pl.*

launch[1] /lɔːntʃ/ *v.t.* lancer. —*n.* lancement *m.* ∼ **(out) into,** se lancer dans. ∼**ing pad,** aire de lancement *f.*

launch[2] /lɔːntʃ/ *n.* (*boat*) vedette *f.*

launder /'lɔːndə(r)/ *v.t.* blanchir.

launderette /lɔːn'dret/ *n.* laverie automatique *f.*

laundry /'lɔːndrɪ/ *n.* (*place*) blanchisserie *f.*; (*clothes*) linge *m.*

laurel /'lɒrəl/ *n.* laurier *m.*

lava /'lɑːvə/ *n.* lave *f.*

lavatory /'lævətrɪ/ *n.* cabinets *m. pl.*

lavender /'lævəndə(r)/ *n.* lavande *f.*

lavish /'lævɪʃ/ *a.* (*person*) prodigue; (*plentiful*) copieux; (*lush*) somptueux. —*v.t.* prodiguer (**on**, à). **~ly** *adv.* copieusement.

law /lɔː/ *n.* loi *f.*; (*profession, subject of study*) droit *m.* **~-abiding** *a.* respectueux des lois. **~ and order**, l'ordre public. **~ful** *a.* légal. **~fully** *adv.* légalement. **~less** *a.* sans loi.

lawcourt /'lɔːkɔːt/ *n.* tribunal *m.*

lawn /lɔːn/ *n.* pelouse *f.*, gazon *m.* **~-mower** *n.* tondeuse à gazon *f.* **~ tennis**, tennis (sur gazon) *m.*

lawsuit /'lɔːsuːt/ *n.* procès *m.*

lawyer /'lɔːjə(r)/ *n.* avocat *m.*

lax /læks/ *a.* négligent; (*morals etc.*) relâché. **~ity** *n.* négligence *f.*

laxative /'læksətɪv/ *n.* laxatif *m.*

lay[1] /leɪ/ *a.* (*non-clerical*) laïque; (*opinion etc.*) d'un profane.

lay[2] /leɪ/ *v.t.* (*p.t.* **laid**) poser, mettre; (*trap*) tendre; (*table*) mettre; (*plan*) former; (*eggs*) pondre. —*v.i.* pondre. **~ aside**, mettre de côté. **~ down**, (dé)poser, (*condition*) (im)poser. **~ hold of**, saisir. **~ off** *v.t.* (*worker*) licencier; *v.i.* (*fam.*) arrêter. **~-off** *n.* licenciement *m.* **~ on**, (*provide*) fournir. **~ out**, (*design*) dessiner; (*display*) disposer; (*money*) dépenser. **~ up**, (*store*) amasser. **~ waste**, ravager.

lay[3] /leɪ/ *see* **lie**[2].

layabout /'leɪəbaʊt/ *n.* fainéant(e) *m. (f.).*

lay-by /'leɪbaɪ/ *n.* (*pl.* **-bys**) petite aire de stationnement *f.*

layer /'leɪə(r)/ *n.* couche *f.*

layman /'leɪmən/ *n.* (*pl.* **-men**) profane *m.*

layout /'leɪaʊt/ *n.* disposition *f.*

laze /leɪz/ *v.i.* paresser.

laz|y /'leɪzɪ/ *a.* (**-ier, -iest**) paresseux. **~iness** *n.* paresse *f.* **~y-bones** *n.* flemmard(e) *m. (f.).*

lead[1] /liːd/ *v.t./i.* (*p.t.* **led**) mener; (*team etc.*) diriger; (*life*) mener; (*induce*) amener. **~ to**, conduire à, mener à. —*n.* avance *f.*; (*clue*) indice *m.*; (*leash*) laisse *f.*; (*theatre*) premier rôle *m.*; (*wire*) fil *m.*; (*example*) exemple *m.* **in the ~**, en tête. **~ away**, emmener. **~ up to**, (*come to*) en venir à; (*precede*) précéder.

lead[2] /led/ *n.* plomb *m.*; (*of pencil*) mine *f.* **~en** *a.* (*sky*) de plomb (*humour*) lourd.

leader /'liːdə(r)/ *n.* chef *m.*; (*of country, club, etc.*) dirigeant(e) *m. (f.)*; (*leading article*) éditorial *m.* **~ship** *n.* direction *f.*

leading /'liːdɪŋ/ *a.* principal. **~ article**, éditorial *m.*

leaf /liːf/ *n.* (*pl.* **leaves**) feuille *f.*; (*of table*) rallonge *f.* —*v.i.* **~ through**, feuilleter. **~y** *a.* feuillu.

leaflet /'liːflɪt/ *n.* prospectus *m.*

league /liːg/ *n.* ligue *f.*; (*sport*) championnat *m.* **in ~ with**, de mèche avec.

leak /liːk/ *n.* fuite *f.* —*v.i.* fuir; (*news: fig.*) s'ébruiter. —*v.t.* répandre; (*fig.*) divulguer. **~age** *n.* fuite *f.* **~y** *a.* qui a une fuite.

lean[1] /liːn/ *a.* (**-er, -est**) maigre. —*n.* (*of meat*) maigre *m.* **~ness** *n.* maigreur *f.*

lean[2] /liːn/ *v.t./i.* (*p.t.* **leaned** *or* **leant** /lent/) (*rest*) (s')appuyer; (*slope*) pencher. **~ out**, se pencher à l'extérieur. **~ over**, (*of person*) se pencher. **~-to** *n.* appentis *m.*

leaning /'liːnɪŋ/ *a.* penché —*n.* tendance *f.*

leap /liːp/ *v.i.* (*p.t.* **leaped** *or* **leapt** /lept/) bondir. —*n.* bond *m.* **~-frog** *n.* saute-mouton *m. invar.*; *v.i.* (*p.t.* **-frogged**) sauter (**over**, par-dessus). **~ year**, année bissextile *f.*

learn /lɜːn/ *v.t./i.* (*p.t.* **learned** *or* **learnt**) apprendre (**to do**, à faire). **~er** *n.* débutant(e) *m. (f.).*

learn|ed /'lɜːnɪd/ *a.* érudit. **~ing** *n.* érudition *f.*, connaissances *f. pl.*

lease /liːs/ *n.* bail *m.* —*v.t.* louer à bail.

leaseback /'liːsbæk/ *n.* cession-bail *f.*

leash /liːʃ/ *n.* laisse *f.*

least /liːst/ *a.* **the ~**, (*smallest amount of*) le moins de; (*slightest*) le *or* la moindre. —*n.* le moins. —*adv.* le moins; (*with adjective*) le *or* la moins. **at ~**, au moins.

leather /'leðə(r)/ *n.* cuir *m.*

leave /liːv/ *v.t.* (*p.t.* **left**) laisser; (*depart from*) quitter. —*n.* (*holiday*) congé *m.*; (*consent*) permission *f.* **be left (over)**, rester. **~ alone**, (*thing*) ne pas toucher à; (*person*) laisser tranquille. **~ behind**, laisser. **~ out**, omettre. **on ~**, (*mil.*) en permission. **take one's ~**, prendre congé (**of**, de).

leavings /'li:vɪŋz/ n. pl. restes m. pl.
Leban|on /'lebənən/ n. Liban m. **~ese**
/-'ni:z/ a. & n. libanais(e) (m. (f.)).
lecher /'letʃə(r)/ n. débauché m. **~ous** a.
lubrique. **~y** n. lubricité f.
lectern /'lektən/ n. lutrin m.
lecture /'lektʃə(r)/ n. cours m., conférence f.; (rebuke) réprimande f.
—v.t./i. faire un cours or une
conférence (à); (rebuke) réprimander.
~r /-ə(r)/ n. conférencier, -ière m., f.,
(univ.) enseignant(e) m. (f.).
led /led/ see **lead**[1].
ledge /ledʒ/ n. (window) rebord m.;
(rock) saillie f.
ledger /'ledʒə(r)/ n. grand livre m.
lee /li:/ n. côté sous le vent m.
leech /li:tʃ/ n. sangsue f.
leek /li:k/ n. poireau m.
leer /lɪə(r)/ v.i. **~** (at), lorgner. —n.
regard sournois m.
leeway /'li:weɪ/ n. (naut.) dérive f.; (fig.)
liberté d'action f. **make up ~**, rattraper
le retard.
left[1] /left/ see **leave**. **~ luggage (office)**,
consigne f. **~-overs** n. pl. restes
m. pl.
left[2] /left/ a. gauche. —adv. à gauche.
—n. gauche f. **~-hand** a. à or de
gauche. **~-handed** a. gaucher. **~-wing**
a. (pol.) de gauche.
leftist /'leftɪst/ n. gauchiste m./f.
leg /leg/ n. jambe f.; (of animal) patte f.;
(of table) pied m.; (of chicken) cuisse f.;
(of lamb) gigot m.; (of journey) étape f.
~-room n. place pour les jambes f. **~-**
warmers n. pl. jambières f. pl.
legacy /'legəsɪ/ n. legs m.
legal /'li:gl/ a. légal; (affairs etc.)
juridique. **~ity** /li:'gælətɪ/ n. légalité f.
~ly adv. légalement.
legalize /'li:gəlaɪz/ v.t. légaliser.
legend /'ledʒənd/ n. légende f. **~ary** a.
légendaire.
leggings /'legɪŋz/ n. pl. collant sans pieds
m.
legib|le /'ledʒəbl/ a. lisible. **~ility**
/-'bɪlətɪ/ n. lisibilité f. **~ly** adv.
lisiblement.
legion /'li:dʒən/ n. légion f. **~naire** n.
légionnaire m. **~naire's disease**,
maladie du légionnaire f.
legislat|e /'ledʒɪsleɪt/ v.i. légiférer. **~ion**
/-'leɪʃn/ n. (body of laws) législation f.;
(law) loi f.
legislat|ive /'ledʒɪslətɪv/ a. législatif.
~ure /-eɪtʃə(r)/ n. corps législatif m.
legitima|te /lɪ'dʒɪtɪmət/ a. légitime. **~cy**
n. légitimité f.

leisure /'leʒə(r)/ n. loisir(s) m. (pl.). **at**
one's ~, à tête reposée. **~ centre**,
centre de loisirs m. **~ly** a. lent; adv.
sans se presser.
lemon /'lemən/ n. citron m.
lemonade /lemə'neɪd/ n. (fizzy)
limonade f.; (still) citronnade f.
lend /lend/ v.t. (p.t. **lent**) prêter;
(contribute) donner. **~ itself to**, se
prêter à. **~er** n. prêteur, -se m., f. **~ing**
n. prêt m.
length /leŋθ/ n. longueur f.; (in time)
durée f.; (section) morceau m. **at ~**, (at
last) enfin. **at (great) ~**, longuement.
~y a. long.
lengthen /'leŋθən/ v.t./i. (s')allonger.
lengthways /'leŋθweɪz/ adv. dans le sens
de la longueur.
lenien|t /'li:nɪənt/ a. indulgent. **~cy** n.
indulgence f. **~tly** adv. avec indulgence.
lens /lenz/ n. lentille f.; (of spectacles)
verre m.; (photo.) objectif m.
lent /lent/ see **lend**.
Lent /lent/ n. Carême m.
lentil /'lentl/ n. (bean) lentille f.
Leo /'li:əʊ/ n. le Lion.
leopard /'lepəd/ n. léopard m.
leotard /'li:ətɑːd/ n. body m.
leper /'lepə(r)/ n. lépreux, -se m., f.
leprosy /'leprəsɪ/ n. lèpre f.
lesbian /'lezbɪən/ n. lesbienne f. —a.
lesbien.
lesion /'li:ʒn/ n. lésion f.
less /les/ a. (in quantity etc.) moins de
(than, que). —adv., n. & prep. moins.
~ than, (with numbers) moins de.
work/etc. **~ than**, travailler/etc. moins
que. **ten pounds**/etc. **~**, dix livres/etc.
de moins. **~ and less**, de moins en
moins. **~er** a. moindre.
lessen /'lesn/ v.t./i. diminuer.
lesson /'lesn/ n. leçon f.
lest /lest/ conj. de peur que or de.
let /let/ v.t. (p.t. **let**, pres. p. **letting**)
laisser; (lease) louer. —v. aux. **~ us**
do, ~'s do, faisons. **~ him do**, qu'il
fasse. **~ me know the results**, informe-
moi des résultats. —n. location f. **~**
alone, (thing) ne pas toucher à;
(person) laisser tranquille; (never
mind) encore moins. **~ down**, baisser;
(deflate) dégonfler; (fig.) décevoir. **~-**
down n. déception f. **~ go** v.t. lâcher;
v.i. lâcher prise. **~ sb. in/out**, laisser or
faire entrer/sortir qn. **~ a dress out**,
élargir une robe. **~ o.s. in for**, (task)
s'engager à; (trouble) s'attirer. **~ off**,
(explode, fire) faire éclater or partir;

(*excuse*) dispenser; (*not punish*) ne pas punir. ~ up, (*fam.*) s'arrêter. ~-up *n.* répit *m.*

lethal /'li:θl/ *a.* mortel; (*weapon*) meurtrier.

letharg|y /'leθədʒɪ/ *n.* léthargie *f.* ~ic /lɪ'θaːdʒɪk/ *a.* léthargique.

letter /'letə(r)/ *n.* lettre *f.* ~-bomb *n.* lettre piégée *f.* ~-box *n.* boîte à *or* aux lettres *f.* ~ing *n.* (*letters*) caractères *m. pl.*

lettuce /'letɪs/ *n.* laitue *f.*, salade *f.*

leukaemia /luː'kiːmɪə/ *n.* leucémie *f.*

level /'levl/ *a.* plat, uni; (*on surface*) horizontal; (*in height*) au même niveau (with, que); (*in score*) à égalité. —*n.* niveau *m.* (**spirit**) ~, niveau à bulle *m.* —*v.t.* (*p.t.* **levelled**) niveler; (*aim*) diriger. **be on the** ~, (*fam.*) être franc. ~ **crossing**, passage à niveau *m.* ~-**headed** *a.* équilibré.

lever /'liːvə(r)/ *n.* levier *m.* —*v.t.* soulever au moyen d'un levier.

leverage /'liːvərɪdʒ/ *n.* influence *f.*

levity /'levɪtɪ/ *n.* légèreté *f.*

levy /'levɪ/ *v.t.* (*tax*) (pré)lever. —*n.* impôt *m.*

lewd /ljuːd/ *a.* (**-er, -est**) obscène.

liable /'laɪəbl/ *a.* **be** ~ **to do**, avoir tendance à faire; pouvoir faire. ~ **to**, (*illness etc.*) sujet à; (*fine*) passible de. ~ **for**, responsable de.

liabilit|y /laɪə'bɪlətɪ/ *n.* responsabilité *f.*, (*fam.*) handicap *m.* ~ies, (*debts*) dettes *f. pl.*

liais|e /lɪ'eɪz/ *v.i.* (*fam.*) faire la liaison. ~on /-ɒn/ *n.* liaison *f.*

liar /'laɪə(r)/ *n.* menteur, -se *m., f.*

libel /'laɪbl/ *n.* diffamation *f.* —*v.t.* (*p.t.* **libelled**) diffamer.

liberal /'lɪbərəl/ *a.* libéral; (*generous*) généreux, libéral. ~ly *adv.* libéralement.

Liberal /'lɪbərəl/ *a.* & *n.* (*pol.*) libéral(e) (*m.* (*f.*)).

liberat|e /'lɪbəreɪt/ *v.t.* libérer. ~ion /-'reɪʃn/ *n.* libération *f.*

libert|y /'lɪbətɪ/ *n.* liberté *f.* **at** ~y **to**, libre de. **take** ~ies, prendre des libertés.

libido /lɪ'biːdəʊ/ *n.* libido *f.*

Libra /'liːbrə/ *n.* la Balance.

librar|y /'laɪbrərɪ/ *n.* bibliothèque *f.* ~ian /-'breərɪən/ *n.* bibliothécaire *m./f.*

libretto /lɪ'bretəʊ/ *n.* (*pl.* -os) (*mus.*) livret *m.*

Libya /'lɪbɪə/ *n.* Libye *f.* ~n *a.* & *n.* libyen(ne) (*m.* (*f.*)).

lice /laɪs/ *see* **louse.**

licence, *Amer.* **license**[1] /'laɪsns/ *n.*

permis *m.*; (*for television*) redevance *f.*; (*comm.*) licence *f.*; (*liberty*: fig.) licence *f.* ~ **plate**, plaque minéralogique *f.*

license[2] /'laɪsns/ *v.t.* accorder un permis à, autoriser.

licentious /laɪ'senʃəs/ *a.* licencieux.

lichen /'laɪkən/ *n.* lichen *m.*

lick /lɪk/ *v.t.* lécher; (*defeat*: *sl.*) rosser. —*n.* coup de langue *m.* ~ **one's chops**, se lécher les babines.

licorice /'lɪkərɪs/ *n.* (*Amer.*) réglisse *f.*

lid /lɪd/ *n.* couvercle *m.*

lido /'laɪdəʊ/ *n.* (*pl.* -os) piscine en plein air *f.*

lie[1] /laɪ/ *n.* mensonge *m.* —*v.i.* (*p.t.* **lied**, *pres. p.* **lying**) (*tell lies*) mentir. **give the** ~ **to**, démentir.

lie[2] /laɪ/ *v.i.* (*p.t.* **lay**, *p.p.* **lain**, *pres. p.* **lying**) s'allonger; (*remain*) rester; (*be*) se trouver, être; (*in grave*) reposer. **be lying**, être allongé. ~ **down**, s'allonger. ~ **in**, **have a** ~-**in**, faire la grasse matinée. ~ **low**, se cacher.

lieu /ljuː/ *n.* **in** ~ **of**, au lieu de.

lieutenant /lef'tenənt, *Amer.* luː'tenənt/ *n.* lieutenant *m.*

life /laɪf/ *n.* (*pl.* **lives**) vie *f.* ~ **cycle**, cycle de vie *m.* ~-**guard** *n.* sauveteur *m.* ~ **insurance**, assurance-vie *f.* ~-**jacket**, ~ **preserver**, *n.* gilet de sauvetage *m.* ~-**size(d)** *a.* grandeur nature *invar.* ~-**style** *n.* style de vie *m.*

lifebelt /'laɪfbelt/ *n.* bouée de sauvetage *f.*

lifeboat /'laɪfbəʊt/ *n.* canot de sauvetage *m.*

lifebuoy /'laɪfbɔɪ/ *n.* bouée de sauvetage *f.*

lifeless /'laɪflɪs/ *a.* sans vie.

lifelike /'laɪflaɪk/ *a.* très ressemblant.

lifelong /'laɪflɒŋ/ *a.* de toute la vie.

lifetime /'laɪftaɪm/ *n.* vie *f.* **in one's** ~, de son vivant.

lift /lɪft/ *v.t.* lever; (*steal*: *fam.*) voler. —*v.i.* (*of fog*) se lever. —*n.* (*in building*) ascenseur *m.* **give a** ~ **to**, emmener (en voiture). ~-**off** *n.* (*aviat.*) décollage *m.*

ligament /'lɪgəmənt/ *n.* ligament *m.*

light[1] /laɪt/ *n.* lumière *f.*; (*lamp*) lampe *f.*; (*for fire, on vehicle, etc.*) feu *m.*; (*headlight*) phare *m.* —*a.* (*not dark*) clair. —*v.t.* (*p.t.* **lit** *or* **lighted**) allumer; (*room etc.*) éclairer; (*match*) frotter. **bring to** ~, révéler. **come to** ~, être révélé. **have you got a** ~?, vous avez du feu? ~ **bulb**, ampoule *f.* ~ **pen**, crayon optique *m.* ~ **up** *v.i.* s'allumer;

v.t. (*room*) éclairer. **~-year** *n.* année lumière *f.*

light[2] /laɪt/ *a.* (**-er, -est**) (*not heavy*) léger. **~-fingered** *a.* chapardeur. **~-headed** *a.* (*dizzy*) qui a un vertige; (*frivolous*) étourdi. **~-hearted** *a.* gai. **~ly** *adv.* légèrement. **~ness** *n.* légèreté *f.*

lighten[1] /'laɪtn/ *v.t.* (*give light to*) éclairer; (*make brighter*) éclaircir.

lighten[2] /'laɪtn/ *v.t.* (*make less heavy*) alléger.

lighter /'laɪtə(r)/ *n.* briquet *m.*; (*for stove*) allume-gaz *m. invar.*

lighthouse /'laɪthaʊs/ *n.* phare *m.*

lighting /'laɪtɪŋ/ *n.* éclairage *m.* **~ technician**, éclairagiste *m./f.*

lightning /'laɪtnɪŋ/ *n.* éclair(s) *m.* (*pl.*), foudre *f.* —*a.* éclair *invar.*

lightweight /'laɪtweɪt/ *a.* léger. —*n.* (*boxing*) poids léger *m.*

like[1] /laɪk/ *a.* semblable, pareil. —*prep.* comme. —*conj.* (*fam.*) comme. —*n.* pareil *m.* **be ~-minded**, avoir les mêmes sentiments. **the ~s of you**, des gens comme vous.

like[2] /laɪk/ *v.t.* aimer (bien). **~s** *n. pl.* goûts *m. pl.* **I should ~**, je voudrais, j'aimerais. **would you ~?**, voulez-vous? **~able** *a.* sympathique.

like|ly /'laɪklɪ/ *a.* (**-ier, -iest**) probable. —*adv.* probablement. **he is ~y to do**, il fera probablement. **not ~y!**, (*fam.*) pas question! **~ihood** *n.* probabilité *f.*

liken /'laɪkən/ *v.t.* comparer.

likeness /'laɪknɪs/ *n.* ressemblance *f.*

likewise /'laɪkwaɪz/ *adv.* de même.

liking /'laɪkɪŋ/ *n.* (*for thing*) penchant *m.*; (*for person*) affection *f.*

lilac /'laɪlək/ *n.* lilas *m.* —*a.* lilas *invar.*

lily /'lɪlɪ/ *n.* lis *m.*, lys *m.* **~ of the valley**, muguet *m.*

limb /lɪm/ *n.* membre *m.* **out on a ~**, isolé (et vulnérable).

limber /'lɪmbə(r)/ *v.i.* **~ up**, faire des exercices d'assouplissement.

limbo /'lɪmbəʊ/ *n.* **be in ~**, (*forgotten*) être tombé dans l'oubli.

lime[1] /laɪm/ *n.* chaux *f.*

lime[2] /laɪm/ *n.* (*fruit*) citron vert *m.*

lime[3] /laɪm/ *n.* **~(-tree)**, tilleul *m.*

limelight /'laɪmlaɪt/ *n.* **in the ~**, en vedette.

limerick /'lɪmərɪk/ *n.* poème humoristique *m.* (*de cinq vers*).

limit /'lɪmɪt/ *n.* limite *f.* —*v.t.* limiter. **~ed company**, société anonyme *f.* **~ation** /-'teɪʃn/ *n.* limitation *f.* **~less** *a.* sans limites.

limousine /'lɪməziːn/ *n.* (*car*) limousine *f.*

limp[1] /lɪmp/ *v.i.* boiter. —*n.* **have a ~**, boiter.

limp[2] /lɪmp/ *a.* (**-er, -est**) mou.

limpid /'lɪmpɪd/ *a.* limpide.

linctus /'lɪŋktəs/ *n.* sirop *m.*

line[1] /laɪn/ *n.* ligne *f.*; (*track*) voie *f.*; (*wrinkle*) ride *f.*; (*row*) rangée *f.*, file *f.*; (*of poem*) vers *m.*; (*rope*) corde *f.*; (*of goods*) gamme *f.*; (*queue: Amer.*) queue *f.* —*v.t.* (*paper*) régler; (*streets etc.*) border. **be in ~ for**, avoir de bonnes chances d'avoir. **in ~ with**, en accord avec. **stand in ~**, faire la queue. **~ up**, (s')aligner; (*in queue*) faire la queue. **~ sth. up**, prévoir qch.

line[2] /laɪn/ *v.t.* (*garment*) doubler; (*fill*) remplir, garnir.

lineage /'lɪnɪɪdʒ/ *n.* lignée *f.*

linear /'lɪnɪə(r)/ *a.* linéaire.

linen /'lɪnɪn/ *n.* (*sheets etc.*) linge *m.*; (*material*) lin *m.*, toile de lin *f.*

liner /'laɪnə(r)/ *n.* paquebot *m.*

linesman /'laɪnzmən/ *n.* (*football*) juge de touche *m.*

linger /'lɪŋgə(r)/ *v.i.* s'attarder; (*smells etc.*) persister.

lingerie /'lænʒərɪ/ *n.* lingerie *f.*

lingo /'lɪŋgəʊ/ *n.* (*pl.* **-os**) (*hum.*, *fam.*) jargon *m.*

linguist /'lɪŋgwɪst/ *n.* linguiste *m./f.*

linguistic /lɪŋ'gwɪstɪk/ *a.* linguistique. **~s** *n.* linguistique *f.*

lining /'laɪnɪŋ/ *n.* doublure *f.*

link /lɪŋk/ *n.* lien *m.*; (*of chain*) maillon *m.* —*v.t.* relier; (*relate*) (re)lier. **~ up**, (*of roads*) se rejoindre. **~age** *n.* lien *m.* **~-up** *n.* liaison *f.*

links /lɪŋks/ *n. invar.* terrain de golf *m.*

lino /'laɪnəʊ/ *n.* (*pl.* **-os**) lino *m.*

linoleum /lɪ'nəʊlɪəm/ *n.* linoléum *m.*

lint /lɪnt/ *n.* (*med.*) tissu ouaté *m.*; (*fluff*) peluche(s) *f.* (*pl.*).

lion /'laɪən/ *n.* lion *m.* **take the ~'s share**, se tailler la part du lion. **~ess** *n.* lionne *f.*

lip /lɪp/ *n.* lèvre *f.*; (*edge*) rebord *m.* **~-read** *v.t./i.* lire sur les lèvres. **pay ~-service to**, n'approuver que pour la forme.

lipsalve /'lɪpsælv/ *n.* baume pour les lèvres *m.*

lipstick /'lɪpstɪk/ *n.* rouge (à lèvres) *m.*

liquefy /'lɪkwɪfaɪ/ *v.t./i.* (se) liquéfier.

liqueur /lɪ'kjʊə(r)/ *n.* liqueur *f.*

liquid /'lɪkwɪd/ *n. & a.* liquide (*m.*). **~ize** *v.t.* passer au mixeur. **~izer** *n.* mixeur *m.*

liquidat|e /'lɪkwɪdeɪt/ v.t. liquider. ~ion /-'deɪʃn/ n. liquidation f. **go into ~ion,** déposer son bilan.

liquor /'lɪkə(r)/ n. alcool m.

liquorice /'lɪkərɪs/ n. réglisse f.

lira /'lɪərə/ n. (pl. **lire** /'lɪəreɪ/ or **liras**) lire f.

lisp /lɪsp/ n. zézaiement m. —v.i. zézayer. **with a ~,** en zézayant.

list[1] /lɪst/ n. liste f. —v.t. dresser la liste de.

list[2] /lɪst/ v.i. (ship) gîter.

listen /'lɪsn/ v.i. écouter. ~ **to,** ~ **in (to),** écouter. ~**er** n. auditeur, -trice m./f.

listless /'lɪstlɪs/ a. apathique.

lit /lɪt/ see **light**[1].

litany /'lɪtəni/ n. litanie f.

liter /'liːtə(r)/ see **litre**.

literal /'lɪtərəl/ a. littéral; (person) prosaïque. ~**ly** adv. littéralement.

literary /'lɪtərəri/ a. littéraire.

litera|te /'lɪtərət/ a. qui sait lire et écrire. ~**cy** n. capacité de lire et écrire f.

literature /'lɪtrətʃə(r)/ n. littérature f.; (fig.) documentation f.

lithe /laɪð/ a. souple, agile.

litigation /lɪtɪ'geɪʃn/ n. litige m.

litre, (Amer.) **liter** /'liːtə(r)/ n. litre m.

litter /'lɪtə(r)/ n. détritus m. pl., papiers m. pl.; (animals) portée f. —v.t. éparpiller; (make untidy) laisser des détritus dans. ~ **bin** n. poubelle f. ~**ed with,** jonché de.

little /'lɪtl/ a. petit; (not much) peu de. —n. peu m. —adv. peu. **a ~,** un peu (de).

liturgy /'lɪtədʒɪ/ n. liturgie f.

live[1] /laɪv/ a. vivant; (wire) sous tension; (broadcast) en direct. **be a ~ wire,** être très dynamique.

live[2] /lɪv/ v.t./i. vivre; (reside) habiter, vivre. ~ **down,** faire oublier. ~ **it up,** mener la belle vie. ~ **on,** (feed o.s. on) vivre de; (continue) survivre. ~ **up to,** se montrer à la hauteur de.

livelihood /'laɪvlɪhʊd/ n. moyens d'existence m. pl.

livel|y /'laɪvlɪ/ a. (-**ier, -iest**) vif, vivant. ~**iness** n. vivacité f.

liven /'laɪvn/ v.t./i. ~ **up,** (s')animer; (cheer up) (s')égayer.

liver /'lɪvə(r)/ n. foie m.

livery /'lɪvərɪ/ n. livrée f.

livestock /'laɪvstɒk/ n. bétail m.

livid /'lɪvɪd/ a. livide; (angry: fam.) furieux.

living /'lɪvɪŋ/ a. vivant. —n. vie f. **make a ~,** gagner sa vie. ~ **conditions,**

conditions de vie f. pl. ~**-room** n. salle de séjour f.

lizard /'lɪzəd/ n. lézard m.

llama /'lɑːmə/ n. lama m.

load /ləʊd/ n. charge f.; (loaded goods) chargement m., charge f.; (weight, strain) poids m. ~**s of,** (fam.) des masses de. —v.t. charger. ~**ed** a. (dice) pipé; (wealthy: sl.) riche.

loaf[1] /ləʊf/ n. (pl. **loaves**) pain m.

loaf[2] /ləʊf/ v.i. ~ **(about),** fainéanter. ~**er** n. fainéant(e) m. (f.).

loam /ləʊm/ n. terreau m.

loan /ləʊn/ n. prêt m.; (money borrowed) emprunt m. —v.t. (lend: fam.) prêter.

loath /ləʊθ/ a. peu disposé **(to, à).**

loath|e /ləʊð/ v.t. détester. ~**ing** n. dégoût m. ~**some** a. dégoûtant.

lobby /'lɒbɪ/ n. entrée f., vestibule m.; (pol.) lobby m., groupe de pression m. —v.t. faire pression sur.

lobe /ləʊb/ n. lobe m.

lobster /'lɒbstə(r)/ n. homard m.

local /'ləʊkl/ a. local; (shops etc.) du quartier. —n. personne du coin f.; (pub: fam.) pub du coin m. ~ **government,** administration locale f. ~**ly** adv. localement; (nearby) dans les environs.

locale /ləʊ'kɑːl/ n. lieu m.

locality /ləʊ'kælətɪ/ n. (district) région f.; (position) lieu m.

localized /'ləʊkəlaɪzd/ a. localisé.

locat|e /ləʊ'keɪt/ v.t. (situate) situer; (find) repérer. ~**ion** /-ʃn/ n. emplacement m. **on ~ion,** (cinema) en extérieur.

lock[1] /lɒk/ n. mèche (de cheveux) f.

lock[2] /lɒk/ n. (of door etc.) serrure f.; (on canal) écluse f. —v.t./i. fermer à clef; (wheels; auto.) (se) bloquer. ~ **in** or **up,** (person) enfermer. ~ **out,** (by mistake) enfermer dehors. ~**-out** n. lockout m. invar. ~**-up** n. (shop) boutique f.; (garage) box m.

locker /'lɒkə(r)/ n. casier m.

locket /'lɒkɪt/ n. médaillon m.

locksmith /'lɒksmɪθ/ n. serrurier m.

locomotion /ləʊkə'məʊʃn/ n. locomotion f.

locomotive /'ləʊkəməʊtɪv/ n. locomotive f.

locum /'ləʊkəm/ n. (doctor etc.) remplaçant(e) m. (f.).

locust /'ləʊkəst/ n. criquet m., sauterelle f.

lodge /lɒdʒ/ n. (house) pavillon (de gardien or de chasse) m.; (of porter) loge f. —v.t. loger; (money, complaint) déposer. —v.i. être logé **(with,** chez);

(*become fixed*) se loger. ∼r /-ə(r)/ n.
locataire m./f., pensionnaire m./f.
lodgings /'lɒdʒɪŋz/ n. chambre
(meublée) f.; (*flat*) logement m.
loft /lɒft/ n. grenier m.
lofty /'lɒftɪ/ a. (**-ier, -iest**) (*tall, noble*)
élevé; (*haughty*) hautain.
log /lɒg/ n. (*of wood*) bûche f. ∼(-**book**),
(*naut.*) journal de bord m.; (*auto.*)
(*équivalent de la*) carte grise f. —v.t.
(*p.t.* **logged**) noter; (*distance*) parcourir. ∼ **on**, entrer. ∼ **off**, sortir.
logarithm /'lɒgərɪðəm/ n. logarithme m.
loggerheads /'lɒgəhedz/ n. pl. **at** ∼, en
désaccord.
logic /'lɒdʒɪk/ a. logique. ∼**al** a. logique.
∼**ally** adv. logiquement.
logistics /lə'dʒɪstɪks/ n. logistique f.
logo /'ləʊgəʊ/ n. (pl. **-os**) (*fam.*)
emblème m.
loin /lɔɪn/ n. (*culin.*) filet m. ∼**s**, reins m.
pl.
loiter /'lɔɪtə(r)/ v.i. traîner.
loll /lɒl/ v.i. se prélasser.
lollipop /'lɒlɪpɒp/ n. sucette f. ∼**y** n.
(*fam.*) sucette f.; (*sl.*) fric m.
London /'lʌndən/ n. Londres m./f. ∼**er**
n. Londonien(ne) m. (f.).
lone /ləʊn/ a. solitaire. ∼**r** /-ə(r)/ n.
solitaire m./f. ∼**some** a. solitaire.
lonely /'ləʊnlɪ/ a. (**-ier, -iest**) solitaire;
(*person*) seul, solitaire.
long¹ /lɒŋ/ a. (**-er, -est**) long. —adv.
longtemps. **how** ∼ **is?**, quelle est la
longueur de?; (*in time*) quelle est la
durée de? **how** ∼**?**, combien de temps?
he will not be ∼, il n'en a pas pour
longtemps. **a** ∼ **time**, longtemps. **as** ∼
so ∼ **as**, pourvu que. **before** ∼, avant
peu. **I no** ∼**er do**, je ne fais plus. ∼-
distance a. (*flight*) sur long parcours;
(*phone call*) interurbain. ∼ **face**,
grimace f. ∼ **johns**, (*fam.*) caleçon
long m. ∼ **jump**, saut en longueur m.
∼-**playing record**, microsillon m. ∼-
range a. à longue portée; (*forecast*) à
long terme. ∼-**sighted** a. presbyte. ∼-
standing a. de longue date. ∼-
suffering a. très patient. ∼-**term** a. à
long terme. ∼ **wave**, grandes ondes f.
pl. ∼-**winded** a. (*speaker etc.*)
verbeux.
long² /lɒŋ/ v.i. avoir bien or très envie
(**for, to**, de). ∼ **for s.o.**, (*pine for*)
languir après qn. ∼**ing** n. envie f.;
(*nostalgia*) nostalgie f.
longevity /lɒn'dʒevətɪ/ n. longévité f.
longhand /'lɒŋhænd/ n. écriture
courante f.

longitude /'lɒndʒɪtjuːd/ n. longitude f.
loo /luː/ n. (*fam.*) toilettes f. pl.
look /lʊk/ v.t./i. regarder; (*seem*) avoir
l'air. —n. regard m.; (*appearance*) air
m., aspect m. (**good**) ∼**s**, beauté f. ∼
after, s'occuper de, soigner. ∼ **at**,
regarder. ∼ **back on**, repenser à. ∼
down on, mépriser. ∼ **for**, chercher. ∼
forward to, attendre avec impatience.
∼ **in on**, passer voir. ∼ **into**, examiner.
∼ **like**, ressembler à, avoir l'air de. ∼
out, faire attention. ∼ **out for**,
chercher; (*watch*) guetter. ∼-**out** n.
(*mil.*) poste de guet m.; (*person*)
guetteur m. **be on the** ∼-**out for**,
rechercher. ∼ **round**, se retourner. ∼
up, (*word*) chercher; (*visit*) passer voir.
∼ **up to**, respecter. ∼-**alike** n. sosie m.
∼**ing-glass** n. glace f.
loom¹ /luːm/ n. métier à tisser m.
loom² /luːm/ v.i. surgir; (*event etc.: fig.*)
paraître imminent.
loony /'luːnɪ/ n. & a. (*sl.*) fou, folle (m.,
f.).
loop /luːp/ n. boucle f. —v.t. boucler.
loophole /'luːphəʊl/ n. (*in rule*)
échappatoire f.
loose /luːs/ a. (**-er, -est**) (*knot etc.*)
desserré; (*page etc.*) détaché; (*clothes*)
ample, lâche; (*tooth*) qui bouge; (*lax*)
relâché; (*not packed*) en vrac; (*inexact*)
vague; (*pej.*) immoral. **at a** ∼ **end**,
(*Amer.*) **at** ∼ **ends**, désœuvré. **come** ∼,
bouger. ∼**ly** adv. sans serrer; (*roughly*)
vaguement.
loosen /'luːsn/ v.t. (*slacken*) desserrer;
(*untie*) défaire.
loot /luːt/ n. butin m. —v.t. piller. ∼**er** n.
pillard(e) m. (f.). ∼**ing** n. pillage m.
lop /lɒp/ v.t. (*p.t.* **lopped**) ∼ **off**, couper.
lop-sided /lɒp'saɪdɪd/ a. de travers.
lord /lɔːd/ n. seigneur m.; (*British title*)
lord m. **the L**∼, le Seigneur. (**good**)
L∼**!**, mon Dieu! ∼**ly** a. noble;
(*haughty*) hautain.
lore /lɔː(r)/ n. traditions f. pl.
lorry /'lɒrɪ/ n. camion m.
lose /luːz/ v.t./i. (*p.t.* **lost**) perdre. **get**
lost, se perdre. ∼**r** /-ə(r)/ n. perdant(e)
m. (f.).
loss /lɒs/ n. perte f. **be at a** ∼, être
perplexe. **be at a** ∼ **to**, être incapable
de. **heat** ∼, déperdition de chaleur f.
lost /lɒst/ see **lose**. —a. perdu. ∼
property, (*Amer.*) ∼ **and found**, objets
trouvés m. pl.
lot¹ /lɒt/ n. (*fate*) sort m.; (*at auction*) lot
m.; (*land*) lotissement m.
lot² /lɒt/ n. **the** ∼, (le) tout m.; (*people*)

tous *m. pl.*, toutes *f. pl.* **a** ∼ **(of)**, ∼**s**
(of), (*fam.*) beaucoup (de). **quite a** ∼
(of), (*fam.*) pas mal (de).
lotion /'ləʊʃn/ *n.* lotion *f.*
lottery /'lɒtəri/ *n.* loterie *f.*
loud /laʊd/ *a.* (**-er, -est**) bruyant, fort.
—*adv.* fort. ∼ **hailer**, portevoix *m.*
invar. **out** ∼, tout haut. ∼**ly** *adv.* fort.
loudspeaker /laʊd'spiːkə(r)/ *n.* haut-
parleur *m.*
lounge /laʊndʒ/ *v.i.* paresser. —*n.* salon
m. ∼ **suit**, costume *m.*
louse /laʊs/ *n.* (*pl.* **lice**) pou *m.*
lousy /'laʊzi/ *a.* (**-ier, -iest**) pouilleux;
(*bad: sl.*) infect.
lout /laʊt/ *n.* rustre *m.*
lovable /'lʌvəbl/ *a.* adorable.
love /lʌv/ *n.* amour *m.*; (*tennis*) zéro *m.*
—*v.t.* aimer; (*like greatly*) aimer
(beaucoup) (**to do**, faire). **in** ∼,
amoureux (**with**, de). ∼ **affair**, liaison
amoureuse *f.* ∼ **life**, vie amoureuse *f.*
make ∼, faire l'amour.
lovely /'lʌvli/ *a.* (**-ier, -iest**) joli,
(*delightful: fam.*) très agréable.
lover /'lʌvə(r)/ *n.* amant *m.*, (*devotee*)
amateur *m.* (**of**, de).
lovesick /'lʌvsɪk/ *a.* amoureux.
loving /'lʌvɪŋ/ *a.* affectueux.
low¹ /ləʊ/ *v.i.* meugler.
low² /ləʊ/ *a. & adv.* (**-er, -est**) bas. —*n.*
(*low pressure*) dépression *f.* **reach a**
(new) ∼, atteindre son niveau le plus
bas. ∼ **in sth.**, à faible teneur en qch. ∼-
calorie *a.* basses-calories. ∼**-cut** *a.*
décolleté. ∼**-down** *a.* méprisable; *n.*
(*fam.*) renseignements *m. pl.* ∼**-fat** *a.*
maigre. ∼**-key** *a.* modéré; (*discreet*)
discret. ∼**-lying** *a.* à faible altitude.
lowbrow /'ləʊbraʊ/ *a.* peu intellectuel.
lower /'ləʊə(r)/ *a & adv. see* **low**². —*v.t.*
baisser. ∼ **o.s.**, s'abaisser.
lowlands /'ləʊləndz/ *n. pl.* plaine(s) *f.*
(*pl.*).
lowly /'ləʊli/ *a.* (**-ier, -iest**) humble.
loyal /'lɔɪəl/ *a.* loyal. ∼**ly** *adv.*
loyalement. ∼**ty** *n.* loyauté *f.*
lozenge /'lɒzɪndʒ/ *n.* (*shape*) losange *m.*;
(*tablet*) pastille *f.*
LP *abbr. see* **long-playing record**.
Ltd. *abbr.* (*Limited*) SA.
lubric|ate /'luːbrɪkeɪt/ *v.t.* graisser,
lubrifier. ∼**ant** *n.* lubrifiant *m.* ∼**ation**
/-'keɪʃn/ *n.* graissage *m.*
lucid /'luːsɪd/ *a.* lucide. ∼**ity** /luː'sɪdəti/
n. lucidité *f.*
luck /lʌk/ *n.* chance *f.* **bad** ∼, malchance
f. **good** ∼!, bonne chance!
luck|y /'lʌki/ *a.* (**-ier, -iest**) qui a de la

chance, heureux; (*event*) heureux;
(*number*) qui porte bonheur. **it's** ∼**y**
that, c'est une chance que. ∼**ily** *adv.*
heureusement.
lucrative /'luːkrətɪv/ *a.* lucratif.
ludicrous /'luːdɪkrəs/ *a.* ridicule.
lug /lʌg/ *v.t.* (*p.t.* **lugged**) traîner.
luggage /'lʌgɪdʒ/ *n.* bagages *m. pl.* ∼-
rack *n.* porte-bagages *m. invar.*
lukewarm /'luːkwɔːm/ *a.* tiède.
lull /lʌl/ *v.t.* (*soothe, send to sleep*)
endormir. —*n.* accalmie *f.*
lullaby /'lʌləbaɪ/ *n.* berceuse *f.*
lumbago /lʌm'beɪgəʊ/ *n.* lumbago *m.*
lumber /'lʌmbə(r)/ *n.* bric-à-brac *m.*
invar.; (*wood*) bois de charpente *m.*
—*v.t.* ∼ **s.o. with**, (*chore etc.*) coller à
qn.
lumberjack /'lʌmbədʒæk/ *n.* (*Amer.*)
bûcheron *m.*
luminous /'luːmɪnəs/ *a.* lumineux.
lump /lʌmp/ *n.* morceau *m.*; (*swelling on
body*) grosseur *f.*; (*in liquid*) grumeau
m. —*v.t.* ∼ **together**, réunir. ∼ **sum**,
somme globale *f.* ∼**y** *a.* (*sauce*)
grumeleux, (*bumpy*) bosselé.
lunacy /'luːnəsi/ *n.* folie *f.*
lunar /'luːnə(r)/ *a.* lunaire.
lunatic /'luːnətɪk/ *n.* fou, folle *m.*, *f.*
lunch /lʌntʃ/ *n.* déjeuner *m.* —*v.i.*
déjeuner. ∼ **box**, cantine *f.*
luncheon /'lʌntʃən/ *n.* déjeuner *m.* ∼
meat, (*approx.*) saucisson *m.* ∼
voucher, chèque-repas *m.*
lung /lʌŋ/ *n.* poumon *m.*
lunge /lʌndʒ/ *n.* mouvement brusque en
avant *m.* —*v.i.* s'élancer (**at**, sur).
lurch¹ /lɜːtʃ/ *n.* **leave in the** ∼, planter
là, laisser en plan.
lurch² /lɜːtʃ/ *v.i.* (*person*) tituber.
lure /lʊə(r)/ *v.t.* appâter, attirer. —*n.*
(*attraction*) attrait *m.*, appât *m.*
lurid /'lʊərɪd/ *a.* choquant, affreux;
(*gaudy*) voyant.
lurk /lɜːk/ *v.i.* se cacher; (*in ambush*)
s'embusquer; (*prowl*) rôder. **a** ∼**ing**
suspicion, un petit soupçon.
luscious /'lʌʃəs/ *a.* appétissant.
lush /lʌʃ/ *a.* luxuriant. —*n.* (*Amer.,
fam.*) ivrogne(sse) *m.* (*f.*).
lust /lʌst/ *n.* luxure *f.*; (*fig.*) convoitise *f.*
—*v.i.* ∼ **after**, convoiter.
lustre /'lʌstə(r)/ *n.* lustre *m.*
lusty /'lʌsti/ *a.* (**-ier, -iest**) robuste.
lute /luːt/ *n.* (*mus.*) luth *m.*
Luxemburg /'lʌksəmbɜːg/ *n.* Luxembourg *m.*
luxuriant /lʌg'zʊəriənt/ *a.* luxuriant.
luxurious /lʌg'zʊəriəs/ *a.* luxueux.

luxury /'lʌkʃərɪ/ n. luxe m. —a. de luxe.
lying /'laɪɪŋ/ see **lie¹**, **lie²**. —n. le mensonge m.
lynch /lɪntʃ/ v.t. lyncher.
lynx /lɪŋks/ n. lynx m.
lyric /'lɪrɪk/ a. lyrique. ⁓s n. pl. paroles f. pl. ⁓**al** a. lyrique. ⁓**ism** /-sɪzəm/ n. lyrisme m.

M

MA abbr. see **Master of Arts**.
mac /mæk/ n. (fam.) imper m.
macaroni /mækə'rəʊnɪ/ n. macaronis m. pl.
macaroon /mækə'ru:n/ n. macaron m.
mace /meɪs/ n. (staff) masse f.
Mach /mɑːk/ n. ⁓ (**number**), (nombre de) Mach m.
machiavellian /mækɪə'velɪən/ a. machiavélique.
machinations /mækɪ'neɪʃnz/ n. pl. machinations f. pl.
machine /mə'ʃiːn/ n. machine f. —v.t. (sew) coudre à la machine; (techn.) usiner. ⁓ **code**, code machine m. ⁓**gun** n. mitrailleuse f.; v.t. (p.t. -**gunned**) mitrailler. ⁓**-readable** a. en langage machine. ⁓ **tool**, machine-outil f.
machinery /mə'ʃiːnərɪ/ n. machinerie f.; (working parts & fig.) mécanisme(s) m. (pl.).
machinist /mə'ʃiːnɪst/ n. (operator) opéralteur, -trice sur machine m., f.; (on sewing-machine) piqueulr, -se m., f.
macho /'mætʃəʊ/ n. (pl. -**os**) macho m. —a. macho invar.
mackerel /'mækrəl/ n. invar. (fish) maquereau m.
mackintosh /'mækɪntɒʃ/ n. imperméable m.
macrobiotic /mækrəʊbaɪ'ɒtɪk/ a. macrobiotique.
mad /mæd/ a. (**madder, maddest**) fou; (foolish) insensé; (dog etc.) enragé; (angry: fam.) furieux. **be ⁓ about**, se passionner pour; (person) être fou de. **drive s.o. ⁓**, exaspérer qn. **like ⁓**, comme un fou. ⁓**ly** adv. (interested, in love, etc.) follement; (frantically) comme un fou. ⁓**ness** n. folie f.
Madagascar /mædə'gæskə(r)/ n. Madagascar f.
madam /'mædəm/ n. madame f.; (unmarried) mademoiselle f.

madden /'mædn/ v.t. exaspérer.
made /meɪd/ see **make**. ⁓ **to measure**, fait sur mesure.
Madeira /mə'dɪərə/ n. (wine) madère m.
madhouse /'mædhaʊs/ n. (fam.) maison de fous f.
madman /'mædmən/ n. (pl. -**men**) fou m.
madrigal /'mædrɪgl/ n. madrigal m.
magazine /mægə'ziːn/ n. revue f., magazine m.; (of gun) magasin m.
magenta /mə'dʒentə/ a. magenta (invar.).
maggot /'mægət/ n. ver m., asticot m. ⁓**y** a. véreux.
magic /'mædʒɪk/ n. magie f. —a. magique. ⁓**al** a. magique.
magician /mə'dʒɪʃn/ n. magicien(ne) m. (f.).
magistrate /'mædʒɪstreɪt/ n. magistrat m.
magnanim|ous /mæg'nænɪməs/ a. magnanime. ⁓**ity** /-ə'nɪmətɪ/ n. magnanimité f.
magnate /'mægneɪt/ n. magnat m.
magnesia /mæg'niːʃə/ n. magnésie f.
magnet /'mægnɪt/ n. aimant m. ⁓**ic** /-'netɪk/ a. magnétique. ⁓**ism** /-ɪzəm/ n. magnétisme m. ⁓**ize** v.t. magnétiser.
magneto /mæg'niːtəʊ/ n. (pl. **os**) magnéto m.
magnificen|t /mæg'nɪfɪsnt/ a. magnifique. ⁓**ce** n. magnificence f.
magnif|y /'mægnɪfaɪ/ v.t. grossir; (sound) amplifier; (fig.) exagérer. ⁓**ication** /-ɪ'keɪʃn/ n. grossissement m.; amplification f. ⁓**ier** n., ⁓**ying glass**, loupe f.
magnitude /'mægnɪtjuːd/ n. (importance) ampleur f.; (size) grandeur f.
magnolia /mæg'nəʊlɪə/ n. magnolia m.
magnum /'mægnəm/ n. magnum m.
magpie /'mægpaɪ/ n. pie f.
mahogany /mə'hɒgənɪ/ n. acajou m.
maid /meɪd/ n. (servant) bonne f.; (girl: old use) jeune fille f.
maiden /'meɪdn/ n. (old use) jeune fille f. —a. (aunt) célibataire; (voyage) premier. ⁓ **name**, nom de jeune fille m. ⁓**hood** n. virginité f. ⁓**ly** a. virginal.
mail¹ /meɪl/ n. poste f.; (letters) courrier m. —a. (bag, van) postal. —v.t. envoyer par la poste. **mail box**, boîte à lettres f. ⁓**ing list**, liste d'adresses f. ⁓ **order**, vente par correspondance f. ⁓ **shot**, publipostage m.
mail² /meɪl/ n. (armour) cotte de mailles f.

mailman /ˈmeɪlmæn/ n. (pl. **-men**) (*Amer.*) facteur m.

maim /meɪm/ v.t. mutiler.

main[1] /meɪn/ a. principal. —n. **in the ~,** en général. **~ line,** grande ligne f. **a ~ road,** une grande route. **~ly** adv. principalement, surtout.

main[2] /meɪn/ n. (**water/gas**) **~,** conduite d'eau/de gaz f. **the ~s,** (*electr.*) le secteur.

mainframe n. unité centrale f.

mainland /ˈmeɪnlənd/ n. continent m.

mainspring /ˈmeɪnsprɪŋ/ n. ressort principal m.; (*motive: fig.*) mobile principal m.

mainstay /ˈmeɪnsteɪ/ n. soutien m.

mainstream /ˈmeɪnstriːm/ n. tendance principale f., ligne f.

maintain /meɪnˈteɪn/ v.t. (*continue, keep, assert*) maintenir; (*house, machine, family*) entretenir; (*rights*) soutenir.

maintenance /ˈmeɪntənəns/ n. (*care*) entretien m.; (*continuation*) maintien m.; (*allowance*) pension alimentaire f.

maisonette /meɪzəˈnet/ n. duplex m.

maize /meɪz/ n. maïs m.

majestic /məˈdʒestɪk/ a. majestueux.

majesty /ˈmædʒəstɪ/ n. majesté f.

major /ˈmeɪdʒə(r)/ a. majeur —n. commandant m. —v.i. **~ in,** (*univ., Amer.*) se spécialiser en. **~ road,** route à priorité f.

Majorca /məˈdʒɔːkə/ n. Majorque f.

majority /məˈdʒɒrətɪ/ n. majorité f. —a. majoritaire. **the ~ of people,** la plupart des gens.

make /meɪk/ v.t./i. (*p.t.* **made**) faire; (*manufacture*) fabriquer; (*friends*) se faire; (*money*) gagner; se faire; (*decision*) prendre; (*destination*) arriver à; (*cause to be*) rendre. **~ s.o. do sth.,** faire faire qch. à qn.; (*force*) obliger qn. à faire qch. —n. fabrication f.; (*brand*) marque f. **be made of,** être fait de. **~ o.s. at home,** se mettre à l'aise. **~ s.o. happy,** rendre qn. heureux. **~ it,** arriver; (*succeed*) réussir. **I ~ it two o'clock,** j'ai deux heures. **I ~ it 150,** d'après moi, ça fait 150. **I cannot ~ anything of it,** je n'y comprends rien. **can you ~ Friday?,** vendredi, c'est possible? **~ as if to,** faire mine de. **~ believe,** faire semblant. **~ believe,** a. feint, illusoire; n. fantaisie f. **~ do,** (*manage*) se débrouiller (**with,** avec). **~ do with,** (*content o.s.*) se contenter de. **~ for,** se diriger vers; (*cause*) tendre à créer. **~**

good v.i. réussir; v.t. compenser; (*repair*) réparer. **~ off,** filer (**with,** avec). **~ out** v.t. distinguer; (*understand*) comprendre; (*draw up*) faire; (*assert*) prétendre; v.i. (*fam.*) se débrouiller. **~ over,** céder (**to,** à); (*convert*) transformer. **~ up** v.t. faire, former; (*story*) inventer; (*deficit*) combler; v.i. se réconcilier. **~ up (one's face),** se maquiller. **~-up** n. maquillage m.; (*of object*) constitution f.; (*psych.*) caractère m. **~ up for,** compenser; (*time*) rattraper. **~ up one's mind,** se décider. **~ up to,** se concilier les bonnes grâces de.

maker /ˈmeɪkə(r)/ n. fabricant m.

makeshift /ˈmeɪkʃɪft/ n. expédient m. —a. provisoire.

making /ˈmeɪkɪŋ/ n. **be the ~ of,** faire le succès de. **he has the ~s of,** il a l'étoffe de.

maladjusted /mæləˈdʒʌstɪd/ a. inadapte.

maladministration /mælədmɪnɪˈstreɪ-ʃn/ n. mauvaise gestion f.

malaise /mæˈleɪz/ n. malaise m.

malaria /məˈleərɪə/ n. malaria f.

Malay /məˈleɪ/ a. & n. malais(e) (m. (f.)). **~sia** n. Malaysia f.

Malaya /məˈleɪə/ n. Malaisie f.

male /meɪl/ a. (*voice, sex*) masculin; (*bot., techn.*) mâle. **~** n. mâle m.

malevolen|t /məˈlevələnt/ a. malveillant. **~ce** n. malveillance f.

malform|ation /mælfɔːˈmeɪʃn/ n. malformation f. **~ed** a. difforme.

malfunction /mælˈfʌŋkʃn/ n. mauvais fonctionnement m. —v.i. mal fonctionner.

malice /ˈmælɪs/ n. méchanceté f.

malicious /məˈlɪʃəs/ a. méchant. **~ly** adv. méchamment.

malign /məˈlaɪn/ a. pernicieux. —v.t. calomnier.

malignan|t /məˈlɪɡnənt/ a. malveillant; (*tumour*) malin. **~cy** n. malveillance f.; malignité f.

malinger /məˈlɪŋɡə(r)/ v.i. feindre la maladie. **~er** n. simulateur, -trice m., f.

mall /mɔːl/ n. (**shopping**) **~,** centre commercial m.

malleable /ˈmælɪəbl/ a. malléable.

mallet /ˈmælɪt/ n. maillet m.

malnutrition /mælnjuːˈtrɪʃn/ n. sous-alimentation f.

malpractice /mælˈpræktɪs/ n. faute professionnelle f.

malt /mɔːlt/ n. malt m. **~ whisky,** whisky pur malt m.

Malt|a /'mɔːltə/ n. Malte f. **~ese** /-'tiːz/ a. & n. maltais(e) (m. (f.)).

maltreat /mæl'triːt/ v.t. maltraiter. **~ment** n. mauvais traitement m.

mammal /'mæml/ n. mammifère m.

mammoth /'mæməθ/ n. mammouth m. —a. monstre.

man /mæn/ n. (pl. **men**) homme m.; (in sports team) joueur m.; (chess) pièce f. —v.t. (p.t. **manned**) pourvoir en hommes; (ship) armer; (guns) servir; (be on duty at) être de service à **~-hour** n. heure de main-d'œuvre f. **~ in the street**, homme de la rue m. **~-made** a. artificiel. **~-sized** a. grand. **~ to man**, d'homme à homme. **~ned space flight**, vol spatial habité m.

manage /'mænɪdʒ/ v.t. diriger; (shop, affairs) gérer; (handle) manier. **I could ~ another drink**, (fam.) je prendrais bien encore un verre. **can you ~ Friday?**, vendredi, c'est possible? —v.i. se débrouiller. **~ to do**, reussir à faire. **~able** a. (tool, size, person, etc.) maniable; (job) faisable. **~ment** n. direction f.; (of shop) gestion f. **managing director**, directeur général m.

manager /'mænɪdʒə(r)/ n. direc|teur, -trice m.f.; (of shop) gérant(e) m.(f.); (of actor) impresario m. **~ess** /-'res/ n. directrice f.; gérante f. **~ial** /-'dʒɪərɪəl/ a. directorial. **~ial staff**, cadres m. pl.

mandarin /'mændərɪn/ n. mandarin m.; (orange) mandarine f.

mandate /'mændeɪt/ n. mandat m.

mandatory /'mændətrɪ/ a. obligatoire.

mane /meɪn/ n. crinière f.

manful /'mænfl/ a. courageux.

manganese /mæŋgə'niːz/ n. manganèse m.

mangetout /mɑnʒ'tuː/ n. mange-tout m. invar.

mangle[1] /'mæŋgl/ n. (for wringing) essoreuse f.; (for smoothing) calandre f.

mangle[2] /'mæŋgl/ v.t. mutiler.

mango /'mæŋgəʊ/ n. (pl. **-oes**) mangue f.

manhandle /'mænhændl/ v.t. maltraiter, malmener.

manhole /'mænhəʊl/ n. trou d'homme m., regard m.

manhood /'mænhʊd/ n. âge d'homme m.; (quality) virilité f.

mania /'meɪnɪə/ n. manie f. **~c** /-ɪæk/ n. maniaque m./f., fou m., folle f.

manic-depressive /'mænɪkdɪ'presɪv/ a & n. maniaco-dépressif(-ive) (m. (f.)).

manicur|e /'mænɪkjʊə(r)/ n. soin des mains m. —v.t. soigner, manucurer. **~ist** n. manucure m./f.

manifest /'mænɪfest/ a. manifeste. —v.t. manifester. **~ation** /-'steɪʃn/ n. manifestation f.

manifesto /mænɪ'festəʊ/ n. (pl. **-os**) manifeste m.

manifold /'mænɪfəʊld/ a. multiple. —n. (auto.) collecteur m.

manipulat|e /mə'nɪpjʊleɪt/ v.t. (tool, person) manipuler. **~ion** /-'leɪʃn/ n. manipulation f.

mankind /mæn'kaɪnd/ n. genre humain m.

manly /'mænlɪ/ a. viril.

manner /'mænə(r)/ n. manière f.; (attitude) attitude f.; (kind) sorte f. **~s**, (social behaviour) manières f. pl. **~ed** a. maniéré.

mannerism /'mænərɪzəm/ n. trait particulier m.

manœuvre /mə'nuːvə(r)/ n. manœuvre f. —v.t./i. manœuvrer.

manor /'mænə(r)/ n. manoir m.

manpower /'mænpaʊə(r)/ n. main-d'œuvre f.

manservant /'mænsɜːvənt/ n. (pl. **menservants**) domestique m.

mansion /'mænʃn/ n. château m.

manslaughter /'mænslɔːtə(r)/ n. homicide involontaire m.

mantelpiece /'mæntlpiːs/ n. (shelf) cheminée f.

manual /'mænjʊəl/ a. manuel. —n. (handbook) manuel m.

manufacture /mænjʊ'fæktʃə(r)/ v.t. fabriquer. —n. fabrication f. **~r** /-ə(r)/ n. fabricant m.

manure /mə'njʊə(r)/ n. fumier m.; (artificial) engrais m.

manuscript /'mænjʊskrɪpt/ n. manuscrit m.

many /'menɪ/ a. & n. beaucoup (de). **a great or good ~**, un grand nombre (de). **~ a**, bien des.

Maori /'maʊrɪ/ a. maori. —n. Maori(e) m. (f.).

map /mæp/ n. carte f.; (of streets etc.) plan m. —v.t. (p.t. **mapped**) faire la carte de. **~ out**, (route) tracer; (arrange) organiser.

maple /'meɪpl/ n. érable m.

mar /mɑː(r)/ v.t. (p.t. **marred**) gâter; (spoil beauty of) déparer.

marathon /'mærəθən/ n. marathon m.

marble /'mɑːbl/ n. marbre m.; (for game) bille f.

March /mɑːtʃ/ n. mars m.

march /mɑ:tʃ/ v.i. (*mil.*) marcher (au pas). ~ **off**/*etc.*, partir/*etc.* allégrement. —v.t. ~ **off**, (*lead away*) emmener. —n. marche f. ~**-past** n. défilé m.

mare /meə(r)/ n. jument f.

margarine /mɑ:dʒə'ri:n/ n. margarine f.

margin /'mɑ:dʒɪn/ n. marge f. ~**al** a. marginal; (*increase etc.*) léger, faible. ~**al seat**, (*pol.*) siège chaudement disputé m. ~**alize** v.t. marginaliser. ~**ally** adv. très légèrement.

marigold /'mærɪgəʊld/ n. souci m.

marijuana /mærɪ'wɑ:nə/ n. marijuana f.

marina /mə'ri:nə/ n. marina f.

marinate /'mærɪneɪt/ v.t. mariner.

marine /mə'ri:n/ a. marin. —n. (*shipping*) marine f.; (*sailor*) fusilier marin m.

marionette /mærɪə'net/ n. marionnette f.

marital /'mærɪtl/ a. conjugal. ~ **status**, situation de famille f.

maritime /'mærɪtaɪm/ a. maritime.

marjoram /'mɑ:dʒərəm/ n. marjolaine f.

mark[1] /mɑ:k/ n. (*currency*) mark m.

mark[2] /mɑ:k/ n. marque f.; (*trace*) trace f., marque f.; (*schol.*) note f.; (*target*) but m. —v.t. marquer; (*exam*) corriger. ~ **out**, délimiter; (*person*) désigner. ~ **time**, marquer le pas. ~**er** n. marque f. ~**ing** n. (*marks*) marques f.pl.

marked /mɑ:kt/ a. marqué. ~**ly**/-ɪdlɪ/ adv. visiblement.

market /'mɑ:kɪt/ n. marché m. —v.t. (*sell*) vendre; (*launch*) commercialiser. ~ **garden**, jardin maraîcher m. ~**place** n. marché m. ~ **research**, étude de marché f. ~ **value**, valeur marchande f. **on the** ~, en vente. ~**ing** n. marketing m.

marksman /'mɑ:ksmən/ n. (*pl.* -**men**) tireur d'élite m.

marmalade /'mɑ:məleɪd/ n. confiture d'oranges f.

maroon /mə'ru:n/ n. bordeaux m. invar. —a. bordeaux invar.

marooned /mə'ru:nd/ a. abandonné; (*snow-bound etc.*) bloqué.

marquee /mɑ:'ki:/ n. grande tente f.; (*awning: Amer.*) marquise f.

marquis /'mɑ:kwɪs/ n. marquis m.

marriage /'mærɪdʒ/ n. mariage m. ~**able** a. nubile, mariable.

marrow /'mærəʊ/ n. (*of bone*) moelle f.; (*vegetable*) courge f.

marr|**y** /'mærɪ/ v.t. épouser; (*give or unite in marriage*) marier. —v.i. se marier. ~**ied** a. marié; (*life*) conjugal. **get** ~**ied**, se marier (**to**, avec).

Mars /mɑ:z/ n. (*planet*) Mars f.

marsh /mɑ:ʃ/ n. marais m. ~**y** a. marécageux.

marshal /'mɑ:ʃl/ n. maréchal m.; (*at event*) membre du service d'ordre m. —v.t. (*p.t.* **marshalled**) rassembler.

marshmallow /mɑ:ʃ'mæləʊ/ n. guimauve f.

martial /'mɑ:ʃl/ a. martial. ~ **law**, loi martiale f.

martyr /'mɑ:tə(r)/ n. martyr(e) m. (f.). —v.t. martyriser. ~**dom** n. martyre m.

marvel /'mɑ:vl/ n. merveille f. —v.i. (*p.t.* **marvelled**) s'émerveiller (**at**, de).

marvellous /'mɑ:vələs/ a. merveilleux.

Marxis|**t** /'mɑ:ksɪst/ a. & n. marxiste (m./f.). ~**m** /-zəm/ n. marxisme m.

marzipan /'mɑ:zɪpæn/ n. pâte d'amandes f.

mascara /mæ'skɑ:rə/ n. mascara m.

mascot /'mæskət/ n. mascotte f.

masculin|**e** /'mæskjʊlɪn/ a. & n. masculin (m.). ~**ity** /-'lɪnɪtɪ/ n. masculinité f.

mash /mæʃ/ n. pâtée f.; (*potatoes: fam.*) purée f. —v.t. écraser. ~**ed potatoes**, purée (de pommes de terre) f.

mask /mɑ:sk/ n. masque m. —v.t. masquer.

masochis|**t** /'mæsəkɪst/ n. masochiste m./f. ~**m** /-zəm/ n. masochisme m.

mason /'meɪsn/ n. (*builder*) maçon m. ~**ry** n. maçonnerie f.

Mason /'meɪsn/ n. maçon m. ~**ic** /mə'sɒnɪk/ a. maçonnique.

masquerade /mɑ:skə'reɪd/ n. mascarade f. —v.i. ~ **as**, se faire passer pour.

mass[1] /mæs/ n. (*relig.*) messe f.

mass[2] /mæs/ n. masse f. v.t./i. (se) masser. ~**-produce** v.t. fabriquer en série. **the** ~**es**, les masses f.pl. **the** ~ **media**, les media m.pl.

massacre /'mæsəkə(r)/ n. massacre m. —v.t. massacrer.

massage /'mæsɑ:ʒ, *Amer.* mə'sɑ:ʒ/ n. massage m. —v.t. masser.

masseu|**r** /mæ'sɜ:(r)/ n. masseur m. ~**se** /-ɜ:z/ n. masseuse f.

massive /'mæsɪv/ a. (*large*) énorme; (*heavy*) massif.

mast /mɑ:st/ n. mât m.; (*for radio, TV*) pylône m.

master /'mɑ:stə(r)/ n. maître m.; (*in secondary school*) professeur m. —v.t. maîtriser. ~**-key** n. passe-partout m. invar. ~**-mind** n. (*of scheme etc.*) cerveau m.; v.t. diriger. **M**~ **of Arts**/*etc.*, titulaire d'une maîtrise ès lettres/*etc. m./f.* ~**-stroke** *n.* coup de maître *m.* ~**y** *n.* maîtrise *f.*

masterly /'mɑːstəlɪ/ *a.* magistral.

masterpiece /'mɑːstəpiːs/ *n.* chef-d'œuvre *m.*

mastiff /'mæstɪf/ *n.* dogue *m.*

masturbat|e /'mæstəbeɪt/ *v.i.* se masturber. ~**ion** /-'beɪʃn/ *n.* masturbation *f.*

mat /mæt/ *n.* (petit) tapis *m.*, natte *f.*; (*at door*) paillasson *m.*

match[1] /mætʃ/ *n.* allumette *f.*

match[2] /mætʃ/ *n.* (*sport*) match *m.*; (*equal*) égal(e) *m.* (*f.*); (*marriage*) mariage *m.*; (*s.o. to marry*) parti *m.* —*v.t.* opposer; (*go with*) aller avec; (*cups etc.*) assortir; (*equal*) égaler. **be a** ~ **for,** pouvoir tenir tête à. —*v.i.* (*be alike*) être assorti. ~**ing** *a.* assorti.

matchbox /'mætʃbɒks/ *n.* boîte à allumettes *f.*

mate[1] /meɪt/ *n.* camarade *m./f.*; (*of animal*) compagnon *m.*, compagne *f.*; (*assistant*) aide *m./f.* —*v.t./i.* (s')accoupler (**with,** avec).

mate[2] /meɪt/ *n.* (*chess*) mat *m.*

material /mə'tɪərɪəl/ *n.* matière *f.*; (*fabric*) tissu *m.*; (*documents, for building*) matériau(x) *m.* (*pl.*). ~**s,** (*equipment*) matériel *m.* —*a.* matériel; (*fig.*) important. ~**istic** /-'lɪstɪk/ *a.* matérialiste.

materialize /mə'tɪərɪəlaɪz/ *v.i.* se matérialiser, se réaliser.

maternal /mə'tɜːnl/ *a.* maternel.

maternity /mə'tɜːnətɪ/ *n.* maternité *f.* —*a.* (*clothes*) de grossesse. ~ **hospital,** maternité *f.* ~ **leave,** congé maternité *m.*

mathematic|s /mæθə'mætɪks/ *n. & n. pl.* mathématiques *f. pl.* ~**ian** /-ə'tɪʃn/ *n.* mathématicien(ne) *m.* (*f.*). ~**al** *a.* mathématique.

maths /mæθs/ (*Amer.* **math** /mæθ/) *n. & n. pl.* (*fam.*) maths *f. pl.*

matinée /'mætɪneɪ/ *n.* matinée *f.*

mating /'meɪtɪŋ/ *n.* accouplement *m.* ~ **season,** saison des amours *f.*

matriculat|e /mə'trɪkjʊleɪt/ *v.t./i.* (s')inscrire. ~**ion** /-'leɪʃn/ *n.* inscription *f.*

matrimon|y /'mætrɪmənɪ/ *n.* mariage *m.* ~**ial** /-'məʊnɪəl/ *a.* matrimonial.

matrix /'meɪtrɪks/ *n.* (*pl.* **matrices** /-ɪsiːz/) matrice *f.*

matron /'meɪtrən/ *n.* (*married, elderly*) dame âgée *f.*; (*in hospital: former use*) infirmière-major *f.* ~**ly** *a.* d'âge mûr; (*manner*) très digne.

matt /mæt/ *a.* mat.

matted /'mætɪd/ *a.* (*hair*) emmêlé.

matter /'mætə(r)/ *n.* (*substance*) matière *f.*; (*affair*) affaire *f.*; (*pus*) pus *m.* —*v.i.* importer. **as a** ~ **of fact,** en fait. **it does not** ~**,** ça ne fait rien. ~**-of-fact** *a.* terre à terre *invar.* **no** ~ **what happens,** quoi qu'il arrive. **what is the** ~**?,** qu'est-ce qu'il y a?

mattress /'mætrɪs/ *n.* matelas *m.*

matur|e /mə'tjʊə(r)/ *a.* mûr. —*v.t./i.* (se) mûrir. ~**ity** *n.* maturité *f.*

maul /mɔːl/ *v.t.* déchiqueter.

Mauritius /mə'rɪʃəs/ *n.* île Maurice *f.*

mausoleum /mɔːsə'lɪəm/ *n.* mausolée *m.*

mauve /məʊv/ *a. & n.* mauve (*m.*).

maverick /'mævərɪk/ *n.* non-conformiste.

maxim /'mæksɪm/ *n.* maxime *f.*

maxim|um /'mæksɪməm/ *a. & n.* (*pl.* **-ima**) maximum (*m.*). ~**ize** *v.t.* porter au maximum.

may /meɪ/ *v. aux.* (*p.t.* **might**) pouvoir. **he** ~/**might come,** il peut/pourrait venir. **you might have,** vous auriez pu. **you** ~ **leave,** vous pouvez partir. ~ **I smoke?,** puis-je fumer? ~ **he be happy,** qu'il soit heureux. **I** ~ *or* **might as well stay,** je ferais aussi bien de rester.

May /meɪ/ *n.* mai *m.* ~ **Day,** le Premier Mai.

maybe /'meɪbɪ/ *adv.* peut-être.

mayhem /'meɪhem/ *n.* (*havoc*) ravages *m. pl.*

mayonnaise /meɪə'neɪz/ *n.* mayonnaise *f.*

mayor /meə(r)/ *n.* maire *m.* ~**ess** *n.* (*wife*) femme du maire *f.*

maze /meɪz/ *n.* labyrinthe *m.*

MBA (*abbr.*) (*Master of Business Administration*) magistère en gestion commerciale.

me /miː/ *pron.* me, m'*; (*after prep.*) moi. (**to**) ~**,** me, m'*. **he knows** ~**,** il me connaît.

meadow /'medəʊ/ *n.* pré *m.*

meagre /'miːgə(r)/ *a.* maigre.

meal[1] /miːl/ *n.* repas *m.*

meal[2] /miːl/ *n.* (*grain*) farine *f.*

mealy-mouthed /miːlɪ'maʊðd/ *a.* mielleux.

mean[1] /miːn/ *a.* (**-er, -est**) (*poor*) misérable; (*miserly*) avare; (*unkind*) méchant. ~**ness** *n.* avarice *f.*; méchanceté *f.*

mean[2] /miːn/ *a.* moyen. —*n.* milieu *m.*; (*average*) moyenne *f.* **in the** ~ **time,** en attendant.

mean[3] /miːn/ *v.t.* (*p.t.* **meant** /ment/)

vouloir dire, signifier; (*involve*) entraîner. **I ∿ that!**, je suis sérieux. **be meant for**, être destiné à. **∿ to do**, avoir l'intention de faire.

meander /mɪ'ændə(r)/ *v.i.* faire des méandres.

meaning /'miːnɪŋ/ *n.* sens *m.*, signification *f.* **∿ful** *a.* significatif. **∿less** *a.* denué de sens.

means /miːnz/ *n.* moyen(s) *m.* (*pl.*). **by ∿ of sth.**, au moyen de qch. —*n. pl.* (*wealth*) moyens financiers *m. pl.* **by all ∿**, certainement. **by no ∿**, nullement.

meant /ment/ *see* **mean²**.

mean|time /'miːntaɪm/, **∿while** *advs.* en attendant.

measles /'miːzlz/ *n.* rougeole *f.*

measly /'miːzlɪ/ *a.* (*sl.*) minable.

measurable /'meʒərəbl/ *a.* mesurable.

measure /'meʒə(r)/ *n.* mesure *f.*; (*ruler*) règle *f.* —*v.t./i.* mesurer. **∿ up to**, être à la hauteur de. **∿d** *a.* mesuré. **∿ment** *n.* mesure *f.*

meat /miːt/ *n.* viande *f.* **∿y** *a.* de viande; (*fig.*) substantiel.

mechanic /mɪ'kænɪk/ *a.* mécanicien(ne) *m.* (*f.*).

mechanic|al /mɪ'kænɪkl/ *a.* mécanique. **∿s** *n.* (*science*) mécanique *f.*; *n. pl.* mécanisme *m.*

mechan|ism /'mekənɪzəm/ *n.* mécanisme *m.* **∿ize** *v.t.* mécaniser.

medal /'medl/ *n.* médaille *f.* **∿list** *n.* médaillé(e) *m.* (*f.*). **be a gold ∿list**, être médaille d'or.

medallion /mɪ'dælɪən/ *n.* (*medal, portrait, etc.*) médaillon *m.*

meddle /'medl/ *v.i.* (*interfere*) se mêler (**in**, de); (*tinker*) toucher (**with**, à). **∿some** *a.* importun.

media /'miːdɪə/ *see* **medium**. —*n. pl.* **the ∿**, les media *m. pl.* **talk to the ∿**, parler à la presse.

median /'miːdɪən/ *a.* médian. —*n.* médiane *f.*

mediat|e /'miːdɪeɪt/ *v.i.* servir d'intermédiaire. **∿ion** /-'eɪʃn/ *n.* médiation *f.* **∿or** *n.* médialteur, -trice *m.*, *f.*

medical /'medɪkl/ *a.* médical; (*student*) en médecine. —*n.* (*fam.*) visite médicale *f.*

medicat|ed /'medɪkeɪtɪd/ *a.* médical. **∿ion** /-'keɪʃn/ *n.* médicaments *m. pl.*

medicin|e /'medsn/ *n.* (*science*) médecine *f.*; (*substance*) médicament *m.* **∿al** /mɪ'dɪsnl/ *a.* médicinal.

medieval /medɪ'iːvl/ *a.* médiéval.

mediocr|e /miːdɪ'əʊkə(r)/ *a.* médiocre. **∿ity** /-'ɒkrətɪ/ *n.* médiocrité *f.*

meditat|e /'medɪteɪt/ *v.t./i.* méditer. **∿ion** /-'teɪʃn/ *n.* méditation *f.*

Mediterranean /medɪtə'reɪnɪən/ *a.* méditerranéen. —*n.* **the ∿**, la Méditerranée *f.*

medium /'miːdɪəm/ *n.* (*pl.* **media**) milieu *m.*; (*for transmitting data etc.*) support *m.*; (*pl.* **mediums**) (*person*) médium *m.* —*a.* moyen.

medley /'medlɪ/ *n.* mélange *m.*; (*mus.*) pot-pourri *m.*

meek /miːk/ *a.* (**-er, -est**) doux.

meet /miːt/ *v.t.* (*p.t.* **met**) rencontrer; (*see again*) retrouver, (*fetch*) (aller) chercher; (*be introduced to*) faire la connaissance de; (*face*) faire face à; (*requirement*) satisfaire. —*v.i.* se rencontrer; (*see each other again*) se retrouver; (*in session*) se réunir.

meeting /'miːtɪŋ/ *n.* réunion *f.*; (*between two people*) rencontre *f.*

megalomania /megələʊ'meɪnɪə/ *n.* mégalomanie *f.* **∿c** /-æk/ *n.* mégalomane *m./f.*

megaphone /'megəfəʊn/ *n.* portevoix *m.* *invar.*

melamine /'meləmiːn/ *n.* mélamine *f.*

melanchol|y /'melənkəlɪ/ *n.* mélancolie *f.* —*a.* mélancolique. **∿ic** /-'kɒlɪk/ *a.* mélancolique.

mellow /'meləʊ/ *a.* (**-er, -est**) (*fruit*) mûr; (*sound, colour*) moelleux, doux; (*person*) mûri. —*v.t./i.* (*mature*) mûrir; (*soften*) (s')adoucir.

melodious /mɪ'ləʊdɪəs/ *a.* mélodieux.

melodrama /'melədrɑːmə/ *n.* mélodrame *m.* **∿tic** /-ə'mætɪk/ *a.* mélodramatique.

melod|y /'melədɪ/ *n.* mélodie *f.* **∿ic** /mɪ'lɒdɪk/ *a.* mélodique.

melon /'melən/ *n.* melon *m.*

melt /melt/ *v.t./i.* (faire) fondre. **∿ing-pot** *n.* creuset *m.*

member /'membə(r)/ *n.* membre *m.* **M∿ of Parliament**, député *m.* **∿ship** *n.* adhésion *f.*; (*members*) membres *m. pl.*; (*fee*) cotisation *f.*

membrane /'membreɪn/ *n.* membrane *f.*

memento /mɪ'mentəʊ/ *n.* (*pl.* **-oes**) (*object*) souvenir *m.*

memo /'meməʊ/ *n.* (*pl.* **-os**) (*fam.*) note *f.*

memoir /'memwɑː(r)/ *n.* (*record, essay*) mémoire *m.*

memorable /'memərəbl/ *a.* mémorable.

memorandum /memə'rændəm/ *n.* (*pl.* **-ums**) note *f.*

memorial /mɪ'mɔːrɪəl/ *n.* monument *m.* —*a.* commémoratif.

memorize /'meməraɪz/ v.t. apprendre par cœur.

memory /'meməri/ n. (mind, in computer) mémoire f.; (thing remembered) souvenir m. **from** ∼, de mémoire. **in** ∼ **of**, à la mémoire de.

men /men/ see **man**.

menac|e /'menəs/ n. menace f.; (nuisance) peste f. —v.t. menacer. ∼**ing** a. menaçant.

menagerie /mɪ'nædʒəri/ n. ménagerie f.

mend /mend/ v.t. réparer; (darn) raccommoder. —n. raccommodage m. ∼ **one's ways**, s'amender. **on the** ∼, en voie de guérison.

menial /'miːnɪəl/ a. servile.

meningitis /menɪn'dʒaɪtɪs/ n. méningite f.

menopause /'menəpɔːz/ n. ménopause f.

menstruation /menstrʊ'eɪʃn/ n. menstruation f.

mental /'mentl/ a. mental; (hospital) psychiatrique. ∼ **block**, blocage m.

mentality /men'tæləti/ n. mentalité f.

menthol /'menθɒl/ n. menthol m. —a. mentholé.

mention /'menʃn/ v.t. mentionner. —n. mention f. **don't** ∼ **it!**, il n'y a pas de quoi!, je vous en prie!

mentor /'mentɔː(r)/ n. mentor m.

menu /'menjuː/ n. (food, on computer) menu m.; (list) carte f.

MEP (abbr.) (member of the European Parliament) député européen m.

mercenary /'mɜːsɪnəri/ a. & n. mercenaire (m.).

merchandise /'mɜːtʃəndaɪz/ n. marchandises f. pl.

merchant /'mɜːtʃənt/ n. marchand m. —a. (ship, navy) marchand. ∼ **bank**, banque de commerce f.

merciful /'mɜːsɪfl/ a. miséricordieux. ∼**ly** adv. (fortunately: fam.) Dieu merci.

merciless /'mɜːsɪlɪs/ a. impitoyable, implacable.

mercury /'mɜːkjʊri/ n. mercure m.

mercy /'mɜːsɪ/ n. pitié f. **at the** ∼ **of**, à la merci de.

mere /mɪə(r)/ a. simple. ∼**ly** adv. simplement.

merest /'mɪərɪst/ a. moindre.

merge /mɜːdʒ/ v.t./i. (se) mêler (**with**, à); (companies: comm.) fusionner. ∼**r** /-ə(r)/ n. fusion f.

meridian /mə'rɪdɪən/ n. méridien m.

meringue /mə'ræŋ/ n. meringue f.

merit /'merɪt/ n. mérite m. —v.t. (p.t. merited) mériter.

mermaid /'mɜːmeɪd/ n. sirène f.

merriment /'merɪmənt/ n. gaieté. f.

merry /'merɪ/ a. (-ier, -iest) gai. **make** ∼, faire la fête. ∼-**go-round** n. manège m. ∼-**making** n. réjouissances f. pl. **merrily** adv. gaiement.

mesh /meʃ/ n. maille f.; (fabric) tissu à mailles m.; (network) réseau m.

mesmerize /'mezməraɪz/ v.t. hypnotiser.

mess /mes/ n. désordre m., gâchis m.; (dirt) saleté f.; (mil.) mess m. —v.t. ∼ **up**, gâcher. —v.i. ∼ **about**, s'amuser; (dawdle) traîner. ∼ **with**, (tinker with) tripoter. **make a** ∼ **of**, gâcher.

message /'mesɪdʒ/ n. message m.

messenger /'mesɪndʒə(r)/ n. messager m.

Messrs /'mesəz/ n. pl. ∼ **Smith**, Messieurs or MM. Smith.

messy /'mesɪ/ a. (-ier, -iest) en désordre; (dirty) sale.

met /met/ see **meet**.

metabolic /metə'bɒlɪk/ adj. métabolique.

metabolism /mɪ'tæbəlɪzəm/ n. métabolisme m.

metal /'metl/ n. métal m. —a. de métal. ∼**lic** /mɪ'tælɪk/ a. métallique; (paint, colour) métallisé.

metallurgy /mɪ'tælədʒɪ, Amer. 'metəlɜːdʒɪ/ n. métallurgie f.

metamorphosis /metə'mɔːfəsɪs/ n. (pl. -phoses /-siːz/) métamorphose f.

metaphor /'metəfə(r)/ n. métaphore f. ∼**ical** /-'fɒrɪkl/ a. métaphorique.

mete /miːt/ v.t. ∼ **out**, donner, distribuer; (justice) rendre.

meteor /'miːtɪə(r)/ n. météore m.

meteorite /'miːtɪəraɪt/ n. météorite m.

meteorolog|y /miːtɪə'rɒlədʒɪ/ n. météorologie f. ∼**ical** /-ə'lɒdʒɪkl/ a. météorologique.

meter¹ /'miːtə(r)/ n. compteur m.

meter² /'miːtə(r)/ n. (Amer.) = **metre**.

method /'meθəd/ n. méthode f.

methodical /mɪ'θɒdɪkl/ a. méthodique.

Methodist /'meθədɪst/ n. & a. méthodiste (m./f.).

methodology /meθə'dɒlədʒɪ/ n. méthodologie f.

methylated /'meθɪleɪtɪd/ a. ∼ **spirit**, alcool à brûler m.

meticulous /mɪ'tɪkjʊləs/ a. méticuleux.

metre /'miːtə(r)/ n. mètre m.

metric /'metrɪk/ a. métrique. ∼**ation** /-'keɪʃn/ n. adoption du système métrique f.

metropol|is /mə'trɒpəlɪs/ n. (city)

métropole f. ~itan /metrə'pɒlɪtən/ a. métropolitain.

mettle /'metl/ n. courage m.

mew /mju:/ n. miaulement m. —v.i. miauler.

mews /mju:z/ n. pl. (dwellings) appartements chic aménagés dans des anciennes écuries m. pl.

Mexic|o /'meksɪkəʊ/ n. Mexique m. ~an a. & n. mexicain(e) (m. (f.)).

miaow /mi:'aʊ/ n. & v.i. = mew.

mice /maɪs/ see mouse.

mickey /'mɪkɪ/ n. take the ~ out of, (sl.) se moquer de.

micro- /'maɪkrəʊ/ pref. micro-.

microbe /'maɪkrəʊb/ n. microbe m.

microchip /'maɪkrəʊtʃɪp/ n. microplaquette f., puce f.

microclimate /'maɪkrəʊklaɪmət/ n. microclimat n.

microcomputer /maɪkrəʊkəm'pju:tə(r)/ n micro(-ordinateur) m.

microcosm /'maɪkrəʊkɒzm/ n. microcosme m.

microfilm /'maɪkrəʊfɪlm/ n. microfilm m.

microlight /'maɪkrəʊlaɪt/ n. U.L.M. m.

microphone /'maɪkrəfəʊn/ n. microphone m.

microprocessor /maɪkrəʊ'prəʊsesə(r)/ n. microprocesseur m.

microscop|e /'maɪkrəskəʊp/ n. microscope m. ~ic /-'skɒpɪk/ a. microscopique.

microwave /'maɪkrəʊweɪv/ n. microonde f. ~ oven, four à micro-ondes m.

mid /mɪd/ a. in ~ air/etc., en plein ciel/etc. in ~ March/etc., à la mimars/etc. in ~ ocean/etc., au milieu de l'océan/etc.

midday /mɪd'deɪ/ n. midi m.

middle /'mɪdl/ a. du milieu; (quality) moyen. —n. milieu m. in the ~ of, au milieu de. ~-aged a. d'un certain âge. M~ Ages, moyen âge m. ~ class, classe moyenne f. ~-class a. bourgeois. M~ East, Proche-Orient m.

middleman /'mɪdlmæn/ n. (pl. -men) intermédiaire m.

middling /'mɪdlɪŋ/ a. moyen.

midge /mɪdʒ/ n. moucheron m.

midget /'mɪdʒɪt/ n. nain(e) m. (f.). —a. minuscule.

Midlands /'mɪdləndz/ n. pl. région du centre de l'Angleterre f.

midnight /'mɪdnaɪt/ n. minuit f.

midriff /'mɪdrɪf/ n. ventre m.

midst /mɪdst/ n. in the ~ of, au milieu de. in our ~, parmi nous.

midsummer /mɪd'sʌmə(r)/ n. milieu de l'été m.; (solstice) solstice d'été m.

midway /mɪdweɪ/ adv. à mi-chemin.

midwife /'mɪdwaɪf/ n. (pl. -wives) sagefemme f.

might¹ /maɪt/ n. puissance f. ~y a. puissant; (very great: fam.) très grand; adv. (fam.) rudement.

might² /maɪt/ see may.

migraine /'mi:greɪn, Amer. 'maɪgreɪn/ n. migraine f.

migrant /'maɪgrənt/ a. & n. (bird) migrateur (m.); (worker) migrant(e) (m. (f.)).

migrat|e /maɪ'greɪt/ v.i. émigrer. ~ion /-ʃn/ n. migration f.

mike /maɪk/ n. (fam.) micro m.

mild /maɪld/ a. (-er, -est) doux; (illness) bénin. ~ly adv. doucement. to put it ~ly, pour ne rien exagérer. ~ness n. douceur f.

mildew /'mɪldju:/ n. moisissure f.

mile /maɪl/ n. mille m. (= 1.6 km.). ~s too big/etc., (fam.) beaucoup trop grand/etc. ~age n. (loosely) kilométrage m.

milestone /'maɪlstəʊn/ n. borne f.; (event, stage: fig.) jalon m.

militant /'mɪlɪtənt/ a. & n. militant(e) (m. (f.)).

military /'mɪlɪtrɪ/ a. militaire.

militate /'mɪlɪteɪt/ v.i. militer.

militia /mɪ'lɪʃə/ n. milice f.

milk /mɪlk/ n. lait m. —a. (product) laitier. —v.t. (cow etc.) traire; (fig.) exploiter. ~ shake, milk-shake m. ~y a. (diet) lacté; (colour) laiteux; (tea etc.) au lait. M~y Way, Voie lactée f.

milkman /'mɪlkmən, Amer. 'mɪlkmæn/ n. (pl. -men) laitier m.

mill /mɪl/ n. moulin m.; (factory) usine f. —v.t. moudre. —v.i. ~ around, tourner en rond; (crowd) grouiller. ~er n. meunier m.

millennium /mɪ'lenɪəm/ n. (pl. -ums) millénaire m.

millet /'mɪlɪt/ n. millet m.

milli- /'mɪlɪ/ pref. milli-.

millimetre /'mɪlɪmi:tə(r)/ n. millimètre m.

milliner /'mɪlɪnə(r)/ n. modiste f.

million /'mɪljən/ n. million m. a ~ pounds, un million de livres. ~aire /-'neə(r)/ n. millionnaire m.

millstone /'mɪlstəʊn/ n. meule f.; (burden: fig.) boulet m.

milometer /maɪ'lɒmɪtə(r)/ n. compteur kilométrique m.

mime /maɪm/ n. (*actor*) mime m./f.; (*art*) (art du) mime m. —v.t./i. mimer.

mimic /'mɪmɪk/ v.t. (*p.t.* **mimicked**) imiter. —n. imitalteur, -trice m., f. ~ry n. imitation f.

mince /mɪns/ v.t. hacher. —n. viande hachée f. ~ **pie**, tarte aux fruits confits f. **not to** ~ **matters**, ne pas mâcher ses mots. ~r /-ə(r)/ n. (*machine*) hachoir m.

mincemeat /'mɪnsmiːt/ n. hachis de fruits confits m. **make** ~ **of**, anéantir, pulvériser.

mind /maɪnd/ n. esprit m.; (*sanity*) raison f.; (*opinion*) avis m. —v.t. (*have charge of*) s'occuper de; (*heed*) faire attention à. **be on s.o.'s** ~, préoccuper qn. **bear that in** ~, ne l'oubliez pas. **change one's** ~, changer d'avis. **make up one's** ~, se décider (**to**, à). **I do not** ~ **the noise**/*etc.*, le bruit/*etc.* ne me dérange pas. **I do not** ~, ça m'est égal. **would you** ~ **checking?**, je peux vous demander de vérifier? ~**ful** a. attentif (**of**, à). ~**less** a. irréfléchi.

minder /'maɪndə(r)/ n. (*for child*) gardien(ne) m. (f.); (*for protection*) ange gardien m.

mine[1] /maɪn/ poss. pron. le mien, la mienne, les mien(ne)s. **it is** ~, c'est à moi *or* le mien.

min|e[2] /maɪn/ n. mine f. —v.t. extraire; (*mil.*) miner. ~**er** n. mineur m. ~**ing** n. exploitation minière f.; a. minier.

minefield /'maɪnfiːld/ n. champ de mines m.

mineral /'mɪnərəl/ n. & a. minéral (m.). ~ **(water)**, (*fizzy soft drink*) boisson gazeuse f. ~ **water**, (*natural*) eau minérale f.

minesweeper /'maɪnswiːpə(r)/ n. (*ship*) dragueur de mines m.

mingle /'mɪŋgl/ v.t./i. (se) mêler (**with**, à).

mingy /'mɪndʒɪ/ a. (*fam.*) radin.

mini- /'mɪnɪ/ pref. mini-.

miniatur|e /'mɪnɪtʃə(r)/ a. & n. miniature (f.). ~**ize** v.t. miniaturiser.

minibus /'mɪnɪbʌs/ n. minibus m.

minicab /'mɪnɪkæb/ n. taxi m.

minim /'mɪnɪm/ n. blanche f.

minim|um /'mɪnɪməm/ a. & n. (*pl.* -**ima**) minimum (m.). ~**al** a. minimal. ~**ize** v.t. minimiser.

minist|er /'mɪnɪstə(r)/ n. ministre m. ~**erial** /-'stɪərɪəl/ a. ministériel. ~**ry** n. ministère m.

mink /mɪŋk/ n. vison m.

minor /'maɪnə(r)/ a. petit, mineur. —n. (*jurid.*) mineur(e) m. (f.).

minority /maɪ'nɒrətɪ/ n. minorité f. —a. minoritaire.

mint[1] /mɪnt/ n. **the M**~, l'Hôtel de la Monnaie m. **a** ~, une fortune. —v.t. frapper. **in** ~ **condition**, à l'état neuf.

mint[2] /mɪnt/ n. (*plant*) menthe f.; (*sweet*) pastille de menthe f.

minus /'maɪnəs/ prep. moins; (*without*: *fam.*) sans. —n. (*sign*) moins m. ~ **sign**, moins m.

minute[1] /'mɪnɪt/ n. minute f. ~**s**, (*of meeting*) procès-verbal m.

minute[2] /maɪ'njuːt/ a. (*tiny*) minuscule; (*detailed*) minutieux.

mirac|le /'mɪrəkl/ n. miracle m. ~**ulous** /mɪ'rækjʊləs/ a. miraculeux.

mirage /'mɪrɑːʒ/ n. mirage m.

mire /maɪə(r)/ n. fange f.

mirror /'mɪrə(r)/ n. miroir m., glace f. —v.t. refléter.

mirth /mɜːθ/ n. gaieté f.

misadventure /mɪsəd'ventʃə(r)/ n. mésaventure f.

misanthropist /mɪs'ænθrəpɪst/ n. misanthrope m./f.

misapprehension /mɪsæprɪ'henʃn/ n. malentendu m.

misbehav|e /mɪsbɪ'heɪv/ v.i. se conduire mal. ~**iour** n. mauvaise conduite f.

miscalculat|e /mɪs'kælkjʊleɪt/ v.t. mal calculer. —v.i. se tromper. ~**ion** /-'leɪʃn/ n. erreur de calcul f.

miscarr|y /mɪs'kærɪ/ v.i. faire une fausse couche. ~**iage** /-ɪdʒ/ n. fausse couche f. ~**iage of justice**, erreur judiciaire f.

miscellaneous /mɪsə'leɪnɪəs/ a. divers.

mischief /'mɪstʃɪf/ n. (*foolish conduct*) espièglerie f.; (*harm*) mal m. **get into** ~, faire des sottises.

mischievous /'mɪstʃɪvəs/ a. espiègle; (*malicious*) méchant.

misconception /mɪskən'sepʃn/ n. idée fausse f.

misconduct /mɪs'kɒndʌkt/ n. mauvaise conduite f.

misconstrue /mɪskən'struː/ v.t. mal interpréter.

misdeed /mɪs'diːd/ n. méfait m.

misdemeanour /mɪsdɪ'miːnə(r)/ n. (*jurid.*) délit m.

misdirect /mɪsdɪ'rekt/ v.t. (*person*) mal renseigner.

miser /'maɪzə(r)/ n. avare m./f. ~**ly** a. avare.

miserable /'mɪzrəbl/ a. (*sad*) malheureux; (*wretched*) misérable; (*unpleasant*) affreux.

misery /ˈmɪzərɪ/ n. (*unhappiness*) malheur m.; (*pain*) souffrances f. pl.; (*poverty*) misère f.; (*person: fam.*) grincheulx, -se m., f.

misfire /mɪsˈfaɪə(r)/ v.i. (*plan etc.*) rater; (*engine*) avoir des ratés.

misfit /ˈmɪsfɪt/ n. inadapté(e) m. (f.).

misfortune /mɪsˈfɔːtʃuːn/ n. malheur m.

misgiving /mɪsˈgɪvɪŋ/ n. (*doubt*) doute m.; (*apprehension*) crainte f.

misguided /mɪsˈgaɪdɪd/ a. (*foolish*) imprudent; (*mistaken*) erroné. **be ∼**, (*person*) se tromper.

mishap /ˈmɪshæp/ n. mésaventure f., contretemps m.

misinform /mɪsɪnˈfɔːm/ v.t. mal renseigner.

misinterpret /mɪsɪnˈtɜːprɪt/ v.t. mal interpréter.

misjudge /mɪsˈdʒʌdʒ/ v.t. mal juger.

mislay /mɪsˈleɪ/ v.t. (*p.t.* **mislaid**) égarer.

mislead /mɪsˈliːd/ v.t. (*p.t.* **misled**) tromper. **∼ing** a. trompeur.

mismanage /mɪsˈmænɪdʒ/ v.t. mal gérer. **∼ment** n. mauvaise gestion f.

misnomer /mɪsˈnəʊmə(r)/ n. terme impropre m.

misplace /mɪsˈpleɪs/ v.t. mal placer; (*lose*) égarer.

misprint /ˈmɪsprɪnt/ n. faute d'impression f., coquille f.

misread /mɪsˈriːd/ v.t. (*p.t.* **misread** /mɪsˈred/) mal lire; (*intentions*) mal comprendre.

misrepresent /mɪsreprɪˈzent/ v.t. présenter sous un faux jour.

miss¹ /mɪs/ v.t./i. manquer; (*deceased person etc.*) regretter. **he ∼es her/Paris/***etc.***,** elle/Paris/*etc.* lui manque. **I ∼ you,** tu me manques. **you're ∼ing the point,** vous n'avez rien compris. **—**n. coup manqué m. **it was a near ∼,** on l'a échappé belle *or* de peu. **∼ out,** omettre. **∼ out on sth,** rater qch.

miss² /mɪs/ n. (*pl.* **misses**) mademoiselle f. (*pl.* mesdemoiselles). **M∼** Smith, Mademoiselle *or* Mlle Smith.

misshapen /mɪsˈʃeɪpən/ a. difforme.

missile /ˈmɪsaɪl/ n. (*mil.*) missile m.; (*object thrown*) projectile m.

missing /ˈmɪsɪŋ/ a. (*person*) disparu; (*thing*) qui manque. **something's ∼,** il manque quelque chose.

mission /ˈmɪʃn/ n. mission f.

missionary /ˈmɪʃənrɪ/ n. missionnaire m./f.

missive /ˈmɪsɪv/ n. missive f.

misspell /mɪsˈspel/ v.t. (*p.t.* **misspelt** *or* **misspelled**) mal écrire.

mist /mɪst/ n. brume f.; (*on window*) buée f. **—**v.t./i. (s')embuer.

mistake /mɪˈsteɪk/ n. erreur f. **—**v.t. (*p.t.* **mistook,** *p.p.* **mistaken**) mal comprendre; (*choose wrongly*) se tromper de. **by ∼,** par erreur. **make a ∼,** faire une erreur. **∼ for,** prendre pour. **∼n** /-ən/ a. erroné. **be ∼n,** se tromper. **∼nly** /-ənlɪ/ adv. par erreur.

mistletoe /ˈmɪsltəʊ/ n. gui m.

mistreat /mɪsˈtriːt/ v.t. maltraiter.

mistress /ˈmɪstrɪs/ n. maîtresse f.

mistrust /mɪsˈtrʌst/ v.t. se méfier de. **—**n. méfiance f.

misty /ˈmɪstɪ/ a. (**-ier, -iest**) brumeux; (*window*) embué.

misunderstand /mɪsʌndəˈstænd/ v.t. (*p.t.* **-stood**) mal comprendre. **∼ing** n. malentendu m.

misuse¹ /mɪsˈjuːz/ v.t. mal employer; (*power etc.*) abuser de.

misuse² /mɪsˈjuːs/ n. mauvais emploi m.; (*unfair use*) abus m.

mitigat|e /ˈmɪtɪgeɪt/ v.t. atténuer. **∼ing circumstances,** circonstances atténuantes f.pl.

mitten /ˈmɪtn/ n. moufle f.

mix /mɪks/ v.t./i. (se) mélanger. n. mélange m. **∼ up,** mélanger; (*bewilder*) embrouiller; (*mistake, confuse*) confondre (with, avec). **∼-up** n. confusion f. **∼ with,** (*people*) fréquenter. **∼er** n. (*culin.*) mélangeur m. **be a good ∼er,** être sociable. **∼er tap,** mélangeur m.

mixed /mɪkst/ a. (*school etc.*) mixte; (*assorted*) assorti. **be ∼-up,** (*fam.*) avoir des problèmes.

mixture /ˈmɪkstʃə(r)/ n. mélange m.; (*for cough*) sirop m.

moan /məʊn/ n. gémissement m. **—**v.i. gémir; (*complain*) grogner. **∼er** n. (*grumbler*) grognon m.

moat /məʊt/ n. douve(s) f. (pl.).

mob /mɒb/ n. (*crowd*) cohue f.; (*gang: sl.*) bande f. **—**v.t. (*p.t.* **mobbed**) assiéger.

mobil|e /ˈməʊbaɪl/ a. mobile. **∼e home,** caravane f. **—**n. mobile m. **∼ity** /-ˈbɪlətɪ/ n. mobilité f.

mobiliz|e /ˈməʊbɪlaɪz/ v.t./i. mobiliser. **∼ation** /-ˈzeɪʃn/ n. mobilisation f.

moccasin /ˈmɒkəsɪn/ n. mocassin m.

mock /mɒk/ v.t./i. se moquer (de). **—**a. faux. **∼-up** n. maquette f.

mockery /ˈmɒkərɪ/ n. moquerie f. **a ∼ of,** une parodie de.

mode /məʊd/ n. (way, method) mode m.;
(fashion) mode f.
model /'mɒdl/ n. modèle m.; (of toy)
modèle réduit m.; (artist's) modèle m.;
(for fashion) mannequin m. —a.
modèle; (car etc.) modèle réduit invar.
—v.t. (p.t. **modelled**) modeler;
(clothes) présenter. —v.i. être mannequin; (pose) poser. ~**ling** n. métier de
mannequin m.
modem /'məʊdem/ n. modem m.
moderate[1] /'mɒdərət/ a. & n. modéré(e)
(m. (f.)). ~**ly** adv. (in moderation)
modérément; (fairly) moyennement.
moderat|**e**[2] /'mɒdəreit/ v.t./i. (se)
modérer. ~**ion** /-'reiʃn/ n. modération
f. **in** ~**ion**, avec modération.
modern /'mɒdn/ a. moderne. ~
languages, langues vivantes f. pl. ~**ize**
v.t. moderniser.
modest /'mɒdist/ a. modeste. ~**y** n.
modestie f.
modicum /'mɒdikəm/ n. **a** ~ **of**, un peu
de.
modif|**y** /'mɒdifai/ v.t. modifier.
~**ication** /-ɪ'keiʃn/ n. modification f.
modular /'mɒdjʊlə(r)/ a. modulaire
modulat|**e** /'mɒdjʊleit/ v.t./i. moduler.
~**ion** /-'leiʃn/ n. modulation f.
module /'mɒdjuːl/ n. module m.
mohair /'məʊheə(r)/ n. mohair m.
moist /mɔist/ a. (**-er**, **-est**) humide,
moite. ~**ure** /'mɔistʃə(r)/ n. humidité
f. ~**urizer** /'mɔistʃəraizə(r)/ n. produit
hydratant.
moisten /'mɔisn/ v.t. humecter.
molar /'məʊlə(r)/ n. molaire f.
molasses /mə'læsiz/ n. mélasse f.
mold /məʊld/ (Amer.) = **mould**.
mole[1] /məʊl/ n. grain de beauté m.
mole[2] /məʊl/ n. (animal) taupe f.
molecule /'mɒlikjuːl/ n. molécule f.
molest /mə'lest/ v.t. (pester) importuner;
(ill-treat) molester.
mollusc /'mɒləsk/ n. mollusque m.
mollycoddle /'mɒlikɒdl/ v.t. dorloter,
chouchouter.
molten /'məʊltən/ a. en fusion.
mom /mɒm/ n. (Amer.) maman f.
moment /'məʊmənt/ n. moment m.
momentar|**y** /'məʊməntri, Amer. -teri/
a. momentané. ~**ily** (Amer. /-'terəli/)
adv. momentanément; (soon: Amer.)
très bientôt.
momentous /mə'mentəs/ a. important.
momentum /mə'mentəm/ n. élan m.
Monaco /'mɒnəkəʊ/ n. Monaco f.
monarch /'mɒnək/ n. monarque m. ~**y**
n. monarchie f.

monast|**ery** /'mɒnəstri/ n. monastère m.
~**ic** /mə'næstik/ a. monastique.
Monday /'mʌndi/ n. lundi m.
monetarist /'mʌnitərist/ n. monétariste
m./f.
monetary /'mʌnitri/ a. monétaire.
money /'mʌni/ n. argent m. ~**s**, sommes
d'argent f. pl. ~**-box** n. tirelire f. ~**-
lender** n. prêteur, -se m., f. ~ **order**,
mandat m. ~**-spinner** n. mine d'or f.
mongrel /'mʌŋgrəl/ n. (chien) bâtard m.
monitor /'mɒnitə(r)/ n. (pupil) chef de
classe m.; (techn.) moniteur m. —v.t.
contrôler; (a broadcast) écouter.
monk /mʌŋk/ n. moine m.
monkey /'mʌŋki/ n. singe m. ~**-nut** n.
cacahuète f. ~**-wrench** n. clef à molette
f.
mono /'mɒnəʊ/ n. (pl. **-os**) mono f. —a.
mono invar.
monochrome /'mɒnəkrəʊm/ a. & n.
(en) noir et blanc (m.).
monogram /'mɒnəgræm/ n. monogramme m.
monologue /'mɒnəlɒg/ n. monologue m.
monopol|**y** /mə'nɒpəli/ n. monopole m.
~**ize** v.t. monopoliser.
monotone /'mɒnətəʊn/ n. ton uniforme
m.
monoton|**ous** /mə'nɒtənəs/ a. mono-
tone. ~**y** n. monotonie f.
monsoon /mɒn'suːn/ n. mousson f.
monst|**er** /'mɒnstə(r)/ n. monstre m.
~**rous** a. monstrueux.
monstrosity /mɒn'strɒsəti/ n. mons-
truosité f.
month /mʌnθ/ n. mois m.
monthly /'mʌnθli/ a. mensuel. —adv.
mensuellement. —n. (periodical) mensuel m.
monument /'mɒnjʊmənt/ n. monument
m. ~**al** /-'mentl/ a. monumental.
moo /muː/ n. meuglement m. —v.i.
meugler.
mooch /muːtʃ/ v.i. (sl.) flâner. —v.t.
(Amer., sl.) se procurer.
mood /muːd/ n. humeur f. **in a good/bad**
~, de bonne/mauvaise humeur. ~**y** a.
d'humeur changeante; (sullen) maussade.
moon /muːn/ n. lune f.
moon|**light** /'muːnlait/ n. clair de lune m.
~**lit** a. éclairé par la lune.
moonlighting /'muːnlaitiŋ/ n. (fam.)
travail au noir m.
moor[1] /mʊə(r)/ n. lande f.
moor[2] /mʊə(r)/ v.t. amarrer. ~**ings** n. pl.
(chains etc.) amarres f. pl.; (place)
mouillage m.

moose /muːs/ n. invar. élan m.

moot /muːt/ a. discutable. —v.t. (question) soulever.

mop /mɒp/ n. balai à franges m. —v.t. (p.t. mopped). ~ (up), éponger. ~ of hair, tignasse f.

mope /məʊp/ v.i. se morfondre.

moped /ˈməʊped/ n. cyclomoteur m.

moral /ˈmɒrəl/ a. moral. —n. morale f. ~s, moralité f. ~ize v.i. moraliser. ~ly adv. moralement.

morale /məˈrɑːl/ n. moral m.

morality /məˈrælətɪ/ n. moralité f.

morass /məˈræs/ n. marais m.

morbid /ˈmɔːbɪd/ a. morbide.

more /mɔː(r)/ a. (a greater amount of) plus de (than, que). —n. & adv. plus (than, que). (some) ~ tea/pens/etc., (additional) encore du thé/des stylos/etc. no ~ bread/etc., plus de pain/etc. I want no ~, I do not want any ~, je n'en veux plus. ~ or less, plus ou moins.

moreover /mɔːˈrəʊvə(r)/ adv. de plus, en outre.

morgue /mɔːg/ n. morgue f.

moribund /ˈmɒrɪbʌnd/ a. moribond.

morning /ˈmɔːnɪŋ/ n. matin m.; (whole morning) matinée f.

Morocc|o /məˈrɒkəʊ/ n. Maroc m. ~an a. & n. marocain(e) (m. (f.)).

moron /ˈmɔːrɒn/ n. crétin(e) m. (f.).

morose /məˈrəʊs/ a. morose.

morphine /ˈmɔːfiːn/ n. morphine f.

Morse /mɔːs/ n. ~ (code), morse m.

morsel /ˈmɔːsl/ n. petit morceau m.; (of food) bouchée f.

mortal /ˈmɔːtl/ a. & n. mortel(le) (m.(f.)). ~ity /mɔːˈtælətɪ/ n. mortalité f.

mortar /ˈmɔːtə(r)/ n. mortier m.

mortgage /ˈmɔːgɪdʒ/ n. crédit immobilier m. —v.t. hypothéquer.

mortify /ˈmɔːtɪfaɪ/ v.t. mortifier.

mortise /ˈmɔːtɪs/ n. ~ lock serrure encastrée f.

mortuary /ˈmɔːtʃərɪ/ n. morgue f.

mosaic /məʊˈzeɪɪk/ n. mosaïque f.

Moscow /ˈmɒskəʊ/ n. Moscou m./f.

Moses /ˈməʊzɪz/ a. ~ basket, moïse m.

mosque /mɒsk/ n. mosquée f.

mosquito /məˈskiːtəʊ/ n. (pl. -oes) moustique m.

moss /mɒs/ n. mousse f. ~y a. moussu.

most /məʊst/ a. (the greatest amount of) le plus de; (the majority of) la plupart de. —n. le plus. —adv. (le) plus; (very) fort. ~ of, la plus grande partie de; (majority) la plupart de. at ~, tout au plus. for the ~ part, pour la plupart. make the ~ of, profiter de. ~ly adv. surtout.

motel /məʊˈtel/ n. motel m.

moth /mɒθ/ n. papillon de nuit m.; (in cloth) mite f. ~-ball n. boule de naphtaline f.; v.t. mettre en réserve. ~-eaten a. mité.

mother /ˈmʌðə(r)/ n. mère f. —v.t. entourer de soins maternels, materner. ~hood n. maternité f. ~-in-law n. (pl. ~s-in-law) belle-mère f. ~-of-pearl n. nacre f. M~'s Day, la fête des mères. ~-to-be n. future maman f. ~ tongue, langue maternelle f.

motherly /ˈmʌðəlɪ/ a. maternel.

motif /məʊˈtiːf/ n. motif m.

motion /ˈməʊʃn/ n. mouvement m.; (proposal) motion f. —v.t./i. ~ (to) s.o. to, faire signe à qn. de. ~less a. immobile. ~ picture, (Amer.) film m.

motivat|e /ˈməʊtɪveɪt/ v.t. motiver. ~ion /-ˈveɪʃn/ n. motivation f.

motive /ˈməʊtɪv/ n. motif m.

motley /ˈmɒtlɪ/ a. bigarré.

motor /ˈməʊtə(r)/ n. moteur m.; (car) auto f. —a. (anat.) moteur; (boat) à moteur. —v.i. aller en auto. ~ bike, (fam.) moto f. ~ car, auto f. ~ cycle, motocyclette f. ~-cyclist n. motocycliste m./f. ~ home, (Amer.) camping-car m. ~ing n. (sport) l'automobile f. ~ized a. motorisé ~ vehicle, véhicule automobile m.

motorist /ˈməʊtərɪst/ n. automobiliste m./f.

motorway /ˈməʊtəweɪ/ n. auto-route f.

mottled /ˈmɒtld/ a. tacheté.

motto /ˈmɒtəʊ/ n. (pl. -oes) devise f.

mould[1] /məʊld/ n. moule m —v.t mouler; (influence) former. ~ing n. (on wall etc.) moulure f.

mould[2] /məʊld/ n. (fungus, rot) moisissure f. ~y a. moisi.

moult /məʊlt/ v.i. muer.

mound /maʊnd/ n. monticule m., tertre m.; (pile: fig.) tas m.

mount[1] /maʊnt/ n. (hill) mont m.

mount[2] /maʊnt/ v.t./i. monter. —n. monture f. ~ up, s'accumuler; (add up) chiffrer (to, à).

mountain /ˈmaʊntɪn/ n. montagne f. ~ bike, (vélo) tout terrain m., vtt m. ~ous a. montagneux.

mountaineer /maʊntɪˈnɪə(r)/ n. alpiniste m./f. ~ing n. alpinisme m.

mourn /mɔːn/ v.t./i. ~ (for), pleurer. ~er n. personne qui suit le cortège funèbre f. ~ing n. deuil m.

mournful /'mɔːnfl/ a. triste.

mouse /maʊs/ n. (pl. mice) souris f.

mousetrap /'maʊstræp/ n. souricière f.

mousse /muːs/ n. mousse f.

moustache /məˈstɑːʃ, Amer. 'mʌstæʃ/ n. moustache f.

mousy /'maʊsɪ/ a. (hair) d'un brun terne; (fig.) timide.

mouth /maʊθ/ n. bouche f.; (of dog, cat, etc.) gueule f. ∼-organ n. harmonica m.

mouthful /'maʊθfʊl/ n. bouchée f.

mouthpiece /'maʊθpiːs/ n. (mus.) embouchure f.; (person: fig.) porte-parole m. invar.

mouthwash /'maʊθwɒʃ/ n. eau dentifrice f.

mouthwatering /'maʊθwɔːtrɪŋ/ a. qui fait venir l'eau à la bouche.

movable /'muːvəbl/ a. mobile.

move /muːv/ v.t./i. remuer, (se) déplacer, bouger; (incite) pousser; (emotionally) émouvoir; (propose) proposer; (depart) partir; (act) agir. ∼ (out), déménager. —n. mouvement m.; (in game) coup m.; (player's turn) tour m.; (procedure: fig.) démarche f.; (house change) déménagement m. ∼ back, (faire) reculer. ∼ forward or on, (faire) avancer. ∼ in, emménager. ∼ over, se pousser. on the ∼, en marche.

movement /'muːvmənt/ n. mouvement m.

movie /'muːvɪ/ n. (Amer.) film m. the ∼s, le cinéma. ∼ camera, (Amer.) caméra f.

moving /'muːvɪŋ/ a. en mouvement; (touching) émouvant.

mow /məʊ/ v.t. (p.p. mowed or mown) (corn etc.) faucher; (lawn) tondre. ∼ down, faucher. ∼er n. (for lawn) tondeuse f.

MP abbr. see Member of Parliament.

Mr /'mɪstə(r)/ n. (pl. Messrs). ∼ Smith, Monsieur or M. Smith.

Mrs /'mɪsɪz/ n. (pl. Mrs). ∼ Smith, Madame or Mme Smith. the ∼ Smith, Mesdames or Mmes Smith.

Ms /mɪz/ n. (title of married or unmarried woman). ∼ Smith, Madame or Mme Smith.

much /mʌtʃ/ a. beaucoup de. —adv. & n. beaucoup.

muck /mʌk/ n. fumier m.; (dirt: fam.) saleté f. —v.i. ∼ about, (sl.) s'amuser. ∼ about with, (sl.) tripoter. ∼ in, (sl.) participer. —v.t. ∼ up, (sl.) gâcher. ∼y a. sale.

mucus /'mjuːkəs/ n. mucus m.

mud /mʌd/ n. boue f. ∼dy a. couvert de boue.

muddle /'mʌdl/ v.t. embrouiller. —v.i. ∼ through, se débrouiller. —n. désordre m., confusion f.; (mix-up) confusion f.

mudguard /'mʌdgɑːd/ n. gardeboue m. invar.

muff /mʌf/ n. manchon m.

muffin /'mʌfɪn/ n. muffin m. (petit pain rond et plat).

muffle /'mʌfl/ v.t. emmitoufler; (sound) assourdir. ∼r /-ə(r)/ n. (scarf) cache-nez m. invar.; (Amer.: auto.) silencieux m.

mug /mʌg/ n. tasse f.; (in plastic, metal) gobelet m.; (for beer) chope f.; (face: sl.) gueule f.; (fool: sl.) idiot(e) m.(f.) —v.t. (p.t. mugged) agresser. ∼ger n. agresseur m. ∼ging n. agression f.

muggy /'mʌgɪ/ a. lourd.

mule /mjuːl/ n. (male) mulet m.; (female) mule f.

mull¹ /mʌl/ v.t. (wine) chauffer.

mull² /mʌl/ v.t. ∼ over, ruminer.

multi- /'mʌltɪ/ pref. multi-.

multicoloured /'mʌltɪkʌləd/ a. multicolore.

multifarious /mʌltɪˈfeərɪəs/ a. divers.

multinational /mʌltɪˈnæʃnəl/ a. & n. multinational(e) (f.).

multiple /'mʌltɪpl/ a. & n. multiple (m.). ∼ sclerosis, sclérose en plaques f.

multipl|y /'mʌltɪplaɪ/ v.t./i. (se) multiplier. ∼ication /-ɪˈkeɪʃn/ n. multiplication f.

multistorey /mʌltɪˈstɔːrɪ/ a. (car park) à étages.

multitude /'mʌltɪtjuːd/ n. multitude f.

mum¹ /mʌm/ a. keep ∼, (fam.) garder le silence.

mum² /mʌm/ n. (fam.) maman f.

mumble /'mʌmbl/ v.t./i. marmotter, marmonner.

mummy¹ /'mʌmɪ/ n. (embalmed body) momie f.

mummy² /'mʌmɪ/ n. (mother: fam.) maman f.

mumps /mʌmps/ n. oreillons m. pl.

munch /mʌntʃ/ v.t./i. mastiquer.

mundane /mʌnˈdeɪn/ a. banal.

municipal /mjuːˈnɪsɪpl/ a. municipal. ∼ity /-ˈpælətɪ/ n. municipalité f.

munitions /mjuːˈnɪʃnz/ n. pl. munitions f. pl.

mural /'mjʊərəl/ a. mural. —n. peinture murale f.

murder /'mɜːdə(r)/ n. meurtre m. —v.t.

assassiner; (*ruin*: *fam.*) massacrer. **~er**
n. meurtrier *m.*, assassin *m.* **~ous** *a.*
meurtrier.

murky /'mɜːkɪ/ *a.* (**-ier, -iest**) (*night,
plans, etc.*) sombre, ténébreux; (*liquid*)
épais, sale.

murmur /'mɜːmə(r)/ *n.* murmure *m.*
—*v.t./i.* murmurer.

muscle /'mʌsl/ *n.* muscle *m.* —*v.i.* **~ in**,
(*sl.*) s'introduire de force (**on,** dans).

muscular /'mʌskjʊlə(r)/ *a.* musculaire;
(*brawny*) musclé.

muse /mjuːz/ *v.i.* méditer.

museum /mjuː'zɪəm/ *n.* musée *m.*

mush /mʌʃ/ *n.* (*pulp, soft food*) bouillie
f. **~y** *a.* mou.

mushroom /'mʌʃrʊm/ *n.* champignon
m. —*v.i.* pousser comme des champi-
gnons.

music /'mjuːzɪk/ *n.* musique *f.* **~al** *a.*
musical; (*instrument*) de musique;
(*talented*) doué pour la musique; *n.*
comédie musicale *f.*

musician /mjuː'zɪʃn/ *n.* musicien(ne) *m.*
(*f.*).

musk /mʌsk/ *n.* musc *m.*

Muslim /'mʊzlɪm/ *a.* & *n.* musulman(e)
(*m. (f.*)).

muslin /'mʌzlɪn/ *n.* mousseline *f.*

mussel /'mʌsl/ *n.* moule *f.*

must /mʌst/ *v. aux.* devoir. **you ~ go,**
vous devez partir, il faut que vous
partiez. **he ~ be old,** il doit être vieux. **I
~ have done it,** j'ai dû le faire. —*n.* **be
a ~,** (*fam.*) être un must.

mustard /'mʌstəd/ *n.* moutarde *f.*

muster /'mʌstə(r)/ *v.t./i.* (se) rassembler.

musty /'mʌstɪ/ *a.* (**-ier, -iest**) (*room,
etc.*) qui sent le moisi; (*smell, taste*) de
moisi.

mutant /'mjuːtənt/ *a.* & *n.* mutant. (*m.*)

mutation /mjuː'teɪʃn/ *n.* mutation *f.*

mute /mjuːt/ *a.* & *n.* muet(te) (*m. (f.*)).
~d /-ɪd/ *a.* (*colour, sound*) sourd,
atténué; (*criticism*) voilé.

mutilate /'mjuːtɪleɪt/ *v.t.* mutiler. **~ion**
/-'leɪʃn/ *n.* mutilation *f.*

mutin|y /'mjuːtɪnɪ/ *n.* mutinerie *f.* —*v.i.*
se mutiner. **~ous** *a.* (*sailor etc.*)
mutiné; (*fig.*) rebelle.

mutter /'mʌtə(r)/ *v.t./i.* marmonner,
murmurer.

mutton /'mʌtn/ *n.* mouton *m.*

mutual /'mjuːtʃʊəl/ *a.* mutuel; (*common
to two or more*: *fam.*) commun. **~ly**
adv. mutuellement.

muzzle /'mʌzl/ *n.* (*snout*) museau *m.*;
(*device*) muselière *f.*; (*of gun*) gueule *f.*
—*v.t.* museler.

my /maɪ/ *a.* mon, ma, *pl.* mes.

myopic /maɪ'ɒpɪk/ *a.* myope.

myself /maɪ'self/ *pron.* moi-même;
(*reflexive*) me, m'*; (*after prep.*) moi.

mysterious /mɪ'stɪərɪəs/ *a.* mystérieux.

mystery /'mɪstərɪ/ *n.* mystère *m.*

mystic /'mɪstɪk/ *a.* & *n.* mystique (*m./f.*)
~al *a.* mystique. **~ism** /-sɪzəm/ *n.*
mysticisme *m.*

mystify /'mɪstɪfaɪ/ *v.t.* laisser perplexe.

mystique /mɪ'stiːk/ *n.* mystique *f.*

myth /mɪθ/ *n.* mythe *m.* **~ical** *a.*
mythique.

mythology /mɪ'θɒlədʒɪ/ *n.* mythologie *f.*

N

nab /næb/ *v.t.* (*p.t.* **nabbed**) (*arrest*: *sl.*)
épingler, attraper.

nag /næg/ *v.t./i.* (*p.t.* **nagged**) critiquer;
(*pester*) harceler.

nagging /'nægɪŋ/ *a.* persistant.

nail /neɪl/ *n.* clou *m.*; (*of finger, toe*)
ongle *m.* —*v.t.* clouer. **~-brush** *n.*
brosse à ongles *f.* **~-file** *n.* lime à ongles
f. **~ polish,** vernis à ongles *m.* **on the
~,** (*pay*) sans tarder, tout de suite.

naïve /naɪ'iːv/ *a.* naïf.

naked /'neɪkɪd/ *a.* nu. **to the ~ eye,** à
l'œil nu. **~ly** *adv.* à nu. **~ness** *n.* nudité
f.

name /neɪm/ *n.* nom *m.*; (*fig.*) réputation
f. —*v.t.* nommer; (*fix*) fixer. **be ~d
after,** porter le nom de. **~less** *a.* sans
nom, anonyme.

namely /'neɪmlɪ/ *adv.* à savoir.

namesake /'neɪmseɪk/ *n.* (*person*)
homonyme *m.*

nanny /'nænɪ/ *n.* nounou *f.* **~-goat** *n.*
chèvre *f.*

nap /næp/ *n.* somme *m.* —*v.i.* (*p.t.*
napped) faire un somme. **catch ~ping,**
prendre au dépourvu.

nape /neɪp/ *n.* nuque *f.*

napkin /'næpkɪn/ *n.* (*at meals*) serviette
f.; (*for baby*) couche *f.*

nappy /'næpɪ/ *n.* couche *f.*

narcotic /nɑː'kɒtɪk/ *a.* & *n.* narcotique
(*m.*).

narrat|e /nə'reɪt/ *v.t.* raconter. **~ion**
/-ʃn/ *n.* narration *f.* **~or** *n.* narra-
teur, -trice *m.*, *f.*

narrative /'nærətɪv/ *n.* récit *m.*

narrow /'nærəʊ/ *a.* (**-er, -est**) étroit.
—*v.t./i.* (se) rétrécir; (*limit*) (se) limiter.
~ down the choices, limiter les choix.

~ly *adv.* étroitement; (*just*) de justesse. ~-**minded** *a.* à l'esprit étroit; (*ideas etc.*) étroit. ~**ness** *n.* étroitesse *f.*

nasal /'neɪzl/ *a.* nasal.

nast|y /'nɑːstɪ/ *a.* (-**ier**, -**iest**) mauvais, désagréable; (*malicious*) méchant. ~**ily** *adv.* désagréablement; méchamment. ~**iness** *n.* (*malice*) méchanceté *f.*

nation /'neɪʃn/ *n.* nation *f.* ~-**wide** *a.* dans l'ensemble du pays.

national /'næʃnəl/ *a.* national. —*n.* ressortissant(e) *m.* (*f.*). ~ **anthem,** hymne national *m.* ~**ism** *n.* nationalisme *m.* ~**ize** *v.t.* nationaliser. ~**ly** *adv.* à l'échelle nationale.

nationality /næʃə'nælətɪ/ *n.* nationalité *f.*

native /'neɪtɪv/ *n.* (*local inhabitant*) autochtone *m./f.*; (*non-European*) indigène *m./f.* —*a.* indigène; (*country*) natal; (*inborn*) inné. **be a** ~ **of,** être originaire de. ~ **language,** langue maternelle *f.* ~ **speaker of French,** personne de langue maternelle française *f.*

Nativity /nə'tɪvətɪ/ *n.* **the** ~, la Nativité *f.*

natter /'nætə(r)/ *v.i.* bavarder.

natural /'nætʃrəl/ *a.* naturel. ~ **history,** histoire naturelle *f.* ~**ist** *n.* naturaliste *m./f.* ~**ly** *adv.* (*normally, of course*) naturellement; (*by nature*) de nature.

naturaliz|e /'nætʃrəlaɪz/ *v.t.* naturaliser. ~**ation** /-'zeɪʃn/ *n.* naturalisation *f.*

nature /'neɪtʃə(r)/ *n.* nature *f.*

naught /nɔːt/ *n.* (*old use*) rien *m.*

naught|y /'nɔːtɪ/ *a.* (-**ier**, -**iest**) vilain, méchant; (*indecent*) grivois. ~**ily** *adv.* mal.

nause|a /'nɔːsɪə/ *n.* nausée *f.* ~**ous** *a.* nauséabond.

nauseate /'nɔːsɪeɪt/ *v.t.* écœurer.

nautical /'nɔːtɪkl/ *a.* nautique.

naval /'neɪvl/ *a.* (*battle etc.*) naval; (*officer*) de marine.

nave /neɪv/ *n.* (*of church*) nef *f.*

navel /'neɪvl/ *n.* nombril *m.*

navigable /'nævɪgəbl/ *a.* navigable.

navigat|e /'nævɪgeɪt/ *v.t.* (*sea etc.*) naviguer sur; (*ship*) piloter. —*v.i.* naviguer. ~**ion** /-'geɪʃn/ *n.* navigation *f.* ~**or** *n.* navigateur *m.*

navvy /'nævɪ/ *n.* terrassier *m.*

navy /'neɪvɪ/ *n.* marine *f.* ~ (**blue**), bleu marine *invar.*

near /nɪə(r)/ *adv.* près. —*prep.* près de. —*a.* proche. —*v.t.* approcher de. **draw** ~, (s')approcher (**to,** de). ~ **by** *adv.* tout près. **N**~ **East,** Proche-Orient *m.*

~ **to,** près de. ~**ness** *n.* proximité *f.* ~-**sighted** *a.* myope.

nearby /nɪə'baɪ/ *a.* proche.

nearly /'nɪəlɪ/ *adv.* presque. **I** ~ **forgot,** j'ai failli oublier. **not** ~ **as pretty/***etc.* **as,** loin d'être aussi joli/*etc.* que.

nearside /'nɪəsaɪd/ *a.* (*auto.*) du côté du passager.

neat /niːt/ *a.* (-**er**, -**est**) soigné, net; (*room etc.*) bien rangé; (*clever*) habile; (*whisky, brandy, etc.*) sec. ~**ly** *adv.* avec soin; habilement. ~**ness** *n.* netteté *f.*

nebulous /'nebjʊləs/ *a.* nébuleux.

necessar|y /'nesəsərɪ/ *a.* nécessaire. ~**ies** *n. pl.* nécessaire *m.* ~**ily** *adv.* nécessairement.

necessitate /nɪ'sesɪteɪt/ *v.t.* nécessiter.

necessity /nɪ'sesətɪ/ *n.* nécessité *f.*; (*thing*) chose indispensable *f.*

neck /nek/ *n.* cou *m.*; (*of dress*) encolure *f.* ~ **and neck,** à égalité.

necklace /'neklɪs/ *n.* collier *m.*

neckline /'neklaɪn/ *n.* encolure *f.*

necktie /'nektaɪ/ *n.* cravate *f.*

nectarine /'nektərɪn/ *n.* brugnon *m.*, nectarine *f.*

need /niːd/ *n.* besoin *m.* —*v.t.* avoir besoin de; (*demand*) demander. **you** ~ **not come,** vous n'êtes pas obligé de venir. ~**less** *a.* inutile. ~**lessly** *adv.* inutilement.

needle /'niːdl/ *n.* aiguille *f.* —*v.t.* (*annoy: fam.*) asticoter, agacer.

needlework /'niːdlwɜːk/ *n.* couture *f.*; (*object*) ouvrage (à l'aiguille) *m.*

needy /'niːdɪ/ *a.* (-**ier**, -**iest**) nécessiteux, indigent.

negation /nɪ'geɪʃn/ *n.* négation *f.*

negative /'negətɪv/ *a.* négatif. —*n.* (*of photograph*) négatif *m.*; (*word*: *gram.*) négation *f.* **in the** ~, (*answer*) par la négative; (*gram.*) à la forme négative. ~**ly** *adv.* négativement.

neglect /nɪ'glekt/ *v.t.* négliger, laisser à l'abandon. —*n.* manque de soins *m.* (**state of**) ~, abandon *m.* ~ **to do,** négliger de faire. ~**ful** *a.* négligent.

négligé /'neglɪʒeɪ/ *n.* négligé *m.*

negligen|t /'neglɪdʒənt/ *a.* négligent. ~**ce** *n.* négligence *f.*

negligible /'neglɪdʒəbl/ *a.* négligeable.

negotiable /nɪ'gəʊʃəbl/ *a.* négociable.

negotiat|e /nɪ'gəʊʃɪeɪt/ *v.t./i.* négocier. ~**ion** /-'eɪʃn/ *n.* négociation *f.* ~**or** *n.* négociateur, -trice *m.*, *f.*

Negr|o /'niːgrəʊ/ *n.* (*pl.* -**oes**) Noir *m.* —*a.* noir; (*art, music*) nègre. ~**ess** *n.* Noire *f.*

neigh /neɪ/ n. hennissement m. —v.i. hennir.

neighbour, Amer. **neighbor** /'neɪbə(r)/ n. voisin(e) m. (f.). ~**hood** n. voisinage m., quartier m. **in the ~hood of**, aux alentours de. ~**ing** a. voisin.

neighbourly /'neɪbəlɪ/ a. amical.

neither /'naɪðə(r)/ a. & pron. aucun(e) des deux, ni l'un(e) ni l'autre. —adv. ni. —conj. (ne) non plus. ~ **big nor small**, ni grand ni petit. ~ **am I coming**, je ne viendrai pas non plus.

neon /'niːɒn/ n. néon m. —a. (lamp etc.) au néon.

nephew /'nevjuː, Amer. 'nefjuː/ n. neveu m.

nerve /nɜːv/ n. nerf m.; (courage) courage m.; (calm) sang-froid m.; (impudence: fam.) culot m. ~**s**, (before exams etc.) le trac m. ~**-racking** a. éprouvant.

nervous /'nɜːvəs/ a. nerveux. **be** or **feel** ~, (afraid) avoir peur. ~ **breakdown**, dépression nerveuse f. ~**ly** adv. (tensely) nerveusement; (timidly) craintivement. ~**ness** n. nervosité f.; (fear) crainte f.

nervy /'nɜːvɪ/ a. = nervous; (Amer., fam.) effronté.

nest /nest/ n. nid m. —v.i. nicher. ~**-egg** n. pécule m.

nestle /'nesl/ v.i. se blottir.

net[1] /net/ n. filet m. —v.t. (p.t. **netted**) prendre au filet. ~**ting** n. (nets) filets m. pl.; (wire) treillis m.; (fabric) voile m.

net[2] /net/ a. (weight etc.) net.

netball /'netbɔːl/ n. netball m.

Netherlands /'neðələndz/ n. pl. **the** ~, les Pays-Bas m. pl.

nettle /'netl/ n. ortie f.

network /'netwɜːk/ n. réseau m.

neuralgia /njʊə'rældʒə/ n. névralgie f.

neuro|sis /njʊə'rəʊsɪs/ n. (pl. **-oses** /-siːz/) névrose f. ~**tic** /-'rɒtɪk/ a. & n. névrosé(e) (m. (f.)).

neuter /'njuːtə(r)/ a. & n. neutre (m.). —v.t. (castrate) castrer.

neutral /'njuːtrəl/ a. neutre. ~ (**gear**), (auto.) point mort m. ~**ity** /-'trælətɪ/ n. neutralité f.

neutron /'njuːtrɒn/ n. neutron m. ~ **bomb**, bombe à neutrons f.

never /'nevə(r)/ adv. (ne) jamais; (not: fam.) (ne) pas. **he** ~ **refuses**, il ne refuse jamais. **I** ~ **saw him**, (fam.) je ne l'ai pas vu. ~ **again**, plus jamais. ~ **mind**, (don't worry) ne vous en faites pas; (it doesn't matter) peu importe. ~**-ending** a. interminable.

nevertheless /ˌnevəðə'les/ adv. néanmoins, toutefois.

new /njuː/ a. (**-er, -est**) nouveau; (brand-new) neuf. ~**-born** a. nouveau-né. ~**-laid egg**, œuf frais m. ~ **moon**, nouvelle lune f. ~ **year**, nouvel an m. **New Year's Day**, le jour de l'an. **New Year's Eve**, la Saint-Sylvestre. **New Zealand**, Nouvelle-Zélande f. **New Zealander**, Néo-Zélandais(e) m. (f.). ~**ness** n. nouveauté f.

newcomer /'njuːkʌmə(r)/ n. nouveau venu m., nouvelle venue f.

newfangled /njuː'fæŋgld/ a. (pej.) moderne, neuf.

newly /'njuːlɪ/ adv. nouvellement. ~**-weds** n. pl. nouveaux mariés m. pl.

news /njuːz/ n. nouvelle(s) f. (pl.); (radio, press) informations f. pl.; (TV) actualités f. pl., informations f. pl. ~ **agency**, agence de presse f. ~**caster**, ~**-reader** ns. présentateur, trice m.,f.

newsagent /'njuːzeɪdʒənt/ n. marchand(e) de journaux m.(f.).

newsletter /'njuːzletə(r)/ n. bulletin m.

newspaper /'njuːzpeɪpə(r)/ n. journal m.

newsreel /'njuːzriːl/ n. actualités f. pl.

newt /njuːt/ n. triton m.

next /nekst/ a. prochain; (adjoining) voisin; (following) suivant. —adv. la prochaine fois; (afterwards) ensuite. —n. suivant(e) m.(f.). ~ **door**, à côté (**to, de**). ~**-door** a. d'à côté. ~ **of kin**, parent le plus proche m. ~ **to**, à côté de.

nib /nɪb/ n. bec m., plume f.

nibble /'nɪbl/ v.t./i. grignoter.

nice /naɪs/ a. (**-er, -est**) agréable, bon; (kind) gentil; (pretty) joli; (respectable) bien invar; (subtle) délicat. ~**ly** adv. agréablement; gentiment; (well) bien.

nicety /'naɪsətɪ/ n. subtilité f.

niche /nɪtʃ, niːʃ/ n. (recess) niche f.; (fig.) place f., situation f.

nick /nɪk/ n. petite entaille f. —v.t. (steal, arrest; sl.) piquer. **in the** ~ **of time**, juste à temps.

nickel /'nɪkl/ n. nickel m.; (Amer.) pièce de cinq cents f.

nickname /'nɪkneɪm/ n. surnom m.; (short form) diminutif m. —v.t. surnommer.

nicotine /'nɪkətiːn/ n. nicotine f.

niece /niːs/ n. nièce f.

nifty /'nɪftɪ/ a. (sl.) chic invar.

Nigeria /naɪ'dʒɪərɪə/ n. Nigéria m./f. ~**n** a. & n. nigérian(e) (m. (f.)).

niggardly /'nɪgədlɪ/ a. chiche.

niggling /'nɪglɪŋ/ a. (*person*) tatillon; (*detail*) insignifiant.

night /naɪt/ n. nuit f.; (*evening*) soir m. —a. de nuit. ~-**cap** n. boisson f. (*avant d'aller se coucher*). ~-**club** n. boîte de nuit f. ~-**dress**, ~-**gown**, ~**ie** ns. chemise de nuit f. ~-**life** n. vie nocturne f. ~-**school** n. cours du soir m. pl. ~-**time** n. nuit f. ~- **watchman** n. veilleur de nuit m.

nightfall /'naɪtfɔ:l/ n. tombée de la nuit f.

nightingale /'naɪtɪŋgeɪl/ n. rossignol m.

nightly /'naɪtlɪ/ a. & adv. (de) chaque nuit or soir.

nightmare /'naɪtmeə(r)/ n. cauchemar m.

nil /nɪl/ n. rien m.; (*sport*) zéro m. —a. (*chances, risk, etc.*) nul.

nimble /'nɪmbl/ a. (-er, -est) agile.

nin|e /naɪn/ a. & n. neuf (m.). ~**th** a. & n. neuvième (m./f.).

nineteen /naɪn'ti:n/ a. & n. dix-neuf (m.). ~**th** a. & n. dix-neuvième (m./f.).

ninet|y /'naɪntɪ/ a. & n. quatre-vingt-dix (m.). ~**tieth** a. & n. quatre-vingt-dixième (m./f.).

nip /nɪp/ v.t./i. (p.t. **nipped**) (*pinch*) pincer; (*rush: sl.*) courir. ~ **out/back/***etc.*, sortir/rentrer/ *etc.* rapidement. —n. pincement m.; (*cold*) fraîcheur f.

nipper /'nɪpə(r)/ n. (*sl.*) gosse m./f.

nipple /'nɪpl/ n. bout de sein m.; (*of baby's bottle*) tétine f.

nippy /'nɪpɪ/ a. (-ier, -iest) (*fam.*) alerte; (*chilly: fam.*) frais.

nitrogen /'naɪtrədʒən/ n. azote m.

nitwit /'nɪtwɪt/ n. (*fam.*) imbécile m./f.

no /nəʊ/ a. aucun(e); pas de. —adv. non. —n. (pl. **noes**) non m. invar. ~ **man/***etc.*, aucun homme/*etc.* ~ **money/time/***etc.*, pas d'argent/de temps/*etc.* ~ **man's land**, no man's land m. ~ **one = nobody**. ~ **smoking/entry**, défense de fumer/ d'entrer. ~ **is there**, personne n'est là. ~ **way!**, (*fam.*) pas question!

nob|le /'nəʊbl/ a. (-er, -est) noble. ~**ility** /-'bɪlətɪ/ n. noblesse f.

nobleman /'nəʊblmən/ n. (pl. -men) noble m.

nobody /'nəʊbədɪ/ pron. (ne) personne. —n. nullité f. **he knows** ~, il ne connaît personne. ~ **is there**, personne n'est là.

nocturnal /nɒk'tɜ:nl/ a. nocturne.

nod /nɒd/ v.t./i. (p.t. **nodded**). ~ (one's head), faire un signe de tête. ~ **off**, s'endormir. —n. signe de tête m.

noise /nɔɪz/ n. bruit m. ~**less** a. silencieux.

nois|y /'nɔɪzɪ/ a. (-ier, -iest) bruyant. ~**ily** adv. bruyamment.

nomad /'nəʊmæd/ n. nomade m./f. ~**ic** /-'mædɪk/ a. nomade.

nominal /'nɒmɪnl/ a. symbolique, nominal; (*value*) nominal. ~**ly** adv. nominalement.

nominat|e /'nɒmɪneɪt/ v.t. nommer; (*put forward*) proposer. ~**ion** /-'neɪʃn/ n. nomination f.

non- /nɒn/ pref. non-. ~-**iron** a. qui ne se repasse pas. ~-**skid** a. antidérapant. ~-**stick** a. à revêtement antiadhésif.

non-commissioned /nɒnkə'mɪʃnd/ a. ~ **officer**, sous-officier m.

non-committal /nɒnkə'mɪtl/ a. évasif.

nondescript /'nɒndɪskrɪpt/ a. indéfinissable.

none /nʌn/ pron. aucun(e). ~ **of us**, aucun de nous. **I have** ~, je n'en ai pas. ~ **of the money was used**, l'argent n'a pas du tout été utilisé. —adv. ~ **too**, (ne) pas tellement. **he is** ~ **the happier**, il n'en est pas plus heureux.

nonentity /nɒ'nentətɪ/ n. nullité f.

non-existent /nɒnɪg'zɪstənt/ a. inexistant.

nonplussed /nɒn'plʌst/ a. perplexe, déconcerté.

nonsens|e /'nɒnsəns/ n. absurdités f. pl. ~**ical** /-'sensɪkl/ a. absurde.

non-smoker /nɒn'sməʊkə(r)/ n. non-fumeur m.

non-stop /nɒn'stɒp/ a. (*train, flight*) direct. —adv. sans arrêt.

noodles /'nu:dlz/ n. pl. nouilles f. pl.

nook /nʊk/ n. (re)coin m.

noon /nu:n/ n. midi m.

noose /nu:s/ n. nœud coulant m.

nor /nɔ:(r)/ adv. ni. —conj. (ne) non plus. ~ **shall I come**, je ne viendrai pas non plus.

norm /nɔ:m/ n. norme f.

normal /'nɔ:ml/ a. normal. ~**ity** /nɔ:'mælətɪ/ n. normalité f. ~**ly** adv. normalement.

Norman /'nɔ:mən/ a. & n. normand(e) (m.(f.)). ~**dy** n. Normandie f.

north /nɔ:θ/ n. nord m. —a. nord invar., du nord. —adv. vers le nord. **N~ America**, Amérique du Nord f. **N~ American** a. & n. nord-américain(e) (m. (f.)). ~-**east** n. nord-est m. ~**erly** /'nɔ:ðəlɪ/ a. du nord. ~**ward** a. au nord. ~**wards** adv. vers le nord. ~-**west** n. nord-ouest m.

northern /'nɔ:ðən/ a. du nord. ~**er** n. habitant(e) du nord m. (f.).

Norw|ay /'nɔ:weɪ/ n. Norvège f. ~**egian**

/nɔːˈwiːdʒən/ *a. & n.* norvégien(ne) (*m.* (*f.*)).

nose /nəʊz/ *n.* nez *m.* —*v.i.* ～ **about,** fouiner.

nosebleed /ˈnəʊzbliːd/ *n.* saignement de nez *m.*

nosedive /ˈnəʊzdaɪv/ *n.* piqué *m.* —*v.i.* descendre en piqué.

nostalg|ia /nɒˈstældʒə/ *n.* nostalgie *f.* ～**ic** *a.* nostalgique.

nostril /ˈnɒstrəl/ *n.* narine *f.*; (*of horse*) naseau *m.*

nosy /ˈnəʊzɪ/ *a.* (**-ier, -iest**) (*fam.*) curieux, indiscret.

not /nɒt/ *adv.* (ne) pas. **I do** ～ **know,** je ne sais pas. ～ **at all,** pas du tout. ～ **yet,** pas encore. **I suppose** ～, je suppose que non.

notable /ˈnəʊtəbl/ *a.* notable. —*n.* (*person*) notable *m.*

notably /ˈnəʊtəblɪ/ *adv.* notamment.

notary /ˈnəʊtərɪ/ *n.* notaire *m.*

notation /nəʊˈteɪʃn/ *n.* notation *f.*

notch /nɒtʃ/ *n.* entaille *f.* —*v.t.* ～ **up,** (*score etc.*) marquer.

note /nəʊt/ *n.* note *f.*; (*banknote*) billet *m.*; (*short letter*) mot *m.* —*v.t.* noter; (*notice*) remarquer.

notebook /ˈnəʊtbʊk/ *n.* carnet *m.*

noted /ˈnəʊtɪd/ *a.* connu (**for,** pour).

notepaper /ˈnəʊtpeɪpə(r)/ *n.* papier à lettres *m.*

noteworthy /ˈnəʊtwɜːðɪ/ *a.* remarquable.

nothing /ˈnʌθɪŋ/ *pron.* (ne) rien. —*n.* rien *m.*; (*person*) nullité *f.* —*adv.* nullement. **he eats** ～, il ne mange rien. ～ **big**/*etc*, rien de grand/*etc*. ～ **else,** rien d'autre. ～ **much,** pas grand-chose. **for** ～, pour rien, gratis.

notice /ˈnəʊtɪs/ *n.* avis *m.*, annonce *f.*; (*poster*) affiche *f.* (**advance**) ～, préavis *m.* **at short** ～, dans des délais très brefs. **give in one's** ～, donner sa démission. —*v.t.* remarquer, observer. ～**board** *n.* tableau d'affichage *m.* **take** ～, faire attention (**of,** à).

noticeabl|e /ˈnəʊtɪsəbl/ *a.* visible. ～**y** *adv.* visiblement.

notif|y /ˈnəʊtɪfaɪ/ *v.t.* (*inform*) aviser; (*make known*) notifier. ～**ication** /-ɪˈkeɪʃn/ *n.* avis *m.*

notion /ˈnəʊʃn/ *n.* idée, notion *f.* ～**s,** (*sewing goods etc.: Amer.*) mercerie *f.*

notor|ious /nəʊˈtɔːrɪəs/ *a.* (tristement) célèbre. ～**iety** /-əˈraɪətɪ/ *n.* notoriété *f.* ～**iously** *adv.* notoirement.

notwithstanding /nɒtwɪθˈstændɪŋ/ *prep.* malgré. —*adv.* néanmoins.

nougat /ˈnuːgɑː/ *n.* nougat *m.*

nought /nɔːt/ *n.* zéro *m.*

noun /naʊn/ *n.* nom *m.*

nourish /ˈnʌrɪʃ/ *v.t.* nourrir. ～**ing** *a.* nourrissant. ～**ment** *n.* nourriture *f.*

novel /ˈnɒvl/ *n.* roman *m.* —*a.* nouveau. ～**ist** *n.* romancier, -ière *m., f.* ～**ty** *n.* nouveauté *f.*

November /nəʊˈvembə(r)/ *n.* novembre *m.*

novice /ˈnɒvɪs/ *n.* novice *m./f.*

now /naʊ/ *adv.* maintenant. —*conj.* maintenant que. **just** ～, maintenant; (*a moment ago*) tout à l'heure. ～ **and again,** ～ **and then,** de temps à autre.

nowadays /ˈnaʊədeɪz/ *adv.* de nos jours.

nowhere /ˈnəʊweə(r)/ *adv.* nulle part.

nozzle /ˈnɒzl/ *n.* (*tip*) embout *m.*; (*of hose*) lance *f.*

nuance /ˈnjuːɑːns/ *n.* nuance *f.*

nuclear /ˈnjuːklɪə(r)/ *a.* nucléaire.

nucleus /ˈnjuːklɪəs/ *n.* (*pl.* **-lei** /-lɪaɪ/) noyau *m.*

nud|e /njuːd/ *a.* nu. —*n.* nu *m.* **in the** ～**e,** tout nu. ～**ity** *n.* nudité *f.*

nudge /nʌdʒ/ *v.t.* pousser du coude. —*n.* coup de coude *m.*

nudis|t /ˈnjuːdɪst/ *n.* nudiste *m./f.* ～**m** /-zəm/ *n.* nudisme *m.*

nuisance /ˈnjuːsns/ *n.* (*thing, event*) ennui *m.*; (*person*) peste *f.* **be a** ～, être embêtant.

null /nʌl/ *a.* nul. ～**ify** *v.t.* infirmer.

numb /nʌm/ *a.* engourdi. —*v.t.* engourdir.

number /ˈnʌmbə(r)/ *n.* nombre *m.*; (*of ticket, house, page, etc.*) numéro *m.* —*v.t.* numéroter; (*count, include*) compter. **a** ～ **of people,** plusieurs personnes. ～ **plate** *n.* plaque d'immatriculation *f.*

numeral /ˈnjuːmərəl/ *n.* chiffre *m.*

numerate /ˈnjuːmərət/ *a.* qui sait calculer.

numerical /njuːˈmerɪkl/ *a.* numérique.

numerous /ˈnjuːmərəs/ *a.* nombreux.

nun /nʌn/ *n.* religieuse *f.*

nurs|e /nɜːs/ *n.* infirmière *f.*, infirmier *m.*; (*nanny*) nurse *f.* —*v.t.* soigner; (*hope etc.*) nourrir. ～**ing home,** clinique *f.*

nursemaid /ˈnɜːsmeɪd/ *n.* bonne d'enfants *f.*

nursery /ˈnɜːsərɪ/ *n.* chambre d'enfants *f.*; (*for plants*) pépinière *f.* (**day**) ～, crèche *f.* ～ **rhyme,** chanson enfantine *f.*, comptine *f.* ～ **school,** (école) maternelle *f.* ～ **slope,** piste facile *f.*

nurture /ˈnɜːtʃə(r)/ *v.t.* élever.

nut /nʌt/ *n.* (*walnut, Brazil nut, etc.*)

noix *f.*; (*hazelnut*) noisette *f.*; (*peanut*)
cacahuète *f.*; (*techn.*) écrou *m.*; (*sl.*)
idiot(e) *m.* (*f.*).

nutcrackers /'nʌtkrækəz/ *n. pl.* casse-
noix *m. invar.*

nutmeg /'nʌtmeg/ *n.* muscade *f.*

nutrient /'njuːtrɪənt/ *n.* substance
nutritive *f.*

nutrit|ion /njuːˈtrɪʃn/ *n.* nutrition *f.*
~**ious** *a.* nutritif.

nuts /nʌts/ *a.* (*crazy*: *sl.*) cinglé.

nutshell /'nʌtʃel/ *n.* coquille de noix *f.* **in
a** ~, en un mot.

nuzzle /'nʌzl/ *v.i.* ~ **up to,** coller son
museau à.

nylon /'naɪlɒn/ *n.* nylon *m.* ~**s,** bas
nylon *m. pl.*

O

oaf /əʊf/ *n.* (*pl.* **oafs**) lourdaud(e) *m.*
(*f.*).

oak /əʊk/ *n.* chêne *m.*

OAP *abbr.* (*old-age pensioner*)
retraité(e) *m.* (*f.*), personne âgée *f.*

oar /ɔː(r)/ *n.* aviron *m.*, rame *f.*

oasis /əʊˈeɪsɪs/ *n.* (*pl.* **oases** /-siːz/) oasis
f.

oath /əʊθ/ *n.* (*promise*) serment *m.*;
(*swear-word*) juron *m.*

oatmeal /'əʊtmiːl/ *n.* farine d'avoine *f.*,
flocons d'avoine *m. pl.*

oats /əʊts/ *n. pl.* avoine *f.*

obedien|t /əˈbiːdɪənt/ *a.* obéissant. ~**ce**
n. obéissance *f.* ~**tly** *adv.* docilement,
avec soumission.

obes|e /əʊˈbiːs/ *a.* obèse. ~**ity** *n.* obésité
f.

obey /əˈbeɪ/ *v.t./i.* obéir (à).

obituary /əˈbɪtʃʊərɪ/ *n.* nécrologie *f.*

object[1] /'ɒbdʒɪkt/ *n.* (*thing*) objet *m.*;
(*aim*) but *m.*, objet *m.*; (*gram.*)
complément (d'objet) *m.* **money**/*etc.* **is
no** ~, l'argent/*etc.* ne pose pas de
problèmes.

object[2] /əbˈdʒekt/ *v.i.* protester. —*v.t.* ~
that, objecter que. ~ **to,** (*behaviour*)
désapprouver; (*plan*) protester contre.
~**ion** /-kʃn/ *n.* objection *f.*; (*drawback*)
inconvénient *m.*

objectionable /əbˈdʒekʃnəbl/ *a.* désagréable.

objectiv|e /əbˈdʒektɪv/ *a.* objectif. —*n.*
objectif *m.* ~**ity** /ɒbdʒekˈtɪvətɪ/ *n.*
objectivité *f.*

obligat|e /'ɒblɪgeɪt/ *v.t.* obliger. ~**ion**
/-'geɪʃn/ *n.* obligation *f.* **under an**
~**ion to s.o.,** redevable à qn. (**for,** de).

obligatory /əˈblɪgətrɪ/ *a.* obligatoire.

oblig|e /əˈblaɪdʒ/ *v.t.* obliger. ~**e to do,**
obliger à faire. ~**ed** *a.* obligé (**to,** de).
~**ed to s.o.,** redevable à qn. ~**ing** *a.*
obligeant. ~**ingly** *adv.* obligeamment.

oblique /əˈbliːk/ *a.* oblique; (*reference
etc.*: *fig.*) indirect.

obliterat|e /əˈblɪtəreɪt/ *v.t.* effacer. ~**ion**
/-'reɪʃn/ *n.* effacement *m.*

oblivion /əˈblɪvɪən/ *n.* oubli *m.*

oblivious /əˈblɪvɪəs/ *a.* (*unaware*) inconscient (**to, of,** de).

oblong /'ɒblɒŋ/ *a.* oblong. —*n.*
rectangle *m.*

obnoxious /əbˈnɒkʃəs/ *a.* odieux.

oboe /'əʊbəʊ/ *n.* hautbois *m.*

obscen|e /əbˈsiːn/ *a.* obscène. ~**ity**
/-enətɪ/ *n.* obscénité *f.*

obscur|e /əbˈskjʊə(r)/ *a.* obscur. —*v.t.*
obscurcir; (*conceal*) cacher. ~**ely** *adv.*
obscurément. ~**ity** *n.* obscurité *f.*

obsequious /əbˈsiːkwɪəs/ *a.* obséquieux.

observan|t /əbˈzɜːvənt/ *a.* observateur.
~**ce** *n.* observance *f.*

observatory /əbˈzɜːvətrɪ/ *n.* observatoire *m.*

observ|e /əbˈzɜːv/ *v.t.* observer;
(*remark*) remarquer. ~**ation** /ɒbzə-
'veɪʃn/ *n.* observation *f.* ~**er** *n.*
observa|teur, -trice *m.*, *f.*

obsess /əbˈses/ *v.t.* obséder. ~**ion** /-ʃn/
n. obsession *f.* ~**ive** *a.* obsédant;
(*psych.*) obsessionnel.

obsolete /'ɒbsəliːt/ *a.* dépassé.

obstacle /'ɒbstəkl/ *n.* obstacle *m.*

obstetric|s /əbˈstetrɪks/ *n.* obstétrique *f.*
~**ian** /ɒbstɪˈtrɪʃn/ *n.* médecin ac-
coucheur *m.*

obstina|te /'ɒbstɪnət/ *a.* obstiné. ~**cy** *n.*
obstination *f.* ~**tely** *adv.* obstinément.

obstruct /əbˈstrʌkt/ *v.t.* (*block*)
boucher; (*congest*) encombrer;
(*hinder*) entraver. ~**ion** /-kʃn/ *n.*
(*act*) obstruction *f.*; (*thing*) obstacle *m.*; (*traffic jam*) encombrement
m.

obtain /əbˈteɪn/ *v.t.* obtenir. —*v.i.* avoir
cours. ~**able** *a.* disponible.

obtrusive /əbˈtruːsɪv/ *a.* importun;
(*thing*) trop en évidence.

obtuse /əbˈtjuːs/ *a.* obtus.

obviate /'ɒbvɪeɪt/ *v.t.* éviter.

obvious /'ɒbvɪəs/ *a.* évident, manifeste.
~**ly** *adv.* manifestement.

occasion /əˈkeɪʒn/ *n.* occasion *f.*; (*big
event*) événement *m.* —*v.t.* occasionner. **on** ~, à l'occasion.

occasional /əˈkeɪʒənl/ a. fait, pris, etc. de temps en temps; (visitor etc.) qui vient de temps en temps. ~ly adv. de temps en temps. **very ~ly,** rarement.

occult /ɒˈkʌlt/ a. occulte.

occupation /ɒkjuˈpeɪʃn/ n. (activity, occupying) occupation f.; (job) métier m., profession f. ~al a. professionnel, du métier. ~al therapy ergothérapie f.

occup|y /ˈɒkjupaɪ/ v.i. occuper. ~ant, ~ier ns. occupant(e) m. (f.).

occur /əˈkɜː(r)/ v.i. (p.t. occurred) se produire; (arise) se présenter. ~ to s.o., venir à l'esprit de qn.

occurrence /əˈkʌrəns/ n. événement m. **a frequent ~,** une chose qui arrive souvent.

ocean /ˈəʊʃn/ n. océan m.

o'clock /əˈklɒk/ adv. **it is six ~/etc.,** il est six heures/etc.

octagon /ˈɒktəgən/ n. octogone m.

octane /ˈɒkteɪn/ n. octane m.

octave /ˈɒktɪv/ n. octave f.

October /ɒkˈtəʊbə(r)/ n. octobre m.

octopus /ˈɒktəpəs/ n. (pl. -puses) pieuvre f.

odd /ɒd/ a. (-er, -est) bizarre; (number) impair; (left over) qui reste; (not of set) dépareillé, (occasional) fait, pris, etc. de temps en temps. ~ **jobs,** menus travaux m. pl. **twenty ~,** vingt et quelques. ~**ity** n. bizarrerie f.; (thing) curiosité f. ~**ly** adv. bizarrement.

oddment /ˈɒdmənt/ n. fin de série f.

odds /ɒdz/ n. pl. chances f. pl.; (in betting) cote f. (on, de). **at ~,** en désaccord. **it makes no ~,** ça ne fait rien. **~ and ends,** des petites choses.

ode /əʊd/ n. ode f.

odious /ˈəʊdɪəs/ a. odieux.

odour, Amer. **odor** /ˈəʊdə(r)/ n. odeur f. ~**less** a. inodore.

of /ɒv, unstressed əv/ prep. de. **of the,** du, de la, pl. des. **of it, of them,** en. **a friend of mine,** un de mes amis. **six of them,** six d'entre eux. **the fifth of June/etc.,** le cinq juin/etc. **a litre of water,** un litre d'eau; **made of steel,** en acier.

off /ɒf/ adv. parti, absent; (switched off) éteint; (tap) fermé; (taken off) enlevé, détaché; (cancelled) annulé. —prep. de. (distant from) éloigné de. **go ~,** (leave) partir; (milk) tourner; (food) s'abimer. **be better ~,** (in a better position, richer) être mieux. **a day ~,** un jour de congé. **20% ~,** une réduction de 20%. **take sth. ~,** (a surface) prendre qch. sur. ~**beat** a. original. **on the ~**

chance (that), au cas où. ~ **colour,** (ill) patraque. ~ **color,** (improper: Amer.) scabreux. ~**licence** n. débit de vins m. ~**line** a. autonome; (switched off) déconnecté. ~**load** v.t. décharger. ~**peak** a. (hours) creux; (rate) des heures creuses. ~**putting** a. (fam.) rebutant. ~**stage** a. & adv. dans les coulisses. ~**white** a. blanc cassé invar.

offal /ˈɒfl/ n. abats m. pl.

offence /əˈfens/ n. délit m. **give ~ to,** offenser. **take ~,** s'offenser (**at,** de).

offend /əˈfend/ v.t. offenser; (fig.) choquer. **be ~ed,** s'offenser (**at,** de). ~**er** n. délinquant(e) m. (f.).

offensive /əˈfensɪv/ a. offensant; (disgusting) dégoûtant; (weapon) offensif. —n. offensive f.

offer /ˈɒfə(r)/ v.t. (p.t. offered) offrir. —n. offre f. **on ~,** en promotion. ~**ing** n. offrande f.

offhand /ɒfˈhænd/ a. désinvolte. —adv. à l'improviste.

office /ˈɒfɪs/ n. bureau m.; (duty) fonction f.; (surgery: Amer.) cabinet m. —a. de bureau. **good ~s,** bons offices m. pl. **in ~,** au pouvoir. ~ **building,** immeuble de bureaux m.

officer /ˈɒfɪsə(r)/ n. (army etc.) officier m.; (policeman) agent m.

official /əˈfɪʃl/ a. officiel. —n. officiel m.; (civil servant) fonctionnaire m./f. ~**ly** adv. officiellement.

officiate /əˈfɪʃɪeɪt/ v.i. (priest) officier; (president) présider.

officious /əˈfɪʃəs/ a. trop zélé.

offing /ˈɒfɪŋ/ n. **in the ~,** en perspective.

offset /ˈɒfset/ v.t. (p.t. -set, pres. p. -setting) compenser.

offshoot /ˈɒfʃuːt/ n. (bot.) rejeton m.; (fig.) ramification f.

offshore /ɒfˈʃɔː(r)/ a. (waters) côtier; (exploration) en mer; (banking) dans les paladis fiscaux.

offside /ɒfˈsaɪd/ a. (sport) hors jeu invar.; (auto.) du côté du conducteur.

offspring /ˈɒfsprɪŋ/ n. invar. progéniture f.

often /ˈɒfn/ adv. souvent. **how ~?,** combien de fois? **every so ~,** de temps en temps.

ogle /ˈəʊgl/ v.t. lorgner.

ogre /ˈəʊgə(r)/ n. ogre m.

oh /əʊ/ int. oh, ah.

oil /ɔɪl/ n. huile f.; (petroleum) pétrole m.; (for heating) mazout m. —v.t. graisser. ~**painting** n. peinture à l'huile f. ~**tanker** n. pétrolier m. ~**y** a. graisseux.

oilfield /'ɔɪlfiːld/ *n.* gisement pétrolifère *m.*

oilskins /'ɔɪlskɪnz/ *n. pl.* ciré *m.*

ointment /'ɔɪntmənt/ *n.* pommade *f.*, onguent *m.*

OK /əʊ'keɪ/ *a. & adv.* (*fam.*) bien.

old /əʊld/ *a.* (-er, -est) vieux; (*person*) vieux, âgé; (*former*) ancien. how ∼ is he?, quel âge a-t-il? he is eight years ∼, il a huit ans. of ∼, jadis. ∼ age, vieillesse *f.* old-age pensioner, retraité(e) *m.* (*f.*) ∼ boy, ancien élève *m.*; (*fellow: fam.*) vieux *m.* ∼er, ∼est, (*son etc.*) aîné. ∼-fashioned *a.* démodé; (*person*) vieux jeu *invar.* ∼ maid, vieille fille *f.* ∼ man, vieillard *m.*, vieux *m.* ∼-time *a.* ancien. ∼ woman, vieille *f.*

olive /'ɒlɪv/ *n.* olive *f.* —*a.* olive *invar.* ∼ oil, huile d'olive *f.*

Olympic /ə'lɪmpɪk/ *a.* olympique. ∼s *n. pl.*, ∼ Games, Jeux olympiques *m. pl.*

omelette /'ɒmlɪt/ *n.* omelette *f.*

omen /'əʊmen/ *n.* augure *m.*

ominous /'ɒmɪnəs/ *a.* de mauvais augure; (*fig.*) menaçant.

omi|t /ə'mɪt/ *v.t.* (*p.t.* omitted) omettre. ∼ssion *n.* omission *f.*

on /ɒn/ *prep.* sur. —*adv.* en avant; (*switched on*) allumé; (*tap*) ouvert; (*machine*) en marche; (*put on*) mis. on foot/time/*etc.*, à pied/l'heure/*etc.* on arriving, en arrivant. on Tuesday, mardi. on Tuesdays, le mardi. walk/*etc.* on, continuer à marcher/*etc.* be on, (*of film*) passer. the meeting/deal is still on, la réunion/le marché est maintenu(e). be on at, (*fam.*) être après. on and off, de temps en temps.

once /wʌns/ *adv.* une fois; (*formerly*) autrefois. —*conj.* une fois que. all at ∼, tout à coup. ∼-over *n.* (*fam.*) coup d'œil rapide *m.*

oncoming /'ɒnkʌmɪŋ/ *a.* (*vehicle etc.*) qui approche.

one /wʌn/ *a. & n.* un(e) (*m.* (*f.*)). —*pron.* un(e) *m.* (*f.*); (*impersonal*) on. ∼ (and only), seul (et unique). a big/red/*etc.* ∼, un(e) grand(e)/rouge/*etc.* this/that ∼, celui-ci/-là, celle-ci/-là. ∼ another, l'un(e) l'autre. ∼-eyed, borgne. ∼-off *a.* (*fam.*), ∼ of a kind, (*Amer.*) unique, exceptionnel. ∼-sided *a.* (*biased*) partial; (*unequal*) inégal. ∼-way *a.* (*street*) à sens unique; (*ticket*) simple.

oneself /wʌn'self/ *pron.* soi-même; (*reflexive*) se.

ongoing /'ɒngəʊɪŋ/ *a.* qui continue à evoluer.

onion /'ʌnjən/ *n.* oignon *m.*

onlooker /'ɒnlʊkə(r)/ *n.* spectalteur, -trice *m.*, *f.*

only /'əʊnlɪ/ *a.* seul. an ∼ son/*etc.*, un fils/*etc.* unique. —*adv. & conj.* seulement. he ∼ has six, il n'en a que six, il en a six seulement. ∼ too, extrêmement.

onset /'ɒnset/ *n.* début *m.*

onslaught /'ɒnslɔːt/ *n.* attaque *f.*

onus /'əʊnəs/ *n.* the ∼ is on me/*etc.*, c'est ma/*etc.* responsabilité (to, de).

onward(s) /'ɒnwəd(z)/ *adv.* en avant.

onyx /'ɒnɪks/ *n.* onyx *m.*

ooze /uːz/ *v.i.* suinter.

opal /'əʊpl/ *n.* opale *f.*

opaque /əʊ'peɪk/ *a.* opaque.

open /'əʊpən/ *a.* ouvert; (*view*) dégagé; (*free to all*) public; (*undisguised*) manifeste; (*question*) en attente. —*v.t./i.* (s')ouvrir; (*of shop, play*) ouvrir. in the ∼ air, en plein air. ∼-ended *a.* sans limite (*de durée etc.*); (*system*) qui peut évoluer. ∼-heart *a.* (*surgery*) à cœur ouvert. keep ∼ house, tenir table ouverte. ∼ out or up, (s')ouvrir. ∼-minded *a.* à l'esprit ouvert. ∼-plan *a.* sans cloisons. ∼ secret, secret de Polichinelle *m.*

opener /'əʊpənə(r)/ *n.* ouvre-boîte(s) *m.*, ouvre-bouteille(s) *m.*

opening /'əʊpənɪŋ/ *n.* ouverture *f.*; (*job*) débouché *m.*, poste vacant *m.*

openly /'əʊpənlɪ/ *adv.* ouvertement.

opera /'ɒpərə/ *n.* opéra *m.* ∼-glasses *n. pl.* jumelles *f. pl.* ∼tic /ɒpə'rætɪk/ *a.* d'opéra.

operat|e /'ɒpəreɪt/ *v.t./i.* opérer; (*techn.*) (faire) fonctionner. ∼e on, (*med.*) opérer. ∼ing theatre, salle d'opération *f.* ∼ion /-'reɪʃn/ *n.* opération *f.* have an ∼ion, se faire opérer. in ∼ion, en vigueur; (*techn.*) en service. ∼or *n.* opéralteur, -trice *m.*, *f.*; (*telephonist*) standardiste *m./f.*

operational /ɒpə'reɪʃənl/ *a.* opérationnel.

operative /'ɒpərətɪv/ *a.* (*med.*) opératoire; (*law etc.*) en vigueur.

operetta /ɒpə'retə/ *n.* opérette *f.*

opinion /ə'pɪnjən/ *n.* opinion *f.*, avis *m.* ∼ated *a.* dogmatique.

opium /'əʊpiəm/ *n.* opium *m.*

opponent /ə'pəʊnənt/ *n.* adversaire *m./f.*

opportune /'ɒpətjuːn/ *a.* opportun.

opportunist /ɒpə'tjuːnɪst/ *n.* opportuniste *m./f.*

opportunity /ɒpə'tjuːnətɪ/ *n.* occasion *f.* (to do, de faire).

oppos|e /ə'pəʊz/ v.t. s'opposer à. **~ed to,** opposé à. **~ing** a. opposé.

opposite /'ɒpəzɪt/ a. opposé. —n. contraire m., opposé m. —adv. en face. —prep. **~ (to),** en face de. **one's ~ number,** son homologue m./f.

opposition /ɒpə'zɪʃn/ n. opposition f.; (mil.) résistance f.

oppress /ə'pres/ v.t. opprimer. **~ion** /-ʃn/ n. oppression f. **~ive** a. (cruel) oppressif; (heat) oppressant. **~or** n. oppresseur m.

opt /ɒpt/ v.i. **~ for,** opter pour. **~ out,** refuser de participer (of, à). **~ to do,** choisir de faire.

optical /'ɒptɪkl/ a. optique. **~ illusion,** illusion d'optique f.

optician /ɒp'tɪʃn/ n. opticien(ne) m. (f.).

optimis|t /'ɒptɪmɪst/ n. optimiste m./f. **~m** /-zəm/ n. optimisme m. **~tic** /-'mɪstɪk/ a. optimiste. **~tically** /-'mɪstɪklɪ/ adv. avec optimisme.

optimum /'ɒptɪməm/ a. & n. (pl. -ima) optimum (m.).

option /'ɒpʃn/ n. choix m., option f.

optional /'ɒpʃənl/ a. facultatif. **~ extras,** accessoires en option m. pl.

opulen|t /'ɒpjʊlənt/ a. opulent. **~ce** n. opulence f.

or /ɔː(r)/ conj. ou; (with negative) ni.

oracle /'ɒrəkl/ n. oracle m.

oral /'ɔːrəl/ a. oral. —n. (examination: fam.) oral m.

orange /'ɒrɪndʒ/ n. (fruit) orange f. —a. (colour) orange invar.

orangeade /ɒrɪndʒ'eɪd/ n. orangeade f.

orator /'ɒrətə(r)/ n. orateur, -trice m., f. **~y** /-trɪ/ n. rhétorique f.

oratorio /ɒrə'tɔːrɪəʊ/ n. (pl. -os) oratorio m.

orbit /'ɔːbɪt/ n. orbite f. —v.t. graviter autour de, orbiter.

orchard /'ɔːtʃəd/ n. verger m.

orchestra /'ɔːkɪstrə/ n. orchestre m. **~ stalls** (Amer.), fauteuils d'orchestre m. pl. **~l** /-'kestrəl/ a. orchestral.

orchestrate /'ɔːkɪstreɪt/ v.t. orchestrer.

orchid /'ɔːkɪd/ n. orchidée f.

ordain /ɔː'deɪn/ v.t. décréter (that, que); (relig.) ordonner.

ordeal /ɔː'diːl/ n. épreuve f.

order /'ɔːdə(r)/ n. ordre m.; (comm.) commande f. —v.t. ordonner; (goods etc.) commander. **in ~,** (tidy) en ordre; (document) en règle; (fitting) de règle. **in ~ that,** pour que. **in ~ to,** pour. **~ s.o. to,** ordonner à qn. de.

orderly /'ɔːdəlɪ/ a. (tidy) ordonné; (not unruly) discipliné. —n. (mil.) planton m.; (med.) garçon de salle m.

ordinary /'ɔːdɪnrɪ/ a. (usual) ordinaire; (average) moyen.

ordination /ɔːdɪ'neɪʃn/ n. (relig.) ordination f.

ore /ɔː(r)/ n. mineral m.

organ /'ɔːgən/ n. organe m.; (mus.) orgue m. **~ist** n. organiste m./f.

organic /ɔː'gænɪk/ a. organique.

organism /'ɔːgənɪzəm/ n. organisme m.

organiz|e /'ɔːgənaɪz/ v.t. organiser. **~ation** /-'zeɪʃn/ n. organisation f. **~er** n. organisateur, -trice m., f.

orgasm /'ɔːgæzəm/ n. orgasme m.

orgy /'ɔːdʒɪ/ n. orgie f.

Orient /'ɔːrɪənt/ n. **the ~,** l'Orient m. **~al** /-'entl/ n. Oriental(e) m. (f.).

oriental /ɔːrɪ'entl/ a. oriental.

orient(at|e) /'ɔːrɪənt(eɪt)/ v.t. orienter. **~ion** /-'teɪʃn/ n. orientation f.

orifice /'ɒrɪfɪs/ n. orifice m.

origin /'ɒrɪdʒɪn/ n. origine f.

original /ə'rɪdʒənl/ a. (first) originel; (not copied) original. **~ity** /-'nælətɪ/ n. originalité f. **~ly** adv. (at the outset) à l'origine; (write etc.) originalement.

originat|e /ə'rɪdʒɪneɪt/ v.i. (plan) prendre naissance. —v.t. être l'auteur de. **~e from,** provenir de; (person) venir de. **~or** n. auteur m.

ornament /'ɔːnəmənt/ n. (decoration) ornement m.; (object) objet décoratif m. **~al** /-'mentl/ a. ornemental. **~ation** /-en'teɪʃn/ n. ornementation f.

ornate /ɔː'neɪt/ a. richement orné.

ornithology /ɔːnɪ'θɒlədʒɪ/ n. ornithologie f.

orphan /'ɔːfn/ n. orphelin(e) m. (f.). —v.t. rendre orphelin. **~age** n. orphelinat m.

orthodox /'ɔːθədɒks/ a. orthodoxe. **~y** n. orthodoxie f.

orthopaedic /ɔːθə'piːdɪk/ a. orthopédique.

oscillate /'ɒsɪleɪt/ v.i. osciller.

ostensibl|e /ɒs'tensəbl/ a. apparent, prétendu. **~y** adv. apparemment, prétendument.

ostentati|on /ɒsten'teɪʃn/ n. ostentation f. **~ous** a. prétentieux.

osteopath /'ɒstɪəpæθ/ n. ostéopathe m./f.

ostracize /'ɒstrəsaɪz/ v.t. frapper d'ostracisme.

ostrich /'ɒstrɪtʃ/ n. autruche f.

other /'ʌðə(r)/ a. autre. —n. & pron. autre m./f. —adv. **~ than,** autrement que; (except) à part. **(some) ~s,** d'autres. **the ~ one,** l'autre m./f.

otherwise /'ʌðəwaɪz/ adv. autrement.

otter /'ɒtə(r)/ n. loutre f.

ouch /aʊtʃ/ int. aïe!

ought /ɔːt/ v. aux. devoir. you ～ to stay, vous devriez rester. he ～ to succeed, il devrait réussir. I ～ to have done it, j'aurais dû le faire.

ounce /aʊns/ n. once f. (= 28.35 g.).

our /'aʊə(r)/ a. notre, pl. nos.

ours /'aʊəz/ poss. le or la nôtre, les nôtres.

ourselves /aʊə'selvz/ pron. nous-mêmes; (reflexive & after prep.) nous.

oust /aʊst/ v.t. évincer.

out /aʊt/ adv. dehors; (sun) levé. be ～, (person, book) être sorti; (light) être éteint; (flower) être épanoui; (tide) être bas; (secret) se savoir; (wrong) se tromper. be ～ to do, être résolu à faire. run/etc. ～, sortir en courant/etc. ～-and-out a. absolu. ～ of, hors de; (without) sans, à court de. ～ of pity/etc., par pitié/etc. made ～ of, fait en or de. take ～ of, prendre dans. 5 ～ of 6, 5 sur 6. ～ of date, démodé; (not valid) périmé. ～ of doors, dehors. ～ of hand, (situation) dont on n'est plus maître. ～ of line, (impertinent: Amer.) incorrect. ～ of one's mind, fou. ～ of order, (broken) en panne. ～ of place, (object, remark) déplacé. ～ of the way, écarté. get ～ of the way! écarte-toi! ～ of work, sans travail. ～-patient n. malade en consultation externe m./f.

outbid /aʊt'bɪd/ v.t. (p.t. -bid, pres. p. -bidding) enchérir sur.

outboard /'aʊtbɔːd/ a. (motor) hors-bord invar.

outbreak /'aʊtbreɪk/ n. (of war etc.) début m.; (of violence, boils) éruption f.

outburst /'aʊtbɜːst/ n. explosion f.

outcast /'aʊtkɑːst/ n. paria m.

outclass /aʊt'klɑːs/ v.t. surclasser.

outcome /'aʊtkʌm/ n. résultat m.

outcrop /'aʊtkrɒp/ n. affleurement m.

outcry /'aʊtkraɪ/ n. tollé m.

outdated /aʊt'deɪtɪd/ a. démodé.

outdo /aʊt'duː/ v.t. (p.t. -did, p.p. -done) surpasser.

outdoor /'aʊtdɔː(r)/ a. de or en plein air. ～s /-'dɔːz/ adv. dehors.

outer /'aʊtə(r)/ a. extérieur. ～ space, espace (cosmique) m.

outfit /'aʊtfɪt/ n. (articles) équipement m.; (clothes) tenue f.; (group: fam.) équipe f. ～ter n. spécialiste de confection m./f.

outgoing /'aʊtgəʊɪŋ/ a. (minister,

tenant) sortant; (sociable) ouvert. ～s n. pl. dépenses f. pl.

outgrow /aʊt'grəʊ/ v.t. (p.t. -grew, p.p. -grown) (clothes) devenir trop grand pour; (habit) dépasser.

outhouse /'aʊthaʊs/ n. appentis m.; (of mansion) dépendance f.; (Amer.) cabinets extérieurs m. pl.

outing /'aʊtɪŋ/ n. sortie f.

outlandish /aʊt'lændɪʃ/ a. bizarre, étrange.

outlaw /'aʊtlɔː/ n. hors-la-loi m. invar. —v.t. proscrire.

outlay /'aʊtleɪ/ n. dépenses f. pl.

outlet /'aʊtlet/ n. (for water, gases) sortie f.; (for goods) débouché m.; (for feelings) exutoire m.

outline /'aʊtlaɪn/ n. contour m.; (summary) esquisse f. (main) ～s, grandes lignes f. pl. —v.t. tracer le contour de; (summarize) exposer sommairement.

outlive /aʊt'lɪv/ v.t. survivre à.

outlook /'aʊtlʊk/ n. perspective f.

outlying /'aʊtlaɪɪŋ/ a. écarté.

outmoded /aʊt'məʊdɪd/ a. démodé.

outnumber /aʊt'nʌmbə(r)/ v.t. surpasser en nombre.

outpost /'aʊtpəʊst/ n. avant-poste m.

output /'aʊtpʊt/ n. rendement m.; (comput.) sortie f. —v.t./i. (comput.) sortir.

outrage /'aʊtreɪdʒ/ n. atrocité f.; (scandal) scandale m. —v.t. (morals) outrager; (person) scandaliser.

outrageous /aʊt'reɪdʒəs/ a. scandaleux, atroce.

outright /aʊt'raɪt/ adv. complètement; (at once) sur le coup; (frankly) carrément. —a. /'aʊtraɪt/ complet; (refusal) net.

outset /'aʊtset/ n. début m.

outside[1] /aʊt'saɪd/ n. extérieur m. —adv. (au) dehors. —prep. en dehors de; (in front of) devant.

outside[2] /'aʊtsaɪd/ a. extérieur.

outsider /aʊt'saɪdə(r)/ n. étranger, -ère m., f.; (sport) outsider m.

outsize /'aʊtsaɪz/ a. grande taille invar.

outskirts /'aʊtskɜːts/ n. pl. banlieue f.

outspoken /aʊt'spəʊkən/ a. franc.

outstanding /aʊt'stændɪŋ/ a. exceptionnel; (not settled) en suspens.

outstretched /'aʊtstretʃt/ a. (arm) tendu.

outstrip /aʊt'strɪp/ v.t. (p.t. -stripped) devancer, surpasser.

outward /'aʊtwəd/ a. & adv. vers l'extérieur; (sign etc.) extérieur;

(*journey*) d'aller. ~**ly** *adv.* extérieurement. ~**s** *adv.* vers l'extérieur.

outweigh /aʊt'weɪ/ *v.t.* (*exceed in
importance*) l'emporter sur.

outwit /aʊt'wɪt/ *v.t.* (*p.t.* -**witted**) duper,
être plus malin que.

oval /'əʊvl/ *n. & a.* ovale (*m.*).

ovary /'əʊvərɪ/ *n.* ovaire *m.*

ovation /ə'veɪʃn/ *n.* ovation *f.*

oven /'ʌvn/ *n.* four *m.*

over /'əʊvə(r)/ *prep.* sur, au-dessus de;
(*across*) de l'autre côté de; (*during*)
pendant; (*more than*) plus de. —*adv.*
(par-)dessus; (*ended*) fini; (*past*) passé;
(*too*) trop; (*more*) plus. **jump**/*etc.* ~,
sauter/*etc.* par-dessus. ~ **the radio,** à la
radio. **ask** ~, inviter chez soi. **he has
some** ~, il lui en reste. **all** ~ (**the
table**), partout (sur la table). ~ **and
above,** en plus de. ~ **and over,** à
maintes reprises. ~ **here,** par ici. ~
there, là-bas.

over- /'əʊvə(r)/ *pref.* sur-, trop.

overall[1] /'əʊvərɔːl/ *n.* blouse *f.* ~**s,**
bleu(s) de travail *m.* (*pl.*).

overall[2] /əʊvər'ɔːl/ *a.* global, d'ensemble; (*length, width*) total. —*adv.*
globalement.

overawe /əʊvər'ɔː/ *v.t.* intimider.

overbalance /əʊvə'bæləns/ *v.t./i.* (faire)
basculer.

overbearing /əʊvə'beərɪŋ/ *a.* autoritaire.

overboard /'əʊvəbɔːd/ *adv.* pardessus
bord.

overbook /əʊvə'bʊk/ *v.t.* accepter trop
de réservations pour.

overcast /'əʊvəkɑːst/ *a.* couvert.

overcharge /əʊvə'tʃɑːdʒ/ *v.t.* ~ **s.o.**
(**for**), faire payer trop cher à qn.

overcoat /'əʊvəkəʊt/ *n.* pardessus *m.*

overcome /əʊvə'kʌm/ *v.t.* (*p.t.* -**came**, *p.p.*
-**come**) triompher de; (*difficulty*) surmonter, triompher de. ~ **by,** accablé de.

overcrowded /əʊvə'kraʊdɪd/ *a.* bondé,
(*country*) surpeuplé.

overdo /əʊvə'duː/ *v.t.* (*p.t.* -**did,** *p.p.*
-**done**) exagérer; (*culin.*) trop cuire. ~
it, (*overwork*) se surmener.

overdose /'əʊvədəʊs/ *n.* overdose *f.*,
surdose *f.*

overdraft /'əʊvədrɑːft/ *n.* découvert *m.*

overdraw /əʊvə'drɔː/ *v.t.* (*p.t.* -**drew,**
p.p. -**drawn**) (*one's account*) mettre à
découvert.

overdrive /'əʊvədraɪv/ *n.* surmultipliée
f.

overdue /əʊvə'djuː/ *a.* en retard;
(*belated*) tardif; (*bill*) impayé.

overestimate /əʊvər'estɪmeɪt/ *v.t.* surestimer.

overexposed /əʊvərɪk'spəʊzd/ *a.* surex-
posé.

overflow[1] /əʊvə'fləʊ/ *v.i.* déborder.

overflow[2] /'əʊvəfləʊ/ *n.* (*outlet*) trop-
plein *m.*

overgrown /əʊvə'grəʊn/ *a.* (*garden
etc.*) envahi par la végétation.

overhang /əʊvə'hæŋ/ *v.t.* (*p.t.* -**hung**)
surplomber. —*v.i.* faire saillie.

overhaul[1] /əʊvə'hɔːl/ *v.t.* réviser.

overhaul[2] /'əʊvəhɔːl/ *n.* révision *f.*

overhead[1] /əʊvə'hed/ *adv.* au dessus; (*in
sky*) dans le ciel.

overhead[2] /'əʊvəhed/ *a.* aérien. ~**s** *n.
pl.* frais généraux *m. pl.* ~ **projector,**
rétroprojecteur *m.*

overhear /əʊvə'hɪə(r)/ *v.t.* (*p.t.* -**heard**)
surprendre, entendre.

overjoyed /əʊvə'dʒɔɪd/ *a.* ravi.

overland *a.* /'əʊvəlænd/, *adv.*
/əʊvə'lænd/ par voie de terre.

overlap /əʊvə'læp/ *v.t./i.* (*p.t.* -**lapped**)
(se) chevaucher.

overleaf /əʊvə'liːf/ *adv.* au verso.

overload /əʊvə'ləʊd/ *v.t.* surcharger.

overlook /əʊvə'lʊk/ *v.t.* oublier,
négliger; (*of window, house*) donner
sur; (*of tower*) dominer.

overly /'əʊvəlɪ/ *adv.* excessivement.

overnight /əʊvə'naɪt/ *adv.* (pendant) la
nuit; (*instantly, fig.*) du jour au
lendemain. —*a.* /'əʊvənaɪt/ (*train etc.*)
de nuit; (*stay etc.*) d'une nuit; (*fig.*)
soudain.

overpay /əʊvə'peɪ/ *v.t.* (*p.t.* -**paid**)
(*person*) surpayer.

overpower /əʊvə'paʊə(r)/ *v.t.* subjuguer; (*opponent*) maîtriser; (*fig.*)
accabler. ~**ing** *a.* irrésistible; (*heat,
smell*) accablant.

overpriced /əʊvə'praɪst/ *a.* trop cher.

overrate /əʊvə'reɪt/ *v.t.* surestimer. ~**d**
/-ɪd/ *a.* surfait.

overreach /əʊvə'riːtʃ/ *v. pr.* ~ **o.s.,** trop
entreprendre.

overreact /əʊvərɪ'ækt/ *v.i.* réagir excessivement.

override /əʊvə'raɪd/ *v.t.* (*p.t.* -**rode**, *p.p.*
-**ridden**) passer outre à. ~**ing** *a.*
prépondérant; (*importance*) majeur.

overripe /'əʊvəraɪp/ *a.* trop mûr.

overrule /əʊvə'ruːl/ *v.t.* rejeter.

overrun /əʊvə'rʌn/ *v.t.* (*p.t.* -**ran,** *p.p.*
-**run,** *pres. p.* -**running**) envahir; (*a
limit*) aller au-delà de. —*v.i.* (*meeting*)
durer plus longtemps que prévu.

overseas /əʊvə'siːz/ *a.* d'outre-mer,

étranger. —*adv.* outre-mer, à l'étranger.

oversee /əʊvə'si:/ *v.t.* (*p.t.* **-saw,** *p.p.* **-seen**) surveiller. ∼**r** /'əʊvəsɪə(r)/ *n.* contremaître *m.*

overshadow /əʊvə'ʃædəʊ/ *v.t.* (*darken*) assombrir; (*fig.*) éclipser.

overshoot /əʊvə'ʃu:t/ *v.t.* (*p.t.* **-shot**) dépasser.

oversight /'əʊvəsaɪt/ *n.* omission *f.*

oversleep /əʊvə'sli:p/ *v.i.* (*p.t.* **-slept**) se réveiller trop tard.

overt /'əʊvɜ:t/ *a.* manifeste.

overtake /əʊvə'teɪk/ *v.t./i.* (*p.t.* **-took,** *p.p.* **-taken**) dépasser; (*vehicle*) doubler, dépasser; (*surprise*) surprendre.

overtax /əʊvə'tæks/ *v.t.* (*strain*) fatiguer; (*taxpayer*) surimposer.

overthrow /əʊvə'θrəʊ/ *v.t.* (*p.t.* **-threw,** *p.p.* **-thrown**) renverser.

overtime /'əʊvətaɪm/ *n.* heures supplémentaires *f. pl.*

overtone /'əʊvətəʊn/ *n.* nuance *f.*

overture /'əʊvətjʊə(r)/ *n.* ouverture *f.*

overturn /əʊvə'tɜ:n/ *v.t./i.* (se) renverser.

overweight /əʊvə'weɪt/ *a.* **be** ∼, peser trop.

overwhelm /əʊvə'welm/ *v.t.* accabler; (*defeat*) écraser; (*amaze*) bouleverser. ∼**ing** *a.* accablant; (*victory*) écrasant; (*urge*) irrésistible.

overwork /əʊvə'wɜ:k/ *v.t./i.* (se) surmener. —*n.* surmenage *m.*

overwrought /əʊvə'rɔ:t/ *a.* à bout.

ow|e /əʊ/ *v.t.* devoir. ∼**ing** *a.* dû. ∼**ing to,** à cause de.

owl /aʊl/ *n.* hibou *m.*

own[1] /əʊn/ *a.* propre. **a house/etc. of one's** ∼, sa propre maison/*etc.*, une maison/*etc.* à soi. **get one's** ∼ **back,** (*fam.*) prendre sa revanche. **hold one's** ∼, bien se défendre. **on one's** ∼, tout seul.

own[2] /əʊn/ *v.t.* posséder. ∼ **up (to),** (*fam.*) avouer. ∼**er** *n.* propriétaire *m./f.* ∼**ership** *n.* possession *f.* (**of,** de); (*right*) propriété *f.*

ox /ɒks/ *n.* (*pl.* **oxen**) bœuf *m.*

oxygen /'ɒksɪdʒən/ *n.* oxygène *m.*

oyster /'ɔɪstə(r)/ *n.* huître *f.*

ozone /'əʊzəʊn/ *n.* ozone *m.* ∼ **layer,** couche d'ozone *f.*

P

pace /peɪs/ *n.* pas *m.*; (*speed*) allure *f.*; —*v.t.* (*room etc.*) arpenter. —*v.i.* ∼

(**up and down**), faire les cent pas. **keep** ∼ **with,** suivre.

pacemaker /'peɪsmeɪkə(r)/ *n.* (*med.*) stimulateur cardiaque *m.*

Pacific /pə'sɪfɪk/ *a.* pacifique. —*n.* ∼ (**Ocean**), Pacifique *m.*

pacifist /'pæsɪfɪst/ *n.* pacifiste *m./f.*

pacif|y /'pæsɪfaɪ/ *v.t.* (*country*) pacifier; (*person*) apaiser. ∼**ier** *n.* (*Amer.*) sucette *f.*

pack /pæk/ *n.* paquet *m.*; (*mil.*) sac *m.*; (*of hounds*) meute *f.*; (*of thieves*) bande *f.*; (*of lies*) tissu *m.* —*v.t.* emballer; (*suitcase*) faire; (*box, room*) remplir; (*press down*) tasser. —*v.i.* ∼ (**one's bags**), faire ses valises. ∼ **into,** (*cram*) (s')entasser dans. ∼ **off,** expédier. **send** ∼**ing,** envoyer promener. ∼**ed** *a.* (*crowded*) bondé. ∼**ed lunch,** repas froid *m.* ∼**ing** *n.* (*action, material*) emballage *m.* ∼**ing case,** caisse *f.*

package /'pækɪdʒ/ *n.* paquet *m.* —*v.t.* empaqueter. ∼ **deal,** forfait *m.* ∼ **tour,** voyage organisé *m.*

packet /'pækɪt/ *n.* paquet *m.*

pact /pækt/ *n.* pacte *m.*

pad[1] /pæd/ *n.* bloc(-notes) *m.*; (*for ink*) tampon *m.* (**launching**) ∼, rampe (de lancement) *f.* —*v.t.* (*p.t.* **padded**) rembourrer; (*text. fig.*) délayer. ∼**ding** *n.* rembourrage *m.*; délayage *m.*

pad[2] /pæd/ *v.i.* (*p.t.* **padded**) (*walk*) marcher à pas feutrés.

paddle[1] /'pædl/ *n.* pagaie *f.* —*v.t.* ∼ **a canoe,** pagayer. ∼**-steamer** *n.* bateau à roues *m.*

paddl|e[2] /'pædl/ *v.i.* barboter, se mouiller les pieds. ∼**ing pool,** pataugeoire *f.*

paddock /'pædək/ *n.* paddock *m.*

paddy(-field) /'pædɪ(fi:ld)/ *n.* rizière *f.*

padlock /'pædlɒk/ *n.* cadenas *m.* —*v.t.* cadenasser.

paediatrician /pi:dɪə'trɪʃn/ *n.* pédiatre *m./f.*

pagan /'peɪɡən/ *a. & n.* païen(ne) (*m.* (*f.*)).

page[1] /peɪdʒ/ *n.* (*of book etc.*) page *f.*

page[2] /peɪdʒ/ *n.* (*in hotel*) chasseur *m.* (*at wedding*) page *m.* —*v.t.* (faire) appeler.

pageant /'pædʒənt/ *n.* spectacle (historique) *m.* ∼**ry** *n.* pompe *f.*

pagoda /pə'ɡəʊdə/ *n.* pagode *f.*

paid /peɪd/ *see* **pay**. —*a.* **put** ∼ **to,** (*fam.*) mettre fin à.

pail /peɪl/ *n.* seau *m.*

pain /peɪn/ n. douleur f. ∼s, efforts m. pl. —v.t. (grieve) peiner. **be in** ∼, souffrir. **take** ∼**s to**, se donner du mal pour. ∼-**killer** n. analgésique m. ∼**less** a. indolore.

painful /'peɪnfl/ a. douloureux; (laborious) pénible.

painstaking /'peɪnzteɪkɪŋ/ a. assidu, appliqué.

paint /peɪnt/ n. peinture f. ∼**s**, (in tube, box) couleurs f. pl. —v.t./i. peindre. ∼**er** n. peintre m. ∼**ing** n. peinture f.

paintbrush /'peɪntbrʌʃ/ n. pinceau m.

paintwork /'peɪntwɜːk/ n. peintures f. pl.

pair /peə(r)/ n. paire f.; (of people) couple m. **a** ∼ **of trousers**, un pantalon. —v.i. ∼ **off**, (at dance etc.) former un couple.

pajamas /pə'dʒɑːməz/ n.pl. (Amer.) pyjama m.

Pakistan /pɑːkɪ'stɑːn/ n. Pakistan. m. ∼**i** a. & n. pakistanais(e) (m. (f.)).

pal /pæl/ n. (fam.) copain, -ine m., f.

palace /'pælɪs/ n. palais m.

palat|e /'pælət/ n. (of mouth) palais m. ∼**able** a. agréable au goût.

palatial /pə'leɪʃl/ a. somptueux.

palaver /pə'lɑːvə(r)/ n. (fuss: fam.) histoire(s) f. (pl.).

pale /peɪl/ a. (-er, -est) pâle. —v.i. pâlir. ∼**ness** n. pâleur f.

Palestin|e /'pælɪstaɪn/ n. Palestine f. ∼**ian** /-'stɪnɪən/ a. & n. palestinien(ne) (m. (f.)).

palette /'pælɪt/ n. palette f.

pall /pɔːl/ v.i. devenir insipide.

pallet /'pælɪt/ n. palette f.

pallid /'pælɪd/ a. pâle.

palm /pɑːm/ n. (of hand) paume f.; (tree) palmier m.; (symbol) palme f. —v.t. ∼ **off**, (thing) refiler, coller (**on**, à); (person) coller. **P**∼ **Sunday**, dimanche des Rameaux.

palmist /'pɑːmɪst/ n. chiromancien(ne) m. (f.).

palpable /'pælpəbl/ a. manifeste.

palpitat|e /'pælpɪteɪt/ v.i. palpiter. ∼**ion** /-'teɪʃn/ n. palpitation f.

paltry /'pɔːltrɪ/ a. (-ier, -iest) dérisoire, piètre.

pamper /'pæmpə(r)/ v.t. dorloter.

pamphlet /'pæmflɪt/ n. brochure f.

pan /pæn/ n. casserole f.; (for frying) poêle f.; (of lavatory) cuvette f. —v.t. (p.t. **panned**) (fam.) critiquer.

panacea /pænə'sɪə/ n. panacée f.

panache /pə'næʃ/ n. panache m.

pancake /'pænkeɪk/ n. crêpe f.

pancreas /'pæŋkrɪəs/ n. pancréas m.

panda /'pændə/ n. panda m. ∼ **car**, voiture pie (de la police) f.

pandemonium /pændɪ'məʊnɪəm/ n. tumulte m., chaos m.

pander /'pændə(r)/ v.i. ∼ **to**, (person, taste) flatter bassement.

pane /peɪn/ n. carreau m., vitre f.

panel /'pænl/ n. (of door etc.) panneau m.; (jury) jury m.; (speakers: TV) invités m. pl. (**instrument**) ∼, tableau de bord m. ∼ **of experts**, groupe d'experts m. ∼**led** a. lambrissé. ∼**ling** n. lambrissage m. ∼**list** n. (TV) invité(e) (de tribune) m. (f.).

pang /pæŋ/ n. pincement au cœur m. ∼**s**, (of hunger, death) affres f. pl. ∼**s of conscience**, remords m. pl.

panic /'pænɪk/ n. panique f. —v.t./ i. (p.t. **panicked**) (s')affoler, paniquer. ∼-**stricken** a. pris de panique, affolé.

panorama /pænə'rɑːmə/ n. panorama m.

pansy /'pænzɪ/ n. (bot.) pensée f.

pant /pænt/ v.i. haleter.

panther /'pænθə(r)/ n. panthère f.

panties /'pæntɪz/ n. pl. (fam.) slip m., culotte f. (de femme).

pantihose /'pæntɪhəʊz/ n. (Amer.) collant m.

pantomime /'pæntəmaɪm/ n. (show) spectacle de Noël m.; (mime) pantomime f.

pantry /'pæntrɪ/ n. office m.

pants /pænts/ n. pl. (underwear: fam.) slip m.; (trousers: fam. & Amer.) pantalon m.

papacy /'peɪpəsɪ/ n. papauté f.

papal /'peɪpl/ a. papal.

paper /'peɪpə(r)/ n. papier m.; (newspaper) journal m.; (exam) epreuve f.; (essay) exposé m.; (wallpaper) papier peint m. (identity) ∼**s** papiers d'identité) m. pl. —v.t. (room) tapisser. **on** ∼, par écrit. ∼-**clip** n. trombone m.

paperback /'peɪpəbæk/ a. & n. ∼ (**book**), livre broché m.

paperweight /'peɪpəweɪt/ n. presse papiers m. invar.

paperwork /'peɪpəwɜːk/ n. paperasserie f.

paprika /'pæprɪkə/ n. paprika m.

par /pɑː(r)/ n. **be below** ∼, ne pas être en forme. **on a** ∼ **with**, à égalité avec.

parable /'pærəbl/ n. parabole f.

parachut|e /'pærəʃuːt/ n. parachute m. —v.i. descendre en parachute. ∼**ist** n. parachutiste m./f.

parade /pə'reɪd/ n. (*procession*) défilé m.; (*ceremony, display*) parade f.; (*street*) avenue f. —v.i. défiler. —v.t. faire parade de.

paradise /'pærədaɪs/ n. paradis m.

paradox /'pærədɒks/ n. paradoxe m. ~**ical** /-'dɒksɪkl/ a. paradoxal.

paraffin /'pærəfɪn/ n. pétrole (lampant) m.; (*wax*) paraffine f.

paragon /'pærəgən/ n. modèle m.

paragraph /'pærəgrɑːf/ n. paragraphe m.

parallel /'pærəlel/ a. parallèle. —n. (*line*) parallèle f.; (*comparison & geog.*) parallèle m. —v.t. (*p.t.* **paralleled**) être semblable à; (*match*) égaler.

paralyse /'pærəlaɪz/ v.t. paralyser.

paraly|sis /pə'ræləsɪs/ n. paralysie f. ~**tic** /pærə'lɪtɪk/ a. & n. paralytique (m./f.).

paramedic /pærə'medɪk/ n. auxiliaire médical(e) m. (f.).

parameter /pə'ræmɪtə(r)/ n. paramètre m.

paramount /'pærəmaʊnt/ a. primordial, fondamental.

paranoi|a /pærə'nɔɪə/ n. paranoïa f. ~**d** a. paranoïaque; (*fam.*) parano *invar*.

parapet /'pærəpɪt/ n. parapet m.

paraphernalia /pærəfə'neɪlɪə/ n. attirail m., équipement m.

paraphrase /'pærəfreɪz/ n. paraphrase f. —v.t. paraphraser.

parasite /'pærəsaɪt/ n. parasite m.

parasol /'pærəsɒl/ n. ombrelle f.; (*on table, at beach*) parasol m.

paratrooper /'pærətruːpə(r)/ n. (*mil.*) parachutiste m/f.

parcel /'pɑːsl/ n. colis m., paquet m. —v.t. (*p.t.* **parcelled**) ~ **out**, diviser en parcelles.

parch /pɑːtʃ/ v.t. dessécher. **be** ~**ed**, (*person*) avoir très soif.

parchment /'pɑːtʃmənt/ n. parchemin m.

pardon /'pɑːdn/ n. pardon m.; (*jurid.*) grâce m. —v.t. (*p.t.* **pardoned**) pardonner (**s.o. for sth.,** qch. à qn.); gracier. **I beg your** ~**,** pardon.

pare /peə(r)/ v.t. (*clip*) rogner; (*peel*) éplucher.

parent /'peərənt/ n. père m., mère f. ~**s,** parents m. pl. ~**al** /pə'rentl/ a. des parents. ~**hood** n. l'état de parent m.

parenthesis /pə'renθəsɪs/ n. (*pl.* **-theses** /-siːz/) parenthèse f.

Paris /'pærɪs/ n. Paris m./f. ~**ian** /pə'rɪzɪən, *Amer.* pə'riːʒn/ a. & n. parisien(ne) (m. (f.)).

parish /'pærɪʃ/ n. (*relig.*) paroisse f.; (*municipal*) commune f. ~**ioner** /pə'rɪʃənə(r)/ n. paroissien(ne) m. (f.).

parity /'pærətɪ/ n. parité f.

park /pɑːk/ n. parc m. —v.t./i. (se) garer; (*remain parked*) stationner. ~**ing-lot** n. (*Amer.*) parking m. ~**ing-meter** n. parcmètre m. ~**ing ticket,** procès-verbal m.

parka /'pɑːkə/ n. parka m./f.

parlance /'pɑːləns/ n. langage m.

parliament /'pɑːləmənt/ n. parlement m. ~**ary** /-'mentrɪ/ a. parlementaire.

parlour, (*Amer.*) **parlor** /'pɑːlə(r)/ n. salon m.

parochial /pə'rəʊkɪəl/ a. (*relig.*) paroissial; (*fig.*) borné, provincial.

parody /'pærədɪ/ n. parodie f. —v.t. parodier.

parole /pə'rəʊl/ n. **on** ~**,** en liberté conditionnelle.

parquet /'pɑːkeɪ/ n. parquet m.

parrot /'pærət/ n. perroquet m.

parry /'pærɪ/ v.t./v.i. (*sport*) parer; (*question etc.*) esquiver. —n. parade f.

parsimonious /pɑːsɪ'məʊnɪəs/ a. parcimonieux.

parsley /'pɑːslɪ/ n. persil m.

parsnip /'pɑːsnɪp/ n. panais m.

parson /'pɑːsn/ n. pasteur m.

part /pɑːt/ n. partie f.; (*of serial*) épisode m.; (*of machine*) pièce f.; (*theatre*) rôle m.; (*side in dispute*) parti m. —a. partiel. —adv. en partie. —v.t./i. (*separate*) (se) séparer. **in** ~**,** en partie. **on the** ~ **of,** de la part de. ~**-exchange** n. reprise f. ~ **of speech,** catégorie grammaticale f. ~**-time** a. & adv. à temps partiel. ~ **with,** se séparer de. **take** ~ **in,** participer à. **in these** ~**s,** dans la région, dans le coin.

partake /pɑː'teɪk/ v.i. (*p.t.* **-took,** *p.p.* **-taken**) participer (**in,** à).

partial /'pɑːʃl/ a. partiel; (*biased*) partial. **be** ~ **to,** avoir une prédilection pour. ~**ity** /-ɪ'ælətɪ/ n. (*bias*) partialité f.; (*fondness*) prédilection f. ~**ly** adv. partiellement.

particip|ate /pɑː'tɪsɪpeɪt/ v.i. participer (**in,** à). ~**ant** n. participant(e) m. (f.). ~**ation** /-'peɪʃn/ n. participation f.

participle /'pɑːtɪsɪpl/ n. participe m.

particle /'pɑːtɪkl/ n. particule f.

particular /pə'tɪkjʊlə(r)/ a. particulier; (*fussy*) difficile; (*careful*) méticuleux. **that** ~ **man,** cet homme-là en particulier. ~**s** n. pl. détails m. pl. **in** ~**,**

en particulier. **∼ly** *adv.* particulièrement.

parting /'pɑ:tɪŋ/ *n.* séparation *f.*; (*in hair*) raie *f.* —*a.* d'adieu.

partisan /pɑ:tɪ'zæn, *Amer.* 'pɑ:tɪzn/ *n.* partisan(e) *m.* (*f.*).

partition /pɑ:'tɪʃn/ *n.* (*of room*) cloison *f.*; (*pol.*) partage *m.*, partition *f.* —*v.t.* (*room*) cloisonner; (*country*) partager.

partly /'pɑ:tlɪ/ *adv.* en partie.

partner /'pɑ:tnə(r)/ *n.* associé(e) *m.* (*f.*); (*sport*) partenaire *m./f.* **∼ship** *n.* association *f.*

partridge /'pɑ:trɪdʒ/ *n.* perdrix *f.*

party /'pɑ:tɪ/ *n.* fête *f.*; (*formal*) réception *f.*; (*for young people*) boum *f.*; (*group*) groupe *m.*, équipe *f.*; (*pol.*) parti *m.*; (*jurid.*) partie *f.* **∼ line,** (*telephone*) ligne commune *f.*

pass /pɑ:s/ *v.t./i.* (*p.t.* **passed**) passer; (*overtake*) dépasser; (*in exam*) être reçu (à); (*approve*) accepter, autoriser; (*remark*) faire; (*judgement*) prononcer; (*law, bill*) voter. **∼ (by),** (*building*) passer devant; (*person*) croiser. —*n.* (*permit*) laissez-passer *m. invar.*; (*ticket*) carte (d'abonnement) *f.*; (*geog.*) col *m.*; (*sport*) passe *f.* **∼ (mark),** (*in exam*) moyenne *f.* **make a ∼ at,** (*fam.*) faire des avances à. **∼ away,** mourir. **∼ out** *or* **round,** distribuer. **∼ out,** (*faint*: *fam.*) s'évanouir. **∼ over,** (*overlook*) passer sur. **∼ up,** (*forego*: *fam.*) laisser passer.

passable /'pɑ:səbl/ *a.* (*adequate*) passable; (*road*) praticable.

passage /'pæsɪdʒ/ *n.* (*way through, text, etc.*) passage *m.*; (*voyage*) traversée *f.*; (*corridor*) couloir *m.*

passenger /'pæsɪndʒə(r)/ *n.* passager, -ère *m., f.*; (*in train*) voyageur, -se *m., f.*

passer-by /pɑ:sə'baɪ/ *n.* (*pl.* **passers-by**) passant(e) *m.* (*f.*).

passing /'pɑ:sɪŋ/ *a.* (*fleeting*) fugitif, passager.

passion /'pæʃn/ *n.* passion *f.* **∼ate** *a.* passionné. **∼ately** *adv.* passionnément.

passive /'pæsɪv/ *a.* passif. **∼ness** *n.* passivité *f.*

Passover /'pɑ:səʊvə(r)/ *n.* Pâque *f.*

passport /'pɑ:spɔ:t/ *n.* passeport *m.*

password /'pɑ:swɜ:d/ *n.* mot de passe *m.*

past /pɑ:st/ *a.* passé; (*former*) ancien. —*n.* passé *m.* —*prep.* au-delà de; (*in front of*) devant. —*adv.* devant. **the ∼ months,** ces derniers mois. **∼ midnight,** minuit passé. **10 ∼ 6,** six heures dix.

pasta /'pæstə/ *n.* pâtes *f. pl.*

paste /peɪst/ *n.* (*glue*) colle *f.*; (*dough*) pâte *f.*; (*of fish, meat*) pâté *m.*; (*jewellery*) strass *m.* —*v.t.* coller.

pastel /'pæstl/ *n.* pastel *m.* —*a.* pastel *invar.*

pasteurize /'pæstʃəraɪz/ *v.t.* pasteuriser.

pastiche /pæ'sti:ʃ/ *n.* pastiche *m.*

pastille /'pæstɪl/ *n.* pastille *f.*

pastime /'pɑ:staɪm/ *n.* passetemps *m. invar.*

pastoral /'pɑ:stərəl/ *a.* pastoral.

pastry /'peɪstrɪ/ *n.* (*dough*) pâte *f.*; (*tart*) pâtisserie *f.*

pasture /'pɑ:stʃə(r)/ *n.* pâturage *m.*

pasty[1] /'pæstɪ/ *n.* petit pâté *m.*

pasty[2] /'peɪstɪ/ *a.* pâteux.

pat /pæt/ *v.t.* (*p.t.* **patted**) tapoter. —*n.* petite tape *f.* —*adv. & a.* à propos; (*ready*) tout prêt.

patch /pætʃ/ *n.* pièce *f.*; (*over eye*) bandeau *m.*; (*spot*) tache *f.*; (*of vegetables*) carré *m.* —*v.t.* **∼ up,** rapiécer; (*fig.*) régler. **bad ∼,** période difficile *f.* **not be a ∼ on,** ne pas arriver à la cheville de. **∼y** *a.* inégal.

patchwork /'pætʃwɜ:k/ *n.* patchwork *m.*

pâté /'pæteɪ/ *n.* pâté *m.*

patent /'peɪtnt/ *a.* patent. —*n.* brevet (d'invention) *m.* —*v.t.* breveter. **∼ leather,** cuir verni *m.* **∼ly** *adv.* manifestement.

paternal /pə'tɜ:nl/ *a.* paternel.

paternity /pə'tɜ:nətɪ/ *n.* paternité *f.*

path /pɑ:θ/ *n.* (*pl.* **-s** /pɑ:ðz/) sentier *m.*, chemin *m.*; (*in park*) allée *f.*; (*of rocket*) trajectoire *f.*

pathetic /pə'θetɪk/ *a.* pitoyable; (*bad*: *fam.*) minable.

pathology /pə'θɒlədʒɪ/ *n.* pathologie *f.*

pathos /'peɪθɒs/ *n.* pathétique *m.*

patience /'peɪʃns/ *n.* patience *f.*

patient /'peɪʃnt/ *a.* patient. —*n.* malade *m./f.*, patient(e) *m.* (*f.*). **∼ly** *adv.* patiemment.

patio /'pætɪəʊ/ *n.* (*pl.* **-os**) patio *m.*

patriot /'pætrɪət, 'peɪtrɪət/ *n.* patriote *m./f.* **∼ic** /-'ɒtɪk/ *a.* patriotique; (*person*) patriote. **∼ism** *n.* patriotisme *m.*

patrol /pə'trəʊl/ *n.* patrouille *f.* —*v.t./i.* patrouiller (dans). **∼ car,** voiture de police *f.*

patrolman /pə'trəʊlmən/ *n.* (*pl.* **-men** /-men/) (*Amer.*) agent de police *m.*

patron /'peɪtrən/ *n.* (*of the arts*) mécène *m.* (*customer*) client(e) *m.* (*f.*). **∼ saint,** saint(e) patron(ne) *m.* (*f.*).

patron|age /'pætrənɪdʒ/ *n.* clientèle *f.*; (*support*) patronage *m.* **∼ize** *v.t.* être client de; (*fig.*) traiter avec condescendance.

patter[1] /'pætə(r)/ *n.* (*of steps*) bruit *m.*; (*of rain*) crépitement *m.*

patter[2] /'pætə(r)/ *n.* (*speech*) baratin *m.*

pattern /'pætn/ *n.* motif *m.*, dessin *m.*; (*for sewing*) patron *m.*; (*procedure*, *type*) schéma *m.*; (*example*) exemple *m.*

paunch /pɔːntʃ/ *n.* panse *f.*

pauper /'pɔːpə(r)/ *n.* indigent(e) *m.* (*f.*), pauvre *m.*, pauvresse *f.*

pause /pɔːz/ *n.* pause *f.* —*v.i.* faire une pause; (*hesitate*) hésiter.

pav|e /peɪv/ *v.t.* paver. **~e the way,** ouvrir la voie (**for,** à). **~ing-stone** *n.* pavé *m.*

pavement /'peɪvmənt/ *n.* trottoir *m.*; (*Amer.*) chaussée *f.*

pavilion /pə'vɪljən/ *n.* pavillon *m.*

paw /pɔː/ *n.* patte *f.* —*v.t.* (*of animal*) donner des coups de patte à; (*touch*: *fam.*) tripoter.

pawn[1] /pɔːn/ *n.* (*chess & fig.*) pion *m.*

pawn[2] /pɔːn/ *v.t.* mettre en gage. —*n.* **in ~,** en gage. **~-shop** *n.* mont-de-piété *m.*

pawnbroker /'pɔːnbrəʊkə(r)/ *n.* prêteur sur gages *m.*

pay /peɪ/ *v.t./i.* (*p.t.* **paid**) payer; (*yield*: *comm.*) rapporter; (*compliment*, *visit*) faire. —*n.* salaire *m.*, paie *f.* **in the ~ of,** à la solde de. **~ attention,** faire attention (**to,** à). **~ back,** rembourser. **~ for,** payer. **~ homage,** rendre hommage (**to,** à). **~ in,** verser (**to,** à). **~ off,** (finir de) payer; (*succeed*: *fam.*) être payant. **~ out,** payer, verser.

payable /'peɪəbl/ *a.* payable.

payment /'peɪmənt/ *n.* paiement *m.*; (*regular*) versement *m.* (*reward*) récompense *f.*

payroll /'peɪrəʊl/ *n.* registre du personnel *m.* **be on the ~ of,** être membre du personnel de.

pea /piː/ *n.* (petit) pois *m.* **~-shooter** *n.* sarbacane *f.*

peace /piːs/ *n.* paix *f.* **~ of mind,** tranquillité d'esprit *f.* **~able** *a.* pacifique.

peaceful /'piːsfl/ *a.* paisible; (*intention*, *measure*) pacifique.

peacemaker /'piːsmeɪkə(r)/ *n.* concilialteur, -trice *m.*, *f.*

peach /piːtʃ/ *n.* pêche *f.*

peacock /'piːkɒk/ *n.* paon *m.*

peak /piːk/ *n.* sommet *m.*; (*of mountain*) pic *m.*; (*maximum*) maximum *m.* **~ hours,** heures de pointe *f. pl.* **~ed cap,** casquette *f.*

peaky /'piːkɪ/ *a.* (*pale*) pâlot; (*puny*) chétif; (*ill*) patraque.

peal /piːl/ *n.* (*of bells*) carillon *m.*; (*of laughter*) éclat *m.*

peanut /'piːnʌt/ *n.* cacahuète *f.* **~s,** (*money*: *sl.*) une bagatelle.

pear /peə(r)/ *n.* poire *f.*

pearl /pɜːl/ *n.* perle *f.* **~y** *a.* nacré.

peasant /'peznt/ *n.* paysan(ne) *m.* (*f.*).

peat /piːt/ *n.* tourbe *f.*

pebble /'pebl/ *n.* caillou *m.*; (*on beach*) galet *m.*

peck /pek/ *v.t./i.* (*food etc.*) picorer; (*attack*) donner des coups de bec (à). —*n.* coup de bec *m.* **a ~ on the cheek,** une bise.

peckish /'pekɪʃ/ *a.* **be ~,** (*fam.*) avoir faim.

peculiar /pɪ'kjuːlɪə(r)/ *a.* (*odd*) bizarre; (*special*) particulier (**to,** à). **~ity** /-'ærətɪ/ *n.* bizarrerie *f.*

pedal /'pedl/ *n.* pédale *f.* —*v.i.* pédaler.

pedantic /pɪ'dæntɪk/ *a.* pédant.

peddle /'pedl/ *v.t.* colporter; (*drugs*) revendre.

pedestal /'pedɪstl/ *n.* piédestal *m.*

pedestrian /pɪ'destrɪən/ *n.* piéton *m.* —*a.* (*precinct*, *street*) piétonnier; (*fig.*) prosaïque. **~ crossing,** passage piétons *m.*

pedigree /'pedɪgriː/ *n.* (*of person*) ascendance *f.*; (*of animal*) pedigree *m.* —*a.* (*cattle etc.*) de race.

pedlar /'pedlə(r)/ *n.* camelot *m.*; (*door-to-door*) colporteulr, -se *m.*, *f.*

pee /piː/ *v.i.* (*fam.*) faire pipi.

peek /piːk/ *v.i. & n.* = **peep**[1].

peel /piːl/ *n.* épluchure(s) *f.* (*pl.*); (*of orange*) écorce *f.* —*v.t.* (*fruit*, *vegetables*) éplucher. —*v.i.* (*of skin*) peler; (*of paint*) s'écailler. **~ings** *n. pl.* épluchures *f. pl.*

peep[1] /piːp/ *v.i.* jeter un coup d'œil (furtif) (**at,** à). —*n.* coup d'œil (furtif) *m.* **~-hole** *n.* judas *m.* **P~ing Tom,** voyeur *m.*

peep[2] /piːp/ *v.i.* (*chirp*) pépier.

peer[1] /pɪə(r)/ *v.i.* **~ (at),** regarder attentivement, scruter.

peer[2] /pɪə(r)/ *n.* (*equal*, *noble*) pair *m.* **~age** *n.* pairie *f.*

peeved /piːvd/ *a.* (*sl.*) irrité.

peevish /'piːvɪʃ/ *a.* grincheux.

peg /peg/ *n.* cheville *f.*; (*for clothes*) pince à linge *f.*; (*to hang coats etc.*) patère *f.*; (*for tent*) piquet *m.* —*v.t.* (*p.t.* **pegged**) (*prices*) stabiliser. **buy off the ~,** acheter en prêt-à-porter.

pejorative /pɪ'dʒɒrətɪv/ *a.* péjoratif.

pelican /'pelıkən/ n. pélican m. **~ crossing,** passage clouté (avec feux de signalisation) m.

pellet /'pelıt/ n. (*round mass*) boulette f.; (*for gun*) plomb m.

pelt[1] /pelt/ n. (*skin*) peau f.

pelt[2] /pelt/ v.t. bombarder (**with,** de). —v.i. pleuvoir à torrents.

pelvis /'pelvıs/ n. (*anat.*) bassin m.

pen[1] /pen/ n. (*for sheep etc.*) enclos m.; (*for baby, cattle*) parc m.

pen[2] /pen/ n. stylo m.; (*to be dipped in ink*) plume f. —v.t. (*p.t.* **penned**) écrire. **~-friend** n. correspondant(e) m. (f.). **~-name** n. pseudonyme m.

penal /'pi:nl/ a. pénal. **~ize** v.t. pénaliser; (*fig.*) handicaper.

penalty /'penltı/ n. peine f.; (*fine*) amende f.; (*sport*) pénalité f.

penance /'penəns/ n. pénitence f.

pence /pens/ *see* **penny.**

pencil /'pensl/ n. crayon m. —v.t. (*p.t.* **pencilled**) crayonner. **~ in,** noter provisoirement. **~-sharpener** n. taille-crayon(s) m.

pendant /'pendənt/ n. pendentif m.

pending /'pendıŋ/ a. en suspens. —*prep.* (*until*) en attendant.

pendulum /'pendjʊləm/ n. pendule m.; (*of clock*) balancier m.

penetrat|e /'penıtreıt/ v.t. (*enter*) pénétrer dans; (*understand, permeate*) pénétrer. —v.i. pénétrer. **~ing** a. pénétrant. **~ion** /-'treıʃn/ n. pénétration f.

penguin /'peŋgwın/ n. manchot m., pingouin m.

penicillin /penı'sılın/ n. pénicilline f.

peninsula /pə'nınsjʊlə/ n. péninsule f.

penis /'pi:nıs/ n. pénis m.

peniten|t /'penıtənt/ a. & n. pénitent(e) (m. (f.)). **~ce** n. pénitence f.

penitentiary /penı'tenʃərı/ n. (*Amer.*) prison f., pénitencier m.

penknife /'pennaıf/ n. (*pl.* **-knives**) canif m.

pennant /'penənt/ n. flamme f.

penniless /'penılıs/ a. sans le sou.

penny /'penı/ n. (*pl.* **pennies** *or* **pence**) penny m.; (*fig.*) sou m.

pension /'penʃn/ n. pension f.; (*for retirement*) retraite f. —v.t. **~ off,** mettre à la retraite. **~ scheme,** caisse de retraite f. **~able** a. qui a droit à une retraite. **~er** n. (**old-age**) **~er,** retraité(e) m. (f.), personne âgée f.

pensive /'pensıv/ a. pensif.

Pentecost /'pentıkɒst/ n. Pentecôte f. **~al** a. pentecôtiste.

penthouse /'penthaʊs/ n. appartement de luxe m. (*sur le toit d'un immeuble*).

pent-up /pent'ʌp/ a. refoulé.

penultimate /pen'ʌltımət/ a. avant-dernier.

people /'pi:pl/ n. pl. gens m. pl., personnes f. pl. —n. peuple m. —v.t. peupler. **English/**etc. **~,** les Anglais/etc. m. pl. **~ say,** on dit,

pep /pep/ n. entrain m. —v.t. **~ up,** donner de l'entrain à. **~ talk,** discours d'encouragement m.

pepper /'pepə(r)/ n. poivre m.; (*vegetable*) poivron m. —v.t. (*culin.*) poivrer. **~y** a. poivré.

peppermint /'pepəmınt/ n. (*plant*) menthe poivrée f.; (*sweet*) bonbon à la menthe m.

per /pɜ:(r)/ prep. par. **~ annum,** par an. **~ cent,** pour cent. **~ kilo/**etc., le kilo/etc. **ten km. ~ hour,** dix km à l'heure,

perceive /pə'si:v/ v.t. percevoir; (*notice*) s'apercevoir de. **~ that,** s'apercevoir que.

percentage /pə'sentıdʒ/ n. pourcentage m.

perceptible /pə'septəbl/ a. perceptible.

percept|ion /pə'sepʃn/ n. perception f. **~ive** /-tıv/ a. pénétrant.

perch /pɜ:tʃ/ n. (*of bird*) perchoir m. —v.i. (se) percher.

percolat|e /'pɜ:kəleıt/ v.t. passer. —v.i. filtrer. **~or** n. cafetière f.

percussion /pə'kʌʃn/ n. percussion f.

peremptory /pə'remptərı/ a. péremptoire.

perennial /pə'renıəl/ a. perpétuel; (*plant*) vivace.

perfect[1] /'pɜ:fıkt/ a. parfait. **~ly** adv. parfaitement.

perfect[2] /pə'fekt/ v.t. parfaire, mettre au point. **~ion** /-kʃn/ n. perfection f. **to ~ion,** à la perfection. **~ionist** /-kʃənıst/ n. perfectionniste m./f.

perforat|e /'pɜ:fəreıt/ v.t. perforer. **~ion** /-'reıʃn/ n. perforation f.; (*line of holes*) pointillé m.

perform /pə'fɔ:m/ v.t. exécuter, faire; (*a function*) remplir; (*mus., theatre*) interpréter, jouer. —v.i. jouer; (*behave, function*) se comporter. **~ance** n. exécution f.; interprétation f.; (*of car, team*) performance f.; (*show*) représentation f.; séance f.; (*fuss*) histoire f. **~er** n. artiste m./f.

perfume /'pɜ:fju:m/ n. parfum m.

perfunctory /pə'fʌŋktərı/ a. négligent, superficiel.

perhaps /pə'hæps/ *adv.* peut-être.
peril /'perəl/ *n.* péril *m.* ~**ous** *a.* périlleux.
perimeter /pə'rɪmɪtə(r)/ *n.* périmètre *m.*
period /'pɪərɪəd/ *n.* période *f.*, époque *f.*; (*era*) époque *f.*; (*lesson*) cours *m.*; (*gram.*) point *m.*; (*med.*) règles *f. pl.* —*a.* d'époque. ~**ic** /-'ɒdɪk/ *a.* périodique. ~**ically** /-'ɒdɪklɪ/ *adv.* périodiquement.
periodical /pɪərɪ'ɒdɪkl/ *n.* périodique *m.*
peripher|y /pə'rɪfərɪ/ *n.* périphérie *f.* ~**al** *a.* périphérique; (*of lesser importance*: *fig.*) accessoire; *n.* (*comput.*) périphérique *m.*
periscope /'perɪskəʊp/ *n.* périscope *m.*
perish /'perɪʃ/ *v.i.* périr; (*rot*) se détériorer. ~**able** *a.* périssable.
perjur|e /'pɜːdʒə(r)/ *v. pr.* ~**e o.s.**, se parjurer. ~**y** *n.* parjure *m.*
perk[1] /pɜːk/ *v.t./i.* ~ **up**, (*fam.*) (se) remonter. ~**y** *a.* (*fam.*) gai.
perk[2] /pɜːk/ *n.* (*fam.*) avantage *m.*
perm /pɜːm/ *n.* permanente *f.* —*v.t.* **have one's hair** ~**ed**, se faire faire une permanente.
permanen|t /'pɜːmənənt/ *a.* permanent. ~**ce** *n.* permanence *f.* ~**tly** *adv.* à titre permanent.
permeable /'pɜːmɪəbl/ *a.* perméable.
permeate /'pɜːmɪeɪt/ *v.t.* imprégner, se répandre dans.
permissible /pə'mɪsəbl/ *a.* permis.
permission /pə'mɪʃn/ *n.* permission *f.*
permissive /pə'mɪsɪv/ *a.* tolérant, laxiste. ~**ness** *n.* laxisme *m.*
permit[1] /pə'mɪt/ *v.t.* (*p.t.* **permitted**) permettre (**s.o. to**, à qn. de), autoriser (**s.o. to**, qn. à).
permit[2] /'pɜːmɪt/ *n.* permis *m.*; (*pass*) laissez-passer *m. invar.*
permutation /pɜːmjʊ'teɪʃn/ *n.* permutation *f.*
pernicious /pə'nɪʃəs/ *a.* nocif, pernicieux; (*med.*) pernicieux.
peroxide /pə'rɒksaɪd/ *n.* eau oxygénée *f.*
perpendicular /pɜːpən'dɪkjʊlə(r)/ *a.* & *n.* perpendiculaire (*f.*).
perpetrat|e /'pɜːpɪtreɪt/ *v.t.* perpétrer. ~**or** *n.* auteur *m.*
perpetual /pə'petʃʊəl/ *a.* perpétuel.
perpetuate /pə'petʃʊeɪt/ *v.t.* perpétuer.
perplex /pə'pleks/ *v.t.* rendre perplexe. ~**ed** *a.* perplexe. ~**ing** *a.* déroutant. ~**ity** *n.* perplexité *f.*
persecut|e /'pɜːsɪkjuːt/ *v.t.* persécuter. ~**ion** /-'kjuːʃn/ *n.* persécution *f.*

persever|e /pɜːsɪ'vɪə(r)/ *v.i.* persévérer. ~**ance** *n.* persévérance *f.*
Persian /'pɜːʃn/ *a.* & *n.* (*lang.*) persan (*m.*). ~ **Gulf**, golfe persique *m.*
persist /pə'sɪst/ *v.i.* persister (**in doing**, à faire). ~**ence** *n.* persistance *f.* ~**ent** *a.* (*cough*, *snow*, *etc.*) persistant; (*obstinate*) obstiné; (*continual*) continuel. ~**ently** *adv.* avec persistance.
person /'pɜːsn/ *n.* personne *f.* **in** ~, en personne. ~**able** *a.* beau.
personal /'pɜːsənl/ *a.* personnel; (*hygiene*, *habits*) intime; (*secretary*) particulier. ~**ly** *adv.* personnellement. ~ **stereo**, baladeur *m.*
personality /pɜːsə'nælətɪ/ *n.* personnalité *f.*; (*on TV*) vedette *f.*
personify /pə'sɒnɪfaɪ/ *v.t.* personnifier.
personnel /pɜːsə'nel/ *n.* personnel *m.*
perspective /pə'spektɪv/ *n.* perspective *f.*
Perspex /'pɜːspeks/ *n.* (P.) plexiglas *m.* (P.).
perspir|e /pə'spaɪə(r)/ *v.i.* transpirer. ~**ation** /-ə'reɪʃn/ *n.* transpiration *f.*
persua|de /pə'sweɪd/ *v.t.* persuader (**to**, de). ~**sion** /-eɪʒn/ *n.* persuasion *f.*
persuasive /pə'sweɪsɪv/ *a.* (*person*, *speech*, *etc.*) persuasif. ~**ly** *adv.* d'une manière persuasive.
pert /pɜːt/ *a.* (*saucy*) impertinent; (*lively*) plein d'entrain. ~**ly** *adv.* avec impertinence.
pertain /pə'teɪn/ *v.i.* ~ **to**, se rapporter à.
pertinent /'pɜːtɪnənt/ *a.* pertinent. ~**ly** *adv.* pertinemment.
perturb /pə'tɜːb/ *v.t.* troubler.
Peru /pə'ruː/ *n.* Pérou *m.* ~**vian** *a.* & *n.* péruvien(ne) (*m.* (*f.*)).
perus|e /pə'ruːz/ *v.t.* lire (attentivement). ~**al** *n.* lecture *f.*
perva|de /pə'veɪd/ *v.t.* imprégner, envahir. ~**sive** *a.* (*mood*, *dust*) envahissant.
pervers|e /pə'vɜːs/ *a.* (*stubborn*) entêté; (*wicked*) pervers. ~**ity** *n.* perversité *f.*
perver|t[1] /pə'vɜːt/ *v.t.* pervertir. ~**sion** *n.* perversion *f.*
perver|t[2] /'pɜːvɜːt/ *n.* perverti(e) *m.* (*f.*), dépravé(e) *m.* (*f.*).
peseta /pə'seɪtə/ *n.* peseta *f.*
pessimis|t /'pesɪmɪst/ *n.* pessimiste *m./f.* ~**m** /-zəm/ *n.* pessimisme *m.* ~**tic** /-'mɪstɪk/ *a.* pessimiste. ~**tically** /-'mɪstɪklɪ/ *adv.* avec pessimisme.
pest /pest/ *n.* insecte *or* animal nuisible *m.*; (*person*: *fam.*) enquiquineur, -se *m.*, *f.*
pester /'pestə(r)/ *v.t.* harceler.

pesticide /'pestɪsaɪd/ n. pesticide m., insecticide m.

pet /pet/ n. animal (domestique) m.; (favourite) chouchou(te) m. (f.). —a. (tame) apprivoisé. —v.t. (p.t. **petted**) caresser; (sexually) peloter. ∼ **hate**, bête noire f. ∼ **name**, diminutif m.

petal /'petl/ n. pétale m.

peter /'piːtə(r)/ v.i. ∼ **out**, (supplies) s'épuiser; (road) finir.

petite /pə'tiːt/ a. (woman) menue.

petition /pɪ'tɪʃn/ n. pétition f. —v.t. adresser une pétition à.

petrify /'petrɪfaɪ/ v.t. pétrifier; (scare: fig.) pétrifier de peur.

petrol /'petrəl/ n. essence f. ∼ **bomb**, cocktail molotov m. ∼ **station**, station-service f. ∼ **tank**, réservoir d'essence.

petroleum /pɪ'trəʊlɪəm/ n. pétrole m.

petticoat /'petɪkəʊt/ n. jupon m.

petty /'petɪ/ a. (-ier, -iest) (minor) petit; (mean) mesquin. ∼ **cash**, petite caisse f.

petulant /'petjʊlənt/ a. irritable. ∼ce n. irritabilité f.

pew /pjuː/ n. banc (d'église) m.

pewter /'pjuːtə(r)/ n. étain m.

phallic /'fælɪk/ a. phallique.

phantom /'fæntəm/ n. fantôme m.

pharmaceutical /faːmə'sjuːtɪkl/ a. pharmaceutique.

pharmac|y /'faːməsɪ/ n. pharmacie f. ∼**ist** n. pharmacien(ne) m. (f.).

pharyngitis /færɪn'dʒaɪtɪs/ n. pharyngite f.

phase /feɪz/ n. phase f. —v.t. ∼ **in/out**, introduire/retirer progressivement.

pheasant /'feznt/ n. faisan m.

phenomen|on /fɪ'nɒmɪnən/ n. (pl. -ena) phénomène m. ∼**al** a. phénoménal.

phew /fjuː/ int. ouf.

phial /'faɪəl/ n. fiole f.

philanderer /fɪ'lændərə(r)/ n. coureur (de femmes) m.

philanthrop|ist /fɪ'lænθrəpɪst/ n. philanthrope m./f. ∼**ic** /-ən'θrɒpɪk/ a. philanthropique.

philatel|y /fɪ'lætəlɪ/ n. philatélie f. ∼**ist** n. philatéliste m./f.

philharmonic /fɪlaː'mɒnɪk/ a. philharmonique.

Philippines /'fɪlɪpiːnz/ n. pl. **the** ∼, les Philippines f. pl.

philistine /'fɪlɪstaɪn, Amer. 'fɪlɪstiːn/ n. philistin m.

philosoph|y /fɪ'lɒsəfɪ/ n. philosophie f. ∼**er** n. philosophe m./f. ∼**ical** /-ə'sɒfɪkl/ a. philosophique; (resigned) philosophe.

phlegm /flem/ n. (med.) mucosité f.

phlegmatic /fleg'mætɪk/ a. flegmatique.

phobia /'fəʊbɪə/ n. phobie f.

phone /fəʊn/ n. téléphone m. —v.t. (person) téléphoner à; (message) téléphoner. —v.i. téléphoner. ∼ **back**, rappeler. **on the** ∼, au téléphone. ∼ **book**, annuaire m. ∼ **box**, ∼ **booth**, cabine téléphonique f. ∼ **call**, coup de fil m. ∼-**in** n. émission à ligne ouverte f.

phonecard /'fəʊnkaːd/ n. télécarte f.

phonetic /fə'netɪk/ a. phonétique.

phoney /'fəʊnɪ/ a. (-ier, -iest) (sl.) faux. —n. (person: sl.) charlatan m. **it's a** ∼, (sl.) c'est faux.

phosphate /'fɒsfeɪt/ n. phosphate m.

phosphorus /'fɒsfərəs/ n. phosphore m.

photo /'fəʊtəʊ/ n. (pl. -os) (fam.) photo f.

photocop|y /'fəʊtəʊkɒpɪ/ n. photocopie f. —v.t. photocopier. ∼**ier** n. photocopieuse f.

photogenic /fəʊtəʊ'dʒenɪk/ a. photogénique.

photograph /'fəʊtəgraːf/ n. photographie f. —v.t. photographier. ∼**er** /fə'tɒgrəfə(r)/ n. photographe m./f. ∼**ic** /-'græfɪk/ a. photographique. ∼**y** /fə'tɒgrəfɪ/ n. (activity) photographie f.

phrase /freɪz/ n. expression f.; (idiom & gram.) locution f. —v.t. exprimer, formuler. ∼-**book** n. guide de conversation m.

physical /'fɪzɪkl/ a. physique. ∼**ly** adv. physiquement.

physician /fɪ'zɪʃn/ n. médecin m.

physicist /'fɪzɪsɪst/ n. physicien(ne) m. (f.).

physics /'fɪzɪks/ n. physique f.

physiology /fɪzɪ'ɒlədʒɪ/ n. physiologie f.

physiotherap|y /fɪzɪəʊ'θerəpɪ/ n. kinésithérapie f. ∼**ist** n. kinésithérapeute m./f.

physique /fɪ'ziːk/ n. constitution f.; (appearance) physique m.

pian|o /pɪ'ænəʊ/ n. (pl. -os) piano m. ∼**ist** /'pɪənɪst/ n. pianiste m./f.

piazza /pɪ'ætsə/ n. (square) place f.

pick[1] /pɪk/ (tool) n. pioche f.

pick[2] /pɪk/ v.t. choisir; (flower etc.) cueillir; (lock) crocheter; (nose) se curer; (pockets) faire. ∼ (**off**), enlever. —n. choix m.; (best) meilleur(e) m. (f.). ∼ **a quarrel with**, chercher querelle à. ∼ **holes in**, relever les défauts de. **the** ∼ **of**, ce qu'il y a de mieux dans. ∼ **off**, (mil.) abattre un à un. ∼ **on**, harceler. ∼ **out**, choisir; (identify) distinguer. ∼ **up** v.t.

ramasser; (*sth. fallen*) relever; (*weight*) soulever; (*habit, passenger, speed, etc.*) prendre; (*learn*) apprendre; *v.i.* s'améliorer. ∿-**me-up** *n.* remontant *m.* ∿-**up** *n.* partenaire de rencontre *m./f.*; (*truck, stylus-holder*) pick-up *m.*

pickaxe /'pɪkæks/ *n.* pioche *f.*

picket /'pɪkɪt/ *n.* (*single striker*) gréviste *m./f.*; (*stake*) piquet *m.* ∿ (**line**), piquet de grève *m.* —*v.t.* (*p.t.* **picketed**) mettre un piquet de grève devant.

pickings /'pɪkɪŋz/ *n. pl.* restes *m. pl.*

pickle /'pɪkl/ *n.* vinaigre *m.*; (*brine*) saumure *f.* ∿s, pickles *m. pl.*; (*Amer.*) concombres *m.pl.* —*v.t.* conserver dans du vinaigre *or* de la saumure. **in a** ∿, (*fam.*) dans le pétrin.

pickpocket /'pɪkpɒkɪt/ *n.* (*thief*) pick-pocket *m.*

picnic /'pɪknɪk/ *n.* pique-nique *m.* —*v.i.* (*p.t.* **picnicked**) piqueniquer.

pictorial /pɪk'tɔːrɪəl/ *a.* illustré.

picture /'pɪktʃə(r)/ *n.* image *f.*; (*painting*) tableau *m.*; (*photograph*) photo *f.*; (*drawing*) dessin *m.*; (*film*) film *m.*; (*fig.*) description *f.*, tableau *m.* —*v.t.* s'imaginer; (*describe*) dépeindre. **the** ∿**s**, (*cinema*) le cinéma. ∿ **book**, livre d'images *m.*

picturesque /pɪktʃə'resk/ *a.* pittoresque.

piddling /'pɪdlɪŋ/ *a.* (*fam.*) dérisoire.

pidgin /'pɪdʒɪn/ *a.* ∿ **English**, pidgin *m.*

pie /paɪ/ *n.* tarte *f.*; (*of meat*) pâté en croûte *m.* ∿ **chart**, camembert *m.*

piebald /'paɪbɔːld/ *a.* pie *invar.*

piece /piːs/ *n.* morceau *m.*; (*of currency, machine, etc.*) pièce *f.* —*v.t.* ∿ (**together**), (r)assembler. **a** ∿ **of advice/furniture/***etc.*, un conseil/meuble/ *etc.* ∿-**work** *n.* travail à la pièce *m.* **go to** ∿**s**, (*fam.*) s'effondrer. **take to** ∿**s**, démonter.

piecemeal /'piːsmiːl/ *a.* par bribes.

pier /pɪə(r)/ *n.* (*promenade*) jetée *f.*

pierce /pɪəs/ *v.t.* percer. ∿**ing** *a.* perçant; (*cold*) glacial.

piety /'paɪətɪ/ *n.* piété *f.*

piffle /'pɪfl/ *n.* (*sl.*) fadaises *f. pl.* ∿**ing** *a.* (*sl.*) insignifiant.

pig /pɪg/ *n.* cochon *m.* ∿-**headed** *a.* entêté.

pigeon /'pɪdʒən/ *n.* pigeon *m.* ∿-**hole** *n.* casier *m.*; *v.t.* classer.

piggy /'pɪgɪ/ *a.* porcin; (*greedy: fam.*) goinfre. ∿-**back** *adv.* sur le dos. ∿ **bank**, tirelire *f.*

pigment /'pɪgmənt/ *n.* pigment *m.* ∿**ation** /-en'teɪʃn/ *n.* pigmentation *f.*

pigsty /'pɪgstaɪ/ *n.* porcherie *f.*

pigtail /'pɪgteɪl/ *n.* natte *f.*

pike /paɪk/ *n. invar.* (*fish*) brochet *m.*

pilchard /'pɪltʃəd/ *n.* pilchard *m.*

pile /paɪl/ *n.* pile *f.*, tas *m.*; (*of carpet*) poils *m.pl.* —*v.t.* ∿ (**up**), (*stack*) empiler. —*v.i.* ∿ **into**, s'empiler dans. ∿ **up,** (*accumulate*) (s')accumuler. **a** ∿ **of**, (*fam.*) un tas de. ∿-**up** *n.* (*auto.*) carambolage *m.*

piles /paɪlz/ *n. pl.* (*fam.*) hémorroïdes *f. pl.*

pilfer /'pɪlfə(r)/ *v.t.* chaparder. ∿**age** *n.* chapardage *m.*

pilgrim /'pɪlgrɪm/ *n.* pèlerin *m.* ∿**age** *n.* pèlerinage *m.*

pill /pɪl/ *n.* pilule *f.*

pillage /'pɪlɪdʒ/ *n.* pillage *m.* —*v.t.* piller. —*v.i.* se livrer au pillage.

pillar /'pɪlə(r)/ *n.* pilier *m.* ∿-**box** *n.* boîte à *or* aux lettres *f.*

pillion /'pɪljən/ *n.* siège arrière *m.* **ride** ∿, monter derrière.

pillory /'pɪlərɪ/ *n.* pilori *m.*

pillow /'pɪləʊ/ *n.* oreiller *m.*

pillowcase /'pɪləʊkeɪs/ *n.* taie d'oreiller *f.*

pilot /'paɪlət/ *n.* pilote *m.* —*a.* pilote. —*v.t.* (*p.t.* **piloted**) piloter. ∿-**light** *n.* veilleuse *f.*

pimento /pɪ'mentəʊ/ *n.* (*pl.* -os) piment *m.*

pimp /pɪmp/ *n.* souteneur *m.*

pimple /'pɪmpl/ *n.* bouton *m.* ∿**y** *a.* boutonneux.

pin /pɪn/ *n.* épingle *f.*; (*techn.*) goupille *f.* —*v.t.* (*p.t.* **pinned**) épingler, attacher; (*hold down*) clouer. **have** ∿**s and needles**, avoir des fourmis. ∿ **s.o. down**, (*fig.*) forcer qn. à se décider. ∿-**point** *v.t.* repérer, définir. ∿ **up**, afficher. ∿-**up** *n.* (*fam.*) pin-up *f. invar.*

pinafore /'pɪnəfɔː(r)/ *n.* tablier *m.*

pincers /'pɪnsəz/ *n. pl.* tenailles *f. pl.*

pinch /pɪntʃ/ *v.t.* pincer; (*steal: sl.*) piquer. —*v.i.* (*be too tight*) serrer. —*n.* (*mark*) pinçon *m.*; (*of salt*) pincée *f.* **at a** ∿, au besoin.

pincushion /'pɪnkʊʃn/ *n.* pelote à épingles *f.*

pine¹ /paɪn/ *n.* (*tree*) pin *m.* ∿-**cone** *n.* pomme de pin *f.*

pine² /paɪn/ *v.i.* ∿ **away**, dépérir. ∿ **for**, languir après.

pineapple /'paɪnæpl/ *n.* ananas *m.*

ping /pɪŋ/ *n.* bruit métallique *m.*

ping-pong /'pɪŋpɒŋ/ *n.* ping-pong *m.*

pink /pɪŋk/ *a. & n.* rose (*m.*).

pinnacle /'pɪnəkl/ *n.* pinacle *m.*

pint /paɪnt/ n. pinte f. (*imperial = 0.57 litre; Amer. = 0.47 litre*).

pioneer /paɪə'nɪə(r)/ n. pionnier m. —v.t. être le premier à faire, utiliser, étudier, *etc.*

pious /'paɪəs/ a. pieux.

pip[1] /pɪp/ n. (*seed*) pépin m.

pip[2] /pɪp/ n. (*sound*) top m.

pipe /paɪp/ n. tuyau m.; (*of smoker*) pipe f.; (*mus.*) pipeau m. —v.t. transporter par tuyau. **~- cleaner** n. cure-pipe m. **~ down**, se taire. **~-dream** n. chimère f.

pipeline /'paɪplaɪn/ n. pipeline m. **in the ~**, en route.

piping /'paɪpɪŋ/ n. tuyau(x) m. (*pl.*). **~ hot**, très chaud.

piquant /'pi:kənt/ a. piquant.

pique /pi:k/ n. dépit m.

pira|te /'paɪərət/ n. pirate m. —v.t. pirater. **~cy** n. piraterie f.

Pisces /'paɪsi:z/ n. les Poissons m. pl.

pistachio /pɪ'stæʃɪəʊ/ n. (*pl.* -os) pistache f.

pistol /'pɪstl/ n. pistolet m.

piston /'pɪstən/ n. piston m.

pit /pɪt/ n. fosse f., trou m.; (*mine*) puits m.; (*quarry*) carrière f.; (*for orchestra*) fosse f.; (*of stomach*) creux m.; (*of cherry etc.: Amer.*) noyau m. —v.t. (*p.t.* **pitted**) trouer; (*fig.*) opposer. **~ o.s. against**, se mesurer à.

pitch[1] /pɪtʃ/ n. (*tar*) poix f. **~-black** a. d'un noir d'ébène.

pitch[2] /pɪtʃ/ v.t. lancer; (*tent*) dresser. —v.i. (*of ship*) tanguer. —n. degré m.; (*of voice*) hauteur f.; (*mus.*) ton m.; (*sport*) terrain m. **~ed battle**, bataille rangée f. **a high-~ed voice**, une voix aiguë. **~ in**, (*fam.*) contribuer. **~ into**, (*fam.*) s'attaquer à.

pitcher /'pɪtʃə(r)/ n. cruche f.

pitchfork /'pɪtʃfɔːk/ n. fourche à foin f.

pitfall /'pɪtfɔːl/ n. piège m.

pith /pɪθ/ n. (*of orange*) peau blanche f.; (*essence: fig.*) moelle f.

pithy /'pɪθɪ/ a. (-ier, -iest) (*terse*) concis; (*forceful*) vigoureux.

piti|ful /'pɪtɪfl/ a. pitoyable. **~less** a. impitoyable.

pittance /'pɪtns/ n. revenu or salaire dérisoire m.

pity /'pɪtɪ/ n. pitié f.; (*regrettable fact*) dommage m. —v.t. plaindre. **take ~ on**, avoir pitié de. **what a ~**, quel dommage. **it's a ~**, c'est dommage.

pivot /'pɪvət/ n. pivot m. —v.i. (*p.t.* **pivoted**) pivoter.

pixie /'pɪksɪ/ n. lutin m.

pizza /'pi:tsə/ n. pizza f.

placard /'plæka:d/ n. affiche f.

placate /plə'keɪt, Amer. 'pleɪkeɪt/ v.t. calmer.

place /pleɪs/ n. endroit m., lieu m.; (*house*) maison f.; (*seat, rank, etc.*) place f. —v.t. placer; (*an order*) passer; (*remember*) situer. **at** or **to my ~**, chez moi. **be ~d**, (*in race*) se placer. **change ~s**, changer de place. **in the first ~**, d'abord. **out of ~**, déplacé. **take ~**, avoir lieu. **~-mat** n. set m.

placenta /plə'sentə/ n. placenta m.

placid /'plæsɪd/ a. placide.

plagiar|ize /'pleɪdʒəraɪz/ v.t. plagier. **~ism** n. plagiat m.

plague /pleɪg/ n. peste f.; (*nuisance: fam.*) fléau m. —v.t. harceler.

plaice /pleɪs/ n. invar. carrelet m.

plaid /plæd/ n. tissu écossais m.

plain /pleɪn/ a. (-er, -est) clair; (*candid*) franc; (*simple*) simple; (*not pretty*) sans beauté; (*not patterned*) uni. —adv. franchement. —n. plaine f. **~ chocolate**, chocolat noir. **in ~ clothes**, en civil. **~ly** adv. clairement; franchement; simplement. **~ness** n. simplicité f.

plaintiff /'pleɪntɪf/ n. plaignant(e) m. (f.).

plaintive /'pleɪntɪv/ a. plaintif.

plait /plæt/ v.t. tresser, natter. —n. tresse f., natte f.

plan /plæn/ n. projet m., plan m.; (*diagram*) plan m. —v.t. (*p.t.* **planned**) prévoir, projeter; (*arrange*) organiser; (*design*) concevoir; (*economy, work*) planifier. —v.i. faire des projets. **~ to do**, avoir l'intention de faire.

plane[1] /pleɪn/ n (*tree*) platane m.

plane[2] /pleɪn/ n. (*level*) plan m.; (*aeroplane*) avion m. —a. plan.

plane[3] /pleɪn/ n. (*tool*) rabot m. —v.t. raboter.

planet /'plænɪt/ n. planète f. **~ary** a. planétaire.

plank /plæŋk/ n. planche f.

plankton /'plæŋktn/ n. plancton m.

planning /'plænɪŋ/ n. (*pol., comm.*) planification f. **family ~**, planning familial m. **~ permission**, permis de construire m.

plant /plɑ:nt/ n. plante f.; (*techn.*) matériel m.; (*factory*) usine f. —v.t. planter; (*bomb*) (dé)poser. **~ation** /-'teɪʃn/ n. plantation f.

plaque /plɑ:k/ n. plaque f.

plasma /'plæzmə/ n. plasma m.

plaster /'plɑ:stə(r)/ n. plâtre m.; (*adhesive*) sparadrap m. —v.t. plâtrer; (*cover*) tapisser (**with**, de). **in ~**, dans

le plâtre. **~ of Paris,** plâtre à mouler *m.*
~er *n.* plâtrier *m.*
plastic /'plæstɪk/ *a.* en plastique; (*art,
substance*) plastique. —*n.* plastique *m.*
~ surgery, chirurgie esthétique *f.*
Plasticine /'plæstɪsiːn/ *n.* (P.) pâte à
modeler *f.*
plate /pleɪt/ *n.* assiette *f.*; (*of metal*)
plaque *f.*; (*gold or silver dishes*)
vaisselle plate *f.*; (*in book*) gravure *f.*
—*v.t.* (*metal*) plaquer. **~ful** *n.* (*pl.*
-fuls) assiettée *f.*
plateau /'plætəʊ/ *n.* (*pl.* -eaux /-əʊz/)
plateau *m.*
platform /'plætfɔːm/ *n.* (*in classroom,
hall, etc.*) estrade *f.*; (*for speaking*)
tribune *f.*; (*rail.*) quai *m.*; (*of bus &
pol.*) plate-forme *f.*
platinum /'plætɪnəm/ *n.* platine *m.*
platitude /'plætɪtjuːd/ *n.* platitude *f.*
platonic /plə'tɒnɪk/ *a.* platonique.
platoon /plə'tuːn/ *n.* (*mil.*) section *f.*
platter /'plætə(r)/ *n.* plat *m.*
plausible /'plɔːzəbl/ *a.* plausible.
play /pleɪ/ *v.t./i.* jouer; (*instrument*)
jouer de; (*record*) passer; (*game*) jouer
à; (*opponent*) jouer contre; (*match*)
disputer. —*n.* jeu *m.*; (*theatre*) pièce *f.*
~-act *v.i.* jouer la comédie. **~ down,**
minimiser. **~-group, ~-school** *ns.*
garderie *f.* **~-off** *n.* (*sport*) belle *f.* **~
on,** (*take advantage of*) jouer sur. **~ on
words,** jeu de mots *m.* **~ed out,** épuisé.
~-pen *n.* parc *m.* **~ safe,** ne pas
prendre de risques. **~ up,** (*fam.*) créer
des problèmes (à). **~ up to,** flatter. **~er**
n. joueur, -se *m.*, *f.*
playboy /'pleɪbɔɪ/ *n.* play-boy *m.*
playful /'pleɪfl/ *a.* enjoué; (*child*) joueur.
~ly *adv.* avec espièglerie.
playground /'pleɪgraʊnd/ *n.* cour de
récréation *f.*
playing /'pleɪɪŋ/ *n.* jeu *m.* **~-card** *n.*
carte à jouer *f.* **~-field** *n.* terrain de
sport *m.*
playmate /'pleɪmeɪt/ *n.* camarade *m./f.*,
copain, -ine *m.*, *f.*
plaything /'pleɪθɪŋ/ *n.* jouet *m.*
playwright /'pleɪraɪt/ *n.* dramaturge
m./f.
plc *abbr.* (*public limited company*) SA.
plea /pliː/ *n.* (*entreaty*) supplication *f.*;
(*reason*) excuse *f.*; (*jurid.*) défense *f.*
plead /pliːd/ *v.t./i.* (*jurid.*) plaider; (*as
excuse*) alléguer. **~ for,** (*beg for*)
implorer. **~ with,** (*beg*) implorer.
pleasant /'pleznt/ *a.* agréable. **~ly** *adv.*
agréablement.
please /pliːz/ *v.t./i.* plaire (à), faire plaisir

(à). —*adv.* s'il vous *or* te plaît. **~ o.s.,
do as one ~s,** faire ce qu'on veut. **~d**
a. content (**with,** de). **pleasing** *a.*
agréable.
pleasur|e /'pleʒə(r)/ *n.* plaisir *m.* **~able**
a. très agréable.
pleat /pliːt/ *n.* pli *m.* —*v.t.* plisser.
plebiscite /'plebɪsɪt/ *n.* plébiscite *m.*
pledge /pledʒ/ *n.* (*token*) gage *m.*; (*fig.*)
promesse *f.* —*v.t.* promettre; (*pawn*)
engager.
plentiful /'plentɪfl/ *a.* abondant.
plenty /'plentɪ/ *n.* abondance *f.* **~ (of),**
(*a great deal*) beaucoup (de); (*enough*)
assez (de).
pleurisy /'plʊərəsɪ/ *n.* pleurésie *f.*
pliable /'plaɪəbl/ *a.* souple.
pliers /'plaɪəz/ *n. pl.* pince(s) *f.* (*pl.*).
plight /plaɪt/ *n.* triste situation *f.*
plimsoll /'plɪms(ə)l/ *n.* chaussure de gym
f.
plinth /plɪnθ/ *n.* socle *m.*
plod /plɒd/ *v.i.* (*p.t.* plodded) avancer
péniblement *or* d'un pas lent; (*work*)
bûcher. **~der** *n.* bûcheur, -se *m.*, *f.*
~ding *a.* lent.
plonk /plɒŋk/ *n.* (*sl.*) pinard *m.* —*v.t.* **~
down,** poser lourdement.
plot /plɒt/ *n.* complot *m.*; (*of novel etc.*)
intrigue *f.* **~ (of land),** terrain *m.*
—*v.t./i.* (*p.t.* plotted) comploter; (*mark
out*) tracer.
plough /plaʊ/ *n.* charrue *f.* —*v.t./i.*
labourer. **~ back,** réinvestir. **~ into,**
rentrer dans. **~ through,** avancer
péniblement dans.
plow /plaʊ/ *n. & v.t./i.* (*Amer.*) =
plough.
ploy /plɔɪ/ *n.* (*fam.*) stratagème *m.*
pluck /plʌk/ *v.t.* cueillir; (*bird*) plumer;
(*eyebrows*) épiler; (*strings: mus.*)
pincer. —*n.* courage *m.* **~ up courage,**
prendre son courage à deux mains. **~y**
a. courageux.
plug /plʌg/ *n.* (*of cloth, paper, etc.*)
tampon *m.*; (*for sink etc.*) bonde *f.*;
(*electr.*) fiche *f.*, prise *f.* —*v.t.* (*p.t.*
plugged) (*hole*) boucher; (*publicize:
fam.*) faire du battage autour de. —*v.i.*
~ away, (*work: fam.*) bosser. **~ in,**
brancher. **~-hole** *n.* vidange *f.*
plum /plʌm/ *n.* prune *f.* **~ job,** travail en
or *m.* **~ pudding,** (plum-)pudding *m.*
plumb /plʌm/ *adv.* tout à fait. —*v.t.*
(*probe*) sonder. **~-line** *n.* fil à plomb *m.*
plumb|er /'plʌmə(r)/ *n.* plombier *m.*
~ing *n.* plomberie *f.*
plum|e /pluːm/ *n.* plume(s) *f.* (*pl.*).
~age *n.* plumage *m.*

plummet /ˈplʌmɪt/ v.i. (p.t. **plummeted**) tomber, plonger.

plump /plʌmp/ a. (-er, -est) potelé, dodu. —v.i. ~ **for,** choisir. ~**ness** n. rondeur f.

plunder /ˈplʌndə(r)/ v.t. piller. —n. (act) pillage m.; (goods) butin m.

plunge /plʌndʒ/ v.t./i. (dive, thrust) plonger; (fall) tomber. —n. plongeon m.; (fall) chute f. **take the** ~, se jeter à l'eau.

plunger /ˈplʌndʒə(r)/ n. (for sink etc.) ventouse f.; débouchoir m.

plural /ˈplʊərəl/ a. pluriel; (noun) au pluriel. —n. pluriel m.

plus /plʌs/ prep. plus. —a. (electr. & fig.) positif. —n. signe plus m.; (fig.) atout m. **ten** ~, plus de dix.

plush(y) /plʌʃ(ɪ)/ a. somptueux.

ply /plaɪ/ v.t. (tool) manier; (trade) exercer. —v.i. faire la navette. ~ **s.o. with drink,** offrir continuellement à boire à qn.

plywood /ˈplaɪwʊd/ n. contreplaqué m.

p.m. /piːˈem/ adv. de l'après-midi or du soir.

pneumatic /njuːˈmætɪk/ a. pneumatique. ~ **drill,** marteau-piqueur m.

pneumonia /njuːˈməʊnɪə/ n. pneumonie f.

PO abbr. see **Post Office.**

poach /pəʊtʃ/ v.t./i. (game) braconner; (staff) débaucher; (culin.) pocher. ~**er** n. braconnier m.

pocket /ˈpɒkɪt/ n. poche f. —a. de poche. —v.t. empocher. **be out of** ~, avoir perdu de l'argent. ~**book** n. (notebook) carnet m.; (wallet: Amer.) portefeuille m.; (handbag: Amer.) sac à main m. ~**money** n. argent de poche m.

pock-marked /ˈpɒkmɑːkt/ a. (face etc.) grêlé.

pod /pɒd/ n. (peas etc.) cosse f.; (vanilla) gousse f.

podgy /ˈpɒdʒɪ/ a. (-ier, -iest) dodu.

poem /ˈpəʊɪm/ n. poème m.

poet /ˈpəʊɪt/ n. poète m. ~**ic** /-ˈetɪk/ a. poétique.

poetry /ˈpəʊɪtrɪ/ n. poésie f.

poignant /ˈpɔɪnjənt/ a. poignant.

point /pɔɪnt/ n. point m.; (tip) pointe f.; (decimal point) virgule f.; (meaning) sens m., intérêt m.; (remark) remarque f. ~**s,** (rail.) aiguillage m. —v.t. (aim) braquer; (show) indiquer. —v.i. indiquer du doigt (at or to s.o., qn.). ~ **out that, make the** ~ **that,** faire remarquer que. **good** ~**s,** qualités f. pl. **make a** ~ **of doing,** ne pas manquer de faire. **on**

the ~ **of,** sur le point de. ~**blank** a. & adv. à bout portant. ~ **in time,** moment m. ~ **of view,** point de vue m. ~ **out,** signaler. **to the** ~, pertinent. **what is the** ~?, à quoi bon?

pointed /ˈpɔɪntɪd/ a. pointu; (remark) lourd de sens.

pointer /ˈpɔɪntə(r)/ n. (indicator) index m.; (dog) chien d'arrêt m.; (advice: fam.) tuyau m.

pointless /ˈpɔɪntlɪs/ a. inutile.

poise /pɔɪz/ n. équilibre m.; (carriage) maintien m.; (fig.) assurance f. ~**d** a. en équilibre; (confident) assuré. ~**d for,** prêt à.

poison /ˈpɔɪzn/ n. poison m. —v.t. empoisonner. ~**ous** a. (substance etc.) toxique; (plant) vénéneux; (snake) venimeux.

poke /pəʊk/ v.t./i. (push) pousser; (fire) tisonner; (thrust) fourrer. —n. (petit) coup m. ~ **about,** fureter. ~ **fun at,** se moquer de. ~ **out,** (head) sortir.

poker[1] /ˈpəʊkə(r)/ n. tisonnier m.

poker[2] /ˈpəʊkə(r)/ n. (cards) poker m.

poky /ˈpəʊkɪ/ a. (-ier, -iest) (small) exigu; (slow: Amer.) lent.

Poland /ˈpəʊlənd/ n. Pologne f.

polar /ˈpəʊlə(r)/ a. polaire. ~ **bear,** ours blanc m.

polarize /ˈpəʊləraɪz/ v.t. polariser.

Polaroid /ˈpəʊlərɔɪd/ n. (P.) polaroïd (P.) m.

pole[1] /pəʊl/ n. (fixed) poteau m.; (rod) perche f.; (for flag) mât m. ~**-vault** n. saut à la perche m.

pole[2] /pəʊl/ n. (geog.) pôle m.

Pole /pəʊl/ n. Polonais(e) m. (f.).

polemic /pəˈlemɪk/ n. polémique f.

police /pəˈliːs/ n. police f. —v.t. faire la police dans. ~ **state,** état policier m. ~ **station,** commissariat de police m.

police|man /pəˈliːsmən/ n. (pl. -men) agent de police m. ~**woman** (pl. -women) femme-agent f.

policy[1] /ˈpɒlɪsɪ/ n. politique f.

policy[2] /ˈpɒlɪsɪ/ n. (insurance) police (d'assurance) f.

polio(myelitis) /ˈpəʊlɪəʊ(maɪəˈlaɪtɪs)/ n. polio(myélite) f.

polish /ˈpɒlɪʃ/ v.t. polir; (shoes, floor) cirer. —n. (for shoes) cirage m.; (for floor) encaustique f.; (for nails) vernis m.; (shine) poli m.; (fig.) raffinement m. ~ **off,** finir en vitesse. ~ **up,** (language) perfectionner. ~**ed** a. raffiné.

Polish /ˈpəʊlɪʃ/ a. polonais. —n. (lang.) polonais m.

polite /pə'laɪt/ a. poli. **~ly** adv.
poliment. **~ness** n. politesse f.
political /pə'lɪtɪkl/ a. politique.
politician /pɒlɪ'tɪʃn/ n. homme politique
m., femme politique f.
politics /'pɒlətɪks/ n. politique f.
polka /'pɒlkə, Amer. 'pəʊlkə/ n. polka f.
~ dots, pois m. pl.
poll /pəʊl/ n. scrutin m.; (survey)
sondage m. —v.t. (votes) obtenir. **go to
the ~s,** aller aux urnes. **~ing-booth** n.
isoloir m. **~ing station,** bureau de vote
m.
pollen /'pɒlən/ n. pollen m.
pollut|e /pə'luːt/ v.t. polluer. **~ion** /-ʃn/
n. pollution f.
polo /'pəʊləʊ/ n. polo m. **~ neck,** col
roulé m. **~ shirt,** polo m.
polyester /pɒlɪ'estə(r)/ n. polyester m.
polygamy /pə'lɪgəmɪ/ n. polygamie f.
polytechnic /pɒlɪ'teknɪk/ n. institut
universitaire de technologie m.
polythene /'pɒlɪθiːn/ n. polythène m.,
polyéthylène m.
pomegranate /'pɒmɪgrænɪt/ n. (fruit)
grenade f.
pomp /pɒmp/ n. pompe f.
pompon /'pɒmpɒn/ n. pompon m.
pomp|ous /'pɒmpəs/ a. pompeux.
~osity /-'pɒsətɪ/ n. solennité f.
pond /pɒnd/ n. étang m.; (artificial)
bassin m.; (stagnant) mare f.
ponder /'pɒndə(r)/ v.t./i. réfléchir (à),
méditer (sur).
ponderous /'pɒndərəs/ a. pesant.
pong /pɒŋ/ n. (stink: sl.) puanteur f.
—v.i. (sl.) puer.
pony /'pəʊnɪ/ n. poney m. **~-tail** n.
queue de cheval f.
poodle /'puːdl/ n. caniche m.
pool[1] /puːl/ n. (puddle) flaque f.; (pond)
étang m.; (of blood) mare f.; (for
swimming) piscine f.
pool[2] /puːl/ n. (fund) fonds commun m.,
(of ideas) réservoir m.; (of typists) pool
m.; (snooker) billard américain m. **~s,**
pari mutuel sur le football m. —v.t.
mettre en commun.
poor /pɔː(r)/ a. (-er, -est) pauvre; (not
good) médiocre, mauvais. **~ly** adv.
mal; a. malade.
pop[1] /pɒp/ n. (noise) bruit sec m.
—v.t./i. (p.t. popped) (burst) crever; (put) mettre. **~ in/out/off,**
entrer/sortir/partir. **~ over,** faire un
saut (to see s.o., chez qn.). **~ up,** surgir.
pop[2] /pɒp/ n. (mus.) musique pop f. —a.
pop invar.
popcorn /'pɒpkɔːn/ n. pop-corn m.

pope /pəʊp/ n. pape m.
poplar /'pɒplə(r)/ n. peuplier m.
poppy /'pɒpɪ/ n. pavot m.; (wild)
coquelicot m.
popsicle /'pɒpsɪkl/ n. (P.) (Amer.) glace
à l'eau f.
popular /'pɒpjʊlə(r)/ a. populaire; (in
fashion) en vogue. **be ~ with,** plaire à.
~ity /-'lærətɪ/ n. popularité f. **~ize** v.t.
populariser. **~ly** adv. communément.
populat|e /'pɒpjʊleɪt/ v.t. peupler. **~ion**
/-'leɪʃn/ n. population f.
populous /'pɒpjʊləs/ a. populeux.
porcelain /'pɔːsəlɪn/ n. porcelaine f.
porch /pɔːtʃ/ n. porche m.
porcupine /'pɔːkjʊpaɪn/ n. (rodent)
porc-épic m.
pore[1] /pɔː(r)/ n. pore m.
pore[2] /pɔː(r)/ v.i. **~ over,** étudier
minutieusement.
pork /pɔːk/ n. (food) porc m.
pornograph|y /pɔː'nɒgrəfɪ/ n. por-
nographie f. **~ic** /-ə'græfɪk/ a.
pornographique.
porous /'pɔːrəs/ a. poreux.
porpoise /'pɔːpəs/ n. marsouin m.
porridge /'pɒrɪdʒ/ n. porridge m.
port[1] /pɔːt/ n. (harbour) port m. **~ of
call,** escale f.
port[2] /pɔːt/ n. (left: naut.) bâbord m.
port[3] /pɔːt/ n. (wine) porto m.
portable /'pɔːtəbl/ a. portatif.
portal /'pɔːtl/ n. portail m.
porter[1] /'pɔːtə(r)/ n. (carrier) porteur m.
porter[2] /'pɔːtə(r)/ n. (door-keeper)
portier m.
portfolio /pɔːt'fəʊlɪəʊ/ n. (pl. -os) (pol.,
comm.) portefeuille m.
porthole /'pɔːthəʊl/ n. hublot m.
portico /'pɔːtɪkəʊ/ n. (pl. -oes) portique
m.
portion /'pɔːʃn/ n. (share, helping)
portion f.; (part) partie f.
portly /'pɔːtlɪ/ a. (-ier, -iest) corpulent
(et digne).
portrait /'pɔːtrɪt/ n. portrait m.
portray /pɔː'treɪ/ v.t. représenter. **~al** n.
portrait m., peinture f.
Portug|al /'pɔːtjʊgl/ n. Portugal m.
~uese /-'giːz/ a. & n. invar.
portugais(e) (m. (f.)).
pose /pəʊz/ v.t./i. poser. —n. pose f. **~
as,** (expert etc.) se poser en.
poser /'pəʊzə(r)/ n. colle f.
posh /pɒʃ/ a. (sl.) chic invar.
position /pə'zɪʃn/ n. position f.; (job,
state) situation f. —v.t. placer.
positive /'pɒzətɪv/ a. (test, help, etc.)
positif; (sure) sûr, certain; (real) réel,

vrai. ∼**ly** *adv.* positivement; (*absolutely*) complètement.

possess /pə'zes/ *v.t.* posséder. ∼**ion** /-ʃn/ *n.* possession *f.* **take** ∼**ion of**, prendre possession de. ∼**or** *n.* possesseur *m.*

possessive /pə'zesɪv/ *a.* possessif.

possib|le /'pɒsəbl/ *a.* possible. ∼**ility** /-'bɪlətɪ/ *n.* possibilité *f.*

possibly /'pɒsəblɪ/ *adv.* peut-être. **if I** ∼ **can**, si cela m'est possible. **I cannot** ∼ **leave**, il m'est impossible de partir.

post¹ /pəʊst/ *n.* (*pole*) poteau *m.* —*v.t.* ∼ **(up)**, (*a notice*) afficher.

post² /pəʊst/ *n.* (*station, job*) poste *m.* —*v.t.* poster; (*appoint*) affecter.

post³ /pəʊst/ *n.* (*mail service*) poste *f.*; (*letters*) courrier *m.* —*a.* postal. —*v.t.* (*put in box*) poster; (*send*) envoyer (par la poste). **catch the last** ∼, attraper la dernière levée. **keep** ∼**ed**, tenir au courant. ∼**box** *n.* boîte à *or* aux lettres *f.* ∼ **code** *n.* code postal *m.* **P**∼ **Office**, postes *f. pl.*; (*in France*) Postes et Télécommunications *f. pl.* ∼ **office**, bureau de poste *m.*, poste *f.*

post- /pəʊst/ *pref.* post-.

postage /'pəʊstɪdʒ/ *n.* tarif postal *m.*, frais de port *m.pl.*

postal /'pəʊstl/ *a.* postal. ∼ **order**, mandat *m.* ∼ **worker**, employé(e) des postes *m.* (*f.*).

postcard /'pəʊstkɑːd/ *n.* carte postale *f.*

poster /'pəʊstə(r)/ *n.* affiche *f.*; (*for decoration*) poster *m.*

posterior /pɒ'stɪərɪə(r)/ *n.* postérieur *m.*

posterity /pɒ'sterətɪ/ *n.* postérité *f.*

postgraduate /pəʊst'grædʒʊət/ *n.* étudiant(e) de troisième cycle *m.* (*f.*).

posthumous /'pɒstjʊməs/ *a.* posthume. ∼**ly** *adv.*, à titre posthume.

postman /'pəʊstmən/ *n.* (*pl.* -men) facteur *m.*

postmark /'pəʊstmɑːk/ *n.* cachet de la poste *m.*

postmaster /'pəʊstmɑːstə(r)/ *n.* receveur des postes *m.*

post-mortem /pəʊst'mɔːtəm/ *n.* autopsie *f.*

postpone /pə'spəʊn/ *v.t.* remettre. ∼**ment** *n.* ajournement *m.*

postscript /'pəʊskrɪpt/ *n.* (*to letter*) post-scriptum *m. invar.*

postulate /'pɒstjʊleɪt/ *v.t.* postuler.

posture /'pɒstʃə(r)/ *n.* posture *f.* —*v.i.* (*affectedly*) prendre des poses.

post-war /'pəʊstwɔː(r)/ *a.* d'après-guerre.

pot /pɒt/ *n.* pot *m.*; (*for cooking*) marmite *f.*; (*drug: sl.*) marie-jeanne *f.*

—*v.t.* (*plants*) mettre en pot. **go to** ∼, (*sl.*) aller à la ruine. ∼**-belly** *n.* gros ventre *m.* **take** ∼ **luck**, tenter sa chance. **take a** ∼**-shot at**, faire un carton sur.

potato /pə'teɪtəʊ/ *n.* (*pl.* -oes) pomme de terre *f.*

poten|t /'pəʊtnt/ *a.* puissant; (*drink*) fort. ∼**cy** *n.* puissance *f.*

potential /pə'tenʃl/ *a. & n.* potentiel (*m.*). ∼**ly** *adv.* potentiellement.

pot-hol|e /'pɒthəʊl/ *n.* (*in rock*) caverne *f.*; (*in road*) nid de poule *m.* ∼**ing** *n.* spéléologie *f.*

potion /'pəʊʃn/ *n.* potion *f.*

potted /'pɒtɪd/ *a.* (*plant etc.*) en pot; (*preserved*) en conserve; (*abridged*) condensé.

potter¹ /'pɒtə(r)/ *n.* potier *m.* ∼**y** *n.* (*art*) poterie *f.*; (*objects*) poteries *f.pl.*

potter² /'pɒtə(r)/ *v.i.* bricoler.

potty /'pɒtɪ/ *a.* (-ier, -iest) (*crazy: sl.*) toqué.— *n.* pot *m.*

pouch /paʊtʃ/ *n.* poche *f.*; (*for tobacco*) blague *f.*

pouffe /puːf/ *n.* pouf *m.*

poultice /'pəʊltɪs/ *n.* cataplasme *m.*

poult|ry /'pəʊltrɪ/ *n.* volaille *f.* ∼**erer** *n.* marchand de volailles *m.*

pounce /paʊns/ *v.i.* bondir (**on**, sur). —*n.* bond *m.*

pound¹ /paʊnd/ *n.* (*weight*) livre *f.* (= 454 g.); (*money*) livre *f.*

pound² /paʊnd/ *n.* (*for dogs, cars*) fourrière *f.*

pound³ /paʊnd/ *v.t.* (*crush*) piler; (*bombard*) pilonner. —*v.i.* frapper fort; (*of heart*) battre fort; (*walk*) marcher à pas lourds.

pour /pɔː(r)/ *v.t.* verser. —*v.i.* couler, ruisseler (**from**, de); (*rain*) pleuvoir à torrents. ∼ **in/out**, (*people*) arriver/sortir en masse. ∼ **off** *or* **out**, vider. ∼**ing rain**, pluie torrentielle *f.*

pout /paʊt/ *v.t./i.* ∼ **(one's lips)**, faire la moue. —*n.* moue *f.*

poverty /'pɒvətɪ/ *n.* misère *f.*, pauvreté *f.*

powder /'paʊdə(r)/ *n.* poudre *f.* —*v.t.* poudrer. ∼**ed** *a.* en poudre. ∼**y** *a.* poudreux. ∼**-room** *n.* toilettes pour dames *f. pl.*

power /'paʊə(r)/ *n.* puissance *f.*; (*ability, authority*) pouvoir *m.*; (*energy*) énergie *f.*; (*electr.*) courant *m.* ∼ **cut**, coupure de courant *f.* ∼**ed by**, fonctionnant à; (*jet etc.*) propulsé par. ∼**less** *a.* impuissant. ∼ **point**, prise de courant *f.* ∼**-station** *n.* centrale électrique *f.*

powerful /'paʊəfl/ *a.* puissant. ∼**ly** *adv.* puissamment.

practicable /'præktɪkəbl/ a. praticable.
practical /'præktɪkl/ a. pratique. ∼ity
/-'kælətɪ/ n. sens or aspect pratique m.
∼ joke, farce f.
practically /'præktɪklɪ/ adv. pratiquement.
practice /'præktɪs/ n. pratique f.; (of
profession) exercice m.; (sport)
entraînement m.; (clients) clientèle f. be
in ∼, (doctor, lawyer) exercer. in ∼,
(in fact) en pratique; (well-trained) en
forme. out of ∼, rouillé. put into ∼,
mettre en pratique.
practis|e /'præktɪs/ v.t./i. (musician,
typist, etc.) s'exercer (à); (sport)
s'entraîner (à); (put into practice)
pratiquer; (profession) exercer. ∼ed a.
expérimenté. ∼ing a. (Catholic etc.)
pratiquant.
practitioner /præk'tɪʃənə(r)/ n. prati-
cien(ne) m. (f.).
pragmatic /præg'mætɪk/ a. prag-
matique.
prairie /'preərɪ/ n. (in North America)
prairie f.
praise /preɪz/ v.t. louer. —n. éloge(s) m.
(pl.), louange(s) f. (pl.).
praiseworthy /'preɪzwɜːðɪ/ a. digne
d'éloges.
pram /præm/ n. voiture d'enfant f.,
landau m.
prance /prɑːns/ v.i. caracoler.
prank /præŋk/ n. farce f.
prattle /'prætl/ v.i. jaser.
prawn /prɔːn/ n. crevette rose f.
pray /preɪ/ v.i. prier.
prayer /preə(r)/ n. prière f.
pre- /priː/ pref. pré-.
preach /priːtʃ/ v.t./i. prêcher. ∼ at or to,
prêcher. ∼er n. prédicateur m.
preamble /priː'æmbl/ n. préambule m.
pre-arrange /priːə'reɪndʒ/ v.t. fixer à
l'avance.
precarious /prɪ'keərɪəs/ a. précaire.
precaution /prɪ'kɔːʃn/ n. précaution f.
∼ary a. de précaution.
preced|e /prɪ'siːd/ v.t. précéder. ∼ing a.
précédent.
precedence /'presɪdəns/ n. priorité f.; (in
rank) préséance f.
precedent /'presɪdənt/ n. précédent m.
precept /'priːsept/ n. précepte m.
precinct /'priːsɪŋkt/ n. enceinte f.;
(pedestrian area) zone f.; (district:
Amer.) circonscription f.
precious /'preʃəs/ a. précieux. —adv.
(very: fam.) très.
precipice /'presɪpɪs/ n. (geog.) à-pic m.
invar.; (fig.) précipice m.

precipitat|e /prɪ'sɪpɪteɪt/ v.t. (person,
event, chemical) précipiter. —a. /-ɪtət/
précipité. ∼ion /-'teɪʃn/ n. précipitation
f.
précis /'preɪsɪs/ n. invar. précis m.
precis|e /prɪ'saɪs/ a. précis; (careful)
méticuleux. ∼ely adv. précisément.
∼ion /-'sɪʒn/ n. précision f.
preclude /prɪ'kluːd/ v.t. (prevent)
empêcher; (rule out) exclure.
precocious /prɪ'kəʊʃəs/ a. précoce.
preconc|eived /priːkən'siːvd/ a. pré-
conçu. ∼eption n. préconception f.
pre-condition /priːkən'dɪʃn/ n. condition requise f.
predator /'predətə(r)/ n. prédateur m.
∼y a. rapace.
predecessor /'priːdɪsesə(r)/ n. prédécesseur m.
predicament /prɪ'dɪkəmənt/ n. mauvaise situation or passe f.
predict /prɪ'dɪkt/ v.t. prédire. ∼able a.
prévisible. ∼ion /-kʃn/ n. prédiction f.
predispose /priːdɪ'spəʊz/ v.t. prédisposer (to do, à faire).
predominant /prɪ'dɒmɪnənt/ a. prédominant. ∼ly adv. pour la plupart.
predominate /prɪ'dɒmɪneɪt/ v.i. prédominer.
pre-eminent /priː'emɪnənt/ a. pré-
éminent.
pre-empt /priː'empt/ v.t. (buy) acquérir
d'avance; (stop) prévenir. ∼ive a.
preventif.
preen /priːn/ v.t. (bird) lisser. ∼ o.s.,
(person) se bichonner.
prefab /'priːfæb/ n. (fam.) bâtiment
préfabriqué m. ∼ricated /-'fæbrɪk-
eɪtɪd/ a. préfabriqué.
preface /'prefɪs/ n. préface f.
prefect /'priːfekt/ n. (pupil) élève
chargé(e) de la discipline m.(f.);
(official) préfet m.
prefer /prɪ'fɜː(r)/ v.t. (p.t. preferred)
préférer (to do, faire). ∼able
/'prefrəbl/ a. préférable. ∼ably adv. de
préférence.
preferen|ce /'prefrəns/ n. préférence f.
∼tial /-ə'renʃl/ a. préférentiel.
prefix /'priːfɪks/ n. préfixe m.
pregnan|t /'pregnənt/ a. (woman)
enceinte; (animal) pleine. ∼cy n. (of
woman) grossesse f.
prehistoric /priːhɪ'stɒrɪk/ a. préhistorique.
prejudge /priː'dʒʌdʒ/ v.t. préjuger de;
(person) juger d'avance.
prejudice /'predʒʊdɪs/ n. préjugé(s) m.
(pl.); (harm) préjudice m. —v.t.

(*claim*) porter préjudice à; (*person*) prévenir. ∼**d** *a.* partial; (*person*) qui a des préjugés.

preliminar|y /prɪ'lɪmɪnərɪ/ *a.* préliminaire. ∼**ies** *n. pl.* préliminaires *m. pl.*

prelude /'preljuːd/ *n.* prélude *m.*

pre-marital /priː'mærɪtl/ *a.* avant le mariage.

premature /'premətjʊə(r)/ *a.* prématuré.

premeditated /priː'medɪteɪtɪd/ *a.* prémédité.

premier /'premɪə(r)/ *a.* premier. —*n.* premier ministre *m.*

première /'premɪeə(r)/ *n.* première *f.*

premises /'premɪsɪz/ *n. pl.* locaux *m. pl.* **on the** ∼, sur les lieux.

premiss /'premɪs/ *n.* prémisse *f.*

premium /'priːmɪəm/ *n.* prime *f.* **be at a** ∼, faire prime.

premonition /priːmə'nɪʃn/ *n.* prémonition *f.*, pressentiment *m.*

preoccup|ation /priːɒkjʊ'peɪʃn/ *n.* préoccupation *f.* ∼**ied** /-'ɒkjʊpaɪd/ *a.* préoccupé.

prep /prep/ *n.* (*work*) devoirs *m.pl.* ∼ **school = preparatory school.**

preparation /prepə'reɪʃn/ *n.* préparation *f.* ∼**s**, préparatifs *m. pl.*

preparatory /prɪ'pærətrɪ/ *a.* préparatoire. ∼ **school,** école primaire privée *f.*; (*Amer.*) école secondaire privée *f.*

prepare /prɪ'peə(r)/ *v.t./i.* (se) préparer (**for,** à). **be** ∼**d for,** (*expect*) s'attendre à ∼**d to,** prêt à.

prepay /priː'peɪ/ *v.t.* (*p.t.* **-paid**) payer d'avance.

preponderance /prɪ'pɒndərəns/ *n.* prédominance *f.*

preposition /prepə'zɪʃn/ *n.* préposition *f.*

preposterous /prɪ'pɒstərəs/ *a.* absurde, ridicule.

prerequisite /priː'rekwɪzɪt/ *n.* condition préalable *f.*

prerogative /prɪ'rɒɡətɪv/ *n.* prérogative *f.*

Presbyterian /prezbɪ'tɪərɪən/ *a. & n.* presbytérien(ne) (*m.* (*f.*)).

prescri|be /prɪ'skraɪb/ *v.t.* prescrire. ∼**ption** /-ɪpʃn/ *n.* prescription *f.*; (*med.*) ordonnance *f.*

presence /'prezns/ *n.* présence *f.* ∼ **of mind,** présence d'esprit *f.*

present[1] /'preznt/ *a.* présent. —*n.* présent *m.* **at** ∼, à présent. **for the** ∼, pour le moment. ∼**-day** *a.* actuel.

present[2] /'preznt/ *n.* (*gift*) cadeau *m.*

present[3] /prɪ'zent/ *v.t.* présenter; (*film, concert, etc.*) donner. ∼ **s.o. with,** offrir à qn. ∼**able** *a.* présentable. ∼**ation** /prezn'teɪʃn/ *n.* présentation *f.* ∼**er** *n.* présentalteur, -trice *m., f.*

presently /'prezntlɪ/ *adv.* bientôt; (*now: Amer.*) en ce moment.

preservative /prɪ'zɜːvətɪv/ *n.* (*culin.*) agent de conservation *m.*

preserv|e /prɪ'zɜːv/ *v.t.* préserver; (*maintain & culin.*) conserver. —*n.* réserve *f.*; (*fig.*) domaine *m.*; (*jam*) confiture *f.* ∼**ation** /prezə'veɪʃn/ *n.* conservation *f.*

preside /prɪ'zaɪd/ *v.i.* présider. ∼ **over,** présider.

presiden|t /'prezɪdənt/ *n.* président(e) *m.* (*f.*). ∼**cy** *n.* présidence *f.* ∼**tial** /-'denʃl/ *a.* présidentiel.

press /pres/ *v.t./i.* (*button etc.*) appuyer (sur); (*squeeze*) presser; (*iron*) repasser; (*pursue*) poursuivre. —*n.* (*newspapers, machine*) presse *f.*; (*for wine*) pressoir *m.* **be** ∼**ed for,** (*time etc.*) manquer de. ∼ **for sth.,** faire pression pour avoir qch. ∼ **s.o. to do sth.,** pousser qn. à faire qch. ∼ **conference/cutting,** conférence/coupure de presse *f.* ∼ **on,** continuer (**with sth.,** qch.). ∼ **release,** communiqué de presse *m.* ∼**-stud** *n.* bouton-pression *m.* ∼**-up** *n.* traction *f.*

pressing /'presɪŋ/ *a.* pressant.

pressure /'preʃə(r)/ *n.* pression *f.* —*v.t.* faire pression sur. ∼**-cooker** *n.* cocotte-minute *f.* ∼ **group,** groupe de pression *m.*

pressurize /'preʃəraɪz/ *v.t.* (*cabin etc.*) pressuriser; (*person*) faire pression sur.

prestige /pre'stiːʒ/ *n.* prestige *m.*

prestigious /pre'stɪdʒəs/ *a.* prestigieux.

presumably /prɪ'zjuːməblɪ/ *adv.* vraisemblablement.

presum|e /prɪ'zjuːm/ *v.t.* (*suppose*) présumer. ∼**e to,** (*venture*) se permettre de. ∼**ption** /-'zʌmpʃn/ *n.* présomption *f.*

presumptuous /prɪ'zʌmptʃʊəs/ *a.* présomptueux.

pretence, (*Amer.*) **pretense** /prɪ'tens/ *n.* feinte *f.*, simulation *f.*; (*claim*) prétention *f.*; (*pretext*) prétexte *m.*

pretend /prɪ'tend/ *v.t./i.* faire semblant (**to do,** de faire). ∼ **to,** (*lay claim to*) prétendre à.

pretentious /prɪ'tenʃəs/ *a.* prétentieux.

pretext /'priːtekst/ *n.* prétexte *m.*

pretty /'prɪtɪ/ *a.* (**-ier, -iest**) joli. —*adv.* assez. ∼ **much,** presque.

prevail /prɪ'veɪl/ v.i. prédominer; (win) prévaloir. ~ **on,** persuader (**to do,** de faire). ~**ing** a. actuel; (wind) dominant.

prevalen|t /'prevələnt/ a. répandu. ~**ce** n. fréquence f.

prevent /prɪ'vent/ v.t. empêcher (**from doing,** de faire). ~**able** a. évitable. ~**ion** /-enʃn/ n. prévention f. ~**ive** a. préventif.

preview /'pri:vju:/ n. avant-première f.; (fig.) aperçu m.

previous /'pri:vɪəs/ a. précédent, antérieur. ~ **to,** avant. ~**ly** adv. précédemment, auparavant.

pre-war /'pri:wɔː(r)/ a. d'avant-guerre.

prey /preɪ/ n. proie f. —v.i. ~ **on,** faire sa proie de; (worry) préoccuper. **bird of** ~, rapace m.

price /praɪs/ n. prix m. —v.t. fixer le prix de. ~**less** a. inestimable; (amusing: sl.) impayable.

pricey /'praɪsɪ/ a. (fam.) coûteux.

prick /prɪk/ v.t. (with pin etc.) piquer. —n. piqûre f. ~ **up one's ears,** dresser l'oreille.

prickl|e /'prɪkl/ n. piquant m.; (sensation) picotement m. ~**y** a. piquant; (person) irritable.

pride /praɪd/ n. orgueil m.; (satisfaction) fierté f. —v. pr. ~ **o.s. on,** s'enorgueillir de. ~ **of place,** place d'honneur f.

priest /pri:st/ n. prêtre m. ~**hood** n. sacerdoce m. ~**ly** a. sacerdotal.

prig /prɪg/ n. petit saint m., pharisien(ne) m. (f.). ~**gish** a. hypocrite.

prim /prɪm/ a. (**primmer, primmest**) guindé, méticuleux.

primar|y /'praɪmərɪ/ a. (school, elections, etc.) primaire; (chief, basic) premier, fondamental. —n. (pol.: Amer.) primaire m. ~**ily** Amer. /-'merɪlɪ/ adv. essentiellement.

prime[1] /praɪm/ a. principal, premier; (first-rate) excellent. **P~ Minister,** Premier Ministre m. **the ~ of life,** la force de l'âge.

prime[2] /praɪm/ v.t. (pump, gun) amorcer; (surface) apprêter. ~**r**[1] /-ə(r)/ n. (paint etc.) apprêt m.

primer[2] /'praɪmə(r)/ n. (school-book) premier livre m.

primeval /praɪ'mi:vl/ a. primitif.

primitive /'prɪmɪtɪv/ a. primitif.

primrose /'prɪmrəʊz/ n. primevère (jaune) f.

prince /prɪns/ n. prince m. ~**ly** a. princier.

princess /prɪn'ses/ n. princesse f.

principal /'prɪnsəpl/ a. principal. —n. (of school etc.) directeur, -trice m., f. ~**ly** adv. principalement.

principle /'prɪnsəpl/ n. principe m. **in/on** ~, en/par principe.

print /prɪnt/ v.t. imprimer; (write in capitals) écrire en majuscules. —n. (of foot etc.) empreinte f.; (letters) caractères m. pl.; (photograph) épreuve f.; (engraving) gravure f. **in** ~, disponible. **out of** ~, épuisé. ~**-out** n. listage m. ~**ed matter,** imprimés m. pl.

print|er /'prɪntə(r)/ n. (person) imprimeur m.; (comput.) imprimante f. ~**ing** n. impression f.

prior[1] /'praɪə(r)/ a. précédent. ~ **to,** prep. avant (de).

prior[2] /'praɪə(r)/ n. (relig.) prieur m. ~**y** n. prieuré m.

priority /praɪ'ɒrətɪ/ n. priorité f. **take** ~, avoir la priorité (**over,** sur).

prise /praɪz/ v.t. forcer. ~ **open,** ouvrir en forçant.

prism /'prɪzəm/ n. prisme m.

prison /'prɪzn/ n. prison f. ~**er** n. prisonnier, -ière m., f. ~ **officer,** gardien(ne) de prison m. (f.).

pristine /'prɪsti:n/ a. primitif; (condition) parfait.

privacy /'prɪvəsɪ/ n. intimité f., solitude f.

private /'praɪvɪt/ a. privé; (confidential) personnel; (lessons, house, etc.) particulier; (ceremony) intime. —n. (soldier) simple soldat m. **in** ~, en privé; (of ceremony) dans l'intimité. ~**ly** adv. en privé; dans l'intimité; (inwardly) intérieurement.

privation /praɪ'veɪʃn/ n. privation f.

privet /'prɪvɪt/ n. (bot.) troène m.

privilege /'prɪvəlɪdʒ/ n. privilège m. ~**d** a. privilégié. **be** ~**d to,** avoir le privilège de.

privy /'prɪvɪ/ a. ~ **to,** au fait de.

prize /praɪz/ n. prix m. —a. (entry etc.) primé; (fool etc.) parfait. —v.t. (value) priser. ~**-fighter** n. boxeur professionnel m. ~**-winner** n. lauréat(e) m. (f.); (in lottery etc.) gagnant(e) m. (f.).

pro /prəʊ/ n. **the** ~**s and cons,** le pour et le contre.

pro- /prəʊ/ pref. pro-.

probab|le /'prɒbəbl/ a. probable. ~**ility** /-'bɪlətɪ/ n. probabilité f. ~**ly** adv. probablement.

probation /prə'beɪʃn/ n. (testing) essai m.; (jurid.) liberté surveillée f. ~**ary** a. d'essai.

probe /prəʊb/ n. (device) sonde f.; (fig.)

enquête *f.* —*v.t.* sonder. —*v.i.* ⌒ **into,** sonder.

problem /'prɒbləm/ *n.* problème *m.* —*a.* difficile. ⌒**atic** /-'mætɪk/ *a.* problématique.

procedure /prə'siːdʒə(r)/ *n.* procédure *f.*; (*way of doing sth.*) démarche à suivre *f.*

proceed /prə'siːd/ *v.i.* (*go*) aller, avancer; (*pass*) passer (**to,** à); (*act*) procéder. ⌒ (**with**), (*continue*) continuer. ⌒ **to do,** se mettre à faire. ⌒**ing** *n.* procédé *m.*

proceedings /prə'siːdɪŋz/ *n. pl.* (*discussions*) débats *m. pl.*; (*meeting*) réunion *f.*; (*report*) actes *m. pl.*; (*jurid.*) poursuites *f. pl.*

proceeds /'prəʊsiːdz/ *n. pl.* (*profits*) produit *m.*, bénéfices *m. pl.*

process /'prəʊses/ *n.* processus *m.*; (*method*) procédé *m.* —*v.t.* (*material, data*) traiter. **in** ⌒, en cours. **in the** ⌒ **of doing,** en train de faire.

procession /prə'seʃn/ *n.* défilé *m.*

procl|aim /prə'kleɪm/ *v.t.* proclamer. ⌒**amation** /prɒklə'meɪʃn/ *n.* proclamation *f.*

procrastinate /prə'kræstɪneɪt/ *v.i.* différer, tergiverser.

procreation /prəʊkrɪ'eɪʃn/ *n.* procréation *f.*

procure /prə'kjʊə(r)/ *v.t.* obtenir.

prod /prɒd/ *v.t./i.* (*p.t.* **prodded**) pousser. —*n.* poussée *f.*, coup *m.*

prodigal /'prɒdɪɡl/ *a.* prodigue.

prodigious /prə'dɪdʒəs/ *a.* prodigieux.

prodigy /'prɒdɪdʒɪ/ *n.* prodige *m.*

produc|e[1] /'prɒdjuːs/ *v.t./i.* produire; (*bring out*) sortir; (*show*) présenter; (*cause*) provoquer; (*theatre, TV*) mettre en scène; (*radio*) réaliser; (*cinema*) produire. ⌒**er** *n.* metteur en scène *m.*; réalisateur *m.*; producteur *m.* ⌒**tion** /-'dʌkʃn/ *n.* production *f.*; mise en scène *f.*; réalisation *f.*

produce[2] /'prɒdjuːs/ *n.* (*food etc.*) produits *m. pl.*

product /'prɒdʌkt/ *n.* produit *m.*

productiv|e /prə'dʌktɪv/ *a.* productif. ⌒**ity** /prɒdʌk'tɪvətɪ/ *n.* productivité *f.*

profan|e /prə'feɪn/ *a.* sacrilège; (*secular*) profane. ⌒**ity** /-'fænətɪ/ *n.* (*oath*) juron *m.*

profess /prə'fes/ *v.t.* professer. ⌒ **to do,** prétendre faire.

profession /prə'feʃn/ *n.* profession *f.* ⌒**al** *a.* professionnel; (*of high quality*) de professionnel; (*person*) qui exerce une profession libérale; *n.* professionnel(le) *m.* (*f.*).

professor /prə'fesə(r)/ *n.* professeur (titulaire d'une chaire) *m.*

proficien|t /prə'fɪʃnt/ *a.* compétent. ⌒**cy** *n.* compétence *f.*

profile /'prəʊfaɪl/ *n.* profil *m.*

profit /'prɒfɪt/ *n.* profit *m.*, bénéfice *m.* —*v.i.* (*p.t.* **profited**). ⌒ **by,** tirer profit de. ⌒**able** *a.* rentable.

profound /prə'faʊnd/ *a.* profond. ⌒**ly** *adv.* profondément.

profus|e /prə'fjuːs/ *a.* abondant. ⌒**e in,** (*lavish in*) prodigue de. ⌒**ely** *adv.* en abondance; (*apologize*) avec effusion. ⌒**ion** /-ʒn/ *n.* profusion *f.*

progeny /'prɒdʒənɪ/ *n.* progéniture *f.*

program /'prəʊɡræm/ *n.* (*Amer.*) = **programme.** (**computer**) ⌒, programme *m.* —*v.t.* (*p.t.* **programmed**) programmer. ⌒**mer** *n.* programmeur, -se *m.*, *f.* ⌒**ming** *n.* (*on computer*) programmation *f.*

programme /'prəʊɡræm/ *n.* programme *m.*; (*broadcast*) émission *f.*

progress[1] /'prəʊɡres/ *n.* progrès *m.* (*pl.*). **in** ⌒, en cours. **make** ⌒, faire des progrès. ⌒ **report,** compte-rendu *m.*

progress[2] /prə'ɡres/ *v.i.* (*advance, improve*) progresser. ⌒**ion** /-ʃn/ *n.* progression *f.*

progressive /prə'ɡresɪv/ *a.* progressif; (*reforming*) progressiste. ⌒**ly** *adv.* progressivement.

prohibit /prə'hɪbɪt/ *v.t.* interdire (**s.o. from doing,** à qn. de faire).

prohibitive /prə'hɪbətɪv/ *a.* (*price etc.*) prohibitif.

project[1] /prə'dʒekt/ *v.t.* projeter. —*v.i.* (*jut out*) être en saillie. ⌒**ion** /-kʃn/ *n.* projection *f.*; saillie *f.*

project[2] /'prɒdʒekt/ *n.* (*plan*) projet *m.*; (*undertaking*) entreprise *f.*; (*schol.*) dossier *m.*

projectile /prə'dʒektaɪl/ *n.* projectile *m.*

projector /prə'dʒektə(r)/ *n.* (*cinema etc.*) projecteur *m.*

proletari|at /prəʊlɪ'teərɪət/ *n.* prolétariat *m.* ⌒**an** *a.* prolétarien; *n.* prolétaire *m./f.*

prolifera|te /prə'lɪfəreɪt/ *v.i.* proliférer. ⌒**ion** /-'reɪʃn/ *n.* prolifération *f.*

prolific /prə'lɪfɪk/ *a.* prolifique.

prologue /'prəʊlɒɡ/ *n.* prologue *m.*

prolong /prə'lɒŋ/ *v.t.* prolonger.

promenade /prɒmə'nɑːd/ *n.* promenade *f.* —*v.t./i.* (se) promener.

prominen|t /'prɒmɪnənt/ *a.* (*projecting*) proéminent; (*conspicuous*) bien en vue; (*fig.*) important. ⌒**ce** *n.* proéminence *f.*; importance *f.* ⌒**tly** *adv.* bien en vue.

promiscu|ous /prəˈmɪskjʊəs/ a. qui a plusieurs partenaires; (*pej.*) de mœurs faciles. **~ity** /promɪˈskjuːətɪ/ n. les partenaires multiples; (*pej.*) liberté de mœurs f.

promis|e /ˈpromɪs/ n. promesse f. —v.t./i. promettre. **~ing** a. prometteur; (*person*) qui promet.

promot|e /prəˈməʊt/ v.t. promouvoir; (*advertise*) faire la promotion de. **~ion** /-ˈməʊʃn/ n. (*of person, sales, etc.*) promotion f.

prompt /prompt/ a. rapide; (*punctual*) à l'heure, ponctuel. —adv. (*on the dot*) pile. —v.t. inciter; (*cause*) provoquer; (*theatre*) souffler (son rôle) à. **~er** n. souffleur, -se m., f. **~ly** adv. rapidement; ponctuellement. **~ness** n. rapidité f.

prone /prəʊn/ a. couché sur le ventre. **~ to**, prédisposé à.

prong /proŋ/ n. (*of fork*) dent f.

pronoun /ˈprəʊnaʊn/ n. pronom m.

pron|ounce /prəˈnaʊns/ v.t. prononcer. **~ouncement** n. déclaration f. **~unciation** /-ʌnsɪˈeɪʃn/ n. prononciation f.

pronounced /prəˈnaʊnst/ a. (*noticeable*) prononcé.

proof /pruːf/ n. (*evidence*) preuve f.; (*test, trial copy*) épreuve f.; (*of liquor*) teneur en alcool f. —a. **~ against**, à l'épreuve de.

prop[1] /prop/ n. support m. —v.t. (*p.t.* **propped**). **~ (up)**, (*support*) étayer; (*lean*) appuyer.

prop[2] /prop/ n. (*theatre, fam.*) accessoire m.

propaganda /propəˈgændə/ n. propagande f.

propagat|e /ˈpropəgeɪt/ v.t./i. (se) propager. **~ion** /-ˈgeɪʃn/ n. propagation f.

propane /ˈprəʊpeɪn/ n. propane m.

propel /prəˈpel/ v.t. (*p.t.* **propelled**) propulser. **~ling pencil**, porte-mine m. invar.

propeller /prəˈpelə(r)/ n. hélice f.

proper /ˈpropə(r)/ a. correct, bon; (*seemly*) convenable; (*real*) vrai; (*thorough: fam.*) parfait. **~ noun**, nom propre m. **~ly** adv. correctement, comme il faut; (*rightly*) avec raison.

property /ˈpropətɪ/ n. propriété f.; (*things owned*) biens m. pl., propriété f. —a. immobilier, foncier.

prophecy /ˈprofəsɪ/ n. prophétie f.

prophesy /ˈprofəsaɪ/ v.t./i. prophétiser. **~ that,** prédire que.

prophet /ˈprofɪt/ n. prophète m. **~ic** /prəˈfetɪk/ a. prophétique.

proportion /prəˈpɔːʃn/ n. (*ratio, dimension*) proportion f.; (*amount*) partie f. **~al, ~ate** adjs. proportionnel.

proposal /prəˈpəʊzl/ n. proposition f.; (*of marriage*) demande en mariage f.

propos|e /prəˈpəʊz/ v.t. proposer. —v.i. **~e to,** faire une demande en mariage à. **~e to do,** se proposer de faire. **~ition** /propəˈzɪʃn/ n. proposition f.; (*matter: fam.*) affaire f.; v.t. (*fam.*) faire des propositions malhonnêtes à.

propound /prəˈpaʊnd/ v.t. (*theory etc.*) proposer.

proprietor /prəˈpraɪətə(r)/ n. propriétaire m./f.

propriety /prəˈpraɪətɪ/ n. (*correct behaviour*) bienséance f.

propulsion /prəˈpʌlʃn/ n. propulsion f.

prosaic /prəˈzeɪɪk/ a. prosaïque.

proscribe /prəˈskraɪb/ v.t. proscrire.

prose /prəʊz/ n. prose f.; (*translation*) thème m.

prosecut|e /ˈprosɪkjuːt/ v.t. poursuivre. **~ion** /-ˈkjuːʃn/ n. poursuites f. pl. **~or** n. procureur m.

prospect[1] /ˈprospekt/ n. perspective f.; (*chance*) espoir m. **a job with ~s**, un travail avec des perspectives d'avenir.

prospect[2] /prəˈspekt/ v.t./i. prospecter. **~or** n. prospecteur m.

prospective /prəˈspektɪv/ a. (*future*) futur; (*possible*) éventuel.

prospectus /prəˈspektəs/ n. prospectus m.; (*univ.*) guide m.

prosper /ˈprospə(r)/ v.i. prospérer.

prosper|ous /ˈprospərəs/ a. prospère. **~ity** /-ˈsperətɪ/ n. prospérité f.

prostate /ˈprosteɪt/ n. prostate f.

prostitut|e /ˈprostɪtjuːt/ n. prostituée f. **~ion** /-ˈtjuːʃn/ n. prostitution f.

prostrate /ˈprostreɪt/ a. (*prone*) à plat ventre; (*submissive*) prosterné; (*exhausted*) prostré.

protagonist /prəˈtægənɪst/ n. protagoniste m.

protect /prəˈtekt/ v.t. protéger. **~ion** /-kʃn/ n. protection f. **~or** n. protecteur, -trice m., f.

protective /prəˈtektɪv/ a. protecteur; (*clothes*) de protection.

protégé /ˈprotɪʒeɪ/ n. protégé m. **~e** n. protégée f.

protein /ˈprəʊtiːn/ n. protéine f.

protest[1] /ˈprəʊtest/ n. protestation f. **under ~,** en protestant.

protest[2] /prəˈtest/ v.t./i. protester. **~er** n. (*pol.*) manifestant(e) m. (f.).

Protestant /'prɒtɪstənt/ a. & n. protestant(e) (m. (f.)).

protocol /'prəʊtəkɒl/ n. protocole m.

prototype /'prəʊtətaɪp/ n. prototype m.

protract /prə'trækt/ v.t. prolonger, faire traîner. ∼ed a. prolongé.

protractor /prə'træktə(r)/ n. (for measuring) rapporteur m.

protrude /prə'truːd/ v.i. dépasser.

proud /praʊd/ a. (-er, -est) fier, orgueilleux. ∼ly adv. fièrement.

prove /pruːv/ v.t. prouver. —v.i. ∼ (to be) easy/etc., se révéler facile/etc. ∼ o.s., faire ses preuves. ∼n a. prouvé.

proverb /'prɒvɜːb/ n. proverbe m. ∼ial /prə'vɜːbɪəl/ a. proverbial.

provide /prə'vaɪd/ v.t. fournir (s.o. with sth., qch. à qn.). —v.i. ∼ for, (allow for) prévoir; (guard against) parer à; (person) pourvoir aux besoins de.

provided /prə'vaɪdɪd/ conj. ∼ that, à condition que

providence /'prɒvɪdəns/ n. providence f.

providing /prə'vaɪdɪŋ/ conj. = **provided**.

provinc|e /'prɒvɪns/ n. province f.; (fig.) compétence f. ∼ial /prə'vɪnʃl/ a. & n. provincial(e) (m. (f.)).

provision /prə'vɪʒn/ n. (stock) provision f.; (supplying) fourniture f.; (stipulation) disposition f. ∼s, (food) provisions f. pl.

provisional /prə'vɪʒənl/ a. provisoire. ∼ly adv. provisoirement.

proviso /prə'vaɪzəʊ/ n. (pl. -os) condition f., stipulation f.

provo|ke /prə'vəʊk/ v.t. provoquer. ∼cation /prɒvə'keɪʃn/ f. ∼cative /-'vɒkətɪv/ a. provocant.

prow /praʊ/ n. proue f.

prowess /'praʊɪs/ n. prouesse f.

prowl /praʊl/ v.i. rôder. —n. be on the ∼, rôder. ∼er n. rôdeur, -se m., f.

proximity /prɒk'sɪmətɪ/ n. proximité f.

proxy /'prɒksɪ/ n. by ∼, par procuration.

prud|e /pruːd/ n. prude f. ∼ish a. prude.

pruden|t /'pruːdnt/ a. prudent. ∼ce n. prudence f. ∼tly adv. prudemment.

prune¹ /pruːn/ n. pruneau m.

prune² /pruːn/ v.t. (cut) tailler.

pry¹ /praɪ/ v.i. être indiscret. ∼ into, fourrer son nez dans.

pry² /praɪ/ v.t. (Amer.) = **prise**.

psalm /sɑːm/ n. psaume m.

pseudo- /'sjuːdəʊ/ pref. pseudo-.

pseudonym /'sjuːdənɪm/ n. pseudonyme m.

psoriasis /sə'raɪəsɪs/ n. psoriasis m.

psyche /'saɪkɪ/ n. psyché f.

psychiatr|y /saɪ'kaɪətrɪ/ n. psychiatrie f. ∼ic /-ɪ'ætrɪk/ a. psychiatrique. ∼ist n. psychiatre m./f.

psychic /'saɪkɪk/ a. (phenomenon etc.) métapsychique; (person) doué de télépathie.

psychoanalys|e /saɪkəʊ'ænəlaɪz/ v.t. psychanalyser. ∼t /-ɪst/ n. psychanalyste m./f.

psychoanalysis /saɪkəʊə'næləsɪs/ n. psychanalyse f.

psycholog|y /saɪ'kɒlədʒɪ/ n. psychologie f. ∼ical /-ə'lɒdʒɪkl/ a. psychologique. ∼ist n. psychologue m./f.

psychopath /'saɪkəʊpæθ/ n. psychopathe m./f.

psychosomatic /saɪkəʊsə'mætɪk/ a. psychosomatique.

psychotherap|y /saɪkəʊ'θerəpɪ/ n. psychothérapie f. ∼ist n. psychothérapeute m./f.

pub /pʌb/ n. pub m.

puberty /'pjuːbətɪ/ n. puberté f.

public /'pʌblɪk/ a. public; (library etc.) municipal. in ∼, en public. ∼ address system, sonorisation f. (dans un lieu public). ∼ house, pub m. ∼ relations, relations publiques f. pl. ∼ school, école privée f.; (Amer.) école publique f. ∼ servant, fonctionnaire m./f. ∼-spirited a. dévoué au bien public. ∼ transport, transports en commun m. pl. ∼ly adv. publiquement.

publican /'pʌblɪkən/ n. patron(ne) de pub m. (f.).

publication /pʌblɪ'keɪʃn/ n. publication f.

publicity /pʌb'lɪsətɪ/ n. publicité f.

publicize /'pʌblɪsaɪz/ v.t. faire connaître au public.

publish /'pʌblɪʃ/ v.t. publier. ∼er n. éditeur m. ∼ing n. édition f.

puck /pʌk/ n. (ice hockey) palet m.

pucker /'pʌkə(r)/ v.t./i. (se) plisser.

pudding /'pʊdɪŋ/ n. dessert m.; (steamed) pudding m. black ∼, boudin m. rice ∼, riz au lait m.

puddle /'pʌdl/ n. flaque d'eau f.

pudgy /'pʌdʒɪ/ a. (-ier, -iest) dodu.

puerile /'pjʊəraɪl/ a. puéril.

puff /pʌf/ n. bouffée f. —v.t./i. souffler. ∼ at, (cigar) tirer sur. ∼ out, (swell) (se) gonfler.

puffy /'pʌfɪ/ a. gonflé.

pugnacious /pʌg'neɪʃəs/ a. batailleur, combatif.

pug-nosed /'pʌgnəʊzd/ a. camus.

pull /pʊl/ v.t./i. tirer; (muscle) se

froisser. —*n.* traction *f.*; (*fig.*) attraction *f.*; (*influence*) influence *f.* **give a ～**, tirer. **～ a face**, faire une grimace. **～ one's weight**, faire sa part du travail. **～ s.o.'s leg**, faire marcher qn. **～ apart**, mettre en morceaux. **～ away**, (*auto.*) démarrer. **～ back** *or* **out**, (*withdraw*) (se) retirer. **～ down**, baisser; (*building*) démolir. **～ in**, (*enter*) entrer; (*stop*) s'arrêter. **～ off**, enlever; (*fig.*) réussir. **～ out**, (*from bag etc.*) sortir; (*extract*) arracher; (*auto.*) déboîter. **～ over**, (*auto.*) se ranger. **～ round** *or* **through**, s'en tirer. **～ o.s. together**, se ressaisir. **～ up**, remonter; (*uproot*) déraciner; (*auto.*) (s')arrêter.

pulley /ˈpʊlɪ/ *n.* poulie *f.*

pullover /ˈpʊləʊvə(r)/ *n.* pull(-over) *m.*

pulp /pʌlp/ *n.* (*of fruit*) pulpe *f.*; (*for paper*) pâte à papier *f.*

pulpit /ˈpʊlpɪt/ *n.* chaire *f.*

pulsate /pʌlˈseɪt/ *v.i.* battre.

pulse /pʌls/ *n.* (*med.*) pouls *m.*

pulverize /ˈpʌlvəraɪz/ *v.t.* (*grind, defeat*) pulvériser.

pummel /ˈpʌml/ *v.t.* (*p.t.* **pummelled**) bourrer de coups.

pump¹ /pʌmp/ *n.* pompe *f.* —*v.t./i.* pomper; (*person*) soutirer des renseignements à. **～ up**, gonfler.

pump² /pʌmp/ *n.* (*plimsoll*) tennis *m.*; (*for dancing*) escarpin *m.*

pumpkin /ˈpʌmpkɪn/ *n.* potiron *m.*

pun /pʌn/ *n.* jeu de mots *m.*

punch¹ /pʌntʃ/ *v.t.* donner un coup de poing à; (*perforate*) poinçonner; (*a hole*) faire. —*n.* coup de poing *m.*; (*vigour: sl.*) punch *m.*; (*device*) poinçonneuse *f.* **～-drunk** *a.* sonné. **～-line**, chute *f.* **～-up** *n.* (*fam.*) bagarre *f.*

punch² /pʌntʃ/ *n.* (*drink*) punch *m.*

punctual /ˈpʌŋktʃʊəl/ *a.* à l'heure; (*habitually*) ponctuel. **～ity** /-ˈælətɪ/ *n.* ponctualité *f.* **～ly** *adv.* à l'heure; ponctuellement.

punctuat|e /ˈpʌŋktʃʊeɪt/ *v.t.* ponctuer. **～ion** /-ˈeɪʃn/ *n.* ponctuation *f.*

puncture /ˈpʌŋktʃə(r)/ *n.* (*in tyre*) crevaison *f.* —*v.t./i.* crever.

pundit /ˈpʌndɪt/ *n.* expert *m.*

pungent /ˈpʌndʒənt/ *a.* âcre.

punish /ˈpʌnɪʃ/ *v.t.* punir (**for sth.**, de qch.). **～able** *a.* punissable (**by**, de). **～ment** *n.* punition *f.*

punitive /ˈpjuːnɪtɪv/ *a.* punitif.

punk /pʌŋk/ *n.* (*music, fan*) punk *m.*; (*person: Amer., fam.*) salaud *m.*

punt¹ /pʌnt/ *n.* (*boat*) bachot *m.*

punt² /pʌnt/ *v.i.* (*bet*) parier.

puny /ˈpjuːnɪ/ *a.* (**-ier, -iest**) chétif.

pup(py) /ˈpʌp(ɪ)/ *n.* chiot *m.*

pupil /ˈpjuːpl/ *n.* (*person*) élève *m./f.*; (*of eye*) pupille *f.*

puppet /ˈpʌpɪt/ *n.* marionnette *f.*

purchase /ˈpɜːtʃəs/ *v.t.* acheter (**from s.o.**, à qn.). —*n.* achat *m.* **～r** /-ə(r)/ *n.* acheteu|r, -se *m.*, *f.*

pur|e /pjʊə(r)/ *a.* (**-er, -est**) pur. **～ely** *adv.* purement. **～ity** *n.* pureté *f.*

purgatory /ˈpɜːgətrɪ/ *n.* purgatoire *m.*

purge /pɜːdʒ/ *v.t.* purger (**of**, de). —*n.* purge *f.*

purif|y /ˈpjʊərɪfaɪ/ *v.t.* purifier. **～ication** /-ɪˈkeɪʃn/ *n.* purification *f.*

purist /ˈpjʊərɪst/ *n.* puriste *m./f.*

puritan /ˈpjʊərɪtən/ *n.* puritain(e) *m.* (*f.*). **～ical** /-ˈtænɪkl/ *a.* puritain.

purple /ˈpɜːpl/ *a.* & *n.* violet (*m.*).

purport /pəˈpɔːt/ *v.t.* **～ to be**, (*claim*) prétendre être.

purpose /ˈpɜːpəs/ *n.* but *m.*; (*fig.*) résolution *f.* **on ～**, exprès. **～-built** *a.* construit spécialement. **to no ～**, sans résultat.

purr /pɜː(r)/ *n.* ronronnement *m.* —*v.i.* ronronner.

purse /pɜːs/ *n.* porte-monnaie *m. invar.*; (*handbag: Amer.*) sac à main *m.* —*v.t.* (*lips*) pincer.

pursue /pəˈsjuː/ *v.t.* poursuivre. **～r** /-ə(r)/ *n.* poursuivant(e) *m.* (*f.*).

pursuit /pəˈsjuːt/ *n.* poursuite *f.*; (*fig.*) activité *f.*, occupation *f.*

purveyor /pəˈveɪə(r)/ *n.* fournisseur *m.*

pus /pʌs/ *n.* pus *m.*

push /pʊʃ/ *v.t./i.* pousser; (*button*) appuyer sur; (*thrust*) enfoncer; (*recommend: fam.*) proposer avec insistance. —*n.* poussée *f.*; (*effort*) gros effort *m.*; (*drive*) dynamisme *m.* **be ～ed for**, (*time etc.*) manquer de. **be ～ing thirty**/ *etc.*, (*fam.*) friser la trentaine/*etc.* **give the ～ to**, (*sl.*) flanquer à la porte. **～ s.o. around**, bousculer qn. **～ back**, repousser. **～-chair** *n.* poussette *f.* **～er** *n.* revendeu|r, -se (de drogue) *m.*, *f.* **～ off**, (*sl.*) filer. **～ on**, continuer. **～-over** *n.* jeu d'enfant *m.* **～ up**, (*lift*) relever; (*prices*) faire monter. **～-up** *n.* (*Amer.*) traction *f.* **～y** *a.* (*fam.*) autoritaire.

pushing /ˈpʊʃɪŋ/ *a.* arriviste.

puss /pʊs/ *n.* (*cat*) minet(te) *m.* (*f.*).

put /pʊt/ *v.t./i.* (*p.t.* **put**, *pres. p.* **putting**) mettre, placer; poser; (*question*) poser. **～ the damage at a million**, estimer les dégâts à un million; **I'd put it at a thousand**, je dirais un millier. ～ **sth. tactfully,** dire qch. avec tact. ～ **across,** communiquer. ～ **away,** ranger; *(fig.)* enfermer. ～ **back,** remettre; *(delay)* retarder. ～ **by,** mettre de côté. ～ **down,** (dé)poser; *(write)* inscrire; *(pay)* verser; *(suppress)* réprimer. ～ **forward,** *(plan)* soumettre. ～ **in,** *(insert)* introduire; *(fix)* installer; *(submit)* soumettre. ～ **in for,** faire une demande de. ～ **off,** *(postpone)* renvoyer à plus tard; *(disconcert)* déconcerter; *(displease)* rebuter. ～ **s.o. off sth.,** dégoûter qn. de qch. ～ **on,** *(clothes, radio)* mettre; *(light)* allumer; *(speed, accent, weight)* prendre. ～ **out,** sortir; *(stretch)* (é)tendre; *(extinguish)* éteindre; *(disconcert)* déconcerter; *(inconvenience)* déranger. ～ **up,** lever, remonter; *(building)* construire; *(notice)* mettre; *(price)* augmenter; *(guest)* héberger; *(offer)* offrir. ～**up job,** coup monté *m.* ～ **up with,** supporter.

putt /pʌt/ *n. (golf)* putt *m.*

putter /'pʌtə(r)/ *v.i. (Amer.)* bricoler.

putty /'pʌtɪ/ *n.* mastic *m.*

puzzle /'pʌzl/ *n.* énigme *f.*; *(game)* casse-tête *m. invar.*; *(jigsaw)* puzzle *m.* —*v.t.* rendre perplexe. —*v.i.* se creuser la tête.

pygmy /'pɪgmɪ/ *n.* pygmée *m.*

pyjamas /pə'dʒɑːməz/ *n. pl.* pyjama *m.*

pylon /'paɪlɒn/ *n.* pylône *m.*

pyramid /'pɪrəmɪd/ *n.* pyramide *f.*

Pyrenees /pɪrə'niːz/ *n. pl.* **the** ～, les Pyrénées *f. pl.*

python /'paɪθn/ *n.* python *m.*

Q

quack¹ /kwæk/ *n. (of duck)* coin-coin *m. invar.*

quack² /kwæk/ *n.* charlatan *m.*

quad /kwɒd/ *(fam.)* = **quadrangle, quadruplet.**

quadrangle /'kwɒdræŋgl/ *(of college) n.* cour *f.*

quadruped /'kwɒdrʊped/ *n.* quadrupède *m.*

quadruple /kwɒ'druːpl/ *a. & n.* quadruple (*m.*). —*v.t./i.* quadrupler. ～**ts** /-plɪts/ *n. pl.* quadruplé(e)s *m. (f.) pl.*

quagmire /'kwægmaɪə(r)/ *n. (bog)* bourbier *m.*

quail /kweɪl/ *n. (bird)* caille *f.*

quaint /kweɪnt/ *a.* **(-er, -est)** pittoresque; *(old)* vieillot; *(odd)* bizarre. ～**ness** *n.* pittoresque *m.*

quake /kweɪk/ *v.i.* trembler. —*n. (fam.)* tremblement de terre *m.*

Quaker /'kweɪkə(r)/ *n.* quaker(esse) *m. (f.).*

qualification /kwɒlɪfɪ'keɪʃn/ *n.* diplôme *m.*; *(ability)* compétence *f.*; *(fig.)* réserve *f.*, restriction *f.*

qualif|y /'kwɒlɪfaɪ/ *v.t.* qualifier; *(modify: fig.)* mettre des réserves à; *(statement)* nuancer. —*v.i.* obtenir son diplôme (**as,** de); *(sport)* se qualifier; *(fig.)* remplir les conditions requises. ～**ied** *a.* diplômé; *(able)* qualifié (**to do,** pour faire); *(fig.)* conditionnel; *(success)* modéré. ～**ying** *a. (round)* éliminatoire; *(candidates)* qualifiés.

qualit|y /'kwɒlətɪ/ *n.* qualité *f.* ～**ative** /-ɪtətɪv/ *a.* qualitatif.

qualm /kwɑːm/ *n.* scrupule *m.*

quandary /'kwɒndərɪ/ *n.* embarras *m.*, dilemme *m.*

quantit|y /'kwɒntətɪ/ *n.* quantité *f.* ～**ative** /-ɪtətɪv/ *a.* quantitatif.

quarantine /'kwɒrəntiːn/ *n. (isolation)* quarantaine *f.*

quarrel /'kwɒrəl/ *n.* dispute *f.*, querelle *f.* —*v.i. (p.t.* **quarrelled)** se disputer ～**some** *a.* querelleur.

quarry¹ /'kwɒrɪ/ *n. (prey)* proie *f.*

quarry² /'kwɒrɪ/ *n. (excavation)* carrière *f.* —*v.t.* extraire.

quart /kwɔːt/ *n. (approx.)* litre *m.*

quarter /'kwɔːtə(r)/ *n.* quart *m.*; *(of year)* trimestre *m.*; *(25 cents: Amer.)* quart de dollar *m.*; *(district)* quartier *m.* ～**s,** logement(s) *m. (pl.)* —*v.t.* diviser en quatre; *(mil.)* cantonner **from all** ～**s,** de toutes parts. ～**final** *n.* quart de finale *m.* ～**ly** *a.* trimestriel; *adv.* trimestriellement.

quartermaster /'kwɔːtəmɑːstə(r)/ *n. (mil.)* intendant *m.*

quartet /kwɔː'tet/ *n.* quatuor *m.*

quartz /kwɔːts/ *n.* quartz *m.* —*a. (watch etc.)* à quartz.

quash /kwɒʃ/ *v.t. (suppress)* étouffer; *(jurid.)* annuler.

quasi- /'kweɪsaɪ/ *pref.* quasi-.

quaver /'kweɪvə(r)/ *v.i.* trembler, chevroter. —*n. (mus.)* croche *f.*

quay /kiː/ *n. (naut.)* quai *m.* ～**side** *n. (edge of quay)* quai *m.*

queasy /'kwiːzɪ/ *a. (stomach)* délicat. **feel** ～, avoir mal au cœur.

queen /kwiːn/ *n.* reine *f.*; *(cards)* dame *f.* ～ **mother,** reine mère *f.*

queer /kwɪə(r)/ a. (**-er, -est**) étrange; (*dubious*) louche; (*ill*) patraque.· —n. (*sl.*) homosexuel m.

quell /kwel/ v.t. réprimer.

quench /kwentʃ/ v.t. éteindre; (*thirst*) étancher; (*desire*) étouffer.

query /ˈkwɪərɪ/ n. question f. —v.t. mettre en question.

quest /kwest/ n. recherche f.

question /ˈkwestʃən/ n. question f. —v.t. interroger; (*doubt*) mettre en question, douter de. **a ~ of money,** une question d'argent. **in ~,** en question. **no ~ of,** pas question de. **out of the ~,** hors de question. **~ mark,** point d'interrogation m.

questionable /ˈkwestʃənəbl/ a. discutable.

questionnaire /kwestʃəˈneə(r)/ n. questionnaire m.

queue /kjuː/ n. queue f. —v.i. (*pres. p.* **queuing**) faire la queue.

quibble /ˈkwɪbl/ v.i. ergoter.

quick /kwɪk/ a. (**-er, -est**) rapide. —adv. vite. —n. **a ~ one,** (*fam.*) un petit verre. **cut to the ~,** piquer au vif. **be ~,** (*hurry*) se dépêcher. **have a ~ temper,** s'emporter facilement. **~ly** adv. rapidement, vite. **~-witted** a. vif.

quicken /ˈkwɪkən/ v.t./i. (s')accélérer.

quicksand /ˈkwɪksænd/ n. **~(s),** sables mouvants m. pl.

quid /kwɪd/ n. invar. (*sl.*) livre f.

quiet /ˈkwaɪət/ a. (**-er, -est**) (*calm, still*) tranquille; (*silent*) silencieux; (*gentle*) doux; (*discreet*) discret. —n. tranquillité f. **keep ~,** se taire. **on the ~,** en cachette. **~ly** adv. tranquillement; silencieusement; doucement; discrètement. **~ness** n. tranquillité f.

quieten /ˈkwaɪətn/ v.t./i. (se) calmer.

quill /kwɪl/ n. plume (d'oie) f.

quilt /kwɪlt/ n. édredon m. (**continental**) **~,** couette f. —v.t. matelasser.

quinine /ˈkwɪniːn, Amer. ˈkwaɪnaɪn/ n. quinine f.

quintet /kwɪnˈtet/ n. quintette m.

quintuplets /kwɪnˈtjuːplɪts/ n. pl. quintuplé(e)s m. (f.) pl.

quip /kwɪp/ n. mot piquant m.

quirk /kwɜːk/ n. bizarrerie f.

quit /kwɪt/ v.t. (*p.t.* **quitted**) quitter. —v.i. abandonner; (*resign*) démissionner. **~ doing,** (*cease:* Amer.) cesser de faire.

quite /kwaɪt/ adv. tout à fait, vraiment; (*rather*) assez. **~ (so)!,** parfaitement! **~ a few,** un assez grand nombre (de).

quits /kwɪts/ a. quitte (**with,** envers). **call it ~,** en rester là.

quiver /ˈkwɪvə(r)/ v.i. trembler.

quiz /kwɪz/ n. (pl. **quizzes**) test m.; (*game*) jeu-concours m. —v.t. (*p.t.* **quizzed**) questionner.

quizzical /ˈkwɪzɪkl/ a. moqueur.

quorum /ˈkwɔːrəm/ n. quorum m.

quota /ˈkwəʊtə/ n. quota m.

quotation /kwəʊˈteɪʃn/ n. citation f.; (*price*) devis m.; (*stock exchange*) cotation f. **~ marks,** guillemets m. pl.

quote /kwəʊt/ v.t. citer; (*reference:* comm.) rappeler; (*price*) indiquer; (*share price*) coter. —v.i. **~ for,** faire un devis pour. **~ from,** citer. —n. (*estimate*) devis; (*fam.*) = quotation. **in ~s,** (*fam.*) entre guillemets.

quotient /ˈkwəʊʃnt/ n. quotient m.

R

rabbi /ˈræbaɪ/ n. rabbin m.

rabbit /ˈræbɪt/ n. lapin m.

rabble /ˈræbl/ n. (*crowd*) cohue f. **the ~,** (*pej.*) la populace.

rabid /ˈræbɪd/ a. enragé.

rabies /ˈreɪbiːz/ n. (*disease*) rage f.

race[1] /reɪs/ n. course f. —v.t. (*horse*) faire courir; (*engine*) emballer. **~ (against),** faire la course à. —v.i. courir; (*rush*) foncer. **~-track** n. piste f.; (*for horses*) champ de courses m.

race[2] /reɪs/ n. (*group*) race f. —a. racial; (*relations*) entre les races.

racecourse /ˈreɪskɔːs/ n. champ de courses m.

racehorse /ˈreɪshɔːs/ n. cheval de course m.

racial /ˈreɪʃl/ a. racial.

racing /ˈreɪsɪŋ/ n. courses f. pl. **~ car,** voiture de course f.

racis|t /ˈreɪsɪst/ a. & n. raciste (m./f.). **~m** /-zəm/ n. racisme m.

rack[1] /ræk/ n. (*shelf*) étagère f.; (*pigeonholes*) casier m.; (*for luggage*) porte-bagages m. invar.; (*for dishes*) égouttoir m.; (*on car roof*) galerie f. —v.t. **~ one's brains,** se creuser la cervelle.

rack[2] /ræk/ n. **go to ~ and ruin,** aller à la ruine; (*building*) tomber en ruine.

racket[1] /ˈrækɪt/ n. raquette f.

racket[2] /ˈrækɪt/ n. (*din*) tapage m.; (*dealings*) combine f.; (*crime*) racket m. **~eer** /-əˈtɪə(r)/ n. racketteur m.

racy /'reɪsɪ/ *a.* (**-ier, -iest**) fougueux, piquant; (*Amer.*) risqué.

radar /'reɪdɑ:(r)/ *n.* radar *m.* —*a.* (*system etc.*) radar *invar.*

radial /'reɪdɪəl/ *a.* (*tyre*) à carcasse radiale.

radian|t /'reɪdɪənt/ *a.* rayonnant. ∼**ce** *n.* éclat *m.* ∼**tly** *adv.* avec éclat.

radiat|e /'reɪdɪeɪt/ *v.t.* dégager. —*v.i.* rayonner (**from**, de). ∼**ion** /-'eɪʃn/ *n.* rayonnement *m.*; (*radioactivity*) radiation *f.*

radiator /'reɪdɪeɪtə(r)/ *n.* radiateur *m.*

radical /'rædɪkl/ *a.* radical. —*n.* (*person: pol.*) radical(e) *m.* (*f.*).

radio /'reɪdɪəʊ/ *n.* (*pl.* **-os**) radio *f.* —*v.t.* (*message*) envoyer par radio; (*person*) appeler par radio.

radioactiv|e /reɪdɪəʊ'æktɪv/ *a.* radioactif. ∼**ity** /-'tɪvətɪ/ *n.* radioactivité *f.*

radiographer /reɪdɪ'ɒɡrəfə(r)/ *n.* radiologue *m./f.*

radish /'rædɪʃ/ *n.* radis *m.*

radius /'reɪdɪəs/ *n.* (*pl.* **-dii** /-dɪaɪ/) rayon *m.*

raffle /'ræfl/ *n.* tombola *f.*

raft /rɑ:ft/ *n.* radeau *m.*

rafter /'rɑ:ftə(r)/ *n.* chevron *m.*

rag[1] /ræɡ/ *n.* lambeau *m.*, loque *f.*; (*for wiping*) chiffon *m.*; (*newspaper*) torchon *m.* **in** ∼**s**, (*person*) en haillons; (*clothes*) en lambeaux. ∼ **doll,** poupée de chiffon *f.*

rag[2] /ræɡ/ *v.t.* (*p.t.* **ragged**) (*tease: sl.*) taquiner. —*n.* (*univ., sl.*) carnaval *m.* (*pour une œuvre de charité*).

ragamuffin /'ræɡəmʌfɪn/ *n.* va-nu-pieds *m. invar.*

rage /reɪdʒ/ *n.* rage *f.*, fureur *f.* —*v.i.* rager; (*storm, battle*) faire rage. **be all the** ∼, faire fureur.

ragged /'ræɡɪd/ *a.* (*clothes, person*) loqueteux; (*edge*) déchiqueté.

raging /'reɪdʒɪŋ/ *a.* (*storm, fever, etc.*) violent.

raid /reɪd/ *n.* (*mil.*) raid *m.*; (*by police*) rafle *f.*; (*by criminals*) hold-up *m. invar.* — *v.t.* faire un raid *or* une rafle *or* un hold-up dans. ∼**er** *n.* (*person*) bandit *m.*, pillard *m.* ∼**ers** *n. pl.* (*mil.*) commando *m.*

rail /reɪl/ *n.* (*on balcony*) balustrade *f.*; (*stairs*) main courante *f.*, rampe *f.*; (*for train*) rail *m.*; (*for curtain*) tringle *f.* **by** ∼, par chemin de fer.

railing /'reɪlɪŋ/ *n.* ∼**s,** grille *f.*

railroad /'reɪlrəʊd/ *n.* (*Amer.*) = **railway.**

railway /'reɪlweɪ/ *n.* chemin de fer *m.* ∼

line, voie ferrée *f.* ∼**man** *n.* (*pl.* **-men**) cheminot *m.* ∼ **station,** gare *f.*

rain /reɪn/ *n.* pluie *f.* —*v.i.* pleuvoir. ∼ **forest,** forêt (humide) tropicale *f.* ∼**storm** *n.* trombe d'eau *f.* ∼**-water** *n.* eau de pluie *f.*

rainbow /'reɪnbəʊ/ *n.* arc-en-ciel *m.*

raincoat /'reɪnkəʊt/ *n.* imperméable *m.*

rainfall /'reɪnfɔ:l/ *n.* précipitation *f.*

rainy /'reɪnɪ/ *a.* (**-ier, -iest**) pluvieux; (*season*) des pluies.

raise /reɪz/ *v.t.* lever; (*breed, build*) élever; (*question etc.*) soulever; (*price etc.*) relever, (*money etc.*) obtenir; (*voice*) élever. —*n.* (*Amer.*) augmentation *f.*

raisin /'reɪzn/ *n.* raisin sec *m.*

rake[1] /reɪk/ *n.* râteau *m.* —*v.t.* (*garden*) ratisser; (*search*) fouiller dans. ∼ **in,** (*money*) amasser. ∼**-off** *n.* (*fam.*) profit *m.* ∼ **up,** (*memories, past*) remuer.

rake[2] /reɪk/ *n.* (*man*) débauché *m.*

rally /'rælɪ/ *v.t./i.* (*strength*) reprendre; (*after illness*) aller mieux. —*n.* rassemblement *m.*; (*auto.*) rallye *m.*; (*tennis*) échange *m.* ∼ **round,** venir en aide.

ram /ræm/ *n.* bélier *m.* —*v.t.* (*p.t.* **rammed**) (*thrust*) enfoncer; (*crash into*) emboutir, percuter.

RAM /ræm/ *abbr.* (*random access memory*) mémoire vive *f.*

rambl|e /'ræmbl/ *n.* randonnée *f.* —*v.i.* faire une randonnée. ∼**e on,** parler (sans cesse), divaguer. ∼**er** *n.* randonneur, -se, *m.*, *f.* ∼**ing** *a.* (*speech*) décousu.

ramification /ræmɪfɪ'keɪʃn/ *n.* ramification *f.*

ramp /ræmp/ *n.* (*slope*) rampe *f.*; (*in garage*) pont de graissage *m.*

rampage[1] /ræm'peɪdʒ/ *v.i.* se livrer à des actes de violence, se déchaîner.

rampage[2] /'ræmpeɪdʒ/ *n.* **go on the** ∼ = **rampage**[1].

rampant /'ræmpənt/ *a.* **be** ∼, (*disease etc.*) sévir, être répandu.

rampart /'ræmpɑ:t/ *n.* rempart *m.*

ramshackle /'ræmʃækl/ *a.* délabré.

ran /ræn/ *see* **run.**

ranch /rɑ:ntʃ/ *n.* ranch *m.*

rancid /'rænsɪd/ *a.* rance.

rancour /'ræŋkə(r)/ *n.* rancœur *f.*

random /'rændəm/ *a.* fait, pris, *etc.* au hasard, aléatoire (*techn.*). —*n.* **at** ∼, au hasard.

randy /'rændɪ/ *a.* (**-ier, -iest**) (*fam.*) excité, en chaleur.

rang /ræŋ/ *see* **ring**[2].

range /reɪndʒ/ n. (*distance*) portée f.; (*of aircraft etc.*) rayon d'action m.; (*series*) gamme f.; (*scale*) échelle f.; (*choice*) choix m.; (*domain*) champ m.; (*of mountains*) chaîne f.; (*stove*) cuisinière f. —v.i. s'étendre; (*vary*) varier.

ranger /ˈreɪndʒə(r)/ n. garde forestier m.

rank[1] /ræŋk/ n. rang m.; (*grade*: mil.) grade m., rang m. —v.t./i. ~ **among,** compter parmi. **the ~ and file,** les gens ordinaires.

rank[2] /ræŋk/ a. (**-er, -est**) (*plants*: pej.) luxuriant; (*smell*) fétide; (*complete*) absolu.

rankle /ˈræŋkl/ v.i. ~ **with s.o.,** rester sur le cœur à qn.

ransack /ˈrænsæk/ v.t. (*search*) fouiller; (*pillage*) saccager.

ransom /ˈrænsəm/ n. rançon f. —v.t. rançonner; (*redeem*) racheter. **hold to** ~, rançonner.

rant /rænt/ v.i. tempêter.

rap /ræp/ n. petit coup sec m. —v.t./i. (*p.t.* **rapped**) frapper.

rape /reɪp/ v.t. violer. —n. viol m.

rapid /ˈræpɪd/ a. rapide. ~**ity** /rəˈpɪdəti/ n. rapidité f. ~**s** n. pl. (*of river*) rapides m. pl.

rapist /ˈreɪpɪst/ n. violeur m.

rapport /ræˈpɔː(r)/ n. rapport m.

rapt /ræpt/ a. (*attention*) profond. ~ **in,** plongé dans.

raptur|e /ˈræptʃə(r)/ n. extase f. ~**ous** a. (*person*) en extase; (*welcome etc.*) frénétique.

rar|e[1] /reə(r)/ a. (**-er, -est**) rare. ~**ely** adv. rarement. ~**ity** n. rareté f.

rare[2] /reə(r)/ a. (**-er, -est**) (*culin.*) saignant.

rarefied /ˈreərɪfaɪd/ a. raréfié.

raring /ˈreərɪŋ/ a. ~ **to,** (*fam.*) impatient de.

rascal /ˈrɑːskl/ n. coquin(e) m. (f.).

rash[1] /ræʃ/ n. (*med.*) éruption f., rougeurs f. pl.

rash[2] /ræʃ/ a. (**-er, -est**) imprudent. ~**ly** adv. imprudemment. ~**ness** n. imprudence f.

rasher /ˈræʃə(r)/ n. tranche (de lard) f.

raspberry /ˈrɑːzbrɪ/ n. framboise f.

rasping /ˈrɑːspɪŋ/ a. grinçant.

rat /ræt/ n. rat m. —v.i. (*p.t.* **ratted**). ~ **on,** (*desert*) lâcher; (*inform on*) dénoncer. ~ **race,** foire d'empoigne f.

rate /reɪt/ n. (*ratio, level*) taux m.; (*speed*) allure f.; (*price*) tarif m. ~**s,** (*taxes*) impôts locaux m. pl. —v.t. évaluer; (*consider*) considérer; (*deserve*: Amer.) mériter. —v.i. ~ **as,** être

considéré comme. **at any ~,** en tout cas. **at the ~ of,** (*on the basis of*) à raison de.

ratepayer /ˈreɪtpeɪə(r)/ n. contribuable m./f.

rather /ˈrɑːðə(r)/ adv. (*by preference*) plutôt; (*fairly*) assez, plutôt; (*a little*) un peu. **I would ~ go,** j'aimerais mieux partir. ~ **than go,** plutôt que de partir.

ratif|y /ˈrætɪfaɪ/ v.t. ratifier. ~**ication** /-ɪˈkeɪʃn/ n. ratification f.

rating /ˈreɪtɪŋ/ n. classement m.; (*sailor*) matelot m.; (*number*) indice m. **the ~s,** (*TV*) l'audimat (P.).

ratio /ˈreɪʃɪəʊ/ n. (*pl.* **-os**) proportion f.

ration /ˈræʃn/ n. ration f. —v.t. rationner.

rational /ˈræʃənl/ a. rationnel; (*person*) raisonnable.

rationalize /ˈræʃənəlaɪz/ v.t. tenter de justifier; (*organize*) rationaliser.

rattle /ˈrætl/ v.i. faire du bruit; (*of bottles*) cliqueter. —v.t. secouer; (*sl.*) agacer. —n. bruit (de ferraille) m.; cliquetis m.; (*toy*) hochet m. ~ **off,** débiter en vitesse.

rattlesnake /ˈrætlsneɪk/ n. serpent à sonnette m., crotale m.

raucous /ˈrɔːkəs/ a. rauque.

raunchy /ˈrɔːntʃɪ/ a. (**-ier, -iest**) (*Amer., sl.*) cochon.

ravage /ˈrævɪdʒ/ v.t. ravager. ~**s** /-ɪz/ n. pl. ravages m. pl.

rav|e /reɪv/ v.i. divaguer; (*in anger*) tempêter. ~**e about,** s'extasier sur. ~**ings** n. pl. divagations f. pl.

raven /ˈreɪvn/ n. corbeau m.

ravenous /ˈrævənəs/ a. vorace. **I am ~,** je meurs de faim.

ravine /rəˈviːn/ n. ravin m.

raving /ˈreɪvɪŋ/ a. ~ **lunatic,** fou furieux m., folle furieuse f.

ravioli /rævɪˈəʊlɪ/ n. ravioli m. pl.

ravish /ˈrævɪʃ/ v.t. (*rape*) ravir. ~**ing** a. (*enchanting*) ravissant.

raw /rɔː/ a. (**-er, -est**) cru; (*not processed*) brut; (*wound*) à vif; (*immature*) inexpérimenté. **get a ~ deal,** être mal traité. ~ **materials,** matières premières f. pl.

ray /reɪ/ n. (*of light etc.*) rayon m. ~ **of hope,** lueur d'espoir f.

raze /reɪz/ v.t. (*destroy*) raser.

razor /ˈreɪzə(r)/ n. rasoir m. ~**-blade** n. lame de rasoir f.

re /riː/ prep. concernant.

re- /riː/ pref. re-, ré-, r-.

reach /riːtʃ/ v.t. atteindre, arriver à; (contact) joindre; (hand over) passer. —v.i. s'étendre. —n. portée f. ∼ for, tendre la main pour prendre. within ∼ of, à portée de; (close to) à proximité de.

react /rɪˈækt/ v.i. réagir.

reaction /rɪˈækʃn/ n. réaction f. ∼ary a. & n. réactionnaire (m./f.).

reactor /rɪˈæktə(r)/ n. réacteur m.

read /riːd/ v.t./i. (p.t. read /red/) lire; (fig.) comprendre; (study) étudier; (of instrument) indiquer. —n. (fam.) lecture f. ∼ about s.o., lire un article sur qn. ∼ out, lire à haute voix. ∼able a. agréable or facile à lire. ∼ing n. lecture f.; indication f. ∼ing-glasses pl. n. lunettes pour lire f. pl. ∼ing-lamp n. lampe de bureau f. ∼-out n. affichage m.

reader /ˈriːdə(r)/ n. lecIteur, -trice m., f. ∼ship n. lecteurs m. pl.

readily /ˈredɪlɪ/ adv. (willingly) volontiers; (easily) facilement.

readiness /ˈredɪnɪs/ n. empressement m. in ∼, prêt (for, à).

readjust /riːəˈdʒʌst/ v.t. rajuster. —v.i. se réadapter (to, à).

ready /ˈredɪ/ a. (-ier, -iest) prêt; (quick) prompt. —n. at the ∼, tout prêt. ∼-made a. tout fait. ∼ money, (argent) liquide m. ∼ reckoner, barème m. ∼-to-wear a. prêt-à-porter.

real /rɪəl/ a. vrai, véritable, réel. —adv. (Amer., fam.) vraiment. ∼ estate, biens fonciers m. pl.

realis|t /ˈrɪəlɪst/ n. réaliste m./f. ∼m /-zəm/ n. réalisme m. ∼tic /-ˈlɪstɪk/ a. réaliste. ∼tically /-ˈlɪstɪklɪ/ adv. avec réalisme.

reality /rɪˈælətɪ/ n. réalité f.

realiz|e /ˈrɪəlaɪz/ v.t. se rendre compte de, comprendre; (fulfil, turn into cash) réaliser; (price) atteindre. ∼ation /-ˈzeɪʃn/ n. prise de conscience f.; réalisation f.

really /ˈrɪəlɪ/ adv. vraiment.

realtor /ˈrɪəltə(r)/ n. (Amer.) agent immobilier m.

realm /relm/ n. royaume m.

reap /riːp/ v.t. (crop, field) moissonner; (fig.) récolter.

reappear /riːəˈpɪə(r)/ v.i. réapparaître, reparaître.

reappraisal /riːəˈpreɪzl/ n. réévaluation f.

rear[1] /rɪə(r)/ n. arrière m., derrière m. —a. arrière invar., de derrière. ∼-view mirror, rétroviseur m.

rear[2] /rɪə(r)/ v.t. (bring up, breed) élever. —v.i. (horse) se cabrer. ∼ one's head, dresser la tête.

rearguard /ˈrɪəgɑːd/ n. (mil.) arrière-garde f.

rearm /riːˈɑːm/ v.t./i. réarmer.

rearrange /riːəˈreɪndʒ/ v.t. réarranger.

reason /ˈriːzn/ n. raison f. —v.i. raisonner. it stands to ∼ that, de toute évidence. we have ∼ to believe that, on a tout lieu de croire que. there is no ∼ to panic, il n'y a pas de raison de paniquer. ∼ with, raisonner. everything within ∼, tout dans les limites normales. ∼ing n. raisonnement m.

reasonable /ˈriːznəbl/ a. raisonnable.

reassur|e /riːəˈʃʊə(r)/ v.t. rassurer. ∼ance n. réconfort m.

rebate /ˈriːbeɪt/ n. remboursement (partiel) m.; (discount) rabais m.

rebel[1] /ˈrebl/ n. & a. rebelle (m./f.).

rebel[2] /rɪˈbel/ v.i. (p.t. rebelled) se rebeller. ∼lion n. rébellion f. ∼lious a. rebelle.

rebound /rɪˈbaʊnd/ v.i. rebondir. ∼ on, (backfire) se retourner contre. — /ˈriːbaʊnd/ n. rebond m.

rebuff /rɪˈbʌf/ v.t. repousser. —n. rebuffade f.

rebuild /riːˈbɪld/ v.t. reconstruire.

rebuke /rɪˈbjuːk/ v.t. réprimander. —n. réprimande f., reproche m.

rebuttal /rɪˈbʌtl/ n. réfutation f.

recall /rɪˈkɔːl/ v.t. (to s.o., call back) rappeler; (remember) se rappeler. —n. rappel m.

recant /rɪˈkænt/ v.i. se rétracter.

recap /ˈriːkæp/ v.t./i. (p.t. recapped) (fam.) récapituler. —n. (fam.) récapitulation f.

recapitulat|e /riːkəˈpɪtʃʊleɪt/ v.t./i. récapituler. ∼ion /-ˈleɪʃn/ n. récapitulation f.

recapture /riːˈkæptʃə(r)/ v.t. reprendre; (recall) recréer.

reced|e /rɪˈsiːd/ v.i. s'éloigner. his hair is ∼ing, son front se dégarnit. ∼ing a. (forehead) fuyant.

receipt /rɪˈsiːt/ n. (written) reçu m.; (of letter) réception f. ∼s, (money: comm.) recettes f. pl.

receive /rɪˈsiːv/ v.t. recevoir. ∼r /-ə(r)/ n. (of stolen goods) receleur, -se m., f.; (telephone) combiné m.

recent /ˈriːsnt/ a. récent. ∼ly adv. récemment.

receptacle /rɪˈseptəkl/ n. récipient m.

reception /rɪˈsepʃn/ n. réception f. give s.o. a warm ∼, donner un accueil chaleureux à qn. ∽**ist** *n.* réceptionniste *m./f.*

receptive /rɪ'septɪv/ *a.* réceptif.

recess /rɪ'ses/ *n.* (*alcove*) renfoncement *m.*; (*nook*) recoin *m.*; (*holiday*) vacances *f. pl.*; (*schol., Amer.*) récréation *f.*

recession /rɪ'seʃn/ *n.* récession *f.*

recharge /ri:'tʃɑ:dʒ/ *v.t.* recharger.

recipe /'resəpɪ/ *n.* recette *f.*

recipient /rɪ'sɪpɪənt/ *n.* (*of honour*) récipiendaire *m.*; (*of letter*) destinataire *m./f.*

reciprocal /rɪ'sɪprəkl/ *a.* réciproque.

reciprocate /rɪ'sɪprəkeɪt/ *v.t.* offrir en retour. —*v.i.* en faire autant.

recital /rɪ'saɪtl/ *n.* récital *m.*

recite /rɪ'saɪt/ *v.t.* (*poem, lesson, etc.*) réciter; (*list*) énumérer.

reckless /'reklɪs/ *a.* imprudent. ∽**ly** *adv.* imprudemment.

reckon /'rekən/ *v.t./i.* calculer; (*judge*) considérer; (*think*) penser. ∽ **on/with,** compter sur/avec. ∽**ing** *n.* calcul(s) *m.* (*pl.*).

reclaim /rɪ'kleɪm/ *v.t.* (*seek return of*) réclamer; (*land*) défricher; (*flooded land*) assécher.

reclin|e /rɪ'klaɪn/ *v.i.* être étendu. ∽**ing** *a.* (*person*) étendu; (*seat*) à dossier réglable.

recluse /rɪ'klu:s/ *n.* reclus(e) *m.* (*f.*), ermite *m.*

recognition /rekəg'nɪʃn/ *n.* reconnaissance *f.* **beyond** ∽, méconnaissable. **gain** ∽, être reconnu.

recognize /'rekəgnaɪz/ *v.t.* reconnaître.

recoil /rɪ'kɔɪl/ *v.i.* reculer (**from,** devant).

recollect /rekə'lekt/ *v.t.* se souvenir de, se rappeler. ∽**ion** /-kʃn/ *n.* souvenir *m.*

recommend /rekə'mend/ *v.t.* recommander. ∽**ation** /-'deɪʃn/ *n.* recommandation *f.*

recompense /'rekəmpens/ *v.t.* (ré)compenser. —*n.* récompense *f.*

reconcil|e /'rekənsaɪl/ *v.t.* (*people*) réconcilier; (*facts*) concilier. ∽**e o.s. to,** se résigner à. ∽**iation** /-sɪlɪ'eɪʃn/ *n.* réconciliation *f.*

recondition /ri:kən'dɪʃn/ *v.t.* remettre à neuf, réviser.

reconn|oitre /rekə'nɔɪtə(r)/ *v.t.* (*pres. p.* **-tring**) (*mil.*) reconnaître. ∽**aissance** /rɪ'kɒnɪsns/ *n.* reconnaissance *f.*

reconsider /ri:kən'sɪdə(r)/ *v.t.* reconsidérer. —*v.i.* se déjuger.

reconstruct /ri:kən'strʌkt/ *v.t.* reconstruire; (*crime*) reconstituer.

record[1] /rɪ'kɔ:d/ *v.t./i.* (*in register, on tape, etc.*) enregistrer; (*in diary*) noter. ∽ **that,** rapporter que. ∽**ing** *n.* enregistrement *m.*

record[2] /'rekɔ:d/ *n.* (*report*) rapport *m.*; (*register*) registre *m.*; (*mention*) mention *f.*; (*file*) dossier *m.*; (*fig.*) résultats *m. pl.*; (*mus.*) disque *m.*; (*sport*) record *m.* (**criminal**) ∽, casier judiciaire *m.* —*a.* record *invar.* **off the** ∽, officieusement. ∽**-holder** *n.* détenlteur, -trice du record *m.*, *f.* ∽**-player** *n.* électrophone *m.*

recorder /rɪ'kɔ:də(r)/ *n.* (*mus.*) flûte à bec *f.*

recount /rɪ'kaʊnt/ *v.t.* raconter.

re-count /ri:'kaʊnt/ *v.t.* recompter.

recoup /rɪ'ku:p/ *v.t.* récupérer.

recourse /rɪ'kɔ:s/ *n.* recours *m.* **have** ∽ **to,** avoir recours à.

recover /rɪ'kʌvə(r)/ *v.t.* récupérer. —*v.i.* se remettre; (*med.*) se rétablir; (*economy*) se redresser. ∽**y** *n.* récupération *f.*; (*med.*) rétablissement *m.*

recreation /rekrɪ'eɪʃn/ *n.* récréation *f.* ∽**al** *a.* de récréation.

recrimination /rɪkrɪmɪ'neɪʃn/ *n.* contre-accusation *f.*

recruit /rɪ'kru:t/ *n.* recrue *f.* —*v.t.* recruter. ∽**ment** *n.* recrutement *m.*

rectang|le /'rektæŋgl/ *n.* rectangle *m.* ∽**ular** /-'tæŋgjʊlə(r)/ *a.* rectangulaire.

rectif|y /'rektɪfaɪ/ *v.t.* rectifier. ∽**ication** /-ɪ'keɪʃn/ *n.* rectification *f.*

recuperate /rɪ'kju:pəreɪt/ *v.t.* récupérer. —*v.i.* (*med.*) se rétablir.

recur /rɪ'kɜ:(r)/ *v.i.* (*p.t.* **recurred**) revenir, se répéter.

recurren|t /rɪ'kʌrənt/ *a.* fréquent. ∽**ce** *n.* répétition *f.*, retour *m.*

recycle /ri:'saɪkl/ *v.t.* recycler.

red /red/ *a.* (**redder, reddest**) rouge; (*hair*) roux. —*n.* rouge *m.* **in the** ∽, en déficit. **roll out the** ∽ **carpet for,** recevoir en grande pompe. **Red Cross,** Croix-Rouge *f.* ∽**-handed** *a.* en flagrant délit. ∽ **herring,** fausse piste *f.* ∽**-hot** *a.* brûlant. **the** ∽ **light,** le feu rouge *m.* ∽ **tape,** paperasserie *f.*, bureaucratie *f.*

redcurrant /red'kʌrənt/ *n.* groseille *f.*

redden /'redn/ *v.t./i.* rougir.

reddish /'redɪʃ/ *a.* rougeâtre.

redecorate /ri:'dekəreɪt/ *v.t.* (*repaint etc.*) repeindre, refaire.

redeem /rɪ'di:m/ *v.t.* racheter. ∽**ing quality,** qualité qui rachète les défauts *f.* **redemption** *n.* /rɪ'dempʃn/ rachat *m.*

redeploy /ri:dɪ'plɔɪ/ *v.t.* réorganiser; (*troops*) répartir.

redirect /ri:daɪə'rekt/ *v.t.* (*letter*) faire suivre.

redness /'rednɪs/ *n.* rougeur *f.*

redo /ri:'du:/ *v.t.* (*p.t.* **-did**, *p.p.* **-done**) refaire.

redolent /'redələnt/ *a.* ~ **of,** qui évoque.

redouble /rɪ'dʌbl/ *v.t.* redoubler.

redress /rɪ'dres/ *v.t.* (*wrong etc.*) redresser. —*n.* réparation *f.*

reduc|e /rɪ'dju:s/ *v.t.* réduire; (*temperature etc.*) faire baisser. ~**tion** /rɪ'dʌkʃn/ *n.* réduction *f.*

redundan|t /rɪ'dʌndənt/ *a.* superflu; (*worker*) licencié. **make** ~, licencier. ~**cy** *n.* licenciement *m.*; (*word, phrase*) pléonasme *m.*

reed /ri:d/ *n.* (*plant*) roseau *m.*; (*mus.*) anche *f.*

reef /ri:f/ *n.* récif *m.*, écueil *m.*

reek /ri:k/ *n.* puanteur *f.* —*v.i.* ~ (**of**), puer.

reel /ri:l/ *n.* (*of thread*) bobine *f.*; (*of film*) bande *f.*; (*winding device*) dévidoir *m.* —*v.i.* chanceler. —*v.t.* ~ **off,** réciter.

refectory /rɪ'fektərɪ/ *n.* réfectoire *m.*

refer /rɪ'fɜ:(r)/ *v.t./i.* (*p.t.* **referred**). ~ **to,** (*allude to*) faire allusion à; (*concern*) s'appliquer à; (*consult*) consulter; (*submit*) soumettre à; (*direct*) renvoyer à.

referee /refə'ri:/ *n.* arbitre *m.*; (*for job*) répondant(e) *m.* (*f.*). —*v.t.* (*p.t.* **refereed**) arbitrer.

reference /'refrəns/ *n.* référence *f.*; (*mention*) allusion *f.*; (*person*) répondant(e) *m.* (*f.*). **in** *or* **with** ~ **to,** en ce qui concerne; (*comm.*) suite à. ~ **book,** ouvrage de référence *m.*

referendum /refə'rendəm/ *n.* (*pl.* **-ums**) référendum *m.*

refill[1] /ri:fɪl/ *v.t.* remplir (à nouveau); (*pen etc.*) recharger.

refill[2] /'ri:fɪl/ *n.* (*of pen, lighter, lipstick*) recharge *f.*

refine /rɪ'faɪn/ *v.t.* raffiner. ~**d** *a.* raffiné. ~**ment** *n.* raffinement *m.*; (*techn.*) raffinage *m.* ~**ry** /-ərɪ/ *n.* raffinerie *f.*

reflate /ri:'fleɪt/ *v.t.* relancer.

reflect /rɪ'flekt/ *v.t.* refléter; (*of mirror*) réfléchir, refléter. —*v.i.* réfléchir (**on,** à). ~ **on s.o.,** (*glory etc.*) (faire) rejaillir sur qn.; (*pej.*) donner une mauvaise impression de qn. ~**ion** /-kʃn/ *n.* réflexion *f.*; (*image*) reflet *m.* **on** ~**ion,** réflexion faite. ~**or** *n.* réflecteur *m.*

reflective /rɪ'flektɪv/ *a.* réfléchissant.

reflex /'ri:fleks/ *a. & n.* réflexe (*m.*).

reflexive /rɪ'fleksɪv/ *a.* (*gram.*) réfléchi.

reform /rɪ'fɔ:m/ *v.t.* réformer. —*v.i.* (*person*) s'amender. —*n.* réforme *f.* ~**er** *n.* réformateur, -trice *m.*, *f.*

refract /rɪ'frækt/ *v.t.* réfracter.

refrain[1] /rɪ'freɪn/ *n.* refrain *m.*

refrain[2] /rɪ'freɪn/ *v.i.* s'abstenir (**from,** de).

refresh /rɪ'freʃ/ *v.t.* rafraîchir; (*of rest etc.*) ragaillardir, délasser. ~**ing** *a.* (*drink*) rafraîchissant; (*sleep*) réparateur. ~**ments** *n. pl.* rafraîchissements *m. pl.*

refresher /rɪ'freʃə(r)/ *a.* (*course*) de perfectionnement.

refrigerat|e /rɪ'frɪdʒəreɪt/ *v.t.* réfrigérer. ~**or** *n.* réfrigérateur *m.*

refuel /ri:'fju:əl/ *v.t./i.* (*p.t.* **refuelled**) (se) ravitailler.

refuge /'refju:dʒ/ *n.* refuge *m.* **take** ~, se réfugier.

refugee /refjʊ'dʒi:/ *n.* réfugié(e) *m.* (*f.*).

refund /rɪ'fʌnd/ *v.t.* rembourser. —*n.* /'ri:fʌnd/ remboursement *m.*

refurbish /ri:'fɜ:bɪʃ/ *v.t.* remettre à neuf.

refus|e[1] /rɪ'fju:z/ *v.t./i.* refuser. ~**al** *n.* refus *m.*

refuse[2] /'refju:s/ *n.* ordures *f. pl.*

refute /rɪ'fju:t/ *v.t.* réfuter.

regain /rɪ'geɪn/ *v.t.* retrouver; (*lost ground*) regagner.

regal /'ri:gl/ *a.* royal, majestueux.

regalia /rɪ'geɪlɪə/ *n. pl.* (*insignia*) insignes (royaux) *m. pl.*

regard /rɪ'gɑ:d/ *v.t.* considérer. —*n.* considération *f.*, estime *f.* ~**s** *n. pl.* amitiés *f. pl.* **in this** ~, à cet égard. **as** ~**s,** ~**ing** *prep.* en ce qui concerne.

regardless /rɪ'gɑ:dlɪs/ *adv.* quand même. ~ **of,** sans tenir compte de.

regatta /rɪ'gætə/ *n.* régates *f. pl.*

regenerat|e /rɪ'dʒenəreɪt/ *v.t.* régénérer. ~**ion** /-'reɪʃn/ *n.* régénération *f.*

regen|t /'ri:dʒənt/ *n.* régent(e) *m.* (*f.*). ~**cy** *n.* régence *f.*

regime /reɪ'ʒi:m/ *n.* régime *m.*

regiment /'redʒɪmənt/ *n.* régiment *m.* ~**al** /-'mentl/ *a.* d'un régiment. ~**ation** /-en'teɪʃn/ *n.* discipline excessive *f.*

region /'ri:dʒən/ *n.* région *f.* **in the** ~ **of,** environ. ~**al** *a.* régional.

regist|er /'redʒɪstə(r)/ *n.* registre *m.* —*v.t.* enregistrer; (*vehicle*) immatriculer; (*birth*) déclarer; (*letter*) recommander; (*indicate*) indiquer; (*express*) exprimer. —*v.i.* (*enrol*) s'inscrire; (*fig.*) être compris. ~**er office,** bureau d'état civil *m.* ~**ration** /-'streɪʃn/ *n.* enregistrement *m.*; inscription *f.*; (*vehicle document*) carte

grise *f.* ~**ration (number),** (*auto.*)
numéro d'immatriculation *m.*

registrar /redʒɪ'strɑ:(r)/ *n.* officier de
l'état civil *m.*; (*univ.*) secrétaire général
m.

regret /rɪ'gret/ *n.* regret *m.* —*v.t.* (*p.t.*
regretted) regretter (**to do,** de faire).
~**fully** *adv.* à regret. ~**table** *a.*
regrettable, fâcheux. ~**tably** *adv.*
malheureusement; (*small, poor, etc.*)
fâcheusement.

regroup /ri:'gru:p/ *v.t./i.* (se) regrouper.

regular /'regjʊlə(r)/ *a.* régulier; (*usual*)
habituel; (*thorough: fam.*) vrai. —*n.*
(*fam.*) habitué(e) *m.* (*f.*). ~**ity**
/-'lærətɪ/ *n.* régularité *f.* ~**ly** *adv.*
régulièrement.

regulat|e /'regjʊleɪt/ *v.t.* régler. ~**ion**
/-'leɪʃn/ *n.* réglage *m.*; (*rule*) règlement *m.*

rehabilitat|e /ri:ə'bɪlɪteɪt/ *v.t.* réadapter;
(*in public esteem*) réhabiliter. ~**ion**
/-'teɪʃn/ *n.* réadaptation *f.*; réhabilita-
tion *f.*

rehash[1] /ri:'hæʃ/ *v.t.* remanier.

rehash[2] /'ri:hæʃ/ *n.* réchauffé *m.*

rehears|e /rɪ'hɜ:s/ *v.t./i.* (*theatre*)
répéter. ~**al** *n.* répétition *f.*

re-heat /ri:'hi:t/ *v.t.* réchauffer.

reign /reɪn/ *n.* règne *m.* —*v.i.* régner
(**over,** sur).

reimburse /ri:ɪm'bɜ:s/ *v.t.* rembourser.

rein /reɪn/ *n.* rêne *f.*

reindeer /'reɪndɪə(r)/ *n. invar.* renne *m.*

reinforce /ri:ɪn'fɔ:s/ *v.t.* renforcer.
~**ment** *n.* renforcement *m.* ~**ments** *n.*
pl. renforts *m. pl.* ~**d concrete,** béton
armé *m.*

reinstate /ri:ɪn'steɪt/ *v.t.* réintégrer,
rétablir.

reiterate /ri:'ɪtəreɪt/ *v.t.* réitérer.

reject[1] /rɪ'dʒekt/ *v.t.* (*offer, plea, etc.*)
rejeter; (*book, goods, etc.*) refuser.
~**ion** /-kʃn/ *n.* rejet *m.*; refus *m.*

reject[2] /'ri:dʒekt/ *n.* (article de) rebut *m.*

rejoic|e /rɪ'dʒɔɪs/ *v.i.* se réjouir. ~**ing** *n.*
réjouissance *f.*

rejuvenate /rɪ'dʒu:vəneɪt/ *v.t.* rajeunir.

relapse /rɪ'læps/ *n.* rechute *f.* —*v.i.*
rechuter. ~ **into,** retomber dans.

relate /rɪ'leɪt/ *v.t.* raconter; (*associate*)
rapprocher. —*v.i.* ~ **to,** se rapporter à;
(*get on with*) s'entendre avec. ~**d** /-ɪd/
a. (*ideas etc.*) lié. ~**d to s.o.,** parent(e)
de qn.

relation /rɪ'leɪʃn/ *n.* rapport *m.*; (*person*)
parent(e) *m.* (*f.*). ~**ship** *n.* lien de
parenté *m.*; (*link*) rapport *m.*; (*affair*)
liaison *f.*

relative /'relətɪv/ *n.* parent(e) *m.* (*f.*).
—*a.* relatif; (*respective*) respectif. ~**ly**
adv. relativement.

relax /rɪ'læks/ *v.t./i.* (*less tense*) (se)
relâcher; (*for pleasure*) (se) détendre.
~**ation** /ri:læk'seɪʃn/ *n.* relâchement
m.; détente *f.* ~**ing** *a.* délassant.

relay[1] /'ri:leɪ/ *n.* relais *m.* ~ **race,** course
de relais *f.*

relay[2] /rɪ'leɪ/ *v.t.* relayer.

release /rɪ'li:s/ *v.t.* libérer; (*bomb*)
lâcher; (*film*) sortir; (*news*) publier;
(*smoke*) dégager; (*spring*) déclencher.
—*n.* libération *f.*; sortie *f.*; (*record*)
nouveau disque *m.* (*of pollution*)
émission *f.*

relegate /'relɪgeɪt/ *v.t.* reléguer.

relent /rɪ'lent/ *v.i.* se laisser fléchir.
~**less** *a.* impitoyable.

relevan|t /'reləvənt/ *a.* pertinent. **be** ~**t
to,** avoir rapport à. ~**ce** *n.* pertinence *f.*,
rapport *m.*

reliab|le /rɪ'laɪəbl/ *a.* sérieux, sûr;
(*machine*) fiable. ~**ility** /-'bɪlətɪ/ *n.*
sérieux *m.*; fiabilité *f.*

reliance /rɪ'laɪəns/ *n.* dépendance *f.*;
(*trust*) confiance *f.*

relic /'relɪk/ *n.* relique *f.* ~**s,** (*of past*)
vestiges *m. pl.*

relief /rɪ'li:f/ *n.* soulagement *m.* (**from,**
à); (*assistance*) secours *m.*; (*outline,
design*) relief *m.* ~ **road,** route de
délestage *f.*

relieve /rɪ'li:v/ *v.t.* soulager; (*help*)
secourir; (*take over from*) relayer.

religion /rɪ'lɪdʒən/ *n.* religion *f.*

religious /rɪ'lɪdʒəs/ *a.* religieux.

relinquish /rɪ'lɪŋkwɪʃ/ *v.t.* abandonner;
(*relax hold of*) lâcher.

relish /'relɪʃ/ *n.* plaisir *m.*, goût *m.*;
(*culin.*) assaisonnement *m.* —*v.t.*
savourer; (*idea etc.*) aimer.

relocate /ri:ləʊ'keɪt/ *v.t.* (*company*)
déplacer; (*employee*) muter. —*v.i.* se
déplacer, déménager.

reluctan|t /rɪ'lʌktənt/ *a.* fait, donné, *etc.*
à contrecœur. ~ **to,** peu disposé à. ~**ce**
n. répugnance *f.* ~**tly** *adv.* à contrecœur.

rely /rɪ'laɪ/ *v.i.* ~ **on,** compter sur;
(*financially*) dépendre de.

remain /rɪ'meɪn/ *v.i.* rester. ~**s** *n. pl.*
restes *m. pl.*

remainder /rɪ'meɪndə(r)/ *n.* reste *m.*;
(*book*) invendu soldé *m.*

remand /rɪ'mɑ:nd/ *v.t.* mettre en
détention préventive. —*n.* **on** ~**,** en
détention préventive.

remark /rɪ'mɑ:k/ *n.* remarque *f.* —*v.t.*

remarquer. —*v.i.* ⁓ **on,** faire des commentaires sur. ⁓**able** *a.* remarquable.

remarry /riːˈmæri/ *v.i.* se remarier.

remed|y /ˈremədi/ *n.* remède *m.* —*v.t.* remédier à. ⁓**ial** /riˈmiːdiəl/ *a.* (*class etc.*) de rattrapage; (*treatment*: *med.*) curatif.

rememb|er /riˈmembə(r)/ *v.t.* se souvenir de, se rappeler. ⁓**er to do,** ne pas oublier de faire. ⁓**rance** *n.* souvenir *m.*

remind /riˈmaɪnd/ *v.t.* rappeler (**s.o. of sth.,** qch. à qn.). ⁓ **s.o. to do,** rappeler à qn. qu'il doit faire. ⁓**er** *n.* (*letter, signal*) rappel *m.*

reminisce /remiˈnis/ *v.i.* évoquer ses souvenirs. ⁓**nces** *n. pl.* réminiscences *f. pl.*

reminiscent /remiˈnisnt/ *a.* ⁓ **of,** qui rappelle, qui évoque.

remiss /riˈmis/ *a.* négligent

remission /riˈmiʃn/ *n* rémission *f.*; (*jurid.*) remise (de peine) *f.*

remit /riˈmit/ *v.t* (*p.t.* **remitted**) (*money*) envoyer; (*debt*) remettre. ⁓**tance** *n.* paiement *m.*

remnant /ˈremnənt/ *n.* reste *m.*, débris *m.*; (*trace*) vestige *m.*; (*of cloth*) coupon *m*

remodel /riːˈmɒdel/ *v.t.* (*p.t.* **remodelled**) remodeler.

remorse /riˈmɔːs/ *n.* remords *m.* (*pl.*). ⁓**ful** *a.* plein de remords. ⁓**less** *a.* implacable.

remote /riˈməʊt/ *a.* (*place, time*) lointain; (*person*) distant; (*slight*) vague. ⁓ **control,** télécommande *f.* ⁓**ly** *adv.* au loin; vaguement. ⁓**ness** *n.* éloignement *m.*

removable /riˈmuːvəbl/ *a.* (*detachable*) amovible.

remov|e /riˈmuːv/ *v.t.* enlever; (*lead away*) emmener; (*dismiss*) renvoyer; (*do away with*) supprimer. ⁓**al** *n* enlèvement *m.*; renvoi *m.*; suppression *f.*; (*from house*) déménagement *m.* ⁓**al men,** déménageurs *m. pl.* ⁓**er** *n.* (*for paint*) décapant *m*

remunerat|e /riˈmjuːnəreit/ *v.t.* rémunérer. ⁓**ion** /-ˈreiʃn/ *n.* rémunération *f.*

rename /riːˈneim/ *v.t.* rebaptiser.

render /ˈrendə(r)/ *v.t.* (*give, make*) rendre; (*mus.*) interpréter. ⁓**ing** *n.* interprétation *f.*

rendezvous /ˈrɒndeivuː/ *n.* (*pl.* **-vous** /-vuːz/) rendez-vous *m. invar.*

renegade /ˈrenigeid/ *n.* renégat(e) *m.* (*f.*).

renew /riˈnjuː/ *v.t.* renouveler; (*resume*) reprendre. ⁓**able** *a.* renouvelable. ⁓**al** *n.* renouvellement *m.*; reprise *f.*

renounce /riˈnaʊns/ *v.t.* renoncer à; (*disown*) renier.

renovat|e /ˈrenəveit/ *v.t.* rénover. ⁓**ion** /-ˈveiʃn/ *n.* rénovation *f.*

renown /riˈnaʊn/ *n.* renommée *f.* ⁓**ed** *a.* renommé.

rent /rent/ *n.* loyer *m.* —*v.t.* louer. **for** ⁓, à louer. ⁓**al** *n.* prix de location *m.*

renunciation /rinʌnsiˈeiʃn/ *n.* renonciation *f.*

reopen /riːˈəʊpən/ *v.t./i.* rouvrir. ⁓**ing** *n.* réouverture *f.*

reorganize /riːˈɔːgənaiz/ *v.t.* réorganiser.

rep /rep/ *n.* (*comm., fam.*) représentant(e) *m.* (*f.*).

repair /riˈpeə(r)/ *v.t.* réparer. —*n.* réparation *f.* **in good/bad** ⁓, en bon/mauvais état. ⁓**er** *n.* réparateur *m.*

repartee /repɑːˈtiː/ *n.* repartie *f.*

repatriat|e /riːˈpætrieit/ *v.t.* rapatrier. ⁓**ion** /-ˈeiʃn/ *n.* rapatriement *m.*

repay /riːˈpei/ *v.t.* (*p.t.* **repaid**) rembourser; (*reward*) récompenser. ⁓**ment** *n.* remboursement *m.*; récompense *f.* **monthly** ⁓**ments,** mensualités *f. pl.*

repeal /riˈpiːl/ *v.t.* abroger, annuler. —*n.* abrogation *f.*

repeat /riˈpiːt/ *v.t./i.* répéter; (*renew*) renouveler. —*n.* répétition *f.*; (*broadcast*) reprise *f.* ⁓ **itself,** ⁓ **o.s.,** se répéter.

repeatedly /riˈpiːtidli/ *adv.* à maintes reprises.

repel /riˈpel/ *v.t.* (*p.t.* **repelled**) repousser. ⁓**lent** *a.* repoussant.

repent /riˈpent/ *v.i.* se repentir (**of,** de). ⁓**ance** *n.* repentir *m.* ⁓**ant** *a.* repentant.

repercussion /riːpəˈkʌʃn/ *n.* répercussion *f.*

repertoire /ˈrepətwɑː(r)/ *n.* répertoire *m.*

repertory /ˈrepətri/ *n.* répertoire *m.* ⁓ (**theatre**), théâtre de répertoire *m.*

repetit|ion /repiˈtiʃn/ *n.* répétition *f.* ⁓**ious** /-ˈtiʃəs/, ⁓**ive** /riˈpetətiv/ *adjs.* plein de répétitions.

replace /riˈpleis/ *v.t.* remettre; (*take the place of*) remplacer. ⁓**ment** *n.* remplacement *m.* (**of,** de); (*person*) remplaçant(e) *m.* (*f.*); (*new part*) pièce de rechange *f.*

replay /ˈriːplei/ *n.* (*sport*) match rejoué *m.*; (*recording*) répétition immédiate *f.*

replenish /riˈpleniʃ/ *v.t.* (*refill*) remplir; (*renew*) renouveler.

replica /ˈreplikə/ *n.* copie exacte *f.*

reply /rɪˈplaɪ/ v.t./i. répondre. —n. réponse f.

report /rɪˈpɔːt/ v.t. rapporter, annoncer (**that**, que); (notify) signaler; (denounce) dénoncer. —v.i. faire un rapport. ～ (**on**), (news item) faire un reportage sur. ～ **to**, (go) se présenter chez. —n. rapport m.; (in press) reportage m.; (schol.) bulletin m.; (sound) détonation f. ～**edly** adv. selon ce qu'on dit.

reporter /rɪˈpɔːtə(r)/ n. reporter m.

repose /rɪˈpəʊz/ n. repos m.

repossess /riːpəˈzes/ v.t. reprendre.

represent /reprɪˈzent/ v.t. représenter. ～**ation** /-ˈteɪʃn/ n. représentation f. **make ～ations to**, protester auprès de.

representative /reprɪˈzentətɪv/ a. représentatif, typique (**of**, de). —n. représentant(e) m. (f.).

repress /rɪˈpres/ v.t. réprimer. ～**ion** /-ʃn/ n. répression f. ～**ive** a. répressif.

reprieve /rɪˈpriːv/ n. (delay) sursis m.; (pardon) grâce f. —v.t. accorder un sursis à; gracier.

reprimand /ˈreprɪmɑːnd/ v.t. réprimander. —n. réprimande f.

reprint /ˈriːprɪnt/ n. réimpression f.; (offprint) tiré à part m.

reprisals /rɪˈpraɪzlz/ n. pl. représailles f. pl.

reproach /rɪˈprəʊtʃ/ v.t. reprocher (**s.o. for sth.**, qch. à qn.). —n. reproche m. ～**ful** a. de reproche, réprobateur. ～**fully** adv. avec reproche.

reproduc|e /riːprəˈdjuːs/ v.t./i. (se) reproduire. ～**tion** /-ˈdʌkʃn/ n. reproduction f. ～**tive** /-ˈdʌktɪv/ a. reproducteur.

reptile /ˈreptaɪl/ n. reptile m.

republic /rɪˈpʌblɪk/ n. république f. ～**an** a. & n. républicain(e) (m. (f.)).

repudiate /rɪˈpjuːdɪeɪt/ v.t. répudier; (treaty) refuser d'honorer.

repugnan|t /rɪˈpʌɡnənt/ a. répugnant. ～**ce** n. répugnance f.

repuls|e /rɪˈpʌls/ v.t. repousser. ～**ion** /-ʃn/ n. répulsion f. ～**ive** a. repoussant.

reputable /ˈrepjʊtəbl/ a. honorable, de bonne réputation.

reputation /repjʊˈteɪʃn/ n. réputation f.

repute /rɪˈpjuːt/ n. réputation f. ～**d** /-ɪd/ a. réputé. ～**dly** /-ɪdlɪ/ adv. d'après ce qu'on dit.

request /rɪˈkwest/ n. demande f. —v.t. demander (**of, from**, à). ～ **stop**, arrêt facultatif m.

requiem /ˈrekwɪem/ n. requiem m.

require rɪˈkwaɪə(r) v.t. (of thing) demander; (of person) avoir besoin de; (demand, order) exiger. ～**d** a. requis. ～**ment** n. exigence f.; (condition) condition (requise) f.

requisite /ˈrekwɪzɪt/ a. nécessaire. —n. chose nécessaire f. ～**s**, (for travel etc.) articles m. pl.

requisition /rekwɪˈzɪʃn/ n. réquisition f. —v.t. réquisitionner.

re-route /riːˈruːt/ v.t. dérouter.

resale /ˈriːseɪl/ n. revente f.

rescind /rɪˈsɪnd/ v.t. annuler.

rescue /ˈreskjuː/ v.t. sauver. —n. sauvetage m. (**of**, de); (help) secours m. ～**r** /-ə(r)/ n. sauveteur m.

research /rɪˈsɜːtʃ/ n. recherche(s) f.(pl.). —v.t./i. faire des recherches (sur). ～**er** n. chercheur, -se m., f.

resembl|e /rɪˈzembl/ v.t. ressembler à. ～**ance** n. ressemblance f.

resent /rɪˈzent/ v.t. être indigné de, s'offenser de. ～**ful** a. plein de ressentiment, indigné. ～**ment** n. ressentiment m.

reservation /rezəˈveɪʃn/ n. réserve f.; (booking) réservation f.; (Amer.) réserve (indienne) f. **make a ～**, réserver.

reserve /rɪˈzɜːv/ v.t. réserver. —n. (reticence, stock, land) réserve f.; (sport) remplaçant(e) m. (f.). **in ～**, en réserve. **the ～s**, (mil.) les réserves f. pl. ～**d** a. (person, room) réservé.

reservist /rɪˈzɜːvɪst/ n. (mil.) réserviste m.

reservoir /ˈrezəvwɑː(r)/ n. (lake, supply, etc.) réservoir m.

reshape /riːˈʃeɪp/ v.t. remodeler.

reshuffle /riːˈʃʌfl/ v.t. (pol.) remanier. —n. (pol.) remaniement (ministériel) m.

reside /rɪˈzaɪd/ v.i. résider.

residen|t /ˈrezɪdənt/ a. résidant. **be ～t**, résider. —n. habitant(e) m. (f.); (foreigner) résident(e) m. (f.); (in hotel) pensionnaire m./f. ～**ce** n. résidence f.; (of students) foyer m. **in ～ce**, (doctor) résidant; (students) au foyer.

residential /rezɪˈdenʃl/ a. résidentiel.

residue /ˈrezɪdjuː/ n. résidu m.

resign /rɪˈzaɪn/ v.t. abandonner; (job) démissionner de. —v.i. démissionner. ～ **o.s. to**, se résigner à. ～**ation** /rezɪɡˈneɪʃn/ n. résignation f.; (from job) démission f. ～**ed** a. résigné.

resilien|t /rɪˈzɪlɪənt/ a. élastique; (person) qui a du ressort. ～**ce** n. élasticité f.; ressort m.

resin /'rezɪn/ n. résine f.

resist /rɪ'zɪst/ v.t./i. résister (à). ∼ance n. résistance f. ∼ant a. (med.) rebelle; (metal) résistant.

resolut|e /'rezəluːt/ a. résolu. ∼ion /-'luːʃn/ n. résolution f.

resolve /rɪ'zɒlv/ v.t. résoudre (**to do**, de faire). —n. résolution f. ∼d a. résolu (**to do**, à faire).

resonan|t /'rezənənt/ a. résonnant. ∼ce n. résonance f.

resort /rɪ'zɔːt/ v.i. ∼ **to**, avoir recours à. —n. (recourse) recours m.; (place) station f. **In the last** ∼, en dernier ressort.

resound /rɪ'zaʊnd/ v.i. retentir (**with**, de). ∼ing a. retentissant.

resource /rɪ'sɔːs/ n. (expedient) ressource f. ∼s, (wealth etc.) ressources f. pl. ∼ful a. ingénieux. ∼fulness n. ingéniosité f.

respect /rɪ'spekt/ n. respect m.; (aspect) égard m. —v.t. respecter. **with** ∼ **to**, à l'égard de, relativement à. ∼ful a. respectueux.

respectab|le /rɪ'spektəbl/ a. respectable. ∼ility /-'bɪlətɪ/ n. respectabilité f. ∼ly adv. convenablement.

respective /rɪ'spektɪv/ a. respectif. ∼ly adv. respectivement.

respiration /respə'reɪʃn/ n. respiration f.

respite /'resp(a)ɪt/ n. répit m.

resplendent /rɪ'splendənt/ a. resplendissant.

respond /rɪ'spɒnd/ v.i. répondre (**to**, à) ∼ **to**, (react to) réagir à.

response /rɪ'spɒns/ n. réponse f.

responsib|le /rɪ'spɒnsəbl/ a. responsable: (job) qui comporte des responsabilités. ∼ility /-'bɪlətɪ/ n. responsabilité f. ∼ly adv. de façon responsable.

responsive /rɪ'spɒnsɪv/ a. qui réagit bien. ∼ **to**, sensible à.

rest¹ /rest/ v.t./i. (se) reposer; (lean) (s')appuyer (**on**, sur); (be buried, lie) reposer. —n. (repose) repos m.; (support) support m. **have a** ∼, se reposer; (at work) prendre une pause. ∼-room n. (Amer.) toilettes f. pl.

rest² /rest/ v.i. (remain) demeurer. —n. (remainder) reste m. (**of**, de). **the** ∼ (**of the**), (others, other) les autres. **it** ∼s **with him to**, il lui appartient de.

restaurant /'restərɒnt/ n. restaurant m.

restful /'restfl/ a. reposant.

restitution /restɪ'tjuːʃn/ n. (for injury) compensation f.

restive /'restɪv/ a. rétif.

restless /'restlɪs/ a. agité. ∼ly adv. avec agitation, fébrilement.

restor|e /rɪ'stɔː(r)/ v.t. rétablir; (building) restaurer. ∼**e sth. to s.o.**, restituer qch. à qn. ∼ation /restə'reɪʃn/ n. rétablissement m.; restauration f. ∼er n. (art) restaura|teur, -trice m., f.

restrain /rɪ'streɪn/ v.t. contenir. ∼ **s.o. from**, retenir qn. de. ∼ed a. (moderate) mesuré; (in control of self) maître de soi. ∼t n. contrainte f.; (moderation) retenue f.

restrict /rɪ'strɪkt/ v.t. restreindre. ∼ion /-kʃn/ n. restriction f. ∼ive a. restrictif.

restructure /riː'strʌktʃə(r)/ v.t. restructurer.

result /rɪ'zʌlt/ n. résultat m. —v.i. résulter. ∼ **in**, aboutir à.

resum|e /rɪ'zjuːm/ v.t./i. reprendre. ∼ption /rɪ'zʌmpʃn/ n. reprise f.

résumé /'rezjuːmeɪ/ n. résumé m.; (of career: Amer.) CV m., curriculum vitae m.

resurgence /rɪ'sɜːdʒəns/ n. réapparition f.

resurrect /rezə'rekt/ v.t. ressusciter. ∼ion /-kʃn/ n. résurrection f.

resuscitate /rɪ'sʌsɪteɪt/ v.t. réanimer.

retail /'riːteɪl/ n. détail m. —a & adv. au détail. —v.t./i. (se) vendre (au détail). ∼er n. détaillant(e) m. (f.).

retain /rɪ'teɪn/ v.t. (hold back, remember) retenir; (keep) conserver.

retaliat|e /rɪ'tælɪeɪt/ v.i. riposter. ∼ion /-'eɪʃn/ n. représailles f. pl.

retarded /rɪ'tɑːdɪd/ a. arriéré.

retch /retʃ/ v.i. avoir un haut-le-cœur.

retentive /rɪ'tentɪv/ a. (memory) fidèle. ∼ **of**, qui retient

rethink /riː'θɪŋk/ v.t. (p.t. **rethought**) repenser.

reticen|t /'retɪsnt/ a. réticent. ∼ce n. réticence f.

retina /'retɪnə/ n. rétine f.

retinue /'retɪnjuː/ n. suite f.

retire /rɪ'taɪə(r)/ v.i. (from work) prendre sa retraite; (withdraw) se retirer; (go to bed) se coucher. v.t. mettre à la retraite. ∼d a. retraité. ∼ment n. retraite f.

retiring /rɪ'taɪərɪŋ/ a. réservé.

retort /rɪ'tɔːt/ v.t./i. répliquer. —n. réplique f.

retrace /riː'treɪs/ v.t. ∼ **one's steps**, revenir sur ses pas.

retract /rɪ'trækt/ v.t./i. (se) rétracter.

retrain /riː'treɪn/ v.t./i. (se) recycler.

retread /riː'tred/ n. pneu rechapé m.

retreat /rɪ'triːt/ v.i. (mil.) battre en retraite. —n. retraite f.

retrial /riːˈtraɪəl/ *n.* nouveau procès *m.*

retribution /retrɪˈbjuːʃn/ *n.* châtiment *m.*; (*vengeance*) vengeance *f.*

retriev|e /rɪˈtriːv/ *v.t.* (*recover*) récupérer; (*restore*) rétablir; (*put right*) réparer. **~al** *n.* récupération *f.*; (*of information*) recherche documentaire *f.* **~er** *n.* (*dog*) chien d'arrêt *m.*

retrograde /ˈretrəgreɪd/ *a.* rétrograde —*v.i.* rétrograder.

retrospect /ˈretrəspekt/ *n.* **in ~**, rétrospectivement.

return /rɪˈtɜːn/ *v.i.* (*come back*) revenir; (*go back*) retourner; (*go home*) rentrer. —*v.t.* (*give back*) rendre; (*bring back*) rapporter; (*send back*) renvoyer; (*put back*) remettre. —*n.* retour *m.*; (*yield*) rapport *m.* **~s**, (*comm.*) bénéfices *m. pl.* **in ~ for**, en échange de. **~ journey**, voyage de retour *m.* **~ match**, match retour *m.* **~ ticket**, aller-retour *m.*

reunion /riːˈjuːnɪən/ *n.* réunion *f.*

reunite /riːjuːˈnaɪt/ *v.t.* réunir.

rev /rev/ *n.* (*auto., fam.*) tour *m.* —*v.t./i.* (*p.t.* **revved**). **~ (up)**, (*engine: fam.*) (s')emballer.

revamp /riːˈvæmp/ *v.t.* rénover.

reveal /rɪˈviːl/ *v.t.* révéler; (*allow to appear*) laisser voir. **~ing** *a.* révélateur.

revel /ˈrevl/ *v.i.* (*p.t.* **revelled**) faire bombance. **~ in**, se délecter de. **~ry** *n.* festivités *f.*

revelation /revəˈleɪʃn/ *n.* révélation *f.*

revenge /rɪˈvendʒ/ *n.* vengeance *f.*; (*sport*) revanche *f.* —*v.t.* venger.

revenue /ˈrevənjuː/ *n.* revenu *m.*

reverberate /rɪˈvɜːbəreɪt/ *v.i.* (*sound, light*) se répercuter.

revere /rɪˈvɪə(r)/ *v.t.* révérer. **~nce** /ˈrevərəns/ *n.* vénération *f.*

reverend /ˈrevərənd/ *a.* révérend.

reverent /ˈrevərənt/ *a.* respectueux.

reverie /ˈrevərɪ/ *n.* rêverie *f.*

revers|e /rɪˈvɜːs/ *a.* contraire, inverse. —*n.* contraire *m.*; (*back*) revers *m.*, envers *m.*; (*gear*) marche arrière *f.* —*v.t.* (*situation, bracket, etc.*) renverser; (*order*) inverser; (*decision*) annuler. —*v.i.* (*auto.*) faire marche arrière. **~al** *n.* renversement *m.*; (*of view*) revirement *m.*

revert /rɪˈvɜːt/ *v.i.* **~ to**, revenir à.

review /rɪˈvjuː/ *n.* (*inspection, magazine*) revue *f.*; (*of book etc.*) critique *f.* —*v.t.* passer en revue; (*situation*) réexaminer; faire la critique de. **~er** *n.* critique *m.*

revis|e /rɪˈvaɪz/ *v.t.* réviser; (*text*) revoir. **~ion** /-ɪʒn/ *n.* révision *f.*

revitalize /riːˈvaɪtəlaɪz/ *v.t.* revitaliser, revivifier.

reviv|e /rɪˈvaɪv/ *v.t.* (*person, hopes*) ranimer; (*play*) reprendre; (*custom*) rétablir. —*v.i.* se ranimer. **~al** *n.* (*resumption*) reprise *f.*; (*of faith*) renouveau *m.*

revoke /rɪˈvəʊk/ *v.t.* révoquer.

revolt /rɪˈvəʊlt/ *v.t./i.* (se) révolter. —*n.* révolte *f.*

revolting /rɪˈvəʊltɪŋ/ *a.* dégoûtant.

revolution /revəˈluːʃn/ *n.* révolution *f.* **~ary** *a.* & *n.* révolutionnaire (*m./f.*). **~ize** *v.t.* révolutionner.

revolv|e /rɪˈvɒlv/ *v.i.* tourner. **~ing door**, tambour *m.*

revolver /rɪˈvɒlvə(r)/ *n.* revolver *m.*

revulsion /rɪˈvʌlʃn/ *n.* dégoût *m.*

reward /rɪˈwɔːd/ *n.* récompense *f.* —*v.t.* récompenser (**for**, de). **~ing** *a.* rémunérateur; (*worthwhile*) qui (en) vaut la peine.

rewind /riːˈwaɪnd/ *v.t.* (*p.t.* **rewound**) (*tape, film*) rembobiner.

rewire /riːˈwaɪə(r)/ *v.t.* refaire l'installation électrique de.

reword /riːˈwɜːd/ *v.t.* reformuler.

rewrite /riːˈraɪt/ *v.t.* récrire.

rhapsody /ˈræpsədɪ/ *n.* rhapsodie *f.*

rhetoric /ˈretərɪk/ *n.* rhétorique *f.* **~al** /rɪˈtɒrɪkl/ *a.* (de) rhétorique; (*question*) de pure forme.

rheumati|c /ruːˈmætɪk/ *a.* (*pain*) rhumatismal; (*person*) rhumatisant. **~sm** /ˈruːmətɪzəm/ *n.* rhumatisme *m.*

rhinoceros /raɪˈnɒsərəs/ *n.* (*pl.* **-oses**) rhinocéros *m.*

rhubarb /ˈruːbɑːb/ *n.* rhubarbe *f.*

rhyme /raɪm/ *n.* rime *f.*; (*poem*) vers *m. pl.* —*v.t./i.* (faire) rimer.

rhythm /ˈrɪðəm/ *n.* rythme *m.* **~ic(al)** /ˈrɪðmɪk(l)/ *a.* rythmique.

rib /rɪb/ *n.* côte *f.*

ribald /ˈrɪbld/ *a.* grivois.

ribbon /ˈrɪbən/ *n.* ruban *m.* **in ~s**, (*torn pieces*) en lambeaux.

rice /raɪs/ *n.* riz *m.*

rich /rɪtʃ/ *a.* (**-er, -est**) riche. **~es** *n. pl.* richesses *f. pl.* **~ly** *adv.* richement. **~ness** *n.* richesse *f.*

rickety /ˈrɪkɪtɪ/ *a.* branlant.

ricochet /ˈrɪkəʃeɪ/ *n.* ricochet *m.* —*v.i.* (*p.t.* **ricocheted** /-ʃeɪd/) ricocher.

rid /rɪd/ *v.t.* (*p.t.* **rid**, *pres. p.* **ridding**) débarrasser (**of**, de). **get ~ of**, se débarrasser de.

riddance /ˈrɪdns/ *n.* **good ~!**, bon débarras!

ridden /ˈrɪdn/ *see* **ride**.

riddle[1] /'rɪdl/ *n.* énigme *f.*

riddle[2] /'rɪdl/ *v.t.* ~ **with,** (*bullets*) cribler de; (*mistakes*) bourrer de.

ride /raɪd/ *v.i.* (*p.t.* **rode,** *p.p.* **ridden**) aller (à bicyclette, à cheval, *etc.*); (*in car*) rouler. ~ **(a horse),** (*go riding as sport*) monter (à cheval). —*v.t.* (*a particular horse*) monter; (*distance*) parcourir. —*n.* promenade *f.*, tour *m.*; (*distance*) trajet *m.* **give s.o. a ~,** (*Amer.*) prendre qn. en voiture. **go for a ~,** aller faire un tour (à bicyclette, à cheval, *etc.*). ~**r** /-ə(r)/ *n.* cavallier, -ière *m., f.,* (*in horse race*) jockey *m.*; (*cyclist*) cycliste *m./f.*; (*motorcyclist*) motocycliste *m./f.*; (*in document*) annexe *f.*

ridge /rɪdʒ/ *n.* arête *f.*, crête *f.*

ridicule /'rɪdɪkjuːl/ *n.* ridicule *m.* —*v.t.* ridiculiser.

ridiculous /rɪ'dɪkjʊləs/ *a.* ridicule.

riding /'raɪdɪn/ *n.* équitation *f.*

rife /raɪf/ *a.* **be ~,** être répandu, sévir. ~ **with,** abondant en.

riff-raff /'rɪfræf/ *n.* canaille *f.*

rifle /'raɪfl/ *n.* fusil *m.* —*v.t.* (*rob*) dévaliser.

rift /rɪft/ *n.* (*crack*) fissure *f.*; (*between people*) désaccord *m.*

rig[1] /rɪg/ *v.t.* (*p.t.* **rigged**) (*equip*) équiper. ~ (*for oil*) derrick *m.* ~ **out,** habiller. ~**-out** *n.* (*fam.*) tenue *f.* ~ **up,** (*arrange*) arranger.

rig[2] /rɪg/ *v.t.* (*p.t.* **rigged**) (*election, match, etc.*) truquer.

right /raɪt/ *a.* (*morally*) bon; (*fair*) juste; (*best*) bon, qu'il faut; (*not left*) droit. **be ~,** (*person*) avoir raison (**to,** de); (*calculation, watch*) être exact. —*n.* (*entitlement*) droit *m.*; (*not left*) droite *f.*; (*not evil*) le bien. —*v.t.* (*a wrong, sth. fallen, etc.*) redresser. —*adv.* (*not left*) à droite; (*directly*) tout droit; (*exactly*) bien, juste; (*completely*) tout (à fait). **be in the ~,** avoir raison. **by ~s,** normalement. **on the ~,** à droite. **put ~,** arranger, rectifier. ~ **angle,** angle droit *m.* ~ **away,** tout de suite. ~**-hand** *a.* à or de droite. ~**-hand man,** bras droit *m.* ~**-handed** *a.* droitier. ~ **now,** (*at once*) tout de suite; (*at present*) en ce moment. ~ **of way,** (*auto.*) priorité *f.* ~**-wing** *a.* (*pol.*) de droite.

righteous /'raɪtʃəs/ *a.* (*person*) vertueux; (*cause, anger*) juste.

rightful /'raɪtfl/ *a.* légitime. ~**ly** *adv.* à juste titre.

rightly /'raɪtlɪ/ *adv.* correctement; (*with reason*) à juste titre.

rigid /'rɪdʒɪd/ *a.* rigide. ~**ity** /rɪ'dʒɪdətɪ/ *n.* rigidité *f.*

rigmarole /'rɪgmərəʊl/ *n.* charabia *m.*; (*procedure*) comédie *f.*

rig|our /'rɪgə(r)/ *n.* rigueur *f.* ~**orous** *a.* rigoureux.

rile /raɪl/ *v.t.* (*fam.*) agacer.

rim /rɪm/ *n.* bord *m.*; (*of wheel*) jante *f.* ~**med** *a.* bordé.

rind /raɪnd/ *n.* (*on cheese*) croûte *f.*; (*on bacon*) couenne *f.*; (*on fruit*) écorce *f.*

ring[1] /rɪn/ *n.* anneau *m.*; (*with stone*) bague *f.*; (*circle*) cercle *m.*; (*boxing*) ring *m.*; (*arena*) piste *f.* —*v.t.* entourer; (*word in text etc.*) entourer d'un cercle. (**wedding**) ~, alliance *f.* ~ **road,** périphérique *m.*

ring[2] /rɪn/ *v.t./i.* (*p.t.* **rang,** *p.p.* **rung**) sonner; (*of words etc.*) retentir. —*n.* sonnerie *f.* **give s.o. a ~,** donner un coup de fil à qn. ~ **the bell,** sonner. ~ **back,** rappeler. ~ **off,** raccrocher. ~ **up,** téléphoner (à). ~**ing** *n.* (*of bell*) sonnerie *f.* ~**ing tone,** tonalité *f.*

ringleader /'rɪnliːdə(r)/ *n.* chef *m.*

rink /rɪnk/ *n.* patinoire *f.*

rinse /rɪns/ *v.t.* rincer. ~ **out,** rincer. —*n.* rinçage *m.*

riot /'raɪət/ *n.* émeute *f.*; (*of colours*) orgie *f.* —*v.i.* faire une émeute. **run ~,** se déchaîner. ~**er** *n.* émeutier, -ière *m., f.*

riotous /'raɪətəs/ *a.* turbulent.

rip /rɪp/ *v.t./i.* (*p.t.* **ripped**) (se) déchirer. —*n.* déchirure *f.* **let ~,** (*not check*) laisser courir. ~ **off,** (*sl.*) rouler. ~**-off** *n.* (*sl.*) vol *m.*

ripe /raɪp/ *a.* (**-er, -est**) mûr. ~**ness** *n.* maturité *f.*

ripen /'raɪpən/ *v.t./i.* mûrir.

ripple /'rɪpl/ *n.* ride *f.*, ondulation *f.*; (*sound*) murmure *m.* —*v.t./i.* (*water*) (se) rider.

rise /raɪz/ *v.i.* (*p.t.* **rose,** *p.p.* **risen**) (*go upwards, increase*) monter, s'élever; (*stand up, get up from bed*) se lever; (*rebel*) se soulever; (*sun, curtain*) se lever; (*water*) monter. —*n.* (*slope*) pente *f.*; (*of curtain*) lever *m.*; (*increase*) hausse *f.*; (*in pay*) augmentation *f.*; (*progress, boom*) essor *m.* **give ~ to,** donner lieu à. ~ **up,** se soulever. ~**r** /-ə(r)/ *n.* **be an early ~r,** se lever tôt.

rising /'raɪzɪn/ *n.* (*revolt*) soulèvement *m.* —*a.* (*increasing*) croissant; (*price*) qui monte; (*tide*) montant; (*sun*) levant. ~ **generation,** nouvelle génération *f.*

risk /rɪsk/ *n.* risque *m.* —*v.t.* risquer. **at**

~, menacé. ~ **doing,** (*venture*) se risquer à faire. ~**y** *a.* risqué.

rissole /'rɪsəʊl/ *n.* croquette *f.*

rite /raɪt/ *n.* rite *m.* **last** ~**s,** derniers sacrements *m. pl.*

ritual /'rɪtʃʊəl/ *a.* & *n.* rituel (*m.*).

rival /'raɪvl/ *n.* rival(e) *m.* (*f.*). —*a.* rival; (*claim*) opposé. —*v.t.* (*p.t.* **rivalled**) rivaliser avec. ~**ry** *n.* rivalité *f.*

river /'rɪvə(r)/ *n.* rivière *f.*; (*flowing into sea & fig.*) fleuve *m.* —*a.* (*fishing, traffic, etc.*) fluvial.

rivet /'rɪvɪt/ *n.* (*bolt*) rivet *m.* —*v.t.* (*p.t.* **riveted**) river, riveter. ~**ing** *a.* fascinant.

Riviera /rɪvɪ'eərə/ *n.* **the (French)** ~, la Côte d'Azur.

road /rəʊd/ *n.* route *f.*; (*in town*) rue *f.*; (*small*) chemin *m.* —*a.* (*sign, safety*) routier. **the** ~ **to,** (*glory etc.: fig.*) le chemin de. ~**-block** *n.* barrage routier *m.* ~**- hog** *n.* chauffard *m.* ~**-map** *n.* carte routière *f.* ~**-works** *n. pl.* travaux *m. pl.*

roadside /'rəʊdsaɪd/ *n.* bord de la route *m.*

roadway /'rəʊdweɪ/ *n.* chaussée *f.*

roadworthy /'rəʊdwɜːðɪ/ *a.* en état de marche.

roam /rəʊm/ *v.i.* errer. —*v.t.* (*streets, seas, etc.*) parcourir.

roar /rɔː(r)/ *n.* hurlement *m.*; rugissement *m.*; grondement *m.* —*v.t./i.* hurler; (*of lion, wind*) rugir; (*of lorry, thunder*) gronder. ~ **with laughter,** rire aux éclats.

roaring /'rɔːrɪŋ/ *a.* (*trade, success*) très gros. ~ **fire,** belle flambée *f.*

roast /rəʊst/ *v.t./i.* rôtir. —*n.* (*roast or roasting meat*) rôti *m.* —*a.* rôti. ~ **beef,** rôti de bœuf *m.*

rob /rɒb/ *v.t.* (*p.t.* **robbed**) voler (**s.o. of sth.,** qch. à qn.); (*bank, house*) dévaliser; (*deprive*) priver (**of,** de). ~**ber** *n.* voleur, -se *m., f.* ~**bery** *n.* vol *m.*

robe /rəʊb/ *n.* (*of judge etc.*) robe *f.*; (*dressing-gown*) peignoir *m.*

robin /'rɒbɪn/ *n.* rouge-gorge *m.*

robot /'rəʊbɒt/ *n.* robot *m.*

robust /rəʊ'bʌst/ *a.* robuste.

rock[1] /rɒk/ *n.* roche *f.*; (*rock face, boulder*) rocher *m.*; (*hurled stone*) pierre *f.*; (*sweet*) sucre d'orge *m.* **on the** ~**s,** (*drink*) avec des glaçons; (*marriage*) en crise. ~**-bottom** *a.* (*fam.*) très bas. ~**-climbing** *n.* varappe *f.*

rock[2] /rɒk/ *v.t./i.* (se) balancer; (*shake*) (faire) trembler; (*child*) bercer. —*n.* (*mus.*) rock *m.* ~**ing-chair** *n.* fauteuil à bascule *m.*

rockery /'rɒkərɪ/ *n.* rocaille *f.*

rocket /'rɒkɪt/ *n.* fusée *f.*

rocky /'rɒkɪ/ *a.* (**-ier, -iest**) (*ground*) rocailleux; (*hill*) rocheux; (*shaky: fig.*) branlant.

rod /rɒd/ *n.* (*metal*) tige *f.*; (*for curtain*) tringle *f.*; (*wooden*) baguette *f.*; (*for fishing*) canne à pêche *f.*

rode /rəʊd/ *see* **ride.**

rodent /'rəʊdnt/ *n.* rongeur *m.*

rodeo /rəʊ'deɪəʊ, *Amer.* 'rəʊdɪəʊ/ *n.* (*pl.* **-os**) rodéo *m.*

roe[1] /rəʊ/ *n.* œufs de poisson *m. pl.*

roe[2] /rəʊ/ *n.* (*pl.* **roe** *or* **roes**) (*deer*) chevreuil *m.*

rogue /rəʊg/ *n.* (*dishonest*) bandit, voleur, -se *m., f.*; (*mischievous*) coquin(e) *m.* (*f.*). ~**ish** *a.* coquin.

role /rəʊl/ *n.* rôle *m.* ~**-playing** *n.* jeu de rôle *m.*

roll /rəʊl/ *v.t./i.* rouler. ~ (**about**), (*child, dog*) se rouler. —*n.* rouleau *m.*; (*list*) liste *f.*; (*bread*) petit pain *m.*; (*of drum, thunder*) roulement *m.*; (*of ship*) roulis *m.* **be** ~**ing (in money),** (*fam.*) rouler sur l'or. ~**-bar** *n.* arceau de sécurité *m.* ~**-call** *n.* appel *m.* ~**ing-pin** *n.* rouleau à pâtisserie *m.* ~ **out,** étendre. ~ **over,** (*turn over*) se retourner. ~ **up** *v.t.* (*sleeves*) retrousser; *v.i.* (*fam.*) s'amener.

roller /'rəʊlə(r)/ *n.* rouleau *m.* ~**-blind** *n.* store *m.* ~**-coaster** *n.* montagnes russes *f. pl.* ~**-skate** *n.* patin à roulettes *m.*

rollicking /'rɒlɪkɪŋ/ *a.* exubérant.

rolling /'rəʊlɪŋ/ *a.* onduleux.

ROM (*abbr.*) (*read-only memory*) mémoire morte *f.*

Roman /'rəʊmən/ *a.* & *n.* romain(e) (*m.* (*f.*)). ~ **Catholic** *a.* & *n.* catholique (*m./f.*). ~ **numerals,** chiffres romains *m. pl.*

romance /rə'mæns/ *n.* roman d'amour *m.*; (*love*) amour *m.*; (*affair*) idylle *f.*; (*fig.*) poésie *f.*

Romania /rəʊ'meɪnɪə/ *n.* Roumanie *f.* ~**n** *a.* & *n.* roumain(e) (*m.* (*f.*)).

romantic /rə'mæntɪk/ *a.* (*of love etc.*) romantique; (*of the imagination*) romanesque. ~**ally** *adv.* (*behave*) en romantique.

romp /rɒmp/ *v.i.* s'ébattre; (*fig.*) réussir. —*n.* **have a** ~, s'ébattre.

roof /ruːf/ *n.* (*pl.* **roofs**) toit *m.*; (*of tunnel*) plafond *m.*; (*of mouth*) palais *m.* —*v.t.* recouvrir. **~ing** *n.* toiture *f.* **~rack** *n.* galerie *f.* **~-top** *n.* toit *m.*

rook[1] /rʊk/ *n.* (*bird*) corneille *f.*

rook[2] /rʊk/ *n.* (*chess*) tour *f.*

room /ruːm/ *n.* pièce *f.*; (*bedroom*) chambre *f.*; (*large hall*) salle *f.*; (*space*) place *f.* **~-mate** *n.* camarade de chambre *m./f.* **~y** *a.* spacieux; (*clothes*) ample.

roost /ruːst/ *n.* perchoir *m.* —*v.i.* percher. **~er** /ˈruːstə(r)/ *n.* coq *m.*

root[1] /ruːt/ *n.* racine *f.*, (*source*) origine *f.* —*v.t./i.* (s')enraciner. **~ out**, extirper. **~er**, prendre racine. **~less** *a.* sans racines.

root[2] /ruːt/ *v.i.* **~ about**, fouiller. **~ for**, (*Amer., fam.*) encourager.

rope /rəʊp/ *n.* corde *f.* —*v.t.* attacher. **know the ~s**, être au courant. **~ in**, (*person*) enrôler.

rosary /ˈrəʊzərɪ/ *n.* chapelet *m.*

rose[1] /rəʊz/ *n.* (*flower*) rose *f.*; (*colour*) rose *m.*; (*nozzle*) pomme *f.*

rose[2] /rəʊz/ *see* **rise**.

rosé /ˈrəʊzeɪ/ *n.* rosé *m.*

rosette /rəʊˈzet/ *n.* (*sport*) cocarde *f.*; (*officer's*) rosette *f.*

roster /ˈrɒstə(r)/ *n.* liste (de service) *f.*, tableau (de service) *m.*

rostrum /ˈrɒstrəm/ *n.* (*pl.* **-tra**) tribune *f.*; (*sport*) podium *m.*

rosy /ˈrəʊzɪ/ *a.* (**-ier, -iest**) rose; (*hopeful*) plein d'espoir.

rot /rɒt/ *v.t./i.* (*p.t.* **rotted**) pourrir. —*n.* pourriture *f.*; (*nonsense: sl.*) bêtises *f. pl.*, âneries *f. pl.*

rota /ˈrəʊtə/ *n.* liste (de service) *f.*

rotary /ˈrəʊtərɪ/ *a.* rotatif.

rotate /rəʊˈteɪt/ *v.t./i.* (faire) tourner; (*change round*) alterner. **~ing** *a.* tournant. **~ion** /-ʃn/ *n.* rotation *f.*

rote /rəʊt/ *n.* **by ~**, machinalement.

rotten /ˈrɒtn/ *a.* pourri; (*tooth*) gâté; (*bad: fam.*) mauvais, sale.

rotund /rəʊˈtʌnd/ *a.* rond.

rouge /ruːʒ/ *n.* rouge (à joues) *m.*

rough /rʌf/ *a.* (**-er, -est**) (*manners*) rude; (*to touch*) rugueux; (*ground*) accidenté; (*violent*) brutal; (*bad*) mauvais; (*estimate etc.*) approximatif; (*diamond*) brut. —*adv.* (*live*) à la dure; (*play*) brutalement. —*n.* (*ruffian*) voyou *m.* —*v.t.* **~ it**, vivre à la dure. **~-and-ready** *a.* (*solution etc.*) grossier (mais efficace). **~-and-tumble** *n.* mêlée *f.* **~ out**, ébaucher. **~ paper**, papier brouillon *m.* **~ly** *adv.* rudement;

(*approximately*) à peu près. **~ness** *n.* rudesse *f.*; brutalité *f.*

roughage /ˈrʌfɪdʒ/ *n.* fibres (alimentaires) *f. pl.*

roulette /ruːˈlet/ *n.* roulette *f.*

round /raʊnd/ *a.* (**-er, -est**) rond. —*n.* (*circle*) rond *m.*; (*slice*) tranche *f.*; (*of visits, drinks*) tournée *f.*; (*mil.*) ronde *f.*; (*competition*) partie *f.*, manche *f.*; (*boxing*) round *m.*; (*of talks*) série *f.* —*prep.* autour de. —*adv.* autour. (*object*) arrondir; (*corner*) tourner. **go or come ~ to**, (*a friend etc.*) passer chez. **I'm going ~ the corner**, je vais juste à côté. **enough to go ~**, assez pour tout le monde. **go the ~s**, circuler. **she lives ~ here** elle habite par ici. **~ about**, (*near by*) par ici; (*fig.*) à peu près. **~ of applause**, applaudissements *m. pl.* **~ off**, terminer. **~ the clock**, vingt-quatre heures sur vingt- quatre. **~ trip**, voyage aller-retour *m.* **~ up**, rassembler. **~-up** *n.* rassemblement *m.*; (*of suspects*) rafle *f.*

roundabout /ˈraʊndəbaʊt/ *n.* manège *m.*; (*for traffic*) rond-point (à sens giratoire) *m.* —*a.* indirect.

rounders /ˈraʊndəz/ *n.* sorte de baseball *f.*

roundly /ˈraʊndlɪ/ *adv.* (*bluntly*) franchement.

rouse /raʊz/ *v.t.* éveiller; (*wake up*) réveiller. **be ~ed**, (*angry*) être en colère. **~ing** *a.* (*speech, music*) excitant; (*cheers*) frénétique.

rout /raʊt/ *n.* (*defeat*) déroute *f.* —*v.t.* mettre en déroute.

route /ruːt/ *n.* itinéraire *m.*, parcours *m.*; (*naut., aviat.*) route *f.*

routine /ruːˈtiːn/ *n.* routine *f.* —*a.* de routine. **daily ~**, travail quotidien *m.*

rove /rəʊv/ *v.t./i.* errer (dans). **~ing** *a.* (*life*) vagabond.

row[1] /rəʊ/ *n.* rangée *f.*, rang *m.* **in a ~**, (*consecutive*) consécutif.

row[2] /rəʊ/ *v.i.* ramer; (*sport*) faire de l'aviron. —*v.t.* faire aller à la rame. **~ing** *n.* aviron *m.* **~(ing)-boat** *n.* bateau à rames *m.*

row[3] /raʊ/ *n.* (*noise: fam.*) tapage *m.*; (*quarrel; fam.*) engueulade *f.* —*v.i.* (*fam.*) s'engueuler.

rowdy /ˈraʊdɪ/ *a.* (**-ier, -iest**) tapageur. —*n.* voyou *m.*

royal /ˈrɔɪəl/ *a.* royal. **~ly** *adv.* (*treat, live, etc.*) royalement.

royalty /ˈrɔɪəltɪ/ *n.* famille royale *f.* **~ies**, droits d'auteur *m. pl.*

rub /rʌb/ *v.t./i.* (*p.t.* **rubbed**) frotter.

—*n.* friction *f.* ∼ **it in,** insister là-dessus. ∼ **off on,** déteindre sur. ∼ **out,** (s')effacer.

rubber /'rʌbə(r)/ *n.* caoutchouc *m.*; (*eraser*) gomme *f.* ∼ **band,** élastique *m.* ∼ **stamp,** tampon *m.* ∼-**stamp** *v.t.* approuver. ∼y *a.* caoutchouteux.

rubbish /'rʌbɪʃ/ *n.* (*refuse*) ordures *f. pl.*; (*junk*) saletés *f. pl.*; (*fig.*) bêtises *f. pl.* ∼y *a.* sans valeur.

rubble /'rʌbl/ *n.* décombres *m. pl.*

ruby /'ru:bɪ/ *n.* rubis *m.*

rucksack /'rʌksæk/ *n.* sac à dos *m.*

rudder /'rʌdə(r)/ *n.* gouvernail *m.*

ruddy /'rʌdɪ/ *a.* (**-ier, -iest**) coloré, rougeâtre; (*damned: sl.*) fichu.

rude /ru:d/ *a.* (**-er, -est**) impoli, grossier; (*improper*) indécent; (*shock, blow*) brutal. ∼**ly** *adv.* impoliment. ∼**ness** *n.* impolitesse *f.*; indécence *f.*; brutalité *f.*

rudiment /'ru:dɪmənt/ *n.* rudiment *m.* ∼**ary** /-'mentrɪ/ *a.* rudimentaire.

rueful /'ru:fl/ *a.* triste.

ruffian /'rʌfɪən/ *n.* voyou *m.*

ruffle /'rʌfl/ *v.t.* (*hair*) ébouriffer; (*clothes*) froisser; (*person*) contrarier. —*n.* (*frill*) ruche *f.*

rug /rʌg/ *n.* petit tapis *m.*

Rugby /'rʌgbɪ/ *n.* ∼ (**football**), rugby *m.*

rugged /'rʌgɪd/ *a.* (*surface*) rude, rugueux; (*ground*) accidenté; (*character, features*) rude.

ruin /'ru:ɪn/ *n.* ruine *f.* —*v.t.* (*destroy*) ruiner; (*damage*) abîmer; (*spoil*) gâter. ∼**ous** *a.* ruineux.

rule /ru:l/ *n.* règle *f.*; (*regulation*) règlement *m.*; (*pol.*) gouvernement *m.* —*v.t.* gouverner; (*master*) dominer; (*decide*) décider. —*v.i.* régner. **as a** ∼, en règle générale. ∼ **out,** exclure. ∼**d paper,** papier réglé *m.* ∼**r** /-ə(r)/ *n.* dirigeant(e) *m.* (*f.*), gouvernant *m.*; (*measure*) règle *f.*

ruling /'ru:lɪŋ/ *a.* (*class*) dirigeant; (*party*) au pouvoir. —*n.* décision *f.*

rum /rʌm/ *n.* rhum *m.*

rumble /'rʌmbl/ *v.i.* gronder; (*stomach*) gargouiller. —*n.* grondement *m.*; gargouillement *m.*

rummage /'rʌmɪdʒ/ *v.i.* fouiller.

rumour, (*Amer.*) **rumor** /'ru:mə(r)/ *n.* bruit *m.*, rumeur *f.* **there's a** ∼ **that,** le bruit court que.

rump /rʌmp/ *n.* (*of horse etc.*) croupe *f.*; (*of fowl*) croupion *m.*; (*steak*) romsteck *m.*

rumpus /'rʌmpəs/ *n.* (*uproar: fam.*) chahut *m.*

run /rʌn/ *v.i.* (*p.t.* **ran,** *p.p.* **run,** *pres. p.* **running**) courir; (*flow*) couler; (*pass*) passer; (*function*) marcher; (*melt*) fondre; (*extend*) s'étendre; (*of bus etc.*) circuler; (*of play*) se jouer; (*last*) durer; (*of colour in washing*) déteindre; (*in election*) être candidat. —*v.t.* (*manage*) diriger; (*event*) organiser; (*risk, race*) courir; (*house*) tenir; (*blockade*) forcer; (*temperature, errand*) faire; (*comput.*) exécuter. —*n.* course *f.*; (*journey*) parcours *m.*; (*outing*) promenade *f.*; (*rush*) ruée *f.*; (*series*) série *f.*; (*in cricket*) point *m.* **have the** ∼ **of,** avoir à sa disposition. **in the long** ∼, avec le temps. **on the** ∼, en fuite. ∼ **across,** rencontrer par hasard. ∼ **away,** s'enfuir. ∼ **down,** descendre en courant; (*of vehicle*) renverser; (*production*) réduire progressivement; (*belittle*) dénigrer. **be** ∼ **down,** (*weak etc.*) être sans forces *or* mal fichu. ∼ **in,** (*vehicle*) roder. ∼ **into,** (*hit*) heurter. ∼ **off,** (*copies*) tirer. ∼-**of-the-mill** *a.* ordinaire. ∼ **out,** (*be used up*) s'épuiser; (*of lease*) expirer. ∼ **out of,** manquer de. ∼ **over,** (*of vehicle*) écraser; (*details*) revoir. ∼ **through** sth., regarder qch. rapidement. ∼ **sth. through** sth., passer qch. à travers qch. ∼ **up,** (*bill*) accumuler. **the** ∼-**up to,** la période qui précède.

runaway /'rʌnəweɪ/ *n.* fugitif, -ve *m.*, *f.* —*a.* fugitif; (*horse, vehicle*) fou; (*inflation*) galopant.

rung¹ /rʌŋ/ *n.* (*of ladder*) barreau *m.*

rung² /rʌŋ/ *see* **ring**².

runner /'rʌnə(r)/ *n.* coureulr, -se *m.*, *f.* ∼ **bean,** haricot (grimpant) *m.* ∼-**up** *n.* second(e) *m.* (*f.*).

running /'rʌnɪŋ/ *n.* course *f.*; (*of business*) gestion *f.*; (*of machine*) marche *f.* —*a.* (*commentary*) suivi; (*water*) courant. **be in the** ∼ **for,** être sur les rangs pour. **four days/etc.** ∼, quatre jours/etc. de suite.

runny /'rʌnɪ/ *a.* (*nose*) qui coule.

runt /rʌnt/ *n.* avorton *m.*

runway /'rʌnweɪ/ *n.* piste *f.*

rupture /'rʌptʃə(r)/ *n.* (*breaking, breach*) rupture *f.*; (*med.*) hernie *f.* —*v.t./i.* (se) rompre. ∼ **o.s.,** se donner une hernie.

rural /'rʊərəl/ *a.* rural.

ruse /ru:z/ *n.* (*trick*) ruse *f.*

rush¹ /rʌʃ/ *n.* (*plant*) jonc *m.*

rush² /rʌʃ/ *v.i.* (*move*) se précipiter; (*be in a hurry*) se dépêcher. —*v.t.* faire, envoyer, *etc.* en vitesse; (*person*) bousculer; (*mil.*) prendre d'assaut. —*n.*

ruée *f.*; (*haste*) bousculade *f.* **in a ~,** pressé. **~-hour** *n.* heure de pointe *f.*

rusk /rʌsk/ *n.* biscotte *f.*

russet /'rʌsɪt/ *a.* roussâtre, roux.

Russia /'rʌʃə/ *n.* Russie *f.* **~n** *a.* & *n.* russe (*m./f.*); (*lang.*) russe *m.*

rust /rʌst/ *n.* rouille *f.* —*v.t./i.* rouiller. **~-proof** *a.* inoxydable. **~y** *a.* (*tool, person, etc.*) rouillé.

rustic /'rʌstɪk/ *a.* rustique.

rustle /'rʌsl/ *v.t./i.* (*leaves*) (faire) bruire; (*steal: Amer.*) voler. **~ up,** (*food etc.: fam.*) préparer.

rut /rʌt/ *n.* ornière *f.* **be in a ~,** rester dans l'ornière.

ruthless /'ruːθlɪs/ *a.* impitoyable. **~ness** *n.* cruauté *f.*

rye /raɪ/ *n.* seigle *m.*; (*whisky*) whisky *m.* (*à base de seigle*).

S

sabbath /'sæbəθ/ *n.* (*Jewish*) sabbat *m.*; (*Christian*) dimanche *m.*

sabbatical /sə'bætɪkl/ *a.* (*univ.*) sabbatique.

sabot|age /'sæbətɑːʒ/ *n.* sabotage *m.* —*v.t.* saboter. **~eur** /-'tɜː(r)/ *n.* saboteulr, -se *m.*, *f.*

saccharin /'sækərɪn/ *n.* saccharine *f.*

sachet /'sæʃeɪ/ *n.* sachet *m.*

sack[1] /sæk/ *n.* (*bag*) sac *m.* —*v.t.* (*fam.*) renvoyer. **get the ~,** (*fam.*) être renvoyé. **~ing** *n.* toile à sac *f.*; (*dismissal: fam.*) renvoi *m.*

sack[2] /sæk/ *v.t.* (*plunder*) saccager.

sacrament /'sækrəmənt/ *n.* sacrement *m.*

sacred /'seɪkrɪd/ *a.* sacré.

sacrifice /'sækrɪfaɪs/ *n.* sacrifice *m.* —*v.t.* sacrifier.

sacrileg|e /'sækrɪlɪdʒ/ *n.* sacrilège *m.* **~ious** /-'lɪdʒəs/ *a.* sacrilège.

sad /sæd/ *a.* (**sadder, saddest**) triste. **~ly** *adv.* tristement; (*unfortunately*) malheureusement. **~ness** *n.* tristesse *f.*

sadden /'sædn/ *v.t.* attrister.

saddle /'sædl/ *n.* selle *f.* —*v.t.* (*horse*) seller. **~ s.o. with,** (*task, person*) coller à qn. **in the ~,** bien en selle. **~-bag** *n.* sacoche *f.*

sadis|t /'seɪdɪst/ *n.* sadique *m./f.* **~m** /-zəm/ *n.* sadisme *m.* **~tic** /sə'dɪstɪk/ *a.* sadique.

safari /sə'fɑːrɪ/ *n.* safari *m.*

safe /seɪf/ *a.* (**-er, -est**) (*not dangerous*) sans danger; (*reliable*) sûr; (*out of danger*) en sécurité; (*after accident*) sain et sauf; (*wise: fig.*) prudent. —*n.* coffre-fort *m.* **to be on the ~ side,** pour être sûr. **in ~ keeping,** en sécurité. **~ conduct,** sauf-conduit *m.* **~ from.** à l'abri de. **~ly** *adv.* sans danger; (*in safe place*) en sûreté.

safeguard /'seɪfgɑːd/ *n.* sauvegarde *f.* —*v.t.* sauvegarder.

safety /'seɪftɪ/ *n.* sécurité *f.* **~-belt** *n.* ceinture de sécurité *f.* **~-pin** *n.* épingle de sûreté *f.* **~-valve** *n.* soupape de sûreté *f.*

saffron /'sæfrən/ *n.* safran *m.*

sag /sæg/ *v.i.* (*p.t.* **sagged**) s'affaisser, fléchir. **~ging** *a.* affaissé.

saga /'sɑːgə/ *n.* saga *f.*

sage[1] /seɪdʒ/ *n.* (*herb*) sauge *f.*

sage[2] /seɪdʒ/ *a.* & *n.* sage (*m.*).

Sagittarius /sædʒɪ'teərɪəs/ *n.* le Sagittaire.

said /sed/ *see* **say**.

sail /seɪl/ *n.* voile *f.*; (*journey*) tour en bateau *m.* —*v.i.* naviguer; (*leave*) partir; (*sport*) faire de la voile; (*glide*) glisser. —*v.t.* (*boat*) piloter. **~ing-boat, ~ing-ship** *ns.* bateau à voiles *m.*

sailor /'seɪlə(r)/ *n.* marin *m.*

saint /seɪnt/ *n.* saint(e) *m.* (*f.*). **~ly** *a.* (*person, act, etc.*) saint.

sake /seɪk/ *n.* **for the ~ of,** pour, pour l'amour de.

salad /'sæləd/ *n.* salade *f.* **~-dressing** *n.* vinaigrette *f.*

salami /sə'lɑːmɪ/ *n.* salami *m.*

salar|y /'sælərɪ/ *n.* traitement *m.*, salaire *m.* **~ied** *a.* salarié.

sale /seɪl/ *n.* vente *f.* **~s,** (*at reduced prices*) soldes *m. pl.* **~s assistant,** (*Amer.*) **~s clerk,** vendeulr, -se *m.*, *f.* **for ~,** à vendre. **on ~,** en vente; (*at a reduced price: Amer.*) en solde. **~-room** *n.* salle des ventes *f.*

saleable /'seɪləbl/ *a.* vendable.

sales|man /'seɪlzmən/ *n.* (*pl.* **-men**) (*in shop*) vendeur *m.*; (*traveller*) représentant *m.* **~woman** *n.* (*pl.* **-women**) vendeuse *f.*; représentante *f.*

salient /'seɪlɪənt/ *a.* saillant.

saline /'seɪlaɪn/ *a.* salin. —*n.* sérum physiologique *m.*

saliva /sə'laɪvə/ *n.* salive *f.*

sallow /'sæləʊ/ *a.* (**-er, -est**) (*complexion*) jaunâtre.

salmon /'sæmən/ *n. invar.* saumon *m.*

salon /'sælɒn/ *n.* salon *m.*

saloon /sə'luːn/ *n.* (*on ship*) salon *m.*; (*bar: Amer.*) bar *m.*, saloon *m.* **~ (car),** berline *f.*

salt /sɔːlt/ n. sel m. —a. (culin.) salé; (water) de mer. —v.t. saler. **~-cellar** n. salière f. **~y** a. salé.

salutary /'sæljʊtrɪ/ a. salutaire.

salute /sə'luːt/ n. (mil.) salut m. —v.t. saluer. —v.i. faire un salut.

salvage /'sælvɪdʒ/ n. sauvetage m.; (of waste) récupération f.; (goods) objets sauvés m. pl. —v.t. sauver; (for re-use) récupérer.

salvation /sæl'veɪʃn/ n. salut m.

salvo /'sælvəʊ/ n. (pl. -oes) salve f.

same /seɪm/ a. même (as, que). —pron. the **~**, le or la même, les mêmes. at the **~** time, en même temps. the **~** (thing), la même chose.

sample /'sɑːmpl/ n. échantillon m.; (of blood) prélèvement m. —v.t. essayer; (food) goûter.

sanatorium /sænə'tɔːrɪəm/ n. (pl. -iums) sanatorium m.

sanctify /'sæŋktɪfaɪ/ v.t. sanctifier.

sanctimonious /sæŋktɪ'məʊnɪəs/ a. (person) bigot; (air, tone) de petit saint.

sanction /'sæŋkʃn/ n. sanction f. —v.t. sanctionner.

sanctity /'sæŋktətɪ/ n. sainteté f.

sanctuary /'sæŋktʃʊərɪ/ n. (relig.) sanctuaire m.; (for animals) réserve f.; (refuge) asile m.

sand /sænd/ n. sable m. **~s**, (beach) plage f. —v.t. sabler. **~-castle** n. château de sable m. **~-pit**, (Amer.) **~-box** n. bac à sable m.

sandal /'sændl/ n. sandale f.

sandpaper /'sændpeɪpə(r)/ n. papier de verre m. —v.t. poncer.

sandstone /'sændstəʊn/ n. grès m.

sandwich /'sænwɪdʒ/ n. sandwich m. —v.t. **~ed between**, pris en sandwich entre. **~ course,** stage de formation continue à mi-temps m.

sandy /'sændɪ/ a. sablonneux, de sable; (hair) blond roux invar.

sane /seɪn/ a. (-er, -est) (view etc.) sain; (person) sain d'esprit. **~ly** adv. sainement.

sang /sæŋ/ see **sing**.

sanitary /'sænɪtrɪ/ a. (clean) hygiénique; (system etc.) sanitaire. **~ towel,** (Amer.) **~ napkin,** serviette hygiénique f.

sanitation /sænɪ'teɪʃn/ n. hygiène (publique) f.; (drainage etc.) système sanitaire m.

sanity /'sænətɪ/ n. santé mentale f.; (good sense: fig.) bon sens m.

sank /sæŋk/ see **sink**.

Santa Claus /'sæntəklɔːz/ n. le père Noël m.

sap /sæp/ n. (of plants) sève f. —v.t. (p.t. **sapped**) (undermine) saper.

sapphire /'sæfaɪə(r)/ n. saphir m.

sarcas|m /'sɑːkæzəm/ n. sarcasme m. **~tic** /sɑː'kæstɪk/ a. sarcastique.

sardine /sɑː'diːn/ n. sardine f.

Sardinia /sɑː'dɪnɪə/ n. Sardaigne f.

sardonic /sɑː'dɒnɪk/ a. sardonique.

sash /sæʃ/ n. (on uniform) écharpe f.; (on dress) ceinture f. **~-window** n. fenêtre à guillotine f.

sat /sæt/ see **sit**.

satanic /sə'tænɪk/ a. satanique.

satchel /'sætʃl/ n. cartable m.

satellite /'sætəlaɪt/ n. & a. satellite (m.). **~ dish,** antenne parabolique f.

satin /'sætɪn/ n. satin m.

satir|e /'sætaɪə(r)/ n. satire f. **~ical** /sə'tɪrɪkl/ a. satirique.

satisfactor|y /sætɪs'fæktərɪ/ a. satisfaisant. **~ily** adv. d'une manière satisfaisante.

satisf|y /'sætɪsfaɪ/ v.t. satisfaire; (convince) convaincre. **~action** /-'fækʃn/ n. satisfaction f. **~ying** a. satisfaisant.

satsuma /sæt'suːmə/ n. mandarine f.

saturat|e /'sætʃəreɪt/ v.t. saturer. **~ed** a. (wet) trempé. **~ion** /-'reɪʃn/ n. saturation f.

Saturday /'sætədɪ/ n. samedi m.

sauce /sɔːs/ n. sauce f.; (impudence: sl.) toupet m.

saucepan /'sɔːspən/ n. casserole f.

saucer /'sɔːsə(r)/ n. soucoupe f.

saucy /'sɔːsɪ/ a. (-ier, -iest) impertinent; (boldly smart) coquin.

Saudi Arabia /saʊdɪə'reɪbɪə/ n. Arabie Séoudite f.

sauna /'sɔːnə/ n. sauna m.

saunter /'sɔːntə(r)/ v.i. flâner.

sausage /'sɒsɪdʒ/ n. saucisse f.; (pre-cooked) saucisson m.

savage /'sævɪdʒ/ a. (fierce) féroce; (wild) sauvage. —n. sauvage m./f. —v.t. attaquer férocement. **~ry** n. sauvagerie f.

sav|e /seɪv/ v.t. sauver; (money) économiser; (time) (faire) gagner; (keep) garder; (prevent) éviter (from, de). —n. (football) arrêt m. —prep. sauf. **~er** n. épargnant(e) m. (f.). **~ing** n. (of time, money) économie f. **~ings** n. pl. économies f. pl.

saviour, (Amer.) **savior** /'seɪvɪə(r)/ n. sauveur m.

savour, (Amer.) **savor** /'seɪvə(r)/ n.

saveur _f._ —_v.t._ savourer. ~y _a._ (_tasty_)
savoureux; (_culin._) salé.

saw[1] /sɔː/ _see_ **see**[1].

saw[2] /sɔː/ _n._ scie _f._ —_v.t._ (_p.t._ **sawed**,
_p.p._ **sawn** /sɔːn/ _or_ **sawed**) scier.

sawdust /'sɔːdʌst/ _n._ sciure _f._

saxophone /'sæksəfəʊn/ _n._ saxophone
_m._

say /seɪ/ _v.t./i._ (_p.t._ **said** /sed/) dire;
(_prayer_) faire. —_n._ **have a** ~, dire son
mot; (_in decision_) avoir voix au
chapitre. **I** ~!, dites donc!

saying /'seɪɪŋ/ _n._ proverbe _m._

scab /skæb/ _n._ (_on sore_) croûte _f._;
(_blackleg_: _fam._) jaune _m._

scaffold /'skæfəʊld/ _n._ (_gallows_)
échafaud _m._ ~**ing** /-əldɪŋ/ _n._ (_for
workmen_) échafaudage _m._

scald /skɔːld/ _v.t._ (_injure_, _cleanse_)
ébouillanter. —_n._ brûlure _f._

scale[1] /skeɪl/ _n._ (_of fish_) écaille _f._

scale[2] /skeɪl/ _n._ (_for measuring_, _size_,
etc.) échelle _f._; (_mus._) gamme _f._; (_of
salaries_, _charges_) barème _m._ **on a
small**/_etc._ ~, sur une petite/_etc._ échelle.
~ **model**, maquette _f._ —_v.t._ (_climb_)
escalader. ~ **down**, réduire (propor-
tionnellement).

scales /skeɪlz/ _n. pl._ (_for weighing_)
balance _f._

scallop /'skɒləp/ _n._ coquille Saint-
Jacques _f._

scalp /skælp/ _n._ cuir chevelu _m._ —_v.t._
(_mutilate_) scalper.

scalpel /'skælp(ə)l/ _n._ scalpel _m._

scamper /'skæmpə(r)/ _v.i._ courir, trotter.
~ **away**, détaler.

scampi /'skæmpɪ/ _n. pl._ grosses
crevettes _f. pl._, gambas _f. pl._

scan /skæn/ _v.t._ (_p.t._ **scanned**) scruter;
(_quickly_) parcourir; (_poetry_) scander;
(_of radar_) balayer. —_n._ (_ultrasound_)
échographie _f._

scandal /'skændl/ _n._ (_disgrace_, _outrage_)
scandale _m._; (_gossip_) cancans _m. pl._
~**ous** _a._ scandaleux.

scandalize /'skændəlaɪz/ _v.t._ scandaliser.

Scandinavia /skændɪ'neɪvɪə/ _n._ Scandinavie _f._ ~**n** _a._ & _n._ scandinave
(_m./f._).

scant /skænt/ _a._ insuffisant.

scant|y /'skæntɪ/ _a._ (**-ier**, **-iest**) in-
suffisant; (_clothing_) sommaire. ~**ily**
adv. insuffisamment. ~**ily dressed**, à
peine vêtu.

scapegoat /'skeɪpgəʊt/ _n._ bouc émissaire _m._

scar /'skɑː(r)/ _n._ cicatrice _f._ —_v.t._ (_p.t._
scarred) marquer d'une cicatrice; (_fig._)
marquer.

scarc|e /skeəs/ _a._ (**-er**, **-est**) rare. **make
o.s.** ~**e**, (_fam._) se sauver. ~**ity** _n._ rareté
_f._, pénurie _f._

scarcely /'skeəslɪ/ _adv._ à peine.

scare /'skeə(r)/ _v.t._ faire peur à. —_n._
peur _f._ **be** ~**d**, avoir peur. **bomb** ~,
alerte à la bombe _f._

scarecrow /'skeəkrəʊ/ _n._ épouvantail _m._

scarf /skɑːf/ _n._ (_pl._ **scarves**) écharpe _f._;
(_over head_) foulard _m._

scarlet /'skɑːlət/ _a._ écarlate. ~ **fever**,
scarlatine _f._

scary /'skeərɪ/ _a._ (**-ier**, **-iest**) (_fam._) qui
fait peur, effrayant.

scathing /'skeɪðɪŋ/ _a._ cinglant.

scatter /'skætə(r)/ _v.t._ (_throw_) éparpiller, répandre; (_disperse_) disperser.
—_v.i._ se disperser. ~**brain** _n._ écer-
velé(e) _m._ (_f._).

scavenge /'skævɪndʒ/ _v.i._ fouiller (dans
les ordures). ~**r** /-ə(r)/ _n._ (_vagrant_)
personne qui fouille dans les ordures _f._

scenario /sɪ'nɑːrɪəʊ/ _n._ (_pl._ **-os**) scénario
_m._

scene /siːn/ _n._ scène _f._; (_of accident_,
crime) lieu(x) _m._ (_pl._); (_sight_) spectacle
_m._; (_incident_) incident _m._ **behind the**
~**s**, en coulisse. **to make a** ~, faire un
esclandre.

scenery /'siːnərɪ/ _n._ paysage _m._;
(_theatre_) décor(s) _m._ (_pl._).

scenic /'siːnɪk/ _a._ pittoresque.

scent /sent/ _n._ (_perfume_) parfum _m._;
(_trail_) piste _f._ —_v.t._ flairer; (_make
fragrant_) parfumer.

sceptic /'skeptɪk/ _n._ sceptique _m./f._ ~**al**
_a._ sceptique. ~**ism** /-sɪzəm/ _n._
scepticisme _m._

schedule /'ʃedjuːl, _Amer._ 'skedʒʊl/ _n._
horaire _m._; (_for job_) planning _m._ —_v.t._
prévoir. **behind** ~, en retard. **on** ~,
(_train_) à l'heure; (_work_) dans les temps.
~**d flight**, vol régulier _m._

scheme /skiːm/ _n._ plan _m._; (_dishonest_)
combine _f._; (_fig._) arrangement _m._ —_v.i._
intriguer. **pension** ~, caisse de retraite
_f._ ~**r** /-ə(r)/ _n._ intrigant(e) _m._ (_f._).

schism /'sɪzəm/ _n._ schisme _m._

schizophrenic /skɪtsəʊ'frenɪk/ _a._ & _n._
schizophrène (_m./f._).

scholar /'skɒlə(r)/ _n._ érudit(e) _m._ (_f._)
~**ly** _a._ érudit. ~**ship** _n._ érudition _f._;
(_grant_) bourse _f._

school /skuːl/ _n._ école _f._; (_secondary_)
lycée _m._; (_of university_) faculté _f._ —_a._
(_age_, _year_, _holidays_) scolaire. —_v.t._
(_person_) éduquer; (_animal_) dresser.

∼ing n. (*education*) instruction f.; (*attendance*) scolarité f.

school|boy /'sku:lbɔɪ/ n. écolier m. ∼girl n. écolière f.

school|master /'sku:lmɑːstə(r)/, ∼mistress, ∼teacher ns. (*primary*) instituteur, -trice m., f.; (*secondary*) professeur m.

schooner /'sku:nə(r)/ n. goélette f.

sciatica /saɪ'ætɪkə/ n. sciatique f.

scien|ce /'saɪəns/ n. science f. ∼ce fiction, science-fiction f. ∼tific /-'tɪfɪk/ a. scientifique.

scientist /'saɪəntɪst/ n. scientifique m./f.

scintillate /'sɪntɪleɪt/ v.i. scintiller; (*person: fig.*) briller.

scissors /'sɪzəz/ n. pl. ciseaux m. pl.

scoff[1] /skɒf/ v.i. ∼ at, se moquer de.

scoff[2] /skɒf/ v.t. (*eat: sl.*) bouffer.

scold /skəʊld/ v.t. réprimander. ∼ing n. réprimande f.

scone /skɒn/ n. petit pain au lait m., galette f.

scoop /sku:p/ n. (*for grain, sugar*) pelle (à main) f.; (*for food*) cuiller f.; (*ice cream*) boule f.; (*news*) exclusivité f. —v.t. (*pick up*) ramasser. ∼ out, creuser. ∼ up, ramasser.

scoot /sku:t/ v.i. (*fam.*) filer.

scooter /'sku:tə(r)/ n. (*child's*) trottinette f.; (*motor cycle*) scooter m.

scope /skəʊp/ n. étendue f.; (*competence*) compétence f.; (*opportunity*) possibilité(s) f. (*pl.*).

scorch /skɔːtʃ/ v.t. brûler, roussir. ∼ing a. brûlant, très chaud.

score /skɔː(r)/ n. score m.; (*mus.*) partition f. —v.t. marquer; (*success*) remporter. —v.i. marquer un point; (*football*) marquer un but; (*keep score*) compter les points. a ∼ (of), (*twenty*) vingt. on that ∼, à cet égard. ∼ out, rayer. ∼-board n. tableau m. ∼r /-ə(r)/ n. (*sport*) marqueur m.

scorn /skɔːn/ n. mépris m. —v.t. mépriser. ∼ful a. méprisant. ∼fully adv. avec mépris.

Scorpio /'skɔːpɪəʊ/ n. le Scorpion.

scorpion /'skɔːpɪən/ n. scorpion m.

Scot /skɒt/ n. Écossais(e) m. (f.). ∼tish a. écossais.

Scotch /skɒtʃ/ a. écossais. —n. whisky m., scotch m.

scotch /skɒtʃ/ v.t. mettre fin à.

scot-free /skɒt'fri:/ a. & adv. sans être puni; (*gratis*) sans payer.

Scotland /'skɒtlənd/ n. Écosse f.

Scots /skɒts/ a. écossais. ∼man n. Écossais m. ∼woman n. Écossaise f.

scoundrel /'skaʊndrəl/ n. vaurien m., bandit m., gredin(e) m. (f.).

scour[1] /'skaʊə(r)/ v.t. (*pan*) récurer. ∼er n. tampon à récurer m.

scour[2] /'skaʊə(r)/ v.t. (*search*) parcourir.

scourge /skɜːdʒ/ n. fléau m.

scout /skaʊt/ n. (*mil.*) éclaireur m. —v.i. ∼ around (for), chercher.

Scout /skaʊt/ n. (*boy*) scout m., éclaireur m. ∼ing n. scoutisme m.

scowl /skaʊl/ n. air renfrogné m. —v.i. faire la tête (at, à).

scraggy /'skrægɪ/ a. (-ier, -iest) décharné, efflanqué.

scram /skræm/ v.i. (*sl.*) se tirer.

scramble /'skræmbl/ v.i. (*clamber*) grimper. —v.t. (*eggs*) brouiller. —n. bousculade f., ruée f. ∼ for, bousculer pour avoir.

scrap[1] /skræp/ n. petit morceau m. ∼s, (*of metal, fabric, etc.*) déchets m. pl.; (*of food*) restes m. pl. —v.t. (*p.t. scrapped*) mettre au rebut; (*plan etc.*) abandonner. ∼-book n. album m. on the ∼-heap, mis au rebut. ∼-iron n. ferraille f. ∼-paper n. brouillon m. ∼py, a. fragmentaire.

scrap[2] /skræp/ n. (*fight: fam.*) bagarre f., dispute f.

scrape /skreɪp/ v.t. racler, gratter; (*graze*) érafler. —v.i. (*rub*) frotter. —n. raclement m.; éraflure f. in a ∼, dans une mauvaise passe. ∼ through, réussir de justesse. ∼ together, réunir. ∼r /-ə(r)/ n. racloir m.

scratch /skrætʃ/ v.t./i. (se) gratter; (*with claw, nail*) griffer; (*graze*) érafler; (*mark*) rayer. —n. éra flure f. start from ∼, partir de zéro. up to ∼, au niveau voulu.

scrawl /skrɔːl/ n. gribouillage m. —v.t./i. gribouiller.

scrawny /'skrɔːnɪ/ a. (-ier, -iest) décharné, émacié.

scream /skriːm/ v.t./i. crier, hurler. —n. cri (perçant) m.

scree /skriː/ n. éboulis m.

screech /skriːtʃ/ v.i. (*scream*) hurler; (*of brakes*) grincer. —n. hurlement m.; grincement m.

screen /skriːn/ n. écran m.; (*folding*) paravent m. —v.t. masquer; (*protect*) protéger; (*film*) projeter; (*candidates*) filtrer; (*med.*) faire subir un test de dépistage. ∼ing n. projection f.

screenplay /'skriːnpleɪ/ n. scénario m.

screw /skruː/ n. vis f. —v.t. visser. ∼ up, (*eyes*) plisser; (*ruin: sl.*) bousiller.

screwdriver /'skru:draɪvə(r)/ n. tournevis m.

screwy /'skru:ɪ/ a. (-ier, -iest) (crazy: sl.) cinglé.

scribble /'skrɪbl/ v.t./i. griffonner. —n. griffonnage m.

scribe /skraɪb/ n. scribe m.

script /skrɪpt/ n. écriture f.; (of film) scénario m.; (of play) texte m. ∼-writer n. scénariste m./f.

Scriptures /'skrɪptʃəz/ n. pl. the ∼, l'Écriture (sainte) f.

scroll /skrəʊl/ n. rouleau m. —v.t./i. (comput.) (faire) défiler.

scrounge /skraʊndʒ/ v.t. (meal) se faire payer; (steal) chiper. —v.i. (beg) quémander. ∼ money from, taper. ∼r /-ə(r)/ n. parasite m.; (of money) tapeur, -se m., f.

scrub[1] /skrʌb/ n. (land) broussailles f. pl.

scrub[2] /skrʌb/ v.t./i. (p.t. **scrubbed**) nettoyer (à la brosse), frotter. —n. nettoyage m.

scruff /skrʌf/ n. by the ∼ of the neck, par la peau du cou.

scruffy /'skrʌfɪ/ a. (-ier, -iest) (fam.) miteux, sale.

scrum /skrʌm/ n. (Rugby) mêlée f.

scruple /'skru:pl/ n. scrupule m.

scrupulous /'skru:pjʊləs/ a. scrupuleux. ∼ly adv. scrupuleusement. ∼ly clean, impeccable.

scrutin|**y** /'skru:tɪnɪ/ n. examen minutieux m. ∼ize v.t. scruter.

scuba-diving /'sku:bədaɪvɪŋ/ n. plongée sous-marine f.

scuff /skʌf/ v.t. (scratch) érafler.

scuffle /'skʌfl/ n. bagarre f.

sculpt /skʌlpt/ v.t./i. sculpter. ∼or n. sculpteur m. ∼ure /-tʃə(r)/ n. sculpture f.; v.t./i. sculpter.

scum /skʌm/ n. (on liquid) écume f.; (people: pej.) racaille f.

scurf /sk3:f/ n. pellicules f. pl.

scurrilous /'skʌrɪləs/ a. grossier, injurieux, venimeux.

scurry /'skʌrɪ/ v.i. courir (for, pour chercher). ∼ off, filer.

scuttle[1] /'skʌtl/ v.t. (ship) saborder.

scuttle[2] /'skʌtl/ v.i. ∼ away, se sauver, filer.

scythe /saɪð/ n. faux f.

sea /si:/ n. mer f. —a. de (la) mer, marin. **at** ∼, en mer. **by** ∼, par mer. ∼-**green** a. vert glauque invar. ∼-**level** n. niveau de la mer m. ∼ **shell**, coquillage m. ∼**shore** n. rivage m.

seaboard /'si:bɔ:d/ n. littoral m.

seafarer /'si:feərə(r)/ n. marin m.

seafood /'si:fu:d/ n. fruits de mer m. pl.

seagull /'si:gʌl/ n. mouette f.

seal[1] /si:l/ n. (animal) phoque m.

seal[2] /si:l/ n. sceau m.; (with wax) cachet m. —v.t. sceller; cacheter; (stick down) coller. ∼**ing-wax** n. cire à cacheter f. ∼ **off**, (area) boucler.

seam /si:m/ n. (in cloth etc.) couture f.; (of coal) veine f.

seaman /'si:mən/ n. (pl. -**men**) marin m.

seamy /'si:mɪ/ a. ∼ side, côté sordide m.

seance /'seɪɑ:ns/ n. séance de spiritisme f.

seaplane /'si:pleɪn/ n. hydravion m.

seaport /'si:pɔ:t/ n. port de mer m.

search /s3:tʃ/ v.t./i. fouiller; (study) examiner. —n. fouille f.; (quest) recherche(s) f. (pl.). **in** ∼ **of**, à la recherche de. ∼ **for**, chercher. ∼-**party** n. équipe de secours f. ∼-**warrant** n. mandat de perquisition f. ∼**ing** a. (piercing) pénétrant.

searchlight /'s3:tʃlaɪt/ n. projecteur m.

seasick /'si:sɪk/ a. **be** ∼, avoir le mal de mer.

seaside /'si:saɪd/ n. bord de la mer m.

season /'si:zn/ n. saison f. —v.t. assaisonner. **in** ∼, de saison. ∼**able** a. qui convient à la saison. ∼**al** a. saisonnier. ∼**ing** n. assaisonnement m. ∼-**ticket** n. carte d'abonnement f.

seasoned /'si:znd/ a. expérimenté.

seat /si:t/ n. siège m.; (place) place f.; (of trousers) fond m. —v.t. (put) placer; (have seats for) avoir des places assises pour. **be** ∼**ed**, **take a** ∼, s'asseoir. ∼-**belt** n. ceinture de sécurité f.

seaweed /'si:wi:d/ n. algues f. pl.

seaworthy /'si:w3:ðɪ/ a. en état de naviguer.

secateurs /sekə't3:z/ n. pl. sécateur m.

sece|**de** /sɪ'si:d/ v.i. faire sécession. ∼**ssion** /-eʃn/ n. sécession f.

seclu|**de** /sɪ'klu:d/ v.t. isoler. ∼**ded** a. isolé. ∼**sion** /-ʒn/ n. solitude f.

second[1] /'sekənd/ a. deuxième, second. —n. deuxième m./f., second(e) m. (f.); (unit of time) seconde f. ∼**s**, (goods) articles de second choix m. pl. —adv. (in race etc.) en seconde place. —v.t. (proposal) appuyer. ∼-**best** a. de second choix, numéro deux invar. ∼-**class** a. de deuxième classe. **at** ∼ **hand**, de seconde main. ∼-**hand** a. & adv. d'occasion; (on clock) trotteuse f. ∼-**rate** a. médiocre. **have** ∼ **thoughts**, avoir des doutes, changer d'avis. **on** ∼ **thoughts**, (Amer.) **on** ∼ **thought**, à la réflexion. ∼**ly** adv. deuxièmement.

second² /sɪ'kɒnd/ *v.t.* (*transfer*) détacher (to, à). ∼**ment** *n.* détachement *m.*

secondary /'sekəndrɪ/ *a.* secondaire. ∼ **school,** lycée *m.*, collège *m.*

secrecy /'si:krəsɪ/ *n.* secret *m.*

secret /'si:krɪt/ *a.* secret. —*n.* secret *m.* in ∼, en secret. ∼**ly** *adv.* en secret, secrètement.

secretariat /sekrə'teərɪət/ *n.* secrétariat *m.*

secretar|y /'sekrətrɪ/ *n.* secrétaire *m./f.* **S∼y of State,** ministre *m.*; (*Amer.*) ministre des Affaires étrangères *m.* ∼**ial** /-'teərɪəl/ *a.* (*work etc.*) de secrétaire.

secret|e /sɪ'kri:t/ *v.t.* (*med.*) sécréter. ∼**ion** /-ʃn/ *n.* sécrétion *f.*

secretive /'si:krətɪv/ *a.* cachottier.

sect /sekt/ *n.* secte *f.* ∼**arian** /-'teərɪən/ *a.* sectaire.

section /'sekʃn/ *n.* section *f.*; (*of country, town*) partie *f.*; (*in store*) rayon *m.*; (*newspaper column*) rubrique *f.*

sector /'sektə(r)/ *n.* secteur *m.*

secular /'sekjʊlə(r)/ *a.* (*school etc.*) laïque; (*art, music, etc.*) profane.

secure /sɪ'kjʊə(r)/ *a.* (*safe*) en sûreté; (*in mind*) tranquille; (*psychologically*) sécurisé; (*firm*) solide; (*against attack*) sûr; (*window etc.*) bien fermé. —*v.t.* attacher; (*obtain*) s'assurer; (*ensure*) assurer. ∼**ly** *adv.* solidement; (*safely*) en sûreté.

security /sɪ'kjʊərətɪ/ *n.* (*safety*) sécurité *f.*; (*for loan*) caution *f.* ∼ **guard,** vigile *m.*

sedan /sɪ'dæn/ *n.* (*Amer.*) berline *f.*

sedate¹ /sɪ'deɪt/ *a.* calme.

sedat|e² /sɪ'deɪt/ *v.t.* donner un sédatif à. ∼**ion** /-ʃn/ *n.* sédation *f.*

sedative /'sedətɪv/ *n.* sédatif *m.*

sedentary /'sedntrɪ/ *a.* sédentaire.

sediment /'sedɪmənt/ *n.* sédiment *m.*

sedition /sɪ'dɪʃn/ *n.* sédition *f.*

seduce /sɪ'dju:s/ *v.t.* séduire. ∼**r** /-ə(r)/ *n.* séducteur, -trice *m.*, *f.*

seduct|ion /sɪ'dʌkʃn/ *n.* séduction *f.* ∼**ive** /-tɪv/ *a.* séduisant.

see¹ /si:/ *v.t./i.* (*p.t.* **saw,** *p.p.* **seen**) voir; (*escort*) (r)accompagner. ∼ **about** or **to,** s'occuper de. ∼ **through,** (*task*) mener à bonne fin; (*person*) deviner (le jeu de). ∼ **(to it) that,** veiller à ce que. **see you (soon)!,** à bientôt! ∼**ing that,** vu que.

see² /si:/ *n.* (*of bishop*) évêché *m.*

seed /si:d/ *n.* graine *f.*; (*collectively*) graines *f. pl.*; (*origin: fig.*) germe *m.*; (*tennis*) tête de série *f.* **go to ∼,** (*plant*) monter en graine; (*person*) se laisser aller. ∼**ling** *n.* plant *m.*

seedy /'si:dɪ/ *a.* (**-ier, -iest**) miteux.

seek /si:k/ *v.t.* (*p.t.* **sought**) chercher. ∼ **out,** aller chercher.

seem /si:m/ *v.i.* sembler. ∼**ingly** *adv.* apparemment.

seemly /'si:mlɪ/ *adv.* convenable.

seen /si:n/ *see* **see¹**.

seep /si:p/ *v.i.* (*ooze*) suinter. ∼ **into,** s'infiltrer dans. ∼**age** *n.* suintement *m.*; infiltration *f.*

see-saw /'si:sɔ:/ *n.* balançoire *f.*, tape-cul *m.* —*v.t.* osciller.

seethe /si:ð/ *v.i.* ∼ **with,** (*anger*) bouillir de; (*people*) grouiller de.

segment /'segmənt/ *n.* segment *m.*; (*of orange*) quartier *m.*

segregat|e /'segrɪgeɪt/ *v.t.* séparer. ∼**ion** /-'geɪʃn/ *n.* ségrégation *f.*

seize /si:z/ *v.t.* saisir; (*take possession of*) s'emparer de. —*v.i.* ∼ **on,** (*chance etc.*) saisir. ∼ **up,** (*engine etc.*) se gripper.

seizure /'si:ʒə(r)/ *n.* (*med.*) crise *f.*

seldom /'seldəm/ *adv.* rarement.

select /sɪ'lekt/ *v.t.* choisir, sélectionner. —*a.* choisi; (*exclusive*) sélect. ∼**ion** /-kʃn/ *n.* sélection *f.*

selective /sɪ'lektɪv/ *a.* sélectif.

self /self/ *n.* (*pl.* **selves**) (*on cheque*) moi-même. **the ∼,** le moi *m. invar.* **your good ∼,** vous-même.

self- /self/ *pref.* ∼**-assurance** *n.* assurance *f.* ∼**-assured** *a.* sûr de soi. ∼**-catering** *a.* où l'on fait la cuisine soi-même. ∼**-centred,** (*Amer.*) ∼**-centered** *a.* égocentrique. ∼**-coloured,** (*Amer.*) ∼**-colored** *a.* uni. ∼**-confidence** *n.* confiance en soi *f.* ∼**-confident** *a.* sûr de soi. ∼**-conscious** *a.* gêné, timide. ∼**-contained** *a.* (*flat*) indépendant. ∼**-control** *n.* maîtrise de soi *f.* ∼**-defence** *n.* autodéfense *f.*; (*jurid.*) légitime défense *f.* ∼**-denial** *n.* abnégation *f.* ∼**-employed** *a.* qui travaille à son compte. ∼**-esteem** *n.* amour-propre *m.* ∼**-evident** *a.* évident. ∼**-government** *n.* autonomie *f.* ∼**-indulgent** *a.* qui se permet tout. ∼**-interest** *n.* intérêt personnel *m.* ∼**-portrait** *n.* autoportrait *m.* ∼**-possessed** *a.* assuré. ∼**-reliant** *a.* indépendant. ∼**-respect** *n.* respect de soi *m.*, dignité *f.* ∼**-righteous** *a.* satisfait de soi. ∼**-sacrifice** *n.* abnégation *f.* ∼**-satisfied** *a.* content de soi. ∼**-seeking** *a.* égoïste. ∼**-service** *n. & a.* libre-service (*m.*). ∼**-styled** *a.* soi-disant. ∼**-sufficient** *a.* indépendant. ∼**-willed** *a.* entêté.

selfish /'selfıʃ/ a. égoïste; (motive) intéressé. ∼ness n. égoïsme m.

selfless /'selflıs/ a. désintéressé.

sell /sel/ v.t./i. (p.t. sold) (se) vendre. ∼-by date, date limite de vente f. be sold out of, n'avoir plus de. ∼ off, liquider. ∼-out, n. trahison f. it was a ∼-out, on a vendu tous les billets. ∼ up, vendre son fonds, sa maison, etc. ∼er n. vendeulr, -se m., f.

Sellotape /'seləʊteıp/ n. (P.) scotch m. (P.).

semantic /sı'mæntık/ a. sémantique. ∼s n. sémantique f.

semaphore /'seməfɔ:(r)/ n. signaux à bras m. pl.; (device: rail.) sémaphore m.

semblance /'sembləns/ n. semblant m.

semen /'si:mən/ n. sperme m.

semester /sı'mestə(r)/ n. (univ., Amer.) semestre m.

semi- /'semı/ pref. semi-, demi-.

semibreve /'semıbri:v/ n. (mus.) ronde f.

semicirc|le /'semıs3:kl/ n. demi-cercle m. ∼ular /-'s3:kjʊlə(r)/ a. en demi-cercle.

semicolon /semı'kəʊlən/ n. point-virgule m.

semiconductor /semıkən'dʌktə(r)/ n. semi-conducteur n.

semi-detached /semı'dıtætʃt/ a. ∼ house, maison jumelle f.

semifinal /semı'faınl/ n. demi-finale f.

seminar /'semına:(r)/ n. séminaire m.

seminary /'semınərı/ n. séminaire m.

semiquaver /'semıkweıvə(r)/ n. (mus.) double croche f.

Semit|e /'si:maıt, Amer. 'semaıt/ n. Sémite m./f. ∼ic /sı'mıtık/ a. sémite; (lang.) sémitique.

semolina /semə'li:nə/ n. semoule f.

senat|e /'senıt/ n. sénat m. ∼or /-ətə(r)/ n. sénateur m.

send /send/ v.t./i. (p.t. sent) envoyer. ∼ away, (dismiss) renvoyer. ∼ (away or off) for, commander (par la poste). ∼ back, renvoyer. ∼ for, (person, help) envoyer chercher. ∼ a player off, renvoyer un joueur. ∼-off n. adieux chaleureux m. pl. ∼ up, (fam.) parodier. ∼er n. expéditeur, -trice m., f.

senil|e /'si:naıl/ a. sénile. ∼ity /sı'nılətı/ n. sénilité f.

senior /'si:nıə(r)/ a. plus âgé (to, que); (in rank) supérieur; (teacher, partner) principal. —n. aîné(e) m. (f.); (schol.) grand(e) m. (f.). ∼ citizen, personne âgée f. ∼ity /-'ɒrətı/ n. priorité d'âge

f.; supériorité f.; (in service) ancienneté f.

sensation /sen'seıʃn/ n. sensation f. ∼al a. (event) qui fait sensation; (wonderful) sensationnel.

sense /sens/ n. sens m.; (sensation) sensation f.; (mental impression) sentiment m.; (common sense) bon sens m. ∼s, (mind) raison f. —v.t. (pres)sentir. make ∼, avoir du sens. make ∼ of, comprendre. ∼less a. stupide; (med.) sans connaissance.

sensibilit|y /sensə'bılətı/ n. sensibilité f. ∼ics, susceptibilité f.

sensible /'sensəbl/ a. raisonnable, sensé; (clothing) fonctionnel.

sensitiv|e /'sensətıv/ a. sensible (to, à); (touchy) susceptible. ∼ity /-'tıvətı/ n. sensibilité f.

sensory /'sensərı/ a. sensoriel.

sensual /'senʃʊəl/ a. sensuel. ∼ity /-'ælətı/ n. sensualité f.

sensuous /'senʃʊəs/ a. sensuel.

sent /sent/ see send.

sentence /'sentəns/ n. phrase f.; (decision: jurid.) jugement m., condamnation f.; (punishment) peine f. —v.t. ∼ to, condamner à.

sentiment /'sentımənt/ n. sentiment m.

sentimental /sentı'mentl/ a. sentimental. ∼ity /-'tælətı/ n. sentimentalité f.

sentry /'sentrı/ n. sentinelle f.

separable /'sepərəbl/ a. séparable.

separate[1] /'seprət/ a. séparé, différent; (independent) indépendant. ∼s n. pl. coordonnés m. pl. ∼ly adv. séparément.

separat|e[2] /'sepəreıt/ v.t./i. (se) séparer. ∼ion /-'reıʃn/ n. séparation f.

September /sep'tembə(r)/ n. septembre m

septic /'septık/ a. (wound) infecté. ∼ tank, fosse septique f.

sequel /'si:kwəl/ n. suite f.

sequence /'si:kwəns/ n. (order) ordre m.; (series) suite f.; (of film) séquence f.

sequin /'si:kwın/ n. paillette f.

serenade /serə'neıd/ n. sérénade f. —v.t. donner une sérénade à.

seren|e /sı'ri:n/ a. serein. ∼ity /-enətı/ n. sérénité f.

sergeant /'sɑ:dʒənt/ n. (mil.) sergent m.; (policeman) brigadier m.

serial /'sıərıəl/ n. (story) feuilleton m. —a. (number) de série.

series /'sıərı:z/ n. invar. série f.

serious /'sıərıəs/ a. sérieux; (very bad, critical) grave, sérieux. ∼ly adv. sérieusement, gravement. take ∼ly, prendre au sérieux. ∼ness n. sérieux m.

sermon /'sɜːmən/ n. sermon m.

serpent /'sɜːpənt/ n. serpent m.

serrated /sɪ'reɪtɪd/ a. (edge) en dents de scie.

serum /'sɪərəm/ n. (pl. -a) sérum m.

servant /'sɜːvənt/ n. domestique m./f.; (of God etc.) serviteur m.

serve /sɜːv/ v.t./i. servir; (undergo, carry out) faire; (of transport) desservir. —n. (tennis) service m. ∼ as/to, servir de/à. ∼ its purpose, remplir sa fonction.

service /'sɜːvɪs/ n. service m.; (maintenance) révision f.; (relig.) office m. ∼s, (mil.) forces armées f. pl. —v.t. (car etc.) réviser. of ∼ to, utile à. ∼ area, (auto.) aire de services f. ∼ charge, service m. ∼ station, station-service f.

serviceable /'sɜːvɪsəbl/ a. (usable) utilisable; (useful) commode; (durable) solide.

serviceman /'sɜːvɪsmən/ n. (pl. -men) militaire m.

serviette /sɜːvɪ'et/ n. serviette f.

servile /'sɜːvaɪl/ a. servile.

session /'seʃn/ n. séance f.; (univ.) année (universitaire) f.; (univ., Amer.) semestre m.

set /set/ v.t. (p.t. **set**, pres. p. **setting**) mettre; (put down) poser, mettre; (limit etc.) fixer; (watch, clock) régler; (example, task) donner; (for printing) composer; (in plaster) plâtrer. —v.i. (of sun) se coucher; (of jelly) prendre. —n. (of chairs, stamps, etc.) série f.; (of knives, keys, etc.) jeu m.; (of people) groupe m.; (TV, radio) poste m.; (style of hair) mise en plis f.; (theatre) décor m.; (tennis) set m.; (mathematics) ensemble m. —a. fixe; (in habits) régulier; (meal) à prix fixe; (book) au programme. ∼ against sth., opposé à. be ∼ on doing, être résolu à faire. ∼ about or to, se mettre à. ∼ back, (delay) retarder; (cost: sl.) coûter. ∼-back n. revers m. ∼ fire to, mettre le feu à. ∼ free, libérer. ∼ in, (take hold) s'installer, commencer. ∼ off or out, partir. ∼ off, (mechanism, activity) déclencher; (bomb) faire éclater. ∼ out, (state) exposer; (arrange) disposer. ∼ out to do sth., entreprendre de faire qch. ∼ sail, partir. ∼ square, équerre f. ∼ to, (about to) sur le point de. ∼-to n. querelle f. ∼ to music, mettre en musique. ∼ up, (establish) fonder, établir; (launch) lancer. ∼-up n. (fam.) affaire f.

settee /se'tiː/ n. canapé m.

setting /'setɪŋ/ n. cadre m.

settle /'setl/ v.t. (arrange, pay) régler; (date) fixer; (nerves) calmer. —v.i. (come to rest) se poser; (live) s'installer. ∼ down, se calmer; (become orderly) se ranger. ∼ for, accepter. ∼ in, s'installer. ∼ up (with), régler. ∼r /-ə(r)/ n. colon m.

settlement /'setlmənt/ n. règlement m. (of, de); (agreement) accord m.; (place) colonie f.

seven /'sevn/ a. & n. sept (m.). ∼th a. & n. septième (m./f.).

seventeen /sevn'tiːn/ a. & n. dix-sept (m.). ∼th a. & n. dix-septième (m./f.).

sevent|y /'sevntɪ/ a. & n. soixante-dix (m.). ∼ieth a. & n. soixante-dixième (m./f.).

sever /'sevə(r)/ v.t. (cut) couper; (relations) rompre. ∼ance n. (breaking off) rupture f. ∼ance pay, indemnité de licenciement f.

several /'sevrəl/ a. & pron. plusieurs.

sever|e /sɪ'vɪə(r)/ a. (-er, -est) sévère; (violent) violent; (serious) grave. ∼ely adv. sévèrement; gravement. ∼ity /sɪ'verətɪ/ n. sévérité f.; violence f.; gravité f.

sew /səʊ/ v.t./i. (p.t. **sewed**, p.p. **sewn** or **sewed**) coudre. ∼ing n. couture f. ∼ing-machine n. machine à coudre f.

sewage /'sjuːɪdʒ/ n. eaux d'égout f. pl., vidanges f. pl.

sewer /'suːə(r)/ n. égout m.

sewn /səʊn/ see **sew**.

sex /seks/ n. sexe m. —a. sexuel. have ∼, avoir des rapports (sexuels). ∼ maniac, obsédé(e) sexuel(le) m. (f.). ∼y a. sexy invar.

sexist /'seksɪst/ a. & n. sexiste (m./f.).

sextet /seks'tet/ n. sextuor m.

sexual /'seksʊəl/ a. sexuel. ∼ intercourse, rapports sexuels m. pl. ∼ity /-'ælətɪ/ n. sexualité f.

shabb|y /'ʃæbɪ/ a. (-ier, -iest) (place, object) minable, miteux; (person) pauvrement vêtu; (mean) mesquin. ∼ily adv. (dress) pauvrement; (act) mesquinement.

shack /ʃæk/ n. cabane f.

shackles /'ʃæklz/ n. pl. chaînes f. pl.

shade /ʃeɪd/ n. ombre f.; (of colour, opinion) nuance f.; (for lamp) abat-jour m.; (blind: Amer.) store m. a ∼ bigger/etc., légèrement plus grand/etc. —v.t. (of person etc.) abriter; (of tree) ombrager.

shadow /'ʃædəʊ/ n. ombre f. —v.t. (follow) filer. S∼ Cabinet, cabinet fantôme *m.* ∼**y** *a.* ombragé; (*fig.*) vague.

shady /'ʃeɪdɪ/ *a.* (**-ier, -iest**) ombragé; (*dubious*: *fig.*) louche.

shaft /ʃɑːft/ *n.* (*of arrow*) hampe *f.*; (*axle*) arbre *m.*; (*of mine*) puits *m.*; (*of light*) rayon *m.*

shaggy /'ʃægɪ/ *a.* (**-ier, -iest**) (*beard*) hirsute; (*hair*) broussailleux; (*animal*) à longs poils.

shake /ʃeɪk/ *v.t.* (*p.t.* **shook**, *p.p.* **shaken**) secouer; (*bottle*) agiter; (*house, belief, etc.*) ébranler. —*v.i.* trembler. —*n.* secousse *f.* ∼ **hands with**, serrer la main à. ∼ **off**, (*get rid of*) se débarrasser de. ∼ **one's head**, (*in refusal*) dire non de la tête. ∼ **up**, (*disturb, rouse, mix contents of*) secouer. ∼**-up** *n.* (*upheaval*) remaniement *m.*

shaky /'ʃeɪkɪ/ *a.* (**-ier, -iest**) (*hand, voice*) tremblant; (*table etc.*) branlant; (*weak*: *fig.*) faible.

shall /ʃæl, *unstressed* ʃ(ə)l/ *v. aux.* **I** ∼ **do**, je ferai. **we** ∼ **do**, nous ferons.

shallot /ʃə'lɒt/ *n.* échalote *f.*

shallow /'ʃæləʊ/ *a.* (**-er, -est**) peu profond; (*fig.*) superficiel.

sham /ʃæm/ *n.* comédie *f.*; (*person*) imposteur *m.*; (*jewel*) imitation *f.* —*a.* faux; (*affected*) feint. —*v.t.* (*p.t.* **shammed**) feindre.

shambles /'ʃæmblz/ *n. pl.* (*mess*: *fam.*) désordre *m.*, pagaille *f.*

shame /ʃeɪm/ *n.* honte *f.* —*v.t.* faire honte à. **it's a** ∼, c'est dommage. ∼**ful** *a.* honteux. ∼**fully** *adv.* honteusement. ∼**less** *a.* éhonté.

shamefaced /'ʃeɪmfeɪst/ *a.* honteux.

shampoo /ʃæm'puː/ *n.* shampooing *m* —*v.t* faire un shampooing à, shampooiner.

shandy /'ʃændɪ/ *n.* panaché *m.*

shan't /ʃɑːnt/ = **shall not**.

shanty /'ʃæntɪ/ *n.* (*shack*) baraque *f.* ∼ **town**, bidonville *m.*

shape /ʃeɪp/ *n.* forme *f.* —*v.t.* (*fashion, mould*) façonner; (*future etc.*: *fig.*) déterminer. —*v.i.* ∼ **up**, (*plan etc.*) prendre tournure *or* forme; (*person etc.*) faire des progrès. ∼**less** *a.* informe.

shapely /'ʃeɪplɪ/ *a.* (**-ier, -iest**) (*leg, person*) bien tourné.

share /ʃeə(r)/ *n.* part *f.*; (*comm.*) action *f.* —*v.t./i.* partager; (*feature*) avoir en commun. ∼**-out** *n.* partage *m.*

shareholder /'ʃeəhəʊldə(r)/ *n.* actionnaire *m./f.*

shark /ʃɑːk/ *n.* requin *m.*

sharp /ʃɑːp/ *a.* (**-er, -est**) (*knife etc.*) tranchant; (*pin etc.*) pointu; (*point*) aigu; (*acute*) vif; (*sudden*) brusque; (*dishonest*) peu scrupuleux. —*adv.* (*stop*) net. **six o'clock**/*etc.* ∼, six heures/*etc.* pile. —*n.* (*mus.*) dièse *m.* ∼**ly** *adv.* (*harshly*) vivement; (*suddenly*) brusquement.

sharpen /'ʃɑːpən/ *v.t.* aiguiser; (*pencil*) tailler. ∼**er** *n.* (*for pencil*) taille-crayon(s) *m.*

shatter /'ʃætə(r)/ *v.t./i.* (*glass etc.*) (faire) voler en éclats, (se) briser; (*upset, ruin*) anéantir.

shav|e /ʃeɪv/ *v.t./i.* (se) raser. —*n.* **have a** ∼**e**, se raser. ∼**en** *a.* rasé. ∼**er** *n.* rasoir électrique *m.* ∼**ing-brush** *n.* blaireau *m.* ∼**ing-cream** *n.* crème à raser *f.*

shaving /'ʃeɪvɪŋ/ *n.* copeau *m.*

shawl /ʃɔːl/ *n.* châle *m.*

she /ʃiː/ *pron.* elle. —*n.* femelle *f.*

sheaf /ʃiːf/ *n.* (*pl.* **sheaves**) gerbe *f.*

shear /ʃɪə(r)/ *v.t.* (*p.p.* **shorn** *or* **sheared**) (*sheep etc.*) tondre. ∼ **off**, se détacher.

shears /ʃɪəz/ *n. pl.* cisaille(s) *f.* (*pl.*).

sheath /ʃiːθ/ *n.* (*pl.* **-s** /ʃiːðz/) gaine *f.*, fourreau *m.*; (*contraceptive*) préservatif *m.*

sheathe /ʃiːð/ *v.t.* rengainer.

shed[1] /ʃed/ *n.* remise *f.*

shed[2] /ʃed/ *v.t.* (*p.t.* **shed**, *pres. p.* **shedding**) perdre; (*light, tears*) répandre.

sheen /ʃiːn/ *n.* lustre *m.*

sheep /ʃiːp/ *n. invar.* mouton *m.* ∼**-dog** *n.* chien de berger *m.*

sheepish /'ʃiːpɪʃ/ *a.* penaud. ∼**ly** *adv.* d'un air penaud.

sheepskin /'ʃiːpskɪn/ *n.* peau de mouton *f.*

sheer /ʃɪə(r)/ *a.* pur (*et simple*); (*steep*) à pic; (*fabric*) très fin. —*adv.* à pic, verticalement.

sheet /ʃiːt/ *n.* drap *m.*; (*of paper*) feuille *f.*; (*of glass, ice*) plaque *f.*

sheikh /ʃeɪk/ *n.* cheik *m.*

shelf /ʃelf/ *n.* (*pl.* **shelves**) rayon *m.* étagère *f.* **on the** ∼, (*person*) laissé pour compte.

shell /ʃel/ *n.* coquille *f.*; (*on beach*) coquillage *m.*; (*of building*) carcasse *f.*; (*explosive*) obus *m.* —*v.t.* (*nut etc.*) décortiquer; (*peas*) écosser; (*mil.*) bombarder.

shellfish /'ʃelfɪʃ/ *n. invar.* (*lobster etc.*) crustacé(s) *m.* (*pl.*); (*mollusc*) coquillage(s) *m.* (*pl.*).

shelter /'ʃeltə(r)/ *n.* abri *m.* —*v.t./i.* (s')abriter; (*give lodging to*) donner asile à. ∼**ed** *a.* (*life etc.*) protégé.

shelve /ʃelv/ v.t. (plan etc.) laisser en suspens, remettre à plus tard.

shelving /'ʃelvɪŋ/ n. (shelves) rayonnage(s) m. (pl.).

shepherd /'ʃepəd/ n. berger m. —v.t. (people) guider. ~'s **pie**, hachis Parmentier m.

sherbet /'ʃɜːbət/ n. jus de fruits m.; (powder) poudre acidulée f.; (water-ice: Amer.) sorbet m.

sheriff /'ʃerɪf/ n. shérif m.

sherry /'ʃerɪ/ n. xérès m.

shield /ʃiːld/ n. bouclier m.; (screen) écran m. —v.t. protéger.

shift /ʃɪft/ v.t./i. (se) déplacer, bouger; (exchange, alter) changer de. —n. changement m.; (workers) équipe f.; (work) poste m.; (auto.: Amer.) levier de vitesse m. **make ~,** se debrouiller. **~ work,** travail par roulement.

shiftless /'ʃɪftlɪs/ a. paresseux.

shifty /'ʃɪftɪ/ a. (-ier, -iest) louche.

shilling /'ʃɪlɪŋ/ n. shilling m.

shilly-shally /'ʃɪlɪʃælɪ/ v.i. hésiter, balancer.

shimmer /'ʃɪmə(r)/ v.i. chatoyer. —n. chatoiement m.

shin /ʃɪn/ n. tibia m.

shine /ʃaɪn/ v.t./i. (p.t. **shone** /ʃɒn/) (faire) briller. —n. éclat m., brillant m. **~ one's torch** or **the light (on),** éclairer.

shingle /'ʃɪŋɡl/ n. (pebbles) galets m. pl.; (on roof) bardeau m.

shingles /'ʃɪŋɡlz/ n. pl. (med.) zona m.

shiny /'ʃaɪnɪ/ a. (-ier, -iest) brillant.

ship /ʃɪp/ n. bateau m., navire m. —v.t. (p.t. **shipped**) transporter; (send) expédier; (load) embarquer. **~ment** n. cargaison f., envoi m. **~per** n. expéditeur m. **~ping** n. (ships) navigation f., navires m. pl.

shipbuilding /'ʃɪpbɪldɪŋ/ n. construction navale f.

shipshape /'ʃɪpʃeɪp/ adv. & a. parfaitement en ordre.

shipwreck /'ʃɪprek/ n. naufrage m. **~ed** a. naufragé. **be ~ed,** faire naufrage.

shipyard /'ʃɪpjɑːd/ n. chantier naval m.

shirk /ʃɜːk/ v.t. esquiver. **~er** n. tire-au-flanc m. invar.

shirt /ʃɜːt/ n. chemise f.; (of woman) chemisier m. **in ~-sleeves,** en bras de chemise.

shiver /'ʃɪvə(r)/ v.i. frissonner. —n. frisson m.

shoal /ʃəʊl/ n. (of fish) banc m.

shock /ʃɒk/ n. choc m., secousse f.; (electr.) décharge f.; (med.) choc m.

—a. (result) choc invar.; (tactics) de choc. —v.t. choquer. **~ absorber,** amortisseur m. **be a ~er,** (fam.) être affreux. **~ing** a. choquant; (bad: fam.) affreux. **~ingly** adv. (fam.) affreusement.

shodd|y /'ʃɒdɪ/ a. (-ier, -iest) mal fait, mauvais. **~ily** adv. mal.

shoe /ʃuː/ n. chaussure f., soulier m.; (of horse) fer (à cheval) m.; (in vehicle) sabot (de frein) m. —v.t. (p.t. **shod** /ʃɒd/, pres. p. **shoeing**) (horse) ferrer. **~ repairer,** cordonnier m. **on a ~string,** avec très peu d'argent.

shoehorn /'ʃuːhɔːn/ n. chausse-pied m.

shoelace /'ʃuːleɪs/ n. lacet m.

shoemaker /'ʃuːmeɪkə(r)/ n. cordonnier m.

shone /ʃɒn/ see **shine**.

shoo /ʃuː/ v.t. chasser.

shook /ʃʊk/ see **shake**.

shoot /ʃuːt/ v.t. (p.t. **shot**) (gun) tirer un coup de; (missile, glance) lancer; (kill, wound) tuer, blesser (d'un coup de fusil, de pistolet, etc.); (execute) fusiller; (hunt) chasser; (film) tourner. —v.i. tirer (**at,** sur). —n. (bot.) pousse f. **~ down,** abattre. **~ out,** (rush) sortir en vitesse. **~ up,** (spurt) jaillir; (grow) pousser vite. **hear ~ing,** entendre des coups de feu. **~ing-range** n. stand de tir m. **~ing star,** étoile filante f.

shop /ʃɒp/ n. magasin m., boutique f.; (workshop) atelier m. —v.i. (p.t. **shopped**) faire ses courses. **~ around,** comparer les prix. **~ assistant,** vendeulr, -se m., f. **~-floor** n. (workers) ouvriers m. pl. **~ per** n. acheteulr, -se m., f. **~-soiled,** (Amer.) **~-worn** adjs. abîmé. **~ steward,** délégué(e) syndical(e) m. (f.). **~ window,** vitrine f.

shopkeeper /'ʃɒpkiːpə(r)/ n. commerçant(e) m. (f.).

shoplift|er /'ʃɒplɪftə(r)/ n. voleulr, -se à l'étalage m., f. **~ing** n. vol à l'étalage m.

shopping /'ʃɒpɪŋ/ n. (goods) achats m. pl. **go ~,** faire ses courses. **~ bag,** sac à provisions m. **~ centre,** centre commercial m.

shore /ʃɔː(r)/ n. rivage m.

shorn /ʃɔːn/ see **shear**. —a. **~ of,** dépouillé de.

short /ʃɔːt/ a. (-er, -est) court; (person) petit; (brief, bref; (curt) brusque. **be ~ (of),** (lack) manquer (de). —adv. (stop) net. —n. (electr.) court-circuit m.; (film) court-metrage m. **~s,**

(*trousers*) short *m*. ～ **of money**, à court d'argent. **I'm two** ～, il m'en manque deux. ～ **of doing sth**, à moins de faire qch. **everything** ～ **of**, tout sauf. **nothing** ～ **of**, rien de moins que. **cut** ～, écourter. **cut s.o.** ～, couper court à qn. **fall** ～ **of**, ne pas arriver à. **he is called Tom for** ～, son diminutif est Tom. **in** ～, en bref. ～**-change** *v.t.* (*cheat*) rouler. ～ **circuit**, court-circuit *m*. ～**-circuit** *v.t.* court-circuiter. ～ **cut**, raccourci *m*. ～**-handed** *a*. à court de personnel. ～ **list**, liste des candidats choisis *f*. ～**-lived** *a*. éphémère. ～**-sighted** *a*. myope. ～**-staffed** *a*. à court de personnel. ～ **story**, nouvelle *f*. ～**-term** *a*. à court terme. ～ **wave**, ondes courtes *f. pl*.

shortage /'ʃɔːtɪdʒ/ *n*. manque *m*.

shortbread /'ʃɔːtbred/ *n*. sablé *m*.

shortcoming /'ʃɔːtkʌmɪŋ/ *n*. défaut *m*.

shorten /'ʃɔːtn/ *v.t.* raccourcir.

shortfall /'ʃɔːtfɔːl/ *n*. déficit *m*.

shorthand /'ʃɔːthænd/ *n*. sténo(graphie) *f*. ～ **typist**, sténodactylo *f*.

shortly /'ʃɔːtlɪ/ *adv*. bientôt.

shot /ʃɒt/ *see* **shoot**. —*n*. (*firing, attempt, etc.*) coup de feu *m*.; (*person*) tireur *m*.; (*bullet*) balle *f*.; (*photograph*) photo *f*.; (*injection*) piqûre *f*. **like a** ～, comme une flèche. ～**-gun** *n*. fusil de chasse *m*.

should /ʃʊd, *unstressed* ʃəd/ *v.aux.* devoir. **you** ～ **help me**, vous devriez m'aider. **I** ～ **have stayed**, j'aurais dû rester. **I** ～ **like to**, j'aimerais bien. **if he** ～ **come**, s'il vient.

shoulder /'ʃəʊldə(r)/ *n*. épaule *f*. —*v.t.* (*responsibility*) endosser; (*burden*) se charger de. ～**-bag** *n*. sac à bandoulière *m*. ～**-blade** *n*. omoplate *f*. ～**-pad** *n*. épaulette *f*.

shout /ʃaʊt/ *n*. cri *m*. —*v.t./i.* crier. ～ **at**, engueuler. ～ **down**, huer.

shove /ʃʌv/ *n*. poussée *f*. —*v.t./i.* pousser; (*put: fam.*) ficher. ～ **off**, (*depart: fam.*) se tirer.

shovel /'ʃʌvl/ *n*. pelle *f*. —*v.t.* (*p.t.* **shovelled**) pelleter.

show /ʃəʊ/ *v.t.* (*p.t.* **showed**, *p.p.* **shown**) montrer; (*of dial, needle*) indiquer; (*put on display*) exposer; (*film*) donner; (*conduct*) conduire. —*v.i.* (*be visible*) se voir. —*n*. démonstration *f*.; (*ostentation*) parade *f*.; (*exhibition*) exposition *f*., salon *m*.; (*theatre*) spectacle *m*.; (*cinema*) séance *f*. **for** ～, pour l'effet. **on** ～, exposé. ～**-down** *n*. épreuve de force *f*. ～**-jumping** *n*. con-

cours hippique *m*. ～ **off** *v.t.* étaler; *v.i.* poser, crâner. ～**-off** *n*. poseur, -se *m., f*. ～**-piece** *n*. modèle du genre *m*. ～ **s.o. in/out**, faire entrer/sortir qn. ～ **up**, (faire) ressortir; (*appear: fam.*) se montrer. ～**ing** *n*. performance *f*.; (*cinema*) séance *f*.

shower /'ʃaʊə(r)/ *n*. (*of rain*) averse *f*.; (*of blows etc.*) grêle *f*.; (*for washing*) douche *f*. —*v.t.* ～ **with**, couvrir de. —*v.i.* se doucher. ～ **y** *a*. pluvieux.

showerproof /'ʃaʊəpruːf/ *a*. imperméable.

showmanship /'ʃəʊmənʃɪp/ *n*. art de la mise en scène *m*.

shown /ʃəʊn/ *see* **show**.

showroom /'ʃəʊrʊm/ *n*. salle d'exposition *f*.

showy /'ʃəʊɪ/ *a*. (**-ier**, **-iest**) voyant; (*manner*) prétentieux.

shrank /ʃræŋk/ *see* **shrink**.

shrapnel /'ʃræpn(ə)l/ *n*. éclats d'obus *m. pl*.

shred /ʃred/ *n*. lambeau *m*.; (*least amount: fig.*) parcelle *f*. —*v.t.* (*p.t.* **shredded**) déchiqueter; (*culin.*) râper. ～**der** *n*. destructeur de documents *m*.

shrew /ʃruː/ *n*. (*woman*) mégère *f*.

shrewd /ʃruːd/ *a*. (**-er**, **-est**) astucieux. ～**ness** *n*. astuce *f*.

shriek /ʃriːk/ *n*. hurlement *m*. —*v.t./i.* hurler.

shrift /ʃrɪft/ *n*. **give s.o. short** ～, traiter qn. sans ménagement.

shrill /ʃrɪl/ *a*. strident, aigu.

shrimp /ʃrɪmp/ *n*. crevette *f*.

shrine /ʃraɪn/ *n*. (*place*) lieu saint *m*.; (*tomb*) châsse *f*.

shrink /ʃrɪŋk/ *v.t./i.* (*p.t.* **shrank**, *p.p.* **shrunk**) rétrécir; (*lessen*) diminuer. ～ **from**, reculer devant. ～**age** *n*. rétrécissement *m*.

shrivel /'ʃrɪvl/ *v.t./i.* (*p.t.* **shrivelled**) (se) ratatiner.

shroud /ʃraʊd/ *n*. linceul *m*. —*v.t.* (*veil*) envelopper.

Shrove /ʃrəʊv/ *n*. ～ **Tuesday**, Mardi gras *m*.

shrub /ʃrʌb/ *n*. arbuste *m*. ～**bery** *n*. arbustes *m. pl*.

shrug /ʃrʌg/ *v.t.* (*p.t.* **shrugged**). ～ **one's shoulders**, hausser les épaules. —*n*. haussement d'épaules *m*. ～ **sth. off**, réagir avec indifférence à qch.

shrunk /ʃrʌŋk/ *see* **shrink**. ～**en** *a*. rétréci; (*person*) ratatiné.

shudder /'ʃʌdə(r)/ *v.i.* frémir. —*n*. frémissement *m*.

shuffle /'ʃʌfl/ *v.t.* (*feet*) traîner; (*cards*)

battre. —*v.i.* traîner les pieds. —*n.* démarche traînante *f.*

shun /ʃʌn/ *v.t.* (*p.t.* **shunned**) éviter, fuir.

shunt /ʃʌnt/ *v.t.* (*train*) aiguiller.

shush /ʃʊʃ/ *int.* (*fam.*) chut.

shut /ʃʌt/ *v.t.* (*p.t.* **shut**, *pres. p.* **shutting**) fermer. —*v.i.* se fermer; (*of shop, bank, etc.*) fermer. ∼ **down** *or* **up**, fermer. ∼**-down** *n.* fermeture *f.* ∼ **in** *or* **up**, enfermer. ∼ **up** *v.i.* (*fam.*) se taire; *v.t.* (*fam.*) faire taire.

shutter /'ʃʌtə(r)/ *n.* volet *m.*; (*photo.*) obturateur *m.*

shuttle /'ʃʌtl/ *n.* (*bus etc.*) navette *f.* —*v.i.* faire la navette. —*v.t.* transporter. ∼ **service**, navette *f.*

shuttlecock /'ʃʌtlkɒk/ *n.* (*badminton*) volant *m.*

shy /ʃaɪ/ *a.* (**-er, -est**) timide. —*v.i.* reculer. ∼**ness** *n.* timidité *f.*

Siamese /saɪə'miːz/ *a.* siamois.

sibling /'sɪblɪŋ/ *n.* frère *m.*, sœur *f.*

Sicily /'sɪsɪlɪ/ *n.* Sicile *f.*

sick /sɪk/ *a.* malade; (*humour*) macabre. **be** ∼, (*vomit*) vomir. **be** ∼ **of**, en avoir assez *or* marre de. **feel** ∼, avoir mal au cœur. ∼**-bay** *n.* infirmerie *f.* ∼**-leave** *n.* congé maladie *m.* ∼**-pay** *n.* assurance-maladie *f.* ∼**room** *n.* chambre de malade *f.*

sicken /'sɪkən/ *v.t.* écœurer. —*v.i.* **be** ∼**ing for**, (*illness*) couver.

sickle /'sɪkl/ *n.* faucille *f.*

sickly /'sɪklɪ/ *a.* (**-ier, -iest**) (*person*) maladif; (*taste, smell, etc.*) écœurant.

sickness /'sɪknɪs/ *n.* maladie *f.*

side /saɪd/ *n.* côté *m.*; (*of road, river*) bord *m.*; (*of hill*) flanc *m.*; (*sport*) équipe *f.* —*a.* latéral. —*v.i.* ∼ **with**, se ranger du côté de. **on the** ∼, (*extra*) en plus; (*secretly*) en catimini. ∼ **by side**, côte à côte. ∼**-car** *n.* side-car *m.* ∼**-effect** *n.* effet secondaire *m.* ∼**-saddle** *adv.* en amazone. ∼**-show** *n.* petite attraction *f.* ∼**-step** *v.t.* (*p.t.* **-stepped**) éviter. ∼**-street** *n.* rue laterale *f.* ∼**-track** *v.t.* faire dévier de son sujet.

sideboard /'saɪdbɔːd/ *n.* buffet *m.* ∼**s**, (*whiskers: sl.*) pattes *f. pl.*

sideburns /'saɪdbɜːnz/ *n. pl.* pattes *f. pl.*, rouflaquettes *f. pl.*

sidelight /'saɪdlaɪt/ *n.* (*auto.*) veilleuse *f.*, lanterne *f.*

sideline /'saɪdlaɪn/ *n.* activité secondaire *f.*

sidewalk /'saɪdwɔːk/ *n.* (*Amer.*) trottoir *m.*

side|ways /'saɪdweɪz/, ∼**long** *adv. & a.* de côté.

siding /'saɪdɪŋ/ *n.* voie de garage *f.*

sidle /'saɪdl/ *v.i.* avancer furtivement (**up to,** vers).

siege /siːdʒ/ *n.* siège *m.*

siesta /sɪ'estə/ *n.* sieste *f.*

sieve /sɪv/ *n.* tamis *m.*; (*for liquids*) passoire *f.* —*v.t.* tamiser.

sift /sɪft/ *v.t.* tamiser. —*v.i.* ∼ **through,** examiner.

sigh /saɪ/ *n.* soupir *m.* —*v.t./i.* soupirer.

sight /saɪt/ *n.* vue *f.*; (*scene*) spectacle *m.*; (*on gun*) mire *f.* —*v.t.* apercevoir. **at** *or* **on** ∼, à vue. **catch** ∼ **of,** apercevoir. **in** ∼, visible. **lose** ∼ **of,** perdre de vue.

sightsee|ing /'saɪtsiːɪŋ/ *n.* tourisme *m.* ∼**r** /-ə(r)/ *n.* touriste *m./f.*

sign /saɪn/ *n.* signe *m.*; (*notice*) panneau *m.* —*v.t./i.* signer. ∼ **language,** (*for deaf*) langage des sourds-muets *m.* ∼ **on,** (*when unemployed*) s'inscrire au chômage. ∼ **up,** (s')enrôler.

signal /'sɪɡnəl/ *n.* signal *m.* —*v.t.* (*p.t.* **signalled**) communiquer (par signaux); (*person*) faire signe à. ∼**-box** *n.* poste d'aiguillage *m.*

signalman /'sɪɡnəlmən/ *n.* (*pl.* **-men**) (*rail.*) aiguilleur *m.*

signatory /'sɪɡnətrɪ/ *n.* signataire *m./f.*

signature /'sɪɡnətʃə(r)/ *n.* signature *f.* ∼ **tune,** indicatif musical *m.*

signet-ring /'sɪɡnɪtrɪŋ/ *n.* chevalière *f.*

significan|t /sɪɡ'nɪfɪkənt/ *a.* important; (*meaningful*) significatif. ∼**ce** *n.* importance *f.*; (*meaning*) signification *f.* ∼**tly** *adv.* (*much*) sensiblement.

signify /'sɪɡnɪfaɪ/ *v.t.* signifier.

signpost /'saɪnpəʊst/ *n.* poteau indicateur *m.*

silence /'saɪləns/ *n.* silence *m.* —*v.t.* faire taire. ∼**r** /-ə(r)/ *n.* (*on gun, car*) silencieux *m.*

silent /'saɪlənt/ *a.* silencieux; (*film*) muet. ∼**ly** *adv.* silencieusement.

silhouette /ˌsɪluː'et/ *n.* silhouette *f.* —*v.t.* **be** ∼**d against,** se profiler contre.

silicon /'sɪlɪkən/ *n.* silicium *m.* ∼ **chip,** microplaquette *f.*

silk /sɪlk/ *n.* soie *f.* ∼**en,** ∼**y** *adjs.* soyeux.

sill /sɪl/ *n.* rebord *m.*

silly /'sɪlɪ/ *a.* (**-ier, -iest**) bête, idiot.

silo /'saɪləʊ/ *n.* (*pl.* **-os**) silo *m.*

silt /sɪlt/ *n.* vase *f.*

silver /'sɪlvə(r)/ *n.* argent *m.*; (*silverware*) argenterie *f.* —*a.* en argent, d'argent. ∼ **wedding,** noces d'argent *f. pl.* ∼**y** *a.* argenté; (*sound*) argentin.

silversmith /'sɪlvəsmɪθ/ n. orfèvre m.

silverware /'sɪlvəweə(r)/ n. argenterie f.

similar /'sɪmɪlə(r)/ a. semblable (**to**, à). ∿**ity** /-ə'lærəti/ n. ressemblance f. ∿**ly** adv. de même.

simile /'sɪmɪlɪ/ n. comparaison f.

simmer /'sɪmə(r)/ v.t./i. (soup etc.) mijoter; (water) (laisser) frémir; (smoulder: fig.) couver. ∿ **down**, se calmer.

simper /'sɪmpə(r)/ v.i. minauder. ∿**ing** a. minaudier.

simpl|e /'sɪmpl/ a. (**-er**, **-est**) simple. ∿**e-minded** a. simple d'esprit. ∿**icity** /-'plɪsəti/ n. simplicité f. ∿**y** adv. simplement; (absolutely) absolument.

simplif|y /'sɪmplɪfaɪ/ v.t. simplifier. ∿**ication** /-ɪ'keɪʃn/ n. simplification f.

simplistic /sɪm'plɪstɪk/ a. simpliste.

simulat|e /'sɪmjʊleɪt/ v.t. simuler. ∿**ion** /-'leɪʃn/ n. simulation f.

simultaneous /sɪml'teɪnɪəs, Amer. saɪml'teɪnɪəs/ a. simultané. ∿**ly** adv. simultanément.

sin /sɪn/ n. péché m. —v.i. (p.t. **sinned**) pécher.

since /sɪns/ prep. & adv. depuis. —conj. depuis que; (because) puisque. ∿ **then**, depuis.

sincer|e /sɪn'sɪə(r)/ a. sincère. ∿**ely** adv. sincèrement. ∿**ity** /-'serəti/ n. sincérité f.

sinew /'sɪnjuː/ n. tendon m. ∿**s**, muscles m. pl.

sinful /'sɪnfl/ a. (act) coupable, qui constitue un péché; (shocking) scandaleux.

sing /sɪŋ/ v.t./i. (p.t. **sang**, p.p. **sung**) chanter. ∿**er** n. chanteur, -se m., f.

singe /sɪndʒ/ v.t. (pres. p. **singeing**) brûler légèrement, roussir.

single /'sɪŋgl/ a. seul; (not double) simple; (unmarried) célibataire; (room, bed) pour une personne; (ticket) simple. —n. (ticket) aller simple m.; (record) 45 tours m. invar. ∿**s**, (tennis) simple m. ∿**s bar**, bar pour les célibataires m.—v.t. ∿ **out**, choisir. **in** ∿ **file**, en file indienne. ∿**-handed** a. sans aide. ∿**-minded** a. tenace. ∿ **parent**, parent seul m. **singly** adv. un à un.

singlet /'sɪŋglɪt/ n. maillot de corps m.

singsong /'sɪŋsɒŋ/ n. **have a** ∿, chanter en chœur. —a. (voice) monotone.

singular /'sɪŋgjʊlə(r)/ n. singulier m. —a. (uncommon & gram.) singulier; (noun) au singulier. ∿**ly** adv. singulièrement.

sinister /'sɪnɪstə(r)/ a. sinistre.

sink /sɪŋk/ v.t./i. (p.t. **sank**, p.p. **sunk**) (faire) couler; (of ground, person) s'affaisser; (well) creuser; (money) investir. —n. (in kitchen) évier m.; (wash-basin) lavabo m. ∿ **in**, (fig.) être compris. ∿ **into** v.t. (thrust) enfoncer dans; v.i. (go deep) s'enfoncer dans. ∿ **unit**, bloc-évier m.

sinner /'sɪnə(r)/ n. pécheur, -eresse m., f.

sinuous /'sɪnjʊəs/ a. sinueux.

sinus /'saɪnəs/ n. (pl. **-uses**) (anat.) sinus m.

sip /sɪp/ n. petite gorgée f. —v.t. (p.t. **sipped**) boire à petites gorgées.

siphon /'saɪfn/ n. siphon m. —v.t. ∿ **off**, siphonner.

sir /sɜː(r)/ n. monsieur m. **Sir**, (title) Sir m.

siren /'saɪərən/ n. sirène f.

sirloin /'sɜːlɔɪn/ n. faux-filet m., aloyau m.; (Amer.) romsteck m.

sissy /'sɪsɪ/ n. personne efféminée f.; (coward) dégonflé(e) m. (f.).

sister /'sɪstə(r)/ n. sœur f.; (nurse) infirmière en chef f. ∿**-in-law** (pl. ∿**s-in-law**) belle-sœur f. ∿**ly** a. fraternel.

sit /sɪt/ v.t./i. (p.t. **sat**, pres. p. **sitting**) (s')asseoir; (of committee etc.) siéger. ∿ (**for**), (exam) se présenter à. **be** ∿**ting**, être assis. ∿ **around**, ne rien faire. ∿ **down**, s'asseoir. ∿ **in on** a meeting, assister à une réunion pour écouter. ∿**-in** n. sit-in m. invar. ∿**ting** n. séance f.; (in restaurant) service m. ∿**ting-room** n. salon m.

site /saɪt/ n. emplacement m. (**building**) ∿, chantier m. —v.t. placer, construire, situer.

situat|e /'sɪtʃʊeɪt/ v.t. situer. **be** ∿**ed**, être situé. ∿**ion** /-'eɪʃn/ n. situation f.

six /sɪks/ a. & n. six (m.). ∿**th** a. & n. sixième (m./f.).

sixteen /sɪk'stiːn/ a. & n. seize (m.). ∿**th** a. & n. seizième (m./f.).

sixt|y /'sɪkstɪ/ a. & n. soixante (m.). ∿**ieth** a. & n. soixantième (m./f.).

size /saɪz/ n. dimension f.; (of person, garment, etc.) taille f.; (of shoes) pointure f.; (of sum, salary) montant m.; (extent) ampleur f. —v.t. ∿ **up**, (fam.) jauger, juger. ∿**able** a. assez grand.

sizzle /'sɪzl/ v.i. grésiller.

skate[1] /skeɪt/ n. invar. (fish) raie f.

skat|e[2] /skeɪt/ n. patin m. —v.i. patiner. ∿**er** n. patineur, -se m., f. ∿**ing** n. patinage m. ∿**ing-rink** n. patinoire f.

skateboard /'skeɪtbɔːd/ n. skateboard m., planche à roulettes f.

skelet|on /'skelɪtən/ n. squelette m. ～**on crew** or **staff**, effectifs minimums m. pl. ～**al** a. squelettique.

sketch /sketʃ/ n. esquisse f., croquis m.; (*theatre*) sketch m. —v.t. faire un croquis de, esquisser. —v.i. faire des esquisses. ～ **out**, esquisser. ～ **pad**, bloc à dessins.

sketchy /'sketʃɪ/ a. (**-ier, -iest**) sommaire, incomplet.

skew /skjuː/ n. **on the** ～, de travers. ～**whiff** a. (*fam.*) de travers.

skewer /'skjʊə(r)/ n. brochette f.

ski /skiː/ n. (*pl.* **-is**) ski m. —a. de ski. —v.i. (*p.t.* **ski'd** or **skied**, *pres. p.* **skiing**) skier; (*go skiing*) faire du ski. ～ **jump**, saut à skis m. ～ **lift**, remontepente m. ～**er** n. skieulr, -se m., f. ～**ing** n. ski m.

skid /skɪd/ v.i. (*p.t.* **skidded**) déraper. —n. dérapage m.

skilful /'skɪlfl/ a. habile.

skill /skɪl/ n. habileté f.; (*craft*) métier m. ～**s**, aptitudes f. pl. ～**ed** a. habile; (*worker*) qualifié.

skim /skɪm/ v.t. (*p.t.* **skimmed**) écumer; (*milk*) écrémer; (*pass or glide over*) effleurer. —v.i. ～ **through**, parcourir.

skimp /skɪmp/ v.t./i. ～ (**on**), lésiner (sur).

skimpy /'skɪmpɪ/ a. (**-ier, -iest**) (*clothes*) étriqué; (*meal*) chiche.

skin /skɪn/ n. peau f. —v.t. (*p.t.* **skinned**) (*animal*) écorcher; (*fruit*) éplucher. ～**-diving** n. plongée sousmarine f. ～**-tight** a. collant.

skinflint /'skɪnflɪnt/ n. avare m./f.

skinny /'skɪnɪ/ a. (**-ier, -iest**) maigre, maigrichon.

skint /skɪnt/ a. (*sl.*) fauché.

skip[1] /skɪp/ v.i. (*p.t.* **skipped**) sautiller; (*with rope*) sauter à la corde. —v.t. (*page, class, etc.*) sauter. —n. petit saut m. ～**ping-rope** n. corde à sauter f.

skip[2] /skɪp/ n. (*container*) benne f.

skipper /'skɪpə(r)/ n. capitaine m.

skirmish /'skɜːmɪʃ/ n. escarmouche f., accrochage m.

skirt /skɜːt/ n. jupe f. —v.t. contourner. ～**ing-board** n. plinthe f.

skit /skɪt/ n. sketch satirique m.

skittle /'skɪtl/ n. quille f.

skive /skaɪv/ v.i. (*sl.*) tirer au flanc.

skivvy /'skɪvɪ/ n. (*fam.*) boniche f.

skulk /skʌlk/ v.i. (*move*) rôder furtivement; (*hide*) se cacher.

skull /skʌl/ n. crâne m. ～**-cap** n. calotte f.

skunk /skʌŋk/ n. (*animal*) mouffette f.; (*person*: *sl.*) salaud m.

sky /skaɪ/ n. ciel m. ～**-blue** a. & n. bleu ciel a. & m. *invar.*

skylight /'skaɪlaɪt/ n. lucarne f.

skyscraper /'skaɪskreɪpə(r)/ n. gratteciel m. *invar.*

slab /slæb/ n. plaque f., bloc m.; (*of paving-stone*) dalle f.

slack /slæk/ a. (**-er, -est**) (*rope*) lâche; (*person*) négligent; (*business*) stagnant; (*period*) creux. —n. **the** ～, (*in rope*) du mou —v.t./i. (se) relâcher.

slacken /'slækən/ v.t./i. (se) relâcher; (*slow*) (se) ralentir.

slacks /slæks/ n. pl. pantalon m.

slag /slæg/ n. scories f. pl. ～**-heap** n. crassier m.

slain /sleɪn/ see **slay**.

slake /sleɪk/ v.t. étancher.

slalom /'slɑːləm/ n. slalom m.

slam /slæm/ v.t./i. (*p.t.* **slammed**) (*door etc.*) claquer; (*throw*) flanquer; (*criticize*: *sl.*) critiquer. —n. (*noise*) claquement m.

slander /'slɑːndə(r)/ n. diffamation f., calomnie f. —v.t. diffamer, calomnier. ～**ous** a. diffamatoire.

slang /slæŋ/ n. argot m. ～**y** a. argotique.

slant /slɑːnt/ v.t./i. (faire) pencher; (*news*) présenter sous un certain jour. —n. inclinaison f.; (*bias*) angle m. ～**ed** a. partial. **be** ～**ing**, être penché.

slap /slæp/ v.t. (*p.t.* **slapped**) (*strike*) donner une claque à; (*face*) gifler; (*put*) flanquer. —n. claque f.; gifle f. —adv. tout droit. ～**-happy** a. (*carefree*: *fam.*) insouciant; (*dazed*: *fam.*) abruti. ～**-up meal**, (*sl.*) gueuleton m.

slapdash /'slæpdæʃ/ a. fait, qui travaille etc. n'importe comment.

slapstick /'slæpstɪk/ n. grosse farce f.

slash /slæʃ/ v.t. (*cut*) taillader; (*sever*) trancher; (*fig.*) réduire (radicalement). —n. taillade f.

slat /slæt/ n. (*in blind*) lamelle f.; (*on bed*) latte f.

slate /sleɪt/ n. ardoise f. —v.t. (*fam.*) critiquer, éreinter.

slaughter /'slɔːtə(r)/ v.t. massacrer; (*animals*) abattre. —n. massacre m.; abattage m.

slaughterhouse /'slɔːtəhaʊs/ n. abattoir m.

Slav /slɑːv/ a. & n. slave (m./f.). ～**onic** /slə'vɒnɪk/ a. (*lang.*) slave.

slave /sleɪv/ n. esclave m./f. —v.i. trimer. ～**-driver** n. négrlier, -ière m., f. ～**ry** /-ərɪ/ n. esclavage m.

slavish /'sleɪvɪʃ/ a. servile.

slay /sleɪ/ v.t. (p.t. slew, p.p. slain) tuer.

sleazy /'sliːzɪ/ a. (-ier, -iest) (fam.) sordide, miteux.

sledge /sledʒ/ n. luge f.; (horse-drawn) traîneau m. ∼-hammer n. marteau de forgeron m.

sleek /sliːk/ a. (-er, -est) lisse, brillant; (manner) onctueux.

sleep /sliːp/ n. sommeil m. —v.i. (p.t. slept) dormir; (spend the night) coucher. —v.t. loger. go to ∼, s'endormir. ∼ in, faire la grasse matinée. ∼er n. dormeur, -se m., f.; (beam: rail) traverse f.; (berth) couchette f. ∼ing-bag n. sac de couchage m. ∼ing pill, somnifère m. ∼less a. sans sommeil. ∼-walker n. somnambule m./f.

sleep|y /'sliːpɪ/ a. (-ier, -iest) somnolent. be ∼y, avoir sommeil. ∼ily adv. à moitié endormi.

sleet /sliːt/ n. neige fondue f.; (coat of ice: Amer.) verglas m. —v.i. tomber de la neige fondue.

sleeve /sliːv/ n. manche f.; (of record) pochette f. up one's ∼, en réserve. ∼less a. sans manches.

sleigh /sleɪ/ n. traîneau m.

sleight /slaɪt/ n. ∼ of hand, prestidigitation f.

slender /'slendə(r)/ a. mince, svelte; (scanty: fig.) faible.

slept /slept/ see sleep.

sleuth /sluːθ/ n. limier m.

slew¹ /sluː/ v.i. (turn) virer.

slew² /sluː/ see slay.

slice /slaɪs/ n. tranche f. —v.t. couper (en tranches).

slick /slɪk/ a. (unctuous) mielleux; (cunning) astucieux. —n. (oil) ∼, nappe de pétrole f., marée noire f.

slide /slaɪd/ v.t./i. (p.t. slid) glisser. —n. glissade f.; (fall: fig.) baisse f.; (in playground) toboggan m.; (for hair) barrette f.; (photo.) diapositive f. ∼ into, (go silently) se glisser dans. ∼-rule n. règle à calcul f. sliding a. (door, panel) à glissière, à coulisse. sliding scale, échelle mobile f.

slight /slaɪt/ a. (-er, -est) petit, léger; (slender) mince; (frail) frêle. —v.t. (insult) offenser. —n. affront m. ∼est a. moindre. ∼ly adv. légèrement, un peu.

slim /slɪm/ a. (slimmer, slimmest) mince. —v.i. (p.t. slimmed) maigrir. ∼ness n. minceur f.

slim|e /slaɪm/ n. boue (visqueuse) f.; (on river-bed) vase f. ∼y a. boueux; vaseux; (sticky, servile) visqueux.

sling /slɪŋ/ n. (weapon, toy) fronde f.; (bandage) écharpe f. —v.t. (p.t. slung) jeter, lancer.

slip /slɪp/ v.t./i. (p.t. slipped) glisser. —n. faux pas m.; (mistake) erreur f.; (petticoat) combinaison f.; (paper) fiche f. give the ∼ to, fausser compagnie à. ∼ away, s'esquiver. ∼-cover n. (Amer.) housse f. ∼ into, (go) se glisser dans; (clothes) mettre. ∼ of the tongue, lapsus m. ∼ped disc, hernie discale f. ∼-road n. bretelle f. ∼ s.o.'s mind, échapper à qn. ∼-stream n. sillage m. ∼ up, (fam.) gaffer. ∼-up n. (fam.) gaffe f.

slipper /'slɪpə(r)/ n. pantoufle f.

slippery /'slɪpərɪ/ a. glissant.

slipshod /'slɪpʃɒd/ a. (person) négligent; (work) négligé.

slit /slɪt/ n. fente f. —v.t. (p.t. slit, pres. p. slitting) couper, fendre.

slither /'slɪðə(r)/ v.i. glisser.

sliver /'slɪvə(r)/ n. (of cheese etc.) lamelle f.; (splinter) éclat m.

slob /slɒb/ n. (fam.) rustre m.

slobber /'slɒbə(r)/ v.i. baver.

slog /slɒg/ v.t. (p.t. slogged) (hit) frapper dur. —v.i. (work) trimer. —n. (work) travail dur m.; (effort) gros effort m.

slogan /'sləʊgən/ n. slogan m.

slop /slɒp/ v.t./i. (p.t. slopped) (se) répandre. ∼s n. pl. eaux sales f. pl.

slop|e /sləʊp/ v.i. être en pente; (of handwriting) pencher. —n. pente f.; (of mountain) flanc m. ∼ing a. en pente.

sloppy /'slɒpɪ/ a. (-ier, -iest) (ground) détrempé; (food) liquide; (work) négligé; (person) négligent; (fig.) sentimental.

slosh /slɒʃ/ v.t. (fam.) répandre; (hit: sl.) frapper. —v.i. patauger.

slot /slɒt/ n. fente f. —v.t./i. (p.t. slotted) (s')insérer. ∼-machine n. distributeur automatique m.; (for gambling) machine à sous f.

sloth /sləʊθ/ n. paresse f.

slouch /slaʊtʃ/ v.i. avoir le dos voûté; (move) marcher le dos voûté.

slovenl|y /'slʌvnlɪ/ a. débraillé. ∼iness n. débraillé m.

slow /sləʊ/ a. (-er, -est) lent. —adv. lentement. —v.t./i. ralentir. be ∼, (clock etc.) retarder. in ∼ motion, au ralenti. ∼ly adv. lentement. ∼ness n. lenteur f.

slow|coach /'sləʊkəʊtʃ/, (Amer.) ∼poke ns. lambin(e) m. (f.).

sludge /slʌdʒ/ *n.* gadoue *f.*, boue *f.*

slug /slʌg/ *n.* (*mollusc*) limace *f.*; (*bullet*) balle *f.*; (*blow*) coup *m.*

sluggish /'slʌgɪʃ/ *a.* lent, mou.

sluice /sluːs/ *n.* (*gate*) vanne *f.*

slum /slʌm/ *n.* taudis *m.*

slumber /'slʌmbə(r)/ *n.* sommeil. *m.* —*v.i.* dormir.

slump /slʌmp/ *n.* effondrement *m.*; baisse *f.*; (*in business*) marasme *m.* —*v.i.* (*collapse, fall limply*) s'effondrer; (*decrease*) baisser.

slung /slʌŋ/ *see* **sling**.

slur /slɜː(r)/ *v.t./i.* (*p.t.* **slurred**) (*spoken words*) mal articuler. —*n.* bredouillement *m.*; (*discredit*) atteinte *f.* (**on**, à).

slush /slʌʃ/ *n.* (*snow*) neige fondue *f.* ~ **fund**, fonds servant à des pots-de-vin *m.* ~**y** *a.* (*road*) couvert de neige fondue.

slut /slʌt/ *n.* (*dirty*) souillon *f.*; (*immoral*) dévergondée *f.*

sly /slaɪ/ *a.* (**slyer, slyest**) (*crafty*) rusé; (*secretive*) sournois. —*n.* **on the** ~, en cachette. ~**ly** *adv.* sournoisement.

smack[1] /smæk/ *n.* tape *f.*; (*on face*) gifle *f.* —*v.t.* donner une tape à; gifler. —*adv.* (*fam.*) tout droit.

smack[2] /smæk/ *v.i.* ~ **of sth.**, (*have flavour*) sentir qch.

small /smɔːl/ *a.* (**-er, -est**) petit. —*n.* ~ **of the back**, creux des reins *m.* —*adv.* (*cut etc.*) menu. ~**ness** *n.* petitesse *f.* ~ **ads**, petites annonces *f. pl.* ~ **businesses**, les petites entreprises. ~ **change**, petite monnaie *f.* ~ **talk**, menus propos *m. pl.* ~**-time** *a.* petit, peu important.

smallholding /'smɔːlhəʊldɪŋ/ *n.* petite ferme *f.*

smallpox /'smɔːlpɒks/ *n.* variole *f.*

smarmy /'smɑːmɪ/ *a.* (**-ier, -iest**) (*fam.*) obséquieux, patelin.

smart /smɑːt/ *a.* (**-er, -est**) élégant; (*clever*) astucieux, intelligent; (*brisk*) rapide. —*v.i.* (*of wound etc.*) brûler. ~**ly** *adv.* élégamment. ~**ness** *n.* élégance *f.*

smarten /'smɑːtn/ *v.t./i.* ~ (**up**), embellir. ~ (**o.s.**) **up**, se faire beau; (*tidy*) s'arranger.

smash /smæʃ/ *v.t./i.* (se) briser, (se) fracasser; (*opponent, record*) pulvériser. —*n.* (*noise*) fracas *m.*; (*blow*) coup *m.*; (*fig.*) collision *f.*

smashing /'smæʃɪŋ/ *a.* (*fam.*) formidable, épatant.

smattering /'smætərɪŋ/ *n.* **a** ~ **of**, des notions de.

smear /smɪə(r)/ *v.t.* (*stain*) tacher; (*coat*) enduire; (*discredit*: *fig.*) entacher. —*n.* tache *f.* ~ **test**, frottis *m.*

smell /smel/ *n.* odeur *f.*; (*sense*) odorat *m.* —*v.t./i.* (*p.t.* **smelt** *or* **smelled**) sentir. ~ **of**, sentir. ~**y** *a.* malodorant, qui pue.

smelt[1] /smelt/ *see* **smell**.

smelt[2] /smelt/ *v.t.* (*ore*) fondre.

smil|e /smaɪl/ *n.* sourire. —*v.i.* sourire. ~**ing** *a.* souriant.

smirk /smɜːk/ *n.* sourire affecté *m.*

smith /smɪθ/ *n.* forgeron *m.*

smithereens /smɪðə'riːnz/ *n. pl.* **to** *or* **in** ~, en mille morceaux.

smitten /'smɪtn/ *a.* (*in love*) épris (**with**, de).

smock /smɒk/ *n.* blouse *f.*

smog /smɒg/ *n.* brouillard mélangé de fumée *m.*, smog *m.*

smoke /sməʊk/ *n.* fumée *f.* —*v.t./i.* fumer. **have a** ~, fumer. ~**d** *a.* fumé. ~**less** *a.* (*fuel*) non polluant. ~**r** /-ə(r)/ *n.* fumeur, -se *m., f.* ~**-screen** *n.* écran de fumée *m.*; (*fig.*) manœuvre de diversion *f.* **smoky** *a.* (*air*) enfumé.

smooth /smuːð/ *a.* (**-er, -est**) lisse; (*movement*) régulier; (*manners, cream*) onctueux; (*flight*) sans turbulence; (*changes*) sans heurt. —*v.t.* lisser. ~ **out**, (*fig.*) faire disparaître. ~**ly** *adv.* facilement, doucement.

smother /'smʌðə(r)/ *v.t.* (*stifle*) étouffer; (*cover*) couvrir.

smoulder /'sməʊldə(r)/ *v.i.* (*fire, discontent, etc.*) couver.

smudge /smʌdʒ/ *n.* tache *f.* —*v.t./i.* (se) salir, (se) tacher.

smug /smʌg/ *a.* (**smugger, smuggest**) suffisant. ~**ly** *adv.* avec suffisance. ~**ness** *n.* suffisance *f.*

smuggl|e /'smʌgl/ *v.t.* passer (en contrebande). ~**er** *n.* contrebandier, -ière *m., f.* ~**ing** *n.* contrebande *f.*

smut /smʌt/ *n.* saleté *f.* ~**ty** *a.* indécent.

snack /snæk/ *n.* casse-croûte *m. invar.* ~**-bar** *n.* snack(-bar) *m.*

snag /snæg/ *n.* difficulté *f.*, inconvénient *m.*; (*in cloth*) accroc *m.*

snail /sneɪl/ *n.* escargot *m.* **at a** ~'**s pace**, à un pas de tortue.

snake /sneɪk/ *n.* serpent *m.*

snap /snæp/ *v.t./i.* (*p.t.* **snapped**) (*whip, fingers, etc.*) (faire) claquer; (*break*) (se) casser net; (*say*) dire sèchement. —*n.* claquement *m.*; (*photograph*) instantané *m.*; (*press-stud*: *Amer.*) bouton-pression *m.* —*a.* soudain. ~ **at**, (*bite*) happer; (*angrily*) être cassant avec. ~ **up**, (*buy*) sauter sur.

snappy /'snæpɪ/ a. (-ier, -iest) (*brisk*: *fam.*) prompt, rapide. **make it ~,** (*fam.*) se dépêcher.

snapshot /'snæpʃɒt/ n. instantané m., photo f.

snare /sneə(r)/ n. piège m.

snarl /snɑːl/ v.i. gronder (en montrant les dents). —n. grondement m. **~-up,** n. embouteillage m.

snarl /snɑːl/ v.i. gronder (en montrant les dents). —n. grondement m. **~-up** n. embouteillage m.

snatch /snætʃ/ v.t. (*grab*) saisir; (*steal*) voler. **~ from s.o.,** arracher à qn. —n. (*theft*) vol m.; (*short part*) fragment m.

sneak /sniːk/ v.i. aller furtivement. —n. (*schol.*, *sl.*) rapporteur, -se m., f. **~y** a. sournois.

sneakers /'sniːkəz/ n. pl. (*shoes*) tennis m. pl.

sneaking /'sniːkɪŋ/ a. caché.

sneer /snɪə(r)/ n. ricanement m. —v.i. ricaner.

sneeze /sniːz/ n. éternuement m. —v.i. éternuer.

snide /snaɪd/ a. (*fam.*) narquois.

sniff /snɪf/ v.t./i. renifler. —n. reniflement m.

snigger /'snɪgə(r)/ n. ricanement m. —v.i. ricaner.

snip /snɪp/ v.t. (*p.t.* **snipped**) couper. —n. morceau coupé m.; (*bargain*: *sl.*) bonne affaire f.

snipe /snaɪp/ v.i. canarder. **~r** /-ə(r)/ n. tireur embusqué m.

snippet /'snɪpɪt/ n. bribe f.

snivel /'snɪvl/ v.i. (*p.t.* **snivelled**) pleurnicher.

snob /snɒb/ n. snob m./f. **~bery** n. snobisme m. **~bish** a. snob invar.

snooker /'snuːkə(r)/ n. (*sorte de*) jeu de billard m.

snoop /snuːp/ v.i. (*fam.*) fourrer son nez partout. **~ on,** espionner.

snooty /'snuːtɪ/ a. (-ier, -iest) (*fam.*) snob invar., hautain.

snooze /snuːz/ n. petit somme m. —v.i. faire un petit somme.

snore /snɔː(r)/ n. ronflement m. —v.i. ronfler.

snorkel /'snɔːkl/ n. tuba m.

snort /snɔːt/ n. grognement m. —v.i. (*person*) grogner; (*horse*) s'ébrouer.

snotty /'snɒtɪ/ a. morveux.

snout /snaʊt/ n. museau m.

snow /snəʊ/ n. neige f. —v.i. neiger. **be ~ed under with,** être submergé de. **~-bound** a. bloqué par la neige. **~-drift** n. congère f. **~-plough** n. chasse-neige m.

invar. **~-shoe** n. raquette f. **~y** a. neigeux.

snowball /'snəʊbɔːl/ n. boule de neige f. —v.i. faire boule de neige.

snowdrop /'snəʊdrɒp/ n. perce-neige m./f. invar.

snowfall /'snəʊfɔːl/ n. chute de neige f.

snowflake /'snəʊfleɪk/ n. flocon de neige m.

snowman /'snəʊmæn/ n. (*pl.* **-men**) bonhomme de neige m.

snowstorm /'snəʊstɔːm/ n. tempête de neige f.

snub /snʌb/ v.t. (*p.t.* **snubbed**) (*person*) snober; (*offer*) repousser. —n. rebuffade f.

snub-nosed /'snʌbnəʊzd/ a. au nez retroussé.

snuff[1] /snʌf/ n. tabac à priser m.

snuff[2] /snʌf/ v.t. (*candle*) moucher.

snuffle /'snʌfl/ v.i. renifler.

snug /snʌg/ a. (**snugger, snuggest**) (*cosy*) comfortable; (*tight*) bien ajusté; (*safe*) sûr.

snuggle /'snʌgl/ v.i. se pelotonner.

so /səʊ/ adv. si, tellement; (*thus*) ainsi. —conj. donc, alors. **so am I,** moi aussi. **so good/etc. as,** aussi bon/etc. que. **so does he,** lui aussi. **that is so,** c'est ça. **I think so,** je pense que oui. **five or so,** environ cinq. **so-and-so** n. un(e) tel(le) m. (f.); (*sl.*) so as to, de manière à. **so-called** a. soi-disant invar. **~ far,** jusqu'ici. **so long!,** (*fam.*) à bientôt! **so many, so much,** tant (de). **so-so** a. & adv. comme ci comme ça. **so that,** pour que.

soak /səʊk/ v.t./i. (faire) tremper (**in,** dans). **~ in** or **up,** absorber. **~ing** a. trempé.

soap /səʊp/ n. savon m. —v.t. savonner. **~ opera,** feuilleton m. **~ powder,** lessive f. **~y** a. savonneux.

soar /sɔː(r)/ v.i. monter (en flèche).

sob /sɒb/ n. sanglot m. —v.i. (*p.t.* **sobbed**) sangloter.

sober /'səʊbə(r)/ a. qui n'est pas ivre; (*serious*) sérieux; (*colour*) sobre. —v.t./i. **~ up,** dessoûler.

soccer /'sɒkə(r)/ n. (*fam.*) football m.

sociable /'səʊʃəbl/ a. sociable.

social /'səʊʃl/ a. social; (*gathering*, *life*) mondain. —n. réunion (amicale) f., fête f. **~ly** adv. socialement; (*meet*) en société. **~ security,** aide sociale f.; (*for old age*: *Amer.*) pension (de retraite) f. **~ worker,** assistant(e) social(e) m. (f.).

socialis|t /'səʊʃəlɪst/ n. socialiste m./f. **~m** /-zəm/ n. socialisme m.

socialize /'səʊʃəlaɪz/ v.i. se mêler aux autres. **~ with,** fréquenter.

society /sə'saɪətɪ/ n. société f.
sociolog|y /səʊsɪ'ɒlədʒɪ/ n. sociologie f.
~**ical** /-ə'lɒdʒɪkl/ a. sociologique. ~**ist**
n. sociologue m./f.
sock[1] /sɒk/ n. chaussette f.
sock[2] /sɒk/ v.t. (hit: sl.) flanquer un coup
(de poing) à.
socket /'sɒkɪt/ n. cavité f.; (for lamp)
douille f.; (electr.) prise (de courant) f.;
(of tooth) alvéole f.
soda /'səʊdə/ n. soude f. ~**(-pop)**,
(Amer.) soda m. ~**(-water)**, soda m.,
eau de Seltz f.
sodden /'sɒdn/ a. détrempé.
sodium /'səʊdɪəm/ n. sodium m.
sofa /'səʊfə/ n. canapé m., sofa m.
soft /sɒft/ a. (-er, -est) (gentle, lenient)
doux; (not hard) doux, mou; (heart,
wood) tendre; (silly) ramolli; (easy: sl.)
facile. ~ **drink**, boisson non alcoolisée
f. ~**ly** adv. doucement. ~**ness** n.
douceur f. ~ **spot**, faible m.
soften /'sɒfn/ v.t./i. (se) ramollir; (tone
down, lessen) (s')adoucir.
software /'sɒftweə(r)/ n. (for computer)
logiciel m.
softwood /'sɒftwʊd/ n. bois tendre
m.
soggy /'sɒgɪ/ a. (-ier, -iest) détrempé;
(bread etc.) ramolli.
soil[1] /sɔɪl/ n. sol m., terre f.
soil[2] /sɔɪl/ v.t./i. (se) salir.
solar /'səʊlə(r)/ a. solaire.
sold /səʊld/ see **sell**. —a. ~ **out**, épuisé.
solder /'sɒldə/, Amer. 'sɒdər/ n.
soudure f. —v.t. souder. ~**ing iron**, fer
à souder m.
soldier /'səʊldʒə(r)/ n. soldat m. —v.i.
~ **on**, (fam.) persévérer.
sole[1] /səʊl/ n. (of foot) plante f.; (of shoe)
semelle f.
sole[2] /səʊl/ n. (fish) sole f.
sole[3] /səʊl/ a. unique, seul. ~**ly** adv.
uniquement.
solemn /'sɒləm/ a. (formal) solennel;
(not cheerful) grave. ~**ity** /sə'lemnətɪ/
n. solennité f. ~**ly** adv. solennellement;
gravement.
solicit /sə'lɪsɪt/ v.t. (seek) solliciter.
—v.i. (of prostitute) racoler.
solicitor /sə'lɪsɪtə(r)/ n. avoué m.
solid /'sɒlɪd/ a. solide; (not hollow)
plein; (gold) massif; (mass) compact;
(meal) substantiel. —n. solide m. ~**s**,
(food) aliments solides m. pl. ~**-state**
a. à circuits intégrés. ~**ity** /sə'lɪdətɪ/ n.
solidité f. ~**ly** adv. solidement.
solidarity /sɒlɪ'dærətɪ/ n. solidarité f.
solidify /sə'lɪdɪfaɪ/ v.t./i. (se) solidifier.

soliloquy /sə'lɪləkwɪ/ n. monologue m.,
soliloque m.
solitary /'sɒlɪtrɪ/ a. (alone, lonely)
solitaire; (only, single) seul.
solitude /'sɒlɪtjuːd/ n. solitude f.
solo /'səʊləʊ/ n. (pl. -os) solo m. —a.
(mus.) solo invar.; (flight) en solitaire.
~**ist** n. soliste m./f.
solstice /'sɒlstɪs/ n. solstice m.
soluble /'sɒljʊbl/ a. soluble.
solution /sə'luːʃn/ n. solution f.
solv|e /sɒlv/ v.t. résoudre. ~**able** a.
soluble.
solvent /'sɒlvənt/ a. (comm.) solvable.
—n. (dis)solvant m.
sombre /'sɒmbə(r)/ a. sombre.
some /sʌm/ a. (quantity, number) du, de
l'*, de la, des; (unspecified, some or other)
un(e), quelque; (a little) un peu de; (a
certain) un(e) certain(e), quelque;
(contrasted with others) quelques,
certain(e)s. —pron. quelques-un(e)s;
(certain quantity of it or them) en; (a little)
un peu. —adv. (approximately) quelque.
pour ~ **milk**, versez du lait. **buy** ~
flowers, achetez des fleurs. ~ **people like
them**, il y a des gens qui les aiment. ~ **of
my friends**, quelques amis à moi. **he
wants** ~, il en veut. ~ **book (or other)**, un
livre (quelconque), quelque livre. ~ **time
ago**, il y a un certain temps.
somebody /'sʌmbədɪ/ pron. quelqu'un.
—n. **be a** ~, être quelqu'un.
somehow /'sʌmhaʊ/ adv. d'une manière
ou d'une autre; (for some reason) je ne
sais pas pourquoi.
someone /'sʌmwʌn/ pron. & n. =
somebody.
someplace /'sʌmpleɪs/ adv. (Amer.) =
somewhere.
somersault /'sʌməsɔːlt/ n. culbute f.
—v.i. faire la culbute.
something /'sʌmθɪŋ/ pron. & n. quelque
chose (m.). ~ **good/etc.** quelque chose
de bon/etc. ~ **like**, un peu comme.
sometime /'sʌmtaɪm/ adv. un jour. —a.
(former) ancien. ~ **in June**, en juin.
sometimes /'sʌmtaɪmz/ adv. quelquefois, parfois.
somewhat /'sʌmwɒt/ adv. quelque peu,
un peu.
somewhere /'sʌmweə(r)/ adv. quelque
part.
son /sʌn/ n. fils m. ~**-in-law** n. (pl. ~**s-
in-law**) beau-fils m., gendre m.
sonar /'səʊnɑː(r)/ n. sonar m.
sonata /sə'nɑːtə/ n. sonate f.
song /sɒŋ/ n. chanson f. **going for a** ~, à
vendre pour une bouchée de pain.

sonic /'sɒnɪk/ *a.* ~ **boom,** bang supersonique *m.*

sonnet /'sɒnɪt/ *n.* sonnet *m.*

sonny /'sʌnɪ/ *n.* (*fam.*) fiston *m.*

soon /suːn/ *adv.* (**-er, -est**) bientôt; (*early*) tôt. **I would** ~**er stay,** j'aimerais mieux rester. ~ **after,** peu après. ~**er or later,** tôt ou tard.

soot /sʊt/ *n.* suie *f.* ~**y** *a.* couvert de suie.

sooth|e /suːð/ *v.t.* calmer. ~**ing** *a.* (*remedy, words, etc.*) calmant.

sophisticated /sə'fɪstɪkeɪtɪd/ *a.* raffiné; (*machine etc.*) sophistiqué.

sophomore /'sɒfəmɔː(r)/ *n.* (*Amer.*) étudiant(e) de seconde année *m.* (*f.*).

soporific /sɒpə'rɪfɪk/ *a.* soporifique.

sopping /'sɒpɪŋ/ *a.* trempé.

soppy /'sɒpɪ/ *a.* (**-ier, -iest**) (*fam.*) sentimental; (*silly: fam.*) bête.

soprano /sə'prɑːnəʊ/ *n.* (*pl.* **-os**) (*voice*) soprano *m.*; (*singer*) soprano *m./f.*

sorcerer /'sɔːsərə(r)/ *n.* sorcier *m.*

sordid /'sɔːdɪd/ *a.* sordide.

sore /sɔː(r)/ *a.* (**-er, -est**) douloureux; (*vexed*) en rogne (**at, with,** contre). —*n.* plaie *f.*

sorely /'sɔːlɪ/ *adv.* fortement.

sorrow /'sɒrəʊ/ *n.* chagrin *m.* ~**ful** *a.* triste.

sorry /'sɒrɪ/ *a.* (**-ier, -iest**) (*regretful*) désolé (**to, de; that,** que); (*wretched*) triste. **feel** ~ **for,** plaindre. ~**!,** pardon!

sort /sɔːt/ *n.* genre *m.*, sorte *f.*, espèce *f.*; (*person: fam.*) type *m.* —*v.t.* ~ (**out**), (*classify*) trier. **what** ~ **of?,** quel genre de? **be out of** ~**s,** ne pas être dans son assiette. ~ **out,** (*tidy*) ranger; (*arrange*) arranger; (*problem*) régler.

SOS /esəʊ'es/ *n.* SOS *m.*

soufflé /'suːfleɪ/ *n.* soufflé *m.*

sought /sɔːt/ *see* **seek.**

soul /səʊl/ *n.* âme *f.* ~**-destroying** *a.* démoralisant.

soulful /'səʊlfl/ *a.* plein de sentiment, très expressif.

sound[1] /saʊnd/ *n.* son *m.*, bruit *m.* —*v.t./i.* sonner; (*seem*) sembler (**as if,** que). ~ **a horn,** klaxonner. ~ **harrier,** mur du son *m.* ~ **like,** sembler être. ~**-proof** *a.* insonorisé; *v.t.* insonoriser. ~**-track** *n.* bande sonore *f.*

sound[2] /saʊnd/ *a.* (**-er, -est**) solide; (*healthy*) sain; (*sensible*) sensé. ~ **asleep,** profondément endormi. ~**ly** *adv.* solidement; (*sleep*) profondément.

sound[3] /saʊnd/ *v.t.* (*test*) sonder. ~ **out,** sonder.

soup /suːp/ *n.* soupe *f.*, potage *m.* **in the** ~, (*sl.*) dans le pétrin.

sour /'saʊə(r)/ *a.* (**-er, -est**) aigre. —*v.t./i.* (s')aigrir.

source /sɔːs/ *n.* source *f.*

south /saʊθ/ *n.* sud *m.* —*a.* sud *invar.*, du sud. —*adv.* vers le sud. **S**~ **Africa/America,** Afrique/Amérique du Sud *f.* **S**~ **African** *a. & n.* sud-africain(e) (*m.* (*f.*)). **S**~ **American** *a. & n.* sud-américain(e) (*m.* (*f.*)). ~**-east** *n.* sud-est *m.* ~**erly** /'sʌðəlɪ/ *a.* du sud. ~**ward** *a.* au sud. ~**wards** *adv.* vers le sud. ~**-west** *n.* sud-ouest *m.*

southern /'sʌðən/ *a.* du sud. ~**er** *n.* habitant(e) du sud *m.* (*f.*).

souvenir /suːvə'nɪə(r)/ *n.* (*thing*) souvenir *m.*

sovereign /'sɒvrɪn/ *n. & a.* souverain(e) (*m.* (*f.*)). ~**ty** *n.* souveraineté *f.*

Soviet /'səʊvɪət/ *a.* soviétique. **the** ~ **Union,** l'Union soviétique *f.*

sow[1] /səʊ/ *v.t.* (*p.t.* **sowed,** *p.p.* **sowed** *or* **sown**) (*seed etc.*) semer; (*land*) ensemencer.

sow[2] /saʊ/ *n.* (*pig*) truie *f.*

soya, soy /'sɔɪə, sɔɪ/ *n.* ~ **bean,** graine de soja *f.* ~ **sauce,** sauce soja *f.*

spa /spɑː/ *n.* station thermale *f.*

space /speɪs/ *n.* espace *m.*; (*room*) place *f.*; (*period*) période *f.* —*a.* (*research etc.*) spatial. —*v.t.* ~ (**out**), espacer.

space|craft /'speɪskrɑːft/ *n. invar.*, ~**ship** *n.* engin spatial *m.*

spacesuit /'speɪssuːt/ *n.* scaphandre *m.*

spacious /'speɪʃəs/ *a.* spacieux.

spade[1] /speɪd/ *n.* (*large, for garden*) bêche *f.*; (*child's*) pelle *f.*

spade[2] /speɪd/ *n.* (*cards*) pique *m.*

spadework /'speɪdwɜːk/ *n.* (*fig.*) travail préparatoire *m.*

spaghetti /spə'getɪ/ *n.* spaghetti *m. pl.*

Spa|in /speɪn/ *n.* Espagne *f.* ~**niard** /'spænɪəd/ *n.* Espagnol(e) *m.* (*f.*). ~**nish** /'spænɪʃ/ *a.* espagnol; *n.* (*lang.*) espagnol *m.*

span[1] /spæn/ *n.* (*of arch*) portée *f.*; (*of wings*) envergure *f.*; (*of time*) durée *f.* —*v.t.* (*p.t.* **spanned**) enjamber; (*in time*) embrasser.

span[2] /spæn/ *see* **spick.**

spaniel /'spænɪəl/ *n.* épagneul *m.*

spank /spæŋk/ *v.t.* donner une fessée à. ~**ing** *n.* fessée *f.*

spanner /'spænə(r)/ *n.* (*tool*) clé (plate) *f.*; (*adjustable*) clé à molette *f.*

spar /spɑː(r)/ *v.i.* (*p.t.* **sparred**) s'entraîner (à la boxe).

spare /speə(r)/ *v.t.* épargner; (*do without*) se passer de; (*afford to give*) donner, accorder; (*use with restraint*) ménager. —*a.* en réserve; (*surplus*) de trop; (*tyre, shoes, etc.*) de rechange; (*room, bed*) d'ami. —*n.* ~ (**part**), pièce de rechange *f.* ~ **time**, loisirs *m. pl.* **are there any** ~ **tickets?** y a-t-il encore des places?

sparing /'speərɪŋ/ *a.* frugal. ~ **of**, avare de. ~**ly** *adv.* en petite quantité.

spark /spɑːk/ *n.* étincelle *f.* —*v.t.* ~ **off**, (*initiate*) provoquer. ~(**ing**)-**plug** *n.* bougie *f.*

sparkle /'spɑːkl/ *v.i.* étinceler. —*n.* étincellement *m.*

sparkling /'spɑːklɪŋ/ *a.* (*wine*) mousseux, pétillant; (*eyes*) pétillant.

sparrow /'spærəʊ/ *n.* moineau *m.*

sparse /spɑːs/ *a.* clairsemé. ~**ly** *adv.* (*furnished etc.*) peu.

spartan /'spɑːtn/ *a.* spartiate.

spasm /'spæzəm/ *n.* (*of muscle*) spasme *m.*; (*of coughing, anger, etc.*) accès *m.*

spasmodic /spæz'mɒdɪk/ *a.* intermittent.

spastic /'spæstɪk/ *n.* handicapé(e) moteur *m.* (*f.*).

spat /spæt/ *see* **spit**[1].

spate /speɪt/ *n.* **a** ~ **of**, (*letters etc.*) une avalanche de.

spatter /'spætə(r)/ *v.t.* éclabousser (**with**, de).

spatula /'spætjʊlə/ *n.* spatule *f.*

spawn /spɔːn/ *n.* frai *m.*, œufs *m. pl.* —*v.t.* pondre. —*v.i.* frayer.

speak /spiːk/ *v.i.* (*p.t.* **spoke**, *p.p.* **spoken**) parler. —*v.t.* (*say*) dire; (*language*) parler. ~ **up**, parler plus fort.

speaker /'spiːkə(r)/ *n.* (*in public*) orateur *m.*; (*pol.*) président; (*loudspeaker*) baffle *m.* **be a French/a good**/*etc.* ~, parler français/bien/*etc.*

spear /spɪə(r)/ *n.* lance *f.*

spearhead /'spɪəhed/ *n.* fer de lance *m.* —*v.t.* (*lead*) mener.

spearmint /'spɪəmɪnt/ *n.* menthe verte *f.* —*a.* à la menthe.

spec /spek/ *n.* **on** ~, (*as speculation*: *fam.*) à tout hasard.

special /'speʃl/ *a.* spécial; (*exceptional*) exceptionnel. ~**ity** /-ɪ'ælətɪ/, (*Amer.*) ~**ty** *n.* spécialité *f.* ~**ly** *adv.* spécialement.

specialist /'speʃəlɪst/ *n.* spécialiste *m.*/*f.*

specialize /'speʃəlaɪz/ *v.i.* se spécialiser (**in**, en). ~**d** *a.* spécialisé.

species /'spiːʃiːz/ *n. invar.* espèce *f.*

specific /spə'sɪfɪk/ *a.* précis, explicite. ~**ally** *adv.* explicitement; (*exactly*) précisément.

specif|**y** /'spesɪfaɪ/ *v.t.* spécifier. ~**ication** /-ɪ'keɪʃn/ *n.* spécification *f.*; (*details*) prescriptions *f. pl.*

specimen /'spesɪmɪn/ *n.* spécimen *m.*, échantillon *m.*

speck /spek/ *n.* (*stain*) (petite) tache *f.*; (*particle*) grain *m.*

speckled /'spekld/ *a.* tacheté.

specs /speks/ *n. pl.* (*fam.*) lunettes *f. pl.*

spectacle /'spektəkl/ *n.* spectacle *m.* ~**s**, lunettes *f. pl.*

spectacular /spek'tækjʊlə(r)/ *a.* spectaculaire.

spectator /spek'teɪtə(r)/ *n.* specta|teur, -trice *m.,f.*

spectre /'spektə(r)/ *n.* spectre *m.*

spectrum /'spektrəm/ *n.* (*pl.* **-tra**) spectre *m.*; (*of ideas etc.*) gamme *f.*

speculat|**e** /'spekjʊleɪt/ *v.i.* s'interroger (**about**, sur); (*comm.*) spéculer. ~**ion** /-'leɪʃn/ *n.* conjectures *f. pl.*; (*comm.*) spéculation *f.* ~**or** *n.* spécula|teur, -trice *m.,f.*

speech /spiːtʃ/ *n.* (*faculty*) parole *f.*; (*diction*) élocution *f.*; (*dialect*) langage *m.*; (*address*) discours *m.* ~**less** *a.* muet (**with**, de).

speed /spiːd/ *n.* (*of movement*) vitesse *f.*; (*swiftness*) rapidité *f.* —*v.i.* (*p.t.* **sped** /sped/) aller vite; (*p.t.* **speeded**) (*drive too fast*) aller trop vite. ~ **limit**, limitation de vitesse *f.* ~ **up**, accélérer; (*of pace*) s'accélérer. ~**ing** *n.* excès de vitesse *m.*

speedboat /'spiːdbəʊt/ *n.* vedette *f.*

speedometer /spiː'dɒmɪtə(r)/ *n.* compteur (de vitesse) *m.*

speedway /'spiːdweɪ/ *n.* piste pour motos *f.*; (*Amer.*) autodrome *m.*

speed|**y** /'spiːdɪ/ *a.* (**-ier, -iest**) rapide. ~**ily** *adv.* rapidement.

spell[1] /spel/ *n.* (*magic*) charme *m.*, sortilège *m.*; (*curse*) sort *m.*

spell[2] /spel/ *v.t.*/*i.* (*p.t.* **spelled** *or* **spelt**) écrire; (*mean*) signifier. ~ **out**, épeler; (*explain*) expliquer. ~**ing** *n.* orthographe *f.* ~**ing mistake**, faute d'orthographe *f.*

spell[3] /spel/ *n.* (courte) période *f.*

spend /spend/ *v.t.* (*p.t.* **spent**) (*money*) dépenser (**on**, pour); (*time, holiday*) passer; (*energy*) consacrer (**on**, à). —*v.i.* dépenser.

spendthrift /'spendθrɪft/ *n.* dépens|ier, -ière *m.,f.*

spent /spent/ *see* **spend**. —*a.* (*used*) utilisé; (*person*) épuisé.

sperm /spɜːm/ *n.* (*pl.* **sperms** *or* **sperm**)

(*semen*) sperme *m.*; (*cell*) spermatozoïde *m.* ~**icide** *n.* spermicide *m.*

spew /spju:/ *v.t./i.* vomir.

sphere /sfɪə(r)/ *n.* sphère *f.*

spherical /'sferɪkl/ *a.* sphérique.

spic|e /spaɪs/ *n.* épice *f.*; (*fig.*) piquant *m.* ~**y** *a.* épicé; piquant.

spick /spɪk/ *a.* ~ **and span**, impeccable, d'une propreté parfaite.

spider /'spaɪdə(r)/ *n.* araignée *f.*

spiel /ʃpi:l/ (*Amer.*) spi:l/ *n.* baratin *m.*

spik|e /spaɪk/ *n.* (*of metal etc.*) pointe *f.* ~**y** *a.* garni de pointes.

spill /spɪl/ *v.t.* (*p.t.* **spilled** *or* **spilt**) renverser, répandre.   *v.i.* se répandre. ~ **over**, déborder.

spin /spɪn/ *v.t./i.* (*p.t.* **spun**, *pres. p.* **spinning**) (*wool, web, of spinner*) filer; (*turn*) (faire) tourner; (*story*) débiter.   *—n.* (*movement, excursion*) tour *m.* ~ **out**, faire durer. ~**-drier** *n.* essoreuse *f.* ~**ning-wheel** *n.* rouet *m.* ~**-off** *n.* avantage accessoire *m.*; (*by product*) dérivé *m.*

spinach /'spɪnɪdʒ/ *n.* (*plant*) épinard *m.*; (*as food*) épinards *m. pl.*

spinal /'spaɪnl/ *a.* vertébral. ~ **cord**, moelle épinière *f.*

spindl|e /'spɪndl/ *n.* fuseau *m.* ~**y** *a.* filiforme, grêle.

spine /spaɪn/ *n.* colonne vertébrale *f.*; (*prickle*) piquant *m.*

spineless /'spaɪnlɪs/ *a.* (*fig.*) sans caractère, mou, lâche.

spinster /'spɪnstə(r)/ *n.* célibataire *f.*; (*pej.*) vieille fille *f.*

spiral /'spaɪərəl/ *a.* en spirale; (*staircase*) en colimaçon. *n.* spirale *f.* —*v.i.* (*p.t.* **spiralled**) (*prices*) monter (en flèche).

spire /'spaɪə(r)/ *n.* flèche *f.*

spirit /'spɪrɪt/ *n.* esprit *m.*; (*boldness*) courage *m.* ~**s**, (*morale*) moral *m.*; (*drink*) spiritueux *m. pl.* —*v.t.* ~ **away**, faire disparaître. ~**-level** *n.* niveau à bulle *m.*

spirited /'spɪrɪtɪd/ *a.* fougueux.

spiritual /'spɪrɪtʃʊəl/ *a.* spirituel. —*n.* (*song*) (negro-)spiritual *m.*

spit[1] /spɪt/ *v.t./i.* (*p.t.* **spat** *or* **spit**, *pres. p.* **spitting**) cracher; (*of rain*) crachiner. —*n.* crachat(s) *m.* (*pl.*) ~ **out**, cracher. **the** ~**ting image of**, le portrait craché *or* vivant de.

spit[2] /spɪt/ *n.* (*for meat*) broche *f.*

spite /spaɪt/ *n.* rancune *f.* —*v.t.* contrarier. **in** ~ **of**, malgré. ~**ful** *a.* méchant, rancunier. ~**fully** *adv.* méchamment.

spittle /'spɪtl/ *n.* crachat(s) *m.* (*pl.*).

splash /splæʃ/ *v.t.* éclabousser. —*v.i.* faire des éclaboussures. ~ (**about**), patauger. —*n.* (*act, mark*) éclaboussure *f.*; (*sound*) plouf *m.*; (*of colour*) tache *f.*

spleen /spli:n/ *n.* (*anat.*) rate *f.*

splendid /'splendɪd/ *a.* magnifique, splendide.

splendour /'splendə(r)/ *n.* splendeur *f.*, éclat *m.*

splint /splɪnt/ *n.* (*med.*) attelle *f.*

splinter /'splɪntə(r)/ *n.* éclat *m.*; (*in finger*) écharde *f.* ~ **group**, groupe dissident *m.*

split /splɪt/ *v.t./i.* (*p.t.* **split**, *pres. p.* **splitting**) (se) fendre; (*tear*) (se) déchirer; (*divide*) (se) diviser; (*share*) partager. —*n.* fente *f.*; déchirure *f.*; (*share: fam.*) part *f.*, partage *m.*; (*quarrel*) rupture *f.*; (*pol.*) scission *f.* ~ **up**, (*couple*) rompre. **a** ~ **second**, un rien de temps. ~ **one's sides**, se tordre (de rire).

splurge /splɜ:dʒ/ *v.i.* (*fam.*) faire de folles dépenses.

splutter /'splʌtə(r)/ *v.i.* crachoter; (*stammer*) bafouiller; (*engine*) tousser; (*fat*) crépiter.

spoil /spɔɪl/ *v.t.* (*p.t.* **spoilt** *or* **spoiled**) (*pamper*) gâter; (*ruin*) abîmer; (*mar*) gâcher, gâter. —*n.* ~(**s**), (*plunder*) butin *m.* ~**- sport** *n.* trouble-fête *m./f. invar.*

spoke[1] /spəʊk/ *n.* rayon *m.*

spoke[2], **spoken** /spəʊk, 'spəʊkən/ *see* **speak**.

spokesman /'spəʊksmən/ *n.* (*pl.* **-men**) porte-parole *m. invar.*

sponge /spʌndʒ/ *n.* éponge *f.* —*v.t.* éponger. —*v.i.* ~ **on**, vivre aux crochets de. ~**-bag** *n.* trousse de toilette *f.* ~**-cake** *n.* génoise *f.* ~**r** /-ə(r)/ *n.* parasite *m.* **spongy** *a.* spongieux.

sponsor /'spɒnsə(r)/ *n.* (*of concert*) parrain *m.*, sponsor *m.*; (*surety*) garant *m.*; (*for membership*) parrain *m.*, marraine *f.* —*v.t.* parrainer, sponsoriser; (*member*) parrainer. ~**ship** *n.* patronage *m.*; parrainage *m.*

spontane|ous /spɒn'teɪnɪəs/ *a.* spontané. ~**ity** /-tə'ni:əti/ *n.* spontanéité *f.* ~**ously** *adv.* spontanément.

spoof /spu:f/ *n.* (*fam.*) parodie *f.*

spool /spu:l/ *n.* bobine *f.*

spoon /spu:n/ *n.* cuiller *f.* ~**-feed** *v.t.* (*p.t.* **-fed**) nourrir à la cuiller; (*help: fig.*) mâcher la besogne à. ~**ful** *n.* (*pl.* **-fuls**) cuillerée *f.*

sporadic /spə'rædɪk/ *a.* sporadique.

sport /spɔːt/ n. sport m. (**good**) ∼, (*person*: *sl.*) chic type m. —v.t. (*display*) exhiber, arborer. ∼s car/coat, voiture/veste de sport f. (*fam.*) sportif.

sporting /'spɔːtɪŋ/ a. sportif. **a** ∼ **chance,** une assez bonne chance.

sports|man /'spɔːtsmən/ n. (pl. **-men**) sportif m. ∼**manship** n. sportivité f. ∼**woman** n. (pl. **-women**) sportive f.

spot /spɒt/ n. (*mark*, *stain*) tache f.; (*dot*) point m.; (*in pattern*) pois m.; (*drop*) goutte f.; (*place*) endroit m.; (*pimple*) bouton m. —v.t. (*p.t.* **spotted**) (*fam.*) apercevoir. **a** ∼ **of,** (*fam.*) un peu de. **be in a** ∼, (*fam.*) avoir un problème. **on the** ∼, sur place; (*without delay*) sur le coup. ∼ **check,** contrôle à l'improviste m. ∼**ted** a. tacheté; (*fabric*) à pois. ∼**ty** a. (*skin*) boutonneux.

spotless /'spɒtlɪs/ a. impeccable.

spotlight /'spɒtlaɪt/ n. (*lamp*) projecteur m., spot m.

spouse /spaʊs/ n. époux m., épouse f.

spout /spaʊt/ n. (*of vessel*) bec m.; (*of liquid*) jet m. —v.i. jaillir. **up the** ∼, (*ruined*: *sl.*) fichu.

sprain /spreɪn/ n. entorse f., foulure f. —v.t. ∼ **one's wrist/**etc., se fouler le poignet/etc.

sprang /spræŋ/ see **spring**.

sprawl /sprɔːl/ v.i. (*town*, *person*, etc.) s'étaler. —n. étalement m.

spray[1] /spreɪ/ n. (*of flowers*) gerbe f.

spray[2] /spreɪ/ n. (*water*) gerbe d'eau f.; (*from sea*) embruns m. pl.; (*device*) bombe f., atomiseur m. —v.t. (*surface*, *insecticide*) vaporiser; (*plant* etc.) arroser; (*crops*) traiter.

spread /spred/ v.t./i. (*p.t.* **spread**) (*stretch*, *extend*) (s')étendre; (*news*, *fear*, etc.) (se) répandre; (*illness*) (se) propager; (*butter* etc.) (s')étaler. —n. propagation f.; (*of population*) distribution f.; (*paste*) pâte à tartiner f.; (*food*) belle table f. ∼**-eagled** a. bras et jambes écartés.

spreadsheet /'spredʃiːt/ n. tableur m.

spree /spriː/ n. **go on a** ∼, (*have fun*: *fam.*) faire la noce.

sprig /sprɪg/ n. (*shoot*) brin m.; (*twig*) brindille f.

sprightly /'spraɪtlɪ/ a. (**-ier**, **-iest**) alerte, vif.

spring /sprɪŋ/ v.i. (*p.t.* **sprang**, *p.p.* **sprung**) bondir. —v.t. faire, annoncer, etc. à l'improviste (**on**, à). —n. bond m.; (*device*) ressort m.; (*season*) printemps m.; (*of water*) source f. ∼**-clean** v.t.

nettoyer de fond en comble. ∼ **from,** provenir de. ∼ **onion,** oignon blanc m. ∼ **up,** surgir.

springboard /'sprɪŋbɔːd/ n. tremplin m.

springtime /'sprɪŋtaɪm/ n. printemps m.

springy /'sprɪŋɪ/ a. (**-ier**, **-iest**) élastique.

sprinkle /'sprɪŋkl/ v.t. (*with liquid*) arroser (**with**, de); (*with salt*, *flour*) saupoudrer (**with**, de). ∼ **sand/**etc., répandre du sable/etc. ∼**r** /-ə(r)/ n. (*in garden*) arroseur m.; (*for fires*) extincteur (à déclenchement) automatique m.

sprinkling /'sprɪŋklɪŋ/ n. (*amount*) petite quantité f.

sprint /sprɪnt/ v.i. (*sport*) sprinter. —n. sprint m. ∼**er** n. sprinteur/, -se m., f.

sprout /spraʊt/ v.t./i. pousser. —n. (*on plant* etc.) pousse f. (**Brussels**) ∼**s,** choux de Bruxelles m. pl.

spruce[1] /spruːs/ a. pimpant. —v.t. ∼ **o.s. up,** se faire beau.

spruce[2] /spruːs/ n. (*tree*) épicéa m.

sprung /sprʌŋ/ see **spring**. —a. (*mattress* etc.) à ressorts.

spry /spraɪ/ a. (**spryer**, **spryest**) alerte, vif.

spud /spʌd/ n. (*sl.*) patate f.

spun /spʌn/ see **spin**.

spur /spɜː(r)/ n. (*of rider*, *cock*, etc.) éperon m.; (*stimulus*) aiguillon m. —v.t. (*p.t.* **spurred**) éperonner. **on the** ∼ **of the moment,** sous l'impulsion du moment.

spurious /'spjʊərɪəs/ a. faux.

spurn /spɜːn/ v.t. repousser.

spurt /spɜːt/ v.i. jaillir; (*fig.*) accélérer. —n. jet m.; (*at work*) coup de collier m.

spy /spaɪ/ n. espion(ne) m. (f.). —v.i. espionner. —v.t. apercevoir. ∼ **on,** espionner. ∼ **out,** reconnaître.

squabble /'skwɒbl/ v.i. se chamailler. —n. chamaillerie f.

squad /skwɒd/ n. (*of soldiers* etc.) escouade f.; (*sport*) équipe f.

squadron /'skwɒdrən/ n. (*mil.*) escadron m.; (*aviat.*) escadrille f.; (*naut.*) escadre f.

squal|id /'skwɒlɪd/ a. sordide. ∼**or** n. conditions sordides f. pl.

squall /skwɔːl/ n. rafale f.

squander /'skwɒndə(r)/ v.t. (*money*, *time*, etc.) gaspiller.

square /skweə(r)/ n. carré m.; (*open space in town*) place f.; (*instrument*) équerre f. —a. carré; (*honest*) honnête; (*meal*) solide; (*fam.*) ringard. (**all**) ∼, (*quits*) quitte. —v.t. (*settle*) régler. —v.i. (*agree*) cadrer (**with**, avec). ∼ **up**

to, faire face à. **~ metre**, mètre carré *m.*
~ly *adv.* carrément.

squash /skwɒʃ/ *v.t.* écraser; (*crowd*) serrer. —*n.* (*game*) squash *m.*; (*marrow*: *Amer.*) courge *f.* **lemon ~**, citronnade *f.* **orange ~**, orangeade *f.* **~y** *a.* mou.

squat /skwɒt/ *v.i.* (*p.t.* **squatted**) s'accroupir. —*a.* (*dumpy*) trapu. **~ in a house**, squatteriser une maison. **~ter** *n.* squatter *m.*

squawk /skwɔːk/ *n.* cri rauque *m.* —*v.i.* pousser un cri rauque.

squeak /skwiːk/ *n.* petit cri *m.*, (*of door etc.*) grincement *m.* —*v.i.* crier; grincer. **~y** *a.* grinçant.

squeal /skwiːl/ *n.* cri aigu *m.* —*v.i.* pousser un cri aigu. **~ on**, (*inform on*: *sl.*) dénoncer.

squeamish /ˈskwiːmɪʃ/ *a.* (trop) délicat, facilement dégoûté.

squeeze /skwiːz/ *v.t.* presser; (*hand, arm*) serrer; (*extract*) exprimer (**from,** de); (*extort*) soutirer (**from,** à). —*v.i.* (*force one's way*) se glisser. —*n.* pression *f.*; (*comm.*) restrictions de crédit *f. pl.*

squelch /skweltʃ/ *v.i.* faire flic flac. —*v.t.* (*suppress*) supprimer.

squid /skwɪd/ *n.* calmar *m.*

squiggle /ˈskwɪɡl/ *n.* ligne onduleuse *f.*

squint /skwɪnt/ *v.i.* loucher; (*with half-shut eyes*) plisser les yeux. —*n.* (*med.*) strabisme *m.*

squire /ˈskwaɪə(r)/ *n.* propriétaire terrien *m.*

squirm /skwɜːm/ *v.i.* se tortiller.

squirrel /ˈskwɪrəl, *Amer.* ˈskwɜːrəl/ *n.* écureuil *m.*

squirt /skwɜːt/ *v.t./i.* (*faire*) jaillir. —*n.* jet *m.*

stab /stæb/ *v.t.* (*p.t.* **stabbed**) (*with knife etc.*) poignarder. —*n.* coup (de couteau) *m.* **have a ~ at sth.**, essayer de faire qch.

stabilize /ˈsteɪbəlaɪz/ *v.t.* stabiliser.

stable[1] /ˈsteɪbl/ *a.* (**-er, -est**) stable. **~ility** /stəˈbɪlətɪ/ *n.* stabilité *f.*

stable[2] /ˈsteɪbl/ *n.* écurie *f.* **~-boy** *n.* lad *m.*

stack /stæk/ *n.* tas *m.* —*v.t.* **~ (up)**, entasser, empiler.

stadium /ˈsteɪdɪəm/ *n.* stade *m.*

staff /stɑːf/ *n.* personnel *m.*; (*in school*) professeurs *m. pl.*; (*mil.*) état-major *m.*; (*stick*) bâton *m.* —*v.t.* pourvoir en personnel.

stag /stæɡ/ *n.* cerf *m.* **have a ~-party**, enterrer sa vie de garçon.

stage /steɪdʒ/ *n.* (*theatre*) scène *f.*; (*phase*) stade *m.*, étape *f.*; (*platform in hall*) estrade *f.* —*v.t.* mettre en scène; (*fig.*) organiser. **go on the ~**, faire du théâtre. **~-coach** *n.* (*old use*) diligence *f.* **~ door**, entrée des artistes *f.* **~ fright**, trac *m.* **~-manage** *v.t.* monter, organiser. **~-manager** *n.* régisseur *m.*

stagger /ˈstæɡə(r)/ *v.i.* chanceler. —*v.t.* (*shock*) stupéfier; (*holidays etc.*) étaler. **~ing** *a.* stupéfiant.

stagnant /ˈstæɡnənt/ *a.* stagnant.

stagnat|**e** /stæɡˈneɪt/ *v.i.* stagner. **~ion** /-ʃn/ *n.* stagnation *f.*

staid /steɪd/ *a.* sérieux.

stain /steɪn/ *v.t.* tacher; (*wood etc.*) colorer. —*n.* tache *f.*; (*colouring*) colorant *m.* **~ed glass window**, vitrail *m.* **~less steel**, acier inoxydable *m.* **~ remover**, détachant *m.*

stair /steə(r)/ *n.* marche *f.* **the ~s**, l'escalier *m.*

stair|**case** /ˈsteəkeɪs/, **~way** *ns.* escalier *m.*

stake /steɪk/ *n.* (*post*) pieu *m.*; (*wager*) enjeu *m.* —*v.t.* (*area*) jalonner; (*wager*) jouer. **at ~**, en jeu. **~ a claim to**, revendiquer.

stale /steɪl/ *a.* (**-er, -est**) pas frais; (*bread*) rassis; (*smell*) de renfermé; (*news*) vieux. **~ness** *n.* manque de fraîcheur *m.*

stalemate /ˈsteɪlmeɪt/ *n.* (*chess*) pat *m.*; (*fig.*) impasse *f.*

stalk[1] /stɔːk/ *n.* (*of plant*) tige *f.*

stalk[2] /stɔːk/ *v.i.* marcher de façon guindée. —*v.t.* (*prey*) traquer.

stall /stɔːl/ *n.* (*in stable*) stalle *f.*; (*in market*) éventaire *m.* **~s**, (*theatre*) orchestre *m.* —*v.t./i.* (*auto.*) caler. **~ (for time)**, temporiser.

stallion /ˈstæljən/ *n.* étalon *m.*

stalwart /ˈstɔːlwət/ *n.* (*supporter*) partisan(e) fidèle *m.* (*f.*).

stamina /ˈstæmɪnə/ *n.* résistance *f.*

stammer /ˈstæmə(r)/ *v.t./i.* bégayer. —*n.* bégaiement *m.*

stamp /stæmp/ *v.t./i.* **~ (one's foot)**, taper du pied. —*v.t.* (*letter etc.*) timbrer. —*n.* (*for postage, marking*) timbre *m.*; (*mark, fig.*) sceau *m.* **~-collecting** *n.* philatélie *f.* **~ out**, supprimer.

stampede /stæmˈpiːd/ *n.* fuite désordonnée *f.*; (*rush*: *fig.*) ruée *f.* —*v.i.* s'enfuir en désordre; se ruer.

stance /stæns/ *n.* position *f.*

stand /stænd/ *v.i.* (*p.t.* **stood**) être *or* se tenir (debout); (*rise*) se lever; (*be* *situated*) se trouver; (*rest*) reposer; (*pol.*) être candidat (**for**, à). —*v.t.* mettre (debout); (*tolerate*) supporter. —*n.* position *f.*; (*mil.*) résistance *f.*; (*for lamp etc.*) support *m.*; (*at fair*) stand *m.*; (*in street*) kiosque *m.*; (*for spectators*) tribune *f.*; (*jurid., Amer.*) barre *f.* **make a ~**, prendre position. **~ a chance,** avoir une chance. **~ back,** reculer. **~ by** *or* **around,** ne rien faire. **~ by,** (*be ready*) se tenir prêt; (*promise, person*) rester fidèle à. **~-by** *a.* de réserve; *n.* **be a ~-by,** être de réserve. **~ down,** se désister. **~ for,** représenter; (*fam.*) supporter. **~ in for,** remplacer. **~-in** *n.* remplaçant(e) *m.* (*f.*). **~ in line,** (*Amer.*) faire la queue. **~-offish** *a.* (*fam.*) distant. **~ out,** (*be conspicuous*) ressortir. **~ to reason,** être logique. **~ up,** se lever. **~ up for,** défendre. **~ up to,** résister à.

standard /'stændəd/ *n.* norme *f.*; (*level*) niveau (voulu) *m.*; (*flag*) étendard *m.* **~s,** (*morals*) principes *m. pl.* —*a.* ordinaire. **~ lamp,** lampadaire *m.* **~ of living,** niveau de vie *m.*

standardize /'stændədaɪz/ *v.t.* standardiser.

standing /'stændɪŋ/ *a.* debout *invar.*; (*army, offer*) permanent. —*n.* position *f.*, réputation *f.*; (*duration*) durée *f.* **~ order,** prélèvement bancaire *m.* **~ room,** places debout *f. pl.*

standpoint /'stændpɔɪnt/ *n.* point de vue *m.*

standstill /'stændstɪl/ *n.* **at a ~,** immobile. **bring/come to a ~,** (s')immobiliser.

stank /stæŋk/ *see* **stink.**

stanza /'stænzə/ *n.* strophe *f.*

staple[1] /'steɪpl/ *n.* agrafe *f.* —*v.t.* agrafer. **~r** /-ə(r)/ *n.* agrafeuse *f.*

staple[2] /'steɪpl/ *a.* principal, de base.

star /stɑ:(r)/ *n.* étoile *f.*; (*famous person*) vedette *f.* —*v.t.* (*p.t.* **starred**) (*of film*) avoir pour vedette. —*v.i.* **~ in,** être la vedette de. **~dom** *n.* célébrité *f.*

starboard /'stɑ:bəd/ *n.* tribord *m.*

starch /stɑ:tʃ/ *n.* amidon *m.*; (*in food*) fécule *f.* —*v.t.* amidonner. **~y** *a.* féculent; (*stiff*) guindé.

stare /steə(r)/ *v.i.* **~ at,** regarder fixement. —*n.* regard fixe *m.*

starfish /'stɑ:fɪʃ/ *n.* étoile de mer *f.*

stark /stɑ:k/ *a.* (**-er, -est**) (*desolate*) désolé; (*severe*) austère; (*utter*) complet; (*fact etc.*) brutal. —*adv.* complètement.

starling /'stɑ:lɪŋ/ *n.* étourneau *m.*

starlit /'stɑ:lɪt/ *a.* étoilé.

starry /'stɑ:rɪ/ *a.* étoilé. **~-eyed** *a.* naïf, (*trop*) optimiste.

start /stɑ:t/ *v.t./i.* commencer; (*machine*) (se) mettre en marche; (*fashion etc.*) lancer; (*cause*) provoquer; (*jump*) sursauter; (*of vehicle*) démarrer. —*n.* commencement *m.*, début *m.*; (*of race*) départ *m.*; (*lead*) avance *f.*; (*jump*) sursaut *m.* **~ to do,** commencer *or* se mettre à faire. **~ off doing,** commencer par faire. **~ out,** partir. **~ up a business,** lancer une affaire. **~er** *n.* (*auto.*) démarreur *m.*; (*runner*) partant *m.*; (*culin.*) entrée *f.* **~ing point,** point de départ *m.* **~ing tomorrow,** à partir de demain.

startle /'stɑ:tl/ *v.t.* (*make jump*) faire tressaillir; (*shock*) alarmer.

starv|e /stɑ:v/ *v.i.* mourir de faim. —*v.t.* affamer; (*deprive*) priver. **~ation** /-'veɪʃn/ *n.* faim *f.*

stash /stæʃ/ *v.t.* (*hide: sl.*) cacher.

state /steɪt/ *n.* état *m.*; (*pomp*) apparat *m.* **S~,** (*pol.*) État *m.* —*a.* d'État, de l'État; (*school*) public. —*v.t.* affirmer (**that,** que); (*views*) exprimer; (*fix*) fixer. **the S~s,** les États-Unis. **get into a ~,** s'affoler.

stateless /'steɪtlɪs/ *a.* apatride.

stately /'steɪtlɪ/ *a.* (**-ier, -iest**) majestueux. **~ home,** château *m.*

statement /'steɪtmənt/ *n.* déclaration *f.*; (*of account*) relevé *m.*

statesman /'steɪtsmən/ *n.* (*pl.* **-men**) homme d'État *m.*

static /'stætɪk/ *a.* statique. —*n.* (*radio, TV*) parasites *m. pl.*

station /'steɪʃn/ *n.* station *f.*; (*rail.*) gare *f.*; (*mil.*) poste *m.*; (*rank*) condition *f.* —*v.t.* poster, placer. **~ed at** *or* **in,** (*mil.*) en garnison à. **~ wagon,** (*Amer.*) break *m.*

stationary /'steɪʃənrɪ/ *a.* immobile, stationnaire; (*vehicle*) à l'arrêt.

stationer /'steɪʃnə(r)/ *n.* papetier, -ière *m.*, *f.* **~'s shop,** papeterie *f.* **~y** *n.* papeterie *f.*

statistic /stə'tɪstɪk/ *n.* statistique *f.* **~s,** statistique *f.* **~al** *a.* statistique.

statue /'stætʃu:/ *n.* statue *f.*

stature /'stætʃə(r)/ *n.* stature *f.*

status /'steɪtəs/ *n.* (*pl.* **-uses**) situation *f.*, statut *m.*; (*prestige*) standing *m.* **~ quo,** statu quo *m.*

statut|e /'stætʃu:t/ *n.* loi *f.* **~es,** (*rules*) statuts *m. pl.* **~ory** /-ʊtrɪ/ *a.* statutaire; (*holiday*) légal.

staunch /stɔ:ntʃ/ *a.* (**-er, -est**) (*friend etc.*) loyal, fidèle.

stave /steɪv/ n. (mus.) portée f. —v.t. ~
off, éviter, conjurer.

stay /steɪ/ v.i. rester; (spend time)
séjourner; (reside) loger. —v.t.
(hunger) tromper. —n. séjour m. ~
away from, (school etc.) ne pas aller à.
~ **behind/on/late/**etc., rester. ~
in/out, rester à la maison/dehors. ~ **up**
(late), veiller, se coucher tard.

stead /sted/ n. **stand s.o. in good** ~, être
bien utile à qn.

steadfast /'stedfɑːst/ a. ferme.

stead|y /'stedɪ/ a. **(-ier, -iest)** stable;
(hand, voice) ferme; (regular) régulier;
(staid) sérieux. —v.t. maintenir, assurer; (calm) calmer. ~**ily** adv. fermement; régulièrement.

steak /steɪk/ n. steak m., bifteck m.; (of
fish) darne f.

steal /stiːl/ v.t./i. (p.t. **stole,** p.p. **stolen**)
voler (**from s.o.,** à qn.).

stealth /stelθ/ n. **by** ~, furtivement. ~**y**
a. furtif.

steam /stiːm/ n. vapeur f.; (on glass)
buée f. —v.t. (cook) cuire à la vapeur;
(window) embuer. —v.i. fumer. ~
engine n. locomotive à vapeur f. ~
iron, fer à vapeur m. ~**y** a. humide.

steam|er /'stiːmə(r)/ n. (culin.) cuit-
vapeur m.; (also ~**ship**) (bateau à)
vapeur m.

steamroller /'stiːmrəʊlə(r)/ n. rouleau
compresseur m.

steel /stiːl/ n. acier m. —v. pr. ~ **o.s.,**
s'endurcir, se cuirasser. ~ **industry,**
sidérurgie f.

steep[1] /stiːp/ v.t. (soak) tremper. ~**ed in,**
(fig.) imprégné de.

steep[2] /stiːp/ a. **(-er, -est)** raide, rapide;
(price: fam.) excessif. ~**ly** adv. **rise**
~**ly,** (slope, price) monter rapidement.

steeple /'stiːpl/ n. clocher m.

steeplechase /'stiːpltʃeɪs/ n. (race)
steeple(-chase) m.

steer[1] /stɪə(r)/ n. (ox) bouvillon m.

steer[2] /stɪə(r)/ v.t. diriger; (ship)
gouverner; (fig.) guider. —v.i. (in ship)
gouverner. ~ **clear of,** éviter. ~**ing** n.
(auto.) direction f. ~**ing-wheel** n.
volant m.

stem[1] /stem/ n. tige f.; (of glass) pied m.
—v.i. (p.t. **stemmed**). ~ **from,**
provenir de.

stem[2] /stem/ v.t. (p.t. **stemmed**) (check,
stop) endiguer, contenir.

stench /stentʃ/ n. puanteur f.

stencil /'stensl/ n. pochoir m.; (for
typing) stencil m. —v.t. (p.t. **stencilled**)
(document) polycopier.

stenographer /ste'nɒɡrəfə(r)/ n.
(Amer.) sténodactylo f.

step /step/ v.i. (p.t. **stepped**) marcher,
aller. —v.t. ~ **up,** augmenter. —n. pas
m.; (stair) marche f.; (of train)
marchepied m.; (action) mesure f. ~**s,**
(ladder) escabeau m. **in** ~, au pas;
(fig.) conforme (**with,** à). ~ **down,**
(resign) démissionner; (from ladder)
descendre. ~ **forward,** (faire un) pas en
avant. ~ **up,** (pressure) augmenter. ~
in, (intervene) intervenir. ~**-ladder** n.
escabeau m. ~**ping-stone** n. (fig.)
tremplin m.

step|brother /'stepbrʌðə(r)/ n. demi-
frère m. ~**daughter** n. belle-fille f.
~**father** n. beau-père m. ~**mother** n.
belle-mère f. ~**sister** n. demi-sœur f.
~**son** n. beau-fils m.

stereo /'sterɪəʊ/ n. (pl. **-os**) stéréo f.;
(record-player) chaîne stéréo f. —a.
stéréo invar. ~**phonic** /-ə'fɒnɪk/ a.
stéréophonique.

stereotype /'sterɪətaɪp/ n. stéréotype m.
~**d** a. stéréotypé.

steril|e /'steraɪl, Amer. 'sterəl/ a. stérile.
~**ity** /stə'rɪlətɪ/ n. stérilité f.

steriliz|e /'sterəlaɪz/ v.t. stériliser.
~**ation** /-'zeɪʃn/ n. stérilisation f.

sterling /'stɜːlɪŋ/ n. livre(s) sterling f.
(pl.). —a. sterling invar.; (silver) fin;
(fig.) excellent.

stern[1] /stɜːn/ a. **(-er, -est)** sévère.

stern[2] /stɜːn/ n. (of ship) arrière m.

steroid /'sterɔɪd/ n. stéroïde m.

stethoscope /'steθəskəʊp/ n. stéthoscope m.

stew /stjuː/ v.t./i. cuire à la casserole.
—n. ragoût m. ~**ed fruit,** compote f.
~**ed tea,** thé trop infusé m. ~**-pan** n.
cocotte f.

steward /stjʊəd/ n. (of club etc.)
intendant m.; (on ship etc.) steward m.
~**ess** /-'des/ n. hôtesse f.

stick[1] /stɪk/ n. bâton m.; (for walking)
canne f.

stick[2] /stɪk/ v.t. (p.t. **stuck**) (glue) coller;
(thrust) enfoncer; (put: fam.) mettre;
(endure: sl.) supporter. —v.i. (adhere)
coller, adhérer; (to pan) attacher;
(remain: fam.) rester; (be jammed) être
coincé. **be stuck with s.o.,** (fam.) se
farcir qn. ~**-in-the-mud** n. encroûté(e)
m. (f.). ~ **at,** persévérer dans. ~ **out**
v.t. (head etc.) sortir; (tongue) tirer; v.i.
(protrude) dépasser. ~ **to,** (promise
etc.) rester fidèle à. ~ **up for,** (fam.)
défendre. ~**ing-plaster** n. sparadrap m.

sticker /'stɪkə(r)/ n. autocollant m.

stickler /'stɪklə(r)/ *n.* **be a** ~ **for,** insister sur.

sticky /'stɪkɪ/ *a.* (**-ier, -iest**) poisseux; (*label, tape*) adhésif.

stiff /stɪf/ *a.* (**-er, -est**) raide; (*limb, joint*) ankylosé; (*tough*) dur; (*drink*) fort; (*price*) élevé; (*manner*) guindé. ~ **neck,** torticolis *m.* ~**ness** *n.* raideur *f.*

stiffen /'stɪfn/ *v.t./i.* (se) raidir.

stifle /'staɪfl/ *v.t./i.* étouffer.

stigma /'stɪgmə/ *n.* (*pl.* **-as**) stigmate *m.* ~**tize** *v.t.* stigmatiser.

stile /staɪl/ *n.* échalier *m.*

stiletto /stɪ'letəʊ/ *a. & n.* (*pl.* **-os**) ~**s,** ~ **heels** talons aiguille.

still[1] /stɪl/ *a.* immobile; (*quiet*) calme, tranquille. —*n.* silence *m.* —*adv.* encore, toujours; (*even*) encore; (*nevertheless*) tout de même. **keep** ~**!,** arrête de bouger! ~ **life,** nature morte *f.*

still[2] /stɪl/ *n.* (*apparatus*) alambic *m.*

stillborn /'stɪlbɔːn/ *a.* mort-né.

stilted /'stɪltɪd/ *a.* guindé.

stilts /stɪlts/ *n. pl.* échasses *f. pl.*

stimulate /'stɪmjʊleɪt/ *v.t.* stimuler. ~**ant** *n.* stimulant *m.* ~**ation** /-'leɪʃn/ *n.* stimulation *f.*

stimulus /'stɪmjʊləs/ *n.* (*pl.* **-li** /-laɪ/) (*spur*) stimulant *m.*

sting /stɪŋ/ *n.* piqûre *f.*; (*organ*) dard *m.* —*v.t./i.* (*p.t.* **stung**) piquer. ~**ing** *a.* (*fig.*) cinglant.

stingy /'stɪndʒɪ/ *a.* (**-ier, -iest**) avare (**with,** de).

stink /stɪŋk/ *n.* puanteur *f.* —*v.i.* (*p.t.* **stank** *or* **stunk,** *p.p.* **stunk**). ~ (**of**), puer. —*v.t.* ~ **out,** (*room etc.*) empester.

stinker /'stɪŋkə(r)/ *n.* (*thing: sl.*) vacherie *f.*; (*person: sl.*) vache *f.*

stint /stɪnt/ *v.i.* ~ **on,** lésiner sur. —*n.* (*work*) tour *m.*

stipulate /'stɪpjʊleɪt/ *v.t.* stipuler. ~**ion** /-'leɪʃn/ *n.* stipulation *f.*

stir /stɜː(r)/ *v.t./i.* (*p.t.* **stirred**) (*move*) remuer; (*excite*) exciter. —*n.* agitation *f.* ~ **up,** (*trouble etc.*) provoquer.

stirrup /'stɪrəp/ *n.* étrier *m.*

stitch /stɪtʃ/ *n.* point *m.*; (*in knitting*) maille *f.*; (*med.*) point de suture *m.*; (*muscle pain*) point de côté *m.* —*v.t.* coudre. **be in** ~**es,** (*fam.*) avoir le fou rire.

stoat /stəʊt/ *n.* hermine *f.*

stock /stɒk/ *n.* réserve *f.*; (*comm.*) stock *m.*; (*financial*) valeurs *f. pl.*; (*family*) souche *f.*; (*soup*) bouillon *m.* —*a.* (*goods*) courant. —*v.t.* (*shop etc.*) approvisionner; (*sell*) vendre. —*v.i.* ~

up, s'approvisionner (**with,** de). ~**-car** *n.* stock-car *m.* ~ **cube,** bouillon-cube *m.* S~ **Exchange,** ~ **market,** Bourse *f.* ~ **phrase,** cliché *m.* ~**-taking** *n.* (*comm.*) inventaire *m.* **in** ~, en stock. **we're out of** ~, il n'y en a plus. **take** ~, (*fig.*) faire le point.

stockbroker /'stɒkbrəʊkə(r)/ *n.* agent de change *m.*

stocking /'stɒkɪŋ/ *n.* bas *m.*

stockist /'stɒkɪst/ *n.* stockiste *m.*

stockpile /'stɒkpaɪl/ *n.* stock *m.* —*v.t.* stocker; (*arms*) amasser.

stocky /'stɒkɪ/ *a.* (**-ier, -iest**) trapu.

stodge /stɒdʒ/ *n.* (*fam.*) aliment(s) lourd(s) *m.* (*pl.*). ~**y** *a.* lourd.

stoic /'stəʊɪk/ *n.* stoïque *m./f.* ~**al** *a.* stoïque. ~**ism** /-sɪzəm/ *n.* stoïcisme *m.*

stoke /stəʊk/ *v.t.* (*boiler, fire*) garnir, alimenter.

stole[1] /stəʊl/ *n.* (*garment*) étole *f.*

stole[2], **stolen** /stəʊl, 'stəʊlən/ *see* **steal.**

stolid /'stɒlɪd/ *a.* flegmatique.

stomach /'stʌmək/ *n.* estomac *m.*; (*abdomen*) ventre *m.* —*v.t.* (*put up with*) supporter. ~**-ache** *n.* mal à l'estomac *or* au ventre *m.*

stone /stəʊn/ *n.* pierre *f.*; (*pebble*) caillou *m.*; (*in fruit*) noyau *m.*; (*weight*) 6.350 kg. —*a.* de pierre. —*v.t.* lapider; (*fruit*) dénoyauter. ~**e-cold/-deaf,** complètement froid/sourd. ~**y** *a.* pierreux. ~**y-broke** *a.* (*sl.*) fauché.

stonemason /'stəʊnmeɪsn/ *n.* maçon *m.*, tailleur de pierre *m.*

stood /stʊd/ *see* **stand.**

stooge /stuːdʒ/ *n.* (*actor*) comparse *m./f.*; (*fig.*) fantoche *m.*, laquais *m.*

stool /stuːl/ *n.* tabouret *m.*

stoop /stuːp/ *v.i.* (*bend*) se baisser; (*condescend*) s'abaisser. —*n.* **have a** ~, être voûté.

stop /stɒp/ *v.t./i.* (*p.t.* **stopped**) arrêter (**doing,** de faire); (*moving, talking*) s'arrêter; (*prevent*) empêcher (**from,** de); (*hole, leak, etc.*) boucher; (*of pain, noise, etc.*) cesser; (*stay: fam.*) rester. —*n.* arrêt *m.*; (*full stop*) point *m.* ~ **off,** s'arrêter. ~ **up,** boucher. ~(**-over**), halte *f.*; (*port of call*) escale *f.* ~**-light** *n.* (*on vehicle*) stop *m.* ~**-watch** *n.* chronomètre *m.*

stopgap /'stɒpgæp/ *n.* bouche-trou *m.* —*a.* intérimaire.

stoppage /'stɒpɪdʒ/ *n.* arrêt *m.*; (*of work*) arrêt de travail *m.*; (*of pay*) retenue *f.*

stopper /'stɒpə(r)/ *n.* bouchon *m.*

storage /'stɔːrɪdʒ/ *n.* (*of goods, food, etc.*) emmagasinage *m.* ~ **heater,**

radiateur électrique à accumulation *m.*
~ **space,** espace de rangement *m.*
store /stɔː(r)/ *n.* réserve *f.*; (*warehouse*)
entrepôt *m.*; (*shop*) grand magasin *m.*;
(*Amer.*) magasin *m.* —*v.t.* (*for future*)
mettre en réserve; (*in warehouse, mind*)
emmagasiner. **have in ~ for,** réserver
à. **set ~ by,** attacher du prix à. **~-room**
n. réserve *f.*
storey /'stɔːrɪ/ *n.* étage *m.*
stork /stɔːk/ *n.* cigogne *f.*
storm /stɔːm/ *n.* tempête *f.*, orage *m.*
—*v.t.* prendre d'assaut. —*v.i.* (*rage*)
tempêter. **~y** *a.* orageux.
story /'stɔːrɪ/ *n.* histoire *f.*; (*in press*)
article *m.*; (*storey: Amer.*) étage *m.* ~
book, livre d'histoires *m.* **~-teller** *n.*
conteur, -se *m.*, *f.*; (*liar: fam.*)
menteur, -se *m.*, *f.*
stout /staʊt/ *a.* (**-er, -est**) corpulent;
(*strong*) solide. —*n.* bière brune *f.*
~ness *n.* corpulence *f.*
stove /stəʊv/ *n.* (*for cooking*) cuisinière
f.; (*heater*) poêle *m.*
stow /stəʊ/ *v.t.* ~ **away,** (*put away*)
ranger; (*hide*) cacher. —*v.i.* voyager
clandestinement.
stowaway /'stəʊəweɪ/ *n.* passager, -ère
clandestin(e) *m.*, *f.*
straddle /'strædl/ *v.t.* être à cheval sur,
enjamber.
straggle /'strægl/ *v.i.* (*lag behind*)
traîner en désordre. **~r** /-ə(r)/ *n.*
traînard(e) *m.* (*f.*).
straight /streɪt/ *a.* (**-er, -est**) droit; (*tidy*)
en ordre; (*frank*) franc. —*adv.* (*in
straight line*) droit; (*direct*) tout droit.
—*n.* ligne droite *f.* ~ **ahead** *or* **on,** tout
droit. ~ **away,** tout de suite. ~ **face,**
visage sérieux *m.* **get sth.** ~, mettre
qch. au clair. ~ **off,** (*fam.*) sans hésiter.
straighten /'streɪtn/ *v.t.* (*nail, situation,
etc.*) redresser; (*tidy*) arranger.
straightforward /streɪt'fɔːwəd/ *a.* honnête; (*easy*) simple.
strain[1] /streɪn/ *n.* (*breed*) race *f.*;
(*streak*) tendance *f.*
strain[2] /streɪn/ *v.t.* (*rope, ears*) tendre;
(*limb*) fouler; (*eyes*) fatiguer; (*muscle*)
froisser; (*filter*) passer; (*vegetables*)
égoutter; (*fig.*) mettre à l'épreuve.
—*v.i.* fournir des efforts. —*n.* tension
f.; (*fig.*) effort *m.* **~s,** (*tune: mus.*)
accents *m. pl.* **~ed** *a.* forcé; (*relations*)
tendu. **~er** *n.* passoire *f.*
strait /streɪt/ *n.* détroit *m.* **~s,** détroit *m.*;
(*fig.*) embarras *m.* **~-jacket** *n.*
camisole de force *f.* **~-laced** *a.* collet
monté *invar.*

strand /strænd/ *n.* (*thread*) fil *m.*, brin
m.; (*lock of hair*) mèche *f.*
stranded /'strændɪd/ *a.* (*person*) en
rade; (*ship*) échoué.
strange /streɪndʒ/ *a.* (**-er, -est**) étrange;
(*unknown*) inconnu. **~ly** *adv.* étrange-
ment. **~ness** *n.* étrangeté *f.*
stranger /'streɪndʒə(r)/ *n.* inconnu(e) *m.*
(*f.*).
strangle /'stræŋgl/ *v.t.* étrangler.
stranglehold /'stræŋglhəʊld/ *n.* **have a
~ on,** tenir à la gorge.
strap /stræp/ *n.* (*of leather etc.*) courroie
f.; (*of dress*) bretelle *f.*; (*of watch*)
bracelet *m.* —*v.t.* (*p.t.* **strapped**)
attacher.
strapping /'stræpɪŋ/ *a.* costaud.
stratagem /'strætədʒəm/ *n.* stratagème
m.
strategic /strə'tiːdʒɪk/ *a.* stratégique.
strategy /'strætədʒɪ/ *n.* stratégie *f.*
stratum /'strɑːtəm/ *n.* (*pl.* **strata**)
couche *f.*
straw /strɔː/ *n.* paille *f.* **the last ~,** le
comble.
strawberry /'strɔːbrɪ/ *n.* fraise *f.*
stray /streɪ/ *v.i.* s'égarer; (*deviate*)
s'écarter. —*a.* perdu; (*isolated*) isolé.
—*n.* animal perdu *m.*
streak /striːk/ *n.* raie *f.*, bande *f.*; (*trace*)
trace *f.*; (*period*) période *f.*; (*tendency*)
tendance *f.* —*v.t.* (*mark*) strier. —*v.i.*
filer à toute allure. **~y** *a.* strié.
stream /striːm/ *n.* ruisseau *m.*; (*current*)
courant *m.*; (*flow*) flot *m.*; (*in schools*)
classe (de niveau) *f.* —*v.i.* ruisseler
(**with,** de); (*eyes, nose*) couler.
streamer /'striːmə(r)/ *n.* (*of paper*)
serpentin *m.*; (*flag*) banderole *f.*
streamline /'striːmlaɪn/ *v.t.* rationaliser.
~d *a.* (*shape*) aérodynamique.
street /striːt/ *n.* rue *f.* ~ **lamp,** réverbère
m. ~ **map,** plan des rues *m.*
streetcar /'striːtkɑː(r)/ *n.* (*Amer.*)
tramway *m.*
strength /streŋθ/ *n.* force *f.*; (*of wall,
fabric, etc.*) solidité *f.* **on the ~ of,** en
vertu de.
strengthen /'streŋθn/ *v.t.* renforcer,
fortifier.
strenuous /'strenjʊəs/ *a.* énergique;
(*arduous*) ardu; (*tiring*) fatigant. **~ly**
adv. énergiquement.
stress /stres/ *n.* accent *m.*; (*pressure*)
pression *f.*; (*med.*) stress *m.* —*v.t.*
souligner, insister sur.
stretch /stretʃ/ *v.t.* (*pull taut*) tendre;
(*arm, leg*) étendre; (*neck*) tendre;
(*clothes*) étirer; (*truth etc.*) forcer.

—*v.i.* s'étendre; (*of person, clothes*) s'étirer. —*n.* étendue *f.*; (*period*) période *f.*; (*of road*) tronçon *m.* —*a.* (*fabric*) extensible. **~ one's legs**, se dégourdir les jambes. **at a ~,** d'affilée.

stretcher /'stretʃə(r)/ *n.* brancard *m.*

strew /stru:/ *v.t.* (*p.t.* **strewed**, *p.p.* **strewed** *or* **strewn**) (*scatter*) répandre; (*cover*) joncher.

stricken /'strɪkən/ *a.* **~ with**, frappé *or* atteint de.

strict /strɪkt/ *a.* (**-er, -est**) strict. **~ly** *adv.* strictement. **~ness** *n.* sévérité *f.*

stride /straɪd/ *v.i.* (*p.t.* **strode**, *p.p.* **stridden**) faire de grands pas. —*n.* grand pas *m.*

strident /'straɪdnt/ *a.* strident.

strife /straɪf/ *n.* conflit(s) *m.* (*pl.*).

strike /straɪk/ *v.t.* (*p.t.* **struck**) frapper; (*blow*) donner; (*match*) frotter; (*gold etc.*) trouver. —*v.i.* faire grève; (*attack*) attaquer; (*clock*) sonner. —*n.* (*of workers*) grève *f.*; (*mil.*) attaque *f.*; (*find*) découverte *f.* **on ~,** en grève. **~ off** *or* **out**, rayer. **~ up a friendship,** lier amitié (**with,** avec).

striker /'straɪkə(r)/ *n.* gréviste *m./f.*; (*football*) buteur *m.*

striking /'straɪkɪŋ/ *a.* frappant.

string /strɪŋ/ *n.* ficelle *f.*; (*of violin, racket, etc.*) corde *f.*; (*of pearls*) collier *m.*; (*of lies etc.*) chapelet *m.* —*v.t.* (*p.t.* **strung**) (*thread*) enfiler. **the ~s,** (*mus.*) les cordes. **~ bean**, haricot vert *m.* **pull ~s,** faire jouer ses relations, faire marcher le piston. **~ out,** (s')échelonner. **~ed** *a.* (*instrument*) à cordes. **~y** *a.* filandreux.

stringent /'strɪndʒənt/ *a.* rigoureux, strict.

strip¹ /strɪp/ *v.t./i.* (*p.t.* **stripped**) (*undress*) (se) déshabiller; (*machine*) démonter; (*deprive*) dépouiller. **~per** *n.* strip-teaseuse *f.*; (*solvent*) décapant *m.* **~-tease** *n.* strip-tease *m.*

strip² /strɪp/ *n.* bande *f.* **comic ~,** bande dessinée *f.* **~ light,** néon *m.*

stripe /straɪp/ *n.* rayure *f.*, raie *f.* **~d** *a.* rayé.

strive /straɪv/ *v.i.* (*p.t.* **strove**, *p.p.* **striven**) s'efforcer (**to,** de).

strode /strəʊd/ *see* **stride**.

stroke¹ /strəʊk/ *n.* coup *m.*; (*of pen*) trait *m.*; (*swimming*) nage *f.*; (*med.*) attaque *f.*, congestion *f.* **at a ~,** d'un seul coup.

stroke² /strəʊk/ *v.t.* (*with hand*) caresser. —*n.* caresse *f.*

stroll /strəʊl/ *v.i.* flâner. —*n.* petit tour *m.* **~ in**/*etc.*, entrer/*etc.* tranquillement. **~er** *n.* (*Amer.*) poussette *f.*

strong /strɒŋ/ *a.* (**-er, -est**) fort; (*shoes, fabric, etc.*) solide. **be fifty**/*etc.* **~,** être au nombre de cinquante/*etc.* **~-box** *n.* coffre-fort *m.* **~-minded** *a.* résolu. **~-room** *n.* chambre forte *f.* **~ly** *adv.* (*greatly*) fortement; (*with energy*) avec force; (*deeply*) profondément.

stronghold /'strɒŋhəʊld/ *n.* bastion *m.*

strove /strəʊv/ *see* **strive**.

struck /strʌk/ *see* **strike**. —*a.* **~ on,** (*sl.*) impressionné par.

structur|e /'strʌktʃə(r)/ *n.* (*of cell, poem, etc.*) structure *f.*; (*building*) construction *f.* **~al** *a.* structural; de (la) construction.

struggle /'strʌgl/ *v.i.* lutter, se battre. —*n.* lutte *f.*; (*effort*) effort *m.* **have a ~ to,** avoir du mal à.

strum /strʌm/ *v.t.* (*p.t.* **strummed**) (*banjo etc.*) gratter de.

strung /strʌŋ/ *see* **string**. —*a.* **~ up,** (*tense*) nerveux.

strut /strʌt/ *n.* (*support*) étai *m.* —*v.i.* (*p.t.* **strutted**) se pavaner.

stub /stʌb/ *n.* bout *m.*; (*of tree*) souche *f.*; (*counterfoil*) talon *m.* —*v.t.* (*p.t.* **stubbed**). **~ one's toe,** se cogner le doigt de pied. **~ out,** écraser.

stubble /'stʌbl/ *n.* (*on chin*) barbe de plusieurs jours *f.*; (*remains of wheat*) chaume *m.*

stubborn /'stʌbən/ *a.* opiniâtre, obstiné. **~ly** *adv.* obstinément. **~ness** *n.* opiniâtreté *f.*

stubby /'stʌbɪ/ *a.* (**-ier, -iest**) (*finger*) épais; (*person*) trapu.

stuck /stʌk/ *see* **stick**². —*a.* (*jammed*) coincé. **I'm ~,** (*for answer*) je sèche. **~-up** *a.* (*sl.*) prétentieux.

stud¹ /stʌd/ *n.* clou *m.*; (*for collar*) bouton *m.* —*v.t.* (*p.t.* **studded**) clouter. **~ded with,** parsemé de.

stud² /stʌd/ *n.* (*horses*) écurie *f.* **~(-farm)** *n.* haras *m.*

student /'stju:dnt/ *n.* (*univ.*) étudiant(e) *m.* (*f.*); (*schol.*) élève *m./f.* —*a.* (*restaurant, life, residence*) universitaire.

studied /'stʌdɪd/ *a.* étudié.

studio /'stju:dɪəʊ/ *n.* (*pl.* **-os**) studio *m.* **~ flat,** studio *m.*

studious /'stju:dɪəs/ *a.* (*person*) studieux; (*deliberate*) étudié. **~ly** *adv.* (*carefully*) avec soin.

study /'stʌdɪ/ *n.* étude *f.*; (*office*) bureau *m.* —*v.t./i.* étudier.

stuff /stʌf/ *n.* substance *f.*; (*sl.*) chose(s) *f.* (*pl.*). —*v.t.* rembourrer; (*animal*) empailler; (*cram*) bourrer; (*culin.*)

farcir; (*block up*) boucher; (*put*)
fourrer. ~ing *n.* bourre *f.*; (*culin.*) farce
f.

stuffy /'stʌfɪ/ *a.* (-ier, -iest) mal aéré;
(*dull: fam.*) vieux jeu *invar.*

stumble /'stʌmbl/ *v.i.* trébucher. ~e
across *or* on, tomber sur. ~ing-block
n. pierre d'achoppement *f.*

stump /stʌmp/ *n.* (*of tree*) souche *f.*; (*of
limb*) moignon *m.*; (*of pencil*) bout *m.*

stumped /stʌmpt/ *a.* (*baffled: fam.*)
embarrassé.

stun /stʌn/ *v.t.* (*p.t.* stunned) étourdir;
(*bewilder*) stupéfier.

stung /stʌŋ/ *see* sting.

stunk /stʌŋk/ *see* stink.

stunning /'stʌnɪŋ/ *a.* (*delightful: fam.*)
sensationnel.

stunt[1] /stʌnt/ *v.t.* (*growth*) retarder. ~ed
a. (*person*) rabougri.

stunt[2] /stʌnt/ *n.* (*feat: fam.*) tour de
force *m.*; (*trick: fam.*) truc *m.*;
(*dangerous*) cascade *f.* ~man *n.*
cascadeur *m.*

stupefy /'stju:pɪfaɪ/ *v.t.* abrutir; (*amaze*)
stupéfier.

stupendous /stju:'pendəs/ *a.* prodigieux, formidable.

stupid /'stju:pɪd/ *a.* stupide, bête. ~ity
/-'pɪdətɪ/ *n.* stupidité *f.* ~ly *adv.*
stupidement, bêtement.

stupor /'stju:pə(r)/ *n.* stupeur *f.*

sturdy /'stɜ:dɪ/ *a.* (-ier, -iest) robuste.
~iness *n.* robustesse *f.*

stutter /'stʌtə(r)/ *v.i.* bégayer. —*n.*
bégaiement *m.*

sty[1] /staɪ/ *n.* (*pigsty*) porcherie *f.*

sty[2] /staɪ/ *n.* (*on eye*) orgelet *m.*

style /staɪl/ *n.* style *m.*; (*fashion*) mode
f.; (*sort*) genre *m.*; (*pattern*) modèle *m.*
—*v.t.* (*design*) créer. do sth. in ~e,
faire qch. avec classe. ~e s.o.'s hair,
coiffer qn. ~ist *n.* (*of hair*) coiffeur,
-se *m.*, *f.*

stylish /'staɪlɪʃ/ *a.* élégant.

stylized /'staɪlaɪzd/ *a.* stylisé.

stylus /'staɪləs/ *n.* (*pl.* -uses) (*of record-
player*) saphir *m.*

suave /swɑ:v/ *a.* (*urbane*) courtois;
(*smooth: pej.*) doucereux.

sub- /sʌb/ *pref.* sous-, sub-.

subconscious /sʌb'kɒnʃəs/ *a.* & *n.*
inconscient (*m.*), subconscient (*m.*).
~ly *adv.* inconsciemment.

subcontract /sʌbkən'trækt/ *v.t.* sous-
traiter.

subdivide /sʌbdɪ'vaɪd/ *v.t.* subdiviser.

subdue /səb'dju:/ *v.t.* (*feeling*)
maîtriser; (*country*) subjuguer. ~d *a.*

(*weak*) faible; (*light*) tamisé; (*person,
criticism*) retenu.

subject[1] /'sʌbdʒɪkt/ *a.* (*state etc.*)
soumis. —*n.* sujet *m.*; (*schol., univ.*)
matière *f.*; (*citizen*) ressortissant(e) *m.*
(*f.*), sujet(te) *m.* (*f.*). ~-matter *n.*
contenu *m.* ~ to, soumis à; (*liable to,
dependent on*) sujet à.

subject[2] /səb'dʒekt/ *v.t.* soumettre.
~ion /-kʃn/ *n.* soumission *f.*

subjective /səb'dʒektɪv/ *a.* subjectif.

subjunctive /səb'dʒʌŋktɪv/ *a.* & *n.*
subjonctif (*m.*).

sublet /sʌb'let/ *v.t.* sous-louer.

sublime /sə'blaɪm/ *a.* sublime.

submarine /sʌbmə'ri:n/ *n.* sousmarin *m.*

submerge /səb'mɜ:dʒ/ *v.t.* submerger.
—*v.i.* plonger.

submissive /səb'mɪsɪv/ *a.* soumis.

submit /səb'mɪt/ *v.t./i.* (*p.t.* submitted)
(se) soumettre (to, à). ~ssion *n.*
soumission *f.*

subordinate[1] /sə'bɔ:dɪnət/ *a.* subalterne;
(*gram.*) subordonné. —*n.* subor-
donné(e) *m.* (*f.*).

subordinate[2] /sə'bɔ:dɪneɪt/ *v.t.* subor-
donner (to, à).

subpoena /səb'pi:nə/ *n.* (*pl.* -as) (*jurid.*)
citation *f.*, assignation *f.*

subroutine /'sʌbru:ti:n/ *n.* sous-
programme *m.*

subscribe /səb'skraɪb/ *v.t./i.* verser (de
l'argent) (to, à). ~ to, (*loan, theory*)
souscrire à; (*newspaper*) s'abonner à,
être abonné à. ~r /-ə(r)/ *n.* abonné(e)
m. (*f.*).

subscription /səb'skrɪpʃn/ *n.* souscrip-
tion *f.*; abonnement *m.*; (*membership
dues*) cotisation *f.*

subsequent /'sʌbsɪkwənt/ *a.* (*later*)
ultérieur; (*next*) suivant. ~ly *adv.* par la
suite.

subside /səb'saɪd/ *v.i.* (*land etc.*)
s'affaisser; (*flood, wind*) baisser. ~nce
/-əns/ *n.* affaissement *m.*

subsidiary /səb'sɪdɪərɪ/ *a.* accessoire.
—*n.* (*comm.*) filiale *f.*

subsidy /'sʌbsədɪ/ *n.* subvention *f.* ~ize
/-ɪdaɪz/ *v.t.* subventionner.

subsist /səb'sɪst/ *v.i.* subsister. ~ence *n.*
subsistance *f.*

substance /'sʌbstəns/ *n.* substance *f.*

substandard /sʌb'stændəd/ *a.* de qualité
inférieure.

substantial /səb'stænʃl/ *a.* considérable;
(*meal*) substantiel. ~ly *adv.* con-
sidérablement.

substantiate /səb'stænʃɪeɪt/ *v.t.* justifier,
prouver.

substitut|e /ˈsʌbstɪtjuːt/ n. succédané m.; (*person*) remplaçant(e) m. (*f.*). —v.t. substituer (**for,** à). **~ion** /-ˈtjuːʃn/ n. substitution f.

subterfuge /ˈsʌbtəfjuːdʒ/ n. subterfuge m.

subterranean /sʌbtəˈreɪnɪən/ a. souterrain.

subtitle /ˈsʌbtaɪtl/ n. sous-titre m.

subtle /ˈsʌtl/ a. (**-er, -est**) subtil. **~ty** n. subtilité f.

subtotal /sʌbˈtəʊtl/ n. total partiel m.

subtract /səbˈtrækt/ v.t. soustraire. **~ion** /-kʃn/ n. soustraction f.

suburb /ˈsʌbɜːb/ n. faubourg m., banlieue f. **~s,** banlieue f. **~an** /səˈbɜːbən/ a. de banlieue.

suburbia /səˈbɜːbɪə/ n. la banlieue.

subversive /səbˈvɜːsɪv/ a. subversif.

subver|t /səbˈvɜːt/ v.t. renverser. **~sion** /-ʃn/ n. subversion f.

subway /ˈsʌbweɪ/ n. passage souterrain m.; (*Amer.*) métro m.

succeed /səkˈsiːd/ v.i. réussir (**in doing,** à faire). —v.t. (*follow*) succéder à. **~ing** a. suivant.

success /səkˈses/ n. succès m., réussite f.

successful /səkˈsesfl/ a. réussi, couronné de succès; (*favourable*) heureux; (*in exam*) reçu. **be ~ in doing,** réussir à faire. **~ly** adv. avec succès.

succession /səkˈseʃn/ n. succession f. **in ~,** de suite.

successive /səkˈsesɪv/ a. successif. **six ~ days,** six jours consécutifs.

successor /səkˈsesə(r)/ n. successeur m.

succinct /səkˈsɪŋkt/ a. succinct.

succulent /ˈsʌkjʊlənt/ a. succulent.

succumb /səˈkʌm/ v.i. succomber.

such /sʌtʃ/ a. & pron. tel(le), tel(le)s; (*so much*) tant (de). —adv. si. **~ a book**/*etc.*, un tel livre/*etc.* **~ books**/*etc.*, de tels livres/*etc.* **~ courage**/*etc.*, tant de courage/*etc.* **~ a big house,** une si grande maison. **~ as,** comme, tel que. **as ~,** en tant que tel. **there's no ~ thing,** ça n'existe pas. **~-and-such** a. tel ou tel.

suck /sʌk/ v.t. sucer. **~ in** or **up,** aspirer. **~er** n. (*rubber pad*) ventouse f.; (*person: sl.*) dupe f.

suction /ˈsʌkʃn/ n. succion f.

sudden /ˈsʌdn/ a. soudain, subit. **all of a ~,** tout à coup. **~ly** adv. subitement, brusquement. **~ness** n. soudaineté f.

suds /sʌdz/ n. pl. (*froth*) mousse de savon f.

sue /suː/ v.t. (*pres. p.* **suing**) poursuivre (en justice).

suede /sweɪd/ n. daim m.

suet /ˈsuːɪt/ n. graisse de rognon f.

suffer /ˈsʌfə(r)/ v.t./i. souffrir; (*loss, attack, etc.*) subir. **~er** n. victime f., malade m./f. **~ing** n. souffrance(s) f. (*pl.*).

suffice /səˈfaɪs/ v.i. suffire.

sufficient /səˈfɪʃnt/ a. (*enough*) suffisamment de; (*big enough*) suffisant. **~ly** adv. suffisamment.

suffix /ˈsʌfɪks/ n. suffixe m.

suffocat|e /ˈsʌfəkeɪt/ v.t./i. suffoquer. **~ion** /-ˈkeɪʃn/ n. suffocation f.; (*med.*) asphyxie f.

suffused /səˈfjuːzd/ a. **~ with,** (*light, tears*) baigné de.

sugar /ˈʃʊgə(r)/ n. sucre m. —v.t. sucrer. **~y** a. sucré.

suggest /səˈdʒest/ v.t. suggérer. **~ion** /-tʃn/ n. suggestion f.

suggestive /səˈdʒestɪv/ a. suggestif. **be ~ of,** suggérer.

suicid|e /ˈsuːɪsaɪd/ n. suicide m. **commit ~e,** se suicider. **~al** /-ˈsaɪdl/ a. suicidaire.

suit /suːt/ n. costume m.; (*woman's*) tailleur m.; (*cards*) couleur f. —v.t. convenir à; (*of garment, style, etc.*) aller à; (*adapt*) adapter. **~ability** n. (*of action etc.*) à-propos m.; (*of candidate*) aptitude(s) f. (*pl.*). **~able** a. qui convient (**for,** à), convenable. **~ably** adv. convenablement. **~ed** a. (**well**) **~ed,** (*matched*) bien assorti. **~ed to,** fait pour, apte à.

suitcase /ˈsuːtkeɪs/ n. valise f.

suite /swiːt/ n. (*rooms, retinue*) suite f.; (*furniture*) mobilier m.

suitor /ˈsuːtə(r)/ n. soupirant m.

sulfur /ˈsʌlfər/ n. (*Amer.*) = **sulphur.**

sulk /sʌlk/ v.i. bouder. **~y** a. boudeur, maussade.

sullen /ˈsʌlən/ a. maussade. **~ly** adv. d'un air maussade.

sulphur /ˈsʌlfə(r)/ n. soufre m. **~ic** /-ˈfjʊərɪk/ a. **~ic acid,** acide sulfurique m.

sultan /ˈsʌltən/ n. sultan m.

sultana /sʌlˈtɑːnə/ n. raisin de Smyrne m., raisin sec m.

sultry /ˈsʌltrɪ/ a. (**-ier, -iest**) étouffant, lourd; (*fig.*) sensuel.

sum /sʌm/ n. somme f.; (*in arithmetic*) calcul m. —v.t./i. (*p.t.* **summed**). **~ up,** résumer, récapituler; (*assess*) évaluer.

summar|y /ˈsʌmərɪ/ n. résumé m. —a. sommaire. **~ize** v.t. résumer.

summer /ˈsʌmə(r)/ n. été m. —a. d'été. **~-time** n. (*season*) été m. **~y** a. estival.

summit /'sʌmɪt/ *n.* sommet *m.* ∼ **(conference),** (*pol.*) (conférence *f.* au) sommet *m.*

summon /'sʌmən/ *v.t.* appeler; (*meeting, s.o. to meeting*) convoquer. ∼ **up,** (*strength, courage, etc.*) rassembler.

summons /'sʌmənz/ *n.* (*jurid.*) assignation *f.* —*v.t.* assigner.

sump /sʌmp/ *n.* (*auto.*) carter *m.*

sumptuous /'sʌmptʃʊəs/ *a.* somptueux, luxueux.

sun /sʌn/ *n.* soleil *m.* —*v.t.* (*p.t.* **sunned**) ∼ **o.s.,** se chauffer au soleil. ∼**-glasses** *n. pl.* lunettes de soleil *f. pl.* ∼**-roof** *n.* toit ouvrant *m.* ∼**-tan** *n.* bronzage *m.* ∼**-tanned** *a.* bronzé.

sunbathe /'sʌnbeɪð/ *v.i.* prendre un bain de soleil.

sunburn /'sʌnbɜːn/ *n.* coup de soleil *m.* ∼**t** *a.* brûlé par le soleil.

Sunday /'sʌndɪ/ *n.* dimanche *m.* ∼ **school,** catéchisme *m.*

sundial /'sʌndaɪəl/ *n.* cadran solaire *m.*

sundown /'sʌndaʊn/ *n.* = **sunset.**

sundr|y /'sʌndrɪ/ *a.* divers. ∼**ies** *n. pl.* articles divers *m. pl.* **all and** ∼**y,** tout le monde.

sunflower /'sʌnflaʊə(r)/ *n.* tournesol *m.*

sung /sʌŋ/ *see* **sing.**

sunk /sʌŋk/ *see* **sink.**

sunken /'sʌŋkən/ *a.* (*ship etc.*) submergé; (*eyes*) creux.

sunlight /'sʌnlaɪt/ *n.* soleil *m.*

sunny /'sʌnɪ/ *a.* (**-ier, -iest**) (*room, day, etc.*) ensoleillé.

sunrise /'sʌnraɪz/ *n.* lever du soleil *m.*

sunset /'sʌnset/ *n.* coucher du soleil *m.*

sunshade /'sʌnʃeɪd/ *n.* (*lady's*) ombrelle *f.*; (*awning*) parasol *m.*

sunshine /'sʌnʃaɪn/ *n.* soleil *m.*

sunstroke /'sʌnstrəʊk/ *n.* insolation *f.*

super /'suːpə(r)/ *a.* (*sl.*) formidable.

superb /suː'pɜːb/ *a.* superbe.

supercilious /suːpə'sɪlɪəs/ *a.* hautain, dédaigneux.

superficial /suːpə'fɪʃl/ *a.* superficiel. ∼**ity** /-ɪ'ælətɪ/ *n.* caractère superficiel *m.* ∼**ly** *adv.* superficiellement.

superfluous /suː'pɜːflʊəs/ *a.* superflu.

superhuman /suːpə'hjuːmən/ *a.* surhumain.

superimpose /suːpərɪm'pəʊz/ *v.t.* superposer (on, à).

superintendent /suːpərɪn'tendənt/ *n.* direct|eur, -trice *m.*, *f.*; (*of police*) commissaire *m.*

superior /suː'pɪərɪə(r)/ *a.* & *n.* supérieur(e) (*m.* (*f.*)). ∼**ity** /-'ɒrətɪ/ *n.* supériorité *f.*

superlative /suː'pɜːlətɪv/ *a.* suprême. —*n.* (*gram.*) superlatif *m.*

superman /'suːpəmæn/ *n.* (*pl.* **-men**) surhomme *m.*

supermarket /'suːpəmɑːkɪt/ *n.* supermarché *m.*

supernatural /suːpə'nætʃrəl/ *a.* surnaturel.

superpower /'suːpəpaʊə(r)/ *n.* superpuissance *f.*

supersede /suːpə'siːd/ *v.t.* remplacer, supplanter.

supersonic /suːpə'sɒnɪk/ *a.* supersonique.

superstiti|on /suːpə'stɪʃn/ *n.* superstition *f.* ∼**ous** *a.* superstitieux.

superstore /'suːpəstɔː(r)/ *n.* hypermarché *m.*

supertanker /'suːpətæŋkə(r)/ *n.* pétrolier géant *m.*

supervis|e /'suːpəvaɪz/ *v.t.* surveiller, diriger. ∼**ion** /-'vɪʒn/ *n.* surveillance *f.* ∼**or** *n.* surveillant(e) *m.* (*f.*); (*shop*) chef de rayon *m.*; (*firm*) chef de service *m.* ∼**ory** /-'vaɪzərɪ/ *a.* de surveillance.

supper /'sʌpə(r)/ *n.* dîner *m.*; (*late at night*) souper *m.*

supple /'sʌpl/ *a.* souple.

supplement[1] /'sʌplɪmənt/ *n.* supplément *m.* ∼**ary** /-'mentrɪ/ *a.* supplémentaire.

supplement[2] /'sʌplɪment/ *v.t.* compléter.

supplier /sə'plaɪə(r)/ *n.* fournisseur *m.*

suppl|y /sə'plaɪ/ *v.t.* fournir; (*equip*) pourvoir; (*feed*) alimenter (with, en). —*n.* provision *f.*; (*of gas etc.*) alimentation *f.* ∼**ies,** (*food*) vivres *m. pl.*; (*material*) fournitures *f. pl.* ∼**y teacher,** (*professeur*) suppléant(e) *m.* (*f.*).

support /sə'pɔːt/ *v.t.* soutenir; (*family*) assurer la subsistance de; (*endure*) supporter. —*n.* soutien *m.*, appui *m.*; (*techn.*) support *m.* ∼**er** *n.* partisan(e) *m.* (*f.*); (*sport*) supporter *m.* ∼**ive** *a.* qui soutient et encourage.

suppos|e /sə'pəʊz/ *v.t./i.* supposer. **be** ∼**ed to do,** être censé faire, devoir faire. ∼**ing he comes,** supposons qu'il vienne. ∼**ition** /sʌpə'zɪʃn/ *n.* supposition *f.*

supposedly /sə'pəʊzɪdlɪ/ *adv.* soi-disant, prétendument.

suppress /sə'pres/ *v.t.* (*put an end to*) supprimer; (*restrain*) réprimer; (*stifle*) étouffer. ∼**ion** /-ʃn/ *n.* suppression *f.*; répression *f.*

suprem|e /suː'priːm/ *a.* suprême. ∼**acy** /-eməsɪ/ *n.* suprématie *f.*

surcharge /'sɜːtʃɑːdʒ/ n. prix supplémentaire m.; (tax) surtaxe f.; (on stamp) surcharge f.

sure /ʃɔː(r)/ a. (-er, -est) sûr. —adv. (Amer., fam.) pour sûr. **make ~ of,** s'assurer de. **make ~ that,** vérifier que. **~ly** adv. sûrement.

surety /ʃɔːrətɪ/ n. caution f.

surf /sɜːf/ n. (waves) ressac m. **~ing** n. surf m.

surface /'sɜːfɪs/ n. surface f. —a. superficiel. —v.t. revêtir. —v.i. faire surface; (fig.) réapparaître. **~ mail,** courrier maritime m.

surfboard /'sɜːfbɔːd/ n. planche de surf f.

surfeit /'sɜːfɪt/ n. excès m. (**of,** de).

surge /sɜːdʒ/ v.i. (of crowd) déferler; (of waves) s'enfler; (increase) monter. —n. (wave) vague f.; (rise) montée f.

surgeon /'sɜːdʒən/ n. chirurgien m.

surg|ery /'sɜːdʒərɪ/ n. chirurgie f.; (office) cabinet m.; (session) consultation f. **need ~ery,** devoir être opéré. **~ical** a. chirurgical. **~ical spirit,** alcool à 90 degrés m.

surly /'sɜːlɪ/ a. (-ier, -iest) bourru.

surmise /sə'maɪz/ v.t. conjecturer. —n. conjecture f.

surmount /sə'maʊnt/ v.t. (overcome, cap) surmonter.

surname /'sɜːneɪm/ n. nom de famille m.

surpass /sə'pɑːs/ v.t. surpasser.

surplus /'sɜːpləs/ n. surplus m. —a. en surplus.

surpris|e /sə'praɪz/ n. surprise f. —v.t. surprendre. **~ed** a. surpris (at, de). **~ing** a. surprenant. **~ingly** adv. étonnamment.

surrender /sə'rendə(r)/ v.i. se rendre. —v.t. (hand over) remettre; (mil.) rendre. —n. (mil.) reddition f.; (of passport etc.) remise f.

surreptitious /sʌrəp'tɪʃəs/ a. subreptice, furtif.

surround /sə'raʊnd/ v.t. entourer; (mil.) encercler. **~ing** a. environnant. **~ings** n. pl. environs m. pl.; (setting) cadre m.

surveillance /sɜː'veɪləns/ n. surveillance f.

survey[1] /sə'veɪ/ v.t. (review) passer en revue; (inquire into) enquêter sur; (building) inspecter. **~or** n. expert (géomètre) m.

survey[2] /'sɜːveɪ/ n. (inquiry) enquête f.; inspection f.; (general view) vue d'ensemble f.

survival /sə'vaɪvl/ n. survie f.; (relic) vestige m.

surviv|e /sə'vaɪv/ v.t./i. survivre (à). **~or** n. survivant(e) m. (f.).

susceptib|le /sə'septəbl/ a. sensible (**to,** à). **~le to,** (prone to) prédisposé à. **~ility** /-'bɪlətɪ/ n. sensibilité f.; prédisposition f.

suspect[1] /sə'spekt/ v.t. soupçonner; (doubt) douter de.

suspect[2] /'sʌspekt/ n. & a. suspect(e) (m. (f.)).

suspen|d /sə'spend/ v.t. (hang, stop) suspendre; (licence) retirer provisoirement. **~ded sentence,** condamnation avec sursis f. **~sion** n. suspension f.; retrait provisoire m. **~sion bridge,** pont suspendu m.

suspender /sə'spendə(r)/ n. jarretelle f. **~s,** (braces: Amer.) bretelles f. pl. **~ belt,** porte-jarretelles m.

suspense /sə'spens/ n. attente f.; (in book etc.) suspense m.

suspicion /sə'spɪʃn/ n. soupçon m.; (distrust) méfiance f.

suspicious /sə'spɪʃəs/ a. soupçonneux; (causing suspicion) suspect. **be ~ of,** (distrust) se méfier de. **~ly** adv. de façon suspecte.

sustain /sə'steɪn/ v.t. supporter; (effort etc.) soutenir; (suffer) subir.

sustenance /'sʌstɪnəns/ n. (food) nourriture f.; (quality) valeur nutritive f.

swab /swɒb/ n. (pad) tampon m.

swagger /'swægə(r)/ v.i. (walk) se pavaner, parader.

swallow[1] /'swɒləʊ/ v.t./i. avaler. **~ up,** (absorb, engulf) engloutir.

swallow[2] /'swɒləʊ/ n. hirondelle f.

swam /swæm/ see **swim.**

swamp /swɒmp/ n. marais m. —v.t. (flood, overwhelm) submerger. **~y** a. marécageux.

swan /swɒn/ n. cygne m. **~-song** n. (fig.) chant du cygne m.

swank /swæŋk/ n. (behaviour: fam.) épate f., esbroufe f.; (person: fam.) crâneur, -se m., f. —v.i. (show off: fam.) crâner.

swap /swɒp/ v.t./i. (p.t. **swapped**) (fam.) échanger. —n. (fam.) échange m.

swarm /swɔːm/ n. (of insects, people) essaim m. —v.i. fourmiller. **~ into** or **round,** (crowd) envahir.

swarthy /'swɔːðɪ/ a. (-ier, -iest) noiraud; (complexion) basané.

swastika /'swɒstɪkə/ n. (Nazi) croix gammée f.

swat /swɒt/ v.t. (p.t. **swatted**) (fly etc.) écraser.

sway /sweɪ/ v.t./i. (se) balancer; (influence) influencer. —n. balancement m.; (rule) empire m.

swear /sweə(r)/ *v.t./i.* (*p.t.* **swore,** *p.p.*
sworn) jurer (**to sth.,** de qch.). ～ **at,**
injurier. ～ **by sth.,** (*fam.*) ne jurer que
par qch. ～**-word** *n.* juron *m.*

sweat /swet/ *n.* sueur *f.* —*v.i.* suer. ～-
shirt *n.* sweat-shirt *m.* ～**y** *a.* en sueur.

sweater /'swetə(r)/ *n.* pull-over *m.*

swede /swi:d/ *n.* rutabaga *m.*

Swed|e /swi:d/ *n.* Suédois(e) *m.* (*f.*).
～**en** *n.* Suède *f.* ～**ish** *a.* suédois; *n.*
(*lang.*) suédois *m.*

sweep /swi:p/ *v.t./i.* (*p.t.* **swept**) balayer;
(*carry away*) emporter, entraîner;
(*chimney*) ramoner. —*n.* coup de balai
m.; (*curve*) courbe *f.*; (*mouvement*)
geste *m.*, mouvement *m.*; (*for chim-
neys*) ramonneur *m.* ～ **by,** passer
rapidement *or* majestueusement. ～
out, balayer. ～**er** *n.* (*for carpet*) balai
mécanique *m.*; (*football*) arrière volant
m. ～**ing** *a.* (*gesture*) large; (*action*) qui
va loin; (*statement*) trop général.

sweet /swi:t/ *a.* (**-er, -est**) (*not sour,
pleasant*) doux; (*not savoury*) sucré;
(*charming*: *fam.*) gentil. —*n.* bonbon
m.; (*dish*) dessert *m.*; (*person*) chéri(e)
m. (*f.*). **have a ～ tooth,** aimer les
sucreries. ～ **corn,** maïs *m.* ～ **pea,** pois
de senteur *m.* ～ **shop,** confiserie *f.* ～**ly**
adv. gentiment. ～**ness** *n.* douceur *f.*;
goût sucré *m.*

sweeten /'swi:tn/ *v.t.* sucrer; (*fig.*)
adoucir. ～**er** *n.* édulcorant *m.*

sweetheart /'swi:tha:t/ *n.* petit(e) ami(e)
m. (*f.*); (*term of endearment*) chéri(e)
m. (*f.*).

swell /swel/ *v.t./i.* (*p.t.* **swelled,** *p.p.*
swollen *or* **swelled**) (*increase*) grossir;
(*expand*) (se) gonfler; (*of hand, face*)
enfler. —*n.* (*of sea*) houle *f.* —*a.*
(*fam.*) formidable. ～**ing** *n.* (*med.*)
enflure *f.*

swelter /'sweltə(r)/ *v.i.* étouffer. ～**ing** *a.*
étouffant.

swept /swept/ *see* **sweep**.

swerve /swɜ:v/ *v.i.* faire un écart.

swift /swift/ *a.* (**-er, -est**) rapide. —*n.*
(*bird*) martinet *m.* ～**ly** *adv.* rapidement.
～**ness** *n.* rapidité *f.*

swig /swig/ *v.t.* (*p.t.* **swigged**) (*drink*:
fam.) lamper. —*n.* (*fam.*) lampée *f.*,
coup *m.*

swill /swil/ *v.t.* rincer; (*drink*) lamper.
—*n.* (*pig-food*) pâtée *f.*

swim /swim/ *v.i.* (*p.t.* **swam,** *p.p.* **swum,**
pres. p. **swimming**) nager; (*be dizzy*)
tourner. —*v.t.* traverser à la nage;
(*distance*) nager. —*n.* baignade *f.* **go
for a ～,** aller se baigner. ～**mer** *n.*

nageur, -se *m.*, *f.* ～**ming** *n.* natation *f.*
～**ming-bath,** ～**ming-pool** *ns.* piscine
f. ～**-suit** *n.* maillot (de bain) *m.*

swindle /'swindl/ *v.t.* escroquer. —*n.*
escroquerie *f.* ～**r** /-ə(r)/ *n.* escroc *m.*

swine /swain/ *n. pl.* (*pigs*) pourceaux *m.
pl.* —*n. invar.* (*person*: *fam.*) salaud *m.*

swing /swiŋ/ *v.t./i.* (*p.t.* **swung**) (se)
balancer; (*turn round*) tourner; (*of
pendulum*) osciller. —*n.* balancement
m.; (*seat*) balançoire *f.*; (*of opinion*)
revirement *m.* (**towards,** en faveur de);
(*mus.*) rythme *m.* **be in full ～,** battre
son plein. ～ **round,** (*of person*) se
retourner.

swingeing /'swindʒiŋ/ *a.* écrasant.

swipe /swaip/ *v.t.* (*hit*: *fam.*) frapper;
(*steal*: *fam.*) piquer. —*n.* (*hit*: *fam.*)
grand coup *m.*

swirl /swɜ:l/ *v.i.* tourbillonner. —*n.*
tourbillon *m.*

swish /swiʃ/ *v.i.* (*hiss*) siffler, cingler
l'air. —*a.* (*fam.*) chic *invar.*

Swiss /swis/ *a.* suisse. —*n. invar.*
Suisse(sse) *m.* (*f.*).

switch /switʃ/ *n.* bouton (électrique) *m.*,
interrupteur *m.*; (*shift*) changement *m.*,
revirement *m.* —*v.t.* (*transfer*) transférer; (*exchange*) échanger (**for,**
contre); (*reverse positions of*) changer
de place. ～ **trains**/*etc.*, (*change*)
changer de train/*etc.* —*v.i.* (*go over*)
passer. ～ **off,** éteindre. ～ **on,** mettre,
allumer.

switchback /'switʃbæk/ *n.* montagnes
russes *f. pl.*

switchboard /'switʃbɔ:d/ *n.* (*telephone*)
standard *m.*

Switzerland /'switsələnd/ *n.* Suisse *f.*

swivel /'swivl/ *v.t./i.* (*p.t.* **swivelled**)
(faire) pivoter.

swollen /'swəʊlən/ *see* **swell**.

swoon /swu:n/ *v.i.* se pâmer.

swoop /swu:p/ *v.i.* (*bird*) fondre;
(*police*) faire une descente, foncer. —*n.*
(*police raid*) descente *f.*

sword /sɔ:d/ *n.* épée *f.*

swore /swɔ:(r)/ *see* **swear**.

sworn /swɔ:n/ *see* **swear**. —*a.* (*enemy*)
juré; (*ally*) dévoué.

swot /swɒt/ *v.t./i.* (*p.t.* **swotted**) (*study*:
sl.) bûcher. —*n.* (*sl.*) bûcheur, -se *m.*, *f.*

swum /swʌm/ *see* **swim**.

swung /swʌŋ/ *see* **swing**.

sycamore /'sikəmɔ:(r)/ *n.* (*maple*)
sycomore *m.*; (*Amer.*) platane *m.*

syllable /'siləbl/ *n.* syllabe *f.*

syllabus /'siləbəs/ *n.* (*pl.* **-uses**) (*schol.,
univ.*) programme *m.*

symbol /'sɪmbl/ *n.* symbole *m.* ~**ic(al)** /-'bɒlɪk(l)/ *a.* symbolique. ~**ism** *n.* symbolisme *m.*

symbolize /'sɪmbəlaɪz/ *v.t.* symboliser.

symmetr|y /'sɪmətrɪ/ *n.* symétrie *f.* ~**ical** /sɪ'metrɪkl/ *a.* symétrique.

sympathize /'sɪmpəθaɪz/ *v.i.* ~ **with**, (*pity*) plaindre; (*fig.*) comprendre les sentiments de. ~**r** /ə(r)/ *n.* sympathisant(e) *m.* (*f.*).

sympath|y /'sɪmpəθɪ/ *n.* (*pity*) compassion *f.*; (*fig.*) compréhension *f.*; (*solidarity*) solidarité *f.*; (*condolences*) condoléances *f. pl.* **be in** ~**y with**, comprendre, être en accord avec. ~**etic** /-'θetɪk/ *a.* compatissant; (*fig.*) compréhensif. ~**etically** /-'θetɪklɪ/ *adv.* avec compassion; (*fig.*) avec compréhension.

symphon|y /'sɪmfənɪ/ *n.* symphonie *f.* —*a.* symphonique. ~**ic** /-'fɒnɪk/ *a.* symphonique.

symposium /sɪm'pəʊzɪəm/ *n.* (*pl.* -**ia**) symposium *m.*

symptom /'sɪmptəm/ *n.* symptôme *m.* ~**atic** /-'mætɪk/ *a.* symptomatique (**of**, de).

synagogue /'sɪnəgɒg/ *n.* synagogue *f.*

synchronize /'sɪŋkrənaɪz/ *v.t.* synchroniser.

syndicate /'sɪndɪkət/ *n.* syndicat *m.*

syndrome /'sɪndrəʊm/ *n.* syndrome *m.*

synonym /'sɪnənɪm/ *n.* synonyme *m.* ~**ous** /sɪ'nɒnɪməs/ *a.* synonyme.

synopsis /sɪ'nɒpsɪs/ *n.* (*pl.* -**opses** /-siːz/) résumé *m.*

syntax /'sɪntæks/ *n.* syntaxe *f.*

synthesis /'sɪnθəsɪs/ *n.* (*pl.* -**theses** /-siːz/) synthèse *f.*

synthetic /sɪn'θetɪk/ *a.* synthétique.

syphilis /'sɪfɪlɪs/ *n.* syphilis *f.*

Syria /'sɪrɪə/ *n.* Syrie *f.* ~**n** *a.* & *n.* syrien(ne) (*m.* (*f.*)).

syringe /sɪ'rɪndʒ/ *n.* seringue *f.*

syrup /'sɪrəp/ *n.* (*liquid*) sirop *m.*; (*treacle*) mélasse raffinée *f.* ~**y** *a.* sirupeux.

system /'sɪstəm/ *n.* système *m.*; (*body*) organisme *m.*; (*order*) méthode *f.* ~**s analyst**, analyste-programmeulr, -se *m.*, *f.* ~**s disk**, disque système *m.*

systematic /sɪstə'mætɪk/ *a.* systématique.

T

tab /tæb/ *n.* (*flap*) languette *f.*, patte *f.*;

(*loop*) attache *f.*; (*label*) étiquette *f.*; (*Amer.*, *fam.*) addition *f.* **keep** ~**s on**, (*fam.*) surveiller.

table /'teɪbl/ *n.* table *f.* —*v.t.* présenter; (*postpone*) ajourner. —*a.* (*lamp*, *wine*) de table. **at** ~, à table. **lay** *or* **set the** ~, mettre la table. ~**-cloth** *n.* nappe *f.* ~**mat** *n.* dessous-de-plat *m. invar.*; (*cloth*) set *m.* ~ **of contents**, table des matières *f.* ~ **tennis**, ping-pong *m.*

tablespoon /'teɪblspuːn/ *n.* cuiller à soupe *f.* ~**ful** *n.* (*pl.* ~**fuls**) cuillerée à soupe *f.*

tablet /'tæblɪt/ *n.* (*of stone*) plaque *f.*; (*drug*) comprimé *m.*

tabloid /'tæblɔɪd/ *n.* tabloïd *m.* **the** ~ **press**, la presse populaire.

taboo /tə'buː/ *n.* & *a.* tabou (*m.*).

tabulator /'tæbjʊleɪtə(r)/ *n.* (*on typewriter*) tabulateur *m.*

tacit /'tæsɪt/ *a.* tacite.

taciturn /'tæsɪtɜːn/ *a.* taciturne.

tack /tæk/ *n.* (*nail*) broquette *f.*; (*stitch*) point de bâti *m.*; (*course of action*) voie *f.* —*v.t.* (*nail*) clouer; (*stitch*) bâtir; (*add*) ajouter. —*v.i.* (*naut.*) louvoyer.

tackle /'tækl/ *n.* équipement *m.*, matériel *m.*; (*football*) plaquage *m.* —*v.t.* (*problem etc.*) s'attaquer à; (*football player*) plaquer.

tacky /'tækɪ/ *a.* (-**ier**, -**iest**) poisseux, pas sec; (*shabby*, *mean*: *Amer.*) moche.

tact /tækt/ *n.* tact *m.* ~**ful** *a.* plein de tact. ~**fully** *adv.* avec tact. ~**less** *a.* qui manque de tact. ~**lessly** *adv.* sans tact.

tactic /'tæktɪk/ *n.* tactique *f.* ~**s** *n.* & *n. pl.* tactique *f.* ~**al** *a.* tactique.

tactile /'tæktaɪl/ *a.* tactile.

tadpole /'tædpəʊl/ *n.* têtard *m.*

tag /tæg/ *n.* (*label*) étiquette *f.*; (*end piece*) bout *m.*; (*phrase*) cliché *m.* —*v.t.* (*p.t.* **tagged**) étiqueter; (*join*) ajouter. —*v.i.* ~ **along**, (*fam.*) suivre.

tail /teɪl/ *n.* queue *f.*; (*of shirt*) pan *m.* ~**s**, (*coat*) habit *m.* ~**s!**, (*tossing coin*) pile! —*v.t.* (*follow*) filer. —*v.i.* ~ **away** *or* **off**, diminuer. ~**-back** *n.* (*traffic*) bouchon *m.* ~**-end** *n.* fin *f.*, bout *m.* ~**gate** *n.* hayon arrière *m.*

tailcoat /'teɪlkəʊt/ *n.* habit *m.*

tailor /'teɪlə(r)/ *n.* tailleur *m.* —*v.t.* (*garment*) façonner (*fig.*) adapter. ~**made** *a.* fait sur mesure. ~**-made for**, (*fig.*) fait pour.

tainted /'teɪntɪd/ *a.* (*infected*) infecté; (*decayed*) gâté; (*fig.*) souillé.

take /teɪk/ *v.t./i.* (*p.t.* **took**, *p.p.* **taken**) prendre; (*carry*) (ap)porter (**to**, à);

(*escort*) accompagner, amener; (*contain*) contenir; (*tolerate*) supporter; (*prize*) remporter; (*exam*) passer; (*choice*) faire; (*precedence*) avoir. ~ **sth. from s.o.**, prendre qch. à qn. ~ **sth. from a place**, prendre qch. d'un endroit. ~ **s.o. home**, ramener qn. chez lui. **be ~n by** *or* **with**, être impressionné par. **be ~n ill**, tomber malade. **it ~s time/courage**/*etc.* **to**, il faut du temps/du courage/*etc.* pour. ~ **after**, ressembler à. ~ **apart**, démonter. ~ **away**, (*object*) emporter; (*person*) emmener; (*remove*) enlever (**from**, à). **~-away** *n.* (*meal*) plat à emporter *m.*; (*shop*) restaurant qui fait des plats à emporter *m.* ~ **back**, reprendre; (*return*) rendre; (*accompany*) raccompagner; (*statement*) retirer. ~ **down**, (*object*) descendre; (*notes*) prendre. ~ **in**, (*object*) rentrer; (*include*) inclure; (*cheat*) tromper; (*grasp*) saisir. ~ **it that**, supposer que. ~ **off** *v.t.* enlever; (*mimic*) imiter; *v.i.* (*aviat.*) décoller. **~-off** *n.* imitation *f.*; (*aviat.*) décollage *m.* ~ **on**, (*task, staff, passenger, etc.*) prendre; (*challenger*) relever le défi de. ~ **out**, sortir; (*stain etc.*) enlever. ~ **over** *v.t.* (*factory, country, etc.*) prendre la direction de; (*firm: comm.*) racheter; *v.i.* (*of dictator*) prendre le pouvoir. ~ **over from**, (*relieve*) prendre la relève de; (*succeed*) prendre la succession de; **~-over** *n.* (*pol.*) prise de pouvoir *f.*; (*comm.*) rachat *m.* ~ **part**, participer (**in**, à). ~ **place**, avoir lieu. ~ **sides**, prendre parti (**with**, pour). ~ **to**, se prendre d'amitié pour; (*activity*) prendre goût à. ~ **to doing**, se mettre à faire. ~ **up**, (*object*) monter; (*hobby*) se mettre à; (*occupy*) prendre; (*resume*) reprendre. ~ **up with**, se lier avec.

takings /'teɪkɪŋz/ *n. pl.* recette *f.*

talcum /'tælkəm/ *n.* talc *m.* ~ **powder**, talc *m.*

tale /teɪl/ *n.* conte *m.*; (*report*) récit *m.*; (*lie*) histoire *f.*

talent /'tælənt/ *n* talent *m* ~**ed** *a* doué, qui a du talent.

talk /tɔːk/ *v.t./i.* parler; (*say*) dire; (*chat*) bavarder. —*n.* conversation *f.*, entretien *m.*; (*words*) propos *m. pl.*; (*lecture*) exposé *m.* ~ **into doing**, persuader de faire. ~ **over**, discuter (de). **~-show** *n.* talk-show *m.* **~er** *n.* causeur, -se *m., f.* **~ing-to** *n.* (*fam.*) réprimande *f.*

talkative /'tɔːkətɪv/ *a.* bavard.

tall /tɔːl/ *a.* (**-er**, **-est**) (*high*) haut;

(*person*) grand. ~ **story**, (*fam.*) histoire invraisemblable *f.*

tallboy /'tɔːlbɔɪ/ *n.* commode *f.*

tally /'tælɪ/ *v.i.* correspondre (**with**, à), s'accorder (**with**, avec).

tambourine /tæmbə'riːn/ *n.* tambourin *m.*

tame /teɪm/ *a.* (**-er**, **-est**) apprivoisé; (*dull*) insipide. —*v.t.* apprivoiser; (*lion*) dompter. ~**r** /-ə(r)/ *n.* dompteur, -se *m., f.*

tamper /'tæmpə(r)/ *v.i.* ~ **with**, toucher à, tripoter; (*text*) altérer.

tampon /'tæmpɒn/ *n.* (*med.*) tampon hygiénique *m.*

tan /tæn/ *v.t./i.* (*p.t.* **tanned**) bronzer; (*hide*) tanner. —*n.* bronzage *m.* —*a.* marron clair *invar.*

tandem /'tændəm/ *n* (*bicycle*) tandem *m.* **in ~**, en tandem.

tang /tæŋ/ *n.* (*taste*) saveur forte *f.*; (*smell*) odeur forte *f.*

tangent /'tændʒənt/ *n.* tangente *f.*

tangerine /tændʒə'riːn/ *n.* mandarine *f.*

tangible /'tændʒəbl/ *a.* tangible.

tangle /'tæŋgl/ *v.t.* enchevêtrer. —*n.* enchevêtrement *m.* **become ~d**, s'enchevêtrer.

tango /'tæŋgəʊ/ *n.* (*pl.* **-os**) tango *m.*

tank /tæŋk/ *n.* réservoir *m.*; (*vat*) cuve *f.*; (*for fish*) aquarium *m.*; (*mil.*) char *m.*, tank *m.*

tankard /'tæŋkəd/ *n.* chope *f.*

tanker /'tæŋkə(r)/ *n.* camionciterne *m.*; (*ship*) pétrolier *m.*

tantaliz|e /'tæntəlaɪz/ *v.t.* tourmenter. **~ing** *a.* tentant.

tantamount /'tæntəmaʊnt/ *a.* **be ~ to**, équivaloir à.

tantrum /'tæntrəm/ *n.* crise de colère *or* de rage *f.*

tap[1] /tæp/ *n.* (*for water etc.*) robinet *m.* —*v.t.* (*p.t.* **tapped**) (*resources*) exploiter; (*telephone*) mettre sur table d'écoute. **on ~**, (*fam.*) disponible.

tap[2] /tæp/ *v.t./i.* (*p.t.* **tapped**) frapper (doucement). —*n.* petit coup *m.* **~-dance** *n* claquettes *f pl*

tape /teɪp/ *n.* ruban *m.*; (*sticky*) ruban adhésif *m.* (**magnetic**) ~, bande (magnétique) *f.* —*v.t.* (*tie*) attacher; (*stick*) coller; (*record*) enregistrer. **~-measure** *n.* mètre (à) ruban *m.* **~-recorder**, magnétophone *m.*

taper /'teɪpə(r)/ *n.* (*for lighting*) bougie *f.* —*v.t./i.* (s')effiler. ~ **off**, (*diminish*) diminuer. **~ed**, **~ing** *adjs.* (*fingers etc.*) effilé, fuselé; (*trousers*) étroit du bas.

tapestry /'tæpɪstrɪ/ n. tapisserie f.

tapioca /tæpɪ'əʊkə/ n. tapioca m.

tar /tɑː(r)/ n. goudron m. —v.t. (p.t. **tarred**) goudronner.

tardy /'tɑːdɪ/ a. (**-ier, -iest**) (slow) lent; (belated) tardif.

target /'tɑːgɪt/ n. cible f.; (objective) objectif m. —v.t. prendre pour cible.

tariff /'tærɪf/ n. (charges) tarif m.; (on imports) tarif douanier m.

Tarmac /'tɑːmæk/ n. (P.) macadam (goudronné) m.; (runway) piste f.

tarnish /'tɑːnɪʃ/ v.t./i. (se) ternir.

tarpaulin /tɑː'pɔːlɪn/ n. bâche goudronnée f.

tarragon /'tærəgən/ n. estragon m.

tart[1] /tɑːt/ a. (**-er, -est**) acide.

tart[2] /tɑːt/ n. tarte f.; (prostitute; sl.) poule f. —v.t. ~ **up**, (pej., sl.) embellir (sans le moindre goût).

tartan /'tɑːtn/ n. tartan m. —a. écossais.

tartar /'tɑːtə(r)/ n. tartre m. ~ **sauce**, sauce tartare f.

task /tɑːsk/ n. tâche f., travail m. **take to** ~, réprimander. ~ **force**, détachement spécial m.

tassel /'tæsl/ n. gland m., pompon m.

taste /teɪst/ n. goût m. —v.t. (eat, enjoy) goûter; (try) goûter à; (perceive taste of) sentir le goût de. —v.i. ~ **of** or **like**, avoir un goût de. **have a** ~ **of**, (experience) goûter de. ~**less** a. sans goût; (fig.) de mauvais goût.

tasteful /'teɪstfl/ a. de bon goût. ~**ly** adv. avec goût.

tasty /'teɪstɪ/ a. (**-ier, -iest**) délicieux, savoureux.

tat /tæt/ see **tit**[2].

tatter|s /'tætəz/ n. pl. lambeaux m. pl. ~**ed** /'tætəd/ a. en lambeaux.

tattoo[1] /tə'tuː/ n. (mil.) spectacle militaire m.

tattoo[2] /tə'tuː/ v.t. tatouer. —n. tatouage m.

tatty /'tætɪ/ a. (**-ier, -iest**) (shabby: fam.) miteux, minable.

taught /tɔːt/ see **teach**.

taunt /tɔːnt/ v.t. railler. —n. raillerie f. ~**ing** a. railleur.

Taurus /'tɔːrəs/ n. le Taureau.

taut /tɔːt/ a. tendu.

tavern /'tævn/ n. taverne f.

tawdry /'tɔːdrɪ/ a. (**-ier, -iest**) (showy) tape-à-l'œil invar.

tax /tæks/ n. taxe f., impôt m.; (on income) impôt m. —v.t. imposer; (put to test: fig.) mettre à l'épreuve. ~**able** a. imposable. ~**ation** /-'seɪʃn/ n. imposition f.; (taxes) impôts m. pl.

~**-collector** n. percepteur m. ~**-deductible** a. déductible d'impôts. ~ **disc**, vignette f. ~**-free** a. exempt d'impôts. ~**ing** a. (fig.) éprouvant. ~ **haven** paradis fiscal m. ~ **inspector**, inspecteur des impôts m. ~ **relief**, dégrèvement fiscal m. ~ **return**, déclaration d'impôts f.

taxi /'tæksɪ/ n. (pl. **-is**) taxi m. —v.i. (p.t. **taxied**, pres. p. **taxiing**) (aviat.) rouler au sol. ~**-cab** n. taxi m. ~ **rank**, (Amer.) ~ **stand**, station de taxi f.

taxpayer /'tækspeɪə(r)/ n. contribuable m./f.

tea /tiː/ n. thé m.; (snack) goûter m. ~**-bag** n. sachet de thé m. ~**-break** n. pause-thé f. ~**-leaf** n. feuille de thé f. ~**-set** n. service à thé m. ~**-shop** n. salon de thé m. ~**-towel** n. torchon m.

teach /tiːtʃ/ v.t. (p.t. **taught**) apprendre (**s.o. sth.**, qch. à qn.); (in school) enseigner (**s.o. sth.**, qch. à qn.). —v.i. enseigner. ~**er** n. professeur m.; (primary) instituteur, -trice m., f.; (member of teaching profession) enseignant(e) m. (f.). ~**ing** n. enseignement m.; a. pédagogique; (staff) enseignant.

teacup /'tiːkʌp/ n. tasse à thé f.

teak /tiːk/ n. (wood) teck m.

team /tiːm/ n. équipe f.; (of animals) attelage m. —v.i. ~ **up**, faire équipe (**with**, avec). ~**-work** n. travail d'équipe m.

teapot /'tiːpɒt/ n. théière f.

tear[1] /teə(r)/ v.t./i. (p.t. **tore**, p.p. **torn**) (se) déchirer; (snatch) arracher (**from**, à); (rush) aller à toute vitesse. —n. déchirure f.

tear[2] /tɪə(r)/ n. larme f. **in** ~**s**, en larmes. ~**-gas** n. gaz lacrymogène m.

tearful /'tɪəfl/ a. (voice) larmoyant; (person) en larmes. ~**ly** adv. en pleurant, les larmes aux yeux.

tease /tiːz/ v.t. taquiner. —n. (person: fam.) taquin(e) m. (f.).

teaspoon /'tiːspuːn/ n. petite cuiller f. ~**ful** n. (pl. **-fuls**) cuillerée à café f.

teat /tiːt/ n. (of bottle, animal) tétine f.

technical /'teknɪkl/ a. technique. ~**ity** /-'kælətɪ/ n. détail technique m. ~**ly** adv. techniquement.

technician /tek'nɪʃn/ n. technicien(ne) m. (f.).

technique /tek'niːk/ n. technique f.

technolog|y /tek'nɒlədʒɪ/ n. technologie f. ~**ical** /-ə'lɒdʒɪkl/ a. technologique.

teddy /'tedɪ/ a. ~ **bear**, ours en peluche m.

tedious /'ti:dɪəs/ *a.* fastidieux.

tedium /'ti:dɪəm/ *n.* ennui *m.*

tee /ti:/ *n.* (*golf*) tee *m.*

teem[1] /ti:m/ *v.i.* (*swarm*) grouiller (**with**, de).

teem[2] /ti:m/ *v.i.* ~ (**with rain**), pleuvoir à torrents.

teenage /'ti:neɪdʒ/ *a.* (d')adolescent. ~d *a.* adolescent. ~r /-ə(r)/ *n.* adolescent(e) *m.* (*f.*).

teens /ti:nz/ *n. pl.* **in one's** ~, adolescent.

teeny /'ti:nɪ/ *a.* (**-ier, -iest**) (*tiny: fam.*) minuscule.

teeter /'ti:tə(r)/ *v.i.* chanceler.

teeth /ti:θ/ *see* **tooth**.

teeth|**e** /ti:ð/ *v.i.* faire ses dents. ~**ing troubles**, (*fig.*) difficultés initiales *f. pl.*

teetotaller /ti:'təʊtlə(r)/ *n.* personne qui ne boit pas d'alcool *f.*

telecommunications /telɪkəmju:nɪ'keɪʃnz/ *n. pl.* télécommunications *f. pl.*

telegram /'telɪgræm/ *n* télégramme *m*

telegraph /'telɪgrɑ:f/ *n.* télégraphe *m.* —*a.* télégraphique ~**ic** /-'græfɪk/ *a* télégraphique.

telepath|**y** /tɪ'lepəθɪ/ *n.* télépathie *f.* ~**ic** /telɪ'pæθɪk/ *a.* télépathique.

telephone /'telɪfəʊn/ *n.* téléphone *m.* —*v.t.* (*person*) téléphoner à; (*message*) téléphoner. —*v.i.* téléphoner. ~ **book**, annuaire *m.* ~**-box** *n.*, ~ **booth**, cabine téléphonique *f.* ~ **call**, coup de téléphone *m.* ~ **number**, numéro de téléphone *m.*

telephonist /tɪ'lefənɪst/ *n.* (*in exchange*) téléphoniste *m./f.*

telephoto /telɪ'fəʊtəʊ/ *a.* ~ **lens**, téléobjectif *m.*

telescop|**e** /'telɪskəʊp/ *n.* télescope *m.* —*v.t./i.* (se) télescoper. ~**ic** /-'skɒpɪk/ *a.* télescopique.

teletext /'telɪtekst/ *n.* télétexte *m.*

televise /'telɪvaɪz/ *v.t.* téléviser.

television /'telɪvɪʒn/ *n.* télévision *f.* ~ **set**, poste de télévision *m.*

telex /'teleks/ *n.* télex *m.* *v.t.* envoyer par télex.

tell /tel/ *v.t.* (*p.t.* **told**) dire (**s.o. sth.**, qch à qn.); (*story*) raconter; (*distinguish*) distinguer. —*v.i.* avoir un effet; (*know*) savoir. ~ **of**, parler de. ~ **off**, (*fam.*) gronder. ~**-tale** *n.* rapporteu|r, -se *m.*, *f.*; *a.* révélateur. ~ **tales**, rapporter.

teller /'telə(r)/ *n.* (*in bank*) caissier, -ière *m.*, *f.*

telling /'telɪŋ/ *a.* révélateur.

telly /'telɪ/ *n.* (*fam.*) télé *f.*

temerity /tɪ'merətɪ/ *n.* témérité *f.*

temp /temp/ *n.* (*temporary employee: fam.*) intérimaire *m./f.* —*v.i.* faire de l'intérim.

temper /'tempə(r)/ *n.* humeur *f.*; (*anger*) colère *f.* —*v.t.* (*metal*) tremper; (*fig.*) tempérer. **lose one's** ~, se mettre en colère.

temperament /'temprəmənt/ *n.* tempérament *m.* ~**al** /-'mentl/ *a.* capricieux; (*innate*) inné.

temperance /'tempərəns/ *n.* (*in drinking*) tempérance *f.*

temperate /'tempərət/ *a.* tempéré.

temperature /'temprətʃə(r)/ *n.* température *f.* **have a** ~, avoir (de) la fièvre *or* de la température.

tempest /'tempɪst/ *n.* tempête *f.*

tempestuous /tem'pestʃʊəs/ *a.* (*meeting etc.*) orageux.

template /'templ(e)ɪt/ *n.* patron *m.*

temple[1] /'templ/ *n.* temple *m.*

temple[2] /'templ/ *n.* (*of head*) tempe *f.*

tempo /'tempəʊ/ *n.* (*pl.* **-os**) tempo *m.*

temporal /'tempərəl/ *a.* temporel.

temporar|**y** /'tempərɪ/ *a.* temporaire, provisoire. ~**ily** *adv.* temporairement, provisoirement.

tempt /tempt/ *v.t.* tenter. ~ **s.o. to do**, donner envie à qn. de faire. ~**ation** /-'teɪʃn/ *n.* tentation *f.* ~**ing** *a.* tentant.

ten /ten/ *a. & n.* dix (*m.*).

tenable /'tenəbl/ *a.* défendable.

tenac|**ious** /tɪ'neɪʃəs/ *a.* tenace. ~**ity** /-æsətɪ/ *n.* ténacité *f.*

tenancy /'tenənsɪ/ *n.* location *f.*

tenant /'tenənt/ *n.* locataire *m./f.*

tend[1] /tend/ *v.t.* s'occuper de.

tend[2] /tend/ *v.i.* ~ **to**, (*be apt to*) avoir tendance à.

tendency /'tendənsɪ/ *n.* tendance *f.*

tender[1] /'tendə(r)/ *a.* tendre; (*sore, painful*) sensible. ~**ly** *adv.* tendrement. ~**ness** *n.* tendresse *f.*

tender[2] /'tendə(r)/ *v.t.* offrir, donner. —*v.i.* faire une soumission. —*n.* (*comm.*) soumission *f.* **be legal** ~, (*money*) avoir cours. **put sth. out to** ~, faire un appel d'offres pour qch.

tendon /'tendən/ *n.* tendon *m.*

tenement /'tenəmənt/ *n.* maison de rapport *f.*, H.L.M. *m./f.*; (*slum: Amer.*) taudis *m.*

tenet /'tenɪt/ *n.* principe *m.*

tenner /'tenə(r)/ *n.* (*fam.*) billet de dix livres *m.*

tennis /'tenɪs/ *n.* tennis *m.* —*a.* de tennis ~ **shoes**, tennis *m. pl.*

tenor /'tenə(r)/ *n.* (*meaning*) sens général *m.*; (*mus.*) ténor *m.*

tense[1] /tens/ *n.* (*gram.*) temps *m.*

tense[2] /tens/ *a.* (**-er, -est**) tendu. —*v.t.* (*muscles*) tendre, raidir. —*v.i.* (*of face*) se crisper. **⁓ness** *n.* tension *f.*

tension /'tenʃn/ *n.* tension *f.*

tent /tent/ *n.* tente *f.*

tentacle /'tentəkl/ *n.* tentacule *m.*

tentative /'tentətɪv/ *a.* provisoire; (*hesitant*) timide. **⁓ly** *adv.* provisoirement; timidement.

tenterhooks /'tentəhʊks/ *n. pl.* **on ⁓,** sur des charbons ardents.

tenth /tenθ/ *a. & n.* dixième (*m./f.*).

tenuous /'tenjʊəs/ *a.* ténu.

tenure /'tenjʊə(r)/ *n.* (*in job, office*) (période de) jouissance *f.* **have ⁓,** être titulaire.

tepid /'tepɪd/ *a.* tiède.

term /tɜːm/ *n.* (*word, limit*) terme *m.*; (*of imprisonment*) temps; (*in school etc.*) trimestre *m.*; (*Amer.*) semestre *m.* **⁓s,** conditions *f. pl.* —*v.t.* appeler, **on good/bad ⁓s,** en bons/mauvais termes. **in the short/long ⁓,** à court/long terme **come to ⁓s,** arriver à un accord. **come to ⁓s with sth.,** accepter qch. **⁓ of office,** (*pol.*) mandat *m.*

terminal /'tɜːmɪnl/ *a.* terminal, final; (*med.*) en phase terminale. —*n.* (*oil, computer*) terminal *m.*; (*rail.*) terminus *m.*; (*electr.*) borne *f.* (**air**) **⁓,** aérogare *f.*

terminat|e /'tɜːmɪneɪt/ *v.t.* mettre fin à. —*v.i.* prendre fin. **⁓ion** /-'neɪʃn/ *n.* fin *f.*

terminology /tɜːmɪ'nɒlədʒɪ/ *n.* terminologie *f.*

terminus /'tɜːmɪnəs/ *n.* (*pl.* **-ni** /-naɪ/) (*station*) terminus *m.*

terrace /'terəs/ *n.* terrasse *f.*; (*houses*) rangée de maisons contiguës *f.* **the ⁓s,** (*sport*) les gradins *m. pl.*

terracotta /terə'kɒtə/ *n.* terre cuite *f.*

terrain /te'reɪn/ *n.* terrain *m.*

terribl|e /'terəbl/ *a.* affreux, atroce. **⁓y** *adv.* affreusement; (*very*) terriblement.

terrier /'terɪə(r)/ *n.* (*dog*) terrier *m.*

terrific /tə'rɪfɪk/ *a.* (*fam.*) terrible. **⁓ally** /-klɪ/ *adv.* (*very: fam.*) terriblement; (*very well: fam.*) terriblement bien.

terrif|y /'terɪfaɪ/ *v.t.* terrifier. **be ⁓ied of,** avoir très peur de.

territorial /terɪ'tɔːrɪəl/ *a.* territorial.

territory /'terɪtərɪ/ *n.* territoire *m.*

terror /'terə(r)/ *n.* terreur *f.*

terroris|t /'terərɪst/ *n.* terroriste *m./f.* **⁓m** /-zəm/ *n.* terrorisme *m.*

terrorize /'terəraɪz/ *v.t.* terroriser.

terse /tɜːs/ *a.* concis, laconique.

test /test/ *n.* examen *m.*, analyse *f.*; (*of goods*) contrôle *m.*; (*of machine etc.*) essai *m.*; (*in school*) interrogation *f.*; (*of strength etc.: fig.*) épreuve *f.* —*v.t.* examiner, analyser; (*check*) contrôler; (*try*) essayer; (*pupil*) donner une interrogation à; (*fig.*) éprouver. **driving ⁓,** (épreuve *f.* du) permis de conduire *m.* **⁓ match,** match international *m.* **⁓ pilot** pilote d'essai *m.* **⁓-tube** *n.* éprouvette *f.*

testament /'testəmənt/ *n.* testament *m.* **Old/New T⁓,** Ancien/Nouveau Testament *m.*

testicle /'testɪkl/ *n.* testicule *m.*

testify /'testɪfaɪ/ *v.t./i.* témoigner (**to,** de). **⁓ that,** témoigner que.

testimony /'testɪmənɪ/ *n.* témoignage *m.*

testy /'testɪ/ *a.* grincheux.

tetanus /'tetənəs/ *n.* tétanos *m.*

tetchy /'tetʃɪ/ *a.* grincheux.

tether /'teðə(r)/ *v.t.* attacher. —*n.* **at the end of one's ⁓,** à bout.

text /tekst/ *n.* texte *m.*

textbook /'tekstbʊk/ *n.* manuel *m.*

textile /'tekstaɪl/ *n. & a.* textile (*m.*).

texture /'tekstʃə(r)/ *n.* (*of paper etc.*) grain *m.*; (*of fabric*) texture *f.*

Thai /taɪ/ *a. & n.* thaïlandais(e) (*m.* (*f.*)). **⁓land** *n.* Thaïlande *f.*

Thames /temz/ *n.* Tamise *f.*

than /ðæn, *unstressed* ðən/ *conj.* que, qu'*; (*with numbers*) de. **more/less ⁓ ten,** plus/moins de dix.

thank /θæŋk/ *v.t.* remercier. **⁓s** *n. pl.* remerciements *m. pl.* **⁓ you!, you!,** merci! **⁓s!,** (*fam.*) merci! **⁓s to,** grâce à. **T⁓sgiving (Day),** (*Amer.*) jour d'action de grâces *m.* (*fête nationale*).

thankful /'θæŋkfl/ *a.* reconnaissant (**for,** de). **⁓ly** *adv.* (*happily*) heureusement.

thankless /'θæŋklɪs/ *a.* ingrat.

that /ðæt, *unstressed* ðət/ *a. pl.* **those** ce *or* cet*, cette. **those,** ces. —*pron.* ce *or* c'*, cela, ça. **⁓ (one),** celui-là, celle-là. **those (ones),** ceux-là, celles-là. —*adv.* si, aussi. —*rel. pron.* (*subject*) qui; (*object*) que, qu'*. —*conj.* que, qu'*. **⁓ boy,** ce garçon (*with emphasis*) ce garçon-là. **⁓ is,** c'est. **⁓ is (to say),** c'est-à-dire. **after ⁓,** après ça *or* cela. **the day ⁓,** le jour où. **the man ⁓ married her,** l'homme qui l'a épousée. **the man ⁓ she married,** l'homme qu'elle a épousé. **the car ⁓ I came in,** la voiture dans laquelle je suis venu. **⁓ big,** grand comme ça. **⁓ many, ⁓ much,** tant que ça.

thatch /θætʃ/ *n.* chaume *m.* **⁓ed** *a.* en chaume. **⁓ed cottage,** chaumière *f.*

thaw /θɔː/ *v.t./i.* (faire) dégeler; (*snow*) (faire) fondre. —*n.* dégel *m.*

the /*before vowel* ðɪ, *before consonant* ðə, *stressed* ðiː/ *a.* le *or* l'*, la *or* l'*, *pl.* les. **of** ~, **from** ~, du, de l'*, de la, *pl.* des. **to** ~, **at** ~, au, à l'*, à la, *pl.* aux. ~ **third of June,** le trois juin.

theatre /'θɪətə(r)/ *n.* théâtre *m.*

theatrical /θɪ'ætrɪkl/ *a.* théâtral.

theft /θeft/ *n.* vol *m.*

their /ðeə(r)/ *a.* leur, *pl.* leurs.

theirs /ðeəz/ *poss. pron.* le *or* la leur, les leurs.

them /ðem, *unstressed* ðəm/ *pron.* les; (*after prep.*) eux, elles. **(to)** ~, leur. **I know** ~, je les connais.

theme /θiːm/ *n.* thème *m.* ~ **song,** (*in film etc.*) chanson principale *f.*

themselves /ðəm'selvz/ *pron.* eux-mêmes, elles-mêmes; (*reflexive*) se; (*after prep.*) eux, elles.

then /ðen/ *adv.* alors; (*next*) ensuite, puis; (*therefore*) alors, donc.   *a.* d'alors. **from** ~ **on,** dès lors.

theolog|y /θɪ'ɒlədʒɪ/ *n.* théologie *f.* ~**ian** /θɪə'ləʊdʒən/ *n.* théologien(ne) *m.* (*f.*).

theorem /'θɪərəm/ *n.* théorème *m.*

theor|y /'θɪərɪ/ *n.* théorie *f.* ~**etical** /-'retɪkl/ *a.* théorique.

therapeutic /θerə'pjuːtɪk/ *a.* thérapeutique.

therapy /'θerəpɪ/ *n.* thérapie *f.*

there /ðeə(r)/ *adv.* là; (*with verb*) y; (*over there*) là-bas. —*int.* allez. **he goes** ~, il y va. **on** ~, là-dessus. ~ **is,** ~ **are,** il y a; (*pointing*) voilà. ~, ~!, allons, allons! ~**abouts** *adv.* par là. ~**after** *adv.* par la suite. ~**by** *adv.* de cette manière.

therefore /'ðeəfɔː(r)/ *adv.* donc.

thermal /'θɜːml/ *a.* thermique.

thermometer /θə'mɒmɪtə(r)/ *n.* thermomètre *m.*

thermonuclear /θɜːməʊ'njuːklɪə(r)/ *a.* thermonucléaire.

Thermos /'θɜːməs/ *n.* (P.) thermos *m./f. invar.* (P.).

thermostat /'θɜːməstæt/ *n.* thermostat *m.*

thesaurus /θɪ'sɔːrəs/ *n.* (*pl.* -**ri** /-raɪ/) dictionnaire de synonymes *m.*

these /ðiːz/ *see* **this**.

thesis /'θiːsɪs/ *n.* (*pl.* **theses** /-siːz/) thèse *f.*

they /ðeɪ/ *pron.* ils, elles; (*emphatic*) eux, elles; (*people in general*) on.

thick /θɪk/ *a.* (-**er,** -**est**) épais; (*stupid*) bête; (*friends: fam.*) très lié. —*adv.* = **thickly.** —*n.* **in the** ~ **of,** au plus gros

de. ~**ly** *adv.* (*grow*) dru; (*spread*) en couche épaisse. ~**ness** *n.* épaisseur *f.* ~-**skinned** *a.* peu sensible.

thicken /'θɪkən/ *v.t./i.* (s')épaissir.

thickset /θɪk'set/ *a.* trapu.

thief /θiːf/ *n.* (*pl.* **thieves**) voleur, -se *m.*, *f.*

thigh /θaɪ/ *n.* cuisse *f.*

thimble /'θɪmbl/ *n.* dé (à coudre) *m.*

thin /θɪn/ *a.* (**thinner, thinnest**) mince; (*person*) maigre, mince; (*sparse*) clairsemé; (*fine*) fin. —*adv.* = **thinly.** —*v.t./i.* (*p.t.* **thinned**) (*liquid*) (s')éclaircir. ~ **out,** (*in quantity*) (s')éclaircir. ~**ly** *adv.* (*slightly*) légèrement. ~**ner** *n.* diluant *m.* ~**ness** *n.* minceur *f.*; maigreur *f.*

thing /θɪŋ/ *n.* chose *f.* ~**s,** (*belongings*) affaires *f. pl.* **the best** ~ **is to,** le mieux est de. **the (right)** ~, ce qu'il faut (**for s.o.,** à qn.).

think /θɪŋk/ *v.t./i.* (*p.t.* **thought**) penser (**about, of,** à); (*carefully*) réfléchir (**about, of,** à); (*believe*) croire. **I** ~ **so,** je crois que oui. ~ **better of it,** se raviser. ~ **nothing of,** trouver naturel de. ~ **of,** (*hold opinion of*) penser de. **I'm** ~**ing of going,** je pense que j'irai peut-être. ~ **over,** bien réfléchir à. ~-**tank** *n.* comité d'experts *m.* ~ **up,** inventer. ~**er** *n.* penseur, -se *m.*, *f.*

third /θɜːd/ *a.* troisième. —*n.* troisième *m/f*; (*fraction*) tiers *m.* ~**ly** *adv.* troisièmement. ~-**rate** *a.* très inférieur. **T**~ **World,** Tiers-Monde *m.*

thirst /θɜːst/ *n.* soif *f.* ~**y** *a.* **be** ~**y,** avoir soif. **make** ~**y,** donner soif à.

thirteen /θɜː'tiːn/ *a.* & *n.* treize (*m.*). ~**th** *a.* & *n.* treizième (*m./f.*).

thirt|y /'θɜːtɪ/ *a.* & *n.* trente (*m.*). ~**ieth** *a.* & *n.* trentième (*m./f.*).

this /ðɪs/ *a.* (*pl.* **these**) ce *or* cet*, cette, **these,** ces. —*pron.* ce *or* c'*, ceci. ~ **(one),** celui-ci, celle-ci. **these (ones),** ceux-ci, celles-ci. ~ **boy,** ce garçon; (*with emphasis*) ce garçon-ci. ~ **is a mistake,** c'est une erreur. ~ **is the book,** voici le livre. ~ **is my son,** je vous présente mon fils. ~ **is Anne speaking,** c'est Anne à l'appareil. **after** ~, après ceci.

thistle /'θɪsl/ *n.* chardon *m.*

thorn /θɔːn/ *n.* épine *f.* ~**y** *a.* épineux.

thorough /'θʌrə/ *a.* consciencieux; (*deep*) profond; (*cleaning, washing*) à fond. ~**ly** *adv.* (*clean, study, etc.*) à fond; (*very*) tout à fait.

thoroughbred /'θʌrəbred/ *n.* (*horse etc.*) pur-sang *m. invar.*

thoroughfare /'θʌrəfeə(r)/ *n.* grande artère *f.*

those /ðəʊz/ *see* that.

though /ðəʊ/ *conj.* bien que. —*adv.* (*fam.*) cependant.

thought /θɔːt/ *see* think. —*n.* pensée *f.*; (*idea*) idée *f.*

thoughtful /'θɔːtfl/ *a.* pensif; (*considerate*) attentionné. ~**ly** *adv.* pensivement; avec considération.

thoughtless /'θɔːtlɪs/ *a.* étourdi. ~**ly** *adv.* étourdiment.

thousand /'θaʊznd/ *a. & n.* mille (*m. invar.*). ~**s of**, des milliers de.

thrash /θræʃ/ *v.t.* rosser; (*defeat*) écraser. ~ **about**, se débattre. ~ **out**, discuter à fond.

thread /θred/ *n.* (*yarn & fig.*) fil *m.*; (*of screw*) pas *m.* —*v.t.* enfiler. ~ **one's way**, se faufiler.

threadbare /'θredbeə(r)/ *a.* râpé.

threat /θret/ *n.* menace *f.*

threaten /'θretn/ *v.t./i.* menacer (**with**, de). ~**ingly** *adv.* d'un air menaçant.

three /θriː/ *a. & n.* trois (*m.*). ~-**dimensional** *a.* en trois dimensions.

thresh /θreʃ/ *v.t.* (*corn etc.*) battre.

threshold /'θreʃəʊld/ *n.* seuil *m.*

threw /θruː/ *see* throw.

thrift /θrɪft/ *n.* économie *f.* ~**y** *a.* économe.

thrill /θrɪl/ *n.* émotion *f.*, frisson *m.* —*v.t.* transporter (de joie). —*v.i.* frissonner (de joie). **be** ~**ed**, être ravi. ~**ing** *a.* excitant.

thriller /'θrɪlə(r)/ *n.* livre *or* film à suspense *m.*

thriv|e /θraɪv/ *v.i.* (*p.t.* **thrived** *or* **throve**, *p.p.* **thrived** *or* **thriven**) prospérer. **he** ~**es on it**, cela lui réussit. ~**ing** *a.* prospère.

throat /θrəʊt/ *n.* gorge *f.* **have a sore** ~, avoir mal à la gorge.

throb /θrɒb/ *v.i.* (*p.t.* **throbbed**) (*wound*) causer des élancements; (*heart*) palpiter; (*fig.*) vibrer. —*n.* (*pain*) élancement *m.*; palpitation *f.* ~**bing** *a.* (*pain*) lancinant.

throes /θrəʊz/ *n. pl.* **in the** ~ **of**, au milieu de, aux prises avec.

thrombosis /θrɒm'bəʊsɪs/ *n.* thrombose *f.*

throne /θrəʊn/ *n.* trône *m.*

throng /θrɒŋ/ *n.* foule *f.* —*v.t.* (*streets etc.*) se presser dans. —*v.i.* (*arrive*) affluer.

throttle /'θrɒtl/ *n.* (*auto.*) accélérateur *m.* —*v.t.* étrangler.

through /θruː/ *prep.* à travers; (*during*) pendant; (*by means or way of, out of*) par; (*by reason of*) grâce à, à cause de. —*adv.* à travers; (*entirely*) jusqu'au bout. —*a.* (*train etc.*) direct. **be** ~, (*finished*) avoir fini. **come** *or* **go** ~, (*cross, pierce*) traverser. **I'm putting you** ~, je vous passe votre correspondant.

throughout /θruː'aʊt/ *prep.* ~ **the country**/*etc.*, dans tout le pays/*etc.* ~ **the day**/*etc.*, pendant toute la journée/*etc.* —*adv.* (*place*) partout; (*time*) tout le temps.

throw /θrəʊ/ *v.t.* (*p.t.* **threw**, *p.p.* **thrown**) jeter, lancer; (*baffle: fam.*) déconcerter. —*n.* jet *m.*; (*of dice*) coup *m.* ~ **a party**, (*fam.*) faire une fête. ~ **away**, jeter. ~-**away** *a.* à jeter. ~ **off**, (*get rid of*) se débarrasser de. ~ **out**, jeter; (*person*) expulser; (*reject*) rejeter. ~ **over**, (*desert*) plaquer. ~ **up**, (*one's arms*) lever; (*resign from*) abandonner; (*vomit: fam.*) vomir.

thru /θruː/ *prep., adv. & a.* (*Amer.*) = **through**.

thrush /θrʌʃ/ *n.* (*bird*) grive *f.*

thrust /θrʌst/ *v.t.* (*p.t.* **thrust**) pousser. —*n.* poussée *f.* ~ **into**, (*put*) enforcer dans, mettre dans. ~ **upon**, (*force on*) imposer à.

thud /θʌd/ *n.* bruit sourd *m.*

thug /θʌg/ *n.* voyou *m.*, bandit *m.*

thumb /θʌm/ *n.* pouce *m.* —*v.t.* (*book*) feuilleter. ~ **a lift**, faire de l'auto-stop. ~-**index**, répertoire à onglets *m.*

thumbtack /'θʌmtæk/ *n.* (*Amer.*) punaise *f.*

thump /θʌmp/ *v.t./i.* cogner (sur); (*of heart*) battre fort. —*n.* grand coup *m.* ~**ing** *a.* (*fam.*) énorme.

thunder /'θʌndə(r)/ *n.* tonnerre *m.* —*v.i.* (*weather, person, etc.*) tonner. ~ **past**, passer dans un bruit de tonnerre. ~**y** *a.* orageux.

thunderbolt /'θʌndəbəʊlt/ *n.* coup de foudre *m.*; (*event: fig.*) coup de tonnerre *m.*

thunderstorm /'θʌndəstɔːm/ *n.* orage *m.*

Thursday /'θɜːzdɪ/ *n.* jeudi *m.*

thus /ðʌs/ *adv.* ainsi.

thwart /θwɔːt/ *v.t.* contrecarrer.

thyme /taɪm/ *n.* thym *m.*

thyroid /'θaɪrɔɪd/ *n.* thyroïde *f.*

tiara /tɪ'ɑːrə/ *n.* diadème *m.*

tic /tɪk/ *n.* tic (nerveux) *m.*

tick[1] /tɪk/ *n.* (*sound*) tic-tac *m.*; (*mark*) coche *f.*; (*moment: fam.*) instant *m.* —*v.i.* faire tic-tac. —*v.t.* ~ (**off**), cocher. ~ **off**, (*fam.*) réprimander. ~

over, (*engine, factory*) tourner au ralenti.

tick² /tɪk/ *n.* (*insect*) tique *f.*

ticket /'tɪkɪt/ *n.* billet *m.*; (*for bus, cloakroom, etc.*) ticket *m.*; (*label*) étiquette *f.* ∼-**collector** *n.* contrôleur, -se *m.*, *f.* ∼-**office** *n.* guichet *m.*

tickle /'tɪkl/ *v.t.* chatouiller; (*amuse*: *fig.*) amuser. —*n.* chatouillement *m.*

ticklish /'tɪklɪʃ/ *a.* chatouilleux.

tidal /'taɪdl/ *a.* qui a des marées. ∼ **wave,** raz-de-marée *m. invar.*

tiddly-winks /'tɪdlɪwɪŋks/ *n.* (*game*) jeu de puce *m.*

tide /taɪd/ *n.* marée *f.*; (*of events*) cours *m.* —*v.t.* ∼ **over,** dépanner.

tidings /'taɪdɪŋz/ *n. pl.* nouvelles *f. pl.*

tid|y /'taɪdɪ/ *a.* (**-ier, -iest**) (*room*) bien rangé; (*appearance, work*) soigné; (*methodical*) ordonné; (*amount*: *fam.*) joli. —*v.t./i.* ranger. ∼**y o.s.,** s'arranger. ∼**ily** *adv.* avec soin. ∼**iness** *n.* ordre *m.*

tie /taɪ/ *v.t.* (*pres. p.* **tying**) attacher, nouer; (*a knot*) faire; (*link*) lier. —*v.i.* (*darts etc.*) finir à égalité de points; (*football*) faire match nul; (*in race*) être ex aequo. —*n.* attache *f.*; (*necktie*) cravate *f.*; (*link*) lien *m.*; égalité (de points) *f.*; match nul *m.* ∼ **down,** attacher; (*job*) bloquer. ∼ **s.o. down to,** (*date*) forcer qn. à respecter. ∼ **in with,** être lié à. ∼ **up,** attacher; (*money*) immobiliser; (*occupy*) occuper. ∼-**up** *n.* (*link*) lien *m.*; (*auto., Amer.*) bouchon *m.*

tier /tɪə(r)/ *n.* étage *m.*, niveau *m.*; (*in stadium etc.*) gradin *m.*

tiff /tɪf/ *n.* petite querelle *f.*

tiger /'taɪɡə(r)/ *n.* tigre *m.*

tight /taɪt/ *a.* (**-er, -est**) (*clothes*) étroit, juste; (*rope*) tendu; (*lid*) solidement fixé; (*control*) strict; (*knot, collar, schedule*) serré; (*drunk*: *fam.*) ivre. —*adv.* (*hold, sleep, etc.*) bien; (*squeeze*) fort. ∼ **corner,** situation difficile *f.* ∼-**fisted** *a.* avare. ∼**ly** *adv.* bien; (*squeeze*) fort.

tighten /'taɪtn/ *v.t./i.* (se) tendre; (*bolt etc.*) (se) resserrer; (*control etc.*) renforcer. ∼ **up on,** se montrer plus strict à l'égard de.

tightrope /'taɪtrəʊp/ *n.* corde raide *f.* ∼ **walker,** funambule *m./f.*

tights /taɪts/ *n. pl.* collant *m.*

tile /taɪl/ *n.* (*on wall, floor*) carreau *m.*; (*on roof*) tuile *f.* —*v.t.* carreler; couvrir de tuiles.

till¹ /tɪl/ *v.t.* (*land*) cultiver.

till² /tɪl/ *prep. & conj.* = **until.**

till³ /tɪl/ *n.* caisse (enregistreuse) *f.*

tilt /tɪlt/ *v.i./i.* pencher. —*n.* (*slope*) inclinaison *f.* (**at**) **full** ∼, à toute vitesse.

timber /'tɪmbə(r)/ *n.* bois (de construction) *m.*; (*trees*) arbres *m. pl.*

time /taɪm/ *n.* temps *m.*; (*moment*) moment *m.*; (*epoch*) époque *f.*; (*by clock*) heure *f.*; (*occasion*) fois *f.*; (*rhythm*) mesure *f.* ∼**s,** (*multiplying*) fois *f. pl.* —*v.t.* choisir le moment de; (*measure*) minuter; (*sport*) chronométrer. **any** ∼, n'importe quand. **behind the** ∼**s,** en retard sur son temps. **for the** ∼ **being,** pour le moment. **from** ∼ **to time,** de temps en temps. **have a good** ∼, s'amuser. **in no** ∼, en un rien de temps. **in** ∼, à temps; (*eventually*) avec le temps. **a long** ∼, longtemps. **on** ∼, à l'heure. **what's the** ∼?, quelle heure est-il? ∼ **bomb,** bombe à retardement *f.* ∼-**honoured** *a.* consacré (par l'usage). ∼-**lag** *n.* décalage *m.* ∼-**limit** *n.* délai *m.* ∼-**scale** *n.* délais fixés *m. pl.* ∼ **off,** du temps libre. ∼ **zone,** fuseau horaire *m.*

timeless /'taɪmlɪs/ *a.* éternel.

timely /'taɪmlɪ/ *a.* à propos.

timer /'taɪmə(r)/ *n.* (*for cooker etc.*) minuteur *m.*; (*on video*) programmateur; (*culin.*) compte-minutes *m. invar.*; (*with sand*) sablier *m.*

timetable /'taɪmteɪbl/ *n.* horaire *m.*

timid /'tɪmɪd/ *a.* timide; (*fearful*) peureux. ∼**ly** *adv.* timidement.

timing /'taɪmɪŋ/ *n.* (*measuring*) minutage *m.*; (*moment*) moment *m.*; (*of artist*) rythme *m.*

tin /tɪn/ *n.* étain *m.*; (*container*) boîte *f.* ∼-(**plate**), fer blanc *m.* —*v.t.* (*p.t.* **tinned**) mettre en boîte. ∼ **foil,** papier d'aluminium *m.* ∼**ny** *a.* métallique. ∼-**opener** *n.* ouvre-boîte(s) *m.*

tinge /tɪndʒ/ *v.t.* teinter (**with,** de). —*n.* teinte *f.*

tingle /'tɪŋɡl/ *v.i.* (*prickle*) picoter. —*n.* picotement *m.*

tinker /'tɪŋkə(r)/ *n.* rétameur *m.* —*v.i.* ∼ (**with**), bricoler.

tinkle /'tɪŋkl/ *n.* tintement *m.*; (*fam.*) coup de téléphone *m.*

tinsel /'tɪnsl/ *n.* cheveux d'ange *m. pl.*, guirlandes de Noël *f. pl.*

tint /tɪnt/ *n.* teinte *f.*; (*for hair*) shampooing colorant *m.* —*v.t.* (*glass, paper*) teinter.

tiny /'taɪnɪ/ *a.* (**-ier, -iest**) minuscule, tout petit.

tip¹ /tɪp/ *n.* bout *m.*; (*cover*) embout *m.* ∼**ped cigarette,** cigarette (à bout) filtre *f.*

tip² /tɪp/ v.t./i. (p.t. **tipped**) (tilt) pencher; (overturn) (faire) basculer; (pour) verser; (empty) déverser; (give money) donner un pourboire à. —n. (money) pourboire m.; (advice) tuyau m.; (for rubbish) décharge f. ~ **off,** prévenir. ~**-off** n. tuyau m. (pour prévenir).

tipsy /'tɪpsɪ/ a. un peu ivre, gris.

tiptoe /'tɪptəʊ/ n. **on** ~, sur la pointe des pieds.

tiptop /'tɪptɒp/ a. (fam.) excellent.

tir|e|¹ /'taɪə(r)/ v.t./i. (se) fatiguer. ~**e of,** se lasser de. ~**eless** a. infatigable. ~**ing** a. fatigant.

tire² /'taɪə(r)/ n. (Amer.) pneu m.

tired /'taɪəd/ a. fatigué. **be** ~ **of,** en avoir assez de.

tiresome /'taɪəsəm/ a. ennuyeux.

tissue /'tɪʃuː/ n. tissu m.; (handkerchief) mouchoir en papier m. ~**-paper** n. papier de soie m.

tit¹ /tɪt/ n. (bird) mésange f.

tit² /tɪt/ n. **give** ~ **for tat,** rendre coup pour coup.

titbit /'tɪtbɪt/ n. friandise f.

titillate /'tɪtɪleɪt/ v.t. exciter.

title /'taɪtl/ n. titre m. ~**-deed** n. titre de propriété m. ~**-role** n. rôle principal m.

titter /'tɪtə(r)/ v.i. rigoler.

titular /'tɪtjʊlə(r)/ a. (ruler etc.) nominal.

to /tuː, unstressed tə/ prep. à; (towards) vers; (of attitude) envers. —adv. **push** or **pull to,** (close) fermer. **to France**/etc., en France/etc. **to town,** en ville. **to Canada**/etc., au Canada/etc. **to the baker's**/etc., chez le boulanger/etc. **the road/door**/etc. **to,** la route/ porte/etc. de. **to me/her**/etc., me/ lui/etc. **to do/ sit**/etc., faire/s'asseoir/etc. **I wrote to tell her,** j'ai écrit pour lui dire. **I tried to help you,** j'ai essayé de t'aider. **ten to six,** (by clock) six heures moins dix. **go to and fro,** aller et venir. **husband**/etc. **-to-be** n. futur mari/etc. m.

toad /təʊd/ n. crapaud m.

toadstool /'təʊdstuːl/ n. champignon (vénéneux) m.

toast /təʊst/ n. pain grillé m., toast m.; (drink) toast m. —v.t. (bread) faire griller; (drink to) porter un toast à; (event) arroser. ~**er** n. grille-pain m. invar.

tobacco /tə'bækəʊ/ n. tabac m.

tobacconist /tə'bækənɪst/ n. marchand(e) de tabac m. (f.). ~**'s shop,** tabac m.

toboggan /tə'bɒgən/ n. toboggan m., luge f.

today /tə'deɪ/ n. & adv. aujourd'hui (m.).

toddler /'tɒdlə(r)/ n. tout(e) petit(e) enfant m.(f).

toddy /'tɒdɪ/ n. (drink) grog m.

toe /təʊ/ n. orteil m.; (of shoe) bout m. —v.t. ~ **the line,** se conformer. **on one's** ~**s,** vigilant. ~**-hold** n. prise (précaire) f.

toffee /'tɒfɪ/ n. caramel m. ~**-apple** n. pomme caramélisée f.

together /tə'geðə(r)/ adv. ensemble; (at same time) en même temps. ~ **with,** avec. ~**ness** n. camaraderie f.

toil /tɔɪl/ v.i. peiner. —n. labeur m.

toilet /'tɔɪlɪt/ n. toilettes f. pl.; (grooming) toilette f. ~**-paper** n. papier hygiénique m. ~**-roll** n. rouleau de papier hygiénique m. ~ **water,** eau de toilette f.

toiletries /'tɔɪlɪtrɪz/ n. pl. articles de toilette m. pl.

token /'təʊkən/ n. témoignage m., marque f.; (voucher) bon m.; (coin) jeton m. —a. symbolique.

told /təʊld/ see **tell.** —a. **all** ~, (all in all) en tout.

tolerabl|e /'tɒlərəbl/ a. tolérable; (not bad) passable. ~**y** adv. (work, play, etc.) passablement.

toleran|t /'tɒlərənt/ a. tolérant (of, à l'égard de). ~**ce** n. tolérance f. ~**tly** adv. avec tolérance.

tolerate /'tɒləreɪt/ v.t. tolérer.

toll¹ /təʊl/ n. péage m. **death** ~, nombre de morts m. **take its** ~, (of age) faire sentir son poids.

toll² /təʊl/ v.i. (of bell) sonner.

tom /tɒm/, ~**-cat** ns. matou m.

tomato /tə'mɑːtəʊ, Amer. tə'meɪtəʊ/ n. (pl. **-oes**) tomate f.

tomb /tuːm/ n. tombeau m.

tombola /tɒm'bəʊlə/ n. tombola f.

tomboy /'tɒmbɔɪ/ n. garçon manqué m.

tombstone /'tuːmstəʊn/ n. pierre tombale f.

tomfoolery /tɒm'fuːlərɪ/ n. âneries f. pl., bêtises f. pl.

tomorrow /tə'mɒrəʊ/ n. & adv. demain (m.). ~ **morning/night,** demain matin/soir. **the day after** ~, après-demain.

ton /tʌn/ n. tonne f. (= 1016 kg.). **(metric)** ~, tonne f. (= 1000 kg.). ~**s of,** (fam.) des masses de.

tone /təʊn/ n. ton m.; (of radio, telephone, etc.) tonalité f. —v.t. ~ **down,** atténuer. —v.i. ~ **in,**

s'harmoniser (**with**, avec). ～**-deaf** *a.* qui n'a pas d'oreille. ～ **up**, (*muscles*) tonifier.

tongs /tɒŋz/ *n. pl.* pinces *f. pl.*; (*for sugar*) pince *f.*; (*for hair*) fer *m.*

tongue /tʌŋ/ *n.* langue *f.* ～**-tied** *a.* muet. ～**-twister** *n.* phrase difficile à prononcer *f.* **with one's** ～ **in one's cheek,** ironiquement.

tonic /'tɒnɪk/ *n.* (*med.*) tonique *m.* —*a.* (*effect*, *accent*) tonique *m.* ～ (**water**), tonic *m.*

tonight /tə'naɪt/ *n.* & *adv.* cette nuit (*f.*); (*evening*) ce soir (*m.*).

tonne /tʌn/ *n.* (*metric*) tonne *f.*

tonsil /'tɒnsl/ *n.* amygdale *f.*

tonsillitis /tɒnsɪ'laɪtɪs/ *n.* amygdalite *f.*

too /tuː/ *adv.* trop; (*also*) aussi. ～ **many** *a.* trop de; *n.* trop. ～ **much** *a.* trop de; *adv.* & *n.* trop.

took /tʊk/ *see* **take**.

tool /tuːl/ *n.* outil *m.* ～**-bag** *n.* trousse à outils *f.*

toot /tuːt/ *n.* coup de klaxon *m.* —*v.t./i.* ～ (**the horn**), klaxonner.

tooth /tuːθ/ *n.* (*pl.* **teeth**) dent *f.* ～**less** *a.* édenté.

toothache /'tuːθeɪk/ *n.* mal de dents *m.*

toothbrush /'tuːθbrʌʃ/ *n.* brosse à dents *f.*

toothcomb /'tuːθkəʊm/ *n.* peigne fin *m.*

toothpaste /'tuːθpeɪst/ *n.* dentifrice *m.*, pâte dentifrice *f.*

toothpick /'tuːθpɪk/ *n.* cure-dent *m.*

top[1] /tɒp/ *n.* (*highest point*) sommet *m.*; (*upper part*) haut *m.*; (*upper surface*) dessus *m.*; (*lid*) couvercle *m.*; (*of bottle, tube*) bouchon *m.*; (*of beer bottle*) capsule *f.*; (*of list*) tête *f.* —*a.* (*shelf etc.*) du haut; (*floor*) dernier, (*in rank*) premier; (*best*) meilleur; (*distinguished*) éminent; (*maximum*) maximum. —*v.t.* (*p.t.* **topped**) (*exceed*) dépasser; (*list*) venir en tête de. **from** ～ **to bottom,** de fond en comble. **on** ～ **of,** sur; (*fig.*) en plus de. ～ **hat,** haut-de-forme *m.* ～**-heavy** *a.* trop lourd du haut. ～**-level** *a.* du plus haut niveau. ～**notch** *a.* excellent. ～**-quality** *a.* de la plus haute qualité. ～ **secret,** ultrasecret. ～ **up,** remplir. ～**ped with,** surmonté de; (*cream etc.*: *culin.*) nappé de.

top[2] /tɒp/ *n.* (*toy*) toupie *f.*

topic /'tɒpɪk/ *n.* sujet *m.*

topical /'tɒpɪkl/ *a.* d'actualité.

topless /'tɒplɪs/ *a.* aux seins nus.

topple /'tɒpl/ *v.t./i.* (faire) tomber, (faire) basculer.

topsy-turvy /tɒpsɪ'tɜːvɪ/ *adv.* & *a.* sens dessus dessous.

torch /tɔːtʃ/ *n.* (*electric*) lampe de poche *f.*; (*flaming*) torche *f.*

tore /tɔː(r)/ *see* **tear**[1].

torment[1] /'tɔːment/ *n.* tourment *m.*

torment[2] /tɔː'ment/ *v.t.* tourmenter; (*annoy*) agacer.

torn /tɔːn/ *see* **tear**[1].

tornado /tɔː'neɪdəʊ/ *n.* (*pl.* **-oes**) tornade *f.*

torpedo /tɔː'piːdəʊ/ *n.* (*pl.* **-oes**) torpille *f.*, —*v.t.* torpiller.

torrent /'tɒrənt/ *n.* torrent *m.* ～**ial** /tə'renʃl/ *a.* torrentiel.

torrid /'tɒrɪd/ *a.* (*climate etc.*) torride; (*fig.*) passionné.

torso /'tɔːsəʊ/ *n.* (*pl.* **-os**) torse *m.*

tortoise /'tɔːtəs/ *n.* tortue *f.*

tortoiseshell /'tɔːtəsʃel/ *n.* (*for ornaments etc.*) écaille *f.*

tortuous /'tɔːtʃʊəs/ *a.* tortueux.

torture /'tɔːtʃə(r)/ *n.* torture *f.*, supplice *m.* —*v.t.* torturer. ～**r** /-ə(r)/ *n.* tortionnaire *m.*

Tory /'tɔːrɪ/ *n.* tory *m.* —*a.* tory (*f. invar.*).

toss /tɒs/ *v.t.* jeter, lancer; (*shake*) agiter. —*v.i.* s'agiter. ～ **a coin,** ～ **up,** tirer à pile ou face (**for,** pour).

tot[1] /tɒt/ *n.* petit(e) enfant *m.(f.)*; (*glass: fam.*) petit verre *m.*

tot[2] /tɒt/ *v.t.* (*p.t.* **totted**) ～ **up,** (*fam.*) additionner.

total /'təʊtl/ *a.* total. —*n.* total *m.* —*v.t.* (*p.t.* **totalled**) (*find total of*) totaliser; (*amount to*) s'élever à. ～**ity** /-'tælətɪ/ *n.* totalité *f.* ～**ly** *adv.* totalement.

totalitarian /təʊtælɪ'teərɪən/ *a.* totalitaire.

totter /'tɒtə(r)/ *v.i.* chanceler.

touch /tʌtʃ/ *v.t./i.* toucher; (*of ends, gardens, etc.*) se toucher; (*tamper with*) toucher à. —*n.* (*sense*) toucher *m.*; (*contact*) contact *m.*; (*of colour*) touche *f.*; (*football*) touche *f.* **a** ～ **of,** (*small amount*) un peu de. **get in** ～ **with,** contacter. **lose** ～, perdre contact. **be out of** ～, n'être plus dans le coup. ～**-and-go** *a.* douteux. ～ **down,** (*aviat.*) atterrir. ～**-line** *n.* (ligne de) touche *f.* ～ **off,** (*explode*) faire partir; (*cause*) déclencher. ～ **on,** (*mention*) aborder. ～ **up,** retoucher.

touchdown /'tʌtʃdaʊn/ *n.* atterrissage *m.*; (*sport, Amer.*) but *m.*

touching /'tʌtʃɪŋ/ *a.* touchant.

touchstone /'tʌtʃstəʊn/ *n.* pierre de touche *f.*

touchy /'tʌtʃɪ/ a. susceptible.

tough /tʌf/ a. (-er, -est) (*hard, difficult*) dur; (*strong*) solide; (*relentless*) acharné. —n. ~ (**guy**), dur m. ~ **luck!**, (*fam.*) tant pis! ~**ness** n. dureté f.; solidité f.

toughen /'tʌfn/ v.t. (*strengthen*) renforcer; (*person*) endurcir.

toupee /'tuːpeɪ/ n. postiche m.

tour /tʊə(r)/ n. voyage m.; (*visit*) visite f.; (*by team etc.*) tournée f. —v.t. visiter. **on** ~, en tournée. ~ **operator**, voyagiste m.

tourism /'tʊərɪzəm/ n. tourisme m.

tourist /'tʊərɪst/ n. touriste m./f. —a. touristique. ~ **office**, syndicat d'initiative m.

tournament /'tɔːnəmənt/ n. (*sport & medieval*) tournoi m.

tousle /'taʊzl/ v.t. ébouriffer.

tout /taʊt/ v.i. ~ (**for**), racoler. —v.t. (*sell*) revendre. —n. racoleulr, -se m.,f.; revendeulr, -se m., f.

tow /təʊ/ v.t. remorquer. —n. remorque f. **on** ~, en remorque. ~ **away**, (*vehicle*) (faire) enlever. ~-**path** n. chemin de halage m. ~ **truck**, dépanneuse f.

toward(s) /tə'wɔːd(z), *Amer.* tɔːd(z)/ prep. vers; (*of attitude*) envers.

towel /'taʊəl/ n. serviette f.; (*teatowel*) torchon m. ~**ling** n. tissu-éponge m.

tower /'taʊə(r)/ n. tour f. —v.i. ~ **above**, dominer. ~ **block**, tour f., immeuble m. ~**ing** a. très haut.

town /taʊn/ n. ville f. **go to** ~, (*fam.*) mettre le paquet. ~ **council**, conseil municipal m. ~ **hall**, hôtel de ville m.

toxic /'tɒksɪk/ a. toxique.

toxin /'tɒksɪn/ n. toxine f.

toy /tɔɪ/ n. jouet m. —v.i. ~ **with**, (*object*) jouer avec; (*idea*) caresser.

toyshop /'tɔɪʃɒp/ n. magasin de jouets m.

trace /treɪs/ n. trace f. —v.t. suivre or retrouver la trace de; (*draw*) tracer; (*with tracing-paper*) décalquer; (*relate*) retracer.

tracing /'treɪsɪŋ/ n. calque m. ~-**paper** n. papier-calque m. invar.

track /træk/ n. (*of person etc.*) trace f., piste f.; (*path, race-track & of tape*) piste f.; (*on disc*) plage f.; (*of rocket etc.*) trajectoire f.; (*rail.*) voie f. —v.t. suivre la trace or la trajectoire de. **keep** ~ **of**, suivre. ~ **down**, (*find*) retrouver; (*hunt*) traquer. ~ **suit**, survêtement m.; (*with sweatshirt*) jogging m.

tract[1] /trækt/ n. (*land*) étendue f.; (*anat.*) appareil m.

tract[2] /trækt/ n. (*pamphlet*) tract m.

tractor /'træktə(r)/ n. tracteur m.

trade /treɪd/ n. commerce m.; (*job*) métier m.; (*swap*) échange m. —v.i. faire du commerce. —v.t. échanger. ~ **deficit**, déficit commercial m. ~ **in**, (*used article*) faire reprendre. ~-**in** n. reprise f. ~ **mark**, marque de fabrique f.; (*name*) marque déposée f. ~-**off** n. (*fam.*) compromis m. ~ **on**, (*exploit*) abuser de. ~ **union**, syndicat m. ~ **unionist** n. syndicaliste m./f. ~**r** /-ə(r)/ n. négociant(e) m. (f.), commerçant(e) m. (f.).

tradesman /'treɪdzmən/ n. (pl. -men) commerçant m.

trading /'treɪdɪŋ/ n. commerce m. ~ **estate**, zone industrielle f.

tradition /trə'dɪʃn/ n. tradition f. ~**al** a. traditionnel.

traffic /'træfɪk/ n. trafic m.; (*on road*) circulation f. —v.i. (*p.t.* **trafficked**) trafiquer (**in**, de). ~ **circle**, (*Amer.*) rond-point m. ~ **cone**, cône de délimitation de voie m. ~ **jam**, embouteillage m. ~-**lights** n. pl. feux (de circulation) m. pl. ~ **warden**, contractuel(le) m. (f.).

tragedy /'trædʒədɪ/ n. tragédie f.

tragic /'trædʒɪk/ a. tragique.

trail /treɪl/ v.t./i. traîner; (*of plant*) ramper; (*track*) suivre. —n. (*of powder etc.*) traînée f.; (*track*) piste f.; (*beaten path*) sentier m. ~ **behind**, traîner.

trailer /'treɪlə(r)/ n. remorque f.; (*caravan: Amer.*) caravane f.; (*film*) bande-annonce f.

train /treɪn/ n. (*rail.*) train m.; (*underground*) rame f.; (*procession*) file f.; (*of dress*) traîne f. —v.t. (*instruct, develop*) former; (*sportsman*) entraîner; (*animal*) dresser; (*ear*) exercer; (*aim*) braquer. —v.i. recevoir une formation; s'entraîner. ~**ed** a. (*skilled*) qualifié; (*doctor etc.*) diplômé. ~**er** n. (*sport*) entraîneulr, -se m., f. ~**ers**, (*shoes*) chaussures de sport f. pl. ~**ing** n. formation f.; entraînement m.; dressage m.

trainee /treɪ'niː/ n. stagiaire m./f.

traipse /treɪps/ v.i. (*fam.*) traîner.

trait /treɪ(t)/ n. trait m.

traitor /'treɪtə(r)/ n. traître m.

tram /træm/ n. tram(way) m.

tramp /træmp/ v.i. marcher (d'un pas lourd). —v.t. parcourir. —n. pas lourds m. pl.; (*vagrant*) clochard(e) m. (f.); (*Amer., sl.*) dévergondée f.; (*hike*) randonnée f.

trample /'træmpl/ v.t./i. ~ (on), piétiner; (fig.) fouler aux pieds.

trampoline /'træmpəli:n/ n. (canvas sheet) trampoline m.

trance /trɑ:ns/ n. transe f.

tranquil /'træŋkwɪl/ a. tranquille. ~lity /-'kwɪlətɪ/ n. tranquillité f.

tranquillizer /'træŋkwɪlaɪzə(r)/ n. (drug) tranquillisant m.

transact /træn'zækt/ v.t. traiter. ~ion /-kʃn/ n. transaction f.

transatlantic /trænzət'læntɪk/ a. transatlantique.

transcend /træn'send/ v.t. transcender. ~ent a. transcendant.

transcript /'trænskrɪpt/ n. (written copy) transcription f.

transfer¹ /træns'fɜ:(r)/ v.t. (p.t. **transferred**) transférer; (power) faire passer. —v.i. être transféré. ~ the **charges**, (telephone) téléphoner en PCV.

transfer² /'trænsfɜ:(r)/ n. transfert m ; (of power) passation f.; (image) décalcomanie f.; (sticker) autocollant m.

transform /træns'fɔ:m/ v.t. transformer. ~ation /-ə'meɪʃn/ n. transformation f. ~er n. (electr.) transformateur m.

transfusion /træns'fju:ʒn/ n. (of blood) transfusion f.

transient /'trænzɪənt/ a. transitoire, éphémère.

transistor /træn'zɪstə(r)/ n. (device, radio set) transistor m.

transit /'trænsɪt/ n. transit m.

transition /træn'zɪʃn/ n. transition f. ~al a. transitoire.

transitive /'trænsətɪv/ a. transitif.

transitory /'trænsɪtərɪ/ a. transitoire.

translat|e /trænz'leɪt/ v.t. traduire. ~ion /-ʃn/ n. traduction f. ~or n. traducteur, -trice m., f.

translucent /trænz'lu:snt/ a. translucide.

transmi|t /trænz'mɪt/ v.t. (p.t. **transmitted**) (pass on etc.) transmettre; (broadcast) émettre. ~ssion n. transmission f.; émission f. ~tter n. émetteur m.

transparen|t /træns'pærənt/ a. transparent. ~cy n. transparence f.; (photo.) diapositive f.

transpire /træn'spaɪə(r)/ v.i. s'avérer; (happen: fam.) arriver.

transplant¹ /træns'plɑ:nt/ v.t. transplanter; (med.) greffer.

transplant² /'trænsplɑ:nt/ n. transplantation f.; greffe f.

transport¹ /træn'spɔ:t/ v.t. (carry, delight) transporter. ~ation /-'teɪʃn/ n. transport m.

transport² /'trænspɔ:t/ n. (of goods, delight, etc.) transport m.

transpose /træn'spəʊz/ v.t. transposer.

transverse /'trænzvɜ:s/ a. transversal.

transvestite /trænz'vestaɪt/ n. travesti(e) m. (f.).

trap /træp/ n. piège m. —v.t. (p.t. **trapped**) (jam, pin down) coincer; (cut off) bloquer; (snare) prendre au piège. ~per n. trappeur m.

trapdoor /træp'dɔ:(r)/ n. trappe f.

trapeze /trə'pi:z/ n. trapèze m.

trappings /'træpɪŋz/ n. pl. (fig.) signes extérieurs m. pl., apparat m.

trash /træʃ/ n. (junk) saleté(s) f. (pl.); (refuse) ordures f. pl.; (nonsense) idioties f. pl. ~-can n. (Amer.) poubelle f. ~y a. qui ne vaut rien, de mauvaise qualité.

trauma /'trɔ:mə/ n. traumatisme m. ~tic /-'mætɪk/ a. traumatisant.

travel /'trævl/ v.i. (p.t. **travelled**, Amer. **traveled**) voyager; (of vehicle, bullet, etc.) aller. —v.t. parcourir. —n. voyage(s) m. (pl.). ~ **agent**, agent de voyage m. ~ler n. voyageur, -se m., f. ~ler's cheque, chèque de voyage m. ~ling n. voyage(s) m. (pl.). ~ sickness, mal des transports m.

travesty /'trævəstɪ/ n. parodie f., simulacre m. —v.t. travestir.

trawler /'trɔ:lə(r)/ n. chalutier m.

tray /treɪ/ n. plateau m.; (on office desk) corbeille f.

treacher|ous /'tretʃərəs/ a. traître. ~ly adv. traîtreusement.

treachery /'tretʃərɪ/ n. traîtrise f.

treacle /'tri:kl/ n. mélasse f.

tread /tred/ v.i. (p.t. **trod**, p.p. **trodden**) marcher (on, sur). —v.t. parcourir (à pied); (soil: fig.) fouler. —n. démarche f.; (sound) (bruit m. de) pas m. pl.; (of tyre) chape f. ~ sth. into, (carpet) étaler qch. sur (avec les pieds).

treason /'tri:zn/ n. trahison f.

treasure /'treʒə(r)/ n. trésor m. —v.t. attacher une grande valeur à; (store) conserver. ~r /-ə(r)/ n. trésorier, -ière m., f.

treasury /'treʒərɪ/ n. trésorerie f. **the** **T~**, le ministère des Finances.

treat /tri:t/ v.t. traiter; (consider) considérer. —n. (pleasure) plaisir m., régal m.; (present) gâterie f. (food) régal m. ~ **s.o. to sth.**, offrir qch. à qn.

treatise /'tri:tɪz/ n. traité m.

treatment /'tri:tmənt/ n. traitement m.

treaty /'tri:tı/ n. (*pact*) traité m.

treble /'trebl/ a. triple. —v.t./i. tripler.
—n. (*voice*: *mus.*) soprano m. ~e clef,
clé de sol f. ~y adv. triplement.

tree /tri:/ n. arbre m. ~-top n. cime (d'un
arbre) f.

trek /trek/ n. voyage pénible m.; (*sport*)
randonnée f. —v.i. (*p.t.* **trekked**)
voyager (péniblement); (*sport*) faire de
la randonnée.

trellis /'trelıs/ n. treillage m.

tremble /'trembl/ v.i. trembler.

tremendous /trı'mendəs/ a. énorme;
(*excellent*: *fam.*) fantastique. ~ly adv.
fantastiquement.

tremor /'tremə(r)/ n. tremblement m.
(**earth**) ~, secousse (sismique) f.

trench /trentʃ/ n. tranchée f.

trend /trend/ n. tendance f.; (*fashion*)
mode f. ~-setter n. lanceur, -se de
mode m., f. ~y a. (*fam.*) dans le vent.

trepidation /trepı'deıʃn/ n. (*fear*)
inquiétude f.

trespass /'trespəs/ v.i. s'introduire sans
autorisation (**on**, dans). ~er n. intrus(e)
m. (f.).

tresses /'tresız/ n. pl. chevelure f.

trestle /'tresl/ n. tréteau m. ~-table n.
table à tréteaux f.

tri- /traı/ pref. tri-.

trial /'traıəl/ n. (*jurid.*) procès m.; (*test*)
essai m.; (*ordeal*) épreuve f. **go on** ~,
passer en jugement. ~ **and error**,
tâtonnements m. pl. ~ **run**, galop
d'essai m.

triangle /'traıæŋgl/ n. triangle m.
~**ular** /-'æŋgjʊlə(r)/ a. triangulaire.

tribe /traıb/ n. tribu f. ~**al** a. tribal.

tribulation /trıbjʊ'leıʃn/ n. tribulation f.

tribunal /traı'bju:nl/ n. tribunal m.;
(*mil.*) commission f.

tributary /'trıbjʊtərı/ n. affluent m.

tribute /'trıbju:t/ n. tribut m. **pay** ~ **to**,
rendre hommage à.

trick /trık/ n. astuce f., ruse f.; (*joke*, *feat
of skill*) tour m.; (*habit*) manie f. —v.t
tromper. **do the** ~, (*fam.*) faire
l'affaire.

trickery /'trıkərı/ n. ruse f.

trickle /'trıkl/ v.i. dégouliner. ~ **in/out**,
arriver *or* partir en petit nombre. —n.
filet m.; (*fig.*) petit nombre m.

tricky /'trıkı/ a. (*crafty*) rusé; (*problem*)
délicat, difficile.

tricycle /'traısıkl/ n. tricycle m.

trifle /'traıfl/ n. bagatelle f.; (*cake*)
diplomate m. —v.i. ~ **with**, jouer avec.
a ~, (*small amount*) un peu.

trifling /'traıflıŋ/ a. insignifiant.

trigger /'trıgə(r)/ n. (*of gun*) gâchette f.,
détente f. —v.t. ~ (**off**), (*initiate*)
déclencher.

trilby /'trılbı/ n. (*hat*) feutre m.

trim /trım/ a. (**trimmer, trimmest**) net,
soigné; (*figure*) svelte. —v.t. (*p.t.*
trimmed) (*cut*) couper légèrement;
(*hair*) rafraîchir; (*budget*) réduire. —n.
(*cut*) coupe légère f.; (*decoration*)
garniture f. **in** ~, en bon ordre; (*fit*) en
forme. ~ **with**, (*decorate*) orner de.
~**ming(s)** n. (pl.) garniture(s) f. (pl.).

Trinity /'trınətı/ n. Trinité f.

trinket /'trıŋkıt/ n. colifichet m.

trio /'tri:əʊ/ n. (pl. -**os**) trio m.

trip /trıp/ v.t./i. (*p.t.* **tripped**) (faire)
trébucher; (*go lightly*) marcher d'un pas
léger. —n. (*journey*) voyage m.;
(*outing*) excursion f.; (*stumble*) faux
pas m.

tripe /traıp/ n. (*food*) tripes f. pl.;
(*nonsense*: *sl.*) bêtises f. pl.

triple /'trıpl/ a. triple. —v.t./i. tripler.
~**ts** /-plıts/ n. pl. triplé(e)s m. (f.) pl.

tripod /'traıpɒd/ n. trépied m.

trite /traıt/ a. banal.

triumph /'traıəmf/ n. triomphe m. —v.i.
triompher (**over**, de). ~**al** /-'ʌmfl/ a.
triomphal. ~**ant** /-'ʌmfənt/ a. triom-
phant, triomphal. ~**antly** /-'ʌmfəntlı/
adv. en triomphe.

trivial /'trıvıəl/ a. insignifiant. ~**ize** v.t.
considérer comme insignifiant.

trod, trodden /trɒd, 'trɒdn/ *see* **tread**.

trolley /'trɒlı/ n. chariot m. (**tea-**)~,
table roulante f. ~-**bus** n. trolleybus m.

trombone /trɒm'bəʊn/ n. (*mus.*) trombone m.

troop /tru:p/ n. bande f. ~**s**, (*mil.*)
troupes f. pl. —v.i. ~ **in/out**,
entrer/sortir en bande. ~**er** n. soldat de
cavalerie m. ~**ing the colour**, le salut
au drapeau.

trophy /'trəʊfı/ n. trophée m.

tropic /'trɒpık/ n. tropique m. ~**s**,
tropiques m. pl. ~**al** a. tropical.

trot /trɒt/ n. trot m. —v.i. (*p.t.* **trotted**)
trotter. **on the** ~, (*fam.*) de suite. ~
out, (*produce*: *fam.*) sortir; (*state*:
fam.) formuler.

trouble /'trʌbl/ n. ennui(s) m. (pl.),
difficulté(s) f. (pl.); (*pains*, *effort*) mal
m., peine f. ~(**s**), ennuis m. pl.; (*unrest*)
conflits m. pl. —v.t./i. (*bother*) (se)
déranger; (*worry*) ennuyer. **be in** ~,
avoir des ennuis. **go to a lot of** ~, se
donner du mal. **what's the** ~?, quel est
le problème? ~**d** a. inquiet; (*period*)

agité. ∼-**maker** n. provocalteur, -trice
m., f. ∼-**shooter** n. personne appelée
pour désamorcer une crise.

troublesome /'trʌblsəm/ a. ennuyeux,
pénible.

trough /trɒf/ n. (*drinking*) abreuvoir m.;
(*feeding*) auge f. ∼ (**of low pressure**),
dépression f.

trounce /traʊns/ v.t. (*defeat*) écraser;
(*thrash*) rosser.

troupe /truːp/ n. (*theatre*) troupe f.

trousers /'traʊzəz/ n. pl. pantalon m.
short ∼, culotte courte f.

trousseau /'truːsəʊ/ n. (pl. -s /-əʊz/) (*of
bride*) trousseau m.

trout /traʊt/ n. invar. truite f.

trowel /'traʊəl/ n. (*garden*) déplantoir
m.; (*for mortar*) truelle f.

truan|t /'truːənt/ n. absentéiste m./f.;
(*schol.*) élève absent(e) sans permission
m.(f.). **play** ∼**t**, sécher les cours. ∼**cy** n.
absentéisme m.

truce /truːs/ n. trève f.

truck /trʌk/ n. (*lorry*) camion m.; (*cart*)
chariot m.; (*rail.*) wagon m., plateforme
f. ∼-**driver** n. camionneur m.

truculent /'trʌkjʊlənt/ a. agressif.

trudge /trʌdʒ/ v.i. marcher péniblement,
se traîner.

true /truː/ a. (-er, -est) vrai; (*accurate*)
exact; (*faithful*) fidèle.

truffle /'trʌfl/ n. truffe f.

truly /'truːlɪ/ adv. vraiment; (*faithfully*)
fidèlement; (*truthfully*) sincèrement.

trump /trʌmp/ n. atout m. —v.t. ∼ **up**,
inventer. ∼ **card**, atout m.

trumpet /'trʌmpɪt/ n. trompette f.

truncate /trʌŋ'keɪt/ v.t. tronquer.

trundle /'trʌndl/ v.t./i. rouler bruyam
ment.

trunk /trʌŋk/ n. (*of tree, body*) tronc m.;
(*of elephant*) trompe f.; (*box*) malle f.;
(*auto., Amer.*) coffre m. ∼**s**, (*for
swimming*) slip de bain m. ∼-**call** n.
communication interurbaine f. ∼-**road**
n. route nationale f.

truss /trʌs/ n. (*med.*) bandage herniaire
m. —v.t. (*fowl*) trousser.

trust /trʌst/ n. confiance f.; (*association*)
trust m. —v.t. avoir confiance en. —v.i.
∼ **in** or **to**, s'en remettre à. **in** ∼, en
dépôt. **on** ∼, de confiance. ∼ **s.o. with**,
confier à qn. ∼**ed** a. (*friend etc.*)
éprouvé, sûr. ∼**ful**, ∼**ing** adjs. confiant.
∼**y** a. fidèle.

trustee /trʌs'tiː/ n. administrateur, -trice
m., f.

trustworthy /'trʌstwɜːðɪ/ a. digne de
confiance.

truth /truːθ/ n. (pl. -s /truːðz/) vérité f.
∼**ful** a. (*account etc.*) véridique;
(*person*) qui dit la vérité. ∼**fully** adv.
sincèrement.

try /traɪ/ v.t./i. (p.t. **tried**) essayer; (*be a
strain on*) éprouver; (*jurid.*) juger. —n.
(*attempt*) essai m.; (*Rugby*) essai m. ∼
on or **out**, essayer. ∼ **to do**, essayer de
faire. ∼**ing** a. éprouvant.

tsar /zɑː(r)/ n. tsar m.

T-shirt /'tiːʃɜːt/ n. tee-shirt m.

tub /tʌb/ n. baquet m., cuve f.; (*bath:
fam.*) baignoire f.

tuba /'tjuːbə/ n. tuba m.

tubby /'tʌbɪ/ a. (-ier, -iest) dodu.

tub|e /tjuːb/ n. tube m.; (*railway: fam.*)
métro m.; (*in tyre*) chambre à air f.
∼**ing** n. tubes m. pl.

tuberculosis /tjuːbɜːkjʊ'ləʊsɪs/ n. tuber-
culose f.

tubular /'tjuːbjʊlə(r)/ a. tubulaire.

tuck /tʌk/ n. (*fold*) rempli m., (re)pli m.
—v.t. (*put away, place*) ranger; (*hide*)
cacher. —v.i. ∼ **in** or **into**, (*eat: sl.*)
attaquer. ∼ **in**, (*shirt*) rentrer; (*blanket,
person*) border. ∼-**shop** n. (*schol.*)
boutique à provisions f.

Tuesday /'tjuːzdɪ/ n. mardi m.

tuft /tʌft/ n. (*of hair etc.*) touffe f.

tug /tʌg/ v.t. (p.t. **tugged**) tirer fort (sur).
—v.i. tirer fort. —n. (*boat*) remorqueur
m. ∼ **of war**, jeu de la corde tirée m.

tuition /tjuː'ɪʃn/ n. cours m. pl.; (*fee*)
frais de scolarité m. pl.

tulip /'tjuːlɪp/ n. tulipe f.

tumble /'tʌmbl/ v.i. (*fall*) dégringoler.
—n. chute f. ∼-**drier** n. séchoir à linge
(à air chaud) m. ∼ **to**, (*realize: fam.*)
piger.

tumbledown /'tʌmbldaʊn/ a. délabré,
en ruine.

tumbler /'tʌmblə(r)/ n. gobelet m.

tummy /'tʌmɪ/ n. (*fam.*) ventre m.

tumour /'tjuːmə(r)/ n. tumeur f.

tumult /'tjuːmʌlt/ n. tumulte m. ∼**uous**
/-'mʌltʃʊəs/ a. tumultueux.

tuna /'tjuːnə/ n. invar. thon m.

tune /tjuːn/ n. air m. —v.t. (*engine*)
régler; (*mus.*) accorder. —v.i. ∼ **in**
(to), (*radio, TV*) écouter. **be in** ∼/**out of**
∼, (*instrument*) être accordé/désac-
cordé; (*singer*) chanter juste/faux. ∼**ful**
a. mélodieux. **tuning-fork** n. diapason
m. ∼ **up**, (*orchestra*) accorder leurs
instruments.

tunic /'tjuːnɪk/ n. tunique f.

Tunisia /tjuː'nɪzɪə/ n. Tunisie f. ∼**n** a. &
n. tunisien(ne) (m. (f.)).

tunnel /'tʌnl/ n. tunnel m.; (*in mine*)

galerie *f*. —*v.i.* (*p.t.* **tunnelled**) creuser un tunnel (**into**, dans).

turban /'tɜːbən/ *n.* turban *m*.

turbine /'tɜːbaɪn/ *n.* turbine *f*.

turbo /'tɜːbəʊ/ *n.* turbo *m*.

turbulen|t /'tɜːbjʊlənt/ *a.* turbulent. **~ce** *n.* turbulence *f*.

tureen /tjʊˈriːn/ *n.* soupière *f*.

turf /tɜːf/ *n.* (*pl.* turf *or* turves) gazon *m*. —*v.t.* **~ out**, (*sl.*) jeter dehors. **the ~**, (*racing*) le turf.

turgid /'tɜːdʒɪd/ *a.* (*speech*, *style*) boursouflé, ampoulé.

Turk /tɜːk/ *n.* Turc *m*., Turque *f*. **~ey** *n.* Turquie *f*. **~ish** *a.* turc; *n.* (*lang.*) turc *m*.

turkey /'tɜːkɪ/ *n.* dindon *m*., dinde *f*.; (*as food*) dinde *f*.

turmoil /'tɜːmɔɪl/ *n.* trouble *m*., chaos *m*. **in ~**, en ébullition.

turn /tɜːn/ *v.t./i.* tourner; (*of person*) se tourner; (*to other side*) retourner; (*change*) (se) transformer (**into**, en); (*become*) devenir; (*deflect*) détourner; (*milk*) tourner. —*n.* tour *m*.; (*in road*) tournant *m*.; (*of mind*, *events*) tournure *f*.; (*illness*: *fam.*) crise *f*. **do a good ~**, rendre service. **in ~**, à tour de rôle. **speak out of ~**, commettre une indiscrétion. **take ~s**, se relayer. **~ against**, se retourner contre. **~ away** *v.i.* se détourner; *v.t.* (*avert*) détourner; (*refuse*) refuser; (*send back*) renvoyer. **~ back** *v.i.* (*return*) retourner; (*vehicle*) faire demi-tour; *v.t.* (*fold*) rabattre. **~ down**, refuser; (*fold*) rabattre; (*reduce*) baisser. **~ in**, (*go to bed*: *fam.*) se coucher. **~ off**, (*light etc.*) éteindre; (*engine*) arrêter; (*tap*) fermer; (*of driver*) tourner. **~-off** *n.* (*auto.*) embranchement *m*. **~ on**, (*light etc.*) allumer; (*engine*) allumer; (*tap*) ouvrir. **~ out** *v.t.* (*light*) éteindre; (*empty*) vider; (*produce*) produire; *v.i.* (*transpire*) s'avérer; (*come*: *fam.*) venir. **~-out** *n.* assistance *f*. **~ over**, (se) retourner. **~ round**, (*person*) se retourner. **~-round** *n.* revirement *m*. **~ up** *v.i.* arriver; (*be found*) se retrouver; *v.t.* (*find*) déterrer; (*collar*) remonter. **~-up** *n.* (*of trousers*) revers *m*.

turning /'tɜːnɪŋ/ *n.* rue (latérale) *f*.; (*bend*) tournant *m*. **~-point** *n.* tournant *m*.

turnip /'tɜːnɪp/ *n.* navet *m*.

turnover /'tɜːnəʊvə(r)/ *n.* (*pie*, *tart*) chausson *m*.; (*money*) chiffre d'affaires *m*.

turnpike /'tɜːnpaɪk/ *n.* (*Amer.*) autoroute à péage *f*.

turnstile /'tɜːnstaɪl/ *n.* (*gate*) tourniquet *m*.

turntable /'tɜːnteɪbl/ *n.* (*for record*) platine *f*., plateau *m*.

turpentine /'tɜːpəntaɪn/ *n.* térébenthine *f*.

turquoise /'tɜːkwɔɪz/ *a.* turquoise *invar*.

turret /'tʌrɪt/ *n.* tourelle *f*.

turtle /'tɜːtl/ *n.* tortue (de mer) *f*. **~-neck** *a.* à col montant, roulé.

tusk /tʌsk/ *n.* (*tooth*) défense *f*.

tussle /'tʌsl/ *n.* bagarre *f*., lutte *f*.

tutor /'tjuːtə(r)/ *n.* précepteur, -trice *m*., *f*.; (*univ.*) direclteur, -trice d'études *m*., *f*.

tutorial /tjuːˈtɔːrɪəl/ *n.* (*univ.*) séance d'études *or* de travaux pratiques *f*.

tuxedo /tʌkˈsiːdəʊ/ *n.* (*pl.* **-os**) (*Amer.*) smoking *m*.

TV /tiːˈviː/ *n.* télé *f*.

twaddle /'twɒdl/ *n.* fadaises *f. pl*.

twang /twæŋ/ *n.* (*son*: *mus.*) pincement *m*.; (*in voice*) nasillement *m*. —*v.t./i.* (faire) vibrer.

tweed /twiːd/ *n.* tweed *m*.

tweezers /'twiːzəz/ *n. pl.* pince (à épiler) *f*.

twel|ve /twelv/ *a.* & *n.* douze (*m*.). **~fth** *a.* & *n.* douzième (*m./f*.). **~ve (o'clock)**, midi *m*. *or* minuit *m*.

twent|y /'twentɪ/ *a.* & *n.* vingt (*m*.). **~ieth** *a.* & *n.* vingtième (*m./f*.).

twice /twaɪs/ *adv.* deux fois.

twiddle /'twɪdl/ *v.t./i.* **~ (with)**, (*fiddle with*) tripoter. **~ one's thumbs**, se tourner les pouces.

twig¹ /twɪg/ *n.* brindille *f*.

twig² /twɪg/ *v.t./i.* (*p.t.* **twigged**) (*understand*: *fam.*) piger.

twilight /'twaɪlaɪt/ *n.* crépuscule *m*. —*a.* crépusculaire.

twin /twɪn/ *n.* & *a.* jum|eau, -elle (*m.*, *f.*). —*v.t.* (*p.t.* **twinned**) jumeler. **~ning** *n.* jumelage *m*.

twine /twaɪn/ *n.* ficelle *f*. —*v.t./i.* (*wind*) (s')enlacer.

twinge /twɪndʒ/ *n.* élancement *m*.; (*remorse*) remords *m*.

twinkle /'twɪŋkl/ *v.i.* (*star etc.*) scintiller; (*eye*) pétiller. —*n.* scintillement *m*.; pétillement *m*.

twirl /twɜːl/ *v.t./i.* (faire) tournoyer.

twist /twɪst/ *v.t.* tordre; (*weave together*) entortiller; (*roll*) enrouler; (*distort*) déformer. —*v.i.* (*rope etc.*) s'entortiller; (*road*) zigzaguer. —*n.* torsion *f*.;

(*in rope*) tortillon *m*.; (*in road*) tournant *m*.; (*of events*) tournure *f*., tour *m*.

twit /twɪt/ *n*. (*fam*.) idiot(e) *m*. (*f*.).

twitch /twɪtʃ/ *v.t./i*. (se) contracter nerveusement. —*n*. (*tic*) tic *m*.; (*jerk*) secousse *f*.

two /tuː/ *a. & n*. deux (*m*.). **in** *or* **of ~ minds**, indécis. **put ~ and two together**, faire le rapport. **~-faced** *a*. hypocrite. **~fold** *a*. double; *adv*. au double. **~-piece** *n* (*garment*) deux-pièces *m. invar*.

twosome /ˈtuːsəm/ *n*. couple *m*.

tycoon /taɪˈkuːn/ *n*. magnat *m*.

tying /ˈtaɪɪŋ/ *see* **tie**.

type /taɪp/ *n*. (*example*) type *m*.; (*kind*) genre *m*., sorte *f*.; (*person: fam*.) type *m*.; (*print*) caractères *m. pl.* —*v.t./i*. (*write*) taper (à la machine). **~-cast** *a*. catégorisé (**as**, comme).

typescript /ˈtaɪpskrɪpt/ *n*. manuscrit dactylographié *m*.

typewrit|er /ˈtaɪpraɪtə(r)/ *n*. machine à écrire *f*. **~ten** /-ɪtn/ *a*. dactylographié.

typhoid /ˈtaɪfɔɪd/ *n*. **~** (**fever**), typhoïde *f*.

typhoon /taɪˈfuːn/ *n*. typhon *m*.

typical /ˈtɪpɪkl/ *a*. typique. **~ly** *adv*. typiquement.

typify /ˈtɪpɪfaɪ/ *v.t*. être typique de.

typing /ˈtaɪpɪŋ/ *n*. dactylo(graphie) *f*.

typist /ˈtaɪpɪst/ *n*. dactylo *f*.

tyrann|y /ˈtɪrənɪ/ *n*. tyrannie *f*. **~ical** /tɪˈrænɪkl/ *a*. tyrannique.

tyrant /ˈtaɪərənt/ *n*. tyran *m*.

tyre /ˈtaɪə(r)/ *n*. pneu *m*.

U

ubiquitous /juːˈbɪkwɪtəs/ *a*. omniprésent, qu'on trouve partout.

udder /ˈʌdə(r)/ *n*. pis *m*., mamelle *f*.

UFO /ˈjuːfəʊ/ *n*. (*pl*. **-Os**) OVNI *m*.

Uganda /juːˈɡændə/ *n*. Ouganda *m*.

ugl|y /ˈʌɡlɪ/ *a*. (**-ier, -iest**) laid. **~iness** *n*. laideur *f*.

UK *abbr. see* **United Kingdom**.

ulcer /ˈʌlsə(r)/ *n*. ulcère *m*.

ulterior /ʌlˈtɪərɪə(r)/ *a*. ultérieur. **~ motive**, arrière-pensée *f*.

ultimate /ˈʌltɪmət/ *a*. dernier, ultime; (*definitive*) définitif; (*basic*) fondamental. **~ly** *adv*. à la fin; (*in the last analysis*) en fin de compte.

ultimatum /ʌltɪˈmeɪtəm/ *n*. (*pl*. **-ums**) ultimatum *m*.

ultra- /ˈʌltrə/ *pref*. ultra-.

ultrasound /ˈʌltrəsaʊnd/ *n*. ultrason *m*.

ultraviolet /ʌltrəˈvaɪələt/ *a*. ultraviolet.

umbilical /ʌmˈbɪlɪkl/ *a*. **~ cord**, cordon ombilical *m*.

umbrella /ʌmˈbrelə/ *n*. parapluie *m*.

umpire /ˈʌmpaɪə(r)/ *n*. (*sport*) arbitre *m*. —*v.t*. arbitrer.

umpteen /ˈʌmptiːn/ *a*. (*many: sl*.) un tas de. **~th** *a*. (*fam*.) énième.

UN *abbr*. (*United Nations*) ONU *f*.

un- /ʌn/ *pref*. in-, dé(s)-, non, peu, mal, sans.

unabated /ʌnəˈbeɪtɪd/ *a*. non diminué, aussi fort qu'avant.

unable /ʌnˈeɪbl/ *a*. incapable; (*through circumstances*) dans l'impossibilité (**to do**, de faire).

unacceptable /ʌnəkˈseptəbl/ *a*. inacceptable, inadmissible.

unaccountabl|e /ʌnəˈkaʊntəbl/ *a*. (*strange*) inexplicable. **~y** *adv*. inexplicablement.

unaccustomed /ʌnəˈkʌstəmd/ *a*. inaccoutumé. **~ to**, peu habitué à.

unadulterated /ʌnəˈdʌltəreɪtɪd/ *a*. (*pure, sheer*) pur.

unaided /ʌnˈeɪdɪd/ *a*. sans aide.

unanim|ous /juːˈnænɪməs/ *a*. unanime. **~ity** /-əˈnɪmətɪ/ *n*. unanimité *f*. **~ously** *adv*. à l'unanimité.

unarmed /ʌnˈɑːmd/ *a*. non armé.

unashamed /ʌnəˈʃeɪmd/ *a*. éhonté. **~ly** /-ɪdlɪ/ *adv*. sans vergogne.

unassuming /ʌnəˈsjuːmɪŋ/ *a*. modeste, sans prétention.

unattached /ʌnəˈtætʃt/ *a*. libre.

unattainable /ʌnəˈteɪnəbl/ *a*. inaccessible.

unattended /ʌnəˈtendɪd/ *a*. (*laissé*) sans surveillance.

unattractive /ʌnəˈtræktɪv/ *a*. peu séduisant, laid; (*offer*) peu intéressant.

unauthorized /ʌnˈɔːθəraɪzd/ *a*. non autorisé.

unavailable /ʌnəˈveɪləbl/ *a*. pas disponible.

unavoidabl|e /ʌnəˈvɔɪdəbl/ *a*. inévitable. **~y** *adv*. inévitablement.

unaware /ʌnəˈweə(r)/ *a*. **be ~ of**, ignorer. **~s** /-eəz/ *adv*. au dépourvu.

unbalanced /ʌnˈbælənst/ *a*. (*mind, person*) déséquilibré.

unbearable /ʌnˈbeərəbl/ *a*. insupportable.

unbeat|able /ʌnˈbiːtəbl/ *a*. imbattable. **~en** *a*. non battu.

unbeknown(st) /ʌnbɪˈnəʊn(st)/ *a*. **~(st) to**, (*fam*.) à l'insu de.

unbelievable /ʌnbɪ'liːvəbl/ a. incroyable.

unbend /ʌn'bend/ v.i. (p.t. unbent) (relax) se détendre.

unbiased /ʌn'baɪəst/ a. impartial.

unblock /ʌn'blɒk/ v.t. déboucher.

unborn /ʌn'bɔːn/ a. futur, à venir.

unbounded /ʌn'baʊndɪd/ a. illimité.

unbreakable /ʌn'breɪkəbl/ a. incassable.

unbridled /ʌn'braɪdld/ a. débridé.

unbroken /ʌn'brəʊkən/ a. (intact) intact; (continuous) continu.

unburden /ʌn'bɜːdn/ v. pr. ~ o.s., (open one's heart) s'épancher.

unbutton /ʌn'bʌtn/ v.t. déboutonner.

uncalled-for /ʌn'kɔːldfɔː(r)/ a. injustifié, superflu.

uncanny /ʌn'kænɪ/ a. (-ier, -iest) étrange, mystérieux.

unceasing /ʌn'siːsɪŋ/ a. incessant.

unceremonious /ʌnserɪ'məʊnɪəs/ a. sans façon, brusque.

uncertain /ʌn'sɜːtn/ a. incertain. be ~ whether, ne pas savoir exactement si (to do, on doit faire). ~ty n. incertitude f.

unchanged /ʌn'tʃeɪndʒd/ a. inchangé. ~ing a. immuable.

uncivilized /ʌn'sɪvɪlaɪzd/ a. barbare.

uncle /'ʌŋkl/ n. oncle m.

uncomfortable /ʌn'kʌmftəbl/ a. (thing) peu confortable; (unpleasant) désagréable. feel or be ~, (person) être mal à l'aise.

uncommon /ʌn'kɒmən/ a. rare. ~ly adv. remarquablement.

uncompromising /ʌn'kɒmprəmaɪzɪŋ/ a. intransigeant.

unconcerned /ʌnkən'sɜːnd/ a. (indifferent) indifférent (by, à).

unconditional /ʌnkən'dɪʃənl/ a. inconditionnel.

unconscious /ʌn'kɒnʃəs/ a. sans connaissance, inanimé; (not aware) inconscient (of, de) —n. inconscient m. ~ly adv. inconsciemment.

unconventional /ʌnkən'venʃənl/ a. peu conventionnel.

uncooperative /ʌnkəʊ'ɒpərətɪv/ a. peu coopératif.

uncork /ʌn'kɔːk/ v.t. déboucher.

uncouth /ʌn'kuːθ/ a. grossier.

uncover /ʌn'kʌvə(r)/ v.t. découvrir.

undecided /ʌndɪ'saɪdɪd/ a. indécis.

undefinable /ʌndɪ'faɪnəbl/ a. indéfinissable.

undeniable /ʌndɪ'naɪəbl/ a. indéniable, incontestable.

under /'ʌndə(r)/ prep. sous; (less than) moins de; (according to) selon. —adv. au-dessous. ~ age, mineur. ~ it/there, là-dessous. ~-side n. dessous m. ~ way, (in progress) en cours; (on the way) en route.

under- /'ʌndə(r)/ pref. sous-.

undercarriage /'ʌndəkærɪdʒ/ n. (aviat.) train d'atterrissage m.

underclothes /'ʌndəkləʊðz/ n. pl. sous-vêtements m. pl.

undercoat /'ʌndəkəʊt/ n. (of paint) couche de fond f.

undercover /'ʌndə'kʌvə(r)/ (agent, operation) a. secret.

undercurrent /'ʌndəkʌrənt/ n. courant (profond) m.

undercut /ʌndə'kʌt/ v.t. (p.t. undercut, pres. p. undercutting) (comm.) vendre moins cher que.

underdeveloped /ʌndədɪ'veləpt/ a. sous-développé.

underdog /'ʌndədɒg/ n. (pol.) opprimé(e) m. (f.); (socially) déshérité(e) m. (f.).

underdone /'ʌndədʌn/ a. pas assez cuit; (steak) saignant.

underestimate /ʌndər'estɪmeɪt/ v.t. sous-estimer.

underfed /ʌndə'fed/ a. sous-alimenté.

underfoot /ʌndə'fʊt/ adv. sous les pieds.

undergo /ʌndə'gəʊ/ v.t. (p.t. -went, pp. -gone) subir.

undergraduate /ʌndə'grædʒʊət/ n. étudiant(e) (qui prépare la licence) m. (f.).

underground[1] /ʌndə'graʊnd/ adv. sous terre.

underground[2] /'ʌndəgraʊnd/ a. souterrain; (secret) clandestin. —n. (rail.) métro m.

undergrowth /'ʌndəgrəʊθ/ n. sous-bois m. invar.

underhand /'ʌndəhænd/ a. (deceitful) sournois.

under|lie /ʌndə'laɪ/ v.t. (p.t. -lay, p.p. -lain, pres. p. -lying) sous-tendre. ~lying a. fondamental.

underline /ʌndə'laɪn/ v.t. souligner.

undermine /ʌndə'maɪn/ v.t. (cliff, society, etc.) miner, saper.

underneath /ʌndə'niːθ/ prep. sous. —adv. (en) dessous.

underpaid /ʌndə'peɪd/ a. sous-payé.

underpants /'ʌndəpænts/ n. pl. (man's) slip m.

underpass /'ʌndəpɑːs/ n. (for cars, people) passage souterrain m.

underprivileged /ˌʌndə'prɪvəlɪdʒd/ a.
défavorisé.

underrate /ˌʌndə'reɪt/ v.t. sous-estimer.

undershirt /'ʌndəʃɜːt/ n. (Amer.) maillot (de corps) m.

undershorts /'ʌndəʃɔːts/ n. pl. (Amer.)
caleçon m.

underskirt /'ʌndəʃkɜːt/ n. jupon m.

understand /ˌʌndə'stænd/ v.t./i. (p.t.
-stood) comprendre. ~able a. compréhensible. ~ing a. compréhensif; n.
compréhension f.; (agreement) entente
f.

understatement /'ʌndəsteɪtmənt/ n.
litote f. that's an ~, c'est en deçà de la
vérité.

understudy /'ʌndəstʌdɪ/ n. (theatre)
doublure f.

undertake /ˌʌndə'teɪk/ v.t. (p.t. -took,
p.p. -taken) entreprendre; (responsibility) assumer. ~e to, s'engager à. ~ing
n. (task) entreprise f.; (promise)
promesse f.

undertaker /'ʌndəteɪkə(r)/ n. entrepreneur de pompes funèbres m.

undertone /'ʌndətəʊn/ n. in an ~, à mi-
voix.

undervalue /ˌʌndə'væljuː/ v.t. sous-
évaluer.

underwater /ˌʌndə'wɔːtə(r)/ a sous-
marin. —adv. sous l'eau.

underwear /'ʌndəweə(r)/ n. sous-
vêtements m. pl.

underwent /ˌʌndə'went/ see undergo.

underworld /'ʌndəwɜːld/ n. (of crime)
milieu m., pègre f.

undeserved /ˌʌndɪ'zɜːvd/ a. immérité.

undesirable /ˌʌndɪ'zaɪərəbl/ a. peu
souhaitable; (person) indésirable.

undies /'ʌndɪz/ n. pl. (female underwear; fam.) dessous m pl

undignified /ʌn'dɪgnɪfaɪd/ a. qui
manque de dignité, sans dignité.

undisputed /ˌʌndɪ'spjuːtɪd/ a. incon-
testé.

undistinguished /ˌʌndɪ'stɪŋgwɪʃt/ a.
médiocre.

undo /ʌn'duː/ v.t. (p.t. -did, p.p. -done
/-dʌn/) défaire, détacher; (a wrong)
réparer. leave ~ne, ne pas faire.

undoubted /ʌn'daʊtɪd/ a. indubitable.
~ly adv. indubitablement.

undreamt /ʌn'dremt/ a. ~ of, insoup-
çonné, inimaginable.

undress /ʌn'dres/ v.t./i. (se) déshabiller.
get ~ed, se déshabiller.

undue /ʌn'djuː/ a. excessif. ~ly adv.
excessivement.

undulate /'ʌndjʊleɪt/ v.i. onduler.

undying /ʌn'daɪɪŋ/ a. éternel.

unearth /ʌn'ɜːθ/ v.t. déterrer.

unearthly /ʌn'ɜːθlɪ/ a. mystérieux. ~
hour, (fam.) heure indue f.

uneasy /ʌn'iːzɪ/ a. (ill at ease) mal à
l'aise; (worried) inquiet; (situation)
difficile.

uneducated /ʌn'edʒʊkeɪtɪd/ a. (person)
inculte; (speech) populaire.

unemploy|ed /ʌnɪm'plɔɪd/ a. en
chômage. ~ment n. chômage m.
~ment benefit, allocations de chômage
f. pl.

unending /ʌn'endɪŋ/ a. interminable,
sans fin.

unequal /ʌn'iːkwəl/ a. inégal. ~led a.
inégalé.

unerring /ʌn'ɜːrɪŋ/ a. infaillible.

uneven /ʌn'iːvn/ a. inégal.

uneventful /ʌnɪ'ventfl/ a. sans incident.

unexpected /ʌnɪk'spektɪd/ a. inattendu,
imprévu. ~ly adv. subitement; (arrive)
à l'improviste.

unfailing /ʌn'feɪlɪŋ/ a. constant, continuel; (loyal) fidèle.

unfair /ʌn'feə(r)/ a. injuste. ~ness n.
injustice f.

unfaithful /ʌn'feɪθfl/ a. infidèle.

unfamiliar /ʌnfə'mɪlɪə(r)/ a. inconnu,
peu familier. be ~ with, ne pas
connaître.

unfashionable /ʌn'fæʃənəbl/ a.
(clothes) démodé. it's ~ to, ce n'est pas
à la mode de.

unfasten /ʌn'fɑːsn/ v.t. défaire.

unfavourable /ʌn'feɪvərəbl/ a. défavo-
rable.

unfeeling /ʌn'fiːlɪŋ/ a. insensible.

unfinished /ʌn'fɪnɪʃt/ a. inachevé.

unfit /ʌn'fɪt/ a. (med.) peu en forme;
(unsuitable) impropre (for, à). ~ to,
(unable) pas en état de.

unflinching /ʌn'flɪntʃɪŋ/ a. (fearless)
intrépide.

unfold /ʌn'fəʊld/ v.t. déplier; (expose)
exposer. —v.i. se dérouler.

unforeseen /ʌnfɔː'siːn/ a. imprévu.

unforgettable /ʌnfə'getəbl/ a. inoubliable.

unforgivable /ʌnfə'gɪvəbl/ a. impardonnable, inexcusable.

unfortunate /ʌn'fɔːtʃʊnət/ a. malheureux; (event) fâcheux. ~ly adv.
malheureusement.

unfounded /ʌn'faʊndɪd/ a. (rumour
etc.) sans fondement.

unfriendly /ʌn'frendlɪ/ a. peu amical,
froid.

ungainly /ʌn'geɪnlɪ/ a. gauche.

ungodly /ʌnˈgɒdlɪ/ *a.* impie. ∼ **hour,** (*fam.*) heure indue *f.*

ungrateful /ʌnˈgreɪtfl/ *a.* ingrat.

unhapp|y /ʌnˈhæpɪ/ *a.* (**-ier, -iest**) malheureux, triste; (*not pleased*) mécontent (**with,** de). ∼**ily** *adv.* malheureusement. ∼**iness** *n.* tristesse *f.*

unharmed /ʌnˈhɑːmd/ *a.* indemne, sain et sauf.

unhealthy /ʌnˈhelθɪ/ *a.* (**-ier, -iest**) (*climate etc.*) malsain; (*person*) en mauvaise santé.

unheard-of /ʌnˈhɜːdɒv/ *a.* inouï.

unhinge /ʌnˈhɪndʒ/ *v.t.* (*person, mind*) déséquilibrer.

unholy /ʌnˈhəʊlɪ/ *a.* (**-ier, -iest**) (*person, act, etc.*) impie; (*great*: *fam.*) invraisemblable.

unhook /ʌnˈhʊk/ *v.t.* décrocher; (*dress*) dégrafer.

unhoped /ʌnˈhəʊpt/ *a.* ∼ **for,** inespéré.

unhurt /ʌnˈhɜːt/ *a.* indemne.

unicorn /ˈjuːnɪkɔːn/ *n.* licorne *f.*

uniform /ˈjuːnɪfɔːm/ *n.* uniforme *m.* —*a.* uniforme. ∼**ity** /-ˈfɔːmətɪ/ *n.* uniformité *f.* ∼**ly** *adv.* uniformément.

unif|y /ˈjuːnɪfaɪ/ *v.t.* unifier. ∼**ication** /-ɪˈkeɪʃn/ *n.* unification *f.*

unilateral /juːnɪˈlætrəl/ *a.* unilatéral.

unimaginable /ʌnɪˈmædʒɪnəbl/ *a.* inimaginable.

unimportant /ʌnɪmˈpɔːtnt/ *a.* peu important.

uninhabited /ʌnɪnˈhæbɪtɪd/ *a.* inhabité.

unintentional /ʌnɪnˈtenʃənl/ *a.* involontaire.

uninterest|ed /ʌnˈɪntrəstɪd/ *a.* indifférent (**in,** à). ∼**ing** *a.* peu intéressant.

union /ˈjuːnɪən/ *n.* union *f.*; (*trade union*) syndicat *m.* ∼**ist** *n.* syndiqué(e) *m.* (*f.*). **U**∼ **Jack,** drapeau britannique *m.*

unique /juːˈniːk/ *a.* unique. ∼**ly** *adv.* exceptionnellement.

unisex /ˈjuːnɪseks/ *a.* unisexe.

unison /ˈjuːnɪsn/ *n.* **in** ∼, à l'unisson.

unit /ˈjuːnɪt/ *n.* unité *f.*; (*of furniture etc.*) élément *m.*, bloc *m.* ∼ **trust,** (*équivalent d'une*) SICAV *f.*

unite /juːˈnaɪt/ *v.t./i.* (s')unir. **U**∼**d Kingdom,** Royaume-Uni *m.* **U**∼**d Nations,** Nations Unies *f. pl.* **U**∼**d States (of America),** États-Unis (d'Amérique) *m. pl.*

unity /ˈjuːnətɪ/ *n.* unité *f.*; (*harmony*: *fig.*) harmonie *f.*

universal /juːnɪˈvɜːsl/ *a.* universel.

universe /ˈjuːnɪvɜːs/ *n.* univers *m.*

university /juːnɪˈvɜːsətɪ/ *n.* université *f.*

—*a.* universitaire; (*student, teacher*) d'université.

unjust /ʌnˈdʒʌst/ *a.* injuste.

unkempt /ʌnˈkempt/ *a.* négligé.

unkind /ʌnˈkaɪnd/ *a.* pas gentil, méchant. ∼**ly** *adv.* méchamment.

unknowingly /ʌnˈnəʊɪŋlɪ/ *adv.* sans le savoir, inconsciemment.

unknown /ʌnˈnəʊn/ *a.* inconnu. —*n.* **the** ∼, l'inconnu *m.*

unleash /ʌnˈliːʃ/ *v.t.* déchaîner.

unless /ənˈles/ *conj.* à moins que.

unlike /ʌnˈlaɪk/ *a.* (*brothers etc.*) différents. —*prep.* à la différence de; (*different from*) très différent de.

unlikel|y /ʌnˈlaɪklɪ/ *a.* improbable. ∼**ihood** *n.* improbabilité *f.*

unlimited /ʌnˈlɪmɪtɪd/ *a.* illimité.

unlisted /ʌnˈlɪstɪd/ *a.* (*comm.*) non inscrit à la cote; (*Amer.*) qui n'est pas dans l'annuaire.

unload /ʌnˈləʊd/ *v.t.* décharger.

unlock /ʌnˈlɒk/ *v.t.* ouvrir.

unluck|y /ʌnˈlʌkɪ/ *a.* (**-ier, -iest**) malheureux; (*number*) qui porte malheur. ∼**ily** *adv.* malheureusement.

unmarried /ʌnˈmærɪd/ *a.* célibataire, qui n'est pas marié.

unmask /ʌnˈmɑːsk/ *v.t.* démasquer.

unmistakable /ʌnmɪˈsteɪkəbl/ *a.* (*voice etc.*) facilement reconnaissable; (*clear*) très net.

unmitigated /ʌnˈmɪtɪgeɪtɪd/ *a.* (*absolute*) absolu.

unmoved /ʌnˈmuːvd/ *a.* indifférent (**by,** à), insensible (**by,** à).

unnatural /ʌnˈnætʃrəl/ *a.* pas naturel, anormal.

unnecessary /ʌnˈnesəsərɪ/ *a.* inutile; (*superfluous*) superflu.

unnerve /ʌnˈnɜːv/ *v.t.* troubler.

unnoticed /ʌnˈnəʊtɪst/ *a.* inaperçu.

unobtainable /ʌnəbˈteɪnəbl/ *n.* impossible à obtenir.

unobtrusive /ʌnəbˈtruːsɪv/ *a.* (*person, object*) discret.

unofficial /ʌnəˈfɪʃl/ *a.* officieux.

unorthodox /ʌnˈɔːθədɒks/ *a.* peu orthodoxe.

unpack /ʌnˈpæk/ *v.t.* (*suitcase etc.*) défaire; (*contents*) déballer. —*v.i.* défaire sa valise.

unpalatable /ʌnˈpælətəbl/ *a.* (*food, fact, etc.*) désagréable.

unparalleled /ʌnˈpærəleld/ *a.* incomparable.

unpleasant /ʌnˈpleznt/ *a.* désagréable (**to,** avec).

unplug /ʌn'plʌg/ v.t. (electr.) débrancher; (unblock) déboucher.

unpopular /ʌn'pɒpjʊlə(r)/ a. impopulaire. ~ with, mal vu de.

unprecedented /ʌn'presɪdentɪd/ a. sans précédent.

unpredictable /ʌnprɪ'dɪktəbl/ a. imprévisible.

unprepared /ʌnprɪ'peəd/ a. non préparé; (person) qui n'a rien préparé. be ~ for, (not expect) ne pas s'attendre à.

unpretentious /ʌnprɪ'tenʃəs/ a. sans prétention(s).

unprincipled /ʌn'prɪnsəpld/ a. sans scrupules.

unprofessional /ʌnprə'feʃənl/ a. (work) d'amateur; (conduct) contraire au code professionel.

unpublished /ʌn'pʌblɪʃt/ a. inédit.

unqualified /ʌn'kwɒlɪfaɪd/ a. non diplômé; (success etc.) total. be ~ to, ne pas être qualifié pour.

unquestionabl|e /ʌn'kwestʃənəbl/ a. incontestable. ~y adv. incontestablement.

unravel /ʌn'rævl/ v.t. (p.t. unravelled) démêler, débrouiller.

unreal /ʌn'rɪəl/ a. irréel.

unreasonable /ʌn'ri:znəbl/ a. déraisonnable, peu raisonnable.

unrecognizable /ʌnrekəg'naɪzəbl/ a. méconnaissable.

unrelated /ʌnrɪ'leɪtɪd/ a. (facts) sans rapport (to, avec).

unreliable /ʌnrɪ'laɪəbl/ a. peu sérieux; (machine) peu fiable.

unremitting /ʌnrɪ'mɪtɪŋ/ a. (effort) acharné; (emotion) inaltérable.

unreservedly /ʌnrɪ'zɜ:vɪdlɪ/ adv. sans réserve.

unrest /ʌn'rest/ n. troubles m. pl.

unrivalled /ʌn'raɪvld/ a. sans égal, incomparable.

unroll /ʌn'rəʊl/ v.t. dérouler.

unruffled /ʌn'rʌfld/ a. (person) qui n'a pas perdu son calme.

unruly /ʌn'ru:lɪ/ a. indiscipliné.

unsafe /ʌn'seɪf/ a. (dangerous) dangereux; (person) en danger.

unsaid /ʌn'sed/ a. leave ~, passer sous silence.

unsatisfactory /ʌnsætɪs'fæktərɪ/ a. peu satisfaisant.

unsavoury /ʌn'seɪvərɪ/ a. désagréable, répugnant.

unscathed /ʌn'skeɪðd/ a. indemne.

unscheduled /ʌn'ʃedju:ld, Amer. ʌn-'skedju:ld/ a. pas prévu.

unscrew /ʌn'skru:/ v.t. dévisser.

unscrupulous /ʌn'skru:pjʊləs/ a. sans scrupules, malhonnête.

unseemly /ʌn'si:mlɪ/ a. inconvenant, incorrect, incongru.

unseen /ʌn'si:n/ a. inaperçu. —n. (translation) version f.

unsettle /ʌn'setl/ v.t. troubler. ~d a. (weather) instable.

unshakeable /ʌn'ʃeɪkəbl/ a. (person, belief, etc.) inébranlable.

unshaven /ʌn'ʃeɪvn/ a. pas rasé.

unsightly /ʌn'saɪtlɪ/ a. laid.

unskilled /ʌn'skɪld/ a. inexpert; (worker) non qualifié.

unsociable /ʌn'səʊʃəbl/ a. insociable, farouche.

unsophisticated /ʌnsə'fɪstɪkeɪtɪd/ a. peu sophistiqué, simple.

unsound /ʌn'saʊnd/ a. peu solide. of ~ mind, fou.

unspeakable /ʌn'spi:kəbl/ a. indescriptible; (bad) innommable.

unspecified /ʌn'spesɪfaɪd/ a. indéterminé.

unstable /ʌn'steɪbl/ a. instable.

unsteady /ʌn'stedɪ/ a. (step) chancelant; (ladder) instable; (hand) mal assuré.

unstuck /ʌn'stʌk/ a. décollé. come ~, (fail: fam.) échouer.

unsuccessful /ʌnsək'sesfl/ a. (result, candidate) malheureux; (attempt) infructueux. be ~, ne pas réussir (in doing, à faire).

unsuit|able /ʌn'su:təbl/ a. qui ne convient pas (for, à), peu approprié. ~ed a. inapte (to, à).

unsure /ʌn'ʃɔ:(r)/ a. incertain.

unsuspecting /ʌnsə'spektɪŋ/ a. qui ne se doute de rien.

unsympathetic /ʌnsɪmpə'θetɪk/ a. (unhelpful) peu compréhensif; (unpleasant) antipathique.

untangle /ʌn'tæŋgl/ v.t. démêler.

untenable /ʌn'tenəbl/ a. intenable.

unthinkable /ʌn'θɪŋkəbl/ a. impensable, inconcevable.

untid|y /ʌn'taɪdɪ/ a. (-ier, -iest) (person) désordonné; (clothes, hair, room) en désordre; (work) mal soigné. ~ily adv. sans soin.

untie /ʌn'taɪ/ v.t. (knot, parcel) défaire; (person) détacher.

until /ən'tɪl/ prep. jusqu'à. not ~, pas avant. —conj. jusqu'à ce que; (before) avant que.

untimely /ʌn'taɪmlɪ/ a. inopportun; (death) prématuré.

untold /ʌn'təʊld/ a. incalculable.

untoward /ʌntə'wɔ:d/ a. fâcheux.

untrue /ʌn'truː/ a. faux.
unused[1] /ʌn'juːzd/ a. (*new*) neuf; (*not in use*) inutilisé.
unused[2] /ʌn'juːst/ a. ～ **to**, peu habitué à.
unusual /ʌn'juːʒʊəl/ a. exceptionnel; (*strange*) insolite, étrange. ～**ly** adv. exceptionnellement.
unveil /ʌn'veɪl/ v.t. dévoiler.
unwanted /ʌn'wɒntɪd/ a. (*useless*) superflu; (*child*) non désiré.
unwelcome /ʌn'welkəm/ a. fâcheux; (*guest*) importun.
unwell /ʌn'wel/ a. indisposé.
unwieldy /ʌn'wiːldɪ/ a. difficile à manier.
unwilling /ʌn'wɪlɪŋ/ a. peu disposé (**to**, à); (*victim*) récalcitrant. ～**ly** adv. à contrecœur.
unwind /ʌn'waɪnd/ v.t./i. (*p.t.* **unwound** /ʌn'waʊnd/) (se) dérouler; (*relax: fam.*) se détendre.
unwise /ʌn'waɪz/ a. imprudent.
unwittingly /ʌn'wɪtɪŋlɪ/ adv. involontairement.
unworkable /ʌn'wɜːkəbl/ a. (*plan etc.*) irréalisable.
unworthy /ʌn'wɜːðɪ/ a. indigne.
unwrap /ʌn'ræp/ v.t. (*p.t.* **unwrapped**) ouvrir, défaire.
unwritten /ʌn'rɪtn/ a. (*agreement*) verbal, tacite.
up /ʌp/ adv. en haut, en l'air; (*sun, curtain*) levé; (*out of bed*) levé, debout; (*finished*) fini. **be up,** (*level, price*) avoir monté. —prep. (*a hill*) en haut de; (*a tree*) dans; (*a ladder*) sur. —v.t. (*p.t.* **upped**) augmenter. **come** *or* **go up,** monter. **up in the bedroom,** là-haut dans la chambre. **up there,** là-haut. **up to,** jusqu'à; (*task*) à la hauteur de. **it is up to you,** ça dépend de vous (**to,** de). **be up to sth.,** (*able*) être capable de qch.; (*do*) faire qch.; (*plot*) faire qch. **be up to,** (*in book*) en être à. **be up against,** faire face à. **be up in,** (*fam.*) s'y connaître en. **feel up to doing,** (*able*) être de taille à faire. **have ups and downs,** connaître des hauts et des bas. **up-and-coming** a. prometteur. **up-market** a. haut-de-gamme. **up to date,** moderne; (*news*) récent.
upbringing /'ʌpbrɪŋɪŋ/ n. éducation f.
update /ʌp'deɪt/ v.t. mettre à jour.
upgrade /ʌp'greɪd/ v.t. (*person*) promouvoir; (*job*) revaloriser.
upheaval /ʌp'hiːvl/ n. bouleversement m.
uphill /ʌp'hɪl/ a. qui monte; (*fig.*) difficile. —adv. **go** ～, monter.

uphold /ʌp'həʊld/ v.t. (*p.t.* **upheld**) maintenir.
upholster /ʌp'həʊlstə(r)/ v.t. (*pad*) rembourrer; (*cover*) recouvrir. ～**y** n. (*in vehicle*) garniture f.
upkeep /'ʌpkiːp/ n. entretien m.
upon /ə'pɒn/ prep. sur.
upper /'ʌpə(r)/ a. supérieur. —n. (*of shoe*) empeigne f. **have the** ～ **hand,** avoir le dessus. ～ **class,** aristocratie f. ～**most** a. (*highest*) le plus haut.
upright /'ʌpraɪt/ a. droit. —n. (*post*) montant m.
uprising /'ʌpraɪzɪŋ/ n. soulèvement m., insurrection f.
uproar /'ʌprɔː(r)/ n. tumulte m.
uproot /ʌp'ruːt/ v.t. déraciner.
upset[1] /ʌp'set/ v.t. (*p.t.* **upset**, *pres. p.* **upsetting**) (*overturn*) renverser; (*plan, stomach*) déranger; (*person*) contrarier, affliger. —a. peiné.
upset[2] /'ʌpset/ n. dérangement m.; (*distress*) chagrin m.
upshot /'ʌpʃɒt/ n. résultat m.
upside-down /ʌpsaɪd'daʊn/ adv. (*in position, in disorder*) à l'envers, sens dessus dessous.
upstairs /ʌp'steəz/ adv. en haut. —a. (*flat etc.*) d'en haut.
upstart /'ʌpstɑːt/ n. (*pej.*) parvenu(e) m. (*f.*).
upstream /ʌp'striːm/ adv. en amont.
upsurge /'ʌpsɜːdʒ/ n. recrudescence f.; (*of anger*) accès m.
uptake /'ʌpteɪk/ n. **be quick on the** ～, comprendre vite.
uptight /ʌp'taɪt/ a. (*tense: fam.*) crispé; (*angry: fam.*) en colère.
upturn /'ʌptɜːn/ n. amélioration f.
upward /'ʌpwəd/ a. & adv., ～**s** adv. vers le haut.
uranium /jʊ'reɪnɪəm/ n. uranium m.
urban /'ɜːbən/ a. urbain.
urbane /ɜː'beɪn/ a. courtois.
urchin /'ɜːtʃɪn/ n. garnement m.
urge /ɜːdʒ/ v.t. conseiller vivement (**to do,** de faire). —n. forte envie f. ～ **on,** (*impel*) encourager.
urgen|t /'ɜːdʒənt/ a. urgent; (*request*) pressant. ～**cy** n. urgence f.; (*of request, tone*) insistance f. ～**tly** adv. d'urgence.
urinal /jʊə'raɪnl/ n. urinoir m.
urin|e /'jʊərɪn/ n. urine f. ～**ate** v.i. uriner.
urn /ɜːn/ n. urne f.; (*for tea, coffee*) fontaine f.
us /ʌs, *unstressed* əs/ pron. nous. **(to) us,** nous.

US *abbr. see* **United States.**

USA *abbr. see* **United States of America**.

usable /'juːzəbl/ *a.* utilisable.

usage /'juːsɪdʒ/ *n.* usage *m.*

use[1] /juːz/ *v.t.* se servir de, utiliser; (*consume*) consommer. ~ **up**, épuiser. ~**r** /-ə(r)/ *n.* usager *m.* ~**r-friendly** *a.* facile d'emploi.

use[2] /juːs/ *n.* usage *m.*, emploi *m.* **in** ~, en usage. **it is no** ~ **shouting/etc.**, ça ne sert à rien de crier/etc. **make** ~ **of**, se servir de. **of** ~, utile.

used[1] /juːzd/ *a.* (*second-hand*) d'occasion.

used[2] /juːst/ *p.t.* **he** ~ **to do**, il faisait (autrefois), il avait l'habitude de faire. —*a.* ~ **to**, habitué à.

use|ful /'juːsfl/ *a.* utile. ~**fully** *adv.* utilement. ~**less** *a.* inutile; (*person*) incompétent.

usher /'ʌʃə(r)/ *n.* (*in theatre, hall*) placeur *m.* —*v.t.* ~ **in**, faire entrer. ~**ette** *n.* ouvreuse *f.*

USSR *abbr.* (*Union of Soviet Socialist Republics*) URSS *f.*

usual /'juːʒʊəl/ *a.* habituel, normal. **as** ~, comme d'habitude. ~**ly** *adv.* d'habitude.

usurp /juːˈzɜːp/ *v.t.* usurper.

utensil /juːˈtensl/ *n.* ustensile *m.*

uterus /'juːtərəs/ *n.* utérus *m.*

utilitarian /juːtɪlɪˈteərɪən/ *a.* utilitaire.

utility /juːˈtɪlətɪ/ *n.* utilité *f.* (**public**) ~, service public *m.*

utilize /'juːtɪlaɪz/ *v.t.* utiliser.

utmost /'ʌtməʊst/ *a.* (*furthest, most intense*) extrême. **the** ~ **care/etc.**, (*greatest*) le plus grand soin/etc. —*n.* **do one's** ~, faire tout son possible.

Utopia /juːˈtəʊpɪə/ *n.* utopie *f.* ~**n** *a.* utopique.

utter[1] /'ʌtə(r)/ *a.* complet, absolu. ~**ly** *adv.* complètement.

utter[2] /'ʌtə(r)/ *v.t.* proférer; (*sigh, shout*) pousser. ~**ance** *n.* déclaration *f.* **give** ~**ance to**, exprimer.

U-turn /'juːtɜːn/ *n.* demi-tour *m.*

V

vacan|t /'veɪkənt/ *a.* (*post*) vacant; (*seat etc.*) libre; (*look*) vague. ~**cy** *n.* (*post*) poste vacant *m.*; (*room*) chambre disponible *f.*

vacate /vəˈkeɪt, *Amer.* 'veɪkeɪt/ *v.t.* quitter.

vacation /veɪˈkeɪʃn/ *n.* (*Amer.*) vacances *f. pl.*

vaccinat|e /'væksɪneɪt/ *v.t.* vacciner. ~**ion** /-'neɪʃn/ *n.* vaccination *f.*

vaccine /'væksiːn/ *n.* vaccin *m.*

vacuum /'vækjʊəm/ *n.* (*pl.* -**cuums** *or* -**cua**) vide *m.* ~ **cleaner**, aspirateur *m.* ~ **flask**, bouteille thermos *f.* (P.). ~-**packed** *a.* emballé sous vide.

vagabond /'væɡəbɒnd/ *n.* vagabond(e) *m.* (*f.*).

vagina /vəˈdʒaɪnə/ *n.* vagin *m.*

vagrant /'veɪɡrənt/ *n.* vagabond(e) *m.* (*f.*), clochard(e) *m.* (*f.*).

vague /veɪɡ/ *a.* (-**er**, -**est**) vague; (*outline*) flou. **be** ~ **about**, ne pas préciser. ~**ly** *adv.* vaguement.

vain /veɪn/ *a.* (-**er**, -**est**) (*conceited*) vaniteux; (*useless*) vain. **in** ~, en vain. ~**ly** *adv.* en vain.

valentine /'væləntaɪn/ *n.* (*card*) carte de la Saint-Valentin *f.*

valet /'vælɪt, 'væleɪ/ *n.* (*manservant*) valet de chambre *m.*

valiant /'vælɪənt/ *a.* courageux.

valid /'vælɪd/ *a.* valable. ~**ity** /vəˈlɪdətɪ/ *n.* validité *f.*

validate /'vælɪdeɪt/ *v.t.* valider.

valley /'vælɪ/ *n.* vallée *f.*

valour, (*Amer.*) **valor** /'vælə(r)/ *n.* courage *m.*

valuable /'væljʊəbl/ *a.* (*object*) de valeur; (*help etc.*) précieux. ~**s** *n. pl.* objets de valeur *m. pl.*

valuation /væljʊˈeɪʃn/ *n.* expertise *f.*; (*of house*) évaluation *f.*

value /'væljuː/ *n.* valeur *f.* —*v.t.* (*appraise*) évaluer; (*cherish*) attacher de la valeur à. ~ **added tax**, taxe à la valeur ajoutée *f.*, TVA *f.* ~**d** *a.* estimé. ~**r** /-ə(r)/ *n.* expert *m.*

valve /vælv/ *n.* (*techn.*) soupape *f.*; (*of tyre*) valve *f.*; (*radio*) lampe *f.*

vampire /'væmpaɪə(r)/ *n.* vampire *m.*

van /væn/ *n.* (*vehicle*) camionnette *f.*; (*rail.*) fourgon *m.*

vandal /'vændl/ *n.* vandale *m./f.* ~**ism** /-əlɪzəm/ *n.* vandalisme *m.*

vandalize /'vændəlaɪz/ *v.t.* abîmer, détruire, saccager.

vanguard /'vænɡuːd/ *n.* (*of army, progress, etc.*) avant-garde *f.*

vanilla /vəˈnɪlə/ *n.* vanille *f.*

vanish /'vænɪʃ/ *v.i.* disparaître.

vanity /'vænətɪ/ *n.* vanité *f.* ~ **case**, mallette de toilette *f.*

vantage-point /'vɑːntɪdʒpɔɪnt/ *n.* (*place*) excellent point de vue *m.*

vapour /'veɪpə(r)/ *n.* vapeur *f.*

vari|able /'veərɪəbl/ a. variable. ~**ation** /-'eɪʃn/ n. variation f. ~**ed** /-ɪd/ a. varié.

variance /'veərɪəns/ n. at ~, en désaccord (**with,** avec).

variant /'veərɪənt/ a. différent. —n. variante f.

varicose /'værɪkəʊs/ a. ~ **veins,** varices f. pl.

variety /və'raɪətɪ/ n. variété f.; (*entertainment*) variétés f. pl.

various /'veərɪəs/ a. divers. ~**ly** adv. diversement.

varnish /'vɑ:nɪʃ/ n. vernis m. —v.t. vernir.

vary /'veərɪ/ v.t./i. varier.

vase /vɑ:z, Amer. veɪs/ n. vase m.

vast /vɑ:st/ a. vaste, immense. ~**ly** adv. infiniment, extrêmement. ~**ness** n. immensité f.

vat /væt/ n. cuve f.

VAT /vi:eɪ'ti:, væt/ abbr. (*value added tax*) TVA f.

vault[1] /vɔ:lt/ n. (*roof*) voûte f.; (*in bank*) chambre forte f.; (*tomb*) caveau m.; (*cellar*) cave f.

vault[2] /vɔ:lt/ v.t./i. sauter. —n. saut m.

vaunt /vɔ:nt/ v.t. vanter.

VCR abbr. see **video cassette recorder.**

VDU abbr. see **visual display unit.**

veal /vi:l/ n. (*meat*) veau m.

veer /vɪə(r)/ v.i. tourner, virer.

vegan /'vi:gən/ a. & n. végétalien(ne) (m. (f.)).

vegetable /'vedʒtəbl/ n. légume m. —a. végétal. ~ **garden,** (jardin) potager m.

vegetarian /vedʒɪ'teərɪən/ a. & n. végétarien(ne) (m. (f.)).

vegetate /'vedʒɪteɪt/ v.i. végéter.

vegetation /vedʒɪ'teɪʃn/ n. végétation f.

vehement /'vi:əmənt/ a. véhément. ~**ly** adv. avec véhémence.

vehicle /'vi:ɪkl/ n. véhicule m.

veil /veɪl/ n. voile m. —v.t. voiler.

vein /veɪn/ n. (*in body, rock*) veine f.; (*on leaf*) nervure f. (*mood*) esprit m.

velocity /vɪ'lɒsətɪ/ n. vélocité f.

velvet /'velvɪt/ n. velours m.

vending-machine /'vendɪŋməʃi:n/ n. distributeur automatique m.

vendor /'vendə(r)/ n. vendeulr, -se m., f.

veneer /və'nɪə(r)/ n. placage m.; (*appearance: fig.*) vernis m.

venerable /'venərəbl/ a. vénérable.

venereal /və'nɪərɪəl/ a. vénérien.

venetian /və'ni:ʃn/ a. ~ **blind,** jalousie f.

vengeance /'vendʒəns/ n. vengeance f. **with a** ~, furieusement.

venison /'venɪzn/ n. venaison f.

venom /'venəm/ n. venin m. ~**ous** /'venəməs/ a. venimeux.

vent[1] /vent/ n. (*in coat*) fente f.

vent[2] /vent/ n. (*hole*) orifice m.; (*for air*) bouche d'aération f. —v.t. (*anger*) décharger (**on,** sur). **give** ~ **to,** donner libre cours à.

ventilat|e /'ventɪleɪt/ v.t. ventiler. ~**ion** /-'leɪʃn/ n. ventilation f. ~**or** n. ventilateur m.

ventriloquist /ven'trɪləkwɪst/ n. ventriloque m./f.

venture /'ventʃə(r)/ n. entreprise f. —v.t./i. (se) risquer.

venue /'venju:/ n. lieu de rencontre or de rendez-vous m.

veranda /və'rændə/ n. véranda f.

verb /vɜ:b/ n. verbe m.

verbal /'vɜ:bl/ a. verbal.

verbatim /vɜ:'beɪtɪm/ adv. textuellement, mot pour mot.

verdict /'vɜ:dɪkt/ n. verdict m.

verge /vɜ:dʒ/ n. bord m. —v.i. ~ **on,** friser, frôler. **on the** ~ **of doing,** sur le point de faire.

verif|y /'verɪfaɪ/ v.t. vérifier. ~**ication** /-ɪ'keɪʃn/ n. vérification f.

vermicelli /vɜ:mɪ'selɪ/ n. vermicelle(s) m. (pl.).

vermin /'vɜ:mɪn/ n. vermine f.

vermouth /'vɜ:məθ/ n. vermouth m.

vernacular /və'nækjʊlə(r)/ n. langue f.; (*regional*) dialecte m.

versatil|e /'vɜ:sətaɪl, Amer. 'vɜ:sətl/ a. (*person*) aux talents variés; (*mind*) souple. ~**ity** /-'tɪlətɪ/ n. souplesse f. **her** ~**ity,** la variété de ses talents.

verse /vɜ:s/ n. strophe f.; (*of Bible*) verset m.; (*poetry*) vers m. pl.

versed /vɜ:st/ a. ~ **in,** versé dans.

version /'vɜ:ʃn/ n. version f.

versus /'vɜ:səs/ prep. contre.

vertebra /'vɜ:tɪbrə/ n. (pl. -**brae** /-bri:/) vertèbre f.

vertical /'vɜ:tɪkl/ a. vertical. ~**ly** adv. verticalement.

vertigo /'vɜ:tɪgəʊ/ n. vertige m.

verve /vɜ:v/ n. fougue f.

very /'verɪ/ adv. très. —a. (*actual*) même. **the** ~ **day**/etc., le jour/etc. même. **at the** ~ **end,** tout à la fin. **the** ~ **first,** le tout premier. ~ **much,** beaucoup.

vessel /'vesl/ n. (*duct, ship*) vaisseau m.

vest /vest/ n. maillot de corps m.; (*waistcoat: Amer.*) gilet m.

vested /'vestɪd/ a. ~ **interests,** droits acquis m. pl., intérêts m. pl.

vestige /'vestɪdʒ/ n. vestige m.

vestry /'vestrɪ/ n. sacristie f.

vet /vet/ n. (fam.) vétérinaire m./f. —v.t. (p.t. **vetted**) (candidate etc.) examiner (de près).

veteran /'vetərən/ n. vétéran m. (**war**) ~, ancien combattant m.

veterinary /'vetərɪnərɪ/ a. vétérinaire. ~ **surgeon**, vétérinaire m./f.

veto /'viːtəʊ/ n. (pl. **-oes**) veto m.; (right) droit de veto m. —v.t. mettre son veto à.

vex /veks/ v.t. contrarier, irriter. ~**ed question**, question controversée f.

via /'vaɪə/ prep. via, par.

viable /'vaɪəbl/ a. (baby, plan, firm) viable.

viaduct /'vaɪədʌkt/ n. viaduc m.

vibrant /'vaɪbrənt/ a. vibrant.

vibrat|e /vaɪ'breɪt/ v.t./i. (faire) vibrer. ~**ion** /-ʃn/ n. vibration f.

vicar /'vɪkə(r)/ n. pasteur m. ~**age** n. presbytère m.

vicarious /vɪ'keərɪəs/ a. (emotion) ressenti indirectement.

vice[1] /vaɪs/ n. (depravity) vice m.

vice[2] /vaɪs/ n. (techn.) étau m.

vice- /vaɪs/ pref. vice-.

vice versa /'vaɪsɪ'vɜːsə/ adv. vice versa.

vicinity /vɪ'sɪnətɪ/ n. environs m. pl. **in the ~ of**, aux environs de.

vicious /'vɪʃəs/ a. (spiteful) méchant; (violent) brutal. ~ **circle**, cercle vicieux m. ~**ly** adv. méchamment, brutalement.

victim /'vɪktɪm/ n. victime f.

victimiz|e /'vɪktɪmaɪz/ v.t. persécuter, martyriser. ~**ation** /-'zeɪʃn/ n. persécution f.

victor /'vɪktə(r)/ n. vainqueur m.

Victorian /vɪk'tɔːrɪən/ a. & n. victorien(ne) (m. (f.)).

victor|y /'vɪktərɪ/ n. victoire f. ~**ious** /-'tɔːrɪəs/ a. victorieux.

video /'vɪdɪəʊ/ a. (game, camera) vidéo invar. —n. (recorder) magnétoscope m.; (film) vidéo f. ~ **cassette**, vidéocassette f. ~ (**cassette**) **recorder**, magnétoscope m. —v.t. (programme) enregistrer.

videotape /'vɪdɪəʊteɪp/ n. bande vidéo f. —v.t. (programme) enregistrer; (wedding) filmer avec une caméra vidéo.

vie /vaɪ/ v.i. (pres. p. **vying**) rivaliser (**with**, avec).

view /vjuː/ n. vue f. —v.t. (watch) regarder; (consider) considérer (**as**, comme); (house) visiter. **in my ~**, à mon avis. **in ~ of**, compte tenu de. **on ~**, exposé. **with a ~ to**, dans le but de.

~**er** n. (TV) téléspectal|teur, -trice m., f.; (for slides) visionneuse f.

viewfinder /'vjuːfaɪndə(r)/ n. viseur m.

viewpoint /'vjuːpɔɪnt/ n. point de vue m.

vigil /'vɪdʒɪl/ n. veille f.; (over sick person, corpse) veillée f.

vigilan|t /'vɪdʒɪlənt/ a. vigilant. ~**ce** n. vigilance f.

vig|our, (Amer.) **vigor** /'vɪgə(r)/ n. vigueur f. ~**orous** a. vigoureux.

vile /vaɪl/ a. (base) infâme, vil; (bad) abominable, exécrable.

vilify /'vɪlɪfaɪ/ v.t. diffamer.

villa /'vɪlə/ n. villa f., pavillon m.

village /'vɪlɪdʒ/ n. village m. ~**r** /-ə(r)/ n. villageois(e) m. (f.).

villain /'vɪlən/ n. scélérat m., bandit m.; (in story etc.) méchant m. ~**y** n. infamie f.

vindicat|e /'vɪndɪkeɪt/ v.t. justifier. ~**ion** /-'keɪʃn/ n. justification f.

vindictive /vɪn'dɪktɪv/ a. vindicatif.

vine /vaɪn/ n. vigne f.

vinegar /'vɪnɪgə(r)/ n. vinaigre m.

vineyard /'vɪnjəd/ n. vignoble m.

vintage /'vɪntɪdʒ/ n. (year) année f., millésime m. —a. (wine) de grand cru; (car) d'époque.

vinyl /'vaɪnɪl/ n. vinyle m.

viola /vɪ'əʊlə/ n. (mus.) alto m.

violat|e /'vaɪəleɪt/ v.t. violer. ~**ion** /-'leɪʃn/ n. violation f.

violen|t /'vaɪələnt/ a. violent. ~**ce** n. violence f. ~**tly** adv. violemment, avec violence.

violet /'vaɪələt/ n. (bot.) violette f.; (colour) violet m. —a. violet.

violin /vaɪə'lɪn/ n. violon m. ~**ist** n. violoniste m./f.

VIP /viːaɪ'piː/ abbr. (very important person) personnage de marque m.

viper /'vaɪpə(r)/ n. vipère f.

virgin /'vɜːdʒɪn/ n. (woman) vierge f. —a. vierge. **be a ~**, (woman, man) être vierge. ~**ity** /və'dʒɪnətɪ/ n. virginité f.

Virgo /'vɜːgəʊ/ n. la Vierge.

viril|e /'vɪraɪl, Amer. 'vɪrəl/ a. viril. ~**ity** /vɪ'rɪlətɪ/ n. virilité f.

virtual /'vɜːtʃʊəl/ a. vrai. **a ~ failure**/etc., pratiquement un échec/etc. ~**ly** adv. pratiquement.

virtue /'vɜːtʃuː/ n. (goodness, chastity) vertu f.; (merit) mérite m. **by** or **in ~ of**, en raison de.

virtuos|o /vɜːtʃʊ'əʊsəʊ/ n. (pl. **-si** /-siː/) virtuose m./f. ~**ity** /-'ɒsətɪ/ n. virtuosité f.

virtuous /'vɜːtʃʊəs/ a. vertueux.

virulent /'vɪrʊlənt/ a. virulent.

virus /'vaɪərəs/ n. (pl. **-uses**) virus m.
visa /'viːzə/ n. visa m.
viscount /'vaɪkaʊnt/ n. vicomte m.
viscous /'vɪskəs/ a. visqueux.
vise /vaɪs/ n. (Amer.) étau m.
visib|le /'vɪzəbl/ a. (discernible, obvious) visible. ∼**ility** /-'bɪləti/ n. visibilité f. ∼**ly** adv. visiblement.
vision /'vɪʒn/ n. vision f.
visionary /'vɪʒənəri/ a. & n. visionnaire (m./f.).
visit /'vɪzɪt/ v.t. (p.t. visited) (person) rendre visite à; (place) visiter. —v.i. être en visite. —n. (tour, call) visite f.; (stay) séjour m. ∼**or** n. visiteu|r, -se m., f.; (guest) invité(e) m. (f.); (in hotel) client(e) m. (f.).
visor /'vaɪzə(r)/ n. visière f.
vista /'vɪstə/ n. perspective f.
visual /'vɪʒʊəl/ a. visuel. ∼ **display unit,** visuel m., console de visualisation f. ∼**ly** adv. visuellement.
visualize /'vɪʒʊəlaɪz/ v.t. se représenter; (foresee) envisager.
vital /'vaɪtl/ a. vital. ∼ **statistics,** (fam.) mensurations f. pl.
vitality /vaɪ'tæləti/ n. vitalité f.
vitally /'vaɪtəli/ adv. extrêmement.
vitamin /'vɪtəmɪn/ n. vitamine f.
vivac|ious /vɪ'veɪʃəs/ a. plein d'entrain, animé. ∼**ity** /-'æsəti/ n. vivacité f., entrain m.
vivid /'vɪvɪd/ a. vif; (graphic) vivant. ∼**ly** adv. vivement; (describe) de façon vivante.
vivisection /vɪvɪ'sekʃn/ n. vivisection f.
vocabulary /və'kæbjʊləri/ n. vocabulaire m.
vocal /'vəʊkl/ a. vocal; (person: fig.) qui s'exprime franchement. ∼ **cords,** cordes vocales f. pl. ∼**ist** n. chanteu|r, -se m., f.
vocation /və'keɪʃn/ n. vocation f. ∼**al** a. professionnel.
vociferous /və'sɪfərəs/ a. bruyant.
vodka /'vɒdkə/ n. vodka f.
vogue /vəʊg/ n. (fashion, popularity) vogue f. **in** ∼, en vogue.
voice /vɔɪs/ n. voix f. —v.t. (express) formuler.
void /vɔɪd/ a. vide (**of,** de); (not valid) nul. —n. vide m.
volatile /'vɒlətaɪl/ Amer. 'vɒlətl/ a. (person) versatile; (situation) variable.
volcan|o /vɒl'keɪnəʊ/ n. (pl. -oes) volcan m. ∼**ic** /-ænɪk/ a. volcanique.
volition /və'lɪʃn/ n. **of one's own** ∼, de son propre gré.

volley /'vɒli/ n. (of blows etc., in tennis) volée f.; (of gunfire) salve f. ∼**-ball** n. volley(-ball) m.
volt /vəʊlt/ n. (electr.) volt m. ∼**age** n. voltage m.
voluble /'vɒljʊbl/ a. volubile.
volume /'vɒljuːm/ n. volume m.
voluntar|y /'vɒləntəri/ a. volontaire; (unpaid) bénévole. ∼**ily** /-trəli, Amer. -'terəli/ adv. volontairement.
volunteer /vɒlən'tɪə(r)/ n. volontaire m./f. —v.i. s'offrir (**to do,** pour faire); (mil.) s'engager comme volontaire. —v.t. offrir.
voluptuous /və'lʌptʃʊəs/ a. voluptueux.
vomit /'vɒmɪt/ v.t./i. (p.t. vomited) vomir. —n. vomi(ssement) m.
voracious /və'reɪʃəs/ a. vorace.
vot|e /vəʊt/ n. vote m.; (right) droit de vote m. —v.t./i. voter. ∼ (**in**), (person) élire. ∼**er** n. électeur, -trice m., f. ∼**ing** n. vote m. (**of,** de); (poll) scrutin m.
vouch /vaʊtʃ/ v.i. ∼ **for,** se porter garant de, répondre de.
voucher /'vaʊtʃə(r)/ n. bon m.
vow /vaʊ/ n. vœu m. —v.t. (loyalty etc.) jurer (**to,** à). ∼ **to do,** jurer de faire.
vowel /'vaʊəl/ n. voyelle f.
voyage /'vɔɪɪdʒ/ n. voyage (par mer) m.
vulgar /'vʌlgə(r)/ a. vulgaire. ∼**ity** /-'gærəti/ n. vulgarité f.
vulnerab|le /'vʌlnərəbl/ a. vulnérable. ∼**ility** /-'bɪləti/ n. vulnérabilité f.
vulture /'vʌltʃə(r)/ n. vautour m.

W

wad /wɒd/ n. (pad) tampon m.; (bundle) liasse f.
wadding /'wɒdɪŋ/ n. rembourrage m., ouate f.
waddle /'wɒdl/ v.i. se dandiner.
wade /weɪd/ v.i. ∼ **through,** (mud etc.) patauger dans; (book: fig.) avancer péniblement dans.
wafer /'weɪfə(r)/ n. (biscuit) gaufrette f.; (relig.) hostie f.
waffle[1] /'wɒfl/ n. (talk: fam.) verbiage m. —v.i. (fam.) divaguer.
waffle[2] /'wɒfl/ n. (cake) gaufre f.
waft /wɒft/ v.i. flotter. —v.t. porter.
wag /wæg/ v.t./i. (p.t. wagged) (tail) remuer.
wage[1] /weɪdʒ/ v.t. (campaign) mener. ∼ **war,** faire la guerre.

wage² /weɪdʒ/ n. (weekly, daily) salaire m. ~s, salaire m. ~-earner n. salarié(e) m. (f.).

wager /'weɪdʒə(r)/ n. (bet) pari m. —v.t. parier (that, que).

waggle /'wægl/ v.t./i. remuer.

wagon /'wægən/ n. (horse-drawn) chariot m.; (rail.) wagon (de marchandises) m.

waif /weɪf/ n. enfant abandonné(e) m.(f.).

wail /weɪl/ v.i. (utter cry or complaint) gémir. —n. gémissement m.

waist /weɪst/ n. taille f.

waistcoat /'weɪskəʊt/ n. gilet m.

wait /weɪt/ v.t./i. attendre. —n. attente f. I can't ~, je n'en peux plus d'impatience. let's ~ and see, attendons voir. while you ~, sur place. ~ for, attendre. ~ on, servir. ~ing-list n. liste d'attente f. ~ing-room n. salle d'attente f.

wait|er /'weɪtə(r)/ n. garçon m., serveur m. ~ress n. serveuse f.

waive /weɪv/ v.t. renoncer à

wake¹ /weɪk/ v.t./i. (p.t. woke, p.p. woken). ~ (up), (se) réveiller.

wake² /weɪk/ n. (track) sillage m. in the ~ of, (after) à la suite de.

waken /'weɪkən/ v.t./i. (se) réveiller, (s')éveiller.

Wales /weɪlz/ n. pays de Galles m.

walk /wɔːk/ v.i. marcher; (not ride) aller à pied; (stroll) se promener. —v.t. (streets) parcourir; (distance) faire à pied; (dog) promener. —n. promenade f., tour m.; (gait) (dé)marche f.; (pace) marche f., pas m.; (path) allée f. ~ of life, condition sociale f. ~ out, (go away) partir; (worker) faire grève. ~-out n. grève surprise f. ~ out on, abandonner. ~-over n. victoire facile f.

walker /'wɔːkə(r)/ n. (person) marcheur, -se m., f.

walkie-talkie /wɔːkɪ'tɔːkɪ/ n. talkie-walkie m.

walking /'wɔːkɪŋ/ n. marche (à pied) f. —a. (corpse, dictionary: fig.) vivant. ~-stick n. canne f.

Walkman /'wɔːkmən/ n. (P.) Walkman (P.) m., baladeur m.

wall /wɔːl/ n. mur m.; (of tunnel, stomach, etc.) paroi f. —a. mural. —v.t. (city) fortifier. go to the ~, (firm) faire faillite.

wallet /'wɒlɪt/ n. portefeuille m.

wallflower /'wɔːlflaʊə(r)/ n. (bot.) giroflée f.

wallop /'wɒləp/ v.t. (p.t. walloped) (hit:

sl.) taper sur. —n. (blow: sl.) grand coup m.

wallow /'wɒləʊ/ v.i. se vautrer.

wallpaper /'wɔːlpeɪpə(r)/ n. papier peint m. —v.t. tapisser.

walnut /'wɔːlnʌt/ n. (nut) noix f.; (tree) noyer m.

walrus /'wɔːlrəs/ n. morse m.

waltz /wɔːls/ n. valse f. —v.i. valser.

wan /wɒn/ a. pâle, blême.

wand /wɒnd/ n. baguette (magique) f.

wander /'wɒndə(r)/ v.i. errer; (stroll) flâner; (digress) s'écarter du sujet; (in mind) divaguer. ~er n. vagabond(e) m. (f.).

wane /weɪn/ v.i. décroître. —n. on the ~, (strength, fame, etc.) en déclin; (person) sur son déclin.

wangle /'wæŋgl/ v.t. (obtain: sl.) se débrouiller pour avoir.

want /wɒnt/ v.t. vouloir (to do, faire); (need) avoir besoin de (doing, d'être fait); (ask for) demander. —v.i. ~ for, manquer de. —n. (need, poverty) besoin m.; (desire) désir m.; (lack) manque m. I ~ you to do it, je veux que vous le fassiez. for ~ of, faute de. ~ed a. (criminal) recherché par la police.

wanting /'wɒntɪŋ/ a. be ~, manquer (in, de).

wanton /'wɒntən/ a. (cruelty) gratuit; (woman) impudique.

war /wɔː(r)/ n. guerre f. at ~, en guerre. on the ~-path, sur le sentier de la guerre.

ward /wɔːd/ n. (in hospital) salle f.; (minor: jurid.) pupille m./f.; (pol.) division électorale f. —v.t. ~ off, (danger) prévenir; (blow, anger) détourner.

warden /'wɔːdn/ n. directeur, -trice m., f.; (of park) gardien(ne) m. (f.). (traffic) ~, contractuel(le) m. (f.).

warder /'wɔːdə(r)/ n. gardien (de prison) m.

wardrobe /'wɔːdrəʊb/ n. (place) armoire f.; (clothes) garde-robe f.

warehouse /'weəhaʊs/ n. (pl. -s /-haʊzɪz/) entrepôt m.

wares /weəz/ n. pl. (goods) marchandises f. pl.

warfare /'wɔːfeə(r)/ n. guerre f.

warhead /'wɔːhed/ n. ogive f.

warily /'weərɪlɪ/ adv. avec prudence.

warm /wɔːm/ a. (-er, -est) chaud; (hearty) chaleureux. be or feel ~, avoir chaud. it is ~, il fait chaud. —v.t./i. ~ (up), (se) réchauffer; (food) chauffer; (liven up) (s')animer; (exercise)

s'échauffer. **~-hearted** *a.* chaleureux.
~ly *adv.* (*wrap up etc.*) chaudement;
(*heartily*) chaleureusement. **~th** *n.*
chaleur *f.*

warn /wɔːn/ *v.t.* avertir, prévenir. **~ s.o.
off sth.,** (*advise against*) mettre qn. en
garde contre qch.; (*forbid*) interdire
qch. à qn. **~ing** *n.* avertissement *m.*;
(*notice*) avis *m.* **without ~ing,** sans
prévenir. **~ing light,** voyant *m.* **~ing
triangle,** triangle de sécurité *m.*

warp /wɔːp/ *v.t./i.* (*wood etc.*) (se)
voiler; (*pervert*) pervertir.

warrant /'wɒrənt/ *n.* (*for arrest*)
mandat (d'arrêt) *m.*; (*comm.*) autorisation *f.* —*v.t.* justifier.

warranty /'wɒrəntɪ/ *n.* garantie *f.*

warring /'wɔːrɪŋ/ *a.* en guerre.

warrior /'wɒrɪə(r)/ *n.* guerrlier, -ière *m.*,
f.

warship /'wɔːʃɪp/ *n.* navire de guerre *m.*

wart /wɔːt/ *n.* verrue *f.*

wartime /'wɔːtaɪm/ *n.* **in ~,** en temps de
guerre.

wary /'weərɪ/ *a.* (**-ier, -iest**) prudent.

was /wɒz, *unstressed* wəz/ *see* **be.**

wash /wɒʃ/ *v.t./i.* (se) laver; (*flow over*)
baigner. —*n.* lavage *m.*; (*clothes*)
lessive *f.*; (*of ship*) sillage *m.* **have a ~,**
se laver. **~-basin** *n.* lavabo *m.* **~-cloth**
n. (*Amer.*) gant de toilette *m.* **~ down,**
(*meal*) arroser. **~ one's hands of,** se
laver les mains de. **~ out,** (*cup etc.*)
laver; (*stain*) (faire) partir. **~-out** *n.*
(*sl.*) fiasco *m.* **~-room** *n.* (*Amer.*)
toilettes *f. pl.* **~ up,** faire la vaisselle;
(*Amer.*) se laver. **~able** *a.* lavable.
~ing *n.* lessive *f.* **~ing-machine** *n.*
machine à laver *f.* **~ing-powder** *n.*
lessive *f.* **~ing-up** *n.* vaisselle *f.*;
~ing-up liquid, produit pour la
vaisselle *m.*

washed-out /wɒʃt'aʊt/ *a.* (*faded*)
délavé; (*tired*) lessivé; (*ruined*)
anéanti.

washer /'wɒʃə(r)/ *n.* rondelle *f.*

wasp /wɒsp/ *n.* guêpe *f.*

wastage /'weɪstɪdʒ/ *n.* gaspillage *m.*
some ~, (*in goods, among candidates,
etc.*) du déchet.

waste /weɪst/ *v.t.* gaspiller; (*time*) perdre.
—*v.i.* **~ away,** dépérir. —*a.* superflu;
(*product*) de rebut. —*n.* gaspillage *m.*;
(*of time*) perte *f.*; (*rubbish*) déchets *m.
pl.* **lay ~,** dévaster. **~ disposal unit,**
broyeur d'ordures *m.* **~** (**land**),
(*desolate*) terre désolée *f.*; (*unused*)
terre inculte *f.*; (*in town*) terrain vague
m. **~ paper,** vieux papiers *m. pl.* **~-**

paper basket, corbeille (à papier) *f.* **~-
pipe** *n.* vidange *f.*

wasteful /'weɪstfl/ *a.* peu économique;
(*person*) gaspilleur.

watch /wɒtʃ/ *v.t./i.* (*television*) regarder;
(*observe*) observer; (*guard, spy on*)
surveiller; (*be careful about*) faire
attention à. —*n.* (*for telling time*)
montre *f.*; (*naut.*) quart. **be on the ~,**
guetter. **keep ~ on,** surveiller. **~-dog**
n. chien de garde *m.* **~ out,** (*take care*)
faire attention (**for,** à). **~ out for,**
guetter. **~-tower** *n.* tour de guet *f.* **~ful**
a. vigilant.

watchmaker /wɒtʃmeɪkə(r)/ *n.* hor-
logler, -ère *m.*, *f.*

watchman /'wɒtʃmən/ *n.* (*pl.* **-men**) (*of
building*) gardien *m.*

water /'wɔːtə(r)/ *n.* eau *f.* —*v.t.* arroser.
—*v.i.* (*of eyes*) larmoyer. **my/his/**etc.
mouth ~s, l'eau me/lui/etc. vient à la
bouche. **by ~,** en bateau. **~-bottle** *n.*
bouillotte *f.* **~-closet** *n.* waters *m. pl.*
~-colour *n.* couleur pour aquarelle *f.*;
(*painting*) aquarelle *f.* **~ down,** couper
(d'eau); (*tone down*) édulcorer. **~
heater,** chauffe-eau *m.* **~-ice** *n.* sorbet
m. **~-lily** *n.* nénuphar *m.* **~-main** *n.*
canalisation d'eau *f.* **~-melon** *n.*
pastèque *f.* **~-pistol** *n.* pistolet à eau *m.*
~ polo, water-polo *m.* **~ power,**
énergie hydraulique *f.* **~-skiing** *n.* ski
nautique *m.*

watercress /'wɔːtəkres/ *n.* cresson (de
fontaine) *m.*

waterfall /'wɔːtəfɔːl/ *n.* chute d'eau *f.*,
cascade *f.*

watering-can /'wɔːtərɪŋkæn/ *n.* arrosoir
m.

waterlogged /'wɔːtəlɒgd/ *a.* imprégné
d'eau; (*land*) détrempé.

watermark /'wɔːtəmɑːk/ *n.* (*in paper*)
filigrane *m.*

waterproof /'wɔːtəpruːf/ *a.* (*material*)
imperméable.

watershed /'wɔːtəʃed/ *n.* (*in affairs*)
tournant décisif *m.*

watertight /'wɔːtətaɪt/ *a.* étanche.

waterway /'wɔːtəweɪ/ *n.* voie navigable
f.

waterworks /'wɔːtəwɜːks/ *n.* (*place*)
station hydraulique *f.*

watery /'wɔːtərɪ/ *a.* (*colour*) délavé;
(*eyes*) humide; (*soup*) trop liquide;
(*tea*) faible.

watt /wɒt/ *n.* watt *m.*

wav|e /weɪv/ *n.* vague *f.*; (*in hair*)
ondulation *f.*; (*radio*) onde *f.*; (*sign*)
signe *m.* —*v.t.* agiter. —*v.i.* faire signe

(de la main); (*move in wind*) flotter. ~y
a. (*line*) onduleux; (*hair*) ondulé.
wavelength /'weɪvleŋθ/ *n.* (*radio & fig.*)
longueur d'ondes *f.*
waver /'weɪvə(r)/ *v.i.* vaciller.
wax[1] /wæks/ *n.* cire *f.*; (*for skis*) fart *m.*
—*v.t.* cirer; farter; (*car*) astiquer. ~en,
~y *adjs.* cireux.
wax[2] /wæks/ *v.i.* (*of moon*) croître.
waxwork /'wækswɜːk/ *n.* (*dummy*)
figure de cire *f.*
way /weɪ/ *n.* (*road, path*) chemin *m.* (**to,**
de); (*distance*) distance *f.*; (*direction*)
direction *f.*; (*manner*) façon *f.*; (*means*)
moyen *m.*; (*particular*) égard *m.* ~s,
(*habits*) habitudes *f. pl.* —*adv.* (*fam.*)
loin. **be in the** ~, bloquer le passage;
(*hindrance*: *fig.*) gêner (qn.). **be on
one's** *or* **the** ~, être sur son *or* le
chemin. **by the** ~, à propos. **by the**
~**side,** au bord de la route. **by** ~ **of,**
comme; (*via*) par. **go out of one's** ~, se
donner du mal pour. **in a** ~, dans un
sens. **make one's** ~ **somewhere,** se
rendre quelque part. **push one's** ~
through, se frayer un passage. **that** ~,
par là. **this** ~, par ici. ~ **in,** entrée *f.* ~
out, sortie *f.* ~-**out** *a.* (*strange*: *fam.*)
original.
waylay /'weɪleɪ/ *v.t.* (*p.t.* -**laid**) (*assail*)
assaillir; (*stop*) accrocher.
wayward /'weɪwəd/ *a.* capricieux.
WC /dʌb(ə)ljuːˈsiː/ *n.* w.-c. *m. pl.*
we /wiː/ *pron.* nous.
weak /wiːk/ *a.* (-**er, -est**) faible;
(*delicate*) fragile. ~ly *adv.* faiblement;
a. faible. ~**ness** *n.* faiblesse *f.*; (*fault*)
point faible *m.* **a** ~**ness for,** (*liking*) un
faible pour.
weaken /'wiːkən/ *v.t.* affaiblir —*v.i.*
s'affaiblir, faiblir.
weakling /'wiːklɪŋ/ *n.* gringalet *m.*
wealth /welθ/ *n.* richesse *f.*; (*riches,
resources*) richesses *f. pl.*; (*quantity*)
profusion *f.*
wealthy /'welθɪ/ *a.* (-**ier, -iest**) riche.
—*n.* **the** ~, les riches *m. pl.*
wean /wiːn/ *v.t.* (*baby*) sevrer.
weapon /'wepən/ *n.* arme *f.*
wear /weə(r)/ *v.t.* (*p.t.* **wore,** *p.p.* **worn**)
porter; (*put on*) mettre; (*expression
etc.*) avoir. —*v.i.* (*last*) durer. ~ (**out**),
(s')user. —*n.* usage *m.*; (*damage*) usure
f.; (*clothing*) vêtements *m. pl.* ~ **down,**
user. ~ **off,** (*colour, pain*) passer. ~
on, (*time*) passer. ~ **out,** (*exhaust*)
épuiser.
wear|y /'wɪərɪ/ *a.* (-**ier, -iest**) fatigué, las;
(*tiring*) fatigant. —*v.i.* ~**y of,** se lasser

de. ~**ily** *adv.* avec lassitude. ~**iness** *n.*
lassitude *f.*, fatigue *f.*
weasel /'wiːzl/ *n.* belette *f.*
weather /'weðə(r)/ *n.* temps *m.* —*a.*
météorologique. —*v.t.* (*survive*)
réchapper de *or* à. **under the** ~,
patraque. ~-**beaten** *a.* tanné. ~
forecast, météo *f.* ~-**vane** *n.* girouette
f.
weathercock /'weðəkɒk/ *n.* girouette *f.*
weave /wiːv/ *v.t./i.* (*p.t.* **wove,** *p.p.*
woven) tisser; (*basket etc.*) tresser;
(*move*) se faufiler. —*n.* (*style*) tissage
m. ~**r** /-ə(r)/ *n.* tisserand(e) *m.* (*f.*).
web /web/ *n.* (*of spider*) toile *f.*; (*fabric*)
tissu *m.*; (*on foot*) palmure *f.* ~**bed** *a.*
(*foot*) palmé. ~**bing** *n.* (*in chair*)
sangles *f. pl.*
wed /wed/ *v.t.* (*p.t.* **wedded**) épouser.
—*v.i.* se marier. ~**ded to,** (*devoted to*:
fig.) attaché à.
wedding /'wedɪŋ/ *n.* mariage *m.* ~-**ring**
n. alliance *f.*
wedge /wedʒ/ *n.* coin *m.*; (*under wheel
etc.*) cale *f.* —*v.t.* caler; (*push*)
enfoncer; (*crowd*) coincer.
Wednesday /'wenzdɪ/ *n.* mercredi *m.*
wee /wiː/ *a.* (*fam.*) tout petit.
weed /wiːd/ *n.* mauvaise herbe *f.* —*v.t./i.*
désherber. ~-**killer** *n.* désherbant *m.* ~
out, extirper. ~**y** *a.* (*person*: *fig.*)
faible, maigre.
week /wiːk/ *n.* semaine *f.* **a** ~
today/tomorrow, aujourd'hui/ demain
en huit. ~**ly** *adv.* toutes les semaines; *a.*
& *n.* (*periodical*) hebdomadaire (*m.*).
weekday /'wiːkdeɪ/ *n.* jour de semaine *m.*
weekend /wiːk'end/ *n.* week-end *m.*, fin
de semaine *f.*
weep /wiːp/ *v.t./i.* (*p.t.* **wept**) pleurer (**for
s.o.,** qn.). ~**ing willow,** saule pleureur
m.
weigh /weɪ/ *v.t./i.* peser. ~ **anchor,** lever
l'ancre. ~ **down,** lester (avec un poids);
(*bend*) faire plier; (*fig.*) accabler. ~ **up,**
(*examine*: *fam.*) calculer.
weight /weɪt/ *n.* poids *m.* **lose/put on** ~,
perdre/prendre du poids. ~**lessness** *n.*
apesanteur *f.* ~-**lifting** *n.* haltérophilie
f. ~**y** *a.* lourd; (*subject etc.*) de poids.
weighting /'weɪtɪŋ/ *n.* indemnité *f.*
weir /wɪə(r)/ *n.* barrage *m.*
weird /wɪəd/ *a.* (-**er, -est**) mystérieux;
(*strange*) bizarre.
welcome /'welkəm/ *a.* agréable; (*timely*)
opportun. **be** ~, être le *or* la
bienvenu(e), être les bienvenu(e)s.
you're ~!, (*after thank you*) il n'y a pas
de quoi! ~ **to do,** libre de faire. —*int.*

soyez le *or* la bienvenu(e), soyez les
bienvenu(e)s. —*n.* accueil *m.* —*v.t.*
accueillir; (*as greeting*) souhaiter la
bienvenue à; (*fig.*) se réjouir de.
weld /weld/ *v.t.* souder. —*n.* soudure *f.*
~**er** *n.* soudeur *m.* ~**ing** *n.* soudure *f.*
welfare /'welfeə(r)/ *n.* bien-être *m.*; (*aid*)
aide sociale *f.* **W**~ **State,** État-
providence *m.*
well[1] /wel/ *n.* (*for water, oil*) puits *m.*; (*of
stairs*) cage *f.*
well[2] /wel/ *adv.* (**better, best**) bien. —*a.*
bien *invar.* **as** ~, *aussi.* **be** ~, (*healthy*)
aller bien. —*int.* eh bien; (*surprise*)
tiens. **do** ~, (*succeed*) réussir. ~-
behaved *a.* sage. ~-**being** *n.* bien-être
m. ~-**built** *a.* bien bâti. ~-**disposed** *a.*
bien disposé. ~ **done!,** bravo! ~-
dressed *a.* bien habillé. ~-**heeled** *a.*
(*fam.*) nanti. ~-**informed** *a.* bien
informé. ~-**known** *a.* (bien) connu. ~-
meaning *a.* bien intentionné. ~ **off,**
aisé, riche. ~-**read** *a.* instruit. ~-
spoken *a.* qui parle bien. ~-**to-do** *a.*
riche. ~-**wisher** *n.* admiralteur, -trice
m., f.
wellington /'welɪŋtən/ *n.* (*boot*) botte de
caoutchouc *f.*
Welsh /welʃ/ *a.* gallois. —*n.* (*lang.*)
gallois *m.* ~**man** *n.* Gallois *m.* ~
rabbit, croûte au fromage *f.* ~**woman**
n. Galloise *f.*
welsh /welʃ/ *v.i.* ~ **on,** (*debt, promise*)
ne pas honorer.
welterweight /'weltəweɪt/ *n.* poids mi-
moyen *m.*
wench /wentʃ/ *n.* (*old use*) jeune fille *f.*
wend /wend/ *v.t.* ~ **one's way,** se
diriger, aller son chemin.
went /went/ *see* go.
wept /wept/ *see* weep.
were /wɜ:(r), *unstressed* wə(r)/ *see* be.
west /west/ *n.* ouest *m.* **the W**~, (*pol.*)
l'Occident *m.* —*a.* d'ouest. —*adv.* vers
l'ouest. **the W**~ **Country,** le sud-ouest
(de l'Angleterre). **W**~ **Germany,**
Allemagne de l'Ouest *f.* **W**~ **Indian** *a.*
& *n.* antillais(e) (*m.* (*f.*)). **the W**~
Indies, les Antilles *f. pl.* ~**erly** *a.*
d'ouest. ~**ern** *a.* de l'ouest; (*pol.*) oc-
cidental; *n.* (*film*) western *m.* ~**erner** *n.*
occidental(e) *m.* (*f.*). ~**ward** *a.* à
l'ouest. ~**wards** *adv.* vers l'ouest.
westernize /'westənaɪz/ *v.t.* occiden-
taliser.
wet /wet/ *a.* (**wetter, wettest**) mouillé;
(*damp, rainy*) humide; (*paint*) frais.
—*v.t.* (*p.t.* **wetted**) mouiller. —*n.* **the**
~, l'humidité *f.*; (*rain*) la pluie *f.* **get**

~, se mouiller. ~ **blanket,** rabat-joie
m. invar. ~**ness** *n.* humidité *f.* ~ **suit,**
combinaison de plongée *f.*
whack /wæk/ *n.* (*fam.*) grand coup *m.*
—*v.t.* (*fam.*) taper sur.
whacked /wækt/ *a.* (*fam.*) claqué.
whacking /'wækɪŋ/ *a.* énorme.
whale /weɪl/ *n.* baleine *f.*
wham /wæm/ *int.* vlan.
wharf /wɔ:f/ *n.* (*pl.* **wharfs**) (*for ships*)
quai *m.*
what /wɒt/ *a.* (*in questions*) quel(le),
quel(le)s. —*pron.* (*in questions*)
qu'est-ce qui; (*object*) (qu'est-ce) que
or qu'*; (*after prep.*) quoi; (*that which*)
ce qui; (*object*) ce que, ce qu'*. —*int.*
quoi, comment. ~ **date?,** quelle date?
~ **time?,** à quelle heure? ~ **happened?,** qu'est-ce qui s'est passé? ~ **he
did he say?,** qu'est-ce qu'il a dit? ~ **he
said,** ce qu'il a dit. ~ **is important,** ce
qui est important. ~ **is it?,** qu'est-ce
que c'est? ~ **you need,** ce dont vous
avez besoin. ~ **a fool**/*etc.,* quel
idiot/*etc.* ~ **about me/him**/*etc.*?, et
moi/lui/*etc.* ~ **about doing?,** si on
faisait? ~ **for?,** pourquoi?
whatever /wɒt'evə(r)/ *a.* ~ **book**/*etc.,*
quel que soit le livre/*etc.* —*pron.* (*no
matter what*) quoi que, quoi qu'*;
(*anything that*) tout ce qui; (*object*) tout
ce que *or* qu'*. ~ **happens,** quoi qu'il
arrive. ~ **happened?,** qu'est-ce qui est
arrivé? ~ **the problems,** quels que
soient les problèmes. ~ **you want,** tout
ce que vous voulez. **nothing** ~, rien du
tout.
whatsoever /wɒtsəʊ'evər/ *a.* & *pron.* =
whatever.
wheat /wi:t/ *n.* blé *m.*, froment *m.*
wheedle /'wi:dl/ *v.t.* cajoler.
wheel /wi:l/ *n.* roue *f.* —*v.t.* pousser.
—*v.i.* tourner. **at the** ~, (*of vehicle*) au
volant; (*helm*) au gouvernail. ~ **and
deal,** faire des combines.
wheelbarrow /'wi:lbærəʊ/ *n.* brouette *f.*
wheelchair /'wi:ltʃeə(r)/ *n.* fauteuil
roulant *m.*
wheeze /wi:z/ *v.i.* siffler (en respirant).
—*n.* sifflement *m.*
when /wen/ *adv.* & *pron.* quand. —*conj.*
quand, lorsque. **the day/moment** ~, le
jour/moment où.
whenever /wen'evə(r)/ *conj.* & *adv.* (*at
whatever time*) quand; (*every time that*)
chaque fois que.
where /weə(r)/ *adv., conj., & pron.* où;
(*whereas*) alors que; (*the place that*) là
où. ~**abouts** *adv.* (à peu prés) où; *n.*

s.o.'s ~abouts, l'endroit où se trouve qn. ~by adv. par quoi. ~upon adv. sur quoi.

whereas /weər'æz/ conj. alors que.

wherever /weər'evə(r)/ conj. & adv. où que; (everywhere) partout où; (anywhere) (là) où; (emphatic where) où donc.

whet /wet/ v.t. (p.t. **whetted**) (appetite, desire) aiguiser.

whether /'weðə(r)/ conj. si. **not know ~,** ne pas savoir si. **~ I go or not,** que j'aille ou non.

which /wɪtʃ/ a. (in questions) quel(le), quel(le)s. —pron. (in questions) lequel, laquelle, lesquel(le)s; (the one or ones that) celui (celle, ceux, celles) qui; (object) celui (celle, ceux, celles) que or qu'*; (referring to whole sentence, = and that) ce qui; (object) ce que, ce qu'*; (after prep.) lequel/etc. —rel. pron. qui; (object) que, qu'*. **~ house?,** quelle maison? **~ (one) do you want?,** lequel voulez-vous? **~ are ready?,** lesquels sont prêts? **the bird ~ flies,** l'oiseau qui vole. **the hat ~ he wears,** le chapeau qu'il porte. **of ~, from ~,** duquel/etc. **to ~, at ~,** auquel/etc. **the book of ~,** le livre dont or duquel. **after ~,** après quoi. **she was there, ~ surprised me,** elle était là, ce qui m'a surpris.

whichever /wɪtʃ'evə(r)/ a. **~ book/etc.,** quel que soit le livre/etc. que or qui. **take ~ book you wish,** prenez le livre que vous voulez. —pron. celui (celle, ceux, celles) qui or que.

whiff /wɪf/ n. (puff) bouffée f.

while /waɪl/ n. moment m. —conj. (when) pendant que; (although) bien que; (as long as) tant que. —v.t. **~ away,** (time) passer.

whilst /waɪlst/ conj. = while.

whim /wɪm/ n. caprice m.

whimper /'wɪmpə(r)/ v.i. geindre, pleurnicher. —n. pleurnichement m.

whimsical /'wɪmzɪkl/ a. (person) capricieux; (odd) bizarre.

whine /waɪn/ v.i. gémir, se plaindre. —n. gémissement m.

whip /wɪp/ n. fouet m. —v.t. (p.t. **whipped**) fouetter; (culin.) fouetter, battre; (seize) enlever brusquement. —v.i. (move) aller en vitesse. **~-round** n. (fam.) collecte f. **~ out,** (gun etc.) sortir. **~ up,** exciter; (cause) provoquer; (meal: fam.) préparer.

whirl /wɜːl/ v.t./i. (faire) tourbillonner. —n. tourbillon m.

whirlpool /'wɜːlpuːl/ n. (in sea etc.) tourbillon m.

whirlwind /'wɜːlwɪnd/ n. tourbillon (de vent) m.

whirr /wɜː(r)/ v.i. vrombir.

whisk /wɪsk/ v.t. (snatch) enlever or emmener brusquement; (culin.) fouetter. —n. (culin.) fouet m.; (broom, brush) petit balai m. **~ away,** (brush away) chasser.

whisker /'wɪskə(r)/ n. poil m. **~s,** (man's) barbe f., moustache f.; (sideboards) favoris m. pl.

whisky /'wɪskɪ/ n. whisky m.

whisper /'wɪspə(r)/ v.t./i. chuchoter. —n. chuchotement m.; (rumour: fig.) rumeur f., bruit m.

whistle /'wɪsl/ n. sifflement m.; (instrument) sifflet m. —v.t./i. siffler. **~ at or for,** siffler.

Whit /wɪt/ a. **~ Sunday,** dimanche de Pentecôte m.

white /waɪt/ a. (-er, -est) blanc. —n. blanc m.; (person) blanc(he) m. (f.). **~ coffee,** café au lait m. **~-collar worker,** employé(e) de bureau m. (f.). **~ elephant,** objet, projet, etc. inutile m. **~ lie,** pieux mensonge m. **W~ Paper,** livre blanc m. **~ness** n. blancheur f.

whiten /'waɪtn/ v.t./i. blanchir.

whitewash /'waɪtwɒʃ/ n. blanc de chaux m. —v.t. blanchir à la chaux; (person: fig.) blanchir.

whiting /'waɪtɪŋ/ n. invar. (fish) merlan m.

Whitsun /'wɪtsn/ n. la Pentecôte f.

whittle /'wɪtl/ v.t. **~ down,** tailler (au couteau); (fig.) réduire.

whizz /wɪz/ v.i. (p.t. **whizzed**) (through air) fendre l'air; (hiss) siffler; (rush) aller à toute vitesse. **~-kid** n. jeune prodige m.

who /huː/ pron. qui.

whodunit /huː'dʌnɪt/ n. (story: fam.) roman policier m.

whoever /huː'evə(r)/ pron. (no matter who) qui que ce soit qui or que; (the one who) quiconque. **tell ~ you want,** dites-le à qui vous voulez.

whole /həʊl/ a. entier; (intact) intact. **the ~ house/etc.,** toute la maison/ etc. —n. totalité f.; (unit) tout m. **on the ~,** dans l'ensemble. **~-hearted** a., **~-heartedly** adv. sans réserve.

wholefoods /'həʊlfuːdz/ n. pl. aliments naturels et diététiques m. pl.

wholemeal /'həʊlmiːl/ a. **~ bread,** pain complet m.

wholesale /'həʊlseɪl/ *n.* gros *m.* —*a.* (*firm*) de gros; (*fig.*) systématique. —*adv.* (*in large quantities*) en gros; (*buy or sell one item*) au prix de gros; (*fig.*) en masse. ∼**r** /-ə(r)/ *n.* grossiste *m./f.*

wholesome /'həʊlsəm/ *a.* sain.

wholewheat /'həʊlhwiːt/ *a.* = **wholemeal.**

wholly /'həʊlɪ/ *adv.* entièrement.

whom /huːm/ *pron.* (*that*) que, qu'*; (*after prep. & in questions*) qui. **of** ∼, dont. **with** ∼, avec qui.

whooping cough /'huːpɪŋkɒf/ *n.* coqueluche *f.*

whopping /'wɒpɪŋ/ *a.* (*sl.*) énorme.

whore /hɔː(r)/ *n.* putain *f.*

whose /huːz/ *pron. & a.* à qui, de qui. ∼ **hat is this?**, ∼ **is this hat?**, à qui est ce chapeau? ∼ **son are you?**, de qui êtes-vous le fils? **the man** ∼ **hat I see,** l'homme dont *or* de qui je vois le chapeau.

why /waɪ/ *adv.* pourquoi. —*int.* eh bien, ma parole, tiens. **the reason** ∼, la raison pour laquelle.

wick /wɪk/ *n.* (*of lamp etc.*) mèche *f.*

wicked /'wɪkɪd/ *a.* méchant, mauvais, vilain. ∼**ly** *adv.* méchamment. ∼**ness** *n.* méchanceté *f.*

wicker /'wɪkə(r)/ *n.* osier *m.* ∼**work** *n.* vannerie *f.*

wicket /'wɪkɪt/ *n.* guichet *m.*

wide /waɪd/ *a.* (**-er, -est**) large; (*ocean etc.*) vaste. —*adv.* (*fall etc.*) loin du but. **open** ∼, ouvrir tout grand. ∼ **open,** grand ouvert. ∼**-angle lens** grand-angle *m.* ∼ **awake,** éveillé. ∼**ly** *adv.* (*spread, space*) largement; (*travel*) beaucoup; (*generally*) généralement; (*extremely*) extrêmement.

widen /'waɪdn/ *v.t./i.* (s')élargir.

widespread /'waɪdspred/ *a.* très répandu.

widow /'wɪdəʊ/ *n.* veuve. *f.* ∼**ed** *a.* (*man*) veuf; (*woman*) veuve. **be** ∼**ed,** (*become widower or widow*) devenir veuf *or* veuve. ∼**er** *n.* veuf *m.*

width /wɪdθ/ *n.* largeur *f.*

wield /wiːld/ *v.t.* (*axe etc.*) manier; (*power: fig.*) exercer.

wife /waɪf/ *n.* (*pl.* **wives**) femme *f.*, épouse *f.* ∼**ly** *a.* d'épouse.

wig /wɪg/ *n.* perruque *f.*

wiggle /'wɪgl/ *v.t./i.* remuer; (*hips*) tortiller; (*of worm*) se tortiller.

wild /waɪld/ *a.* (**-er, -est**) sauvage; (*sea, enthusiasm*) déchaîné; (*mad*) fou; (*angry*) furieux. —*adv.* (*grow*) à l'état

sauvage. ∼**s** *n. pl.* régions sauvages *f. pl.* **run** ∼, (*free*) courir en liberté. ∼**goose chase,** fausse piste *f.* ∼**ly** *adv.* violemment; (*madly*) follement.

wildcat /'waɪldkæt/ *a.* ∼ **strike,** grève sauvage *f.*

wilderness /'wɪldənɪs/ *n.* désert *m.*

wildlife /'waɪldlaɪf/ *n.* faune *f.*

wile /waɪl/ *n.* ruse *f.*, artifice *m.*

wilful /'wɪlfl/ *a.* (*intentional, obstinate*) volontaire.

will[1] /wɪl/ *v. aux.* **he** ∼ **do/you** ∼ **sing/etc.**, (*future tense*) il fera/tu chanteras/etc. ∼ **you have a coffee?**, voulez-vous prendre un café?

will[2] /wɪl/ *n.* volonté *f.*; (*document*) testament *m.* —*v.t.* (*wish*) vouloir. **at** ∼, quand *or* comme on veut. ∼**-power** *n.* volonté *f.* ∼ **o.s. to do,** faire un effort de volonté pour faire.

willing /'wɪlɪŋ/ *a.* (*help, offer*) spontané; (*helper*) bien disposé. ∼ **to,** disposé à. ∼**ly** *adv.* (*with pleasure*) volentiers; (*not forced*) volontairement. ∼**ness** *n.* empressement *m.* (**to do,** à faire); (*goodwill*) bonne volonté *f.*

willow /'wɪləʊ/ *n.* saule *m.*

willy-nilly /'wɪlɪ'nɪlɪ/ *adv.* bon gré mal gré.

wilt /wɪlt/ *v.i.* (*plant etc.*) dépérir.

wily /'waɪlɪ/ *a.* (**-ier, -iest**) rusé.

win /wɪn/ *v.t./i.* (*p.t.* **won,** *pres. p.* **winning**) gagner; (*victory, prize*) remporter; (*fame, fortune*) acquérir, trouver. —*n.* victoire *f.* ∼ **round,** convaincre.

winc|e /wɪns/ *v.i.* se crisper, tressaillir. **without** ∼**ing,** sans broncher.

winch /wɪntʃ/ *n.* treuil *m.* —*v.t.* hisser au treuil.

wind[1] /wɪnd/ *n.* vent *m.*; (*breath*) souffle *m.* —*v.t.* essouffler. **get** ∼ **of,** avoir vent de. **in the** ∼, dans l'air. ∼**cheater,** (*Amer.*) ∼**breaker** *ns.* blouson *m.* ∼ **instrument,** instrument à vent *m.* ∼**swept** *a.* balayé par les vents.

wind[2] /waɪnd/ *v.t./i.* (*p.t.* **wound**) (s')enrouler; (*of path, river*) serpenter. ∼ (**up**), (*clock etc.*) remonter. ∼ **up,** (*end*) (se) terminer. ∼ **up in hospital,** finir à l'hôpital. ∼**ing** *a.* (*path*) sinueux.

windfall /'wɪndfɔːl/ *n.* fruit tombé *m.*; (*money: fig.*) aubaine *f.*

windmill /'wɪndmɪl/ *n.* moulin à vent *m.*

window /'wɪndəʊ/ *n.* fenêtre *f.*; (*glass pane*) vitre *f.*; (*in vehicle, train*) vitre *f.*; (*in shop*) vitrine *f.*; (*counter*) guichet *m.* ∼**-box** *n.* jardinière *f.* ∼**-cleaner** *n.*

laveur de carreaux *m.* **~-dresser** *n.*
étalagiste *m./f.* **~-ledge** *n.* rebord de (la)
fenêtre *m.*; **~-shopping** *n.* lèche-
vitrines *m.* **~-sill** *n.* (*inside*) appui de
(la) fenêtre *m.*; (*outside*) rebord de (la)
fenêtre *m.*

windpipe /'windpaip/ *n.* trachée *f.*

windscreen /'windskri:n/, (*Amer.*)
windshield /'windʃi:ld/ *n.* pare-brise
m. invar. **~ washer,** lave-glace *m.* **~
wiper,** essuie-glace *m.*

windsurf|ing /'windsɜ:fiŋ/ *n.* planche à
voile *f.* **~er** *n.* véliplanchiste *m./f.*

windy /'windi/ *a.* (**-ier, -iest**) venteux. **it
is ~,** il y a du vent.

wine /wain/ *n.* vin *m.* **~-cellar** *n.* cave (à
vin) *f.* **~-grower** *n.* viticulteur *m.* **~-
growing** *n.* viticulture *f.; a.* viticole. **~
list,** carte des vins *f.* **~-tasting** *n.*
dégustation de vins *f.* **~ waiter,**
sommelier *m.*

wineglass /'waingla:s/ *n.* verre à vin *m.*

wing /wiŋ/ *n.* aile *f.* **~s,** (*theatre*)
coulisses *f. pl.* **under one's ~,** sous son
aile. **~ mirror,** rétroviseur extérieur *m.*
~ed *a.* ailé. **~er** *n.* (*sport*) ailier *m.*

wink /wiŋk/ *v.i.* faire un clin d'œil;
(*light, star*) clignoter. —*n.* clin d'œil
m.; clignotement *m.*

winner /'winə(r)/ *n.* (*of game*) ga
gnant(e) *m.* (*f.*); (*of fight*) vainqueur
m.

winning /'winiŋ/ *see* **win.** —*a.* (*number,
horse*) gagnant; (*team*) victorieux;
(*smile*) engageant. **~s** *n. pl.* gains *m. pl.*

wint|er /'wintə(r)/ *n.* hiver *m.* —*v.i.*
hiverner. **~ry** *a.* hivernal.

wipe /waip/ *v.t.* essuyer. —*v i* **~ up,**
essuyer la vaisselle. —*n.* coup de
torchon *or* d'éponge *m.* **~ off** *or* **out,**
essuyer. **~ out,** (*destroy*) anéantir;
(*remove*) effacer.

wir|e /'waiə(r)/ *n.* fil *m.*; (*Amer.*)
télégramme *m.* **~e netting,** grillage *m.*
~ing *n.* (*electr.*) installation électrique
f.

wireless /'waiəlis/ *n.* radio *f.*

wiry /'waiəri/ *a.* (**-ier, -iest**) (*person*)
nerveux et maigre.

wisdom /'wizdəm/ *n.* sagesse *f.*

wise /waiz/ *a.* (**-er, -est**) prudent, sage;
(*look*) averti. **~ guy,** (*fam.*) petit malin
m. **~ man,** sage *m.* **~ly** *adv.*
prudemment.

wisecrack /'waizkræk/ *n.* (*fam.*) mot
d'esprit *m.*, astuce *f.*

wish /wiʃ/ *n.* (*specific*) souhait *m.*, vœu
m.; (*general*) désir *m.* —*v.t.* souhaiter,
vouloir, désirer (**to do,** faire); (*bid*)

souhaiter. —*v.i.* **~ for,** souhaiter. **I ~
he'd leave,** je voudrais bien qu'il parte.
best ~es, (*in letter*) amitiés *f. pl.*; (*on
greeting card*) meilleurs vœux *m. pl.*

wishful /'wiʃfl/ *a.* **it's ~ thinking,** on se
fait des illusions.

wishy-washy /'wiʃiwɒʃi/ *a.* fade.

wisp /wisp/ *n.* (*of smoke*) volute *f.*

wistful /'wistfl/ *a.* mélancolique.

wit /wit/ *n.* intelligence *f.*; (*humour*)
esprit *m.*; (*person*) homme d'esprit *m.*,
femme d'esprit *f.* **be at one's ~'s** *or*
~s' end, ne plus savoir que faire.

witch /witʃ/ *n.* sorcière *f.* **~craft** *n.*
sorcellerie *f.*

with /wið/ *prep.* avec; (*having*) à;
(*because of*) de; (*at house of*) chez. **the
man ~ the beard,** l'homme à la barbe.
fill/etc. ~, remplir/*etc.* de. **pleased/
shaking/etc. ~,** content/frémissant/
etc. de. **~ it,** (*fam.*) dans le vent.

withdraw /wið'drɔ:/ *v t /i* (*p.t.*
withdrew, *p.p.* **withdrawn**) (se) retirer.
~al *n.* retrait *m.* **~n** *a.* (*person*)
renfermé.

wither /'wiðə(r)/ *v.t./i.* (se) flétrir. **~ed**
a. (*person*) desséché.

withhold /wið'həuld/ *v.t.* (*p.t.* **withheld**)
refuser (de donner); (*retain*) retenir;
(*conceal, not tell*) cacher (**from,** à).

within /wi'ðin/ *prep. & adv.* à l'intérieur
(de); (*in distances*) à moins de. **~ a
month,** (*before*) avant un mois. **~
sight,** en vue.

without /wi'ðaut/ *prep.* sans. **~ my
knowing,** sans que je sache.

withstand /wið'stænd/ *v.t.* (*p.t.*
withstood) résister à.

witness /'witnis/ *n.* témoin *m.*;
(*evidence*) témoignage *m.* —*v.t.* être le
témoin de, voir; (*document*) signer.
bear ~ to, témoigner de. **~ box** *or*
stand, barre des témoins *f.*

witticism /'witisizəm/ *n.* bon mot *m.*

witt|y /'witi/ *a.* (**-ier, -iest**) spirituel.
~iness *n.* esprit *m.*

wives /waivz/ *see* **wife.**

wizard /'wizəd/ *n.* magicien *m.*; (*genius:
fig.*) génie *m.*

wobbl|e /'wɒbl/ *v.i.* (*of jelly, voice,
hand*) trembler; (*stagger*) chanceler;
(*of table, chair*) branler. **~y** *a.*
tremblant; branlant.

woe /wəu/ *n.* malheur *m.*

woke, woken /wəuk, 'wəukən/ *see*
wake[1].

wolf /wulf/ *n.* (*pl.* **wolves**) loup *m.* —*v.t.*
(*food*) engloutir. **cry ~,** crier au loup.
~-whistle *n.* sifflement admiratif *m.*

woman /'wʊmən/ n. (pl. **women**) femme f. **~ doctor,** femme médecin f. **~ driver,** femme au volant f. **~ friend,** amie f. **~hood** n. féminité f. **~ly** a. féminin.

womb /wuːm/ n. utérus m.

women /'wɪmɪn/ see **woman**.

won /wʌn/ see **win**.

wonder /'wʌndə(r)/ n. émerveillement m.; (thing) merveille f. —v.t. se demander (**if,** si). —v.i. s'étonner (**at,** de); (reflect) songer (**about,** à). **it is no ~,** ce or il n'est pas étonnant (**that,** que).

wonderful /'wʌndəfl/ a. merveilleux. **~ly** adv. merveilleusement; (work, do, etc.) à merveille.

won't /wəʊnt/ = **will not.**

woo /wuː/ v.t. (woman) faire la cour à; (please) chercher à plaire à.

wood /wʊd/ n. bois m. **~ed** a. boisé. **~en** a. en or de bois; (stiff: fig.) raide, comme du bois.

woodcut /'wʊdkʌt/ n. gravure sur bois f.

woodland /'wʊdlənd/ n. région boisée f., bois m. pl.

woodpecker /'wʊdpekə(r)/ n. (bird) pic m., pivert m.

woodwind /'wʊdwɪnd/ n. (mus.) bois m. pl.

woodwork /'wʊdwɜːk/ n. (craft, objects) menuiserie f.

woodworm /'wʊdwɜːm/ n. (larvae) vers (de bois) m. pl.

woody /'wʊdɪ/ a. (wooded) boisé; (like wood) ligneux.

wool /wʊl/ n. laine f. **~len** a. de laine. **~lens** n. pl. lainages m. pl. **~ly** a. laineux; (vague) nébuleux; n. (garment: fam.) lainage m.

word /wɜːd/ n. mot m.; (spoken) parole f., mot m.; (promise) parole f.; (news) nouvelles f. pl. —v.t. rédiger. **by ~ of mouth,** de vive voix. **give/keep one's ~,** donner/tenir sa parole. **have a ~ with,** parler à. **in other ~s,** autrement dit. **~ processor,** machine de traitement de texte f. **~ing** n. termes m. pl.

wordy /'wɜːdɪ/ a. verbeux.

wore /wɔː(r)/ see **wear**.

work /wɜːk/ n. travail m.; (product, book, etc.) œuvre f., ouvrage m.; (building etc. work) travaux m. pl. **~s,** (techn.) mécanisme m.; (factory) usine f. —v.t./i. (of person) travailler; (shape, hammer, etc.) travailler; (techn.) (faire) fonctionner; (faire) marcher; (land, mine) exploiter; (of drug etc.) agir. **~ s.o.,** (make work) faire

travailler qn. **~-force** n. main-d'œuvre f. **~ in,** (s')introduire. **~-load** n. travail (à faire) m. **~ off,** (get rid of) se débarrasser de. **~ out** v.t. (solve) résoudre; (calculate) calculer; (elaborate) élaborer; v.i. (succeed) marcher; (sport) s'entraîner. **~-station** n. poste de travail m. **~-to-rule** n. grève du zèle f. **~ up** v.t. développer; v.i. (to climax) monter vers. **~ed up,** (person) énervé.

workable /'wɜːkəbl/ a. réalisable.

workaholic /wɜːkə'hɒlɪk/ n. (fam.) bourreau de travail m.

worker /'wɜːkə(r)/ n. travailleur, -se m., f.; (manual) ouvrier, -ière m., f.

working /'wɜːkɪŋ/ a. (day, lunch, etc.) de travail. **~s** n. pl. mécanisme m. **~ class,** classe ouvrière f. **~-class** a. ouvrier. **in ~ order,** en état de marche.

workman /'wɜːkmən/ n. (pl. **-men**) ouvrier m. **~ship** n. maîtrise f.

workshop /'wɜːkʃɒp/ n. atelier m.

world /wɜːld/ n. monde m. —a. (power etc.) mondial; (record etc.) du monde. **best in the ~,** meilleur au monde. **~-wide** a. universel.

worldly /'wɜːldlɪ/ a. de ce monde, terrestre. **~-wise** a. qui a l'expérience du monde.

worm /wɜːm/ n. ver m. —v.t. **~ one's way into,** s'insinuer dans. **~-eaten** a. (wood) vermoulu; (fruit) véreux.

worn /wɔːn/ see **wear**. —a. usé. **~-out** a. (thing) complètement usé; (person) épuisé.

worr|y /'wʌrɪ/ v.t./i. (s')inquiéter. —n. souci m. **~ied** a. inquiet. **~ier** n. inquiet, -iète m., f.

worse /wɜːs/ a. pire, plus mauvais. —adv. plus mal. —n. pire m. **be ~ off,** perdre.

worsen /'wɜːsn/ v.t./i. empirer.

worship /'wɜːʃɪp/ n. (adoration) culte m. —v.t. (p.t. **worshipped**) adorer. —v.i. faire ses dévotions. **~per** n. (in church) fidèle m./f.

worst /wɜːst/ a. pire, plus mauvais. —adv. (**the**) **~,** (sing etc.) le plus mal. —n. **the ~** (one), (person, object) le or la pire. **the ~** (thing), (être) le pire (**that,** que). **get the ~ of it,** (be defeated) avoir le dessous.

worsted /'wʊstɪd/ n. worsted m.

worth /wɜːθ/ a. **be ~,** valoir. **it is ~ waiting/etc.,** ça vaut la peine d'attendre/etc. —n. valeur f. **ten pence ~ of,** (pour) dix pence de. **it is ~ (one's) while,** ça (en) vaut la peine. **~less** a. qui ne vaut rien.

worthwhile /wɜːθ'waɪl/ *a.* qui (en) vaut la peine.

worthy /'wɜːðɪ/ *a.* (**-ier, -iest**) digne (**of,** de); (*laudable*) louable. —*n.* (*person*) notable *m.*

would /wʊd, *unstressed* wəd/ *v. aux.* he ∼ **do/you** ∼ **sing/**etc., (*conditional tense*) il ferait/tu chanterais/etc. **he** ∼ **have done,** il aurait fait. **I** ∼ **come every day,** (*used to*) je venais chaque jour. **I** ∼ **like some tea,** je voudrais du thé. ∼ **you come here?**, voulez-vous venir ici? **he** ∼**n't come,** il a refusé de venir. ∼**be** *a.* soi-disant.

wound[1] /wuːnd/ *n.* blessure *f.* —*v.t.* blesser. the ∼**ed,** les blessés *m. pl.*

wound[2] /waʊnd/ *see* **wind**[2].

wove, woven /wəʊv, 'wəʊvn/ *see* weave.

wow /waʊ/ *int.* mince (alors).

wrangle /'ræŋgl/ *v.i.* se disputer. —*n.* dispute *f.*

wrap /ræp/ *v.t.* (*p.t.* **wrapped**). ∼ (**up**), envelopper. *v.i.* ∼ **up,** (*dress warmly*) se couvrir. —*n.* châle *m.* ∼**ped up in,** (*engrossed*) absorbé dans. ∼**per** *n.* (*of book*) jaquette *f.*; (*of sweet*) papier *m.* ∼**ping** *n.* emballage *m.*; ∼**ping paper,** papier d'emballage *m.*

wrath /rɒθ/ *n.* courroux *m.*

wreak /riːk/ *v.t.* ∼ **havoc,** (*of storm etc.*) faire des ravages.

wreath /riːθ/ *n.* (*pl.* ∼**s** /-ðz/) (*of flowers, leaves*) couronne *f.*

wreck /rek/ *n.* (*sinking*) naufrage *m.*; (*ship, remains, person*) épave *f.*; (*vehicle*) voiture accidentée *or* délabrée *f.* —*v.t.* détruire; (*ship*) provoquer le naufrage de. ∼**age** *n.* (*pieces*) débris *m. pl.*; (*wrecked building*) décombres *m. pl.*

wren /ren/ *n.* roitelet *m.*

wrench /rentʃ/ *v.t.* (*pull*) tirer sur; (*twist*) tordre; (*snatch*) arracher (**from,** à). —*n.* (*tool*) clé *f.*

wrest /rest/ *v.t.* arracher (**from,** à).

wrestl|e /'resl/ *v.i.* lutter, se débattre (**with,** contre). ∼**er** *n.* lutteur, -se *m., f.*; catcheur, -se *m., f.* ∼**ing** *n.* lutte *f.* (**all-in**) ∼**ing,** catch *m.*

wretch /retʃ/ *n.* malheureu|x, -se *m., f.*; (*rascal*) misérable *m./f.*

wretched /'retʃɪd/ *a.* (*pitiful, poor*) misérable; (*bad*) affreux.

wriggle /'rɪgl/ *v.t./i.* (se) tortiller.

wring /rɪŋ/ *v.t.* (*p.t.* **wrung**) (*twist*) tordre; (*clothes*) essorer. ∼ **out of,** (*obtain from*) arracher à. ∼**ing wet,** trempé (jusqu'aux os).

wrinkle /'rɪŋkl/ *n.* (*crease*) pli *m.*; (*on skin*) ride *f.* —*v.t./i.* (se) rider.

wrist /rɪst/ *n.* poignet *m.* ∼**-watch** *n.* montre-bracelet *f.*

writ /rɪt/ *n.* acte judiciaire *m.*

write /raɪt/ *v.t./i.* (*p.t.* **wrote,** *p.p.* **written**) écrire. ∼ **back,** répondre. ∼ **down,** noter. ∼ **off,** (*debt*) passer aux profits et pertes; (*vehicle*) considérer bon pour la casse. ∼**-off** *n.* perte totale *f.* ∼ **up,** (*from notes*) rédiger. ∼**-up** *n.* compte rendu *m.*

writer /'raɪtə(r)/ *n.* auteur *m.*, écrivain *m.* ∼ **of,** auteur de.

writhe /raɪð/ *v.i.* se tordre.

writing /'raɪtɪŋ/ *n.* écriture *f.* ∼(**s**), (*works*) écrits *m. pl.* **in** ∼, par écrit. ∼**-paper** *n.* papier à lettres *m.*

written /'rɪtn/ *see* **write**.

wrong /rɒŋ/ *a.* (*incorrect, mistaken*) faux, mauvais; (*unfair*) injuste; (*amiss*) qui ne va pas; (*clock*) pas à l'heure. **be** ∼, (*person*) avoir tort (**to,** de); (*be mistaken*) se tromper. —*adv.* mal. —*n.* injustice *f.*; (*evil*) mal *m.* —*v.t.* faire (du) tort à. **be in the** ∼, avoir tort. **go** ∼, (*err*) se tromper; (*turn out badly*) mal tourner; (*vehicle*) tomber en panne. **it is** ∼ **to,** (*morally*) c'est mal de. **what's** ∼?, qu'est-ce qui ne va pas? **what is** ∼ **with you?**, qu'est-ce que vous avez? ∼**ly** *adv.* mal; (*blame etc.*) à tort.

wrongful /'rɒŋfl/ *a.* injustifié, injuste. ∼**ly** *adv.* à tort.

wrote /rəʊt/ *see* **write**.

wrought /rɔːt/ *a.* ∼ **iron,** fer forgé *m.*

wrung /rʌŋ/ *see* **wring**.

wry /raɪ/ *a.* (**wryer, wryest**) (*smile*) désabusé, forcé. ∼ **face,** grimace *f.*

X

xerox /'zɪərɒks/ *v.t.* photocopier.

Xmas /'krɪsməs/ *n.* Noël *m.*

X-ray /'eksreɪ/ *n.* rayon X *m.*; (*photograph*) radio(graphie) *f.* —*v.t.* radiographier.

xylophone /'zaɪləfəʊn/ *n.* xylophone *m.*

Y

yacht /jɒt/ *n.* yacht *m.* ∼**ing** *n.* yachting *m.*

yank /jæŋk/ *v.t.* tirer brusquement. —*n.* coup brusque *m.*

Yank /jæŋk/ n. (fam.) Américain(e) m. (f.), Amerloque m./f.

yap /jæp/ v.i. (p.t. **yapped**) japper.

yard¹ /jɑːd/ n. (measure) yard m. (= 0.9144 metre).

yard² /jɑːd/ n. (of house etc.) cour f.; (garden: Amer.) jardin m.; (for storage) chantier m., dépôt m.

yardstick /'jɑːdstɪk/ n. mesure f.

yarn /jɑːn/ n. (thread) fil m.; (tale: fam.) (longue) histoire f.

yawn /jɔːn/ v.i. bâiller. —n. bâillement m. ⁓ing a. (gaping) béant.

year /jɪə(r)/ n. an m., année f.; **school/tax/**etc. ⁓, année sco-laire/fiscale/etc. **be ten/**etc. ⁓**s old,** avoir dix/etc. ans. ⁓**-book** n. annuaire m. ⁓**ly** a. annuel; adv. annuelle-ment.

yearn /jɜːn/ v.i. avoir bien or très envie (**for, to,** de). ⁓**ing** n. envie f.

yeast /jiːst/ n. levure f.

yell /jel/ v.t./i. hurler. —n. hurlement m.

yellow /'jeləʊ/ a. jaune; (cowardly: fam.) froussard. —n. jaune m.

yelp /jelp/ n. (of dog etc.) jappement m. —v.i. japper.

yen /jen/ n. (desire) grande envie f.

yes /jes/ adv. oui; (as answer to negative question) si. —n. oui m. invar.

yesterday /'jestədɪ/ n. & adv. hier (m.).

yet /jet/ adv. encore; (already) déjà. —conj. pourtant, néanmoins.

yew /juː/ n. (tree, wood) if m.

Yiddish /'jɪdɪʃ/ n. yiddish m.

yield /jiːld/ v.t. (produce) produire, rendre; (profit) rapporter; (surrender) céder. —v.i. (give way) céder. —n. rendement m.

yoga /'jəʊgə/ n. yoga m.

yoghurt /'jɒgət, Amer. 'jəʊgərt/ n. yaourt m.

yoke /jəʊk/ n. joug m.

yokel /'jəʊkl/ n. rustre m.

yolk /jəʊk/ n. jaune (d'œuf) m.

yonder /'jɒndə(r)/ adv. là-bas.

you /juː/ pron. (familiar form) tu, pl. vous; (polite form) vous; (object) te, t'*, pl. vous; (polite) vous; (after prep.) toi, pl. vous; (polite) vous; (indefinite) on; (object) vous; (polite) vous; (indefinite) on; (object) vous; (polite) vous. **I gave ⁓ a pen,** je vous ai donné un stylo. **I know ⁓,** je te connais; je vous connais.

young /jʌŋ/ a. (-er, -est) jeune. —n. (people) jeunes m. pl.; (of animals) petits m. pl. ⁓**er** a. (brother etc.) cadet.

⁓**est** a. **my ⁓est brother,** le cadet de mes frères.

youngster /'jʌŋstə(r)/ n. jeune m./f.

your /jɔː(r)/ a. (familiar form) ton, ta, pl. tes; (polite form, & familiar form pl.) votre, pl. vos.

yours /jɔːz/ poss. pron. (familiar form) le tien, la tienne, les tien(ne)s; (polite form, & familiar form pl.) le or la vôtre, les vôtres. ⁓**s faithfully/sincerely,** je vous prie d'agréer/de croire en l'expression de mes sentiments les meilleurs.

yoursel|**f** /jɔː'self/ pron. (familiar form) toi-même; (polite form) vous-même; (reflexive & after prep.) te, t'*; vous. ⁓**ves** pron. pl. vous-mêmes; (reflexive) vous.

youth /juːθ/ n. (pl. -s /-ðz/) jeunesse f.; (young man) jeune m. ⁓ **club,** centre de jeunes m. ⁓ **hostel,** auberge de jeunesse f. ⁓**ful** a. juvénile, jeune.

yo-yo /'jəʊjəʊ/ n. (pl. -os) (P.) yo-yo m. invar. (P.).

Yugoslav /'juːgəslɑːv/ a. & n. Yougo-slave (m./f.) ⁓**ia** /-'slɑːvɪə/ n. Yougo-slavie f.

yuppie /'jʌpɪ/ n. yuppie m.

Z

zany /'zeɪnɪ/ a. (-ier, -iest) farfelu.

zap /zæp/ v.t. (fam.) (kill) descendre; (comput.) enlever; (TV) zapper.

zeal /ziːl/ n. zèle m.

zealous /'zeləs/ a. zélé. ⁓**ly** a. zèle.

zebra /'zebrə, 'ziːbrə/ n. zèbre m. ⁓ **crossing,** passage pour piétons m.

zenith /'zenɪθ/ n. zénith m.

zero /'zɪərəʊ/ n. (pl. -os) zéro m. ⁓ **hour,** l'heure H f.

zest /zest/ n. (gusto) entrain m.; (spice: fig.) piment m.; (of orange or lemon peel) zeste m.

zigzag /'zɪgzæg/ n. zigzag m. —a. & adv. en zigzag. —v.i. (p.t. **zigzagged**) zigzaguer.

zinc /zɪŋk/ n. zinc m.

Zionism /'zaɪənɪzəm/ n. sionisme m.

zip /zɪp/ n. (vigour) allant m. ⁓**(-fast-ener),** fermeture éclair f. (P.). —v.t. (p.t. **zipped**) fermer avec une fermeture éclair (P.). —v.i. aller à toute vitesse. **Zip code,** (Amer.) code postal m.

zipper /'zɪpə(r)/ n. (Amer.) = **zip (-fastener).**

zither /'zɪðə(r)/ *n.* cithare *f.*

zodiac /'zəʊdɪæk/ *n.* zodiaque *m.*

zombie /'zɒmbɪ/ *n.* mort(e) vivant(e) *m.* (*f.*); (*fam.*) automate *m.*

zone /zəʊn/ *n.* zone *f.*

zoo /zu:/ *n.* zoo *m.*

zoolog|y /zəʊ'ɒlədʒɪ/ *n.* zoologie *f.*

~ical /-ə'lɒdʒɪkl/ *a.* zoologique. **~ist** *n.* zoologiste *m./f.*

zoom /zu:m/ *v.i.* (*rush*) se précipiter. **~ lens,** zoom *m.* **~ off** *or* **past,** filer (comme une flèche).

zucchini /zu:'ki:nɪ/ *n. invar.* (*Amer.*) courgette *f.*

French Verb Tables

Notes The conditional may be formed by substituting the following endings for those of the future: *ais* for *ai* and *as*, *ait* for *a*, *ions* for *ons*, *iez* for *ez*, *aient* for *ont*. The present participle is formed (unless otherwise indicated) by substituting *ant* for *ons* in the first person plural of the present tense (e.g. *finissant* and *donnant* may be derived from *finissons* and *donnons*). The imperative forms are (unless otherwise indicated) the same as the second persons singular and plural and the first person plural of the present tense. The second person singular does not take *s* after *e* or *a* (e.g. *donne, va*), except when followed by *y* or *en* (e.g. *vas-y*).

Regular verbs:

1. in *-er* (e.g. **donn|er**)

   Present. ⁓e, ⁓es, ⁓e, ⁓ons, ⁓ez, ⁓ent.
   Imperfect. ⁓ais, ⁓ais, ⁓ait, ⁓ions, ⁓iez, ⁓aient.
   Past historic. ⁓ai, ⁓as, ⁓a, ⁓âmes, ⁓âtes, ⁓èrent.
   Future. ⁓erai, ⁓eras, ⁓era, ⁓erons, ⁓erez, ⁓eront.
   Present subjunctive. ⁓e, ⁓es, ⁓e, ⁓ions, ⁓iez, ⁓ent.
   Past participle. ⁓é.

2. in *-ir* (e.g. **fin|ir**)

   Pres. ⁓is, ⁓is, ⁓it, ⁓issons, ⁓issez, ⁓issent.
   Impf. ⁓issais, ⁓issais, ⁓issait, ⁓issions, ⁓issiez, ⁓issaient.
   Past hist. ⁓is, ⁓is, ⁓it, ⁓îmes, ⁓ites, ⁓irent.
   Fut. ⁓irai, ⁓iras, ⁓ira, ⁓irons, ⁓irez, ⁓iront.
   Pres. sub. ⁓isse, ⁓isses, ⁓isse, ⁓issions, ⁓issiez, ⁓issent.
   Past part. ⁓i.

3. in *-re* (e.g. **vend|re**)

   Pres. ⁓s, ⁓s, ⁓, ⁓ons, ⁓ez, ⁓ent.
   Impf. ⁓ais, ⁓ais, ⁓ait, ⁓ions, ⁓iez, ⁓aient.
   Past hist. ⁓is, ⁓is, ⁓it, ⁓îmes, ⁓ites, ⁓irent.
   Fut. ⁓rai, ⁓ras, ⁓ra, ⁓rons, ⁓rez, ⁓ront.
   Pres. sub. ⁓e, ⁓es, ⁓e, ⁓ions, ⁓iez, ⁓ent.
   Past part. ⁓u.

Peculiarities of *-er* verbs:

In verbs in *-cer* (e.g. **commencer**) and *-ger* (e.g. **manger**), *c* becomes *ç* and *g* becomes *ge* before *a* and *o* (e.g. commença, commençons; mangea, mangeons).

In verbs in *-yer* (e.g. **nettoyer**), *y* becomes *i* before mute *e* (e.g. nettoie, nettoierai). Verbs in *-ayer* (e.g. **payer**) may retain *y* before mute *e* (e.g. paye or paie, payerai or paierai).

In verbs in *eler* (e.g. **appeler**) and in *-eter* (e.g. **jeter**), *l* becomes *ll* and *t* becomes *tt* before a syllable containing mute *e* (e.g. appelle, appellerai; jette, jetterai). In the verbs **celer, ciseler, congeler, déceler, démanteler, écarteler, geler, marteler, modeler,** and **peler,** and in the verbs **acheter, crocheter, fureter, haleter** and **racheter,** *e* becomes *è* before a syllable containing mute *e* (e.g. cèle, cèlerai; achète, achèterai).

In verbs in which the penultimate syllable contains mute *e* (e.g. **semer**) or *é* (e.g. **révéler**), both *e* and *é* become *è* before a syllable containing mute *e* (e.g. sème, sèmerai; révèle). However, in the verbs in which the penultimate syllable contains *é*, *é* remains unchanged in the future and conditional (e.g. révélerai).

Irregular verbs:

At least the first persons singular and plural of the present tense are shown. Forms not listed may be derived from these. Though the base form of the imperfect, future, and present subjunctive may be irregular, the endings of these tenses are as shown in the regular verb section. Only the first person singular of these tenses is given in most cases. The base form of the past historic may also be irregular but the endings of this tense shown in the verbs below fall (with few exceptions) into the 'u' category, listed under **être** and **avoir**, and the 'i' category shown under **finir** and **vendre** in the regular verb section. Only the first person singular of the past historic is listed in most cases.

Additional forms appear throughout when these cannot be derived from the forms given or when it is considered helpful to list them. Only those irregular verbs judged to be the most useful are shown in the tables.

abattre *as* BATTRE.

accueillir *as* CUEILLIR.

acquérir
- *Pres.* acquiers, acquérons, acquièrent.
- *Impf.* acquérais. ● *Past hist.* acquis. ● *Fut.* acquerrai. ● *Pres. sub.* acquière. ● *Past part.* acquis.

admettre *as* METTRE.

aller
- *Pres.* vais, vas, va, allons, allez, vont. ● *Fut.* irai. ● *Pres. sub.* aille, allions.

apercevoir *as* RECEVOIR.

apparaître *as* CONNAÎTRE.

appartenir *as* TENIR.

apprendre *as* PRENDRE.

asseoir
- *Pres.* assieds, asseyons, asseyent. ● *Impf.* asseyais. ● *Past hist.* assis. ● *Fut.* assiérai. ● *Pres. sub.* asseye. ● *Past part.* assis.

atteindre
- *Pres.* atteins, atteignons, atteignent. ● *Impf.* atteignais. ● *Past hist.* atteignis. ● *Fut.* atteindrai. ● *Pres. sub.* atteigne. ● *Past part.* atteint.

avoir
- *Pres.* ai, as, a, avons, avez, ont. ● *Impf.* avais. ● *Past hist.* eus, eut, eûmes, eûtes, eurent. ● *Fut.* aurai. ● *Pres. sub.* aie, aies, ait, ayons, ayez, aient. ● *Past part.* eu. ● *Imp.* aie, ayons, ayez.

battre
- *Pres.* bats, bat, battons, battez, battent.

boire
- *Pres.* bois, buvons, boivent. ● *Impf.* buvais. ● *Past hist.* bus. ● *Pres. sub.* boive, buvions. ● *Past part.* bu.

bouillir
- *Pres.* bous, bouillons, bouillent. ● *Impf.* bouillais. ● *Pres. sub.* bouille.

combattre *as* BATTRE.

commettre *as* METTRE.

comprendre *as* PRENDRE.

concevoir *as* RECEVOIR.

conclure
- *Pres.* conclus, concluons, concluent. ● *Past hist.* conclus. ● *Past part.* conclu.

conduire
- *Pres.* conduis, conduisons, conduisent. ● *Impf.* conduisais. ● *Past hist.* conduisis. ● *Pres. sub.* conduise. ● *Past part.* conduit.

connaître
- *Pres.* connais, connaît, connaissons. ● *Impf.* connaissais. ● *Past hist.* connus. ● *Pres. sub.* connaisse. ● *Past part.* connu.

construire *as* CONDUIRE.

contenir *as* TENIR.

contraindre *as* ATTEINDRE (except *ai* replaces *ei*).

contredire *as* DIRE, except ● *Pres.* vous contredisez.

convaincre *as* VAINCRE.

convenir *as* TENIR.

corrompre *as* ROMPRE.

coudre
- *Pres.* couds, cousons, cousent. ● *Impf.* cousais. ● *Past hist.* cousis. ● *Pres. sub.* couse. ● *Past part.* cousu.

courir
- *Pres.* cours, courons, courent. ● *Impf.* courais. ● *Past hist.* courus. ● *Fut.* courrai. ● *Pres. sub.* coure. ● *Past part.* couru.

couvrir
- *Pres.* couvre, couvrons. ● *Impf.* couvrais. ● *Pres. sub.* couvre. ● *Past part.* couvert.

craindre *as* ATTEINDRE (except *ai* replaces *ei*).

croire
- *Pres.* crois, croit, croyons, croyez, croient. ● *Impf.* croyais. ● *Past hist.* crus. ● *Pres. sub.* croie, croyions. ● *Past part.* cru.

croître
- *Pres.* crois, croît, croissons. ● *Impf.* croissais. ● *Past hist.* crûs. ● *Pres. sub.* croisse. ● *Past part.* crû, crue.

cueillir
- *Pres.* cueille, cueillons. ● *Impf.* cueillais. ● *Fut.* cueillerai. ● *Pres. sub.* cueille.

débattre *as* BATTRE.

décevoir *as* RECEVOIR.
découvrir *as* COUVRIR.
décrire *as* ÉCRIRE.
déduire *as* CONDUIRE.
défaire *as* FAIRE.
détenir *as* TENIR.
détruire *as* CONDUIRE.
devenir *as* TENIR.
devoir ● *Pres.* dois, devons, doivent. ● *Impf.* devais. ● *Past hist.* dus. ● *Fut.* devrai. ● *Pres. sub.* doive. ● *Past part.* dû, due.
dire ● *Pres.* dis, dit, disons, dites, disent. ● *Impf.* disais. ● *Past hist.* dis. ● *Past part.* dit.
disparaître *as* CONNAÎTRE.
dissoudre ● *Pres.* dissous, dissolvons. ● *Impf.* dissolvais. ● *Pres. sub.* dissolve. ● *Past part.* dissous, dissoute.
distraire *as* EXTRAIRE.
dormir ● *Pres.* dors, dormons. ● *Impf.* dormais. ● *Pres. sub.* dorme.
écrire ● *Pres.* écris, écrivons. ● *Impf.* écrivais. ● *Past hist.* écrivis. ● *Pres. sub.* écrive. ● *Past part.* écrit.
élire *as* LIRE.
émettre *as* METTRE.
s'enfuir *as* FUIR.
entreprendre *as* PRENDRE.
entretenir *as* TENIR.
envoyer ● *Fut.* enverrai.
éteindre *as* ATTEINDRE.
être ● *Pres.* suis, es, est, sommes, êtes, sont. ● *Impf.* étais. ● *Past hist.* fus, fut, fûmes, fûtes, furent. ● *Fut.* serai. ● *Pres. sub.* sois, soit, soyons, soyez, soient. ● *Pres. part.* étant. ● *Past part.* été. ● *Imp.* sois, soyons, soyez.
exclure *as* CONCLURE.
extraire ● *Pres.* extrais, extrayons. ● *Impf.* extrayais. ● *Pres. sub.* extraie. ● *Past part.* extrait.
faire ● *Pres.* fais, fait, faisons, faites, font. ● *Impf.* faisais. ● *Past hist.* fis. ● *Fut.* ferai. ● *Pres. sub.* fasse. ● *Past part.* fait.

falloir (impersonal) ● *Pres.* faut. ● *Impf.* fallait. ● *Past hist.* fallut. ● *Fut.* faudra. ● *Pres. sub.* faille. ● *Past part.* fallu.
feindre *as* ATTEINDRE.
fuir ● *Pres.* fuis, fuyons, fuient. ● *Impf.* fuyais. ● *Past hist.* fuis. ● *Pres sub.* fuie. ● *Past part.* fui.
inscrire *as* ÉCRIRE.
instruire *as* CONDUIRE.
interdire *as* DIRE, except ● *Pres.* vous interdisez.
interrompre *as* ROMPRE.
intervenir *as* TENIR.
introduire *as* CONDUIRE.
joindre *as* ATTEINDRE (except *oi* replaces *ei*).
lire ● *Pres.* lis, lit, lisons, lisez, lisent. ● *Impf.* lisais. ● *Past hist.* lus. ● *Pres. sub.* lise. ● *Past part.* lu.
luire ● *Pres.* luis, luisons. ● *Impf.* luisais. ● *Past hist.* luisis. ● *Pres. sub.* luise. ● *Past part.* lui.
maintenir *as* TENIR.
maudire ● *Pres.* maudis, maudissons. ● *Impf.* maudissais. ● *Past hist.* maudis. ● *Pres. sub.* maudisse. ● *Past part.* maudit.
mentir *as* SORTIR (except *en* replaces *or*).
mettre ● *Pres.* mets, met, mettons, mettez, mettent. ● *Past hist.* mis. ● *Past part.* mis.
mourir ● *Pres.* meurs, mourons, meurent. ● *Impf.* mourais. ● *Past hist.* mourus. ● *Fut.* mourrai. ● *Pres. sub.* meure, mourions. ● *Past part.* mort.
mouvoir ● *Pres.* meus, mouvons, meuvent. ● *Impf.* mouvais. ● *Fut.* mouvrai. ● *Pres. sub.* meuve, mouvions. ● *Past part.* mû, mue.
naître ● *Pres.* nais, naît, naissons. ● *Impf.* naissais. ● *Past hist.* naquis. ● *Pres. sub.* naisse. ● *Past part.* né.
nuire *as* LUIRE.

obtenir *as* TENIR.
offrir, ouvrir *as* COUVRIR.
omettre *as* METTRE.
paraître *as* CONNAÎTRE.
parcourir *as* COURIR.
partir *as* SORTIR (except *ar* replaces *or*).
parvenir *as* TENIR.
peindre *as* ATTEINDRE.
percevoir *as* RECEVOIR.
permettre *as* METTRE.
plaindre *as* ATTEINDRE (except *ai* replaces *ei*).
plaire ● *Pres.* plais, plaît, plaisons. ● *Impf.* plaisais. ● *Past hist.* plus. ● *Pres. sub.* plaise. ● *Past part.* plu.
pleuvoir (impersonal) ● *Pres.* pleut. ● *Impf.* pleuvait. ● *Past hist.* plut. ● *Fut.* pleuvra. ● *Pres. sub.* pleuve. ● *Past part.* plu.
poursuivre *as* SUIVRE.
pourvoir *as* VOIR, except ● *Fut.* pourvoirai
pouvoir ● *Pres.* peux, peut, pouvons, pouvez, peuvent. ● *Impf.* pouvais. ● *Past hist.* pus. ● *Fut.* pourrai. ● *Pres. sub.* puisse. ● *Past part.* pu.
prédire *as* DIRE, except ● *Pres.* vous prédisez.
prendre ● *Pres.* prends, prenons, prennent. ● *Impf.* prenais. ● *Past hist.* pris. ● *Pres. sub.* prenne, prenions. ● *Past part.* pris.
prescrire *as* ÉCRIRE.
prévenir *as* TENIR.
prévoir *as* VOIR, except ● *Fut.* prévoirai.
produire *as* CONDUIRE.
promettre *as* METTRE.
provenir *as* TENIR.
recevoir ● *Pres.* reçois, recevons, reçoivent. ● *Impf.* recevais. ● *Past hist.* reçus. ● *Fut.* recevrai. ● *Pres. sub.* reçoive, recevions. ● *Past part.* reçu.
reconduire *as* CONDUIRE.
reconnaître *as* CONNAÎTRE.
reconstruire *as* CONDUIRE.
recouvrir *as* COUVRIR.
recueillir *as* CUEILLIR.

redire *as* DIRE.
réduire *as* CONDUIRE.
refaire *as* FAIRE.
rejoindre *as* ATTEINDRE (except *oi* replaces *ei*).
remettre *as* METTRE.
renvoyer *as* ENVOYER.
repartir *as* SORTIR (except *ar* replaces *or*).
reprendre *as* PRENDRE.
reproduire *as* CONDUIRE.
résoudre ● *Pres.* résous, résolvons. ● *Impf.* résolvais. ● *Past hist.* résolus. ● *Pres. sub.* résolve. ● *Past part.* résolu.
ressortir *as* SORTIR.
restreindre *as* ATTEINDRE.
retenir, revenir *as* TENIR.
revivre *as* VIVRE.
revoir *as* VOIR.
rire ● *Pres.* ris, rit, rions, riez, rient. ● *Impf.* riais. ● *Past hist.* ris. ● *Pres. sub.* rie, riions. ● *Past part.* ri.
rompre *as* VENDRE (regular), except ● *Pres.* il rompt.
satisfaire *as* FAIRE.
savoir ● *Pres.* sais, sait, savons, savez, savent. ● *Impf.* savais. ● *Past hist.* sus. ● *Fut.* saurai. ● *Pres. sub.* sache, sachions. ● *Pres. part.* sachant. ● *Past part.* su. ● *Imp.* sache, sachons, sachez.
séduire *as* CONDUIRE.
sentir *as* SORTIR (except *en* replaces *or*).
servir ● *Pres.* sers, servons. ● *Impf.* servais. ● *Pres. sub.* serve.
sortir ● *Pres.* sors, sortons. ● *Impf.* sortais. ● *Pres. sub.* sorte.
souffrir *as* COUVRIR.
soumettre *as* METTRE.
soustraire *as* EXTRAIRE.
soutenir *as* TENIR.
suffire ● *Pres.* suffis, suffisons. ● *Impf.* suffisais. ● *Past hist.* suffis. ● *Pres. sub.* suffise. ● *Past part.* suffi.
suivre ● *Pres.* suis, suivons. ● *Impf.* suivais. ● *Past hist.* suivis. ● *Pres. sub.* suive. ● *Past part.* suivi.

surprendre *as* PRENDRE.

survivre *as* VIVRE.

taire
- *Pres.* tais, taisons.
- *Impf.* taisais. ● *Past hist.* tus. ● *Pres. sub.* taise.
- *Past part.* tu.

teindre *as* ATTEINDRE.

tenir
- *Pres.* tiens, tenons, tiennent. ● *Impf.* tenais.
- *Past hist.* tins, tint, tînmes, tîntes, tinrent.
- *Fut.* tiendrai. ● *Pres. sub.* tienne. ● *Past part.* tenu.

traduire *as* CONDUIRE.

traire *as* EXTRAIRE.

transmettre *as* METTRE.

vaincre
- *Pres.* vaincs, vainc, vainquons. ● *Impf.* vainquais. ● *Past hist.* vainquis. ● *Pres. sub.* vainque. ● *Past part.* vaincu.

valoir
- *Pres.* vaux, vaut, valons, valez, valent. ● *Impf.* valais. ● *Past hist.* valus.
- *Fut.* vaudrai. ● *Pres. sub.* vaille. ● *Past part.* valu.

venir *as* TENIR.

vivre
- *Pres.* vis, vit, vivons, vivez, vivent. ● *Impf.* vivais. ● *Past hist.* vécus.
- *Pres. sub.* vive. ● *Past part.* vécu.

voir
- *Pres.* vois, voyons, voient. ● *Impf.* voyais.
- *Past hist.* vis. ● *Fut.* verrai. ● *Pres. sub.* voie, voyions. ● *Past part.* vu.

vouloir
- *Pres.* veux, veut, voulons, voulez, veulent.
- *Impf.* voulais. ● *Past hist.* voulus. ● *Fut.* voudrai. ● *Pres. sub.* veuille, voulions. ● *Past part.* voulu. ● *Imp.* veuille, veuillons, veuillez.